The author's writing style is the best feature of the book and of the chapters. It is simple, engaging, and connective. It is an easy read and has an entertaining style that will appeal to my students.
JAMES SWENSON, MINNESOTA STATE UNIVERSITY, MOORHEAD

The way the entire text is written is refreshing. Expected content is covered and then some. The additional chapter on entrepreneurship and innovation is a deal maker for me.
MARK FENTON, UNIVERSITY OF WISCONSIN-STOUT

I strongly applaud the approach since I agree that critical thinking skills are the key to organizational success.
HERBERT SHERMAN, LIU, BROOKLYN

I like the writing style and feel the students would be more apt to read it. I think there is focus on more relevant topics, some topics are expanded that are not in my text. Honestly it just seems much more interesting!
ANN SNELL, TULANE UNIVERSITY

The style throughout is conversation and casual, while still business like. It is easy and engaging to read.
ALLEN AMASON, UNIVERSITY OF GEORGIA

The ethics and responsibility chapter was excellent. It provides better descriptions and detail than other books I have seen. The examples were clear, the writing made the chapter easy to read, and the graphics and boxes were helpful.
RYAN ATKINS, UNIVERSITY OF GEORGIA

Very well written, easy read for students with relevant real world examples that students will readily understand. The book also provides a variety of ways to apply the material presented, taking into consideration different learning styles.
DR. ANDREA SMITH-HUNTER, SIENA COLLEGE

I really did like the system approach used throughout the chapters that I reviewed. That approach is a huge positive for me. It is unique and very helpful as a framework for discussing management.
CHARLENE DYKMAN, UNIVERSITY OF ST. THOMAS

This textbook's competitive advantage is that it looks at systems and critical thinking. The chapters are each written to best cover the topics. Students are challenged to look at what influences organizations and how decisions are made. The content is highly relevant to traditional students.
ROBERT ELIASON, JAMES MADISON UNIVERSITY

Writing style was superb--more interesting and involving that any principles of management textbook I have read. It just draws the reader in, like a well written novel, yet imparts management key principles that all management texts wish to do. From the chapters I have reviewed, I am ready to adopt this textbook for my courses right now.
VERL ANDERSON, DIXIE STATE COLLEGE

Fresh, new, nicely done.
HARRY CANDLER, JR., VALENCIA COLLEGE

These materials offer a different yet comprehensive approach to understanding management, uniting traditional structural elements with an increasingly significant emphasis on critical thinking and systems thinking.
WILLIAM MARTELLO, ST. EDWARD'S UNIVERSITY

I think this is one of the few texts that were written specifically at the PoM student level and it is a clean break from the standard 'kitchen sink' mode. What I mean by that is that the text is very well thought out and it shows in both the content coverage and presentation.
JEREMY STAFFORD, UNIVERSITY OF NORTH ALABAMA

This text is understandable and leads to classroom discussion better than any I have seen. Using role playing and believable and identifiable scenarios is a great approach.
HARRY CANDLER, JR., VALENCIA COLLEGE

Not just significantly better than my current text, but significantly better than any principles of management text I have read.
VERL ANDERSON, DIXIE STATE COLLEGE

Yes, it is a "fresh" look and provides an improved insight over the traditional approaches. It is thought provoking and should challenge student learning.
ANTHONY NARSING, MIDDLE GEORGIA STATE COLLEGE

BRIEF CONTENTS

MANAGEMENT

WileyPLUS with ORION

Based on cognitive science, *WileyPLUS* with ORION provides students with a personal, adaptive learning experience so they can build their proficiency on topics and use their study time most effectively.

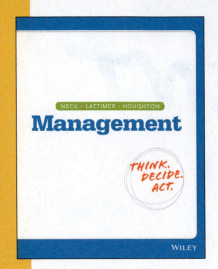

NECK · LATTIMER · HOUGHTON

Management

THINK.
DECIDE.
ACT.

WILEY

BEGIN

Unique to ORION, students **BEGIN** by taking a quick diagnostic for any chapter. This will determine each student's baseline proficiency on each topic in the chapter. Students see their individual diagnostic report to help them decide what to do next with the help of ORION's recommendations.

PRACTICE

For each topic, students can either **STUDY**, or **PRACTICE**. Study directs students to the specific topic they choose in *WileyPLUS*, where they can read from the e-textbook or use the variety of relevant resources available there. Students can also practice, using questions and feedback powered by ORION's adaptive learning engine. Based on the results of their diagnostic and ongoing practice, ORION will present students with questions appropriate for their current level of understanding, and will continuously adapt to each student to help build proficiency.

MAINTAIN

ORION includes a number of reports and ongoing recommendations for students to help them **MAINTAIN** their proficiency over time for each topic.

Students can easily access ORION from multiple places within *WileyPLUS*. It does not require any additional registration, and there will not be any additional charge for students using this adaptive learning system.

ABOUT THE ADAPTIVE ENGINE

ORION includes a powerful algorithm that feeds questions to students based on their responses to the diagnostic and to the practice questions. Students who answer questions correctly at one difficulty level will soon be given questions at the next difficulty level. If students start to answer some of those questions incorrectly, the system will present questions of lower difficulty. The adaptive engine also takes into account other factors, such as reported confidence levels, time spent on each question, and changes in response options before submitting answers.

The questions used for the adaptive practice are numerous and are not found in the WileyPLUS assignment area. This ensures that students will not be encountering questions in ORION that they may also encounter in their WileyPLUS assessments.

ORION also offers a number of reporting options available for instructors, so that instructors can easily monitor student usage and performance.

WileyPLUS with ORION helps students learn by learning about them.™

MANAGEMENT

Christopher P. Neck, Ph.D.
Arizona State University

Charles L. Lattimer
Cooperative Leadership Institute

Jeffery D. Houghton, Ph.D.
West Virginia University

WILEY

VICE PRESIDENT & EXECUTIVE PUBLISHER	George Hoffman
EXECUTIVE EDITOR	Lisé Johnson
DEVELOPMENTAL EDITOR	Susan McLaughlin
PROJECT EDITOR	Brian Baker
EDITORIAL ASSISTANT	Jacqueline Hughes
EDITORIAL OPERATIONS MANAGER	Yana Mermel
DIRECTOR OF MARKETING	Amy Scholz
SENIOR MARKETING MANAGER	Kelly Simmons
MARKETING ASSISTANT	Marissa Carroll
SENIOR CONTENT MANAGER	Dorothy Sinclair
SENIOR PRODUCTION MANAGER	Valerie Vargas
SENIOR PRODUCT DESIGNER	Allison Morris
MEDIA SPECIALIST	Elena Santa Maria
SENIOR PHOTO EDITOR	Mary Ann Price
PHOTO RESEARCHER	Susan McLaughlin
DESIGN DIRECTOR	Harry Nolan
SENIOR DESIGNER	Tom Nery

This book was set in 10/12 Kepler by MPS Limited and printed and bound by Courier. The cover was printed by Courier.

This book is printed on acid free paper. ∞

Founded in 1807, John Wiley & Sons, Inc. has been a valued source of knowledge and understanding for more than 200 years, helping people around the world meet their needs and fulfill their aspirations. Our company is built on a foundation of principles that include responsibility to the communities we serve and where we live and work. In 2008, we launched a Corporate Citizenship Initiative, a global effort to address the environmental, social, economic, and ethical challenges we face in our business. Among the issues we are addressing are carbon impact, paper specifications and procurement, ethical conduct within our business and among our vendors, and community and charitable support. For more information, please visit our website: www.wiley.com/go/citizenship.

978-1-118-74954-8 (BRV)
978-1-118-74956-2 (IE)

Printed in the United States of America

10 9 8 7 6 5 4 3 2 1

We dedicate Management *to all of our students who have believed in us, inspired us, and encouraged us to try new ways of teaching.*

ABOUT THE AUTHORS

Courtesy Arizona State University

CHRISTOPHER P. NECK

Dr. Christopher P. Neck is currently an associate professor of management at Arizona State University, where he holds the title "University Master Teacher." From 1994 to 2009, he was part of the Pamplin College of Business faculty at Virginia Tech. He received his Ph.D. in management from Arizona State University and his MBA from Louisiana State University. Neck is author of the books *Fit To Lead: The Proven 8-Week Solution for Shaping Up Your Body, Your Mind, and Your Career* (St. Martin's Press, 2004; Carpenter's Sons Publishing, 2012), *Mastering Self-Leadership: Empowering Yourself for Personal Excellence*, 6th edition (Pearson, 2013), *The Wisdom of Solomon at Work* (Berrett-Koehler, 2001), *For Team Members Only: Making Your Workplace Team Productive and Hassle-Free* (Amacom Books, 1997), and *Medicine for the Mind: Healing Words to Help You Soar*, 4th edition (Wiley, 2012).

Dr. Neck's research specialties include employee/executive fitness, self-leadership, leadership, group decision-making processes, and self-managing teams. He has contributed to over 90 publications in the form of books, chapters, and articles in various journals. Some of the outlets in which Neck's work has appeared include *Organizational Behavior and Human Decision Processes, The Journal of Organizational Behavior, The Academy of Management Executive, Journal of Applied Behavioral Science, The Journal of Managerial Psychology, Executive Excellence, Human Relations, Human Resource Development Quarterly, Journal of Leadership Studies, Educational Leadership, and The Commercial Law Journal.*

Due to Neck's expertise in management, he has been cited in numerous national publications, including the *Washington Post, The Wall Street Journal*, the *Los Angeles Times*, the *Houston Chronicle*, and the *Chicago Tribune*. Additionally, each semester, Neck teaches an introductory management course to a single class of anywhere from 500 to 1,000 students.

Dr. Neck was the recipient of the "2007 Business Week Favorite Professor Award. He is featured on www.businessweek.com as one of the approximately 20 professors from across the world to receive this award.

CHARLES L. LATTIMER

Courtesy Charles L. Lattimer

Charles is the CEO and founder of the Cooperative Leadership Institute, a private leadership and management development company founded at Virginia Tech. As a keynote speaker, executive coach, leadership guide, and technology entrepreneur, Charles has directed and designed international and enterprise-level organizational development and training programs for the past 15 years. He has over a decade of experience in designing, developing, and delivering programs and strategic planning solutions for thousands of executives to ensure sustainable results through a balanced approach to management.

Charles regularly speaks about all areas of leadership capacity development, entrepreneurship, courage in business, innovation, creativity, learning organizations, and systems thinking. He has designed development programs for managers and executives from Akridge, Alpha Pharmaceuticals, B. F. Saul Company, Club Corporation of America (ClubCorp), e5 Systems, General Electric, LPGA's Duramed Tour, LTD Management, Marriott, U. S. Foreign Service Institute, Virginia Tech, Wal-Mart, Whole Child Learning Company, local governments, schools systems, and many others. Charles has lifetime memberships in Phi Beta Kappa and Phi Kappa Phi and is President Emeritus of Virginia Tech's Phi Beta Kappa chapter.

JEFFERY D. HOUGHTON

Alex Wilson, WVU College of Business and Economics

Dr. Jeffery D. Houghton completed his Ph.D. in management at Virginia Tech and is currently an associate professor of management at West Virginia University. He previously held faculty positions at Abilene Christian University (TX) and Lipscomb University (TN). Prior to pursuing a full-time career in academics, he worked in the banking industry as a loan officer and branch manager.

A member of the honor society Phi Kappa Phi, Dr. Houghton's research specialties include human behavior, motivation, personality, leadership, and self-leadership. Dr. Houghton has presented his research at various professional meetings and has published more than 30 peer-reviewed journal articles and book chapters.

In addition to his research activities, Dr. Houghton has done consulting and conducted training seminars for companies, including the Federal Bureau of Investigations (FBI), Pfizer Pharmaceuticals, and the Bruce Hardwood Floors Company. In his spare time, he enjoys traveling, classic mystery novels, racquetball, mountain biking, and snow skiing. Finally, he has trained for and completed two marathons: the Marine Corps Marathon in Washington, D.C., and the Dallas White Rock Marathon in Dallas, TX.

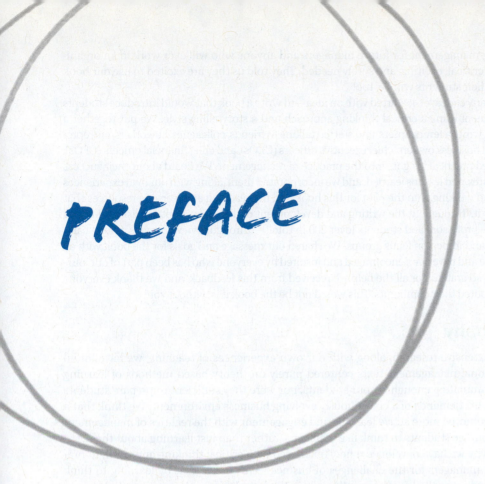

PREFACE

An innovative and very contemporary way of teaching management.
—Douglas M. McCabe, Georgetown University

I think your using the systems approach to critical thinking is a great thing. Getting students thinking critically from a systems perspective and looking at the intended and unintended consequences of decisions is much needed.
—Kenneth J. Harris, Indiana University Southeast

Writing style was superb—more interesting and involving than any principles of management textbook I have read. It just draws the reader in, like a well-written novel, yet imparts management key principles that all management texts wish to do.
—Verl Anderson, Dixie State College

We would like to offer a warm welcome to instructors and students to *Management*. In a rapidly changing business world, this is an exhilarating time for 21st-century managers! Globalization and technological innovation has revolutionized every aspect of our daily lives, changing the way we work and learn. Today's managers need to be equipped with the right skills to deal with the growing number of challenges facing them within this uncertain economic climate. Dealing with the competition, coping with ethical dilemmas, identifying and hiring talent, managing diversity, building sustainability, and adapting to the latest technology are just a few of the many challenges that today's managers face.

This book is designed to give you a better idea of what management really is, who the most successful managers are, how to become a great manager, and how to think critically. It is our hope that this book will help prepare you for these challenges and support you in your future careers as managers.

We have been told that it's not very often a book reviews the way this one has, and we have been humbled and honored by the feedback we have received as we wrote and revised this text. From the start of this project, professors told us that we were on to something. Our critical thinking approach, novel style of writing, systems thinking emphasis, and coverage of Positive Psychology got their attention, and they were sure that it would get their students' attention, too. They told us that it was truly different from any introductory management book they had used or reviewed before. And they said that a new and unique approach to teaching management for future managers and anyone who will ever work in an organization was critical, exciting, and sorely needed. They told us they are excited to use our book and think their students will be, too!

As with any endeavor, it started with an idea—to write a book that would introduce students to management using a critical thinking approach and a storytelling style. We put together a prospectus, wrote a few chapters, and started talking to friends, colleagues, coworkers, entrepreneurs, small business owners, chief executive officers (CEOs), and chief financial officers (CFOs), and gathered practical insights into the practice of management. We heard about their success stories, failures, and lessons learned, and we incorporated them, along with our own experiences teaching and working, into the plan for this book and the teaching and learning resources that accompany it. Throughout the writing and development of the manuscript, we listened to our customers—professors and students (over 200 in total!)—through reviews, emails, phone calls, and virtual and in-person focus groups. We shared our message and goals for the book with all these people and have been encouraged and inspired by everyone who has been part of our journey. We are so grateful for all the help we received from this feedback, and we thank everyone who contributed their comments. This would not be the book it is without you!

Philosophy

Based on extensive research, along with our own experiences of teaching, we have found that traditional management texts centered purely on theory-based methods of learning were not stimulating enough for our students, nor were they sufficient to prepare students for the real-life demands of a continuously evolving business environment. We think that a text that promoted more active learning and engagement with the realities of management would encourage students to think like managers, rather than just learning about them.

This is why we have developed a new text based on a critical thinking approach, to prepare future managers for the challenges of business. We believe that by learning to think critically, students will play a more active role in the learning process, engage with the content, and really understand what it is like to be a manager. And our ideas are supported by a national market segmentation survey that Wiley conducted with principles of management professors. Over 80 percent of those surveyed said the number one thing that students need to learn is how to think critically.

Our goal is to show you that the study of management is exciting and stimulating. To illustrate this, we have included several management stories, based on real-life scenarios, that describe epic failures, risings and fallings, overnight successes, poetic justices, dilemmas, and plain, hardworking people that find meaningful ways to make a difference. We believe that a storytelling approach inspires students to think critically by putting themselves in the place of a manager to resolve management dilemmas.

Pedagogy

The content of *Management* is based on sound pedagogical foundations that aim to support students in learning quickly and efficiently.

As educators, our goals are to:

- Help students realize that management is extremely relevant to each and every one of them . . . that management begins with each of them . . . that before we can manage others, we have to learn to manage ourselves, and that, ultimately, management is relevant to us all.

- Challenge our students to embrace all types of organizations, from start-ups to large corporations, and to understand that effective management is essential for all employees in every type of organization.

- Improve our students' critical thinking skills. Why? Because research shows that employers want and value employees who can think critically.

- Enhance our students' understanding of current organizational issues that affect businesses, society, and individuals.

- Inspire lifelong learning about management that stretches beyond the duration of a single management course.

Our approach incorporates a balance between the following characteristics:

- Management theory and real life experience.
- Historical teachings and current trends and theories.
- Self-management and managing an organization.
- Providing information and allowing students to formulate their own questions.
- The four functions of management.

Critical Thinking

Increasingly used in business as a problem-solving tool, the critical thinking approach is a powerful analytical method that helps managers to consider intended and unintended consequences of behaviors on their teams, organizations, and communities. Organizations need managers who think independently, without judgment and bias; predict patterns of behaviors and processes; and ask the right questions: "How?" and "Why?" versus just "What?" in order to make effective and thoughtful decisions.

To support the teaching of critical thinking skills, we draw from several management theories such as systems thinking and Positive Psychology, providing students with systems archetypes, research, and management stories to illustrate the relationship between the facets of each theory. The management stories are based on real-life case studies and scenarios which we feel really help to demonstrate the application of critical thinking. Some of the characters you will meet include Chris Heppler, a new manager from the Dolphin Resort & Hotel, whose mission is to save a family business from bankruptcy; newly appointed chief of police Robin Richardson, who sets out to revolutionize the Metropolitan Police Department (MPD) in Washington D.C.; Julian Wales, group leader of Upstream Fisheries, whose goal is to increase productivity and motivation through leadership; and university friends Katy Johnson, Fred Arters, and Lisa Fang, who leave their respective jobs to begin a new entrepreneurial venture together.

We feel strongly that once the art of critical thinking is mastered, it can become a very powerful tool that can be applied to many different scenarios.

Take the issue of sustainability, for example. Events of the past few decades have resulted in increased demand for corporate accountability and social responsibility, even as managers are realizing the benefits of finding new ways to balance the needs of stockholders, employees, and communities. We believe that through critical thinking, young managers can contribute to building a more sustainable and responsible global marketplace by making logical decisions based on evidence and reason.

Content and Organization

Management incorporates a learning model based on critical thinking that captures the imagination of the students, transporting them into real-life work dilemmas to better prepare them for their future careers. The chapter content is current, timely, and structured to promote flow and accessibility.

Part One: Introduction

Two chapters introduce management, beginning with the challenges facing today's managers, followed by the origins of management. They are Chapter 1, "Management in the 21st Century," and Chapter 2, "The Evolution of Management."

Part Two: Sustaining: A Balanced Approach to Management

Four chapters discuss the environment within which managers work, in the context of critical thinking and sustainability. They are Chapter 3, "Critical Thinking for Managers," Chapter 4, "Organizations and Change Management," Chapter 5, "Diversity in a Global Economy," and Chapter 6, "Ethics and Social Responsibility."

Part Three: Planning

Three chapters cover decision making, goal setting, and strategy design, all within a framework of one comprehensive management story. They are Chapter 7, "Making Better Decisions," Chapter 8, "Setting Goals," and Chapter 9, "Designing Strategies."

Part Four: Organizing

Three chapters explore how managers organize structures, individuals, and teams, through a new management story. They are Chapter 10, "Organizational Structures," Chapter 11, "The Human Side of Management," and Chapter 12, "Managing Team Performance."

Part Five: Leading

Three chapters illustrate leadership within another original management story. They are Chapter 13, "Managers as Leaders," Chapter 14, "Understanding Individual Behavior," and Chapter 15, "Communicating and Motivating Others."

Part Six: Controlling

Two chapters discuss how managers exercise controls within a business environment, as portrayed by another innovative management story. They are Chapter 16, "Information and Operations," and Chapter 17, "Performance Development."

Part Seven: The Future of Management

The final chapter, "Entrepreneurship and Innovation," combines many elements of the previous chapters and follows the journey of a group of entrepreneurs and the challenges they face along the way.

Management Stories

For this book, we have created several rich, extended management stories that enable students to engage critically with the exciting complexities of the real world. These narratives serve two key purposes: 1) offer fully imagined characters and relationships that reflect actual challenges and opportunities that managers encounter, and 2) provide sufficiently rich contexts to practice critical thinking skills usefully, in ways that mimic actual workplace dynamics. We firmly believe that a sustained, compelling narrative helps students move beyond the mere memorization of terms and concepts to a critical understanding that lasts beyond the final exam.

Voices of Management

In the "Voices of Management" feature, we use interviews with real-life managers and leaders to augment the learning and storytelling style for each chapter. These interviews were researched or conducted during the development of the chapter, so as to increase the relevance of each manager's perspectives.

Research @ Work

In the "Research @ Work" feature, we balance key research in the field of management with current topics of interest to practicing managers by synthesizing leading academic journal research. Each "Research @ Work" box is accompanied by a "Critical Thinking in the Classroom" exercise to further promote active engagement.

Chapter Exercises

We have designed exercises and examples that activate management principles for college students to build valuable experience and increase skills through decision-oriented challenges that relate specifically to the business environment and student organizations. Students will have unparalleled access to management and leadership tools and resources that real-world professionals use to increase personal and team performance.

Key Terms

Throughout the chapter, key terms are defined within the narrative and highlighted where they first appear. The definitions of each key term are repeated in the "Additional Resources" section at the end of each chapter.

In Review and Self-Tests

For each chapter, we include traditional chapter review materials: a recap of the chapter content, organized by learning objective, and a self-test that includes multiple-choice, fill-in-the-blank, and short-answer questions, with an answer key.

Teaching and Learning Resources

Annotated Instructor's Edition With teaching notes prepared by author Jeffrey D. Houghton, the Annotated Instructor's Edition includes a Lecture Enhancer for each section of the book. Lecture Enhancers are section outlines designed to stimulate deeper discussion, energize the class, and improve learning through reinforcement and application.

WileyPLUS *WileyPLUS* is a research-based, online environment for effective teaching and learning that now includes an adaptive learning experience that guides students as they build their proficiency on topics. Based on cognitive science, *WileyPLUS* with ORION helps students learn by learning about them.

Instructor's Manual The *Instructor's Manual,* written by Jeffery Houghton, offers helpful teaching ideas. It has advice on course development, sample assignments, and recommended activities. It also offers chapter-by-chapter text highlights, learning objectives, lecture outlines, class exercises, lecture notes, and tips on using cases. Because the Instructor's Manual was written by one of the textbook's authors, it matches perfectly with the book.

Test Bank This comprehensive Test Bank, written by Jeffery Houghton and available on the instructor portion of the *Management 1e* website, includes true/false, multiple-choice, and short-essay questions that vary in degree of difficulty. All the questions are tagged to learning objectives and difficulty. The Respondus Test Bank allows instructors to modify and add questions to the master bank and to customize their exams. Because the Test Bank was written by one of the textbook's authors, professors can be assured that it is consistent with the structure and style of the book.

Practice Quizzes This online study guide, with quizzes of varying levels of difficulty written by Jeffery Houghton, helps students evaluate their progress through each chapter. It is available on the student portion of the *Management 1e* website. Because the Practice Quizzes were written by one of the textbook's authors, they match with each chapter of the book.

Pre- and Post-Lecture Quizzes Included in *WileyPLUS*, the Pre- and Post-Lecture Quizzes focus on the key terms and concepts. They can be used as stand-alone quizzes or in combination to evaluate students' progress before and after lectures.

PowerPoint Presentation Slides This robust set of Microsoft PowerPoint slides can be accessed on the instructor portion of the *Management 1e* website. Lecture notes accompany each slide.

Management in Action Videos One video per chapter presents the major themes of each chapter, both with the authors of the textbook and with industry insiders.

Lecture Launcher Videos Short video clips developed from CBS News source materials provide an excellent starting point for lectures or for general class discussion. Teaching Notes are available, with video summaries and quiz and discussion questions.

Personal Response System The Personal Response System (PRS) questions for each chapter are designed to spark classroom discussion and debate. For more information on PRS, please contact your local Wiley sales representative.

ACKNOWLEDGMENTS

The authors would like to thank all those people who have supported our efforts in writing this book. There are a plethora of people who contributed to making this text a reality. First, we'd like to thank Emma Murray for her amazing talents, as she served as the best content editor an author team could ever have. We also want to thank Shelley Smith for her above-and-beyond efforts to keep us on track, as well as keeping the book afloat throughout the writing process. We'd also like to thank our respective deans, Amy Hillman at Arizona State (W. P. Carey School of Business) and Jose "Zito" Sartarelli at West Virginia University's College of Business & Economics, for their support for this project. We'd like to thank our department heads (Gerry Keim, Arizona State, and Joyce Heames, West Virginia University) for their encouragement as well. Chris Neck would also like to thank Fred Corey (Vice Provost, Dean of University College and Director of the School of Letters and Sciences at Arizona State University) for his steadfast support and encouragement to excel in the classroom.

In addition, we would like to thank the fine folks at Wiley for bringing this book to fruition. Our dream of creating an innovative management textbook and ancillary package has become a reality due to our amazing, energetic and encouraging executive editor, Lise Johnson. She has been a champion for this book and our ideas (and there were many!), every step of the way. We can't thank her enough for her dedication and support. Susan McLaughlin, our talented developmental editor, pushed us to explore new ideas and kept us on track to write the best book possible. Brian Baker, our project editor, made sure that everything that needed to happen did indeed happen, and kept all of us on track. We appreciate all of his hard work, creativity, and attention to detail. We are also grateful to Maria Guarascio from Wiley.

Designer Tom Nery came up with an elegant and contemporary look for this book that visually brings to life our ideas more than we could have ever imagined. Valerie Vargas and Edward J. Dionne, our organized and efficient production editors, kept us on track. Jackie Hughes, editorial assistant, took care of a myriad of tasks during the development of the manuscript with an energy and enthusiasm that was inspiring. Kelly Simmons, our marketing manager, did a great job coordinating the promotion of our book, from organizing focus groups to overseeing all of the professor outreach efforts. And we would like to thank our families for "living without us" as we worked diligently on completing this textbook.

Additionally, there are a number of folks at Wiley that helped make this book happen, including:

George Hoffman, *Vice President and Executive Publisher*

Allison Morris, *Senior Product Designer*

Yana Mermel, *Editorial Operations Manager*

Elena Santa Maria, *Senior Media Specialist*

Amy Scholz, *Director of Marketing*

Mary Ann Price, *Senior Photo Researcher*

Marissa Carroll, *Marketing Assistant*

Harry Nolan, *Design Director*

Dorothy Sinclair, *Senior Content Manager*

Maria Danzilo

Rhea Siegel

We would also like to thank the following colleagues, who gave invaluable feedback at various stages of this book with their constructive feedback:

Manuscript Reviewers

Ryan Atkins, *University of Georgia*

Larry Able, *Johnson County Community College*

Allen Amason, *University of Georgia*

Lydia Anderson, *Fresno City College*

Verl Anderson, *Dixie State College*

Randall Andre, *Winona State University*

Bonnie Bachman, *Missouri University of Science and Technology*

Reuel Barksdale, *Columbus State Community College*

William Becker, *Texas Christian University*

Ellen Benowitz, *Mercer County Community College*

Tony Bledsoe, *Meredith College*

Queen Esther Booker, *Minnesota State University*

Paula Buchanan, *Jacksonville State University*

Harry Candler, *Valencia College*

Diana Carmel, *Golden West College*

Glen Chapuis, *St. Charles Community College*

Frank Christopian, *Brevard Community College*

Gary Corona, *Florida State College*

Brad Cox, *Midlands Technical College*

Suzanne Crampton, *Grand Valley State University*

Tom Craven, *York College of Pennsylvania*

Joseph DeFilippe, *Suffolk County Community College*

Gregory Dickens, *Sam Houston State University*

Michael Drafke, *College of DuPage*

Charlene Dykman, *University of St. Thomas*

Bob Eliason, *James Madison University*

Cassandra Elrod, *Missouri University of Science and Technology*

Rodney Erakovich, *Texas Wesleyan University*

David Feller, *Brevard Community College*

Mark Fenton, *University of Wisconsin*

Janice Gates, *Western Illinois University*

Terry Girdon, *Pennsylvania College of Technology*

Michael Gordon, *Rutgers State University*

Susan Greer, *Horry-Georgetown Technical College*

Kenneth Harris, *Indiana University Southeast*

Karen H. Hawkins, *Miami Dade College*

Linda Hefferin, *Elgin Community College*

Sherman Herbert, *Long Island University*

Nathan Himmelstein, *Essex County College*

Peter Holland, *Napa Valley College*

Phil Holleran, *Mitchell Community College*

Jenni Hunt, *Southern Illinois University*

Chip Izard, *Richland College*

David Jalajas, *Long Island University*

Janice Karlen, *CUNY, LaGuardia Community College*

David Kalicharan, *Nova Southeastern University*

George Kelley, *Eerie Community College*

Angela Kiser, *University of the Incarnate Word*

Susan Kowalewski, *D'Youville College*

John Leblanc, *Cedarville University*

Beverly Little, *Horry-Georgetown Technical College*

Emilio Lopez, *Eastfield College*

Denise Lorenz, *Wake Technical Community College*

Richards Lynn, *Johnson County Community College*

Ralph Marra, *Stony Brook University*

Daniel Marrone, *Farmingdale State College*

William Martello, *St. Edwards University*

David Matthews, *SUNY Adirondack*

Jeanne McNett, *Assumption College*

Catherine Michael, *St. Edwards University*

Amy Mickel, *California State University*

Elouise Mintz, *St. Louis University*

Susan Monaco, *Molloy College*

John Myers, *Jefferson College*

Anthony Narsing, *Middle Georgia State College*

Steven Nichols, *Metropolitan Community College*

Lisa Nieman, *Indiana Wesleyan University*

Lizzie Ngwenya-Scoburgh, *University of Cincinnati*

John Okpara, *Bloomsburg University*

Nathan Oliver, *University of Alabama*

Dianna Parker, *Ozarks Technical Community College*

Nicholas Peppes, *St. Louis Community College*

Alan Platt, *Florida Gulf Coast University*

Patrizia Porrini, *Long Island University*

Tracy Porter, *Cleveland State University*

Jessica Reyes, *Temple College*

David Ruderman, *University of Colorado*

Paul Salada, *Fayetteville Technical Community College*

Trent Salvaggio, *College of Charleston*

Kelly Schultz, *University of Wisconsin*

Michael Shaner, *St. Louis University*

Sarah Shepler, *Ivy Tech Terre Haute*

Marc Siegall, *California State University*

Lisa Slevitch, *Oklahoma State University*

Andrea Smith-Hunter, *Siena College*

Ann Snell, *Tulane University*

Rieann Spence-Gale, *Northern Virginia Community College*
Jeremy Stafford, *University of North Alabama*
Alice Stewart, *North Carolina A&T State University*
Charlotte Sutton, *Auburn University*
James Swenson, *Minnesota State University*
Marguerite Teubner, *Nassau Community College*
Ronald Thomas, *Oakton Community College*

Itoe Valentine, *Albany Technical College*
Maria Vitale, *Brandman University*
Anita Vorreyer, *Georgia Gwinnett College*
Robert Waris, *University of Missouri*
Dennis Williams, *Pennsylvania College of Technology*
Dilek Yunlu, *Northern Illinois University*
Mary Zellmer-Bruhn, *University of Minnesota*

Message Testing

Verl Anderson, *Dixie State College*
Lydia Anderson, *Fresno City College*
Bonnie Bachman, *Missouri University of Science and Technology*
Karen Bangs, *Cal Poly San Luis Obispo*
William Becker, *Texas Christian University*
Ellen Benowitz, *Mercer County Community College*
Edward Bewayo, *Montclair State University*
Tony Bledsoe, *Meredith College*
Melvin Blumberg, *Penn State*
Glen Chapuis, *Saint Charles Community College*
Frank Christopian, *Brevard Community College and Rollins College*
Thomas Craven, *York College of Pennsylvania*
Paul Croitoru, *Wilbur Wright College*
Joseph DeFilippe, *Suffolk County Community College*
Michael Drafke, *College of DuPage*
Cassandra Elrod, *Missouri University of Science and Technology*
Raymond Gibney, *Penn State*
Terry Girdon, *Pennsylvania College of Technology*
Nathan Himelstein, *Essex County College*
Peter Holland, *Napa Valley College*
David Jalajas, *Long Island University*
Susan Kowalewski, *D'Youville College*
Emilio Lopez, *Eastfield College*
Denise Lorenz, *Wake Technical Community College*

William Martello, *St. Edward's University*
Catherine Michael, *St. Edward's University*
Larry Michaelsen, *University of Central Missouri*
Elouise Mintz, *Saint Louis University*
Susan Monaco, *Molloy College*
Diane Nelson, *Washington State University*
Lizzie Ngwenya-Scoburgh, *University of Cincinnati*
Lisa Nieman, *Indiana Wesleyan University*
John Okpara, *Bloomsburg University of Pennsylvania*
Nicholas Peppes, *St. Louis Community College*
David Ruderman, *University of Colorado Denver*
Mike Shaner, *Saint Louis University*
Sarah Shepler, *Ivy Tech*
Marc Siegall, *California State University*
Lisa Slevitch, *Oklahoma State University*
Paul Smith, *Missouri University of Science and Technology*
Andrea Smith-Hunter, *Siena College*
Ann Snell, *Tulane University*
Marguerite Teubner, *Nassau Community College*
Ronald Thomas, *Oakton Community College*
Itoe Valentine, *Albany Technical College*
Tim Waid, *University of Missouri*
Dennis Williams, *Pennsylvania College of Technology*

Focus Group Participants

Elsa Anaya, *Palo Alto College*
Harry Bernstein, *Essex County College*
Kenneth Harris, *Indiana University Southeast*
Thomas Mobley, *Miami University Middletown*
Miles Smayling, *Minnesota State University*
Laurie Taylor-Hamm, *California State University*

Darrell Coleman, *University of Utah*
Randy Kidd, *Longview Community College*
David Wilhelm, *Metropolitan Community College*
Xia Zhao, *California State University*
Mitch Zimmer, *Penn State*

Principles of Management Summit Attendees

Bob Eliason, *James Madison University*
Michael Gordon, *Rutgers University*
Harrychand Kalicharan, *University of Maryland University College*
Nathan Oliver, *University of Alabama*

Paul Salada, *Fayetteville Tech Community College*
Trent Salvaggio, *College of Charleston*
Jeremy Stafford, *University of North Alabama*
Alice Stewart, *North Carolina A&T University*
Charlotte Sutton, *Auburn University*

Academic Advisory Board

Dean Cleavenger, *University of Central Florida*
William Furrell, *Moorpark College*
Melanie Hilburn, *Lonestar College*
Nathan Himelstein, *Essex County College*
Moronke Oke, *Grand Canyon University*

Paul Salada, *Fayetteville Tech Community College*
Mike Shaner, *St. Louis University*
Marc Siegall, *California State University*
Tim Waid, *University of Missouri*
Sheila Webber, *Suffolk University*

Private Industry Advisory Board

Robert Adler, *Terrapin Management*
Timothy Beres, *CNA*

Anthony Beverina, *Digital Sandbox*
Bobby Christian, *Impact Enterprises*

Kim Drumgo, *Blue Cross Blue Shield*
Jim Flowers, *VT KnowledgeWorks*
Pat Horner, *E5 Systems*
Chuck Jones, *Thundermist Community Centers*
Ken Kovach, *B. F. Saul Company*
Cathy Lanier, *Metropolitan Police Department Washington DC*
Camye Mackey, *B. F. Saul Company Hotel Division*
David Makarsky, *Gold Key/PHR*

Patrick Matthews, *Rackspace*
John McCann, *Partners in Performance*
Donald Norris, Ph.D., *Strategic Initiatives*
Richard Rodgers, *Resource Network*
Scott Shilling, *E5 Systems*
Keith Smith, *Riverside Health Long-Term Division*
Ric Stroup, *E5 Systems*
Michael Woodhead, *Gold Key/PHR*

Independent Industry Reviewers

David Attardi, Jennifer Barton, Frank Beamer, Timothy Beres, Anthony Beverina, Kimberly Carlson, Ph.D., Bobby Christian, Candice Clemenz, Ph.D., Alex Coburn, Chuck DeSantis, Melanie Flagg, Jim Flowers, Christine Gilmore, Joan Hirt, Pat Horner, Ph.D., Jack Kimbell, Benjamin Knapp, Ph.D., Cathy Lanier, Craig Lambert, Camye Mackey, David Makarsky, James Martin, Ph.D., Nancy Martini, Patrick Matthews, John McCann, Patrick McCarthy, Amy McNally, Joe W. Meredith, Ph.D., Jeffery Mitchell, Donald Norris, Ph.D., Steve Picarde, Jr., Richard Rodgers, Peggy Fang Roe, Steven Schneider, Starr Shafer, Ph.D., Scott Shilling, Thomas Snediker, Ric Stroup, Joel Williams, Ph.D., and Christopher Zobel, Ph.D.

BRIEF CONTENTS

CONTENTS

PART ONE
Introduction

5 | Diversity in a Global Economy   116

PART THREE
Planning

PART FOUR Organizing

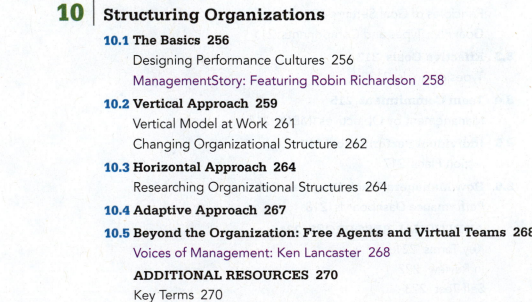

PART FIVE
Leading

15 | Communicating and Motivating Others 372

PART SIX
Controlling

PART SEVEN
The Future of Management

PART ONE

Introduction

CHAPTER ONE

MANAGEMENT IN THE 21ST CENTURY

CHAPTER OUTLINE

Learning Objectives

By the end of the chapter, you will be able to:

1.1 | Define management.

1.2 | Describe a manager's four major tasks: planning, organizing, leading, and controlling.

1.3 | Describe sustaining as a balanced approach to management.

1.4 | Correlate managers' tasks with the organizational roles that they play.

1.5 | Compare and contrast different types of organizations, managers, and the decisions they make.

1.6 | Explain the purpose of organizational values, mission, and vision.

1.7 | Demonstrate how focusing on skills and strengths leads to success as a manager.

ADDITIONAL RESOURCES

KEY TERMS
IN REVIEW
SELF-TEST
CHAPTER EXERCISES
ANSWER KEYS

JP Greenwood/Getty Images

INTRODUCTION

There is one light bulb inside a room. You are outside the room and unable to see if the light is on or off. In front of you, there are three switches, all of them set to an "off" position. Your challenge is to find out which of the three switches controls the light bulb inside the room—yet you are permitted to enter the room only once. How do you figure out which switch controls the light bulb?

What skills do you think you would need to solve this riddle? To solve the riddle, we need to adopt a new way of thinking that allows us to delve deeper beneath the surface and find the most rational solution. This is called **critical thinking**, which is the ability to diagnose situations and predict patterns of behaviors, which result in better decision making.

While there are a plethora of critical thinking definitions out there, most if not all include the ability of a person to use his or her intelligence, knowledge and skills to question and carefully explore situations to arrive at thoughtful conclusions based on evidence and reason. A critical thinker is able to put aside biases and view situations from different perspectives to ultimately improve his or her understanding of the world.[1]

Let's return to the above mentioned riddle. Using our critical thinking skills here involves asking the right questions, evaluating the information provided, gathering evidence, and drawing from our reasoning and existing knowledge to reach an objective and logical solution. When we follow this process, we have a greater chance of solving the puzzle. So what's the answer? Turn two of the switches on and leave one switch off, and wait about a minute.

Then, turn one switch from on to off. Enter the room and feel the light bulb. If the bulb is lit, then it is controlled by the switch you left on, obviously. If the bulb is warm but unlit, then you can deduce that it is controlled by the last switch you turned off. If the bulb is cold and unlit, then it is the switch that you left in the off position the whole time.[2]

Yet, critical thinking is not simply good for solving riddles; it can be applied to every facet of daily life, from trying to solve a math problem to assessing whether a job is right for you. In today's workplace, it is fast becoming one of the most important skills that employers look for in 21st-century managers.

Why is critical thinking important? A multitude of research shows that critical thinkers will enjoy more success in education, the workplace, and life in general because the more we can critically think, the more we can handle difficult situations and make the right decisions.

The following data supports the impact of critical thinking in the workplace:

1. When more than 400 senior human resources (HR) professionals were asked in a survey to name the most important skill their employees will need in the next five years, critical thinking ranked the highest—beating out innovation and information technology.[3]

Critical thinking The ability to diagnose situations and predict patterns of behaviors, which result in better decision making.

© Bart Coenders / iStockphoto

2. Senior executive-development professionals report that future leaders are lacking chiefly in strategic thinking skills—which are closely related to critical thinking skills.[4]

3. A 2009 study by Ones and Dilchert found that the most successful senior executives (compared to the less successful ones) scored higher on critical thinking skills.[5]

So, why are critical thinking skills so important for today's managers? The process of globalization brings about many new challenges for managers who need to adapt quickly and meet customer and market expectations. Managers in the 21st century recognize that decisions have complex cause and effects, and that they need to think critically by asking the right questions and suspending judgment or bias to solve problems. Some of the main challenges facing managers today are dealing with a fluctuating and uncertain economic climate, keeping up with the latest technological developments, identifying and hiring talent, keeping up with (and staying ahead of) the competition, managing diversity, and adapting to an ever-changing company culture. Managers have a multitude of decisions to make every day, and each of them must be made carefully to ensure a successful outcome. Critical thinking will help managers make the best choices for their companies; their roles involve the need to evaluate, analyze, and conceptualize information constantly to reach a clear understanding of the organization within which they are working. Successful managers apply their skills and strengths to diagnose and anticipate the consequences of their decisions. These judgment calls affect the performance of an organization; but equally important, these actions determine outcomes for both internal and external environments.

Given this contention that critical thinking is essential to our managerial lives, the question that arises is, how do we learn to think critically?

Critical thinking is both a concept and a process. Conceptually, *critical* refers to importance and *thinking* to analysis. Managers with strong critical thinking skills know what challenges and opportunities are important to spend time analyzing. One of the main roles of managers is to prioritize their time and resources to solve problems as they are happening and prevent similar problems from occurring in the future.

The process of critical thinking will provide you with the tools to visualize the many forces affecting any given business situation and how your decisions as a manager may have effects beyond the immediate situation. These forces change human, material, and information behaviors.

The generally accepted critical thinking methodology addresses this in seven steps (Figure 1-1): observe (recognize the behavior), interpret (understand the cause and effects of behavior), analyze (investigate the causes and effects of behavior), infer (propose paths to change behavior), evaluate (assess the consequences of changing behavior), explain (justify a change to behavior), and meta-think (consider the process used to propose this behavior change).[6]

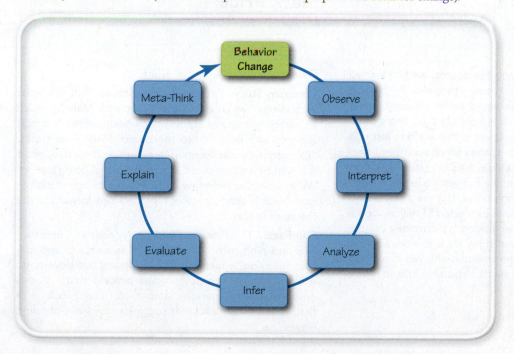

Figure 1-1

Seven Steps to Changing Behavior with Critical Thinking
Managers follow the seven steps of critical thinking, which include analyzing, observing, and evaluating, to initiate behavioral change.

LECTURE ENHANCER:

1.1 What Is Management?

✓ **Management** is the process of working with people and distributing an organization's resources to achieve goals efficiently and effectively.

✓ The four things every organization needs to be successful:
1) Access to resources
2) Effective leaders
3) Competent employees
4) Interested consumers/advocates

• **What do managers do?**
  o People-focused vs. technically-focused

• **How is management both art and science?**
  o People-focused duties are "art of management"
    ✓ Collaborating and communicating with a team to pursue a goal
  o Technically-focused duties are "science of management"
    ✓ Observing and gathering the necessary information to achieve set goals

For example, suppose that you are an HR manager specializing in employee relations. One day, a member of the company staff comes to you and accuses another employee of bullying. As you don't have all the facts, you must use critical thinking skills to investigate the real source of the problem. First, it is important to *observe* the situation objectively, suspending all bias and judgment. You might begin by conducting fact-finding interviews with other members of the staff to assess the level of bullying and take people's statements. This will help you to *interpret* the causes and effects of the bullying behavior on other employees. If you find sufficient evidence to establish that bullying is taking place in the workplace, then you might *analyze* these effects and *infer* a way to deal with the behavior. You could fire the bully, but what if this particular employee is excellent at his job? Maybe his absence would severely affect the rest of the team's performance. In such a case, you might *evaluate* the situation and assess the consequences of trying to change his behavior. You might *explain* to your boss why you believe that an attempt to change the behavior might be justified. Finally, you will need to *meta-think* by devising a process to instigate this behavior change. One option might include arranging a meeting with the accuser and the person suspected of bullying to see if some sort of resolution could be reached. There are many outcomes that could arise from this situation, and critical thinking will help you to find the most appropriate solution.

Over the course of this book, we will explore situations that are inspired by actual events. By the end, you will be able to recognize problematic symptoms, diagnose situations, recommend alternative paths, and make better choices using critical thinking tools. In the sections that cover each of the four management functions, stories span multiple chapters, offering you the chance to fully immerse yourself in situations that accurately reflect the complexity of real life and address challenges that you will find in the workplace.

1.1 | WHAT IS MANAGEMENT?

1.1 **Define** management.

Management is the process of working with people and distributing an organization's resources to achieve goals efficiently and effectively. Mark Price, CEO of Firewire Surfboards, consulted with a lot of people when deciding how to use the company's resources

Voices of Management

Mark Price,
CEO, Firewire Surfboards[7]

When I started with Firewire Surfboards, we had a small team with big, global dreams—to make the highest performance surfboard in the world using environmentally friendly materials. With this goal in front of us, our team came up with a way to get the best surfers in the world to just ride our boards one time and give us their feedback. They loved the product. One of the top surfers in the world starting surfing [with] our board, and we caught the biggest wave of our lives.

Sure, there were some tough times, but the team stayed motivated, and last year, our sales exceeded $1 million for the first time. It is great to finally be making good money, but the most fulfilling thing I have done in my life is to work with this team to raise awareness for the environment. We all feel like we are preserving the oceans and the sport we love so much.

Company Profile
Name: Firewire Surfboards
Founded: 2005 in Australia

Owner: Gordon "Grubby" Clark

Company Story: Firewire Surfboards uses "Future Shapes Technology" when designing surfboards. Materials such as parabolic balsa (a lightweight wood) are used to add strength and flexibility to the board. Mark Price states: "Our company was founded by surfers, and our daily effort is driven by and centered around the act of going surfing. We're stoked on what we've been able to accomplish in an incredibly short space of time and look forward to the Future of Shape."

Fun Facts: The Firewire philosophy features, "unorthodox and high-tech materials such as bamboo and carbon . . . and the fact that [the company] has developed a high-capacity computer-aided process that includes environmentally friendly lamination. The result is a featherweight product that suggests new ways of riding waves." ■

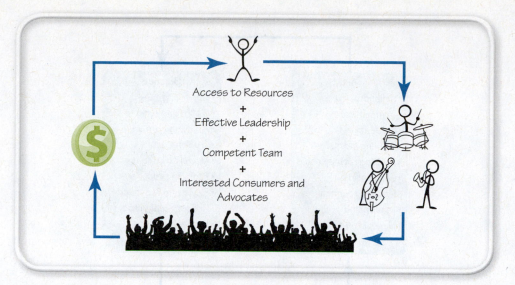

Figure 1-2
Success Factors for Organizations
Organizations need four main factors to be successful, including access to resources and effective leadership.

and successfully launch its new surfboard worldwide. Firewire achieved this goal by building a loyal team that came together during the tough times, running a financially healthy company that created jobs, protecting the environment by using renewable materials in their manufacturing process, and launching an innovative and direct appeal to customers.[8]

In this textbook, you'll learn and practice the critical skills that managers need to build and maintain healthy and sustainable organizations. Successful managers who understand and appropriately apply management principles can create positive change for people both inside and outside their organizations. These principles are constantly evolving to better meet the four things every organization needs to be successful: 1) access to resources—primarily money and talent, 2) effective leaders, 3) competent employees, and 4) interested consumers or advocates.[9] (Figure 1-2)

To demonstrate the difference that managers can make in building and sustaining successful organizations, we'll present managers and leaders who work in a variety of companies, as well as the people who work with them. Their challenges and successes, and the lessons they've learned from their careers, will introduce you to many different types of organizations and management styles. But most important, you'll gain an understanding of what managers do and how they help their organizations achieve their goals.

What Do Managers Do?

Every type of company needs managers—from scheduling film crews for a Hollywood movie to deciding who should be promoted to run a new Citibank branch office in Hong Kong, managers have a pivotal role in ensuring that decisions are made. Managers might conduct a web demonstration of the company's latest cell phone or choose which video games to put into production for next season. They might set up a conference to sell existing clients on the latest iPhone application or instruct volunteers on how to clean up a contaminated waterway. What would a day look like for one of these managers? Since we've already met him, let's take a look at a day in the life of Mark Price.

Mark Price's day is typical for a manager. He has a great deal of information to communicate, feedback to gather, decisions to make, meetings to host with clients, and motivation to offer the team. Price might begin his day surfing with the director of marketing and get to the office just before 9:00 a.m. But don't let the casual start to his workday fool you. His day quickly gets busy, and it usually includes six to nine meetings, calls to regional sales teams, web demos for new customers, a tour of a manufacturing facility, and a review of designs for next year's product offering. This sounds like a lot to fit into a workday, doesn't it? Managers are always busy, as many people rely on their feedback, perspectives, and decisions to complete their own daily tasks. As you will learn in this book, managers' activities are both people-focused and technically focused. Their tasks fall into four main

• **How do managers make a difference?**
o "3 P's" – people, profit, planet
   ✓ *People* – invest in wellness programs, training and education, retirement accounts, healthcare benefits, career advancement opportunities, and flexible environments
   ✓ *Profit* – ensure company is financially healthy so it can offer employees stable jobs, hire new college graduates, reward investors, and support local and global causes
   ✓ *Planet* – protecting and supporting the environment and community to ensure that the organization is still around in 100 years
o **Corporate Social Responsibility** is an organization's self-defined commitment to the health and well-being of the local and global community beyond its legal obligations
   ✓ Milton Friedman – maximize shareholders' wealth
o Managers that build sustainable organizations do so by balancing needs and results for people, profit, and the planet.

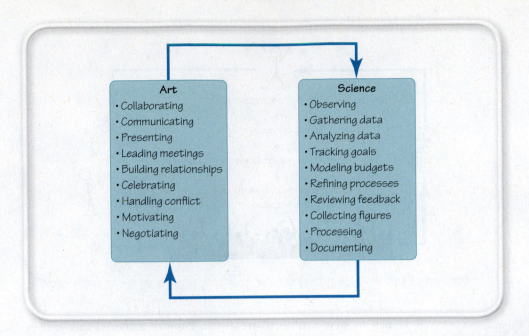

Figure 1-3
The Art and Science of Management
Management can be both people-focused (art) and technical (science).

Art
- Collaborating
- Communicating
- Presenting
- Leading meetings
- Building relationships
- Celebrating
- Handling conflict
- Motivating
- Negotiating

Science
- Observing
- Gathering data
- Analyzing data
- Tracking goals
- Modeling budgets
- Refining processes
- Reviewing feedback
- Collecting figures
- Processing
- Documenting

categories which will be discussed a little later in this chapter: planning, organizing, leading, and controlling.

How Is Management Both an Art and a Science?

Managers collaborate and communicate with their team to pursue a goal. This task could include setting up and leading monthly sales meetings to look at progress, organizing and hosting a celebration for an employee who has completed 10 years of service, or presenting the company's quarterly results to the media. We often describe this people-focused side of a manager's duties as the "art of management."

Another side of the management job is equally exciting but more technical. Tasks in this category might include testing a new manufacturing process to reduce energy costs at a plant, using an online program to track employees' progress on developing a new product, or reviewing customer feedback to decide whether to continue providing a service that is losing money. In general, we can think of these more technical activities as the "science of management." Of course, as Figure 1-3 demonstrates, effective managers must balance the people-focused and technical sides of their jobs.[10]

But managers don't just get things done. They have a unique opportunity to *make a difference* in organizations, communities, and people's lives. This is not a new phenomenon, but a long tradition that began over 100 years ago. Consider Ford Motor Company, known throughout its long history for its innovation of interchangeable parts, assembly-line techniques, and automobile mass production. On January 5, 1914, the company announced its plan to give $10 million to 26,000 employees in a profit-sharing program in recognition of the commitment made by its employees when the company began to run its plant 24 hours a day. The company released the following statement: "It is our belief that social justice begins at home. We want those who have helped us to produce this great institution and are helping maintain it to share our prosperity."[11] Managers have the ability to make a difference, not only within the boundaries of the company itself but within the lives of their employees.

How Do Managers Make a Difference?

Increasingly, managers focus on more than just profits. Instead, they look at how their practices affect their *triple* bottom line, defined as the "3 P's": people, profit, and planet.[12] Taking a balanced approach to these three areas has yielded great results by enabling companies to recruit happy and talented employees, increase revenue, create new jobs, and attract new customers. One company that has successfully adopted this approach is Patagonia, a firm headquartered in Ventura, California, that was originally founded in 1965 to sell mountain-climbing equipment, but expanded its products to clothing for outdoor enthusiasts in the 1970s.[13] The chief executive officer (CEO), Yvon Chouinard, the top manager in the organization, has established a very high standard for making a difference. Let's take a look at how Chouinard applies the 3 P's to Patagonia, in order to "cause the least harm while doing business."[14]

People How would you like a job where you could set your own work schedule, based on your passions and interests? Want to go mountain climbing on pretty days in the fall, or go skiing after a perfect snow? This is exactly what Patagonia asks its employees to do. Why? Because Chouinard knows that happy, loyal employees who are also expert outdoors people offer customers better service and product recommendations. That is good business. Management can make a difference through *people* by investing in wellness programs, training and education, retirement accounts, healthcare benefits, career advancement opportunities, and flexible environments where work is fun, engaging, meaningful, and productive. Patagonia even goes one step further. Any employee can volunteer his or her time with an organization that supports environmental causes, and Patagonia will pay full salary and benefits for the duration.[15] Clearly, if a company wants to make a difference, it must encourage and support its employees to make a difference for their community and the planet. A question worth asking here is, "This sounds great, but does it make good financial sense? Can you actually make any money with this philosophy?" Let's answer that next.

©John Norris / Corbis

Profit To make a difference through *profit*, managers make sure that their company is financially healthy so it can offer employees stable jobs, hire new college graduates, reward investors, and support local and global causes. We've established that Patagonia is a fun place to work that encourages its employees to do good things for the planet, but this goal is possible only if the company has the money to support its beliefs. Let's look at Patagonia's financial health. By delivering reliable products that people want and carefully managing its resources, the company earns over $300 million in revenues a year and profits of about $30 million annually. Chouinard has committed 10 percent of Patagonia's profits to fund grants to nonprofit organizations focused on the environment, so that's about $3 million each year. Of course, this all sounds remarkable, but now we may wonder: "Why is supporting or protecting the environment important to the health of the company? Isn't that just a 'feel good' thing to do?"

Planet It won't surprise you that Chouinard doesn't look at it that way. At Patagonia, protecting and supporting the environment is about ensuring that the company will be around 100 years from now, along with people to buy its products. Focusing on the planet is actually broader than simply caring about the environment. To make a difference for the *planet*, companies must concentrate on communities and causes as well. Organizations do not operate in a vacuum. They need vital local communities where their employees live, healthy towns where people can get services and goods from around the world, and clean, renewable resources to ensure that these communities can thrive over the long term.

By working to protect communities, causes, and the environment, Patagonia's managers are yielding significant value for the organization through increased employee morale, greater customer loyalty, and a positive public image. Consider this: Patagonia's managers "contract out to mills and factories worldwide, [and] they select companies that share their values, including fair treatment of workers, and environmentally sound business practices." This practice ensures that Chouinard's business philosophy of making a difference is carried out not just at Patagonia, but among its suppliers in communities all around the world.

"Making a difference" or "doing well by doing good" is the fulfillment of **Corporate Social Responsibility (CSR)**, an organization's self-defined commitment to the health and well-being of the local and global community beyond its legal obligations. However, not every organization or manager agrees that companies should be strongly socially responsible. U.S. economist Milton Friedman (1912–2006) famously said that the only responsibility of

Corporate social responsibility
An organization's self-defined commitment to the health and well-being of the local and global community, beyond its legal obligation.

LECTURE ENHANCER:

1.2 The Four Management Functions
✓ Henri Fayol's principles: planning, organizing, commanding, coordinating, controlling
✓ *Traditional view* – management functions are separate steps in linear process
✓ *Today view* – management functions are overlapping and interconnected
• **Planning** is the process of setting goals for the future, designing appropriate strategies, and deciding on the actions and resources needed to achieve success.
   o Working towards a specific destination is imperative to being successful in business.
   o Organizational planning has evolved from a centralized activity - performed only by a handful of top managers - to a process that starts with management's clear sense of the company's purpose, which it communicates directly to its customers, employees, and communities.
• **Organizing** is the process of orchestrating people, actions, resources, and decisions to achieve goals.
   o Once a plan is in place, a team of people must be assembled to implement the plan.

a for-profit company is to maximize the amount of money it can make for the stockholders who own a piece of the firm.[16] It was up to these individuals, then, to do good privately.

What is the mainstream view of U.S. business? In 2007, more than 300 of the *Financial Times* Global 500 companies submitted CSR Reports.[17] For Chouinard, the reason for reporting the firm's social responsibility was very clear: "Only those businesses operating with a sense of urgency . . . constantly evolving, open to diversity and new ways of doing things, are going to be here 100 years from now." With 67 percent of global businesses wanting to ensure a healthier society, it appears that Patagonia is not alone in its quest. Managers that build sustainable organizations do so by balancing needs and results for people, profit, and the planet.

1.2 | THE FOUR MANAGEMENT FUNCTIONS

1.2 | Describe a manager's four major tasks: planning, organizing, leading, and controlling.

Whatever managers do and however they make a difference, we can categorize their actions by using four distinct management functions. Henri Fayol (1841–1925) a French mining engineer and management theorist in the early twentieth century, proposed that managers had five administrative functions: planning, organizing, commanding, coordinating, and controlling.[18] In the 1970s, management writers streamlined these to four: planning, organizing, leading, and controlling. Since then, as work environments have evolved rapidly, managers' roles have expanded, but those four functions are still relevant when describing the work and responsibilities of managers today.

That said, managers today must embrace dramatic fluctuations in the economy, technology innovations, cultural dynamics in a global marketplace, and a changing workforce. The traditional view of management sees the management functions as separate steps in a linear process (Figure 1-4). Today, however, to ensure that organizations can respond quickly to change, managers need to see them as overlapping and interconnected. Why? To keep up with the speed of communication, production, and service, managers must often do all these functions simultaneously.

Planning

Planning The process of setting goals for the future, designing strategies, and deciding on the actions and resources needed to achieve success.

Working toward a specific destination is imperative to being successful in business. Defining what the organization wants to achieve and how it will get there is called *planning*. **Planning** is the process of setting goals for the future, designing appropriate strategies, and deciding on the actions and resources needed to achieve success. Amazon.com, for instance, took

Figure 1-4

Management Functions: Traditional View vs. Today's Approach
Today's approach to management takes a strikingly different tack from the traditional view of management functions.

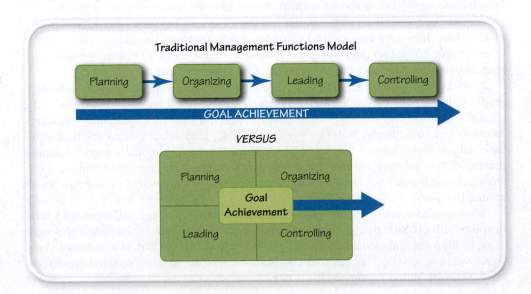

on a competitor, the giant low-price retailer Wal-Mart, by engaging in a price war for many consumer products.[19]

Organizational planning has evolved over time from a centralized activity performed only by a handful of top managers in the company to a process that starts with management's clear sense of the company's purpose, which it communicates directly to its customers, employees, and communities. When Howard Schultz founded Starbucks and began setting his goals for the company's future, his purpose was to create a "third place" between home and work, where the customer's experience was as important as the coffee. With a direction this clear, the smaller goals and strategies he needed to achieve became obvious. Starbucks stores feature relaxing music, comfortable chairs, and warm, inviting interiors that are consistent (though not identical) across thousands of stores. But even a successful company like Starbucks, if it loses its commitment to these fundamentals, can begin to feel disconnected from its customers, employees, and communities.[20]

When Starbucks suffered a decline in sales revenue, many wondered why. Many believe that the company's financial losses were due to their pricing strategy. As Starbucks grew more successful, it had replaced some of its cheaper (yet popular) products with more expensive ones. Many customers questioned the higher prices they were paying for sandwiches, bagels, and coffee, and simply went somewhere else. Starbucks tried to generate more revenue by selling knick-knacks and promotional music. Eventually this strategy had the unintended consequence of obscuring the idea of the "third place" experience. How did Starbucks respond? The company rehired Schultz, who had retired as CEO, and began reinventing the customer experience, but with a plan very different from the original one. Instead of a small number of top managers making decisions for thousands of others, Starbucks assigned individual store managers with the task of understanding their specific customers, employees, and communities and designing specific goals and strategies to meet their needs. This planning process, through which the company attempts to respond to local needs and keep a consistent product and service, will define whether Starbucks can reconnect with customers and increase its revenue.[21]

Mandel Ngan /AFP / Getty Images Inc

- **Leading** is the process of effectively motivating and communicating with people to achieve goals.
  o Understanding what motivates employee behavior and communicating effectively with a diverse team are even more critical for a manager when the team experiences a setback or disappointment.
- **Controlling** is the process of monitoring activities, measuring results and comparing them with goals, and correcting performance when necessary.

Organizing

Once the plan is in place, as a manager you might be asked to assemble a team of people to implement it. This is **organizing**, the process of orchestrating people, actions, resources, and decisions to achieve goals.

At the film animation studio Pixar, a manager will have a number of responsibilities when it comes to preparing for an upcoming film. This includes the following phases: voice talent begins recording; editorial team makes preliminary videotape; art department creates the look and feel of sets and characters; models are sculpted; sets are dressed; shots are laid out; shots are animated; sets and characters are shaded; lighting completes the look; computer data is rendered; and final touches are added. The organizing process for the $92 million film *The Incredibles*, for example, took hundreds of people years to complete and was critical to creating a movie that met Pixar's high quality standards and creative vision. Thanks to superb management, the project was kept within its time and budget constraints.[22]

> **Organizing** The process of orchestrating people, actions, resources, and decisions to achieve goals.

Leading

Planning and organizing are essential functions of management. Any seasoned manager will tell you, however, that things rarely go as planned, and that organizing is a continuous process. A manager's greatest opportunity to ensure that activities go as planned is through **leading**: the process of effectively motivating and communicating with people to achieve goals. When it comes to large projects, it can be difficult for employees and team members to realize the importance of their individual roles within the process. Understanding what motivates employee behavior and communicating effectively with a diverse team are even

> **Leading** The process of effectively motivating and communicating with people to achieve goals.

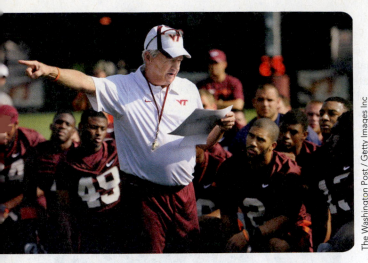

The Washington Post / Getty Images Inc

more critical for a manager when the team experiences a setback or disappointment.

Let's look at a sports example: October 25, 2007 was a cold, rainy Thursday night. The number 3–ranked Virginia Tech Hokies football team was playing Boston College's Eagles at home, and ESPN was televising the game to a national audience. Virginia Tech was winning 10–0, with two minutes left and serious hopes for a national championship season. But in those final minutes, Boston scored 14 points, upending the Hokies' aspirations. This was surely not the plan. What does a leader do in this moment?

In the locker room after the game, Virginia Tech's head coach Frank Beamer brought everyone together and said, "What happened out there tonight was a devastating loss, a heartbreaking loss. But people are going to remember this football team not by what happened out there on the football field tonight, but by how we finish this season. We can't make this loss everything. If we work hard, practice tough, and care for each other, we will make it through this."

It was a clear leadership moment. Beamer's powerful communications skills motivated the team by encouraging them to focus on what lay ahead. In business, dramatic moments like this are rare, but we can imagine a manager needing to motivate a sales team at an auto dealership after several months of a sluggish economy, or communicating the needs of a community hit by a hurricane by inspiring a group of volunteers to aid in cleanup efforts. Virginia Tech went on to win the Atlantic Coast Conference championship that year—an extraordinary accomplishment.[23]

Controlling

So, you have the *plan*. Everything is *organized*. You are *leading* the team. Things are getting done.

Are the right things getting done in the right way, and in the manner you anticipated and expected? Let's take another look at Pixar and how it ensures that its films get completed on time, within the budget approved during the planning process, and meeting the high quality standards that audiences expect. This function is **controlling**—the process of monitoring activities, measuring results and comparing them with goals, and correcting performance when necessary.

Just one small part of developing *The Incredibles* was producing the special effects, such as the dust that came up around the character Dash's feet as he ran. In fact, the movie required the design and creation of hundreds of such effects. The technical director creating the dust effect works in a team of 15–20 artists and has an immediate supervisor who reviews the team's work. The art director ensures the quality of the effect; the movie director approves the work as consistent with the artistic vision; and finally a producer makes sure that not too much time is spent developing any one effect. This balancing act ensures that the hundreds of effects are achieved in the film with the human and financial resources available to the producer and director. Knowing that things rarely go as planned or organized, managers on the film meet regularly (most likely every day) to review progress, analyze artists' renderings, make adjustments to production schedules, reallocate funding from one budget to another, and approve or redo work based on Pixar's quality standards.[24]

You should now have a solid understanding of the functions and examples that represent the things that managers do during any given workday. But if a manager understands the functions and effectively executes them, does that ensure long-term success for the organization? Not necessarily. Indeed, for the past decade, managers and management theorists have struggled to understand why organizations that have been run by competent managers have, nevertheless, failed.

Disney/Pixar/Photofest

1.3 | SUSTAINING: A BALANCED APPROACH TO MANAGEMENT

1.3 | **Describe** sustaining as a balanced approach to management.

Jeffrey R. Immelt, the CEO of General Electric (GE), begins and ends each annual meeting of GE's officers and senior managers by reemphasizing the company's primary principle of integrity: "GE's business success is built on our reputation with all stakeholders for lawful and ethical behavior."[25] Taking our cue from this principle, we will now discuss how a *balanced approach* to management can ensure that organizations are both effective in the short and long term. Immelt presents *unethical behavior* as one challenge that can prevent a company from surviving over the long term. Other threats faced by organizations include limited natural resources, uneducated workforces, rising energy costs, global political instability, and economic turbulence. Effective managers today understand these threats and approach every function in full consideration of the consequences of their decisions on their organization, community, and environment.

© PUNIT PARANJPE/Reuters/Corbis

This balanced approach to management is called **sustaining**, which means seeing, analyzing, and designing systems to achieve long-term organizational, community, and environmental health. Before managers decide on goals, coordinate activities, motivate their team to do great things, or measure how their organization is progressing toward achievement (the four functions), they must be sure that the balanced approach of sustaining underpins all their critical thought and decision making (Figure 1-5). As Immelt suggests, sustaining goes beyond corporate social responsibility and encompasses ethical decision making and behavior.[26] To create sustainable organizations, successful managers see the organization as a system that is connected to the internal and external environment, where their responsibilities are to think through, analyze, and design the systems of behaviors and processes that help the organization achieve its goals.

At GE, for example, Immelt, through continuous written and oral communications, charges the company's business leaders with the responsibility of maintaining integrity within their division's operations. This message is reinforced by incorporating global standards of integrity into business policies and practices as often as possible. GE plant managers and manufacturing leaders are held directly responsible for health, environmental, and safety issues within their divisions. Quarterly reports tracking key indicators such as accident rates are compiled into a master matrix that compares the performance of each plant. Because the master report ultimately is sent to Immelt for review, being in the bottom quartile of the rankings can be a great incentive for improvement.[27]

One goal of the *sustaining* approach to management is to create, build, and continuously nurture trust among customers, employees, and communities. Without this, organizations find it difficult, if not impossible, to operate. It's sobering to realize how much time and effort it can take to build trust, yet how quickly it can be lost. In 1994, Immelt's predecessor, Jack Welch, reportedly vomited shortly after hearing about a $300 million loss created by one unethical trader.[28]

Sustaining Seeing, analyzing, and designing systems to achieve long-term organizational, community, and environmental health.

LECTURE ENHANCER:
1.4 Management Roles
- Henry Mintzberg's managerial roles: interpersonal, informational, and decisional roles.
  - ✓ *Interpersonal roles* are when managers build relationships with people they work with and act as a public symbol for the many people they represent.
  - ✓ *Interpersonal roles* require managers to gather, assess, and communicate information to individuals and teams in support of the organization's values, mission, vision, and goals.
  - ✓ In *decisional roles*, managers are responsible for making judgments and decisions based on available information and analysis of the situation.
- Table 1-1: Henry Mintzberg's Management Roles

Figure 1-5
A Balanced Approach to Management
Managers must consider a sustaining approach before implementing the four functions of management.

Once we explore the evolution of management, we will fully discuss the balanced approach of sustaining, followed by the major management functions of *planning, organizing, leading,* and *controlling*. The four functions of management, based on the balanced approach of sustaining, provide the structure of this textbook. As our discussion of GE suggests, Jeffrey Immelt has demonstrated several of the roles and skills that managers must adopt to be successful decision makers. Let's explore another popular theory that focuses on organizing the discipline of management: roles.

Managerial roles Organizational expectations that determine the actions of managers, including *interpersonal, informational,* and *decisional* roles.

Interpersonal roles Managerial roles in which managers build relationships with the people they work with and act as a public symbol for the many people they represent.

Informational roles Managerial roles in which managers gather, assess, and communicate information to individuals and teams in support of the organization's values, mission, vision, and goals.

Decisional roles Managerial roles in which managers are responsible for making judgments and decisions based on available information and analysis of the situation.

1.4 | *MANAGEMENT ROLES*

1.4 | Correlate managers' tasks with the organizational roles that they play.

Henry Mintzberg (b. 1939), management researcher, strategy theorist, and author of *The Nature of Managerial Work*, has been observing managers in their organizational environments since the late 1960s. Based on his observations outlined in Table 1-1, he suggests that we can describe a manager's work most accurately in terms of **managerial roles**, or organizational expectations that determine the actions of managers, including *interpersonal, informational,* and *decisional* roles. In **interpersonal roles**, managers build relationships with the people they work with and act as a public symbol for the many people they represent. **Informational roles** require managers to gather, assess, and communicate information to individuals and teams in support of the organization's values, mission, vision, and goals. And in **decisional roles**, managers are responsible for making judgments and decisions based on available information and analysis of the situation. Mintzberg observed that managers were required to act as figureheads, analyze and monitor data, and understand information so the organization can pursue goals and maximize resources effectively.[29]

Table 1-1	Henry Mintzberg's Management Roles	
Categories	**Roles**	**Example Actions**
Interpersonal *Manager's actions that include symbolic, public-facing activities.*	Figurehead	• Speaking or being present at ceremonial events, hosting guests (e.g., vendors, clients, or potential employees)
	Leader	• Motivating and influencing employees' behaviors, train and mentor employees
	Liaison	• Keeping up information links internally and externally to the organization
Informational *Manager's actions relating to gathering, assessing, and communicating information.*	Monitor	• Gathering data and information, studying industry papers, reading reports, maintaining interpersonal relationships
	Disseminator	• Sending messages (email, text, and voice), writing memos, forwarding relevant information
	Spokesperson	• Making speeches, citing the organization's position on a subject
Decisional *Manager's actions that include making judgments and decisions based on situations and information gathered.*	Entrepreneur	• Identifying new business opportunities, nurturing new projects or initiatives, selling new business
	Disturbance handler	• Working through employee conflict, conducting efforts during a crisis, interpreting and responding to internal and external change
	Resource allocator	• Approving and setting budgets, deciding the beneficiaries of internal resources, setting priorities
	Negotiation	• Mediating discussions with unions, protecting the organization's interests, bargaining and agreeing to supplier deals

Source: Adapted from H. Mintzberg, *The Nature of Managerial Work* (Englewood Cliffs, NJ: Prentice Hall, 1980).

We will focus on examples of management functions throughout this book, but it is also notable to recognize the importance of Mintzberg's role theory and explore how it applies to managers.

1.5 | *MANAGERS AT WORK*

1.5 | **Compare and contrast** different types of organizations, managers, and the decisions they make.

Management's primary functions are consistent across organizations, but the types of organizations where they work can differ dramatically based on employee and manager attitudes, beliefs, decision-making styles, availability of resources, purpose, and tolerance of risk, to name just a few factors. Let's look into the different types of organizations and the internal and external forces that their managers negotiate.

Types of Organizations

An **organization** is an entity formed and structured to achieve goals. In Chapter 4, we will take an in-depth look at organizations, but as a form of introduction, let's look at some examples of sizes and types of organizations. In the United States, there are three business sizes: small, mid-size, and large, defined by the number of people they employ. **Small organizations** have fewer than 100 employees, **mid-size organizations** between 100 and 500, and **large organizations** more than 500 employees (see Figures 1-6 and 1-7). Represented in all these size categories are start-ups, multinational corporations, growth companies, non-profit organizations, and student organizations.

Start-up Companies While at Stanford University, Ph.D. computer science students Larry Page and Sergey Brin developed a set of algorithms as part of a research project that they called BackRub. BackRub allowed people to quickly find web pages relevant to their requests for information. The two friends soon realized that running a search engine required a huge amount of computer resources, as well as over half the university's bandwidth. In fact, their work regularly brought down Stanford's Internet connection.[30] However, thanks to the support of the university staff, they were able to gain access to

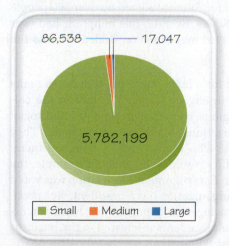

Figure 1-6
Organization Sizes by Number in the United States
Small businesses represent the greatest number of organizations in the United States.

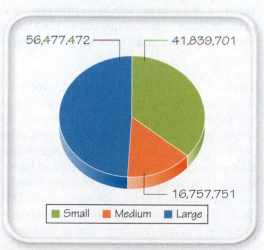

Figure 1-7
Organization Sizes by Number of Paid Employees in the United States
Small and large businesses have the greatest number of paid employees in the United States.

LECTURE ENHANCER:
1.5 Managers at Work
• **Types of Organizations**
✓ An **organization** is an entity formed and structured to achieve goals.
  ➤ *Small* organizations have fewer than 100 employees
  ➤ *Mid-size* organizations have between 100 and 500 employees
  ➤ *Large* organizations have more than 500 employees
✓ Figure 1-6 shows organization sizes by number in the U.S.
  ➤ Small businesses represent the most number of organizations in U.S.
✓ Figure 1-7 depicts organization sizes by number of paid employees in the U.S.
  ➤ Small and large businesses represent the most number of paid employees in the U.S.

Organization An entity formed and structured to achieve goals.

Small organizations Organizations with fewer than 100 employees.

Mid-size organizations Organizations with between 100 and 500 employees.

Large organizations Organizations with more than 500 employees.

✓ **Startup companies** are newly formed organizations with limited or no operational history.
✓ **Multinational companies** have operations in multiple countries, usually more than 10,000 employees, and design, develop, and sell products and services to customers all over the world.
✓ **Growth companies** increase its annual revenue faster than its competitors.
✓ **Non-profit organizations** are required by the IRS to reinvest all profits back into the organization, as opposed to distributing the money to investors or employees.
✓ **Student organizations** are groups formed to further engage students in the college experience through academic, political, religious, sports, environmental, and social action.
• **Types of Managers**
o Traditional organizations are formed hierarchically with a few senior managers at the top and a proportionally greater number of lower-level managers below who are responsible for daily tasks and actions of staff.

David Strick/Redux Pictures

the resources they needed to complete their study. It was out of this initial research project that Google was born. As the new search engine grew in popularity on campus, it began to attract more widespread attention. In August 1998, Brin and Page met with Andy Bechtolsheim, co-founder of Sun Microsystems, who gave the friends a check for $100,000. One month later, Page and Brin formed a company called Google Inc. and set up operations in a friend's garage. This is a classic story of a **start-up company**: a newly formed organization with limited or no operational history.[31]

Multinational Corporations Fast-forward to today and consider how Google has grown into a *multinational corporation*. A **multinational corporation** has operations in multiple countries, usually employs more than 10,000 people, and designs, develops, and sells products and services to customers all over the world. Today, you can access Google in nearly 40 languages, and it has almost 20,000 employees with offices in China, Europe, North America, Middle East, South America, and Russia.[32]

Growth Companies A **growth company** is an organization that increases its annual revenue faster than its competitors. Imagine managing a company that has 4,056 percent revenue growth in only five years. That is exactly what flat-panel TV manufacturer Vizio accomplished between its founding in 2002 and 2007. Vizio's revenues grew from $46 million to over $3 billion between 2004 and 2012. Founder and CEO William Wang talks about how the company got started and the importance of managing resources in a growth company: "We started the company with $600,000. I borrowed some money from my parents, mortgaged my house, and had a couple of friends who helped me. When I started, I worked 14 hours a day. I've cut down on that. I work 8 hours a day."[33]

Nonprofit Organizations **Nonprofit organizations** are required by the Internal Revenue Service (IRS) to reinvest all profits back into the organization, as opposed to distributing that money to investors or employees. Religious organizations, charities, arts organizations, and free health clinics are all nonprofits.[34] When Wendy Kopp was a senior at Princeton University, she wrote her undergraduate thesis about how she believed that recent college graduates would be interested in serving low-income communities if a teaching corps existed for them to join. After graduation, she raised $2.5 million to found Teach for America in 1990. In its first year, Teach for America signed up over 500 people to teach in six communities across the United States. By 2012, this nonprofit had over 10,000 volunteers and 28,000 alumni and had served over 3 million students across the country.[35]

Student Organizations It is not uncommon for a large university to have as many as 500 **student organizations**, groups formed to engage students further in the college experience through academic, political, religious, sports, environmental, and social action. Why are we highlighting student organizations in a management book? They provide great opportunities for college students who want to practice management, take on leadership responsibilities, and build their résumés. In 2006, for example, the Indiana University chapter of Business Careers in Entertainment Association was voted the best student organization on campus. This organization has a president, vice presidents, and directors and seeks "to provide internships, job opportunities, hands-on experience, and career information to undergraduate students interested in the business end of the entertainment industry." With almost 30 positions on its executive board, this organization gives students a number of opportunities to participate and get valuable management experience.[36] Throughout this book, we will explore student organizations through case studies and exercises in which you can investigate and practice management.

Start-up company A newly formed organization with limited or no operational history.

Multinational corporation An organization with operations in multiple countries, usually more than 10,000 employees, and designs, develops, and sells products and services to customers all over the world.

Growth company An organization that increases its annual revenue faster than its competitors.

Nonprofit organizations Organizations that are required by the Internal Revenue Service (IRS) to reinvest all profits back into the organization, as opposed to distributing that money to investors or employees.

Student organization An organization formed to engage students further in the college experience through academic, political, religious, sports, environmental, and social action.

✓ Managers are organized into *top managers, middle managers,* and *first-line managers*
 ➤ *Top managers* set the organization's direction and make decisions that impact everybody.
 ➤ *Middle managers* report to upper management and direct the work of first-line managers;

Table 1-2 Types of Managers

Types	Titles	Decisions	Time Frames
Top managers *Set the organization's direction and makes decisions that affect everyone.*	CEO President Executive director Director General manager Executive vice president	Establish partnerships Approve significant purchases Approve strategic plans Commit resources for new opportunities	Daily, weekly, monthly, quarterly, annually, decades
Middle managers *Direct the work of first-line managers and are responsible for divisions or departments.*	Vice president Assistant vice president Manager	Assign financial and human resources Allocate budget resources Set production and service offerings	Daily, weekly, monthly, quarterly, annually
First-line managers *Direct daily activities for producing goods and services.*	Associate director Project manager Coordinator Assistant manager Team leader	Set employee schedules Hire and promote staff Change processes to improve daily tasks and actions	Daily, weekly, monthly

Source: Adapted from T. V. Bonoma and J.C. Lawler, "Chutes and Ladders: Growing the General Manager," *Sloan Management Review* (Spring 1989): 27–37.

Types of Managers

Both the functions and roles of managers provide a thoughtful framework to consider the craft of management, yet most organizations refer to managers by *type*, so people inside and outside the organization can better understand each manager's decision-making power and scope of authority. Traditional organizations are formed hierarchically (like a pyramid), with a few senior managers at the top and a proportionally greater number of lower-level managers below who are responsible for daily tasks and actions of staff. This structure is designed to ensure that lines of communication, authority, and reporting responsibilities are clear to everyone.

We can organize managers as *top managers, middle managers, and first-line managers.* Each type makes decisions with different time horizons, from days to decades. **Top managers** set the organization's direction and make decisions that affect everybody. **Middle managers** report to upper management and direct the work of first-line managers; they are also responsible for divisions or departments. And **first-line managers** direct daily activities for producing goods and services. For example, a top manager might choose to partner with another company to launch a new software product, which could affect the organization for five to seven years or longer. A first-line manager at a retail store might settle on how to schedule employee work hours most effectively over a holiday season, which could have an impact on the organization for two to three weeks.[37] Table 1-2 provides a breakdown of types of managers, their typical titles, the kinds of decisions they make, and the time frames of those decisions.

1.6 | *VALUES, MISSION, AND VISION*

1.6 | Explain the purpose of organizational values, mission, and vision.

Up to this point, we've explored management's functions, roles, types, and success factors. Now let's put these components into context. Inside organizations, managers find and create forces that determine how people interact and what they are expected to do.

also responsible for divisions and departments.

> *First-line managers* direct daily activities for producing goods and services

o Table 1-2 provides a breakdown of types of managers, their typical titles, the kinds of decisions they make, and the timeframes of those decisions.

Top managers Managers who set the organization's direction and make decisions that affect everybody.

Middle managers Managers who direct the work of first-line managers and are responsible for divisions or departments.

First-line managers Managers who direct daily activities for producing goods and services.

LECTURE ENHANCER:

1.6 Values, Mission, and Vision
- An organization's *values, mission,* and *vision* shape decision making, product and services, beliefs, and relationships with people inside and outside the organization.
- *Values, mission,* and *vision* are the philosophical statements and beliefs managers use to allocate resources, provide consistent feedback to

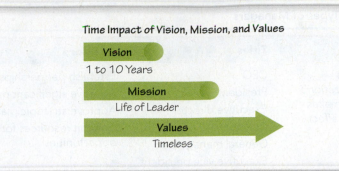

Figure 1-8
Values, Mission, and Vision Time Frames
Vision, mission, and values can be differentiated based on the time impact on the organization.

employees, make decisions, and foster organizational culture.
- Figure 1-8 organizes the three internal forces by the timeline of their impact on the organization.
  ✓ *Values* are beliefs that shape employee and organizational behaviors and are intended to be timeless.
  ✓ A *mission* is an organization's central purpose intended to generate value in the marketplace

Values Beliefs that shape employee and organizational behaviors and are intended to be timeless.

Mission An organization's central purpose intended to generate value in the marketplace (for-profit) or community (nonprofit) and which lasts for the life of the leader.

Figure 1-9
Comparing Kroger and Whole Foods Market Values
Kroger and Whole Foods Market's value statements tell us a lot about the company's priorities relating to service, products, and their relationship with the community.

These forces—values, mission, and vision—shape decision making, products and services, beliefs, and relationships with people inside and outside the organization. They provide consistent and predictable environments in which employees and clients can work and do business.

Values, mission, and vision are the philosophical statements and beliefs that managers use to allocate resources, provide consistent feedback to employees, make decisions, and foster organizational culture, which is the company's atmosphere and expectations that emerge in response to its philosophies and beliefs—"how we do things around here." In Figure 1-8, these three internal forces are organized by the time frame of their impact on the organization: timeless, lifetime of the leader, and 1–10 years.[38]

Organizational **values** are beliefs that shape employee and organizational behaviors and are intended to be timeless. As a consumer, can we experience the effect of different company values? Can you see the differences between the two companies shown in Figure 1-9?

Mission is an organization's central purpose, intended to generate value in the marketplace (for-profit) or community (nonprofit), which lasts for the life of the leader. In Figure 1-10, we look at two companies with different missions operating in the same industry. Now, think about Starbucks Coffee. This organization sells strong, bold coffee for an extraordinary price, gives its customers a place to sit and be comfortable for hours without

Kroger	Whole Foods Market
Honesty – Doing the right thing and telling the truth	Selling the highest-quality natural and organic products available
Integrity – Living our values in all we do, united approach to how we do business and treat each other	Satisfying and delighting our customers, supporting team member happiness and excellence
Respect – Valuing opinions, property, and perspectives of others	Creating wealth through profits and growth, caring about our communities and our environment
Diversity – Reflecting a workplace that includes a variety of people from different backgrounds and cultures, diversity of opinions and thoughts	Creating ongoing win-win partnerships with our suppliers
Safety – Watching out for others, being secure and safe in you workplace	Promoting the health of our stakeholders through healthy eating education
Inclusion – Your voice matters, working together works, encouraging everyone's involvement, being the best person you can be	

Dunkin' Donuts

Starbucks Coffee

Joe Raedle / Getty Images

© Massimo Borchi / Corbis

Mission Statements

Deliver innovative product choices at the right price served fresh, meeting the needs of people who are busy living.

To inspire and nurture the human spirit—one person, one cup, and one neighborhood at a time.

Figure 1-10

Compare Starbucks Coffee and Dunkin' Donuts Missions

Starbucks Coffee and Dunkin' Donuts missions are quite different. This has led each company to create unique products and services that attract different kinds of customers.

interruption, and puts inspirational quotes on its cups to give customers something to ponder. Consider the traditional coffee shop business model before Starbucks entered the market. This model offers customers regular coffee, minimal store atmosphere, hard seats, and grab-and-go food that's ultra-convenient. It's Dunkin' Donuts. What's the difference?[39] Mission.

By consistently holding to the values of the company, the organization's leadership defines its mission and projects its **vision**, a description of an optimal future 1–10 years from now. Let's look at Microsoft and Apple Computers, two companies that compete and have two distinct stated visions for their companies (Figure 1-11). How do these differing visions change the products and services that you have seen from each company? Does each company seem to be achieving its vision?

Values, mission, and vision are the forces that managers, depending on their type, can control and shape directly. What are the forces that are outside of managers' control that determine the conditions in which companies must operate?

or community, which lasts for the life of the leader.

✓ A *vision* is a description of an optimal future one to ten years from now.

• Values, mission, and vision are the forces that managers can directly control and shape.

Vision A description of an optimal future 1–10 years from now.

Microsoft

Apple

Torian Dixon/iStockphoto

cotesbastien/iStockphoto

Vision Statements

Create experiences that combine the magic of software with the power of Internet services across a world of devices.

To make a contribution to the world by making tools for the mind that advance humankind.

Figure 1-11

Compare Microsoft and Apple's Visions

Visions shape how companies innovate, where they spend their resources, and what customers attract. Can you connect the difference in these two companies' vision statements and their products?

Effectiveness The level to which people or organizations achieve agreed-upon goals.

Efficiency Using the smallest amount of resources to achieve the greatest output.

effectiveness and efficiency through other people and systems, and they are successful when they accomplish this objective.
✓ **Effectiveness** is the level to which people or organizations achieve agreed-upon goals.
✓ **Efficiency** is using the smallest amount of resources to achieve the greatest output.
  ➤ Organizations and managers need both of these elements to be successful, but must keep a balance between the two.
• **Skills** are the degree to which a person can effectively and efficiently complete a particular task, interaction, or process.
  ✓ Three types of skills determine managers' success or failure in carrying out their responsibilities – *conceptual, technical,* and *relational.*
  ✓ Figure 1-12 shows how the type of manager you are affects how important each skill is to accomplishing your goals.
    ➤ *Conceptual skills* are the ability to think through complex

Skills The talents or abilities that enable a person to complete a particular task, interaction, or process effectively and efficiently.

1.7 | SUCCESSFUL MANAGEMENT

1.7 | Demonstrate how focusing on skills and strengths leads to success as a manager.

We have looked at what managers *actually* do, but it is equally important to discuss what they *should* do. Managers are expected to continuously seek ways to increase effectiveness and efficiency through other people and systems, and they are successful when they accomplish this objective. **Effectiveness** is the level to which people or organizations achieve agreed-upon goals, and **efficiency** means using the smallest amount of resources to achieve the greatest output.

Organizations and managers need both effectiveness and efficiency to be successful, but it is the balance of these two ideals that managers constantly monitor. Let's look at an example of a start-up company that sells specialty rugby shirts and wants to conduct 100 percent of its business online. With very limited financial resources, the company's management has to make a critical decision of balancing efficiency and effectiveness when it comes to developing its website. The most *efficient* process to build the company's website might be to hire a friend who designs websites on the weekends. With this strategy, the company would have a marginal website operational in a couple of weeks that does not have the attractive design qualities of its competitors, but as it has been built for almost nothing, the company can start making money in a very short period of time. The most *effective* process to launch the company's website might be to hire a professional design firm that will also help make sure the website is recognized by search engines, such as Google, Yahoo!, and Bing. This could cost 10 times more money and take a few months to launch, but the expected revenue would be much higher. This is an example of one of the classic dilemmas that managers face.

Many organizations believe that managers can achieve superior results if they learn how to do their jobs better. GE spends almost $1 billion every year on developing its managers; its top 191 managers have spent 12 months in training over the past 15 years. Jack Welch, former CEO of the firm, once said, "At GE, our core product is management. We build great managers around here. Now all I need to do is find them good businesses to run."[40] Only a few organizations can afford to spend a billion dollars on training their managers, but most approach developing their managers in similar ways. Let's look at building skills and focusing on strengths as a common, fundamental process to developing successful management practices.

Skills

Skills are talents or abilities that enable a person to complete a particular task, interaction, or process effectively and efficiently. Three types of skills determine managers' success or failure in carrying out their responsibilities, whether at the top level of the firm or on the front lines: *conceptual, technical,* and *relational.* Although the type of manager you are affects how important each skill is to accomplishing your goals, all managers use all three of these skills, as shown in Figure 1-12.

Figure 1-12
Skills Required by Types of Managers
Top managers need a higher level of conceptual skills than middle or first-line managers; middle managers require a greater degree of relational skills; and first-line managers need to possess more technical skills.

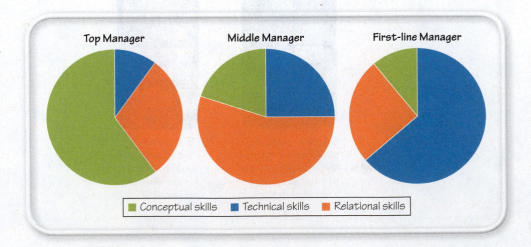

Top Manager | Middle Manager | First-line Manager

■ Conceptual skills ■ Technical skills ■ Relational skills

Let's consider how these skills apply. **Conceptual skills** are the ability to think through complex systems and problems. How hard could it be to make *one* surfboard? At Firewire Surfboard, it takes 14 days, 10 suppliers from five countries, and 20 employees. For the business to be profitable and provide customers with a good price, management has to see the big picture and at the same time be able to think through the details at each point in the process.

Suppose one of Firewire's suppliers, let's call it Float My Boat, shared Firewire's commitment to making a difference. It offers an ecologically sound foam product that costs $25 more per surfboard than competitors' components—a substantial difference. Most managers would likely seek out cheaper foam. But suppose Firewire's managers did some research and found that Float My Boat offers three additional products that they also can use, cutting the cost difference to only $5. Using conceptual skills, they can make a decision compatible with their organization's desire to support environmental causes and keep profits at a healthy level.

Technical skills are the ability to perform job-specific tasks. Imagine that Starbucks has just hired you to be a store manager. After your first three months, you will go through a seven-week management training program.

What skills will you acquire there? Training may include learning how to do the following:

- Access the company intranet
- Complete financial reports
- Hire and train new employees
- Ensure quality for the store's 87,000 possible beverage combinations
- Schedule employees
- Organize inventory
- Clean and maintain the expensive beverage machines and equipment
- Respond to customer concerns and employee complaints
- Complete and submit quarterly performance reports

These are a few of the job-specific tasks that managers at Starbucks might be expected to perform.

Relational skills are the ability to collaborate and communicate with others. Ever wonder who founded Birkenstocks USA, the company that imports those comfortable sandals? It was a woman named Margot Fraser, who first saw the odd-looking shoes on a trip to Europe. She got a $6,000 loan from the bank to start her company and by 2009 had turned it into a $50 million business. How? Fraser credits her company's success to the relationships that she built with the manufacturing company in Germany.[41]

When Birkenstock USA was just getting started and was distributing sandals through a few health stores across the country, the company's manufacturers in Germany were reluctant to make any changes or upgrades to their shoes. Unable to convince Mr. Birkenstock that purple suede, popular in the United States at the time, was a good idea, she built a relationship with a woman on the manufacturing floor, who made sure that Fraser got her wish and manufactured purple suede Birkenstocks for the U.S. market. Just imagine the impact of a relationship with *one person* on the manufacturing floor halfway around the world.[42] This is the power of collaborating and communicating.

Strengths

Strengths are the skills in which managers demonstrate the greatest aptitude. After more than 30 years of research, Marcus Buckingham and Donald O. Clifton found that professionals who focused primarily on their strengths were more successful than those who spent more time trying to fix their weaknesses. In their book *Now, Discover Your Strengths*, they offer the example of legendary composer and songwriter Cole Porter.

Conceptual skills The ability to think through complex systems and problems.

systems and problems; can make a decision compatible with their organization's desire to support environmental causes and keep profits at a healthy level.

➤ *Technical skills* are the ability to perform job-specific tasks.
➤ *Relational skills* are the ability to collaborate and communicate with others.

Technical skills The ability to perform job-specific tasks.

- **Strengths** are the skills in which managers demonstrate the greatest aptitude.
  ✓ Research demonstrates that managers who focus on the skills at which they are already very good will someday have the opportunity to be great.
  ✓ Managers must recognize and understand their own key strengths and endeavor to ascertain and nurture the strengths of others.
  ✓ "Positive Psychology" explores ways to help people recognize their positive traits or strengths, and nurture them to their full potential.

Relational skills The ability to collaborate and communicate with others effectively.

Steve Finn / Getty Images

➤ Can be used as a tool
to enhance the working
environment by encouraging,
rewarding, and motivating
employees.

✓ Research has shown that there is
a notable shift in organizations
from a traditional problem-solving
model to a more sustainable one.

• **Systems Thinking**

✓ Managers have the potential to
take a systematic approach to
critical thinking, which will change
the mindset, adjust behaviors,
and use existing skills to enhance
strengths within.

✓ Applying a systems approach
to critical thinking and adopting
the principles of Positive
Psychology will give managers
a clearer understanding of how

Positive Psychology A field of
psychology that helps people
define and cultivate their personal
strengths, so they can thrive and
flourish with a sense of purpose
through challenging work.

the organization functions, make
better decisions, and have the
ability to encourage and motivate
their employees, which in turn
will help boost morale, increase
loyalty, and make the workplace
happy and productive.

Porter's strength was his ability to write wonderful melodies and perfect lyrics. However, creating believable characters and plots in his Broadway musicals were not his strong suit. Many people choose to work hard on improving their weaknesses, but not Porter. Instead, Porter pursued an aggressive yet counterintuitive strategy for managing his weaknesses. Porter believed that if he focused on refining his skills as a songwriter, audiences would overlook his weaknesses. His strategy worked. Driven by sophisticated melodies and clever lyrics as opposed to well-developed plots and characters, Porter's musicals (including *Anything Goes* and *Kiss Me Kate*) have become classics. Research demonstrates that managers who focus on the skills at which they are already very good at will someday have the opportunity to achieve greatness.[43]

As we have explored, management is both an art and a science; where managers must learn to juggle people skills with technical skills. Indeed, we might say that the real skill in management is achieving a balance between these two major functions. To do this, managers must recognize and understand their own key strengths and endeavor to ascertain and nurture the strengths of others. So, how can managers apply this skill to bringing out the best in themselves and their employees?

Over the past 10 years, a new branch of psychology has emerged. First introduced by Martin Seligman and Mihaly Csikszentmihalyi, **Positive Psychology** explores ways to help people recognize their positive traits or strengths and nurture them to their full potential. Traditionally, psychology has been rooted in mental illness; that is, looking for what is wrong with a patient and then attempting to fix the problem. However, Seligman and Csikszentmihalyi, believed that psychology could be used in a different way: to help people define and cultivate the strengths within them, and thrive and flourish as a result.

Dr. Barbara Fredrickson, a research psychologist in the study of positive emotions and an advocate of Positive Psychology, has created a "broaden-and-build" positive psychological approach.[44] According to this theory, positive emotions such as joy and happiness serve to broaden or expand our awareness and encourage us to think more creatively, while negative emotions actually narrow or restrict our behavior. More and more organizations are beginning to explore the potential of Positive Psychology as a tool to enhance the working environment by encouraging, rewarding, and motivating employees.[45]

Arguably, one of the more difficult challenges that managers have to face since the inception of globalization is a change in mindset. With this new era comes a need for a new vision: to find unique ways to tackle this ever-changing world and become less reliant on the "old ways" of doing things. Managers need to make room for a different paradigm about how the world works. But changing our way of thinking does not happen overnight. Indeed, any kind of change is often perceived as a threat. In a sense, our mindset is programmed to maintain a deep set of beliefs that form our perspective about the world around us. In the past, organizations relied solely on a problem-solving model that focused on "fixing" people's weaknesses rather than building on their strengths. However, as many companies have discovered, in an environment that is constantly in flux, this model has its limitations. The latest organizational behavioral research has shown that there is a notable shift in organizations from a traditional problem-solving model to a more sustainable one. Although shifting our way of thinking is a challenging process, it is entirely possible.

The environmental scientist, teacher, and writer Donella Meadows believed that we all have the power to "self-organize" or change and create new systems; and the ability to discover areas of intervention in a system to instigate shifts and changes. By identifying "leverage points" in the system (i.e., the areas within a system), "where a small change could lead to a large shift in behavior," we all have the ability to mold and adjust the system.[46] With the help of new management theories such as Systems Thinking, which we will explore in Chapter 3, we have the potential to take a systemic approach to critical thinking, which will help to change our mindset, adjust our behaviors, and use our existing skills to enhance strengths within ourselves and others.

© Hero Images / Corbis

As we discuss in future chapters, by applying a systems approach to critical thinking and adopting the principles of Positive Psychology, managers will have a clearer understanding of how the organization functions, make better decisions, and have the ability to encourage and motivate their employees, which in turn will help to boost morale, increase loyalty, and make the workplace a happy and productive one. All of this will have a notable impact on both the internal and external environment, as well as the ever-important bottom line.

Throughout this text, we are presenting a number of case studies and scenarios to demonstrate the application of critical thinking. Some of the characters you will meet include Chris, a new manager from the Dolphin Resort and Hotel, whose mission is to save a family business from bankruptcy; newly appointed chief of police Robin Richardson, who sets out to revolutionize the Metropolitan Police Department (MPD) in Washington D.C.; Julian Wales, group leader of Upstream Fisheries, whose goal is to increase productivity and motivation through leadership; and university friends Katy, Fred, and Lisa, who leave their respective jobs to begin a new entrepreneurial venture together.

By now, you should have a fundamental understanding of management, where managers work, the forces they contend with inside and outside the organization, and how each person can seek to become a more successful manager. It's worth repeating that managers are expected to boost effectiveness and efficiency for their organizations. As they do, managers face opportunities and challenges each day that they need to overcome.

As you continue through this textbook and explore new management concepts, theories, and practices, remember to ask yourself: "Wherever I'm working, how might I as a manager *make a difference* for my organization, the local and global community, and the people I have an opportunity to work with?" That's where successful management begins.

Case**Snapshot**

Chapter 1 Case: Management in the 21st Century: Facebook can be found on pg. 462

ADDITIONAL RESOURCES

KEY TERMS

Conceptual skills The ability to think through complex systems and problems. (p. 21)

Controlling The process of monitoring activities, measuring results and comparing them with goals, and correcting performance when necessary. (p. 12)

Corporate social responsibility An organization's self-defined commitment to the health and well-being of the local and global community, beyond its legal obligation. (p. 9)

Critical thinking The ability to diagnose situations and predict patterns of behaviors, which result in better decision making. (p. 4)

Decisional roles Managerial roles in which managers are responsible for making judgments and decisions based on available information and analysis of the situation. (p. 14)

Effectiveness The level to which people or organizations achieve agreed-upon goals. (p. 20)

Efficiency Using the smallest amount of resources to achieve the greatest output. (p. 20)

First-line managers Managers who direct daily activities for producing goods and services. (p. 17)

Growth company An organization that increases its annual revenue faster than its competitors. (p. 16)

Informational roles Managerial roles in which managers gather, assess, and communicate information to individuals and teams in support of the organization's values, mission, vision, and goals. (p. 14)

Interpersonal roles Managerial roles in which managers build relationships with the people they work with and act as a public symbol for the many people they represent. (p. 14)

Large organizations Organizations with more than 500 employees. (p. 15)

Leading The process of effectively motivating and communicating with people to achieve goals. (p. 11)

Management The process of working with people and distributing an organization's resources to achieve goals efficiently and effectively. (p. 6)

Managerial roles Organizational expectations that determine the actions of managers, including *interpersonal*, *informational*, and *decisional* roles. (p. 14)

Middle managers Managers who direct the work of first-line managers and are responsible for divisions or departments. (p. 17)

Mid-size organizations Organizations with between 100 and 500 employees. (p. 15)

Mission An organization's central purpose intended to generate value in the marketplace (for-profit) or community (nonprofit) and which lasts for the life of the leader. (p. 18)

Multinational corporation An organization with operations in multiple countries, usually more than 10,000 employees, and designs, develops, and sells products and services to customers all over the world. (p. 16)

Nonprofit organizations Organizations that are required by the Internal Revenue Service (IRS) to reinvest all profits back into the organization, as opposed to distributing that money to investors or employees. (p. 16)

Organization An entity formed and structured to achieve goals. (p. 15)

Organizing The process of orchestrating people, actions, resources, and decisions to achieve goals. (p. 11)

Planning The process of setting goals for the future, designing strategies, and deciding on the actions and resources needed to achieve success. (p. 12)

Positive Psychology A field of psychology that helps people define and cultivate their personal strengths, so they can thrive and flourish with a sense of purpose through challenging work. (p. 22)

Relational skills The ability to collaborate and communicate effectively with others. (p. 21)

Skills Talents or abilities that enable a person to complete a particular task, interaction, or process effectively and efficiently. (p. 20)

Small organizations Organizations with fewer than 100 employees. (p. 15)

Start-up company A newly formed organization with limited or no operational history. (p. 16)

Student organization An organization formed to engage students further in the college experience through academic, political, religious, sports, environmental, and social action. (p. 16)

Sustaining Seeing, analyzing, and designing systems to achieve long-term organizational, community, and environmental health. (p. 13)

Technical skills The ability to perform job-specific tasks. **(p. 21)**
Top managers Managers who set the organization's direction and make decisions that affect everybody. **(p. 17)**

Values Beliefs that shape employee and organizational behaviors and are intended to be timeless. **(p. 18)**
Vision A description of an optimal future 1–10 years from now. **(p. 19)**

IN REVIEW

1.1 | Define management.

Management is the process of working with people and distributing resources to achieve goals efficiently and effectively. *Effectiveness* is the level to which people or organizations achieve agreed-upon goals, and *efficiency* is using the smallest amount of resources to achieve the greatest output.

1.2 | Describe a manager's four major tasks: planning, organizing, leading, and controlling.

The four management functions are planning, organizing, leading, and controlling. *Planning* is defining what the organization wants to achieve, which includes setting goals for the future, designing strategies, and deciding the actions and resources needed to achieve success. *Organizing* means orchestrating people, actions, resources, and decisions to achieve goals. Managers have the greatest opportunity to ensure that events occur as planned or better than planned by *leading*, effectively motivating and communicating with people to achieve goals. Asking whether the right things are getting done in the right way and in the manner that you anticipated is *controlling*, which includes measuring and monitoring activities, comparing results with goals, and correcting performance.

1.3 | Describe sustaining as a balanced approach to management.

The purpose of the *sustaining* approach to management is sustainable organizations, achieved through managers' ability to see, analyze, and design systems that seek organizational, community, and environmental stability.

1.4 | Correlate managers' tasks with the organizational roles that they play.

Mintzberg identifies three categories of management roles: *interpersonal*, including symbolic, public-facing activities; *informational*, gathering, assessing, and communicating information; and *decisional*, making judgments and decisions based on situations and gathered information.

1.5 | Compare and contrast different types of organizations, managers and the decisions they make.

An organization is an entity formed and structured to achieve goals. It can be a small, mid-sized, or large company. A variety of different types of organizations and businesses can fall into these various size categories. A *start-up company* is a newly formed organization. A *growth company* increases annual revenue faster than its competitors. *Multinational corporations* usually have thousands of employees and operate all around the world. *Nonprofit organizations* are required by the IRS to reinvest all profits back into the organization, as opposed to distributing it to investors or employees. Examples include religious organizations, charities, arts organizations, and free health clinics. *Student organizations* are intended to engage students further in the college experience. Their focus can be academic, political, religious, sports, environmental, or social. *Top managers* set the organization's direction and make decisions that affect everybody; *middle managers* direct the work of first-line managers and are responsible for divisions or departments; and *first-line managers*, who direct daily activities for producing goods and services.

1.6 | Explain the purpose of organizational values, mission, and vision.

Organizational *values* are beliefs that shape employee and organizational behaviors and are intended to be timeless. *Mission* is an organization's central purpose intended to generate value in the marketplace (for-profit) or community (nonprofit) and lasts for the life of the leader. By consistently holding to the values of the company, the organization's leadership defines the mission and sets forth a *vision*, a descriptive picture of an optimal future 1–10 years from now.

1.7 | Demonstrate how focusing on skills and strengths leads to success as a manager.

Skills are talents or abilities that enable a person to complete a particular task, interaction, or process effectively and efficiently. Three types of management skills are conceptual, technical, and relational. *Strengths* are skills for which managers demonstrate the greatest aptitude. Research demonstrates that managers who focus on existing strengths earn the opportunity to be great in those skills one day.

SELF-TEST

1.1 | Define management

1. *Management* is the process of working with people and distributing an organization's resources to achieve goals _____

a. Profitably and ethically
b. Efficiently and effectively
c. Quickly and cheaply
d. For the benefit of shareholders
e. None of the above

2. Managers have the ability to "make a difference" through a balanced approach to:
   a. Employee and customer satisfaction
   b. Doing well by doing good
   c. The triple bottom line of people, profit, and planet
   d. Efficiency and effectiveness
   e. Values, mission, and vision

3. Using examples, compare and contrast the "art" and "science" of management.

4. Organizations are legally required to have *Corporate Social Responsibility* programs.
   a. True   b. False

5. U.S. economist Milton Friedman famously stated that:
   a. The only responsibility of a for-profit company is to maximize the amount of money that can be made for shareholders.
   b. Organizations have to establish trust with employees, communities, and shareholders to operate effectively.
   c. The earth's resources are limited and it is the responsibility of all organizations to conserve.
   d. A company can afford to lose a lot of money, but not one shred of reputation.

1.2 | Describe a manager's four major tasks: planning, organizing, leading, and controlling.

6. Give an example of how Starbucks' planning process has changed over the past decade.

7. During what function do managers have the greatest opportunity to ensure things go as planned and possibly even better?
   a. Planning   b. Organizing   c. Leading   d. Controlling

8. Illustrate how the management function of controlling was used at Pixar to make *The Incredibles*.

9. Diagram the four management functions and their relationship to goal achievement.

1.3 | Describe sustaining as a balanced approach to management.

10. Explain how sustaining provides a balanced approach to management.

1.4 | Correlate managers' tasks with the organizational roles that they play.

11. To which of Mintzberg's 10 management roles does each of the following correspond?
    a. Sit down with two team members to discuss an ongoing argument that has started to interfere with performance.
    b. Present the company's quarterly financial results to the media.
    c. Train new employees to complete monthly performance reports.
    d. Reallocate budget resources to increase the marketing budget for one of the company's services.
    e. Host conference call with top management to update them on sales projections.
    f. Attend an award dinner where the CEO of the company will accept a community award on behalf of the company.

1.5 | Compare and contrast different types of organizations, managers and the decisions they make.

12. Compare and contrast start-up companies with growth companies.

13. Contrast for-profit and nonprofit organizations.

14. Decide what type of manager should make the following decisions.
    a. Set employee schedules.
       Top manager   Middle manager   First-line manager
    b. Allocate budget resources.
       Top manager   Middle manager   First-line manager
    c. Hire staff.
       Top manager   Middle manager   First-line manager
    d. Prioritize financial resources.
       Top manager   Middle manager   First-line manager
    e. Establish partnerships.
       Top manager   Middle manager   First-line manager

1.6 | Explain the purpose of organizational values, mission, and vision.

15. Match each of the following internal factors with the time frame of its impact.
Values	1–10 years
Mission	Timeless
Vision	Life of leader

1.7 | Demonstrate how focusing on skills and strengths leads to success as a manager.

16. Summarize the theory that Marcus Buckingham and Donald O. Clifton propose in *Now, Discover Your Strengths*.

CHAPTER EXERCISES

The "Orange Effect"

Exercise Purpose In this real-world-inspired scenario, you'll consider how a manager might use team member strengths, negotiate internal and external dynamics, and take behaviors into account when making decisions.

Characters

Sterling Montgomery, Student Government Association (SGA) president

Behaviors: Builds and uses relationships to get work done. Talks a lot and enthusiastically persuades and motivates others. Good intuitive understanding of interpersonal relations. Strongly independent in putting forth his own ideas, which are innovative and original. Fights back hard when challenged. Strong sense of urgency. Focused on goals and the people he needs to get there, not details or plans.

Skill Strengths (in descending order): 1) Relational, 2) Conceptual, 3) Technical

Julie Simmons, SGA secretary

Behaviors: Relatively formal and reserved. Requires some "proof" to build trust in new people. Attention to detail; follows through on tasks to ensure completion. Thinks about what needs to be done and how to do it well and generally follows the plan. More focused on technical matters than social ones. Consistent and thoughtful. Not inclined to change.

Skill Strengths (in descending order): 1) Technical, 2) Conceptual, 3) Relational

Leslie Harris, SGA treasurer

Behaviors: Connects quickly with others. Strongly motivated to build and uses relationships to get work done. Talks a lot. Enthusiastically persuades and motivates others by adjusting his message. Very collaborative, works almost exclusively with and through others. Socially focused, he naturally empathizes with people, easily seeing their point of view. Teaches and shares. Often puts team/company goals before his own personal goals.

Skill Strengths (in descending order): 1) Relational, 2) Technical, 3) Conceptual

Situation Overview

Sterling Montgomery, the new president of the Student Government Association (SGA) at Washington Technology Institute (WTI), is ready to set a new standard for how the SGA can bring student and alumni communities together to support campus spirit through sports. Sterling believes that the basketball team already provides great energy on campus, and if he could make this energy more visible, alumni would get more involved in campus life. This could be his legacy—his real chance to make an impact.

Here's his idea. Sterling has heard that Ohio State University sells *tens of thousands* of colorful, team-inspired T-shirts for each football game. He thought, "If we could just do 1/10 of their results, I'd be a hero!" He calls a meeting with Julie and Leslie to discuss his new vision for bringing students, faculty, staff, and alumni together—to have all attendees at WTI basketball games wearing T-shirts in the *same* school color. The school colors are orange and white, so Sterling called his new initiative "the Orange Effect."

The Meeting During the meeting, Sterling wants to get consensus from the team to move forward with the Orange Effect idea; create a plan, including next steps to take; and assign tasks to the most appropriate person. Although the three of them know each other well, the meeting does not go as Sterling hoped. He met resistance from one of the team members, who wanted to do a lot more homework before committing and was reluctant to launch a new program, as opposed to continuing with an existing program. Explore the background information and following questions to see what might have gone wrong.

Background Information

WTI's Mission Through its focus on teaching and learning, research and discovery, and outreach and engagement, WTI creates, conveys, and applies knowledge to expand personal growth and opportunity, advance social and community development, foster economic competitiveness, and improve the quality of life.

WTI's Vision Work with administration, faculty, staff, alumni, and students to bring the university to a top-tier academic ranking. We will accomplish this by ensuring that all our major constituencies are collaborating to increase research funding, foster collective school spirit, and drive up the value of education at WTI.

WTI's Values Innovation, integrity, social impact, resource results, and personal transformation

Questions

1. In what ways is Sterling's vision for "Orange Effect" consistent or inconsistent with the university's mission, vision, and values?

2. Based on their behaviors, which team member do you think was resistant to Sterling's idea in the meeting, and why?

3. After agreeing to include information gathering as a part of the initial plan, Sterling has persuaded Julie and Leslie to move forward with the Orange Effect plan. The team has come up with the following list of tasks to complete by the next meeting. Who should be responsible for each task, and why? (Hint: if the answer is not clear based on skill strengths, consider the impact of the person's dominant behaviors.)

Task #1 Contact student government presidents at other schools with similar programs, collect information about how they made their programs successful, and organize this feedback into a spreadsheet so the team can write a plan.

    Sterling   Julie   Leslie

Task #2 Meet with T-shirt companies and negotiate the best possible price.

    Sterling   Julie   Leslie

Task #3 Prepare the budget for the first year of the program, with detailed supporting data.

    Sterling   Julie   Leslie

Task #4 Host a dinner meeting with the president of the Alumni Boosters to garner support for the program and get a commitment from the boosters to promote the T-shirts in their newsletter.

    Sterling   Julie   Leslie

Task #5 Write a plan for how volunteers will receive, sell, and distribute the T-shirts.

    Sterling   Julie   Leslie

Task #6 Find five volunteers to help run the program this year.

    Sterling   Julie   Leslie

Task #7 Get sample T-shirts and ask students which shirts they would most likely buy at basketball games and what price they would be willing to pay.

    Sterling   Julie   Leslie

Task #8 Based on information gathered, write a description of the Orange Effect plan to present to the university president.

Sterling   Julie   Leslie

Task #9 Meet with the university president to present the Orange Effect plan for approval.

Sterling   Julie   Leslie

Role of a Lifetime

Brian Troy, West Coast Area Manager for the Red Cross, has just mobilized his team and a large group of volunteers to respond to a wildfire that spread rapidly across southern California. Circle the role in Mintzberg's theory that best matches the actions that Brian took the first week after the hurricane.

Paul J. Richards/Getty Images Inc

1. Two of the engineers assessing the damage to a bridge that crosses a bay strongly disagree about whether to reopen the roadway. They have stopped talking. Brian invites them both for coffee to discuss the situation, so that the engineers can come to a consensus decision.

Figurehead	Leader	Liaison	Monitor	Disseminator
Spokesperson	Entrepreneur	Disturbance handler	Resource allocator	Negotiator

2. Brian speaks at a press conference for local television stations and newspapers to update the media on how the Red Cross is working with local officials to provide response services for families displaced from their homes.

Figurehead	Leader	Liaison	Monitor	Disseminator
Spokesperson	Entrepreneur	Disturbance handler	Resource allocator	Negotiator

3. Brian receives a report from the federal government that outlines expected aid, funding, and National Guard participation. He forwards this to his team members.

Figurehead	Leader	Liaison	Monitor	Disseminator
Spokesperson	Entrepreneur	Disturbance handler	Resource allocator	Negotiator

4. After three hours of evaluating how the Red Cross can have the greatest impact on the recovery efforts, Brian calls the executive team of Red Cross to give them his preliminary recommendations.

Figurehead	Leader	Liaison	Monitor	Disseminator
Spokesperson	Entrepreneur	Disturbance handler	Resource allocator	Negotiator

5. The mayor invites Brian to stand behind her at a national press conference to demonstrate to the world that recovery efforts are organized and moving forward.

Figurehead	Leader	Liaison	Monitor	Disseminator
Spokesperson	Entrepreneur	Disturbance handler	Resource allocator	Negotiator

6. Brian meets with a national account executive from Enterprise Rent-a-Car to get the best price on 250 rental cars for families with no transportation.

Figurehead	Leader	Liaison	Monitor	Disseminator
Spokesperson	Entrepreneur	Disturbance handler	Resource allocator	Negotiator

Check your answers in the "Answer Key" section.

Just the Right Type

Digital Sandbox, a risk management and anti-terrorism software company, has seen extraordinary growth over the past decade in response to turbulent market, political, and environmental conditions. In just a few years, the company has grown from a small team of four friends to almost 100 employees. During a management meeting, the company's president, Anthony Beverina, lists major management activities and needs to make a decision on how to best assign those activities and decision-making responsibilities based on the types of managers.

Directions: Circle the type of manager that you would associate with the following tasks, actions, and decisions.

1. The company has a major project to do for the Port Authority of New York. Which manager should organize the tasks of each of the team members and set work schedules between now and project completion?

Top manager   Middle manager   First-line manager

2. As the number of clients has increased, the company's telephone support group has begun having trouble keeping up. Someone needs to identify software programs to purchase and decide what kinds of support will still be handled over the phone. Existing clients should still feel as though they can talk to a real person when they phone in. Who should make this call?

Top manager   Middle manager   First-line manager

3. No More Risk Software Co. offers a complementary product, and its CEO has offered to sell the company to Digital Sandbox. Who should assess the market opportunity that this purchase might offer?

Top manager   Middle manager   First-line manager

4. With a new government project just approved, the company needs to hire a project manager and coordinator for government services. Who should take on this task?

   Top manager   Middle manager   First-line manager

5. The budgets were approved in January, and it is now August. The company had thought it would need to spend $50,000 to build a new website, but a friend of Anthony's just started a web design company and did the whole project for $20,000. Who should decide what to do with the $30,000 that was not spent?

   Top manager   Middle manager   First-line manager

Check your answers in the "Answer Key" section.

ANSWER KEYS

Chapter Exercises

The "Orange Effect"

1. Sterling's idea for the "Orange Effect" program is consistent with the university's mission and vision, with not such a clear connection to values. In the mission statement, the university states its commitment to "outreach and engagement." This could certainly include connecting with alumni as an outreach effort and further engaging students through a large, highly visible project. More than anything else, "Orange Effect" seems squarely focused on the university's vision to "foster collective school spirit."

2. Based on her list of dominant behaviors, it would make sense that Julie might be resistant to launching a new program right out of the gate. Her need to be detail-oriented and resistance to change could provide a significant barrier to launching the "Orange Effect" program. It would have been a very good idea for Sterling to have a conversation with Julie before the meeting and include her early in the planning process. As opposed to presenting a fully developed idea, Sterling could exchange ideas with Julie and ask that they both gather some more information before presenting thoughts at the officer's meeting.

3. Although there are a few doable combinations, we suggest the following distribution of tasks for the officer team: *Task #1*—Leslie, *Task #2*—Sterling, *Task #3*—Julie, *Task #4*—Sterling, *Task #5*—Julie, *Task #6*—Leslie, *Task #7*—Leslie, *Task #8*—Julie, *Task #9*—Sterling.

Role of a Lifetime

1. Disturbance handler
2. Spokesperson
3. Disseminator
4. Disseminator
5. Figurehead
6. Negotiator

Just the Right Type

1. First-line manager
2. Middle manager
3. Middle manager
4. Middle manager
5. Top manager

Self-Test

1. b. Efficiently and effectively
2. c. People, profit, and planet
3. The art of management refers to the things that managers do to collaborate and communicate in pursuit of an organizational goal, such as setting up and leading a monthly sales meeting. The science of management refers to technically focused activities, such as tracking data to ensure quality on an assembly line.

4. b. False

5. a. The only responsibility of a for-profit company is to maximize the amount of money that can be made for shareholders.

6. Store managers must understand and listen to customers so that the store can reflect the local culture and community.

7. c. Leading

8. Controlling was used to ensure that the quality of effects was consistent with the director's vision and within the budget constraints.

9.

10. Without ethical and socially responsible decision making, the other management functions cannot be properly executed.

11. a—Disturbance handler, b—Spokesperson, c—Leader, d—Resource allocator, e—Disseminator, f—Figurehead

12. A start-up company does not have an operating history, compared to a growth company, which has a track record and increases its revenues faster than industry standards or competitors

13. For-profit organizations distribute profits to shareholders and employees, compared to nonprofits that must reinvest all surplus resources back into the organization

14. a. First-line manager, b. Middle manager, c. First-line manager, d. Middle manager, e. Top manager

15. Values—Timeless, Mission—Life of leader, Vision—1–10 Years

16. When managers focus on the skills where they are strongest, they will see greater performance results than when they focus more on their weaknesses.

CHAPTER TWO

THE EVOLUTION OF MANAGEMENT

Learning Objectives

By the end of the chapter, you will be able to:

2.1 | Describe the historical foundations of management.

2.2 | Explain the beginning of modern management theory and education.

2.3 | Outline the progression of the quantitative approach to management.

2.4 | Outline the progression of the humanistic approach to management.

2.5 | Interpret the factors that led to a balanced approach to management.

ADDITIONAL RESOURCES

KEY TERMS
IN REVIEW
SELF-TEST
CHAPTER EXERCISE
SELF-ASSESSMENT
SELF-TEST
ANSWER KEY

JP Greenwood/Getty Images

"The past reminds us of timeless human truths and allows for the perpetuation of cultural traditions that can be nourishing; it contains examples of mistakes to avoid, preserves the memory of alternatives ways of doing things, and is the basis for self-understanding . . ."

—*Bettina Drew*

LECTURE ENHANCER:

2.1 The Historical Foundations of Management
- Adam Smith, Scottish economist and philosopher; author of *The Wealth of Nations*
  - ➤ Division of labor could increase production by having workers specialize on a task.
- *Dartmouth College v. Woodward* gave corporations rights that were similar to those of individuals and provided the context for the modern corporation.

2.1 | THE HISTORICAL FOUNDATIONS OF MANAGEMENT

2.1 Describe the historical foundations of management.

In Chapter 1, we explored critical thinking and how important it is for 21st-century managers. Although some believe the theory of critical thinking is a relatively new concept, it can in fact be traced back 2,500 years to the time of Socrates, the Greek philosopher. Socrates questioned the beliefs of authority figures and found that even those in positions of high power did not have all the answers. Refusing to accept the thoughts and ideas of others at face value, Socrates looked beyond the surface to delve into the deeper realities of reason and logic. Plato and Aristotle followed suit, and the adoption of critical thinking spread through the Middle Ages, the Renaissance, and right up to today.[1]

In this chapter, we have included some of history's greatest managers and how they used critical thinking skills to question the "norm" and establish a better way of running their businesses. Each of these managers gathered evidence and used reasoning and existing knowledge in order to form objective and logical viewpoints. Let's take a look at the evolution of management and the impact made by these critical thinkers on organizations throughout the ages.

What can managers learn about courage and success from the evolution of management theory and practice? In business, history has more to do with forging the future than looking back. So where did modern business get its start? The genesis of management can be found in early civilizations; from the Egyptians erecting the pyramids to the Chinese Empire building the Great Wall of China. Here, we will focus on the development of management practices, the origins of which can be traced back to the Declaration of Independence.[2]

Imagine the economic and business landscape of the early United States. Small regional economies were driven by self-employed artisans and small, family-owned shops. Collaborative networks of towns and communities were slowly forming a national economy.[3] As machines began to transform the economy, production migrated from homes to factories. This shift transformed these patched-together, fragile economies of self-employed individuals and family businesses into the globally integrated, national economy we have today. How did management facilitate this economic revolution? Two moments in history initiated modern management practice: Adam Smith's book *The Wealth of Nations* and the Industrial Revolution.

Wealth of a Nation

In 1776, prominent critical thinker Adam Smith (1723–1790), a Scottish economist and philosopher, published *The Wealth of Nations,* which argued that *division of labor* could increase production by having workers specialize on a task. Let's say that it takes 18 tasks or steps to make one pin. By analyzing the production process, Smith suggested that 10 employees, each completing all the tasks needed to make a pin, might make only 20 pins in a day, or 200 total. In contrast, those same employees, each specializing in no more than a couple of tasks and working together, could manufacture 48,000 pins in the same amount of time. When workers focus on completing a limited number of tasks, it is referred to as *specialization.* If you were an 18th-century pin manager selling pins for 5 cents each, the economics of *specialization* were simple to understand, and the numbers were very compelling.[4]

The Corporation

This concept, known as "division of labor," gave self-employed and family-owned businesses a model for expanding their enterprises and creating more wealth. This expansion also created greater political power for business owners. In the late 18th century, businesses were still subject to the direct control of government, and these burgeoning enterprises sought legal protection and autonomy. *Corporations,* a type of organization, are *legal* entities formed and structured to achieve goals with special protections for owners. In 1819, the U.S. Supreme Court ruling in the *Dartmouth College v. Woodward* case gave corporations rights that were similar to those of individuals, providing the context for the modern corporation.[5]

2.2 | *DISCOVERING AND TEACHING MANAGEMENT THEORY*

2.2 | Explain the beginning of modern management theory and education.

Let's imagine the rapid growth that occurred over the past two centuries, allowing today's managers to collaborate with teams across the globe, to manufacture products using parts from multiple countries and cultures, and to build customer relationships using the Internet as a medium. In 1800, there were no roads, railways, intricate canal systems, or phones, and it was easier to cross the Atlantic Ocean than travel halfway across your state. Today, a manager can email millions of stakeholders with the touch of a button, build collaborative communities online through Facebook, Twitter, and LinkedIn, ship a package around the world within days, or deliver a ton of goods 40 miles away in less than an hour. The rapid development of infrastructure and factories was made possible through Smith's *division of labor.* But the application of Smith's theories also created an avalanche of complexities for managers and workers; specifically, it was difficult to identify who was *responsible* for certain activities and who had the *authority* to make decisions when problems arose. With so many new systems, technologies, and infrastructures changing how organizations operated, how did managers use critical thinking skills to make sense of these changes and take advantage of them?

Bureaucratic Management: Max Weber

One of the initial theories for management came from a scholar seeking to understand capitalism, an economic system that is defined by private ownership. Max Weber (1864–1920), German sociologist and economist, asked why certain European countries were successful at implementing this system and others were not. Weber said that he witnessed

LECTURE ENHANCER:

2.2 Discovering and Teaching Management Theory
- Max Weber, German sociologist and economist
  - ✓ **Bureaucracy**—a form of organization marked by the division of labor, managerial hierarchy, rules and regulations, and impersonality.
    - o Weber's characteristics of bureaucracy sought to bring humanity to the workplace, where workers could rely on the rules and controls of the organization, not necessarily the whims of the people managing them.
    - o Table 2-1: Max Weber's Characteristics of Bureaucracy
- Henri Fayol
  - ✓ **Administrative theory**—identifies the functions of management in an organization and the principles needed to make sense of a complex set of organizational tasks.
    - o Fayol linked motivated and satisfied employees to successful management.
    - o Table 2-2: Evolution of Fayol's Principles
- Joseph Wharton, philanthropist and co-founder of Bethlehem Steel Corporation
  - ➤ Recognized the need for American managers to have a way to share experiences and to train the next generation of managers.

the "spirit of capitalism" in 1904, when he visited several prominent cities in the United States, where innovation and competition were encouraged.[6] Weber noted that "U.S. manufacturing and marketing had grown from small stores and owner-managed businesses to large professionally managed firms that were bound together by an intercontinental network of communication and transportation."[7] This was in stark contrast to the capitalistic practices in his home country of Germany, where small groups of powerful people controlled prices and distribution.

Bureaucracy A form of organization marked by division of labor, managerial hierarchy, rules and regulations, and impersonality.

Weber defined the ideal management of an organization as a **bureaucracy**, a form of organization marked by the division of labor, managerial hierarchy, rules and regulations, and impersonality (see Table 2-1). In business today, the term *bureaucracy* is often used to describe an organizational structure, usually the government, which operates with the greatest number of rules and the least amount of effort, motivation, and sense of

Table 2-1	**Max Weber's Characteristics of Bureaucracy**	
Characteristics	**Advantages**	**Disadvantages and Distortions**
Division of Labor	Managers increased production over 2,000% (as per Smith's pin economics), and workers knew exactly what they were supposed to do through specialization.	Managers took this concept to an extreme and began overanalyzing work to increase efficiency. Workers became bored and tired; as a result, they began to underperform, often on purpose.
Managerial Hierarchy	Managers had confidence in their responsibility and authority in the organization, and employees knew who they reported to and had the authority to make decisions.	Managers mistook authority for power, and used the power of their position for personal gain. Employees with bad bosses felt like they had no recourse because of their supervisors' legitimate authority.
Formal Selection	Managers needed to consider the skills necessary to complete the tasks of a job and ensure that the best possible candidates were identified. Employees were more likely to be successful in the position because they were selected based on their skills and strengths that matched with the job.	Managers overlooked good candidates because they did not have the requisite experience for the job, instead of spending the time to train and nurture a potentially great performer. Employees were disqualified from selection because of lack of experience.
Career Orientation	Managers were invested in the long-term welfare of the people that worked for them, and employees did not feel like a replacement part on a machine.	Managers and employees felt entitled to their jobs regardless of job performance.
Formal Rules and Controls	Managers could document the best way to accomplish tasks and share those expectations with employees. Employees understood the parameters of their work and what the organization needed them to accomplish.	Managers could create a rule for everything, which built an organizational culture that lacked creativity and innovation. Employees stopped trying to improve their tasks, although they were in the best position to do so, because they simply followed the rules.
Impersonality	Managers focused on the responsibility and authority of their position, not their personal desires and likes. Employees would not have to be subjected to the whims of their managers.	Managers mistook this for being cruel, distant, aloof, and fear-inducing. Employees became afraid to approach management and express new ideas or opinions.

Source: Adapted from C. A. Rodrigues, "Fayol's 14 Principles of Management Then and Now: A Framework for Managing Today's Organizations Effectively," *Management Decision* 39, no. 10 (2001): 880–889.

urgency. Weber thought of bureaucracy quite differently, as the ultimate state of organizational and managerial excellence, defined by six model characteristics: division of labor, managerial hierarchy, formal selection, career orientation, formal rules and controls, and impersonality.[8] This became the intellectual basis for many theories that follow in this chapter. Often misunderstood, Weber's characteristics of bureaucracy sought to bring humanity to the workplace, where workers could rely on the rules and controls of the organization, not necessarily the whims of the people managing them.

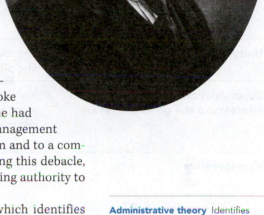

Administrative Management: Henri Fayol

Predating Weber's theoretical findings, Henri Fayol had created another theory of management. In the 1860s, Fayol, a mining engineer, observed the need for managers to gain both *responsibility* and *authority* through a greater set of skills than those that simply increased production output and quality.[9] He also saw a need for management theory, which for him was "a collection of principles, rules, methods, and procedures tried and checked by general experience." This need was apparent when the mine where he worked shut down because a horse broke its leg. The mine's manager was not present, and no one else at the mine had the authority to procure another draft horse. Everything stopped. Management failed. For Fayol, this was a failure due to poor planning and organization and to a communication disconnect between management and employees.[10] Following this debacle, Fayol implemented a team concept for miners and shifted decision-making authority to these work groups.

Fayol's ideas became the foundation for **administrative theory**, which identifies the functions of management in an organization and the principles needed to make sense of a complex set of organizational tasks. Fayol's views incorporated some of Weber's *bureaucracy* theory, where legitimate authority was inherent in a position and organizational hierarchy attempted to create order—a rules-based approach that disregarded the personal needs of individual workers. However, Fayol linked motivated and satisfied employees to successful management, a departure from Weber. This led to his original concept of the "functions of management": planning, organizing, command, coordination, and control. Beyond the functions of management, Fayol noticed a need for managers to have principles by which they conducted their functions. These principles were not meant to be an exhaustive list; moreover, Fayol began to call for studying the *art of management*—"there is nothing rigid in or absolute in management affairs, it is all a question of proportion. Principles are flexible and capable of adaptation to every need; it is a matter of how to make use of them, which is a difficult art requiring intelligence, experience, decision, and proportion."[11] Table 2-2 shows Fayol's original principles and how they have changed in today's practice.

The theories of Weber and Fayol, along with Fayol's principles, gave management educators a base of knowledge to begin teaching the workforce of the 20th century. In 1881, Joseph Wharton, philanthropist and cofounder of Bethlehem Steel Corporation, recognized the need for American managers to have a way to share experiences and to train the next generation of managers. He funded the Wharton School of Finance and Economy at the University of Pennsylvania, the first successful undergraduate school of business. Here, managers, scholars, and governments began the quest to understand, refine, and optimize management practices to create competitive advantages for organizations and countries.[12]

Administrative theory Identifies the functions of management in an organization and the principles needed to make sense of a complex set of organizational tasks.

Table 2-2 The Evolution of Fayol's Principles

Principles	Fayol's Intent	Today's Practice
Division of work	Workers specialize in one task or a few tasks.	Employees are encouraged to generalize their activities to create diverse contributions.
Authority	Managers hold the power.	Employees are empowered.
Discipline	Managers implement formal rules and controls.	Employees work in teams where the pressure to perform is self- or peer-induced.
Unity of command	Workers have one boss.	Employees could have one boss, many bosses, or no bosses, depending on the culture of the company and the situation.
Unity of direction	Employees work for one manager with one plan.	Employees work with managers on multiple plans.
Subordination of individual interests to the general interest	*Shared purpose* means that employees are committed to the organization's direction.	*Shared purpose* means that the organization and employees are committed to their mutual direction.
Remuneration	Employees receive reasonably based pay for reasonable performance.	Employees receive performance-based pay for creating expected and unexpected value for the organization.
Centralization	Employees take orders from a hierarchal management.	Employees participate in decision making and are expected to decide the best course of action on an *ad hoc* basis.
Scalar chain (line of authority)	Communication is controlled with a top-down approach.	Communication is open and shared freely, when and where possible.
Order	Internal information is used to control activities.	Internal information is used to control and coordinate activities.
Equity	Managers earn employees' commitment through kindness.	Managers earn employees' commitment through shared purpose, thus a sense of ownership.
Stability of tenure of personnel	Managers train employees when they start working for the organization and then continuously encourage them to stay.	Managers train and develop employees continuously so they will want to stay.
Initiative	Managers create the direction of the company and tell employees to go there.	Employees create the direction of the company and managers and employees go there together.
Esprit de corps	Managers avoid conflict to keep worker attitude high.	Managers look for productive conflict to grow the organization, creating worker trust.

2.3 | THE QUANTITATIVE APPROACH

2.3 | Outline the progression of the quantitative approach to management.

Charles Babbage (1792–1871), inventor of the first mechanical computer, was also interested in questions of management, particularly the inefficiencies that he observed in the modern factory.[13] He found that specialization led to bored workers, and bored workers decreased productivity. Workers being subjected to the same monotonous tasks, day after day, led to unprofitable behaviors for companies and demotivating conditions for employees. In a manufacturing environment, speed is critical. The faster everybody performs, the more goods can be produced and the more money can be made.

Workers began to test management by performing as slowly as possible while giving their supervisors the impression that they were working fast. This is known as **soldiering**. Two types of soldiering were observed: workers were said to be doing *natural soldiering* when they were simply "taking it easy," as opposed to *systemic soldiering*, when workers consciously and deliberately underworked. Natural soldiering could be easily addressed by inspiring and motivating the team, but systemic soldiering was emerging as a negative phenomenon in the 19th century.[14]

So what was Babbage's solution? He conducted *time studies*, documenting the amount of time that it took workers to complete tasks, so he could better understand the amount of performance that was reasonable to expect from workers. There were certainly critics of this practice. Luddites (workers who opposed the threat of technology and machines to their jobs) rebelled against the emergence of manufacturing and Babbage timing their efforts. In response, Babbage suggested that managers implement profit-sharing, so that employees could benefit directly from maximizing production. This began the **quantitative approach** to management—applying objective methods to enhance decision making. This approach became practice through **management science**, using statistics, mathematics, and other quantitative methods to improve efficiencies.[15]

Scientific Management: Frederick W. Taylor

As a manager at the Midvale Steel Company, critical thinker Frederick W. Taylor (1856–1915) observed soldiering among his workers.[16] By observing his team, and analyzing the information he had gathered, he suspected that the team was underperforming at about a third less than their potential, and felt that both managers and workers bore responsibility. Heated debates between managers and workers regarding "a fair day's work for a fair day's pay" were common. From this atmosphere of unproductive conflict, Taylor sought to create a reliable system to solve these problems—a science for management.[17] This *classical perspective* sought to make organizations and workers operate as efficiently as possible.

Continuing Charles Babbage's efforts to create an equitable workplace where both owners' and workers' needs were met, Taylor started conducting his own time studies in 1881. Armed with a stopwatch, scale, and tape, he meticulously weighed materials, measured distances that workers walked to conduct a task, and the exact time it took to complete each step of an activity. In contrast to the earlier work of Babbage, which described worker activity, Taylor's time studies searched for new ways to improve performance through a scientific, quantitative approach.[18] This was revolutionary at the time; suddenly, managers could break down a job into basic movements, understand what performance standards were possible, and set expectations for each employee.

This focus on analyzing and synthesizing the flow of work to maximize productivity is called **scientific management**. Taylor sought "the ultimate standardization of all elements surrounding and accompanying a job,"[19] including methods, materials, and machines. Applied in the wrong way, this approach often had the unintended implication of diminishing Taylor's concern for the worker, for he focused his concern for workers by advocating improving incentives, much like Babbage, and a new management methodology he called the **task-management system**, a combination of setting performance standards, selecting the best worker for the job, and building good relations between managers and employees.

Soldiering A way that workers tested management by performing as slowly as possible while giving their supervisors the impression that they were working fast.

Quantitative approach Applying objective methods to enhance decision making.

Management science Using statistics, mathematics, and other quantitative methods to improve efficiencies.

Scientific management Using a quantitative approach to analyzing and synthesizing the flow of work to maximize productivity.

Task-management system A combination of setting performance standards, selecting the best worker for the job, and building good relations between managers and employees.

Table 2-3	Four Basic Principles

Frederick Taylor's Principles	
Principle #1	Develop a quantifiable, scientific way to measure performance.
Principle #2	Select workers based on scientific methods.
Principle #3	Train employees based on measurable standards.
Principle #4	Work closely, side by side, with employees.

Task-Management System Frederick Taylor defined management as "knowing exactly what you want men to do, and then seeing that they do it in the best and cheapest way." He also believed that "the relations between employers and men form without question the most important part of [management]".[20] These philosophies became the guiding principles of the task-management system. First, he separated "planning" work from "performing" tasks, and created four principles of scientific management that defined the task-management system[21] (see Table 2-3).

Harrington Emerson (1853–1931) became the first "efficiency engineer," a title that he created for himself. As a management consultant, Emerson focused on many of the same principles as Taylor's task-management model and incentive system. Within a couple of years of working with the Atchison, Topeka, and Santa Fe Railroad, Emerson saw great success with his client, improving manufacturing output by 57 percent, cutting costs 36 percent, and increasing the pay of workers by 14.5 percent.[22] Although he was inspired by and took advantage of the scientific management methods of his time, Emerson saw a better way.

Much like the managers who felt subjugated by Taylor's removal of their authority, Emerson believed that line-level management needed to maintain unity of command, but he also thought that they should have access to the specialized knowledge that was necessary to operate the day's large and ever-growing corporations.[23] Here was his solution. First, he created a chief of staff position that would oversee the activities of four subdivisions: 1) employee relations; 2) machines, tools, and equipment; 3) materials, including purchasing, handling, and inventory; and 4) records and accounting. Next, Emerson gave full authority to line-level managers to lead the activities of workers, with the added benefit of access to staff with specialized knowledge.[24] With this simple evolution of Taylor's task-management model, Emerson successfully transformed how most companies organized staff and line-level management.

These advances earned Emerson a title that he probably would not have felt comfortable giving himself—the High Priest of Efficiency. In addition to his revolutionary staff model, he made significant strides in cost accounting, which had been merely descriptive, meaning that records were kept solely based on money that was spent and earned.[25] Emerson implemented cost accounting processes that estimated costs *before work started,* giving managers another tool to set standards and ideals for performance. This evolution of thought parallels the change in perspectives from Babbage's to Taylor's time studies, where managers were now expected to understand the possibilities of performance, as opposed to simply observing and documenting what had been performed.

In Emerson's 1913 book *The Twelve Principles of Efficiency,* he articulated a new set of principles for management, based on observation and understanding what is possible to achieve, which became the historical blueprint for the art and science of management.[26] His first five principles define the art of management and dealing with people. By shifting a manager's attention to seeking ideal performance, Emerson established the concept of *goals,* which became his first management principle, "clearly defined ideals." He understood that ideals were realistic only when they were developed and understood by both managers and employees. To achieve his first principle, he created his second principle, where he implored managers to look everywhere in the operation, regardless of position, for the best perspectives to help the team achieve the ideal performance standard. This required management to select, hire, and retain the most knowledgeable staff to support first-line managers, which was his third principle. Likely inspired by Weber's work on bureaucracy, Emerson wanted to balance the open discussion between managers and employees through his fourth principle, which sought discipline through adherence to rules. In his fifth and final principle relating to people, he set the standard for employee-employer fairness.

The last seven principles of Emerson's management manifesto dealt with the science of management, with easily measurable processes and methods. Easy to follow, these seven principles were keeping accurate, timely, and permanent records; planning activities; standards and timing for tasks; "standardized conditions"; "standardized operations"; written documentation for processes; and rewards for achieving ideal efficiency.[27] (For more, see Table 2-4.)

Motion Studies: Frank B. Gilbreth

Frank B. Gilbreth (1868–1924), a contemporary of Taylor, sought a much more detailed approach to efficiency than observed in Taylor's time studies, measuring motion in units as small as 1/1,000 of a minute. As a journeyman bricklayer and the slowest one on the job, he began to break down and understand each and every movement needed to lay *one* brick.

o William E. Deming, statistician for U.S. Census Bureau
✓ **Plan-Do-Act**—it is a manager's job to distinguish between real problems and trivial mishaps that happen day-to-day
➤ Predominant theme in the qualitative approach to management through the 1980s.
➤ Many quality programs were introduced based on the principles outlined by Deming and Juran
■ Lean manufacturing, Total Quality Management (TQM), Six Sigma

Table 2-4	Evolution of Management Theory from Weber to Fayol to Emerson	
Emerson	**Fayol**	**Weber**
Clearly defined ideals	Unity of direction	NA
Discipline	Discipline	NA
The fair deal	Equity	NA
Reliable, immediate, and adequate records	Order	Formal rules and controls
Standards and schedules	Order	Formal rules and controls
Standardized conditions	Order	Formal rules and controls
Standardized operations	Order	Formal rules and controls
Written standard-practice instructions	Order	Formal rules and controls
Dispatching	Centralization	NA
Efficiency-reward	Remuneration	NA
Common sense	NA	NA
Competent counsel	NA	NA
NA	Division of work	Division of labor
NA	Scalar chain (line of authority)	Managerial hierarchy
NA	Subordination of individual interests to the general interest	Formal selection
NA	Stability of tenure of personnel	Career orientation
NA	Authority	Impersonality
NA	Initiative	NA
NA	Unity of command	NA
NA	Esprit de corps	NA

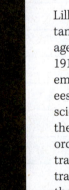

Gilbreth determined that exactly 18 motions of the hand were used to lay one brick. By designing new working methods, such as building a shelf at the right height to save the bricklayer bending down and creating innovative types of scaffolding, he was able to reduce that number to six.[28] At the time, a journeyman was expected to lay 175 bricks in a day—after reducing the number of motions to lay one brick to 6, Gilbreth could lay 350.[29] Not only did Gilbreth improve the efficiency of the bricklayers, but the quality of their work was better as well. In addition, thanks to the new working methods, the men were no longer as fatigued as they had once been.

With this understanding of creating efficiency, Gilbreth started his own construction business, eventually employing over 10,000 workers all over the world. As his business and reputation grew, Gilbreth decided he wanted to evolve scientific management. Management challenges in factories were much more complex than the task of laying a brick, so Gilbreth set forth to apply *motion studies,* where he used a motion-picture camera to capture the step-by-step movements that were taken to complete a task.[30] This method was employed wherever possible and applicable—in such widely varying areas as surgery, nursing, golf, and baseball.

By applying scientific management methods, Gilbreth's motion studies sought efficiencies by orchestrating the maximum results for the least worker effort. With their smallest physical movements being analyzed, what must workers have thought? At the time, there was no one better to study the psychological impact on workers than Frank Gilbreth's wife and collaborator, psychologist Lillian Gilbreth.

Scientific Management and the Mind: Lillian M. Gilbreth

Lillian M. Gilbreth (1878–1972) was a first-rate scholar and management consultant. Her ability to connect scientific management to "the psychology of management" secured her place in the annals as a great management thinker. In her 1912 doctoral thesis, *The Psychology of Management,* she studied the perceptions, emotions, and thoughts of managers, and how these affected work and employees. Consistent with the motion studies of her husband and the efforts of Taylor's scientific management, Lillian Gilbreth centered her attention on understanding the precise workings of the manager's mind so that behaviors could be taught and orchestrated. In her analysis, she compared three historical types of management: traditional, transitory, and scientific. *Traditional* management depended on centralized authority. *Transitory* represented the confused shift between central authority and manager-employee cooperation. And *scientific* management relied on positive manager-employee relationships, which could be maximized by refining methods for employee selection, incentives, and welfare. This work made Lillian Gilbreth a pioneer in the field of *human resource management,* as it bridged theorists' dual focus on profit and people and made the seemingly intangible visible.[31]

Visualizing Management: Henry Gantt

Babbage, Taylor, and Frank Gilbreth specialized in observing and documenting the visible, making it possible to eventually set ideals, or goals, for performance. Lillian Gilbreth observed and documented the invisible workings of the mind, or psychology, in order to create ideal environments for managers and employees to establish productive performance-based relationships. Many other invisible forces affected the day-to-day management of production as well. What might managers gain from observing, documenting, and making these dynamics visible, with the intent to create new performance standards?

This was the managerial quest of Henry L. Gantt (1861–1919). A mechanical engineer, Gantt joined the Midvale Steel Company in 1872, where he met and worked with Taylor. Using the philosophies that he learned from Taylor, Gantt became a management consultant in 1901. His methods and advice were not always embraced by his clients. At Sayles

Table 2-5 Gantt's Management Color Performance

| | | | | | Performance Standard of 175 Bricks Laid per Day | | | | |
Workers	Mon	Tues	Wed	Thur	Fri	Mon	Tues	Wed	Thur
John	142	201	187	133	192	125	152	200	220
Alan	199	190	150	124	220	180	192	168	173
Neville	178	180	190	198	129	127	112	125	135
Loren	171	175	173	176	178	177	181	177	170

Bleacheries, a textile plant in Rhode Island, both management and employees refused to go along with Gantt's recommendation and the employees went on *strike*, which is when employees stop work in pursuit of a concession from management. In an attempt to restore order, Gantt hired new employees and quickly taught them their tasks and "habits of industry," which we now refer to as *training*. These "habits" of *industriousness* and *cooperation* were behaviors that could be observed, documented, standardized, and idealized.[32] Yet, the internal forces that determined these habits were invisible; training sought to make them visible.

Another dynamic that managers must contend with every day is *time*. Before he could solve the challenge of visualizing time, for many years Gantt had refined methods for visualizing performance standards.[33] For example, if a worker was expected to lay 175 bricks a day, Gantt introduced color so that managers could quickly assess performance, with black indicating that the employee was meeting or exceeding performance standards, and red indicating failure to meet expectations. If you were Gilbreth, managing 10,000 employees on hundreds of job sites, this would have been a marvelous breakthrough in terms of efficiency, as you would now have the necessary data to analyze performance (see Table 2-5).

These progressive methods established Gantt as a management consultant of the first order. His talent for graphically representing performance was sought after by the U.S. Army in World War I, for whom he worked from 1914 to 1918. At the time, the army was an organizational mess: "plants [were] scattered all over the nation, shipments were late, [and] warehouses were crowded or disorganized."[34] Eventually, Gantt had an insight that would change how managers viewed projects forever. He noted, "We have all been wrong in scheduling on a basis of quantities; the essential element in the situation is *time*, and this should be the basis in laying out any program."

Let's put this in context. A bricklaying job has three primary operational tasks: material delivery, bricklaying, and cleanup. Managers had previously measured tasks independently: the quantity of materials sent, the number of bricks that were laid in a day, and the amount of waste removed from the job site. Though this method was probably sufficient for simple projects, it led to chaos in the complex environment of the growing corporation, and especially the U.S. Army, because these tasks are dependent on each other in time. For instance, if the bricks and mortar were supposed to be on the job site on Monday but did not arrive until Thursday, the bricklayers could not work until Friday, where they had originally planned on starting Tuesday.

Chaos resulted when a manager was planning and organizing hundreds of tasks and had no way of visualizing when a project was behind schedule. Gantt introduced the progress chart, which would be later known as the *Gantt Progress Chart* and has been described as "the most notable contribution to the art of management made in this generation."[35] This simple solution to a complex problem broke down tasks by planned time to perform and actual time to perform. This provided managers with immediate visual feedback as to when a project was behind schedule and required corrective attention.[36] See Figure 2-1 for an illustration of a Gantt chart.

Scientific management, including time studies, motion studies, and worker incentives, combined with advances in graphically representing performance, gave managers many methods to increase worker productivity. At the same time, *mass production*—the production of large quantities of a product requiring the standardization of processes and

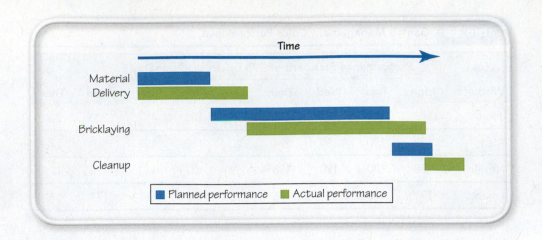

Figure 2-1

A Bricklaying Week, with Planned and Actual Performance

The Gantt progress chart allows managers to plan and schedule projects, estimate the length of time that a project should take, decide the required resources, and arrange the order of tasks.

parts—was becoming common practice and setting new standards for production. Remember Smith's concept of division of labor, where different employees were responsible for different tasks in the manufacturing process? Based on this theory, the ideal state of efficiency would be when each part created by each employee was exactly the same, so the assembly of those parts would take the least amount of time, and an amount that could be predicted. The endless pursuit of this ideal state of efficiency became the *quality movement.*

Quality Movement

At the turn of the century, cars were still only for the wealthy, but the masses yearned to own them, too, either to get places more quickly or to rid the streets of the stench of horse manure. In 1899, Henry Ford (1863–1947) founded the Detroit Automobile Company, which closed down operations only two years later due to poor quality and high prices. Learning from his mistakes, Ford founded the Ford Motor Company in 1903 with a passion to create a high-quality car that was affordable for the masses. In 1908, the Ford Motor Company introduced the Model T, an automobile that cost $825. Over the course of the next 10 years, the company sold 472,000 Model Ts, which retailed for $360 per car. By 1927, the Ford Motor Company had produced and sold more than 15 million cars.[37] How did they do it? Quality.

The American Society for Quality suggests that "quality has two meanings: 1) the characteristics of a product or service that bear on its ability to satisfy stated or implied needs; 2) a product or service free of deficiencies."[38] For the Ford Motor Company, this meant that they needed to produce a car that met the needs of the American middle class (their customers), with as few defects as possible. To accomplish this, the company invented a process for manufacturing called the *assembly line*, where parts are added sequentially to construct a product faster. This process was sped up dramatically by designing and manufacturing *interchangeable parts*. These were parts that were of such a high quality that they appeared to be identical. Through advances in quality, through the assembly line and interchangeable parts, the build time for a Ford Model-T dropped from days to 93 minutes.[39]

The United States and its allies in World War II used the advances made at the Ford Motor Company to produce airplanes and weapons quickly, cheaply, and in great numbers. Indeed, refining production was a critical component in increasing output during the war, but the management needs of the military exceeded those of civilian management. Military managers needed to lead global production and distribution, with very defined goals that had to be achieved. *Operations research* became a central management theme during World War II, in an attempt to establish a quantitative rationale for decisions that would lead to goal achievement.

During the war, William E. Deming (1900–1993) a statistician from the U.S. Census Bureau known for his use of mathematics to improve operational processes, was called on to help engineers improve their efficiency and effectiveness. In 1947, after the conclusion of the war, Deming went to Japan to help set up the country's census process. Curious, he immersed himself in the culture of Japan, including theater and conversations with local business executives. These conversations led to an invitation in 1950 by the Union of Japanese Scientists and Engineers (JUSE) to speak on his statistical methods for quality. His impact was extraordinary in Japan: only one year later, the country established the Deming Prize, a national quality award for businesses.[40]

One of the primary philosophies of the quality movement is the ongoing effort to improve a process, method, service, or product, called *continuous improvement*. Deming referred to this as "Plan-Do-Act," and suggested that a manager's job was to distinguish between real problems and trivial mishaps that happen on a day-to-day basis. By focusing on the big problems first, managers would be more likely to fix the 20 percent of operational ineffectiveness that causes 80 percent of the quality problems.

Deming and a colleague, Joseph M. Juran (1904–2008), suggested using statistical methods combined with planning, organizing, and controlling to lead companywide quality efforts. Establishing teams called *quality circles*, companies in Japan (most notably Toyota) brought together knowledge specialists, supervisors, and workers to continuously discuss ways to improve. In addition, all workers were given permission to stop the assembly in the plant if they noticed a problem.[41] Quality in Japan's manufacturing became the premier standard for the world. Yet, given that both Deming and Juran were Americans, why did Japan's quality standards begin to exceed U.S. carmakers?

An NBC television program in 1980, *If Japan Can . . . Why Can't We?* asked a similar question. Deming was a guest on the program, and U.S. manufacturing companies were embarrassed by his answer. During the previous 30 years, Deming was largely ignored by U.S. companies, and throughout his interview on the NBC show, he made it clear that U.S. management was to blame.[42] Within days, his phone began to ring with calls from Ford Motor Company and General Motors (GM), who were having their worst financial performance since World War II. Never very popular with U.S. car executives, Deming was nearly banned from GM for yelling at its president at the time, Jim McDonald, in front of GM workers and executives, "Who is responsible for quality problems? You are!" To underscore his philosophy that quality started at the top of an organization, Deming famously walked off stage after Ford's CEO at the time, Donald Peterson introduced Deming as a speaker to a group of senior staff members and announced that he would rejoin them after lunch. When Peterson asked where Deming was going, Deming retorted, "If this isn't important enough for you, it's not important enough for me." Peterson cancelled his meetings and joined the group.[43] U.S. business started to listen.

The quality movement was the predominant theme in the qualitative approach to management through the 1980s. Many quality programs were introduced based on the principles outlined by Deming and Juran; these included *lean manufacturing*, *Total Quality Management* (TQM), and *Six Sigma*, which was founded at Motorola and popularized by General Electric (GE). In contrast to production management, the quality movement understood the need for every employee in the company, regardless of role, to participate in the problem-solving efforts to achieve stated goals.[44]

© Bettmann/CORBIS

2.4 | THE HUMANISTIC APPROACH

2.4 | Outline the progression of the humanistic approach to management.

When scientific management began to place rigid expectations on workers, it's fair to say that employees were not happy about it. Joseph Wharton, businessman and management education pioneer, once asked Frederick Taylor to consult for Bethlehem Iron Company (later called Bethlehem Steel) to decrease costs and improve overall efficiency.

that extended beyond work hours; resulting in increased productivity.
- **Conflict**
  - ➤ Mary Parker Follett - argued that the American notion of individual rights over the interests and well-being of the group was counterproductive.
  - ➤ "The Group Principle"— the whole of the group is comprised of equally weighted and integrated individual differences.
- **Conflict Resolution—Figure 2-2**
  1) **Group Submission**— everyone sits silent for a moment, and to avoid conflict says, "okay, fine, let's do that"
  2) **Struggle for Victory** - one or two people push back and demand that a picnic is more appropriate for a corporate event, with one of the two sides eventually winning, typically the most stubborn

Humanistic approach A focus on the human side of management in response to negative worker response to scientific management principles.

  3) **Compromise**—often seen as the most desirable outcome; one or two people push back and demand that the picnic is more appropriate for a corporate event, with eventually someone suggesting an enclosed tent with catered food at a local park.
  4) **Integration**—Follett's ideal state of conflict resolution; one or two people push back and demand that a picnic is more appropriate, and through further discussion and adherence to the merits of each individual's idea, the group decides to set up a large barbeque pit for grilling with picnic tables adjacent to a large tent equipped with games and extra seating.
    - ➤ *Constructive conflict*— positive outcomes for group conflict emerge when individual ideals remain intact and become a part of a "single whole."
- **Motivation**
  - ➤ Douglas McGregor— management professor at MIT that stated that managers build effective and ineffective relationships with employees based on one of two primary

In 1899, during his stint at the company, the price of pig-iron, a type of crude iron, soared. This increased demand for high-quality iron, and Bethlehem sold 10,000 tons of its iron in a short period of time. This also increased demand on workers to load the iron onto railcars. Workers at this time were earning by "piece rate"—meaning they were paid for how much "pig-iron" they loaded, which were iron ingots or moulds that each weighed 92 pounds. Taylor and his team selected the 10 best workers at Bethlehem and asked these men to work at "maximum speed" for one day. They loaded a staggering 75 long tons (2,240 pounds) in one day, compared to the usual 12.5 long tons expected by average workers. They were physically exhausted. With this new data, Taylor and his team created a new performance and pay plan at Bethlehem. The "first-class" workers were expected to load 45 long tons a day, almost quadruple the previous expectation. These workers would be paid $.0375 per long ton or $1.85 a day, which represented a 60 percent raise in pay.[45] Certainly management and shareholders saw great value in the new system—but what about the worker?

As scientific management became popular, laborers organized into *labor unions* to bargain collectively for worker rights. The unions saw scientific management as an emerging evil in the burgeoning capitalistic economy; as companies applied Taylor's methods, the first-class workers kept their jobs, but many others lost theirs. Union leaders petitioned Congress to investigate Taylor and scientific management methods. The phrase *first-class worker* invited particular scrutiny that started a monumental argument between William B. Wilson, the chairman of a special committee of the U.S. House of Representatives looking into the matter, and Taylor.[46] The phrase suggested that the other workers were disposable, and the public debate brought scientific management and its impact on people to the forefront of national discussion in management. An increasingly disgruntled workforce, as well as management eager to avoid strikes, brought about the **humanistic approach**, which focused on the human side of management.

Hawthorne Studies

Hawthorne Works, a division of the Western Electric Company and the sole supplier of telephone parts to AT&T, was a special place to work in the mid-1920s. Athletic and social programs, savings and stock plans, a restaurant with discount meals, and other generous benefits defined the Hawthorne culture, and employee morale was high.[47] This became the context for one of the most cited management studies in the modern era (revered by some, but criticized by others). The Hawthorne Studies, conducted between 1924 and 1932, seemingly verified that employees were motivated by many factors, not just money, and that group dynamics had an impact on employee morale and performance.

Illumination Study (1924–1927) Led by Dugald C. Jackson, electrical engineering professor at the Massachusetts Institute of Technology (MIT) and in collaboration with the Council on Industrial Lighting, the Illumination Study had the simple objective of observing the effect of lighting on worker productivity. Researchers selected two teams of participants with equal performance records and experience. One team was the control group (no change in their lighting conditions), and the other team was the variable group (their lighting conditions would change). What the researchers found was baffling and inconclusive: In the variable group, their performance increased with any change in the lighting conditions, regardless of the brightness of the room or whether the lighting went up or down, dark or light. This led researchers to two unsatisfying conclusions: 1) there was no correlation between lighting and performance output, and, by default, 2) performance productivity must have multiple factors. The MIT researchers and company employees were intrigued by the unpredictable outcome of the study and sought to set up another study to understand the multiple factors that could be affecting productivity.[48]

Relay-Assembly Test Room Study (1927–1932) In 1927, the research team, now led by Homer Hibarger and Charles E. Snow, was energized to understand these factors and went about assessing the effects of work conditions on employee productivity, including breaks, meals, and length of workday. This time, the researchers selected five women for the study who assembled relays.[49] Invited to a separate observation room, the women were asked to produce relays at a "comfortable pace" and assured that any increase from their previous, "normal" output would be "returned to them entirely." During the first several months, the researchers introduced many changes in the work conditions: two 5-minute breaks, six 5-minute breaks, two 10-minute breaks, and even free lunch at the company restaurant. No one could have predicted what happened next—regardless of the change, productivity increased. Seemingly, all that was required to increase productivity was to change work conditions in some way. Could this be possible?

After a year, the researchers changed their strategy and removed all breaks, the work week was increased from 40 to 48 hours, and the assemblers had to bring their own lunch. Performance output actually increased overall, but it declined on an hourly basis. When breaks were reinstituted a month later, performance increased to its best output in the study. After physical and mental examinations, the research team concluded that fatigue was not a cause of the performance increase; rather, breaks offered the team time to socialize, which improved "attitude." At this point, both the researchers and workers were coming to conclusions as to why the performance had increased. The research team identified five major reasons, "in order of importance: 1) working in a small group, 2) a less restrictive and friendlier supervisory style, 3) increased earnings, 4) the novelty of being a study participant, and 5) attention given to the assemblers by company officials and the researchers."[50] The assembly workers gave two reasons: "[The study room and research environment] was fun," and they liked the friendlier supervisory style.[51]

Women in the Relay Assembly Test Room, ca. 1930. Western Electric Company Hawthorne Studies Collection. Baker Library Historical Collections, Harvard Business School.

The Interviewing Program (1925–1932) Interviewing was a component of the research that offered insights into worker attitudes. When the study was initiated, researchers using the *directive method* asked questions that could easily be answered "yes" or "no," such as "Are you satisfied with your work?"[52] After about four years, the research team was not yielding the information needed to help analyze which work conditions had the greatest impact. They needed a different perspective.

G. Elton Mayo (1880–1949), a professor at Harvard University, brought an approach to the interviews that clarified findings and inspired a new management theory. Mayo was already known for his theory that management could not be reduced to individual independently operating factors, such as incentive pay; instead, he proposed an industrial "psychology of the total situation." Upon visiting Hawthorne, he recommended that the research team use a *non-directive* interview method, which would encourage workers to share their overall feelings and experiences.[53]

Something delightful happened. As researchers built relationships with the workers, becoming genuinely interested in their concerns and aspirations, the workers, no longer intimidated by authority, began to relax and establish friendships in their group that extended beyond work hours. This bred group cooperation and loyalty, which increased productivity. The interviewing program became the methodology for teaching supervisors how to talk with employees, to learn about their personal lives, and, most important, to listen.[54,55] In short, for the first time, a management theory gave managers permission to treat workers as *people* and to approach groups informally.

Conflict: Mary Parker Follett

According to the Hawthorne studies, working groups increased performance in a more informal environment, where they could express themselves with each other and the leader and be heard. For Mary Parker Follett (1868–1933), however, simply looking at group dynamics,

assumptions of human nature: Theory X or Theory Y.

✓ **Theory X**—a negative view of the worker that states that people do not like to work; therefore, workers need to be coerced, told what to do, and intimidated.

✓ **Theory Y**—a positive view of the worker that states that people enjoy the mental and physical purpose that work provides; therefore, when participating in a group with a shared commitment, people will direct themselves and look for ways to expand their personal contributions and responsibilities

■ **Table 2-6: Theory X and Theory Y**

✓ **Behavioral management**—relies on understanding individual behaviors, decisions, and attitudes to motivate employees

absent their relationship to authority, was not enough. A political philosopher, Follet argued that the American notion of individual rights over the interests and well-being of the group was counterproductive.[56] "When we say that there is the One which comes *from* the Many, this does not mean that the One is *above* the Many." This one line sums up a philosophy that she then applied to conflict resolution, leadership, authority, and power. She introduced the concept of "the group principle," where the whole of the group is comprised of equally weighted and integrated individual differences.[57] In the business world of measuring tapes, assembly lines, Weber's bureaucracy, Taylor's task management, and single lines of authority, this was a revolutionary idea.

Conflict Resolution Where are power dynamics in groups most apparent? Conflict. Have you ever been a part of a group project that one person "takes over"? For example, let's say that you are a part of a five-person team asked to set up a customer appreciation event for your company. The company president's only request is that the event include family fun and take place on a Saturday afternoon in September. In the first meeting, the group would like to decide on theme and location. About an hour into the conversation, many ideas have been presented, from a bowling tournament to a picnic. In the past 15 minutes, one of the group members has repeatedly said, "We have a lot of salary sitting around this table. I've got a lot of work to do. Let's make a decision." This person finally erupts in frustration and suggests, "Okay, this is taking too much time. Let's just do the bowling tournament. The bowling alley will handle most of the logistics, and we don't have to worry about it raining. And, we can hand out trophies—people love to win something."

In Follett's *Creative Experience*, she suggests that there are four possible outcomes to this scenario (as outlined in Figure 2-2: 1) group submission—the group sits silently for a moment, and to avoid conflict, everyone says, "OK, fine, let's do that"; 2) *struggle for victory*—one or two people push back and demand that a picnic is more appropriate for a corporate event, with one of the two sides (typically the most stubborn one) eventually winning; 3) *compromise*— one or two people push back and demand that the picnic is more appropriate for a corporate event, with eventually someone suggesting an enclosed tent with catered food at a local park; and 4) *integration*—Follett's ideal state of conflict resolution—one or two people push back and demand that the picnic is more appropriate, and through further discussion and adherence to the merits of each individual's idea, the group decides to set up a large barbecue pit for grilling, with picnic tables adjacent to a large tent equipped with games and extra seating. In Follett's view, integration is the ideal state of conflict resolution, but unfortunately, most groups settle for compromise.

This anecdote demonstrates Follett's *constructive conflict* concept, where positive outcomes for group conflict emerge when individual ideals remain intact and become a part of a "single whole."[58]

Figure 2-2
Visualization of Follett's Conflict Resolution Model, Where "A" Asserts a Position of Power
Follett's conflict resolution model illustrates the power dynamics between groups where person A asserts a position of power.

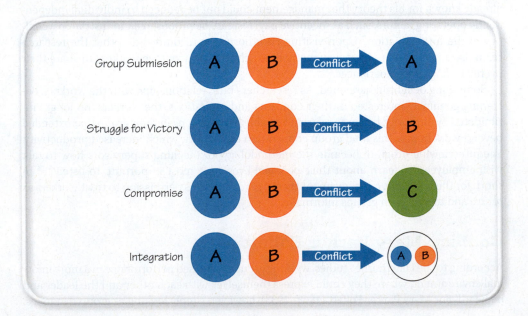

Power with People Using scientific management, managers typically tried to keep workers happy through pay incentives tied to performance output. Unfortunately, by focusing on pay incentives, managers were not seeing workers as people with complex sets of needs. Follett's constructive conflict philosophy recognized individual complexity and sought ways for groups to embrace and incorporate each person's needs. Why did businesses listen to Follett, a female political philosopher, in the "scientific management" frenzy of the 1920s and 1930s? Remember, informal groups with good attitudes are more productive, meaning greater profits, as shown in the Hawthorne Studies. Follett's philosophies challenged the premise that owners had an interest and laborers had an interest, which were sometimes amenable but always in discord. But doesn't somebody's interest have to prevail? Isn't business a constant back-and-forth of gaining and losing power—the economy is bad, so management can demand more work for less pay; times are good again, so labor needs to get back what it appears to have lost?

Follett saw this reality, but she did not accept it as a foregone conclusion—"Labor and [management] can never be reconciled as long as labor persists in thinking that there is a [management] point of view and [management] thinks there is a labor point of view. There is not. These are imaginary wholes which must be broken up before [management] and labor can cooperate."[59] Here, she is asking business managers to reconsider their power over labor by clarifying their interests and fully understanding labor's interests, thus creating a relationship between management and workers where they create common interest, a shared ideal. This shift in perspective required managers to share the planning, organizing, and *leading* of the organization *with* labor. This was "power with people" not "power over people."

Motivation: Douglas McGregor

But wasn't Follett missing something? Didn't workers dislike working and managers enjoy authority? Douglas McGregor (1906–1964), management professor at MIT and later president of Antioch University, thought differently: "A manager who believes that people in general are lazy, untrustworthy, and antagonistic towards him will make very different decisions [from] a manager who regards people generally as cooperative and friendly." Having studied management in an academic setting for decades, it wasn't until his actual management experience as president of a university that he realized that "a leader cannot avoid the exercise of authority any more than he can avoid responsibility for what happens to his organization."

In *The Human Side of Enterprise*, McGregor states that managers build effective and ineffective relationships with employees based on one of two primary assumptions of human nature: *Theory X* or *Theory Y*, as seen in Table 2-6. **Theory X** is a negative view of the worker stating that people do not like to work; therefore, workers need to be coerced, told what to do, and intimidated. Otherwise, left on their own, workers will soldier, or, worse yet, do nothing at all. **Theory Y** is a positive view of the worker stating that people enjoy the mental and physical purpose that work provides; therefore, when participating in a group with a shared commitment, people will direct themselves and look for ways to expand their personal contributions and responsibilities.[60] Obviously a student of Follett's work, McGregor suggested that an organization where management and employees applied Theory Y as a system of beliefs could "achieve their own goals best by directing their efforts toward the success of the enterprise."[61] This changed the role and authority of management in that

Theory X A negative view of the worker stating that people do not like to work; therefore, workers need to be coerced, told what to do, and intimidated.

Theory Y A positive view of the worker stating that people enjoy the mental and physical purpose that work provides; therefore, when participating in a group with a shared commitment, people will direct themselves and look for ways to expand their personal contributions and responsibilities.

Table 2-6	Theory X and Theory Y	
	Theory X	**Theory Y**
Premise	People don't like to work.	People enjoy the sense of purpose provided by work.
Managerial Action	Coerce and intimidate employees into getting the job done.	Motivate and nurture employees; facilitate creation of a shared group purpose.
Locus of Power	Managers have power over employees.	Managers share power with employees.

Research@Work

Theory Y in Practice[62]

It's easy to assume that old theories cease to be relevant as we learn new and better ways of managing. However, there is a growing school of thought that believes that McGregor's theories are widely used in practice and may even have universal application.

In their article "McGregor's Legacy: The Evolution and Current Application of Theory Y Management," authors P. F. Sorensen and M. Minahan believe that McGregor's Theory Y is far from irrelevant. In fact, they have found a link between Theory Y and appreciative inquiry (AI), which is an organizational approach that focuses on the organization's strengths and how they can be improved, rather than trying to fix its weaknesses. The belief is that people are more likely to be motivated toward achieving a goal if they are given the opportunity to make things better.

Professor's Response

What's most exciting about this research is the idea that the application of Theory Y might well be useful in all cultural contexts. That could be a useful tool for understanding and managing international businesses and increasingly diverse workforces.

Manager's Response

I can certainly see how Theory Y ideas work well for certain personality types and certain positions, but frankly, there are some jobs that just aren't that inspiring, and there are some people who really aren't motivated by anything other than their paycheck. So while I can see that Theory Y might often be relevant, I don't think I'd call it universal, in my experience.

Critical Thinking in the Classroom

If you were a manager, which premise would you feel was most beneficial in the workplace, Theory X or Theory Y? And what managerial action would you take to apply it to your employees?

2.5 The Balanced Approach

✓ **Contingency (Situational) Theory**—different organizations, situations, and contexts require different approaches

- **Cooperation**
  - ➤ Chester Barnard—believed that inefficient organizations were doomed to fail through continued entropy

> **Behavioral management**
> Understanding individual behaviors, decisions, and attitudes to motivate employees.

✓ **Entropy**—loss of social and market-based energy leading to the decline of the system

✓ **Negative entropy**—social and market-based energy that builds or maintains a system

> **Contingency (or situational) theory** A management theory that states that different organizations, situations, and contexts require different approaches.

power was shared, but the manager had a responsibility to nurture and motivate employees by paying attention to their best intentions and actions. The results were individual and group goal-pursuing behaviors nurtured, inspired, and directed by management. Theorists and practitioners call this *motivation*.

The philosophies and practices that initiated in the interview rooms at Hawthorne where Mayo opened a conversation, the political situations where Follett questioned the productivity of authority, and the university boardrooms that McGregor led, all brought forth a new dimension to management—people. This qualitative approach to management theory created the field of *human resources*, which continues to formalize processes, methods, and manager training so that people in an organization can meet their needs to be motivated and to achieve goals. From this approach, the **behavioral management** perspective relies on understanding individual behaviors, decisions, and attitudes to motivate employees. Where does this leave scientific management, quality, and the overall quantitative approach to management?

2.5 | THE BALANCED APPROACH

2.5 | Interpret the factors that led to a balanced approach to management.

Management theorists in the mid-20th century began to recognize that each of the historical management approaches had something useful to offer. What managers needed to do was to recognize what approach would be most effective in a particular situation and be flexible enough to change approaches as needed. Called **contingency (or situational) theory**, this states that different organizations, situations, and contexts require different approaches.[63] Contingency theory laid the groundwork for the *balanced approach* that is emerging in management practice today. Management theory, responding to the forces of technology, capitalism, and globalization, required a new model to rethink the roles and responsibilities of employees, managers, and organizations today. This model needed the discipline of the quantitative approach, with its determination to continuously improve processes and methods, *and* the perspective of the qualitative approach, with its understanding of motivation and a manager's power and authority. These ways of thinking about management have come together to form a balanced approach to management theory.

Cooperation: Chester I. Barnard

Chester I. Barnard (1886–1961), college dropout, experienced executive, and management theorist, saw organizations and their systems as being comprised of three components: 1) "willingness of members to cooperate"; 2) "a common purpose"; and 3) "members able to communicate with each other."[64] Barnard believed that inefficient organizations were doomed to fail through continued **entropy**, or loss of social and market-based energy leading to the decline of the system. Therefore, the manager's responsibility and authority is to establish **negative entropy**, social and market-based energy that builds or maintains a system. Where does this energy come from?

Barnard states that management is affected by forces inside and outside the organization. Managers can achieve effective and efficient systems by understanding how to maintain an *equilibrium* of these forces and their relationship to the organization, including management, employees, shareholders, customers, and suppliers. In contrast to Follett's view of power and authority, Barnard saw this "equilibrium" as a **cooperative system**, in which organizations are effective and efficient when managers control and influence people's behaviors by modifying their motives.[65] He believed that individuals had the right to join a cooperative system, and the primary benefit to the individual was the collective power to accomplish something greater than one could do alone—build a car, lay a transcontinental rail system, or design the iPod. However, Barnard agreed with Follett that the interests of individuals need to be compatible with the interests of the organization. If not, that individual employee would become unmotivated, lose interest, and stop participating. Therefore, it was the individual, the employee, that gave authority to management, not the other way around.

Barnard's theories benefited from his extensive experience as an executive at AT&T and as the president of several nonprofit organizations. These experiences, combined with his concept of cooperative systems, led to Barnard's ideas on the "function of an executive," which were threefold: 1) "to provide a system of communication," 2) "to promote the securing of essential efforts," and 3) "to formulate and define purpose."[66] He compared the role of manager to the body's central nervous system, whose function is to transmit information continuously to enable all other parts to perform.

Systems: Jay W. Forrester

In 1956, engineering professor Jay W. Forrester became a management faculty member in MIT's new Sloan School of Management, primarily because he thought it would be an "interesting challenge to look at what an engineering background could mean to management." Forrester took on a problem faced by GE managers, who were "puzzled why their household appliance plants in Kentucky were sometimes working three and four shifts, and then a few years later, half the people would be laid off." Forrester drew a conceptual system of GE's inventory as it related to the company's decision to hire or lay off employees, a method that became known as *system dynamics*. System dynamics allowed Forrester to show the management team at GE a simulation that demonstrated unintended consequences of their hiring practices. His findings enabled managers to connect faulty decision-making practices to instability in the number of people employed at their factories. System dynamics sought to enable managers to achieve "equilibrium" and stability in their organizations.

Using words like *equilibrium* and analogies such as the central nervous system, Barnard and Forrester were both biologists at heart. It would take another biologist to create the theory that would enable management theorists to understand, plan, and organize in a global economy defined by computers and information. The Austrian biologist Ludwig

---

✓ **Cooperative system—** organizations that are effective and efficient when managers control and influence people's behaviors by modifying their motives.
• **Systems**
  ➤ Jay Forrester—drew a conceptual system of GE's inventory, as it related to the company's decision to hire or lay

Entropy The loss of social and market-based energy, leading to the decline of an organization.

Negative entropy Social and market-based energy that builds or maintains a system.

Cooperative system A kind of equilibrium in which organizations are effective and efficient when managers control and influence people's behaviors by modifying their motives.

off employees, known as system dynamics
  ➤ **General Systems Theory (GST)**
    1) a study of organizations must make an observation of the whole; the interdependent sub-systems make up the whole system
    2) organizations seek a state of equilibrium
    3) organizations are "open systems"

Subsystem Smaller, interdependent systems that make up the whole system.

Open systems Systems that have the power to change and be changed by external and internal forces.

von Bertalanffy (1901–1972) looked for a way to describe and understand real world activities, based on his theoretical comprehension of organisms and biological life forms. These studies uncovered the General Systems Theory (GST). He observed three factors that were consistent among a multitude of disciplines, not just management: 1) a study of organizations must make an observation of the whole (i.e., the interdependent **subsystems**, smaller interdependent systems that make up the whole system); 2) organizations seek a state of equilibrium; and 3) organizations are **open systems**—they have the power to change and be changed by external and internal forces.[67] Much like Follett's shifting of power away from people toward the situation, Forrester encourages modern theorists to see management as a series of ever-changing social systems with limitations and dependencies on environments.

We now have a good understanding of how the concept of management has evolved over the centuries, together with the different challenges faced by managers over several generations. Each era gives rise to a new set of management theories, from a quantitative approach to a humanistic approach to theorists applying all historical lessons learned for a balanced analytical process that leads to better decisions. This evolution in theory requires contemporary managers to apply similar critical thinking methods, which take into account an interconnected system of cooperative stakeholders. In the next chapter, we will explore the importance and practicalities of a systems approach to critical thinking and its relevance within the daily functions of 21st-century managers.

Case**Snapshot**

Chapter 2 Case: The Evolution of Management: Valve Corporation can be found on pg. 463

ADDITIONAL RESOURCES

KEY TERMS

Administrative theory Identifies the functions of management in an organization and the principles needed to make sense of a complex set of organizational tasks. **(p. 35)**

Behavioral management Understanding individual behaviors, decisions, and attitudes to motivate employees. **(p. 48)**

Bureaucracy A form of organization marked by division of labor, managerial hierarchy, rules and regulations, and impersonality. **(p. 34)**

Cooperative system A kind of equilibrium in which organizations are effective and efficient when managers control and influence people's behaviors by modifying their motives. **(p. 49)**

Contingency (or situational) theory A management theory that states that different organizations, situations, and contexts require different approaches. **(p. 48)**

Entropy The loss of social and market-based energy, leading to the decline of an organization. **(p. 49)**

Humanistic approach A focus on the human side of management in response to negative worker response to scientific management principles. **(p. 44)**

Management science Using statistics, mathematics, and other quantitative methods to improve efficiencies. **(p. 37)**

Negative entropy Social and market-based energy that builds or maintains a system. **(p. 49)**

Open systems Systems that have the power to change and be changed by external and internal forces. **(p. 50)**

Quantitative approach Applying objective methods to enhance decision making. **(p. 37)**

Scientific management Using a quantitative approach to analyzing and synthesizing the flow of work to maximize productivity. **(p. 37)**

Soldiering A way that workers tested management by performing as slowly as possible, while giving their supervisors the impression that they were working fast. **(p. 37)**

Subsystem Smaller, interdependent systems that make up the whole system. **(p. 50)**

Task-management system A combination of setting performance standards, selecting the best worker for the job, and building good relations between managers and employees. **(p. 37)**

Theory X A negative view of the worker that states that people do not like to work; therefore, workers need to be coerced, told what to do, and intimidated. **(p. 47)**

Theory Y A positive view of the worker that states that people enjoy the mental and physical purpose that work provides; therefore, when participating in a group with a shared commitment, people will direct themselves and look for ways to expand their personal contributions and responsibilities. **(p. 47)**

IN REVIEW

2.1 | Describe the historical foundations of management.

Two moments in history initiated the theories and practices of modern management: 1) the concept of *division of labor*, as argued in Adam Smith's *The Wealth of Nations*, and 2) the Industrial Revolution. *Division of labor* suggested that manufacturing could increase productivity by having workers specialize in tasks, as opposed to being responsible for activities in the assembly or making of a product. The division of labor helped lead to the development of *corporations*, which are legal entities formed and structured to achieve goals with special protection for owners.

2.2 | Explain the beginning of modern management theory and education.

Two early management theorists were Max Weber and Henri Fayol. In Weber's theory of bureaucracy, power was embedded in organizational roles and rules, rather than in individual people, thus protecting workers from the whims of their managers. Fayol's administrative theory built on Weber's work, linking motivated and satisfied employees to successful management. These theoretical advances provided a curriculum framework for higher education. In 1881, Joseph Wharton, philanthropist and cofounder of Bethlehem Steel Corporation, funded the Wharton School of Finance and Economy at the University of Pennsylvania, the first successful undergraduate school of business.

2.3 | Outline the progression of the quantitative approach to management.

The quantitative approach attempted to improve performance by applying objective methods to decision making. Frederick W. Taylor (1856–1915), an innovator of this approach, sought to create a reliable system to solve the problems facing managers through scientific application. Using a quantitative approach to analyzing and synthesizing the flow of work to maximize productivity is scientific management. Taylor created the task-management system and "functional foremanship." Harrington Emerson, in his 1913 book *The Twelve Principles of Efficiency,* articulated a new set of principles for management based on observation and understanding what is possible to achieve. By shifting a manager's attention to seeking an ideal performance, Emerson established the concept of *goals,* which became his first management principle, "clearly defined ideals." Where Taylor's time studies measured movements in feet, weight in pounds, and time in seconds, Frank Gilbreth wanted to help workers with the motions of their tasks by removing wasteful movements. Lillian Gilbreth expanded the scope of scientific management by studying the movements of the mind. To help visualize these scientific performance results, Henry Gantt contributed to the evolution of the quantitative approach through visualization techniques that are still used today.

2.4 | Outline the progression of the humanistic approach to management.

The *humanistic approach* to management was a direct response to a workforce who resented and resisted scientific management. Using innovative methods, researchers in the Hawthorne Studies group showed the positive effects that good interpersonal relationships between management and labor had on productivity. Political philosopher Mary Parker Follett developed methods of improving group dynamics, including non-intuitive approaches to conflict resolution that "integrated" individual interests. Her work inspired Douglas McGregor, who proposed *Theory X,* in which it is assumed that people do not like to work and must be coerced into doing so; and *Theory Y,* in which it is assumed that people enjoy working in a group with a shared purpose and will self-motivate.

2.5 | Interpret the factors that led to a balanced approach to management.

Chester I. Barnard's theories laid the foundation for a balanced approach to management. He believed organizations and their systems were comprised of three components: 1) "willingness of members to cooperate," 2) "a common purpose," and 3) "members able to communicate with each other." This focus on organizations as systems fed into the work of Ludwig von Bertalanffy, who created "general system theory" and observed three factors that were consistent among a multitude of disciplines: 1) a study of organizations must make an observation of the whole (i.e., the interdependent subsystems that make up the organization); 2) organizations seek a state of equilibrium; and 3) organizations are open systems—organizations have the power to change and be changed by external and internal forces.

SELF-TEST

2.1 | Describe the historical foundations of management.

1. When workers focus on completing a limited number of tasks, it is referred to as:
   a. task focus
   b. specialization
   c. limited production
   d. industrialization

2. Explain how Adam Smith's *The Wealth of Nations* influenced the foundations of management thought.

2.2 | Explain the beginning of modern management theory and education.

3. A form of organization marked by the division of labor, managerial hierarchy, rules and regulations, and impersonality is:
   a. democracy
   b. theocracy
   c. bureaucracy
   d. aristocracy

4. What important lessons did Henri Fayol learn from a horse's broken leg?

2.3 | Outline the progression of the quantitative approach to management.

5. The quantitative approach to management involves applying subjective methods to enhance decision making.
   a. True
   b. False

6. A focus on *analyzing* and *synthesizing* the flow of work to maximize productivity is called:
   a. scientific management
   b. synthesis management
   c. management by analysis
   d. management by objectives

7. What are Taylor's four principles of scientific management that defined the task-management system?

8. What was the purpose of Frank Gilbreth's motion studies?

9. A Gantt Progress Chart provides managers with immediate visual feedback as to when a project is behind schedule and requires corrective attention.
   a. True
   b. False

2.4 | Outline the progression of the humanistic approach to management.

10. The Hawthorne Studies, conducted between 1924 and 1932, seemingly verified that money had the most important impact on employee morale and performance.
    a. True
    b. False

11. Explain Mary Parker Follett's constructive conflict concept.

12. A Theory Y perspective of human nature assumes that:
    a. people do not like to work
    b. workers need to be coerced, told what to do, and intimidated
    c. left on their own, workers will soldier
    d. people will direct themselves and look for ways to expand responsibilities

2.5 | Interpret the factors that led to a balanced approach to management.

13. _____ states that different organizations, situations, and contexts require different approaches.
    a. Contingency (or situational) theory
    b. Behavioral theory
    c. Differential theory
    d. Disintegration theory

14. Explain Chester I. Barnard's concept of a cooperative system.

15. An open system is one that has the power to change and be changed by external and internal forces.
    a. True
    b. False

CHAPTER EXERCISE

The Legacy of Scientific Management

Scientific management is still with us today. The legacy of scientific management lives on in the form of modern, fast, and efficient assembly lines. Scientific management techniques are used in every field, from fast food to surgery to job design, selection, and training.

A. List some general ways in which scientific management principles are incorporated into our modern world:

_____

_____

_____

B. Provide some specific examples of how scientific management concepts are being applied in various industries (such as manufacturing, fast food, medical, etc.)

_____

_____

_____

C. What are some ways in which scientific management concepts and principles affect your personal life on a daily basis?

_____

_____

_____

SELF-ASSESSMENT

Are you a Theory X or Theory Y Manager?

Douglas McGregor created and developed Theory X and Theory Y as contrasting concepts of human motivation at the Sloan School of Management at MIT in the 1960s. The following assessment will help you to understand whether you are likely to take more of a Theory X or Theory Y perspective on management.

Choose the statement that best describes your feelings:

1. Employees are inherently:
   a. lazy
   b. ambitious

2. Employees tend to:
   a. avoid work if they can
   b. seek out and accept responsibilities

3. Most workers believe that work:
   a. is distasteful
   b. can be as natural as play

4. Workers should be:
   a. closely supervised
   b. allowed to use their natural creativity to solve problems

5. In most organizations:
   a. comprehensive systems of control should be developed
   b. employees' talents are underutilized

6. _____ should be used to gain employee compliance and commitment.
   a. Threats and coercion
   b. Self-direction and self-control

7. Most people:
   a. are only out for themselves
   b. want to do well at work

Scoring:

A. Count the number of times you selected choice "a" and write it here: _____

B. Count the number of times you selected choice "b" and write it here: _____

C. If your score on line A is higher, you tend to take a Theory X perspective on management. If your score on line B is higher, you tend to take more of a Theory Y perspective on management.

SELF-TEST ANSWER KEY

1. b.

2. Smith argued that *division of labor* could increase production by having workers specialize on a task. The division of labor helped lead to the development of *corporations,* which are legal entities formed and structured to achieve goals with special protection for owners.

3. c.

4. A draft horse at a mine broke its leg. The mine's manager was not present, and no one else at the mine had the authority to procure another horse, causing production to stop. Fayol believed that this failure occurred due to poor planning and organization and to a communication disconnect between management and employees. Fayol implemented a team concept for miners and shifted decision-making authority to these work groups. Fayol's ideas became the foundation for his administrative theory, which identifies the functions of management and other important management concepts.

5. b. False. It involves applying *objective* methods to enhance decision making. This approach became practice through management science, using statistics, mathematics, and other quantitative methods to improve efficiencies.

6. a.

7.   **Frederick Taylor's Principles**

Principle #1	Develop a quantifiable, scientific way to measure performance.
Principle #2	Select workers based on scientific methods.
Principle #3	Train employees based on measurable standards.
Principle #4	Work closely, side by side, with employees.

8. Gilbreth used a motion-picture camera to capture step-by-step movements that were taken to complete a task. By applying scientific management methods, Gilbreth's motion studies sought efficiencies by producing the maximum results with the least worker effort.

9. a. True

10. b. False. The Hawthorne Studies, conducted between 1924 and 1932, seemingly verified that employees were motivated by *many* factors, not just money, and that group dynamics had an impact on employee morale and performance.

11. According to Follett, positive outcomes for group conflict emerge when individual ideals remain intact and become a part of a "single whole." Her philosophy recognized individual complexity and sought ways for groups to embrace and incorporate each person's needs.

12. d.

13. a.

14. According to Barnard, a cooperative system is one in which managers control and influence people's behaviors by modifying their motives.

15. a. True

Notes

_____

_____

_____

_____

PART TWO

Sustaining:
A Balanced Approach
to Management

CHAPTER THREE

CRITICAL THINKING FOR MANAGERS

Learning Objectives

By the end of the chapter, you will be able to:

3.1 | Explain how managers use a systems approach to critical thinking to achieve results.

3.2 | Illustrate how systems diagrams are used to show cause-and-effect relationships.

3.3 | Show how systems balance and reinforce their behavior over time.

3.4 | Analyze system discrepancies to determine a manager's intervention.

3.5 | Diagram the eight most common systems archetypes that managers can expect to encounter.

ADDITIONAL RESOURCES

KEY TERMS

IN REVIEW

SELF-TEST

CHAPTER EXERCISE

SELF-ASSESSMENT

SELF-TEST ANSWER KEYS

SELF-ASSESSMENT ANSWER KEY

JP Greenwood/Getty Images

3.1 | HOW MANAGERS APPLY CRITICAL THINKING TO MAKE A DIFFERENCE

3.1 | Explain how managers use a systems approach to critical thinking to achieve results.

LECTURE ENHANCER:

3.1 How Managers Apply Critical Thinking to Make a Difference

✓ A **systems approach** to critical thinking involves looking at an organization as a whole; that is, as a set of interrelated parts (people, processes and structures) and understanding how these parts influence one another.

✓ **Systems thinking** was popularized in Peter Senge's book *The Fifth Discipline.*

✓ Senge believes that by seeing an organization as a whole "system", or a set of inter-related elements, rather than as a number of separate parts, managers are better able to understand the underlying structure and apply the principles of systems theory to solve and correct problems.

✓ The **five main disciplines** described by Senge include:

1) *personal mastery,* which involves focus, patience and holding on to our vision

2) *mental models* which are the perceptions we form about the world around us and how they shape our behavior

3) *building a shared vision,* where we share our vision of the future with others in order to inspire and motivate

4) *team learning* where we open up a dialogue with our team members in order to encourage a free-flow of thoughts and ideas

5) and finally, *systems thinking* which is *the fifth discipline* that integrates the other four disciplines.

In Chapter 2, we explored the evolution of management and the different business approaches that arose through each era. Each of these management approaches and theories was highly relevant at the time. Some of them continue to be applicable in organizations today. However, we live in a culturally and financially connected world where most countries are affected by other countries' behaviors and market conditions. In other words, the world itself is a system where economics, politics, culture, and international relations have an impact not just on one country, but on a global level. This is why a systems approach to critical thinking, as discussed in Chapters 1 and 2, is gaining ground as an innovative way of approaching the current challenges facing managers today.

A systems approach to critical thinking allows managers to fully visualize the "interconnected set of elements that is coherently organized in a way that achieves something."[1] It involves looking at an organization as a whole (a set of interrelated parts, such as people, processes, and structures that are all dependent on each other) and understanding how these parts influence each other.

Understanding and using a systems approach to critical thinking requires a real paradigm shift. When it comes to problem solving, managers are used to linear business models that identify a problem, fix it, and then move on. A systems approach encourages us to see an organization as a fluid arrangement of many different parts, such as employees, teams, and departments, all of which depend on each other. The role of a manager is to look at these interconnected systems as a whole to understand the importance of each part and how it contributes to the organization. A systems approach holds that "we must look beyond individual mistakes or bad luck to understand important problems. We must look beyond personalities and events. We must look into the underlying structures which shape individual actions and create the conditions where types of events become likely."[2] It encourages us to look beyond perceived weaknesses, use and enhance strengths, and avoid the blame culture to ascertain the real root of the problem.

The following example illustrates what happens when managers fail to understand how an organization functions and the consequences of not seeing the bigger picture. A company experiences a drop in sales due to an economic recession. Senior management decides to terminate middle manager positions, resulting in several families losing their income. These families then rely on local, state, and federal help, straining public resources. The company expects more production and results from the remaining managers and employees with no additional compensation, which leads to lower employee satisfaction. When the economy begins to recover, these dissatisfied managers and employees find other jobs. The company is surprised and attempts to find replacements, and the stress of the recent events encourages some senior managers to retire. Having terminated most of the company's middle management, the organization now lacks the ability to function properly, or even sustain itself. An exaggeration? This is an actual example from a billion-dollar organization with experienced and well-intentioned leaders. Because they did not foresee the possible consequences of their decisions, these managers made choices that had negative impacts inside and outside the organization.

This theory of **systems thinking** was popularized as a practical tool for managers in Peter Senge's seminal text *The Fifth Discipline*.[3] An American scientist and senior lecturer at the Massachusetts Institute of Technology (MIT), Senge believes that by learning to see an organization as a whole "system," or a set of interrelated elements rather than a number of separate parts, managers are better able to understand the underlying structure and apply the principles of systems theory to address existing issues and prevent those issues from recurring in the future.

> **Systems thinking** A methodology of analysis that managers use to understand interconnected cause-and-effect relationships that change organizational behaviors and dynamics.

The five main disciplines described by Senge include 1) personal mastery, which involves focus, patience, and holding on to our vision; 2) mental models, which are the perceptions we form about the world around us and how they shape our behavior; 3) building a structure where we share our vision of the future with others to inspire and motivate; 4) team learning, where we open up a dialogue with our team members to encourage a free flow of thoughts and ideas; 5) and finally, systems thinking, which integrates the previous four disciplines.

As Senge explains, "Systems thinking also needs the disciplines of building shared vision, mental models, team learning, and personal mastery to realize its potential. Building shared vision fosters a commitment to the long term. Mental models focus on the openness needed to unearth shortcomings in our present ways of seeing the world. Team learning develops the skills of groups of people to look for the larger picture beyond individual perspectives. And personal mastery fosters the personal motivation to continually learn how our actions affect our world."[4]

Senge believes that many organizations are hampered by a number of "disabilities" which stunt growth and productivity. For example, people who see themselves as mere "cogs in the wheel" of a company will fail to make any proactive changes, as they believe that they have very little influence. There may also be a pervading blame culture, when people point fingers at others or their competition when things go awry, which leads to inertia; or people take a short-term view that impedes their ability to see the big picture.

According to Senge, organizations should ideally be "learning organizations," which are

". . . organizations where people continually expand their capacity to create the results they truly desire, where new and expansive patterns of thinking are nurtured, where collective aspiration is set free, and where people are continually learning to see the whole together."[5]

Voices of Management

Michael Woodhead, Vice President of Business Development, EscapeWire[6]

My clients require fast solutions, innovative ideas, and a real partner in the marketplace. Ten years ago, there was a lot of talk about solving problems with clients. In my opinion, the greatest change in that conversation is a shift to possibility. Companies and their managers want to know what is possible. I think I know why . . .

Solving a problem somehow suggests looking back at how we did it yesterday and solving the pain of today. Creating possibilities solves today's pain with an eye on the future. The companies that I work with that do that best are winning in this highly competitive market environment.

Company Profile

Name: EscapeWire Solutions

CEO: Mike Beecher

Company Story: EscapeWire provides solutions and services for clients nationwide. Our innovative use of emerging technologies allows us to build IT solutions that are of the highest quality and meet the flexibility and mobility needs of most businesses.

Critical Thinking in the Classroom

If you were a manager of EscapeWire, how would you perceive the "shift to possibility" as beneficial to your clients? ∎

LECTURE ENHANCER:

3.2 Seeing Systems with Diagrams

• **How are systems diagrams used to show cause and effect relationships?**

✓ **Stocks and flow diagrams**
  o Systems have two basic components: stocks and flows.
  o **Stocks** are material or information that accumulates over time (e.g., trees in a forest, money in a bank account)
  o **Flows** are physical or informational forces that increase or decrease stocks
  o An **inflow** increases stock, while an **outflow** decreases stock.

Behavior over time (BOT) diagrams A visual tool that allows managers to see the change in measurements across a span of time.

Stocks Material or information that can be measured.

Inflows Increase the value of a stock measurement.

Outflows Decrease the value of a stock measurement.

  o A *water reservoir* represents a good example of a system with stocks and flows.
    ■ The stock is the amount of water in the reservoir
    ■ Inflows of rain and rivers increase the stock of water, while outflows via evaporation or discharge decrease the stock of water
✓ **Behavior over time diagrams**
  o Systems are dynamic and change over time as stocks and flows increase and decrease
  o A student's bank account serves as good example of how we can understand a system's behavior over time

Figure 3-1

Basic System of Stock and Flow
A basic stock and flow diagram illustrating inflows and outflows.

By adopting the five disciplines, of which systems thinking is the cornerstone, managers will be able to build organizations where everybody shares in a vision, works together as a team, and creates an environment that inspires continuous learning and an effortless free flow of ideas.

3.2 | SEEING SYSTEMS WITH DIAGRAMS

3.2 | Illustrate how systems diagrams are used to show cause-and-effect relationships.

An important part of systems theory is the application of system dynamics, first introduced in the 1950s by Jay Forrester (see Chapter 2) as a way of understanding the underlying problems within organizations. This involves using diagrams and models to highlight different aspects of system behavior. The two main systems diagrams adopted by managers are *stock and flow diagrams*, and **behavior over time (BOT) diagrams**. Let's consider each of these.

Stock and Flow Diagrams

Systems have two basic components: stocks and flows. In systems theory, **stocks** mean material, or information that has accumulated over time. Stocks can be physical items such as trees in a forest, water in a reservoir, and money in a bank account; or they can be non-physical elements such as the level of satisfaction you have doing a job and the amount of empathy you have for others. **Flows** are the physical or informational forces that increase or decrease stocks. An **inflow** increases stock, and an **outflow** decreases stock.[7] Figure 3-1 shows a basic system of stock and flows. Notice the empty clouds on either end. These are placeholders indicating that the source of the inflow and the deposit of the outflow are not known or are not being considered.

Let's look at a reservoir as an example of a system. In a reservoir, the *stock* is the amount of water it contains. *Inflows* of rain and rivers can increase the stock of water, and *outflows* through evaporation and discharge decrease the stock of water. Figure 3-2 illustrates this example, showing two different inflows and two different outflows. Notice again the empty clouds. They mean that in this figure, we are not considering where the river is coming from or where the extra water is being discharged. It is important to remember that all systems diagrams necessarily simplify reality.

Let's add a little complexity to this diagram and consider more carefully one component—the inflow from the river. You can see from this simple example how you can use a stock and flow diagram to understand the following better:

• The forces (flows) affecting a particular stock
• The causes and effects of a particular inflow or outflow, and
• How different stocks and flows are interconnected in a system.

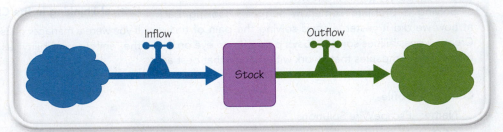

Source: Adapted from Figure 1 in *Thinking in Systems: A Primer,* Copyright © 2008 by Donella Meadows et al., with permission by Chelsea Green Publishing (chelseagreen.com).

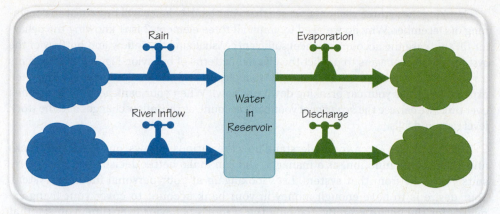

Figure 3-2
System with Multiple Flows
A system with multiple flows, using the water in a reservoir as an example.

Source: D. H. Meadows, *Thinking in Systems: A Primer*, D. Wright, ed. (White River Junction, VT: Chelsea Green Publishing Company, 2008): 19.

Behavior Over Time (BOT) Diagrams

Systems are dynamic. That is, they change over time as stocks and flows increase and decrease. Understanding how systems will change in response to alterations in stocks and flows is a key component in using systems thinking as a decision-making tool. Let's consider another example: your personal financial system. In this case, the stock is the amount of money in your bank account. You have an inflow of income from your summer job, and an outflow of money to pay for living expenses as shown in Figure 3-3.

We can visualize how this system will behave over time using a graph in which we represent the *inflow*, the *outflow*, and the *stock* level. To keep things simple, we will presume a few things: 1) you started with $0; and 2) you made $3,000 a month in June, July, and August; and, finally 3) you have fixed monthly expenses of $1,500. The graph appears in Figure 3-4.

- o Understanding how a system behaves over time can help to facilitate changes and adjustments to the system
- o **Discrepancy** is the difference between the desired and actual stock levels in a system
- o **Delay** refers to the idea that changes to a system may take time to have an effect

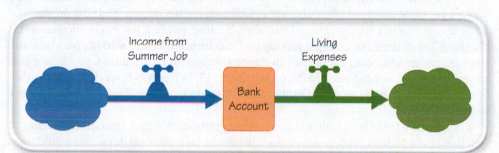

Figure 3-3
Bank Account Represented as a System
A system showing how money flows in and out of a bank account.

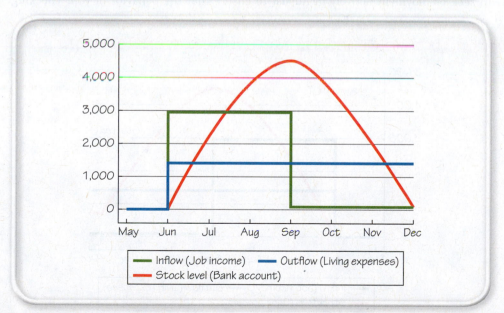

Figure 3-4
Graph Diagram of System Behavior
A figure illustrating system behavior over time on a bank account.

Source: L. Booth Sweeney, and J. D. Sterman, "Bathtub Dynamics: Initial Results of a Systems Thinking Inventory," *System Dynamics Review* 16, vol. 4 (2000): 249–294.

Graphing these three elements, we see that your bank balance will be zero at the beginning of December. Why do we need to graph all three elements? Isn't knowing the behavior (in this case the account balance) sufficient? Visualizing the inflow and outflow of the system allows managers to predict the delayed patterns of behavior. Figure 3-4 represents a very simple system, without adding the complexities of interest (inflow) or unexpected expenses, such as your car breaking down (outflow). When your bank account is graphed over time, we can see the *behavior* of your bank account, as the inflow changes and the stock level rises and falls.

System Change Once you understand how the various inflows, outflows, and stocks affect a system's function, as a manager, you can make better decisions to get the results you want from that system. Let's look again at your personal financial system. Your desire is to have enough money in your bank account to cover your living expenses for the entire year. By mapping the system's behavior over time, you see that your bank account will be empty by the end of November. There is a *discrepancy* between your desired stock level and the actual stock level. Seeing that discrepancy motivates you to change. So what can you do? You've identified one inflow (summer job income) and one outflow (living expenses). Working with just these two flows, you have three options: increase the inflow (work more), decrease the outflow (eat out less), or do a little of both. But let's say that you've already trimmed your living expenses as much as possible, and you don't see any way to make more money over the summer. In that case, you might decide to add a new inflow, such as picking up a part-time job during the school year.

Looking at your graph, you might think that you could start working your part-time job on December 1, when your bank account is slated to hit zero. But that decision would not accommodate the lag time, or *delay*, that is inherent in any system change. **Delay** means that any change to the system, whether from external forces or from intentional decisions, takes time to have an effect. Let's say that you started working on December 1. When would you get your first paycheck? Probably not until the end of the month. And that means your bank account would still be zero in December, because you had not made allowances for the delay. To continue our example, let's say that you are interested in working part-time and have the potential to earn $1,500/month during the semester. In addition, you have a goal of getting an account balance of $750 by November 15. In Figure 3-5, we demonstrate that you would need to begin work by October 15. How might managers use this theory to make better decisions?

Let's assume that the summer employment opportunity is no longer available, so you will need time to look for a position, and this could take 30 to 60 days. You would need to seek employment actively in August to ensure that the behavior of your checking

> **Delay** Refers to the time a force, internal or external, takes to have an effect on system behavior.

Figure 3-5
Delayed Behavior in a System
The effects of delayed behavior in a system.

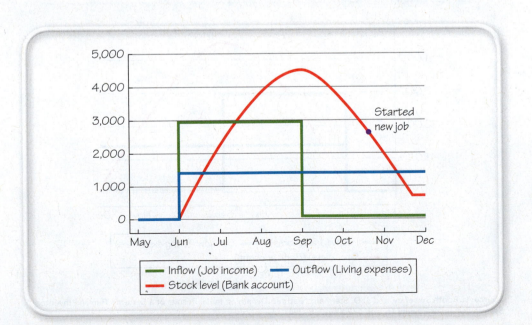

account was at a desirable equilibrium in November. The ability to diagnose and predict these system behaviors allows managers to make more effective decisions, such as allocating resources, hiring employees, marketing products and services, training staff to increase quality, investing in growth, and expanding an organization's capacity to serve customers.

3.3 | SYSTEMS BEHAVIORS AND FEEDBACK LOOPS

3.3 | Show how systems balance and reinforce their behavior over time.

To our systems diagrams of stocks, flows, and discrepancies, we can add **feedback loops**, reactionary forces that cause fluctuations in behavior. A **balancing loop** seeks stabilization or an equilibrium. It counteracts a force of change in an effort to keep stock at the same level. An example of equilibrium in a balancing loop is room temperature, where a glass of ice water or cup of hot tea over time will warm or cool—homing in on the room temperature. You can then adjust the thermostat, which alters the equilibrium higher or lower. After a delay in behavior, both the glass and cup of water then stabilizes in relationship to the new room temperature as illustrated in Figure 3-6. A **reinforcing loop**, on the other hand, encourages and amplifies change that increases or decreases a stock. An example of amplification in reinforcing loops is practicing a musical instrument. The more you practice playing the piano, the prettier the sounds produced, and the more you enjoy listening to the music you play. This encourages you to practice even more, thus increasing your skill, the beauty of the music, and your appreciation of playing and listening. In Figure 3-6, balancing loops are identified in the diagrams as B, and reinforcing loops are signified by R.

LECTURE ENHANCER:

3.3 Systems Behaviors and Feedback Loops

- **How do systems balance and reinforce their behavior over time?**
- ✓ **Feedback loops** are reactionary forces that cause fluctuations in behavior
  - o A **balancing loop** seeks stabilization or equilibrium in an effort to keep stock at the same level (e.g., a cup of hot tea cooling toward room temperature)

Feedback loop A reactionary force that causes fluctuations in behavior.

Balancing loop A reactionary force that seeks stabilization toward a stock level equilibrium, typically a goal or desired state.

Reinforcing loop A self-multiplying reactionary force that amplifies change in a stock level.

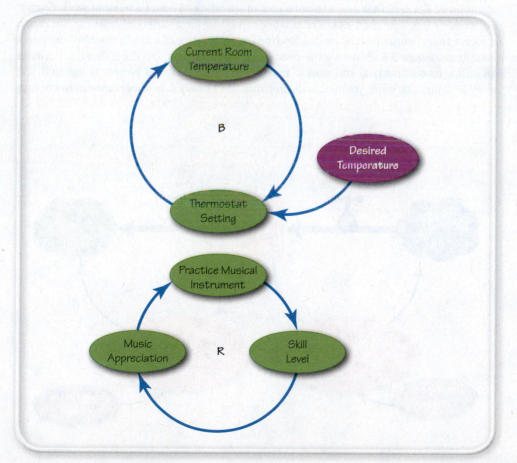

Figure 3-6

Balancing and Reinforcing Loops
Room temperature is a balancing loop, which can be adjusted using a thermostat to reach the desired temperature. A musical instrument, which when practiced increases the skill level and music appreciation of the player, illustrates a reinforcing loop B, balancing loop; R, reinforcing loop.

Systems Behavior

To explore feedback loops further, let's revisit an earlier example. While you are in college, your bank account probably goes up and down depending on the sum of your outflows and inflows. In reality, you can adjust the inflow of your account by working another shift at your job and the outflow of your account by taking a cross-country road trip with friends. Or, better yet, your bank account might be interest-bearing, which will increase the inflow without you doing anything. The causes of these fluctuations are the feedback loops, occurring when the inflow or outflow *behaves* due to the level of stock.

Balancing Behavior Let's say your goal is to have $9,000 (the equivalent of setting a thermostat for a desired room temperature) by the end of August, and you go on a cross-country trip with friends for the last two weeks of July. At the time of your departure, you have $4,500 in your account. For those two weeks, you do not make your normal $1,500, and you spend $1,500 while you are gone. When you return from your trip, you notice that the stock level of your bank account is lower than desired. To reach your goal, you must increase the inflow to your bank account by an additional $6,000. This encourages you to work double shifts until you have a desired level of cash stored. When a feedback loop tries to achieve stability or a goal, this is called a *balancing loop* (shown in Figure 3-7). This example also shows us that feedback loops have levels of *intensity*, which if controllable, can be altered to achieve a desirable outcome. This means that if your bank account is too low, you can create the intensity of the factors that affect "income from summer job," which means working more hours, resulting in a *stronger intensity* for this feedback loop. If you work more hours, presumably you will need to change the intensity of factors that affect "living expenses," which means taking fewer vacations with friends, resulting in a *weaker intensity* for this feedback loop.

In business, examples of systems will become more complex, but the same principles apply. One common phrase used in organizations is "work-life balance," referring to people's needs to stabilize their time spent at work and their time spent with friends, family, and community. For you, that might mean a goal of spending 48 hours a week at work. Spending more or less time than 48 hours at work can occur for a variety of reasons: you coach a soccer team, work projects are due, and/or long-term care of a family member demands your focus. Figure 3-8 illustrates the concept of work-life balance. The difference between an inflow or outflow goal and sum of flow is a **discrepancy**. If a project is due and you work 59 hours one week, you have a discrepancy of 11 hours. It is important not to confuse

Discrepancy The difference between an inflow or outflow sum of flow, relative to an equilibrium or desired state.

Figure 3-7
System with Balancing Loop
A balancing loop showing the effects of income on a bank account and living expenses B, balancing loop.

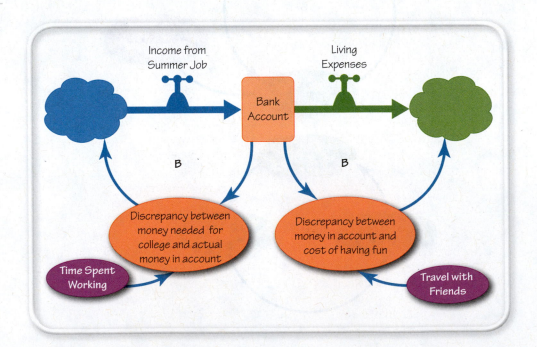

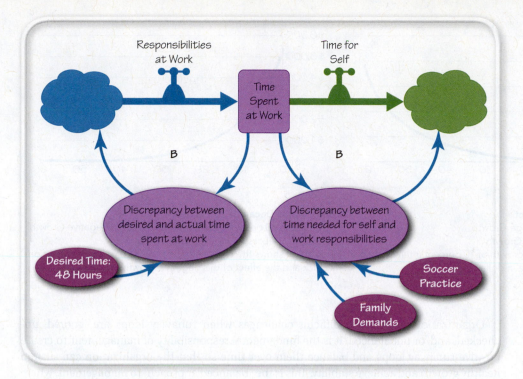

Figure 3-8
**System Showing "Work-Life"
Balance**
A system showing the
discrepancies between
responsibilities at work and
making time for yourself
B, balancing loop.

a goal with a purpose. The *goal* of your time spent at work is 48 hours. So, what is the purpose of this "work-life balance" system? Presumably, you equate a healthy balancing of time between your personal and work lives to happiness. The purpose of this system, then, is to achieve a stable happiness.

Runaway Behavior Now let's say that in addition to your bank account, you have a trust fund that your very generous Uncle Albert set up for you when you were 5 years old. This trust fund earns interest and is a stock that you cannot touch until you are 25 years old, so it is not affecting the level of your bank account. Uncle Albert lets you choose between two options. He will set aside either 1) $5,000 earning 10 percent interest or 2) $10,000 earning 5 percent interest. In 20 years, if you went with option 1, you would have $33,637.50; and with option 2, you would have $26,532.98. After 20 years, you would have 26 percent more money, so if you chose option 1, you did quite well. What if you completely forget about this money until you receive a bank notice when you retire at the age of 65? How much money would each option offer you? After 60 years, option 1 increases the level of your trust fund to $1,522,408.20; in comparison, option 2 will have a level of only $186,791.86. After 60 years, you will have 815 percent more money choosing option 1, which is a great example of amplification! *Compounding* is when money made through interest is added to the stock and earns future interest, which is then added to the stock to earn future interest, and so on. This is called a *runaway or reinforcing loop*, where feedback becomes self-multiplying or amplifying to the level of stock. Rarely is a system left unbalanced, where a runaway loop is allowed to increase exponentially, unless it is ignored—like forgetting about your trust fund until you are 65. **Exponential growth or decay** is when a stock increases or decreases relative to its size. Interest is a runaway loop that leads to exponential growth or decay, as illustrated in Figures 3-9 and 3-10.

Runaway loops can produce positive and negative self-multiplying effects. We have discussed the positive results of runaway behavior, but what about the negative consequences? Consider what would happen when runaway behavior directly depletes a limited resource. The classic example in society today is fossil fuels. Societies around the world are becoming more industrialized, which often leads to more energy usage. With a limited resource such as oil, this behavior could eventually lead to a depletion in the world's supply of fossil fuel to nearly zero.

Exponential growth or decay
When a stock increases or
decreases relative to its size,
wherein the stock is self-multiplying.

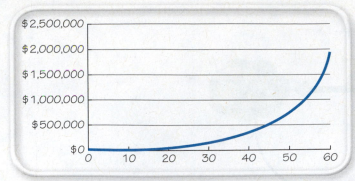

Figure 3-9
Exponential Growth of 10 Percent
0 percent to 60 percent—Percentage Growth
$0–$2,500,000—Dollars of Interest Growth
This graph shows the exponential growth of 10 percent interest on a stock and the effect of this increase in dollars.

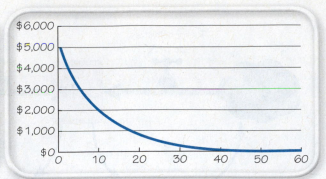

Figure 3-10
Exponential Decay of 10 Percent
0 percent to 60 percent—Percentage of Decay (Negative Growth)
$0 to $6,000—Loss in Dollars (Negative Growth)
This graph shows the exponential decay of 10 percent interest on a stock and the effect of this negative growth in dollars.

Organizations experience difficult challenges when runaway loops are ignored, unchecked, and/or unbalanced. It is the fundamental responsibility of management to create positive runaway loops and balance them over time so that the organization can sustain healthy growth and achieve stability. This is the "balanced approach" to management, where managers continuously change the system when necessary.[8]

LECTURE ENHANCER:

3.4 Analyzing Systems and Knowing What to Change

✓ **Causal loops**
  o Managers often need to see the whole system in order to predict patterns of behavior
  o **Causal loop diagrams** map out the structure of a system and show how the components of a system interact with each other, allowing managers to visualize discrepancies, systemically view behavior, and make decisions.

✓ **Building a culture of change**
  o Managers create a culture for healthy change when they:
  1) understand the company's mission
  2) comprehend the purpose of its subsystems
  3) acknowledge the imbalances or discrepancies that feedback loops are imposing on the subsystem's purpose
  4) design a plan to achieve balance
  5) communicate to all relevant employees a subsystem's purpose and discrepancies.

3.4 | ANALYZING SYSTEMS AND KNOWING WHAT TO CHANGE

3.4 | **Analyze** system discrepancies to determine a manager's intervention.

Now that you have a fundamental understanding of how systems work, let's look at another example. Amazon, the world's largest online retailer, saves energy costs by removing the bulbs in the vending machines, saving the company a significant amount of money. Amazon also has a "cloud computing" initiative, where instead of storing information on one computer for people to retrieve (also called a *computer server*), this information is stored on multiple servers.[9] Cloud computing offers people the ability to access applications and services over the Internet from anywhere in the world, rather than through traditional network access.[10]

Cloud computing allows a large number of "requests" to be sent to multiple computers, so that no single computer gets overwhelmed. In 2009, Amazon's "cloud" had 1.8 million servers, with customer demand that could increase that number to 5.4 million in 2010.[11] What does this have to do with the vending machines? At Amazon, energy consumption is a subsystem of the company (a system). Computer servers use energy, and a lot more of it than vending machines do. Both servers and vending machines have an impact on this subsystem, one greater than the other. Management at Amazon has the ability to unscrew the lightbulbs from the vending machines with no noticeable effect on company performance. Conversely, as more customers demand cloud computing services, management will continue to add computer servers.[12] This will predictably increase energy consumption and costs, which will grow at a greater rate than management's ability to find lightbulbs to unscrew.[13]

What can managers do to balance the company's need to grow and provide shareholder value *and* contain energy costs and usage? First, let's create this system one step at a time, starting with the stock and flows. The stock of this system is energy cost, with the inflow and outflow being usage and savings, respectively. Next, in analyzing a management system, we need to ask, "Is there a runaway loop necessary for the company to achieve growth?" Let's add a runaway loop from *cost of energy* (the stock) to *usage* (the inflow). Next, we need to know the system's purpose. For you as a manager and leader, this is a vital task because the system's purpose affects your team's behavior and, as a result, how the system behaves. We will say that the purpose of this system is to stabilize the company's energy costs. The goal is to have these costs represent the same percentage of expenses in 10 years that they are today. Before we add more feedback loops, this is the time to consider all the factors that affect this loop—specifically, *goals* or *discrepancies*. In this example, the primary factor affecting this runaway loop is cloud computing growth. We know that the company's purpose is to have "energy costs represent the same percentage of company expenses in 10 years that they are today." Now, as a manager, you might ask, "To achieve the purpose of this system, is there a feedback loop that can balance the exponential effects of growth in cloud computing (a runaway loop)?" This question becomes the inspiration for a "balanced approach" to organizational change.

To stabilize the impact of a runaway feedback loop, a manager must introduce a balancing loop that continuously seeks the goal of the subsystem. In this example, we need to increase the intensity of savings (outflow) to compensate for the growth in usage (inflow). This will then require the addition of a balancing loop, which influences savings. What factors might affect the intensity of savings? Two ideas are unscrewing lightbulbs (low intensity) and purchasing renewable energy (potentially high intensity). In this example, we can assume that the manager responsible for building the cloud computing business for Amazon is not also overseeing the energy budget. As we said before, there are not enough lightbulbs for Amazon to unscrew, so management will likely consider purchasing renewable energy sources. In fact, there are two popular ideas that have proposed at Amazon to create renewable energy for computer server farms: water dams (hydroelectric) and cow manure (biofuel).

Causal Loops

In rapidly changing environments, managers also need to see the "whole system" to predict patterns of behavior. Causal loop diagrams map out the structure of a system and show how the components of a system interact with each other. They allow managers to visualize discrepancies and provide managers a systemic view of a behavior, which enables them to make decisions. Figure 3-11 shows an example of a causal loop diagram using the "Amazon Energy Budget System."

Throughout this book, we will explore causal loop diagrams and stock and flow diagrams for predicting behaviors and consequences that managers make or consider for change.

Building a Culture of Change

Organizations go through continuous change. Managers create a culture for healthy change when they clearly 1) understand the company's mission, 2) comprehend the purpose of its subsystems, 3) acknowledge the imbalances or discrepancies that feedback loops are imposing on the subsystem's purpose, 4) design a plan to achieve balance, and 5) communicate to all relevant employees a subsystem's purpose and discrepancies.

The Amazon energy management quandary is a classic example of why different divisions, or subsystems, in a company should communicate with one another. The two managers responsible for cloud computing and energy management need to understand the purpose and goal of their respective subsystems (divisions or business units) to help achieve balance for the overall system (the company). This mutual understanding gives each manager the knowledge they need to know when and how to change the behavior of their subsystem. This reasoning allows managers to communicate effectively why change is necessary to internal and external stakeholders.[14] (Table 3-1 demonstrates this approach.)

In the next chapter, we will further explore how managers deal with cultural and organizational changes taking place within their internal and external environments.

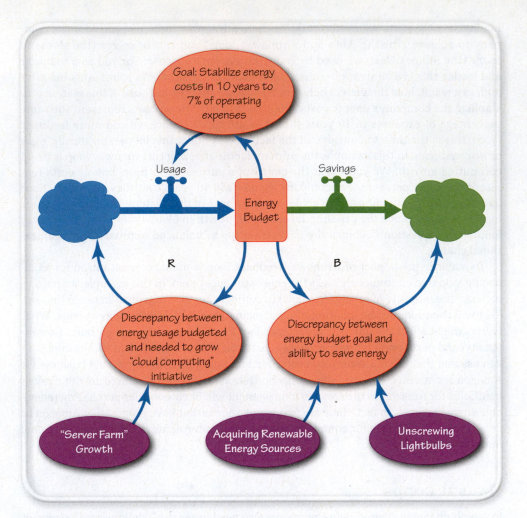

Figure 3-11

Seeing Systems: Amazon's Energy Budget System
A causal loop diagram using Amazon's Energy Budget System to show the discrepancies between usage, growth, resources, and the ability to save energy B, balancing loop; R, reinforcing loop.

LECTURE ENHANCER:

3.5 Common Systems Patterns

• **The Eight Most Common System Archetypes That Managers Can Expect To Encounter**

  o **Limits to growth systems archetype**—"The harder we run, the more we seem to stay in the same place."

  o **Shifting the burden systems archetype**—"Look here, this solution has worked so far! What do you mean there's trouble down the road?"

  o **Eroding goals systems archetype**—"It's okay if our performance standards slide a little, just until the crisis is over…"

  o **Escalation systems archetype**—"If our opponent would only slow down, then we could stop fighting this battle and get some other things done."

  o **Success to the successful systems archetype**

Systems archetypes Peter Senge's classification of common patterns of complex problems that managers encounter.

Table 3-1 Reasons for Change Management

Top Five Reasons Managers Should Change
1. Goal for growth in one subsystem makes it implausible to achieve stability in another
2. Intensity of balancing loop not sufficient to curb behavior in runaway loop
3. Purpose of subsystem inconsistent with mission of system
4. Organization does not have the talent, customers, or suppliers to achieve goals
5. Capacity to inflow or outflow exceeds the environment's ability to saturate or evaporate resources to and from the system

3.5 | COMMON SYSTEMS PATTERNS

3.5 Diagram the eight most common systems archetypes that managers can expect to encounter.

In the previous section, we explored system dynamics as a useful method for managers to assess the functions and behavior of complex systems. The early study of system dynamics allowed other systems thinking researchers to expand on the recurring underlying problems affecting organizations and how they might be resolved. In *The Fifth Discipline*, Senge outlines some of these problems or "disabilities" that impede the performance of an organization, resulting in stagnation, and lack of productivity. Through Systems Theory, Senge classifies these complex problems into eight predictable patterns called **systems archetypes**.[15]

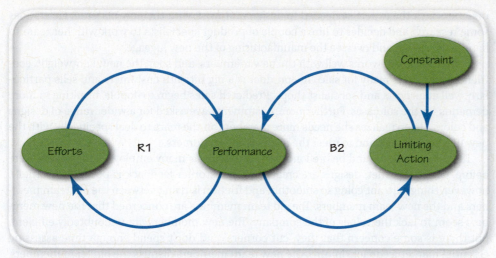

Figure 3-12
Limits to Growth Systems Archetype
This shows limits to growth on work efforts and performance where the growth process is impeded by constraints that limit progress B, balancing loop; R, reinforcing loop.

Managers can use these archetypes as effective tools for establishing the underlying reasons for recurring problems. Once the patterns of behavior are revealed, managers can then take steps to resolve the issue and break the pattern before it becomes embedded in the system structure. The following section provides an example of each of the eight systems archetypes, which are **Limits to Growth**, **Shifting the Burden**, **Eroding Goals**, **Escalation**, **Success to the Successful**, **Tragedy of the Commons**, **Fixes That Fail**, and **Growth and Underinvestment.**

Senge's Eight Archetypes

1. Limits to Growth

"The harder we run, the more we seem to stay in the same place."[16]

Many organizations experience rapid growth for a certain period of time before coming to a seemingly inexplicable halt. Generally, this happens because the process of growth, caused by a "reinforcing feedback process," has come up against a balancing process that can slow down the rate of improvement or even cause the business to come to a standstill.

The cycle begins when a process has proved so successful that certain problems go unnoticed or management reinforces the situation by relying too much on the "old way of doing things" instead of addressing the issues. This is mainly because the management and employees are so caught up with the accelerating growth or expansion of the company that a "reinforcing feedback" process occurs, where each individual buys into an "If it ain't broke, don't fix it" approach. However, the more they rely on the same business model, the more static the business becomes.

Recognizing and understanding the factors that are causing these limits to growth and development, as shown in Figure 3-12, is essential when an organization reaches a bump in the road. Many managers compensate with this faltering growth by pushing themselves and the team even harder to restore the company to its former glory. However, this method only results in tired, overworked employees and potentially a lowering of morale. By addressing the underlying reasons for the limitations, the source of the problem can be removed and the company's balance restored.

Helen's Story Helen works as a product manager for a successful, high-quality luggage manufacturing company. She firmly believes that the success of the company is based upon its core values, which include quality, customer satisfaction, and innovation. Every employee in the company is expected to adhere to the company's values and performance standards.

Lately, her team has been trying to find ways to make their suitcases more eco-friendly. Although the team has some good ideas about how to manufacture the new product, its members lack the expertise needed to design and work with the new material. Helen does some research and decides to hire a couple of product specialists to work with her team to handle the design and oversee the manufacturing of the new luggage.

At first, the team works well with the new members, and soon the new, lightweight, eco-friendly luggage is ready for sale. The product is a big hit with customers and sells particularly well at airports and specialist shops. Predicted sales begin to double, resulting in more demands for the suitcases. Furthermore, customers have asked for a wider range of designs and colors. Helen realizes she needs more members on the team to deal specifically with the new luggage product and to meet the needs of the customers.

The team expands, and before long there are twice as many employees than there were before. Orders are met, designs are created, and customer feedback is positive. Internally, however, things are not going so smoothly, and friction is rising between the old team members and the new team members. The old team members are concerned that the new members seem to lack the values of the company. The new members are undoubtedly efficient, but there is some concern that they "cut corners" and don't spend enough time assessing essential market feedback. In turn, the new team members dismiss the old team members' suggestions that they follow "the old way of doing things."

Helen notices the divisions within the team, but she puts the dissension down to competition; the most important thing is that the team performs and continues to make money for the company. As the company's profit grows, she pushes the team to work even harder to meet demand. She is so caught up with meeting the financial goals that she fails to notice the effect of the extra pressure on the team members. They grow further and further apart until, eventually, communication breaks down altogether, leading to confusion and failure to fulfill orders. It is not long before sales begin to drop, customers complain about quality, morale hits rock bottom, and disgruntled employees start to leave. Helen realizes that if she wants to save the new product from extinction, she must find a solution.

Helen sits down with her boss to discuss the plummeting financial figures and analyze what has happened and how they can remove the limitations to growth. One of the major underlying reasons for the falling team performance is the growing distance and tension between the old and new team members. Helen suggests that they call a meeting to address the internal friction and try to find ways to reconcile the team. Helen's boss agrees: they need to find some way of boosting morale, and get the team excited about the new product once more. In the end, they hold some team-building events, and contests, with the winners receiving a set of luggage as a prize. The relationship between the team members gradually improves, and so does the company performance. Problem solved; but Helen continues to keep a close eye on her staff and makes sure she addresses any other potential issues before they escalate.

2. Shifting the Burden

> "Look here, this solution has worked so far! What do you mean there's trouble down the road?"[17]

Shifting the Burden shown in Figure 3-13 occurs when people use quick fixes when resolving an underlying problem that seems too time-consuming, difficult, or costly to address fully. Because the fix seems to work initially, it is used repeatedly. However, as the fundamental issue still exists, these "fixes" are usually only short-term solutions; it is inevitable that the situation will worsen over the long term and produce unwanted side effects further down the road.

Another example of Shifting the Burden is when organizations bring in outside "interveners" to help resolve a problem. Again, this can be useful in the short term—the external team identifies and solves the issue and once more restores balance and order to organizational processes. The disadvantage to hiring external help is that the existing employees fail to learn the skills that could help them to fix the problem themselves, which fosters dependency on the outside teams whenever the issue recurs.

The key here is to find a long-term, enduring solution to the problem rather than relying on a quick fix. At best, the Shifting the Burden method should be used only to buy time while a lasting solution is being put in place.

Tony's Story When Tony founded a start-up business selling gourmet pet food, he was extremely excited. Within the first year, business was booming, and orders were coming

---

Shifting the Burden archetypes
A systems pattern, similar to "Fixes that Fail," where managers use short-term fixes that result in long-term problems, typically by using non-sustainable resources to address a challenge.

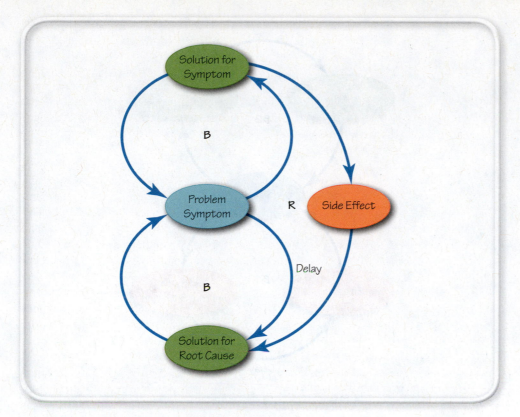

Figure 3-13
Shifting the Burden Systems Archetype
This diagram shows shifting the burden of solving problems to external forces, resulting in delays and other side effects B, balancing loop; R, reinforcing loop.

in fast. However, by the second year, sales had started to taper off, and Tony was getting concerned. Looking at the database, he saw that the company was selling well to existing customers, but it had been months since they had any new customers. Tony reasoned that his sales and marketing team were too busy with their existing customer base to stump for new business, so he elected to contract external help for a couple of months.

At first, the outside sales team made great strides in attracting new customers. They designed a better strategy, defined a different target market, and built a new sales system. Soon, the company was getting more orders than ever before, and business was really taking off.

Two months later, the contract with the outside sales team was up, and Tony had to let the team leave. Suddenly, business began to decline again due to a number of glitches. As the existing sales team had never learned how to use the new system, they had no idea how to correct errors or mend system breakdowns. Orders were lost or delayed, and customers began to complain. Furthermore, unlike the external team, Tony's own team had never established any kind of relationship with the new clients and did not know how to cater to their needs.

As business began to go downhill, Tony realized that shifting the burden to another team had worked in the short term but had brought about a new set of problems in its place. Consequently, he started to look for a long-term solution to prevent his company from going under.

Tony reasoned that the main problem was lack of knowledge: his existing team had no idea how to work the new system implemented by the external team, nor did they have a good understanding of how to deal with the new target customer base. Immediately, Tony introduced a range of training sessions and held open forums to answer any questions or concerns. Three months later, armed with their new knowledge, and reassured by the managerial support, the team began to perform much better. Within six months, Tony's gourmet pet-food business had started to make a profit once again.

3. Eroding Goals

"It's okay if our performance standards slide a little, just until the crisis is over . . ."[18]

Eroding Goals archetypes A systems pattern where managers impose short-term solutions, leading to the decline of long-term goals.

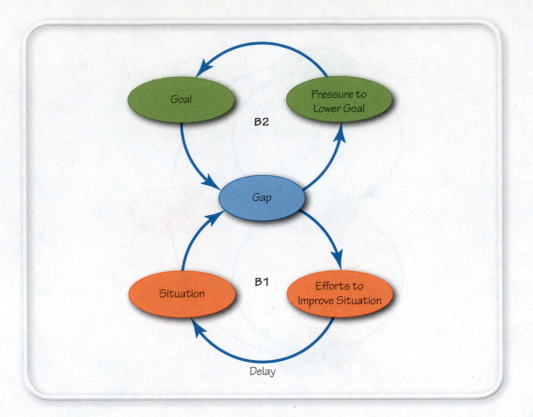

Figure 3-14
Eroding Goals Systems Archetype
A Shifting the Burden concept where a short-term solution is put in place, leading to the erosion of a long-term goal B, balancing loop; R, reinforcing loop.

Eroding Goals shown in Figure 3-14 is another case of shifting the burden. Too much dependence on relieving the symptom rather than the underlying problem by employing easy fixes and short-term solutions will have a negative impact on long-term fundamental goals.

In this uncertain economy, it is easy for a company to fall prey to accepting lower performance levels. By making comparisons to other struggling organizations in the same industry, managers can perceive their falling standards and slipping goals as "good enough under the circumstances." Once more, the balancing feedback loop is overcome by the reinforcing feedback loop. In other words, if managers and employees accept this goal-slipping process and allow for lowering performance standards rather than taking corrective action, then the balance will shift and business will continue to decline gradually.

There is a choice between allowing goals to slip and improving the situation. Organizations can avoid the pitfalls of the goal-eroding trap by maintaining absolute performance standards regardless of whatever crisis they may be facing, or how the economy is performing. Indeed, if the perception shifts from "well, we've done our best under the circumstances," to "let's see this as a temporary setback and find ways to improve performance," then the company will achieve its goals in a much shorter time.

Seline's Story Seline is a physician in a large hospital in Florida. Her job includes treating patients, forming diagnoses, and communicating with other departments when a patient needs specialized care. When Seline refers a patient to another department or hospital for cardiology or respiratory care, for example, she needs an efficient way of sharing information.

Fortunately, a couple of years ago, one of her hospital's goals was to invest in the latest IT healthcare systems and technology, which allow each department to exchange accurate information about a patient with other departments and hospitals quickly and efficiently. Seline is an advocate of this product and works closely with other hospitals to teach them how to use the technology. For the past two years, Seline has championed this technology, doing demonstrations and exalting the benefits of the system. In many cases, her efforts have paid off, and she has succeeded in persuading hospitals to use the new technology.

In spite of her success, however, a few hospitals in the area have been slow to employ the system. This means that when Seline or other doctors need to send a patient to another hospital for further treatment, instead of using the system, they must handwrite everything, which is time consuming and prone to errors.

As the economy dips, some of the hospitals that use the system start to view it as an unnecessary expense. Seline's boss has also started to instigate budget cuts, which include the decision not to renew the contract with the software company that leases the system to the hospital. Seline is told that this is only a temporary measure until the hospital gets back on its feet.

Seline and the other doctors resort to writing patient diagnoses manually once more, leading to loss of patient records and general confusion. As Seline observes performance standards slipping within her own hospital as well as others, she realizes that she needs to figure out how she is going to weather the storm and if she can help maintain the hospital's original objective.

Seline decides that she needs to convince her boss to bring back the new system, so she sets up a meeting with him for the following week. She spends the next few days analyzing and gathering information to prepare for the discussion. By using charts and statistics, Seline is able to show her boss how performance standards have declined as a direct result of taking away the system. She is also able to report a higher level of negative patient feedback since the software has been decommissioned. Seline's boss responds that while the situation is not ideal, the hospital simply does not have the budget for the system. Anticipating this response, Seline outlines a plan where they could keep the system but introduce cost savings elsewhere, such as encouraging hospital staff to turn off lights and computers when they go home, which would bring about significant savings. She also suggests holding a weekly brainstorming session with the staff so they can put forward ideas on how the hospital could save money in other areas. Impressed by Seline's proposal, her boss puts her in charge of a new initiative to implement cost-cutting measures—and he promises that if they work, he will reintroduce the system. Three months later, the system is back up and running, and performance levels improve once more.

4. Escalation

> "If our opponent would only slow down, then we could stop fighting this battle and get some other things done."[19]

Escalation shown in Figure 3-15 takes place when competition between two individuals or organizations gets completely out of hand, leading to a "lose-lose" situation. Of course, healthy competition is imperative for businesses to survive, but when it becomes overly aggressive, there can only be negative results. When one party launches an attack, the other side inevitably sees this as a threat and fights back, leading to a snowball effect. This often occurs when companies have price wars, where one company lowers its prices to compete with another company in the same industry. The other company ends up reducing its prices to compete, the first company responds in kind again, and so on, until both companies are losing profits.

Escalation can be avoided if managers look for ways for both sides to achieve their goals. This involves cooperation, mutual understanding, and open discussion.

Escalation archetypes A systems pattern where two competing interests eventually take irrational actions against one another, resulting in a "lose-lose" situation.

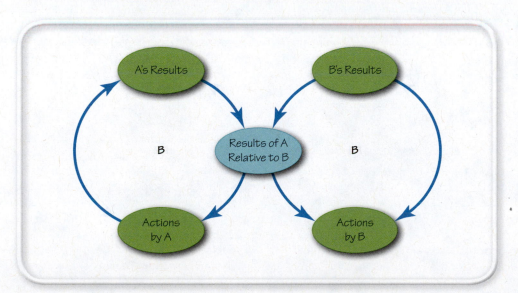

Figure 3-15
Escalation Systems Archetype
One individual or organization aggressively competes against another individual or organization, leading to escalation B, balancing loop.

Jamal's Story Jamal is an entrepreneur and an inventor. Having recently patented his ideas and received endorsement from a number of investors, Jamal can't wait to build his start-up company and put it on the road to success. The first invention that Jamal will use to test the market is a three-wheeled scooter for adults and children. Safe, lightweight, and affordable, the scooter quickly flies off the shelves, and Jamal is delighted to find himself inundated with orders.

Within a year, however, another growth company that specializes in bicycles manufactures its own three-wheeled scooter, almost identical to Jamal's invention, and starts to sell it at a lower price. When sales start to fall and Jamal's fledgling company begins to struggle, he panics and lowers the price to match his competitor's price. Eager to increase market share, Jamal's competitor drops the price even further. As this pattern continues over several years, both companies suffer a blow to their bottom line. Customers begin to become suspicious of such "cheap" products, and soon the survival of the scooter and the companies themselves are called into question.

Facing bankruptcy, Jamal has to find a way to save his invention, restore investor faith, and build up his company once more. He knows that at this critical point, he has nothing to lose by arranging a meeting with his biggest adversary. To his surprise, Jamal's competitor is interested in discussing ways in which both businesses can break free of the pattern and thrive once again. They agree that they need to differentiate rather than being in direct competition with each other. Jamal confesses that he has a number of other inventions that he would like to market, and his competitor reassures him that he intends to focus solely on bicycle manufacturing in the future. As for the three-wheeled scooter, the two parties agree to sell it at the same price in each of their stores. In the end, Jamal's new inventions take his business in an entirely different direction from his competitor's, and his company gets back on track once again.

5. Success to the Successful

The Success to the Successful paradigm shown in Figure 3-16 occurs when two efforts or activities compete for the same resources. The more success one effort achieves the more support it gets, to the detriment of the other. Again, this is another example of a lose-lose situation. One party is thriving and the other is struggling. However, as they are competing for the same resource, it is only a matter of time before that resource becomes limited or runs out altogether, leading to loss for both parties.

The key here is to strike a balance between the two activities. Ascertain the reasons why the other party is struggling and try to make the resource accessible to both. If the resource is already under pressure, then find ways to distribute it evenly or present another alternative.

Marielle and Rachael's Story Marielle and Rachael have known each other since childhood; they went to the same schools, achieved similar academic results, and attended the same

Success to the Successful archetypes A systems pattern where two efforts compete for the same resources, and the more successful effort today gets more support, regardless of future potential of the competing effort.

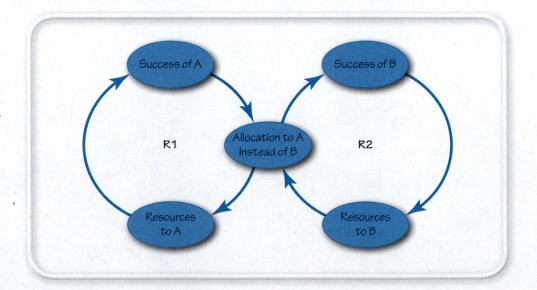

Figure 3-16
Success to the Successful Systems Archetype
Two activities compete for the same resources. One activity becomes more successful, depriving the other of support and resources R, reinforcing loop.

university. Both have a passion for the hotel industry, and each graduated with honors in hotel management. When they both got jobs as trainee hotel managers at one of the world's most luxurious hotels, Marielle and Rachael were excited. They joked about which one of them would climb the career ladder quicker.

On their first day, the new trainees found out that they would both be reporting to the same manager. Marielle and Rachael exchanged a look: the pressure was really on now; they would be competing against each other. Their first few weeks went well. They worked hard and worked well together on tasks, and soon both stood out in the eyes of their manager.

One day, Rachael receives some bad news; her grandfather has passed away. Devastated, Rachael flies home to attend the funeral, and she is gone for almost a week. During her absence, the hotel experiences a minor fire. Marielle jumps into action and makes sure that all the guests are out of their rooms and brought to safety. Marielle's boss is so impressed with her ability to take initiative, together with her impressive work performance, that he puts her up for promotion.

When Rachael returns, she notices a distinct camaraderie between her manager and Marielle. She becomes frustrated that her suggestions never seem to be taken into account, and she is constantly assigned the more menial tasks, while Marielle gets the more rewarding assignments. When she tries to talk to her manager about the situation, she is waved away or told that she is being paranoid. As time goes by, Rachael feels that she is being pushed further and further out; either the situation needs to improve or she will have to get another job.

As Rachael's manager is unable to see her point of view, Rachael feels that she has no other recourse but to go to the executive hotel manager to explain the situation. To her relief, the executive manager is sympathetic to her plight and suggests that Rachael work for a different manager in the hotel, where she would be carrying out duties that would not necessarily overlap with her previous role. Rachael agrees to try out the new approach and finds her new boss supportive and encouraging and her new responsibilities interesting and varied. As they are not in direct competition any longer, Rachael and Marielle are able to maintain their friendship, and both become fully qualified hotel managers in the same amount of time.

6. Tragedy of the Commons

"There used to be plenty for everyone. Now things are getting tough. If I'm going to earn any profit this year, I'll have to work harder."[20]

Tragedy of the Commons shown in Figure 3-17 occurs when individuals use a common limited resource purely for their own gain, without paying attention to the effects that they are having on it.[21] The more they use it, the less resource they have, until eventually the resource is depleted. Competing companies that continue to mine for the same natural resources until they are in danger of running out is an example of a tragedy of the commons.

Managers can address this problem of regulating the available resource by gaining input from the individuals who use it.

Max's Story Max is a senior manager for a large car manufacturing company and is responsible for managing the company's suppliers. One of his main responsibilities is to monitor the company's oil manufacturers to ensure that the oil is made to exact specifications and delivered on time by the suppliers.

When the company decides to manufacture its own oil, engineered specifically for its own type of car, Max is delighted. He reasons that the firm can gain market share by improving on the quality of the oil, as well as providing the customer with a unique product. Max realizes he will have to liaise even more closely with the oil supplier to get the blend just right.

Although the idea is top secret, information about it leaks out. Suddenly a local rival company copies the idea and makes its own unique brand of oil. As both companies rely on the same oil resource, significant pressure is put on the suppliers to deliver.

Within a few years, both companies are thriving: customers are satisfied with the enhanced quality of the engine oil and don't seem to mind paying a higher premium for it. Rising market share, increased profit, and a reduction in internal expenditure means that business is booming. However, the suppliers begin to fall behind on their orders and warn

Tragedy of the Commons archetypes A systems pattern where multiple efforts are competing for the same resource, where self-interest overrides a collective solution.

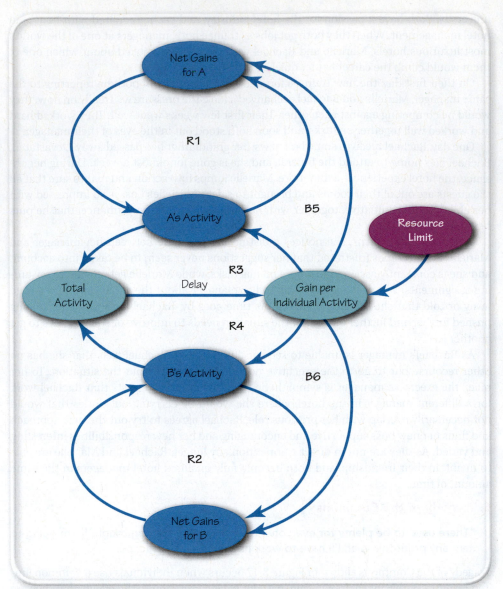

Figure 3-17
Tragedy of the Commons Systems Archetype
Individuals use common limited resources until the resources are diminished or eradicated altogether B, balancing loop; R, reinforcing loop.

Diagram labels: Net Gains for A, A's Activity, Resource Limit, Total Activity, Delay, Gain per Individual Activity, B's Activity, Net Gains for B, R1, R2, R3, R4, B5, B6

Source: From D. Kim, *Systems Archetypes II* (Waltham, MA: Pegasus Communications, Inc., 1994). Printed with permission by the author, Dr. Daniel H. Kim (dhkim@alum.edu).

their clients that the oil supply is becoming significantly depleted. Yet, both companies continue to place orders to manufacture their unique brands of oil until one day, there is no oil left. Almost instantly, revenues drop, customer orders go unfilled, and staff is let go. Shocked that the company has used up their entire supply of a natural resource, Max vows to find a solution to the situation.

On further investigation, Max feels that the problem that has led to the oil scarcity lies in lack of regulation. Max's company and its rival did not regulate the amount of oil that they were using, nor did they heed the warnings from the suppliers. Max eventually finds an oil alternative that is superior to the one they originally manufactured, and business slowly returns to normal. This time, he makes sure that the company regulates its supply and even holds talks at other companies to encourage them to use regulation and educate them about the dangers of overusing natural resources.

7. Fixes That Fail

"It always seemed to work before; why isn't it working now?"

When an urgent problem arises, managers are tempted to address the matter as quickly as possible by putting in a solution to fix the issue. Many times, however, this fix is merely a short-term solution and does not fully correct the problem in the long term, leading to adverse consequences in the future. This is called Fixes That Fail, as illustrated in Figure 3-18.

Fixes That Fail archetypes A systems pattern where managers use short-term fixes that result in long-term problems, typically significantly worse than the original challenge.

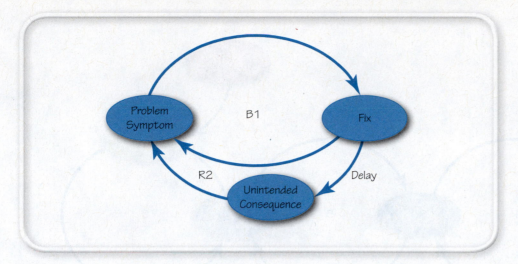

Figure 3-18
Fixes That Fail Systems Archetype
Short-term fixes can have unintended consequences and cause more problems in the long run B, balancing loop; R, reinforcing loop.

Focusing on the long term instead of the short term by implementing a fundamental solution that will have longer-lasting effects helps managers to avoid quick fixes.

Jane's Story Jane works for a top healthcare company in New York City. As finance manager, she is responsible for the overall budget. When the company starts losing revenue, the CEO of the company turns to Jane to see how it can mitigate the loss against the existing budget. Jane starts by investigating the expenses of each department to see if she can find the weak link in the chain. After a few days, it is clear that the sales department is overspending more than the other areas, and so it is dangerously close to exhausting its allocated budget for the year.

On further investigation, it appears that some of the employees have been expensing items that do not fall under the acceptable expense limits. When she questions a senior salesperson, Bill, about his habit of expensing high-priced lunches, he tells her that they were business lunches, and that as far as he was concerned, the company ought to pay for the client as well as himself. Jane tries to explain that the lunch bills were far above the allocated budget and he would have to cut down on the business lunches and find a different way for himself and his sales team to conduct meetings. Bill refuses to comply and tells Jane that business lunches are a fundamental part of being in sales.

Jane is frustrated. As far as she is concerned, the only way she can cut costs, balance the books, and get the budget back on track is to lay down the law with the sales department: either dismiss some of them or give them an ultimatum to cut down on expenses. When the sales team still refuses to comply, Jane makes the decision to fire the main offenders without consulting her boss.

Within a month, Jane is pleased to find that by getting rid of the "troublemakers," the departmental budget was back on track. However, without the extra staff, sales revenue is down. Jane has to hire new salespeople to replace the others, but finds that wages have risen. She will have to factor in higher salaries for the new employees, which will have a severe impact on her budget.

When Jane is called into a meeting with the CEO, she fears the worst—and she is right. Angry that Jane used a quick-fix approach without consulting him, he immediately gives Jane her notice. Jane is disappointed and upset at losing her job, but not surprised; she knew she could have handled the situation differently. Maybe if she had held a meeting with the sales team explaining the effect of overspending on the bottom line, and asked them to introduce new initiatives in which the sales department could reduce its spending, there might have been a different outcome. More important, she should have kept her boss fully informed of her actions.

8. Growth and Underinvestment

"Well, we used to be the best, and we'll be the best again, but right now, we have to conserve our resources and not overinvest."[22]

Growth and Underinvestment archetypes A systems pattern where managers reduce resource allocation to increase profits temporarily or to avoid risk, with the unintended consequence of losing its equilibrium in the marketplace.

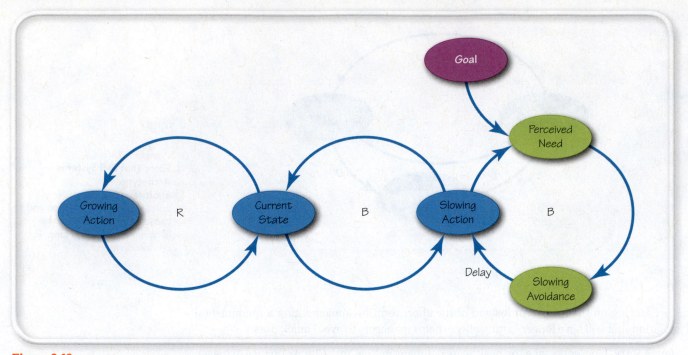

Figure 3-19

Growth and Underinvestment Systems Archetype

Companies that underinvest remain in their current state, leading to stagnation and unfulfilled goals B, balancing loop; R, reinforcing loop.

In these economically challenging times, many organizations tend to batten down the hatches and avoid exposure to "risky" expenditures. Plenty of companies have experienced meteoric growth, only to fall into bankruptcy not long thereafter. Some companies grow too rapidly and fail to meet rising demand. Underinvestment is just as risky as overinvestment if an organization is to maintain its equilibrium in the marketplace. If managers let performance standards slide so they can conserve resources, then the company is on a slippery slope to lower expectations and can lead to a potential collapse. Figure 3-19 illustrates the concept of growth and underinvestment.

To address the balance, managers need to determine if there is capacity for investment and real potential for growth. They need to stay focused on the original vision of the company, work hard to attain these goals, and maintain performance standards to achieve success. Blaming the economy, competition, or internal staff for the slowing of growth will only lead to deterioration and poor morale.

Peter's Story Peter is the owner and manager of a small boutique hotel in Cape Cod. The hotel has 12 rooms, a gourmet restaurant, and stellar customer service. Awarded a five-star rating (out of five) in its first year of business, the hotel is in first place among all the other small hotels in the area. The hotel enjoys a comfortable annual profit and attracts repeat and new business, year after year. Often, Peter has to turn away customers, as the rooms fill up quickly.

One summer, another boutique hotel springs up about a mile away from Peter's hotel. It has almost double the number of rooms as Peter's hotel, as well as a kitchen run by a top chef, and a swimming pool. Soon, Peter's hotel is losing customers to its rival, and profits are beginning to erode. When Peter looks at the books, he realizes that there is potential for his hotel to expand or at least add a few improvements. However, he is worried that he might drive his existing customers away by closing the hotel for a couple of months to make the necessary adjustments and so he decides to sit tight.

In the meantime, business slows down, the staff members are bored, and without the usual number of guests, they have less to do. The quality of their service begins to suffer. When a hotel inspector threatens to downgrade the hotel from A to C, Peter realizes he needs to act quickly to prevent his business from slipping away.

Peter sends an email out to all his regular guests, informing them of the hotel's temporary closure, and he promises them an upgraded facility and a complimentary lunch the next time they come to stay. When the hotel reopens two months later, it includes deluxe, renovated rooms, a refurbished restaurant and menu, and new features that differentiate itself from its rivals: concierge service, free mineral water, WiFi, and luxurious guest robes. Within six months, Peter's hotel is more popular than ever.

Over the course of the following chapters, we will apply a systems approach to critical thinking so that we can design and visualize how all the factors outlined in this chapter interact. You will be able to assess systems archetypes and visualize systems that become a blueprint for management decisions, which stabilize organizations to achieve predictable and desirable outcomes. We will use this skill throughout the remainder of the book as a practical tool for analyzing management challenges and opportunities.

From here, this book will guide you through today's management thought, as it seeks to find a balanced approach to decision making. As management theorists Gary Hamel and Bill Breen say in their book *The Future of Management*, "Look around you: what things have demonstrated their adaptability across decades, centuries, and eons? What sets the benchmark for adaptability? From my vantage point, life, markets, democracies, faith, and cities all seem surprisingly adaptable. They must become the role models for 21st century [management]."[23] These role models of adaptability are complex and durable systems, designed by communities of critical thinkers.

Case**Snapshot**

Chapter 3 Case: Critical Thinking for Managers:
Airbnb can be found on pg. 464

ADDITIONAL RESOURCES

KEY TERMS

Balancing loop A reactionary force that seeks stabilization toward a stock level equilibrium, typically a goal or desired state. **(p. 63)**

Behavior over time (BOT) diagrams A visual tool that allows managers to see the change in measurements across a span of time. **(p. 60)**

Delay Refers to the time a force, internal or external, takes to have an effect on system behavior. **(p. 62)**

Discrepancy The difference between an inflow or outflow sum of flow, relative to an equilibrium or desired state. **(p. 64)**

Eroding Goals archetype A systems pattern where managers impose short-term solutions, leading to the decline of long-term goals. **(p. 71)**

Escalation archetype A systems pattern where two competing interests eventually take irrational actions against one another, resulting in a "lose-lose" situation. **(p. 73)**

Exponential growth or decay When a stock increases or decreases relative to its size, wherein the stock is self-multiplying. **(p. 65)**

Feedback loop A reactionary force that causes fluctuations in behavior. **(p. 63)**

Fixes That Fail archetype A systems pattern where managers use short-term fixes that result in long-term problems, typically significantly worse than the original challenge. **(p. 76)**

Growth and Underinvestment archetype A systems pattern where managers reduce resource allocation to increase profits temporarily or to avoid risk, with the unintended consequence of losing its equilibrium in the marketplace. **(p. 77)**

Inflows Increase the value of a stock measurement. **(p. 60)**

Limits to Growth archetype A systems pattern where an external or internal force restricts the ability to expand a service or product offering, **(p. 69)**

Outflows Decrease the value of a stock measurement. **(p. 60)**

Reinforcing loops A self-multiplying reactionary force that amplifies change in a stock level. **(p. 63)**

Shifting the Burden archetype A systems pattern, similar to "Fixes that Fail," where managers use short-term fixes that result in long-term problems, typically by using non-sustainable resources to address a challenge. **(p. 70)**

Stocks Material or information that can be measured. **(p. 60)**

Success to the Successful archetype A systems pattern where two efforts compete for the same resources, and the more successful effort today gets more support, regardless of future potential of the competing effort. **(p. 74)**

Systems archetypes Peter Senge's classification of common patterns of complex problems that managers encounter. **(p. 69)**

Systems thinking A methodology of analysis that managers use to understand interconnected cause-and-effect relationships that change organizational behaviors and dynamics. **(p. 59)**

Tragedy of the Commons archetype A systems pattern where multiple efforts are competing for the same resource, where self-interest overrides a collective solution. **(p. 75)**

IN REVIEW

3.1 | Explain how managers use systems thinking to achieve results.

With the help of systems thinking, we have the potential to change our mindset, adjust our behaviors, and use our existing skills to enhance strengths within ourselves and others. Systems thinking allows managers to understand and analyze the "interconnected set of elements that is coherently organized in a way that achieves something."

3.2 | Illustrate how systems diagrams are used to show cause-and-effect relationships.

Two kinds of systems diagrams that managers use in their work, each highlighting a different aspect of system behavior, are *stock and flow diagrams*, and *behavior over time (BOT) diagrams*. Stocks are material or information that can be measured, such as trees in a forest, water in a reservoir, electricity produced, money in a bank account, or satisfaction doing a job. Flows are the physical or informational forces that increase or decrease stocks. An *inflow* increases stock, and an *outflow* decreases stock.

You can see from this simple example how you can use a stock and flow diagram to better understand:

- The forces (flows) affecting a particular stock;
- The causes and effects of a particular inflow or outflow; and,
- How different stocks and flows are interconnected in a system.

BOT diagrams help managers visualize the changes and the way the stock level rises and falls. Once you understand how the various inflows, outflows, and stocks affect a system's function, then as a manager, you can make better decisions to get the results you want from that system over time. When there is a *discrepancy* between your desired stock level and the actual stock level, that discrepancy motivates change.

3.3 | **Show** how systems balance and reinforce their behavior over time.

Balancing loops are reactionary forces that seek stabilization toward a stock level equilibrium, typically a goal or desired state. *Reinforcing loops* are self-multiplying reactionary forces that amplify change in a stock level. Organizations experience difficult challenges when runaway loops are ignored, unchecked, and unbalanced. It is the fundamental responsibility of management to create positive runaway loops and balance them over time so that the organization can sustain healthy growth and achieve stability. This is the "balanced approach" to management, where managers continuously change the system when necessary.

3.4 | **Analyze** system discrepancies to determine a manager's intervention.

To stabilize the impact of a runaway feedback loop, a manager must introduce a balancing loop to seek the goal of the subsystem continuously. Visualizing discrepancies in a stock and flow diagram enables managers to make specific policy-based decisions. In rapidly changing environments, managers also need to see the "whole system," to predict patterns of behavior. Causal loop diagrams provide managers with a systemic view of a behavior, which is helpful in understanding more complex relationships between variables.

3.5 | **Diagram** the eight most common systems archetypes that managers can expect to encounter.

In *The Fifth Discipline*, Peter Senge outlines the "disabilities" that impede the performance of an organization, resulting in stagnation and lack of productivity. Through Systems Theory, Senge classifies these complex problems into eight predictable patterns, called *systems archetypes*, that managers encounter: Limits to Growth, Shifting the Burden, Eroding Goals, Escalation, Success to the Successful, Tragedy of the Commons, Fixes That Fail, and Growth and Underinvestment.

SELF-TEST

3.1 | **Explain** how managers use a systems approach to critical thinking to achieve results.

1. The ability to see an organization as a whole "system," or a set of inter-related elements rather than a number of separate parts, is known as:
   a. Interconnectedness
   b. Systems thinking
   c. Big picture thinking
   d. Interrelatedness

2. Describe the five main disciplines described by Peter Senge.

3.2 | **Illustrate** how systems diagrams are used to show cause-and-effect relationships.

3. _____ are the physical or informational forces that increase or decrease stocks.
   a. Flows
   b. Dynamics
   c. Power bases
   d. Dispositions

3.3 | **Show** how systems balance and reinforce their behavior over time.

4. Explain the difference between a balancing and reinforcing feedback loop.

5. The difference between an inflow or outflow goal and sum of flow is known as a discrepancy.
   a. True
   b. False

3.4 | **Analyze** system discrepancies to determine a manager's intervention.

6. Explain how Amazon uses systems thinking to cut energy costs.

7. _____ map out the structure of a system and show how the components of a system interact with each other.

3.5 | **Diagram** the eight most common systems archetypes that managers can expect to encounter.

8. Which of the following is *not* one of Senge's eight most common system archetypes that managers can expect to encounter?
   a. Limits to Growth
   b. Shifting the Burden
   c. Escalation
   d. Tragedy of the Commons
   e. Overachievement

CHAPTER EXERCISE

Aliens at the Ballpark

Suppose that an alien delegation is visiting Earth to observe and better understand human customs, practices, and norms. You have been asked to serve as tour guide for the aliens on a trip to a professional baseball game. Upon arrival at the ballpark, the aliens become quite confused and have many questions for you. You find it surprisingly difficult to explain baseball, a game you understand quite well, to the aliens. For example, how would you answer the following questions:

1. What is a game?
2. What is a team?
3. Why are there no female players in the game?
4. Why do people in the stadium get so excited about watching other people play a game?

5. Why can't the people in bleachers go down on the field and play too?
6. Why are winning and losing so important?

Thinking like a tour guide for an alien delegation will help you to become a more effective critical thinker. Looking at something the way that an outsider unfamiliar with the process might can help you to realize that much of what we do and how we think are based on deeply imbedded assumptions and values. Our basic values and ways of doing things may appear less logical and "correct" when viewed from the perspective of an alien. Trying to think like an alien tour guide can help you to think critically when addressing challenges and solving problems.

SELF-ASSESSMENT

Critical Thinking Skills

"Between truth and lie are images and ideas we imagine and think are real, that paralyze our imagination and our thinking in our effort to conserve them."
— R. D. Laing

One of the greatest challenges to critical thinking involves self-imposed constraints that are not actually part of the problem that we are facing. Riddles are often difficult because we impose constraints on our thinking that are not part of the stated problem. Test your critical thinking skills by trying to solve the following classic riddles (see answers on the following page):

1. **Two Masked Men** One evening, a man leaves home and starts running. He runs for a while and then makes a left turn. He runs some more before making another left turn. After running a while longer, he makes another left turn. As he approaches home, he encounters two masked men. Why is he not alarmed?

2. **Three Bags of Gold** You have three bags full of gold pieces. One bag contains fake gold pieces that weigh 1 ounce more than the genuine gold pieces, which weigh 1 pound each. You have a penny scale and just one penny. How can you determine which bag contains the fake gold?

3. **The Missing Dollar** Three guests decide to share a hotel room. The clerk says the bill is $30, so each guest pays $10. The clerk later realizes that the bill should have been $25. Therefore, he gives $5 to the bellhop to return to the guests. On the way to the room, the bellhop realizes that he cannot divide the money equally. As the guests didn't know they would be getting a refund, the bellhop decides to just give each guest $1 and keep $2 for himself. Each guest got $1 back: so now each guest only paid $9; bringing the total paid to $27. The bellhop has $2. If the guests originally paid $30, what happened to the remaining $1?

SELF-TEST ANSWER KEYS

1. b.
2. 1) personal mastery, which involves focus, patience and holding on to our vision; 2) mental models, which are the perceptions that we form about the world around us and how they shape our behavior; 3) building a shared vision, where we share our vision of the future with others to inspire and motivate; 4) team learning where we open up a dialogue with our team members to encourage a free flow of thoughts and ideas; 5) systems thinking, which integrates the other four disciplines.

3. a.
4. A *balancing loop* seeks stabilization or an equilibrium. It counteracts a force of change in an effort to keep stock at the same level. An example of equilibrium in a balancing loop is room temperature, where a glass of ice water or cup of hot tea over time will warm or cool—homing in on the room temperature. A *reinforcing loop,* on the other hand, encourages and amplifies change that increases or decreases a stock. An example of amplification in reinforcing loops is practicing a musical instrument. The more you practice playing the piano, the prettier the sounds you make and the more you enjoy listening to the music that you play.

5. a. True.
6. Amazon saves energy costs by removing the bulbs in the vending machines, saving the company a significant amount of money. Amazon also has a "cloud computing" initiative, where instead of storing information on one computer for people to retrieve (also called a *computer server*), this information is stored on multiple computer servers.

7. Causal loop diagrams
8. e.

SELF-ASSESSMENT ANSWER KEY

Riddle Solutions:

1. **Two Masked Men** You are playing baseball and have just hit a home run. The masked men are the umpire and the catcher.

2. **Three Bags of Gold** Take one gold piece from the first bag, two pieces from the second bag, and three pieces from the third bag. Place all six pieces on the scale and insert the penny. If the pieces weigh 6 pounds and 1 ounce, the fake gold is in the first bag. If the pieces weigh 6 pounds and 2 ounces, the fake gold is in the second bag. If the pieces weigh 6 pounds and 3 ounces, the fake gold is in the third bag.

3. **The Missing Dollar** The initial payment of $30 is accounted for, as the clerk takes $25, the bellhop takes $2, and the guests get a $3 refund. It adds up. After the refund has been applied, we only have to account for a payment of $27. Again, the clerk keeps $25 and the bellhop gets $2. This also adds up. There is no reason to add the $2 and $27—the $2 is contained within the $27 already. Thus, the addition is meaningless (mixing cost and cash). Instead, the $2 should be subtracted from the $27 to get the revised bill of $25.

Notes

CHAPTER FOUR

ORGANIZATIONS AND CHANGE MANAGEMENT

INSIDE THIS CHAPTER

ManagementStory:
Featuring **Katy Johnson, Fred Arters, and Lisa Fang**

Learning Objectives

By the end of the chapter, you will be able to:

4.1 | Illustrate how internal influences create unique types of cultures.

4.2 | Describe and compare general and specific external environments.

4.3 | Explain how managers analyze challenges and opportunities in organizations.

4.4 | Summarize the common reasons why managers change how their organizations operate.

4.5 | Summarize how managers change organizations by intervening in systems.

ADDITIONAL RESOURCES

KEY TERMS
IN REVIEW
SELF-TEST
CHAPTER EXERCISE
SELF-ASSESSMENT
SELF-TEST
ANSWER KEY

JP Greenwood/Getty Images

85

INTRODUCTION

University of Texas (UT) students Katy Johnson, Fred Arters, and Lisa Fang have been friends since they met sophomore year at a student organization meeting for young leaders.[1] In addition to their shared student experiences, they have something exciting in common—within the past week, they each received job offer letters to enter management training programs. Katy, finishing a double major in marketing and chemistry, is excited that multinational electricity company Reliable Energy offered her a fuel marketing management position located in Houston, Texas, which is close to her family. Fred majored in computer science with a minor in management, and he can't wait to begin his career at a gaming company called Perfect Planet Interactive in California, with operations based in Europe. And Lisa, with a major in information systems and a minor in marketing, landed her "dream job" at Hannah's, one of the world's largest online retailers, specializing in women's products, located in Los Angeles.

Up until now, their experiences at UT have been similar, with shared courses, student organizations, and extracurricular activities. In this chapter, we will follow these three young managers as they go through their training programs and first major job assignments. These stories will highlight how managers use critical thinking to 1) create unique experiences and expectations for employees, 2) respond to controllable and uncontrollable influences outside the company, and 3) adapt to create new products and services for customers to ensure the sustainability of the organization. By the end of the chapter, you will be able to chart an organization and understand the forces that affect its ability to change and be competitive in ever-evolving environments.

Internal and External Environments

There are two different types of environments that managers must deal with when operating an organization: internal and external. An *internal environment* corresponds to the forces inside an organization, and an *external environment* is made up of forces outside an organization. Depending on the environment and its forces, managers can have direct, moderate, or little power to effect change. Regardless of their level of influence, it is the responsibility of managers to understand and respond effectively to these forces, which means that managers must decide how to focus their attention to maximize long-term organizational performance as outlined in Figure 4-1.

Let's explore where managers have historically focused their attention. There have been three stages of modern capitalism that have shaped how managers respond to an organization's internal and external environments: management-focused, shareholder-focused, and customer-focused.[2] The management-focused era began in the early 20th century with the advent of scientific management and human resources management, as discussed in Chapter 2. This approach to capitalism inspired managers to maximize performance through a focus on the internal environment of an organization. You will recall from Chapter 1 that the next era, shareholder-focused management, was ushered in by Milton Friedman's treatise in the 1960s, where creating value for the owners of the company became the focus of management.[3]

Management in the United States began to apply these principles in the mid-1970s and early 1980s, when Jack Welch, the former CEO of General Electric (GE), famously shifted the

LECTURE ENHANCER:

Introduction

- **Internal vs. External Environment**
  ✓ **Internal environment—** corresponds to the forces inside an organization
  ✓ **External environment—**made up of forces outside an organization
    ➤ Figure 4-1 Organizational Environments & Managers' Power to Affect Them

- **Three Stages of Modern Capitalism**
  ✓ **Management-Focused—** inspired managers to maximize performance through a focus on the internal environment of an organization
  ✓ **Shareholder-Focused—**creating value for the owners of the company is the main focus of management
  ✓ **Customer-Focused—**able to sell to customers as well as form collaborative relationships with them

General External Environment
(All Organizations)
Technology - Political - Legal
Economy - Resources - Sociocultural

Specific External Environment
(Industry-Specific)
Customers - Talent - Suppliers
Competitors - Advocacy - Regulation

Internal Environment
(Organization-Specific)
Slogans - Stories - Symbols
Rituals - Ceremonies - Heroes

Power to Change

Figure 4-1
Organizational Environments and Managers' Power to Affect Them
Different types of organizational environments.

LECTURE ENHANCER:

4.1 Internal Environment

• Culture
  ✓ **Organizational culture**—a collection of beliefs that individuals and groups share to help their organization respond to environmental forces and changes
  ✓ Experienced on two different levels
    ✓ *Conscious*—things that can be seen or heard in the organization (i.e. dress codes, mission statements, slogans, office furniture)
    ✓ *Unconscious*—things that are felt and thought by employees (i.e. beliefs, perceptions, and values)

company to a "profits-first focus."[4] In the beginning of the 21st century, managers and investors began to reconsider the wisdom of the "profit-first focus" because, ironically, investors made more money from 1933 to 1976 than from 1977 to 2008, with average annual returns of 7.6 percent and 5.9 percent, respectively.[5] We briefly discussed the impact that the Internet browser had on communication in Chapter 2, where businesses not only have the luxury of selling to millions of customers but are able to form collaborative relationships with their customers as well. This has changed how managers build value for their organizations, resulting in customer-focused capitalism.

4.1 | INTERNAL ENVIRONMENT

4.1 | Illustrate how internal influences create unique types of cultures.

A company's **internal environment** comprises the forces inside the organization that affect how managers set expectations, how employees perform their roles, and how the company interacts with stakeholders and responds to the external environment. These forces include everything from behaviors of individuals to the facility and offices where employees perform. Because of the broad impact on how an organization operates, effective managers ensure that the internal environment of the company is consistent with its mission and values. This focus on internal environment happens well before employees start their positions. Most successful organizations understand that selecting employees who are well suited to adapt to the internal environment of the company is essential. The internal environment of the company is experienced immediately by all employees and successful managers.

Culture and Its Characteristics

Organizational culture is a collection of beliefs that individuals and groups share to help their organization respond to environmental forces and changes. From the time you submit an application to your first day on the job to leading a large project team, culture guides

Internal environment The forces inside an organization that affect how the managers set expectations, how employees perform their roles, and how the company interacts with stakeholders and responds to external environments.

Organizational culture A collection of beliefs that individuals and groups share to help their organization respond to environmental forces and changes.

> **Slogan** A repetitive phrase intended to support an organization's culture, mission, vision, or values.

> **Story** A narrative, usually fictionalized or enhanced over time, based on actual organizational experiences.

Figure 4-2
How Employees Experience Organizational Culture
Conscious and unconscious components of organizational culture.

your behaviors and decision making to ensure that they are consistent with management's expectations.[6] Culture is experienced on two different levels: *conscious* and *unconscious*. Conscious aspects of culture include the things that can be seen or heard openly in the organization, including dress codes, mission statements, slogans chanted at meetings, and even the office furniture.[7] For example, on Lisa's first day at Hannah's, she was given a tour of a fulfillment center. She had already noticed the company's attention to detail, so Lisa was surprised to see that some of the offices were unlit. When she asked about this, one of the managers explained that the company uses motion sensor lighting that goes off at a certain time, usually around 5 p.m. This not only saved the company thousands of dollars in electricity but encouraged staff to leave at the end of the day rather than working overtime. Lisa was impressed with Hannah's sensible approach to cost-cutting and was especially relieved to find that the company also worked toward achieving a work-life balance for their employees.

The unlit offices are a visual, *conscious* element that supports an *unconscious* aspect of Hannah's culture. Unconscious components of a culture refer to the beliefs, perceptions, and values of an organization—the things that employees feel or think. The dark offices at Hannah's represent an *unconscious* level of culture that supports, as an example, energy conservation and frugality. Successful managers understand the need to support what the organization feels and thinks with visual and spoken indications as outlined in Figure 4-2.

Slogans, Stories, and Symbols

Walking through the halls at Perfect Planet Interactive, Fred was beginning to wonder whether he was going to fit in. There was an odd combination of eccentric, individualistic personalities and an inclusive, private community. Over the course of the morning, Fred heard at least a dozen times that he should focus on the "Planet Power" and he would be just fine. "Planet Power" is a **slogan**, a repetitive phrase intended to support an organization's culture, mission, vision, or values. "Planet Power" is reflected in Perfect Planet Interactive's value of committment to strong, high-quality products. Throughout the course of the day, Fred saw symbols and heard stories that supported the company's values and beliefs. **Stories** are narratives, usually fictionalized or enhanced over time, based on actual organizational experiences.

One story that Fred enjoyed involved the launch of Galaxy Millennium, a game he remembered standing in line for the day after Christmas and which he played nonstop though New Year's Eve with a friend. One developer told him that after the launch of Galaxy Millennium, the team had taken three months trying to come up with ideas for

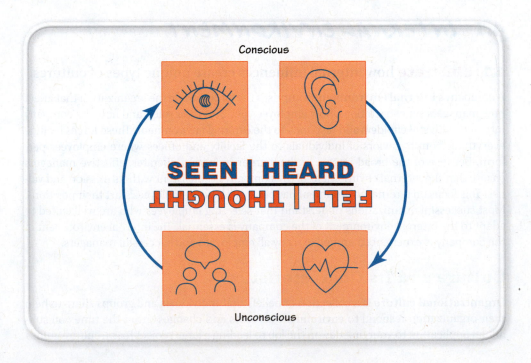

the next game that they would make. The team had lived and breathed the Galaxy Millennium game to such a degree that there was a consensus that no one on the team was interested in ever working on it again, even though their most loyal customers were already asking for a sequel. But as the months passed, the team began to talk about all the things that they wish they could have done to make Galaxy Millennium an even better game. The team was also excited about the feedback from customers, and sales of the game were breaking industry records. In a meeting, one of the team leaders asked the group members to stay focused on the company values of committing to quality and being passionate about their work. He also wanted to know if they believed that the company could learn and grow by developing a sequel to their best-selling game—thus, Galaxy Millennium II was born.

By the end of the day, Fred was getting more comfortable with the internal environment and was feeling that he had made the right decision to take this job. On his way out, his new team leader stopped him for a little quiz: "What was the one thing that every person you met today had in common, including staff in the cafeteria, receptionists, graphic designers, sales representatives, and computer programmers?" By asking this question, his new boss was quizzing Fred about the company's **symbols**—events, situations, objects, people, or other artifacts that provide greater meaning to the organization. Without giving Fred time to think about it, the boss answered his own question: "We are all geeks and gamers!" The team leader was not joking. The values of Perfect Planet Interactive require all employees to play and be passionate about computer games and encourages every person to embrace their inner geek.

Symbol An event, situation, object, person, or other artifact that provides greater meaning to the organization.

Rituals and Ceremonies

Before joining Reliable Energy, Katy knew the company had a reputation. It was known as a tough place to work, where profit came first and fun was nonexistent. This was reinforced when Katy sat down for her first meeting with her boss. The 23-year veteran of Reliable Energy made it clear: "If you survive here during the next 20–30 years, you will probably have 10–15 different jobs and learn every aspect of this business. There are three things you need to know in order to be successful here: 1) document everything, 2) safety is a top priority, and finally, 3) we are here to make our shareholders money." Her boss went on to explain the company ritual of writing memos. **Rituals** are formalized activities intended to communicate and teach the organization's culture.[8] Clearly, the company's culture of documentation is supported by writing memos. The ritual of memo-writing has the intended consequence of ensuring that decisions are well considered, formally approved, and shared broadly in the organization.[9]

Ritual A formalized activity intended to communicate and teach the organization's culture.

To say that Reliable Energy was not a fun place to work was probably an exaggeration. Later in the day, hundreds of employees gathered in the company cafeteria to eat the biggest cake Katy had ever seen. What was the celebration? The management team at one of the company's refineries was being recognized for Reliable Energy's "Safety First" award, celebrating over 10 years of safety in the organization. In addition to the cash bonuses and cake, there was a feeling of festivity and pride. This was the first year that a local team had won this award, and the occasion was attended by the top executives, including the company's CEO. Such **ceremonies** are events that provide one or more stakeholders with a sense of purpose and meaning connected to the organization and are powerful tools for managers to reinforce the mission and objectives of the company, especially when it involves recognizing excellence in front of peers and senior management.[10] When senior management attends ceremonies like the Safety First Award event, employee pride and commitment grows.

Ceremony An event that provides one or more stakeholders with a sense of purpose and meaning connected to the organization.

Heroes

In business, as in life, people need to believe in something greater than themselves in order to handle the anxiety that comes with change, barriers, growth, and loss. We have just examined how different organizational cultures use everything from slogans like "Safety First" to stories that exemplify the determination of the company to adhere to its values, as demonstrated in Perfect Planet Interactive's commitment to build Galaxy

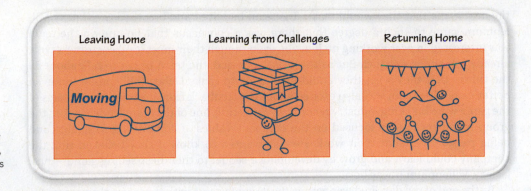

Figure 4-3

The Stages of a Hero's Journey
The hero ventures into the world, faces new challenges, and returns home triumphant.

Leaving Home   Learning from Challenges   Returning Home

Hero A real or imagined person who represents an ideal performer specific to the organizational culture.

Millennium II. **Heroes** are real or imaginary people who represent an ideal performer specific to the organizational culture, and these people help managers demonstrate to employees the determination to succeed in a particular organizational context. In *The Hero with a Thousand Faces*, 20th-century philosopher Joseph Campbell showed the hero's journey as universal and having three stages: 1) leaving home for adventure, 2) facing barriers that question success, and 3) returning home successful (Figure 4-3).[11]

At lunch, Lisa asked if she would ever meet Hannah's founder and CEO, Hannah Mills. The eyes of her fellow employees lit up, and stories of Mills filled the air. Clearly, they regarded their boss as a hero. The rise to success of Hannah Mills also mirrors the stages, described by Campbell, of a hero's journey. Mills left her modest home in Vallejo, San Francisco, to attend Harvard University. After graduation, she joined a Wall Street firm and was quickly promoted to senior vice president. While she was there, Hannah had the idea to sell eco-friendly beauty care products over the Internet and, from there, started one of the first major online retail companies exclusively for women. After quitting her Wall Street job, Mills and her family left their New York City home and relocated to Los Angeles. Not long after she moved, Mills rented a small office in a warehouse close to her home. There, she set up a couple of computers and got to work. Three months later, the company had sales of $30,000 a week. However, with such rapid growth, Mills knew she couldn't keep this up alone, so she rented some office space, hired a marketing and IT team, and forged ahead with Hannah's.

However, five years later, the company was facing serious financial challenges. Although they had $2 billion in revenue, they had lost $300 million in the previous quarter alone. The following year, Hannah's had its worst year ever and posted a $1.5 billion loss.

Mills knew that she had to employ a different strategy to turn the company around or else it would fall into bankruptcy. Her plan was to lead the company through significant change by completely altering its business model. Mills realized that one of the problems with her original model was that her range of products was too narrow. Women were used to having more choices. She decided to expand their online offerings and sell products from other well-known women's companies. Just one year later, Hannah's began to experience success once more, with sales taking off and its first annual profit of $5 million. Several years after her landmark decision, in the middle of one of the worst economic recessions in history, Hannah's successfully launched a revolutionary skincare product which put the company in the big leagues. In 10 years, the value of Hannah's grew 300 percent, to almost $70 billion. This is a hero's story.

LECTURE ENHANCER:

4.2 External Environments
✓ **External environments**—the specific and general factors outside of an organization that can change how it operates

External environments The specific and general factors outside an organization that can change how it operates.

4.2 | EXTERNAL ENVIRONMENTS

4.2 Describe and compare general and specific external environments.

We just discussed internal environments, where managers have direct power to effect change. **External environments** are the specific and general factors outside an organization that can change how it operates. In this section, we will examine external environments, from specific to general, or the forces where managers have only moderate to little power in effecting change. A common mistake made by managers is not focusing on the external environment because it appears to be separate from the operation of the organization. Let's look at how managers effectively (and sometimes ineffectively) act in response to their external environment and the resulting consequences from those decisions.

4.3 | SPECIFIC ENVIRONMENT

4.3 Explain how managers analyze challenges and opportunities in organizations.

An organization's **specific environment** is the industry-focused part of the external environment that directly affects an organization's operations and performance. The dimensions of a specific environment include customers, talent, suppliers, competitors, advocacy, and regulation. These dimensions are the forces outside the organization where management can build relationships and attempt to persuade change to the benefit of the organization. Examples in the following section show how, as managers become more customer-focused, customers can often become the company's talent, get frustrated, and form an advocacy group against the business's practices or demand regulation to force an organization to change. We'll also examine how managers make different decisions relative to their specific environment when they are shareholder-focused. These investigations lead us to analyze a logical question, "What are managers' responsibilities to monitor and build relationships with the dimensions of their specific environments?"

Customers

It was Monday morning, and Lisa had been at Hannah's for three weeks. She loved her new job, but her time so far had been spent learning and reading everything about the company. She wanted to be a part of the action and do something. One day, Lisa's team leader asked her, "Have you ever had 'wrap rage'?" Lisa became nervous and wondered if she had done something wrong. He continued, "Well, let me tell you . . . I bought my kid a science lab play set for her birthday. You actually had to be a brain surgeon to get this thing open! By the time I figured out how to open her present, I had two cuts on my hand, a stack of about 100 wire ties, and a heaping pile of shredded plastic. After all of that, I realized the two most important pieces were missing. My daughter went outside to play with her friends, and I tried to figure out how to stuff all of this junk back in the original box to bring back to the store. At that very moment, I had wrap rage! I want you to go work with Doug on the 'Wrap Rage Team' for the next couple of months." Intrigued at her new assignment, Lisa went along to Doug's team to learn all there was about "wrap rage" and how it affected Hannah's customers. Guess what one of the biggest complaints Hannah's gets from its customers? Having to deal with plastic cases and bubble wrap! So why do manufacturers make it so difficult to open products? As an example, Wal-Mart, the world's largest retailer who loses upwards of $3 billion because of theft, purposely makes some packages difficult to open.[12] They realized if packages were difficult to open, they are less likely to be stolen.

As an online retailer, however, Hannah's does not have to worry about shoplifters and related theft. Indeed, Hannah's has a customer advantage over competitors like Wal-Mart, as it provides the company with a unique opportunity to address customers' needs and increase their satisfaction. Which package in Figure 4-4 would you rather open?

There are three ways that managers respond to customer needs: reactive engagement, proactive engagement, and interactive engagement. Hannah's "frustration-free" effort is an example of **reactive engagement**, where management monitors positive and negative customer feedback through surveys and customer communications and improves its products and services accordingly. **Proactive engagement** is when a company creates a product or service as an alternative to enhance the customer's experience.[13] If Hannah's encouraged its customers to purchase products in "frustration-free" packaging, this would be an instance of proactive engagement. As technology enables companies to cost-effectively build relationships with customers, organizations are no longer just listening to customers—they are collaborating with them to develop future products and services. This is called **interactive engagement**.

LECTURE ENHANCER:

4.3 Specific Environment

✓ **Specific environment**—the industry-specific part of the external environment that directly impacts an organization's operations and performance

• **Customers**
➤ Figure 4-4: Frustration-Free Packaging Customer Service Strategy

Specific environment The industry-focused part of the external environment that directly affects an organization's operations and performance.

✓ **Reactive engagement**—management monitors positive and negative customer feedback through surveys and customer communications, and improves products and services accordingly

✓ **Proactive engagement**—when a company creates a product or service as an alternative to enhance the customer's experience

✓ **Interactive engagement**—building relationships with customers; organizations collaborate with customers to develop future products and services

• **Talent**
✓ **Talent**—people who have the skills, knowledge, creativity, and relationships necessary to optimize an organization's performance

✓ **Crowdsourcing**—companies that employ the efforts of its customers and the public to innovate and further its mission

• **Advocacy**
✓ **Advocacy group**—set of people dedicated to instituting change based on their concern or interests
■ Greenpeace International

Reactive engagement Monitoring positive and negative customer feedback and improving the organization's products and services accordingly.

Proactive engagement Creating a product or service as an alternative to enhance the customer's experience.

Interactive engagement Collaborating with consumers to develop future products and services.

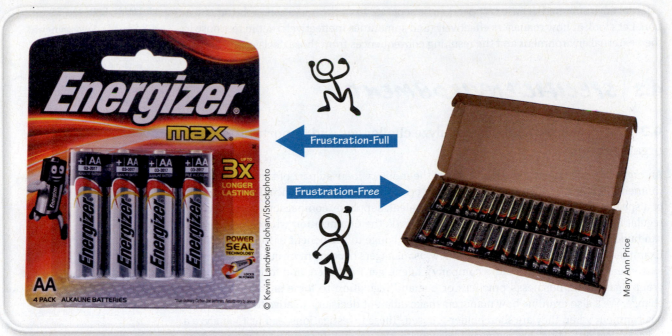

Figure 4-4
Frustration-Free Packaging Customer Service Strategy
Different types of packaging can either be frustration-full or frustration-free.

Talent

Talent refers to the people who have the skills, knowledge, creativity, and relationships necessary to optimize an organization's performance. In 2013, unemployment hovered at around 7.5 percent, yet Manpower's 2013 Talent Shortage Survey showed that 35 percent of employers felt like there was a shortage of talent.[14] What does this really mean? In 2013, there were approximately 12 million people out of work. Inconsistent with this statistic, there were also 4 million job openings, for which companies could not find qualified people to hire. This paradox is called the *talent war*. In 2020, the United States could face having to fill 10 to 14 million job openings in science-, technology-, engineering-, and mathematics-related positions, as unemployment is projected to stabilize around 5 percent.[15] Because of this, identifying and hiring talent has emerged as a challenge for managers, and companies have a broader view of the talent necessary to be competitive in a global marketplace. Management now relies on talent *inside* and *outside* the organization, primarily employees and customers. Given the competition to identify qualified people, how do managers find talent?

Fred did well in school, but he did not get recruited by Perfect Planet Interactive as a result of passing his résumé around a career fair, like many of his friends who were also recruited by organizations. He loves playing Planet Wars, a popular Perfect Planet Interactive game that sold 4 million copies in the first month of its release. Fans of Planet Wars play this game with and against each other over the Internet and form a dedicated community committed to the company and its products. Fred was identified as a potential employee after a map that he designed and submitted for the game caught the attention of Perfect Planet Interactive's management. By using the company's product and participating in its online community, Fred proved that he had already gained a good grasp of the company's internal environment and had played a part in its culture.

Another example of finding talent comes from Cisco Systems, who hosted a competition called the I-Prize. The purpose of the contest was to discover new strategies that the company could use to bring in $1 billion worth of new business. The winner would receive $250,000 under the condition that they would agree to give Cisco the idea and full ownership. In the end, more than 2,500 innovators from 104 countries submitted some 1,200 distinct ideas. So, what did Cisco say was the biggest benefit of the competition? The answer might surprise you. Guido Jouret, chief technology officer of Cisco's Emerging Technologies Group, said: "What we gained was invaluable. We learned how people around the world think about

Cisco and the markets we ought to be pursuing. We [also] learned that if you ask, you can reach a worldwide audience of smart, passionate people eager to help you drive innovation."[16] When companies employ the efforts of its customers and the public to innovate and further its mission, this is called **crowdsourcing**. This and other types of interactive engagement are other ways that managers identify passionate and qualified candidates in today's workforce.[17] But what happens when this passion turns against the organization?

Courtesy Cisco Systems, Inc.

Advocacy

An **advocacy group** is a set of people dedicated to instituting change based on their concerns or interests. Greenpeace International, an environmental advocacy group, explains that it "exists because this fragile earth deserves a voice. It needs solutions. It needs change. It needs action."[18] On April 15, 2010, Greenpeace staged a protest in front of British Petroleum (BP) headquarters in Calgary, Canada, to condemn a proposed oil sands development in Northern Alberta. To argue their position, the group sharply criticized BP for its involvment in tar sands as a viable energy source and its resulting marketing campaign, in which the company had created a new logo and slogan, "Beyond Petroleum." Greenpeace protested using signs painted with the words, "Broken Promises," as it believed that BP had reneged on its promise of "Beyond Petroleum" by excavating tar sands oil, which the group claimed posed a threat to the environment. However, on this day, the advocacy group was getting more criticism than support from those walking past, who questioned the environmental safety of the signs they were using. According to one passerby, "The yellow poles that they are using are made of plastic. The paint is petroleum based. So I would suggest they do some research on their protest prior to them protesting." The event was reported by Canadian Broadcast Centre (CBC) News, but not many people noticed.[19]

Advocacy groups use a wide array of media and communication tactics to voice their concerns: television, radio, on-the-street protests, Facebook, Twitter, blogs, and YouTube. Each of these can be used for a variety of purposes. In some cases, advocacy groups simply have a goal of providing factual information so consumers can make informed decisions. They may be raising money to support a particular cause.[20] The above-mentioned protest is an example of an advocacy group trying to convince a company to change an aspect of their business plan. Another method that can be used in an attempt to change the actions of a specific organization is to convince other consumers not to purchase a company's products and services; this is called a **boycott**.

Katy, who had just applied for a position at Reliable Energy, was not aware of this small protest in Canada on April 15, 2010. Some scoffed at the protesters. On April 20, however, Katy and many people around the world certainly took notice when the Deepwater Horizon oil well operated by BP exploded and sank into the Gulf of Mexico, killing 11 workers and creating an environmental catastrophe that took months to clean up. Two months later, as Katy begins her career at Reliable Energy, there is good news and bad news. The good news is that the company has seen an increase in gas stations that want to drop their BP affiliation and carry the Reliable Energy brand. The bad news is that the U.S. government instituted a moratorium on deepwater drilling, which investors fear could hurt profits. Although Reliable Energy had nothing to do with the Deepwater Horizon explosion and the subsequent oil spill, the entire energy industry was

> **Crowdsourcing** Employing the efforts of customers and the public to innovate and further an organization's mission.

> **Advocacy group** A set of people dedicated to instituting change based on their concerns or interests.

> **Boycott** An attempt by an individual or group to change the actions of an organization by convincing other consumers not to purchase its products or services.

SCOTT OLSON/REUTERS/NewsCom

affected by this event.[21] This is an example of how an unexpected turn of events can make a big difference to a business.

Suppliers

In reality, the oil spill in the Gulf of Mexico had little effect on the supply of oil available in the world. On a personal level, Katy was anticipating higher gas prices because of the oil spill, so she budgeted more for travel expenses as she moved her things to Houston from her college apartment. Actually, gas prices stayed about the same, but she found that some local businesses had suffered from the effects of the oil spill. For example, Katy's local fish restaurant, Poppy's, was struggling to find enough oysters to satisfy customer demand. The once-abundant shellfish had suddenly become a precious commodity.

Suppliers provide companies with the external resources needed to operate, including money, material, people, and information. Restaurants like Poppy's need food, financing, linens, temporary workers during the holidays, beverages, cleaning chemicals, and many other things to run their business. Each of their suppliers has suppliers, too. For example, Poppy's buys its seafood from a vendor that gets fish directly from fishing boats. When the oil spill prevented fishing boats in the gulf from fishing and farming oyster beds, the company that supplies Poppy's needed to find a new supplier for its oysters, and was considering a vendor from the Chesapeake Bay area in the mid-Atlantic as outlined in Figure 4-5.

> **Suppliers** Entities that provide an organization with the external resources that it needs to operate, including money, materials, people, and information.

Regulation

Regulations are rules set by external governing bodies that dictate standards and procedures for industries, businesses, and professionals. Almost every industry and business has rules that oversee their practices. Managers must understand these rules to operate ethically and legally. In most cases, government agencies, commissions, and industry associations set standards that organizations must abide by in order to operate. Oyster farmers, seafood wholesalers, and restaurants must each abide by regulations set by federal, state, and local agencies and commissions. As an example, oyster farmers in Louisiana must obtain licenses for their business, vehicles, and gear. The state of Louisiana states that "oysters may be taken from public grounds by dredgers, scrapers, and tongs. Dredges and scrapers used to remove oysters can be no longer than

> **Regulations** Rules set by external governing bodies that dictate standards and procedures for industries, businesses, and professionals.

Figure 4-5
Suppliers in the Restaurant Industry
Oyster farmers supply seafood wholesalers, who in turn supply restaurants.

Video Game Age Rating Systems Compared

	EARLY CHILDHOOD	EVERYONE	EVERYONE 10+	TEEN	MATURE 17+	ADULTS ONLY 18+	RATING PENDING
	eC CONTENT RATED BY ESRB	**E** CONTENT RATED BY ESRB	**E10+** CONTENT RATED BY ESRB	**T** CONTENT RATED BY ESRB	**M** CONTENT RATED BY ESRB	**A** CONTENT RATED BY ESRB	**RP** CONTENT RATED BY ESRB
	No objectional material	No objectional material	Cartoon, fantasy or mild violence, mild language and/or minimal suggestive themes	Violence, suggestive themes, crude humor, minimal blood, simulated gambling and/or infrequent strong language	Intense violence, blood and gore, sexual content, and/or strong language	Intense violence and/or graphic sexual content and nudity	
ESRB/CTIA	3+	6+	10+	13+	17+	18+	Rating pending
Apple iOS	4+*	4+*	9+	12+	17+	17+	Not available until rated
Google Android	Everyone	Everyone	Low maturity	Medium maturity**	High maturity***	High maturity	Not available until rated

*Must not ask for location. **References to drugs, alcohol and/or tobacco ***Focus on drug use/sale, alcohol and/or tobacco.

six feet in width measured along the tooth bar. The dredge teeth shall be no longer than five inches in length, and there shall be no more than seven dredges in use on any one vessel."[22] These types of regulations can become expensive for companies, especially small businesses. Federal regulations cost U.S. businesses $1.75 million annually, or over $8,000 per employee.[23]

With the threat of additional expense, industries sometimes choose to self-regulate. Have you ever wondered who rates movies G, PG, PG-13, R, or NC-17? The answer: parents. In an effort not to have government involvement in "freedom of speech and expression," the Motion Picture Association of America (MPAA) decided to regulate itself. It enlists a panel of parents to review and rate every film formally released in the United States. The MPAA states that "the purpose of the ratings system is to provide clear, concise advance information to parents about film content so parents can determine what movies are appropriate for their kids while preserving freedom of expression for filmmakers and the film industry."[24] In 1994, the video game industry also took steps to self-regulate, implementing a rating system. Although there has been some controversy over the violent nature of some of the video games and their apparent negative influence on minors, a recent survey carried out by the consumer protection agency, the Federal Trade Commission (FTC), shows that self-regulation within the gaming industry has been more effective than other media; for example, minors are more likely to be sold explicit music and R-rated movies than adult-rated video games.[25]

Government Activism However, there are times when companies work together with the government in order to seek solutions to a number of financial problems. For example, during the financial crisis of 2008, government and business worked together to solve issues that neither entity could solve alone. This is not a new phenomenon. Over half a century ago, Frank Abrams, former chair of Standard Oil, drew the following conclusion: "Maximizing shareholder returns will continue to be the primary responsibility of managers, but to achieve that goal, they will work with government more directly than we have witnessed at any time since World War II."[26] Today, government takes an active role in encouraging business through tax credits and other incentives to behave in ways

Table 4-1 Government Activism by Industry

Industry	Government's Involvement
Financial Services	• Lends banks money to create stability in the market. • In certain cases, takes ownership stakes. • Regulations to align financial institution's interests with the public's. • Anticipated future involvement: require banks to have more money relative to their debt, more disclosures/transparency, and restrictions on financial instruments called derivatives.
Housing	• The U.S. government is guaranteeing or taking over a large percentage of outstanding mortgage loans. • Provide incentives for lenders and borrowers to refinance their home loans at subsidized rates. • Anticipated future involvement: more oversight of lenders.
Insurance	• The U.S. government became a major investor in insurance markets. • Subsidize lower-income individuals and families to help them afford private health insurance. • Affordable Healthcare Act.
Automobiles	• Countries around the world are providing their automakers with loans and taking ownership positions. • Supply funds to develop fuel-efficient cars. • Anticipated future involvement: incentives to favor domestic automakers over foreign.
Energy	• Countries around the world are subsidizing the development of non-carbon-based energies. • U.S. spending billions of dollars each year. • Pledge to double the country's capacity to generate wind, solar, and geothermal power. • Anticipated future involvement: modernize systems for transmitting electricity.
Healthcare	• Many countries have nationalized healthcare; the United States highly regulates the industry. • Require companies over a certain size to either insure their employees or pay into a national healthcare pool. • Affordable Healthcare Act.
Pharmaceutical	• The United States uses its purchasing power to negotiate lower drug prices for the public.
Telecom/Information Technology	• Subsidizing great broadband coverage, especially for rural areas. • Anticipated future involvement: influence intellectual property, privacy, and intelligence gathering in the industry.

Adapted from Robert Reich, "Government in Your Business," *Harvard Business Review* 87 (July–August 2010): 94–99.

Government activism
Government's active role in encouraging business to behave in ways that are in the public interest through tax credits and other incentives.

that are in the public interest. This is called **government activism**, detailed in Table 4-1. For example, according to economist Robert Reich, "U.S. Department of Energy is guaranteeing loans to small businesses that want to implement alternative-energy projects but would otherwise have trouble financing them; their lenders will be repaid even if the projects go belly-up."[27]

Competitors

On November 21, 2007, Amazon launched the Kindle, which sold out in 5½ hours. At the time of the launch, the Kindle was the first electronic book product enabled with a non-glare screen for easier reading and cell phone technology for easier downloading of books. When a company builds a product or service where there is no competition, it is called a *blue ocean* strategy, and the company is said to be "first to market."[28] By 2010, several competitors had started selling products that challenged Amazon's dominant position: Sony's

Voices of Management

Jean-Francois Zobrist,
CEO, FAVI[29]

The first think that Jean Francois Zobrist did when he started at FAVI, a French company that manufactures auto parts for companies like Volvo and Fiat, was to dissolve all the FAVI hierarchies. "I came in the day after I became CEO, and gathered the people. I told them, 'tomorrow when you come to work, you do not work for me or for a boss. You work for your customer. I don't pay you. They do. Every customer has its own factory now. You do what is needed for the customer.'"

Instead of having a dozen different departments, each responsible for one aspect of work, Zobrist created 20 teams, each responsible for one customer, and everything related to the work for that customer, from human resources to product development. The result has been that employees are more focused on the actual quality of their work than on competing with their coworkers—with no job titles or promotions, it only makes sense to work together.

Plenty of people are skeptical about Zobrist's approach. But FAVI's work is consistently of high quality. When one customer asked to audit FAVI's procedures, says Zobrist, "They were not pleased, because we had no measurement system for tracking late orders—nothing in place, no plan, no process, no structure in case of delay. They [had been] a customer for over 10 years, so I say, 'In that time, have we ever been late?' They say, 'No.' I say, Have we ever been early?' They say again, 'No.' And so I ask them why they want me to measure things that do not exist."

Critical Thinking in the Classroom

How do you view Zobrist's approach to management? Would you apply this strategy in your company? If not, why not? ∎

Reader, Apple's iPad, Barnes and Noble's Nook, Border's Kobo eReader, and dozens of tablet computers.

When companies face competition, managers attempt to understand the features and benefits of their competitors' products and services, including strengths and weaknesses. This is called a *competitive analysis*, which helps managers respond to their competitors' actions in the market.[30] Now that many companies have developed handheld electronic devices intended for reading books, Amazon has changed its approach by selling and developing new versions of the Kindle based on competitive analysis. Being first to market has its advantages, but it does not ensure long-term success. By 2013, the iPad had an 82 percent share of US and Canadian tablet web traffic compared with a 6.5 percent share for the Kindle Fire.[31]

4.4 | GENERAL ENVIRONMENT

4.4 Summarize the common reasons why managers change how their organizations operate.

Some things are out of a manager's control, but they still greatly affect the organization and how it must operate. We have explored specific environments, where the impact of forces is relative to their industry. For example, when an oil spill damages fishing and oyster beds, oysters become scarce, and consequently, restaurant managers must either increase prices or remove items from the menu. **General environments** are external forces that affect *all organizations* participating in an economy, where managers have little or no power to effect change. These forces include political and legal, resource availability, economic, technological, and sociocultural. We will discuss these in the order in which managers are required to deal with these forces to accommodate the interests of their organizations, arranged from the most impact to the least.

Politics and Laws

Unlike *industry-specific* regulations, which we discussed earlier in this chapter, *political* and *legal* forces relate to most, if not all, businesses. Managers are required to understand and

General environment External forces that affect all organizations participating in an economy, where managers have little or no power to effect change.

Table 4-2   Federal Legislation Affecting Business and Managers

People

Legislation	Primary Purpose	Impact on Managers	President Signed
Civil Rights Act of 1964	To outlaw discrimination based on race and gender in schools, housing, and hiring.	Managers had to ensure that their businesses did not discriminate in their hiring practices or in their service practices.	Lyndon B. Johnson (D)
Occupational Safety and Health Act of 1970	To ensure employees have safe conditions to work, free from hazards that are recognizable and addressable.	Identify areas of potential risk and take proactive steps to remove or minimize hazards	Richard M. Nixon (R)
Consumer Product Safety Act of 1972	Established the Consumer Products Safety Commission (CPSC) to develop safety and product recall standards for consumer products.	Identify products and processes that will fall under CPSC regulations and address issues to minimize liability	Richard M. Nixon (R)
Americans with Disabilities Act (ADA) of 1990	Provides that people with disabilities will not face discrimination in the workplace, be provided access to all public places, and be provided access to telecommunications services.	Issues with public access to disabled people must be addressed, including physical structures and telecommunications services	George H. W. Bush (R)

Profit

Legislation	Purpose	Impact on Managers	President Signed
Economic Espionage Act of 1996	Made the theft or misappropriation of trade secrets a federal crime.	Managers must ensure that none of their products or services are misappropriated, including those from foreign sources.	William J. Clinton (D)
Electronic Signatures in Global and National Commerce Act of 2000	Legalized the use of electronic signatures in interstate and international commerce.	Makes the transfer of funds, products, and services across state or national boundaries easier, but also creates security issues that need to be addressed.	William J. Clinton (D)
Sarbanes-Oxley Act of 2002 (SOX)	Set new and enhanced standards of financial disclosure for publicly traded companies and accounting firms.	Managers must keep and maintain accurate and honest financial records, as well as the records of any third-party accounting firms	George W. Bush (R)

Planet

Legislation	Purpose	Impact on Managers	President Signed
Clean Air Act of 1963	Mandated the Environmental Protection Agency (EPA) to develop regulations to protect the public from airborne contaminates that pose a safety hazard.	Managers must be proactive in diagnosing and solving emissions problems.	Lyndon B. Johnson (D)
National Environmental Policy Act of 1969	Set up the President's Council on Environmental Quality, as well as setting procedural standards for federal government agencies to set up environmental assessments (EAs) and environmental impact statements (EIAs).	Governmental agencies must conduct thorough investigations into their impact on the environment.	Richard M. Nixon (R)
Clean Water Act of 1972	Mandated the elimination of releasing high amounts of toxic substances into public waters and mandated standards for surface water pollution for human sports and recreation.	Managers must be proactive in diagnosing and solving water-based pollutant problems.	Richard M. Nixon (R)
Pollution Prevention Act of 1990	Required the EPA to establish an Office of Pollution Prevention to coordinate a pollution prevention strategy, as well as mandating manufacturing facilities to report annually on source reduction and recycling.	Managers must maintain or implement waste reduction programs as part of their business practices.	George H. W. Bush (R)

abide by the constraints of these legislative acts, which means that managers must spend time and money ensuring that their personal decisions and the behaviors of their teams are consistent with these mandates. All organizations, with some exceptions based on the size of the company, are required to follow federal laws and rules intended to change business behavior in the interest of people, profit, and planet. Contrary to popular opinion, federal legislation that is considered "anti-business," meaning that it mandates how organizations operate, is neither a Republican or Democratic party issue; both parties have contributed to major legislative acts over the past several decades, as shown in Table 4-2.

In 2010, the U.S. Supreme Court decided in a 5–4 ruling that corporations could not be limited in the amount that they spent to support political causes relating to business interests. This decision, known as *Citizens United,* "held that corporations are covered by the First Amendment [granting these entities free speech]." In his dissenting opinion, Justice John Paul Stevens suggested that lawmakers (i.e., U.S. Congress) "consider requiring corporations to disclose how they intended to spend shareholders' money or to put such spending to a shareholder vote." This ruling allows managers to participate actively in voicing the interests of their businesses in context of political campaigns. This is a departure from business's traditional relationship with politics, and this legal ruling will have an impact on the legislation that affects businesses in the future.[32] In Chapter 5, we will discuss how political uncertainty can present managers with complex challenges.

Resources

One certain challenge that businesses face today is resource availability and scarcity. There are three categories of resources that affect how businesses operate globally: food, energy, and water.[33] To understand fully the challenge that organizations and businesses face, let's look at future demand for these resources. The primary factor determining demand for these resources is *world population,* which is currently approximately 7 billion people, with the greatest population density in Asia and India[34] (see Figure 4-6). The rate of population growth

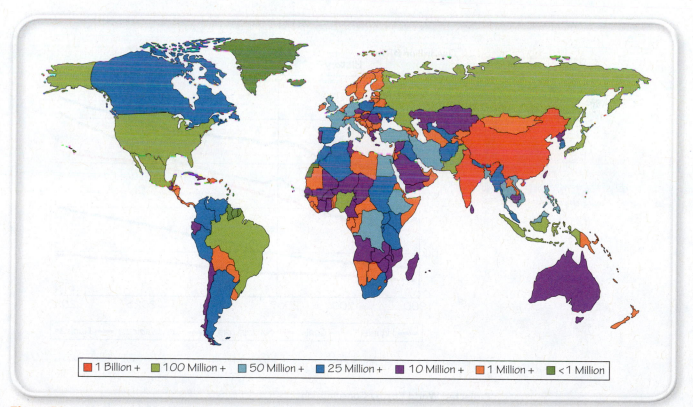

Figure 4-6
Population Density by Country
The world's population density per country.

| ■ 1 Billion + | ■ 100 Million + | ■ 50 Million + | ■ 25 Million + | ■ 10 Million + | ■ 1 Million + | ■ <1 Million |

is currently about 1 percent a year; if this continues, the world's population will double in 70 years. You can watch the world population grow minute by minute, by checking the Population Clock on the U.S. Census Bureau website (census.gov/main/www/popclock.html).[35]

Food *One-sixth* of the world's population is undernourished—that is, over 1 billion people go hungry every day. Hunger causes low energy, slow thinking, and loss of hope.[36] These are physical, cognitive, and emotional states that are consistent with poor workplace performance. In a business environment that depends heavily on cognitive talent, organizations around the world have a lot to gain by ensuring that people are nourished and healthy.

Energy "The energy crisis is real. It is worldwide. It is a clear and present danger to our nation. These are facts and we simply must face them." U.S. president Jimmy Carter proclaimed this challenge in his 1979 "Crisis of Confidence" speech. What progress has been made in the past three decades to address this "clear and present danger"? In 2010, the U.S. Energy Information Administration (EIA) stated that in 2035, the world was expected to consume 49 percent more energy than 2007 consumption levels.[37] One might assume that this is not an issue, *if* the energy consumed is renewable. Unfortunately, the EIA suggests that the world will continue to use non-renewable energy at about the same rate in 2035 as it does in 2010, as shown in Figure 4-7.

The UNEP-led Green Economy Initiative (GEI) articulates barriers and opportunities that managers and organizations face because of the continuing energy demands on limited resources. Launched in late 2008, the GEI's objective is to promote investment in green sectors and help more environmentally unfriendly countries become greener.[38] By greening production processes, implementing new policy reforms and regulation changes, and seizing international trade opportunities with other countries, the GEI has assisted over 30 developing countries and least developed countries with the transition to a green

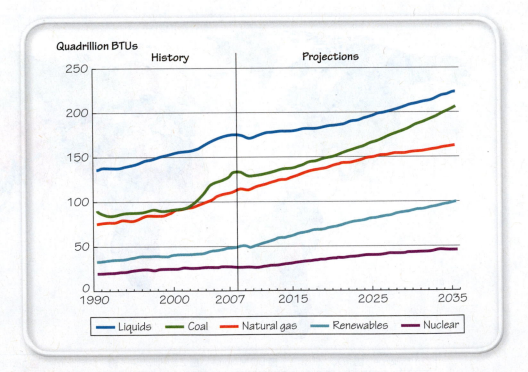

Figure 4-7
Projected World Energy Consumption
Non-renewable energy consumption is expected to continue over the next two decades.

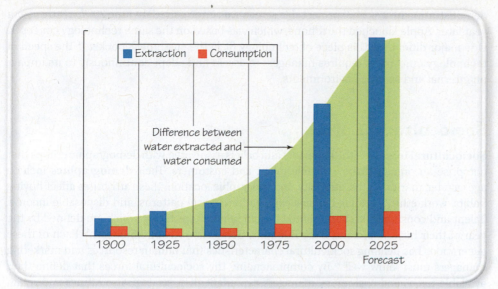

Difference between water extracted and water consumed

| Extraction | Consumption |

1900 1925 1950 1975 2000 2025
Forecast

Source: E. Beinhocker, I. Davis, and L. Mendonca, "The 10 Trends You Have to Watch," *Harvard Business Review* (July–August 2009): 55–60.

Figure 4-8
Global Industrial Waste of Water
Shows the projected forecast for water consumption and waste.

economy. Assisting countries to become more green builds sustainability and reduces the exploitation of natural resources.[39]

Water Businesses rely on water as a primary resource for operating. In addition to drinking water and sewage, water is used in business as a coolant or solvent and to produce electricity. Water is a limited resource, and businesses continue to increase the amount of water that the world extracts relative to consumption as outlined in Figure 4-8.

Peter Paul van de Wijs, global issues management leader at The Dow Chemical Company, says that "40% of Dow sites around the world will experience some degree of freshwater stress by 2025."[40] To help companies like Dow understand and address their water usage and needs, the World Business Council for Sustainable Development (WBCSD) has developed the "Global Water Tool," an online application that allows companies to keep track of their water usage.[41]

Technology

Every year, 1,000 of the most influential leaders from across the world, including Bill Gates, and Google founders Larry Page and Sergey Brin, assemble by invitation-only and attend the Technology, Entertainment, and Design (TED) conference.[42] Why do these prominent people go to the TED conference? They do this to see and understand the latest innovations from around the world in technology, in art, and in solving social problems. In February 2006, Jeffery Han, a research scientist at New York University, received a standing ovation from the esteemed crowd for his technology innovation. Han led the team that invented an "interface-free, touch-driven computer screen." This innovation allows users to navigate their digital experience by pinching, sliding, and spreading their fingers across the screen. Han's

Steve Juvetson/Wikimedia Commons

demonstration on a 4' × 3' projectable screen was impressive.[43] In June 2007, a little over a year later, Apple launched the iPhone, which was based on the same technology concepts. One major difference: this piece of technology fit in the customer's pocket.[44] The speed of technology innovation requires managers to assess and adapt continuously to its impact on internal and specific environments.

Sociocultural Forces

Sociocultural forces are the behaviors and beliefs associated with demographic groups that comprise an organization's available talent and customers. Their **demographics** include age, gender, marital status, ethnicity, and geographic location; these attributes affect buying habits, work ethic, work-life balance expectations, travel patterns, and disposable income. Talent and consumers are represented by four generations today, which are defined by the year of their births: Veterans, Baby Boomers, Generation X, and Millenials.[45] Each of these generations has defining sociocultural characteristics that human resources and marketing managers must know well.[46] By comprehending the sociocultural forces that define their available talent and customers, managers can adapt their strategies to attract and retain employees or sell to and keep customers. In Table 4-3, we outline the attitudes and beliefs that determine the behavior patterns of these generations.

Economy

An **economy** is an orchestrated system of talent, resources, and money with the purpose to create and distribute products and services. For organizations, managers need money to acquire resources and hire talent to achieve the company's goals. When the economy is doing well, it is easier for managers to get money from banks, investors, or stock markets. Stock markets are primarily intended to coordinate transactions where owners can sell a piece, or share, of their company to investors. Depending on a company's perceived future performance and the confidence of buyers, investors buy and sell a company's stock, increasing and decreasing its stock price. What do we mean by perceived future performance and confidence?[47]

As an example, Apple's stock price on January 5, 2007, was $85. Steve Jobs, Apple's CEO at the time, announced that the company would soon introduce a new product, the iPhone, on January 9, 2007, which promised to "reinvent the phone." Investors liked what they heard. By January 12, 2007, Apple's stock price was selling for $94. Therefore, if you bought

ROLF NVENNENBERND/EPA /NewsCom

1,000 shares of Apple's stock on January 5 and sold it one week later, you would have earned approximately $9,000 (less fees, etc.); in other words, your investment would have increased by 10 percent.[48] Remember that Jobs had only *announced* the iPhone at that point; the product itself did not launch until June 2007.

Managers typically look at stock market indexes as a benchmark for measuring the economy. These indexes are basically a combination of company stocks intended to represent how the overall stock market (or economy) is doing. The major market indexes in the United States are the Dow Jones Industrial Average, NASDAQ Composite, and S&P 500. The Dow Jones Industrial Average index, founded by then-editor of the *Wall Street Journal* Charles

Table 4-3	Sociocultural Characteristics by Generation

Veterans: 1922–1945	
Work Ethics/Values	Hard Work; Respect Authority; Sacrifice; Duty Before Fun; Adhere to Rules
Work Is . . .	An Obligation
Leadership Style	Directive; Command-and-Control
Interactive Style	Individual
Communication Style	Formal; Written
Feedback and Rewards	No News Is Good News; Satisfaction in a Job Well Done
Messages That Motivate	Your Experience Is Respected
Work and Family Life	No Balance; Work to Survive

Baby Boomers: 1946–1964	
Work Ethics/Values	Workaholics; Work Efficiently; Crusading Causes; Personal Fulfillment; Desire Quality; Question Authority
Work Is . . .	An Exciting Adventure
Leadership Style	Consensual; Collegial
Interactive Style	Team Player; Loves Meetings
Communication Style	In Person
Feedback and Rewards	Money; Title Recognition
Messages That Motivate	You Are Valued; You Are Needed
Work and Family Life	No Balance; Work to Live

Generation X: 1965–1980	
Work Ethics/Values	Eliminate the Task; Self-Reliance; Want Structure and Direction; Skeptical
Work Is . . .	A Difficult Challenge; A Contract
Leadership Style	Everyone Is the Same; Challenge Others; Ask Why?
Interactive Style	Entrepreneur
Communication Style	Direct; Immediate
Feedback and Rewards	Freedom = Best Reward; Sorry to Interrupt, but How Am I Doing?
Messages that Motivate	Do It Your Way; Forget the Rules
Work and Family Life	Balance

Millenials: 1981–2000	
Work Ethics/Values:	Multitasking; Tenacity; Entrepreneurial; Tolerant; Goal-Oriented; What's Next?
Work is . . .	A Means to an End; Fulfillment
Leadership Style	The Young Leaders Century
Interactive Style	Participate
Communication Style	Email, Voice Mail
Feedback and Rewards	Whenever I Want It; At the Push of a Button; Meaningful Work
Messages that Motivate	Working with Other Bright and Creative People
Work and Family Life	Balance

G. Hammill, "Mixing and Managing Four Generations of Employees," *FDU Magazine Online*, Winter/Spring 2005, http://www.fdu.edu/newspubs/magazine/05ws/generations.htm; and Johnson Controls, "Generation Y and the Workplace Annual Report 2010"; http://www.johnsoncontrols.com/publish/etc/medialib/jci/be/global_workplace_innovation/oxygenz.Par.41451.File.dat/Oxygenz%20Report%20-%202010.pdf.

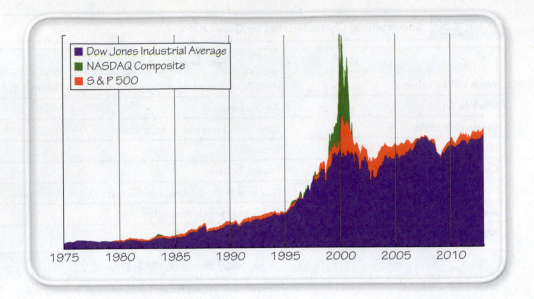

Figure 4-9
Historical View of the Major Stock Indexes
The rise and fall of major market indexes.

- Dow Jones Industrial Average
- NASDAQ Composite
- S & P 500

1975 1980 1985 1990 1995 2000 2005 2010

Dow, represents 30 large company stocks.[49] The NASDAQ Composite index represents over 3,000 company stocks, primarily signifying growth and technology.[50] The S&P 500 represents 500 large U.S. company stocks.[51] Figure 4-9 shows these three indexes over the past few decades. What do you notice? Probably the big green spike from 1997 to 2002! During this time, the economy experienced the "Internet boom," followed by the "Internet bust," where technology stocks increased then decreased dramatically. The "green spike" is the NASDAQ Composite rising and falling accordingly.

Gross domestic product (GDP) is the value of what a country produces on an annual basis, representing the size of its economy. GDP is represented as a total number (nominal) or per person (capita). Comparing the world's economies by each country's total GDP and their per capita amount, we see a very different story as shown in Figure 4-10. What do you see? Do you notice that not all the countries that have large nominal GDPs have large per-capita GDPs? This is good and bad for those countries: *bad* because its citizens on a per-person basis are not prospering in comparison to others around the world; and *good* because they have extraordinary growth opportunities.[52]

In order, the largest economies are the European Union, the United States, China, Japan, India, Russia, and Brazil. Over the past two decades, the Internet and e-commerce have enabled these and all other countries around the world to exchange services easily, leading to rapid expansion of economies, in particular Brazil, Russia, India, and China (BRIC, pronounced "brick"). The impact of international economies and business practices have on managers will be discussed in further detail in Chapter 5. So, how do GDPs and the world economy affect managers?

To answer this question, let's go back and revisit Katy, Fred, and Lisa. What if these three new managers had graduated in 2001? A few months after graduation, they probably would have finished their job orientations and manager training programs at Reliable Energy, Perfect Planet Interactive, and Hannah's, respectively. On the fateful day of September 11, 2001, when terrorists flew airplanes into the World Trade Center towers in New York City, the stock markets did not open, and they remained closed until September 17. When the markets reopened, the Dow Jones industrial average declined by 7.1 percent in one day, the largest single-day decline in history. The Dow Jones would decline by 14.3 percent over the course of the following week, which meant $1.4 trillion in value lost for the U.S. economy. During that week, Reliable Energy and Hannah's stock would have fallen. However, as Perfect Planet Interactive maintains operations in Europe, its stock might have *risen* by almost 10 percent in the two weeks following the terrorist attack. This is because the gaming company's stock is traded on the Paris Stock Exchange, which was probably perceived by investors as safer than the U.S. economic market at that time—a powerful example of how politics and confidence affect the economy.

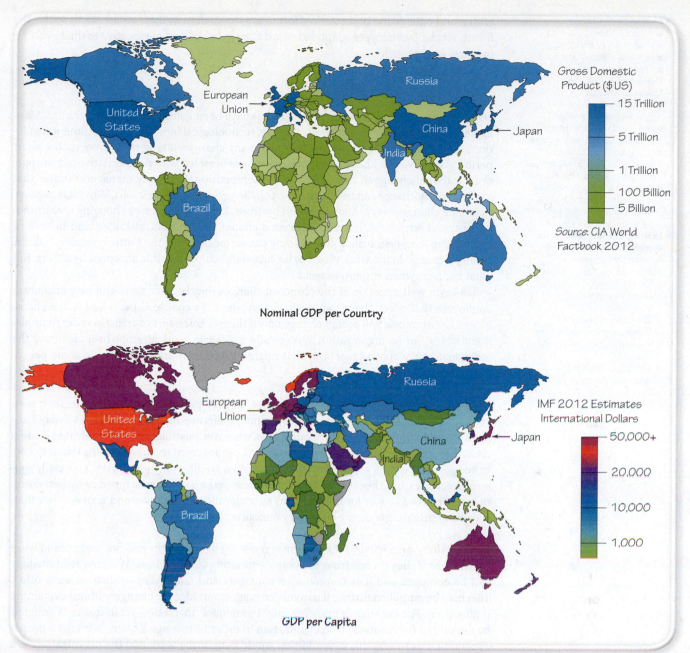

Nominal GDP per Country

GDP per Capita

Figure 4-10

World Economies—Nominal Versus Per-Capita GDP

Nominal GDP per country and GDP per capita.

4.5 | HOW DO MANAGERS CHANGE ORGANIZATIONS?

4.5 | Summarize how managers change organizations by intervening in systems.

Change management means achieving goals by altering behaviors or processes in response to environmental forces.[53] Managers have a unique role in organizations to see and understand the overall internal and external environments and design ways for their teams to change behaviors in order to achieve organizational goals and missions. As we explored in Chapter 3, Systems Theory can help managers to understand the changes that are occurring

LECTURE ENHANCER:

4.5 How Do Managers Change Organizations?
✓ **Change management**—achieving goals by altering behaviors or processes in response to environmental forces

Change management Achieving goals by altering behaviors or processes in response to environment forces.

within and outside the organization, formulate the goals that they would like to set for the future, and help employees adapt and adjust their behavior and perspective to their evolving business environment.

Resistance to Change[54]

Over the last couple of decades, organizations have been going through rapid change. Managers are now challenged with new products, technological innovation, government regulations, and a fluctuating workforce. With so many changes taking place over such a short period of time, we could argue that managers have been left with no alternative but to apply organizational change to keep ahead of the competition. Yet, many managers confess that implementing change can be one the most challenging parts of their jobs. Why? It is because enforcing change is very much a human business. It not only involves changing ideas, innovations, and structures, but also requires a change in mindsets, attitudes, and behaviors, challenging long-held beliefs and in some cases transforming the entire company culture. In short, change in the workforce can be successful only when it is accepted by others. But what happens when employees resist?

However well intentioned the proposed changes may be, managers still may encounter employees that reject change altogether, even when the change is perceived as beneficial. Indeed, some people will accept change only if there is some sort of crisis. In order to implement change in an organization successfully, managers must attempt to understand the individual behaviors and reactions that might lead to resistance. So, why do some people resist change?

Personal Threat Some people fear change, as they perceive it as a threat to their own personal interests. For example, due to economic factors, many organizations today have been forced to implement austerity measures wherever possible. The days of flying business class, huge bonuses, lavish corporate occasions, complimentary food and drink, and tickets to sought-after events are a thing of the past. As a result, many employees, especially top-level executives, have become resentful that these perks have been stripped away, perceiving these cutbacks as a way for the company to undermine their power and status rather than accepting them as necessary budgetary measures.

Uncertainty and Mistrust People may resist change when they do not understand what it means or if they do not trust the person initiating the new idea. Working relationships can be complex, and it is common for managers and employees to distrust each other. This may be amplified further if a manager suggests an idea for change without explaining it effectively. For example, a manager might announce that a new team leader is going to be appointed from outside the organization in order to manage a team. Without a proper explanation as to why this new addition would benefit the team and the organization as a whole, rumours could surface and people might feel threatened, leading to suspicion, mistrust, and doubt.

© Otmar Winterleitner/iStockphoto

Fear and Doubt About Abilities People who have a low tolerance for change have a fear that they do not possess the required skills and abilities to cope with the new changes. For example, with the introduction of new technology, many longstanding employees may struggle to embrace such new innovations in such a short period of time.

Clashing Perspectives There can also be a disparity between how change is assessed by different people. Differences of opinion may arise between those initiating the idea and those who are expected to accept the change. For example, a company has two databases that effectively do the same thing, yet they are run by two different departments headed by two senior managers. The logical solution would be to streamline the databases to perform one function.

However, this situation can give rise to political behavior, where one manager perceives the merger of the databases as a useful cost-saving and efficient initiative, whereas the other may see it as a threat to his power and authority. The latter then may argue against the merger by coming up with all sorts of reasons why it would not work, thus delaying it or preventing it from happening altogether, leading to in-house battles and power struggles.

The Art of Persuasion

There are a number of ways that managers can deal with those who resist change. Some managers choose to provide emotional support to their employees in order to address the underlying fear associated with change. In certain instances, managers may give stressed-out employees some time off or an option to work from home, away from the office environment. They may also provide additional training to employees who are having difficulty learning the skills required to cope with the new approach.

In other situations, managers may offer financial incentives, such as a wage increase or higher benefits, to persuade dissenters to embrace the change. This type of bargaining is more commonly used with companies that have strong unions that have the power to accept or reject the proposed change. Others might use a form of manipulation by enlisting support from top management in order to endorse the change, or co-opt a popular individual to take an active role in the decision-making process. The reasoning here is that people will be more inclined to accept an idea when it is initiated by respected leaders.

In more extreme circumstances, managers may use coercion to force employees to accept change—to the point of using the threat of job loss if they don't comply. This is a risky move, as it can kill morale, cause resentment, and in some cases, create mass rebellion.

Most managers use a combination of the approaches described above in order to manage resisters, but these methods are by no means foolproof. However, by formulating a clear strategy for change, analyzing the reasons behind the resistance, and choosing specific methods to deal with different dissenters, managers will have a better chance of overcoming many of the obstacles that stand in the way of progress.

Driving and Restraining Forces[55]

Force-Field Analysis is based on the work of Kurt Lewin, who believed that there are two main competing forces at play that influence change. Driving forces help to provide motivation toward achieving a goal, whereas restraining forces or barriers to change impede the progress of the goal. In order to implement a change, driving forces must be increased while ensuring that restraining forces are decreased.

Managers can use Force-Field Analysis as an aid in the decision-making process by analyzing the forces for and against change. Once identfied, managers can make a decision as to whether the change should be implemented, and how they might go about mitigating any potential resistance. For example, say that you are the manager of a start-up company that produces personalized, handmade handbags. Customers register online and enter the details of the designs they would like displayed on their own unique handbag. Business is good, but you realize your competitors seem to be getting their product to their customers much faster than you are. The CEO of the company suggests implementing new manufacturing equipment that will help speed up the process. While the design will still be handmade, the bags themselves will be manufactured by a new machine.

As manager, you conduct a force-field analysis to assess the need for change and the potential obstacles that you might need to overcome before the change is made. First, you look at the driving forces or the reasons why the company needs to make some changes: the manufacturing equipment will help speed up the production process and get the handbags to consumers more quickly, making the business more competitive. However, you may also have to plan for some barriers to change; for example, your staff may feel threatened by the new equipment and fear they will be replaced by machines. They may also worry that they lack the skills and abilities to operate the new technology. There is also the cost of installing new equipment—can the company afford it, and if so, what cost benefits will it produce?

Identifying both driving and restraining forces allows managers to decide a strategy for implementing the change as smoothly as possible. Once the change initiative is signed off, managers must prepare their staff for the changes ahead.

Stages of Change[56]

One of the toughest functions of a manager is convincing people to accept change, especially when managers deal with so many different behaviors and personalities. Organizational development theory suggests following three stages of change: unfreezing, changing, and refreezing, in order to secure commitment and buy-in from employees.

Unfreezing *Unfreezing* is the process by which managers inform their staff of the change and why it is needed. People are more likely to adjust their attitudes and behaviors to support change when they understand the reasoning behind it, as well as the potentially negative implications that might arise should the company remain static. Some organizations use change agents, or organizational development specialists who help facilitate change by identifying problems and presenting them to management. As change agents come from outside the company, they provide more objective diagnoses of the existing problems that helps managers "unfreeze" their traditional, learned behaviors and adopt a new perspective.

Changing Once "unfrozen," the change agent implements *changing*, a strategy for employees to help reinforce the need for change. For example, some managers might create a vision and use a wide range of communication channels to deliver the new plans for change to the firm's employees. Managers could reinforce the idea further by holding town hall meetings and setting up training programs designed to help employees learn the new skills required to meet the change.

Refreezing The final stage is *refreezing*, which is when people embrace the change and adopt the behaviors and attitudes needed to generate successful results. During this phase, managers might reward employees for their commitment and their participation in making the change happen.

Leading Change[57]

In addition to Force-Field Analysis, and the freezing/changing/refreezing method, managers can draw from the following steps in order to implement change effectively.

Putting the Pressure On Managers must communicate a sense of urgency to their employees to implement speedier change. This is especially significant when companies are experiencing some sort of crisis that needs to be addressed quickly.

Forming a Guiding Coalition People are more likely to buy in to an idea when they are involved in its implementation. A coalition comprised of a management team to lead the change effort can have a tremendously powerful effect in encouraging others to embrace the change, especially when the group is supported by the CEO.

Creating a Vision One of the first tasks of the coalition group is to create a vision of what the organization is trying to achieve. This vision must be clear, easily understood, and inspirational to others.

Using Widespread Communication Communication is key when delivering a strategy for change. Managers can use visual presentations, hold meetings, and create webinars that can be accessed by every employee in the organization to promote their message for change. In situations where a new product, or technology initiative is being introduced, training programs help educate employees and provide them with the skills they need to handle the new technology. Armed with sufficient education and training, employees are more likely to be motivated toward achieving the company's goal.

Overcoming Obstacles Although creating a vision, and optimizing the communication channels available to promote the vision are important, both efforts will be futile if other employees resist the change or present obstacles that block progress. Managers must identify the obstacles and the reasons behind them and remove them as quickly as possible to drive the change forward.

Celebrating Short-Term Wins Large-scale change often takes years before the end result is achieved. Without acknowledging achievements along the way, the project could lose momentum. So it is important that managers establish milestones along the way, and reward performance by celebrating with respective teams when they achieve their objectives.

Assessing the Transformation Process Change is a continuous process, where modifications must be evaluated and reassessed constantly to make any necessary adjustments. Managers can learn from each stage of the change process and apply those lessons to future projects.

Instilling Change in the Corporate Culture Managers know change is successful when it becomes part of the corporate culture. However, organizations that experience a major cultural shift may still be subject to a few naysayers that may undermine the change and set back progress. In order for new attitudes and behaviors to become ingrained into the culture, managers must take steps to show employees the benefits of the change and how it has improved the organization.

But how do managers change the structure of a system that is simply not functioning as well as it should? Systems theorists such as Jay Forrester and Donella Meadows at the Massachusetts Institute of Technology (MIT) believe in the power of different types of leverage points or "places in the system where a small change could lead to a large shift in behavior."[58] Meadows cites 12 leverage points, ranging from highest effect to lowest effect. Positive and negative feedback loops, delays, reinforcing feedback loops, and balancing feedback loops (as discussed in Chapter 3) are all examples of leverage points. They all have the capability to set off a whole change of events, similar to a butterfly effect, where small changes can result in large outcomes, if they are managed properly. But finding and managing these points is no easy feat; indeed, when managers do find them, they might even end up pushing for change in entirely the wrong direction. Why is this? When we first look at a system structure, we tend to perceive the clearest and most obvious problem. Take the leverage point of parameters, and let's ascribe it to crime, as one example. If we were to consider what it would take to rid society of criminal activity altogether, we might try and resolve this by hiring more police and investing in more public safety programs. However, history has shown that regardless of how much we spend on crime-fighting, crime still exists. So, even if we find a supposed solution, it is unlikely to change behavior in the long term. These types of parameters are the lowest on the list of leverage points because even when identified, they will not help to make any sort of long-lasting change.

In Chapter 3, we explored the example of a reservoir as a system. When there is an increase in the inflow of water, the outflow of water decreases, making the system stable. In this sense, the water acts as a buffer between the reservoir overflowing or running out altogether. However, a reservoir can contain only so much water, and any variation in climate or even the onset of natural disasters can upset the delicate balance. Buffers are another type of low leverage point, but like parameters, they can help to improve a system but are unable to change it immeasurably. And what if the water in the reservoir, which is a stock and flow

Research@Work

structure, becomes polluted? We might think that building a water treatment plant is the obvious solution, but this would require serious expenditure.

With so many complex activities taking place in the system, it can be difficult to spot the difference between low leverage points and high leverage points. One of the most destructive forces to a system is lack of data. For example, if you don't know the reservoir is polluted, how can you do anything about it? When we are equipped with new information, we have the power to change the system. Yes, it might be expensive to build a water treatment plant, but if enough people get together to raise awareness, then it might give rise to new initiatives for treating the pollution problem. Of course, although effective, this sort of leverage point is not the most popular: as history dictates, the powers that be aren't known for their tolerance of mass uprisings. Just as accessibility to information is a powerful leverage point, so is knowledge of the rules or boundaries that exist in the system. Once managers have a clear idea of the rules, they have the ability to challenge or even change them.

As introduced in Chapter 3, self-organization, which involves the creation of entirely new systems, is one of the most powerful functions of systems. Evolution and social revolution are examples of self-organization. A system that can fluctuate and change has the highest chance of survival. However, this does not mean that it is invincible. Whole ecosystems have been wiped out through erroneous interventions by humans into nature. An even higher leverage point than self-organization is goals. What if the goal of the very highest powers was to focus on the environment, and address the issues of pollution, climate change, and extinction? Then every leverage point discussed so far would fall under the umbrella of this goal: everybody would be kept informed, parameters would be removed, and the system's structure would be adapted to this new initiative. It might sound impossible, but one person has the power to shift systems in an entirely different direction, sometimes for better and sometimes for worse.

Yet the most powerful leverage point of all is the ability to shift paradigms and the way that we think about the world. Many of us exist inside the system, following its rules, accepting the information that is passed down, and believing that this is the way that things should be. By transcending these paradigms, we can step outside the system and consider the idea that no paradigm is completely right or true. Only then will managers have the ability to see the system as a whole, successfully determine leverage points, and initiate real and long-lasting change.

In the next chapter, we will explore more challenges facing managers in a global economy and the importance of successfully managing cultural differences and diversity.

Case**Snapshot**

Chapter 4 Case: Organizations and Change Management: AstraZeneca can be found on pg. 465

ADDITIONAL RESOURCES

KEY TERMS

Advocacy group A set of people dedicated to instituting change based on their concerns or interests. **(p. 93)**

Boycott An attempt by an individual or group to change the actions of an organization by convincing other consumers not to purchase its products or services. **(p. 93)**

Ceremony An event that provides one or more stakeholders with a sense of purpose and meaning connected to the organization. **(p. 89)**

Change management Achieving goals by altering behaviors or processes in response to environment forces. **(p. 105)**

Crowdsourcing Employing the efforts of customers and the public to innovate and further an organization's mission. **(p. 93)**

Demographics Sociological characteristics, including age, gender, marital status, ethnicity, and geographic location, which affect buying habits, work ethic, work-life balance expectations, travel patterns, and disposable income. **(p. 102)**

Economy An orchestrated system of talent, resources, and money with the purpose to create and distribute products and services. **(p. 102)**

External environments The specific and general factors outside an organization that can change how it operates. **(p. 90)**

General environment External forces that affect all organizations participating in an economy, where managers have little or no power to effect change. **(p. 97)**

Government activism Government's active role in encouraging business to behave in ways that are in the public interest through tax credits and other incentives. **(p. 96)**

Gross domestic product (GDP) The value of what a country produces on an annual basis, representing the size of its economy. **(p. 104)**

Hero A real or imagined person who represents an ideal performer specific to the organizational culture. **(p. 90)**

Interactive engagement Collaborating with consumers to develop future products and services. **(p. 91)**

Internal environment The forces inside an organization that affect how the managers set expectations, how employees perform their roles, and how the company interacts with stakeholders and responds to external environments. **(p. 87)**

Organizational culture A collection of beliefs that individuals and groups share to help their organization respond to environmental forces and changes. **(p. 87)**

Proactive engagement Creating a product or service as an alternative to enhance the customer's experience. **(p. 91)**

Reactive engagement Monitoring positive and negative customer feedback and improving the organization's products and services accordingly. **(p. 91)**

Regulations Rules set by external governing bodies that dictate standards and procedures for industries, businesses, and professionals. **(p. 94)**

Ritual A formalized activity intended to communicate and teach the organization's culture. **(p. 89)**

Slogan A repetitive phrase intended to support an organization's culture, mission, vision, or values. **(p. 88)**

Sociocultural forces The behaviors and beliefs associated with demographic groups that comprise an organization's available talent and customers. **(p. 102)**

Specific environment The industry-focused part of the external environment that directly affects an organization's operations and performance. **(p. 91)**

Story A narrative, usually fictionalized or enhanced over time, based on actual organizational experiences. **(p. 88)**

Suppliers Entities that provide an organization with the external resources that it needs to operate, including money, materials, people, and information. **(p. 94)**

Symbol An event, situation, object, person, or other artifact that provides greater meaning to the organization. **(p. 89)**

Talent The people who have the skills, knowledge, creativity, and relationships necessary to optimize an organization's performance. **(p. 92)**

IN REVIEW

4.1 | Describe the components that make up an organizational culture.

An organizational culture is a collection of beliefs that individuals and groups share to help their organization respond to environmental forces and changes. Culture is experienced on two different levels: conscious and unconscious. The components of culture include slogans, stories, symbols, rituals, ceremonies, and heroes.

4.2 | Illustrate how internal influences create unique types of cultures.

Managers employ the components of culture to create a specific experience for employees and other stakeholders that establishes consistent expectations. We demonstrated how managers at Perfect Planet Interactive, Hannah's, and Reliable Energy communicated their organizational cultures differently, which led to very unique types of organizations that were well suited for their industries.

4.3 | Describe and compare general and specific external environments.

Specific environment forces include customers, talent, advocacy, suppliers, regulations, and competitors. Specific environments are specific to an organization's industry; therefore, these forces have a tangible effect on operations. General environment forces include politics/laws, resources, technology, sociocultural, and economy. Managers have a limited impact on these influences, which nonetheless can have a dramatic impact on organizations and managers' need to change.

4.4 | Explain how managers analyze challenges and opportunities in organizations.

How do managers know what to change? First, it is vital that a manager understands the mission of the organization and purpose of its subsystems. This allows a manager to understand where process and employee behaviors are inconsistent with purpose. Exponential growth- or decay-driven runaway loops are easily identified, and managers must seek to balance them. Goals and states of stability offer managers targets to adjust behavior.

4.5 | Summarize the common reasons why managers change how their organizations operate.

Organizations go through continuous change, whether management notices or not. By understanding mission and purposes, acknowledging imbalances, designing plans to stabilize the system, and communicating with stakeholders, managers can institute well-considered, positive change for their organizations.

SELF-TEST

4.1 | Describe the components that make up an organizational culture.

1. List the six characteristics of corporate culture.
2. Which of the following reconstructs the stages of a "hero's journey"?
   a. Identifying Resources, Innovation, and Resource Allocation
   b. Idea Generation, Motivation, Success
   c. Plan, Organize, Lead
   d. Leaving Home, Learning from Challenges, Returning Home
   e. None of the above
3. Compare and contrast rituals and ceremonies.

4.2 | Illustrate how internal influences create unique types of cultures.

4. Interpret the significance of Reliable Energy's ceremony to recognize the company's safety award.
5. Describe how employees at Perfect Planet Interactive demonstrate the organizational value of "embracing their inner geek."

4.3 | Describe and compare general and specific external environments.

6. Cite a contemporary example of a *boycott*.
7. Industries are only regulated by external governing bodies.
   a. True
   b. False

8. Explain the impact of government activism on two industries by citing one example for each that is not detailed in this book.
9. Government legislation limiting the behaviors of management in support of the public's interest has primarily been a bipartisan issue.
   a. True
   b. False
10. Predict challenges that a manager might face with Veteran and Millennial generation employees working together on a team.

4.4 | Explain how managers analyze challenges and opportunities in organizations.

11. In the summer job scenario, what feedback loop balances the behavior of "traveling with friends"?
12. Explain the concept of a "balanced approach" to management.
13. Predict the behavior of an energy budget system, with a runaway feedback loop for savings and a low-intensity balancing loop for usage.

4.5 | Summarize the common reasons why managers change how their organizations operate.

14. Which of the "top five reasons managers should change" applies to the Amazon energy budget example? Based on an analysis of the system, formulate a change in behavior to save on energy costs.

CHAPTER EXERCISE

Force Field Analysis

Force Field Analysis is a process for analyzing the factors that drive or restrain a given outcome. It can be a very effective way both to examine a situation and determine the most effective approaches to attain a desired goal.

Instructions:

- In the space provided below, write down a goal that you would like to achieve.

  _____

- Next, consider the forces that are supporting or driving you toward achieving the goal and write these in the spaces provided in the "Driving Forces" arrow below. Write additional driving forces on a separate sheet of paper if necessary.

- Then determine the restraining forces that are holding back your progress toward achieving the goal and write these in the spaces provided in the "Restraining Forces" arrow below. Write additional restraining forces on a separate sheet of paper if necessary.

Driving Forces
1. _____
2. _____
3. _____

Restraining Forces
1. _____
2. _____
3. _____

- Your success in achieving your goal can be assessed in terms of the balance between the driving and restraining forces. The present situation or status quo is determined by the equilibrium between these opposing forces. If you can increase existing or create additional driving forces or reduce or eliminate restraining forces, the situation will change and allow you to make progress toward your goal. Answer the following questions:

1. Consider the restraining forces. Which restraining force is most significantly impeding your progress? If you were to remove it, would you be able to change the situation enough to allow you to meet your goal? What actions would you need to take to remove it? If you can't remove it, what can be done to minimize its effects?

2. Now consider the driving forces. What can you do to increase the influence of the driving forces in order to offset the restraining forces? What new driving forces could you create in order to shift the equilibrium?

- Identify the three most important actions that could shift the equilibrium and allow you to achieve your goal and write them in the spaces below:

  1. _____

  2. _____

  3. _____

- Develop an action plan for implementing each of the actions listed above.

Adapted from Kurt Lewin. *Field Theory in Social Science: Selected Theoretical Papers,* Dorwin Cartwright, ed. Oxford, U.K.: Harpers (1951).

SELF-ASSESSMENT

Openness Toward Change*

For each statement, circle the number that best describes you based on the following scale:

Not at all Accurate	Somewhat Accurate	A little Accurate	Mostly Accurate	Completely Accurate
1	2	3	4	5

1. I would consider myself to be open to the changes that I encounter in my life.

   1   2   3   4   5

2. Right now, I am somewhat resistant to proposed changes in my life.

   1   2   3   4   5

3. I am looking forward to changes that will occur in my life.

   1   2   3   4   5

4. I am quite reluctant to consider changing the way I like to do things.

   1   2   3   4   5

5. I think that future changes will have a positive effect on my life.

   1   2   3   4   5

6. From my perspective, changes in my life will be for the better.

   1   2   3   4   5

7. The changes in my life will be for the worse in terms of the way I get things done.

   1   2   3   4   5

8. I think the changes in my life will have a negative effect on how I will be able to perform.

   1   2   3   4   5

*Adapted from Vernon D. Miller, John R. Johnson, and Jennifer Grau. "Antecedents to willingness to participate in a planned organizational change," *Journal of Applied Communication Research* 22, no. 1 (February 1994): 59–80.

Scoring:

A. Add the numbers that you circled for items 1, 3, 5, 6: _____

B. Add the numbers that you circled for items 2, 4, 7, 8: _____

C. Subtract the number on line B from the number on line A and write it here: _____

Interpretation:

+5 or higher: You are open to change and view it as an opportunity

−4 to +4: You are indifferent to change; it doesn't really bother you but you also don't embrace it

+5 or lower: You are resistant to change and see it as a threat

SELF-TEST ANSWER KEY

1. Slogans, Stories, Symbols, Rituals, Ceremonies, and Heroes.

2. d.

3. Rituals communicate and teach the organizational culture, while ceremonies create a sense of purpose through recognition and celebration.

4. This ceremony celebrated the company's "Safety First" program commitment to safety, by recognizing the team with the best overall company performance.

5. At Perfect Planet Interactive, the company's value of "embracing your inner geek" is demonstrated by every employee having an active passion for gaming.

6. Coca-Cola is currently being boycotted by consumers for depleting groundwater in India.

7. False; industries can also be self-regulating.

8. Housing industry: to stabilize the financial industry, the U.S. government in 2010 announced that it would provide refinancing options for homeowners with home loans less than $729,750. Automobiles: nearly 680,000 cars were replaced with more fuel-efficient vehicles, based on a government supported incentive.

9. False. Legislation over the past four decades has been evenly split between Republican and Democratic presidents.

10. Three dynamics that could lead to team challenges include communication style, leadership style, and work ethic. The Veteran generation is formal in their communications, believes that leadership is earned over time, and works to survive. Conversely, the Millennial generation communicates informally with their peers, using quick and short communications over mobile devices; believes that leadership in a technology-driven world is the domain of young people; and works to live a good life. This could lead to challenging manager situations, including miscommunication, disparity in needs for recognition and power, and inconsistent expectations regarding the time spent physically in the office.

11. The balancing loop that affects the inflow of "income" through a summer job.

12. A "balanced approach" to management refers to the manager's responsibility to ensure that the system and subsystems of an organization achieves long-term stability, with limited adverse effects on itself or interconnected forces. Understanding how to change system dynamics positively is a primary competence for a balanced approach to management.

13. This would create an effect on an organization's energy budget, where it would eventually have a surplus of energy that could be sold to other users. Thus, the energy budget would ultimately stop being an expense and actually make money.

14. "Intensity of balancing loop not sufficient to curb behavior in runaway loop"—in order to find stability in this system, one might recommend investing in alternative, renewable energy sources that the company would purchase. This would increase the intensity of the balancing loop for the outflow of savings, and thus counterbalance the anticipating increase in inflow due the growth projections of cloud computing.

Notes

_____

_____

_____

_____

_____

CHAPTER FIVE

DIVERSITY IN A GLOBAL ECONOMY

CHAPTER OUTLINE

Learning Objectives

By the end of the chapter, you will be able to:

5.1 | Understand how managers organize international businesses.

5.2 | Explain the challenges and opportunities of working with cultural differences.

5.3 | Understand the legal requirements for respecting workforce diversity.

5.4 | Recognize and explain the implications of changing workforce demographics.

5.5 | Interpret the dimensions of diversity as a management strategy to increase innovation, creativity, and performance.

ADDITIONAL RESOURCES

KEY TERMS

IN REVIEW

SELF-TEST

CHAPTER EXERCISE

SELF-ASSESSMENT

SELF-TEST

ANSWER KEY

JP Greenwood/Getty Images

5.1 | MANAGING IN A GLOBAL ECONOMY

5.1 | Understand how managers organize international businesses.

Damian Williams moves away from the whiteboard and looks at the ideas and strategies shared over the past three hours. Four, maybe five, dry-erase-marker colors paint the wall with arrows, circles, and dollar signs for punctuation. For some reason, this chaos seems to make sense to everybody around the table. Four boxes spelling "BRIC" on the board stand out. As we learned in Chapter 4, BRIC stands for "Brazil," "Russia," "India," and "China"—the major emerging economies now competing with and providing services such as software programming to businesses in the United States and European Union (EU).

Williams is the new senior vice president of information systems of Mansfield Exports, and he was hired primarily for his 25 years of experience managing teams in China, Europe, South America, India, and the United States. He has just finished giving the senior management team a lesson on the strengths and weaknesses of outsourcing software development to different regions across the world. Some of his analyses relate to costs, but to the surprise of some team members, the session has become a tutorial on cultural differences, and building diverse teams. As Williams said, "It's all about getting results by leading and managing a diversity of people with trust, respect, and loyalty."

Managers running globalized companies are affected by external political, resource, economic, and social forces that can change management challenges and opportunities significantly. For organizations to achieve results in today's global economy, managers must understand international business practices, including international trade rules, agreements, and legal requirements. This chapter will introduce you to the dynamics that managers should embrace when managing diverse teams, whether a team at a small start-up company in Palo Alto, California, or a multinational team. Many of the same management principles apply to managing diverse teams in the United States and in other countries. These principles rely on managers understanding *culture*.[1] And to be effective, managers need to motivate their teams by understanding their team members' cultural differences, dynamics, and dimensions. They must communicate, motivate, and achieve goals with people of different cultural and ethnic backgrounds, ages, genders, and sexual orientations. As we journey through this chapter, we will explore these factors and ask the question: "Through this cultural understanding, how do managers foster diverse organizations to achieve more effective and efficient results?"

© GlobalStock / iStockphoto

Global Organizations, Trade Rules, and Agreements

Many companies, when they expand internationally, maintain their headquarters in their home country and develop satellite offices elsewhere. This structure is what's known as a **global company**: an organization that has operations in more than one country and its senior management decision making centrally located in one country. In contrast, Mansfield Exports is organized as a **multi-domestic company**: an organization where senior management decision making is distributed across the countries in which it operates. Mansfield Exports didn't start out as a multi-domestic company. In its early days, Mansfield Exports was a small, family-owned business in Chicago that specialized in both **importing**, the process of acquiring products and services from another country; and **exporting**, the process of creating products in one country and selling them in another.

Strategic Partnerships

In order to grow her family's business, the current chief executive officer (CEO) of Mansfield Exports, Jill Mansfield, established a series of *strategic partnerships* with importing/exporting companies in the emerging BRIC economies. **Strategic partnerships** are agreements between two or more organizations to share complementary resources to develop and sell products and services.[2] Each of these partner companies had its own strengths and provided a viable context for translating regional cultures and connecting to existing relationships. Mansfield thought that these strategic partnerships were a brilliantly conceived strategy, yet in the past few years, her company has been embroiled in a series of trade disputes, costing it a lot of money.

The leadership of Mansfield Exports in Chicago and its partners' managers all pleaded ignorance, and Mansfield realized that the company needed to shift its philosophical focus. In 2007, Mansfield Exports decided to buy all four of its strategic partners in Brazil, Russia, India, and China and build a global business based on shared values, mission, and vision. Buying existing or building new businesses in other countries is referred to as **direct foreign investment**. Mansfield recognized the need for Mansfield Exports to build its internal understanding of trade rules and regulations, so she hired Williams to oversee the creation of a global software program to track different government tariffs, quotas, legislation, import standards, and subsidies.

Williams recommended that they take advantage of the resources made available through organizations like the **World Trade Organization (WTO)**, which is responsible for global trade rules between countries.[3] As he discussed the company's needs with Jill Mansfield, Williams saw that the challenges really emerged when Mansfield Exports transformed from a small, family-owned import/export firm to a multi-domestic corporation trying to conduct business in multiple *regional trading zones*. **Regional trading zones** are established through trade agreements among several countries in which trade barriers are reduced or eliminated for member countries.[4] The United States is a member of several such zones, including the **North American Free Trade Agreement (NAFTA)**, an agreement between Canada, Mexico, and the United States intended to remove barriers to trade and investment.[5] On the other side of the Atlantic, the **European Union (EU)** is a political and economic union of 27 European countries that share a common currency, the euro.[6]

For Mansfield Exports, the two additional important trade zones are the Union of South American Nations (UNASUR),[7] which includes Brazil; and the Asian-Pacific Economic Cooperation (APEC),[8] which includes China and Russia. By establishing business centers in each trading zone, Mansfield Exports takes advantage of these agreements, which opens up markets where they conduct business all over the world. Yet this expansion also presents new challenges, as each country and trading zone has different regulations and ways of doing business.

The challenge facing Mansfield Exports was familiar to Williams. As a manager at a small IT firm, he had worked extensively with officials in the **Association of Southeast Asian Nations (ASEAN)**, a cooperative organization of 10 countries in Southeast Asia established to promote economic, political, and social progress throughout the region.[9] As Williams learned early in his career, understanding and respecting the cultural differences of colleagues, clients, and partners was critical to achieving goals.[10] Working with ASEAN,

Global company An organization that has operations in multiple countries and its senior management decision making centrally located in one country.

Multi-domestic company An organization with operations in multiple countries and its senior management decision making distributed across the countries in which it operates.

Importing The organizational process of acquiring products and services from another country.

Exporting The organizational process of creating products in one country and selling them in another.

Strategic partnership An agreement between two or more organizations to share complementary resources to develop and sell products and services.

Direct foreign investment Buying existing or building new businesses in other countries.

World Trade Organization (WTO) The organization responsible for global trade rules between countries.

Regional trading zones Zones established through trade agreements among several countries in which trade barriers are reduced or eliminated for member countries.

North American Free Trade Agreement (NAFTA) An agreement between Canada, Mexico, and the United States intended to remove barriers to trade and investment.

European Union (EU) A political and economic union of 27 European countries that share a common currency, the euro.

Association of Southeast Asian Nations (ASEAN) A cooperative organization of 10 countries in Southeast Asia established to promote economic, political, and social progress throughout the region.

Success to the Successful[11]

Doing business internationally is "more complicated because [of the] language, physical, and cultural considerations," says Ric Stroup, CEO of E5 Systems. "Sometimes we find this difference disadvantages the client in unexpected ways. Because most of our clients don't have the language and cultural skills to build effective relationships with our team in China, they sometime assume that their ideas are the best. As an example, we see clients offer ideas for how to fix a problem. Because they are paying us to complete the work and like their own idea, the client does not spend a lot of time trying to understand other solutions that our team in China is proposing."

The difficulty that Stroup faces with his clients is a classic systems thinking problem, referred to as "Success to the Successful" (see Figure 5-1a). This prime example suggests that "success or failure may be due more to the initial conditions than intrinsic merit."[12] In Stroup's example, he has a client whose idea is not as good as the team in China's, yet the client is paying E5 Systems to develop the project and has little patience with communicating through cultural and language differences. This eventually leads to the client "succeeding" at implementing an inferior solution (see Figure 5-1a). How does E5 Systems work with their clients (see Figure 5-1b) to help understand the need to embrace cultural differences?

Figure 5-1a Success to the Successful

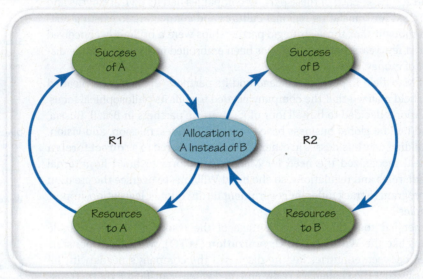

Figure 5-1b Success to the Client!

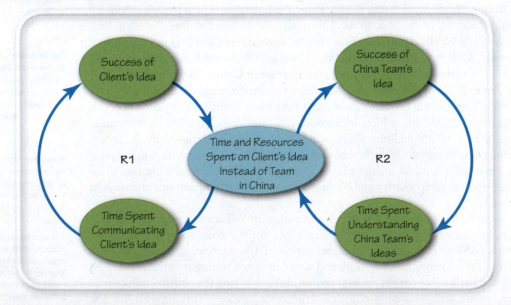

Williams began to understand the complexity of cultural differences and chose to invest only in the emerging engineering workforce of China because diversifying its holdings to Russia and India as well would be too challenging for the small growth company that he worked for at the time. Ultimately, Williams recommended that they build a knowledge base software application based on readily available resources through the WTO and other regional trading zones. The executive team at Mansfield Exports was excited by the possibility of having a shared resource that each of their multi-domestic teams could access.

Yet, based on his recent similar experience, Williams saw the threats facing Mansfield Exports had as much to do with the challenges of managing cultural differences, both internally and externally, as with navigating international rules and regulations. Armed with this information, Williams also offered a temperate assessment of why he thought the company's China subsidiary had become involved in its trade dispute. He believed that it wasn't just a lack of understanding of regulatory knowledge or rules that was causing the problem, but also an unawareness of cultural differences.[13] Mansfield leaned back in her chair and requested that Williams further explain his perspective.

5.2 | CULTURAL DIFFERENCES

5.2 | Explain the challenges and opportunities of working with cultural differences

Those of us with little exposure to other cultures often assume that most of our values and assumptions about how the world works are universal. For example, we figure that people in the United States, China, New Zealand, and Sweden all have similar ideas about what it means to be successful and the ways that businesses and customers should interact. In fact, there is a great deal of variety among cultures about what we consider valuable and how we should interact with each other.[14] In a global economy, being unaware of those differences can lead to embarrassment, lost business, and legal troubles. On the other hand, cultural awareness can facilitate stronger and more profitable business relationships with companies and clients in other countries and a more diverse, flexible, and creative workforce within a single company.[15,16]

Cultural Values and Dynamics

What Williams is suggesting to Mansfield is that she needs to do more than improve her company's understanding of the legal infrastructure that shapes international trade. She also needs to build her firm's **cultural intelligence**—the ability to understand and make effective decisions based on cultural differences.[17] Management typically takes one of three broad approaches to working with cultural differences: ethnocentric, polycentric, or geocentric. In an **ethnocentric** approach to international business, management believes that people who share their cultural values make the best managers. Managers with a **polycentric** attitude believe that managers from a particular country know best how to achieve results in that cultural context. In a **geocentric** business, management seeks talent and best practices from all around the world.[18] How do you think each approach would affect the relationships of Mansfield Exports with its international partners? Given that Mansfield Exports is a multi-domestic company in the import/export business, which approach do you think will be most effective for management?

Dimensions of Culture

As an initial resource for developing her cultural intelligence, Williams suggested that Mansfield look at some of the research done by Dutch sociologist Geert Hofstede and by the Global Leadership and Organizational Behavior Effectiveness (GLOBE) Project. Both Hofstede and GLOBE are interested in how cultural differences affect leadership and management practices. Based on research with over 100,000 IBM employees in 40 different

> **World Trade Organization (WTO)** —responsible for global trade rules between countries
> **Regional trading zones**— established through trade agreements between several countries in which trade barriers are reduced or eliminated for member countries
> **North American Free Trade Agreement (NAFTA)**—an agreement between Canada, Mexico, and the United States intended to remove barrier to trade and investment
> **European Union (EU)**—a political and economic union of 27 European countries, sharing a common currency, the Euro
> **Association of Southeast Asian Nations (ASEAN)**—a cooperative organization of 10 countries in Southeast Asia established to promote economic, political, and social progress throughout the region

LECTURE ENHANCER:

5.2 Cultural Differences
✓ Exhibit A: Success to the Successful
✓ Exhibit B: Success to the Client
• Cultural Values and Dynamics
> **Cultural intelligence (CI)**—the ability to understand and make effective decisions based on cultural differences
> **Ethnocentric**—management believes that people who share their cultural values make the best managers
> **Polycentric**—management believes that managers from a particular country know best how to achieve results in that cultural context

Cultural intelligence A manager's or leader's ability to understand and make effective decisions based on cultural differences.

Ethnocentric An approach to international business in which management believes that people who share their cultural values make the best managers.

Polycentric An approach to international business in which management believes that managers from a particular country know best how to achieve results in that cultural context.

Geocentric An approach to international business in which management seeks talent and best practices from all around the world.

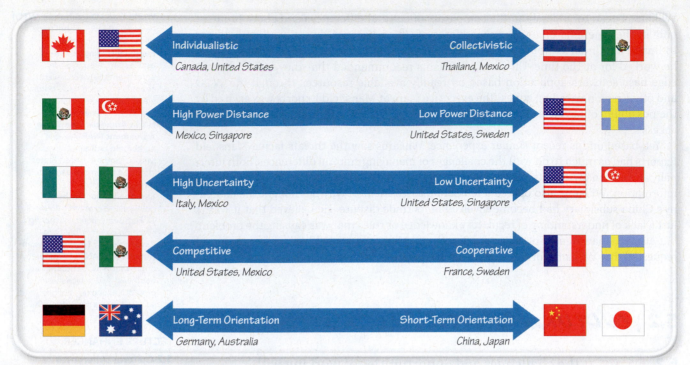

Figure 5-2

Hofstede's Cultural Dimensions

Hofstede's theory of the different cultural dimensions of certain countries.

Global Leadership and Organizational Effectiveness (GLOBE) A network of over 150 researchers from 62 cultures from around the world assembled to study cultural dynamics in leadership and management.

countries, Hofstede identified five value dimensions that varied among different cultures as outlined in Figure 5-2:[19]

1. *Individualism versus collectivism. Individualism* is a social view that values individual freedom and self-expression and assumes that individuals are responsible for their own welfare. *Collectivism,* on the other hand, values the welfare of the group over any one individual and emphasizes the responsibilities of individuals and groups (families and organizations) to each other.

2. *Power distance.* A high ranking on the power distance dimension means that people from that culture accept an unequal distribution of power. A low ranking means that people expect a more equal distribution of power.

3. *Uncertainty avoidance.* The higher the ranking on the uncertainty avoidance scale, the more uncomfortable people are with uncertainty and ambiguity. They are more at ease with conformity and with events that follow an expected structure. Societies with low uncertainty avoidance are more comfortable with a lack of structure and the unexpected.

4. *Competition versus cooperation. Competitive* and *cooperative* refer to whether the society as a whole places greater value on performance, achievement, material success, and contest or on quality of life, collaboration, personal relationships, and group decision making. This dimension is also referred to as "masculine versus feminine."

5. *Long-term versus short-term orientation.* Countries that tend toward long-term orientation are more concerned about the future than the present and value thrift and perseverance. Countries that tend toward short-term orientation, on the other hand, are more concerned with the present and past and value tradition and social obligations.[20]

GLOBE Studies The **Global Leadership and Organizational Effectiveness (GLOBE)** research program is a network of over 150 researchers from 62 cultures around the world. Their goal is to "develop an empirically based theory to describe, understand, and predict the impact of cultural variables on leadership and organizational processes and the effectiveness of these processes."[21] Expanding upon Hofstede's earlier work, the research team identified nine dimensions that collectively describe a culture's disposition. Collecting responses from 17,000 managers at 951 organizations, the researchers found patterns that differentiated cultures, with countries ranking high on a particular dimension exhibiting these behaviors and beliefs more dominantly as outlined in Table 5-1.[22]

Table 5-1 GLOBE Studies[23]

Assertiveness		Humane Orientation	
Tough, confrontational, assertive, and competitive versus modest and tender		Encourage and reward individuals for being fair, altruistic, friendly, generous, caring, and kind to others.	
High-Ranked Countries	**Low-Ranked Countries**	**High-Ranked Countries**	**Low-Ranked Countries**
United States	New Zealand	Malaysia	Germany
Austria	Japan	Ireland	France
Sweden		Philippines	Singapore

In-Group Collectivism		Performance Orientation	
Express pride, loyalty, and cohesiveness in their organizations or families.		Encourages and rewards group members for performance improvement and excellence.	
High-Ranked Countries	**Low-Ranked Countries**	**High-Ranked Countries**	**Low-Ranked Countries**
Iran	Denmark	Singapore	Russia
India	Sweden	Hong Kong	Italy
China	New Zealand	United States	Argentina

Institutional Collectivism		Power Distance	
Encourage and reward collective distribution of resources and collective action.		Expect and agree that power should be unequally shared.	
High-Ranked Countries	**Low-Ranked Countries**	**High-Ranked Countries**	**Low-Ranked Countries**
Sweden	Greece	Russia	Denmark
South Korea	Italy	Thailand	The Netherlands
Japan	Argentina	Spain	Sweden

Gender Egalitarianism		Uncertainty Avoidance	
Maximizes gender role differences.		Rely on social norms, rituals, and bureaucratic practices to alleviate the unpredictability of future events.	
High-Ranked Countries	**Low-Ranked Countries**	**High-Ranked Countries**	**Low-Ranked Countries**
South Korea	Hungary	Switzerland	Russia
Egypt	Poland	Sweden	Greece
China	Denmark	Germany	Venezuela

Future Orientation			
Encourages and rewards . . . planning, investing in the future, and delaying gratification.			
High-Ranked Countries	**Low-Ranked Countries**		
Singapore	Russia		
Switzerland	Argentina		
The Netherlands	Italy		

Universal Cultural Perspectives Once the responses were collected, researchers asked, "Are there attributes and traits that managers from organizations all across the world could agree are positive and negative?" The answer was "yes."[24] The ideal leader or manager, has a universal set of positive attributes as shown in Table 5-2. How might you use the lists of traits to foster personal development?

Table 5-2 Universally Positive Leadership Traits[25]

Universal Positive Traits		
Administrative Skills	Effective Bargainer	Motivational
Communicative	Encouraging	Motive Arouser
Confidence Builder	Excellence-Oriented	Plans Ahead
Coordinator	Foresight	Positive
Decisive	Honest	Team Builder
Dependable	Informed	Trustworthy
Dynamic	Intelligent	Win-win Problem Solver
	Just	

Table 5-3	Universally Negative Leadership Traits[26]	
Universal Negative Traits		
Asocial	Irritable	Uncooperative
Dictatorial	Loner	Non-explicit
Egocentric		Ruthless

The traits and attributes listed above in Table 5-3 are universally viewed as *negative*.

Approaches to Cultural Differences

Understanding cultural differences is about much more than just getting along with different kinds of people. Successful management of diverse cultural attitudes and beliefs can mean the difference between winning and losing a contract, between meeting and missing a deadline, even between life and death. In the 1990s, Korean Airlines had one of the worst safety records in the airline industry. In 1997, a Korean Airline plane crashed in Guam, killing 228 people. Inquiries revealed that a contributing factor to the crash was a cultural mismatch. Most large aircraft are designed and built in Western, low-power-distance societies, with the expectation that there would be little power distance between the two people flying the plane. But South Korea is traditionally a high-power-distance culture, which made it extremely difficult for the copilot to be as direct in communicating the problem as was needed. The result of this cultural mismatch was a fatal accident.[27]

Since then, the CEO of Korean Airlines, Cho Yang-Ho, has worked to overhaul the internal culture of his organization in many ways, including empowering subordinates to speak up. Under Cho's direction, Korean Airlines now has one of the best safety and service records in the industry, and, bolstered by a burgeoning Korean-American population, Korean Airlines has become the largest Asian airline operating in the United States.[28]

Would we expect the same cultural challenge at Lufthansa Airlines, operated in Germany? Consider the following cultural data from Hofstede's online resource as outlined in Figure 5-3 (http://www.geert-hofstede.com/).

Figure 5-3

Hofstede's Cultural Comparison of Germany and South Korea

PDI = High versus Low Power Distance

IDV = Individualistic versus Collectivistic

COP = Competitive versus Cooperative

UAI = High versus Low Uncertainty Avoidance

LTO = Long-term versus Short-term Orientation[29]

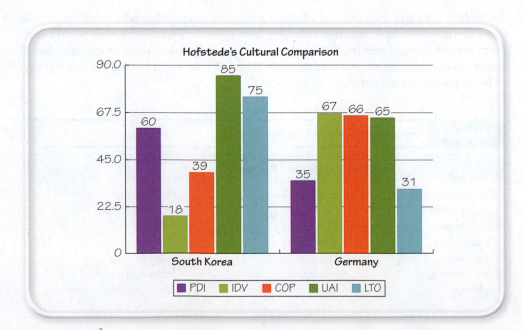

5.3 | LEGAL BASICS FOR MANAGING DIVERSITY

5.3 | **Understand** the legal requirements for respecting workforce diversity.

In addition to cultural dynamics, organizations rely on team members from diverse backgrounds to attract and retain high-quality talent *and* customers. As we discussed earlier, **diversity** is the degree to which an organization represents different cultures. In business, as in life, people experience diversity on two levels. **deep-level diversity** is the degree to which individuals in a group represent differences that cannot be seen, such as personalities, attitudes, values, and perspectives.[30] **Surface-level diversity** is the degree to which individuals in a group represent differences based on visual cues, such as age, ethnicity, and gender.[31] These levels are the layers that explain the *dimensions of diversity*, as shown in Figure 5-4. What responsibilities do managers have when managing a diverse workforce?

Following the 1964 Civil Rights Act, which made racial and sex discrimination illegal, successive presidents issued executive orders requiring **affirmative action**, proactive steps taken by organizations to counteract discrimination against minorities, including women.[32] In addition to the Civil Rights Act, Congress passed the Americans with Disabilities Act (ADA) in 1990 to address discrimination against people with **disabilities**, physical or mental impairments that substantially limit one or more of an individual's major life activities.[33]

Many people believe that **discrimination**, treating individuals or groups unfairly or negatively based on their diversity traits, including sexual orientation, age, ethnicity, gender, or disability, is no longer an issue in the workplace. The situation has improved because organizations have modified their practices, but discrimination does still exist.[34] In business, a **glass ceiling** is an invisible barrier that limits the opportunities for women and minorities to advance to upper-level positions. These barriers exist wherever organizations and management have biases that create an organizational culture of unspoken, and often unrecognized, discrimination.[35] Women, for example, have made great strides in achieving workplace equality, but are still underpaid in comparison to their male counterparts as outlined in Figure 5-5, and underrepresented in upper management roles per Figure 5-6.[36]

But what if the company that you work for advocates organizational policies and practices that hamper your ability to progress? Many organizations are aware of these invisible barriers and are taking proactive steps, including affirmative action, to correct the

Diversity The degree to which an organization represents different cultures.

Deep-level diversity The degree to which individuals in a group represent differences that cannot be seen, such as personalities, attitudes, values, and perspectives.

Surface-level diversity The degree to which individuals in a group represent differences based on visual cues, such as age, ethnicity, and gender.

Affirmative action Proactive steps taken by organizations to counteract discrimination against minorities, including women.

Disabilities Physical or mental impairments that substantially limit one or more of an individual's major life activities.

Discrimination Treating individuals or groups unfairly or negatively based on their diversity traits, including sexual orientation, age, ethnicity, gender, or disability.

Glass ceiling An invisible barrier that limits the opportunities for women and minorities to advance to upper-level positions.

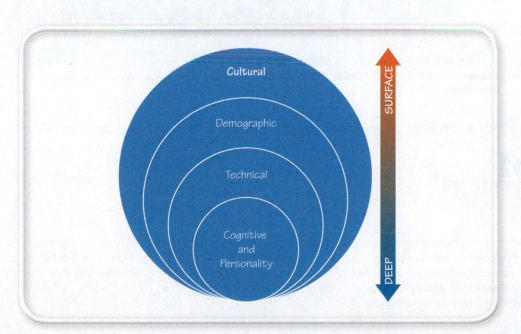

Figure 5-4
Dimensions of Diversity Wheel
There are deep-level and surface-level dimensions of diversity.

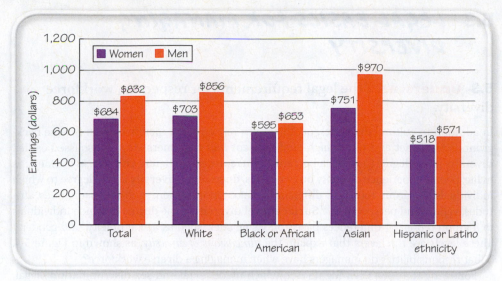

Figure 5-5
The Wage Gap Between Men and Women
Statistics show that men still earn more than women.

Adapted from US Bureau of Labor Statistics, "Highlights of Women's Earnings in 2011," Report 1038, US Department of Labor (October 2012), http://www.bls.gov/cps/cpswom2011.pdf.

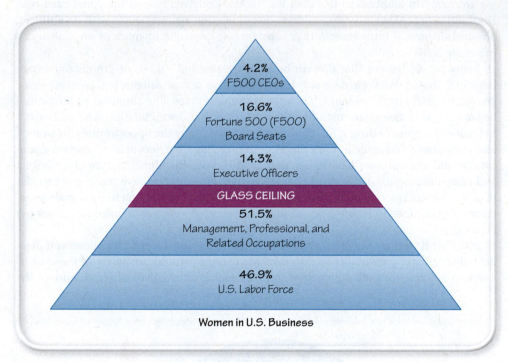

Figure 5-6
Women in U.S. Business
U.S. businesswomen are underpaid in comparison to their male counterparts.

Adapted from "U.S. Women in Business," *Catalyst Research*, July 2013, http://www.catalyst.org/knowledge/us-women-business-0

Voices of Management

Ursula Burns,
CEO, Xerox Corporation

Ursula Burns is the first African American woman to become chairperson of a Fortune 500 company. She has been CEO since 2009. Burns says: "I'm in this job because I believe I earned it through hard work and high performance. Did I get some opportunities early in my career because of my race and gender? Probably. I went to work for a company that was openly seeking to diversify its workforce. So, I imagine race and gender got the hiring guys' attention. And then the rest was really up to me."[37] ■

Research @ Work

Trust[38]

How important is trust in the workplace? Recent studies have demonstrated that trust is strongly correlated to productivity—the greater the trust, the greater the productivity. For example, Boe (2002) reported that productivity, turnover, absenteeism, and motivation are all affected by employee trust. In general, management research has focused primarily on two kinds of trust relationships—between coworkers, and between managers and employees (or leaders and followers).

De Jong and Elfring (2010), after studying 73 long-term teams at a large multinational consulting firm, found a positive correlation between team performance and two trust-building processes: *reflexivity*, or a team's ability to reflect upon and revise their work processes, goals, and strategies openly; and *effort*, or the extent to which team members devote time and energy to team tasks.

Knowing that trust between coworkers leads to better productivity is great, but how can a manager foster that trust? It turns out that leaders can have a great deal of influence on how much employees trust each other. Lau and Liden (2008) found that the more a leader trusted workers, the more coworkers trusted each other. And that correlation turns out to be especially strong during hard times. In other words, when a team is struggling to perform well, a manager's trust in employees has a strong impact on their trust of each other, and that, in turn, helps them to improve their performance.

Trust works in the other direction, too. In Dirks and Ferrin's (2002) research, they found that when people trust their leader, they don't feel the need to "cover their backs," and so are able to devote more time and energy to their actual work. An atmosphere of trust also makes it easier for individuals to develop strong social relationships with each other. Strong personal relationships in the workplace increase the likelihood that individuals will help each other and that they will perform beyond minimum expectations, both of which lead to higher productivity.

Bottom line? Teams in which workers and leaders trust each other and feel themselves to be trusted are productive teams.

Professor's Response

What I find interesting about this research is that it demonstrates the exponential impact of trust—the benefits extend beyond one-to-one relationships. I imagine that this information would encourage managers to be more explicit in their expressions of trust.

Manager's Response

I already cultivate an atmosphere of trust with my team. We're all very comfortable relying on each other. But I can see how it could be helpful to share this with new managers, who sometimes are reluctant to trust their team for fear of looking like they aren't taking on their responsibilities fully.

Critical Thinking in the Classroom

How would you, as a manager, foster a relationship based on trust with your team?

---

underrepresentation of women and minority groups. Some people think this issue was solved 20+ years ago. They feel that there is no longer a need for government to step in and mandate the morality of business and management. But others feel that discrimination, while less common now, nevertheless is still a problem.[39] A divisive issue, affirmative action is passionately argued by two opposing perspectives as shown in Table 5-4.

Table 5-4	The Affirmative Action Controversy[40]
Positions *for* Affirmative Action	**Positions *Against* Affirmative Action**
• The right of an applicant "to equal consideration"	• Severing reward from a "person's character, talents, choices, and abilities"
• The right of the maximally competent to an open position	• "Subordinating merit, conduct, and character to race"
• The right of everyone to equal opportunity	• Disconnecting outcomes from actual liability and damage

The U.S. Equal Employment Opportunity Commission (EEOC) is the government agency charged with "enforcing federal laws that make it illegal to discriminate against a job applicant or an employee because of the person's race, color, religion, sex (including pregnancy), national origin, age (40 or older), disability, or genetic information."[41] In the year 2012, the EEOC reported that there were nearly 100,000 workplace discrimination charges filed, costing organizations $365 million.[42] What are the practical implications of these legislative acts on managers? Table 5-5 lists some of the issues involved.

Table 5-5	A Legal Framework for Diversity in Practice[43]	
A Manager's Responsibility	**Legality of Discrimination**	**Management Examples**
Job Advertisements	It is illegal for an employer to publish a job advertisement that shows a preference for or discourages someone from applying for a job because of his or her race, color, religion, sex (including pregnancy), national origin, age (40 or older), disability, or genetic information.	For example, a "Help Wanted" ad that seeks "females" or "recent college graduates" may discourage men and people over 40 from applying and may violate the law.
Recruitment	It is illegal for an employer to recruit new employees in a way that discriminates against them because of their race, color, religion, sex (including pregnancy), national origin, age (40 or older), disability, or genetic information.	For example, an employer's reliance on word-of-mouth recruitment by its mostly Hispanic workforce may violate the law if the result is that almost all new hires are Hispanic.
Job Referrals	It is illegal for an employer, employment agency, or union to take into account a person's race, color, religion, sex (including pregnancy), national origin, age (40 or older), disability, or genetic information when making decisions about job referrals.	For example, an employer cannot show preference for candidates that go to a certain church.
Job Assignments and Promotions	It is illegal for an employer to make decisions about job assignments and promotions based on an employee's race, color, religion, sex (including pregnancy), national origin, age (40 or older), disability, or genetic information.	For example, an employer may not give preference to employees of a certain race when making shift assignments and may not segregate employees of a particular national origin from other employees or from customers.
Pay and Benefits	It is illegal for an employer to discriminate against an employee in the payment of wages or employee benefits on the bases of race, color, religion, sex (including pregnancy), national origin, age (40 or older), disability, or genetic information. Employee benefits include sick and vacation leave, insurance, access to overtime and overtime pay, and retirement programs.	For example, an employer may not pay Hispanic workers less than African American workers because of their national origin, and men and women in the same workplace must be given equal pay for equal work.
Discipline and Discharge	An employer may not take into account a person's race, color, religion, sex (including pregnancy), national origin, age (40 or older), disability, or genetic information when making decisions about discipline or discharge.	For example, if a white employee and an Asian employee commit a similar offense, an employer may not discipline them differently.
Employment References	It is illegal for an employer to give a negative or false employment reference (or refuse to give a reference) because of a person's race, color, religion, sex (including pregnancy), national origin, age (40 or older), disability, or genetic information.	When an employer is contacted for a reference for a female worker, it may not cite pregnancy or having children as a negative trait.

Table 5-5 Continued

A Manager's Responsibility	Legality of Discrimination	Management Examples
Reasonable Accommodation and Disability	The law requires that an employer provide reasonable accommodation to an employee or job applicant with a disability, unless doing so would cause significant difficulty or expense for the employer. A reasonable accommodation is any change in the workplace (or in the ways things are usually done) to help a person with a disability apply for a job, perform the duties of a job, or enjoy the benefits and privileges of employment.	Reasonable accommodation might include, for example, providing a ramp for a wheelchair user or providing a reader or interpreter for a blind or deaf employee or applicant.
Reasonable Accommodation and Religion	The law requires an employer to provide reasonable accommodation to an employee's religious beliefs or practices, unless doing so would cause difficulty or expense for the employer.	Reasonable accommodation might include, for example, providing structured breaks during the day for prayer or to attend religious services.
Training and Apprenticeship Programs	It is illegal for a training or apprenticeship program to discriminate on the bases of race, color, religion, sex (including pregnancy), national origin, age (40 or older), disability, or genetic information.	For example, an employer may not deny training opportunities to African American employees because of their race.
Terms and Conditions of Employment	The law makes it illegal for an employer to make any employment decision because of a person's race, color, religion, sex (including pregnancy), national origin, age (40 or older), disability, or genetic information.	An employer may not discriminate when it comes to such things as hiring, firing, promotions, and pay. It also means, for example, that an employer may not discriminate when granting breaks, approving leave, assigning work stations, or setting any other term or condition of employment, however small.

From U.S. Equal Employment Opportunity Commission, "Prohibited Employment Policies/Practices"; http://www1.eeoc.gov//laws/practices/index.cfm?renderforprint=1.

5.4 | *TALENT IN A DIVERSE WORKFORCE*

5.4 | Recognize and explain the implications of changing workforce demographics.

Changing Workforce Demographics

Jill Mansfield and her team of executives started working together in the Mansfield family business 20 years ago. Mansfield believes that in the next 12 years, all the senior-level talent and management in the organization will retire. What will be lost and what will be gained when this happens?

Let's say you are manager of a manufacturing plant with a talented and dedicated team. The labor involved is physically demanding, and the average age of your employees is expected to rise to 47 by the year 2020. A consultant recently alerted you that with an aging workforce, you should expect your team members to call in sick more often and for longer periods of time.[44] What do you do? This is the management dilemma that the automotive company BMW faces. Traditionally, companies would fire older workers or offer them early retirement.[45] But for legal and practical reasons, this is no longer an option.[46] By 2020, 25 percent of the U.S. workforce will be aged 55 or older, while workers aged 16–24 will make up only 11 percent of the workforce.[47]

LECTURE ENHANCER:

5.4 Talent in a Diverse Workforce

- Changing Workforce Demographics
  ✓ Figure 5-7: Changing Workplace Age Demographic
  ✓ Figure 5-8: The Biggest Trends for the Workforce You Will Manage
- Outsourcing and Offshoring Talent
  ➤ **Outsourcing**—when an organization hires an outside company to fulfill one or more of its core functions
  ➤ **Offshoring**—when an organization outsources to a company in another country
  ➤ **Professional employee organizations**—offer employee management services to other companies

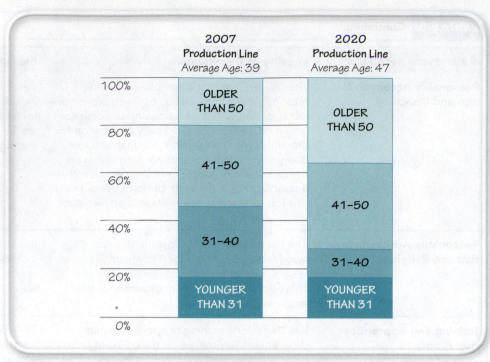

2007 Production Line Average Age: 39	2020 Production Line Average Age: 47
100%	
OLDER THAN 50	
80%	OLDER THAN 50
41–50	
60%	41–50
40%	
31–40	31–40
20%	
YOUNGER THAN 31	YOUNGER THAN 31
0%	

Figure 5-7

Changing Workplace Age Demographics

The average age of production-line workers by percentage in 2007, and projected in 2020.

Source: C. H. Loch, F. J. Sting, N. Bauer, and H. Mauermann, "How BMW Is Defusing the Demographic Time Bomb," *Harvard Business Review*, March 2010, 99–102.

Concerned about a potential production crisis, top managers at a BMW plant in Lower Bavaria, Germany, presented the problem to production managers and asked that they set aside one production line as an experimental line and staff it with workers that represented the mix of ages expected in the local workforce in 2020. That meant that the average age of workers on the line was 47 as outlined in Figure 5-7.[48]

At first, employees were reluctant to participate in the program. Among other things, they feared that that they would be ridiculed by other employees for going on the "pension-ers" line. Aware of resistance to a "top-down" program of this sort, management actively sought out workers' ideas, concerns, questions, and solutions.[49] Ultimately, the line work-ers developed the solutions, including installing wooden floors to reduce joint pain, having adjustable chairs and tables, and using a task rotation schedule to prevent repetitive strain. By bringing together an assortment of ideas from top management, middle management, and line workers, and from people of all ages, BMW achieved its goal with the experimen-tal line: health-related absenteeism dropped from 7 percent to 2 percent, below the plant's average. The line reached BMW's quality goal of 10 defects per million within the first three months, and by 2010, it had achieved zero defects. What about productivity? One of the big worries of an aging workforce is that older workers work more slowly and productivity will decline. But the BMW team discovered that by making employee-recommended changes, workers on the experimental line had no trouble keeping up with increasing production targets.[50]

Aging is one primary concern for managers in the beginning of the 21st century, but this is just one piece of a much larger and more complex puzzle.[51] What dynamics might a manager expect to face in building and growing a company in the next 20 years? Talent in the workforce today is shifting dramatically in terms of ethnicity, age, gender, and required skills.[52] Consider Figure 5-8, which outlines the changing workforce that you will manage.[53] What are some of the new challenges and opportunities that you might encounter with this new diversity of employees and colleagues?

Outsourcing and Offshoring Talent

With so many dynamics to manage and regulations to adhere to, many companies and their management have opted to contract with specialized companies rather than hiring

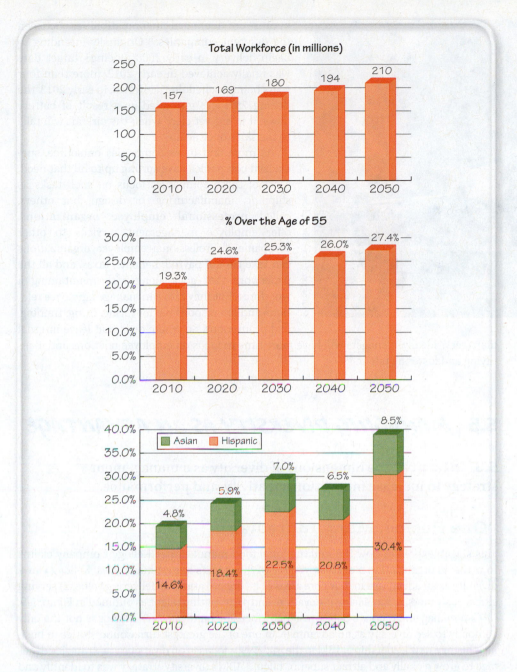

Total Workforce (in millions)

2010: 157
2020: 169
2030: 180
2040: 194
2050: 210

% Over the Age of 55

2010: 19.3%
2020: 24.6%
2030: 25.3%
2040: 26.0%
2050: 27.4%

Asian / Hispanic

2010: Asian 4.8%, Hispanic 14.6%
2020: Asian 5.9%, Hispanic 18.4%
2030: Asian 7.0%, Hispanic 22.5%
2040: Asian 6.5%, Hispanic 20.8%
2050: Asian 8.5%, Hispanic 30.4%

Figure 5-8
The Biggest Trends for the Workforce That You Will Manage[54]
Projection of the percentage of the workforce that will be over the age of 55, and the growth in the population of Asian and Hispanic workers by 2050.

individual talent.[55] Instead of hiring and managing graphic designers, software developers, and accountants, a company might instead contract with a graphic design company, a software development company, and an accounting firm. When an organization hires an outside company to fulfill one or more of its core functions, this is called **outsourcing**. When an organization moves a business process to another country, it is called **offshoring**.

Both outsourcing and offshoring can greatly benefit a company by reducing costs and improving efficiency. But the practices can also cause additional challenges, both within the organization and, in the case of offshoring, in the larger society.[56] Consider, for example, how U.S. companies' tendency to offshore manufacturing has affected communities in the United States whose economies have relied on large, local manufacturing plants. Or consider Boeing's struggles to deliver its newest aircraft, the Boeing 787 Dreamliner. With more than 600 orders for the new, fuel-efficient plane, the launch of the 787 was one of the most successful in airline history.[57] But Boeing soon ran into trouble meeting its production deadlines. With the 787, Boeing decided to outsource much of the design and development work, something that it had not tried before. Rather than improving efficiency and reducing costs, Boeing found that its outsourcing decisions led to costly delays

Outsourcing Hiring an outside company to fulfill one or more of an organization's core functions.

Offshoring Moving a business process to another country.

© Grzegorz Kieca / iStockphoto

because of technical incompatibilities between the different companies.[58] Originally intending to begin delivery in early 2008, Boeing's target date was finally achieved in early 2012, more than four years behind schedule.[59] However, in early 2013, the Boeing 787, was grounded as a result of battery flaws. It is not yet clear when the aircraft will take to the skies once again.

As more and more companies outsource, specialized companies have sprung up to fill that need. Most of these companies focus on such tasks as shipping, manufacturing, or design, but others, called **professional employee organizations**, offer employee management services to other companies.[60] Professional employee organizations can take care of payroll, benefits, taxes, and all the paperwork that goes along with maintaining a workforce. But they also can manage employee relations and are responsible for hiring, firing, training, and promotions. So where does that leave internal managers? Ideally, managers will have more time to focus on employee relations and identifying and fostering talent. [61]

Professional employee organizations Organizations that offer employee management services to other companies.

5.5 | *MANAGING DIVERSITY AS AN ADVANTAGE*

5.5 | Interpret the dimensions of diversity as a management strategy to increase innovation, creativity, and performance.

"One Recipe, Many Ingredients"

This slogan expresses how the mulitnational food manufacturer Kellogg Company claims to make its organization a success. As one of the world's largest businesses, Kellogg views diversity as an advantage in four core areas of its organization: 1) delivering value, 2) serving global customers, 3) increasing innovation, and 4) attracting talent as outlined in Figure 5-9.

Can management create better results by focusing on diversity?[62] Kellogg is not the only company to see diversity as an advantage. In one of the greatest turnaround stories in business history, new leadership at IBM in the mid-1990s focused on diversity as a strategic advantage to grow globally and attract superior talent.[63] IBM's diversity strategy was to identify and understand the differences between the many groups that made up their employee and customer pools. Rather than simply ignoring cultural differences, IBM chose to pursue diversity as a way of developing its internal talent pool and expanding its customer base.[64] They created a management task force for each of eight demographics: Asians, blacks, gays/lesbians/bisexual/transgendered people, Hispanic, Native Americans, people with disabilities, white men, and women.[65] Each task force was charged with answering four specific questions:

What can IBM do to make your constituency feel welcome here? What can IBM do to maximize your constituency's productivity? How can we best serve your constituency as customers? And what organizations should we develop relationships with in order to understand your constituency better?[66]

The changes that IBM implemented based on the task forces' research and recommendations had powerful effects. Not only did they see employee production and job satisfaction improve, but they saw sales to small and medium-sized business, often owned by women and minorities, grow from $10 million in 1998 to hundreds of millions of dollars by today. And by listening to the People with Disabilities task force, IBM was ahead of the game when new regulations required that the federal government prioritize accessibility over cost when awarding federal contracts.[67]

Figure 5-9
Kellogg Company Diversity and Inclusion Business Strategy[68]
Kellogg Company's commitment to diversity can be seen here.

Diversity as a Strategy

At this point, it is time to put together cultural, workforce, and organizational-level diversity into a strategy that managers can apply. Organizations invest in diversity as a strategy because it positively affects creativity and innovation, which increases performance.[69] As in the cases of Kellogg and IBM, effective managers foster organizational cultures that translate to business strategies and policies/practices. The dimensions of diversity affect group and team processes, which have an effect on organizational outcomes.[70] The dimensions that we have discussed in this chapter can be placed in four categories: cultural, demographic, technical, and cognitive. Hofstede's and GLOBE's work provided us with a research-based context to view *cultural* dimensions, reminding managers that understanding cultural differences enables them to achieve more effective outcomes. Then we discussed the changing dynamics of the workforce *demographics*, which provides managers with challenges and opportunities for growth and innovation. In particular, BMW provides us a template for how large organizations can approach the complexity of a changing workforce by broadly gathering perspectives across the organizations and designing technical systems to respond to change.[71]

Organizations and managers that use diversity as an advantage create an internal environment that supports **social integration**, where individuals share and collaborate based on their unique perspective, transforming individuals' cognitive approach to diverse viewpoints.[72] An organization and its management's approach to these dimensions creates a vital part of the company's culture, which then gets translated into business strategy and human resource policies and practices[73] as outlined in Figure 5-10.

Social integration The degree to which individuals in a group share and collaborate based on their unique perspective.

How Diversity Affects Creativity, Innovation, and Performance

Each organization approaches the dimensions of diversity differently, which can dramatically change group and team processes and organizational outcomes.[74] As shown in Figure 5-11, diversity dimensions affect group and team processes, ultimately increasing organizational creativity and innovation by means of communication, conflict, cohesion, and information. Successful managers understand that their team's capacity to be creative and innovative depends upon their ability to communicate, engage in productive conflict, develop cohesion, and realize and share information effectively.[75] This allows organizations

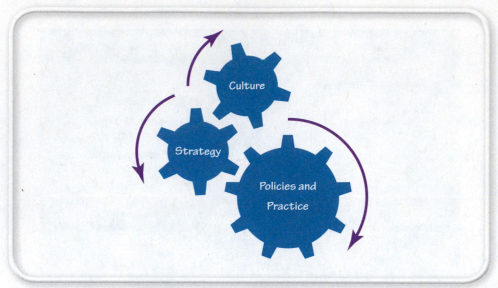

Adapted from T. Kochan et al., "The Effects of Diversity on Business Performance: Report of the Diversity Research Network," *Human Resource Management* 42, vol.1 (2003): 3–21.

Figure 5-10
From Organizational Culture to Practice
Diversity affects culture, which affects strategy, as well as policies and practice.

to create more relevant and/or higher-quality products and services for customers, which directly relates to three outcomes: performance, satisfaction, and turnover. Performance refers to the degree to which the company achieves its goals. Especially true in service organizations, employee satisfaction positively or negatively affects customer satisfaction. Satisfied employees demonstrate positive behaviors, such as being thoughtful, friendly, and optimistic. Positive or negative employee satisfaction translates into positive and negative customer satisfaction, respectively.[76] And satisfied employees have lower levels of turnover than dissatisfied employees[77] as described in Figure 5-11.

Fostering Diversity

Some managers find fostering diversity challenging because it requires letting go of control and embracing something different. What things do managers and the people on their

Figure 5-11
Translating Diversity into Outcomes
The impact of diversity on group and team processes, and the resulting outcomes.

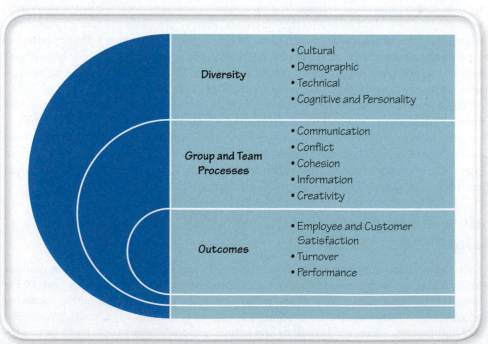

Adapted from T. Kochan et al., "The Effects of Diversity on Business Performance: Report of the Diversity Research Network," *Human Resource Management* 42.1 (2003): 3–21.

Fixes That Fail

Let's illustrate how a strategic advantage also can become a disadvantage if management is not careful.[78] As you will recall in the "Success to the Successful" example, E5 Systems faced the challenge of clients not taking the time to understand innovative solutions provided by the team in China, largely based on cultural and communication differences.

We can use systems thinking, cultural dynamics, and the dimensions of diversity to consider how and when fixes work and fail.[79] Mansfield Exports has set up its organizational structure as a multi-domestic company, wherein most of the decision making occurs in each of its headquarters around the world. Let's say Mansfield Exports has a policy in its Chicago headquarters to have a "town hall" meeting once a month, where all employees have an opportunity to express their opinions and question the decision making of senior executives. In Chicago, this has a positive impact on outcomes, in terms of performance, satisfaction, and turnover. Senior management would like to see this impact at all their headquarters, so the company mandates this policy to each management team around the world.

According to GLOBE Studies research, we can anticipate challenges when this policy is implemented in Russia.[80] Based on the cultural dynamic of power distance, we learn that Russia is one of the highest rated cultures in the world in this area,[81] where the culture "expects and agrees that power should be unequally shared." When the Chicago headquarters mandates this policy, two things might happen: 1) the management team in Russia assumes that the policy mandate is not to be negotiated and therefore implements it, and 2) as town hall meetings don't generally exist in the Russian culture, the policy has the unintended consequence of reducing management and employee satisfaction and increasing company turnover, which significantly decreases performance. (See Figure 5-12, which illustrates these consequences.)

In a "Fixes That Fail" situation like this one, the symptoms of a problem create pressure for a solution. As a result, a solution is quickly implemented that alleviates the symptom. However, the solution itself results in unintended consequences that cause the original symptoms of the problem eventually to recur at a similar, if not worse, level of severity. This causes the application of the same or similar solution, leading to self-reinforcing cycle of "Fixes That Fail."[82]

Figure 5-12 A Doomed Cultural Fix

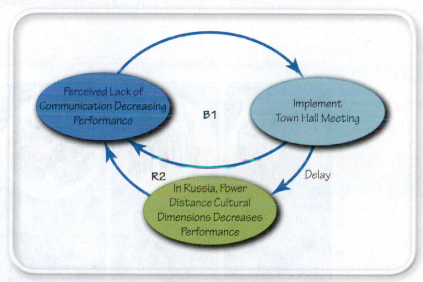

Source: D. Kim, *Systems Archetypes I* (Waltham, MA: Pegasus Communications, Inc., 1994).

teams really control? Regarding diversity, one can control technical and cognitive dimensions only by developing them over time.[83] Some managers make the mistake of attempting to homogenize the cultural and demographic characteristics of their teams in an attempt to match the organization's culture and perceived values. Managers that foster teams with the requisite capacities to develop collectively the technical and cognitive skills to be competitive in the marketplace always benefit from embracing cultural and demographic differences.[84] Why? In a global economy, as IBM and Kellogg Company have experienced, fostering diversity translates into expanded market opportunities because these organizations are increasing their capacity to address customer needs and desires.[85] How do managers build diversity as a strategic advantage for an organization? To begin to answer this question, let's continue our investigation of the Mansfield Exports case.

Williams goes to the whiteboard to make a point. Drawing four circles on the board, he labels them "Brazil," "Russia," "India," and "China." Looking at Mansfield, he concedes, "Clearly, Mansfield Exports chose to build businesses in these markets because they are the four largest emerging economies in the world. In my career, I have done business in each of these countries, and the people and organizational values could not be more different. The challenge you face is 10 percent regulation and rules and 90 percent understanding how to motivate your international teams to embrace the Mansfield Exports culture and to want to collaborate with one another, first by embracing their culture and diversity. Twenty years ago, the offshoring industry looked at the talent in India and China the way that Frederick Taylor looked at workers on an assembly line 100 years ago—simply as part of a machine, not talent to be cared for, nurtured, and fostered over time. Find a way to understand and look after your employees, and Mansfield Exports will be successful."

As a manager, how can Mansfield foster diversity as an advantage? Based on all the principles of culture and diversity discussed in this chapter, Mansfield might apply the following methodology to establish diversity as a strategic advantage for Mansfield Exports: First, build a company culture that embraces diversity as a core tenet. Next, design a business strategy to attract and retain talent to support the organization's culture and to meet client expectations. Then, establish policies and expectations of practices to support the business strategy. Finally, as the author and well-known management consultant Peter Drucker reminds us, nurture individual and group skills and competencies necessary to support the organization's culture, strategy, and policies and practices.[86]

Let's revisit the case analysis of IBM. In Figure 5-13, we show the system of diversity that created a global strategic advantage for the company. In this example, we see how IBM's diversity management philosophy prevents the cultural mishaps that Mansfield could

Figure 5-13

IBM's Diversity as a Strategic Advantage

IBM's strategic approach to diversity.

Adapted from D. A. Thomas, "Diversity as Strategy," *Harvard Business Review*, September 2004, 1–10.

experience by implementing their Chicago town hall meetings in Moscow. This can be prevented if managers understand the intended and unintended consequences as a result of cultural dynamics and diversity dimensions.

You should now have a good grasp of the importance of diversity in the workplace. In the next chapter, we will explore the equally important topic of ethics and social responsibility and how both are crucial to the survival of any business.

Case**Snapshot**

Chapter 5 Case: Diversity in a Global Economy:
Zumba can be found on pg. 466

ADDITIONAL RESOURCES

KEY TERMS

Affirmative action Proactive steps taken by organizations to counteract discrimination against minorities, including women. **(p. 125)**

Association of Southeast Asian Nations (ASEAN) A cooperative organization of 10 countries in Southeast Asia established to promote economic, political, and social progress throughout the region. **(p. 119)**

Cultural intelligence A manager's or leader's ability to understand and make effective decisions based on cultural differences. **(p. 121)**

Deep-level diversity The degree to which individuals in a group represent differences that cannot be seen, such as personalities, attitudes, values, and perspectives. **(p. 125)**

Direct foreign investment Buying existing or building new businesses in other countries. **(p. 119)**

Disabilities Physical or mental impairments that substantially limit one or more of an individual's major life activities. **(p. 125)**

Discrimination Treating individuals or groups unfairly or negatively based on their diversity traits, including sexual orientation, age, ethnicity, gender, or disability. **(p. 125)**

Diversity The degree to which an organization represents different cultures. **(p. 125)**

Ethnocentric An approach to international business in which management believes that people who share their cultural values make the best managers. **(p. 121)**

European Union (EU) A political and economic union of 27 European countries that share a common currency, the euro. **(p. 119)**

Exporting The organizational process of creating products in one country and selling them in another. **(p. 119)**

Geocentric An approach to international business in which management seeks talent and best practices from all around the world. **(p. 121)**

Glass ceiling An invisible barrier that limits the opportunities for women and minorities to advance to upper-level positions. **(p. 125)**

Global company An organization that has operations in multiple countries and its senior management decision making centrally located in one country. **(p. 119)**

Global Leadership and Organizational Effectiveness (GLOBE) A network of over 150 researchers from 62 cultures from around the world assembled to study cultural dynamics in leadership and management. **(p. 122)**

Importing The organizational process of acquiring products and services from another country. **(p. 119)**

Multi-domestic company An organization with operations in multiple countries and its senior management decision making distributed across the countries in which it operates. **(p. 119)**

North American Free Trade Agreement (NAFTA) An agreement between Canada, Mexico, and the United States intended to remove barriers to trade and investment. **(p. 119)**

Offshoring Moving a business process to another country. **(p. 131)**

Outsourcing Hiring an outside company to fulfill one or more of an organization's core functions. **(p. 131)**

Polycentric An approach to international business in which management believes that managers from a particular country know best how to achieve results in that cultural context. **(p. 121)**

Professional employee organizations Organizations that offer employee management services to other companies. **(p. 132)**

Regional trading zones Zones established through trade agreements among several countries in which trade barriers are reduced or eliminated for member countries. **(p. 119)**

Social integration The degree to which individuals in a group share and collaborate based on their unique perspective. **(p. 133)**

Strategic partnership An agreement between two or more organizations to share complementary resources to develop and sell products and services. **(p. 119)**

Surface-level diversity The degree to which individuals in a group represent differences based on visual cues, such as age, ethnicity, and gender. **(p. 125)**

World Trade Organization (WTO) The organization responsible for global trade rules between countries. **(p. 119)**

IN REVIEW

5.1 | Understand how managers organize international businesses.

Many international businesses are organized as either *global companies*, which have operations in more than one country and senior management decision making centrally located in one country, or *multi-domestic companies*, with operations in multiple countries and senior management decision making distributed across the countries in which it operates. Companies may also form *strategic partnerships* with other companies to share complementary resources.

5.2 | Explain the challenges and opportunities of working with cultural differences.

When approaching cultural differences, managers can take one of three approaches: ethnocentric, polycentric, or geocentric. In an *ethnocentric* approach to international business, management believes that people who share their cultural values make the best managers. Managers with a *polycentric* attitude believe that managers from a particular country know best how to achieve results in that cultural context. In a *geocentric* business, management seeks talent and best practices from all around the world.

5.3 | Understand the legal requirements for respecting workforce diversity.

Federal legislation such as the Civil Rights Act of 1964 and the American with Disabilities Act of 1990 (ADA) make it illegal to discriminate against people based on factors like race, gender, ethnicity, age, sexual orientation, etc. Nevertheless, invisible barriers called *glass ceilings* often exist in organizations, which prevent women and minorities from advancing to top-level positions. To address ongoing inequalities, successive presidents have issued executive orders requiring *affirmative action*, proactive steps taken by organizations to counteract discrimination against minorities and women. The value of affirmative action is passionately argued, with some believing that it provides more equal opportunities and others believing that it provides unfair advantages.

5.4 | Recognize and explain the implications of changing workforce demographics.

One of the primary concerns for managers in the 21st century is a rapidly aging workforce. As in the example from BMW, managers will have to seek feedback from employees about what changes can be made in systems originally designed for younger workers in order to continue to meet targets successfully. Managers also will see significant growth in the number of Asian and Hispanic people in the U.S. workforce.

5.5 | Interpret the dimensions of diversity as a management strategy.

Deep-level diversity is the degree to which individuals in a group represent differences that cannot be seen, such as personalities, attitudes, values, and perspectives. *Surface-level diversity* is the degree to which individuals in a group represent differences based on visual cues, such as age, ethnicity, and gender. As in the case of IBM, proactively fostering diversity in the workplace is an effective way to develop internal talent and expand market opportunities.

SELF-TEST

5.1 | Understand how managers organize international businesses.

1. What is the difference between a global company and a multi-domestic company?
2. What are regional trading zones?
3. The United States is NOT a member of which of the following:
   a. NAFTA
   b. UNASUR
   c. EURS
   d. APEC

5.2 | Explain the challenges and opportunities of working with cultural differences.

4. Lack of patience with communicating with people with cultural and language differences may lead to the implementation of an inferior solution simply due to initial conditions and not due to intrinsic merit. This is referred to as a(n) _____ situation.
5. What is cultural intelligence?
6. Which of the following is NOT one of the five cultural value dimensions identified by the Dutch sociologist Geert Hofstede?
   a. Individualism versus Collectivism
   b. Initiative versus Compliance
   c. Competition versus Cooperation
   d. Power Distance
7. Due to cultural differences, there are no universal attributes and traits that managers from across the world can agree are positive and negative.
   a. True
   b. False

5.3 | Understand the legal requirements for respecting workforce diversity.

8. _____ is treating individuals or groups unfairly or negatively based on their diversity traits, including sexual orientation, age, ethnicity, gender, or disability.
9. What U.S. government agency is charged with "enforcing federal laws that make it illegal to discriminate against a job applicant or an employee because of the person's race, color, religion, sex (including pregnancy), national origin, age (40 or older), disability, or genetic information"?

5.4 | Recognize and explain the implications of changing workforce demographics.

10. When faced with the changing demographics of their workforce, a BMW plant in Lower Bavaria chose to implement

a "top-down" program to seek a solution to possible decreased productivity in the future.
a. True
b. False

11. When an organization hires an outside company to fulfill one or more of its core functions, it is called _____. When a business process is moved to another country, it is called _____.

12. What are the benefits and challenges of the practices in Question 11?

5.5 | Interpret the dimensions of diversity as a management strategy to increase innovation, creativity, and performance.

13. What are the four categories that summarize the dimensions of diversity discussed in this chapter?

14. Managers that foster teams with the requisite capacities to develop collectively the technical and cognitive skills to be competitive in the marketplace always benefit from embracing cultural and demographic differences.
a. True
b. False

15. Cultural mishaps are prevented when
a. managers understand the intended and unintended consequences resulting from cultural dynamics and diversity dimensions
b. managers downplay cultural dynamics and diversity dimensions to build teamwork
c. managers ignore cultural dynamics such as *power distance*
d. managers mandate policies for all management teams regardless of cultural dynamics, thus creating unity

CHAPTER EXERCISE

Exploring Hofstede's Cultural Dimensions

This exercise will help you explore intercultural differences by comparing your home country's culture to the culture of another country of interest to you. Based on his research with over 100,000 IBM employees in 40 different countries, Geert Hofstede identified five value dimensions that varied among different cultures: Individualism versus Collectivism (IDV); Power Distance (PDI); Uncertainty Avoidance (UAI); Masculinity versus Femininity (MAS); and Long-term versus Short-term Orientation (LTO).

Instructions:

1. Choose a country to compare to your home country. This country could be the home country of an international student in your class, a country that you have visited or plan to visit, or just a country in which you are interested.

2. Visit the following website: www.geert-hofstede.com/countries .html.

3. Select your home country from the "Select a Country" pull-down menu at the top of the page. Once the page reloads with your home country's information, examine your countries'

scores and the brief discussion of those scores on the site for each of the five dimensions.

4. Now select your comparison country using the "Comparison Country" pull-down menu at the top of the page.

5. On which dimension is your home country most different from the comparison country? On which dimension is your home country most similar to the comparison country?

6. Now use the "Select a Country" pull-down menu to select your comparison country as the primary country and review the brief discussion on the site explaining your comparison country's scores on each of the five dimensions.

7. Based on the information from the website and your own experiences with this country, give some specific examples of how these cultural differences manifest themselves in terms of behaviors in your home country and in the comparison country. If you chose the home country of an international student in your class as your comparison country, ask that person for details about his or her culture relative to the scores on the five dimensions.

SELF-ASSESSMENT

Global Mindset*

A global mindset refers to the extent to which a person is open to and appreciative of cross-cultural diversity. The following brief assessment will help you to determine if you have a global mindset.

For each statement, circle the number that best describes you based on the following scale:

Not at all Accurate	Somewhat Accurate	A little Accurate	Mostly Accurate	Completely Accurate
1	2	3	4	5

1. When I interact with others, national origin never has an impact on how I view their status relative to me.

   1   2   3   4   5

2. I consider myself to be as open to ideas from other countries and cultures as I am to ideas from my own country and culture.

   1   2   3   4   5

3. When I find myself in a new cultural setting, I experience excitement rather than fear and anxiety.

   1   2   3   4   5

4. When I am in another culture, I am sensitive to the cultural differences without becoming a prisoner of these differences.

   1 2 3 4 5

5. When I interact with people from other cultures, it is more important to understanding them as individuals rather than viewing them as representatives of their national cultures.

   1 2 3 4 5

6. I see my values as a hybrid of values acquired from multiple cultures as opposed to just one culture.

   1 2 3 4 5

Scoring:

Add the numbers circled above: _____

Interpretation:

23 and above = You have a strong and well-developed global mindset. You are likely to view cultural diversity as an opportunity.

16 – 22 = You have a moderately developed global mindset. You appreciate cultural differences to some extent, but your vision may still be limited by some of your own cultural norms and values.

15 and below = You have an underdeveloped global mindset. Your perspective is dominated by the values and norms of your own dominant culture, and you may find cultural diversity threatening or intimidating.

*Adapted from Anil K. Gupta, and Vijay Govindarajan, "Cultivating a global mindset," Academy of Management Executive 16, no. 1 (February 2002): 116–126.

SELF-TEST ANSWER KEY

1. A global company is an organization with operations in more than one country and its senior management decision making centrally located in one country. A multi-domestic company is an organization with operations in more than one country and senior management decision making distributed across the countries in which it operates.

2. Regional trading zones are established through trade agreements among several countries in which trade barriers are reduced or eliminated for member countries.

3. c.

4. "Success to the Successful"

5. the ability to understand and make effective decisions based on cultural differences

6. b.

7. b. False. The GLOBE research program found several universal cultural perspectives. See Table 5-2 earlier in this chapter for the leadership traits found to be universally positive and negative.

8. Discrimination

9. The U.S. Equal Employment Opportunity Commission (EEOC)

10. b. False. The company discovered that bringing together a diversity of ideas from top management, middle management, and line workers allowed them to achieve their goals.

11. outsourcing/offshoring

12. Both outsourcing and offshoring can benefit a company greatly by reducing costs and improving efficiency. However, it can have dramatic effects on the surrounding communities and possibly lead to incompatibilities between the different companies.

13. cultural, demographic, technical, and cognitive

14. True

15. a.

Notes

_____

_____

_____

_____

_____

CHAPTER SIX

ETHICS AND SOCIAL RESPONSIBILITY

Learning Objectives

By the end of the chapter, you will be able to:

6.1 | Explain ethics as they relate to the five domains of individuals, organizations, stakeholders, government, and the global community.

6.2 | Demonstrate processes and practices for managing organizational ethics.

6.3 | Describe how businesses approach social responsibility.

6.4 | Explain how organizations seek to prosper through social responsibility.

6.5 | Summarize management's role in building responsible businesses based on ethical decision making.

ADDITIONAL RESOURCES

KEY TERMS
IN REVIEW
SELF-TEST
CHAPTER EXERCISE
SELF-ASSESSMENT
SELF-TEST
ANSWER KEY

JP Greenwood/Getty Images

Ethics The moral principles, values, and beliefs that govern group or individual behavior according to what is right or wrong and what contributes to the balanced good of all stakeholders.

Ethical dilemma A situation in which no choice is entirely right.

Bloomberg / Getty Images Inc

6.1 | WHAT ARE ETHICS?

6.1 Explain ethics as they relate to the five domains of individuals, organizations, stakeholders, government, and the global community.

Going into the national championship tournament, the Oxford University basketball team was undefeated. Clayton M. Christensen played center, which some argue is the most important position on the team. With each game the team won, he faced a growing predicament. Christensen had made the personal decision to never play basketball on Sundays for religious reasons. Looking at the schedule, he realized that if the team made it to the national championship they would play on—you guessed it—a Sunday. When Christensen mentioned his predicament to his coach, he was told that if the team made it to the championships and he didn't play, he would be letting his whole team down. And then, during the semifinals, Christensen's backup dislocated his shoulder. But the team pulled together and won the game. The pressure for Christensen to play in the upcoming national championship game on Sunday was immense. The team had worked all season in preparation for the chance to win the title, and they relied on Christensen. What do you think Christensen should do? Should he keep his promise to himself? Or should he play the championship game for his team and coach—"just this once?"[1]

Ethics are the moral principles, values, and beliefs that govern group or individual behavior according to what is right or wrong and what contributes to the balanced good of all stakeholders. Are ethics as simple as "doing the right thing"? Not always. With his commitment to his religion at odds with his commitment to his team, Christensen faced an **ethical dilemma**—a situation in which no choice is entirely right. Managers face small and large ethical dilemmas regularly. An example of a small dilemma would be whether or not to accept a lavish corporate gift from a client. By accepting it, you could be breaching a client/company code, and it also might be perceived as favoritism. On the other hand, rejecting it might offend the client, who may have wanted to show his gratitude for your hard work. Consider a more difficult ethical dilemma that a manager could face:

> "You are a senior executive in the sales department of a large manufacturing company. A competitor's technological innovation has disrupted your company's production and has plunged profits into the red for the last three quarters. Your boss has made it very clear that if you do not make your profit projections for this quarter, you will be out of a job. One of your staff members makes a suggestion to you about investing in new equipment to monitor and service clients better. After some research, you realize that this investment, if enacted quickly, could increase sales and help the overall health of the company. Each quarter that you wait to implement this equipment will reduce its positive impact, but investing now will cause you to miss your profit projections and lose your job."[2]

As a manager, how might you approach an ethical dilemma like this? What questions could you ask to ensure that you make a well-considered decision? What factors might affect your decision?[3]

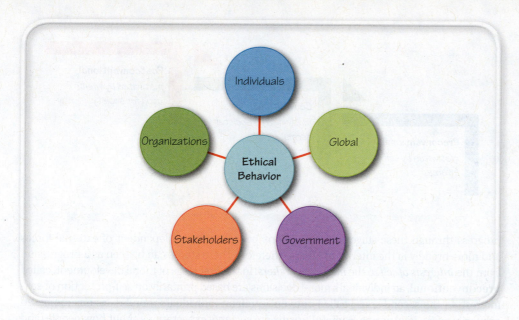

Figure 6-1
Domains of Ethical Decision Making
Managers need to consider the effects of their decision making based on the five domains of ethical behavior.

In this section, we will explore how ethical decisions are made and assess which factors determine those decisions. Additionally, we will explore a framework that managers can rely on to optimize principle-based decision making. Where do ethics originate? As shown in Figure 6-1, there are five domains where ethical behavior is defined: individuals, organizations, stakeholders, governments, and the global community.

In each of these domains, individuals or groups articulate their expectations regarding principles, values, and beliefs that support their perception of what is good for themselves and others. How managers make decisions related to these five domains can ultimately lead to positive or destructive consequences for an organization.

Individuals

In 2000, Enron appeared to be a wildly successful energy trading company, claiming revenues of nearly $101 billion.[4] For six consecutive years, *Fortune* magazine named Enron "America's Most Innovative Company."[5] Kenneth Lay, founder and CEO of Enron Corporation, was said to be "articulate, sophisticated, [and] astute about people" and "nothing less than a corporate visionary."[6] He was even-tempered, could bring conflicted parties together to seek resolution, and contributed to community causes. By all measures, Lay was a leader that captured the hearts and minds of employees and investors.

But Lay also led his team to commit one of the largest corporate fraud cases in U. S. history. Using unethical accounting practices, Enron hid billions of dollars in debt from investors while paying its executives extraordinary salaries and valuable stock options (at least, they were valuable for a while). The most insidious accusations were that at some point, top executives knew that the company would soon be exposed for wrongdoing and sold their stock. At the same time, they encouraged employees to continue buying company stock for their retirement funds and to invest in the company's pension fund. Shareholders lost $74 billion, and over 20,000 employees lost $20 billion in their pension fund. Lay personally liquidated more than $300 million of his personal stocks, while thousands of families lost their entire retirement savings.

Why are some people ethical and others not? Why are some businesses ethical and others not? As described by psychologist Lawrence Kohlberg (1927—1987), individuals go through "stages of moral development" in their lives. His research, outlined in Figure 6-2, suggests that as individuals

governments, and the **global community**.

o **Individuals**
- Psychologist Lawrence Kohlberg suggests that individuals go through three stages of moral development:
  1) *Preconventional*, an individual's moral decisions are based primarily on self-protection or self-interest
  2) *Conventional*, an individual's moral decisions are based primarily on societal norms. *Societal norms* are society's expectations about how people (and organizations) should behave.
  3) *Postconventional*, an individual's moral decisions are based primarily on what he or she believes is good for society as a whole.

David Einsel / Getty Images Inc

Figure 6-2
Kohlberg's Stages of Moral Development
Kohlberg proposes that moral development is a continuous process that takes place throughout our lives.

Postconventional
motivated by what's good for society

Conventional
motivated by societal norms

Preconventional
motivated by self-interest

Preconventional stage In Kohlberg's model, the stage of moral development in which an individual's moral decisions are based primarily on self-protection or self-interest.

Conventional stage In Kohlberg's model, the stage of moral development in which the individual's moral decisions are based primarily on societal norms.

Societal norms Society's expectations about how people (and organizations) should behave.

Postconventional stage In Kohlberg's model, the stage of moral development in which an individual's moral decisions are based primarily on what he or she believes is good for society as a whole.

○ **Organizations**
 ■ *Ben & Jerry's Ice Cream's three-part company mission, consisting of Social, Product, and Economic components,*

progress through these stages, their decisions become more independent of external forces and more broadly in the interest of others. Therefore, these stages can be seen as a progression from the *interests of self* to the *interests of others*. In the first stage of moral development, called **preconventional**, an individual's moral decisions are based primarily on self-protection or self-interest. In the second stage, called **conventional**, an individual's moral decisions are based primarily on societal norms. **Societal norms** are society's expectations about how people (and organizations) should behave. Those who meet those expectations are generally rewarded with social acceptance, while those who don't may be punished by being treated as outsiders. In the final stage of moral development, called **postconventional**, an individual's moral decisions are based primarily on what he or she believes is good for society as a whole.

Let's go back to our original example. When Kenneth Lay, CEO of Enron, publicly encouraged employees to buy company stock, it had the effect of increasing the company's stock value. During this time, Lay sold part of his stock for $300 million. Which of Kohlberg's stages of moral development best describe these decisions? What is the role of an organization to support moral development for managers and employees?

Organizations

In 1968, good friends Ben Cohen and Jerry Greenfield saw an opportunity in Burlington, home of the University of Vermont, to open an ice cream shop. With $12,000 and a correspondence course on how to make ice cream, they opened their first Ben & Jerry's Ice Cream shop in a renovated gas station. From the start, Ben & Jerry's built a corporate culture that was focused on the community: from Free Cone Days and Summer Movie Festivals to political activism and the founding of nonprofit organizations.

The old gas station was demolished by the land owner in 1982, but at that point Ben & Jerry's was well on its way to becoming one of the leading brands of specialty ice cream in the country. Recognizing the threat to their own market share, Pillsbury, owner of Häagen-Dazs ice cream, attempted to limit the distribution of Ben & Jerry's ice cream. Ben & Jerry's responded by suing Pillsbury and launching the famous marketing campaign, "What's the Doughboy Afraid Of?" Ben & Jerry's won the case.

The company's focus on community and a willingness to address big challenges began to define the organization. In 1985, Cohen and Greenfield established the Ben & Jerry's Foundation to support community-oriented projects, funded by 7.5 percent of Ben & Jerry's pretax profits. Their focus did not stop at their local community. In 1988, they helped found 1% For Peace, whose goal was to redirect 1 percent of the national defense budget to peace-promoting projects.[7] That same year, the company launched its three-part mission statement shown in Figure 6-3, consisting of a Product Mission, a Social Mission, and an Economic Mission. Ben & Jerry's company culture was now "official."

© Lou Dematteis / Corbis

Ben and Jerry's Mission

SOCIAL Mission	PRODUCT Mission	ECONOMIC Mission
To operate the company in a way that actively recognizes the central role that business plays in society by initiating innovative ways to improve the quality of life locally, nationally, and internationally.	To make, distribute, and sell the finest-quality, all-natural ice cream and euphoric concoctions with a continued commitment to incorporating wholesome, natural ingredients and promoting business practices that respect the earth and the environment.	To operate the company on a sustainable financial basis of profitable growth, increasing value for our stakeholders and expanding opportunities for development and career growth for our employees.

Source: http://www.benjerry.com/activism/mission-statement/

Figure 6-3
Ben & Jerry's Three-Part Company Mission
Ben and Jerry's company mission had a great impact on the company culture.

What effect did this have on the company? One year after Ben & Jerry's unveiled the company mission, an important change happened inside the company: employees began to organize efforts to make a difference consistent with the company's mission statements, some of which are detailed in Figure 6-4. In 1989, employees organized a program called "Green Teams," whose "primary goal is to foster environmental awareness, education, and action throughout the company."[8] The company's employees had embraced its culture, and Ben & Jerry's subsequent social impact was, and continues to be, both diverse and substantial.

This is an example of **values-based management**, where the company's culture affects employee behavior in ways that are consistent with the organization's mission and values.

provides an excellent example of values-based management
■ *Values-based management* is where the company's culture impacts employee behavior in ways that are consistent with the organization's mission and values.

Values-based management A management style in which the company's culture affects employee behavior in ways that are consistent with the organization's mission and values.

Stakeholders

The effect of Ben & Jerry's focus on their Social, Product, and Economic Missions was felt by a variety of individuals, organizations, and communities around the world. For example, if you

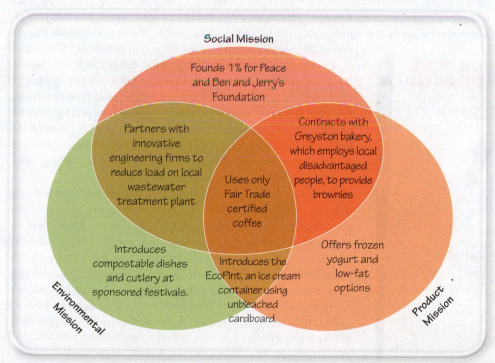

Social Mission

Founds 1% for Peace and Ben and Jerry's Foundation

Partners with innovative engineering firms to reduce load on local wastewater treatment plant

Contracts with Greyston bakery, which employs local disadvantaged people, to provide brownies

Uses only Fair Trade certified coffee

Introduces compostable dishes and cutlery at sponsored festivals.

Introduces the EcoPint, an ice cream container using unbleached cardboard.

Offers frozen yogurt and low-fat options

Environmental Mission

Product Mission

Figure 6-4
Ben & Jerry's Mission Actions
Ben and Jerry's social, product, and economic missions had a global influence on stakeholders.

o **Stakeholders**
■ *Ben & Jerry's stakeholders* are affected by their mission.
■ *Stakeholders* have a direct interest in the organization's behavior and experience the effects of the company's management decisions.
■ Some stakeholders are internal (managers, employees, owners), while some are external (suppliers, customers, shareholders, etc.).
■ An **externality** is a cost (negative) or benefit (positive) that occurs beyond the direct exchange between an organization and its stakeholders.
  • Beekeeping is a classic example of a *positive externality* because although a beekeeper may be in the business of raising bees in

Source: Adapted from "History," *Ben & Jerry's*, http://www.benjerry.com/company/history/

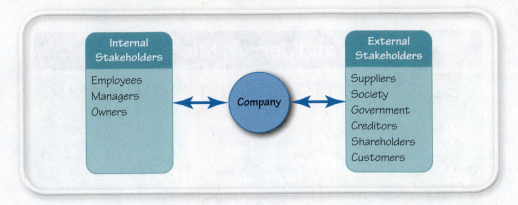

Figure 6-5
Stakeholder Model
Model showing a company's internal and external stakeholders.

order to sell honey and wax, the bees' natural pollinating activities also provides a direct benefit to farmers and gardeners in the area.

Stakeholders Individuals or groups who have a direct interest in an organization's behavior and experience the effects of the company's management decisions.

• Extractive industries such as mining often externalize many of the environmental costs of their processes, leaving the government and local communities to deal with

Externality A cost (negative) or benefit (positive) that occurs beyond the direct exchange between an organization and its stakeholders.

negative externalities such as polluted drinking water and increased flooding.

• The fast-food industry is another that creates some negative externalities,

were a supplier of vanilla beans to the company, your organization was expected to "respect the earth and the environment." The company promoted "Farm Aid," in 1990 a campaign to support and encourage family farms, by printing "Support Farm Aid" on 8 million cups, along with a toll-free phone number to call to offer support and donations. This had consequences for customers, suppliers, communities, and government. All of these constituencies are called **stakeholders**, because they have a direct interest in the organization's behavior and experience the effects of the company's management decisions.[9] Some stakeholders, like managers, employees, and owners, are internal to the organization. That is, they are a part of it. Other stakeholders, such as suppliers, customers, shareholders, the media, creditors, and local and global communities, are external to the organization, but they are still affected by the organization's management decisions. The stakeholder model is shown in Figure 6-5.

Let's assume that all internal and external stakeholders have ethical expectations of the organization. Does a manager's responsibility cease once the interests of all internal and external stakeholders have been addressed sufficiently? From a legal perspective, yes. Yet, organizations have an impact on their stakeholders and society, beyond their stakeholders' interests.

An **externality** is a cost (negative) or benefit (positive) that occurs beyond the direct exchange between an organization and its stakeholders. A classic example of a *positive externality* comes from beekeeping. Although a beekeeper may be in the business of raising bees to sell honey and wax, the bees' natural pollinating activities also provides a direct benefit to farmers and gardeners in the entire area. Extractive industries such as mining often externalize many of the environmental costs of their processes, leaving the government and local communities to deal with negative externalities such as polluted drinking water and increased flooding. Such industries may also create a positive externality by fostering new local businesses that provide support services for the mining company. What are managers' ethical responsibilities when it comes to recognizing and responding to externalities? Sometimes that question is decided by the government through new regulations that force businesses to internalize their negative externalities (that is, to reduce or pay for the negative effects of their processes). Pollution regulations, workers' compensation, and zoning laws are all examples of the government intervening to hold companies accountable for the negative side effects of their businesses. Government intervention isn't always required, however. Many businesses take the initiative to internalize externalities.[10]

Let's look at the fast food industry, which has had a mixed response to the most visible negative externality of their business—poor health. Now, fast food cannot be held solely responsible for increased rates of heart attacks and obesity in the United States, of course, but it is fair to say that its prominence in the American diet is one of many contributing factors. There has been a dramatic increase in fat, salt, and calories in fast food in the past 50 years. McDonald's, for example, has increased its largest serving of French fries from 2.4 ounces to 6 ounces, an increase of 250 percent; and its largest hamburger offering from 1.6 ounces to 8 ounces, a 500 percent increase.[11] We can imagine how this happened. As companies like Wendy's and Burger King began competing for customers, product and marketing

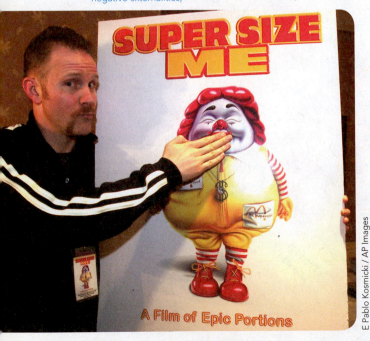

E Pablo Kosmicki / AP Images

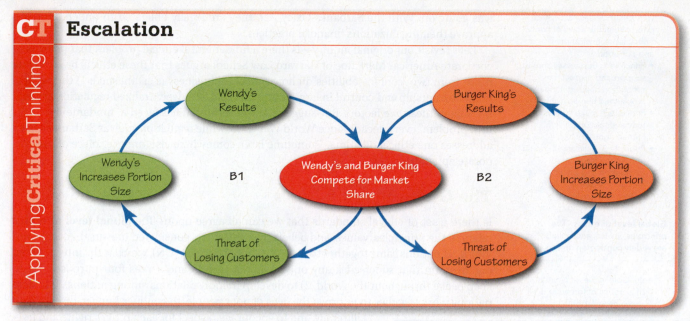

managers expanded meal sizes to increase value. What happened? It worked—but over time, this competition escalated offerings with the unintended externality of serving loyal customers lots of unhealthy food. How long do you imagine such escalation can continue? In 2004, Morgan Spurlock drew attention to the negative externalities of fast food in his documentary *Super Size Me*. The movie graphically demonstrated the horrid effects of a one-month, all-McDonald's diet on Spurlock's health and well-being.[12] Although it denied that the movie was an influence on this decision,[13] McDonald's chose to discontinue its Super Size offerings soon after the release of *Super Size Me*.[14] On the flip side, more and more fast food restaurants are changing the oils used in fryers to reduce the amount of saturated and trans fats in their foods, and there has been an increase in offerings like salads and grilled, rather than fried, chicken.[15] In fact, the more healthy options that one fast food chain offers, the more healthy options other fast food chains choose to offer. Both of these are examples of systems behavior called **escalation**, where there is an increase in an organizational behavior as a direct response to a competitor's behavior.

Governments

What role should the government play in establishing rules and regulations to guide business ethics?[16] Between 2000 and 2010, the U. S. government faced two major disruptions in the business world based on ethical dilemmas: 1) the fall of Enron in 2001, followed soon after by the collapse of WorldCom; and 2) the banking failures of 2008. These two events negatively affected economic markets around the world. This left some wondering, "Is there a fundamental ethical problem that persists in corporate America?"[17] Let's look at these ethical breakdowns and the U. S. government's responses.

Enron fell because of poor ethical decisions made by top managers. Under pressure to show ever-increasing revenues and profits, managers exploited loopholes in accounting requirements, inflating expected revenues and hiding billions of dollars in debt. Such practices made Enron look like a much healthier company than it actually was, which in turn artificially inflated its stock prices. In the end, Enron went bankrupt, its stockholders lost millions of dollars, its employees lost their jobs and much of their retirement savings, and top executives were sentenced with hefty fines and prison terms.[18] The same kinds of poor ethical decisions were also being made in other organizations, with top executives from companies like Tyco and WorldCom being criminally convicted.[19] With such a widespread failure in accounting practices, the U.S. government enacted stricter legal requirements to prevent similar unethical behavior in the future.

In 2002, Congress passed the Sarbanes-Oxley Act, co-sponsored by Sen. Paul Sarbanes (D-MD) and Rep. Michael Oxley (R-OH). The act requires much greater transparency of corporate accounting practices and, perhaps most importantly, holds the chief executive officer (CEO) and chief financial officer (CFO) responsible for the accuracy of their company's financial reporting. No longer can top management claim that they didn't know what

as shown in the 2004 documentary *Super Size Me!*
- However, as one fast food chain offers healthier options, others tend to follow; an example of the *escalation* systems archetype presented in Chapter 3.
o **Governments**
  ■ In 2002, Congress passed the Sarbanes-Oxley Act, co-sponsored by Sen. Paul Sarbanes (D-MD) and Rep.

> **Escalation** An increase in an organizational behavior as a direct response to a competitor's behavior.

Michael Oxley (R-OH), and requiring much greater transparency of corporate accounting practices.
  ■ Mark Roe of Harvard Law School argues that ethical breakdowns result from two "core instabilities" in how American business is established: 1) the separation of ownership and control in large companies, and 2) a decentralized regulation system, and that because of these two factors, the government faces a "fundamental large-firm problem" that will lead to additional corporate lapses.
o **The Globe**
  ■ The **global level of ethics** refers to the principles, values, and beliefs that are widely considered universal.
  ■ The United Nations, created by 51 countries after WWII, established "The Global Compact" for businesses, which "is a strategic policy initiative for businesses that are committed to aligning their operations and strategies

with *ten universally accepted principles* in the areas of human rights, labor, environment and anti-corruption.

- Principle 1: Businesses should support and respect the protection of internationally proclaimed human rights
- Principle 2: make sure that they are not complicit in human rights abuses.
- Principle 3: Businesses should uphold the freedom of association and the effective recognition of the right to collective bargaining;

Global level of ethics The principles, values, and beliefs that are widely considered universal.

- Principle 4: the elimination of all forms of forced and compulsory labor;

Valery Hache / Getty Images Inc

was going on. With the Sarbanes-Oxley Act, they are legally obligated to understand and approve their organization's financial practices.

Let's revisit our original inquiry—Is there a fundamental ethical problem that persists in corporate America? Mark Roe of Harvard Law School argues that these ethical breakdowns result from two "core instabilities" in how American business is established: 1) the separation of ownership and control in large companies and 2) a decentralized regulation system. Because of these two factors, Roe suggests, the government has faced a "fundamental large-firm problem" every decade since World War II. So, while regulation such as Sarbanes-Oxley addresses one ethical dilemma, "sometime later, somewhere else, another piece of the corporate apparatus will fail."[20]

The Globe

Is there a set of ethical standards that we can all agree upon? The **global level of ethics** refers to the principles, values, and beliefs that are widely considered universal. After World War II, 51 nations came together to form the United Nations (UN), which is the international organization that supersedes any one country's agenda and serves four purposes: "1) to keep peace throughout the world, 2) to develop friendly relations among nations, 3) to help nations work together to improve the lives of poor people, to conquer hunger, disease, and illiteracy, and to encourage respect for each other's rights and freedoms, and 4) to be a centre for harmonizing the actions of nations to achieve these goals."[21]

In 2010, UN secretary-general Ban Ki-moon noted, "Businesses and global corporations were stepping up their efforts to become more ethical, sustainable, and responsible at just the right moment … [H]ailing good corporate citizenship [is] one of the keys to overcoming complex and interlinked crisis—from financial market meltdown to environmental degradation—and to unlocking long-term growth and development for all of the United Nations."[22]

What is "good corporate citizenship," and what are the standards that managers and organizations can adhere to? The United Nations established the "Global Compact" for businesses, which "is a strategic policy initiative for businesses that are committed to aligning their operations and strategies with ten universally accepted principles in the areas of human rights, labor, environment, and anti-corruption."[23] As outlined in Table 6-1, these

Table 6-1	10 Principles of the United Nations
Human Rights	**Principle 1:** Businesses should support and respect the protection of internationally proclaimed human rights; and
	Principle 2: make sure that they are not complicit in human rights abuses.
Labor	**Principle 3:** Businesses should uphold the freedom of association and the effective recognition of the right to collective bargaining;
	Principle 4: the elimination of all forms of forced and compulsory labor;
	Principle 5: the effective abolition of child labor; and
	Principle 6: the elimination of discrimination in respect of employment and occupation.
Environment	**Principle 7:** Businesses should support a precautionary approach to environmental challenges;
	Principle 8: undertake initiatives to promote greater environmental responsibility; and
	Principle 9: encourage the development and diffusion of environmentally friendly technologies.
Anti-Corruption	**Principle 10:** Businesses should work against corruption in all its forms, including extortion and bribery.

Source: United Nations, *United Nations Global Compact*, http://www.unglobalcompact.org/aboutthegc/thetenprinciples/index.html.

principles are intended to guide decision making when it comes to answering the question: do my actions respect the rights and legitimate expectations of others?

6.2 | MAKING ETHICAL DECISIONS

6.2 | **Demonstrate** processes and practices for managing organizational ethics.

Jan Wilson was recently hired as the food services director for a professional services company that manages school cafeterias in Nebraska. Young, energetic, and full of new ideas, Wilson's management experience includes coordinating a regional food cooperative, where local organic farmers (including her family) share resources to attract more customers, and managing a commercial kitchen at a conference center. In this new position, Wilson is responsible for all the operating activity associated with over 60 schools across multiple counties, including dozens of suppliers, hundreds of employees, and many active Parent-Teacher Associations (PTAs). Senior management is excited by Wilson's ideas and passion for including healthy menu options for the students and has given her a lot of flexibility in creating new offerings. That said, Wilson vividly remembers that one executive remarked, "I don't care what you do, as long as you increase this region's profit margin."

During the first few months in her new position, Wilson added a "fresh bite" daily meal, which was made with organic local vegetables and meat. School administrators, PTA board members, organic farmers, and senior management noticed these efforts, but their reactions were not all positive. PTA board members liked the "fresh bite" option and wanted the entire menu to be healthier. Organic farmers agreed with the PTA and believed that having an organic menu would be both good for students and the local economy. The school system and Wilson's company shared profits, so administrators and senior management were not impressed because her initial efforts actually decreased profitability. Wilson began to wonder if the "old way" of managing food service was the best way, where unhealthy foods were simply more profitable.

Wanting to get more ideas from staff, Wilson decided to work lunch shifts at the company's best- and worst-performing kitchens for one week. Working at the best-performing kitchen was easy; managers had very detailed systems and provided support during the busy service times. Halfway through the first shift at the company's worst-performing kitchen, however, Wilson was overwhelmed—the line of hungry students was getting longer and longer. Then the kitchen ran out of French fries, with about 250 more students to feed. Fearing a student revolt, Wilson had to be creative. Out of the corner of her eye, she noticed a large pile of carrot sticks toward the end of the food offerings. She quickly moved the carrots to where the French fries normally were placed, found a marker, and made a sign that said, "Fresh Fries!" Not all the students were amused, but something interesting happened after the meal. During a discussion with the kitchen manager about the lunch service, he laughed and said, "That's a record! We have never sold so many carrot sticks in one day." This was the idea that Wilson had been looking for. She looked at the kitchen manager with a smile and asked, "Are you ready for a little experiment?"

During the following month, working with a few of the company's kitchen managers, Wilson led a series of experiments to see if there was connection between where food was placed on the serving line and sales. For example, if a large bowl of apples was the first item students encountered, would more students buy apples? Or, if carrot sticks were presented at eye-level and toward the beginning of the offerings, would more students choose "Fresh Fries" over the French fries sold at the end of the offerings? After a month of experiments, Wilson was convinced that the results clearly showed that by placing foods at certain locations,

© Robert Sciarrino / Corbis

- Principle 5: the effective abolition of child labor; and
- Principle 6: the elimination of discrimination in respect of employment and occupation.
- Principle 7: Businesses should support a precautionary approach to environmental challenges;
- Principle 8: undertake initiatives to promote greater environmental responsibility; and
- Principle 9: encourage the development and diffusion of environmentally friendly technologies.
- Principle 10: Businesses should work against corruption in all its forms, including extortion and bribery.

LECTURE ENHANCER:

6.2 Making Ethical Decisions

✓ **Preliminary Questions for Ethical Decision Making**

○ Is this action consistent with my role and responsibilities?

○ Does my action respect the rights and legitimate expectations of others?

○ Will this decision reflect a best practice for myself and the organization?

○ Is this action compatible with my own deeply held principles?

✓ **Principle-based ethical decisions** are based on one or more of the following principles:

○ **Legal Principle—**Making decisions that follow both the letter and the spirit of the law.

○ **Individual Rights Principle—**Making decisions that do not infringe upon the rights of other people.

○ **Virtuous Principle—**Making decisions that you would be publicly proud of.

○ **Long-Term Principle—**Making decisions that support the

Legal principle Making decisions that follow both the letter and the spirit of the law.

Individual rights principle Making decisions that do not infringe upon the rights of other people.

Virtuous principle Making decisions that you would be publicly proud of.

Long-term principle Making decisions that support the long-term interests of yourself and your organization.

Community principle Making decisions that contribute to the strength and well-being of the community.

Utilitarian principle Making decisions that provide the greatest good to the greatest number (or the least harm to the fewest number).

Distributed justice principle Making decisions that do not harm those who are already disadvantaged.

she could dramatically affect the foods that students purchased. As Wilson designed a plan for how to reorganize where food was placed, she was faced with an ethical dilemma defined by the following options:

- Arrange the food randomly.
- Arrange the food to ensure that students choose healthy food.
- Arrange the food to encourage students to select organic, local offerings, thus supporting her former colleagues and family in the community.
- Arrange the food to generate more profits for the company.
- Arrange the food consistent with how students already eat, supporting their individual rights.

In this case, where there is no right choice, which decision would you make? When faced with an ethical dilemma, how do managers consider all the variables necessary to ensure the "right decision" is made?[24] In the next two sections, we will consider Wilson's ethical dilemma through a variety of contexts and approaches. By the end of this investigation, see if your original decision has changed.

Principles of Ethics

Where should managers begin when considering an ethical dilemma? In Table 6-2, we outline four questions that you could ask yourself to begin the decision-making process. Ethical dilemmas exist when the answers to these questions further complicate the decision. Let's explore these questions for Wilson's case and discover if there is a clear, obvious decision to be made. One apparent conflict is the fact that the best practice for the organization (high-profit, yet unhealthy food) competes with legitimate expectations of others (parents seeking healthier food for students). How do managers reconcile this impasse?

When there is no clearly correct course of action, managers are required to make decisions based on one or more of the following principles: legal, individual, virtuous, long-term self-interest, community, utilitarian, and distributed justice.[25]

- **Legal principle** Making decisions that follow both the letter and the spirit of the law
- **Individual rights principle** Making decisions that do not infringe upon the rights of other people
- **Virtuous principle** Making decisions that you would be publicly proud of
- **Long-term principle** Making decisions that support the long-term interests of yourself and your organization
- **Community principle** Making decisions that contribute to the strength and well-being of the community
- **Utilitarian principle** Making decisions that provide the greatest good to the greatest number (or the least harm to the fewest number)
- **Distributed justice principle** Making decisions that do not harm those who are already disadvantaged

Applying these principles of ethical decision making, if you were Wilson, which choice would you make? Do you choose the principle of virtue over long-term company principle of profit and risk losing your job, where you could presumably continue to have positive

Table 6-2	**Preliminary Questions for Ethical Decision Making**

1. Is this action consistent with my role and responsibilities?
2. Does my action respect the rights and legitimate expectations of others?
3. Will this decision reflect a best practice for myself and the organization?
4. Is this action compatible with my own deeply held principles?

Source: Adapted from L. Paine, R. Deshpande, J. D. Margolis, and K. E. Bettcher, "Up to Code: Does Your Company's Conduct Meet World-Class Standards?" *Harvard Business Review*, December 2005, 122–133.

impact? Do you choose community and utilitarian principles and increase local, organic food offerings, where the greatest number of stakeholders realize positive effects? Once you have made your decision, does it reflect a particular stage of Kohlberg's moral development? We have explored how an individual makes an ethical decision, but how do companies frame these principles so that all managers and employees know the company's expectations of ethical decision making?[26]

Codes of Conduct

Two different organizations may have similar or even identically stated values and beliefs, such as a franchise company, yet employees can make very different ethical choices. Values and beliefs are translated into behaviors based on the principles by which decisions are made. Effective organizations and their managers take a principle-based approach to translating their values and beliefs into standards for behaviors. So that all employees have a consistent set of ethical behavior expectations, organizations publish guidelines called **codes of conduct**.[27] The standards outlined in codes of conduct clearly state behavioral requirements and prohibitions. Table 6-3 shows eight broad categories of ethical standards that most Codes of Conduct address.

Principle-based Management Principle-based management is when an organization proactively connects values and beliefs to behavior expectations, where all stakeholders are continuously made aware of these standards. Reflecting on this section's case, we can see that the choice that Wilson makes will have an impact on the organization. We assumed that she was not given a set of expectations with which to make a decision consistent with the company's values and beliefs. The only guidance she was offered from senior management was to increase profits, which is not unethical. One could argue that ensuring profits allows an organization to retain employees over the long term, which leads to benefits for many stakeholders. How would Wilson's dilemma be different with a clearly stated code of conduct? By removing the guessing associated with Wilson's original dilemma, what is the role of her personal principles?

When organizations support a principle-based management approach, stakeholders become a vital component to decision making. This approach requires that management make decisions regarding the organization's responsibility for each stakeholder. In the next section, we will explore how different organizations interpret their responsibility to external stakeholders.

- ■ Citizenship
- ■ Responsiveness
- ✓ **Principle-based management** is when an organization proactively connects values and beliefs to behavior expectations, where all stakeholders are continuously made aware of these standards.

> **Code of conduct** An organization's guidelines for ethical behavior, also called a "code of ethics."

> **Principle-based management** A management style in which an organization proactively connects values and beliefs to behavior expectations, where all stakeholders are continuously made aware of these standards.

Voices of Management | Lonnie J. Williams, Owner, LJ Building Maintenance, LLC[28]

Why is it important to study management? For Lonnie Williams, the answer is simple: "[I]f you can manage, you can do any business." Williams owns LJ Building Maintenance, LLC a small company of about 50 people. His managerial style is reminiscent of his previous careers in the military and as director of youth services in Topeka, KS. "I expect you to do something, and I follow up on those expectations," explains Williams. "I know none of us are . . . flawless. We all have good and bad days, and I tell my managers, 'If you're having a bad day, just admit you're having a bad day.'"

Williams expects his employees to be as honest with him as he is with them, and he makes a point of understanding where they're coming from, what's happening in both their work and personal lives. "I know more about some of my employees' day-to-day living than some of my friends," he says. "When they have hardships, I try to be a part of that. When they have financial situations, I try to make that a teaching mechanism." And he understands firsthand what kind of work he is asking for. "I don't ask anyone to do anything I haven't done or can't do. I think most people know that because they've seen me work. I've worked beside just about anybody in any building, just to let them know that I still know the business inside and out."

Williams's caring but no-nonsense style has earned him dedicated employees, whose quality of work has helped grow LJ Building Maintenance, LLC, into an award-winning company serving customers in six states. ■

Table 6-3 Codes of Conduct Standards

Standard	Required Behaviors	Prohibited Behaviors
Fiduciary	• Show diligence, candor, loyalty to company • Disclose conflicts of interest • Demonstrate prudence, intelligence, best efforts • Maintain the company's financial health	• Engage in unauthorized self-dealing • Seek self-benefit at expense of company • Demonstrate negligence, carelessness, half-hearted efforts • Accept or offer bribes
Dignity	• Protect human health, safety, privacy, dignity • Respect human rights • Support affirmative action to develop human capacities • Show special concern for the vulnerable	• Engage in coercion, humiliation, invasion of privacy • Cause injury or threaten safety • Use force or violence • Violate human rights
Property	• Respect others' property • Safeguard the company's property • Use the company's property responsibly	• Steal or embezzle • Misappropriate intellectual property • Waste resources • Infringe on others' property
Transparency	• Be accurate, truthful, honest • Present information accurately • Disclose material information in a timely manner • Correct misinformation promptly	• Engage in fraud or deceit • Misrepresent information or intent • Delay presentation of information
Reliability	• Fulfill commitments, promises, contracts, agreements • Commit only to what can be delivered	• Break promises or contracts • Go back on one's word • Make false or misleading promises
Fairness	• Deal fairly in all exchanges • Treat all stakeholders fairly • Offer due process to all stakeholders • Engage in fair competition	• Show preferential or arbitrary treatment • Discriminate unfairly • Use an unfair competitive advantage • Suppress competition
Citizenship	• Respect laws and regulations • Share in maintaining the commons • Cooperate with public officials • Contribute to the civic good • Recognize and respect government's jurisdiction	• Violate the letter or the spirit of the law • Freeload • Cause injury or damage to society or the environment • Improperly participate in politics or government
Responsiveness	• Listen • Respond promptly and fairly to complaints and suggestions • Address the legitimate concerns of others in a timely manner	• Show indifference to legitimate claims and claimants • Neglect serious concerns

Source: Adapted from L. Paine, R. Deshpande, J. D. Margolis, and K. E. Bettcher, "Up to Code: Does Your Company's Conduct Meet World-Class Standards?" *Harvard Business Review*, December 2005, 122–133.

LECTURE ENHANCER:

6.3 Social Responsibility

✓ CLIF Bar is organized around five sustainability aspirations: "sustaining our brands, sustaining our business, sustaining our people, sustaining our community, and sustaining the planet"

✓ Such proactive behaviors that benefit society are referred to as **social responsibility**.

6.3 | SOCIAL RESPONSIBILITY

6.3 | **Describe** how businesses approach social responsibility.

Gary Erickson likes to call it his "epiphany ride." He and his riding partner, Jay, were nearing the end of a 12-hour, 175-mile bike ride. They'd been sustaining themselves on energy bars, but as Erickson faced energy bar number six, he just couldn't bring himself to eat it. He was exhausted, his body desperate for calories, and yet he couldn't choke down one more sawdust-flavored energy bar. He threw it away and downed a six-pack of doughnuts at the first convenience store they came to. Erickson decided right then that there had to be a better option and that he was going to make it.

By 1991, he was ready to launch his new product, an energy bar that he named after his father, Clif. For the CLIF Bar's debut, Erickson chose a large bike show, hoping to convince a few bike shops to carry his product. Within just a few months, seven hundred bike shops were carrying CLIF Bars. The company had $700,000 in revenues the first year, $1.2 million the next, and continued growing at a rate of 50 to 100 percent each year for the next several years. Erickson had an opportunity to sell the company for $120 million, but CLIF Bar would be moved from California to the headquarters of Quaker Oats, in the Midwest. The minute Erickson decided not to sell, he knew he'd made the right choice. He asked his staff to help him create CLIF Bar as the kind of company they wanted to work for, the kind of company they could be even more proud of. That feedback, in conjunction with Erickson's own values, led the organization to commit to five sustainability aspirations that would support the long-term health not only of CLIF Bar, but also of the surrounding communities and the environment.[29]

Chicago Tribune / Getty Images Inc

CLIF Bar is organized around five sustainability aspirations: "sustaining our brands, sustaining our business, sustaining our people, sustaining our community, and sustaining the planet."[30] Those objectives translate into the practices of listening and responding to consumers with new products; controlling growth; paying employees fair wages and providing opportunities to learn and advance; donating time, money, and products to the community; and continually working to reduce their ecological footprint. These proactive behaviors for the benefit of society are referred to as **social responsibility**.[31]

In the upcoming sections, we will explore the following questions: Why would a company's management choose to allocate resources to support these behaviors? Are there social responsibility standards that managers can use to measure their organizations' behaviors? How do different organizations approach social responsibility? Do these activities generate value for investors and shareholders?

Corporate Social Responsibility

Many organizations today have corporate social responsibility (CSR) programs that coordinate the company's efforts to address societal and community challenges as they emerge. Corporations like CLIF Bar actually have social responsibility as a part of the organization's values and mission, but most organizations isolate this function. Because managers and stakeholders are still debating the appropriate role for corporations to take in addressing societal issues, governments and some organizations are beginning to formalize what defines a socially responsible company.[32] So, what is the difference between a for-profit company that is focused on community needs, and nonprofit companies? How do for-profit companies approach social responsibility?

Approaches to Social Responsibility Generally speaking, for-profit companies have the access and flexibility to generate more money. Companies like CLIF Bar and Patagonia, as we discussed in Chapter 1, have concluded that focusing on stakeholders in the decision-making process creates more value for shareholders; therefore, they take a **proactive approach**, where the organization goes beyond industry norms to solve and prevent problems. As a manager, how do you know what is right for your company? To answer this question, shareholders and managers first analyze the company's **articles of incorporation**, which is the legal agreement between shareholders and management that determines the fiduciary duty of management in operating the organization. Most modern corporations make it *optional* for management to consider the interests of all stakeholders beyond just the shareholder. For Leslie Christian, co-founder of Upstream 21, optional was not enough. "There's a provision that says the company may consider the interests of the community and of the employees and the effect on the local economy. We simply changed that requirement from 'may' to 'shall'. It's not enough to say you can consider these interests—you must consider them."[33] Upstream 21 acquires small, privately owned businesses in the Pacific Northwest and operates them as wholly owned subsidiaries. Their mission is to help these companies grow in ways that are socially and environmentally responsible by providing financial and knowledge resources.[34]

This model for changing the legal structure of an organization to recognize formally the social responsibility of a corporation appealed to the founders of the nonprofit organization B Lab, which certifies socially responsible companies. "Certified *B Corporations* are a new type of corporation which uses the power of business to solve social and environmental problems."[35] Organizations that pass a certification test by "[setting] a benchmark for social and environmental impact for good companies" legally change their articles of incorporation to require consideration of all stakeholders.[36]

It is not always easy to determine if an organization is socially responsible as organizations may accept social responsibility to varying degrees. In addition to the *proactive approach* organizations may also take an *accommodative, defensive,* or *reactive* approach. The **accommodative approach** is when an organization accepts responsibility and takes action in response to societal pressures. The **defensive approach** is when an organization accepts responsibility but does only the minimum required. The **reactive approach** is when an organization denies responsibility for social problems and responds only when legally required. With all these approaches to social responsibility, does it pay for businesses to be nice?

Accommodative approach An approach to social responsibility in which an organization accepts responsibility and takes action in response to societal pressures.

Defensive approach An approach to social responsibility in which an organization accepts responsibility but does only the minimum required.

Reactive approach A response to social responsibility in which an organization denies responsibility for social problems and responds only when legally required.

Research@Work

Internal Transparency[37]

Transparency. You hear the word everywhere these days. Politicians and CEOs alike promise greater transparency in response to the many financial scandals of recent years. But what does *transparency* really mean? In the field of management studies, the term refers to the free flow of information within and between an organization and its stakeholders. In a democratic society, the "free flow of information" sounds like an inherently good thing. It is easy to see how transparency with its customers and shareholders can build trust with an organization, but what about internal transparency?

In *Transparency: How Leaders Create a Culture of Candor,* Bennis, Goleman, and O'Toole explain that the free flow of information doesn't mean that all information is accessible by anyone, any time. It makes sense to keep proprietary processes and designs secret, but not to "hoard" information without good reason. But it does mean that "critical information gets to the right person at the right time and for the right reason" (p. 4). For managers, that doesn't just mean sharing information with others. It also means listening carefully and asking the right questions. Subordinates are understandably reluctant to share bad news with their supervisors. But good managers will cultivate a culture in which employees feel safe speaking freely so that they will have the information they need, when they need it, so they can manage effectively.

Professor's Response

What this work does is to expand upon the definition of *transparency* to show that the "free flow of information":

a. Involves both a top-down and down-to-top process (whereas traditional views imply a top-down flow of information)

b. Does NOT mean free flow of ALL information, ANY TIME

Manager's Response

What I find most compelling here is the reminder that the free flow of information isn't just about making sure you get the right information to other people. It's also about making sure that people feel comfortable getting the right information to you, so that you can make well-informed decisions.

Critical Thinking in the Classroom

As a manager, how would you cultivate a trusting relationship with your teams to encourage the free flow of information?

6.4 | HOW DOES SOCIAL RESPONSIBILITY PAY OFF?

6.4 Explain how organizations seek to prosper through social responsibility.

The founders of Pura Vida, John Sage and Chris Dearnley, are **social entrepreneurs**—people who start a business for the dual purpose of profit and societal benefit. The idea for Pura Vida began in 1997, when John Sage met his Harvard classmate Chris Dearnley for their annual golfing reunion. Chris had been telling John about his work with homeless children in Costa Rica and his difficulties in sustaining the funding that he needed to continue that work. John was impressed by the positive changes that Chris was making in these children's lives, and when Chris gave him a bag of coffee that he had bought in Costa Rica for a third of what it would cost in the United States, John had a flash of insight. Why not use the terrific profits that could be realized in the U.S. coffee market to fund the kind of social justice work that Chris was doing in South America? On a handful of paper napkins, John and Chris started sketching a business plan for what would become Pura Vida—a phrase that translates literally as "pure life," but also means "way cool" on the streets of Costa Rica. Pura Vida's mission "is to create good by using capitalism to empower producers, motivate consumers, inspire business leaders, and ultimately serve the poor."

Pura Vida purchases only Fair Trade, organic, shade-grown coffee. Their packaging is made from 100 percent recycled and recyclable materials, and their profits go directly to supporting social justice programs in the areas where the coffee that they buy is grown. All these practices appeal directly to Pura Vida's target market of "values-driven, socially conscious consumers." Pura Vida's big market break came when several colleges expressed interest in their products. The company's management immediately recognized the potential of university contracts and began marketing to colleges. It now has over 70 contracts with universities and colleges across the country and is earning multimillion-dollar revenues. As communities benefit more from social entrepreneurship, consumers and investors are becoming more active in supporting and investing in companies that are socially responsible.[38]

Peter Yates/The New York Times /Redux Pictures

Social Investing

Wayne Silby was attending a retreat on the principle of "right living." Participants were asked, "How can you live your life in a way that is consistent with your values on a day-to-day basis?" That question got Silby thinking: he and his business partner John Guffey had started an investment fund, First Variable Rate Fund, which was doing very well, but their investment strategies were not guided by the same values that guided the rest of Silby's life. Issues like social justice, human rights, and environmentalism were not common topics in investment circles in 1979. But Silby wondered if he could combine successful investment practices with his social values. What would happen if he started a fund that invested solely in companies that had good track records in racial and gender equality, in labor rights, and in environmentalism?[39]

To answer that question, Silby and Guffey joined with Bob Zevin in 1982 to start the Calvert Social Investment Fund. Over the years, it became a highly successful socially responsible investment company that has earned steady returns and influenced many companies to make their business practices more socially responsible. In addition to evaluating companies' financial performance, Calvert screens companies based on seven criteria: "environment; workplace; human rights; Indigenous Peoples' rights; community relations; product safety and impact; and governance/business ethics." Calvert Funds is a for-profit company, but it also founded the Calvert Foundation, a 501(c)(3) nonprofit organization that works on community investment. The investment products offered by the organization generally pay a relatively low rate of interest (between 0 and 3 percent in 2013, compared with the historic

LECTURE ENHANCER:

6.4 How Does Social Responsibility Pay Off?

✓ **Social entrepreneurs** are people who start a business for the dual purpose of profit and societal benefit.

Social entrepreneur Someone who starts a business for the dual purpose of profit and societal benefit.

LECTURE ENHANCER:

6.5 Managing Responsibly Today

✓ **Internalizing Externalities**—when management proactively addresses a negative externality for the benefit of its stakeholders.
  o Working with Michelle Obama, Wal-Mart announced that it would "reformulate thousands of [food] products to make them healthier and push its suppliers to do the same, [in an] effort to combat childhood obesity."

✓ **Building an Ethical Culture**
  o Managers define and foster ethical organizational cultures in two ways:
    1) applying a framework for ethical decision making
    2) ethics training
  o A framework for ethics provides managers with the organizational rituals, stories, and symbols necessary to communicate ethical ideals and expectations.

average of about 9 to 10 percent for the stock market in the United States). People may purchase a Calvert Community Investment Note and select a return rate up to the maximum of 3 percent. When the note matures, the investor receives the amount invested plus interest. Meanwhile, the Calvert Foundation shows that the investment provides a "social return." For example, $10,000 invested at 2 percent over three years yields about $600 (the financial return), but it also "can finance 36 microenterprises creating 50 jobs abroad, or two affordable housing units for low-income families in the U.S."

6.5 | MANAGING RESPONSIBLY TODAY

6.5 | Summarize management's role in building responsible businesses based on ethical decision making.

Managing responsibly in today's business environment requires that managers make principle-based decisions informed by industry and societal standards. As illustrated throughout this chapter, these decisions have intended and unintended consequences that lead to positive and negative externalities. The role of all managers is to behave ethically and responsibly and to build an organizational culture that supports and expects those behaviors for all employees. As a manager, you will be in a unique position to understand the impact that decisions made by your organization and its employees have on all stakeholders.[40] What do you do with this knowledge?

© Christy Bowe / Corbis

Internalizing Externalities

With a 16 percent share of the grocery market[41] and as much as 40 percent in some metropolitan areas,[42] Wal-Mart's product offerings can have a significant effect on the diets of its customers. With encouragement from First Lady Michelle Obama, Wal-Mart's management recognized that if a high percentage of its grocery offerings were high-profit, low-nutrition products, it was externalizing the health costs of such products onto its customers. Working with Obama, Wal-Mart announced that it would "reformulate thousands of [food] products to make them healthier and push its suppliers to do the same, [in an] effort to combat childhood obesity."[43] This is an example of "internalizing an externality," when management proactively addresses a negative externality for the benefit of its stakeholders.

✓ **Ethical Decision Making Framework**
  o An ethical framework has four primary components:
    1) Duties
      o *Perfect duties* are moral obligations that are clearly articulated, such as a contract or verbal agreement (a "promise").
      o *Imperfect duties* are moral obligations that can be interpreted in different ways; for example whether an organization chooses to be more or less socially responsible and to include externalities.

Building an Ethical Culture

Let's go back to the case of Jan Wilson, discussed earlier in the chapter. We examined that case as an ethical dilemma, but how might the Wal-Mart example help us further understand Wilson's challenge? Was her dilemma just about making the right ethical decision?

One can reasonably conclude that Wilson's ethical and social responsibility begins internally within the organization. How might Wilson work with senior management to build an ethical culture for her organization? Managers define and foster ethical organizational cultures in two ways: 1) applying a framework for ethical decision making and 2) ethics training. A framework for ethics provides managers with the organizational rituals, stories, and symbols necessary to communicate ethical ideals and expectations.

Ethical Decision Making Framework Organizations with cultures that specifically communicate standards for ethical behavior have more engaged employees and better performance results than their counterparts. The Wilson case is an appropriate example of this dynamic, where time must be spent considering dilemmas that could be spent focusing on producing results. What makes an organization ethical? Ethical organizations consciously apply a framework through which behavior expectations are continuously communicated and monitored. An ethical framework has four primary components: 1) duties, 2) rights, 3) standards of excellence, and 4) commitments.

Duties can be *perfect* or *imperfect*. **Perfect duties** are moral obligations that are clearly articulated, such as a contract or verbal agreement (a "promise"). **Imperfect duties** are moral obligations that can be interpreted in different ways. For example, whether an organization chooses to be more or less socially responsible and to include externalities. While duties define your moral obligations, **rights** are the behaviors you can expect from others based on their duties. For example, if an organization signs a contract (a duty) to purchase a fleet of used cars from a rental car company, the rental car company has the *right* to expect payment. **Standards of excellence** are an organization's highest expectations of behavior for all employees, including required and prohibited behaviors. Finally, **commitments** are self-defined principles unique to an organization or individual. Commitments are not mandatory behavior or externally expected, yet not fulfilling on these principles can damage one's reputation.

Applying the Framework Effective and higher-performing organizations continuously communicate and apply their ethical framework for legal and performance obligations. There are three progressive steps for this application: 1) understanding the situation, 2) connecting behaviors to standards, and 3) impartial analysis. Let's say that you are in the accounting department for an Internet advertising company. One of the sales managers brings you a $200 restaurant and bar bill from last evening, with the explanation of the expense, "Sales meeting for important client." Later in the day, you overhear one of your colleagues talking about having dinner and drinks with this sales manager last night. What do you do?

To apply the framework, you must first *understand the situation*. Immediately reporting the apparently dishonest behavior could be needlessly damaging to many people because there is not yet enough information to determine the expense's legitimacy. You find out that the sales manager invited your coworker to dinner and drinks because she has family connections with a Fortune 500 company. Once you find out the exact details, it could turn out to be a valid expense. Next, you *connect behaviors to standards*. Reviewing the company's Code of Behavior Standards, you discover that hosting colleagues to discuss sales leads is a legitimate expense. That said, you also note that the company has a policy prohibiting employees from soliciting family members for personal benefit. Now what do you do? Clearly this is an ethical dilemma, because the expense was valid, but the intent of the expense was not. Finally, you are responsible for conducting an *impartial analysis* of the situation, which has three factors—visibility, generality, and legacy. *Visibility* is sometimes referred to as the "newspaper test"—would you feel comfortable if your decision to approve this expense was printed on the front page of tomorrow's newspaper? Also, would you feel comfortable if everyone in the organization made decisions like this? This is the *generality* factor. And finally, *legacy*—if you approved this expense, would you feel comfortable with people remembering you for this decision?[44]

Ethics Training

The examples of behavior that we have discussed so far in this chapter relate to actions that have already occurred. Successful organizations prevent unethical behavior from occurring by effectively training all employees. Management researchers have identified four facets of successful ethics training programs: 1) trainee characteristics, 2) needs assessment, 3) training transfer, and 4) evaluation.[45] Figure 6-6 shows a diagram of the Integrative Framework.

When structuring a training program, the first step is to understand the audience. Before you begin to design a training experience, successful facilitators document the following characteristics about trainees:

Training Characteristics
- What are the trainees' current moral profiles? Where do they reside on Kohlberg's moral development scale? To what degree do they behave with integrity? Are they honest with themselves and others? Are their personalities predisposed to impulsive or deviant behaviors?

Perfect duties Moral obligations that are clearly articulated, such as a contract or verbal agreement.

Imperfect duties Moral obligations that can be interpreted in different ways.

Rights The behaviors you can expect from others based on their duties.

Standards of excellence An organization's highest expectations of behavior for all employees, including required and prohibited behaviors.

Commitments Self-defined principles unique to an organization or individual.

2) Rights are the behaviors you can expect from others, based on their duties.
3) Standards of excellence are an organization's highest expectations of behavior for all employees, including required and prohibited behaviors.
4) Commitments are self-defined principles unique to an organization or individual. Commitments are not mandatory behavior or externally expected, yet not fulfilling on these principles can damage one's reputation.

✓ Applying the Framework
   o There are three progressive steps:
   1) understanding the situation
   2) connecting behaviors to standards
   3) impartial analysis
✓ Ethics Training — Successful organizations prevent unethical behavior from occurring by effectively training all employees.
   o Management researchers have identified four facets of successful ethics training programs:
   1) trainee characteristics
   2) needs assessment
   3) training transfer
   4) evaluation
✓ In the Interests of Self or Others?
   o The "Tragedy of the Commons" system archetypes introduced in Chapter 3 is revisited to address this question
   o If entities pursuing individually beneficial actions do not understand the impact of their actions, the system risks breaking down or losing its value for all involved

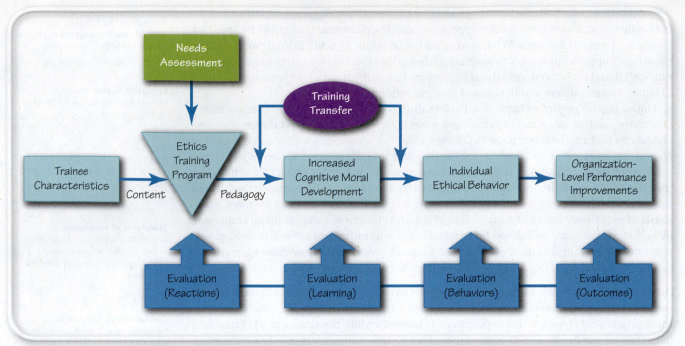

Figure 6-6

An Integrative Framework

The Integrative Framework is often used as a model for ethical training programs to assess and evaluate the behaviors and characteristics of the trainees.

Source: Adapted from D. Wells and M. Schminke, "Ethical Development and Human Resources Training: An Integrative Framework," *Human Resource Management Review* 11 (2001): 135–158.

- How assertive is the audience? More assertive personality traits are linked positively to ethical behavior.
- What is the audience's overall cognitive ability or intelligence level?
- What previous experiences have formed their perspectives on ethical behavior? People exposed to unethical behavior, or victims of it, tend to be more receptive to training programs.
- What are their general demographics, such as age, gender, ethnicity, and personality profiles?

Needs Assessment

- The following assets can be helpful in assessing the audience's need for ethics training: "employee surveys, advisory committees, assessment centers, management requests, exit interviews, and group discussions."[46]
- Conduct an *Ethics Climate Survey* to determine "the prevailing perceptions of typical organizational practices and procedures that have ethical content."[47]
- Clarify program expectations—trainers should clearly state the codes of conduct, standards of excellence, behavioral expectations, and the organizational goal for the training.
- Content should include topics on the fundamentals of ethics knowledge, assertiveness, productivity, and self-leadership.
- Senior management should have access to content that is meaningful and relevant to their roles in the organization.
- The following teaching strategies are effective in ethics training: discussions on dilemmas, personal growth, role-playing, scenario-based games, and interactive simulations.

Training Transfer

- Reinforce that trainees were selected because of their potential to have a positive impact on organizational performance, not as punishment.
- Provide trainees with a pretraining packet that introduces them to the concepts covered.

- Encourage trainees to state clearly what they would like to achieve as a result of the training—a goal for increasing a specific competency.
- Ensure training is similar to the activities and tasks that the audience experiences during a normal workday.
- Performance and ethical behavior increases commensurate to the support and reinforcement of training topics once the trainees return to the workplace.
- When employees return to an ethical environment, training is more likely to lead to behavior change successfully.

Evaluation
- Training evaluation should include four levels: trainee reactions, knowledge/skill tests, positive change in workplace behavior, and organizational performance results.[48]

In the Interests of Self or Others?

What is the risk of managers not acting responsibly or ethically? Is there a dilemma between serving self-defined principles and the interests of others? To answer this question, let's look back at a discussion we began in Chapter 3 on the rapidly growing economies of Brazil, Russia, India, and China. Because the world has limited quantities of food, energy, and water, if all these countries had the same quality of life and consumed these limited resources at the same rate as Americans, how long would it be before these limited resources are depleted? In systems thinking, this "all for one; none for all" behavior pattern is referred to as "Tragedy of the Commons" as shown in Figure 6-7.

In the 17th century, immigrants in New England formed communities that had both private land and shared pastures where cattle could graze, known as *commons*. Over time, these commons were badly maintained and overused, resulting in a useless piece of land for everybody.[49] This became known as the *tragedy of the commons*, which is a common pattern identified in economics and systems thinking. In this behavior pattern, two or more entities "pursue actions which are individually beneficial,"[50] where resources supporting these actions are limited. If entities pursuing individually beneficial actions do not understand the impact of their actions, the system risks breaking down or losing its value for all involved.

Any person living close to a big city understands the consequences of the tragedy of the commons. Organizations that operate on "traditional business hours" expect employees to be in the office from 9 a.m. to 5 p.m., Monday through Friday. For many reasons, this makes a lot of sense: other companies that we work with are open during those times, we all get to spend time with our families at night, and so forth. The problem comes when most companies pursue this action; driving to and from work in bumper-to-bumper traffic can become a nightmare. Like the pasture for raising cattle, the roads are a place to which all community members share access. Yet, if we all expect to use roads at the same time of day, traffic becomes so bad that the system becomes useless. In business, this example translates to any situation where competitors pursue self-serving actions based on limited resources; eventually, all competitors will lose.

Ethical Dilemma Revisited Does this mean that serving the interests of others is managing responsibly? Not necessarily. Based on everything we discussed in this chapter, do you think Clayton Christensen should have played in the championship game? The decision to play in the game would have served the interests of others. Would a decision not to play in the game be principled or selfish? Once he became the captain of the team, didn't he have an obligation to serve the team and organization's interests over his own personal principles? Let's find out what decision Christensen made, why, and if he regretted it.

"I'm a deeply religious man, so I went away and prayed about what I should do. And I got a very clear feeling that I shouldn't break my commitment—so I didn't play in the championship game. In many ways that was a small decision—involving one of several thousand Sundays in my life. In theory, surely I could have crossed over the line just that one time and then not done it again. But looking back on it, resisting the temptation whose logic was 'In this extenuating circumstance, just this once, it's OK' has proven to be one of the most important decisions of my life. Why? My life has been one unending stream of

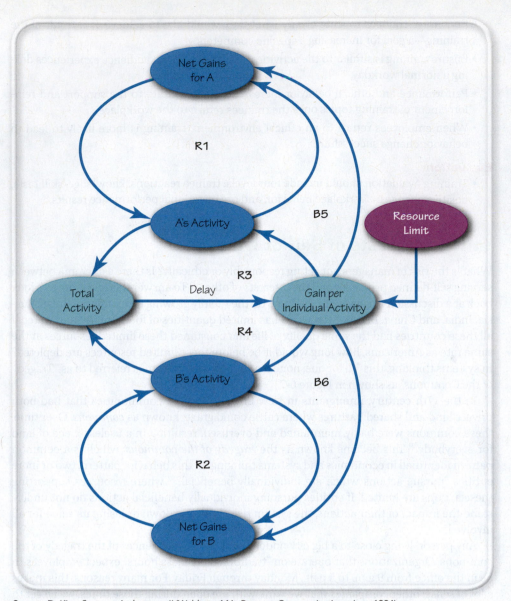

Figure 6-7
Tragedy of the Commons Systems Archetype
Individuals over-use resources for individual gain, until the resource is depleted.

Net Gains for A

R1

A's Activity

B5

Resource Limit

Total Activity

R3

Delay

Gain per Individual Activity

R4

B's Activity

B6

R2

Net Gains for B

Source: D. Kim, *Systems Archetypes II* (Waltham, MA: Pegasus Communications, Inc., 1994).

extenuating circumstances. Had I crossed the line that one time, I would have done it over and over in the years that followed. The lesson I learned from this is that it's easier to hold to your principles 100 percent of the time than it is to hold to them 98 percent of the time. If you give in to 'just this once,' . . . , you'll regret where you end up. You've got to define for yourself what you stand for and draw the line in a safe place."

CaseSnapshot

Chapter 6 Case: Ethics and Social Responsibility: Chipotle can be found on pg. 468

ADDITIONAL RESOURCES

KEY TERMS

Accommodative approach An approach to social responsibility in which an organization accepts responsibility and takes action in response to societal pressures. **(p. 156)**

Articles of incorporation The legal agreement between shareholders and management that determines the fiduciary duty of management in operating the organization. **(p. 155)**

Codes of conduct An organization's guidelines for ethical behavior, also called a "code of ethics." **(p. 153)**

Commitments Self-defined principles unique to an organization or individual. **(p. 159)**

Community principle Making decisions that contribute to the strength and well-being of the community. **(p. 152)**

Conventional stage In Kohlberg's model, the stage of moral development in which the individual's moral decisions are based primarily on societal norms. **(p. 146)**

Defensive approach An approach to social responsibility in which an organization accepts responsibility but does only the minimum required. **(p. 156)**

Distributed justice principle Making decisions that do not harm those who are already disadvantaged. **(p. 152)**

Escalation An increase in an organizational behavior as a direct response to a competitor's behavior. **(p. 149)**

Ethics The moral principles, values, and beliefs that govern group or individual behavior according to what is right or wrong and what contributes to the balanced good of all stakeholders. **(p. 144)**

Ethical dilemma A situation in which no choice is entirely right. **(p. 144)**

Externality A cost (negative) or benefit (positive) that occurs beyond the direct exchange between an organization and its stakeholders. **(p. 148)**

Global level of ethics The principles, values, and beliefs that are widely considered universal. **(p. 150)**

Imperfect duties Moral obligations that can be interpreted in different ways. **(p. 159)**

Individual rights principle Making decisions that do not infringe upon the rights of other people. **(p. 152)**

Legal principle Making decisions that follow both the letter and the spirit of the law. **(p. 152)**

Long-term principle Making decisions that support the long-term interests of yourself and your organization. **(p. 152)**

Perfect duties Moral obligations that are clearly articulated, such as a contract or verbal agreement. **(p. 159)**

Postconventional stage In Kohlberg's model, the stage of moral development in which an individual's moral decisions are based primarily on what he or she believes is good for society as a whole. **(p. 146)**

Preconventional stage In Kohlberg's model, the stage of moral development in which an individual's moral decisions are based primarily on self-protection or self-interest. **(p. 146)**

Principle-based management A management style in which an organization proactively connects values and beliefs to behavior expectations, where all stakeholders are continuously made aware of these standards. **(p. 153)**

Proactive approach An approach to social responsibility in which an organization goes beyond industry norms to solve and prevent problems. **(p. 155)**

Reactive approach A response to social responsibility in which an organization denies responsibility for social problems and responds only when legally required. **(p. 156)**

Rights The behaviors you can expect from others based on their duties. **(p. 159)**

Social entrepreneurs Someone who starts a business for the dual purpose of profit and societal benefit. **(p. 157)**

Social responsibility Proactive behavior by an organization for the benefit of society. **(p. 155)**

Societal norms Society's expectations about how people (and organizations) should behave. **(p. 146)**

Stakeholders Individuals or groups who have a direct interest in an organization's behavior and experience the effects of the company's management decisions. **(p. 148)**

Standards of excellence An organization's highest expectations of behavior for all employees, including required and prohibited behaviors. **(p. 159)**

Utilitarian principle Making decisions that provide the greatest good to the greatest number (or the least harm to the fewest number). **(p. 152)**

Values-based management A management style in which the company's culture affects employee behavior in ways that are consistent with the organization's mission and values. **(p. 147)**

Virtuous principle Making decisions that you would be publicly proud of. **(p. 152)**

IN REVIEW

6.1 | Explain ethics as they relate to the five domains of individuals, organizations, stakeholders, government, and the global community.

As described by psychologist Lawrence Kohlberg (1927–1987), individuals go through three "stages of moral development" in their lives (preconventional, conventional, and postconventional), in which the individual transitions from acting in the interest of the self to acting in the interest of others. An example of ethics in the organizational domain is the case of Ben & Jerry's, which has been giving back to the community since its inception. Ethical behavior towards stakeholders means taking into consideration everyone who will be affected by the organization's behavior. When organizations do not behave ethically, governments must sometimes step in with new regulations. Global ethics are the principles, values, and beliefs that are widely considered universal, such as those upon which the United Nations is founded.

6.2 | Demonstrate processes and practices for managing organizational ethics.

When there is no clearly correct course of action, managers are required to make decisions based on one or more of the following principles: legal, individual, virtuous, long-term self-interest, community, utilitarian, and distributed justice. To assist with ethical decision making, many organizations publish ethical guidelines called *codes of conduct*.

6.3 | Describe how businesses approach social responsibility.

Social responsibility means acting proactively for the benefit of society. Many organizations today have corporate social responsibility (CSR) programs that coordinate the company's efforts to address societal and community challenges as they emerge. In a *proactive approach*, the organization goes beyond industry norms to solve and prevent problems. The *accommodative approach* is when an organization accepts responsibility and takes action in response to societal pressures. The *defensive approach* is when an organization accepts responsibility but does only the minimum required. The *reactive approach* is when an organization denies responsibility for social problems and responds only when legally required.

6.4 | Explain how organizations seek to prosper through social responsibility.

As communities benefit more and more from social entrepreneurship, consumers and investors are becoming more active in supporting and investing in companies that are socially responsible. Socially responsible companies can fill niche markets, as in the case of Pura Vida. Social investment firms like the Calvert Community Investment Fund can make money because of their strict criteria for investment opportunities and their unique appeal to customers.

6.5 | Summarize management's role in building responsible businesses based on ethical decision making.

Managing responsibly in today's business environment requires that managers make principle-based decisions informed by industry and societal standards. In some cases, organizations may decide to address a negative externality proactively by internalizing it, thus benefiting stakeholders. Managers define and foster ethical organizational cultures in two ways: 1) applying a framework for ethical decision making and 2) ethics training.

SELF-TEST

6.1 | Explain ethics as they relate to the five domains of individuals, organizations, stakeholders, government, and the global community.

1. A situation in which no choice is entirely right is called
   a. situational ethics
   b. an ethical dilemma
   c. morality
   d. escalation

2. Name and describe the three stages of individual moral development.

3. An **externality** is a cost (negative) or benefit (positive) that occurs within the direct exchange between an organization and its stakeholders.
   a. True
   b. False

4. With the _____ Act, top management is legally obligated to understand and approve their organization's financial practices.

5. What is the the "Global Compact," established by the United Nations?

6.2 | Demonstrate processes and practices for managing organizational ethics.

6. Which of the following is NOT one of the principles used to make principle-based decisions?
   a. individual rights principle
   b. long-term principle
   c. global principle
   d. community principle

7. A consistent set of ethical behavior expectations, published by organizations and clearly stating behavioral requirements and prohibitions, is called _____.

8. Name two of the eight broad categories of ethical standards that can be addressed by the above.

9. Explain principle-based management.

6.3 | Describe how businesses approach social responsibility.

10. Which of the following is NOT an approach to social responsibility?
    a. accommodative
    b. defensive
    c. transparent
    d. reactive

11. How did Upstream 21 implement a proactive approach to social responsibility?

6.4 | Explain how organizations seek to prosper through social responsibility.

12. As communities benefit more from social entrepreneurship, consumers and investors are becoming more active in supporting and investing in companies that are socially responsible.
    a. True
    b. False

6.5 | Summarize management's role in building responsible businesses based on ethical decision making.

13. What does "internalizing an externality" mean?

14. What are the two ways that managers define and foster ethical organizational cultures?

15. What are the four primary components to an ethical framework?

16. What is the tragedy of the commons?

CHAPTER EXERCISE

Backovers and Backup Cameras: Worth the Cost?

Two-year-old Cameron Gulbransen was fast asleep on a Saturday night when his parents returned home from a dinner with friends. While Cameron's mom, Leslie, was paying the babysitter, Cameron's dad, respected pediatrician Dr. Greg Gulbransen, went back outside to move the family SUV into the driveway. No one realized that Cameron, who had awakened upon hearing his parents' voices, had followed his dad out the front door, dressed in his pajamas and dragging his blue blanket. Cameron walked to the end of the driveway just as Dr. Gulbransen was backing in. "I felt a bump. I didn't know what it was," Dr. Gulbransen later recalled, "Quickly I jumped from the vehicle and saw the most devastating scene of my life. My little Cameron was lying down with his blanket in his hand while bleeding profusely from his head. As a physician, I knew it was the end. I did everything I could do and so did the paramedics. Cameron had died a sudden and horrible death because he was too small for me to see him behind my vehicle."

Sadly, Cameron Gulbransen's story is not uncommon enough. According to KidsandCars.org, approximately 50 children are backed over by vehicles every *week* in the United States. Of those children, 48 are treated in hospital emergency rooms, while at least 2 children are fatally injured every week. More than 100 children age 5 or younger die from backover deaths each year, according to the National Highway Traffic Safety Administration (NHTSA). Tragically, in most of these cases, parents or grandparents are behind the wheel.

Many of these backover deaths could be prevented through the use of backup cameras and/or other technologies that could warn drivers of potential dangers. In fact, the NHTSA is currently in the process of finalizing legislation that will require backup cameras in all cars and trucks sold in the United States. The backup camera technology will increase the price of new cars and trucks by around $200 per vehicle. The NHTSA calculates that the rearview camera proposal will cost consumers between $11.8 million and $19.7 million per life saved.

Instructions: Pair up with someone else in your class. Choose one of the following positions. Have your partner take the opposite position and debate the issue.

Position 1. The U.S. government and the automobile manufacturers have a corporate social responsibility to provide vehicles to consumers that are as safe as possible. Backup cameras should be mandatory because they save lives. All consumers should be willing to pay extra for new vehicles to save lives. You can't place a value on a human life.

Position 2. Backup cameras should not be mandatory. Corporate social responsibility is one thing, but the government and automobile manufacturers can't be expected to mitigate every possible danger associated with vehicles. Cameras should remain optional for those people who have small children, but people who do not have children should not be forced to pay extra for something they don't need. Human life is precious, but $11.8 million and $19.7 million per life saved is an exorbitant cost for consumers to bear. Besides, parents should keep better track of where their children are at all times.

Having debated the issue, which position do you now believe is the most valid? Why? What arguments would you use to convince someone else of your position?

SELF-ASSESSMENT

How Ethical Am I?*

For each statement, circle the number that best describes you based on the following scale:

Not at all Accurate	Somewhat Accurate	A little Accurate	Mostly Accurate	Completely Accurate
1	2	3	4	5

1. I consistently work the hours I'm paid for and avoid using sick leave unless I'm really sick.

    1   2   3   4   5

2. I take full responsibility for my actions, behaviors, and attitudes. I avoid "passing the buck" or blaming others for my problems and mistakes.

    1   2   3   4   5

3. I know and follow *all* of the rules established by my organization.

    1   2   3   4   5

4. When given a task or assignment, I regularly try to do *more* than is expected of me.

    1   2   3   4   5

5. When I see things that need to be done, I do them without waiting for others to take the lead.

    1   2   3   4   5

6. I'm a considerate coworker. I regularly clean up after myself and avoid behaviors that may disturb others or cause them additional work.

    1   2   3   4   5

7. I remember my promises and commitments, and I *keep* them.

    1   2   3   4   5

8. When I'm down, I avoid whining, complaining, or otherwise spreading negative feelings to my coworkers.

    1   2   3   4   5

9. I look for (and seize) opportunities to help my coworkers be successful rather than just "being in it for myself."

    1   2   3   4   5

10. I make an effort to be patient with everyone I work with (and for)—cutting them the same "slack" that I wish for in return.

    1   2   3   4   5

11. I respect and protect my organization's equipment, resources, and facilities—just as if I owned the business and had my personal finances at stake.

    1   2   3   4   5

12. It's critically important for me to always perform with ethics and integrity . . . and I do it!

    1   2   3   4   5

Scoring:

Add the numbers circled above: _____

Interpretation

48 and above = You are a highly ethical person who rarely compromises your ethical standards.

25—47 = You are a moderately ethical person, but you are likely inconsistent in your application of your ethical standards and values.

24 and below = You need to make some substantial improvements in establishing and consistently adhering to your ethical standards and behaviors.

*Adapted from a "Walk the Talk" resource, available at http://www.walkthetalk.com/media/solution_finder/pdf/how_ethical_am_i.pdf.

SELF-TEST ANSWER KEY

1. b.
2. **preconventional**—moral decisions motivated by self-interest; **conventional**—moral decisions motivated by societal norms; **postconventional**—moral decisions are motivated by what's good for society as a whole
3. b. False; this occurs beyond the direct exchange.
4. Sarbanes-Oxley
5. a strategic policy initiative for businesses that are committed to aligning their operations and strategies with 10 universally accepted principles in the areas of human rights, labor, environment, and anti-corruption
6. c.
7. a code of conduct
8. Fiduciary, Dignity, Property, Transparency, Reliability, Fairness, Citizenship, Responsiveness (See Table 6-3 for more information.)
9. When an organization proactively connects values and beliefs to behavior expectations, where all stakeholders are continuously made aware of these standards.
10. c.
11. They made consideration of the interests of all stakeholders, including the community and the local economy, a requirement in their organization instead of an optional consideration.
12. a. True
13. When management proactively addresses a negative externality for the benefit of its stakeholders.
14. applying a framework for ethical decision making, and ethics training
15. duties, rights, standards of excellence, and commitments
16. Two or more entities pursue individually beneficial actions where resources supporting these actions are limited, resulting in possible system breakdown or devaluation for all.

PART THREE

Planning

CHAPTER SEVEN

MAKING BETTER DECISIONS

CHAPTER OUTLINE

Learning Objectives

By the end of this chapter, you will be able to:

7.1 | Describe the seven steps of the decision-making process.

7.2 | Identify problems by analyzing causes and effects.

7.3 | Describe how managers generate alternatives.

7.4 | Predict possible consequences of alternatives.

7.5 | Demonstrate how managers select the most desirable alternative.

7.6 | Describe the manager's role in implementing alternatives.

7.7 | Explain the patterns of behavior and delayed results for decisions made.

ADDITIONAL RESOURCES

KEY TERMS
IN REVIEW
SELF-TEST
CHAPTER EXERCISE
SELF-ASSESSMENT
SELF-TEST
ANSWER KEY

JP Greenwood/Getty Images

INSIDE THIS CHAPTER

ManagementStory:
Featuring **Chris Heppler**

7.1 | DECISIONS THAT MAKE A DIFFERENCE

7.1 | Describe the seven steps of the decision-making process.

"The human being striving for rationality and restricted within the limits of his knowledge has developed some working procedures that partially overcome these difficulties. These procedures consist in assuming that he can isolate from the rest of the world a closed system containing a limited number of variables and a limited range of consequences."[1]

— Herbert Simon, management theorist (1947)

Decisions are not events. If people in organizations could make the absolute "right" choice every time, the role of a manager would be greatly reduced. Decisions are processes, with a beginning, middle, and end. Earlier in this book, we discussed the different dynamics and variables, from internal to external forces, that continuously change the situations that managers and organizations face.[2] To help prepare you for making better decisions inside an organization, we will explore how managers make decisions through in-depth stories inspired by real life events.

Real-life management decisions are much more complicated than books often make them seem. So what will we offer you here? We will present you with a reliable seven-step

Manager Profile

David J. Makarsky
Senior Vice President of Operations, B. F. Saul Hospitality Group

Dave leads the operations team, with the goal of achieving excellence in guest, team member, and owner satisfaction at all of B. F. Saul's properties, which include 14 hotels in the metropolitan Washington, D.C. area as well as three hotels in Florida and one in Michigan. Working with him on the operations team are the regional directors, the corporate director of human resources, the corporate director of food and beverage, and the financial, development, and operations analyst.

Dave joined the B. F. Saul Hospitality Group in 1998 as a regional director for four hotels. Six years into his tenure, he assumed the position of vice president of human resources. Dave's success during his three years in this role yielded a more strategic role for human resources within the organization and ultimately led to his promotion to vice president of operations in 2007. His prior experience

included positions as general manager, regional food and beverage director, regional director of hotel operations, and free-standing restaurant manager. Dave holds a B.S. degree from the Cornell University School of Hotel Administration.

Dave serves on the board of directors for the Dulles Regional Chamber of Commerce. He has served as an "Executive in Residence" for a graduate level Human Resource course in the Department of Hospitality and Tourism at Virginia Tech. For the past two years, Dave has spoken at the HR in Hospitality Conference, which is co-sponsored by *Human Resource Executive* magazine and Cornell University's Schools of Hotel Administration and Industrial and Labor Relations. He has also addressed numerous gatherings of human resource and hospitality professionals in the metropolitan Washington, D.C. region. ∎

decision-making process to make better decisions—but they may not always be the "right" decisions. We will show you how a real team made decisions to recover from poor financial and quality performance. We will give you ways of thinking through complex situations and the opportunity to practice making the well-considered choices required of a manager. Making decisions is the real *art* of management—probably the one element of a manager's job that can clearly determine success or failure.

Why is decision making an art? It is the act of balance. Spend too little time, and decisions often lead to undesirable outcomes; spend too much time, and you can become paralyzed, resulting in lost opportunity and reduced team motivation. If you spend just two minutes choosing classes for next semester, for example, you'll likely end up with classes that don't really fit your needs and schedule. On the other hand, if you spend days agonizing over the decision, the classes you want might fill up and your current schoolwork will suffer from lack of attention.

Managers today have the added benefit (and sometimes liability) of much more data, computers to handle complex sets of variables, and a communication infrastructure to explore thoroughly a vast array of consequences associated with each decision. This often comes at the cost of overanalyzing a situation. In reality, it is impossible to know all the variables. All decisions are necessarily based on incomplete analysis, which is why managers will continue to be responsible for making many judgment calls. Let's look at how a real-world case presented a manager with an array of choices, but not much time to make a difference.

© Ikon Images / Corbis

Types of Decision Making

The following case study is inspired by the real management events of David J. Makarsky, Senior VP of Operations for the B.F. Saul Hospitality Group, discussed in the Manager Profile on the previous page.

In the following case study, we follow fictional character Chris Heppler (based on Dave Makarsky) and his goal to achieve excellence at a hotel based on a small island off the coast of South Carolina.

The Hilton Head Dolphin Resort & Hotel is a unique property on Hilton Head Island, and it's the only hotel with access to the public beach. Herb Cork became the general manager of the Hilton Head Dolphin Resort in 2008, vowing to increase profitability by raising the average daily rate that guests pay for their rooms. Cork was a quiet manager who was fond of financials and the quantitative responsibilities of management. Despite his detailed management style and fondness for numbers, the hotel's profit over the past decade had steadily declined even though there had been an increase in revenue. Kathy Osborne, the owner of the hotel, decided that a change was required. In 2014, she hired a new general manager.

When Kathy Osborne interviewed Chris Heppler, she showed him the resort's revenue and profit numbers for the past five years (see Figure 7-1) and told him that his goal would

✓ **Optimum Decision**—the best possible decision given all the needed information
  ➤ Figure 7-2: Classical Model of Decision Making

• Seven Steps to make better decisions as a manager
  ➤ Figure 7-3: Seven Steps to Better Decision Making

✓ **Adaptive management**—require managers to use critical thinking, collaboration, and reflection skills to make non-programmed decisions

ManagementStory:
Featuring Chris Heppler

Figure 7-1

Hilton Head Dolphin Resort & Hotel Financials
Revenue and profit numbers for the Dolphin Resort over five years.

© Martin Siepmann/imagebroker/Corbis

be to increase the hotel's profit by $500,000 for the following year. As the two of them discussed the graph, Kathy asked Chris how he would explain an increase in revenue over time, coupled with a decrease in profit. Chris indicated that he didn't have an answer, but that he loved the challenge of solving difficult problems. He only had one request: "If I take this position, I want flexibility and your support to make the decisions required to achieve your goal." Kathy agreed, and Chris was hired.

In this chapter, we will explore the process through which managers make decisions with teams and the impact that those decisions can have over time. There are two types of decisions that managers make: *programmed* and *nonprogrammed*. **Programmed decision** are based on preestablished rules in response to a recurring situation.[3] For example, as Chris would discover, the restaurant manager at the Dolphin Resort automatically orders more soda when inventory declines to a predetermined level. So what type of decision did Chris face after Kathy Osborne offered him the position as general manager? As they consider all the alternatives involved in making this underperforming organization successful, Chris and the team at the Dolphin Resort will make a series of **nonprogrammed decision** based on reason and/or intuition in response to a unique situation that requires a tailored decision.[4] These decisions will include refocusing efforts, such as service behaviors—some hotels offer freshly baked cookies for arriving guests—or changing the inventory of the gift shop to appeal to a different demographic. What process should Chris implement with his team to make more successful decisions than his predecessor?

The **classical model** of decision making is a normative model of decision making that leads to an optimum decision, assuming full availability of information, sufficient time, and rationality of the decision maker. An **optimum decision** is the best possible decision given all the needed information. The classical model as shown in Figure 7-2, describes a linear process and assumes that managers will make the "right decisions."

As Herbert Simon suggested in 1947, the assumption that you can isolate "a closed system" from the rest of the world is a faulty theory. As we have explored in previous chapters, systems are open and continuously dynamic; therefore, the decisions that managers make are processes, not events. This is why in a systems approach to critical thinking, we look at diagrams that show interconnected variables and behavior over time.

We will discuss a seven-step process to make *better* decisions as a manager as illustrated in Figure 7-3: 1) identify the problem, 2) analyze the problem and its causes, 3) generate alternatives, 4) evaluate alternatives, 5) choose a path, 6) implement a choice, 7) solicit feedback and analyze results.[5]

Programmed decision A decision based on preestablished rules in response to a recurring situation.

Nonprogrammed decision A decision based on reason and/or intuition in response to a unique situation that requires a tailored decision.

Classical model A normative model of decision making that leads to an optimal decision, assuming full availability of information, sufficient time, and rationality of the decision maker.

Optimum decision The best possible decision given all the needed information.

Figure 7-2
Classical Model of Decision Making
A decision-making model that tells managers how to make a decision based on a variety of assumptions.

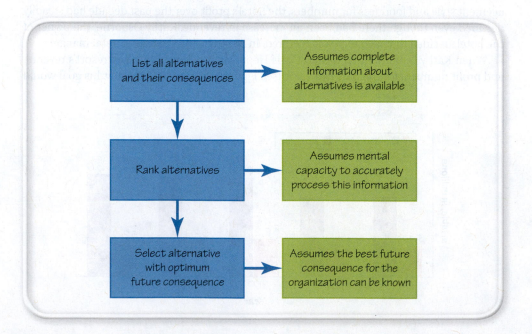

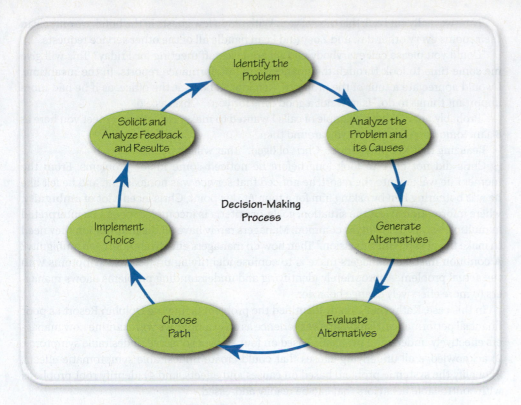

Decision-Making Process

- Identify the Problem
- Analyze the Problem and its Causes
- Generate Alternatives
- Evaluate Alternatives
- Choose Path
- Implement Choice
- Solicit and Analyze Feedback and Results

Figure 7-3
Seven Steps to Better Decision Making
A seven-step process to making better decisions.

Many companies create policies and rules to maximize the number of programmed decisions that managers make in order to reduce the likelihood of error. In a rapidly changing business environment, more businesses are implementing **adaptive management** philosophies for decision making, which require managers to use critical thinking, collaboration, and reflection skills to make nonprogrammed decisions.[6] Let's explore how Chris followed these steps to become more adaptive to systemic forces and to make better decisions.

Adaptive management An approach to decision making that requires managers to use critical thinking, collaboration, and reflection skills to make nonprogrammed decisions.

7.2 | IDENTIFYING AND UNDERSTANDING THE PROBLEM

7.2 | Identify problems by analyzing causes and effects.

When Chris arrived at the Dolphin Resort & Hotel, it was a blustery January morning, with howling winds and freezing rain. The hotel was empty. When he walked into the lobby, he saw no one standing behind the front desk, no one in the gift shop, no one in the restaurant. Chris thought, "Are we closed and somebody forgot to lock the doors?" As he approached the front desk to find a phone, he saw a large bell, with a sign that read, "Ring Bell LOUDLY For Service . . . Thanks!"

Chris rang the bell, and Ken Gold, the resort's director of sales, emerged from a hallway that connected the front-desk area to the management offices.

"Hey! What can I do for you?" Ken seemed impatient for a response.

"Hi, I'm Chris Heppler, the new general manager."

Ken looked surprised. "Oh! I'm Ken Gold, director of sales. We thought you were coming next week. Kathy told us to have the place super clean for your arrival. Sorry things are a little messy—this is the time of year we all catch up on our sleep!"

"Where is everybody?"

"Oh, it's just me, and Zoey Zhang, one of the kitchen staff."

Chris laughed. "You are joking, right?"

LECTURE ENHANCER:

7.2 Identifying and Understanding the Problem

✓ **Ambiguity**—information about the situation, goals, or criteria is incomplete or can be interpreted in multiple ways

- How managers effectively understand problems:
  1. Observe undesirable symptoms
  2. Acknowledge all underlying causes that could create undesirable symptomatic effects
  3. Qualify the systemic problem based on causes and effects
  4. Identify root problems with controllable behaviors that can be readily addressed

- Symptomatic Effects
  ➤ Figure 7-4: Dolphin Resort: Guest Satisfaction Goal
  ✓ **Symptomatic effects**— observable behaviors related to underlying causal variables

- Underlying Causes
  ✓ **Underlying Causes**—the behaviors that lead to a desired or undesired symptomatic effect

Ambiguity Information about the situation, goals, or criteria that is incomplete or can be interpreted in multiple ways.

"No—we really cut back this time of year. With only a few guests in the hotel, we only clean their rooms every other day, and Zoey and I can handle all of the other service requests."

"Could you please call everybody and schedule a staff meeting for Friday? This will give me some time to look through the financials and performance reports. In the meantime, I would appreciate a tour of the property." Ken looked back at the office, as if he had more important things to do. "Is now not a good time for you?" Chris asked.

"Probably not . . . I have a couple of calls I wanted to make. How about I meet you here at 8 a.m. tomorrow? I can show you around then."

Realizing that Ken was serious, Chris obliged. "That will be fine."

Chris did not have to look long before he noticed some major problems. From the moment he walked into the resort, he noticed that service was nonexistent, and he felt like he was bothering Ken by asking him for a tour. At this point, Chris faced a lot of **ambiguity**, where information about the situation, goals, or criteria is incomplete or can be interpreted in multiple ways. Ambiguity is common. Managers rarely have all the information they need to make the best possible decision.[7] Then how do managers effectively approach ambiguity? A common mistake managers make is to confuse identifying undesirable symptoms with the actual problem. Appropriately identifying and understanding problems allows managers to more effectively change behavior.

In this case, Kathy had already identified the problem facing the Dolphin Resort as poor financial performance. Using Chris's experience as an example, we will examine how managers effectively understand problems based on four steps: 1) observe undesirable symptoms, 2) acknowledge all underlying causes that could create undesirable symptomatic effects, 3) qualify the systemic problem based on causes and effects, and 4) identify root problems with controllable behaviors that can be readily addressed.

Symptomatic Effects

After walking around the hotel property for a while, Chris went into the restaurant's kitchen and introduced himself to Zoey Zhang. Warm and friendly, her personality was everything you could hope for in a hotel employee. Chris is confident that with 20 more employees like Zoey, the Hilton Head Dolphin Resort & Hotel is sure to be a success once more.

Friday was Chris's first team meeting with the employees at the resort. After introductions and conversations during a continental breakfast, he started by asking the team a question: "Can anyone tell me how many times in the past five years the hotel has achieved

Voices of Management

Bob Adler[8]
Senior Vice President, Terrapin Management Corporation

Bob Adler found his career path early. When he was 20 years old, he worked for a ski lodge in Big Sky, Montana, and knew immediately that he wanted to work in the hotel industry. He's now senior vice president of hotel operations at Terrapin Management Corporation, in Albuquerque, New Mexico, and has never regretted his early career decision for an instant. But not all choices are so clear. When faced with ambiguity, says Adler, it's best "not to resist change and unfamiliar circumstances, but rather embrace them for the rich opportunities and experiences that unfold when we simply say yes. One of the things I'm most proud of is the choice to accept new challenges and increasing responsibilities whenever presented to me, even

if it felt uncomfortable and included some fear of the unknown." With that attitude, Adler has made a successful career that is still as exciting today as it was when he began 20 years ago.

Adler's advice to students? "Lead with your head and your heart, and always be true to yourself and your values, even when you face resistance. Do the right things and everything will work out well."

Critical Thinking in the Classroom

As a manager, how would you apply Adler's ethos of embracing change while maintaining your own values in the workplace? ∎

Figure 7-4
Dolphin Resort: Guest
Satisfaction Goal
The hotel has suffered a decrease
in guest satifaction over the last
five years.

its quality goal?" A few hands were raised—"Sure. We've achieved that goal every single year. I know that because achieving our quality goal is tied to our annual bonus," said John Johnson, the resort's food and beverage director. "That's correct," Chris said. He paused to draw a graph on a whiteboard (as shown in Figure 7-4) . "Now, can anyone help me understand why the quality goal has *decreased* every year for the past six years?" Once again, a few hands were raised—"We had a really difficult few years financially, and to keep our profit up, Mr. Cork decided not to make capital improvements, like new carpet or dishware. He said it was only fair that we adjust our quality goals for things that we cannot control—like worn carpet," Johnson continued.

Clearly, service quality and its goals are a problem at the Dolphin Resort. That might be the entirety of the problem, requiring a very straightforward solution. Assuming this, Chris could simply raise the quality goals, implement service training programs, and hope that these decisions would solve the problem. Yet in this situation, service quality results and gradually declining quality goals are just **symptomatic effects**, or observable behaviors related to underlying causal variables. If Chris stopped his analysis of the problem here, what else might he miss?

Underlying Causes

Problems are undesirable behaviors. We notice problems by recognizing *symptomatic effects*. To understand the origins of these symptoms, we must then explore and understand the **underlying causes**, the behaviors that lead to a desired or undesired symptomatic effect. There are two ways of understanding and analyzing underlying causes: *systemic* and *policy-based* analysis.

According to systems engineer and consultant Jack Harich, "The important thing is to not stop at intermediate causes. These are plausible and easily found. Working on resolving them *looks* productive and *feels* productive. Intermediate cause solutions may even work for awhile. But until the true root cause is resolved, the system will invariably find a way to circumvent or thwart these solutions, because intermediate causes are symptoms of deeper causes. One must strike at the root."[9] *Systemic* and *policy-based* analyses provide managers with a thorough process to discover and "strike at the root."

Systemic-Based Analysis: To be sure that they ask the right questions and consider the most relevant variables, managers who make better decisions begin understanding a problem through **systemic-based analysis**, which takes into account the array of all known variables associated with a problem and its symptoms, including behavior over time. A common example is gaining and losing body weight. Let's say a person is behaving in all the ways that would logically lead to losing weight, yet is still gaining weight. In seeking help, doctors may run a series of blood tests to measure a broad array of causal variables and analyze an individual's metabolism and health as a systemic problem, which can be a complicated interconnection of variables such as genetic coding, enzymes, disease, thyroid levels, and

Symptomatic effects Observable behaviors related to underlying causal variables.

Underlying causes The behaviors that lead to a desired or undesired symptomatic effect

Systemic-based analysis A method of analyzing a problem that takes into account the array of all known variables associated with a problem and its symptoms, including behavior over time.

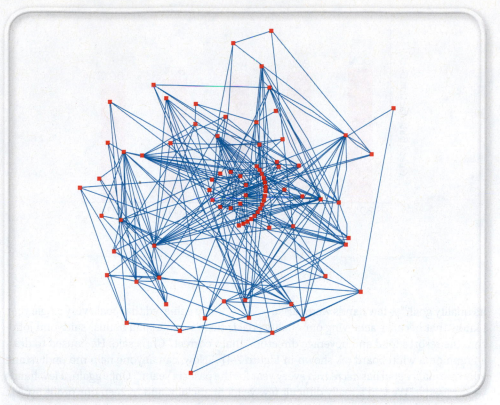

Figure 7-5
A Thaliana Metabolic Network
An organism with an interconnected network of variables.

Source: http://en.wikipedia.org/wiki/File:A_thaliana_metabolic_network.png.

so forth (like the one shown in Figure 7-5) As you can imagine, it would require a doctor to analyze this data and suggest a solution based on a variety of alternatives—herbal remedies, medication, exercise, and/or dietary changes.

Luckily for most of us, we don't need to understand the complicated image in Figure 7-5. That said, managers, like doctors, also have tools to analyze situations systemically to make better decisions. These decisions and consequential behavior can be expressed and understood as an interconnected system of variables. As we discussed briefly in Chapter 3, managers can use systems thinking to analyze the interconnection of variables in order to better predict behaviors and consequences over time. Management theorists and researchers have identified common patterns of behaviors and consequences that managers face, such as customer satisfaction. Figure 7-6 is a systems diagram depicting the major causal variables for customer satisfaction. This diagram provides a holistic view, but it lacks the specificity that would allow a manager to predict a behavior. These frequently occurring patterns that are deemed predictable are referred to as *systems archetypes*.

For instance, over the past several years, the Dolphin Resort's management focused on financial savings and largely ignored service quality. Chris's predecessor, Herb Cork, addressed the issue by incrementally lowering guest satisfaction standards without the owner being aware—unfortunately, a commonly observed pattern of behavior in organizations. This is a classic example of the "Drifting Goals" system archetype, also known as the "Boiled Frog Syndrome" (see Figure 7-7). Boiled Frog Syndrome is often used to describe people who don't react quickly enough or are unaware of the changes going on around them. For example, if a frog is put into hot water, he will jump out, but if he is placed in cold water that is gradually heated up, he will not notice and will end up being boiled to death. This metaphor is often used in businesses that are slow to see the "writing on the wall" and fail to adapt accordingly.

In this systems archetype, the gap between "guest satisfaction goal" and "actual guest satisfaction" is shown. At the Dolphin Resort & Hotel, one of the employees suggested that every year there was pressure to lower the quality goal for two reasons: 1) annual bonuses depended on achieving the goal, 2) lack of capital improvements were blamed for declining service quality or "guest satisfaction." This pressure resulted in the previous general manager lowering the goal, which instigated a downward trend in actual guest satisfaction. This is an example of a systemic-based analysis.

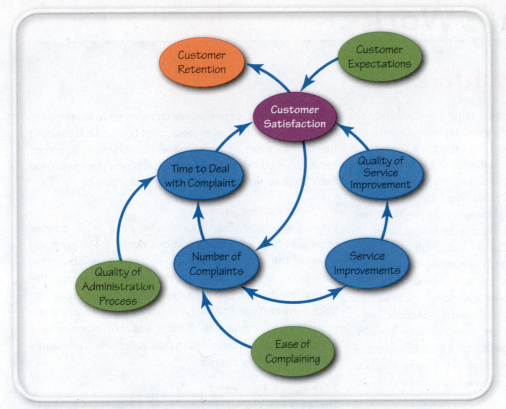

Figure 7-6
Customer Satisfaction
A systems archetype diagram showing the causal variables for customer satisfaction.

Source: M. J. Schroek, "The Next Generation of Balanced Scorecards," *Information Management Magazine*, December 2001; http://www.information-management.com/issues/20011201/4337-1.html.

Policy-Based Analysis Once managers have a systemic understanding of a situation, they can begin to look at specific policies that could be contributing to undesirable effects. Let's return to the weight gain and loss example to explore further how managers get a full understanding of the underlying causes of a problem beyond the full array of variables displayed in a systemic analysis. In the case of weight loss or gain, two primary underlying

Figure 7-7
Drifting Goals Systems Archetype
The "Drifting Goals" system archetype, showing that a short-term solution leads to the erosion of a long-term goal. B, balancing loop.

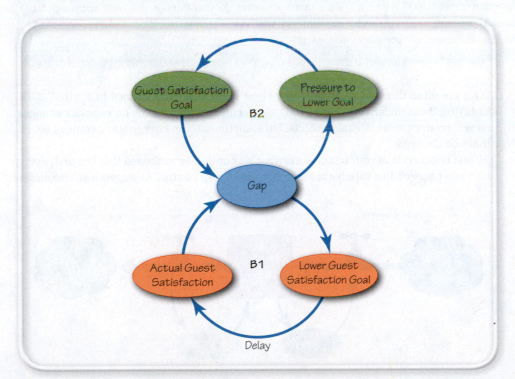

Source: D. Kim, *Systems Archetypes I* (Waltham, MA: Pegasus Communications, 1994).

Research@Work

Effective Intuition[10]

Researchers have repeatedly shown that managers rely on intuition when they need to make a fast decision in a complex situation, and that intuitive decision making is a crucial skill for upper management. But intuition isn't always reliable. In their award-winning article titled "Exploring Intuition and Its Role in Managerial Decision Making," Dane and Pratt (2007) propose some organizational conditions that they believe enable managers to develop *effective* intuition.

Intuitive decisions, say Dane and Pratt, are fast, nonconscious, and involve both emotions and pattern recognition (p. 40). We store patterns in our minds as *schemas*, mental models of how the world works. When we make intuitive decisions, we are drawing, nonconsciously, on our own schemas. The more complex and domain-specific (i.e., expert knowledge about a certain aspect of our own environment) our schemas are, the more effective our intuitive decisions because we have more relevant information at our disposal.

As an example, Dane and Pratt cite Carly Fiorina's ousting from Hewlett-Packard (HP) in 2005. They suggest that although Fiorina had plenty of experience and expertise, it was not domain-specific to HP's organization, so her intuitive decisions were not as effective as they could have been.

So how can organizations develop intuitive decision-making skills in their managers? Dane and Pratt suggest two methods: First, organizations can foster "kind" learning environments, in which feedback is prompt, accurate, and exacting, thus facilitating the development of complex schemas. Second, organizations can commit to strategies to retain managers for longer periods of time, thus facilitating the development of domain-specific schemas. Together, these two methods will help managers form the foundation from which to make effective intuitive decisions.

Professor's Response

What Dane and Pratt contribute here is a deeper understanding of how intuition works by identifying some of the individual and organizational variables that contribute to effective intuitive decisions (namely, the mental models of the managers and organizations can help cultivate conditions necessary for reliable mental models within managers). It suggests that organizations would benefit from developing policies to retain managers for longer periods of time.

Manager's Response

There's a real challenge here to find a balance between the benefits of retaining managers who have developed "domain-specific" knowledge and the benefits of bringing in new managers who have fresh ideas and different experiences to draw from. I'd like to see some research on how different companies have managed this balance and what the effects have been.

Critical Thinking in the Classroom

As a manager, what do you think is the best approach to developing effective intuitive decision making within an organization?

---

causes are often diet and exercise, which affect metabolism as outlined in Figure 7-8. By identifying these underlying causes, individuals can choose to focus on behavior changes that will produce more desirable effects. But sometimes there are variables, some of which cannot be changed.

Upon conclusion of your blood work, what if your doctor explained that the underlying cause was genetic? This variable is very much out of your control. Managers also encounter

Figure 7-8
Policy-based Analysis Using "Stock-and-Flow" Diagram
Both exercise and diet have an effect on metabolism, leading to weight loss or weight gain.

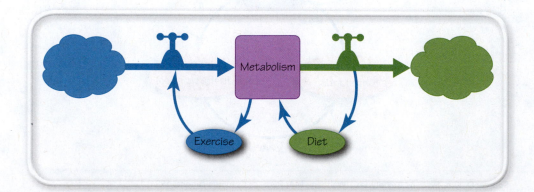

variables that are out of their control. For example, the Windy City Salt Supply Company manufactures and packages road salt for the state of Illinois and other localities. A total of 90 percent of their revenue comes in when bad weather is predicted; therefore, each year, their business depends on the weather, which is 100 percent out of their control.

It would not be a productive decision-making exercise for managers at Windy City Salt Supply Company to think through alternatives for changing the weather. To focus managers on productive decision-making activities, **policy-based analysis** isolates the variables in a system that can truly be addressed through management intervention. Managers use stock-and-flow diagrams to better understand policy-based decisions. As shown in Figure 7-8, someone who wanted the effect of weight loss might identify a lack of exercise as an underlying cause and choose to walk a mile every day and decrease their caloric intake by 20 percent. Managers would love for their problems to be so easily defined! So how do managers know when they have identified the controllable variables that, through intervention, will most likely lead to desirable behaviors?

To answer this question, let's return to the Dolphin Resort & Hotel case. When discussing underlying causes with the team, Chris had only cited two variables—service quality results and quality goals—both of which were appropriate for a systems archetype/systemic analysis. Is it possible that there are more causes that led to poor financial results at the Dolphin Resort? Let's reconsider the systemic view of "customer satisfaction," where the biggest problem of concern (the primary effect here) would be "customer retention" as shown previously in Figure 7-6.

There are three primary underlying causes noted here as well—customer expectations, quality of administration process, and ease of complaining. What could be causing such poor financial results? "Quality of administration processes" and "ease of complaining" can both be addressed through training and new procedures, but Chris doubts that this could be contributing to the entire profit decline. That leaves "customer expectations" for the team to consider. Chris asks the group, "You all know the Dolphin Resort a lot better than I do. What do you think could be causing a guest expectation problem, if there is one?" Wendy, the resort's front-desk manager, walks to a flipchart (see Figure 7-9) in the front of the room, draws a couple of lines, and suggests, "We have been steadily charging guests more and more over the past few years. It seems logical that the more a customer pays, the higher the quality they will expect. If our quality is steadily declining, there is our problem."

The team had spent Friday morning discussing the quality issues at the resort, with everyone agreeing that the most likely cause was "guest expectations." Sensing that the team was exhausted, Chris suggested that the managers consider the team's insights and reconvene on Monday to conclude their policy-based analysis. Chris's biggest challenge was to balance efficiency and effectiveness—spending enough time, but not too much, making a better decision. Let's see how Chris framed this process for his management team.

On Monday, the management team came together in a small meeting room. Chris arrived early and redrew the "guest expectation gap" that Wendy had presented on the flipchart. Beside the diagram, he wrote, "Agreed! But, what does this tell us?"

Policy-based analysis A method of problem analysis that isolates the variables in a system that can truly be addressed through management intervention

Figure 7-9
Front Desk Manager's "Guest Expectation Gap" Explanation
The guest expectation gap between increasing prices and decreasing quality.

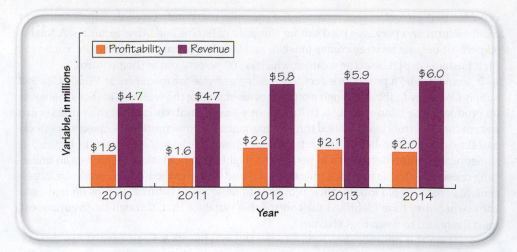

Figure 7-10
Dolphin Resort: Annualized Revenue and Profit
This graph shows increase in revenue versus decrease in profit over five years.

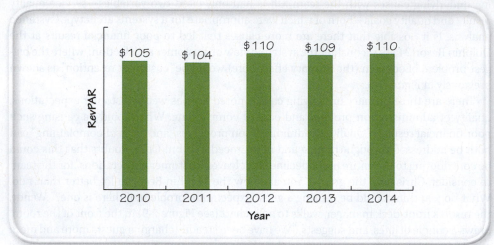

Figure 7-11
Dolphin: RevPAR
Revenue per available room for the Dolphin Resort over five years.

John Johnson spoke up, "Is this why you called me in on my day off? You want us to do your job? Mr. Cork was the best manager of money that I have ever worked with—he counted every cent. When he came to this hotel five years ago, our average daily rate was $70 a night, and now it is almost $100. That is over $20 more than our competitors! No offense, Chris, but you look like you are 18 years old and have no chance of getting better results than an industry veteran like Mr. Cork."

Chris was startled by the outburst. "No offense taken, John. From what I have seen, Mr. Cork was very thorough with the finances here and really watched costs. I admire him for that. But we still have a problem with declining financial performance. Here are a few questions, which I would like to work with you all to figure out . . . If we keep raising our rates, why is our profit decreasing? If our revenue is steadily going up, why is RevPAR* remaining stagnant?" He turns to draw more images on the flipchart as shown in Figures 7-10 and 7-11.

The team agreed that they needed to understand the answers to Chris's questions before they could generate alternatives. After a lively conversation, the group concluded that the major factors associated with the expectation gap were room rate and service quality, which was having an impact on the occupancy percentage. When the room rate and occupancy numbers where collected and drawn on the board (as shown in Figures 7-12 and 7-13), the management team had a lot of questions and comments: "Now I know why our RevPAR has not increased—our occupancy dropped." "Wow, we really dropped our occupancy when we raised our rates." "It seems like we need to go back to 2012—that was a pretty good year."

*(Explanation: RevPAR is a way of measuring performance within the hotel industry. It is an acronym for "revenue per available room," which is a calculation of total revenue divided by all available room nights. For example, if a hotel has 100 rooms available every night of the year, they have 36,500 room nights available. If their RevPAR is $110, the hotel's total revenue would be $4,015,000.)

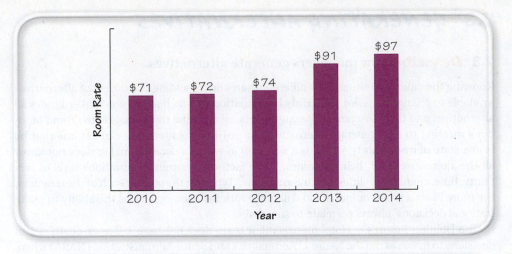

Figure 7-12
Dolphin Resort: Annualized Room Rate
Increase in annual room rate over five years.

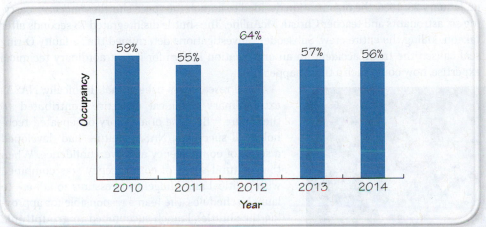

Figure 7-13
Dolphin Resort: Annualized Occupancy Percentage
Percentage of rooms occupied over five years.

(Explanation: Occupancy is the percentage of all room nights available that were sold and occupied by guests.)

The management team began to see that the relationship between the variables of room rate, guest satisfaction, and occupancy was the primary (or root) cause of the problem (as shown in Figure 7-14). Chris and his team needed to understand further how this created an undesirable guest expectation gap and then generate alternatives to intervene. In the next section, we will explore how managers work with their teams to generate alternatives in preparation for selecting a path.

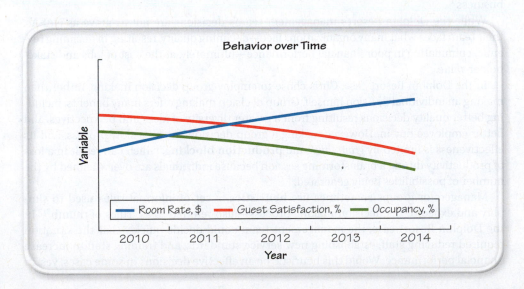

Figure 7-14
Dolphin Resort: Guest Expectation Variables
This graph illustrates the relationships among different variables over five years.

LECTURE ENHANCER:

7.3 Generating Alternatives

✓ **Certainty**—a situation in which a decision-maker knows all alternatives and their outcomes

Certainty A situation in which a decision maker knows all the alternatives and their outcomes.

Uncertainty A situation in which a decision maker does not know all the alternatives and their outcomes.

✓ **Uncertainty**—a situation in which a decision-maker does not know all alternatives and their outcomes

• Three factors that determine a situation's level of certainty:
  1. Time
  2. Cognitive Abilities
  3. Information

7.3 | GENERATING ALTERNATIVES

7.3 | **Describe** how managers generate alternatives.

Knowing the cause of a situation is different than understanding the variety of alternatives available to change behavior. **Certainty** is a situation in which a decision maker knows all alternatives and their outcomes.[11] Because Chris asked for all the managers to attend Monday's meeting to help generate alternatives for possible solutions, we can assume that he is in a state of **uncertainty**, which is a situation in which a decision maker does not know all the alternatives and their outcomes. Three factors determine a situation's level of certainty: time, cognitive abilities, and information.[12] Typically, the greater each of these factors, the more likely a group or individual will make rational decisions. Does the ability to make "rational decisions" always correlate to success?

The Dolphin Resort's & Hotel management team does not have a "life-or-death" set of decisions to make, as did the National Aeronautics and Space Administration (NASA) when, on January 28, 1986, the organization decided to launch the space shuttle *Challenger,* carrying six astronauts and teacher Christa McAuliffe. The shuttle disintegrated 73 seconds after takeoff, killing the entire crew. Subsequent investigations determined that a faulty O-ring seal caused the tragic accident. In an organization known for its extraordinary technical expertise, how could such a thing happen?

NASA

Some researchers believe that, ironically, NASA's extraordinary technical expertise contributed to the failure.[13] Because of a history of repeated technological successes, NASA's culture had developed a sense of complacency and overconfidence. When that cultural sense of complacency was combined with political and budgetary pressures to adhere to launch schedules, the teams responsible for approving the shuttle's launch succumbed to **groupthink**, an unconscious mode of group decision making in which individuals prioritize agreement over analysis.[14] So when engineers raised concerns about the O-ring's ability to seal properly in the cold temperatures of that January day, they were asked to reassess their analysis, which they did. The group agreed with the desired alternative that it was safe to launch. The decision was rationalized by the entire team based on NASA's impressive success record of solving technical problems quickly and efficiently and for having launched successfully in similar temperatures[15] and perhaps the resort going out of business?

While the Dolphin Resort's management team's decisions are not as grave as NASA's, their team faces what many organizations face—declining quality, resulting in declining revenue, culminating in poor financial performance—ultimately, at the cost of jobs and stakeholder value.

In the Dolphin Resort case, Chris chose to employ group decision making, rather than making an individual decision himself. Group decision making offers many benefits, including better quality decisions resulting from a greater diversity of ideas and perspectives, and better employee buy-in. However, making a group decision can be a slow process, and its effectiveness is limited by *groupthink* and **production blocking**, which can result in a loss of productivity during a brainstorming session because individuals are overwhelmed by the number of possibilities being generated.[16]

Managers or groups sometimes use **heuristics**, a set of informal rules used to simplify and expedite the decision-making process—also referred to as "rules of thumb."[17] In the Dolphin Resort case, the management team could decide quickly that the situation required reducing staff, establishing new service standards, and training staff to increase financial performance. Would this heuristic be an effective decision? In some cases, yes. In

Groupthink An unconscious mode of group decision making in which individuals prioritize agreement over analysis.

Production blocking A loss in productivity during a brainstorming session because individuals are overwhelmed by the number of possibilities being generated.

Heuristics A set of informal rules used to simplify and expedite the decision-making process.

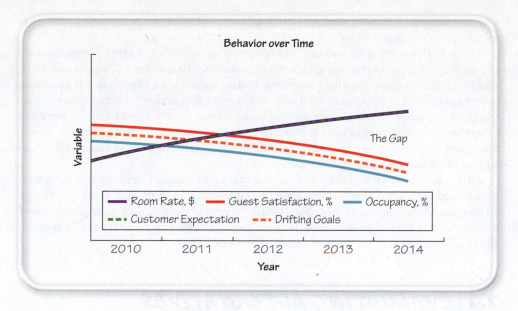

Behavior over Time

Legend:
- Room Rate, $
- Guest Satisfaction, %
- Occupancy, %
- Customer Expectation
- Drifting Goals

The Gap

Years: 2010, 2011, 2012, 2013, 2014

Y-axis: Variable
X-axis: Year

Figure 7-15
Expectation Gap Between Price and Drifting Goals
Expectation gap variables over five years.

this particular case, no, because it would probably be based on the fear of losing additional time and resources through overanalyzing the problem, creating pressure for everyone to agree quickly to a certain path. *Production blocking* and *groupthink* are fear-based dynamics that generally escalate one another—"Why do we have to waste so much time in meetings discussing the problem, instead of solving the issue? We could all be working now!" and "Wendy's comment on 'guest expectations' sounds good to me. Let's just go work on that."

The management team at the Dolphin Resort concluded that the relationship between the variables of room rate, guest satisfaction, and occupancy was the primary (or root) cause of the problem—a negative gap in guests' service expectations. Chris referred the team back to Wendy's original insight that "when you increase price, guests' expectations increase." Chris erased the whiteboard and redrew the diagram, depicting the three expectation gap variables with actual data from the hotel's performance. First, he added a dotted line through "room rate" for "guest expectation," and then a dotted line through "guest satisfaction" and "occupancy" for "drifting goals" (see Figure 7-15).

"Ladies and gentlemen, we need to close this gap." Chris then recommended that the group generate as many alternatives as possible to solve the primary cause of the resort's problem, which they have identified as "the gap." He suggested that the team start with a **brainstorming** session, creating as many alternatives as possible, without making value judgments about any idea. A model of the brainstorming process is shown in Figure 7-16. When managers don't generate and evaluate multiple alternatives, they often end up making poor decisions.[18] As he passed out dry-erase markers to all the managers, Chris explained how the team would conduct their brainstorming—"First, let's create as many possible solutions to closing this gap, and don't worry if the ideas are right or wrong, doable or undoable,

✓ **Groupthink**—an unconscious mode of group decision-making in which individuals prioritize agreement over analysis
✓ **Production blocking**—a loss in productivity during a brainstorming session because individuals are overwhelmed by the number of possibilities being generated
✓ **Heuristics**—a set of informal rules used to simplify and expedite the decision-making process; "rule of thumb"
  ➤ Figure 7-15: Expectation Gap Between Price and Drifting Goals
✓ **Brainstorming**—creating as many alternatives as possible, without making value judgments about any idea
  ➤ Figure 7-16: Brainstorming Model

Brainstorming Creating as many alternatives as possible, without making value judgments about any idea.

Figure 7-16
Brainstorming Model
This brainstorming model is used to generate ideas.

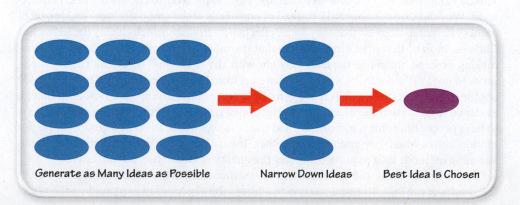

Generate as Many Ideas as Possible   Narrow Down Ideas   Best Idea Is Chosen

silly or otherwise. The more ideas we have, the better. We will then go through a process of selecting the best possibilities."

Group brainstorming techniques, where everybody contributes ideas simultaneously, can be very effective in producing high quality solutions. Researchers Kavadias and Sommer found that in some situations, individual brainstorming is a better choice. If a problem is very specialized, a single individual with expertise in that area will be much more effective than a group of people with an array of backgrounds. On the other hand, a diversity of expertise, skills, and perspectives is beneficial when dealing with a more complex, "cross-functional" problem.[19] Service quality is definitely categorized as a "cross-functional" problem, so Chris made a good process choice here.

After a few minutes of silence, with all the managers staring blurry-eyed at the whiteboard filled with alternatives, it was time to evaluate the merit of each alterative. Within 20 minutes, the management team dismissed 80 percent of the alternatives generated based on relevance or resource restrictions. How do managers effectively sort through a series of viable alternatives to make the best possible decision?

7.4 | *EVALUATING ALTERNATIVES*

7.4 | Predict possible consequences of alternatives.

Evaluating alternatives requires managers to predict and assess the outcomes of each alternative.[20] The degree to which the outcomes of an alternative can be predicted is referred to as **risk**. High-risk environments can lead to anxiety in the decision-making process. The management team at the Dolphin Resort felt the need to make the "right decision," mainly because choosing the wrong alternative could lead to a loss of jobs, including their own. John Johnson, the food and beverage manager, seemed to become even more frustrated as the discussion continued, finally saying, "What if none of these options work? I don't know which path we should take. Am I going to be held responsible for the decisions made here today? Chris decided to refocus the conversation. "Let's not start talking about problems that don't even exist yet. We don't know what decisions we are all comfortable making. Our first task is to take this array of options and select the best small group of options—let's say five to seven options to choose from."

Chris presented two methods for evaluating the merit of the alternatives that the group had generated. With the first method, called **nominal group technique (NGT)**, individuals rate proposed solutions and the total tally determines the final decision.[21] Wendy thought this was a good idea, but she suggested that they invite some of the line-level managers to participate in the process. The second method, called **Delphi technique**, is a method of decision making in which a group of experts propose and question ideas until a consensus is reached.[22] Chris suggested that the team might gain a lot of insights by including a few outside consultants that specialize in service quality. John, still not in a very good mood, suggested that the team had all the knowledge necessary to operate a successful hotel, and that bringing consultants to the table would be insulting.

After listening to the team's perspectives, Chris requested that the team reconvene on Tuesday afternoon with the line-level managers and apply NGT to choose the best path forward. Why did Chris choose NGT instead of one of the other group decision-making techniques? Research suggests that they are all effective in producing high-quality decisions. But Chris recognized that what's important is that the more people participate in the decision-making process, the more satisfied they are with the decision.[23] In Chris's case, it made sense to use NGT since there was already interest from the team in using it. Chris also made another important decision by choosing to use group brainstorming methods. Even though evidence suggests that the most effective method of generating and choosing alternatives is to have people brainstorm individually and then evaluate those ideas as a group, people *feel* more effective when they brainstorm together. The choice to use individual or group brainstorming methods thus requires balancing the quality of ideas against team buy-in.[24]

The next day, Chris invited all the managers, including line-level managers, to discuss the results of the brainstorming session to address the expectation gap problem the resort

Risk The degree to which the outcomes of an alternative can be predicted.

Nominal group technique (NGT) A group decision-making process in which individuals rate proposed solutions and the total tally determines the final decision.

Delphi technique A method of decision making in which a group of experts propose and question ideas until a consensus is reached.

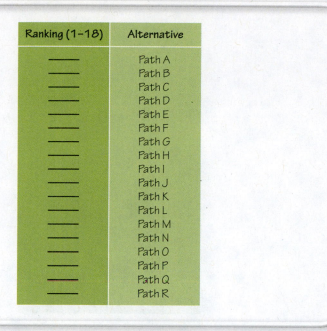

Ranking (1–18)	Alternative
——	Path A
——	Path B
——	Path C
——	Path D
——	Path E
——	Path F
——	Path G
——	Path H
——	Path I
——	Path J
——	Path K
——	Path L
——	Path M
——	Path N
——	Path O
——	Path P
——	Path Q
——	Path R

Figure 7-17
Template for NGT Rating Sheet
An NGT sheet to be completed, with 18 alternatives and their rankings.

was facing. Chris began by sharing the results and passing around a piece of paper with a list of all the possible decisions that the team was considering like the one shown in Figure 7-17.

Chris asked each manager to rank 18 possible alternatives from 1 (best) to 18 (worst). He explained that he would add up the results, with the lowest scores indicating the group's collective recommendations. First, Chris compiled everybody's feedback into a table (Figure 7-18). In order to calculate the results, Chris added up each row and divided that by the number of responses, so for the example of Alternative A, this calculation would be $(3 + 1 + 3 + 5 + 8 + 3 + 3)/7 = 3.714$.

Alternative	Manager # 1	Manager # 2	Manager # 3	Manager # 4	Manager # 5	Manager # 6	Manager # 7
Path A	3	1	3	5	8	3	3
Path B	9	9	9	9	14	12	9
Path C	12	10	14	12	17	19	14
Path D	14	15	12	14	9	15	12
Path E	2	2	2	2	7	2	2
Path F	4	4	4	4	15	4	4
Path G	15	14	15	15	10	14	15
Path H	7	7	6	7	13	7	7
Path I	6	6	7	6	11	6	6
Path J	17	17	18	17	12	17	17
Path K	16	16	16	18	6	18	16
Path L	13	13	13	13	16	13	13
Path M	1	3	1	1	18	1	1
Path N	5	5	5	3	1	5	5
Path O	18	18	17	16	4	16	18
Path P	8	8	11	8	3	8	8
Path Q	11	11	8	11	2	11	11
Path R	10	12	10	10	5	10	10

Figure 7-18
Data from NGT Process
Data showing the results of the NGT process.

Ranking# (Actual Result)	Alternative
3 (3.714)	Path A
11 (10.143)	Path B
15 (14.001)	Path C
12 (13.000)	Path D
1 (2.714)	Path E
5 (5.571)	Path F
14 (14.000)	Path G
7 (7.714)	Path H
6 (6.857)	Path I
18 (16.429)	Path J
16 (15.142)	Path K
13 (13.428)	Path L
2 (3.713)	Path M
4 (4.142)	Path N
17 (15.285)	Path O
8 (7.715)	Path P
9 (9.286)	Path Q
10 (9.571)	Path R

Figure 7-19
Results of NGT Process
Data showing the actual result and its corresponding alternative.

Once Chris made these calculations, he compiled the results for the team to review (see Figure 7-19). When John saw the results, he grumbled, "That is the exact opposite of what I thought we should do. These exercises are ridiculous. Alternative B is okay, but there is no way we should do E—that has never worked for me in the past."

John's attitude is less than helpful. In addition to ego and pride, what other reasons might managers have for dismissing alternatives in the evaluation process? **Prior-hypothesis bias** is when a decision is made based on beliefs or assumptions despite evidence to the contrary—a process that sometimes happens unconsciously.[25] To prevent these decisions, which can perpetuate undesirable effects, managers can apply a third evaluation method called **dialectical inquiry**, in which a proposal and a conflicting counterproposal are given equal consideration.[26] Sensing that the conversation could become unproductive, given John's negative attitude, Chris applied this method and suggested he propose both alternatives to Kathy Osborne for her input. "Given the importance of these top two decisions, and the philosophical and cultural shifts required, I will sit down with Kathy and make these recommendations on the group's behalf and ask her for her insights." So what decisions did the group want to make?

7.5 | PATH SELECTION

7.5 | Demonstrate how managers select the most desirable alternative.

There are three kinds of decision making: *intuitive, optimum,* and *satisficing.* **Intuitive** (also known as, "gut") decisions are based on feelings, previous experience, and existing knowledge.[27] It is typical for managers to encounter situations where there is a limit to the amount of information, time, or resources available—good intuition can be an effective capacity for a manager to possess, but it can be a dangerous quality.[28] If managers rely too much on personal intuition, they risk alienating the team and making mistakes that could have easily been avoided. A traditional approach to decision making suggested that an optimum path was available for each situation. In reality, managers never have *all* the information needed to make the "best decision." Acknowledging that we live in an imperfect world, how do managers consistently make *better* decisions?

Successful managers consistently choose an acceptable solution, rather than the perceived "optimal solution"—a process called **satisficing**. This process balances time,

Prior-hypothesis bias Basing decisions on beliefs or assumptions despite evidence to the contrary.

Dialectical inquiry A method of decision making in which a proposal and a conflicting counterproposal are given equal consideration.

LECTURE ENHANCER:

7.5 Path Selection
• Three Kinds of Decision-Making
✓ Intuitive—decisions are based on feelings, previous experience, and existing knowledge; "gut"
✓ Optimum decision—the best possible decision given all the needed information

Intuitive decision A decision based on feelings, previous experience, and existing knowledge.

Satisficing Choosing an acceptable solution rather than an optimal solution.

information, and the team's ability to consider and implement alternatives.[29] The decisions that managers make are a product of the process models employed. Here, we will discuss two primary decision-making models used by managers. The classical model of decision making is a normative model that leads to an optimal decision, assuming full availability of information, sufficient time, and rationality of decision makers. This model presumes that a manager can make a **reasoned judgment**—a decision based on extensive information gathering, careful analysis, and generation of alternatives—which they can, to a limited degree.[30] The positive consequences of this model, obviously, are well-informed decisions. What are the potential negative outcomes of this model? Managers can become stuck in "analysis paralysis," which is jargon for spending too much time analyzing the problem and not selecting a path, or fool themselves into believing that a "right" path is available in a situation where only *satisficing* paths exist.

The **administrative model** of decision making recognizes the limits of information, time, and individuals and seeks a *satisficing* rather than an optimum solution.[31] By restraining the available time to "one year to produce results," Kathy has forced an administrative model of decision making, for no other reason than time. The Dolphin Resort team is in a state of **bounded rationality**, rational decision making that is limited by time, cognitive abilities, and available information. The negative consequences of this model obviously are not having enough time to gather and analyze information, resulting in making uninformed decisions. A common mistake under these circumstances is **representative bias**, which means generalizing from too small a sample size.[32] The benefits of the administrative model are that it encourages organizations to minimize production loss, be creative and flexible, and continuously change and improve. By seeking a series of small incremental improvements, managers establish change over time, giving all stakeholders time to adapt accordingly. So let's reconvene with Chris and his team to see what paths they are presenting to Kathy.

Kathy seemed more serious than during their previous meetings. "Well, Chris, you have made quite an impression during your brief time at the Dolphin!"

Chris nervously interjected, "I hope that is a good thing."

"Let's just say that it has been like the beginning of *A Tale of Two Cities* with all the calls I have been getting on a daily basis—the best of times; the worst of times. How can I help you today?"

Chris began, "The Dolphin Resort is an amazing property, with a terrific location and great potential. A fundamental change in management philosophy needs to occur before we can be successful here. Here are the top five paths that the team, with my full support, would like to present to you for approval:

- "Focus equally on employee satisfaction, guest satisfaction, owner return on investment, and the environment.
- "Make employee satisfaction our most important priority— Invest in capital improvements: complete a cosmetic renovation before the summer season—primarily painting, carpet, mattresses, linens, and HDTVs.
- "Raise occupancy by approaching the local time-share companies to see if they are interested in purchasing a fixed number of rooms at a lower daily rate. In general, lower the rates at the hotel. The team believes that with a great restaurant, upscale gift shop, and fun activities for the family, the hotel can make even more money. We might even set up a homemade ice cream cart by the pool and walkway to the beach."

"Here is the rationale: the operation was too focused on trying to increase revenue by cutting costs and increasing room rates. Previous management did not spend the resources necessary to continuously make capital improvements and chose not to focus on service quality. With the increased room rates and declining service quality, this created an 'expectation gap,' which had a negative effect on

Petros Tsonis / Shutterstock

✓ **Satisficing**—choosing an acceptable solution rather than an optimal solution

✓ **Reasoned judgment**—a decision based on extensive information

Reasoned judgment A decision based on extensive information gathering, careful analysis, and generation of alternatives.

Administrative model A model of decision making that recognizes the limits of information, time, and individuals and seeks a satisficing rather than an optimum solution.

Bounded rationality Rational decision making that is limited by time, cognitive abilities, and available information.

Representative bias Generalizing from too small a sample size.

gathering, careful analysis, and generation of alternatives
o *Analysis paralysis*—spending too much time analyzing the problem and not selecting a path
✓ **Administrative model**—recognizes the limits of information, time, and individuals and seeks a satisficing rather than optimal solution
✓ **Bounded rationality**—rational decision-making that is limited by time, cognitive abilities, and available information
✓ **Representative bias**—generalizing from too small a sample size

profitability. To systemically address these causes, the team believes the previously stated paths will close this gap and increase the resort's profitability. I would like your support."

After a long pause, Kathy spoke. "Chris, I have defended the decision to hire you on more than one occasion this past week. This is your first general manager position, and I hope you know what you are doing. You have my support, but fair warning—I think your biggest challenge is going to be 'employee satisfaction,' because there are quite a few unhappy people at The Dolphin Resort today."

LECTURE ENHANCER:

7.6 Implementation

✓ Illusion of Control—overestimating one's ability to control events and activities

7.6 | *IMPLEMENTATION*

7.6 | Describe the manager's role in implementing alternatives.

On the drive back to the Dolphin Resort, Chris began thinking about how to get his management team involved in the implementation of the selected alternative. How do managers effectively and efficiently implement a chosen alternative? Do managers need an emotional commitment from others, or should managers expect employees to perform because they are paid to do so?

Despite the positive outcome, Chris was a little disturbed by the meeting with Kathy. He appreciated her support, but he realized that there were probably more than a few managers and employees complaining about him, and he had been on the job less than a month. That could not leave a good impression on Kathy; she was obviously wondering if she had made the right choice in hiring Chris. As he walked back into the lobby, Chris took a deep breath and reminded himself that this was "not about him. And, if these decisions were going to be successful, he would need everyone's full commitment—even those who were against him at this moment. Slowly and surely, all **illusion of control** dissipated from Chris's mind—this is overestimating one's ability to control events and activities—and he thought about Kathy's final suggestion to focus on employee satisfaction.[33]

Managers succeed at implementation when they connect strategy, people, and operations.[34] In the planning section of this book, we thoroughly discuss how managers make decisions about goals, which lead to strategies that are well considered and doable. Having the "right people in the right positions" with well-crafted strategies contributes to employee engagement, and the more engaged people are at work, the better they perform.[35,36] The following sections, including *organizing*, *leading*, and *controlling*, outline management practices relating to people and operations. After Chris announced that Kathy supported the paths selected by the team, he recommended a course of action to secure the overall team's commitment and get all the staff refocused on service quality and growth.

Illusion of control Overestimating one's ability to control events and activities.

LECTURE ENHANCER:

7.7 Feedback and Results

➤ Figure 7-20: Dolphin Resort & Hotel: Process for Feedback & Measuring Results

➤ Figure 7-21: Behavior Over Time Graph for Weight Loss Variables

✓ Reinforcing engine—a system behavior indicative of growth coupled with an unintended consequence in another part of the system
  ➤ Figure 7-22: Systems Archetype—"Limits to Success"
  ➤ Figure 7-23: Delayed Behavior Over Time—"Limits to Success"

✓ Balancing Correction—a system behavior in which long-term problems are created through "short-term fixes"
  ➤ Figure 7-24: Systems Archetype—"Fixes that Fail"
  ➤ Figure 7-25: Delayed Behavior Over Time—"Fixes that Fail"

7.7 | *FEEDBACK AND RESULTS*

7.7 | Explain the patterns of behavior and delayed results for decisions made.

Things are getting done. The painters have arrived, new HDTVs are being installed, and each day a different section of the lobby is closed so the new carpet can be installed. The management and staff at the Dolphin Resort are starting to see results. Now that the team has initiated the implementation of the selected paths, how should the managers ensure that the implementation is yielding the expected results? How much time is reasonable before managers can expect to see results in the operation? What if the alternative paths selected do not effectively address the problem identified by management?

Gathering and analyzing feedback and results is the last step in the decision-making process, but as we have discussed, this process never ends—it is not a single event. What you learn from an honest evaluation of feedback and results tells you if you've actually solved the original problem or created or discovered new ones, and it also suggests ways for continued improvement. To do so, managers must establish clear feedback criteria, gather feedback

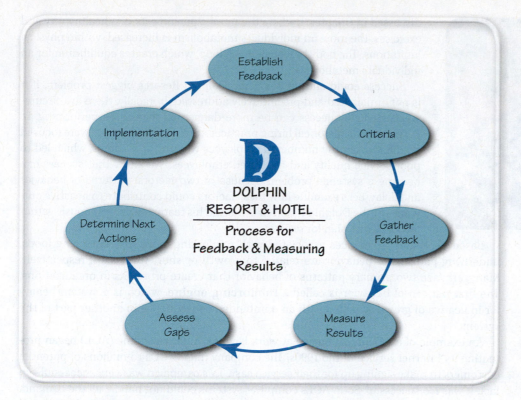

Figure 7-20
Dolphin Resort & Hotel: Process for Feedback & Measuring Results
The process of gathering feedback and analyzing results.

on an ongoing basis, measure the results, assess gaps in expected outcomes, and determine next actions—and then reinitiate implementation and begin the process all over again as outlined in Figure 7-20. Managers who do not consistently gather and evaluate feedback often repeat the same mistakes.[37]

In systems thinking analysis, managers track patterns of behavior associated with variables and understand that there is a delay in altering behavior after decisions have been made. To explain these phenomena, we will revisit the case of a person's weight-loss efforts. Let's say that a person makes a New Year's resolution to eat healthy and to exercise (behaviors associated with the cause), in order to lose 50 pounds (symptomatic effect). When would this person realistically expect to lose 50 pounds? It might take a full year. There is a delay associated with the behaviors of dieting and exercising, and how they change a person's metabolism. In Figure 7-21, we show a person starting an exercise routine one day and consistently maintaining that over time. In addition, this person gradually decreases his caloric intake over time and maintains this intake at a desirable level. We show that this person's weight does not dramatically decrease right away; instead, it decreases over time and then finds equilibrium. This is another example of a reinforcing loop, which we

Figure 7-21
Behavior over Time Graph for Weight-Loss Variables
The effect of weight-loss variables over time.

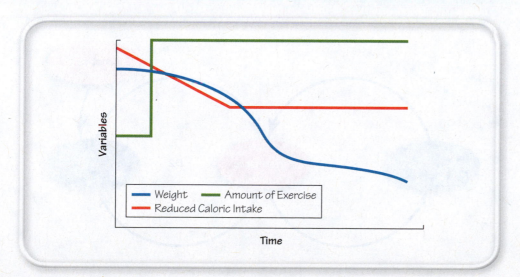

discussed in Chapter 3, where the more a person eats in a healthy way and exercises, the more an individual's metabolism is increased, within physical limitations. The body has a balancing loop, which creates equilibrium for an individual's metabolism.

Success could end up being the Dolphin Resort's biggest problem, if it is not anticipated and preemptively addressed. Ironically, there are circumstances where success can be more dangerous than underperforming. In particular, the historical hiring practices at the Dolphin Resort were focused on minimizing the number of employees working at all times, which led to poor service quality and frustrated employees. We know that success can become a systemic problem because of two factors: patterns of behavior and delay. Let's examine how these factors could contribute to negative outcomes at the Dolphin Resort, if Chris and his team don't continuously gather feedback and plan for results.

Based on the consequences associated with reinforcing loops and balancing loops, underlying patterns of behavior are related to growth or short-term fixes, respectively. Managers face two primary patterns of behavior that create problems in organizations. The first pattern of behavior is called a **reinforcing engine**, which is a system behavior indicative of growth coupled with an unintended consequence in another part of the system.

An example of a reinforcing engine at work is when America Online (AOL) began promoting its Internet service in the 1990s. The company mailed CDs to millions of potential customers to make signing up for their service easy. This campaign was very successful—in fact, it was *too* successful. Soon AOL's computer systems could not handle all the demand, causing new and existing clients to abandon the service. The lesson? Too much of a good thing can be very bad indeed. A possible delayed result is something that Chris and his team need to pay attention to. By lowering rates and raising service quality (efforts), they should expect to increase occupancy dramatically (performance). Without commensurately expanding their service capacity (limiting action and constraint), the Dolphin Resort management team could find themselves in the same negative situation as AOL. This example of a reinforcing engine is based on the systems thinking archetype referred to as "Limits to Success," shown in Figure 7-22.

We can also review this behavioral dynamic in the same way as our earlier "delayed behavior" weight-loss example. In Figure 7-23, we show an example of a hotel that increases service quality and lowers rates, resulting in a greater number of reservations. Here, we show what happens when management fails to expand the operation's capacity to serve the new guests and accommodate the greater occupancy, which leads to declining service quality and reservations—they are all interconnected, yet the effects happen at different times. This pattern of behavior shows us that the Dolphin Resort will need a well-trained staff before it sees an increase in revenue and reservations.

> **Reinforcing engine** A system behavior indicative of growth coupled with an unintended consequence in another part of the system.

Figure 7-22
Systems Archetype—"Limits to Success"
B, balancing loop; R, reinforcing loop.

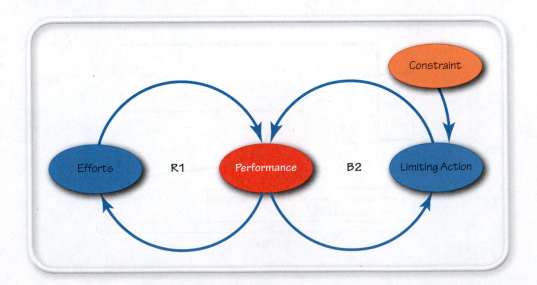

Figure 7-23
Delayed Behavior over
Time—"Limits to Success"

The second pattern of behavior that creates problems in organizations is called a **balancing correction** which is a system behavior in which long-term problems are created through short-term fixes. Let's say that a manufacturing facility has quality problems associated with a complex packaging process (see the B1 section of Figure 7-24). To solve the problem, senior managers continuously ask outside consultants to intervene and provide solutions for the undesirable symptoms that periodically arise. Over time, the line-level managers are not being trained to assess the underlying causes effectively, and they feel like their authority is being undermined. This results in line-level managers and talented employees quitting the company, which compounds the long-term quality issues that the company faces (see the R2 section of Figure 7-24). This example of a balancing correction is based on the systems thinking archetype referred to as "Fixes That Fail."

The Dolphin Resort could also experience the balancing correction pattern of behavior, where a manager applies a short-term fix with long-term unintended consequences. Let's say that Chris applied a short-term fix to the symptom of quality scores by mandating that managers personally address each guest complaint. This might improve service quality in the short term, but the hotel would be at serious risk of losing some of its most talented service staff as they might be frustrated because their days were being occupied with tasks far below their level of expertise and experience, rather than more important matters. In addition, new hotel employees would not have the opportunity to gain the valuable experience associated with serving guests through challenging situations. Over time, this would produce a negative and predictable pattern of behavior, resulting in greater employee turnover and decreased satisfaction, as shown in Figure 7-25.

Balancing correction A system behavior in which long-term problems are created through short-term fixes.

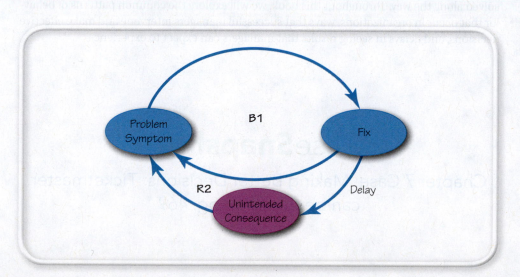

Figure 7-24
Systems Archetype—"Fixes That Fail"
B, balancing loop; R, reinforcing loop.

Figure 7-25
Delayed Behavior over Time—
"Fixes That Fail"

How might these two common types of behavior patterns enable management to identify systemic problems? Both of these patterns of behavior explain a real problem that Chris and his management team might face—service capacity, where growth in occupancy is overtaking the service staff's ability to handle it. Within a couple of months of implementing lower rates, capital improvements and renovations, service training, and a renewed focus on employee satisfaction, both quality scores and reservations at the Dolphin Resort dramatically increased, but the financial results had yet to be realized.

As we discussed earlier in the chapter, managers are at particularly high risk for prior-hypothesis bias when the information they need to make a decision is ambiguous. In such situations, it is very easy for a manager to focus unconsciously on those pieces of information that confirm their prior beliefs—for instance, managers not in full support of a decision may begin resisting the change, claiming that the "old way of doing things" produced better results. The Dolphin Resort team will need the discipline to avoid short-term fixes that could also create a service capacity problem through unwanted employee turnover and engagement problems.

These effective managers see systematic behavior and can predict the consequences and patterns of behavior of their decisions. Not being able to analyze problems systemically can lead to unintended consequences, which we will continue to explore with Chris and his management team. This raises a new set of questions for us to explore. What were the goals and strategies that led to the situation at the Dolphin Resort? How do these factors affect the problems and challenges that managers face? In the next two chapters, we will explore how Chris and the management team established the company's goals and the strategies that led to their success, but not without encountering a series of problems that need to be solved along the way. Throughout this book, we will explore the common patterns of behavior that occur in organizations, ways that successful managers intervene and make effective decisions, and delays in seeing results that managers can expect to experience.

Case**Snapshot**

Chapter 7 Case: Making Better Decisions: Ticketmaster
can be found on pg. 469

ADDITIONAL RESOURCES

KEY TERMS

Adaptive management An approach to decision making that requires managers to use critical thinking, collaboration, and reflection skills to make nonprogrammed decisions. (p.173)

Administrative model A model of decision making that recognizes the limits of information, time, and individuals and seeks a satisficing rather than an optimum solution. (p.187)

Ambiguity Information about the situation, goals, or criteria that is incomplete or can be interpreted in multiple ways. (p.174)

Balancing correction A system behavior in which long-term problems are created through short-term fixes. (p.191)

Bounded rationality Rational decision making that is limited by time, cognitive abilities, and available information. (p.187)

Brainstorming Creating as many alternatives as possible, without making value judgments about any idea. (p.183)

Certainty A situation in which a decision maker knows all the alternatives and their outcomes. (p.182)

Classical model A normative model of decision making that leads to an optimal decision, assuming full availability of information, sufficient time, and rationality of the decision maker. (p.172)

Delphi technique A method of decision making in which a group of experts propose and question ideas until a consensus is reached. (p.184)

Dialectical inquiry A method of decision making in which a proposal and a conflicting counterproposal are given equal consideration. (p.186)

Groupthink A usually unconscious mode of group decision making in which individuals prioritize agreement over analysis. (p.182)

Heuristics A set of informal rules used to simplify and expedite the decision-making process. (p.182)

Illusion of control Overestimating one's ability to control events and activities. (p.188)

Intuitive decision A decision based on feelings, previous experience, and existing knowledge. (p.186)

Nominal group technique (NGT) A group decision-making process in which individuals rate proposed solutions and the total tally determines the final decision. (p.184)

Nonprogrammed decision A decision based on reason and/or intuition in response to a unique situation that requires a tailored decision. (p.172)

Optimum decision The best possible decision given all the needed information. (p.172)

Policy-based analysis A method of problem analysis that isolates the variables in a system that can truly be addressed through management intervention (p.179)

Prior-hypothesis bias Basing decisions on beliefs or assumptions despite evidence to the contrary. (p.186)

Production blocking A loss in productivity during a brainstorming session because individuals are overwhelmed by the number of possibilities being generated. (p.182)

Programmed decision A decision based on preestablished rules in response to a recurring situation. (p.172)

Reasoned judgment A decision based on extensive information gathering, careful analysis, and generation of alternatives. (p.187)

Reinforcing engine A system behavior indicative of growth coupled with an unintended consequence in another part of the system. (p.190)

Representative bias Generalizing from too small a sample size. (p.187)

Risk The degree to which the outcomes of an alternative can be predicted. (p.184)

Satisficing Choosing an acceptable solution rather than an optimal solution. (p.186)

Symptomatic effects Observable behaviors related to underlying causal variables. (p.175)

Systemic-based analysis A method of analyzing a problem that takes into account the array of all known variables associated with a problem and its symptoms, including behavior over time. (p.175)

Uncertainty A situation in which a decision maker does not know all the alternatives and their outcomes. (p.182)

Underlying causes The behaviors that lead to a desired or undesired symptomatic effect (p.175)

IN REVIEW

7.1 | Describe the seven steps of the decision-making process.

There are two types of decisions that managers make: programmed and nonprogrammed. *Programmed decisions* are based on preestablished rules in response to a recurring situation, and *nonprogrammed decisions* are based on reason and/or intuition in response to a unique situation that requires tailored actions. There is a recommended seven-step process to make better decisions as a manager: 1) identify the problem, 2) analyze the problem and its causes, 3) generate alternatives, 4) evaluate alternatives, 5) choose a path, 6) implement a choice, 7) solicit feedback and analyze results.

7.2 | Identify problems by analyzing causes and effects.

Managers effectively understand problems based on four steps: 1) observe undesirable symptoms, 2) acknowledge all primary causes that could create undesirable symptomatic effects, 3) qualify the systemic problem based on causes and effects, and 4) identify root problems with controllable behaviors that can be readily addressed.

There are two ways of understanding and analyzing underlying causes: systemic and policy-based. *Systemic-based analysis* takes into account the array of all known variables associated with a problem and its symptoms, taking into account behavior over time. Managers use causal loop diagrams and systems archetypes to better understand the behavior of variables. To focus managers on productive decision-making activities, *policy-based analysis* isolates the variables in a system that can truly be addressed through management intervention. Managers use stock-and-flow diagrams to better understand policy-based decisions.

7.3 | Describe how managers generate alternatives.

In generating alternative paths to address identified problems, managers should be aware of the negative effects caused by production blocking and groupthink. Yet, when managers don't generate and evaluate alternatives, they often end up making poor decisions. In our scenario, the Dolphin Resort & Hotel management team started with a brainstorming session, creating as many alternatives as possible without making value judgments about any idea.

7.4 | Predict possible consequences of alternatives.

There are two methods for evaluating alternatives. In *nominal group technique (NGT)*, individuals rate proposed solutions and the total tally determines the final decision. This means that everyone's opinions are taken into account, rather than the usual "majority rules" technique which is usually applied to voting. The second method, called the *Delphi technique*, is a method of decision making in which a group of experts propose and question ideas until a consensus is reached. The case team decided to conduct their evaluation of alternatives using the NGT method, where alternatives were individually ranked, tallied, and collectively ranked by a simple calculation.

Sensing some resistance, the general manager must reconcile what other reasons might managers have for dismissing alternatives in the evaluation process. To prevent these decisions, where negative behaviors can perpetuate, managers can apply a third evaluation method called *dialectical inquiry*, in which a proposal and a conflicting counterproposal are given equal consideration.

7.5 | Demonstrate how managers select the most desirable alternative.

There are three ways to select a path: intuitive, optimum, and satisficing. An *intuitive* decision is based on previous experience, feelings, and previous knowledge. An *optimum* decision is the best possible decision given all the needed information. Successful managers consistently adhere to a process in order to choose an acceptable solution, rather than the perceived "optimal solution"—this is called *satisficing*. In reality, managers never have all the needed information to make the "best decision." This process balances time, information, and the ability of the team to consider and implement alternatives.

The decisions that managers make are a product of the process models employed. The two primary decision-making models used by managers include the *classical model* of decision making, which leads to an optimal decision, and the *administrative model* of decision making, which seeks a satisficing rather than an optimal solution.

7.6 | Describe the manager's role in implementing an intervening decision.

Managers succeed at implementation when they connect strategy, people, and operations. They make decisions about goals, resulting in carefully considered and achievable strategies. This must be supported by placing the right people in the right jobs and getting them engaged to enhance their performance.

7.7 | Explain the patterns of behavior and delayed results for decisions made.

Gathering and analyzing feedback and results is the last step in the decision-making process; this process never ends—it is not a single event. What you learn from an honest evaluation of feedback and results tells you if you've actually solved the original problem or created or discovered new ones, and it also suggests ways for continued improvement. Managers must establish clear feedback criteria, gather feedback on an ongoing basis, measure the results, assess gaps in expected outcomes, and determine next actions—and then reinitiate implementation and begin again. Managers that do not consistently gather and evaluate feedback typically repeat the same mistakes.

Managers face two primary patterns of behavior that create problems in organizations. Based on the consequences associated with reinforcing loops and balancing loops, underlying patterns of behavior are related to growth or short-term fixes, respectively. First, a *reinforcing engine* is a system behavior indicative of growth coupled with an unintended consequence in another part of the system. Next, a *balancing correction* is a system behavior in which long-term problems are created through "short-term fixes."

SELF-TEST

7.1 | **Describe** the seven steps of the decision-making process.

1. The typical type of decision for managers to make is a *programmed decision.*
   a. True
   b. False

2. Which of the following statements best describes decision making?
   a. Decision making is more science than art.
   b. Decision making focuses on a specific outcome.
   c. Managers make optimum decisions through a detailed, thorough analysis of all data.
   d. Decision making is a process, not an event.
   e. None of the above

3. Diagram the seven steps of decision making.

7.2 | **Identify** problems by analyzing causes and effects.

4. Contrast the differences between systemic analysis and policy-based analysis.

5. As described in the chapter, what would be a common example of a "root cause" of a problem?
   a. Customer retention
   b. Body metabolism
   c. Feedback response rate
   d. Prior hypothesis
   e. None of the above

6. For the following systems archetype diagram, what negative behavior effect would a manager expect?

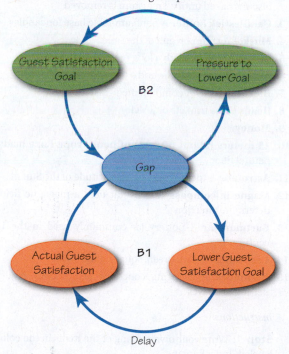

a. Employee turnover
b. Declining guest satisfaction
c. Guest expectation gap
d. Employee satisfaction
e. All of the above

7. Summarize the two primary causal factors of the "guest expectation gap" and the negative consequences that the Dolphin Resort and Hotel experienced because of this gap.

8. Explain why the Dolphin Resort and Hotel experienced a decline in guest satisfaction.

7.3 | **Describe** how managers generate alternatives.

9. Which of the following describes an important component of brainstorming?
   a. An answer to a question is needed quickly.
   b. Lots of ideas are generated, without judgment of merit.
   c. Group consensus is needed.
   d. All of the above

10. Groupthink is the ability for a team to synthesize their thoughts into a more effective alternative path.
    a. True
    b. False

7.4 | **Predict** possible consequences of alternatives.

11. Ranking feedback results is a critical step when applying the Delphi technique.
    a. True
    b. False

12. Choose the situation where a dialectical inquiry would be most effective.
    a. A team cannot decide between two choices.
    b. A manager seeks to understand two positions.
    c. A manager asks questions of team members to anticipate consequences.
    d. None of the above.

13. Describe the three major steps that managers use when they apply the nominal group technique (NGT).

7.5 | **Demonstrate** how managers select the most desirable alternative.

14. Which of the following situations best explains when managers make optimum decisions?
    a. When a thorough process of analysis has been conducted.
    b. As a result of systems-based computer models.
    c. It is not possible to make an optimum decision.
    d. None of the above

15. Defend which model of decision making is best suited for a longstanding, multinational corporation: classical model or administrative model.

16. Argue Chris Heppler's rationale for proposing the five alternative paths for Kathy's approval.

7.6 | Describe the manager's role in implementing an intervening decision.

17. Which of the three following factors should managers connect to successfully implement a selected path?
    a. People, profit, planet
    b. Resources, strategy, goals
    c. Strategy, people, operations
    d. Leading, organizing, controlling

7.7 | Explain the patterns of behavior and delayed results for decisions made.

18. Reconstruct a process for feedback and measuring results.

19. Compare and contrast the two primary patterns of behavior that create problems in organizations.

20. Summarize the relevance of the following behavior over time graph.

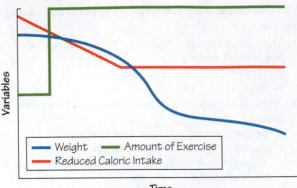

CHAPTER EXERCISE

Individual vs. Group Decision Making: Jamestown 1607*

You are a passenger on one of the three small, English sailing ships captained by Christopher Newport in the spring of 1607. You are approaching the coast of Virginia after a long, wintry voyage across the Atlantic Ocean.

After reaching the coast, you explore up and down the James River in a shallop, or small boat. You had been directed by the Virginia Company of London to find "the true, most wholesome and fertile place" to settle. Finally, you pick the site of Jamestown because it appears defensible, has a deep harbor close to shore, and is covered with walnut, beech, oak, and hickory trees. On May 13, 1607, you are one of 104 weary people to step off the cramped quarters of the three ships onto the swampy lowland. Fear of a massive attack by the Powhatan Indians makes the immediate construction of James Fort more important than building structures for housing. Soon, a triangular wooden wall, or palisade, is built to protect you and the other settlers against future attacks. By the end of June, when Captain Newport returns to England for new supplies, your settlement seems to be well established.

Suddenly, conditions in Jamestown change. Supplies begin to run low and food is spoiling. The weather is turning hot and conditions are very dry. Little or no rain has fallen in weeks, no wells have been dug, and you are forced to drink water from the swamps or river. This water not only carries diseases but is brackish, containing about five times the normal salt that a person should consume. As conditions worsen, men are dying daily. By autumn, disease reduces the number of survivors to fewer than 60. Imagine that you are one of these survivors. You must make some hard decisions in order to survive. Like all living things, you must have food, shelter, and water. You are challenged to choose items that will help you survive. Below you will find a list of 15 items that may have been used in Jamestown during this time. Some of the artifacts have been found in recent archaeological digs. Rank these items from 1 to 15 according to their importance to you and the other settlers. Beside each choice, explain why you gave each item the rank it received and how you plan to use the item to help you survive. Once you've made your own choices, work with your team of settlers to come to consensus. It is a desperate time, and everyone living in Jamestown must agree, not only about the value of these items, but about how to use them as well.

Items that may help you survive in Jamestown:

1. **Flint and striker** A hard gray stone (flint) and a small piece of steel (striker)
2. **Salted pork and hard tack** Meat preserved by salting, and biscuits baked until all moisture is removed
3. **Candlestick holder** A nonflammable base for candles
4. **Musket** A common gun of the time
5. **Sword** A weapon with a long metal blade
6. **Ax** A tool with a handle and a heavy sharp blade
7. **Bleeding bowl** A common medical item
8. **Beads** Glass trinkets or jewelry
9. **Money**
10. **15 meters (about 50 feet) of hemp rope** Rope made of natural fiber
11. **Astrolabe** A tool to measure the altitude of the Sun
12. **Magnetic compass** A tool that uses a magnetic field to determine direction
13. **Bartman jar** A pottery jar commonly used in the 17th century
14. **Case bottle** A dark-green, square, glass bottle
15. **Hammock** A swinging couch or bed, usually made of netting or canvas

Instructions:

Step 1: Write your own ranking of the items in the column labeled "Indiv Ranking."

Step 2: Write your team's ranking of the items in the column labeled "Team Ranking."

Step 3: Write the expert's ranking (provided by your instructor) of the items in the column labeled "Expert Ranking."

Step 4: Calculate the absolute value difference between your individual ranking and the expert's ranking and write that number in the column labeled "Difference Ranking [1–3]."

Step 5: Calculate the absolute value difference between your team ranking and the expert's ranking and write that number in the column labeled "Difference Ranking [2–3]."

*Adapted from an exercise available at http://www.nasa.gov/pdf/166504main_Survival.pdf

Items	Step 1 Indiv Ranking	Step 2 Team Ranking	Step 3 Expert Ranking	Step 4 Difference Ranking [1–3]	Step 5 Difference Ranking [2–3]
Flint and striker					
Salted pork and hard tack					
Candlestick holder					
Musket					
Sword					
Ax					
Bleeding bowl					
Beads					
Money					
15 meters (about 50 feet) of hemp rope					
Astrolabe					
Magnetic compass					
Bartman jar					
Case bottle					
Hammock					
Total the absolute differences of Steps 4 and 5 → (the lower the score, the better)				Your Score	Team Score

Did you score higher as an individual or as a team? Why?

What are some of the advantages of individual decision making?

What are some of the advantages of team decision making?

SELF-ASSESSMENT

Decision-Making Style*

For each statement, circle the number that best describes you based on the following scale:

Not at all Accurate	Somewhat Accurate	A little Accurate	Mostly Accurate	Completely Accurate
1	2	3	4	5

1. I make decisions in a logical and systematic way.

   1   2   3   4   5

2. When making decisions, I rely upon my instincts.

   1   2   3   4   5

3. I often need the assistance of other people when making important decisions.

   1   2   3   4   5

4. I avoid important decisions until the pressure is on.

   1   2   3   4   5

5. I generally make snap decisions.

   1   2   3   4   5

6. My decision making requires careful thought.

   1   2   3   4   5

7. I generally make decisions that feel right to me.

   1   2   3   4   5

8. I rarely make important decisions without consulting other people.

   1   2   3   4   5

9. I postpone decision making whenever possible.

    1   2   3   4   5

10. I often make decisions on the spur of the moment.

    1   2   3   4   5

11. When making decisions, I consider various options in terms of a specific goal.

    1   2   3   4   5

12. When I make decisions, I trust my inner feelings and reactions.

    1   2   3   4   5

13. I use the advice of other people when making decisions.

    1   2   3   4   5

14. I generally make important decisions at the last minute.

    1   2   3   4   5

15. I make quick decisions.

    1   2   3   4   5

Scoring:

Rational Style (add items 1, 6, and 11 and write your score in the blank) _____
The extent to which you search for and logically evaluate alternatives

Intuitive Style (add items 2, 7, and 12 and write your score in the blank) _____
The extent to which you rely on hunches and feelings

Dependent Style (add items 3, 8, and 13 and write your score in the blank) _____
The extent to which you search for advice and direction from others

Avoidant Style (add items 4, 9, and 14 and write your score in the blank) _____
The extent to which you attempt to avoid decision making

Spontaneous Style (add items 5, 10, and 15 and write score in the blank) _____
The extent to which you make decisions quickly

What was your strongest decision-making style? What are the advantages and disadvantages of this style?

What was your weakest decision-making style? What are the advantages and disadvantages of this style?

*Adapted from Susanne G. Scott and Reginald A. Bruce. "Decision-making style: The development and assessment of a new measure," *Educational & Psychological Measurement* 55, no. 5 (October 1995): 818.

SELF-TEST ANSWER KEY

1. b. False.

2. d.

3.

Decision-Making Process: Identify the Problem → Analyze the Problem and its Causes → Generate Alternatives → Evaluate Alternatives → Choose Path → Implement Choice → Solicit and Analyze Feedback and Results →

4. Systemic-based analysis accounts for all the known variables and causes related to a problem, where policy-based analysis focuses only on the relevant variables that are controllable.

5. b.

6. b.

7. The primary causal factors are price and quality—the higher the price, the higher the guest will expect the quality to be. When this gap between high price and lower quality increased, the Dolphin Resort and Hotel's occupancy percentage.

8. Management gradually decreased the guest satisfaction goal, which allowed the actual satisfaction to decline unnoticed over time.

9. b.

10. b; False.

11. b; False.

12. a.

13. 1) Individuals rank paths, 2) all individual ranking averaged, 3) the average rankings are then organized into a group ranking.

14. d.

15. The administrative model for decision making is the understood preferred model for modern corporations because it recognizes the limitations of known variables, yet seeks to apply a reliable process consistently.

16. Here is the rationale: the operation was too focused on trying to increase revenue by cutting costs and increasing room rates. Previous management did not spend the resources necessary to make capital improvements continuously and chose not to focus on service quality. With the increased room rates and declining service quality, this created an "expectation gap" that had a negative effect on profitability. To systemically address these causes, the team believes the previously stated paths will close this gap and increase the resort's profitability.

17. c.

18.

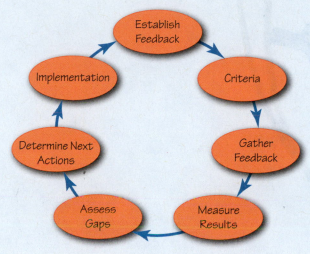

19. First, a *reinforcing engine* is a system behavior indicative of growth coupled with an unintended consequence in another part of the system. Next, a *balancing correction* is a system behavior in which long-term problems are created through short-term fixes. These two patterns are different because a *reinforcing engine* is based on exponential growth or decay behavior that has natural limits, and a *balancing correction* is based on behavior that homes into equilibrium. Each of these patterns is similar in that unintended consequences are delayed.

20. When a person changes his or her exercise and dieting behaviors, a delay exists before results are experienced with regard to weight loss or gain.

Notes

CHAPTER EIGHT

SETTING GOALS

Learning Objectives

By the end of this chapter, you will be able to:

8.1 | Describe the primary goals of an organization.

8.2 | Explain the principles and different types of goal plans in an organization.

8.3 | Outline different types of goals and the characteristics that make them effective.

8.4 | Illustrate how managers secure team-level commitment to goals.

8.5 | Construct action plans consistent with goals to achieve individual-level performance.

8.6 | Describe how managers track progress of goal plans through performance dashboards.

ADDITIONAL RESOURCES

KEY TERMS
IN REVIEW
SELF-TEST
CHAPTER EXERCISE
SELF-ASSESSMENT
SELF-TEST
ANSWER KEY

JP Greenwood/Getty Images

INSIDE THIS CHAPTER

ManagementStory:
Featuring **Chris Heppler**

201

8.1 | SETTING GOALS THAT MAKE A DIFFERENCE

8.1 | Describe the primary goals of an organization.

Setting goals is an essential part of achieving personal and professional success. Yet no goal will succeed without individual or organizational support. This means that managers must believe in what the company is doing and where it is going in order to cement its success. Goals must be set within a strategic framework consisting of mission, vision, and values.

So, why are goals so important? They give us direction, a sense of purpose and achievement, reinforce our beliefs, the ability to reach our full potential, and boost our self-esteem. Yet, like the art of decision making, goal setting is a balancing act. If we set the goal too high, we can fail; if it's too low, we don't achieve the same personal fulfilment. For example, if you set a goal to be fluent in French within a month, this is unlikely to happen, even if you have the greatest gift for languages. However, if you set a more realistic time frame, gather all the resources you will need, remain focused, and practice regularly, it is entirely possible that you will be able to achieve fluency within a reasonable period of time.

The theory of goal setting is arguably one of the most researched topics in management.[1] Hundreds of studies across many countries have taken place in order to examine the effects of goal setting on behavior and motivation. Setting goals is a relatively new concept. Frederick W. Taylor, who we met in Chapter 2, first developed the theory of Scientific Management in the early twentieth century. By studying productivity and performance of the workers through time and motion, Taylor defined the first real goal-setting ideal: encouraging managers to specify tasks, outline the details of the job to the workers, and explain exactly how the task was to be achieved. As a result of this enhanced communication between managers and workers, productivity rose and men began to work more efficiently. However, as we know now, Taylor's plan had its own imperfections, and it caused much controversy at the time.

Indeed, the theory of goal setting has come under much scrutiny ever since. The main debate focuses on "what really motivates people." You might think the answer is obvious: Money! Yet, researchers have found that money alone is not enough to drive employees to achieve high performance. For example, as we discussed in Chapter 7, Chris Heppler, the general manager, found that although the Dolphin Resort & Hotel's performance was tied to the staff annual bonus, the team wasn't particularly motivated to work toward helping save the hotel from potential bankruptcy.

As we explored in Chapter 1, values, mission, and vision shape the beliefs of an organization and its culture. A strong,

Todd Anderson/Disney/ABC/Getty Images Inc

powerful mission statement will be assimilated into the company culture, so that each employee is committed to putting the mission into action in order to ensure the success of the organization. For example, Disney's mission statement is "We create happiness by providing the finest in entertainment for people of all ages, everywhere." [2]

Yet, as we have learned, no mission is complete without a clear vision and strong values. Every company must have a vision of what the organization wants to become in the future. An effective vision inspires and excites employees and makes them feel proud to work for a company. Many organizations translate their vision into a vision statement. For example, Westin Hotel's vision statement is: "Year after year, Westin and its people will be regarded as the best and most sought-after hotel and resort management group in North America." [3]

Managers setting goals must follow the organization's mission, have a clear vision of what they want to achieve, and ensure that the team embraces the core values of what the organization represents. Fostering a strong corporate culture within this framework is the first step toward goal success.

In the previous chapter, we explored the concept of decision making and how managers work through complex situations by using different decision-making models, processes, and systemic-based analysis in order to arrive at a solution they feel is best for the organization. Through a series of decision-making and systemic-based strategies with the hotel staff, Chris identified the areas that he needed to improve in order to achieve the task set for him by Kathy Osborne, the hotel owner. By employing the group decision-making process, Chris and the hotel team produced a number of actions that they believed would help enhance the hotel's dwindling financial performance. With the support of Osborne, as well as the rest of the staff, Chris began to implement those decisions by beginning the refurbishment of the property and focusing on ways to increase employee satisfaction and guest satisfaction.

In this chapter, we will continue to follow Chris's journey in carrying out his assigned goal to save the declining Hilton Head Dolphin Resort & Hotel by increasing its profit by $500,000 for the following year. In order to meet this challenge, Chris must devise a goal plan with his management team, secure staff commitment to the specified goals, construct an action plan in line with them, and track its progress.

As Chris knows, making decisions is just the first step. After a decision has been made and clearly defined, the information has been gathered and analyzed, and the best course of action has been agreed upon, it is time to start the goal-setting process.

In order to get the ball rolling, Chris decides to have one-to-one meetings with each of the staff to assess their commitment to the hotel. He begins with John Johnson, the hotel's food and beverage director (as well as the biggest dissenter to date). Johnson has already made his feelings about his new manager abundantly clear by disagreeing with his decision-making approaches and questioning Chris's judgments and managerial abilities. Chris knows that in order for a goal to succeed, the whole team must be fully committed to it. One weak link in the chain of commitment could set off a series of catastrophic events that would ensure the potential failure of the goal. Chris needs to make sure that John's attitude does not impede the progress at the hotel.

In preparation for the meeting, Chris asks for John's previous year's goal plans for review. As the hotel's food and beverage director, John is responsible for the operation of the hotel restaurant, recruiting and monitoring kitchen and restaurant staff, controlling inventory, and managing revenues and expenses. In line with the attitude of the previous general manager, Herb Cork, John believes that making financial savings is the most important goal. Stating that he "runs a tight ship," John tells Chris that his management of the bottom line profit is second-to-none, which he is certain is "great for the industry."

Chris then suggests that John bring him five departmental goals, excluding John's apparently sole goal of focusing on the numbers. The following day, John enters the meeting room, looking pretty confident. He hands Chris a hastily scribbled piece of paper and sits down, reclining in his chair. Chris reads John's following five goals:

1. To increase the RevPAR (revenue per available room) from $100 to $150 per night
2. Close the restaurant when the hotel has only a few guests
3. Reduce hours of the kitchen staff to save on wages.
4. Shut down hotel altogether outside the summer months
5. No outside involvement; the hotel has been running fine to date and doesn't need outside interference

When Chris finishes reading John's goals, he tries not to let his heart sink too much. It is clear that John has not taken on board any of the new ideas that Chris and the team came up with during the decision-making process. Instead, he has ignored Chris's decisions to focus on service quality and employee satisfaction, as well as investing in refurbishment and considering other partnerships. Furthermore, it is obvious that John is still highly unappreciative of Chris's "outside interference." In fact, most of the goals aren't even related to his own department! Still, he tries not to take John's criticisms personally and rereads his goals once more to see if he can salvage any of his ideas and make at least one of them "S.M.A.R.T."

So, what is a S.M.A.R.T. goal? (See the "S.M.A.R.T. Goals" box to find out.) Popularly, goal setting has been defined as the establishment of *specific, measurable, achievable, relevant* and *time-bound* goals, also known as **S.M.A.R.T goals**.

S.M.A.R.T goals Goals that are specific, measurable, achievable, relevant, and time-bound.

So, let's take John's first goal: "To increase the RevPAR from $100 to $150 per night." Aside from the fact that Chris and the team had agreed that charging guests more for less quality was one of the major pitfalls of the hotel, is there a way for Chris to make John's goal S.M.A.R.T.?

Chris decides to work through John's goal with him, using the S.M.A.R.T. technique. He explains to John that his goal needs to be *specific*. Without wanting to step on his toes too much, Chris suggests that perhaps John should focus on how his own department could contribute toward achieving the goal and how he himself and his staff could participate in the process.

Chris starts by bringing John through some areas of improvement in his department. For example, John, who is in charge of inventory has a habit of ordering more sodas as soon as the inventory declines to a predetermined level, which led to over-ordering and unnecessary expenditure. John, visibly bristling, tells Chris, "I don't see the problem with that—better to have more than run out altogether." Chris explains that there was simply too much soda in stock, and a large majority of it had expired. John says nothing, so Chris goes on to explain how with further analysis of soda consumption, John could easily correct this problem and order enough to cater for the needs of the guests without running out or losing money.

Then Chris asks John if he had any other ideas about how his department could help improve customer service. "Well, as I recall, you said something about baking cookies to welcome guests, but personally I think that's a waste of time and money. I mean, who gives away

CT S.M.A.R.T. Goals

Applying**Critical**Thinking

Specific: Goals need to be specific in order to help you focus on the task at hand. Clearly defined goals help you to decide what to do, why it is important, how it is going to be achieved, and what the result should be.

Measurable: How can you measure a goal if you don't manage it? If you don't set milestones along the way, you will never know if employees are fulfilling their responsibilities in working toward achieving the goal. Conversely, the team will experience uncertainty about their own performance and lose motivation if they have no way of knowing the extent of their progress.

Achievable: Goals must be realistic and attainable. There is no point to setting goals that are too far out of reach or too high above standard performance. A good manager will assess the capability of his employees and set goals that cater to their skills, and perhaps even stretch them a bit, in order to accomplish the objective.

Relevant: Goals must be in line with the company's vision, mission, and values in order to succeed. Employees need to be made aware of their part in contributing to the overall strategy and objectives of the organization. A relevant goal will encourage employees to work toward the goal but not push themselves to the breaking point.

Time-bound: The crucial question to consider here is: When? Setting a time frame for the goal gives employees a firm target to work toward. If the goal is several months or even a year in the future, milestones must be set along the way to assess performance and allow room for feedback. Goals that are not "set in stone" tend to be neglected, as the team has no sense of urgency to complete them.

Critical Thinking in the Classroom: What do you think is the value of S.M.A.R.T. goals within an organization, and how would you apply them as a manager?

free cookies these days?" Patiently, Chris takes John through the concept of customer loyalty and guest expectations, and how making a guest feel valued was a sure-fire way to secure a repeat visit, as well as generating positive word-of-mouth.

"O.K., fine," John says. "But how am I going to get my kitchen staff to bake cookies? There is such a high turnover of staff; I don't know who does what at this stage." Chris replies, "I understand there is a problem with the lack of permanent staff, but we are in the process of addressing that. However, for a goal to succeed, it has to be *measurable*. This means that you will need to monitor your staff and set key milestones along the way to make sure you and the staff are certain about what goes on in the kitchen."

© Images.com/Corbis

"But why should my staff go along with my goal?" John says. "They do their job for four months, pick up a paycheck, and then they are gone. Why should they care?" Chris reminds John that he already had an excellent employee, Zoey Zhang, in the kitchen that cared about the future success of the hotel, and she was sure to help motivate the rest of the staff, given the right support. He also tells John that as a manager and a leader, he needs to emphasize that the goal is *relevant* to every single one of them, and assert that it is in line with the hotel's vision, mission, and values. Furthermore, his staff must be assured that although the goal seems to be challenging at present, it will certainly be *achievable* if everyone works hard and pulls together to make it succeed.

Chris then adds that John would need to set key milestones for his employees over a certain period of time, right up until the goal deadline (*time-bound*), and provide support and feedback along the way.

When Chris finishes taking John through his goal, they both agree that it seems a bit more realistic than it had before. However, John still does not seem convinced that it is actually achievable.

Although exasperated with John's reluctance to commit fully to the hotel's goals, Chris is determined to find out how he can motivate him and get him to work as a team player. To start the process, Chris needs to find out more about John as a person, rather than as just a prickly food and beverage manager who is entirely resistant to change. After a few gentle opening questions about his professional background, John explodes, "Why do you want to know what I've done in the past? I'm sure Kathy Osborne gave you a full summary of my career to date. Again, this is just time wasting. I'll tell you, in my father's day, there wouldn't be any time dedicated to sitting around in meeting rooms for hours talking fluff. He would be out there getting the job done, no questions asked."

Calmly, Chris ventures another question, and asks John what his father does for a living. John replied stiffly, "He started off as a logger when he was only in his teens and then became senior manager of a furniture manufacturer. He was extremely successful."

Chris can't believe his luck. His background research on goal setting highlighted studies and their findings from the logging industry in particular. He feels that, finally, he can relate to John on some level, and hopes that John will reciprocate. So, Chris begins to tell John about the series of studies on goal setting and motivation carried out over the last four decades by Professors Gary Latham and Edwin Locke. He tells him that they had arrived at the conclusion that rather than just using money as an incentive, people were more motivated by challenging, clear goals and achieved more personal satisfaction by overcoming difficult obstacles than doing easier tasks. Apparently, people who were told to "do their best" performed less well than those who were given specific targets.

John listens to Chris without interruption, but he still looks a bit skeptical. So, Chris decides to tell John about a case study that focuses on the wood products industry conducted in the South in the 1960s and 1970s. (See the "Research at Work" box for more details.)

As soon as Chris finishes, John sits straight up in his chair and snaps his fingers. "My father was like one of those workers; he liked a challenge and always wanted to find new ways to improve things. That's why he was so successful." Delighted with John's newfound enthusiasm, Chris says, "So do you understand what I am trying to achieve for the hotel? By setting challenging but not impossible team goals, I believe that each of you has the skill and the capability to make this hotel a success once more. But it is not enough for me to believe in this vision; every team member, including you, John, must be a part of it too."

John nods his head briefly, as if deep in thought. Chris feels this was a good point to end the meeting, and he leaves feeling a little more optimistic about John's attitude going forward.

Research@Work

Increasing Productivity[4]

In 1968, the American Pulpwood Association wanted to increase the productivity among the loggers but wasn't quite sure how to go about it. At the time, companies were dependent on loggers who were mostly self-employed. This meant they could work as often or as little as they wished, and often it was the latter. Although companies had tried to invest in machinery that would reduce their dependency on the loggers, many found they could not afford the expense.

© Dan Lamont/Corbis

In response, researchers carried out an experiment: they put three types of groups of logging supervisors in place; one stayed on site with the loggers but did not set specific goals; the second did not stay on site but did lay out specific goals; and the third both stayed on site and gave specific production goals.

The researchers found that the third group had the greatest increase in productivity. Why? Because the workers knew exactly what to do and the target that needed to be reached, and they benefited from the presence of a supervisor who provided feedback and supported them in their achievement of the goal. As workers became more engaged with the task, absenteeism dropped and the rate of injuries decreased. By attaining a goal that was both challenging and difficult, the workers experienced a sense of great achievement and accomplishment. The experiment proved that workers were more motivated by the presence of an on-site supervisor, as well as being assigned specific production goals.

Next, the researchers addressed the problem of under loading trucks. Loggers tended to limit the amount of logs in each truck, as there were fines imposed if trucks were overloaded. A goal was set to fill the trucks at 94 percent capacity (up from the former average of 60 percent), which was perceived as a "difficult yet attainable goal." The experiment involved six company logging operations in Oklahoma, whose truck drivers belonged to a union and were paid by the hour. Six trucks and six drivers were assigned to each logging operation. The drivers were responsible for ensuring that the trucks were loaded to the maximum legal weight. The net weight of the 36 trucks in the fleet would be collected over a 12-month period. No incentives such as money were promised to the workers, nor were they given any additional training. They were told that if they failed to attain the goal, they would not get any repercussions. Production increased to such a degree that the company saved almost $250,000 over a nine-month period, money that would have been spent on extra trucks to carry the same number of logs to the mill.

So, how did they do it? By being allocated a specific, challenging goal, each worker knew what was expected. Rather than "doing their best," the workers were aware exactly how much each one needed to achieve each day. When the workers reached their targets, they experienced a measure of pride and satisfaction in their work. This, as well as being assured that they would not be punished if they failed to reach the goal, motivated them to carry out the task to its completion.

Time and again, research has proved that the setting of specific and challenging goals led to enhanced work performance, as well as increased job satisfaction for the worker.

Critical Thinking in the Classroom

Imagine that you are the manager of a team of loggers. What approach would you take to boost productivity?

When Goals Go Wrong

We have discussed the conditions and dimensions that lead to successful goal achievement, but there are a number of reasons that goals will fail. In the early 1990s, Sears set a goal for their repair team to charge $147 per hour. This led to the staff overcharging and making unnecessary repairs in order to meet their target. Companies such as Enron and Ford also made similar errors in goal setting. For example, Enron awarded bonuses based on revenue rather than profit, leading the company to its eventual collapse. In the case of Ford, employees were asked to make a new car in an unrealistic deadline, resulting in neglected safety checks and subsequent lawsuits.[5]

© Greg Smith / Corbis

Researchers Locke and Latham outline the pitfalls of goal setting to which individuals and organizations commonly fall prey, including "excessive risk-taking, increases in stress, feelings of failure, using goals as a ceiling for performance, ignoring non-goal areas, short-range thinking, and dishonesty/cheating."[6] Based on this theory, we might conclude that the three companies cited above had fallen prey to some of these pitfalls.

Similarly, Chris had first-hand experience of the departmental pitfalls of the Dolphin Resort & Hotel. The former general manager, Herb Cork, had set a goal to keep profits stable by focusing on financial savings, to the detriment of service quality. So long as he maintained the bottom line, Cork was satisfied with the hotel performance. Similar to the decisions made at Enron, he was more inclined to focus on revenue than profit. Unfortunately, his short-range thinking led to a decline in guest satisfaction and a decrease in profit. The hotel had also fallen prey to excessive risk taking by being fully operational for only four months of the year. As a result, there were very few permanent staff members, which affected any kind of team loyalty or commitment to the hotel. Furthermore, the skeleton staff was expected to multitask and fill a number of roles. For example, Chris was greeted by sales director Ken Gold, who as acting receptionist did not provide the best first impression.

John Johnson could also be accused of using goals as a ceiling for performance and ignoring non-goal areas. So far as he was concerned, he was doing his job just as he was told, by focusing on the financials and performing well enough to pick up his bonus at the end of the year. However, was John entirely to blame for his attitude? After all, Herb Cork tended to micromanage the financials of every department, emphasizing that maintaining the bottom line was the most important function of their roles. With such a narrow view, it appears as if Cork left no room for creativity or change. Chris was especially impressed by one of the kitchen staff, Zoey Zhang, but it does not seem that her manager nurtured her enthusiasm.

It is little wonder that Chris had a challenge on his hands: the management team had never been asked what they thought and how they could contribute to the running of the hotel.

But what about the hotel's owner, Kathy Osborne? Over the course of six years, she had watched the hotel profit steadily decline under the helm of Cork. It is clear that Kathy should have stepped in earlier to address Cork's management technique, yet she had let the situation drift on, presumably in the hope that the hotel would pick up pace again without any intervention. In this sense, we could say that Kathy also suffered from the pitfall of short-range thinking.

Like all aspects of management, goal setting is a people business. The success of the goal depends on the people carrying it out. As we have learned, managers must have commitment from their employees, match skill set to performance, give productive feedback, and strive to make the goal clear and challenging. All these principles stem from a belief in the goal itself. If there is any doubt that the goal will succeed, then it is more likely that it will fail. For example, in organizations, the manager might not buy in fully to the goals of the company, leading to conflict.[7]

Similarly, employees who feel that they simply don't have the ability or skill set to overcome the obstacles and challenges of reaching the goal can also cloud their focus on the

"The Boiled Frog"

Kathy Osborne, the owner of the Dolphin Resort & Hotel, wants to understand how the team came to be so dissatisfied. She felt that employee satisfaction used to be a cornerstone of the Dolphin and kept asking Chris Heppler, "How did we get here?".

Finally, he responded "So gradually, that no one ever noticed." Little by little, employee satisfaction expectations eroded over time, without being noticed on a daily basis, until turnover started to skyrocket, accident reports tripled, and the company faced two harassment lawsuits.

In Systems Thinking, this challenge is the "Drifting Goals" archetype, also known as "The Boiled Frog," illustrated in the graphic shown here. Why a frog? As we mentioned in Chapter 7, if you throw a frog into a boiling pot of water, it will jump out. Yet, if you place that frog in cold water and gradually turn up the heat, it will swim around and not notice until it is too late. (Note: the authors are a bit disturbed by this metaphor, so please don't try this at home!)

Because the Dolphin Resort & Hotel had not been tracking employee satisfaction, Chris demonstrates his point to Kathy by showing her that it was following the same trend that guest satisfaction had experienced. He noted that as the goals were lowered, so were results, as seen here.

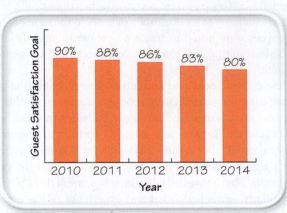

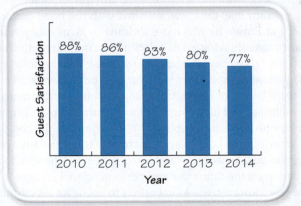

So what is the recommended intervention that a manager should take when a "boiling frog" has been identified? The solution here is straightforward: reset the goal to the highest desirable standard.

Critical Thinking in the Classroom: As a manager, how would you avoid "The Boiled Frog" syndrome taking place within your organization?

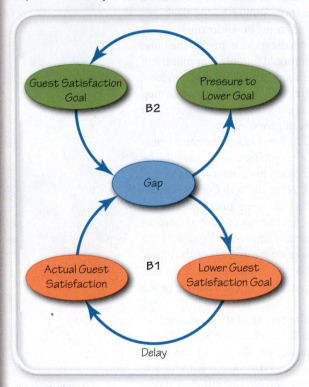

The Boiled Frog

desired outcome.[8] If goal setting is a people business, how will Chris manage the pitfalls at the Dolphin Resort? He has already made a start in securing the commitment from John Johnson, discovered the reasons behind many of the mistakes made by his incumbent, and received full buy-in from Kathy. Yet, his abilities as a manager will be put to a continual test.

However, the application of Positive Psychology and a systems approach to critical thinking can help Chris in setting and completing his goals. Systems theory holds that people who concentrate on the vision of the goal and what it would mean to achieve the result help give clarity to the process. On the other hand, as our first instinct is to look for all the problems that could occur on our journey to completing a task, it is not an easy skill to simply put these concerns aside to focus on the outcome.

It is up to Chris to hold onto the vision, no matter how frustrated he might feel at times, to keep the staff inspired and motivated. By using Positive Psychology, Chris could also assess the skills of the employees, match them to the organizational objectives, share his passion for the goal with them, and help direct their focus on the vision itself.

8.2 | GOAL PLANS

8.2 | Explain the principles and different types of goal plans in an organization.

Principles of Goal Setting

The previous example from the logging industry comes from pioneering research carried out by Latham and Locke on goal setting and motivation. Their goal-setting theory also subscribes to the S.M.A.R.T. approach. In their 1990 book *A Theory of Goal Setting and Task Performance*, the authors outline five main principles of goal setting to motivate workers: Clarity, Challenge, Commitment, Feedback, and Task Complexity.[9]

Clarity Goals must be clear, specific, unambiguous, measurable, and set with a specific time frame for completion. Which is the clearer goal? "I want to write a thesis about sports"; or "I want to write a thesis about the impact of goal setting on sports that will be 100 pages long and completed within three months. Every weekday, I will write at least 3 pages per day until the thesis is finished."

The first example is vague and unclear; there are no timelines set, no specific goals to aspire to, and the topic is ambiguous to say the least. In fact, if you told a friend or a professor that you wanted to write a thesis on sports, they wouldn't understand what you wanted to achieve. However, by clearly defining your goals, as described in the second example, nobody is left in any doubt as to what you are striving to achieve, including yourself. When Chris redefined John's goal to increase room rates, it didn't seem as far-fetched; in fact, it seemed entirely achievable.

Clearly defined goals motivate us—knowing that you have a set task to achieve every day, such as writing at least 3 pages, helps you to engage with the task in order to meet the set deadline. This is why managers set clear goals for their teams: to improve performance and motivate their employees.

Challenge As researchers have discovered through a number of experiments, people are more motivated by challenging goals. In the trucking story from earlier in this chapter, the workers achieved great satisfaction in fulfilling the assigned "difficult, yet attainable" goal.[10]

One of the most important characteristics of goals is the level of challenge. As people are often motivated by achievement, they'll judge a goal based on the significance of the anticipated accomplishment. When you know that what you do will be well received, there's a natural motivation to do a good job. For example, although the workers in the logging case study were not promised any additional monetary compensation for their goal achievement, they were compensated verbally and given positive feedback at regular intervals. Having a supervisor on site who believed in the significance of the goal and conveyed this confidence and feedback to the workers made an enormous difference when it came to achieving the logging challenge.

Indeed, in some cases, workers became so excited by the goal that they started to come up with creative ways to improve the logging system. In this case, we could say that goal setting, presented in the right way, spawns creativity. This was the part of the case study that really inspired John at the Dolphin Resort & Hotel. As he told Chris, his father loved a

LECTURE ENHANCER:
8.2 Goal Plans

- Five Principles of Goal Setting
  1. *Clarity*—must be clear, specific, unambiguous, measurable, and set with a specific timeframe for completion
  2. *Challenge*—people are more motivated by challenging goals
  3. *Commitment*—in order for goals to be achieved, must have full commitment from everyone on the team
  4. *Feedback*—giving timely feedback allows managers to monitor progress as well as address any signs of lapsed enthusiasm or motivation
  5. *Task Complexity*—when setting complex tasks, managers must account for the difficulty of the goal by ensuring workers are given enough time to complete the task and provide the appropriate resources needed to complete the goal

- Goal Plan Types and Components
  ✓ **Business Plan**—a plan that interprets an organizational strategy into a market or community-based opportunity for division or departmental managers
  ✓ **Budget**—the quantitative part of a plan that allocates available financial resources to cover all the improvements
  ✓ **Policy**—a standing plan that describes how an organization and its members should respond to recurring or anticipated situations
  ✓ **Rules & Regulations**—formal descriptions of how specific actions must be carried out
  ✓ **Standing Plan**—a plan designed for repeated use in response to commonly occurring events
  ✓ **Procedure**—another example of a standing plan that provides specific steps to be taken as part of a recurring process or in response to a recurring situation
  ✓ **Directional Plan**—a general, flexible plan that provides guidelines for an organization's long-term goals
  ✓ **Tactical Plan**—plans that cover an intermediate time-scale and enact divisional strategies by allocating people and resources; usually short-term
  ✓ **Operational Plan**—guides the day-to-day production or delivery of an organization's goods and services; can be single-use
  ✓ **Options-based Planning**—a method of planning that preserves flexibility in contexts of uncertainty by investing in several alternative plans

challenge, and he had lots of ideas about how to overcome certain obstacles. John believed that this was the main reason for his father's success.

Commitment: Managers often use the term *buy-in* when it comes to goal setting. This means that in order for goals to be achieved, the manager must have full commitment, or buy-in, from everyone on the team. Typically, people will be more committed to a goal if the task itself is important to them, as well as the outcome, and if they truly believe they can achieve the goal.[11] Chris set up that meeting with John first, as he knew that he would be the toughest person on the team to buy in to his goal.

Employees are much more likely to engage in the goal if they feel they were a part of creating it in the first place. By participating in the goal-setting process, employees have a personal interest in the task and are more willing to work toward achieving it. Giving an order to an employee to "do something," without giving any further explanation, might get the task done, but it is doubtful that the worker will have any personal interest in the task itself or even feel motivated enough to do it repeatedly. This is why it is so important for managers and employees to interact regularly. Goals have a better chance of being achieved if the employees are involved in the decision-making and the planning processes.

However, not everyone on the team might agree with the goal, even if they have been involved from the outset; indeed, it can be difficult to get everyone's buy-in at once. This is why it is essential that the manager is passionate about the goal and communicates with the team in a way that assures them that the goal is in line with organizational values and vision. Employees need to believe that the goal is worthwhile and feel that their contribution will truly make a difference.

Feedback: "So how are we doing?" is a commonly asked question by team members when it comes to measuring goal performance. For instance, if the goal was to make 1,000 auto parts in a week, how would the team know whether they were achieving the objective unless someone else was monitoring their progress and informing them about it?

In addition to planning goals, managers must include feedback, which can be a motivator in and of itself. Through progress reports, managers can clarify expectations, assess the process, adjust it if necessary, and recognize and award good work. As a result, team members will have more incentive to achieve the goals set for them.

> **Long-term plan** A plan that covers time periods of a year or more and is used to achieve future goals.

This is especially important for a **long-term plan**, which is a plan that covers time periods of a year or more and is used to achieve future goals. In many cases, goals that are set quite far in the future can lose momentum. Employees might either put off their allocated tasks, telling themselves they will return to it "closer to the deadline," or simply lose interest altogether.

By giving timely feedback, managers can monitor progress, as well as address any signs of lapsed enthusiasm or motivation. Through progress reports, team members will be able to assess for themselves how they are doing and where they might need to improve performance.

However, managers must also take into account the way they distribute feedback. If Chris told John: "You haven't managed to reach your target this week; you are doing a terrible job. If your poor work continues, you won't have a job soon," it is likely that John would just get up and walk out. For most of us, our work performance is also tied to our self-worth, or self-efficacy.[12] If we are given negative feedback, we might feel upset, angry, discouraged, and disillusioned, which will in turn affect our work performance. Indeed, being consistently critiqued or threatened by a manager will affect any desire to complete future goals and may result in us leaving the company altogether.

Task Complexity: Although Locke and Latham found that people excelled when they were given more challenging tasks, they were careful to advise against allocating tasks that could be too overwhelming. This is particularly relevant to tasks of high complexity, which demand an elevated level of skills.

People who work in a complex environment generally possess the skill set and motivation necessary to carry out their roles. However, if the goal does not account for the complexity of the task, and appropriate measures are not put in place at the beginning to address it, then people might become overworked, pushing themselves to meet the expectations of the goal. Pressure to perform beyond the limits of our ability can really impede performance, leading to a lapse in commitment.

When setting complex tasks, managers must account for the difficulty of the goal by ensuring that workers are given enough time to complete the task or, if they lack the necessary skills, provide them with the appropriate resources to show them how to build a strategy to complete the goal. Without any clarification or definition, John's goal to charge more for rooms is in itself a complex (if not an apparently impossible) task, as it is unlikely that guests will be happy to pay more for a subpar hotel experience. As S.M.A.R.T. dictates, goals must be *achievable* from the outset in order to be successful.

Goal Plan Types and Components

Now that Chris has made a connection, albeit a fragile one, with John Johnson, he is eager to nurture the relationship further. John is a strong personality and something of a leader among the staff. Chris knows that if he can get John fully committed to the goal, then he will be a significant force in persuading the rest of the team to get involved. In light of the off-the-mark goals set by John previously, Chris felt it was important to reiterate the hotel's strategy to inform John fully as to what had been decided in terms of improving the hotel's performance. He also hopes that by fully involving John in the plan, he will be more motivated to working toward the goal.

As a result, Chris informs John of the hotel's **business plan**, which is a plan that interprets an organizational strategy into a market- or community-based opportunity for division or departmental managers. In particular, the hotel's plan sets the following goals:

- Focus equally on employee satisfaction, guest satisfaction, owner return on investment, and the environment
- Make employee satisfaction the most important priority
- Invest in capital improvements: complete a cosmetic renovation before the summer season
- Raise occupancy by approaching the local time-share companies to see if they are interested in purchasing a fixed number of rooms at a lower daily rate
- In general, lower the rates at the hotel and increase revenue through an upgraded gift shop and activities

Silently, John looked through the list, and then said, "How can we afford all these refurbishments to the hotel? Fancy TVs and new carpets and linens . . . Sounds like you are taking money and throwing it down the river." Chris explained to John that he had received full support from Kathy Osborne to carry out the renovations, and that they had worked out a **budget**, which is the quantitative part of a plan that allocates available financial resources, to cover all the improvements. John went back to the list.

"OK, so we have a budget in place. What I want to know is how you are going to get this time-share idea past company policy. Herb Cork made it very clear that the Dolphin Resort would never be affiliated with other partners."

Chris had already been through the company **policy**, which is a standing plan that describes how an organization and its members should respond to recurring or anticipated situations. He knew that there was nothing in there about the hotel engaging in partnerships, and suspected that this was just Cork's personal opinion. Chris handed a copy of the company policy guidelines to John, who grudgingly conceded that there was nothing to stop the hotel from forming new business relationships. "I still don't think it's a good idea, though," he added.

Chris thought that it would be a good idea to bring John through the policy and procedures of the company so he was absolutely clear on the **rules and regulations**, which are formal descriptions of how specific actions must be carried out.

He explained that a policy is a **standing plan**, which is a plan designed for repeated use in response to commonly occurring events. A **procedure** is another example of a standing plan that provides specific steps to be taken as part of a recurring process or in response to a recurring situation. For example, the hotel's policy dictates that employees are to gather at a certain assembly area during a fire drill or in the event of a fire. Managers and employees are expected to carry out the terms of the policy by behaving according to the instructions outlined in the procedure.

Business plan Plans that interpret an organizational strategy into a market- or community-based opportunity for division or departmental managers.

Budget The quantitative part of a plan that allocates available financial resources.

Policy A standing plan that describes how an organization and its members should respond to recurring or anticipated situations.

Rules and regulations Formal descriptions of how specific actions are to be carried out.

Standing plan Plans designed for repeated use in response to commonly occurring events.

Procedure A standing plan that provides the specific steps to be taken as part of a recurring process or in response to a recurring situation.

When John and Chris finish going through the business plan and hotel policy, Chris is pleased to hear that John is becoming a little more interested in the goal-setting process for the hotel. For example, when he grumbled about lowering the hotel rates, Chris thought he detected some passion and felt satisfied that John was slowly coming on board.

The next step is to devise a goal plan. Goal plans are an essential way of committing department, resources, and individuals to a future goal. Once the business plan is in place, managers then identify the appropriate goal plans to best achieve the objectives of the organization.

Chris begins with a **directional plan**, which is a general, flexible plan that provides guidelines for an organization's long-term goals. Directional plans provide focus but they do not include specific objectives or allocate responsibility. They are used to educate employees as to where the organization is going and what it hopes to achieve in the future. Once again, Chris outlines the main objectives of the goal to John, how they want the hotel to perform, and when they expect the goal to be achieved. Confident that John is starting to share the vision, Chris begins to break down the goal plan into specific segments.

Chris said, "First, we need to figure out how we are going to put our goals into action and who is going to help us achieve our objectives. I have devised a tactical plan, which I think will give us a better idea of roles and responsibilities when it comes to carrying out some of our short-term goals."

Tactical plans are plans that cover an intermediate time scale and enact divisional strategies by allocating people and resources. They are directly related to organizational goals. The tactical plan ensures adequate resources and assigns responsibility to each division and individuals involved in the strategy. Tactical plans are usually **short-term plans**, plans that cover one year or less and are used to achieve short-term goals. Chris and John decide that some of the areas that they can address immediately in the food and beverage division are coming up with a unique recipe for the "Dolphin Cookie," which they can offer to guests on arrival once the hotel has been refurbished and is fully open for business in a few weeks' time. They assign Zoey Zhang and the kitchen staff to this goal plan, thinking that her enthusiasm is sure to be reflected in the cookie itself. It is also agreed that Zoey will coordinate with Wendy at the front desk to discuss how the cookies are going to be presented to the guests.

Chris also suggests that sales and marketing could begin researching their competition and assessing potential partnerships with time-share companies, and other related activities. "Maybe you should have a chat with the director of sales, Ken Gold, about that," John offered. Chris tried to hide his surprise at John's suggestion; he had expected another litany of reasons why partnerships were a bad idea. They made a note to assign Ken and his department to the goal of seeking new business relationships.

Next on the list are **operational plans**, which guide the day-to-day production or delivery of an organization's goods and services, and which enact a functional strategy. For example, a sales manager might be instructed to increase the sales of his department by 10 percent by the end of the year. In order to accomplish this task, the manager of that department would assign each individual a goal to meet this requirement. Operational plans can be **single-use**, where a plan developed to achieve a particular goal or in response to an event that is not expected to be repeated. For example, the goal assigned to the sales team described above might be a one-time event—a grand reopening weekend, for example—that probably will not happen again.

Chris assigns John the operational goal of reviewing his inventory, especially the issue of over-ordering soda, and states that he wants to see a 20 percent reduction in beverage expenditure by the end of the year. John agrees to rework the daily checklists for his staff to manage the inventory better.

Between them, Chris and John decide that the food and beverage team will revisit and rewrite the inventory policy for each of the storage areas within the next 30 days. Once they implement the process, they will check back with the cost of goods sold (COGS) every 15 days over the next three quarters and adjust their procedures as necessary. John also suggests rotating the person(s) responsible for the physical inventory count at least twice a week for more accuracy and accountability. Both Chris and John feel that this internal adjustment to the day-to-day operations will allow input from everyone, as well as overall accountability and better control of expenses, which will help increase potential profit. Chris also advises John to check out some different suppliers to see which ones offer the

Directional plan A general, flexible plan that provides guidelines for an organization's long-term goals.

Tactical plans Plans that cover an intermediate time scale and enact divisional strategies by allocating people and resources.

Short-term plan A plan that covers one year or less and is used to achieve short-term goals.

Operational plans Plans that guide the day-to-day production or delivery of an organization's goods and services, and which enact a functional strategy.

Single-use A plan developed to achieve a particular goal or in response to an event that is not expected to be repeated.

better rates. John agrees to involve his kitchen staff in his decisions and to seek their advice about local suppliers.

Finally, Chris brings John through **options-based planning**, which is a method of planning that preserves flexibility in contexts of uncertainty by investing in several alternatives. For example, a health organization may devise a number of response options and solutions to a pandemic, involving media and other health departments and professionals, so it can be resolved as quickly as possible. Chris and John agree that certain contingencies should be put in place in case anything goes awry at the hotel. They go through the hotel's policies on emergencies, security, and other potential hazards and plan alternatives to ensure their guests and employees are fully supported in the event of an unusual occurrence.

When the goal plans are finished, both Chris and John feel like a break, so they both head off to lunch and agree to resume their discussion later that day.

Options-based planning A method of planning that preserves flexibility in contexts of uncertainty by investing in several alternative plans.

Different Types of Plans

Plan Types	Aim Targeted Focus
Business Plan	Organizational Focused
Standby Plan	Common Occurrences Focused
Procedure Plan	Step-by-step Focused
Goal Plan	Future Objective Focused
Directional Plan	More Flexible Long-term Focused
Tactical Plan	More Short-term Focused
Operational Plan	Day-to-day Operations Focused
Options-based Plan	Alternative Flexible Plans Focused

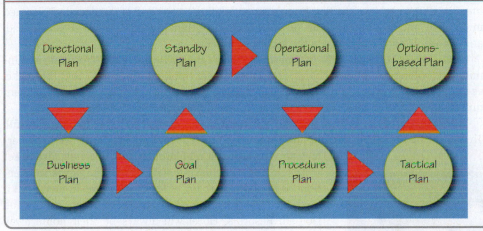

8.3 | EFFECTIVE GOALS

8.3 | Outline different types of goals and the characteristics that make them effective.

Types of Goals

Satisfied with the work that he and John have done on the goal plans, Chris feels it is a good time to address the type of goals that he needs to consider when putting a goal plan into action. As mentioned in section 8.1, goals must be S.M.A.R.T. (specific, measurable,

LECTURE ENHANCER:

8.3 Effective Goals

- Types of Goals
  - ✓ **Distal**—primary or long-term
  - ✓ **Proximal**—short-term goals that increase individuals' ability to reach distal goals by providing motivation and feedback
  - ✓ **Stretch**—a goal that is almost unattainable and requires the full capacity of an individual, manager, team, or organization to accomplish
  - ✓ **Means-end Chain**—an integrated series of goals in which the accomplishment of lower-level goals contributes to the achievement of higher-level goals

Distal goals Primary or long-term goals.

Proximal goals Short-term goals that increase individuals' ability to reach distal goals by providing motivation and feedback.

Stretch goal A goal that is almost unattainable and requires the full capacity of an individual, manager, team, or organization to accomplish.

achievable, relevant, and time-bound) to be effective. Most companies adhere to the S.M.A.R.T. principle, including the goal-setting pioneers Locke and Latham.

To recap what they have discussed, Chris begins by describing the hotel's **distal goals**, which are primary or long-term goals. Again, setting distal goals is a balancing act, and Chris knows that goals set too far in the future have a tendency to lose momentum. To counteract this effect, managers set **proximal goals,** or short-term goals, that increase individuals' ability to reach distal goals by providing motivation and feedback.[13]

Looking at the staff roster and attendance over the four-month peak period of the hotel's occupancy, Chris notices that John has been absent more than any of the other managers. His absences, not to mention his prior displays of lack of team spirit, have been putting a strain on the rest of the team. He is constantly late, he is absent at least three times a month, and he rarely makes team meetings. Although Chris feels more confident that John will perform better in his role in the future, he needs to set a distal goal for John to adhere to. He takes a deep breath and brings John through the staff attendance records, pointing out that his absences exceed the others by a large margin.

Going distinctly red in the face, John says, "I have a life outside this place, you know. I only take time off when the hotel is dead and there is nothing to do." Chris reiterates that things are only going to get busier at the hotel, and year-round, not just for four months; and the staff will need to be committed to the hotel for the goal to succeed.

Then Chris breaks down the distal goal into manageable, specific steps and sets some proximal goals. For example, he tells John that every two weeks, they will meet to assess his absenteeism and lateness. He goes on to say that John should come to him if he is experiencing issues in his personal life that are having an effect on his work attendance and performance. Chris knows that managers who make an effort to uncover the underlying issues of a situation will have a better chance of improving performance in the long term. John crosses his arms, but makes no attempt to argue. Chris feels it is a good idea to move on to the next type of goal.

Chris is a big believer in the **stretch goal**, which is a goal that is almost unattainable and requires the full capacity of an individual, manager, team, or organization to accomplish.[14] One of Chris's favorite examples of a stretch goal is President John F. Kennedy's announcement in 1961 to achieve the first human moon landing by the end of the decade. It seemed impossible, and required a whole new way of creative thinking, but the goal was achieved, and the whole country basked in the accomplishment.

Stretch goals begin with a vision, one that must be shared by the team. If the team is committed, is willing to embrace change and a new way of thinking, and thinks that the goal is as important as you do, there is more chance of the goal being achieved. In short, the team must believe that the seemingly impossible is indeed possible.

However, Chris knows that stretch goals must be set in the right way to be successful. They must be attainable, broken down into specific steps and targets, and have their performance reviewed at regular intervals. Chris decides to set a stretch goal of achieving 100 percent employee satisfaction for the hotel staff for at least two years. In fact, even if the hotel loses a team member to another opportunity, the Dolphin Resort & Hotel will always be their home away from home—guests for life. If they reach their goal after two years, Chris decides they will have a big party, complete with food, games, raffles, prizes, and certificates of recognition to celebrate the achievement, which he hopes will incentivize employees to commit to further difficult challenges. He decides to announce this stretch goal to the team at their next staff meeting.

Let's step away from the Dolphin Resort & Hotel briefly to consider the example of Ryan Hall, a known expert at achieving goals. Hailed as the fastest American-born long-distance runner of all time, Ryan's accomplishments include the fastest half-marathon (59:43 in Houston in 2007) and the fastest marathon (2:04:58 in Boston in 2011) finishes ever achieved by a U.S. runner. Like most distance runners, Ryan

Thomas B. Shea/Getty Images Inc

uses a means-end chain to help him prepare for and complete his races. A **means-end chain** is an integrated series of goals in which the accomplishment of lower-level goals contributes to the achievement of higher-level goals.[15] Runners preparing for a marathon usually follow a training schedule involving daily runs of specified times and distances, cross-training, and days of rest. This integrated series of lower-level, short-term goals provide the foundation and motivation for ultimately achieving the higher goal of completing the marathon within a targeted time. In his book *Running with Joy: My Daily Journey to the Marathon*, Ryan chronicles his 14-week preparation for the 2010 Boston Marathon, providing specific insights into the daily training regimen and means-end chain of this world-class marathoner.[16]

8.4 | *TEAM COMMITMENT*

8.4 | Illustrate how managers secure team-level commitment to goals.

In Chapter 7, Kathy Osborne warned Chris that the biggest challenge that he might face when trying to achieve his objectives was dissatisfied employees. After his first encounter with John Johnson, Chris was only too aware of this issue, but he felt a bit more optimistic after their succession of one-to-one meetings. Now, he needed to tackle the staff as a whole and ensure that they could commit and work as a team.

It was clear that the staff had enjoyed a relaxed environment under the charge of Chris's predecessor, Herb Cork, and was unsettled by this recent change in management. However, Chris had been given the goal of saving the hotel from bankruptcy, and it was his vision that the hotel become successful once more. Chris knew that the team needed to share in this vision and believe in the importance of achieving the goal. He needed full **goal commitment**, which is the motivation and determination needed to achieve a goal.[17] With summer only a few months away, Chris needed to engage the team quickly. For Chris's new efforts to work, he first would have to ensure that all the team members were collectively excited and energized about the transformation of the Dolphin Resort. Chris had been the new general manager for one week when he asked to meet with the entire staff of the Hilton Head Dolphin Resort & Hotel. The meeting took place in the resort's restaurant, with coffee and pastries served. When everyone sat down, he asked, "Are you proud to work here?"

The restaurant was silent for a full minute, which seemed like an eternity. Finally, Suzanne, a server in the restaurant, spoke. "I am proud of my friends here. We have a great time together. After work, we all spend time together, and that makes coming into work a lot easier. Serving people all day is tiring. Guests complaining can really ruin a good day, so having coworkers that are fun is something to be proud of." Many voices echoed her sentiments.

At that moment, Chris knew the challenges he faced were more than he had originally imagined. In order to achieve his goal, he had to get full commitment or buy-in from the staff, and persuade them to share his vision; otherwise, the goal would fail. Luckily, the hotel owner, Kathy Osborne, had promised to give him her full commitment and support, but without the staff on his side, he wouldn't get anywhere. In short, he needed to give the employees at the resort something to believe in. "Okay, let me ask this another way—what do you like or dislike about the resort's mission statement?" Silence. "Does anyone know the mission statement?" Silence. "I have been here for a week and have yet to find one. Let's start by building a mission together. Listen, if we want to achieve Kathy's goal of increasing the hotel's profit by $500,000, we will need to believe in what we are doing together!"

From experience, Chris knew that employees who embraced a company's mission statement were more likely to believe in the goals of the company and actively participate in bringing those goals to fruition.

Having talked it through with the staff, Chris continued to work with Kathy, the team, and hotel stakeholders to define the new "Mission, Vision, and Values of the Dolphin

Goal commitment The motivation and determination needed to achieve a goal.

Figure 8-1
Dolphin Resort & Hotel's Mission and Vision
The mission and BHAG of the Dolphin Resort & Hotel.

Resort & Hotel" shown in Figure 8-1. To show their commitment and enthusiasm for this change, Chris and the management team revealed the resort's new mission statement and Big Hairy Audacious Goal (BHAG) at a party for all the company's stakeholders. BHAG is a term coined by management expert Jim Collins, and it refers to an organization's grandest aspiration for the future, one that differentiates it from all its competitors. The mission statement and BHAG will provide the Dolphin Resort's management team a litmus test for all decisions made in the goal-setting process.

During the party, after Chris announced the mission statement and company BHAG, he spoke with jubilation, "Today is a special day, and I want to introduce you to one more team member! Her name is Dolly, and she is the reason we all have a job here."

At that moment, music started playing and a dancing dolphin erupted through the doors to a cheering crowd. Okay, in reality, some of the people didn't cheer—they were surprised and confused. John Johnson looked especially perplexed.

After the commotion subsided, Dolly the Dolphin stood at the front of the room with Chris as he explained: "When I came here a month ago, I asked the team why they were proud to work here. No one could give me a real answer. So here is our answer—Dolly. She stands for everything we want to be—Dolly is kind, thoughtful, playful, professional, eager to please, and well-trained. Most of all she is proud of what she does—Dolly performs for the sole purpose of bringing happiness to everyone."

Over time, most of the staff became enthusiastic about Dolly, who became their company's mascot. Dolly was a symbol of what they needed to work toward to fulfil the hotel's mission. The slogan "Do it for Dolly" was coined by employees as a form of motivation whenever they encountered an obstacle during their workday.

Management by Objectives (MBO)

Chris was empowered with Kathy's approval and support of the initiatives for the hotel. Now it was up to him to make the team aware of the goal plans and the types of goals that had been set for them in order for the initiatives to be fulfilled. Chris decided to employ a **Management by Objectives (MBO)** technique, which is a method of management in which management and employees agree to specific goals that are then used to evaluate individual performance.[18] Chris felt that the MBO technique would be appropriate to use in this instance, and at the next team meeting, he outlined the hotel's strategy.

Confident that he now had the team's full commitment and buy-in, he made the following motivational speech: "We know what we have to do in order to make the Dolphin Resort & Hotel the best it can be. Now, we have to put those goals into action. Each of you will be assigned a task, deadline, and clear targets to reach along the way. I will be providing you with support and feedback at every step, and of course, I will be here for you should you have any questions or new ideas you feel would enhance our mission."

With the support and positive energy of the team and stakeholders, Chris began to work with the department managers and their different approaches to goal setting. Over the course of many meetings, Chris and the team standardize the goal-designing process to ensure consistency. This includes a standard in which all departments and team members establish S.M.A.R.T. goals and one stretch goal. Once this process is completed, the departmental managers work with team members to begin executing the plan, which includes strategies that will be discussed in the next chapter.

Chris presents this new approach to departmental managers in order to design a process intended to secure the team's commitment and alignment to the resort's new mission, BHAG, S.M.A.R.T. goals, and stretch goals.

Management by Objectives (MBO) A method of management in which management and employees agree to specific goals that are then used to evaluate individual peformance.

8.5 | INDIVIDUAL PERFORMANCE

8.5 | Construct action plans consistent with goals to achieve individual-level performance.

8.5 Individual Performance
• Action Plans
  ✓ **Action Plan**—a specific action, people, and resources needed to accomplish a goal

Action Plans

Chris is excited to see how well the plans are coming together. The staff seemed genuinely motivated, and Dolly the Dolphin is becoming a big hit! When Ken Gold, the director of sales, approached him one day and told him how unhappy he was with one of the goals that had been assigned to him and his team, Chris was surprised.

In line with the goal plans devised with John Johnson, Chris had asked the sales and management team to research the possibility of partnering with a time-share company in the interests of raising occupancy at the hotel. The team had been making progress and had found a local time-share company who was interested in purchasing a fixed number of rooms every night for a daily rate of $45. The next step was for Ken and the team to close the deal and sign a contract with the time-share company. Yet, a couple of weeks had gone by, and the deal had not progressed. When Chris asked the reasons for the delay, he was told that the other company was waiting for their legal department to sign off on the contract. It turns out that this was not the case at all.

Ken told Chris, "Look, we appreciate what you are trying to do here, but I need to do what's best for my team, and I don't think giving rooms away is the way to do it." Chris gestured for him to continue. "As you know, Herb Cork linked our bonuses to our financial performance. Whenever we raised the room rate and met our sales goals, we received a commission. Now, as the room rates for the time-share company have been set at $45, we have no way of increasing our earning potential. We also have received a request for a wedding party that could book out the hotel for an entire weekend in June, but we can't do that if some of the rooms are going to the time-share."

While Chris understood Ken and the team's concerns, he knew he had to address the issue there and then; otherwise, he would have a mutiny on his hands. So he decided to create an **action plan**, which is the specific action, people, and resources needed to accomplish a goal

First, Chris addressed the issue of RevPAR. "Ken, I understand that you and the team have less rooms to sell on a daily basis as a result of some of the rooms going to the time-share company at a set price. However, that just means we need to be more creative with the rooms we already have. I think it is key that we start looking at the days of the week where we can enhance our daily rate to make up the commissions for your team."

Ken replied, "I see what you're saying, Chris, but that doesn't make up for the fact that we are selling less rooms than before." Chris said, "You may have less rooms to sell on a daily basis, but there is also a higher possibility of filling them at a higher rate per night once the hotel is up and running. I would suggest looking into our corporate clients that use the hotel on prime-time nights at higher rates. It might also be a good idea to research our competition and see what they charge for accommodation during festivals, celebrations, and other occasions. Often, the daily rate doubles during peak periods."

Ken nodded slowly, "I guess I could get the team to look at our reports on LNR (local negotiated rates) to help zero in on possible client accounts, and carry out research on our competition."

Chris was relieved when it seemed like Ken was coming around to his ideas. Ken was a valuable member of the staff, and the last thing he wanted was to lose his support. Chris added, "Great idea, Ken! You could also work with other account managers, which should help provide links to corporate clients for social gatherings."

"Yes, that would really help, too!" Ken replied. "But for this to work, Chris, I need the sales team fully on board. We don't hold regular meetings, and morale is low at the moment. Do you think I should set up a weekly meeting to assess the progress of this latest plan?"

Chris said, "Absolutely! Perhaps the first meeting could be a brainstorming session with the entire sales team, where you could devise a sales forecast flow, which will help determine clear opportunities to fill the hotel during premium-price days. Then you could start assigning goals. For example, your account manager could start looking into the LNR accounts for gap weekends that need to be filled and then post package pricing to LNR accounts to fill gap openings; your sales manager can chase leads that have not responded, or check lost business reports to find the reasons why some clients have turned down the Dolphin Resort & Hotel in the past."

After a few more minutes of discussion, Ken decided to set a team meeting for the very next day. They shook hands, and Ken agreed to let Chris know the outcome of the meeting. Chris went away satisfied with how his conversation with Ken had gone. He just hoped that the rest of the sales team would also come around to his and Ken's new approach.

Action plan The specific actions, people, and resources needed to accomplish a goal.

Performance dashboard A visual representation of an organization's strategies and goals, which allow managers to track progress toward metrics and goals immediately.

8.6 | *HOW MANAGERS TRACK PROGRESS*

8.6 Describe how managers track progress of goal plans through performance dashboards.

Performance Dashboards

If you spend enough time on any management team, you will most likely hear a couple of old adages: "The numbers don't lie" and "What gets measured gets done." Most contemporary managers use **performance dashboards** to provide a visual representation of an organization's strategies and goals, which allow managers to track progress toward metrics and goals immediately.[19]

Researchers Robert Kaplan and David Norton designed the enduring "Balanced Scorecard" model shown in Figure 8-2, which has given managers and information system designers a balanced approach to developing performance dashboards. "A *balanced scorecard* augments traditional financial measures with benchmarks for performance in three key nonfinancial areas: 1) a company's relationship with its customers, 2) its key internal processes, and 3) its learning and growth."[20]

This balanced approach starts with continuously and clearly communicating the team's progress. Chris and his management team worked with a local technology company to centralize their performance efforts into a dashboard in a way that was authentic to their mission and goals. This requires measuring different areas of the operation. **Key performance indicators (KPIs)** are measurements that managers identify as vital to the company's performance with regard to financials, internal processes, customers, and learning/growth. By doing this, Chris sought to connect the Dolphin Resort & Hotel's mission and vision into a management practice. This process is called *strategy*, which we will discuss in the next chapter.

Chris and his management team worked with a local technology development company to design and build the Dolphin Resort & Hotel's performance dashboard illustrated in Figure 8-3.

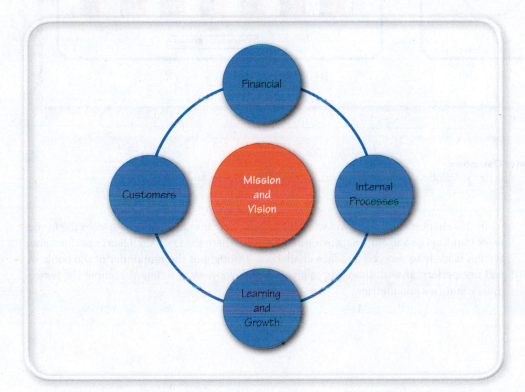

immediately track progress toward metrics and goals
➤ *Balanced Scorecard*—augments traditional financial measures with benchmarks for performance in three key nonfinancial areas
1) A company's relationship with its customers
2) Its key internal processes
3) Its learning and growth
➤ Figure 8-2: A Balanced Scorecard

Key performance indicators (KPIs) Measurements that managers identify as vital to the company's performance.

➤ Key Performance Indicators— measurements that managers identify as vital to the company's performance with regards to financials, internal processes, customers, and learning/growth
➤ Figure 8-3: Dolphin Resort & Hotel Performance Dashboard

Figure 8-2
A Balanced Scorecard
Balanced scorecards include top-line sales (financial), both internal and external (customers), systems and processes (internal processes), and continued development (growth) with continued profit. Each should be included in the overall mission and vision for an organization.

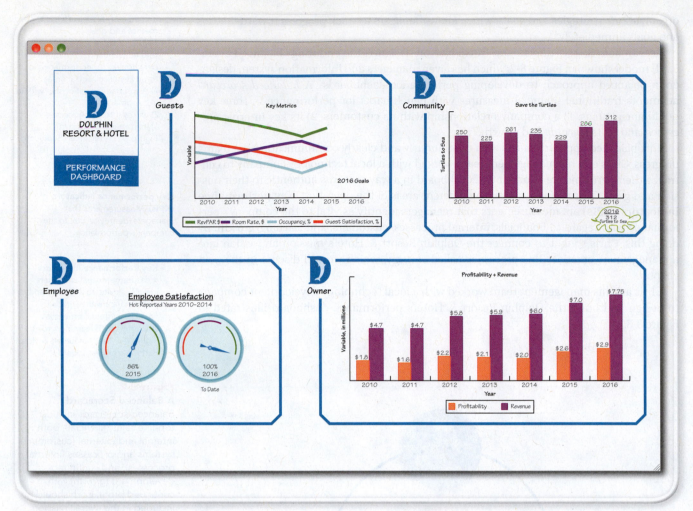

Figure 8-3

Dolphin Resort & Hotel Performance Dashboard

The dashboard includes a graphic matrix for the Dolphin's scorecard of guests, community, employee, and owner.

In this chapter's exercises, you will explore how well this dashboard addresses the framework that Kaplan and Norton provide and analyze where the Dolphin Resort's performance system is likely to succeed and face challenges. Throughout the remainder of the book, we will use performance dashboards to give a high-level view of different companies' performance statuses and metrics.

Chapter 8 Case: Setting Goals:
Spirit Airlines can be found on pg. 470

ADDITIONAL RESOURCES

KEY TERMS

Action plan The specific actions, people, and resources needed to accomplish a goal. **(p. 218)**

Budget The quantitative part of a plan that allocates available financial resources. **(p. 211)**

Business plans Plans that interpret an organizational strategy into a market- or community-based opportunity for division or departmental managers. **(p. 211)**

Directional plan A general, flexible plan that provides guidelines for an organization's long-term goals. **(p. 212)**

Distal goals Primary or long-term goals. **(p. 214)**

Goal commitment The motivation and determination needed to achieve a goal. **(p. 215)**

Key performance indicators (KPIs) Measurements that managers identify as vital to the company's performance. **(p. 219)**

Long-term plan A plan that covers time periods of a year or more and is used to achieve future goals. **(p. 210)**

Management by Objectives (MBO) A method of management in which management and employees agree to specific goals that are then used to evaluate individual peformance. **(p. 217)**

Means-ends chain An integrated series of goals in which the accomplishment of lower-level goals contributes to the achievement of higher-level goals. **(p. 215)**

Operational plans Plans that guide the day-to-day production or delivery of an organization's goods and services, and which enact a functional strategy. **(p. 212)**

Options-based planning A method of planning that preserves flexibility in contexts of uncertainty by investing in several alternative plans. **(p. 213)**

Performance dashboard A visual representation of an organization's strategies and goals, which allow managers to track progress toward metrics and goals immediately. **(p. 218)**

Policy A standing plan that describes how an organization and its members should respond to recurring or anticipated situations. **(p. 211)**

Procedure A standing plan that provides the specific steps to be taken as part of a recurring process or in response to a recurring situation. **(p. 211)**

Proximal goals Short-term goals that increase individuals' ability to reach distal goals by providing motivation and feedback. **(p. 214)**

Rules and regulations Formal descriptions of how specific actions are to be carried out. **(p. 211)**

Short-term plan A plan that covers one year or less and is used to achieve short-term goals. **(p. 212)**

Single-use plan A plan developed to achieve a particular goal or in response to an event that is not expected to be repeated. **(p. 212)**

S.M.A.R.T. goals Goals that are specific, measurable, achievable, relevant, and time-bound. **(p. 204)**

Standing plans Plans designed for repeated use in response to commonly occurring events. **(p. 211)**

Stretch goal A goal that is almost unattainable and requires the full capacity of an individual, manager, team, or organization to accomplish. **(p. 214)**

Tactical plans Plans that cover an intermediate time scale and enact divisional strategies by allocating people and resources. **(p. 212)**

IN REVIEW

8.1 | Describe the primary goals of an organization.

To maximize effectiveness and efficiency, goals must be set within a strategic framework consisting of mission, vision, and values. A strong, powerful mission statement will be assimilated into the company culture, so that each employee is committed to putting the mission into action to ensure the success of the organization.

Managers setting goals must follow the organization's mission, have a clear vision of what they want to achieve, and ensure that the team embraces the core values of what the organization represents. Goal setting has been defined as the establishment of *specific, measurable, achievable, relevant* and *time-bound* goals, also known as "S.M.A.R.T goals."

8.2 | Explain the principles and different types of goal plans in an organization.

The core principles of effective goal setting to motivate workers can be defined into five dimensions: Clarity, Challenge, Commitment, Feedback, and Task Complexity. The framework of these core principles is shaped into different kinds of goal plans to achieve certain objectives.

A *business plan* interprets an organizational strategy into a market or community-based opportunity for division or departmental managers. This business plan then gets translated into many subparts. A *standing plan* is a designed for repeated use in response to commonly occurring events. *Goal plans* are an essential way of committing department, resources, and individuals to a future goal. Once the business plan is in place, managers then identify the appropriate goal plans to best achieve the objectives of the organization.

A *directional plan* is a general, flexible plan that provides guidelines for an organization's long-term goals. Directional plans provide focus but they do not include specific objectives or allocate responsibility. *Tactical plans* then cover an intermediate time scale and enact divisional strategies by allocating people and resources. They are directly related to organizational goals. The tactical plan ensures adequate resources, and assigns responsibility to each division and individuals involved in the strategy. Tactical plans are usually *short-term plans,* which are plans that cover one year or less and are used to achieve short-term goals.

Day-to-day production or delivery of an organization's goods and services are formalized by *operational plans*. Managers use *options-based planning,* which preserves flexibility in contexts of uncertainty by investing in several alternatives.

8.3 | Outline different types of goals and the characteristics that make them effective.

Most companies adhere to the S.M.A.R.T. principle. Chris begins by describing the hotel's *distal goals,* which are primary or long-term goals. Setting distal goals is a balancing act, and goals set too far in the future have a tendency to lose momentum. To counteract this affect, managers set *proximal goals,* or short-term goals that increase individuals' ability to reach distal goals by providing motivation and feedback.

A *stretch goal* is a goal that is almost unattainable and requires the full capacity of an individual, manager, team, or organization to accomplish. A method for helping individuals and teams to achieve such large aspirations is called *means-end chain,* an integrated series of goals in which the accomplishment of lower-level goals contributes to the achievement of higher-level goals.

8.4 | Illustrate how managers secure team-level commitment to goals.

Full *goal commitment* is the motivation and determination needed to achieve the goal.

BHAG is an acronym (spelled out as "Big Hairy Audacious Goal") that refers to an organization's grandest aspiration for the future that differentiates it from all of its competitors. An organization's mission statement and BHAG can provide its management team a litmus test for all decisions made in the goal-setting process.

To ensure accountability, the *Management by Objectives (MBO)* technique is a method of management in which management and employees agree to specific goals that are then used to evaluate individual performance.

8.5 | Construct action plans consistent with goals to achieve individual-level performance.

Chris's change in the efforts on the sales team led to significant team disagreement. While Chris understood the concerns of the sales manager, Ken Gold, and his team, he knew he had to address the issue. He decided to create an *action plan,* which includes the specific action, people, and resources needed to accomplish a goal.

8.6 | Describe how managers track progress of goal plans through performance dashboards.

Managers use *performance dashboards* to provide a visual representation of an organization's strategies and goals, which allow managers to track progress toward metrics and goals immediately. A *balanced scorecard* focuses on three key nonfinancial areas: 1) relationships with customers, 2) key internal processes, and 3) learning and growth.

Key performance indicators (KPIs) are measurements that managers identify as vital to the company's performance with regard to financials, internal processes, customers, and learning/growth.

SELF-TEST

8.1 | **Describe** the primary goals of an organization.

1. Explain the acronym in the term *S.M.A.R.T goals*.

2. People who were told to "do their best" performed better than those who were given specific targets.
   a. True
   b. False

3. Name two of the common goal-setting pitfalls outlined by Locke and Latham.

8.2 | **Explain** the principles and different types of goal plans in an organization.

4. What are the five main principles of goal setting in order to motivate workers outlined by Locke and Latham?

5. The plan that interprets an organizational strategy into a market or community-based opportunity for division or departmental managers is called a _____.
   a. directional plan
   b. transitional plan
   c. business plan
   d. tactical plan

6. Plans that guide the day-to-day production or delivery of an organization's goods and services, and that enact a functional strategy are known as _____.
   a. operational
   b. standby
   c. options-based
   d. transitional

8.3 | **Outline** different types of goals and the characteristics that make them effective.

7. What's the difference between distal goals and proximal goals?

8. A _____ goal is an almost unattainable goal that requires the full capacity of an individual, manager, team, or organization to accomplish.

9. What type of goal is a marathon runner's daily schedule of training, an integrated series of goals in which the accomplishment of lower-level goals contributes to the achievement of higher goals?

8.4 | **Illustrate** how managers secure team-level commitment to goals.

10. Employees who embraced a company's _____ were more likely to believe in the goals of the company and actively participate in bringing those goals to fruition.

11. Describe the Management by Objectives (MBO) technique.

8.5 | **Construct** action plans consistent with goals to achieve individual-level performance.

12. What steps did Chris and his director of sales, Ken, follow to create an action plan for the sales team?

8.6 | **Describe** how managers track progress of goal plans through performance dashboards.

13. What do performance dashboards provide to an organization?

14. Dashboards include measurements that managers identify as vital to the company's performance with regard to financials, internal processes, customers, and learning/growth. These are known as:
    a. RPMs
    b. KPIs
    c. MPHs
    d. PPIs

CHAPTER EXERCISE

Long-Term and Short-Term Goal Setting

Part 1. Write Your Own Obituary

Imagine that you have died. Your obituary is appearing in the local newspaper. What will you have done in your life? What will you have accomplished? How will you be remembered? How will you have affected others? In the space provided here, write your own obituary, focusing on your personal and career accomplishments. You may be as creative and imaginative as you want.

_____

_____

_____

_____

_____

_____

_____

_____

_____

_____

_____

Part 2. Five Years from Now

Where do you see yourself five years from now? What job will you have? What will your salary be? Where will you be living? What hobbies will you have? Will you have a significant other? What new skills or interests will you have developed? In the space provided here, briefly describe how you foresee your situation five years from now.

_____

_____

_____

_____

_____

_____

_____

_____

_____

_____

_____

Writing your own obituary helps you to determine your long-term goals and objectives in life—those things that you would like to do or become. Thinking about where you will be five years from now helps you to consider your short-term goals, those things that will help you progress toward accomplishing your long-term goals.

SELF-ASSESSMENT

Goal Orientation*

For each of the following paired statements, circle the letter next to the statement that best describes you.

1. A. I prefer to do things that I can do well rather than things that I do poorly.
   B. The opportunity to do challenging work is important to me.

2. A. I'm happiest at work when I perform tasks on which I know that I won't make any errors.
   B. When I fail to complete a difficult task, I plan to try harder the next time I work on it.

3. A. The things I enjoy the most are the things I do the best.
   B. I prefer to work on tasks that force me to learn new things.

4. A. The opinions that others have about how well I can do certain things are important to me.
   B. The opportunity to learn new things is important to me.

5. A. I feel smart when I do something without making any mistakes.
   B. I do my best when I'm working on a fairly difficult task.

6. A. I like to be fairly confident that I can successfully perform a task before I attempt it.
   B. I try hard to improve on my past performance.

7. A. I like to work on tasks that I have done well on in the past.
   B. The opportunity to extend the range of my abilities is important to me.

8. A. I feel smart when I can do something better than most other people.
   B. When I have difficulty solving a problem, I enjoy trying different approaches to see which one will work.

Scoring:

Performance Goal Orientation

(Add up the total number of "As" circled above and write that number in the blank.) _____

Individuals with a performance goal orientation strive to demonstrate their competence via their task performance.

Learning Goal Orientation

(Add up the total number of "Bs" circled above and write that number in the blank.) _____

Individuals with a learning goal orientation strive to understand something new or to increase their level of competence in a given activity.

Which goal orientation was dominant for you? How can you use your goal orientation to your advantage to help you accomplish your goals?

*Adapted from Scott B. Button, John E. Mathieu, and Dennis M. Zajac, "Goal Orientation in Organizational Research: A Conceptual and Empirical Foundation," *Organizational Behavior & Human Decision Processes* 67, no. 1 (July 1996): 26–48.

SELF-TEST ANSWER KEY

1. Popularly, goal setting has been defined as the establishment of *specific, measurable, achievable, relevant* and *time-bound* goals, also known as *S.M.A.R.T* goals.

2. b. False. People performed less well without a list of specific targets. According to Latham and Locke, people are more motivated by challenging, clear goals and achieve more personal satisfaction by overcoming more difficult obstacles than performing easier tasks.

3. Answers include excessive risk taking, increases in stress, feelings of failure, using goals as a ceiling for performance, ignoring non-goal areas, short-range thinking, and dishonesty/cheating.

4. Clarity, Challenge, Commitment, Feedback, and Task Complexity

5. c.

6. a.

7. *Distal goals* are primary or long-term goals. *Proximal goals* are short-term goals that increase individuals' ability to reach distal goals by providing motivation and feedback.

8. stretch

9. means-end chain

10. mission statement

11. Management by Objectives (MBO) is a method of management in which management and employees agree to specific goals that are then used to evaluate individual performance.

12. Chris made sure that action was taken immediately instead of waiting for the problem to fester. He helped Ken find some specific steps that he could take to resolve the problem. In addition, they agreed to get input from all the staff during weekly meetings that could help increase buy-in and morale.

13. A visual representation of an organization's strategies and goals, which allow managers to track progress toward metrics and goals immediately.

14. b. KPIs

Notes

_____

_____

_____

_____

_____

_____

_____

_____

_____

_____

_____

_____

_____

_____

CHAPTER NINE

DESIGNING STRATEGIES

Jamie Roach/Shutterstock

Learning Objectives

By the end of this chapter, you will be able to:

9.1 | Explain how businesses use planning to solve problems and make a difference.

9.2 | Distinguish how planning is different at the organizational, divisional, and functional levels of a business.

9.3 | Explain how senior managers develop organizational strategies and business plans.

9.4 | Outline methods that managers use to understand their industries and competitors.

9.5 | Describe how managers assess the organization's capacity to execute proposed business plans.

9.6 | Demonstrate how managers develop divisional strategies and tactical plans.

9.7 | Compare traditional strategic planning models to an event-based approach.

ADDITIONAL RESOURCES

KEY TERMS
IN REVIEW
SELF-TEST
CHAPTER EXERCISES
SELF-ASSESSMENT
SELF-TEST
ANSWER KEY

JP Greenwood/Getty Images

INSIDE THIS CHAPTER

ManagementStory:
Featuring **Chris Heppler**

227

ManagementStory:
Featuring Chris Heppler

9.1 | *HOW MANAGERS PLAN TO MAKE A DIFFERENCE*

9.1 | Explain how businesses use planning to solve problems and make a difference.

> "Strategy is about making choices, trade-offs; it's about deliberately choosing to be different."
>
> — Michael E. Porter

Designing and defining strategies is a continuous process that helps organizations determine what they do, why they should be in business, how they can win and sustain market share, and how they can continually innovate in order to keep ahead of the competition. One of the main responsibilities of managers is to create, present, and implement strategies that will defend the company against the threat of competition, ascertain the best market position, and determine the weaknesses that might make its position vulnerable in the industry. In order to design a successful strategy, managers must use critical thinking to understand the full nature of the competitive forces that are present, and take a holistic, systemic view of the industry structure.

Over the years, we have seen many organizations burst onto the market as a result of their exacting and well-researched strategies; namely, Apple, Microsoft, and other innovative companies saw an opportunity, designed a strategy, and dived in, fully committed to achieving their goals. Being able to diversify in a competitive industry, seeing an opening in the market and continuously staying ahead of the competition would not be possible without a clearly defined, skillfully designed strategy.

In Chapter 8, we explored how general manager Chris Heppler successfully set goals by gaining the support of his team at the Dolphin Resort & Hotel, allocating S.M.A.R.T. and stretch goals to each department, creating a new Big Hairy Audacious Goal (BHAG) and mission statement, and setting a new idea about time-shares in motion. He also had to overcome a number of stumbling blocks in order to achieve his vision, such as dealing with adversaries like John Johnson and getting Ken Gold and the rest of the sales team on board with the time-share partnership. It had been a busy year, yet a fulfilling one.

On the anniversary of his first day as general manager of the Dolphin Resort & Hotel, Chris was making his usual rounds of the hotel grounds. As he walked, memories of the past year swirled through his mind. He remembered how shocked Kathy Osborne, the owner, was when he told her that the Dolphin Resort needed to lower its rates to increase profitability, but the tactic had paid off. Following Chris's conversation with Ken,

Bloomberg / Getty Images Inc

the sales manager at the resort, the sales team had done a fantastic job in closing the deal with a local time-share company, the largest one on Hilton Head Island. Yes, Chris felt very lucky about the way things had worked out; yet his achievements had been more than just luck; he recalled Thomas Jefferson's saying: "I'm a great believer in luck, and I find the harder I work, the more I have of it." By working hard, committing to his vision and goals, and motivating and supporting hotel staff, Chris's efforts to transform the Dolphin Resort have really paid off.

© A330Pilot / iStockphoto

A month later, the contract was signed with the time-share company, which was headed by Paul Reynolds, a local businessman. The Dolphin sales team was delighted with the business arrangement. They agreed that the time-share company would prepurchase 50 rooms, at $45 per room, from the Dolphin Resort every day of the year, and it would be determined each morning that if the time-share company was not going to use the rooms for that day, the hotel could potentially sell the rooms to other guests, with a percentage of the RevPar (revenue per available room) going to the time-share company.

Through the partnership with the time-share company, the number of guests increased. The Dolphin team was delighted with this boost to their customer base, but they also knew that to maintain momentum, they would need to treat these guests so well that they would never want to leave. Initiatives such as welcoming the guests with delicious home-baked cookies, nightly entertainment, a new menu in the refurbished restaurant, free WiFi, new corporate facilities, and a renovated gift shop selling high-quality and quirky Dolphin Resort & Hotel memorabilia had already attracted a large number of new and repeat guests. Chris's ideas were paying off, and the resort was having its most successful year in a long time.

When he walked into the lobby, Chris was surprised when he turned the corner and saw Kathy Osborne sitting in the reception area. This was only the second time he had seen her at the resort in the past year. She was the type of boss who was hands off and did not like to distract the team members or undermine Chris's authority, which he appreciated. At this moment, he could only think about all of the loose tree limbs and trash that she must have seen in the parking lot.

Kathy was carrying a bouquet of flowers, with a card addressed to Chris and the entire staff at the Dolphin Resort & Hotel. The flowers and card were a "thank-you" for the goals reached and outstanding profits achieved during the past year. This was a thoughtful addition to the end-of-year bonuses that she had already approved for every team member, which had been very well received. "Well, are you ready for a new challenge?" Kathy asked as she grinned broadly at Chris. "Are you referring to all of the branches in the parking lot?"

In the newly refurbished lobby of the hotel, Kathy outlined her ideas to Chris. She started off by voicing her concerns about the downturn in the economy; real estate prices had declined sharply on the island. Even with the decline in prices, many investors were hesitant to purchase properties for fear that the economy might not recover for several more years. A year ago, Kathy thought that she would have to get out of the hotel business altogether, but with the Dolphin Resort's stellar performance this past year, her enthusiasm for the business had been renewed.

When the president of Hilton Head National Bank and Trust called her in early January, she was intrigued to learn that the Porpoise Inn, located less than a mile from the Dolphin Resort & Hotel, was going into foreclosure. This was a surprise, as the Porpoise Inn was well equipped with conference facilities, including meeting rooms and private dining rooms, and it had a great reputation. In fact, before the Dolphin Resort had added its own corporate facilities during the refurbishment, it had lost business to the Porpoise Inn when it came to corporate events. Kathy didn't know why the Porpoise Inn

LECTURE ENHANCER:

9.2 Different Levels of Strategy

✓ **Strategy**—a plan of action for achieving goals

✓ **Organizational Strategy**—a corporate-level strategy that addresses the question "what business are we in?" and unites all parts of the organization

✓ **Divisional Strategy**—determines how a business will compete in a particular industry or market

Acquisition When an organization purchases another organization or business in order to grow.

✓ **Functional Strategy**—determines how employees will implement and achieve a tactical plan
➤ Figure 9-1: Connecting "Mission, Vision, & Values" to Strategies and Plans
✓ **Business Plan**—the stated actions and goals that support organizational strategy
✓ **Tactical Plan**—the stated actions and goals that support the divisional strategy

Strategy A plan of action for achieving goals.

Organizational strategy A corporate-level strategy that addresses the question "What business are we in?" and unites all parts of the organization.

Divisional strategy A strategy that determines how a business will compete in a particular industry or market.

Functional strategy A strategy that determines how employees will implement and achieve a tactical plan.

Business plan The stated actions and goals that support the organizational strategy.

Tactical plan The stated actions and goals that support achieving the divisional strategy.

Operational plan The stated actions and goals that support achieving the functional strategy.

was experiencing financial difficulties, but she was interested in finding out how the Dolphin could take advantage of this situation. It was then that she revealed Chris's new challenge.

"Because we are 'such good customers and because of our great performance this past year,' the bank president has agreed to let us make the first offer to purchase the Porpoise Inn and seems willing to accept any fair deal. Chris, I know that we can get this property at a good price, but can we make money? In this uncertain climate, I'm not sure if we can take such a huge risk. It's great that the Dolphin Resort is doing so well, but we are running out of space. Maybe purchasing the Porpoise Inn is a way to address capacity issues. Do you think you could meet with the general manager at the Porpoise Inn and find out why the hotel went into foreclosure and assess whether there is potential for us there?"

Chris had a lot of questions. If Kathy was talking about an **acquisition**, when an organization purchases another organization or business in order to grow, he needed to carry out extensive due diligence to see if this was a viable opportunity for the Dolphin Resort. So, he agreed to spend the upcoming week putting together an analysis and recommendation for Kathy's review.

9.2 | *DIFFERENT LEVELS OF STRATEGY*

9.2 | Distinguish how planning is different at the organizational, divisional, and functional levels of a business.

Chris spends the next week working on a new **strategy**—a plan of action for achieving goals—in preparation for the resort's next phase, and he relished the new challenge. As we have seen, Chris enjoys the planning process, which involves setting goals for the future, designing strategies, and deciding on the actions and resources needed to achieve success. As a result of the planning process, Chris needs to document decisions regarding the required goals, strategies, resource allocation, and actions; these are called *strategic plans*.

There are three levels of strategy: organizational, divisional, and functional.[1] **Organizational strategy** is a corporate-level strategy that addresses the question "What business are we in?" and unites all parts of the organization. As the Dolphin Resort & Hotel is a family business, Chris has to make sure that the new acquisition is in line with Kathy's vision for future success, as well as maintaining the mission to ensure customer and employee satisfaction. He also needs to assess whether the expansion will sustain their strong position in the marketplace. Next, Chris has to look at **divisional strategy**, which determines how a business will compete in a particular industry or market. He will need to assess each division of the hotel, ensure that it is in line with the hotel's vision, and decide which measures will need to be put in place in order to provide for the new acquisition. Finally, Chris designs a **functional strategy**, which determines how employees will implement and achieve a tactical plan. He needs to define a set of rules for the hotel staff in each functional area. With the philosophical foundation of an organization's mission, vision, and values, organizational, divisional, and functional strategies are documented using business, tactical, and operational plans, respectively. See Figure 9-1 for an illustration of how all this is interrelated.

Here, we can define a **business plan** as the stated actions and goals that support organizational strategy, and **tactical** and **operational** plans as the stated actions and goals that support achieving the divisional strategy.

But it isn't enough to simply reflect on the three levels of strategy; Chris has to take an in-depth look at the hotel industry as a whole, assess the competition, and decide whether or not the acquisition of the Porpoise Inn would be a good move for the Dolphin Resort & Hotel in such a tough economic climate. Following Kathy's advice, he picks up the phone and arranges a meeting with Lisa Reynolds, the general manager of the Porpoise Inn.

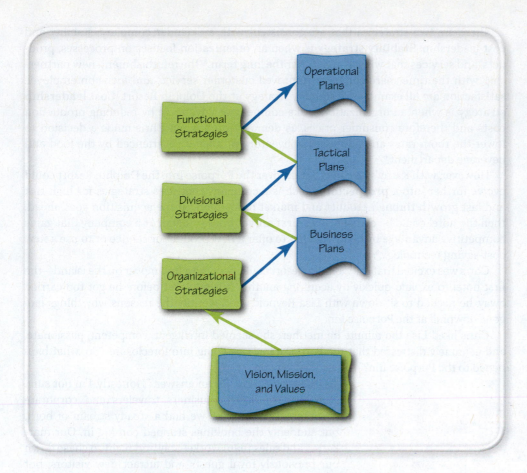

✓ **Operational Plan**—the stated actions and goals that support the functional strategy

LECTURE ENHANCER:

9.3 Organizational Strategies

➤ Organizations are defined by the types of strategies they apply to their business.

➤ Competitive Advantage—the characteristics of an organization's products or services that distinguish it from competitors and provide an advantage in the marketplace

➤ Companies can be categorized as *first movers*, *reactors*, *prospectors*, *defenders*, or *analyzers*.

✓ **Reactor**—a company that does not follow a consistent strategy, but just "reacts" to changes in the environment

✓ **Analyzer**—a company whose strategies seek to maintain existing products and services while pursuing limited innovation

Figure 9-1
Connecting "Mission, Vision, and Values" to Strategies and Plans
Vision, mission, and values stem from plans and strategies.

✓ **Defender**—a company whose strategies support stable growth and continual improvements of existing products and services

✓ **Prospector**—a company that uses strategies for high-risk and fast growth through product and market innovation

Competitive advantage The characteristics of an organization's products or services that distinguish it from competitors and provide an advantage in the marketplace.

Reactor A company that does not follow a consistent strategy but just responds to changes in the environment.

Analyzer A company whose strategies seek to maintain existing products and services while pursuing limited innovation. They often imitate or follow the proven success of prospector organizations.

Defender A company whose strategies support stable growth and continual improvement of existing products and services.

9.3 | ORGANIZATIONAL STRATEGIES

9.3 | Explain how senior managers develop organizational strategies and business plans.

Organizations are defined by the types of strategies that they apply to their business. Business strategies can be classified in many ways, but all of them seek to gain **competitive advantage**, the characteristics of an organization's products or services that distinguish it from competitors and provide an advantage in the marketplace.[2] By following certain types of strategies, companies can be categorized as *first movers*, *reactors*, *prospectors*, *defenders*, or *analyzers*.

Now, let's take a look at how the Dolphin Resort & Hotel has evolved strategically over the past five years. Under Herb Cork's management, we could define the hotel as a **reactor**, which is a company that does not follow a consistent strategy, but just responds to changes in the environment. This is the least effective of all the strategies, and in the case of the Dolphin Resort & Hotel, its lack of progression nearly resulted in bankruptcy.

When Chris joined as general manager of the Dolphin Resort & Hotel, he created a new mission statement and BHAG, which were the foundations of a new strategy. Under his management, the Dolphin Resort started as an **analyzer**, which is a company whose strategies seek to maintain existing products and services while pursuing limited innovation.[3] As we explored in Chapter 8, Chris based many of his suggestions for the Dolphin Resort on his experience in the hotel industry and introduced several measures that had already proved to be successful in other hotels, such as welcoming guests with cookies, arranging a partnership with a local time-share company, and managing cost-effective improvements and renovations to the hotel's divisions.

Thanks to the implementation of goal plans and decision making, the hotel has successfully made the transition from analyzer to **defender**, which is a company whose strategies support stable growth and continual improvement of existing products and services.[4] It is a requirement of the division-level managers to pursue certain strategies consistent with being a defender company.

There are two strategies that are consistent with a defender company: stability and cost leadership. **Stability strategy** is when an organization focuses on processes, products, and services that will sustain it over the long term.[5] The refurbishment, new partnership with the time-share company, improved customer service, and focus on employee satisfaction are all examples of stability strategy at the Dolphin Resort. **Cost leadership strategy** is when an organization seeks competitive advantage by reducing production costs and therefore consumer prices, as demonstrated when Chris made a decision to lower the room rates and address the inventory problems experienced by the food and beverage department.[6]

However, with Kathy's new idea to take over the Porpoise Inn, the Dolphin Resort could evolve further into a **prospector**, which is a company that uses strategies for high-risk and fast growth through product and market innovation.[7] If the acquisition goes ahead, then the hotel could be classified as a **first mover** on the island, or a company that gains competitive advantage by being the first to offer a new product or service or to use a new cost-saving technology.[8]

Chris was excited that the Dolphin Resort could become a first mover on the island—the first hotel to expand quickly by acquiring another business. Yet before he got too carried away, he needed to sit down with Lisa Reynolds and identify the reasons why things had gone downhill at the Porpoise Inn.

Chris liked Lisa the minute he met her: she seemed intelligent, competent, passionate, and genuinely distressed that the Porpoise Inn was going into foreclosure. "So, what happened to the Porpoise Inn?" Chris asked, simply.

© Blend Images/iStockphoto

Lisa seemed lost for an answer. "Honestly, I'm not sure. Our main market is business travelers and corporate events, and in the past we had a steady stream of both, but suddenly the bookings stopped coming in. Our marketing and sales team worked day and night to chase down our previously loyal guests and attract new visitors, but nothing seemed to work. Eventually the number of empty rooms grew and our profits sank."

As Chris talked through the figures with Lisa, he was not encouraged by the hotel's performance. How could you have such a great manager and staff and still suffer such a steady decline? Although Chris had experienced a number of obstacles during his time at the Dolphin Resort, he had remained confident that he could get things back on track. Not wanting to write the opportunity off too soon, Chris forged ahead with assessing the situation to see if acquiring the Porpoise Inn was a viable option.

9.4 | INDUSTRY AND COMPETITIVE ANALYSIS

9.4 | Outline methods that managers use to understand their industries and competition.

Over the next few days, Chris continues to work on the analysis for Kathy. He knows the hotel industry well but realizes that he needs to know it inside out in order to assess the level of risk involved in the acquisition. After his preliminary conversation with Lisa at the Porpoise Inn, Chris conducts an industry and **competitive analysis**, which is the process of assessing and monitoring the competition in order to design more effective strategies.

During the review, he is reminded of the multiple levels of systemic change experienced by the hotel industry, including the impacts from terrorism, pandemics, third-party distributors on the Internet, oversupply developed in an inflated real estate market, shift in business and leisure consumer travel habits, and expanded efficiencies through technology. The most noticeable trend was a steadily declining market for business travel, brought on by technology advances in communication; business meetings all over the world could now be

Voices of Management

Akhil Jain[9]
President, Landmark Hotel Group

"You must start with a perpetual desire to learn, innovate, and be the best in your field. Once armed with that drive, I believe resources to better understand your industry and competition will become self-evident because one cannot be successful in a vacuum; to be successful, we must have intimate knowledge of our industry and the competition around us.

As president of a growing hotel management company, I keep tabs on my industry by religiously reading industry trade magazines, journals, blogs, and websites. I also make it a point to attend annual industry conferences to network with colleagues and gain new perspectives from experts in fields relevant to me.

To truly understand one's competition, there is no substitute for physically touring the competition's facilities and getting to know their people, systems, and processes. I make it a point to personally experience my competitor's hotels in order to understand their strengths and weaknesses. This knowledge becomes critical when developing an effective SWOT analysis for our company and its hotels—an integral component of our strategic planning process."

Company Profile

Name: Landmark Hotel Group

Founded: 1983 in North Carolina

Owner/Founder: Raj Jain

President: Akhil Jain

Company Story: Landmark Hotel Group is a hospitality management company that owns, operates, and develops hotels along the East Coast. The company is founded on the knowledge and understanding that excellent service and a quality product is key to achieving the highest level of performance.

Critical Thinking in the Classroom

What are your views on Akhil Jain's approach to management? What methods would you use to research and better understand your competition? ■

---

conducted virtually. Rising fuel costs were also affecting air travel, making it too expensive for some organizations to justify face-to-face business meetings.

Five Forces Model

To put all of these factors into a clear illustration for Kathy, Chris applies the Five Forces Model outlined in Figure 9-2, that were developed by Harvard University professor and researcher Michael Porter.[10] This analytical model allows managers to assess the major threats that an organization can expect to encounter in an industry. By outlining and proactively responding to these threats, Porter suggests that managers can define more clearly their opportunity to be successful. The Five Forces Model outlines five forces that determine what managers should expect when competing in an industry: power of suppliers, power of buyers, substitute products and services, new entrants, and rivalry.

As Chris goes through all of the collected data, he is lacking reasons as to why the Dolphin Resort & Hotel should buy the Porpoise Inn. The Five Forces Model illustrates the following threats facing the hotel industry:

- Power of suppliers
- Power of buyers (customers)
- Substitute products and services
- New entrants
- Rivalry

Power of Suppliers Chris starts by assessing the ability of their suppliers to increase prices. In Chapter 8, Chris set a goal for John Johnson, the Dolphin's food and beverage director, to check out other suppliers on the island and to see what the cost would be if they switched from one to the other. He notices that the Porpoise Inn uses some of the same suppliers as the Dolphin Resort & Hotel. The acquisition should put them in a good bargaining position with the suppliers, who would, most likely, be eager to retain their contracts with both hotels.

LECTURE ENHANCER:

9.4 Industry and Competitive Analysis

➤ Voices of Management: Akhil Jain—President, Landmark Hotel Group, LLC

✓ **Competitive Analysis**—the process of assessing and monitoring the competition in order to design more effective strategies

● **Five Forces Model**
  ➤ Developed by Harvard University professor and researcher Michael Porter
  ➤ Outlines five forces that determine what managers should expect when competing in an industry
  ➤ Figure 9-2: The Five Forces that Shape Industry Competition
  1. *Power of Suppliers*—the ability of suppliers to increase prices
  2. *Power of Buyers (Customers)*—the ability of customers to drive prices down or switch loyalty to a competitor
  3. *Substitute Products and Services*—the importance of maintaining a unique rand of products and services to retain the customer base
  4. *New Entrants*—the threat of new competitors entering the market
  5. *Rivalry*—a rise of competitors that offer the same products and services

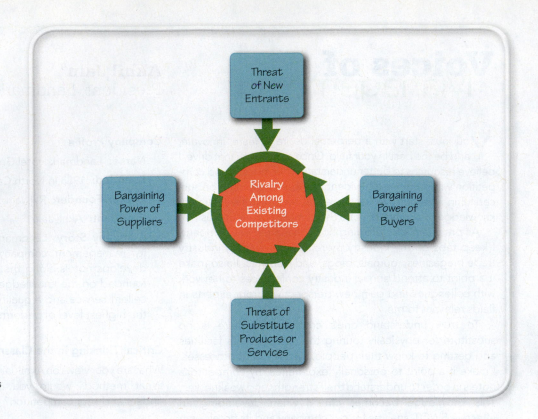

Figure 9-2
The Five Forces That Shape Industry Competition
Continued reinvention and the shaping of a business can be an ongoing process that includes market condition changes, including the competition, economic changes, and changes in the customer base.

- **Knowing the Competition Seven Barriers to Entry**
  1. *Supply-side Economies of Scale*—cost advantages resulting from additional resources
  2. *Demand-side Benefits of Scale*—higher sales resulting from increased customer-base
  3. *Customer Switching Costs*—a reduction in competition due to a higher cost in switching from one product or service to another
  4. *Capital Requirements* – how much investment is needed to maintain operations
  5. *Incumbent Advantages Independent of Size*—an organization's advantages (i.e. capital investment, excellent rapport, loyal staff and customers, etc.)
  6. *Unequal Access to Distribution Channels*—competing on the ability to secure distributors or advertisers
  7. *Restrictive Government Policy*—restriction imposed by government policies

- ✓ **Competitive Inertia**—a tendency to continue with competitive practices that have previously been successful

- ✓ **Barrier to entry**—an obstacle that makes it difficult for an organization to enter a particular market or replicate a competitor's service and product offerings

Power of Buyers (Customers) In the hotel business, customers have all the power. If a hotel has only a few guests at a time, then they drive prices down, as the hotel might need to reduce rates in order to compete. It is also easy for customers to switch from one hotel to the other. Chris knows that guest retention is key when running a hotel business, but they are running out of space at the Dolphin Inn. Here, he concludes that an acquisition of another hotel property will give the Dolphin Inn an opportunity to expand and take in more guests, while maintaining their room rate.

Substitute Products and Services Chris realizes the importance of maintaining a unique range of products and services for his customers. One of the main problems affecting the hotel industry is that videoconferencing has become a substitute for business travel. Corporate clients can now network virtually, substituting a hotel stay with videoconferences held between offices. However, although there is less business travel than before, Chris knows there are still a number of well-attended corporate events that are held every year. By offering WiFi, a state-of-the-art conference room and business center, and a refurbished hotel that offered gourmet food, all in a beautiful setting, Chris feels that the Dolphin Resort & Hotel is taking the right steps toward attracting and retaining their corporate client base. Having reviewed the services offered at the Porpoise Inn, Chris realizes that the Dolphin Resort does not offer a van service for their clients. He makes a note to address this point with Kathy. Chris knows they will have to be continually innovative to maintain this segment of the market.

New Entrants Chris also has to consider the threat of new competitors entering the market. He recently discovered that developers are planning to build a new hotel, the Fisherman's Hotel, about two miles from the Dolphin Resort. The sign on the building site notes a grand opening for the following summer. He has yet to find out the details, but if it matches or even exceeds the services offered by the Dolphin Resort and offers a competitive rate, the new hotel's arrival could weaken their position.

Seven Barriers to Entry Chris makes a note to keep an eye on the potential competitor and stay one step ahead of it wherever possible. Chris also has to consider the seriousness of the threat of entry and how the new hotel might affect the Dolphin Resort & Hotel, as well as the Porpoise Inn, and what they could do to retaliate if it posed a significant threat to their business.

Chris decides to do an assessment of the Fisherman's Hotel by considering seven possible barriers to entry. A **barrier to entry** is an obstacle that makes it difficult for an organization to enter a particular market or replicate a competitor's service and product offerings.[11]

- **Supply-side economies of scale**

  Chris asks around and learns that the Fisherman's Hotel is privately owned, it is not part of a chain, and at least so far, it didn't seem to have any plans to expand once it gets established in the area. If the Dolphin Resort and the Porpoise Inn were to merge, it would give them a competitive advantage over the Fisherman's Hotel, as their economies of scale, or cost advantages resulting from the expansion, would potentially be lower. For example, the merged properties would require double the supplies, which could be bought at a lower bulk rate if they can negotiate better terms from suppliers (which they might be in a better position to do). They would also have more staff in research, marketing, and sales than the Fisherman's Hotel, which would enable them to be more aggressive when it came to attracting new business and retaining customers. Chris concluded that the potential competitor would have to enter the market on a very large scale to be considered a threat to the Dolphin Resort and Porpoise Inn.

- **Demand-side benefits of scale**

  Chris was confident that the Dolphin and the Porpoise Inn were market leaders on the island when it came to offering unique products. Their increasing customer base at the Dolphin Resort was buying items from the gift shop, indulging in the homemade ice cream, and paying higher prices at their much-improved restaurant. As word of mouth spread, Chris was delighted to find the numbers of guests rising every week. He knew that the Dolphin still needed to implement a van service and keep pushing new initiatives to make sure that it maintained its status as one of the island's top hotels. If the merger was to take place, it would also need to invest heavily on branding to let its customers know that the Dolphin and the Porpoise were part of the same hotel group. Chris needed to find out how the Fisherman's Hotel intended to advertise and brand itself in preparation for the big opening next summer.

- **Customer switching costs**

  Often, competition will be reduced if there is a higher cost to switching from one product or service to another. From experience, Chris knew that one of the main challenges facing the hotel industry was when customers went elsewhere because of cost. So far, the Dolphin Resort has competitive room rates, an Olympic-size pool, private beach access, refurbished rooms, free WiFi, complimentary afternoon tea and cookies on arrival, a unique gift shop, a reasonably priced restaurant offering locally grown organic and gourmet food, and a state-of-the-art conference room and business center. Chris was confident that customers would not get the same value for their money if they went to any other hotel on the island. Still, he had to do his due diligence on the Fisherman's Hotel to make sure that it would not rival the Dolphin Resort on rates or amenities.

- **Capital requirements**

  From his experience at other hotels that he had managed and, most recently at the Dolphin Resort, Chris knew how much investment was needed to maintain a hotel and its operation, particularly when much of the upfront capital was spent on advertising and marketing. He felt fortunate that the Dolphin Resort was in such a good financial position that they were even able to consider a merger with another hotel. Chris wondered if the Fisherman's Hotel had the large financial resources necessary to be serious competition for them.

© Sigarru / iStockphoto

- **Incumbent advantages independent of size**

  Although Chris was beginning to realize how a merger with the Porpoise Inn could be a good strategic move, especially when it came to defending the organization against the competition, he also believed that the Dolphin

Resort was strong standing on its own. The resort had capital investment, a healthy bank balance, an excellent rapport with the bank, access to the latest technology, loyal staff and customers, an excellent geographic location, and the potential to expand. "Even if we didn't merge with the Porpoise Inn, the Fisherman's Hotel would have to do a great deal to challenge our position," Chris thought.

- **Unequal access to distribution channels**

Chris knew that the Fisherman's Hotel would need to secure distribution of its services. The previous year, Chris made a deal with several of the local travel agents and tourist offices to give the Dolphin Resort priority when it came to promoting properties to walk-in customers. The marketing department had also succeeded in securing advertising space in local magazines and newspapers and on online travel sites. The Fisherman's Hotel could easily use these forms of distribution to attract new customers, however, and Chris made a note for the marketing department to follow their advertising and branding strategy closely.

- **Restrictive government policy**

Every industry, big or small, is subject to government policies. Typically, the hotel industry is affected by restrictions regarding licensing, foreign investment, and fairly recent restrictive immigration laws, the latter of which have affected the tourist industry. Chris relied on the legal team to make sure that they were kept fully appraised of all existing and potential government policies, and wondered if the Fisherman's Hotel had done the same.

Expected Retaliation To consider the idea of possible retaliation, Chris put himself in the other owner's shoes: if he were building a new hotel and knew that his property was going to have to face serious competition, what kind of reaction might he expect from the incumbent hotel? Concerns would include:

- Whether the incumbent has a large amount of financial resources to fight back, a loyal customer base, and influence over distribution channels
- Whether the incumbent can afford to slash prices to compete with the new hotel and to keep its share of the market
- Whether industry growth is slow, meaning that the only way that the new hotel could attract customers would be by luring them away from the incumbent

As Chris assessed these points, he realized that if he were in the other owner's shoes, he would be pretty worried about the Dolphin Resort and the competition that it would pose. Still, this was not a time to be complacent. Chris needed to brief Kathy and the team about the new hotel and outline a strategy that would keep them ahead of the game whether the Dolphin Resort bought the Porpoise Inn or not.

Rivalry An increase in competitors that offer the same products and services can spell trouble for a business unless it finds some way of differentiating its offerings. While Chris is confident that the Dolphin Resort has a unique selling point in providing private beach access to its guests, he is well aware that in the future, this might not be enough.

This competitive analysis gave Chris new insights into the challenges that the industry must address. He picked up the phone and arranged another meeting with the Porpoise Inn's general manager, Lisa Reynolds, for the next morning.

Chris was impressed by Lisa, and he wanted to forge a business relationship with her. After all, even if they didn't acquire the Porpoise Inn, he may be able to find a place for her at the Dolphin Resort. But first, he had to establish the reasons why such a once-profitable business was close to going under. So he pursued that line of inquiry at their next meeting. "Your main market was business visitors," Chris recapped. "But as we know, business travel has slowed down due to technological innovation and budget constraints. In light of this, did you ever consider going after a different segment of the market?"

"Yes," Lisa said, nodding. "Very recently, we launched a campaign to attract families with children, but it didn't work. In hindsight, we should have carried out the campaign much earlier."

A light bulb went off in Chris's head. He now knew why the Porpoise Inn had gone downhill. For too long, it had focused on its steady flow of business travelers while neglecting other areas of the market. The inn had suffered from **competitive inertia**, which is a tendency to continue competitive practices that had been successful in the past, even if they are less effective in the present.[12] Lisa agreed with this assumption, telling Chris that she regretted not taking action earlier to keep the hotel profitable. After a pause, Chris asked, "So, why do you think your plan to attract families failed?"

Lisa said, "The feedback we received was that families coming to a coastal town expect beach access, which we don't have." Chris replied, "So, if you only had access to a private beach like the Dolphin Resort, you and your team would probably be doing better!" Chris did a quick analysis in his head: for the Porpoise Inn, inaccessibility to the beach was a barrier to entry.

Chris stopped himself. "Wait a minute . . . Maybe we are looking at this opportunity all wrong. Okay, Lisa, are you willing to be *really* creative in order to make Porpoise Inn a success?"

She nodded enthusiastically. "I am willing to try anything that will keep us in business, and keep my team members employed."

9.5 | ORGANIZATIONAL POSITION AND CAPACITY

9.5 | **Describe** how managers assess the organization's capacity to execute proposed business plans.

Chris and Lisa spent the next several days traveling back and forth between the Porpoise Inn and Dolphin Resort exchanging thoughts and ideas. Although he had gained a new understanding of the hotel industry and the local competitors, there were still many questions to be answered: What level of **resources**—the assets, people, processes, and capabilities of an organization[13]—could the Dolphin afford to allocate if they acquired the Porpoise? Would there be enough money to make capital improvements to the property once it was purchased? How would the stakeholders react to such a big venture? Overall, what are the strengths and weaknesses of the Dolphin Resort & Hotel and the Porpoise Inn, and could the organization sustain immediate growth if the two were merged?

To answer these questions effectively, Chris needed to assess the position of the organization and its capacity to move to a more desirable position. An organization's **market position** is an honest assessment about how the company competes in its industry. An organization's **capacity** refers to the financial and human resources available to the company, which will enable or hinder it to achieve goals. In this section, we will explore how managers assess the organization's market position and capacity to execute proposed business plans.

Company Position

The **BCG Matrix**, illustrated in Figure 9-3, is a framework developed by the Boston Consulting Group for evaluating business units according to growth and market share.[14] This tool and process was designed so that managers could quickly categorize their company's position in the industry where it competes, enabling management to assess quickly the validity of its strategies and where to invest resources.

The BCG Matrix is largely based on market share. The higher percentage of the market an organization holds, the higher proportion of the market controlled by that organization. It stands to reason that companies with a high market share make more money than those that have a smaller segment of the market. Chris knew that the Dolphin Resort & Hotel had almost regained its status as the most desirable hotel on the island, and concluded that it had the greatest market share when it came to the hotel industry in the area. However, did this mean that they should be investing in another venture just because they were profitable?

Competitive inertia A tendency to continue with competitive practices that had been successful in the past, even if they are less effective in the present.

LECTURE ENHANCER:
9.5 Organizational Position and Capacity
➤ An organization's market position is an honest assessment about how the company competes in its industry.
➤ An organization's capacity refers to the financial and human resources available to the company, which will enable or hinder it to achieve goals
• Company Position
✓ BCG Matrix—a framework developed by Boston Consulting Group for evaluating business units according to growth and market share
➤ Figure 9-3: BCG Matrix
1. Dogs—low market share and low market growth
2. Cash Cows—high market share and low market growth
3. Stars—high market share and high market growth
4. Question Marks—low market share and high market growth

Resources The assets, people, processes, and capabilities of an organization.

Market position An honest assessment about how the company competes in its industry.

Capacity refers to the financial and human resources available to the company, which will enable or hinder it to achieve goals.

BCG Matrix A framework developed by the Boston Consulting Group for evaluating business units according to growth and market share.

✓ **Growth Strategy**—strategy for increasing revenues, profits, market share, or territories
✓ **SWOT analysis**—a method of assessing an organization's strengths, weaknesses, opportunities, and threats

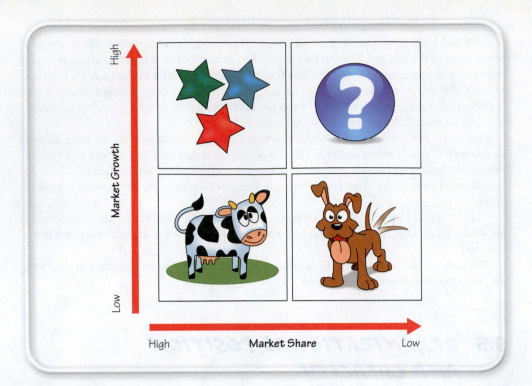

Figure 9-3
BCG Matrix
The four quadrants defined in the matrix include Star, Question Mark, Cash Cow, and Dog.

Growth strategy A strategy for increasing revenue, profits, market share, or territories.

➤ A useful way of defining business strategy and helping to make strategic insights and decisions.
➤ Table 9-1: SWOT Analysis
• **Capabilities and Resources**
✓ **Core capabilities (Core competencies)**—the activities and processes that an organization routinely does well in comparison to its competitors
✓ **Resources**—the assets, people, and processes of an organization
➤ Table 9-2: Dolphin Resort & Hotel vs. Porpoise Inn Capabilities & Resources Analysis
➤ Figure 9-4: Growth and Underinvestment Archetype
➤ Companies that experience rapid growth within a small time period have a tendency to come to a rapid halt, without any clear explanation.

To figure this out, Chris needed to take a look at **growth strategy**, which is a strategy for increasing revenue, profits, market share, or territories.[15] In a high-growth market, where the total business is expanding, it is easier for companies in that realm to build their profits even if their market share remains the same. There is less competition in a high-growth market, as there is enough business for everyone to enjoy. In short, everyone gets a slice of the pie. However, as Chris knows from his study of the Five Forces model, the hotel industry has suffered a number of blows over the past few years, which means it is currently categorized as a low-growth market. Competition is tougher; there is not enough pie to go around, and everybody is fighting for the last slice. Even if companies have high market share, they might end up losing a portion of it through discounting and other competitive measures. Chris needed to work through the matrix to find out which area was most relevant to the Dolphin Resort.

Managers plot market share and growth potential on a 2 × 2 matrix, and the business's position in the matrix determines a strategic recommendation. On the x-axis, a manager plots market share, from low to high, and on the y-axis, growth potential from low to high. There are four quadrants defined in the matrix:

- Dogs
- Cash Cows
- Stars
- Question Marks

Dogs (Low Market Share/Low Market Growth) Dogs are organizations that have very little market presence and barely register on other companies' radars. Unless something major happens in the industry, there is very little chance that Dogs will ever develop into a real competitor, and some might be better off cutting their losses. Companies classified as Dogs must work very hard in order to establish higher growth and to be considered a serious player in the industry.

Cash Cows (High Market Share/Low Market Growth) Cash-cow companies that have high market share also have a high profile, which gives them the flexibility to take advantage of new opportunities. However, if the market isn't growing, the company might be limited in how much it can actually expand. Many cash-cow organizations use this time of low growth to save money in anticipation of the market picking up in the future.

Stars (High Market Share/High Market Growth) Being a Star is probably the optimal position to be in for any organization. With high market share and growth comes significant investment and return. Not only is the company well established, with a high profile and a growing market, it has potential to invest in the future.

Question Marks (Low Market Share/High Market Growth) Question Marks are companies that generate the most questions as to where they going in the future; they have low market share, but they are in the right industry for growth, so they have the potential to make money. Usually, Question Marks will invest heavily in order to achieve Star status. Only time will tell if the Question Marks will become Cash Cows and eventually Stars.

How do managers know where to plot their organization, other than simply guessing? Chris applied a **SWOT analysis**, which is a method of assessing an organization's strengths, weaknesses, opportunities, and threats (abbreviated as SWOT).[16] It is a useful way of defining business strategy and helping to make strategic insights and decisions. Table 9-1 outlines a general set of questions that Chris applied to the Dolphin Resort to complete an honest assessment of the organization's position, and Table 9-2 shows the answers to those questions.

As Chris reviews both tables, he realizes that they provide a useful reminder of some of the areas that he has considered; namely, that they needed a van service in order to compete

> **SWOT analysis** A method of assessing an organization's strengths, weaknesses, opportunities, and threats (abbreviated as SWOT).

Table 9-1	Dolphin Resort SWOT Analysis Questions		
Strengths vs. Competitors (internal)	**Weaknesses vs. Competitors (internal)**	**Opportunities (internal and external)**	**Threats (can't control)**
What does our hotel (department) do well?	What could we improve?	What market trends can we take advantage of?	Are there any threatening weather events that could potentially hurt our business?
How is our physical building a strength?	Building maintenance?	Are there new companies moving in the market?	What is going on in the market that may harm us?
Is our location a strength?	Landscaping?	Is there a company with growth happening?	Which weaknesses can harm us further?
Is our service a strength?	Location?	Is there a hotel undergoing renovations, and therefore fewer rooms in the market?	Do we have a renovation scheduled or any amenity changes coming?
What do our customers say are our strengths?	Amenities?	Are there special events scheduled?	
What do our employees say are our strengths?	Service?	Can any of our strengths better position us with a tough client?	
What is unique about our hotel?	Competitive rates?	Can we market our strengths?	
	Staff levels?		
	Training?		
	Development?		
	Recruitment?		
	On-boarding?		
	What do our customers and vendors say are our weaknesses?		
	What do our employees say?		

Table 9-2 Dolphin Resort Responses to SWOT Analysis Questions

Strengths vs. Competitors (internal)	Weaknesses vs. Competitors (internal)	Opportunities (internal and external)	Threats (can't control)
Our location can easily be found vs. our competition.	Our menu selection, although much improved, could do with some refreshing.	Engage long-term employees in service training and becoming champions of our business.	There is a new enterprise, called the Fisherman's Hotel, opening mid-year.
Our staffing levels are consistent; we have low turnover and easy recruitment.	Our customer service scores are improving but could be better.	Check which of our corporate accounts are requesting van service, and find out the volume potential in revenue vs. van cost and staffing.	The hurricane season is supposed to be bad this year.
We just completed a soft-goods renovation (i.e., an upgrade to linens, carpets, draperies, etc.) in our rooms and public spaces.	We do not have the same capacity as some other local hotels.	There is a hotel nearby that is undergoing renovation and will have to close off part of its building. We could have the opportunity to take on the overflow and the ability to raise rates.	The highway department has scheduled roadwork in front of the hotel in the spring.
We have private access to the beach.	We do not have van service. Employees need more training.		

with some of the other hotels in the area, and that road construction in the future months may affect business. It also did not escape him that the opportunity to take on the overflow of guests from the hotel that was undergoing refurbishment might not happen unless they deal with the capacity issue at the Dolphin Resort.

Once Chris completes the SWOT analysis, he is ready to plot the Dolphin Resort on the BCG Matrix. As the Dolphin is the most profitable hotel on the island, Chris considers that it has a high share of the market, yet it is clear that the hotel industry is facing low growth potential. When Chris applies the BCG Matrix, the framework process affirms the insights that he gained from the industry and competitive analysis, yet it also introduces new questions that require further investigation. According to the matrix, the Dolphin Resort is a Cash Cow. It also determines that the Porpoise Inn is a Dog in its current state. Chris ponders the question: "Should Cash Cows invest in Dogs? If I propose a new strategy to Kathy to transform the Porpoise Inn into another potential Cash Cow by increasing its market share, does the Dolphin Resort have the resources and capabilities to execute the plan?"

Capabilities and Resources

Chris knew that even the best plans fail if organizations are not capable of executing or committing the resources necessary to succeed. The **core capabilities**, of an organization, sometimes referred to as *core competencies*, refers to the activities and processes that an organization routinely does well in comparison to its competitors.[17,18] To analyze the acquisition opportunity effectively, Chris completed a core capabilities and resource analysis for both the Dolphin Resort and the Porpoise Inn. This process is an extension of the SWOT analysis and was conducted using the questions outlined in Table 9-1 to investigate capabilities and resources, respectively.

For each question, Chris worked with staff from both hotels to do due diligence and gather verifiable information. He worked with Lisa on the Porpoise Inn's past and present financial statements, reviewed their management and operations, and requested that the Dolphin Resort's legal team carry out a legal compliance review to ensure that the hotel would be protected from any potential legal problems in the future. Litigation analysis is a particularly important part of the due diligence process; buyers need to be aware of any

Core capabilities Activities and processes that an organization routinely does well in comparison to its competitors; also known as *core competencies*.

Table 9-3	Capabilities and Resources Analysis: Dolphin Hotel & Resort vs. Porpoise Inn

Questions	Dolphin vs. Porpoise
What are the overall biggest expenses and differences in the hotels?	Labor—the organizational chart from fixed expenses on top-line executive salary and structure is more streamlined at the Dolphin vs. at the Porpoise. Porpoise has a larger executive staff vs. line employees, costing more in fixed labor costs in terms of percentage, therefore lowering profit.
How does the Cost Per Occupied Room (CPOR) measure up at each location?	The Dolphin Resort maintains a consistent cost month to month, regardless of occupancy fluctuations. The Porpoise Inn has a rollercoaster model, with month-to-month expenses per occupied room. This variance makes up approximately an additional 5 percent in profit annually.
How do the CPOR and/or % to revenue measure up with regard to utility costs per hotel, as well as to the national average?	The Dolphin Resort's utility costs have increased with the national averages and local utility forecasted costs each year. The Porpoise Inn costs have spiked during the past 18 months. Further investigation is needed to review possible causes, including gas leaks and/or equipment draw on electricity. This equates another 3 percent in lost profits.
How do repairs and maintenance stack up at each location?	Overall, the Porpoise Inn has had several equipment failures and replacement the past 24 months—some items should have been capitalized vs. expensed on the profit and loss statement. The preventative maintenance system (PMS) is far more consistent in the rooms, public space, and back of the house at the Dolphin Resort, requiring less cost on large repairs and items or rooms out of service over time.
Sales and marketing costs typically average at 10 percent of total revenue—how do the two locations compare?	In comparisons, both hotels spend equal dollars per location, but the values in terms of percentage of sales are different. The Porpoise Inn has experienced a decline in top-line revenue but maintained the sales staffing model and marketing plan. Reorganization, rebudgeting, and stronger accountability is needed for the return expected as per the expenses.
Turnover in line employees, training, and development comparisons.	The inconsistent occupancy trends at the Porpoise Inn have made it difficult to staff and train employees properly. The ongoing costs to run ads for placement, along with training fees, have dramatically increased the cost of labor for both the front-of-house and back-of-house employees.

dispute in the past from suppliers, customers, employees, or shareholders that may affect the hotel in the future.[19] The information that Chris gathered is included in Table 9-3.

Once Chris had completed the due diligence process, he put together a strategic plan and was ready to make his formal recommendation to Kathy and the stakeholders to acquire the Porpoise Inn. The major premise of the strategy that he presented was a need to invest, so that the company could continue to grow its profits.

During the presentation, Chris talked through the discoveries that he had made through the Five Forces Model, the BCG Matrix, and his analysis of the Porpoise Inn's potential. He told Kathy that the Dolphin Resort's major challenge to increasing its performance was capacity (segment B3 in Figure 9-4). The hotel was running out of space. With lower rates and higher quality, the resort was now operating at a very high occupancy level, which would likely increase. In order to grow, Chris concluded that the resort needed to invest in more accommodations for their ever-growing client base.

Kathy, who had been silent throughout the presentation, suddenly interjected, "I can see where this is going, Chris. I know our hotel is becoming popular, but our success has been relatively recent. You need to convince me we should spend our hard-earned profits on buying another hotel that has had such poor financial performance. Don't you think this is too much of a risk?" Chris nodded. "I agree that this acquisition could be perceived as a risk, but it might be more of a risk to adopt a 'wait and see' approach." To illustrate his point, Chris put up the systems archetype "Growth and Underinvestment," as illustrated in Figure 9-4, on the screen.

This archetype is similar in concept to the Limits to Growth archetype that we explored in Chapter 3. The theory holds that companies that experience rapid growth within a small

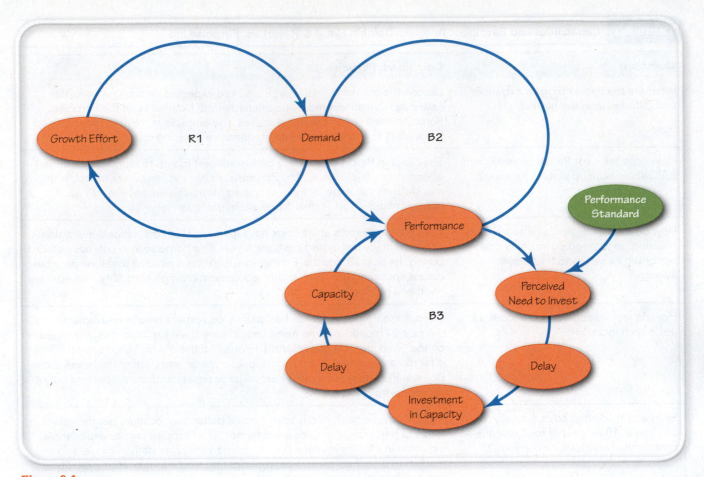

Figure 9-4
Growth and Underinvestment Archetype
Companies that underinvest remain in their current state, leading to stagnation and unfulfilled goals. B, balancing loop; R, reinforcing loop.
Source: D. Kim, *Systems Archetypes I* (Waltham, MA: Pegasus Communications, 1994).

© moncsicsi/iStockphoto

time period have a tendency to come to a rapid halt, without any clear explanation. Chris said, "Kathy, this archetype is to show you the threat of not investing when the time is right. As you can see, our performance is top-notch; we are almost filled to capacity, and demand is the highest it's ever been. Yes, all our achievements look great on paper, but if we delay with moving forward, we will end up running out of rooms, turning guests away, and losing the profit we have fought so hard for. In short, we will have become victims of our own success. All investment is risky, but I passionately believe that this is the right time for the Dolphin Resort & Hotel to expand." Chris stopped to catch his breath, and wondered if he had got a bit carried away with his motivational speech.

Kathy suggested to the stakeholders that they take some time to digest the information, reconvene the following day, and let Chris know the decision they had made. As the boardroom filled up the next morning, Chris couldn't remember a time that he had felt so nervous. Kathy spoke, "OK, Chris, you've convinced me and the rest of the shareholders. Let's do it. Let's buy the Porpoise Inn!" Chris let out a "Whoop!" His well-researched presentation had paid off. He and the team had convinced top management that the acquisition was a good idea. Now all they had to do was make their goal a reality—and then make the reality work.

A few months and a ton of paperwork later, the Dolphin Resort formally acquired the Porpoise Inn, which was subsequently renamed the Dolphin Resort and Porpoise Inn—"the best-valued hotel on Hilton Head Island, with trolley access to our private beach." The "Dolly Trolley" ran continuously from sunrise to 10 p.m. during the busy months of the year, and by request all other times. The newly implemented van service, which transported guests to and from the airport, was also a big hit with the guests. Soon, both hotels were thriving. Paul Reynolds, head of the time-share company, agreed to let the Dolphin Resort place time-share prospects stay at either hotel during the busy season, which allowed the resort and inn to both benefit from this unique arrangement.

9.6 | DIVISIONAL AND FUNCTIONAL STRATEGIES

LECTURE ENHANCER:

9.6 Divisional and Functional Strategies
- ➤ A Balanced Scorecard—Translating Vision into Strategy
- ➤ A Balanced Scorecard—Managing Strategy

9.6 | Demonstrate how managers develop divisional strategies and tactical plans.

It is a year later, and the transition process has been both exciting and difficult. With Chris managing the process, the Porpoise Inn has been fully transitioned into the Dolphin Resort & Hotel's operating policies and procedures. Applying the balanced scorecard approach has allowed the management team to "augment traditional financial measures with benchmarks for performance in three key nonfinancial areas: 1) a company's relationship with its customers, 2) its key internal processes, and 3) its learning and growth."[20] The framework intends to ensure that managers translate vision into strategy and execution of the strategy, both of which are critical to success. (See Research at Work: Seeing the Balanced Scorecard on page 244)

Team members from both hotels have been working well together, and morale is high. In the last year, Chris has only to make one staffing decision. The food and beverage division was doing well, and although John Johnson had come around to the transition, he was still the voice of dissent and tended to debate even the smallest of changes in his area. Chris worried that John's pessimistic nature was having a negative effect on the kitchen and restaurant staff; he also felt that he was spending more time managing John than anybody else. A change had to be made, especially in light of a promotion he was planning for one of the employees.

Chris had been thinking about the positive and creative contributions that Zoey Zhang had made since Chris arrived at the Dolphin Resort & Hotel, and he decided that it was the right time to increase her responsibilities. So he approached her one day and said, "Zoey, how would you like to be joint food and beverage director with John Johnson?" Zoey was taken aback. Chris went on, "We need someone with your passion and ideas in there, and I think you are the perfect choice."

Zoey replied, "I would be delighted, but how does John feel about it?" Chris paused. He had not cleared it with John—or Kathy yet, for that matter. It had just seemed like the perfect time to propose the idea. "I'll talk to John; it will be fine," Chris said. How could it not be fine? With John's expertise and Zoey Zhang's enthusiasm, they were the perfect partnership. He just hoped that Kathy and John would see it that way. That same day, he set up a meeting with Kathy. He told her the staffing decision he had made, albeit without her consent. "In theory, it's a good idea," Kathy said, "But knowing John for all these years, I'm not sure if he is going to take it well. He is a prideful man, and he may consider this a demotion."

Sure enough, John was not pleased about the idea of sharing his directorship with Zoey Zhang. "What have I been doing wrong?" he asked Chris. "Everyone in the division is doing a great job; we have implemented all your suggestions and cost-cutting measures, and everything is going smoothly. Why are you weakening my position by assigning someone to share my job?" Chris explained that rather than taking away from the role, Zoey would enhance it by helping John manage the staff and implement new initiatives. The meeting had been a long one, but eventually John begrudgingly assented. He'll come around, Chris thought, as he walked out of the meeting. He just needs time to get used to the idea.

Over the following months, however, John started to become a smaller presence at weekly team meetings, and eventually he stopped going altogether. Chris noticed his absences, but things were going so well in the food and beverage division that he didn't think much about it. Besides, he had a million other areas to tend to.

Seeing the Balanced Scorecard

As we explored in Chapter 8, researchers Robert Kaplan and David Norton have provided managers a balanced approach to planning through their balanced scorecard.[21] This framework, shown in the illustration, provides managers with a visual tool to translate vision into strategy.

A Balanced Scorecard—Translating Vision into Strategy: Four Perspectives

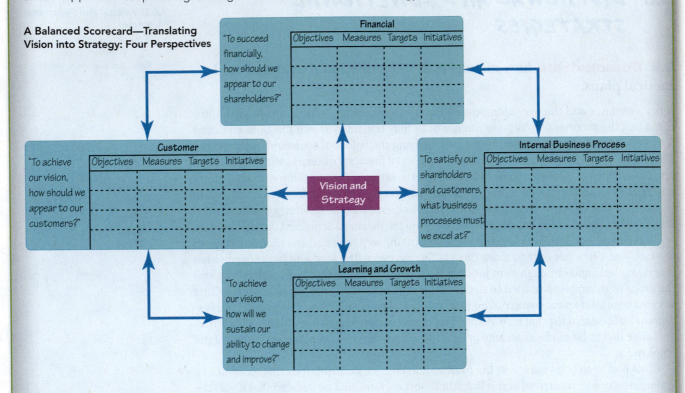

A Balanced Scorecard—Managing Strategy: Four Processes

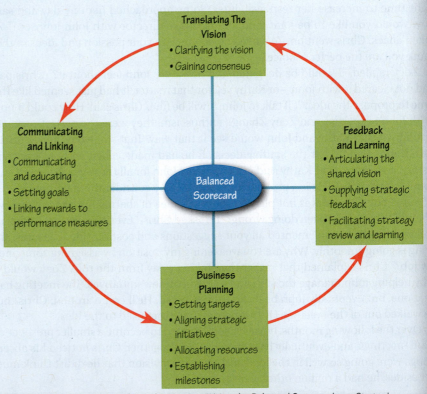

Once managers have turned their company's mission and vision into a strategy, Kaplan and Norton recommend using this exact framework as a tool for achieving results.

Critical Thinking in the Classroom

As a manager, how would you use the balanced scorecard to translate your vision into strategy?

Source: Robert S. Kaplan and David P. Norton, "Using the Balanced Scorecard as a Strategic Management System," *Harvard Business Review* (July 2007): 150–161.

On the one-year anniversary of the acquisition, John Johnson announced his resignation. Chris was disappointed. This was the first employee he had lost under his management, and he immediately blamed himself. Furthermore, John's resignation upset Chris's goal plan for 100 percent employee retention. The rest of the staff at both hotels seemed to be content and were working hard, united in their mission to achieve guest satisfaction and stellar customer service. Yet, he knew the resignation of any longstanding staff member was sure to cause ripples among the staff. Much as he tried, he couldn't persuade John to stay. "Things have changed too much for me here," John explained sadly. "As much as I respect Zoey, I feel I have been replaced."

Following an exhausting two hours of conversation, Chris had to admit defeat and accept that he had lost John Johnson. Not only was John a prideful man, but a stubborn one, and no argument from Chris could persuade him to stay. And Chris could not afford to dwell on the situation for too long. With their calendar full of corporate events coming up, he needed to sort out the staffing issue in the food and beverage division—and fast.

That afternoon, Chris walked into Kathy's office and said, "I have good news and bad news. The bad news is John Johnson has just resigned. The good news is that I think I have the perfect candidate to run the entire food and beverage division."

Kathy looked unsure. "First, I am very sad that John is leaving us; he has been with us from the beginning, and I really thought he was becoming more engaged with his new responsibilities." After a short pause, she said, "What reason did he give for resigning?" Chris cleared his throat, "He felt that his position was threatened with the addition of a new partner." Kathy didn't say anything—she didn't have to. Grateful for not receiving an "I told you so" from Kathy, Chris broke the silence. "I do think I have the answer to the staffing problem," he said.

Kathy replied, "Who do you have in mind to fill his shoes?" Chris smiled. "Zoey Zhang," he replied. "She has performed exceptionally well during her time as John's partner, and I think she is more than ready to take over sole directorship." They both agreed that the hardworking and cheerful Zoey Zhang was the perfect candidate for the position. It was decided that Chris would tell her the good news. He would then make a tactical plan to accomplish all the tasks that needed to be done before corporate event season took off. The rest of the staff also needed to be notified about the change in management and how they could work with Zoey to make the transition as smooth as possible.

9.7 | STRATEGIES FOR PERFORMANCE

9.7 | Compare traditional strategic planning models to an event-based approach.

Over the next year, the Dolphin Resort and the Porpoise Inn collaborated on a series of strategies to execute the company's goals more effectively and address operational challenges that they faced during implementation. The trolley access to the beach soon attracted more families to both hotels, and business was growing fast. However, Chris was noticing a trend: while they were attracting more leisure travelers and families, their corporate client base was declining. This was in spite of investing in a van service. Feedback confirmed his fears: the recession had affected businesses' attitude about travel, and companies were paying for hotel accommodation only when absolutely necessary. This led Chris to believe that to compensate for a lack of corporate clients, they needed to attract more leisure travelers, families in particular, to book the resort for their summer vacation.

Chris had an idea and hoped that Kathy would go for it. As they ran through the latest monthly figures, he pointed out to Kathy that some of their regular corporate clients had cancelled on several occasions. "So, what's the plan, Chris?" she said. Chris told her that while they couldn't do much to repair the effects of the economic recession—in the short term anyway—they could focus on the segment of the market that was bringing them the majority of their business. "I agree," Kathy said. "But how do we increase our family and leisure base? Both the Dolphin Resort and the Porpoise Inn have access to the beach; we already have a gift shop that stocks lots of items for kids; and our menu

LECTURE ENHANCER:

9.7 Strategies for Performance

✓ **Focus Strategy**—when an organization concentrates on specific target market and may use cost leadership and/or differentiation strategies

✓ **Differentiation Strategy**—when an organization seeks competitive advantage by providing goods or services, which are significantly different from the competition

✓ **Vertical Integration**—companies that seek to produce and distribute their supplies

✓ *Backward Integration*—the method of diversification in which an organization begins producing its own supplies

✓ **Diversification Strategy**—risk-reduction strategy in which an organization adds new kinds of goods, services, or business units

✓ *Forward Integration*—the method of diversification in which an organization takes on the distribution and selling of its products

✓ **Renewal Strategy**—a strategy to address declining performance through retrenchment and regrowth

✓ *Retrenchment*—when a company reduces expenses to create financial stability

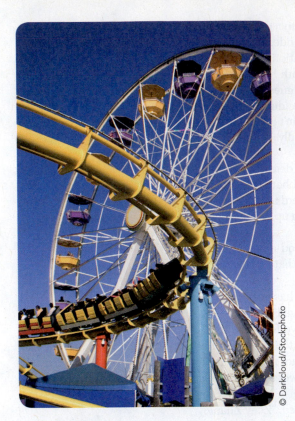

© Darkcloud/iStockphoto

is child-friendly and popular. What more can we do?" Chris replied, "I think we need more ideas, and I think we need to learn from the best." Noting Kathy's look of puzzlement, he clarified his latest idea, "I would like to bring the senior management team on a retreat to San Diego to stay at the world's biggest theme park, Adventure Quest, on a fact-finding expedition."

Kathy took a deep breath and asked Chris his reasoning behind such an elaborate trip. He replied: "At the moment, both the Dolphin Resort and the Porpoise Inn have state-of-the-art meeting rooms and conference facilities for business clients. Those rooms are standing empty for at least three days a week as a result of the slowdown in business travel. I believe we can build a sustainable competitive advantage if we reallocate the unused space in the hotels, thereby transforming them even further into leisure destinations. In order to achieve this, I believe that the team could really reap the benefits of understanding how Adventure Quest creates their guest experience."

As Chris had anticipated, Kathy had lots of questions: Could they afford to fund the trip? How would the rest of the staff function without any senior management in place? Chris explained to her that it would only be a couple of days, and he had chosen a relatively quiet weekend for the retreat. All the departmental heads would have trusted staff members on site to act on their behalf in their absence. As for funding the trip, Chris convinced Kathy that it was a worthwhile investment of their earnings. "Well, you have certainly thought of everything!" Kathy said. "I guess if we want to attract leisure and family travelers, there is no better company to learn from than Adventure Quest."

From the moment the management team walked off the airplane ramp in San Diego, they noticed that the Adventure Quest experience had already started. The airport was filled with murals and statues of Adventure Quest characters, and there were hosts available to help guests begin their vacation. The team was impressed by Adventure Quest's ability to create an immediate, all-encompassing experience for their guests. By the time they arrived at the Adventure Quest hotel, there was a sense of feeling transported to another world where the only rule was to have fun.

The team decided to take a couple of hours to explore and then meet back for dinner at the hotel. As the team sat down, Ken Gold, director of sales and marketing, could not contain his enthusiasm for what he had witnessed in the past two hours. "I can't believe how dedicated Adventure Quest is in immersing their guests in the Adventure Quest world. They seem to make and sell everything here. They even grow their own produce and serve it in the restaurant. I would not be surprised if the fish I ate tonight was caught by a staff person in the lake outside the hotel. They own everything in town. But that is not the most important point. They own and do everything *because* no one else can do it better."

Without realizing it, Ken had summed up Adventure Quest's strategies in one statement. Adventure Quest focused on three types of strategies to run its business: focus, differentiation, and vertical integration. **Focus strategy** is when an organization concentrates on a specific target market and may use cost leadership and/or differentiation strategies.[22] At Adventure Quest, the company focuses entirely on entertainment for families. With this singular focus, the company has the opportunity to cut expenses for lower consumer prices or higher profits. For example, Adventure Quest owns the rights to print all Adventure Quest characters on its merchandise, so it does not pay extra for using that image. Additionally, the company can sell its merchandise at a premium price. This is how cost leadership applies to a focus strategy. **Differentiation strategy** is when an organization seeks competitive advantage by providing goods or services that are significantly different from the competition.[23] The Adventure Quest experience doesn't just begin at the gates of the theme park; it occurs the second that their guests step off the plane in San Diego. That's different. Speaking of "different," why would Adventure Quest want to grow their own produce?

Focus strategy A strategy in which an organization concentrates on a specific target market and may use cost leadership and/or differentiation strategies.

Differentiation strategy A strategy in which an organization seeks competitive advantage by providing goods or services that are significantly different from the competition.

As a result of focus, cost leadership, and differentiation strategies, companies will often seek to produce and distribute their supplies, called **vertical integration**.[24] The method of diversification in which an organization begins producing its own supplies is referred to as *backward integration*. So, in the case of Adventure Quest, growing the produce used in its hotels is backward integration. We could also call this **diversification strategy**, which is a risk-reduction strategy in which an organization adds new kinds of goods, services, or business units.[25] The method of diversification in which an organization takes on the distribution and selling of its products is referred to as *forward integration*. When Adventure Quest opened retail stores in shopping malls and on crowded city streets all over the country to sell movies, clothing, and toys, this is an example of *forward integration*.

The conversation grew more animated, with lofty aspirations of obtaining more land to grow their own produce, and opening Dolphin and Porpoise gift shops and activity centers around the entire island. At this point, Chris needed to refocus the team: "I appreciate the positive energy and creativity of our conversation, but I would like to us to look what we can do today that will bring us closer to the vision first, to find innovative ways to attract more leisure travelers, and second, to maintain our business traveler occupancy. To that end, I would like to hear your opinions on what experience we are offering our guests and how that will need to change in order to attract leisure travelers and their families." To explain his point further, Chris brought the team through the concept of **renewal strategy**, which addresses declining performance through retrenchment and regrowth.[26]

Lisa Reynolds, who had remained as senior manager of the Porpoise Inn, spoke up. "Before the Porpoise Inn was acquired by the Dolphin Resort, I had been working in the hotel industry for six years. For as much as the hotel industry talks about building relationships and a magical experience for guests, what we really want is loyalty on our terms—join our reward program, so that you will feel obligated to come back because of the points you earn. There is nothing magical about that. Here at Adventure Quest, I feel inspired to play and explore, which is very different from most of my family vacations. Our trips generally involve me getting maps from the concierge and a list of the "top 10 things to do with your family on vacation." Next thing you know, we are running around trying to check off our list of things to do." For the remainder of the dinner, the managers of Dolphin Resort and the Porpoise Inn discussed how staying at their hotels could be a more personal experience. The group brainstormed about what really set the Dolphin Resort and Porpoise Inn apart from other hotels and how they could create a unique experience for their guests, just as they themselves were experiencing at Adventure Quest.

Eventually, they decided on one unique factor: The Dolphin Resort and Porpoise Inn was the only truly family-run hotel on the island. Over the next couple of days, the executive team worked together to design a new business model to increase the level of personal service that they provide to their guests to make them feel at home. In a world where technology connects people more than personal contact, the team feels that both business and leisure travelers will be attracted by the "family" approach to service.

Five years later, the Dolphin Resort & Hotel and Porpoise Inn are thriving. By continuously assessing processes and looking for opportunities to improve business performance, Chris and the hotel team have managed to design new, successful strategies and fresh initiatives to meet current trends, and cater for an increasingly demanding customer base. Thanks to Chris's management style, the commitment of the hotel staff, and the unfailing support of Kathy Osborne, the property remains at the top of its game.

> **Vertical integration** A method of diversification in which an organization begins producing its own supplies (backward integration) or takes on the distribution and selling of its products (forward integration).

> **Diversification strategy** A risk-reduction strategy in which an organization adds new kinds of goods, services, or business units.

> **Renewal strategy** A strategy to address declining performance through retrenchment and regrowth.

Case**Snapshot**

Chapter 9 Case: Designing Strategies:
Big Bottom Market can be found on pg. 470

ADDITIONAL RESOURCES

KEY TERMS

Acquisition When an organization purchases another organization or business in order to grow. **(p. 230)**

Analyzer A company whose strategies seek to maintain existing products and services while pursuing limited innovation. They often imitate or follow the proven success of prospector organizations. **(p. 231)**

Barrier to entry An obstacle that makes it difficult for an organization to enter a particular market or replicate a competitor's service and product offerings. **(p. 235)**

BCG Matrix A framework developed by the Boston Consulting Group for evaluating business units according to growth and market share. **(p. 237)**

Business plan The stated actions and goals that support the organizational strategy. **(p. 230)**

Capacity refers to the financial and human resources available to the company, which will enable or hinder it to achieve goals. **(p. 237)**

Competitive advantage The characteristics of an organization's products or services that distinguish it from competitors and provide an advantage in the marketplace. **(p. 231)**

Competitive analysis The process of assessing and monitoring the competition in order to design more effective strategies. **(p. 232)**

Competitive inertia A tendency to continue with competitive practices that had been successful in the past, even if they are less effective in the present. **(p. 237)**

Core capabilities Activities and processes that an organization routinely does well in comparison to its competitors; also known as *core competencies*. **(p. 240)**

Cost leadership strategy A strategy in which an organization seeks competitive advantage by reducing production costs and therefore consumer prices. **(p. 232)**

Defender A company whose strategies support stable growth and continual improvement of existing products and services. **(p. 231)**

Differentiation strategy A strategy in which an organization seeks competitive advantage by providing goods or services that are significantly different from the competition. **(p. 246)**

Diversification strategy A risk-reduction strategy in which an organization adds new kinds of goods, services, or business units. **(p. 247)**

Divisional strategy A strategy that determines how a business will compete in a particular industry or market. **(p.230)**

First mover A company that gains competitive advantage by being the first to offer a new product or service, or to use a new cost-saving technology. **(p. 232)**

Focus strategy A strategy in which an organization concentrates on a specific target market and may use cost leadership and/or differentiation strategies. **(p. 246)**

Functional strategy A strategy that determines how employees will implement and achieve a tactical plan. **(p. 230)**

Growth strategy A strategy for increasing revenue, profits, market share, or territories. **(p. 238)**

Market position An honest assessment about how the company competes in its industry. **(p. 237)**

Operational plan The stated actions and goals that support achieving the functional strategy. **(p. 230)**

Organizational strategy A corporate-level strategy that addresses the question "What business are we in?" and unites all parts of the organization. **(p. 230)**

Prospector A company that uses strategies for high-risk, fast growth through product and market innovation. **(p. 232)**

Reactor A company that does not follow a consistent strategy but just responds to changes in the environment. **(p. 231)**

Renewal strategy A strategy to address declining performance through retrenchment and regrowth. **(p. 247)**

Resources The assets, people, processes, and capabilities of an organization. **(p. 237)**

Stability strategy A strategy in which an organization focuses on processes, products, and services that will sustain it over the long term. **(p. 232)**

Strategy A plan of action for achieving goals. **(p. 230)**

SWOT analysis A method of assessing an organization's strengths, weaknesses, opportunities, and threats (abbreviated as SWOT). **(p. 239)**

Tactical plan The stated actions and goals that support achieving the divisional strategy. **(p. 230)**

Vertical integration A method of diversification in which an organization begins producing its own supplies (backward integration) or takes on the distribution and selling of its products (forward integration). **(p. 247)**

IN REVIEW

9.1 | Explain how businesses use planning to solve problems and make a difference.

Designing and defining strategies is a continuous process that helps organizations determine what they do, why they should be in business, how they can win and sustain market share, and how they can innovate continually to keep ahead of the competition.

To design a successful strategy, managers must understand the full nature of the competitive forces that are present and take a holistic, systemic view of the industry structure. Being able to diversify in a competitive industry, seeing an opening in the market, and continuously staying ahead of the competition would not be possible without a clearly defined, skillfully designed strategy.

9.2 | Distinguish how planning is different at the organizational, divisional, and functional levels of a business.

As a result of the planning process, Chris needs to document decisions regarding goals, strategies, resource allocation, and actions required; these are called *strategic plans*. There are three levels of strategy: organizational, divisional, and functional.

With the philosophical foundation of an organization's mission, vision, and values, organizational, divisional, and functional strategies are documented with business, tactical, and operational plans, respectively.

9.3 | Explain how senior managers develop organizational strategies and business plans.

Business strategies can be classified in many ways, but all of them seek to gain *competitive advantage,* which is the characteristic of an organization's products or services that distinguish it from competitors and provide an advantage in the marketplace. By following certain types of strategies, companies can be categorized as first movers, reactors, prospectors, defenders, or analyzers.

A *reactor* is a company that does not follow a consistent strategy, but just responds to changes in the environment. An *analyzer* is a company whose strategies seek to maintain existing products and services while pursuing limited innovation. A *defender* is a company whose strategies support stable growth and continual improvement of existing products and services. A *prospector* is a company that uses strategies for high-risk, fast growth through product and market innovation.

9.4 | Outline methods that managers use to understand their industries and competitors.

The Five Forces Model outlines five forces that determine what managers should expect when competing in an industry: power of suppliers, power of buyers, substitute products and services, new entrants, and rivalry. Understanding and designing strategies to compete effectively should create a *barrier to entry,* an obstacle that makes it difficult for competing organizations to enter a particular market or replicate a competitor's service and product offerings.

9.5 | Describe how managers assess the organization's capacity to execute proposed business plans.

An organization's market position is an honest assessment about how the company competes in its industry. An organization's capacity refers to the financial and human resources available to the company, which will enable or hinder it to achieve goals.

The *BCG Matrix* is a framework developed by the Boston Consulting Group for evaluating business units according to growth and market share, so that managers could quickly categorize their company's position in the industry where it competes. This enables management to assess quickly the validity of its strategies and where to invest resources.

How do managers know how to figure out their organization's future plans, other than simply guessing? Managers typically apply a *SWOT analysis*, which assesses an organization's strengths, weaknesses, opportunities, and threats. It is a useful way of defining business strategy and helping to make strategic insights and decisions.

9.6 | Demonstrate how managers develop divisional strategies and tactical plans.

Applying the balanced scorecard approach allows the management team to "augment traditional financial measures with benchmarks for performance in three key nonfinancial areas: 1) a company's relationship with its customers, 2) its key internal processes, and 3) its learning and growth." The framework intends to ensure that managers translate vision into strategy and execution of the strategy, both of which are critical to success.

9.7 | Compare traditional strategic planning models to an event-based approach.

Managers typically use three types of strategies to run its business: focus, differentiation, and vertical integration. *Focus strategy* is when an organization concentrates on a specific target market and may use cost leadership and/or differentiation strategies. *Differentiation strategy* is when an organization seeks competitive advantage by providing goods or services, which are significantly different from the competition. As a result of focus, cost leadership, and differentiation strategies, companies will often seek to produce and distribute their supplies, called *vertical integration*. The method of diversification in which an organization begins producing its own supplies is referred to as *backward integration*. This is also called *diversification strategy*, which is a risk-reduction strategy in which an organization adds new kinds of goods, services, or business units. The method of diversification in which an organization takes on the distribution and selling of its products is referred to as *forward integration*.

SELF-TEST

9.1 | Explain how businesses use planning to solve problems and make a difference.

1. One of the main responsibilities of managers is to create, present, and implement _____ that will defend the company against the threat of competition, ascertain the best market position, and determine the weaknesses that might make its position vulnerable in the industry.

2. When an organization purchases another organization or business in order to grow, that is called a(n) _____.

9.2 | Distinguish how planning is different at the organizational, divisional, and functional levels of a business.

3. The three levels of strategy include:
   a. organizational
   b. transitional
   c. functional
   d. (a) and (c)

4. The three levels are strategy are documented with which three types of plans?

9.3 | Explain how senior managers develop organizational strategies and business plans.

5. Strategically, organizations can be defined in three ways. Using those terms, describe the Dolphin Resort under Herb Cork and then how it changed under Chris Heppler.

6. **Stability strategy** is when an organization seeks competitive advantage by reducing production costs and therefore consumer price.
   a. True
   b. False

9.4 | Outline methods that managers use to understand their industries and competitors.

7. What is the Five Forces model?

8. What seven barriers did Chris explore to determine if the new Fisherman's Hotel would weaken the Dolphin Resort's position in the market?

9.5 | Describe how managers assess the organization's capacity to execute proposed business plans.

9. What is the BCG Matrix?

10. A(n) _____ analysis is a method of assessing an organization's strengths, weaknesses, opportunities, and threats

9.6 | Demonstrate how managers develop divisional strategies and tactical plans.

11. The balanced scorecard framework intends to ensure that managers translate vision into strategy and execution of the strategy, both of which are critical to success.
   a. True
   b. False

9.7 | Compare traditional strategic planning models to an event-based approach.

12. When an organization seeks competitive advantage by providing goods or services, which are significantly different from the competition, it's called _____.
   a. vertical integration
   b. diversification strategy
   c. differentiation strategy
   d. forward strategy

CHAPTER EXERCISES

Create a Mission Statement

Instructions:

1. Working by yourself or in a team, choose one of the following companies (or your instructor may assign one to you or your team) and write a mission statement for that company.
   a. FedEx
   b. Google
   c. Apple Computers
   d. Starbucks
   e. Wal-Mart
   f. Ben & Jerry's
   g. Your college or university

2. Compare the mission statement that you wrote with the *actual* mission statement for your company. Your instructor may provide the actual mission statements to you, or you can find them online. Consider the following questions:

   a. Was the mission statement that you wrote longer or shorter than the company's actual mission statement?

   b. Was it more detailed or less detailed than the actual company mission statement?

   c. In what ways did your mission statement differ from the company's actual mission statement?

   d. Did the mission statement that you wrote focus on the same or a different target audience (e.g., employees, customers, shareholders, etc.)?

   e. In what ways was your statement superior to the company's actual mission statement?

   f. In what ways was it inferior?

SELF-ASSESSMENT

Strategic Leadership Skills*

For each statement, circle the number that best describes you based on the following scale:

Not at all Accurate	Somewhat Accurate	A little Accurate	Mostly Accurate	Completely Accurate
1	2	3	4	5

1. I try to anticipate problems before they actually occur.
   1   2   3   4   5

2. I like to challenge the status quo.
   1   2   3   4   5

3. I am good at synthesizing complex information in order to recognize patterns and obtain new insights.
   1   2   3   4   5

4. I don't mind making difficult decisions, even when I don't have complete information.
   1   2   3   4   5

5. I can effectively find common ground and achieve buy-in from those around me, even those with differing perspectives and agendas.
   1   2   3   4   5

6. I try to learn from the past successes and failures of myself and others.
   1   2   3   4   5

7. I can often predict the actions or reactions of my allies and my competitors.
   1   2   3   4   5

8. I enjoy questioning assumptions, both my own and others, and encourage differing perspectives.
   1   2   3   4   5

9. I have an open mind and I am curious about the world around me.
   1   2   3   4   5

10. I consider multiple options before making any important decision.
    1   2   3   4   5

11. I use frequent communication to build trust in those around me.
    1   2   3   4   5

12. I study failures, my own and those of others, in order to find hidden lessons.
    1   2   3   4   5

Scoring:

Add the numbers circled above and write your score in the blank. _____

Interpretation:

48 and above = You have excellent strategic leadership skills. You are effective at engaging in the key strategic leadership skills of anticipating, challenging, interpreting, deciding, aligning, and learning.

25–47 = You have a moderate level of strategic leadership skills and could work toward increasing your skills in this area.

24 and below = You have room to make some substantial improvements in your strategic leadership skills.

*This self-assessment was created based on information presented in Paul J. H. Schoemaker, Steve Krupp, and Samantha Howland. "Strategic Leadership: The Essential Skills." *Harvard Business Review* 91, no. 1 (January 2013): 131–134.

SELF-TEST ANSWER KEY

1. strategies
2. acquisition
3. d.
4. Organizational, divisional, and functional strategies are documented with business, tactical, and operational plans, respectively.
5. Under Herb Cork's management, we could define the hotel as a *reactor*, which is a company that does not follow a consistent strategy, but just responds to changes in the environment. Under Chris's management, the Dolphin Resort started as an *analyzer*, which is a company whose strategies seek to maintain existing products and services while pursuing limited innovation but then successfully made the transition from analyzer to *defender*, which is a company whose strategies support stable growth and continual improvement of existing products and services.
6. b; False. *Cost leadership strategy* is when an organization seeks competitive advantage by reducing production costs and therefore consumer price. *Stability strategy* is when an organization focuses on processes, products, and services that will sustain it over the long term.
7. The Five Forces Model outlines five forces that determine what managers should expect when competing in an industry: power of suppliers, power of buyers, substitute

products and services, new entrants, and rivalry. Managers can then assess the major threats that an organization can expect to encounter in an industry. By outlining and pro-actively responding to these threats, managers can define more clearly their opportunity to succeed.

8. Supply-side economies of scale, demand-side benefits of scale, customer switching costs, capital requirements, incumbent advantages independent of size, unequal access to distribution channels, and restrictive government policy.

9. The *BCG Matrix* is a framework developed by the Boston Consulting Group for evaluating business units according to growth and market share. It allows managers to categorize quickly their company's position in the industry where it competes, enabling management to assess the validity of its strategies and where to invest resources.

10. *SWOT* (Strengths, Weaknesses, Opportunities, Threats)

11. a; True.

12. b.

Notes

_____

_____

_____

_____

_____

_____

_____

_____

_____

_____

_____

_____

_____

_____

_____

_____

_____

PART FOUR

Organizing

CHAPTER TEN

STRUCTURING ORGANIZATIONS

Learning Objectives

By the end of this chapter, you will be able to:

10.1 | Explain how differentiation and integration define performance cultures.

10.2 | Describe how managers vertically organize processes and teams to centralize decision making.

10.3 | Describe how managers horizontally organize processes and teams to distribute decision making throughout the organization.

10.4 | Show how managers combine vertical and horizontal approaches to organizational design in order to be more adaptive.

10.5 | Identify additional resources that contemporary managers use to increase organizational adaptability.

ADDITIONAL RESOURCES

KEY TERMS
IN REVIEW
SELF-TEST
CHAPTER EXERCISES
SELF-ASSESSMENT
SELF-TEST
ANSWER KEY

INSIDE THIS CHAPTER

ManagementStory:
Featuring **Robin Richardson**

JP Greenwood/Getty Images

LECTURE ENHANCER:

10.1 The Basics

✓ **Hierarchy**—a vertically-organized structure of power relationships where the top-level holds the most power and resources
  ➤ Managers issued commands without expecting anything but compliance from their employees.

• **Designing Performance Cultures**
  ➤ Environment, culture, strategy, technology, people, tasks, and processes must all be linked in a cohesive pattern to ensure that operations run smoothly.

> **Hierarchy** A vertically organized structure of power relationships, where the top level holds the most power and resources.

✓ **Differentiation**—the process through which managers divide labor based on tasks and function

✓ **Integration**—horizontal coordination between functions, departments, and organizational activities
  ➤ The success of the organizational structure very much depends on the type of culture that has already been fostered by senior management.
  ➤ In order to be successful, organizations must strike a balance between differentiation and integration.

✓ **Organic Organization**—a highly adaptive structure defined by horizontal integration, distributed decision making, and employees with a high degree of generalization

✓ **Span of Control**—the optimum number of direct reports a person can effectively manage

✓ **Specialization**—focusing a group or individual's activities based on their strength, aptitude, or skills

✓ **Coordination**—the synchronization of organizations' functions in order to ensure efficient use of resources in pursuit of goals and objectives

10.1 | *THE BASICS*

10.1 | Explain how differentiation and integration define performance cultures.

"Every company has two organizational structures: The formal one is written on the charts; the other is the everyday relationship of the men and women in the organization."

—Harold S. Geneen

Designing the perfect organizational structure has been the source of much discussion over the last 200 years. In Chapter 2, we learned about the early theorists of organizational structure, Frederick W. Taylor, Henri Fayol, and Max Weber, and their individual approaches to introducing structural change within different industries. Traditionally, industries were headed up by authoritarian figures that operated within a **hierarchy**, which is a vertically organized structure of power relationships where the top level holds the most power and resources. Figure 10-1 shows a range of hierarchies. These managers issued commands without expecting anything but compliance from their employees. However, the work and studies carried out by the early theorists helped to give these "lowly" workers a voice, and for the first time, the structure started to change from an autocratic environment to a more democratic one.[1]

Although each theory has been widely contested ever since, most will agree that one point has become very clear; every single organization, no matter how big or small, needs some sort of organizational structure in place to be successful. This means having the right manager(s) in place to design a structure that is best suited to the organization and its culture. Therefore, it is essential that each company leader wholly embraces the purpose, values, and vision of the organization and is representative of its cultural values and behaviors.

With so many elements to consider, designing a structure for an organization can be one of the most challenging roles for managers, and there are disastrous consequences if they get it wrong. Poorly designed organizational structures can result in confusion among employees, slow decision making, and a lack of cohesiveness among different departments, leading to reduced teamwork and stress and frustration for managers.

So, why are organizational structures so important? A well-designed structure not only unites the different units of a company but brings it in tune with its underlying principles, core purposes, goals, and objectives. Critical thinking helps managers achieve structural change within their organizations.

Designing Performance Cultures

From the tiniest growth company to the largest financial organization, there are many factors to take into consideration when it comes to designing the appropriate structure. Environment, culture, strategy, technology, people, tasks, and processes must all be linked in a cohesive pattern to ensure that operations run smoothly.

In Chapter 4, we looked at narratives, stories, artifacts, and rituals as symptoms, residues, and tools that managers use to establish and perpetuate culture within the workplace.

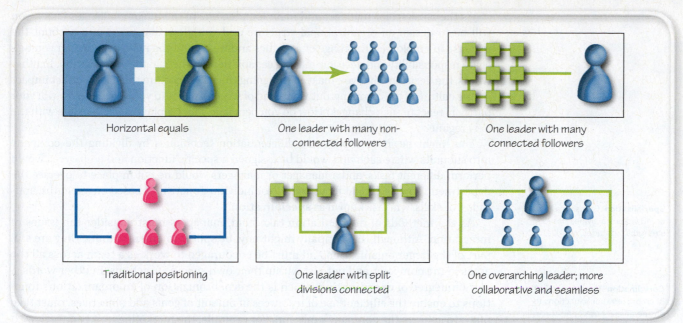

Figure 10-1

Hierarchy Comes in Many States. Here are a few. . .

Organizations can have a range of hierarchical structures.

As we learned, a good corporate culture can foster innovation and productivity and motivate employees to work as a team. But we can also argue that through the creation of an organizational structure, managers can also design a performance culture, consciously or unconsciously, depending on the intensity levels of **differentiation**, the process through which managers divide labor based on tasks and functions; and **integration**, the horizontal coordination between functions, departments, and organizational activities.[2]

In this sense, the success of the organizational structure very much depends on the type of culture that has already been fostered by senior management. Furthermore, structures can be fluid; as the business fluctuates and develops over time, the culture is likely to change, which means that the structure will need to be modified, or even revised altogether, to adapt to both the internal and external changes that are taking place.[3]

But how does an organizational structure adapt to its environment? In order to be successful, organizations must strike a balance between differentiation and integration. Indeed, managers can create an organizational culture based on the intensity levels of how efficient the structure is (differentiation), and how effective it is (integration). We could also argue that it is more important to differentiate by implementing certain structures or processes before initiating the integration process. The idea here is that once an organizational structure is in place, the culture will be more easily determined, leading to a smoother integration of employees who are motivated to achieve the company's goals, vision, and mission.

For example, say that you founded a small business selling novelty gift items. Initially, there are only a few people involved. As you all work together and swap ideas, there might seem little need to design a formal organizational structure; after all, everyone has been fully integrated into the strategy-planning, goal-setting, and decision-making processes ever since the company became operational. This sort of structure is called a *horizontal* or *flat organization*, where there are few levels of hierarchy and everyone is directly involved in all corporate communications.[4] It could also be known as an **organic organization**, a highly adaptive structure defined by horizontal integration, distributed decision making, and employees with a high degree of generalization.[5]

But what happens when the company starts to grow? You might need to take on more employees, deal with more consumer demands, and manage increased levels of inventory. It might become impossible to monitor every single employee and ensure that high standards are being met. As the founder of the organization, your **span of control**, or the number of employees that a person directly manages,[6] might become too much to handle; and you and the original partners might struggle to juggle so many balls in the air.

Differentiation The process through which managers divide labor based on tasks and functions.

Integration Horizontal coordination between functions, departments, and organizational activities.

✓ **Standardization**—a performance context where policies and procedures seek to create uniform results
✓ **Formalization**—the degree of which policies and procedures determine specific jobs and functions
✓ **Delegation**—when a manager grants power and authority to another team member

Organic organization A highly adaptive structure defined by horizontal integration, distributed decision making, and employees with a high degree of generalization.

Span of control The optimum number of direct reports that a person can manage effectively.

As the most senior manager and main founder, one of the major challenges facing you will be to design an organizational structure and workflow that takes into account the increase in employees, the range of activities and tasks, and the manner in which you delegate responsibility and decision-making capabilities to others in the organization. In other words, the decisions that you make in designing the new structure will have a direct impact on the culture of the company. But what kind of structure should you choose? How will your partners react to such changes? How do you persuade your employees to fall in line with the new regime?

You might begin to apply some differentiation techniques by dividing the company into subunits where each unit would be assigned a specific function and employees would perform different tasks, and a manager or managers would be put in place to oversee the department. You also might focus a group or individual's activities based on strengths, aptitudes, or skills, which is known as **specialization**.[7]

As the methods of differentiation take hold, managers must consider the issues of integration. Although the company might now be split into different units, they are still part of the larger organization and must be encouraged to work as a team across all the areas in the company, and not just within their own specific functions. In other words, a certain degree of **coordination** which is the synchronization of an organization's functions to ensure the efficient use of resources in pursuit of goals and objectives, must take place to achieve the company's mission. For example, the marketing unit can work with the sales department to understand the client base; similarly, accounting can work with each of these departments to give them an idea of the budgeted amount that they have at their disposal.

However, no transition is easy, and a number of issues can arise with this change in structure. To help give clarity to the integration process, you may have implemented a level of **standardization**, a performance context where policies and procedures seek to create uniform results; and **formalization**, the degree of which policies and procedures determine specific jobs and functions.[8] Despite these procedures, some employees may feel uneasy; the other partners may become resentful about the new approach to **delegation**, when a manager grants power and authority to another team member,[9] and perceive this as a loss of power; the new employees may not like being "pigeonholed" into specific units, even though they are encouraged to work with other teams; the original employees may be reluctant to integrate the new employees, and so on.

In this chapter, we will look at the different types of organizational structures, the role of managers in designing and adapting them, the challenges arising from implementing differentiation and integration processes; and the factors that determine their ability to change from one structure to another.

Let's begin by looking at a Metropolitan Police Department (MPD) case study based on the real-life experiences of Washington MPD chief of police Cathy L. Lanier. Lanier's efforts to revolutionize the police force are a powerful illustration of the real challenges of designing and changing organizational structures.

Cathy L. Lanier: *Chief of Police, Metropolitan Police Department, Washington, D.C.*[10]

Cathy L. Lanier has spent her entire law enforcement career with the MPD. From the beginning of her career in 1990, Lanier has been in uniformed patrol, where she served as commander of the Fourth District, one of the largest and most diverse residential patrol districts in the city. She also served as the commanding officer of the department's Major Narcotics Branch and Vehicular Homicide Units.

Chief Lanier was named commander of the Special Operations Division (SOD), where, for four years, she managed the Emergency Response Team, Aviation and Harbor Units, Horse Mounted and Canine Units, Special Events/Dignitary Protection Branch, and Civil Disturbance Units. During her tenure as SOD commander, she established the agency's first Homeland Security/Counter-Terrorism Branch and created an agencywide chemical, biological, and radiological response unit known as the Special Threat Action Team.

In 2006, the MPD's Office of Homeland Security and Counter-Terrorism (OHSCT) was created, and Chief Lanier was tapped to be its first commanding officer. A highly respected professional in the areas of homeland security and community policing, she took the lead

---

Specialization Focusing a group or individual's activities based on strengths, aptitudes, or skills.

Coordination The synchronization of an organization's functions to ensure efficient use of resources in pursuit of goals and objectives.

Standardization A performance context where policies and procedures seek to create uniform results.

Formalization The degree of which policies and procedures determine specific jobs and functions.

Delegation When a manager grants power and authority to another team member.

role in developing and implementing coordinated counterterrorism strategies for all units within the MPD and launched Operation TIPP (Terrorist Incident Prevention Program). After assuming the leadership of the MPD on January 2, 2007, Lanier was unanimously confirmed as the chief of police by the Council of the District of Columbia on April 3, 2007.

Chief Lanier is a graduate of the National Academy of the Federal Bureau of Investigation (FBI) and the federal Drug Enforcement Administration's Drug Unit Commanders Academy. She holds bachelor's and master's degrees in management from Johns Hopkins University, and a master's degree in national security studies from the Naval Postgraduate School in Monterey, California. She is certified at the technician level in hazardous materials operations.

In the following case narrative, we will follow Robin Richardson (a fictional character inspired by Cathy L. Lanier) and the challenges that she faces on her quest to transform the MPD into an efficient, technologically savvy, and compassionate organization.

Robert MacPherson/AFP / GettyImages Inc

10.2 | VERTICAL APPROACH

10.2 Describe how managers vertically organize processes and teams to centralize decision making.

When Robin Richardson first joined the MPD, the chief of police was Troy Kimbell. Kimbell came from a long line of police officers: his grandfather, father, and brother were officers. In 1984, the whole family celebrated as Troy was appointed the MPD's chief of police in Washington, D.C. That day, Troy remembered his late father's advice: "Always protect the fellas in blue—without them, who's going to protect the community?"

For the first 10 years of Chief Kimbell's appointment, this advice defined his management style and provided him with several very loyal lieutenants who worked directly for him. Each officer was schooled in the history of the police force and was never left in any doubt about how much of an honor it was to be a part of one of the most storied institutions in the world. The chief and his team wore their badges with pride and regarded them as symbols of ethics and integrity.

Kimbell was an advocate of the **vertical organizational structure**,[11] characterized by hierarchical authority and communication channels and had been in place within the MPD for over a century. Like many law enforcement agencies all over the world, the MPD was a **centralized organization**, a design structure that relies on senior-level managers to collect information broadly[12] in order to make decisions on behalf of the entire company. Within this MPD vertical structure, Kimbell was a commander who had sole **authority**, the implicit and explicit power that a manager or employee has to fulfill an organizational function or role, enabling that person to issue orders to subordinates and expect them to be carried out as quickly as possible. After all, most of the senior staff were ex-military men and ex-marines, and like Kimbell, well into their fifties and sixties. They were from a generation that expected to be given direct orders from their chief. The structure of the MPD is illustrated in Figure 10-2.

Kimbell was more than satisfied with his **chain of command**, a predefined structural order of authority that determines how decisions are made and communicated.[13] Each senior officer was appointed as manager of a team, and each team worked in isolation from the other departments. Each department was split off into separate functions, such as homicide, narcotics, and intelligence units. It was up to the senior managers to run their own teams, issue orders to their staff, solve any problems that arose, and keep the operations running as smoothly as possible. Although he was the sole authority and decision

LECTURE ENHANCER:

10.2 Vertical Approach

✓ **Vertical Organizational Structure**— characterized by hierarchical authority and communication channels

✓ **Centralized Organization**—a design structure that relies on senior level managers to broadly collect information in order to make decisions on behalf of the entire company

✓ **Authority**—the implicit and explicit power that a manager or employee has to fulfill an organizational function or role, enabling them to issue orders to subordinates and

Vertical organizational structure A structure, characterized by hierarchical authority and communication channels.

Centralized organization A design structure that relies on senior-level managers to collect information broadly, in order to make decisions on behalf of the entire company.

Authority The implicit and explicit power that a manager or employee has to fulfill an organizational function or role.

Chain of command A predefined structural order of authority that determines how decisions are made and communicated.

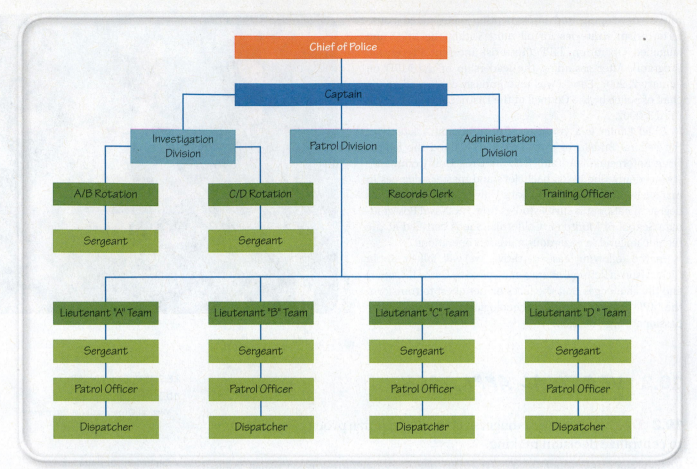

Figure 10-2
Vertical Organizational Model, MPD

expect them to be carried out as quickly as possible
➤ Vertical Organizational Model

✓ **Chain-of-command**—a predefined structural order of authority that determines how decisions are made and communicated

✓ **Corporate Governance**—a compendium of policies intended to

maker, everyone knew better than to approach the chief of police with any minor problems; he left those for the senior managers to resolve. Troy Kimbell could then focus his time on what he did best: giving speeches and making appearances at high-profile events and press conferences to promote the police force and secure its position in the political circles of Washington, D.C.

But in the late 1990s, things began to change. After five years of tight budgets, the department began to hire more officers. By 1999, 200 new recruits had come on board. Comprised mostly of younger officers, this new generation had an attitude that did not make sense to Chief Kimbell. They didn't seem to care about maintaining the status quo, taking orders without question, or following "how things are done around here." In fact, one new officer, Alfonso Diaz, had the audacity to try to schedule a meeting with the chief of police to pass on his ideas about how things could be improved. Kimbell couldn't fathom how the officer had the nerve to bypass his own manager and approach him directly. He never would have imagined subverting the chain of command when he had just joined the force.

It wasn't just Diaz that tried this approach. Soon Kimbell's secretary was inundated with requests from these new officers to set up a meeting with the chief. Eventually, this became such a major issue that Kimbell asked his lieutenants to establish a mentorship program for the new recruits to help acclimate this new generation and teach them a thing or two about the traditional vertical model and the strict chain of command that had existed since the 1800s. These young officers also needed to be schooled in good **corporate governance**, which is a compendium of policies intended to ensure transparency and fulfillment of duties to stakeholders.[14] Examples of stakeholders for the MPD include the mayor, city council, district attorney's office, and some citizens of the community. Kimbell gathered his senior team to help choose somebody to lead the program and act as a **broker**, a trusted intermediary that facilitates mutually agreed-upon outcomes for two or more parties.

After months of discussion, Kimbell's senior team recommended Robin Richardson, a field commander four layers deep in the **organizational chart**, a visual document that communicates how a company is organized,[15] to lead this new mentorship program. Among themselves, the senior team would joke that what these kids needed was someone to pat them on the heads and congratulate them on their creativity while simultaneously putting an end to their newfangled and unrealistic ideas for change.

At first, Chief Kimbell questioned the selection of Robin Richardson, feeling that his senior team was not taking his recommendation for this program seriously. She was, after all, a woman working in a predominantly male environment, and he wasn't sure that the senior team would treat her or the program with enough respect. Although he hoped that the mentorship program would put an end to the continuous breach of the chain of command, he was also curious to find out why the new recruits were so desperate to talk to him. In the end, he finally conceded to the appointment of Field Commander Richardson, but he insisted that Richardson report to him directly and update him weekly regarding the progress of the initiative; he wanted to make sure that the senior team was supporting her enough to drive the program forward.

Three weeks of meetings later, Chief Kimbell walked into his senior leadership meeting and pronounced, "Team, you better watch out—she is going to be your boss one day!" Over the next few years, Chief Kimbell was so impressed by Richardson's efficiency and ability to handle the new recruits that he personally mentored her and encouraged her to continue her education, including sponsoring her to complete her graduate degree in management. In her position, she continued to share news from the field (both good and bad) and make a series of recommendations on how to improve communications across the department.

Often, Chief Kimbell would encourage Richardson to write up any new ideas in a report for senior leadership approval, out of respect for the chain of command. Resenting the implication that the "teacher's pet" was being pushed on them, the senior leadership team would always listen politely and simply never follow up on any of the proposals. In response to recommendations that had taken months for Richardson to prepare, inevitably a one-paragraph memo would be circulated, suggesting that "now just isn't the right time, but thank you very much for your interesting thoughts."

Vertical Model at Work

On September 11, 2001, when the Pentagon was attacked by terrorists, the police department found themselves in the middle of a national security situation. During the crisis, and through the days and weeks that followed, Chief Kimbell's vertical organization stood strong. The police made sure that members of the community did not enter any dangerous areas, controlled traffic so emergency services could get through quickly, and helped with the evacuation process. Kimbell's orders were followed to the letter—and the department's reaction was an example of the efficiency of the vertical organizational structure and the effectiveness of the chain of command. In the media, Kimbell was a hero;

© Bill Vaughan/Sygma / Corbis

Corporate governance A compendium of policies intended to ensure transparency and fulfillment of duties to stakeholders.

Broker A trusted intermediary that facilitates mutually agreed-upon outcomes for two or more parties.

Organizational chart A visual document that communicates how a company is organized.

ensure transparency and fulfillment of duties to stakeholders
✓ **Broker**—a trusted intermediary that facilitates mutually agreed upon outcomes for two or more parties
✓ **Organizational chart**—a visual document that communicates how a company is organized
• **Vertical Model at Work**
  ✓ **Network Organization**—a group of independent companies that organize themselves to appear as a larger entity
• **Changing Organizational Structure**
  ✓ **Unity-of-Command Principle**—a philosophy that each employee reports to and is accountable to only one manager

his ability to remain calm and in control helped stabilize the emotions of the police department and community.

The FBI and newly minted U.S. Department of Homeland Security, impressed by Kimbell's performance during the 9/11 Pentagon attacks, asked him to work with them to integrate functions and communications in preparation for possible future terrorist incidents. Kimbell liked the idea of working with the FBI, realizing it could lead to the setting up a type of **network organization**, a group of independent companies that organize themselves to appear as a larger entity.[16]

When Chief Kimbell brought these recommendations to his senior leadership team, he was met with extraordinary resistance—"Hey, that's the Fed's job. Let them clean up their own mess." With dissension in the ranks, it appeared that Chief Kimbell would need to rely on Commander Richardson to help integrate the department. Some members of the senior team were not pleased when Chief Kimbell announced that Commander Richardson would lead a task force to research and make recommendations for integrating the department with external agencies in order to increase national security.

But Kimbell's days as chief of police were coming to an end. Over the previous decade, Washington, D.C., had slowly evolved into one of the most dangerous cities in the country, with the dubious honor of having the most murders per capita. This had attracted a huge amount of attention to the MPD and its leader. The mayoral election was coming up, and since the chief of police is an appointed position by the mayor, Troy Kimbell knew that he would most likely be replaced.

Mayor Neil Strong thanked Chief Kimbell for his service and affirmed that his replacement would be announced within one month. Kimbell was disappointed but not surprised; the signs had all been there. As the mayor went to the door, Kimbell, who was trying not to show how insulted he was that Strong was not asking him who he thought his successor should be, asked, "Who's your pick to fill my position?"

Strong responded, "I don't know. I am going to work with your assistant and meet with 50 or so officers over next couple of weeks. I am sure they will tell me who should be their leader."

Weeks later, the phone rang in her office on a Friday afternoon, and Robin wondered who could be calling just before she left for the night. "Commander Richardson, this is Mayor Strong. Do you have a moment?"

Robin's heart immediately sank, thinking that a crisis must be underway. "Yes, sir. How can I be of assistance?" Robin could hardly believe it when Mayor Strong told her she was one of the candidates to replace Kimbell as chief of police. But first, he told her, she would need to go through a rigorous interviewing process to prove her ability to do the job. Three weeks of interviews followed before she heard the news.

The first call that she made was to her brother, a fellow officer and her confidant—"Hi, Bobby—this is Robin. You won't believe this. Mayor Strong just called to offer me the chief of police position."

Bobby couldn't contain his excitement. "My little sister! The chief of police!" Robin replied, "No. I turned him down."

"You did what?" Bobby couldn't believe what he was hearing. Robin, trying to calm him down, said, "Well, he told me to think about it over the weekend, but swore me to confidentiality, with the exception of family members. I am just not ready. Bobby, I am not even on the senior team—those guys don't take me seriously. Being their boss will be pure hell." After a moment, Bobby said, "Well, it definitely doesn't sound like my sister, letting those guys scare you away."

Robin had just returned from her night shift when the phone rang. She knew who it was, and she knew what she had to do. Bobby's words made her think twice about rejecting the offer. Perhaps it was time to face up to the challenge and introduce some changes that the MPD badly needed. And 30 days later, the MPD swore in the city's first woman chief of police: Robin Richardson.

Changing Organizational Structure

Respecting the chain of command, Robin had refrained from communicating with the department's senior leaders prior to her appointment. Three hours after the swearing-in ceremony, Robin gathered with her senior team in the main boardroom. Walter "Mac" McNeil was the first to speak. "Mayor Strong certainly didn't ask this group who should be the next chief. Clearly, this is just his way of showing the community that he is capable of making *big* changes. We know that things are going to change around here, and the writing is on the wall—do you want us to resign, or what?"

Aware that all eyes were on her, Robin took a deep breath. "If that is an ultimatum, I guess the answer is "Or what." Are things going to change at MPD? Yes. Are you all invited to be a part of that growth and solution? Yes. Are you expected to agree with me 100 percent of the time? No. Are you expected to respect this office? Yes. If you don't respect the community, our police officers, or me, should you expect to be here much longer? No." Robin raised her eyebrows and asked, "Are there any more questions?" After 30 seconds or so of silence, she continued, "All right—let's get to work."

Of the 12 senior team members in the room that day, 9 were still in their positions almost six months later. Of those managers, Robin believed around 7 of them were 100 percent committed to change, with the remaining people just staying around long enough to say, "I told you so!" So what did Robin do to cause almost half of the senior team to disagree with her?

That first day in the boardroom as chief, Robin had shown the senior team a 10-foot-long banner. Written on it were three words—Communication, Compassion, Computers. Over the course of her career to date, Robin noticed that the communication was poor or nonexistent between the MPD staff and the community; that compassion was severely lacking for victims of crime; and that the MPD had an old-fashioned approach to technology compared to other organizations. It was time for the MPD to make significant changes and catch up with the times.

"We are facing one of the worst crime and murder rates in this country. The community has lost faith and trust in the MPD, as we are not doing enough to protect them. We don't communicate with the community, let alone each other; we show little compassion to victims or their family members when a crime has taken place; and our approach to technology is backward at best," she told the MPD officers and staff at their first official meeting.

Robin paused, trying to ignore the angry stares and folded arms in the room. There was not one senior member who seemed to like what she was saying. Still, she knew that she had to drive her point home and leave them with no doubt as to the changes she intended to implement, and this was the time to do it. She cleared her throat. "The most important asset we have available to us is the community. Yet, we don't talk to them enough. We don't show them we care. And one of the most efficient ways we can do that is with technology. If we have isolated internal systems that are incapable of communicating with each other, we are going to continue to be segregated from the community, which means we will be unable to be a part of the national security solution."

Robin held her iPhone in the air and declared, "From this moment on, every single person in this department and every single person in the community can email me directly and expect a response the same day. Community members will be notified of this new initiative through our virtual noticeboard, and at community meetings, where I will be giving talks regarding the upcoming changes within the MPD. Within the MPD, I have set up an anonymous virtual suggestion box, where every single officer can email me ideas of how we can improve things around here."

Mac was the first to speak. "All of this looks good on paper, but we already have leaders in the field, and you are undermining their authority by encouraging every staff and community member to get involved. You are going to have nothing but chaos! Soldiers need sergeants—if you are not willing to command and control, you will put lives in danger." Several other heads in the room nodded in agreement.

Robin had expected this response, and knew how impassioned the senior officers were about the **Unity-of-Command principle**, which is a philosophy that each employee reports to and is accountable to only one manager.[17] Still, she wanted to nip the argument in the bud as

Unity-of-Command principle A philosophy that each employee reports to and is accountable to only one manager.

© W2 Photography / Corbis

soon as possible. "Mac, we will need to agree to disagree on this. I believe we need to evolve into an organization of 'communication and collaboration,' not 'command and control'—we need to get out into the community."

Before the meeting came to an end, three senior officers had walked out, and by the next morning, they had quit the MPD.

10.3 | *HORIZONTAL APPROACH*

10.3 | Describe how managers horizontally organize processes and teams to distribute decision making throughout the organization.

Chief Richardson could not have anticipated the floodgate of communication and change that would incur over the next several months. She thought it would take much longer to engage the community's interest enough to encourage them to communicate directly with the MPD. Discovering that it was not realistic for her to be the sole responder to every single email from the community, she equipped all cops with an iPhone and instructions that they were to respond to community questions and requests in their district within 24 hours. Over 10,000 community members had joined a mailing list introduced by Robin, and it was proving to be extraordinarily successful. The members would use the mailing list not only to air their grievances, but also to send information to the MPD relating to crimes in the community. Something profound was happening: when the police department was willing to listen, the community was more willing to talk.

To accommodate for this dramatic shift in performance culture, Robin decided to drop her next bombshell—the decision to change the traditional vertical organizational structure to a less hierarchical, more horizontal one. After all, the police were forming relationships with the community members, so why couldn't they form relationships with each other and traverse departmental boundaries when it came to solving crimes? With the existing structure, this simply wasn't possible. The chain of command was too strong.

The police department had always been a centralized organization, and Robin felt it was time to create a more **decentralized structure** and rely on all employees to collect and communicate information to make decisions and recommend changes.[18] Robin set up a meeting with the senior managers for the following week; but first, she needed to prepare for this next big challenge.

Researching Organizational Structures

To frame her argument, Robin headed to the library and read every single management textbook she could get her hands on. She then went online and studied the effects of moving from one structure to another. Next, she called some of her contacts in other MPDs around the country who had successfully restructured their organizations and asked them for feedback. Finally, she contacted Troy Kimbell, the former chief of police and her mentor; she had made a point of staying in touch with him after he left the MPD and valued his advice.

After she gathered all the information, she sat back and thought for a minute. Instinctively, she knew that suggesting a redesign in structure would mean a major upheaval for the MPD culture, and she wanted to have her facts straight. The way she saw it, the MPD had become strictly divided into individual departments that refused to have anything to do with each other. While she was earning her management degree, she had learned all about Systems Theory and wholeheartedly agreed with the concept of seeing an organization as a system composed of many different parts, all of which depend on each other. Now, all she had to do was persuade the senior team to look at these interconnected systems as a whole in order to understand the importance of each part and how all the departments could contribute to the organization if they cooperated with one another.

In order to reengineer the MPD into a horizontal structure, Robin felt that by following a process of **departmentalization**, a design structure that groups together processes and jobs based on functions, products, or customers, she could get the units talking to each other again. Robin learned that there were three main approaches to departmentalization: Functional, divisional, and matrix.[19]

Decentralized structure A design structure that relies on all employees to collect and communicate information, in order to make decisions and recommend changes.

Departmentalization A design structure that groups together processes and jobs based on functions, products, or customers.

A **functional organization** is a hierarchical structure in which employees are managed through clear levels of authority. Although Robin agreed with some of the elements of this design, she felt that the departments were already too concerned with their own functions and had lost sight of the overall mission of the MPD. Rather than the existing vertical hierarchy of authority, she wanted a structure where the employees were involved in the decision-making process and given a certain level of **autonomy**, the level of individual discretion that an employee has to make decisions.

Next, she took a look at the **divisional organization**, a design structure that groups processes and jobs based on clearly defined market segments or geography. For the MPD, this meant that different subunits could be set up under each division. Decision making could take place at the divisional level by managers, and differences of opinion would be resolved without depending on the chief. Robin felt that this design was leading more toward what she visualized for the MPD: a centralized, horizontal organization.

Finally, she turned her attention to the **matrix organization**, a design structure that facilitates horizontal integration and collaboration. A matrix model combines elements of both the functional and the divisional organizations, has dual lines of authority, and is designed to encourage the sharing of information. Robin felt that by using this model, the reporting line would shift dramatically: each function and division would be assigned a manager. When a crime took place, there would be more collaboration between the different departments, as they would be working more closely together. This is the type of organization that she thought would be best for the MPD. Robin was excited to present her thoughts to the senior team.

Robin scheduled a meeting with the team to discuss the changes in the chain of command. Aware that winning them over on this latest change was going to be her biggest challenge to date, she made sure she began her presentation strongly and confidently.

"Over the past few months, we have seen many changes in the MPD. As we know, police officer community approval rates are at an all-time high, and crime and murder rates are beginning to fall. The community is starting to trust the MPD more, which has been pivotal in solving and reducing the amount of crime in our area. In light of this, I think it is time to formally redesign our structure from a vertical organizational structure to a more horizontal, flat one. Personally, I do not believe that a senior title is enough to encourage teams to work together. We need to earn the trust of our staff so we can share ideas and implement new initiatives."

Robin unveiled a chart shown in Figure 10-3 that outlined the new structure. She paused for the fallout, and was not disappointed.

"Hold on a second," yelled Mac. 'Yes, statistics prove that crime is on the decline, and the initiatives we have put in place are working, but why mess with the structure? After all, it has been the traditional police model for over 200 years. If it ain't broke, why fix it?"

Robin replied, "The new chart is not designed to take away power; it is merely a way of encouraging all the teams to work more closely together rather than in isolation. I don't believe there is a single person in this department that can work on their own in any function. And I truly believe this is the best structure for the MPD to move us into the future."

She explained to the team the results of the research that she had done and why this structure would benefit the MPD and the wider community. Yet Mac and some of the others weren't convinced about the new model. "What's the sense of having employees report to two bosses? Surely, that's a case of 'too many cooks in the kitchen'; you will have a mutiny on your hands," he warned.

Several other managers joined in, agreeing with Mac, and although Robin repeated her reasons for the structure change, she knew that it would take longer for them to accept the idea. As the meeting drew to a close, she decided to end things on a positive and confident note: "Extensive research shows that this change is the best thing we can do to ensure the success of the department. Let's give it a chance and see how it works out over time. In the meantime, if you have any other questions, I will be more than happy to discuss them with you."

As the team filed out of the room, she couldn't help but note the number of dissatisfied faces; she knew that words weren't going to be enough. She needed to put her plan into action to prove to the disgruntled managers that a structural change was the right decision for the MPD.

Functional organization A hierarchal structure where employees are managed through clear levels of authority.

Autonomy The level of individual discretion that an employee has to make decisions.

Divisional organization A design structure that groups processes and jobs based on clearly defined market segments or geography.

Matrix organization A design structure that facilitates horizontal integration and collaboration.

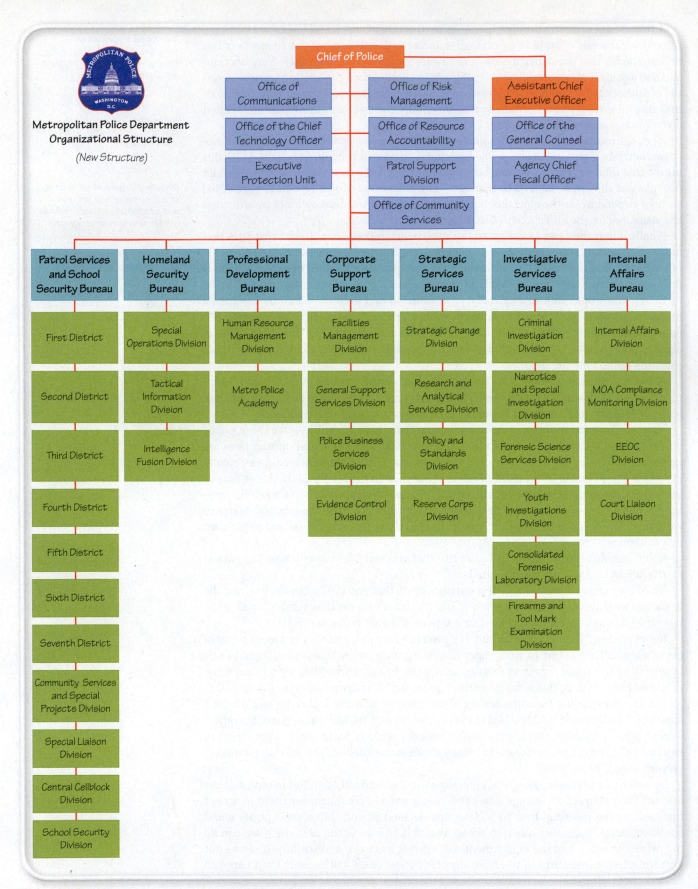

Figure 10-3

Metropolitan Police Department Organizational Structure

The new organizational structure for the Metropolitan Police Department.

LECTURE ENHANCER:

10.4 Adaptive Approach

✓ Accountability—an expectation that team members are responsible for their activities and transparently report outcomes

10.4 | ADAPTIVE APPROACH

10.4 | Show how managers combine vertical and horizontal approaches to organizational design in order to be more adaptive.

It was February 2012, and most of the Occupy Wall Street protests related to the indiscretions on Wall Street and the widening gap between the "haves" and "have nots" had been confined to New York City. One Sunday morning, however, Chief Richardson learned that rallies to "Take Back Our Country" were being planned for Washington, D.C.[20]

Alex Wong / Getty Images Inc

By mid-afternoon, the department's listserv was jammed with thousands of concerned emails. Washington, D.C. residents were worried about the impact of the impending flood of protestors. Following the new departmental protocol and the formally announced matrix structure, every officer was told by his or her divisional and functional manager to respond to every email. Confident that the senior team had everything under control, Robin did not follow up on the number of cops on the street. Because of the new initiative to put more officers on the street, she was sure the community would be well protected against any kind of threat.

Then it happened.

Within a matter of hours of the announcement to "Take Back our Country," thousands of angry protestors poured into Washington, D.C., from all over the country.[21] Tents popped up . . . bonfires began to blaze . . . and the crowd started to protest—calmly at first, but then defiantly. In response to the protesters, many members of the community flooded into the city to hold a counterprotest. When one frustrated community member yelled: "Too bad those tents don't have showers! Maybe you could take a bath and get a job," all hell broke loose. That comment sparked a riot that took the MPD, with military assistance, over six hours to contain. In retrospect, there had not been enough officers on the street to prevent this kind of crisis from occurring.

That night, reporters began to ask Chief Richardson hard questions: "Where were all of the police officers?" Why did it take so long to restore order?" Why did you need to call in the military for help?" And the most difficult question of all: "Are we safe?"

As chief of police, Robin knew she had to take full **accountability**, an expectation that team members are responsible for their activities and must report outcomes transparently, for the incident. With her head held high, she responded, "Last night was my responsibility, and over the next several days, we will be assessing what mistakes were made and how to ensure that we won't repeat them." As she walked away from the press conference, she knew she needed to make sure that an incident like that never happened again.

The first phone call she made was to Troy Kimbell; she asked him, "Chief—where did I go wrong?"

He replied, "Sometimes the new way of doing things seems so good that it's easy to forget the old way worked, too. Chief Richardson, you are in a unique position to be able to do both, almost simultaneously."

Robin understood Kimbell's advice. She had worked so hard to change from the *vertical model* that she had forgotten that it has its place, especially in crisis situations. As chief of police, she should have used her authority to issue direct orders to her officers, quickly get them equipped with riot gear, and send as many of them as possible to the scene of the protest. That would have deflected aggravation between the two camps; she was sure of it. Instead, she had focused on the technology initiatives and had relied too heavily on the other managers to take control, with disastrous consequences. Furthermore, she hadn't yet filled the positions following the resignation of the three senior managers, which left some departments short-staffed. She had taken her eye off the ball.

She realized that she needed a more adaptive approach to the organizational structure that she implemented, where she could use the best aspects of the vertical and the horizontal models to deal with specific situations. To achieve this, she needed to hire more staff,

Accountability An expectation that team members are responsible for their activities and must report outcomes transparently.

reinforce elements of the vertical model, and get buy-in from the senior team. It all sounded pretty daunting, and she knew that she had to prepare herself for the next challenge in the MPD: recruiting and building teams of excellence.

LECTURE ENHANCER:

10.5 Beyond the Organization: Free Agents and Virtual Teams
➤ Voices of Management: Ken Lancaster—Owner, Lancaster Advertising

Free agents Independent workers that supply organizations with talent for projects or time-bound objectives.

Telecommuting A work arrangement in which an employee is given flexibility in terms of work location, and often hours as well.

10.5 | BEYOND THE ORGANIZATION: FREE AGENTS AND VIRTUAL TEAMS

10.5 | Identify additional resources that contemporary managers use to increase organizational adaptability.

Free agents are independent workers that supply organizations with talent for projects or time-bound objectives. Free agents and freelancers are not the only ways that companies are saving money while providing flexibility to their workers. Many companies are employing other types of flexible workforce arrangements, such as telecommuting and virtual teams. **Telecommuting** refers to a work arrangement in which an employee is given flexibility in terms of work location and often hours as well. Corporate leaders often identify telecommuting as a primary tool for attracting and retaining the best and the brightest

Voices of Management

Ken Lancaster
Owner, Lancaster Advertising

Lancaster Advertising, of Lewisville, Texas, has no full-time employees and no offices in which to operate. Sound strange? The company is actually part of a growing trend of staffing positions with "free agents" rather than with traditional full-time workers.[22] The company used to have 15 full-time employees and two office buildings, but today, owner Ken Lancaster contracts with freelancers worldwide and works from his home, boat, or at a coffee shop. "You don't have to worry about someone coming late to work, or if they can't stand you, or about all the payroll taxes and health insurance," says Lancaster.[23] Bryce Davis, one of Lancaster's web designers, contracts with anywhere from 5 to 10 clients at a time and relishes his free agent status: "I enjoy the change of pace. It gives you an opportunity to be creative. . .without stagnating."[24]

More and more companies are moving toward flexible workforce arrangements based on engaging temporary workers, independent contractors, and freelancers in an effort to cut costs, respond more efficiently to fluctuating demands, or to engage workers with specialized skills for short-term projects. "The basic bargain at the center of work used to be, employees gave loyalty and the organization gave security—that bargain is kaput," says Daniel Pink, the author of *Free Agent Nation: The Future of Working for Yourself*.[25] Although the number of contingent workers has risen sharply in recent years as workers have sought increased flexibility and job security, traditional employees still comprise around 90 percent of the workforce.[26]

Despite the freedom that supposedly comes with being a free agent, Stanford University professor Jeffrey Pfeffer points out that some freelancers may feel less freedom due to the opportunity cost associated with time not worked.[27] As Pfeffer explains, people who decide to take contract work assignments to have more flexibility often become obsessed with the "time is money" concept and have trouble taking time away from their jobs because they think about the income opportunities that they are passing up in terms of "billable hours." A possible solution? Pfeffer observes that many individual contractors are asking to be paid by the job rather than by the hour to avoid this situation.[28]

Company Profile

Name: Lancaster Advertising

Owner: Ken Lancaster

Company Story: On Lancaster Advertising's website, they say, "You might say we have the idea of delivering big ideas for small (or medium) budgets built into our DNA. Most of the hundreds of clients we have served since then have been entrepreneur-lead organizations with big ideas and usually less capital than their competition."

Fun Fact: One of Lancaster Advertising's first clients was a pizza parlor that sold all-you-can-eat pizza for $2.99.

Critical Thinking in the Classroom

How do you perceive Ken Lancaster's adoption of flexible workforce arrangements? What would you envisage to be the benefits and pitfalls of this strategy? ∎

employees; indeed, 82 of *Fortune*'s "100 Best Companies to Work For" offer some form of telecommuting to their employees.[29] For example, nearly 20 percent of Delta Air Line's reservation agents now work from home full-time.[30] Delta spends approximately $2,500 to purchase each agent a computer as well as software licenses, but the employees pay for their own phone line. At-home Delta agents are paid less than their call-center counterparts, but they save time and gasoline by not commuting to work, and they enjoy the convenience of working from home.[31]

As flexible work options involving free agents and telecommuting continue to grow, the need to coordinate the efforts of these physically dispersed workers has led to a new type of organizational structure, the virtual team. A **virtual team** refers to a group of employees who work across barriers consisting of time, distance, and organizational boundaries, while being linked together by information and communication technologies. Experts suggest that companies with virtual teams should provide space within the information technology systems for those teams to operate. This space can be used for sharing information about projects, but it should also have a social network component that can allow team members to share information about their personal lives, such as family news. As University of Central Florida professor Eduardo Salas notes, "Within an office setting, co-workers swap stories, talk about their families and share vacation photos. It's being part of the organization and feeling connect with the people you work with. With virtual teams, employers need to provide a way for team members to interact and encourage them to build that sense of community and friendship."[32] As technologies continue to evolve, organizations will likely find new and even more effective ways to reap the benefits of flexible work arrangements such as telecommuting and virtual teams.

Whether employees work as free agents, in virtual teams, or in the office, managers need to ensure that they hire the right people for the right job. In the next chapter, we will follow Robin as she seeks to identify and recruit new talent for the MPD.

✓ **Free Agents**—independent workers that supply organizations with talent for projects or time-bound objectives

✓ **Telecommuting**—a work arrangement in which an employee is given flexibility in terms of work location and hours
  ➤ Corporate leaders often identify telecommuting as a primary tool

Virtual team A group of employees who work across barriers consisting of time, distance, and organizational boundaries, while being linked together by information and communication technologies.

for attracting and retaining the best and the brightest employees.

✓ **Virtual Team**—a group of employees who work across barriers consisting of time, distance, and organizational boundaries, while being linked together by information and communication technologies

CaseSnapshot

Chapter 10 Case: Structuring Organizations:
W.L. Gore & Associates can be found on pg. 472

ADDITIONAL RESOURCES

KEY TERMS

Accountability An expectation that team members are responsible for their activities and must report outcomes transparently. (p. 267)

Authority The implicit and explicit power that a manager or employee has to fulfill an organizational function or role. (p. 259)

Autonomy The level of individual discretion that an employee has to make decisions. (p. 265)

Broker A trusted intermediary that facilitates mutually agreed-upon outcomes for two or more parties. (p. 261)

Centralized organization A design structure that relies on senior-level managers to collect information broadly, in order to make decisions on behalf of the entire company. (p. 259)

Chain of command A predefined structural order of authority that determines how decisions are made and communicated. (p. 259)

Coordination The synchronization of an organization's functions to ensure efficient use of resources in pursuit of goals and objectives. (p. 258)

Corporate governance A compendium of policies intended to ensure transparency and fulfillment of duties to stakeholders. (p. 261)

Decentralized structure A design structure that relies on all employees to collect and communicate information, in order to make decisions and recommend changes. (p. 264)

Delegation When a manager grants power and authority to another team member. (p. 258)

Departmentalization A design structure that groups together processes and jobs based on functions, products, or customers. (p. 264)

Differentiation The process through which managers divide labor based on tasks and functions. (p. 257)

Divisional organization A design structure that groups processes and jobs based on clearly defined market segments or geography. (p. 265)

Formalization The degree of which policies and procedures determine specific jobs and functions. (p. 258)

Free agents Independent workers that supply organizations with talent for projects or time-bound objectives. (p. 268)

Functional organization A hierarchal structure where employees are managed through clear levels of authority. (p. 265)

Hierarchy A vertically organized structure of power relationships, where the top level holds the most power and resources. (p. 256)

Integration Horizontal coordination between functions, departments, and organizational activities. (p. 257)

Matrix organization A design structure that facilitates horizontal integration and collaboration. (p. 265)

Network organization A group of independent companies that organize themselves to appear as a larger entity. (p. 262)

Organizational chart A visual document that communicates how a company is organized. (p. 261)

Organic organization A highly adaptive structure defined by horizontal integration, distributed decision making, and employees with a high degree of generalization. (p. 257)

Span of control The optimum number of direct reports that a person can manage effectively. (p. 257)

Specialization Focusing a group or individual's activities based on strengths, aptitudes, or skills. (p. 258)

Standardization A performance context where policies and procedures seek to create uniform results. (p. 258)

Telecommuting A work arrangement in which an employee is given flexibility in terms of work location, and often hours as well. (p. 268)

Unity-of-Command principle A philosophy that each employee reports to and is accountable to only one manager. (p. 263)

Vertical organizational structure A structure, characterized by hierarchical authority and communication channels. (p. 259)

Virtual team A group of employees who work across barriers consisting of time, distance, and organizational boundaries, while being linked together by information and communication technologies. (p. 269)

IN REVIEW

10.1 | Explain how differentiation and integration define performance cultures.

Managers can design a performance culture, consciously or unconsciously, depending on the intensity levels of differentiation and integration. *Differentiation* is the process through which managers divide labor based on tasks and functions, and *integration* is the horizontal coordination between functions, departments, and organizational activities.

10.2 | Describe how managers vertically organize processes and teams to centralize decision making.

Vertical organizational structures are characterized by hierarchical authority and communication channels. This structure relies on senior-level managers to collect information broadly in order to make decisions on behalf of the entire company. The term *chain of command*, a predefined structural order of authority that determines how decisions are made and communicated, is commonly associated with this type of structure.

10.3 | Describe how managers horizontally organize processes and teams to distribute decision making throughout the organization.

The horizontal organizational structure is categorized as a *decentralized structure*, or one that relies on all employees to collect and communicate information to make decisions and recommend changes.

10.4 | Show how managers combine vertical and horizontal approaches to organizational design in order to be more adaptive.

When managers combine vertical and horizontal approaches, it is known as an *adaptive approach*. This approach takes the best aspects of the vertical and horizontal approaches, and uses them in specific situations.

10.5 | Identify additional resources that contemporary managers use to increase organizational adaptability.

Free agents or freelancers, telecommuting, and virtual teams are all ways to increase an organization's adaptability. *Free agents* are independent workers that supply organizations with talent for projects or time-bound objectives. *Telecommuting* refers to a work arrangement in which an employee is given flexibility in terms of work location and hours. A *virtual team* refers to a group of employees who work across barriers consisting of time, distance, and organizational boundaries, while being linked by information and communication technologies.

SELF-TEST

10.1 | Explain how differentiation and integration define performance cultures.

1. A vertically organized structure of power relationships where the top level holds the most power and resources is referred to as:
   a. A hierarchy
   b. An oligarchy
   c. Decentralized
   d. An organic organization

2. A highly adaptive structure defined by horizontal integration, distributed decision making, and employees with a high degree of generalization is referred to as:
   a. A hierarchy
   b. An oligarchy
   c. Centralized
   d. An organic organization

3. Span of control refers to the maximum number of direct reports that a person can manage effectively.
   a. True.
   b. False.

10.2 | Describe how managers vertically organize processes and teams to centralize decision making.

4. A(n) _____ organizational structure is characterized by hierarchical authority and communication channels.

5. A predefined structural order of authority that determines how decisions are made and communicated is called:
   a. A flow of authority
   b. A chain of command
   c. A chain of management
   d. A flow of power

6. A visual document that communicates how a company is organized is:
   a. An organizational map
   b. An organizational blueprint
   c. An organizational chart
   d. An organizational schematic

7. The Unity-of-Command principle is a philosophy that each manager should manage only one employee.
   a. True.
   b. False.

10.3 | Describe how managers horizontally organize processes and teams to distribute decision making throughout the organization.

8. List and describe the three main approaches to departmentalization.

10.4 | Show how managers combine vertical and horizontal approaches to organizational design in order to be more adaptive.

9. Using the best parts of the vertical and horizontal models to deal with specific situations may allow organizations to be more:
   a. Adaptive
   b. Constructive
   c. Aggressive
   d. Concentrated

10.5 | Identify additional resources that contemporary managers use to increase organizational adaptability.

10. Independent workers that supply organizations with talent for projects or time-bound objectives are known as:
    a. Free thinkers
    b. Free agents
    c. Odd jobbers
    d. Executioners

11. _____ refers to a work arrangement in which an employee is given flexibility in terms of work location and hours.

12. A(n) _____ refers to a group of employees who work across barriers consisting of time, distance, and organizational boundaries, while being linked together by information and communication technologies.

CHAPTER EXERCISES

Create an Organizational Structure

Instructions:

1. Working by yourself or in a team, choose one of the following types of organizations (or your instructor may assign one to you or your team) and create an organizational structure for it. You may be as traditional or creative in your approach as you like.

   a. Airline
   b. Local fast food restaurant
   c. National hotel chain
   d. Professional football franchise
   e. Local lawn care company
   f. College or university
   g. Movie production company

2. Briefly describe your structure and why you chose to design it as you did.

3. Is your structure more centralized or decentralized?

4. Does your stucture have a narrow or wide span of control?

5. Is your structure more organic or more mechanistic?

SELF-ASSESSMENT

Organic vs. Mechanistic

For each of the following paired statements, circle the letter next to the statement that best describes you:

1. A) I prefer organizations in which employees work separately and specialize on a single task.
   B) I prefer organizations in which employees work together and coordinate tasks.

2. A) I prefer organizations in which the authority hierarchy is well defined.
   B) I prefer organizations in which people from across the organization work together in teams and task forces.

3. A) I prefer organizations in which decision making is centralized at the top of the organizational structure.
   B) I prefer organizations in which decision making is delegated to the lower levels of the organizational structure.

4. A) I prefer organizations in which there are extensive rules, standards, and procedures.
   B) I prefer organizations in which work processes are informal and unpredictable.

5. A) I prefer organizations in which there is a lot of formal written communication.
   B) I prefer organizations in which there is a lot of informal face-to-face communication.

6. A) I prefer organizations in which there are fixed duties.
   B) I prefer organizations in which there are adaptable duties.

7. A) I prefer organizations in which there are rigid, hierarchical relationships.
   B) I prefer organizations in which there is both vertical and horizontal collaboration.

Scoring:

Preference for Mechanistic Organizations

(Add up the total number of "As" circled above and write that number in the blank.) _____

Mechanistic organizations tend to have a traditional, centralized, hierarchical, and bureaucratic organizational structure. Mechanistic organizations are often found in industries in which there is little change and little competition.

Preference for Organic Organizations

(Add up the total number of "Bs" circled above and write that number in the blank.) _____

Organic organizations tend to have nontraditional, decentralized organizational structures. Organic organizations are often found in industries characterized by high growth, rapid change, and fierce competition.

SELF-TEST ANSWER KEY

1. a.
2. d.
3. b; False. Span of control refers to the *number* of direct reports that a person manages.
4. Vertical
5. b.
6. c.
7. b; False. The Unity-of-Command principle is a philosophy that each employee reports to and is accountable to only one manager.
8. A *functional organization* is a hierarchical structure in which employees are managed through clear levels of authority. The *divisional organization* involves a design structure that groups processes and jobs based on clearly defined market segments or geography. A *matrix organization* is a design structure that facilitates horizontal integration and collaboration. It combines elements of both the functional and the divisional organizations, has dual lines of authority, and is designed to encourage the sharing of information.
9. a.
10. b.
11. Telecommuting
12. Virtual team

Notes

CHAPTER ELEVEN

THE HUMAN SIDE OF MANAGEMENT

Learning Objectives

By the end of the chapter, you will be able to:

11.1 | Describe how managers make a significant difference by attracting, selecting, and retaining the best available talent within legal requirements.

11.2 | Explain how managers assess human resource needs and select talent to meet demand.

11.3 | Discuss different approaches to increasing organizational performance through the education of employees.

11.4 | Describe how managers retain employees and adjust to turnover.

11.5 | Design a performance development process based on organizational needs.

ADDITIONAL RESOURCES

KEY TERMS
IN REVIEW
SELF-TEST
CHAPTER EXERCISE
SELF-ASSESSMENT
SELF-TEST
ANSWER KEY

INSIDE THIS CHAPTER
ManagementStory:
Featuring **Robin Richardson**

JP Greenwood/Getty Images

LECTURE ENHANCER:

11.1 Human Resource Management

✓ **Human Resources Management—**an organizational function that deals with people-related issues such as recruitment, performance management, benefits, training, employee motivation, safety, and administration while ensuring compliance with employment and labor laws

Human resource management (HRM, or HR) An organizational function that deals with people-related issues such as recruitment, performance management, benefits, training, employee motivation, safety, and administration, while ensuring compliance with employment and labor laws.

✓ **Collective Bargaining—**the process of negotiation between employers and trade unions usually with respect to pay, working hours and working conditions

✓ **Labor Relations—**the relationship between management and the workforce, began to improve significantly

✓ **Equal Employment Opportunity—**every employee has an equal right to advance in a company irrespective of age, sex, race, disability or color

Collective bargaining The process of negotiation between employers and trade unions, usually with respect to pay, working hours, and working conditions.

Labor relations The relationship between management and the workforce.

11.1 | *HUMAN RESOURCE MANAGEMENT*

11.1 | Describe how managers make a significant difference by attracting, selecting, and retaining the best available talent within legal requirements.

"The days of simply maintaining personnel files and advising on hiring, firing, and compensation are long gone for HR professionals. Today they fulfill a variety of roles that require knowledge and competencies in areas that were foreign to them in the past."
—*HR Magazine*[1]

Human resource management (HRM, or HR) is an organizational function that deals with people-related issues such as recruitment, performance management, benefits, training, employee motivation, safety, and administration, while ensuring compliance with employment and labor laws.[2]

In Chapter 2, we learned about the poor treatment of workers during the Industrial Revolution, a time when machines, production volumes, and consumer demands took priority over the well-being of employees. This perception was further confirmed by managers such as Frederick W. Taylor, who adopted a scientific approach to his workforce with the aim of making employees as efficient as the machines they worked with. Although workers would become more effective, they were still subjected to low wages, long hours, and unsafe environments.

Indeed, it was not until the late 1880s that management philosophy began to change. With such poor working conditions, employers were having difficulties in hiring and retaining staff. This led them to believe that there was a direct link between employee satisfaction and productivity. Worker strikes, unions, and general unrest also motivated employers to implement processes that would protect their employees in the workplace. The government followed suit and introduced several laws designed to defend the workers against discrimination and harassment, and introduced reforms to regulate working hours, compensation for injuries, and laws governing child labor.

During the 1920s, a new focus on human relations was born. HR was no longer seen as merely a function of an organization, but a vital part to its commercial success. Time and again, research, such as the Hawthorne Studies, found that the feelings and emotions of the workers were central to their motivation and productivity. In short, it was how they were treated that really mattered. By the 1930s, workers were legally permitted to engage in **collective bargaining**, which is the process of negotiation between employers and trade unions, usually with respect to pay, working hours, and working conditions.[3] In time, **labor relations**, the relationship between management and the workforce, began to improve significantly.[4]

However, it was not until the 1960s and 1970s that the role of HR really took hold. In an era where civil rights took center stage, it became more important than ever for managers to ensure that their employees were treated fairly, equally, and with respect.

More and more, the HR function is being woven into business practices across the board. HR professionals are expected to be well versed in economics, politics, technology, labor laws, health care, sociocultural trends, and many other issues affecting organizations today. In an increasingly complex legal environment, HR managers are challenged with maintaining ethical and financial standards, which involve monitoring employees from the top down to ensure that they are in compliance with government laws and regulations. As the workforce becomes more diverse, companies must adhere to **equal employment opportunity**, a principle stating that every employee has an equal right to advance in a company regardless of age, sex, race, disability, or color.[5]

© Jose Luis Pelaez Inc./Image Source/Corbis

Table 11-1 summarizes some of the U.S equal employment laws that HR managers need to abide by.

Over the last century, HR has evolved to such a degree that it seems impossible for an organization to succeed without an HR department. For instance, when you apply for a job, more often than not, your first contact will be with some area of HR. Similarly, the final stage of your interview process more than likely also will be with HR; and if you get the job, HR staff will be the ones that prepare your offer letter and contract. Throughout your career, HR policies will affect every aspect of your role in an organization, including your salary, training, behavioral conduct, promotions, performance reviews, compensation, and benefits.

It is not only internal policies that are managed by HR, however; indeed, many senior managers consider HR to be an essential part of long-range strategic planning.

Making the Human Side of Management Strategic

In Chapter 4, we explored the phenomenon of talent shortage despite unemployment records showing millions out of work. This means that organizations are struggling to fill positions because they cannot find the right people to match the skills that they are looking for. As a result, competition for talent has become fierce, giving rise to talent wars where companies compete for the most desirable employees. Many companies have adopted the process of **talent management**, a strategic, deliberate approach to attracting new, highly skilled workers and developing the abilities of existing employees to meet current and future organizational objectives.[6]

Managers know that the success of an organization depends on the quality of their employees. They also know that the right talent can give companies an enormous competitive and strategic advantage over rival institutions. Moreover, there is an enormous generational shift taking place:[7] The baby boomers (born between 1945 and 1964) are close to retirement, and organizations need to find the right talent to replace them. However, Generation Y (born between 1981 and 2000) candidates do not necessarily subscribe to the same demands and values as their predecessors. For example, they prefer more flexible working hours, collaboration, and the freedom to introduce new initiatives, and they are not as motivated by money and status. In this age of globalization and technological advancement, it has never been more important to diversify and ensure that businesses stand out from their competition in order to attract this new generation.

As we learned in Chapter 1, critical thinking skills are very much in demand for companies considering new hires. Managers know that innovative, organized people with rare skill sets such as critical thinking add value to products and services and provide something unique that differentiates their company from the competition. As people are an organization's most valuable asset, companies have become more invested in **human capital**, the

Equal employment opportunity A principle stating that every employee has an equal right to advance in a company regardless of age, sex, race, disability, or color.

➤ HR policies affect every aspect of your role in an organization, including your salary, training, behavioral conduct, promotions, performance reviews, compensation and benefits

Talent management A strategic, deliberate approach to attracting new highly skilled workers and developing the abilities of existing employees to meet current and future organizational objectives.

SergeBertasiusPhotography/Shutterstock

Human capital Employee skills and experience gained by education and training that increase the economic value for employers.

Table 11-1   Laws Governing Equal Employment in the United States

Legislation	Primary Purpose	Impact on Managers	President Signed
National Labor Relations Act/ Wagner Act (1935)	Legalized labor organizations, which permitted unions to bargain collectively for better labor conditions, such as improved working hours, health benefits, and higher wages. Created the National Labor Relations Board (NLRB)	Limits the power of employers to fire workers who belong to certain unions, and the ability to put down strikes. Managers have to observe the rights of their employees.	Franklin D. Roosevelt (D)
National Labor Relations Board (NLRB) of 1935	Independent agency of the U.S. government. Set up to conduct unionized elections and investigate unfair business practices. Deals with private-sector businesses only.	Private-sector employers needed to respect the unions and make sure their workers are treated fairly.	Franklin D. Roosevelt (D) Board members are appointed by the president.
Labor-Management Relations Act/ Taft-Hartley Act (1947)	Amendment of National Labor Relations Act. Protected employers' rights to free speech, limited the power of unions to strike, prohibits unfair business practices by unions, and allows union members to reject radical leaders.	Employers do not have to engage in collective bargaining unless they want to. Managers needed to deal with the unrest that followed the act, which was denounced by Truman as the "slave-labor bill."	Harry S. Truman (D) vetoed the act but was overridden by Congress.
Equal Pay Act of 1963	Amendment of Fair Labor Standards Act. Outlaws sex discrimination based on unequal pay for men and women doing similar work.	Managers have to ensure that both the male and female employees in similar roles are paid equally for their work.	John F. Kennedy (D)
Civil Rights Act of 1964	To outlaw discrimination based on race and gender in schools, housing, and hiring.	Managers had to ensure that their businesses did not discriminate in their hiring or in their service practices.	Lyndon B. Johnson (D)
Age Discrimination in Employment Act (ADEA) of 1967	Prohibits discrimination for employees over 40 years of age.	Managers need to ensure that hiring or firing decisions are not based on age.	Lyndon B. Johnson (D)
Occupational Safety and Health Act of 1970	To ensure that employees have safe conditions to work, free from hazards that are recognizable and addressable.	Identify areas of potential risk and take proactive steps to remove or minimize hazards.	Richard M. Nixon (R)
Consumer Product Safety Act of 1972	Established the Consumer Products Safety Commission (CPSC) to develop safety and product recall standards for consumer products.	Identify products and processes that will fall under CPSC regulations and address issues to minimize liability.	Richard M. Nixon (R)
Employee Retirement Income Security Act (ERISA) of 1974	Protects employees by ensuring that funds in their pension plans would still be there when they retired.	Monitors employee benefits and understands the organization's fiduciary responsibility for retirement plans.	Gerald Ford (R)
Americans with Disabilities Act (ADA) of 1990	Provides that persons with disabilities will not face discrimination in the workplace, are provided access to all public places, and have access to telecommunication services.	Issues concerning public access to disabled persons must be addressed, including physical structures and telecommunications services.	George H. W. Bush (R)
Civil Rights Act of 1991	Amendment of Civil Rights Act of 1964. To provide for damages in employment discrimination lawsuits. Shifts the burden of proof to the employer.	Ensures that employment decisions are not based on intentional discrimination such as sex, religion, and disabilities.	George H. W. Bush (R)
Family Medical Leave Act of 1993	Entitles employees up to 12 weeks of unpaid medical leave with fully covered health insurance and full job protection during their absence.	Managers need to ensure that employees are eligible for the leave of absence under the terms specified by the act.	President Bill Clinton (D)

employees' skills and experience gained by education and training that increase the economic value for employers.[8]

This is why HR has become so crucial to strategic planning.[9] Rather than simply hiring and firing, the role of the HR professional has evolved into analyzing information that helps them understand how to find and keep talent, match people to jobs, optimize employee skills, and identify different methods of training.

The HR profession has come a long way since the dehumanizing days of the Industrial Revolution, where employees were treated as little more than cogs in the greasy wheel of production. With the rapid progress of technology and product innovation, it has never been more important for organizations to find the right talent, nurture it, and allow it to flourish while operating within the framework of legal boundaries and equal opportunities.

Chapter 10 introduced us to Robin Richardson, the new chief of police who has been determined to restructure the Metropolitan Police Department (MPD) and transform it into a more efficient, technologically savvy, and compassionate organization. In doing so, she has faced many challenges, including protests from some of her senior staff regarding the changes that she intends to make. Furthermore, following the mishandling of the "Take Back Our Country" riot, Chief Richardson learned a valuable lesson in asserting her authority as a leader, as well as the importance of having the right people in the right place at the right time. In the next section, we will follow Chief Richardson as she addresses the weaknesses in the MPD by identifying and recruiting new talent.

11.2 | *IDENTIFYING TALENT*

11.2 **Explain** how managers assess human resource needs and select talent to meet demand.

As Chief Richardson reflects on the "Take Back Our Country" riot and everything that had gone wrong with the MPD's response to it, she knows that one of the glaring weaknesses in the department is the senior leadership team—mainly because she had not instructed the HR department to fill the positions as previous team members resigned. At the time, she had chosen to reinvest those resources into supporting officers in the field with technology and tools so they were more equipped to deal with challenges as they emerged in the community. This decision had the unintended consequence of leaving the department vulnerable in times of crisis, just when the demands on senior leadership were dramatically increased.

In the post-assessment report developed by the HR department for the mayor's office, Chief Richardson and her team acknowledged that the riot could have been prevented. Averting this outcome in the future, the report stated, would require identifying and selecting senior leadership from within the department and targeting external candidates to join the police force as new recruits each year. Additionally, training and development would be essential to enable the department to behave adaptively as it entered and exited crisis situations.

Chief Richardson now faced the challenge of building a solid leadership team without creating the impression that she was distancing herself from the field. In particular, by not filling the vacant positions, the chief now had a direct reporting line with 18 commanders, captains, and assistant chiefs. The report recommended that she select three of these internal candidates to replace the vacant director positions. This was difficult for Chief Richardson because it seemed to undermine her determination to restructure the chain of command. Now, she would have to select three leaders to recreate the hierarchy that she had worked so hard to dissolve. More important, she knew that she needed help identifying the talent within the police force to fill these positions. Making the wrong choices would cause even more waves within the police department.

- Making the Human Side of Management Strategic
✓ **Talent Management**—a strategic, deliberate approach to attracting new, highly-skilled workers and developing the abilities of existing employees to meet current and future organizational objectives
➤ In this age of globalization and technological advancement, it has never been more important to diversify and ensure that businesses stand out from their competition in order to attract this new generation.
✓ **Human Capital**—the employees' skills and experience gained by education and training that increase the economic value for employers
➤ The role of the HR professional has evolved into analyzing information that helps them understand how to find and keep talent, match people to jobs, optimize employee skills, and identify different methods of training.

LECTURE ENHANCER:

11.2 Identifying Talent

- **Defining and Planning Human Resource Needs**
➤ The role of the HR manager is to analyze the needs of each department, and decide which type of employee would best fit into the culture and possess the skills to enhance the performance of the organization
✓ **Employment-at-Will**—where employees can quit their jobs at any time without any reason, and employers can terminate employees at any time and without any reason

© Jim Smithson/Corbis

There's more to come on how this situation evolves, but first, it's important to discuss HR needs in an organization.

Defining and Planning Human Resource Needs

The HR planning processes of most organizations are essential when it comes to defining the numbers and types of human resources necessary to achieve business goals within a given time frame. The role of the HR manager is to analyze the needs of each department, and decide which type of employee would best fit into the culture and possess the skills to enhance the performance of the organization. With every new hire, HR managers must take into account the law of **employment-at-will**, where employees can quit their jobs at any time without any reason, and employers can terminate employees at any time and without any reason.[10] There are very few reasons why companies would want to enforce this law, as unhappy employees who quit suddenly or are terminated cost firms a great deal of money and inconvenience. It is imperative that HR matches the right people with the right role.

As the hunt for talent becomes more competitive, companies are becoming even more specific when it comes to defining the type of employees they want working for them. In particular, there has been a renewed quest for **knowledge workers**, self-motivated workers who use a variety of skills to enhance their overall understanding of a particular subject or area. These types of employees usually have an excellent educational background, a large amount of experience in a particular field, and add value to the business by introducing new business models, technologies, products, and services. Although knowledge workers tend to be self-motivated, managers still need to monitor their performance and ensure that they are being afforded the same promotional opportunities as the rest of the workforce.

HR managers might also look for **independent contractors**, self-employed individuals or outside businesses that provide services to another entity.[11] Hiring outside contractors can save money. Although their hourly rate tends to be higher than the pay of full-time employees, since contractors do not receive the same benefits, this presents significant cost savings for an organization. In addition, there are not the same problems that might exist when hiring and firing decisions are made—contractors are hired for a specific length of time and for a particular project and then let go once the work is completed. There are also drawbacks to hiring contractors, however. As they are usually short-term hires, they cannot strictly be considered as employees and therefore cannot be managed in the same way. Indeed, some contractors can become resentful if there is too much interference from management. Also, contractors come and go, which can be disruptive and unsettling for the company culture.

Let's return to the MPD case narrative and see how the HR department defines and plans their HR needs.

"Hi, Ken. When you have a few minutes, can you stop by my office?" the chief asks as she pokes her head around the cubicle wall. MPD's assistant chief for HR, Ken Gilmore, nods and tells her he will meet her in her office in a few minutes.

Ken knocks on Chief Richardson's door, "Is now a good time?"

The chief gets up from her chair and points to a sitting area in her office. "Let's sit over here." She begins, "Ken, how much of your time do you spend on solving problems that have already happened? Or, let me ask that another way, how much of your day is spent cleaning up messes?"

Ken folds his hands and answers, "Probably 90 percent of my time, with the other 10 percent spent reminding people of the messes that were made in the past, so we don't repeat them."

Chief Richardson stands up and says, "Exactly! That's the problem—this department has evolved into a culture of solving problems instead of planning for the future."

He responds, "So, let me make sure I understand you correctly. Did you just say that our problem was that we solve problems? If so, you are going to have to help me understand that one."

Chief Richardson laughs. "Okay, let me start over here. Ken, you just told me you spend 90 percent of your time 'putting out fires' and 10 percent of your time looking back at past mistakes to prevent fires. Right?" Ken nods in agreement. The chief sits back down and begins to reframe her vision. "We need to shift our human resources efforts from problem-based to possibility-based. This means that you are going to be the most strategic partner I have on my senior team. Why? Because I believe that with your extensive HR experience, the culture of this entire department has a chance of shifting it from problems to possibilities. That has to start with you and me. Agreed?"

Ken thinks for a minute, and then says, "Traditionally, the MPD HR department has been more of a personnel and administrative function than anything else. We recruit, sort out compensation and benefits, and arrange training for new hires. We have never been asked to do anything more than that. And now you want the department to strategize and implement a new culture of possibilities?"

Chief Richardson asks, "How do you think the HR department is perceived within the MPD?"

Ken laughs, ruefully. "We are known as 'form-fillers'!"

Chief Richardson knew that the HR department didn't get a lot of respect in the MPD, but to hear it from Ken reinforced her beliefs.

"OK, so here's what I want to happen. The whole department is going through a cultural change, and that includes HR. I want your team to be part of the bigger picture. The people in the force are one of our most valuable assets and we have to make sure we get the right candidates who will fit in and embrace the new culture," Richardson explains.

"I like what you are saying. How should we get started? To be quite honest, it does seem a little overwhelming," Ken offers.

Chief Richardson interjects, "It starts with selection and recruitment. How does HR recruit at the moment?"

Ken says, "We usually run an ad in the newspaper; sift through applications, and then conduct interviews. It's not as thorough as I would like it to be, but we have never had a problem with the labor pool."

Chief Richardson nods, "I agree. We've never been short of applicants, but it's quality we need, not quantity. Half our police force will be retiring soon, and a whole new generation is coming in with different skills, attitudes, and expectations. My concern is that there will be a glaring imbalance between the number of experienced officers and new recruits. Working in the police force isn't as attractive as it used to be. Long, uncertain hours and average salaries don't appeal to this current generation and we'll be facing a labor shortage sooner than we think. What we need is change."

Ken says, "Sounds great to me. So, what do you have in mind?"

Chief Richardson replies, "From my analysis, and keeping in mind our average turnover, we have three senior positions that need to be filled internally and 50 external new recruits to hire. I have to believe that if we have the right people in the right positions, 80 percent of our work to change the culture will be done, because the new employees will be carrying forward the new beliefs."

Ken sits up in his seat, and leans forward. To Chief Richardson, it appeared as if Ken was experiencing an epiphany. "What are you thinking, Ken?"

"That this is a great idea! The first thing we should do is re-create our recruitment and selection process. If we do the same things, we are going to get the same results. Give me a week and I will present you with some formal recommendations for recruiting and selecting new candidates."

Chief Richardson has never seen Ken this excited. On his way out of the office, he turns and says enthusiastically, "This is really going to make a difference—I promise you!"

The Abilene Reporter-News, JoyLewis/AP

the qualifications of an individual and evaluate whether they have the skills and abilities to do a job
  ➤ Questions you should ask in an interview
  ➤ Questions to avoid in an interview

• **Selecting Candidates**
✓ **Predictive Validity**—the extent to which a selection test predicts future job performance
✓ **Grievance**—a complaint made by an employee claiming unfair treatment

Internal and External Recruiting

The following week, Ken returns to the chief's office with a series of recommendations to reform their **recruiting**, the process of identifying the best applicants internally or externally for specific roles;[12] and **selection**, the process that assesses the level of skills and abilities possessed by an individual to perform a specific role.[13]

Internal Recruiting Ken begins by discussing the strategy for **internal recruiting**, the method of creating a pool of existing employees who may have the qualifications to fill required job vacancies in an organization.[14]

"Here's what I propose with regard to filling the three senior positions," Ken begins. "I think we will need to fill these roles internally, as I don't think it's good for morale if we look outside for such high-profile roles."

Chief Richardson nods as she imagines the fallout if she appointed three new directors from outside the organization. She was confident that she would find the right people with the skills, talent, and experience to fill those roles, right there within the MPD.

"So, who do you have in mind?" Chief Richardson asks Ken.

Ken presents her with a list of names. "The recruitment team advertised the roles through a new job-posting system on the MPD intranet and the staff bulletin board. These are the applicants we thought best fit the roles."

After reviewing the recommendations, Chief Richardson asks, "These are good choices in terms of experience, but I worry that a number of them won't embrace the new culture we are trying to implement. How will we know they are a cultural fit?"

Ken responds confidently, "Through the interview process . . ."

But the chief isn't sure about his answer. "We need something more dependable than a one- or two-hour interview to vet these candidates, even if they are internal staff. I also want some members of the senior team to interview the candidates for the three available director positions; these are important roles, and the senior team should be involved in the decision-making process."

Ken quickly says, "Got it—let me find a couple of members of the senior team willing to interview the candidates. I will also come up with some options to create a more thorough recruitment process."

External Recruitment Chief Richardson continues with the next point on the agenda: **external recruiting**, the process of creating a pool of qualified applicants outside the organization.[15]

"How are we progressing with the 50 new external recruits we need to breathe more life into this place?" Chief Richardson asked.

"We have reformed our advertising methods significantly," Ken responds. "We have posted on Internet job boards, the MPD website, in the newspaper, through other state law enforcement agencies, and through career fairs. We are also looking into hiring an executive search firm to narrow down the pool of applicants."

Chief Richardson is impressed. "Great news, Ken! Let me know when you have selected the top 50 applicants and can provide some strategies on how we can reform our interviewing process."

They agree to meet the following week.

A few days later, Ken recommends that the department adopt **psychometric tools**, questionnaires or tests that measure an individual's personality, intelligence, and aptitude.[16] He believes they would benefit the interview process by offering management a common understanding of styles and behaviors for existing and potential team members.

"Ken, I'm not a fan of Myers-Briggs type-testing," Chief Richardson replies firmly. "I believe that everything you need to know can be learned by just listening to someone."

Ken offers a few alternatives, shown in Table 11-2.

Using the new recruiting and selection system, over the next two weeks, Ken and Chief Richardson identify six internal candidates, two for each of the three available director positions, which included director of administration, special operations, and operations. The **job description**,[17] a written account of specific tasks, duties and responsibilities required within a particular role, is listed on pages 284-285 for each position:

Recruiting The process of identifying the best applicants internally or externally for specific roles.

Selection The process that assesses the level of skills and abilities possessed by an individual to perform a specific role.

Internal recruiting The process of creating a pool of existing employees who may have the qualifications to fill required job vacancies in an organization.

External recruiting The process of creating a pool of qualified applicants outside the organization.

Psychometric tools Questionnaires or tests that measure an individual's personality, intelligence, and aptitude.

Job description A written account of specific tasks, duties, and responsibilities required within a particular role.

Table 11-2   Examples of Predictive Tools

	Predictive Index (PI)	Myers Briggs (MBTI)	DiSC – DiSC Classic	HPI (Hogan)	Fundamental Interpersonal Relations Orientation – Behavior (Firo-B)	Strength Finder
Publisher Website	www.piworldwide.com	www.cpp.com	www.inscapepublishing.com or www.everythingdisc.com	www.hoganassessments.com	www.psychometrics.com	http://www.strengthsfinder.com/home.aspx
Primary Business Application	• Selection and hiring • Employee engagement • Leadership development • Team effectiveness • Coaching and retention • Succession planning	• Career counseling • Team building • Self/organizational development • Not for selection	• Performance improvement • Conflict resolution • Individual and team development • Relationship building • Not for selection	• Personnel screening and selection • Leadership identification and development • Succession planning • Coaching • Talent management	• Individual or Group • Stand alone or with MBTI • One-on-One Coaching • Team Building • Leadership Development	• Identification of talents and dominant strengths.
Conceptual Background	• Trait theory • Cattell and Eysenck • Closest to 16PF & DiSC	• Jungian typology	• Marston's emotional (DiSC) theory (to measure behavioral styles)	• Based on the Big Five factors of personality—the most prominent, well researched, and current model of personality in existence	• Psychology	• Dr. Donald Clifton and The Standards for Educational and Psychological Testing (American Educational Research Association, American Psychological Association, & National Council on Measurement in Education, 1999
Inventory Design	• Free-choice instrument • 4 primary factors, 2 resultant scales • Approximately 10 minutes to complete; untimed • 67 languages, including Braille	• Forced-choice, 93 items • 20 to 60 minutes to complete • Defines people as psychological "types" (e.g., ESTJ)	• Forced-choice, 28 items • Under 20 minutes to complete • 4 factors	• 206 True/False items • 7 primary scales and 6 occupational scales • 15 to 20 minutes to complete	• 54 multiple choice • Self-paced • Self-scored manually • 15 minutes to complete	• 34 Strength themes measured • On line free assessments • 30 to 60 minutes • The 177-item pairs were based on the theory and research by Selection Research Incorporated and Gallup (Harter, Hayes.
Primary Constructs Measured	• Dominance • Extraversion • Patience • Formality • Decision Making • Response Level • Morale	• 4 dimensions (16 possible types): Extraversion or Introversion Sensing or Intuiting, Thinking or Feeling Judging or Perceiving	• Dominance • Influence • Steadiness • Conscientiousness	• Adjustment • Ambition • Sociability • Interpersonal Sensitivity • Prudence • Inquisitive • Learning Approach	• Three areas measured: Inclusion, Control, Affection	• 34 Talent themes
Technical Quality	• Validated and reliable, No adverse impact • Over 500 validity studies • Primary scales correlate with 16PF and NEO • Significant research since 1970s • Scientific Advisory Board • Follows EEOC guidelines	• Undefined number of validity studies on reported type and best-fit type (selected by participants) • General lack of hard science • Does not appear to follow EEOC guidelines	• Little validity information is provided • Only some of the scales correlate with the 16PF and the MBTI • Does not appear to follow EEOC guidelines	• Validated and reliable, No adverse impact • Over 400 validity studies showing HPI predicts occupational success • Primary scales correlate to other Big Five measures • Significant research since the 1970s • Follows EEOC guidelines	• Little validity information is provided • Case Studies and White Papers • Does not appear to follow EEOC guidelines	• Validity studies completed (numerous) • White Papers and case studies • No shown impact on age and sex differences found • Does not appear to follow EEOC guidelines

Director of Special Operations

I. DEFINITION

Manages and directs the SWAT Response Team and associated resources for the City's Department of Emergency Medical Services; does related work as required.

II. CRITICAL ELEMENTS OF PERFORMANCE:

- Ensures that all departmental policies, rules, and regulations are understood and adhered to by the SWAT team members.
- Acts as a liaison between supervised personnel and the chief of the department or his or her designate.
- Formulates and institutes procedures for the coordinated delivery of emergency medical patient care services.
- Establishes cooperative relationships with all personnel.
- Assumes command of general emergencies and mass casualties.

III. PERFORMANCE STANDARDS:

- Ensures that staffing remains commensurate with manpower with his or her squad.
- Completes evaluations on pilot projects in a timely manner.
- Organizes supervised work units so that resource shortages and scheduling conflicts are avoided.
- Demonstrates comprehension of issues or problems and makes decisions accordingly.
- Communicates clearly and precisely both orally and in writing.
- Works well with volunteers and career staff.

IV. MINIMUM QUALIFICATIONS:

- Graduation from high school, or possess a GED, and supplemented with technical-level courses in EMS.
- Previous supervisory experience or any equivalent combination of experience and training that provides the required knowledge, skills, and abilities.
- All candidates should be free from corrective action in order to be considered for promotion by the chief of EMS or his or her designee.

Director of Administration

I. DEFINITION

The director of administration must be skilled in problem-solving and personnel management; will be responsible for the efficient and orderly operation of the police department.

II. CRITICAL ELEMENTS OF PERFORMANCE:

- Supervises work performed in connection with all aspects of the police operation, including, but not limited to, the prevention, reporting, investigation, prosecution, and analysis of crime.
- Enforcement of all rules, regulations, general orders, and policies and procedures of the police department and the city.
- Provides information, orally and in writing, to superiors and subordinates as requested or as needed.
- Assumes command and control of police operations in the absence of the police chief, including duties as a department spokesperson when required.

III. Performance Standards

- Assists the police chief with managing and directing all aspects of the day-to-day police department operation, including, but not limited to, employment, promotion, policy development, counseling, discipline, litigation, and termination recommendations.
- Provides daily reports to the police chief on department events as they may develop.
- Reviews and approves all requests for training and travel by department personnel.
- Constantly strives to improve the department operation through training and professional development opportunities for subordinates.
- Constantly strives to strengthen department relationships with the community, and encourage positive public relations.
- Drafts, reviews and/or approves departmental correspondence as requested or necessary.

IV. MINIMUM QUALIFICATIONS:

- Must have been a certified law enforcement officer for at least ten (10) years.
- Must be a high school graduate or possess equivalent; college degree preferred.

Director of Operations

I. DEFINITION

The operations officer of the uniformed patrol divisions exercises control over all its members and is responsible for the accomplishment of the police mission through the Operations division of the police department.

II. CRITICAL ELEMENTS OF PERFORMANCE

- Provides control and standardization of all operational procedures, including manpower allocation, scheduling, staffing, organization, methods of patrol, patrol coverage, deployment and special patrol activities; i.e. "directed patrol" and "selective enforcement" programs.
- Production of law enforcement intelligence and supplying the essential information and intelligence requirements of the chief of police.
- Preparing, coordinating, and activating operational plans and orders, reviewing plans and orders of subordinates, and recommending priorities for allocating critical resources of the department.
- Planning, coordinating, and providing budget preparation information for all operations functions of the police department.
- Processing and preparing information for coordinating, advising and planning to assist the chief of police in operations matters.

III. PERFORMANCE STANDARDS

- Review and approve assignments of personnel.
- Observe procedures affecting the operation of her or his division and recommend changes designed to increase its effectiveness.
- Insist that all members of her or his division comply with standard operating procedures, giving special attention to those failures that may jeopardize the safety of officers, the rights and liberties of private persons, and the reputation of the police department.
- Make a frequent inspection of the city at irregular times, noting all violations of laws and ordinances and conditions requiring police attention.
- See that all complaints anywhere in the city are promptly and properly investigated and that appropriate action is taken.
- Provide staff supervision of officers from other divisions who may be on duty in the absence of their own supervising officers.

IV. MINIMUM QUALIFICATIONS

- Must have been a certified law enforcement officer for at least ten (10) years.
- Must be a high school graduate or possess equivalent; college degree preferred.

Ken has chosen Walter "Mac" McNeil to conduct some of the interviews; Chief Richardson is surprised at this choice, given that Mac has been her biggest dissenter to date in her efforts to redesign the structure of the MPD (as discussed in Chapter 10). However, she is pleased that Mac is showing an interest in the recruitment process and hopes that this is a sign he is beginning to come around to the new vision. Selections for the directors of administration and special operations positions are obvious after the first interview—Assistant Chief Jeff Mitchell and Commander Tommy Malone are both veterans of the force and respected by their peers. Jeff Mitchell is a member of Chief Kimbell's legacy leadership team and has been incredibly supportive of Chief Richardson's efforts and changes. He has been proficient at providing daily reports and improving communication between departments. Chief Richardson saw Mitchell as a natural choice for director of administration.

Tommy Malone was a surprise pick for director of special operations. At 34 years old, he would be the youngest director ever in the history of the department, but his commitment to integrating special operations across the functions of the department and ability to communicate with the SWAT team, and external stakeholders made him an excellent choice.

Interviewing Potential Candidates

The MPD follows a rigorous selection process involving interviews and psychometric testing in order to recruit internally and externally. While some companies do not carry out psychometric testing, most companies use **interviews**, meetings or conversations arranged to assess the qualifications of an individual and evaluate whether that person has the skills

> **Interview** A meeting or conversation arranged to assess the qualifications of an individual and evaluate whether that person has the skills and abilities to do a job.

Questions You Should Ask in an Interview:

- How would you describe the company's culture and leadership philosophy?
- Can you please show me some examples of projects that I'd be working on?
- What is the single largest problem facing your staff, and would I be in a position to help you solve this problem?
- What specific qualities and skills are you looking for in the job candidate?
- Is this a new position, or did someone leave? If someone left, why did they leave or what did they go on to do?
- What is the typical career trajectory for a person in this position?
- What would you say are the three most important skills needed to excel in this position?
- Who would be my manager, and will I have the opportunity to meet him or her?
- Why do you like working here?
- What does a typical day or week look like for the person in this position? Is there travel, flextime, etc.?
- How do you see this position contributing to the success of the organization?
- What do you think distinguishes this company from its competitors, both from a public and employee perspective?
- Does the company offer continued education and professional training?
- How can I best contribute to the department?
- What particular achievements would equate to success at this job? What would success look like?
- Are you most interested in a candidate who works independently, on a team, cross-functionally, or through a combination of them all? Can you give me an example?
- What is your ideal communication style with your staff? Do you meet regularly with your team, rely heavily on email, use status reports, or work primarily through other means?
- How do you see me as a candidate for the job in comparison with an ideal candidate?
- Do you have any concerns about me or about my qualifications that may prevent you from selecting me for the job?
- What is the next step? When do you think you will be making a decision?

Subjects and Questions to Avoid in an Interview:

- Information you could have found easily with a quick Google search
- If you can change the job details, the schedule, or the salary
- Multiple questions about the interviewer's background
- Pay, time off, benefits, etc. (Wait until later in the process to inquire about these things.)
- "What does your company do?"
- "If I'm hired, when can I start applying for other positions in the company?"
- How quickly you can be promoted
- "Do you do background checks?"
- About gossip you've heard
- If the company monitors email or Internet usage

and abilities to do a job.[19] As an interview candidate, there are certain dos and don'ts when it comes to asking questions in an interview as shown in Table 11-3.

The last position to be filled in the department is the director of operations. The department has rewritten its mission statement to include the "best-trained officers, compassion, and business systems" as "key success factors" in transforming Washington, D.C. into one of the safest communities in the country. Ken has identified the director of operations as the key to these success factors.

Assistant Chief Susan Taylor and Captain Joel Holcomb are the final candidates for the position. Both of them have strengths that match the job description and the department's performance culture.

Here are the behavioral/style profiles for each candidate according to the results of the psychometric testing:

Operational: Captain Joel Holcomb

- Steady, patient, relaxed, warm, and approachable
- Does best in an unchanging environment; high tolerance for systematic/repetitive work

Andrey Popov/Shutterstock

- Learns by repetition
- Specialist, needs strong structure and book to go by
- Respects and seeks direction from a business plan, professional experience, trusted advisors, and/or management
- Eager to do what is expected, and is conscientious
- Better than average detail work

Venturer: Assistant Chief Susan Taylor

- Self-starter, self-motivator, strong initiative
- Results and goal-oriented, fast worker, intense
- Independent generalist, needs freedom from structure
- Venturesome, risk taker, authoritative, telling
- Drawn to unique ideas, new technologies, innovation
- Will delegate details but not authority
- Creative problem solver, troubleshooter

Selecting Candidates

The interview and selection process helps give managers an idea of *predictive validity*, the extent to which a selection test predicts future job performance.[20]

It is on this basis that Chief Richardson selects Captain Holcomb. Holcomb is both delighted and a little surprised about the appointment. Although he felt he had performed well in the interviews, he had thought Assistant Chief Taylor would get the position on the basis that she had been there longer than he had and was ranked above him.

A couple of days later, it became abundantly clear that Assistant Chief Taylor felt the same way. She takes exception to the decision, claiming gender discrimination, and files a **grievance** with HR, which is a complaint made by an employee claiming unfair treatment.[21] She is basing her grievance on questions asked during her interview.

It is not only interview candidates that need to be careful about the questions they ask during interviews; employers must adhere to federal law and ensure that they do not discriminate against candidates on the basis of sex, race, and other criteria. It transpires that during the interview process, Walter "Mac" McNeill had questioned Taylor, mother of two young children, about her childcare arrangements should the new role require her to work longer and more uncertain hours. This question is in direct violation of the Civil Rights Act of 1964, and Assistant Chief Taylor is convinced that this is the reason she was passed over for the position. Within the grievance letter, she also draws attention to her flawless track record and the excellent performance appraisals that she has received over the course of her career.

During their meeting, Assistant Chief of Human Resources Ken Gilmore promises Taylor that he will review the grievance and provide her with a response within the week. He also makes a note to inform Chief Richardson about Mac's behavior in the interview, as alleged by Taylor. In the meantime, Ken must also oversee the onboarding and training process for the new recruits they have selected for roles within the MPD.

11.3 | TRAINING TALENT

11.3 | Discuss different approaches to increasing organizational performance through the education of employees.

Onboarding Programs

Onboarding is a new employee orientation where workers acquire the skills, knowledge, and behaviors to aid transition into an organization.[22] Whether it is an internal or external employee moving into a new role, a smooth onboarding process is essential in order to integrate employees into the organization successfully. There is nothing more frustrating for

LECTURE ENHANCER:

11.3 Training Talent

- **Onboarding Programs**
  - ✓ **Onboarding**—a new employee orientation where workers acquire the skills, knowledge and behaviors to aid transition into an organization
    - ➤ Top 9 HR Onboarding Success Rituals/Habits
      1. Describe the true job expectations
      2. Give a written plan of employee objectives and responsibilities
      3. Give the employee your undivided attention
      4. Have new hire paper work packet ready
      5. Introduce the new employee to their fellow co-workers
      6. Set up a new hires workstation
      7. Schedule one-on-one meetings with new hires
      8. Clarify company culture
      9. Create balance
- **Types of Training Strategies**
  - ✓ **Training**—to teach new or existing employees the skills necessary to carry out their roles and improve job performance
  - ✓ **Development**—managers help employees learn the skills necessary to carry out their present or future roles

Grievance A complaint made by an employee claiming unfair treatment.

  - ✓ **Cross-Training**—where team members freely share knowledge and provide peer-to-peer mentorship
- **ADDIE for Results**
  - ✓ *Analysis*—define goals and objectives for the program, and identify any existing knowledge or skills, and learning challenges the recruits may have
  - ✓ *Design*—designed visual storyboards, exercises, and other visual aids in order to assist the learning process
  - ✓ *Development*—develop and create the learning materials suggested during the Design phase
  - ✓ *Implementation*—the procedure for training both the teacher and the learner is developed
  - ✓ *Evaluation*—review and evaluate each phase (analyze, design, develop, implement) to make sure you are getting the results you want

Onboarding A new employee orientation where workers acquire the skills, knowledge and behaviors to aid transition into an organization.

new hires than showing up on their first day of work with nobody to greet them, nowhere to work, or being unable to log in to their tablet or smartphone in order to do their jobs. A well-organized onboarding program will help address and, hopefully, avoid these concerns.

Top 10 HR Onboarding Success Rituals/Habits[23]

- Describe the true job expectations—few things are more disappointing to a new employee than the realization that the job he or she was hired to do is vastly different than what the person is actually doing.
- Give a written plan of employee objectives and responsibilities—detail goals, strategy, and expectations of future results, which helps diminish any confusion about a new employee's job functions and instead provides a chance to discuss concerns or new opportunities.
- Give the employee your undivided attention—ignore all phone calls, text messages, emails, or other things that may distract you during orientation sessions. Create a checklist (agenda) of the items you will discuss with the new hire and show them that they have your full attention.
- Have a new hire paperwork packet ready—make sure that all the required administration forms are ready and organized before you start orientation.
- Introduce the new employee to his or her coworkers—give a tour of the offices, cafeteria, grounds, etc.
- Set up a workstation for the new hire—make sure that all the necessary equipment and systems are in place on day one.
- Schedule one-on-one meetings—do this for the first month on a weekly basis, then biweekly during the second 30 days, and then again at 90 days. Check in on new employees frequently to ensure that all of their questions and concerns are being addressed.
- Clarify company culture—avoid confusion by providing the employee with company information regarding dress code, late policies, dating coworkers, etc.
- Create balance—the day of hire and perhaps into the first week of hire, combine onboarding fun time with work time. Help the new hire integrate into the team with a welcome lunch, or a team dinner after working hours. Think beyond the first day—after the first 90 days, sit down for a formal discussion with the new person and gather feedback. Set the ongoing review and development process checkpoints with the person.

Types of Training Strategies

In today's competitive environment, organizations spend billions of dollars every year on **training**, teaching new or existing employees the skills necessary to carry out their roles and improve current job performance.[24] Most companies use training tools to enhance employee **development**, where managers help employees learn the skills necessary to carry out future roles.[25] One popular training method is **cross-training**, where team members freely share knowledge and provide peer-to-peer mentorship.[26] This tool gives employees the opportunities to experience other roles across departments and an understanding of what their colleagues do on a daily basis.

In Ken Gilmore's opinion, the department has always been a sterling example of training for the fundamentals of police work through its "boot camp" approach. The training strategy comprises a mixture of classroom and field training, and has always helped new recruits learn the ropes. Still, he knows the training program is by no means perfect, and he is keen to refine the popular learning theory ADDIE (Analysis, Design, Develop, Implement, and Evaluate)[27], which the MPD employs.

Chief Richardson agrees that there is room for improvement. One concern that she has about the academy training is the way that it instructs the recruits to distance themselves emotionally from the criminals and victims in order to protect themselves from emotional trauma. Chief Richardson doesn't agree that the officers should be emotionally remote, and believes that they should work toward being more empathic and compassionate. She wants to ensure that this message is delivered during the training program.

She believes that the new culture and core values should be based on compassion for the victims and their loved ones regardless of who they are or the nature of the crime. When

Training Teaching new or existing employees the skills necessary to carry out their roles and improve current job performance.

Development Where managers help employees learn the skills necessary to carry out future roles.

Cross-training Where team members freely share knowledge and provide peer-to-peer mentorship.

she expresses understanding and compassion in the field, she finds that not only are the victims and their families grateful for the support, but they are more amenable to communicating with the police department, and in some cases provide the evidence and information necessary to solve the crime. As far as she is concerned, this is the best way for the MPD to bond with the community: show that they have a human side.

When she shares her thoughts with Ken, he suggests that she teach the final section of the onboarding experience, which would include a history of the department ("our tradition"), together with the new culture, values, and what it means to be a compassionate police officer. Ken believes that in order to break the common myth of police officers being stoic and emotionally distant, Chief Richardson will need to give the new recruits permission to show that they care for one another and the members of community.

© Bernd Obermann/Corbis

ADDIE for Results Ken is pleased with the feedback he receives from the training and onboarding programs. His ADDIE approach to training[28] has paid off. Let's discuss the ADDIE model and how Ken designed the onboarding program as a standard approach to training.

The five phases of ADDIE are as follows:

1. Analysis

Ken and his team define goals and objectives for the program, and identify any existing knowledge or skills and learning challenges that the recruits may have. They decide what learning methods are most suitable for their audience and how long the program project is going to last.

2. Design

The team then designs systematic learning objectives. With Chief Richardson's input, Ken and the team designed storyboards, exercises, and other visual aids in order to assist the learning process.

3. Development

The HR team works with the IT and administrative departments to develop and create the learning materials suggested during the design phase.

4. Implementation

During implementation, the procedure for training both the teacher and the learner is developed. Ken wants to make sure that the academy trainers are up to speed with the new onboarding approach and the different ways they will deliver their message to the new recruits. Once the trainers are clear on their roles, he arranges to have the learning materials delivered and distributed to the new recruit.

5. Evaluation

Throughout the program, Ken and his team review and evaluate each phase (analyze, design, develop, implement) to make sure that they are getting the results they want. After the program is finished, they monitor the recruits ensuring that they have the ability to put into action everything they have learned in a working environment. The team also assess feedback for ways to improve the new training system.

11.4 | RETAINING QUALIFIED TALENT

11.4 | Describe how managers retain employees and adjust to turnover.

With so much money, time, energy and resources invested in recruiting and training staff, how do managers keep their talent from going elsewhere? As we discussed earlier, top talent isn't driven by money or power, but the possibility of being a part of something they feel

© Diane Diederich/iStockphoto

passionate about. There are many reasons why employees may be inclined to seek new opportunities, including:

- Always being told what to do and not getting a say in how things are done
- Lack of detailed performance reviews and feedback
- Unwillingness by management to discuss future career development and opportunities
- Being constantly moved from one unfinished project to another
- Being surrounded by people who do not suit the working environment or culture
- A feeling of not fitting in
- Generational differences
- Inadequate training
- Dissatisfaction with the behavior of their boss or management

Affirmative action A purposeful effort taken by an organization to create equal employment opportunities for minority groups and women.

To address these concerns, some organizations have set up support groups to help provide emotional and career support to employees who are unhappy in their current jobs. And many organizations have pursued **affirmative action**, a purposeful effort by an organization to create equal employment opportunities for minority groups and women.[29]

Glass ceiling effect An invisible barrier that keeps women and minorities from moving up the corporate ladder, regardless of qualifications and achievements.

Many companies have adopted mentoring programs that focus on helping employees progress in their careers, in order to bypass the "**glass ceiling effect**," an invisible barrier that keeps women and minorities from moving up the corporate ladder regardless of qualifications and achievements.[30] Organizations also can address these issues by training their managers to provide feedback and detailed performance reviews in order to motivate employees. A good **performance development** strategy manages employee performance and assesses opportunities for growth and development.

Performance development Managing employee performance and assessing opportunities for growth and development.

Planned and Unplanned Turnover

Both Ken and Chief Richardson agree on the number of new recruits they needed on the basis of staffing analysis and average turnover rates. They analyze planned turnover, which involves figuring out which employees were due to retire over the next couple of years. Then they review the level of unplanned turnover by looking at the number of resignations over the previous two years. With these figures in hand, the HR department has a good idea of the number of vacancies they need to fill in order to staff the MPD fully for that year.

Pay and Benefits

Compensation Remuneration in salary or wages to reward employees for their work.

Chief Richardson also asks Ken and the HR team to review **compensation**, the remuneration in salary or wages to reward employees for their work;[31] and **benefits**, non-monetary compensation in the form of health insurance, pensions, paid vacation, etc., which vary depending on the industry and organization.[32] The team finds that many officers resigned because they felt their salary was too low or thought they could get better benefits elsewhere. Chief Richardson instructs the team to conduct due diligence to ensure that the MPD is offering competitive rates and remuneration. She wants to make sure that the staff is being paid fairly and are properly rewarded for their good work.

Benefits Non-monetary compensation in the form of health insurance, pensions, paid vacation, etc., which may vary from industry to industry.

One of the major issues is the confusion over health benefits. A police officer was recently injured on the job, and HR had not been able to come up with the right insurance documentation to cover her hospital visit and follow-up care. This had caused a great deal of stress for the officer and her family. The chief instructs Ken to brief the HR department on the health insurance options and MPD benefits as a whole. Ken agrees, and he promises to retrain his team in that area to avoid any problems in the future.

Employee Engagement

Engaged employees are passionate and enthusiastic about their work and are fully committed to contributing toward the company's success.[33] Indeed, there is a direct link between engagement and retention.[34] Satisfied employees are more likely to stay with a company, which leads to less turnover, more productivity, and greater company loyalty. In contrast,

Research @ Work

Engaging Employees

Research suggests that an employee's immediate supervisor may substantially influence employee engagement, both positively and negatively. A recently released Employee Engagement Survey conducted by the International Association of Business Communicators Research Foundation (IABCRF) and Buck Consultants indicates that 44 percent of the approximately 1,000 communication professionals who responded report that their supervisors strongly increased employee engagement.[35] Another 41 percent said their supervisors strongly decreased employee engagement.

In a related study published in the *Leadership and Organization Development Journal*, researchers Jessica Xu and Helena Cooper Thomas examined the role of organizational leaders in facilitating employee engagement.[36] Their results, based on a sample of employees from a large insurance company in New Zealand, suggest that one of the primary things that leaders can do to increase employee engagement is to support and develop their team members. Their findings also suggest that leaders can increase the engagement of their followers through good decision making, effective task management, displaying integrity, showing high ethical standards, and being open and honest in communications.[37]

Employee recognition is another way that supervisors can increase employee engagement. Although 80 percent of organizations report having formal employee recognition programs, only 31 percent of HR management professionals say that employees are satisfied with the recognition they receive for a job well done.[38]

According to a recent survey on employee recognition conducted by the Society for Human Resource Management (SHRM) and Globoforce, the most common form of employee recognition is for "years of service" (58 percent of respondents), followed by "going above and beyond regular work assignments" (48 percent of respondents) and "boosting the organization's financial bottom line" (43 percent of respondents).[39] Yet the popularity of "years of service" as a focus for employee recognition may not be as effective a tool for employee engagement as some companies might like to think. As Evren Esen, SHRM's survey research manager, points out: "Employee length of service, while important to recognize, is not directly linked with performance and therefore may not have a significant impact on employee engagement and motivation. Employees want to be recognized for the work they do; therefore, specific recognition of their work performance tied to the organization's values and business strategy are generally more meaningful."[40]

Critical Thinking in the Classroom

As a manager, what steps would you take to engage your employees in order to motivate and encourage greater communication?

---

disengaged employees cost employers billions of dollars every year in poor work performance, low productivity, and high levels of absenteeism. Clearly, it is in every company's best interests to ensure that their workforce is committed and invested in the work they do. But how do managers assess the level to which an employee is engaged?

Many organizations use **career surveys**, which are questionnaires that employers use to assess employee satisfaction and career aspirations, in order to tailor development programs and project opportunities that support growth toward these goals.[41] Usually anonymous, these surveys include questions regarding the company's vision and mission statement and how effective their manager is when it comes to training and feedback. The results are then assessed and trends analyzed.

11.5 | *PERFORMANCE DEVELOPMENT*

11.5 | Design a performance development process based on organizational needs.

An **appraisal** is the process of measuring and assessing an employee's performance objectively and providing feedback to that employee.[42] Most managers regard the performance appraisal as essential when it comes to providing them with accurate information about

Career surveys are questionnaires that employers use to assess employee satisfaction and career aspirations, in order to tailor development programs and project opportunities that support growth toward these goals.

LECTURE ENHANCER:

11.5 Performance Development

✓ Appraisal—the process of measuring and assessing an employee's performance objectively

Appraisal The process of measuring and assessing an employee's performance objectively and providing feedback to that employee.

360-degree review Confidential feedback obtained from the performance appraisal about an individual provided by peers, subordinates, and supervisors that is intended to assess training and development needs.

Behaviorally Anchored Rating Scale (BARS) A method that rates employee performance based on specific behaviors relating to a particular role.

employee productivity and performance. In turn, employees benefit from the feedback and learn how to improve their performance through training and development.

Chief Richardson was facing some tough decisions. The appointment of Holcomb over Assistant Chief Taylor as director of operations has caused some divisions in the department. As already noted, Assistant Chief Taylor, highly regarded by her peers, believed that she was more qualified than Holcomb and filed a grievance claiming gender discrimination. Many members of the staff sided with her and openly resented Holcomb as their new director. When Ken Gilmore quizzed Mac about what had actually happened in the interview, Mac admitted asking Taylor about her childcare arrangements. At first, Mac was defensive about his line of questioning, telling Ken he "didn't mean anything by it," but when Ken told him he was in violation of the Civil Rights Act of 1964, he immediately offered to apologize to Taylor.

When Ken discussed the outcome of the meeting with Chief Richardson, she was confused. On the one hand, it was good that Mac was prepared to apologize to Assistant Chief Taylor, but then what? If she accepted the apology and dropped the grievance, she would still be in the same role as before (and presumably still unhappy she had been passed over), and the department would still be split. Yet, how can they ask Holcomb to step down? He was awarded the director title fairly, and perhaps he will win over the team in time. Chief Richardson needs to make sure that she has carried out as much due diligence as possible in order to make her final decision.

Designing Appraisals

One of the points that Assistant Chief Taylor made in her grievance letter was her performance appraisal history, which has been consistently stellar over the course of her career. Chief Richardson asks Ken to review Taylor's performance history together to see if it is as impeccable as Taylor claims.

Ken gets to work. First, he looks at Taylor's **360-degree review**, which is confidential feedback about an individual provided by peers, subordinates, and supervisors intended to assess training and development needs.[43] Ken isn't sure if he is reading the review accurately. He reads it again. Finally, he takes off his glasses and sits back in his chair. The review is flawless. According to Assistant Chief Taylor's colleagues and managers, she is a perfect employee in every way. There are no development issues or suggestions as to how to improve performance. In fact, Assistant Chief Taylor has been given a high rating in every single area of evaluation every year. This sounds great, but Ken is suspicious. In his experience, these kinds of reviews imply that managers are not putting enough effort into conducting the review, and simply are speeding through it by ticking off each box.

There is another way that Ken can find a more accurate description of Taylor's work performance. A **Behaviorally Anchored Rating Scale (BARS)** is a method that rates employee performance based on specific behaviors relating to a particular role.[44]

Immediately, he notes that Taylor has been involved in several specific incidents over the years with regard to lack of communication. Several of her colleagues have given her a lower rating when it comes to the accuracy and timeliness of her verbal and written communication.

Assessing Behaviors and Results

Ken sets up a meeting with Chief Richardson to share his assessment of Taylor's past appraisals with her. The chief reads through the notes and says, "I see two things here: first, that some of our managers have not taken enough time when it comes to completing appraisals, which shows they are not taking them seriously. Second, based on BARS, Assistant Chief Taylor needs to work on her communication skills, which is vital for the role of director of operations."

Ken replies, "Yes, I am going to set up a course for the departmental managers to learn how to conduct performance appraisals properly, and how important they are for the employees."

Making the right staffing decisions is crucial to the success of an organization. Potential employees must be the right fit for the company culture and willing to embrace the organization's mission, values, and work ethic. An important part of being a manager is being involved in the recruitment process; after all, we could argue that a good team reflects on the hiring ability of the manager. In the next chapter, we will look at the different roles and responsibilities fulfilled by managers when leading teams.

Chapter 11 Case: The Human Side of Management: Zappos.com can be found on pg. 473

ADDITIONAL RESOURCES

KEY TERMS

360-degree review Confidential feedback obtained from the performance appraisal about an individual provided by peers, subordinates, and supervisors that is intended to assess training and development needs. **(p.292)**

Affirmative action A purposeful effort taken by an organization to create equal employment opportunities for minority groups and women. **(p.290)**

Appraisal The process of measuring and assessing an employee's performance objectively and providing feedback to that employee. **(p.291)**

Behaviorally Anchored Rating Scale (BARS) A method that rates employee performance based on specific behaviors relating to a particular role. **(p.292)**

Benefits Non-monetary compensation in the form of health insurance, pensions, paid vacation, etc., which may vary from industry to industry. **(p.290)**

Career surveys are questionnaires that employers use to assess employee satisfaction and career aspirations, in order to tailor development programs and project opportunities that support growth toward these goals. **(p.291)**

Collective bargaining The process of negotiation between employers and trade unions, usually with respect to pay, working hours, and working conditions. **(p.276)**

Compensation Remuneration in salary or wages to reward employees for their work. **(p.290)**

Cross-training Where team members freely share knowledge and provide peer-to-peer mentorship. **(p.288)**

Development Where managers help employees learn the skills necessary to carry out future roles. **(p.288)**

Employment-at-will The concept that employees can quit their jobs at any time without any reason, and employers can terminate employees at any time and without any reason. **(p.280)**

Equal employment opportunity A principle stating that every employee has an equal right to advance in a company regardless of age, sex, race, disability, or color. **(p.277)**

External recruiting The process of creating a pool of qualified applicants outside the organization. **(p.282)**

Glass ceiling effect An invisible barrier that keeps women and minorities from moving up the corporate ladder, regardless of qualifications and achievements. **(p.290)**

Grievance A complaint made by an employee claiming unfair treatment. **(p.287)**

Human capital Employee skills and experience gained by education and training that increase the economic value for employers. **(p.277)**

Human resource management (HRM, or HR) An organizational function that deals with people-related issues such as recruitment, performance management, benefits, training, employee motivation, safety, and administration, while ensuring compliance with employment and labor laws.**(p.276)**

Independent contractors Self-employed individuals or independent businesses that provide services to another entity. **(p.280)**

Internal recruiting The process of creating a pool of existing employees who may have the qualifications to fill required job vacancies in an organization. **(p.282)**

Interview A meeting or conversation arranged to assess the qualifications of an individual and evaluate whether that person has the skills and abilities to do a job. **(p.285)**

Job description A written account of specific tasks, duties, and responsibilities required within a particular role. **(p.282)**

Knowledge workers Self-motivated workers that use a variety of skills to enhance their overall understanding of a particular subject or area. **(p.280)**

Labor relations The relationship between management and the workforce. **(p.276)**

Onboarding A new employee orientation where workers acquire the skills, knowledge and behaviors to aid transition into an organization. **(p.287)**

Performance development Managing employee performance and assessing opportunities for growth and development. **(p.290)**

Psychometric tools Questionnaires or tests that measure an individual's personality, intelligence, and aptitude. **(p.282)**

Recruiting The process of identifying the best applicants internally or externally for specific roles. **(p.282)**

Selection The process that assesses the level of skills and abilities possessed by an individual to perform a specific role. **(p.282)**

Talent management A strategic, deliberate approach to attracting new highly skilled workers and developing the abilities of existing employees to meet current and future organizational objectives. **(p.277)**

Training Teaching new or existing employees the skills necessary to carry out their roles and improve current job performance. **(p.288)**

IN REVIEW

11.1 | Describe how managers make a significant difference by attracting, selecting, and retaining the best available talent within legal requirements.

The implementation of a Human Resource Management department is essential in attracting, selecting, and retaining employees. The feelings and emotions of the workers are central to their motivation and productivity. *Human Resources Management (HRM)* is an organizational function that deals with people-related issues such as recruitment, performance management, benefits, training, employee motivation, safety, and administration, while ensuring compliance with employment and labor laws. The role of HR professionals has evolved into analyzing information that helps them understand how to find and keep talent, match people to jobs, optimize employee skills, and identify different methods of training.

11.2 | Explain how managers assess human resource needs and select talent to meet demand.

The role of the HR manager is to analyze the needs of each department and decide which type of employee would best fit into the culture and possess the skills to enhance the performance of the organization. Recruiting can take place either internally or externally. *Internal recruiting* is the method of creating a pool of existing employees who may have the qualifications to fill required job vacancies in an organization. *External recruiting* is the process of creating a pool of qualified applicants outside the organization. *Psychometric tools*, questionnaires or tests that measure an individual's personality, intelligence and aptitude, can be used to filter applicants based on the organization's needs.

Not all companies carry out psychometric testing, but most companies use *interviews*, meetings or conversations arranged to assess the qualifications of an individual and evaluate whether that person has the skills and abilities to do a job. The interview and selection process helps give managers an idea of *predictive validity*, the extent to which a selection test predicts future job performance.

11.3 | Discuss different approaches to increasing organizational performance through the education of employees.

Onboarding is a new employee orientation where workers acquire the skills, knowledge and behaviors to aid transition into an organization. Companies use *training tools* to teach new or existing employees the skills necessary to carry out their roles and improve job performance. One popular training method is *cross-training*, where team members freely share knowledge and provide peer-to-peer mentorship.

11.4 | Describe how managers retain employees and adjust to turnover.

Compensation (remuneration in salary or wages to reward employees for their work) and *benefits* (non-monetary compensation in the form of health insurance, pensions, paid vacation, etc., which may vary from industry to industry) are both examples of how organizations retain employees. Satisfied employees are more likely to stay with a company, which leads to less turnover, more productivity, and greater company loyalty. Managers can increase the engagement of their followers through good decision making, effective task management, displaying integrity, showing high ethical standards, and being open and honest in communications.

11.5 | Design a performance development process based on organizational needs.

An *appraisal* is the process of measuring and assessing an employee's performance objectively and providing feedback to that employee. A *Behaviorally Anchored Rating Scale (BARS)* is a method that rates employee performance based on specific behaviors relating to a particular role.

SELF-TEST

11.1 | Describe how managers make a significant difference by attracting, selecting, and retaining the best available talent within legal requirements.

1. The organizational function that deals with people-related issues, such as recruitment, performance management, benefits, training, employee motivation, safety, and administration while ensuring compliance with employment and labor laws, is:
   a. Organizational development
   b. Information technology (IT)
   c. Human resource management (HRM)
   d. Human relations development (HRD)

2. The concept of equal employment opportunity states that every employee has an equal right to advance in a company regardless of:
   a. Knowledge, skills, and abilities
   b. Qualifications
   c. Work performance
   d. Age, sex, race, disability, or color

3. A strategic, deliberate approach to attracting new, highly skilled workers and developing the abilities of existing employees to meet current and future organizational objectives is:
   a. Talent management
   b. Hiring
   c. Promoting
   d. Compensation

11.2 | **Explain** how managers assess human resource needs and select talent to meet demand.

4. Employment-at-will dictates that employees can quit their jobs at any time and employers can terminate employees at any time, so long as a good reason can be provided.
   a. True
   b. False

5. Compare and contrast the concepts of recruiting and selection.

6. _____ recruiting involves creating a pool of existing employees who may have the qualifications to fill required job vacancies, while _____ recruiting is the process of creating a pool of qualified applicants outside the organization.

7. A(n) _____ is a written account of specific tasks, duties, and responsibilities required within a particular role.

8. To the extent that a selection test predicts future job performance, it is said to have:
   a. Reliability
   b. Variance
   c. Predictive validity
   d. Discretion

11.3 | **Discuss** different approaches to increasing organizational performance through the education of employees.

9. _____ is a new employee orientation where workers acquire the skills, knowledge and behaviors to aid transition into an organization.

10. Explain the difference between training and development.

11. What does the acronym ADDIE stand for?

11.4 | **Describe** how managers retain employees and adjust to turnover.

12. Affirmative action is a legally mandated quota that requires an organization to hire a certain number of minority and women applicants.
    a. True
    b. False

13. _____ is remuneration in the form of salary or wages to reward employees, while _____ is non-monetary remittance in the form of health insurance, pensions, paid vacation, etc., which may vary from industry to industry.

11.5 | **Design** a performance development process based on organizational needs.

14. A performance _____ is the process of measuring and assessing an employee's performance objectively and providing feedback to that employee.
    a. Appraisal
    b. Examination
    c. Test
    d. Development

15. Which of the following tools is used to increase the accuracy of performance appraisals?
    a. Accuracy Insured Performance Appraisals (AIPA)
    b. Behaviorally Anchored Rating Scales (BARS)
    c. Situationally Determined Rating Scales (SDRS)
    d. Performance-Enhanced Measurement Appraisals (PEMA)

CHAPTER EXERCISE

Employee Selection Exercise*

For this exercise, assume that you are employed as an HR consultant for a mid-sized bank. The bank employs 200 tellers across its branches. The following is a partial job description and specification for the bank teller position, based on information obtained from O*Net (the Occupational Information Network Resource Center). O*Net is an online database containing information on hundreds of standardized and occupation-specific descriptors.

Bank Teller Tasks/Duties/Responsibilities

- Cash checks for customers after verification of signatures and sufficient funds in the account
- Receive checks and cash for deposit

- Examine checks for endorsements and verify other information such as dates, bank names and identification
- Enter customers' transactions into computers to record them
- Count currency, coins, and checks received to prepare them for deposit
- Identify transaction mistakes when debits and credits do not balance
- Balance currency, coins, and checks in cash drawers at the end of a shift

Knowledge, Skills, Abilities

- Customer service skills
- Basic math skills

- Knowledge of verification requirements for checks
- Ability to verify signatures and proper identification of customers
- Ability to use accounting software
- High school diploma required; associate's or bachelor's degree preferred
- Previous work experience as a teller or related occupation (cashier, billing clerk) desired

Key Statistics:

- The median 2011 wage for tellers was $11.82 (hourly); $24,590 (annually).
- In 2010, there were approximately 560,000 tellers in the United States.
- Projected growth (2010–2020): Little or no change.

Based on this information, the bank decides that the ideal candidate for this position will possess the following factors:

1. Have at least a high school education (bachelor's or associate's degree desirable).
2. Have experience as a teller or in a related field (cashier, billing clerk).
3. Be able to perform basic math skills related to banking (for example, count currency quickly and accurately and balance a cash drawer correctly).
4. Be knowledgeable of verification requirements for bank transactions (for example, finding errors in checks and using proper identification to authorize transactions).
5. Have good interpersonal skills (for example, speak clearly, make good eye contact, and develop rapport easily).
6. Be motivated to work.

A. Choose the selection methods: Identify which selection method (e.g., résumé, interview, test, role-play exercise, reference check, or personality inventory) you would recommend for each of the six factors listed above. You can use the same selection method more than once if you believe that it is appropriate for more than one factor. Below is an example of how you might justify using an application form as an appropriate selection method for education.

1. **Education**—Selection method: Application form
   Justification: A question on the application form can ask applicants to describe their education. This selection method makes it easy and inexpensive to obtain this information.

2. **Work experience**—Selection method:
   _____
   Justification:

3. **Math skills**—Selection method:
   _____
   Justification:

4. **Verification knowledge**—Selection method:
   _____
   Justification:

5. **Interpersonal skills**—Selection method:
   _____
   Justification:

6. **Work motivation**—Selection method:
   _____
   Justification:

B. Operationalize your assessments: Now that you have identified selection methods for the six factors, you must decide how to score each of these assessments. Based on your responses in part A ("Choose the selection methods"), think about how each factor may be scored and develop a point system for that factor.

A common approach to performing this task is to have some type of numerical rating system that may include one or two minimum requirements. Your task is to develop a rubric (point system) to "score" applicants for each of the six factors. In developing your rubric, review the job description information. The "education" factor is provided for you below. Remember that tellers need to have a high school diploma, according to the job specification. Applicants who do not meet this requirement are rejected. College degrees are preferred and receive more points in the example below.

1. **Education** assessed via application form.
   My assessment:

Points	Highest Level of Education
10	Bachelor's level or higher
6	Associate's degree
3	High school diploma
Reject	Less than high school diploma

2. **Work experience** assessed via _____
   _____
   My assessment:

3. **Math skills** assessed via _____
   _____
   My assessment:

4. **Verification knowledge** assessed via _____
   _____
   My assessment:

5. **Interpersonal skills** assessed via _____
   _____
   My assessment:

6. **Work motivation** assessed via _____
   _____
   My assessment:

C. Apply your assessment systems: Listed below are applicants for the teller position. Based on your answers in part B ("Operationalize your assessments"), score each of the applicants.

Sample applicant information:

	Maria	Lori	Steve	Jenna
Education	Associate's degree	High school diploma	G.E.D.(High school equivalency)	Bachelor's degree
Work experience	4 years as a cashier	1 year as a teller	5 years as a sales clerk at a national retail clothing store chain	Completed a semester-long internship at a bank
Math skills	Very strong	Marginal	Satisfactory	Good
Verification knowledge	Marginal	Strong	Satisfactory	Strong
Interpersonal skills	Very strong	Good	Good	Good
Work motivation	Good	Good	Marginal	Strong

Score the applicants:

	Maria	Lori	Steve	Jenna
Education	6	3	3	10
Work experience				
Math skills				
Verification knowledge				
Interpersonal skills				
Work motivation				

a. Which applicant scored best based on the scores that you entered into the table?

b. What difficulties did you have applying your scoring system?

c. Based on this applicant data, would you make any changes to your rubrics? If yes, please describe.

*Adapted from Marc C. Marchese, "Case Study—Structured Exercises–Employee Selection," The Society for Human Resource Management. **http://www.shrm.org/Education/hreducation/Pages/EmployeeSelection-StructuredExercises.aspx**

SELF-ASSESSMENT

Human Resources Competencies*

The Society for Human Resource Management (SHRM) has developed a competency model for HR professionals. In addition to basic HR technical expertise (that is, the ability to apply basic HR principles and practices in a business context), the model suggests eight behavioral competencies that should allow HR professionals to be successful in their jobs.

Instructions:

The following statements are based on the eight behavioral competencies in the SHRM model. Consider to what extent you are attracted to each of the statements using the following scale:

Not at all Attractive	Somewhat Attractive	A little Attractive	Quite Attractive	Extremely Attractive
1	2	3	4	5

1. Relationship Management—the ability to manage interactions with and between others with the specific goal of providing service and contributing to organizational success.

    1   2   3   4   5

2. Consultation—the art of providing direct guidance to organizational stakeholders (e.g., employees and leaders) seeking expert advice on a variety of situations or circumstances.

    1   2   3   4   5

3. Organizational Leadership and Navigation—the ability to direct initiatives and processes within the organization with agility and to gain buy-in from stakeholders.

    1   2   3   4   5

4. Communication—the ability to exchange and create a free flow of information with and among various stakeholders at all levels of the organization to produce effective outcomes.

    1   2   3   4   5

5. Global and Cultural Effectiveness—the art of managing human resources both within and across borders and cultures.

    1   2   3   4   5

6. Ethical Practice—the integration of core values, integrity, and accountability throughout all organizational and business practices.

    1   2   3   4   5

7. Critical Evaluation—skill in interpreting information (e.g., data, metrics, literature) to determine return on investment (ROI) and organizational impact in making business decisions and/or recommendations.

    1   2   3   4   5

8. Business Acumen—the ability to understand business functions and metrics within the organization and industry.

    1   2   3   4   5

Scoring:

Add the numbers circled above and write your score in the blank. _____

Interpretation:

32 and above = The SHRM HR professional competencies are very attractive to you. You should carefully consider the possibilities of a career in the HR profession.

17–31 = The SHRM HR professional competencies are moderately attractive to you. You should further investigate the HR profession before deciding if a career in the HR field is right for you.

16 and below = The SHRM HR professional competencies hold little attraction for you. You may want to consider a career in another field or discipline.

*Assessment developed based on the SHRM competency model for HR professionals, available at http://www.shrm.org/HRCompetencies/Pages/Model.aspx.

SELF-TEST ANSWER KEY

1. c.
2. d.
3. a.
4. b; False. Employment-at-will dictates that employees can quit their jobs at any time and employers can terminate employees at any time.
5. *Recruiting* is the process of identifying the best applicants internally or externally for specific roles, while *selection* is the process that assesses the level of skills and abilities possessed by an individual to perform a specific role.
6. Internal, external
7. Job description
8. c.

9. Onboarding
10. *Training* teaches new or existing employees the skills necessary to carry out their roles and improve *current* job performance, while *development* helps employees learn the skills necessary to carry out *future* roles.
11. Analysis, Design, Develop, Implement, and Evaluate
12. b; False. Affirmative action is a *purposeful* and *voluntary* effort by an organization to create equal employment opportunities for minority groups and women.
13. Compensation, benefits
14. a.
15. b.

Notes

CHAPTER TWELVE

MANAGING TEAM PERFORMANCE

Learning Objectives

By the end of the chapter, you will be able to:

12.1 | Describe why managers form working groups to achieve results.

12.2 | Explain the characteristics of teams.

12.3 | Explain team dynamics and its relationship to performance.

12.4 | Compare and contrast productive and unhealthy conflict as it relates to organizational results.

12.5 | Develop a strategic plan to increase team performance.

ADDITIONAL RESOURCES

KEY TERMS
IN REVIEW
SELF-TEST
CHAPTER EXERCISE
SELF-ASSESSMENT
SELF-TEST
ANSWER KEY

JP Greenwood/Getty Images

INSIDE THIS CHAPTER

ManagementStory:
Featuring **Robin Richardson**

LECTURE ENHANCER:

12.1 How Teams Make a Difference

✓ **Team**—a purposeful group formed to accomplish a project, task, or goal

➤ Teams can improve company performance, increase productivity and morale, and enhance decision-making.

➤ Ineffective team members, social loafing, high turnover, and personality clashes are all symptoms of a poorly-performing team.

✓ **The Power of Working Groups**

➤ A happy team is a productive team.

> **Team** A purposeful group formed to accomplish a project, task, or goal.

12.1 | *HOW TEAMS MAKE A DIFFERENCE*

12.1 | Describe why managers form working groups to achieve results.

"Teamwork is the ability to work together toward a common vision. The ability to direct individual accomplishments toward organizational objectives. It is the fuel that allows common people to attain uncommon results."

—Andrew Carnegie

In Chapters 7 through 9, we learned how Chris Heppler, general manager of the Hilton Head Dolphin Resort Hotel, used critical thinking to organize and develop a noncommittal group of individuals into a strong, loyal team. We saw them band together and successfully achieve the goals and objectives set by the hotel owner and executive management. So what, exactly, is a team, and why is it so important?

A **team** is a purposeful group formed to accomplish a project, task, or goal.[1] In this age of globalization and heightened competition, it is even more important for organizations to employ teams to help solve cross-disciplinary problems, traverse cultural boundaries, and drive initiatives. Managed in the right way, teams can improve company performance, increase productivity and morale, and enhance decision making. Indeed, teams that are involved in the decision-making process are more likely to have a stronger sense of commitment to the task at hand, and to each other. With so many different personalities, skills, and abilities, a strong team can present a diversity of viewpoints on how to solve problems within the organization.

Well-trained teams fully meet the needs and expectations of customers, leading to greater customer satisfaction. For example, Chris Heppler and his team created new initiatives specifically aimed at improving overall customer satisfaction by introducing complimentary, homemade cookies for their guests, a van service, and impressive conference and family facilities. As a result, the hotel became the most popular choice for visitors to the island.

However, not all teams are successful.[2] Ineffective team members, *social loafing* which occurs when members of a team contribute less effort than they would if they were individually responsible, high turnover, and personality clashes are all symptoms of a poorly performing team. Indeed, most of us can probably cite examples of challenging team experiences. The teamwork mentality is present during our early years, up to when we enter the workforce, and even beyond. In grade schools, middle schools, high schools, and universities, students are encouraged to work together in groups to achieve a common objective. And obviously, most sports could not exist without teamwork.

© Images.com / Corbis

Although teamwork is strongly encouraged, not everyone is enchanted by the idea of working closely with others. For example, say that you are assigned a college project. The class is divided into teams of four, and you are given a deadline of two weeks. Immediately, you see a number of problems with your newly formed team: one of your team members has a reputation for being lazy, casual, and careless about deadlines. As the grade is based on the team's success rather than the individual's, it frustrates you that this "freeloader" or "social loafer" is going to get the same reward as the rest of the team, as he will benefit from everyone's hard work. Furthermore, another person on the team is a real micromanager, who instantly proclaims himself the team leader and proceeds to boss everyone around. This does not sit well with the freeloader, who will more than likely ditch the entire project within a couple of days, leaving you and the other team member (who is, thankfully, quite sensible and efficient) to pick up the pieces. Still, even if you achieve a good grade on the project, most likely it won't be a pleasant experience, and it might make you feel more apprehensive about working with a team again in the future.

Why do we work in teams? Doesn't that mean giving up our independence, our power, and our freedom to choose who we want to work with? These are many of the challenges that employees face when they are organized into teams. But in spite of these concerns, teams can work so long as there is a reason for them to exist in the first place. If they are given a clearly defined purpose, ample resources to carry out the task, and the authority to make decisions, teams can be the most powerful driving force within an organization.[3]

The Power of Teams

Most organizations encourage teamwork because they realize that a team can be more effective in attaining goals, if it is managed the right way.[4] There are very few roles that involve working in a vacuum, and it is largely agreed that more is achieved when individuals collaborate together to accomplish their tasks.[5]

When teams are managed effectively, they become a very powerful force. In a sense, the team takes on a life of its own. As for the team members, they benefit from the feeling of belonging to something greater than themselves and gain positive affirmation from being part of such a powerful process.

In short, a happy team is a productive team. In Chapter 8, we learned how the productivity of loggers in Oklahoma vastly improved due to the implementation of certain management techniques, which resulted in unification toward a common goal.[6] The teams became so motivated by the new techniques that they even put forward suggestions as to how certain areas could be improved—feedback that made the logging process even more efficient. Researchers concluded that teams become more effective at completing complex and creative tasks when they work as a unit.

Similarly, good team collaboration leads to more accurate judgment-based decisions because team members have the freedom and the ability to give each other feedback and provide reasons why a certain idea may or may not work. This leads to faster decision making and higher levels of productivity.

Typically, working groups come together in organizations both formally (by management design) and informally. A **formal team** is a working group formed by an organization's management to achieve specific, agreed-upon strategies, plans, and outcomes. An **informal team** is a working group, generally not intended to be permanent, formed by team members to accomplish self-defined tasks and objectives.

Informal teams can often be set up with a common goal of gathering people together outside the constraints of the working environment (for example, setting up corporate soccer teams or arranging social events). Both formal and informal teams form to accomplish individual tasks or to collaborate on processes (a logical aggregation of tasks) that lead to achieving defined outcomes.

In this chapter, we will continue our insight into the Metropolitan Police Department (MPD) in Washington, D.C., and explore how Chief Robin Richardson transforms the compartmentalized police department into a cohesive environment of working groups.

✓ **Informal team**—a working group formed by team members to accomplish self-defined tasks and objectives, generally not intended to be permanent

Formal team A working group formed by an organization's management to achieve specific, agreed-upon strategies, plans, and outcomes.

Informal team A working group, generally not intended to be permanent, formed by team members to accomplish self-defined tasks and objectives.

Functional team A formal, longstanding working group organized around specific tasks, processes, or roles.

organized around specific tasks, processes, or roles

Cross-functional team A formal, longstanding working group with representation from diverse divisions, departments, and levels of authority.

12.2 | TEAM CHARACTERISTICS

12.2 | Explain the characteristics of teams.

What does an effective team look like? Table 12-1 and Figure 12-1 outline some characteristics of effective teams.

Different Types

In Chapter 10, we learned how managers design organizational structures such as vertical, horizontal, and matrix. Most organizations create formal teams in line with these types of organizational structures.

Like most organizations, the MPD has several types of teams. A **functional team** is a formal, longstanding working group organized around specific tasks, processes, or roles.[7] Functional teams may also be referred to as *vertical* or *command teams*. Typically, departments such as accounting, human resources (HR), and marketing follow a hierarchical structure headed by a manager or managers within a formal chain of command. Within the MPD, teams within operations, special operations, and administration are organized into a functional or vertical structure.

A **cross-functional team** is a formal, longstanding working group with representation from diverse divisions, departments, and levels of authority.[8] Usually, the members represent a wide set of skills, roles, and perspectives. These teams are typically formed to complete complex tasks, solve difficult problems, innovate new products and services, and perform other functions.[9] Cross-functional teams are also known as *horizontal teams*.

Table 12-1	Characteristics of Effective Teams
Clear Purpose	Good teams usually have a clear purpose about what they are doing and how their work contributes to the success of the organization. Team members are fully committed to the vision, mission, goals, and objectives of the team. Without clarity of purpose, team members tend to scatter and follow their own agenda and misguided beliefs, which can lead to team fragmentation.[10]
Good Communication	The team that communicates together stays together. Open discussion and the freedom to air opinions within a comfortable environment helps the team make decisions and aids in the bonding process. Conversely, poor communication leads to conflict and dissatisfaction.[11]
Healthy Conflict	With so many personalities on a team, combined with the pressure to produce results, there is bound to be a measure of conflict. However, in effective teams, disagreements are usually dealt with openly and resolved constructively. This involves a high degree of trust between members. If trust is lacking, then there are bound to be more disputes that can escalate into real battles, leading to divisions within the team.[12]
Effective Decision Making	Effective teams will make decisions based on the general consensus of the team members.[13] However, this does not imply a "majority rules" mentality—if they oppose a decision, members will be allowed to air their views until a satisfactory conclusion is reached.
Accountability	Members hold themselves and each other accountable, rather than blaming managers or any outside influence for mishaps.[14]
Strong Relationships	Team members work on building strong relationships with each other based on trust. They support each other and feel comfortable enough to share their thoughts and concerns.[15]
Commitment	Effective team members fully commit to the project and the rest of the team by arriving on time, meeting deadlines, and taking full responsibility for their roles in the assignment. They focus on what's best for the team rather than their own personal agendas.[16]
Shared Leadership	Good teams will share leadership roles when appropriate, rather than just one person dominating. When leadership is distributed, there is a sense of shared purpose where everyone is given a voice, which helps to improve team morale and performance.[17]

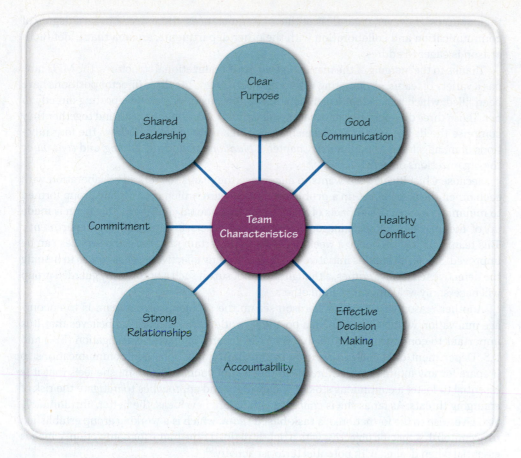

Figure 12-1
Team Characteristics
The key characteristics of effective teams include good communication, shared leadership, and a clear purpose.

These types of teams are particularly important within the MPD. For example, when a crime is committed, a task force of expertise is formed at the scene, consisting of detectives, cops, forensic scientists, and other members of the department. Banding individuals together across departments is a powerful way of ensuring that the crime is resolved as quickly as possible. Similarly, the counterterrorism team is comprised of detectives, SWAT team members, police officers, and MPD management, all working together to defend against terrorist threats. Overseeing these teams is the **management team**, a functional or cross-functional working group of managers formed to plan, organize, lead, and control organizational performance.

A *self-directed* team refers to a team that operates without hierarchical management supervision.[18] Defined by specific outcomes and timetables, members of these teams are responsible for each other's success and are typically rewarded for group performance. As discussed in Chapter 11, *cross-training*, where team members freely share knowledge and provide peer-to-peer mentorship, is a common attribute of these working groups.

As we read in Chapter 10, Chief Richardson stated that no one person could work in isolation in any function within the MPD. However, there are certain areas within the police force that are self-directed and require some autonomy, albeit with supervision. For example, detective teams work autonomously from the rest of the MPD, gathering research from confidential sources and collaborating with one another to help solve a variety of cases. Sharing information with other departments with regard to informants can be a matter of life and death if their identities are revealed, so detectives need to implement the strongest confidentiality measures to protect

✓ **Cross-functional team**—a formal, longstanding working group with representation from diverse divisions, departments, and levels of authority

Management team A functional or cross-functional working group of managers formed to plan, organize, lead, and control organizational performance.

© Rick D'Elia / Corbis

✓ **Management team**—functional or cross-functional working group of managers formed to plan, organize, lead, and control organizational performance

✓ **Self-directed team**—a team that operates without hierarchal management supervision

✓ **Problem-solving team**—a working group formed to minimize the negative impacts of a specific organizational challenge

Problem-solving team A working group formed to minimize the negative impacts of a specific organizational challenge.

✓ **Task-based team**—a working group established to accomplish a specific objective with a tightly defined timeframe for completion, essential when it comes to dealing with potential terrorist activity

✓ **Quality Circle**—a working group comprised of management and staff with the purpose of minimizing performance errors and variance

Task-based team a working group established to accomplish a specific objective, with a tightly defined time frame for completion.

Quality circle A working group comprised of management and staff with the purpose of minimizing performance errors and variance.

✓ **Virtual Teams**—a working group that conducts the majority of its collaborations via electronic communications

• **Size and Roles**
  ➤ There is a clear correlation between team size and performance.

✓ **Social loafing**—occurs when members of a team contribute less effort than they would if they were individually responsible

✓ **Role**—a behavioral and performance expectation that is consciously or unconsciously defined by a group

✓ **Role structure**—a prescribed set of behavioral and performance expectations set for one position or job

✓ **Role ambiguity**—confusion that arises from an employee not understanding the expectations, intentions, or purpose of their position

Virtual team A working group that conducts the majority of its collaborations via electronic communications.

their sources. However, regardless of these circumstances, there needs to be a degree of communication and collaboration with the other departments, an area that Chief Richardson is eager to address.

Thanks to the merging of the matrix and vertical organizational structures, the MPD now has a variety of teams, all operating within the new design. The three director positions have been filled, which means that Chief Richardson now has three people reporting directly to her. Those three directors also have several individuals reporting to them, and together they comprise the department's management team. This working group follows the four functions of management as outlined in Chapter 1: *planning, organizing, leading,* and *controlling* the organization's objectives.

Because Chief Richardson wants to encourage the teams to work in collaboration with each other, she also has set up a **problem-solving team**, which is a working group formed to minimize the negative impacts of a specific organizational challenge.[19] The team is made up of members from the management team and others from across the departments. This team gets together once a week to discuss how certain processes and services can be improved. She feels that this initiative will be particularly effective when it comes to helping the detective team solve crimes, although she is not sure if such a notoriously guarded group will necessarily welcome input from others.

Another reason that Chief Richardson set up the problem-solving team is to encourage innovation within the group. In a post-9/11 world, Chief Richardson believes that it is important to continue her partnership with the Federal Bureau of Investigation (FBI) and U.S. Department of Homeland Security by integrating functions and communications to prepare for any future terrorist threats. In the area of counterterrorism, she feels that it is essential to foster a continuous stream of new ideas and approaches to mitigate the risk of emerging threats. As far as she is concerned, the more new ideas, the better. This initiative also gives rise to the formation of a **task-based team**, which is a working group established to accomplish a specific objective with a tightly defined time frame for completion, which is essential when dealing with potential terrorist activity.[20]

Quality Circle One of the reasons that Assistant Chief Jeff Mitchell was an easy choice for director of administration was because of the results he achieved through his **quality circle**, a working group comprised of management and staff with the purpose of minimizing performance errors and variance.[21]

Mitchell had created the quality circle to address a troubling statistic—they found that only 24 percent of the community trusted the MPD. It was this statistic that prompted Chief Richardson to collaborate with the quality circle and come up with new initiatives as to how these figures could be improved. Chief Richardson had already started to attend community meetings and events to get to know the people they were protecting, as well as to get valuable feedback about the public's views of the MPD. She also made sure that she was present at as many crime scenes as possible to reinforce the message that the MPD took their responsibilities seriously and that they care about the community. Chief Richardson wanted to reach out even further, in order to truly connect with the community.

Based on this premise, the quality circle organized social media technology and email listserves and measured the department's response time to community members, seeking a standard of having every question or comment responded to in less than five minutes. For the first time in the history of the MPD, community members had 24-hour access to the organization. It was then that the public's perspective of the MPD started to change. Within two years, a remarkable 86 percent of community members who responded to a survey about the MPD's communication strategies said that they trusted the MPD.

Virtual Teams As the MPD department is investing heavily in technology enhancements, they have partnered with the Department of Homeland Security and FBI to identify external talent, or a virtual team, to work with their internal Information Technology (IT) team. A **virtual team** is a working group that conducts the majority of its collaborations via electronic communications.[22] The team will work virtually and post updates, targets, and milestones to measure their progress. Chief Richardson makes a note to set up regular meetings with the MPD IT manager to ensure that the teams are working together by sharing ideas and feedback and engaging in successful communication.

Table 12-2   The Impact of Team Size on Team Characteristics and Dynamics

Number of Team Members	Changing Team Characteristics
2–6	Little structure or organization required
7–12	Structure and differentiation of roles begins Face-to-face interaction may become less frequent
13–25	Structure and role differentiation vital Subgroups emerge Face-to-face or virtual interaction for the whole team may become more difficult
26 and above	Positive leadership is vital to success Subgroups form Greater anomymity

(left margin, bottom-to-top arrow) Increasing cohesion

(right margin, top-to-bottom arrow) Increasing tension

✓ **Overload**—behavioral and system strains that occur when expectations for positions or working groups exceed their capacity to perform

➤ **Task Roles**—behaviors that focus on accomplishing work goals, such as providing specific skills and expertise to deliver outcomes and providing project-level organization, including adherence to deadlines and communication exchanges

➤ **Socio-emotional Roles**—behaviors that fulfill the social and emotional needs of team members such as enhancing satisfaction, including recognition and motivation.

Size and Roles

Research has shown a clear correlation between team size and performance.[23] As Table 12-2 shows, smaller teams tend to be more cohesive than larger ones.[24] Teams comprised of less than seven members have the opportunity for all members to get to know each other, and offer a better forum for everyone to contribute to discussions. Yet, teams that are too small might not have the necessary diversity of skills and knowledge or the same ability to come up with a number of new ideas.

However, in teams that are too large, members might not get to know each other to the same degree, and there is more of a likelihood that the members will splinter off into subgroups. In this instance, subgroups can work against each other, leading to arguments and delays in the decision-making process. Because there is more opportunity in bigger teams to hide behind others yet still claim credit for the team's performance, there is also a higher instance of social loafing.[25]

So how do managers know when to adjust the size of a team? Typically, when decision making is slow, there is conflict between team members, and there is little commitment to the task, then it is time to reduce the size of the team. Similarly, if a team lacks the abilities to perform a task or has difficulty generating new initiatives, then it might be time to increase the size of the team.

Different Kinds of Roles The success of a team's performance also depends on the type of **role**, a behavioral and performance expectation that is consciously or unconsciously defined by a group. Table 12.3 describes the cause and effects of different types of roles.

Managers must clearly define roles by implementing a **role structure**, a prescribed set of behavioral and performance expectations for a position or job.[26] If the role lacks clarity, then employees can experience **role ambiguity**, confusion that arises from an employee not understanding the expectations, intentions, or purpose of his or her position.[27]

When managers are assigning roles, they need to be fully aware of the skills and abilities of their employees to play to their strengths and match the right person to the right role. They must also ensure that the role is realistic and manageable to avoid **overload**, behavioral and system strains that occur when expectations for positions or working groups exceed their capacity to perform.[28]

Team member roles may generally be divided into two basic categories:[29]

- Task roles—Behaviors that focus on accomplishing work goals, such as providing specific skills and expertise to deliver outcomes and providing project-level organization, including adherence to deadlines and communication exchanges
- Socioemotional roles—Behaviors that fulfill the social and emotional needs of team members, such as enhancing satisfaction, recognition, and motivation

Managers need to assign appropriate tasks to the right team members and ensure that the team is both motivated and rewarded. When team morale is high, successful results are more likely to follow.

Role A behavioral and performance expectation that is consciously or unconsciously defined by a group.

Role structure A prescribed set of behavioral and performance expectations for a position or job.

Role ambiguity Confusion that arises from an employee not understanding the expectations, intentions, or purpose of his or her position.

Overload Behavioral and system strains that occur when expectations for positions or working groups exceed their capacity to perform.

LECTURE ENHANCER:

12.3 Team Dynamics

➤ Team dynamics are largely unseen forces, but they can influence the way a team operates and performs

✓ **Conformity**—where an individual or group adheres to organizational policies, procedures, cultural dynamics, and performance standards

✓ **Generalization**—an individual or group perspective that is formed through limited data or experiences

• **Forming—Storming—Norming—Performing**

  ✓ **Stages of Group Development**—a four-stage process by which teams become more effective and efficient over time

    1. Forming
      ✓ **Norms**—expectations implicitly or explicitly defined by a group that result in a consistent set of behaviors or beliefs

    2. Storming
      ✓ **Conflict**—resistance or hostility resulting from two or more parties focusing on and attempting to reconcile differing opinions

    3. Norming
      ✓ **Cohesiveness**—the degree to which individuals in a working group exhibit loyalty and norm consistencies
      ✓ **Socialization**—the processes by which individuals attain the knowledge, skills, cultural distinctions, and values to adapt to a group's norms

    4. Performing
      ✓ **Affiliation**—a person's perceived connection to a group, based on purpose, demographics, function, and other intangible dimensions

Conformity The situation where an individual or group adheres to organizational policies, procedures, cultural dynamics, and performance standards.

Generalization An individual or group perspective that is formed through limited data or experiences.

Stages of group development A four-stage process by which teams become more effective and efficient over time; the stages are Forming, Storming, Norming, and Performing.

Norms Expectations implicitly or explicitly defined by a group that result in a consistent set of behaviors or beliefs.

Table 12-3	Role Types Cause and Effects—Individual vs. Manager(s) or Group(s)		
	Cause	**Who Determines or Whom it Affects**	
		Individual	**Manager(s) or Group(s)**
ROLE Type	Behavioral and performance defined	Affected	Determined
ROLE Structure	Behavioral and performance defined	Affected	Determined
ROLE Ambiguity	Unclear and confusion in expectations	Affected	Determined and Affected
ROLE Overload		Affected	Determined and Affected

12.3 | TEAM DYNAMICS

12.3 **Explain** team dynamics and its relationship to performance.

The dynamics between team members can make or break a team. Team dynamics are largely unseen forces, but they can influence the way that a team operates and performs. For example, say that you are part of a team of four, where two people are particularly close friends. This could either have a positive or negative effect on the group: the friends might be close but have an easy, infectious style of communication that encourages the rest of the group to join in; or they may communicate only with each other, which effectively excludes the rest of the team.

Similarly, the organizational structure and behavior of team leaders and management executives can also have an impact on team dynamics. Take the MPD, for example. Prior to Chief Richardson's appointment, the department was run as a hierarchy, with employees treated as subordinates, too afraid to put forward suggestions for fear of breaking the chain of command. There was a high expectation of **conformity**, where an individual or group adheres to organizational policies, procedures, cultural dynamics, and performance standards.[30]

This vertical structure caused tension throughout the department, fostering a culture of mistrust, suspicion, and blame among the employees. Because of their narrow viewpoint, workers were prone to **generalization**, an individual or group perspective that is formed through limited data or experiences. By changing the structure, not only was Chief Richardson improving the culture of the organization, but also the way teams worked and their relationships with one another. However, the smallest incident can threaten the delicate balance of team dynamics, as she soon will discover.

Forming—Storming—Norming—Performing

Often teams follow **stages of group development**, a four-stage process by which teams become more effective and efficient over time.[31] Those stages are Forming, Storming, Norming, and Performing.

Forming This is the first stage of group development, where team members meet each other for the first time and get a feel for the type of team that they have joined. During this time, some **norms**, expectations implicitly or explicitly defined by a group that result in a consistent set of behaviors or beliefs, will be established.[32] Typically, team members use this time to form impressions of their team members and tend to avoid conflict or any kind of serious discussion.

Storming During the second stage, a measure of **conflict**, which is resistance or hostility resulting from two or more parties focusing on and attempting to reconcile differing opinions, may arise.[33] Different personalities might clash, and disagreements erupt about the way the project should be approached. Team members become more opinionated about how the project should be run and use this time to establish their roles within the team. In some cases, teams never leave this second stage, mired in conflict and indecision. Moving out of this stage requires patience and tolerance of other personalities and the ability to avoid judging the behaviors of others.

Norming Conflict has been resolved in this stage, and the team members have settled into their roles. They have come to a mutual agreement about how to achieve their goals and objectives and are committed to the team and its success. This is when group **cohesiveness**, or the degree to which individuals in a working group exhibit loyalty and norm consistencies, is being developed.[34] During this period, **socialization**, the processes by which individuals attain the knowledge, skills, cultural distinctions, and values to adapt to a group's norms, also occurs. [35]

© endopack / iStockphoto

Performing During this final stage, the team is working at its optimal level. Loyalty is high, and each member is invested in achieving the goal. The team operates as a unit and makes decisions almost autonomously. Members also feel a strong **affiliation** with the group, which is a person's perceived connection to a group, based on purpose, demographics, function, and other intangible dimensions.[36]

However, there are many factors that still may negatively affect the team dynamics, which results in the team reverting to earlier stages. These include high turnover, a change in management or leadership, or a clash between new and existing members. This is where managers must be aware of the changing team dynamics and enforce measures to mitigate any impact on performance.

In Chapters 10 and 11, we charted the progress of Chief Richardson and her goal of restructuring the MPD in Washington, D.C., to reduce crime rates and transform the department into a more efficient, and compassionate organization. Her first challenge was to convince senior management to accept a more horizontal structure rather than the vertical model that had been in place for decades. Richardson had her fair share of dissenters, almost to the point of open rebellion. However, through perseverance, new technology initiatives, new recruits, and an inspiring training program, Richardson was able to prove that a different approach was exactly what the MPD needed.

Chief Richardson selected Captain Joel Holcomb as the new director of operations. When the news of his selection was announced, however, there was an immediate internal uproar, as described in Chapter 11. Although many regarded Holcomb as a solid worker, they felt that he came in a distant second to Assistant Chief Susan Taylor, the runner-up for the position. She was an obvious choice, in the minds of many in the department; after all, she had an impeccable record, enjoyed longer tenure with the department, and was widely seen as Holcomb's mentor. When Taylor filed a grievance for gender discrimination based on questions she had been asked during her interview that she thought were unfair and sexist, this further cemented the loyalty of her supporters, who believed that she had been discriminated against for being a mother.

In the days that followed the selection of Director Holcomb, the tension on the newly formed operations team was growing increasingly uncomfortable. Aside from the situation with Assistant Chief Taylor, nobody on the team believed that Holcomb had the leadership abilities or the experience to manage them; he was simply not boss material. When Holcomb held meetings, the team listened politely, but Holcomb could tell from their resigned expressions that they weren't fully engaged. However, he was determined to make the most of his new role and get the team on his side. "They'll accept me eventually, I suppose," he thought miserably.

In the meantime, Taylor accepted her interviewer's apology for asking inappropriate questions. She agreed to remain in her current role for the time being, but she informed Ken

Conflict Resistance or hostility resulting from two or more parties focusing on and attempting to reconcile differing opinions.

Cohesiveness The degree to which individuals in a working group exhibit loyalty and norm consistencies.

Socialization The processes by which individuals attain the knowledge, skills, cultural distinctions, and values to adapt to a group's norms.

Affiliation A person's perceived connection to a group, based on purpose, demographics, function, and other intangible dimensions.

ManagementStory:
Featuring Robin Richardson

Research @ Work

Too Much of a Good Thing? Team Cohesion and Groupthink

Team cohesion is a necessary prerequisite for effective team performance, as indicated by the stages of group development. But is it possible to have too much of a good thing when it comes to team cohesion? The answer is yes!

In the 1970s, Yale University psychologist Irving Janis suggested that a dysfunctional condition called *groupthink* could occur in a team that is too cohesive.[37] According to Janis, groupthink occurs when members of a group, in an effort to preserve harmony and conformity, attempt to reach a consensus decision without critically evaluating ideas and viewpoints while isolating themselves from external perspectives. Individuals within the group either refrain from making suggestions and observations that go against the prevailing group consensus or, if they do attempt to interject a dissenting opinion, they are ignored or shunted aside by the majority of group members. Janis identified some common symptoms of groupthink.

These include 1) social pressure against divergent perspectives, 2) self-censorship of concerns, 3) self-appointed mind guards that screen external information, 4) illusions of morality, 5) illusions of invulnerability, 6) illusions of unanimity, 7) efforts to rationalize, and 8) stereotyped portrayals of enemy leaders.[38] Classic examples of poor team decision making resulting from groupthink include the Bay of Pigs fiasco, a failed U.S. military invasion of Cuba in the 1960s; and the space shuttle *Challenger* disaster in 1986, where seven crew members were killed shortly after launch.[39]

Janis suggested that group cohesion is a primary cause of groupthink.[40] In addition, lapses in ethical behavior, for example, the Watergate scandal, where the Nixon administration tried to cover up a break-in to the Democratic National Committee's offices in the Watergate building in Washington, DC, which sparked a series of events leading to Nixon's resignation in 1974, have often been suggested as a likely outcome of groupthink.[41] Recent research lends some support to these suppositions.

Results from a study based on a sample of 237 public procurement officers showed that social cohesion was positively related to groupthink, which was negatively related to the ethical behavior of the procurement officers.[42] These findings suggest that managers would be well advised to ensure that too much team cohesion does not result in groupthink processes, bad decision making, and unethical behavior.

Critical Thinking in the Classroom

As a manager, how can you guard against too much cohesion in your team that could lead to a groupthink situation?

Gilmore, assistant chief of HR, that she did not intend to stay with the MPD for too much longer—not after everything that had happened.

Over the following weeks, Director Holcomb worked tirelessly to earn the respect of his new team. He organized team events to encourage team-bonding and unity, and while the members participated in the activities, they remained detached. Holcomb also set up one-to-one meetings in an effort to understand their goals and aspirations; yet the discussions felt stilted and tense. The challenge seemed insurmountable. His responsibility was to manage the functional group of police officers in the field; most of which believed he was too inexperienced and that Assistant Chief Taylor deserved his job. One fateful night, an incident took place that would put further obstacles in his path.

Terrell Rhodes, one of the 50 new recruits to the department, was an instant hit. Everyone liked and respected him. With a wife and young child, and his new job, he was living his life's dream. Terrell's dad and grandfather had been an integral part of the police department for decades, and Terrell had always longed to follow in their footsteps. It was only the previous year, just before Chief Richardson began her new position, that Terrance Rhodes, Terrell's father, had accepted the police chief position in neighboring Fairfax County. Many of the long-term MPD employees thought that the mayor might even one day replace Chief Richardson with Terrance Rhodes—he was an exceptional cop and manager.

It was a quiet evening—Terrell's third time patrolling the neighborhoods alone. A car pulled out in front of Terrell, who soon noticed that one headlight was not working. He followed the slow-moving car for a couple of blocks before noticing that its license plate tags had expired. Terrell called for backup before turning on his flashing lights to indicate for the driver of the car to pull over.

When Terrell approached the car, the driver rolled down the window and sat silently with his hands on the wheel. Terrell said, "Sir, I will need to see your driver's license and registration." The driver sat perfectly still. Terrell repeated, "Sir, driver's license and registration, please." Still nothing. Finally, Terrell said, "Sir, could you please turn off the engine and step out of the vehicle?"

The driver swung the door open, and with one quick, heavy push, Terrell Rhodes was on his back. During the struggle, the driver grabbed Terrell's gun. Terrell watched as the driver pulled the trigger on the gun; he felt a shocking blow to the middle of his chest. His attacker dropped the gun, returned to his car, and drove away.

Within seconds, Terrell's backup arrived on the scene and called for an ambulance and additional backup. Within 10 minutes, the scene of the standard traffic stop gone tragically awry was swamped with people, including community members, fellow officers, Assistant Chief Mitchell, and Director Holcomb. Chief Richardson had been called as well, but she was attending a conference 100 miles outside town and would be delayed getting to the crime scene. She gave instructions to Holcomb to handle the situation in her absence.

Officer Terrell Rhodes was still alive, thanks to his bulletproof vest. Director Holcomb quickly took control of the scene, giving concise orders and commands and coordinating all the efforts necessary to catch the suspect. By now, a dozen police were trawling the surrounding area searching for the shooter. The dynamic of the team was focused and calculated—swift and by the book. As Assistant Chief Taylor watched Holcomb perform, she could not help but note how competent he was in an emergency situation. Thanks to his calm, collected manner, the team was operating like a well-oiled machine under his leadership. Maybe she had misjudged him. Still, something wasn't right but she couldn't put her finger on it.

Assistant Chief Taylor watched as Officer Rhodes was loaded into the back of an ambulance, his face ashen, his fingers twitching uncontrollably, and saw the tears streaming down his face from eyes that seemed not to blink. Rhodes was totally alone, flanked only by a medic that had no idea who Terrell Rhodes was or how his family had served the MPD and the community for generations. The rest of the officers on the scene were deftly following Director Holcomb's orders. They were all following standard traditional protocol, but the reaction disturbed Assistant Chief Taylor. In that instant, she realized what it was about Holcomb that bothered her: his communication was excellent, and his knowledge of technology was second to none, but he lacked one vital ingredient: compassion. When Richardson took over as chief, she presented the department with a huge banner that included the three words that summed up her vision for the new culture of the MPD: Computers, Communication, and Compassion. If he didn't embrace this ethos fully, then how could the rest of his team be expected to? "Well, two out of three isn't good enough," Assistant Chief Taylor murmured and jumped into action.

She ran to the back of the ambulance, climbed in, held Terrell's hand, and reassured him, "I am here, Terrell. Don't you worry, I am here. Your father and grandfather are meeting us at the hospital. You are going to be fine. We are all so proud of you."

Holcomb watched as the ambulance drove away. He was angry but decided that he would deal with Assistant Chief Taylor's conduct, which undermined his authority, tomorrow.

12.4 | MANAGING CONFLICT

12.4 | Compare and contrast productive and unhealthy conflict as it relates to organizational results.

Conflict often occurs when environmental forces initiate organizational system changes. This is known as **variation**, the system-level changes that inevitably occur and may require individuals and groups to respond. As we have explored, certain changes such as high turnover, recent appointments, and new team members can affect the team dynamic and serve

LECTURE ENHANCER:

12.4 Managing Conflict

✓ **Variation**—the system-level changes that inevitably occur and may require individuals and groups to respond

• **Addressing Unhealthy Conflict**

• **Encouraging Productive Conflict**

✓ **Negotiation**—the process by which two or more parties with differing objectives, desires, or perspectives go through to find a mutually agreeable solution

• **Key dimensions of "good conflict"**

➤ Conflict can be good when emotion is left out of the equation.

➤ Managers must get buy-in from each team-member on the vision they propose in order to encourage productive debate.

✓ **Teaming**—an adaptive working group formed internally and externally, in order to address unexpected environmental changes, challenges, and opportunities

Variation The system-level changes that inevitably occur that may require individuals and groups to respond.

as a catalyst for unhealthy conflict. If the conflict is mismanaged or simply ignored, the matter tends to escalate, leading to poor morale and ultimately low organizational performance. In the following section, we will see how the appointment of Director Holcomb led to even more conflict as he confronted Assistant Chief Taylor about her behavior at the crime scene where fellow officer Terrell Rhodes was shot.

Addressing Unhealthy Conflict

The next day, Director Holcomb called Assistant Chief Taylor into his office. "I need to discuss an important matter with you," he said grimly. "Yesterday, at the scene of Terrell's shooting we were in the midst of a manhunt. I thought my orders were very clear that we needed all available personnel to ensure that we captured the perpetrator. In direct opposition to my leadership, you climbed into the back of the ambulance and went to the hospital with Terrell. You did not follow orders. If you were in my position, what would you do?"

Taylor sat still for a moment and said very directly, "Well, Director Holcomb, if I were in your position, I would suspend me without pay for three days for insubordination." He paused, stunned by Taylor's answer, and quickly stated, "Okay, you got it. You are suspended for three days without pay, effective immediately."

About two hours later, Ken Gilmore called from Human Resources. "Director Holcomb, I am looking at an Insubordination Suspension form for Assistant Chief Taylor, and I'm confused. Let me offer you a piece of advice . . . Call her. Apologize. And tell her that you made a grave error of judgment."

Holcomb interjected, "Ken, I can't do that. This is a crucial moment in the department, specifically with respect to my leadership as the director of operations. In front of the entire team, she left a crime scene, without permission, to conduct an unauthorized task. That is unacceptable, per our operating procedures and the chain of command. When the department needed her, she was not there."

Ken offered once again, "Joel, between you and me, let this go. I am not approving this request. Per our operating procedures, this will go to the chief for approval, with my candid recommendation to reject your management decision."

"Well, Ken, if this is how the management team stands up for one another, then I guess that's worth knowing. Are you telling me that you would have made a different decision, if you were in my position?"

Ken replied, "Yes, Joel. If I were you, I would be holding a meeting this morning to thank everyone for their service last night and recognize Assistant Chief Taylor for the deep compassion she displayed to one of our finest young rookies."

"Sorry to disappoint you, Ken. I would completely lose my authority with that tactic, which would take away my power as a manager in the future," Holocomb offered.

Ken was exasperated. "Joel, have you actually listened to anything Chief Richardson has said since she took over from Kimbell? She wants the MPD to be more compassionate toward members of the community and each other. Who do you think the department is going to trust and respect more—the rigid dictator or the leader willing to crawl in the back of an ambulance and hold a terrified rookie's hand on the way to the hospital? You will never get authority simply because of your title. People need to trust and respect you."

Ken sighed, "Okay, let's see what the chief says about this."

As predicted, Chief Richardson denied Director Holcomb's suspension recommendation for Taylor. Holcomb proceeded to type up his letter of resignation. Chief Richardson would receive it an hour later.

Encouraging Productive Conflict

Negotiation The process by which two or more parties with differing objectives, desires, or perspectives go through to find a mutually agreeable solution.

Chief Richardson was not surprised that Holcomb had resigned. She was sorry to be losing him, but she knew he was struggling with embracing the new ethos of the MPD and leading his team. She picked up the phone and asked Taylor to join her for a cup of coffee at a local shop. She was ready to start the **negotiation**, the process by which two or more parties with differing objectives, desires, or perspectives go through to find a mutually agreeable solution, and hoped Taylor was open to it as well.[43]

The chief began by saying, "Susan, I heard about what happened last night."

Assistant Chief Susan Taylor, unable to contain her frustration, shot back, "That kid was scared. If I had to do the whole thing over, I would get in that ambulance without a second thought."

Chief Richardson said, "Susan, I wanted to get together with you so that I could apologize. You deserve better from this department and from me. I need you on our team. I made a mistake when I didn't appoint you as director—let me fix it."

Assistant Chief Taylor says, "This is not just about getting the director position. I need to know that we can become a department that fosters a safe community for everybody. I want to know that I have your support for some dramatic cultural changes. All of your technology efforts and tracking numbers for communication response is worthless if we don't give our cops permission to care for each other and our community members."

Richardson was impressed by Taylor's vision: despite being passed over for the position initially, here was an ally who believed in the changes that Richardson had been fighting so hard to implement. But first, Chief Richardson had to clear up one matter that had been nagging her ever since she had read Taylor's performance evaluations as part of reviewing her discrimination complaint. The reviews had been stellar, apart from the issue of communication. Chief Richardson needed to make sure that Assistant Chief Taylor could recognize this as a developmental area, as it was a vital part of the director of operation's role.

"Susan, I wholeheartedly applaud your actions on the night of Terrell's shooting, but do you think it would have helped the situation if you had communicated to Holcomb about what you were trying to do? Maybe then the situation wouldn't have escalated to such a degree."

Assistant Chief Taylor replied, "I admit that it wasn't the smartest thing to just leave my post without giving any kind of reason to the team or the officer in charge. I guess I acted on impulse. Not that I have any regrets, but I think better communication would have helped."

She continued, "I see compassion as a sign of good police work—not as a sign of weakness. Last week, I sat with a mother whose son was shot to death. His body was lying 10 feet from us—blood soaking through the sheets. I had my arms around her and we cried together. Once she could talk, I asked her what had happened. She started telling me everything—all about her son's friends and enemies, and who she thought had shot him. All the while, here were our detectives walking around counting bullet casings and making measurements—that is important stuff, but surely we also need the community as a partner in solving crimes."

Chief Richardson said, somberly, "Susan, I hear you. But I have been struggling to get this message across to the MPD. Although I am grateful for your support, how do we go about telling 1,000 police officers to be more compassionate?

Assistant Chief Taylor thought for a minute. "We don't tell them; we show them. One ambulance at a time . . . one broken-hearted mother at a time . . . we *show* them. And by showing them, we give them permission to care."

On that note, Chief Richardson asked Assistant Chief Taylor if she would be willing to take over the director of operations position. Taylor accepted on the spot. Relieved that the situation had been sorted out, the two women walked back to the office together, ready to make an announcement to the team that they had a new director of operations.

Key Dimensions of "Good Conflict" It might sound like an oxymoron, but conflict can be good. Indeed, its value to the performance of an organization cannot be underestimated. Good conflict can spark new ideas, generate creativity, and motivate employees. So how do organizations facilitate good conflict? Some companies set up training programs to teach their employees conflict resolution methods that help them resolve these issues themselves, rather than passing them on to their managers. However, in the event of a serious conflict, managers still need to intervene and help to find a solution wherever possible.

Conflict can be good when emotion is left out of the equation.[44] Many of us can attest to feeling vengeful toward colleagues and others who we feel have offended us in some way. Yet, this behavior is more destructive than anything else, causing unbearable tension and divisions within teams. For conflict to be productive, managers must get buy-in from each team member on the vision they propose to encourage productive debate. Discussions might become heated as team members jostle to be heard, disagree with each other, and put forward new ideas. But ultimately, the result will be the same: new initiatives, solutions, and perspectives all directed toward achieving the same goal. A debate that focuses on the future, rather than dwelling on the problems of the past, without any backbiting, self-interest, or personal attacks is invaluable. However, it can be beneficial for managers to learn how past conflicts have been resolved to apply the same techniques in the future.

Chief Richardson was so buoyed by resolving her conflict with Assistant Chief Taylor that she felt confident enough to address the issue of the slow crime-solving process within the MPD. To tackle this area, she had decided to adopt a teaming approach. **Teaming** is a process whereby an adaptive working group is formed to address unexpected environmental changes, challenges, and opportunities.[45] It was time for this team to improve its shared understanding of the new strategic direction of the MPD.

As she prepared herself for the meeting, she looked around to make sure that there was full attendance. All the experts from the different functions across the MPD were present, including members of the homicide detective team, forensics, intelligence, narcotics, and the gang unit.

"One of the reasons I have formed this group is to focus on one particular issue that continues to pose a challenge within the MPD. In fact, feedback from the anonymous email group I set up consistently notes their frustration with the MPD's delay in solving crimes. Although the organizational structure and the culture have improved, certain teams are still struggling to work together, which, I feel, is creating conflict."

She waited for the inevitable folding-of-arms-in-defense position, and went on:

"Last week, there was a gang shooting a couple of miles from here. Homicide, have you had any leads?"

One of the detectives replied, "Not yet, Chief, we are still working on it."

Chief Richardson said, "As it was a gang shooting, did you speak to anyone in the gang unit?"

"No, Chief."

"As this particular gang has a reputation for drug dealing, have you spoken to narcotics to see if they have any sources in the area that might know anything?"

"No, Chief."

"What about the Intelligence unit? They might have had a beat officer in that location the night of the shooting—maybe he or she knows something about the murder."

Chief Richardson changed tack. She said, "May I ask why Homicide has not liaised with any of these departments to solve the crime?"

The detective coughed, "I'm going to have to have that conversation with you offline, Chief."

Chief Richardson had predicted this response; Homicide was notorious for their inability to communicate with the other teams, citing their investigations as too high-level for the rest of the MPD. They enjoyed the power and prestige that came with their roles and felt threatened if there was any outside intervention.

Chief Richardson persisted, refusing to be stonewalled. "In the MPD, we must be focused on resolving violence and homicide. We need everybody in this room, as well as the rest of the department, to solve crimes as quickly as possible, for the sake of our reputation and for the safety of our community. To do this, we need to share information, not just internally but outside in the community."

"You know we can't do that, Chief," another homicide detective spoke up. "We are a closed unit—everything we do has to remain top-secret."

A narcotics expert joined in, "I have to say I agree. It is absolutely untenable for Narcotics to share their sources with Homicide or anyone else outside the unit. If their identity is disclosed, their lives will be in real danger, and our information stream cut off for good."

"I understand your concerns," Chief Richardson replied, "but I think I have an idea that might work."

Ignoring the skeptical looks, she went on. "What if we had a database of all our sources that detailed the locations they were in, and which narcotics officer was responsible for that source. Then when a crime occurs, we can contact the responsible officer and get him to contact his source directly. That way, there is no chance of the identity being revealed, and the sources remain protected."

The homicide detective looked like he wanted to say something but remained silent.

Chief Richardson took this as a good sign. After a few more questions, the group decided to reconvene the following week.

Teaming A process whereby an adaptive working group is formed to address unexpected environmental changes, challenges, and opportunities.

Over the coming weeks, Chief Richardson assigned an IT expert to design the database and gave access to only a few of the most senior executives in the organization. As soon as a major crime occurred, she sent an email out to every senior manager in the crime departments outlining the nature of the crime and encouraging them to communicate with one another. At first, the different departments clashed; after all, with so many years of working in isolation, it was difficult for the teams to overcome the different personalities, cultures, values, jargon, and norms particular to each area. Yet each conflict gave rise to new perspectives and creative ideas, as well as a broader view of what they were trying to accomplish.

Over time, the homicide detectives became more comfortable with the new regime. They now had a whole host of resources to develop information and new leads, giving them more time to carry out their work on the street, such as talking to victims' families and gathering evidence. Narcotics became less threatened by the database initiative as well, particularly as access was restricted to a couple of top-level MPD executives.

As communication between the departments improved, crime rates went down. For the first time in years, the MPD got positive press and recognition for their efforts from the community. A sense of pride and passion infiltrated the teams as they realized the difference that they were making in the community. Chief Richardson finally felt that progress was being made, yet she didn't want to be complacent; she knew how easy it would be for some of the team to slip back into the old ways of doing things. In order to maintain this enhanced level of performance, she gathered some of her team to come up with some strategies that would help keep up the momentum.

12.5 | STRATEGIES TO INCREASE PERFORMANCE

12.5 | Develop a strategic plan to increase team performance.

As soon as Assistant Chief Taylor was named the new director of operations, she threw herself into her new role. Working closely with Ken and the chief, they implemented a plan to raise the operational performance of the department to a national standard of excellence. Director Taylor immediately announced plans for a three-pronged approach to transform the department's performance: Effective Meetings, Performance Development, and Recognizing Excellence. The approach is illustrated in Figure 12-2.

LECTURE ENHANCER:
12.5 Strategies to Increase Performance
➤ Effective Meetings
  1. Set a purpose before the meeting.
  2. Don't meet unless there is a purpose.
  3. Ask whether the purpose could be achieved without holding a meeting (i.e., through a memo or e-mail).
  4. Set an agenda and distribute it in advance so that everyone can prepare for the discussion. Use the agenda to stay on track during the meeting.
  5. Set time limits for the meeting, including an exact starting and stopping time.
  6. Find ways to discourage lateness. For example, whoever is late must buy coffee for the team's next meeting.
  7. Designate a record keeper to take notes at each meeting.
  8. Encourage everyone on the team to communicate and air their opinions during the meeting. Comments such as "How do you feel about this?" or "We haven't heard from you yet" may help to facilitate discussion.
  9. Stop the meeting when all agenda items have been discussed so that team members can get back to other important tasks.
➤ Performance Development
  1. Increase identifiability
  2. Promote involvement
  3. Strengthen team cohesion
  4. Provide performance reviews and feedback
  5. Maintain an appropriate team size

Figure 12-2
Effective Meeting Flow Options
Steps for holding effective meetings

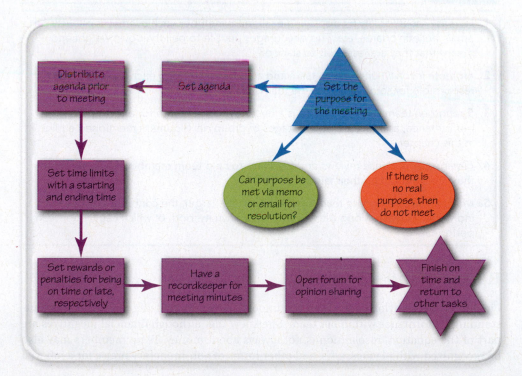

Effective Meetings[46]

Director Taylor knew from personal experience that team meetings could sometimes be a waste of time, dragging on and on without accomplishing anything. However, she also understood that team meetings, when run correctly, can help a team to solve problems, communicate with one another, and provide emotional support. In order to make her team's meetings more enjoyable and productive, Director Taylor suggested the following guidelines:

1. Set a purpose before the meeting.
2. Ask whether the purpose could be achieved without holding a meeting (i.e., through a memo or email).
3. Don't meet unless there is a purpose.
4. Set an agenda and distribute it in advance so that everyone can prepare for the discussion. Use the agenda to stay on track during the meeting.
5. Set time limits for the meeting, including an exact starting and stopping time.
6. Find ways to discourage lateness. For example, whoever is late must buy coffee for the team's next meeting.
7. Designate a recordkeeper to take notes at each meeting.
8. Urge everyone on the team to communicate and air their opinions during the meeting. Comments such as "How do you feel about this?" or "We haven't heard from you yet" may help to facilitate and encourage discussion.
9. Stop the meeting when all agenda items have been discussed so that team members can get back to other important tasks.

Performance Development

Director Taylor also knew that maintaining team performance over time can be a challenge.[47] Many things can detract from effective team performance, including social loafing.[48] In an effort to overcome social loafing and help her team to become more effective, Director Taylor employed the following strategies:[49]

Strategy Implementation Options 1–5

1. *Increase identifiability* by displaying each team member's achievements publicly via email, bulletin boards, etc. This encourages people to pull their own weight and means that they are less likely to slack off.
2. *Promote involvement* in team tasks and activities by making each team member responsible for some aspect of the team's task.
3. *Strengthen team cohesion,* which is a necessary prerequisite for effective team performance, as indicated by the stages of group development mentioned earlier in this chapter.
4. *Provide performance reviews and feedback* to help team members know whether they are contributing their fair share.
5. *Maintain an appropriate team size.* As teams get larger, the contributions of each individual increase, along with feelings of anonymity, both of which can hinder team performance.

Recognizing Excellence

Finally, Director Taylor understood the importance of recognizing and rewarding outstanding performance within her team. She knew that although financial incentives are part of the equation, recognition is not always about money. Team members may also be recognized with plaques, gifts, and other forms of non-monetary praise for a job well done. Director Taylor identified the following techniques for recognizing excellence in her teams:[50]

1. The recognition award should have a *clearly stated purpose* that clearly acknowledges what has been accomplished and why it is important.

2. Recognition awards can be given using *program award levels* that recognize both differing accomplishments and differing levels of contributions.

3. A *nomination procedure* should be established so that peers, supervisors, and/or customers can have input in the recognition process.

4. In terms of *timing*, recognition should be given as closely as possible to the actual event to reinforce the connection between the meritorious actions and the event.

5. The *award presentation* should be a positive and personalized experience that refers to the details of the achievement and makes the winner feel proud.

As the above case study illustrates, a fully functioning team communicates well, freely generates new ideas, and is able to settle conflict in a healthy manner. One of the most important roles of a manager is to ensure that her team is productive and incentivized to work toward achieving a goal. After all, in most instances, a manager is only as good as her team.

Case**Snapshot**

Chapter 12 Case: Managing Team Performance: Pfizer can be found on pg. 474

ADDITIONAL RESOURCES

KEY TERMS

Affiliation A person's perceived connection to a group, based on purpose, demographics, function, and other intangible dimensions. **(p. 309)**

Cohesiveness The degree to which individuals in a working group exhibit loyalty and norm consistencies. **(p. 309)**

Conflict Resistance or hostility resulting from two or more parties focusing on and attempting to reconcile differing opinions. **(p. 309)**

Conformity The situation where an individual or group adheres to organizational policies, procedures, cultural dynamics, and performance standards. **(p. 308)**

Cross-functional team A formal, longstanding working group with representation from diverse divisions, departments, and levels of authority. **(p. 304)**

Formal team A working group formed by an organization's management to achieve specific, agreed-upon strategies, plans, and outcomes. **(p. 303)**

Functional team A formal, longstanding working group organized around specific tasks, processes, or roles. **(p. 304)**

Generalization An individual or group perspective that is formed through limited data or experiences. **(p. 308)**

Informal team A working group, generally not intended to be permanent, formed by team members to accomplish self-defined tasks and objectives. **(p. 303)**

Management team A functional or cross-functional working group of managers formed to plan, organize, lead, and control organizational performance. **(p. 305)**

Negotiation The process by which two or more parties with differing objectives, desires, or perspectives go through to find a mutually agreeable solution. **(p. 312)**

Norms Expectations implicitly or explicitly defined by a group that result in a consistent set of behaviors or beliefs. **(p. 308)**

Overload Behavioral and system strains that occur when expectations for positions or working groups exceed their capacity to perform. **(p. 307)**

Problem-solving team A working group formed to minimize the negative impacts of a specific organizational challenge. **(p. 306)**

Quality circle A working group comprised of management and staff with the purpose of minimizing performance errors and variance. **(p. 306)**

Role ambiguity Confusion that arises from an employee not understanding the expectations, intentions, or purpose of his or her position. **(p. 307)**

Role structure A prescribed set of behavioral and performance expectations for a position or job. **(p. 307)**

Role A behavioral and performance expectation that is consciously or unconsciously defined by a group. **(p. 307)**

Socialization The processes by which individuals attain the knowledge, skills, cultural distinctions, and values to adapt to a group's norms. **(p. 309)**

Stages of group development A four-stage process by which teams become more effective and efficient over time; the stages are Forming, Storming, Norming, and Performing. **(p. 308)**

Task-based team a working group established to accomplish a specific objective, with a tightly defined time frame for completion. **(p. 306)**

Team A purposeful group formed to accomplish a project, task, or goal. **(p. 302)**

Teaming A process whereby an adaptive working group is formed to address unexpected environmental changes, challenges, and opportunities. **(p. 314)**

Variation The system-level changes that inevitably occur that may require individuals and groups to respond. **(p. 311)**

Virtual team A working group that conducts the majority of its collaborations via electronic communications. **(p. 306)**

IN REVIEW

12.1 | Describe why managers form working groups to achieve results.

A team, or working group, is a purposeful group formed to accomplish a project, task, or goal. With so many different personalities, skills and abilities, a strong team can present a diversity of viewpoints on how to solve problems within the organization. For the team members, they benefit from the feeling of belonging to something greater than themselves and gain positive affiliation from being part of such a powerful process. A *formal team* is a working group formed by an organization's management to achieve specific, agreed-upon strategies, plans, and outcomes. An *informal team* is a working group, generally not intended to be permanent, formed by team members to accomplish self-defined tasks and objectives.

12.2 | Explain the characteristics of teams.

Good teams usually have a clear purpose about what they are doing and how their work contributes to the success of the organization. Clear communication helps the team make decisions and aids in the bonding process. Disagreements are usually dealt with openly and resolved constructively. Effective teams will make decisions based on the general consensus of the team members. Members hold themselves and each other accountable, rather than blaming managers or any outside influence for mishaps. Team members work on building strong relationships with each other based on trust. Effective team members fully commit to the project and the rest of the team by arriving on time, meeting deadlines, and taking full responsibility for their role in the assignment. Good teams will share leadership roles when appropriate, rather than just one person dominating.

12.3 | Explain team dynamics and its relationship to performance.

Team dynamics are largely unseen forces, but they can influence the way a team operates and performs. The organizational structure and behavior of team leaders and management executives can also have an impact on team dynamics. Often teams follow *stages of group development,* a four-stage process by which teams become more effective and efficient over time. Those stages are Forming, Storming, Norming, and Performing. *Forming* is the first stage of group development where team members meet each other for the first time and get a feel for the type of team they have joined. *Storming*, the second stage, is when a measure of *conflict*, which is resistance or hostility resulting from two or more parties focusing on and attempting to reconcile differing opinions, may arise. In *Norming*, conflict has been resolved, and the team members are settled into their roles. During the final stage, *Performing*, the team is working at its optimal level. The team operates as a unit and makes decisions almost autonomously.

12.4 | Compare and contrast productive and unhealthy conflict as it relates to organizational results.

High turnover, recent appointments, and new team members can affect the team dynamic and serve as a catalyst for unhealthy conflict. If the conflict is mismanaged or simply ignored, the matter tends to escalate, leading to poor morale and ultimately low organizational performance. Good conflict can spark new ideas, generate creativity, and motivate employees. Companies set up training programs to teach their employees conflict resolution methods that help them to resolve these issues themselves, rather than passing them on to their managers.

12.5 | Develop a strategic plan to increase team performance.

An effective plan for increasing team performance can include various strategies to have more effective meetings, develop team and member performance, and to recognize excellence in the team.

SELF-TEST

12.1 | Describe why managers form working groups to achieve results.

1. What is a team, and why do we have them?

2. A(n) _____ team is a working group formed by an organization's management to achieve specific, agreed-upon strategies, plans, and outcomes, while a(n) _____ team is a working group, generally not intended to be permanent, formed by team members to accomplish self-defined tasks and objectives.

12.2 | Explain the characteristics of teams.

3. Which of the following is *not* one of the characteristics of effective teams?
   a. Clear purpose
   b. Good communication
   c. Healthy conflict
   d. A "majority rules" mentality

4. A formal, longstanding working group with representation from diverse divisions, departments, and levels of authority is a:
   a. Functional team
   b. Cross-functional team
   c. Representative team
   d. Delegated team

5. A problem-solving team operates without hierarchical management supervision.
   a. True
   b. False

6. A working group comprised of management and staff with the purpose of minimizing performance errors and variance is a(n) _____.

12.3 | Explain team dynamics and its relationship to performance.

7. List and define the Stages of Group Development.

8. The degree to which individuals in a working group exhibit loyalty and norm consistencies is:
   a. Socialization
   b. Cohesiveness
   c. Generalization
   d. Dynamism

12.4 | Compare and contrast productive and unhealthy conflict as it relates to organizational results.

9. _____ is the process by which two or more parties with differing objectives, desires, or perspectives go through to find a mutually agreeable solution.

10. What are some of the key dimensions of "good conflict"?

12.5 | Develop a strategic plan to increase team performance.

11. Which of the following is *not* a way to make meetings more effective?
    a. Always move forward with a planned meeting, even if there is no defined purpose.
    b. Set an agenda and distribute it ahead of the meeting.
    c. Set time limits for the meeting.
    d. Find ways to discourage lateness.

12. Although financial incentives are part of the equation, recognition is not always about _____.

CHAPTER EXERCISE

The Shoebox Exercise

This exercise will help you to understand the difference between individual, group, and team performance.

Step 1—Individual Performance. Your instructor will show each individual in the class the inside of a shoebox filled with 30 to 40 miscellaneous items. You will have 3 seconds to observe the items and remember as many of them as you can. The instructor will then ask everyone in the class how many of the items they can remember. Each person will respond with a number of items (without actually naming them) that he or she can remember. Responses are given based on the honor system. Your instructor will record the maximum, minimum, and average number of items on the board or screen.

Step 2—Ad Hoc Group Performance. Now form a group of three to five people with other members of your class. Talk together and come up with a list of items (no duplications) from the box that you can collectively recall. The instructor then asks each group how many items they were able to list and record

the maximum, minimum, and average number of items for the groups on the board or screen.

Step 3—Organized Team Performance. Groups must put away their list of items. You will be allowed to look in the box for another 3 seconds, but this time as an organized team. Your team will have a few minutes to create a strategy and organize your efforts. The instructor will once again record the maximum, minimum, and average number of items for the team on the board or screen.

Discussion Questions

1. Did performance increase from individual to group to team? If so, why? If not, why not?

2. What strategy did your team implement to take advantage of individual member skills and increase performance?

3. In what ways does an organized team effort lead to better results than indivdual effort or simply pooling information and knowledge in a group?

SELF-ASSESSMENT

Team Member Effectiveness*

Consider a class project team on which you were recently a member. For each statement below, circle the number that best describes your best team member, worst team member, and yourself based on the following scale:

Not at all Accurate	Somewhat Accurate	A little Accurate	Mostly Accurate	Completely Accurate
1	2	3	4	5

1. Did a fair share of the work

Best Team Member	1	2	3	4	5
Worst Team Member	1	2	3	4	5
You	1	2	3	4	5

2. Communicated effectively

Best Team Member	1	2	3	4	5
Worst Team Member	1	2	3	4	5
You	1	2	3	4	5

3. Stayed aware of fellow team members' progress

Best Team Member	1	2	3	4	5
Worst Team Member	1	2	3	4	5
You	1	2	3	4	5

4. Expected the team to succeed

Best Team Member	1	2	3	4	5
Worst Team Member	1	2	3	4	5
You	1	2	3	4	5

5. Had the skills and expertise to do excellent work

Best Team Member	1	2	3	4	5
Worst Team Member	1	2	3	4	5
You	1	2	3	4	5

6. Fulfilled responsibilities to the team

Best Team Member	1	2	3	4	5
Worst Team Member	1	2	3	4	5
You	1	2	3	4	5

7. Exchanged information with teammates in a timely fashion

Best Team Member	1	2	3	4	5
Worst Team Member	1	2	3	4	5
You	1	2	3	4	5

8. Came to team meetings prepared

Best Team Member	1	2	3	4	5
Worst Team Member	1	2	3	4	5
You	1	2	3	4	5

9. Assessed whether the team was making progress as expected

Best Team Member	1	2	3	4	5
Worst Team Member	1	2	3	4	5
You	1	2	3	4	5

10. Believed that the team could produce high-quality work

Best Team Member	1	2	3	4	5
Worst Team Member	1	2	3	4	5
You	1	2	3	4	5

11. Had the skills and abilities that were necessary to do a good job

Best Team Member	1	2	3	4	5
Worst Team Member	1	2	3	4	5
You	1	2	3	4	5

12. Provided encouragement to other team members

Best Team Member	1	2	3	4	5
Worst Team Member	1	2	3	4	5
You	1	2	3	4	5

13. Stayed aware of external factors that influenced team performance

Best Team Member	1	2	3	4	5
Worst Team Member	1	2	3	4	5
You	1	2	3	4	5

14. Believed that the team should achieve high standards

Best Team Member	1	2	3	4	5
Worst Team Member	1	2	3	4	5
You	1	2	3	4	5

15. Had enough knowledge of teammates' jobs to fill in if necessary

Best Team Member	1	2	3	4	5
Worst Team Member	1	2	3	4	5
You	1	2	3	4	5

Scoring:

Add up the numbers you circled for your Best Team Member: _____

Add up the numbers you circled for your Worst Team Member: _____

Add up the numbers you circled for yourself: _____

Reflection Questions:

1. What was the greatest strength of your best team member?

2. What was the greatest weakness of your worst team member?

3. In what ways could you help your worst team member to become a more effective teammate?

4. In what ways could you improve your own team performance to become more like the most effective team member?

*Adapted from Misty L. Loughry, Matthew W. Ohland, and D. DeWayne Moore, "Development of a theory-based assessment of team member effectiveness," *Educational And Psychological Measurement* 67, no. 3 (June 2007): 505–524.

SELF-TEST ANSWER KEY

1. A *team* is a purposeful group formed to accomplish a project, task, or goal. If they are given a clearly defined purpose, ample resources to carry out the task, and the authority to make decisions, teams can be the most powerful driving force within an organization.

2. Formal, informal

3. d.

4. b.

5. b; False. A self-directed team operates without hierarchical management supervision.

6. Quality circle

7. *Forming:* This is the first stage of group development where team members meet each other for the first time and get a feel for the type of team that they have joined. *Storming:* During the second stage, a measure of conflict characterized by resistance or hostility resulting from

two or more parties focusing on and attempting to reconcile differing opinions may arise. *Norming:* Conflict has been resolved, and the team members are settled into their roles. *Performing:* During this final stage, the team is working at its optimal level.

8. b.
9. Negotiation
10. Conflict can be good when emotion is left out of the equation. For conflict to be productive, managers must get buy-in from each team member on the vision that he or she proposes to encourage productive debate that focuses on the future, rather than dwelling on the problems of the past without any backbiting, self-interest, or personal attacks.

11. a.
12. Money. Team members may also be recognized with plaques, gifts, and other forms of non-monetary praise for a job well done.

Notes

_____

_____

_____

_____

_____

_____

_____

_____

_____

_____

_____

_____

_____

_____

PART FIVE

Leading

CHAPTER THIRTEEN

MANAGERS AS LEADERS

Learning Objectives

By the end of the chapter, you will be able to:

13.1 | Define leadership in a global context.

13.2 | Explain how managers gain or lose authority in teams and organizations.

13.3 | Distinguish among four basic types of leaders.

13.4 | Demonstrate the progression of leadership thought and practice.

13.5 | Appraise new and emerging leadership perspectives.

ADDITIONAL RESOURCES

KEY TERMS
IN REVIEW
SELF-TEST
CHAPTER EXERCISE
SELF-ASSESSMENT
SELF-TEST
ANSWER KEY

JP Greenwood/Getty Images

INSIDE THIS CHAPTER

ManagementStory:
Featuring **Julian Wales**

> **Leadership** A process of influence aimed at directing behavior toward the accomplishment of objectives.

➤ Not every leader is asked to be a manager, but every manager must be a leader.

• **Leadership in a Global Economy**
  ➤ Companies now are more reliant on innovation, creativity, and getting their products and services to the market quicker.
  ➤ Businesses are cutting costs and distributing their workforces to stay competitive.
    ■ Approximately 2.5 million people work from home.
  ➤ Until fairly recently, face-to-face contact was largely agreed to be the best method of communicating and motivating employees.
    ■ Now, social networking and virtual communication have opened up communication on a global scale.

13.1 | MANAGERS AS LEADERS

13.1 | **Define** leadership in a global context.

"A man who wants to lead the orchestra must turn his back on the crowd."

—Max Lucado

In the previous chapter, we looked at teams and their dynamics. Once the team is formed and working toward a goal, how can a manager motivate the members of a team to achieve better results consistent with the company's mission and strategy? This is **leadership**, the process of influence aimed at directing behavior toward the accomplishment of objectives.[1] Those people who use critical thinking to successfully influence others to get positive organizational results through motivation and communication are referred to as *leaders*.

How do we identify leaders? Close your eyes and picture the ideal leader in your mind. How tall is this person? What gender are they? What ethnicity is this person? How smart is he or she? How does this person act? Is this person good looking? Does this picture change if we vary the criteria slightly? Picture a leader of a technology company. Picture a leader of a nonprofit company that serves underprivileged children. Picture a military leader. Picture a leader of a multinational company. Picture a leader of a start-up company based in a garage with only one other partner.

These images are the icons of leadership, as you define them. Societal norms, influenced by such things as the environment and media, inform how we make assumptions on who can be an effective leader. Is this a false premise? In many ways, yes. Understanding these assumptions and the classically associated images that employees, managers, and companies have regarding leadership can enable you to reconsider how you perceive yourself and others as potential and effective leaders.

Over the past century, management and leadership theory has sought to understand these perceptions and increase organizational performance through improving managers' capacity to lead. Researchers have discovered that leadership enables managers to make a difference in organizations, communities, and people's lives by increasing production, exceeding company profit expectations, keeping employees motivated through tough times, connecting company values to community needs to increase customer loyalty, and inspiring employees to achieve the best possible results given any particular situation.

As an inspirational example, let's meet Kelly Flatley, Founder and former CEO of Bear Naked, the growth company that has made a big difference in the consumer package goods industry.

Kelly Flatley learned during her meteoric rise that leading, one of the primary functions of management, was necessary in order to increase daily production from 100 pounds of granola in her parents' kitchen to over 40,000 pounds a day in a manufacturing facility by 2007.[2] As a manager, overseeing this process required *communicating* the company's philosophy of "unprocess—simplify—enjoy," so all employees, customers, distributors, suppliers, and retailers were *motivated* to help Bear Naked achieve its goal of becoming the number one granola company in the world.[3] Some of the ways that Flatley and the other managers at Bear Naked provide this leadership is by holding daily, weekly, and monthly meetings that are concise and

Voices of Management

Kelly Flatley,
Founder of Bear Naked[4]

I was just out of college and looking for something to be passionate about. After an "ah-ha" moment during a trip to Paris, I realized that in college my roommates and friends loved my granola and more importantly I loved making it for them. When I went home, I started baking granola in my parents' kitchen. This was in 2001. The next eight years were fast, fun, and fulfilling, all culminating in selling the business in 2009 to the Kellogg Company. I was 29 years old.

I don't know that I ever looked in the mirror and said, 'Kelly, you are a leader.' But to effectively manage and grow the business, I had to be. As a manager and leader, I began to believe in the power of the following: 1) believe, 2) work really hard, 3) take risks, 4) learn constantly and from everyone, 5) go with my gut, 6) stick with what I love, 7) be bold, 8) don't listen to the naysayers, and 9) connect my work with my passions. To be able to do these things every day, it boiled down to two things: Trust and Courage. First, I had to trust myself and then build trust in others. Second,

it simply took courage to "go for it" and inspire the people around to believe in the possibility of Bear Naked, as a food and lifestyle philosophy.

Company Profile

Name: Bear Naked (owned by Kellogg Company)

Founded: 2002

Founders: Kelly Flatley and Brendan Synnott

Philosophy: Un-process—simplify—enjoy

Fun Facts: Bear Naked was sold to Kellogg Company in 2009 for approximately $60 million, making both Flatley and Synnott multimillionaires before the age of 30. During the early stage of the company, distributers would not sell them ingredients because the company was too small. They bought so much honey and almonds at their local Costco that they were awarded "Customer of the Month" in 2003. ∎

continuously reinforce the company's philosophy. They give back to the community through a partnership with the Arbor Day Foundation to demonstrate the company's ability to connect actions to their words, and host a national "Live Bear Naked Tour" so that customers, fans, and employees can work together to celebrate the company's philosophy.[5]

Let's look at some of the other things that Kelly Flatley did over the course of a week to motivate and communicate with her team and partners:

A Manager's Calendar . . . Kelly Flatley, Co-Founder of Bear Naked[6]

Monday, 7:00 a.m. Meet with direct reports to share weekend stories about "unprocess—simplify—enjoy," last week's individual and team accomplishments, and specific goals for the coming week.

Monday, 3:00 p.m. Call distributor to thank them for keeping up with increased volume and working with the company on payment terms during their expansion.

Tuesday, 9:30 a.m. Launch quality contest with new manufacturing team in Michigan.

Tuesday, 4:30 p.m. Provide one-on-one coaching and mentorship to a high-performing manager with potential for executive growth.

Wednesday, 11:30 a.m. Impromptu meeting with team to celebrate the company securing a large order from a major grocery-store chain and inform them of the need to increase next month's output by 50 percent.

Wednesday, 6:00 p.m. Send communication to entire team with a plan on how to increase next month's production, without putting unfair burden on any one team member.

Thursday, 8:30 a.m. Host conference call with all managers to see if there are any questions or recommendations regarding the plan sent the previous night.

Thursday, 4:00 p.m. Distribute quality results via email to the entire executive team and recognize the teams that exceeded company standards.

Friday, 4:45 p.m. Surprise visit to the team in California to congratulate them on dramatically improving their quality scores.

Traditionally, "leaders" have been perceived as being different from "managers." Yet, as we have seen through Kelly Flatley's leadership style, to successfully attain an organizational goal, managers must communicate and motivate. It is helpful to realize that not every leader is asked to be a manager, but every manager must be a leader. This makes leadership every manager's business.

Leadership in a Global Economy

During the last decade, the stock market and global economy has been defined by a turbulent series of successes and failures. Companies now are more reliant on innovation, creativity, and getting their products and services to the market quicker. Business competition is fierce, with technology enabling more entrepreneurs to offer consumers greater alternatives. With these environmental forces, businesses are cutting costs and distributing their workforces to stay competitive. Currently, approximately 2.5 million people work from home, with an estimated 40 percent of the U.S. workforce, or 50 million people working from home at least part-time.[7] With these turbulent new dynamics, how do managers adjust and adapt their leadership style to accommodate for these unstable, rapidly changing markets and work conditions? Or, simply put, what is the future of leadership?

Julian Wales has recently been hired as a group leader overseeing the European region for Upstream Fisheries, a company that farm-raises fish using organic food and environmentally friendly practices. The business was set up in response to the alarmingly low levels of fish in the ocean due to aggressive farming and climate change. Known for its strong corporate culture and effective leadership, the company is growing quickly and developing production facilities in a dozen regions around the world. The company's CEO identified the southern tip of Spain as an ideal market region to test a sustainable strategy. This involves reclaiming previously drained wetlands and reflooding them to create a natural ecosystem. As the water comes directly from the ocean, the fish feed on algae and other smaller fish, which helps them grow and multiply. Pollution is nonexistent because the natural plant life filters out chemicals and other pollutants.

It sounds like the perfect plan to promote sustainability and protect the endangered species of fish, yet the initial team has had difficulties producing results. The CEO sees the project in Spain as a core part of the company's future and gives Julian a clear directive, "Produce results now, with no additional resources. Once you show the team can produce, we will invest in new technologies and facility enhancements that your predecessor said the team is requesting. What the team needs is strong leadership—go show them who is in charge."[8]

Julian has been asked to lead a globalized company and motivate the team to achieve successful results. But what does it mean to be a leader? The concept of leadership still remains a highly debated topic. Is there such a thing as a "born leader"? Or is it a learned skill? Are there very few true leaders or are there millions of them dormant around us? The modality of communication has had an impact on leadership and how leaders operate within organizations. Until fairly recently, face-to-face contact was largely agreed to be the best method of communicating and motivating employees. However, with the rapid progression of Internet technologies, organizations are changing the way that they are running their businesses. Social networking and virtual communication have opened up communication on a global scale, and yet they bring about their own challenges. Obstacles such as cultural differences, lack of cohesiveness within teams, and technical difficulties that arise from working over long distances, are all issues that are currently faced by the modern-day leader. As a result, the modality of communication has had a significant impact on leadership styles and behavior, leading to new leadership theory constructs.

Leaders running globalized companies are affected by external political, resource, economic, and social forces that can significantly change management challenges and

LECTURE ENHANCER:

13.2 How Leaders Gain Authority

✓ **Power**—the ability to influence

✓ *Positional Power*—power that is given because they relate to the powers that are granted because of a manager's type and ability to positively or negatively affect someone through resource allocation or disciplinary measures

   ✓ **Legitimate**—the influence that a manager has because of their title inside of an organization or status in a community

   ✓ **Reward**—an influential ability to positively impact a team member through resources, preferred schedules, and additional status

   ✓ **Coercive**—how a manager influences people through the threat of or actual negative consequences for undesired actions

✓ *Personal Power*—powers that are obtained by being perceived as likable and well-informed

© Kristian Buus/In Pictures / Corbis

opportunities. As we discussed in Chapter 5, these principles rely on managers understanding *culture*. And to lead effectively, managers motivate their teams by understanding their team members' cultural differences, dynamics, and dimensions.

For organizations to achieve results in today's global economy, leaders must understand how to communicate, motivate, and achieve goals effectively while working with team members with different cultural and ethnic backgrounds, ages, genders, and sexual orientations. As we journey through this chapter, we will explore these factors and also ask, "Through this cultural understanding, how do leaders apply leadership theory and practice to achieve more effective or efficient results?" This understanding begins with an appreciation of the power that leaders possess.

13.2 | HOW LEADERS GAIN AUTHORITY

13.2 | Explain how managers gain or lose authority in teams and organizations.

When Julian arrives to start his job as a group leader at Upstream Fisheries, he might be expected to wield a certain level of power in order to motivate the team and get them on board with his ideas. **Power** is the ability to influence. Leaders have powers that are given and some that are earned. Most leaders will wield power, but how this power is manifested can differ from leader to leader. The powers that are given are called **positional powers** because they relate to the powers that are granted because of a manager's position and ability to affect someone positively or negatively through resource allocation or disciplinary measures. Managers also have **personal powers** that are obtained by being perceived as likable and well informed.[9] A combination of these powers determine a manager's capacity to have people listen when he or she is communicating and influence the team's actions when they are leading a team in pursuit of a goal. Understanding how to use both positional and personal powers effectively, thoughtfully, and judiciously is essential for managers.

Positional Power

There are three kinds of positional power: *legitimate*, *reward*, and *coercive*. **Legitimate power** refers to the influence that a manager has because of his or her title inside an organization or status in a community. **Reward power** is an influential ability to affect a team member positively through resources, preferred schedules, and additional status. Finally, **coercive power** is the ability that a manager has to influence people through the threat of or actual negative consequences for undesired actions.[10]

Personal Power

There are two kinds of personal power: *referent* and *expert*. **Referent power** is based on a manager's appealing traits or resources, such as charisma or the ability to offer an employee a promotion. **Expert power** is derived from perceived knowledge, skill, or competence, such as a manager, skilled in computer programming, who has expert power within a software development team.[11] An interesting example of personal power is Bill Ford, Jr., chairman of the board of Ford Motor Company.

After graduating from Princeton University and before attending graduate school, Ford worked at the Ford Motor Company in a "variety of positions in manufacturing, sales, marketing, product development and finance."[12] He knew the company from the ground up, an expert power that would later help him gain the respect of his fellow employees. Then on one fateful day, February 1, 1999, the Ford Rouge Powerhouse plant exploded.[13] At the time, Ford, then president and CEO, was at the company's world headquarters, which was close to the burning plant. In a heated conversation with one of his advisors about his desire to go to the plant to offer his support, he was told that "Generals don't go out to the front lines." In a defining moment, Ford snapped back, "Then bust me down to private."[14] This decision captured the hearts of Ford employees and gained him referent power. This is leadership.

✓ **Referent**—is based on a manager's appealing traits or resources, such as charisma or the ability to offer an employee a promotion
✓ **Expert**—derived from perceived knowledge, skill, or competence, such as a manager, skilled in computer programming

Power The ability to influence how others behave. Leaders have powers that are given and some that are earned.

Positional power The influence that is granted because of a manager's type and ability to affect someone positively or negatively through resource allocation or disciplinary measures.

Personal power Influence that is obtained by being perceived as likable and well-informed.

Legitimate power The influence that a manager has because of his or her title inside an organization or status in a community.

Reward power An influential ability to affect a team member positively through resources, preferred schedules, and additional status.

Coercive power The influential ability to influence people through the threat of or actual negative consequences for undesired actions.

Referent power An influence that is based on a manager's appealing traits or resources, such as charisma or the ability to offer an employee a promotion.

Expert power An influence that is derived from perceived knowledge, skill, or competence, such as a manager that is skilled in computer programming has expert power with a software development team.

LECTURE ENHANCER:

13.3 Types of Leaders

✓ **Directive Leadership**—providing specific task-focused directions, giving commands, assigning goals, close supervision and constant follow-up

✓ **Transactional leadership**—focuses on the creation of reward contingencies and exchange relationships resulting in a calculative compliance on the part of followers

Directive leadership involves providing specific, task-focused directions, giving commands, assigning goals, close supervision, and constant follow-up.

Transactional leadership focuses on the creation of reward contingencies and exchange relationships that result in a calculative compliance on the part of followers.

Transformational leadership involves creating and communicating a higher-level vision in a charismatic way that elicits an emotional response and commitment from the followers.

Empowering leadership A style of leadership that emphasizes employee self-influence processes rather than hierarchical control processes and actively encourages followers to take ownership of their own behaviors and work processes.

✓ **Transformational leadership**—creating and communicating a higher-level vision in a charismatic way that elicits an emotional response and commitment from the followers

➤ Max Weber—German sociologist
  ✓ *Charismatic authority*—a person that motivates employees to exceed expected performance through their inspiring behaviors

✓ **Empowering leadership**—emphasizes employee self-influence processes rather than hierarchical control processes and actively encourages followers to take ownership of their own behaviors and work processes
  ✓ *SuperLeadership*—the process of leading others to lead themselves

Leaders hold power in organizations and can have a positive and negative impact on employees and the overall community. In the next section, we will describe specific theories and techniques that enable managers to communicate with and motivate their teams more effectively.

13.3 | TYPES OF LEADERS

13.3 | **Distinguish** among four basic types of leaders.

Through the years, leadership theorists have identified a number of distinct leadership approaches and styles. A considerable portion of this research has been effectively summarized in a typology of leadership approaches originally presented by Charles C. Manz and Henry P. Sims, Jr.,[15] and expanded upon and refined by others.[16] Within this typology, each of four leadership archetypes represents a distinct leadership perspective that is well established within the leadership research.

Directive leadership involves providing specific, task-focused directions, giving commands, assigning goals, close supervision, and constant follow-up. This approach to leadership employs position power or legitimate power to exert influence over followers. **Transactional leadership** focuses on the creation of reward contingencies and exchange relationships that result in a calculative compliance on the part of followers. The transactional leadership approach strives to reinforce desirable behaviors with rewards that are perceived to be equitable and attractive by followers. **Transformational leadership**, often contrasted with transactional leadership, involves creating and communicating a higher-level vision in a charismatic way that elicits an emotional response and commitment from the followers. German sociologist Max Weber (1864–1920) suggested that leaders had *charismatic authority* and were born with "heroism or exemplary character."[17] A charismatic leader in business is a person that motivates employees to exceed expected performance through their inspiring behaviors. Typical transformational leadership traits include vision, inspirational communication/motivation, intellectual stimulation, and individualized consideration. Finally, **empowering leadership** emphasizes employee self-influence processes rather than hierarchical control processes and actively encourages followers to take ownership of their own behaviors and work processes. This approach to leadership has been called "SuperLeadership" and has been defined as the process of leading others to lead themselves.[18]

Let's return to our case study and follow Group Leader Julian Wales as he works to meet his goal of raising morale and boosting production levels at Upstream Fisheries. Julian is eager to get to know the Upstream team and find out what makes them tick. His first objective is to become acquainted with the various leadership styles adopted by each shift team leader and acquire an understanding of how each leader is perceived by the respective team members.

Upstream Fisheries processes 1 million pounds of fish each year and runs three shifts each day, with about 50 employees on each shift. These results are 25 percent less than comparable regional production facilities. Vikas Singh, Liam Nelson, and Maribel Gonzalez are the shift leaders, and all come from the company's successful California facility. The shift leaders were selected by the company's vice president of operations because of their experience with the company and previous successes. All the shift leaders have worked for the company for several years and are close friends. They enjoy working at Upstream and believe that they are making a difference in the industry with the vision for this new project.

The day after his arrival, Julian sits down with team members and shift leaders to get a better understanding of the operation. In preparation for these meetings, Julian had requested that the shift leaders and he take a leadership style self-assessment and share it with the group. These are the findings:

Julian Wales, Upstream Fisheries, Group Leader Julian is unhurried, deliberate, and stable. He usually acts according to an established process. Cooperative, easygoing, and agreeable, he gets on well with others, and is a focused, uncritical listener. A relatively private individual, it takes him some extra time to connect to and trust new people. He's serious, reserved, and not inclined to change.

Vikas Singh, Upstream Fisheries, First-Shift Leader Vikas is careful with rules. He's precise, by the book, fast-paced, and literal when interpreting instructions, schedules, and results. Detail-oriented and thorough, he works to ensure that things don't fall through the cracks, and follows up to ensure that they're done properly and on time. Eager for results, his drive for implementation can lead to him taking control of a situation easily.

Maribel Gonzalez, Upstream Fisheries, Second-Shift Leader As Maribel connects quickly with others, she's open and sharing of herself. She builds and uses relationships to get work done, and enthusiastically persuades and motivates others by considering their points of view and adjusting her delivery. Similar to Vikas, she is also careful with rules and is precise, by the book, fast-paced, and literal when interpreting instructions, schedules and results. Driven to achieve operational efficiencies, she thinks about what needs to be done and how it can be done as fast as possible while maintaining a high-quality outcome. She is also impatient with routines.

Liam Nelson, Upstream Fisheries, Third-Shift Leader Liam connects quickly with others and is motivated to build and use relationships to get work done. Like Maribel, he is open and easily shares information about himself. Expressive, effusive, and outgoing, he talks a lot, and very quickly. He is also collaborative and works almost exclusively with and through others. Relatively independent when taking action on his own ideas, he resourcefully works around most obstacles.

Applying the Leadership Typology

As Julian reads the descriptions to the group, the reaction is much amusement. Judging by the way they are smiling and nodding, all the team members enjoy hearing the descriptions of the shift leaders. During this conversation and a follow-up observation of each shift, Julian concludes the following characteristics for each of the shifts, subordinates, and their three respective leaders:

Directive Leader Vikas—"Dead Head" Vikas is the team leader and believes in a "paint-by-numbers" process, whereby every action and process is clearly explained and posted with pictures and instructions at each microstep on the production line. He takes a directive approach. Team members laugh and groan at how easy and boring it is to do their jobs, saying, "You could be dead in the head and do this job." Vikas obsessively follows up with each team member to increase production, offering detailed advice on how to improve each little step on the production line. In general, the team members like Vikas and believe that he cares about increasing results and doing a good job. However, sometimes they feel like he is disconnected and doesn't really understand how "bloody boring" it is to do their job.

Transactional Leader Maribel—"Cake Walk" The team on Maribel's shift is responsible for transporting the fish from the maze of ponds and conducting a quality assurance test on the production process. Maribel knows this process well and truly enjoys coaching the team for continuous improvement. She takes a transactional approach. At least once a week, she hosts "deep dive" meetings, where the team contributes thoughts on how to improve, and normally at least a couple of their ideas are implemented. A real motivator, Maribel often refers to the complex process as a "piece of cake" and celebrates with a cake party for the team each month if they reach their goals. Her team respects her for taking the time to coach them one-on-one. Recently, she has recommended team members for positions on other shifts, but then she has been criticized when they don't perform the way she had said they would.

Transformational Leader Liam—"Sterling Striker" Liam really cares about his team; he even started the company's soccer team so they could have fun together outside work. He routinely invites the team to join him after their shift at a local pub. He takes a transformational approach to team management. Most fish farms raise fish in tanks inside greenhouses, but Upstream manages hundreds of small outside ponds to produce sustainable fish. This shift is responsible for identifying the best yield from the hundreds of ponds and

Trait perspective A system of ideas that focuses on identifying effective leaders through personal characteristics that are difficult to or cannot be learned.

---

changing the production to accommodate the different fish being processed. This approach has been great for marketing, but difficult for the production team. The company does use procedures to manage this process, but it rarely works, and the shift team is constantly solving problems. The team routinely complains to Vikas after the shift to figure out a better way of managing the process.

Empowering Leader Julian—"Super Leader" After observing all the shifts and talking with team members, Julian struggles to make thoughtful recommendations. Each of the shift leaders brings special talents and perspectives to the company, and he wishes that they could just be wrapped up into one composite leader. Now there's a thought . . .

In an attempt to empower his team with a shared sense of purpose, Julian implements a private social network for all the shifts, where employees can communicate and collaborate with each other. This is akin to having a social media website that only their company employees can access.

When Julian reveals this communication strategy to the shift leaders, he shares his ideas for empowering their behaviors and leadership efforts, where the sum of the leadership team can be significantly greater than each individual. A part of this strategy requires ensuring that each leader has the autonomy and ability to focus on their core strengths. Using the leadership typology as a framework, Julian believes that each of the shift leaders can focus on the leadership approach to which are most inclined, yet he must also ensure that they see and recognize the power and value of each.

Having presented the team with his ideas, Julian discusses the company's mission, performance, and vision, and which member will be the "champion" for each one. Eventually, it is decided that Vikas will be the mission champion. He is responsible for ensuring that the company's mission, which is its commitment to sustainability, is not lost or mitigated because of daily operational challenges. Maribel has agreed to be the performance champion, overseeing the implementation of performance development and recognition systems to ensure financial and operational goal achievement. Finally, Liam is the vision champion, ensuring that the latest technologies and progressive marketing strategies are used. In addition, Liam will be responsible for motivating the employees and monitoring employee turnover. Everyone seems excited by Julian's empowering leadership approach. As Julian explains, "The four of us will continually work together to ensure that every employee has a voice and access to enact positive change for the company. We will be successful when our employees are leading themselves!"

13.4 | *THE EVOLUTION OF LEADERSHIP*

13.4 | Demonstrate the progression of leadership thought and practice.

How has leadership evolved over time? As we have explored, the topic of leadership has been much scrutinized over the last century. The following leadership theories offer managers, like those at Upstream Fisheries, philosophies and practices to apply concepts thoughtfully and change their behavior to create more effective and efficient results.

The Trait Perspective

In the early 20th century, research began to emerge on the topic of leadership, primarily as a result of an interest in determining the attributes of great leaders, such as Mohandas Gandhi, Winston Churchill, Abraham Lincoln, Alexander the Great, and Julius Caesar. These investigations established the **trait perspective**, a system of ideas that focuses on identifying effective leaders through personal characteristics that are difficult to obtain or cannot be learned. Between 1904 and 1974, leadership theorist R. M. Stogdill conducted a series of leadership studies and suggested that there was a significant connection between effective leadership and the following personal traits: achievement, cooperativeness, influence, initiative, insight, persistence, responsibility, self-confidence, sociability, and tolerance.[19]

Although some dismiss these investigations as outdated, modern experts continued to explore the usefulness of these theories. For example, in 1959, R. D. Mann conducted similar studies as Stoghill and identified a strong connection between effective leadership and performance with the following personality traits: adjustment, conservatism, dominance, extraversion, intelligence, and masculinity.[20] Then in 1986, inspired by these developments, researchers R. G. Lord, C. L. DeVader, and G. M. Alliger suggested that dominance, intelligence, and masculinity were traits that followers associated strongly with effective leadership.[21] Lord et al. advanced the conversation on leadership by suggesting that classically associated "Great Man" traits, such as dominance, intelligence, and masculinity, can be seen as discriminatory and, more disturbingly, these trait judgments are being perpetuated by both leaders *and* followers.[22]

"Great Man" Leaders

"A prince should earnestly endeavor to gain the reputation of kindness, clemency, piety, justice, and fidelity to his engagements. He ought to possess all of the qualities but still retain such power over himself as to display their opposites whenever it may be expedient."[23] This quote from Machiavelli's *The Prince* is a classic portrait of the qualities that make up a **"Great Man"** leader, who is a person born into a position of power and authority and seen by some as having a divine right to assume power. Owing to the preponderance of male leaders throughout history, this concept was called "Great Man" leaders, although there has been a significant shift in mentality in recent years owing to the rising numbers of women leaders. Seven common leadership traits have been identified for women leaders, as illustrated in Figure 13-1.[24]

"Great Man" icons are usually associated with royalty, military leaders, religious idols, and politicians such as John F. Kennedy, who came from a prominent, wealthy family. Knowing that most of us are not born into family fortunes and global business empires, this led leadership thinkers to look at the *characteristics* or *personality traits* that leaders seem to be born with. The major leadership traits researched over the past century can be condensed into five dominant traits, as shown in Figure 13-2.

Emotional Intelligence

In an attempt to develop a leadership trait theory that could be tied to measurable organizational results, Daniel Goleman popularized a concept known as *emotional intelligence (EI)* in his 1995 book *Emotional Intelligence: Why It Can Matter More Than IQ.* Similar to the major leadership traits, his studies explore four major emotional factors that drive leadership performance: 1) self-awareness: ability to be aware of our own emotions and make "gut decisions"; 2) self-management: ability to have power over one's own emotions; 3) social awareness: ability to be aware of, comprehend, and react to others'

4. Relationship management—ability to influence and cooperate with others, even through conflict

- **The Behavioral Perspective**
- ✓ **Behavioral Perspective**—connects what managers do and their ability to influence others
  - Focused on *task* and *relationship*
  - ➤ The Ohio State Studies
    - Leaders have two dominant sets of behaviors that predict success—*consideration* and *initiating structure.*
  - ➤ The University of Michigan Studies
    - Studied parallel thoughts with a focus on how leaders' behaviors affected small group performance.

> **"Great Man" leader** A person born into a position of power and authority and seen by some as having a divine right to power.

  - Leaders focus their behavior to achieve group performance in two ways—*employee oriented* and *production oriented*
  - ➤ The Managerial Grid
    - Designed by Robert R. Blake and Jane S. Mouton to demonstrate how managers balance their concerns for *results* and *people* to attain organizational goals
    - Represents leadership into one of five styles: impoverished (1,1), authority-compliance (9,1), middle-of-the-road (5,5), country club (1,9), and team (9,9)
    - Figure 13.3—The Managerial Grid

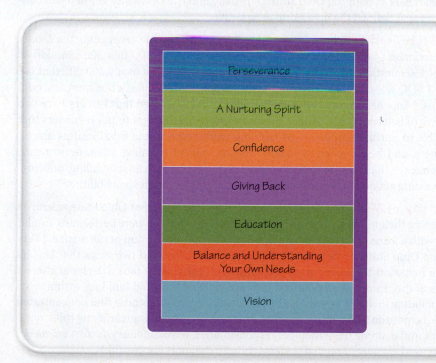

Figure 13-1
Seven Traits of Women Leaders
Women leaders have been identified as possessing seven main leadership traits including perseverance, confidence, and vision.

Perseverance
A Nurturing Spirit
Confidence
Giving Back
Education
Balance and Understanding Your Own Needs
Vision

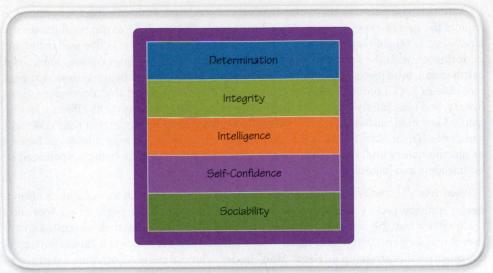

Source: Adapted from P. Northouse, *Leadership: Theory and Practice*, 4th ed. (Thousand Oaks, CA: Sage Publications, 2007), p. 19.

> **Behavioral perspective** The behavioral perspective connects what managers do to their ability to influence others.

emotions; and 4) relationship management: ability to influence and cooperate with others, even through conflict.[25] Some have disregarded Goleman's theories as "pop psychology," but many organizations have benefitted from the EI model.

Overall, the trait perspective has been criticized for being too limited. According to trait theory, to be a leader, you needed to be born into a position and/or have personality characteristics that set you apart.

The Behavioral Perspective

The **behavioral perspective** connects what managers do to their ability to influence others. There are two primary behaviors that researchers have focused on within this perspective: *tasks* (behaviors that help team members achieve goals) and *relationships* (behaviors that enable team members be satisfied with one another and their situation).

The behavioral perspective significantly increased our understanding of how leading applies to all managers. How did leadership thought get past the notion that leaders were born or had certain abilities that allowed them to perform well? During the 1950s, independent researchers at both the Ohio State University and the University of Michigan conducted studies that defined the behavioral perspective.

The Ohio State Studies Researchers at Ohio State conducted a survey using the *Leader Behavior Description Questionnaire*, commonly referred to as LBDQ. This questionnaire is composed of 150 questions and was designed by compiling a list of over 1,800 different behaviors. The LBDQ was completed by hundreds of people in the military, business, and educational fields.[26] So what did the researchers find? They determined that leaders have two dominant sets of behaviors that predict success. *Consideration* refers to the behaviors that leaders exhibit to nurture employees by building trust, respect, and relationships among team members, and being generally likable. The second set is called *initiating structure*, which are behaviors that are oriented around achieving tasks, such as scheduling, prioritizing and organizing actions, and clarifying team member roles and responsibilities.[27]

The University of Michigan Studies During the same time that Ohio State scientists were conducting their research, University of Michigan researchers were performing similar studies, but with a focus on how leaders' behaviors affected small group performance.[28] Very similar to the Ohio State studies, the Michigan research identified two ways that leaders focused their behaviors to achieve group performance. Leaders that took a personal interest in the needs of the team and emphasized interpersonal relationship building within team members, including themselves, were called *employee oriented*. And those that concentrated their behaviors more on task completion activities, such as scheduling, clarifying roles, organizing efforts, and defining team member responsibilities, were called *production oriented*.[29] The study showed *employee-oriented* leaders tended to be more successful.[30]

The Managerial Grid In the early 1960s, management researchers Robert R. Blake and Jane S. Mouton designed the *Managerial Grid* to demonstrate how managers balance their concerns for *results* and *people* to attain organizational goals.[31] This model plots a leader's intensity for results (x-axis) and people (y-axis) from 1 to 9. So if a leader is very concerned about achieving results and not worried about the people on the team, they would score a 9,1 (Results, People). As you can see in Figure 13-3, the Managerial Grid then separates leadership into one of five styles: impoverished (1,1), authority-compliance (9,1), middle-of-the-road (5,5), country club (1,9), and team (9,9).[32]

What do these leadership styles look like in practice? Let's look back at the weekly calendar for Kelly Flatley, founder of Bear Naked; it is clear that she is constantly balancing her concerns for *people* and *results*. It is also clear that the team is not too excited about a new "big order." She was careful to make sure that the announcement of this new order and the need to increase production was immediately followed up with communicating a plan that respected the team's ability to deliver. This is leadership. But we might ask here, "To be an effective leader, is there a right or wrong way to balance management concerns for *people* and *results*?"

To answer this, let's explore what things managers are concerned with when seeking results. In Flatley's week, she focused on ensuring manufacturing quality, measuring workload capacity, establishing new payment terms with a supplier, securing and processing new sales, and expanding the company's production infrastructure. What things did she do to show her concern for the people on her team? She took the time to fly out to California to recognize a team's accomplishments, listen to relevant personal weekend stories from employees, and open lines of communication to get feedback and answer questions on her plans for expanding the team's production capacity. All these things build trust and respect between the team and the leader.

✓ **Transformational Leadership**—uplift and inspire their followers to higher levels of motivation and commitment by creating and communicating a charismatic vision
  ■ Achieved through *idealized influence and inspiration, intellectual stimulation, and individualized consideration*
✓ **Charismatic Leadership**—motivate employees to exceed expected performance through inspiring behaviors
➤ Empowering Leadership
✓ **Empowering Leadership**—encourages followers to take greater responsibility for their own behaviors resulting in a deeper level of commitment based on ownership.
➤ Self-Leadership
✓ **Self-Leadership**—as a process through which people influence themselves to achieve the self-direction and self-motivation necessary to perform
  ■ Divided into three categories: *behavior-focused strategies, natural reward strategies, and constructive thought strategies*

Figure 13-3
The Managerial Grid
The managerial grid determines leadership style by plotting the way leaders balance concern for results and concern for people.

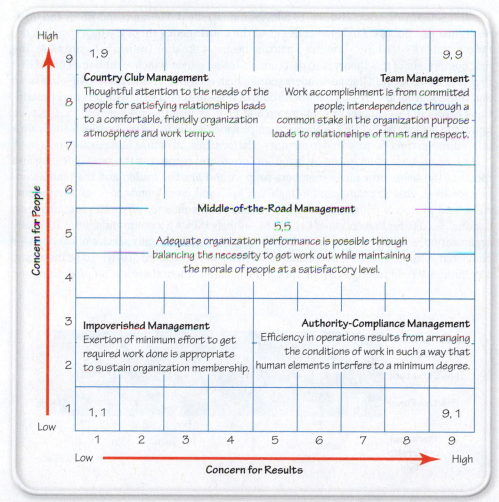

Source: From Robert R. Blake and Anne Adams McCanse, *Grid Solutions*, Copyright © 1991

© EDUARDO MUNOZ/Reuters /Corbis

The Contingency Perspective

So far, we have explored two early leadership perspectives that evolved in the early part of the last century that focused on identifying the traits, characteristics, and behaviors, resulting in effective leadership. However, in a rapidly changing world, with companies and organizations continuously in flux, there is no such thing as one best leadership approach that will be effective in all situations. Indeed, most organizations require multiple leadership styles to function effectively. Building a common language of these approaches is requisite to sustainable organizational leadership. Beginning in the 1960s, researchers have provided a number of contingency theories of leadership that continue to help today's leaders navigate their teams and businesses into the future. **Ursula Burns, Chief Executive Officer Xerox Corporation**

In July 2009, an African-American woman was named CEO of a Fortune 500 company for the first time. While this was a historic occasion in business history, the Xerox Corporation's welcome party for Ursula Burns was brief. The company's previous year had seen revenues drop by 18 percent, and its stock price fell by 50 percent, compounded with debt over $9 billion and greatly weakened opportunities to sell its core hardware products.[33] This is not to suggest that the previous leader produced poor results. The previous CEO, Anne Mulcahy, successfully led the company through near bankruptcy (from losing $273 million in 2000 to earning $91 million in 2005), government investigations, and fierce and rapidly growing competition.[34] In 2009, to Mulcahy's credit, she recognized that the situation called for new leadership given her seniority, and her protégé, Burns, was ready for the challenge.[35] How can leadership theory help us understand this challenge more clearly?

Fiedler's Contingency Theory To address management dilemmas, industrial and organizational psychologist Fred Fiedler designed the **contingency theory**, which matches the most suitable leadership style with a particular business situation (shown in Figure 13-4). The first component of this theory is to determine a leader's style, which is measured on a *Least Preferred Coworker (LPC)* scale. Leaders scoring high on the scale are *relationship motivated*, and those scoring low are *task motivated*; both of these are consistent with previous descriptions earlier in this chapter of relationship and task- or result-focused behaviors. Once we know the leader's style, Fiedler's theory then provides a way to determine the leader's situation through three factors: leader-member relations, task structure, and position power.

Leader-member relations can be "good" or "poor" and represents the general feeling and mood of the team, how much members support and like the leader, and the team's confidence level. *Task structure* can be "high" or "low" and corresponds to level of structure, rules, and protocols defined to complete a task.[36] For a director of youth programs for a regional Society for Prevention of Cruelty to Animals (SPCA), a nonprofit animal advocacy organization, a *high-structured task* would be organizing community service obligations for convicted youth to volunteer at the animal shelter. A *low-structured task* would be managing a community fund-raising event at a local music store where there are no predetermined

> **Contingency theory** A way of thinking that matches the most suitable leadership style with a particular business situation.

Figure 13-4
Fiedler's Contingency Model
Fiedler's contingency model matches different leadership styles with different business situations.

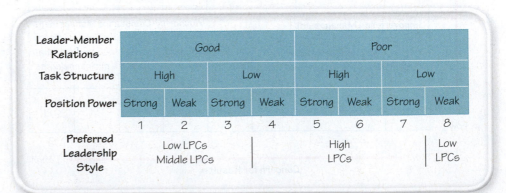

Leader-Member Relations	Good				Poor			
Task Structure	High		Low		High		Low	
Position Power	Strong	Weak	Strong	Weak	Strong	Weak	Strong	Weak
	1	2	3	4	5	6	7	8
Preferred Leadership Style	Low LPCs Middle LPCs				High LPCs			Low LPCs

Source: Adapted from F. E. Fiedler, *A Theory of Leadership Effectiveness* (New York: McGraw-Hill, 1967).

336 *CHAPTER THIRTEEN* **Managers as Leaders**

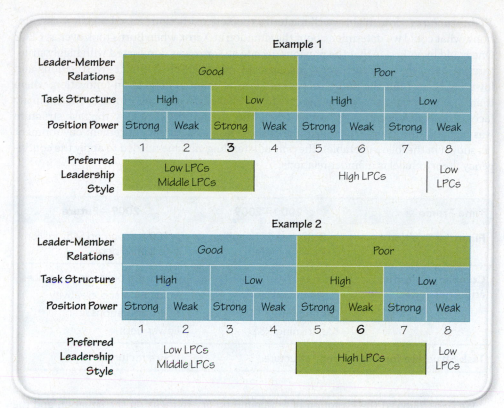

Example 1

Leader-Member Relations	Good				Poor			
Task Structure	High		Low		High		Low	
Position Power	Strong	Weak	Strong	Weak	Strong	Weak	Strong	Weak
	1	2	**3**	4	5	6	7	8
Preferred Leadership Style	Low LPCs Middle LPCs				High LPCs			Low LPCs

Example 2

Leader-Member Relations	Good				Poor			
Task Structure	High		Low		High		Low	
Position Power	Strong	Weak	Strong	Weak	Strong	Weak	Strong	Weak
	1	2	3	4	5	**6**	7	8
Preferred Leadership Style	Low LPCs Middle LPCs				High LPCs			Low LPCs

Figure 13-5
Contingency Model Examples
Contingency model example that catergorizes situational variables on a scale of 1-8.

Source: Adapted from F. E. Fiedler, *A Theory of Leadership Effectiveness* (New York: McGraw-Hill, 1967).

outcomes or procedures to follow.[37] *Position power* can be "strong" or "weak" and refers to the legitimate influences that the leader has, such as position in the company, and their ability to reward or discipline team members.

Applying Contingency Theory So how does this work? Once you assess the three situational variables, the model categorizes the situation on a scale of 1–8. As shown in the first example in Figure 13-5, if a situation has GOOD leader-member relations, LOW task structure, and a leader with STRONG position power, the model categorizes this situation as a 3, which would recommend a Low or Middle LPC leadership style (i.e., task-driven). In the second example, if a situation has POOR leader-member relations, HIGH task structure, and a leader with WEAK position power, the model categorizes this situation as 6, which would recommend a High LPC leadership style (i.e., relationship-driven).[38]

Mulcahy is known as a "charismatic leader;" Burns is a mechanical engineer, celebrated problem solver, and "known for being very frank." For this example, let's assume that Mulcahy scored high on the LPC scale, meaning that she is relationship driven, and Burns scored low on the LPC scale, or is task driven. A medium LPC score refers to a balanced leadership style. How about power? This is easy; being the CEO gives both Mulcahy and Burns "strong power" as a leader. These results are shown in the following table.

Name	Anne Mulcahy	Ursula Burns
Leader Icon	Charismatic leader	Transformative leader
Described As . . .	"a problem-solving optimist who can . . . bring the required players to the table and keep [them] inspired."	"being very frank" and a celebrated problem solver.
LPC Scale	High (Relationship-driven)	Low (Task-driven)
Position Power	Strong	Strong
Member Relations	?	?

Task Structures How might we characterize the Xerox situation? Based on a few assumptions, what could we determine about the situation at Xerox when Burns took over as CEO? One could hypothesize that the previous decade at Xerox was dominated with highly structured tasks for the CEO, such as refinancing debt, managing government investigations, and lowering costs.[39] But the future success of Xerox is going to depend on innovation, where there are many right and wrong answers to the challenges and opportunities the company faces. Consequently, let's suggest that when Mulcahy ran the company, the task structure was high, but the future would be more of a low-task-structure management environment (as shown in the following table). The only outstanding variable needed to apply the contingency theory model is member relations.

Time Frame	2000—2009	2009—Future
Financial Position	In 2000, lost $273 million, $19 billion in debt	In 2009 . . . earned $485 million; $9 billion in debt
Company Priorities and Challenges	Refinancing debt Government investigations Cutting jobs Maintaining R&D	Transform products to services Innovation and creativity Keep operations lean Lower debt
Task Structure for CEO	High structure	Low structure

We have followed the evolution of leadership theory to focus on the situation and the mood of the team, and ensuring that the right leader is matched with the current circumstance. What might be missing? What about the future—the goal or goals the team faces? And what should the leader do when the team hits an obstacle? We have looked at the characteristics of a leader, but what about the characteristics of the team members?

Situational Leadership Model The situational leadership model suggests that different workplace scenarios and levels of follower readiness require different leadership styles. Developed in 1969 by management experts Dr. Paul Hersey and Ken Blanchard, the model focuses on two behavioral dimensions of leadership. The first dimension is *directive* and refers to leader behaviors that enable the team to achieve goals through clear directions, planning tasks, organizing and prioritizing team member actions, and defining a foreseeable path to success. The second dimension, *supportive*, relates to behaviors that encourage positive interpersonal relationships and ensure that the team members are comfortable with the current circumstance. Situational leadership suggests that leaders can achieve better results when they correctly assess their employee's competence and commitment to achieving a goal, referred to as *development level*, and adjust attention levels to being more or less *directive* and *supportive*.[40]

Similar to the Managerial Grid, the situational leadership model, based on these two dimensions, plots four leadership styles as outlined in Figure 13-6: delegating (S4), supporting (S3), coaching (S2), and directing (S1).[41] However, the situational leadership model is fundamentally different from earlier theories for a couple of reasons: 1) it takes into account the followers' readiness, or development level, to achieve a goal, and 2) based on the team's or individual employee's development level, the model suggests that certain leader behaviors are more effective.

Path-Goal Theory Path-goal theory focuses on leadership behaviors that motivate a team through clarification, support, and removal of barriers in pursuit of a goal.[42] Different from the situational leadership model and the contingency theory, path-goal theory seeks to match a leader's style with what the team needs in order to be motivated.[43] This theory has a lot of variables, but its premise is simple. The team is on a path to achieving a goal. The team will hit obstacles in their pursuit of the goal. These barriers can diminish the team's motivation to continue to work to achieve the goal. The leader defines the goal, clarifies the path, removes barriers, and offers support to keep the team motivated as outlined in Figure 13-7.[44]

Path-goal theory A theory that identifies leadership behaviors that motivate a team through clarification, support, and removal of barriers in pursuit of a goal.

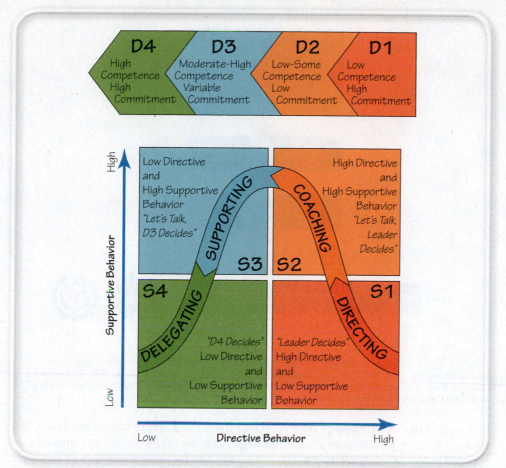

Figure 13-6
Situational Leadership Model
Situational Leadership Model suggesting four leadership styles for managers to use depending on the situation.

Source: From K Blanchard, P. Zigarmi, and D. Zigarmi, *Leadership and the One-Minute Manager: Increasing Effectiveness Through Situational Leadership* (New York: William Morrow, 1985).

There are three major factors that researchers have identified that influence the team's motivation: leader behaviors, team member characteristics, and task characteristics as outlined in Figure 13-8. The leader's behaviors are organized into four categories, including *directive, supportive, participative,* and *achievement-oriented. Team member characteristics* determine how a leader is perceived by the team. These characteristics consist of a team member's *need for affiliation, preference for structure, desire for control,* and *self-perceived level of task ability.* Finally, task characteristics, including *task design, system authority,* and *group norms,* are other factors that can influence the team's motivation.[45]

For path-goal theory to be most useful, leaders cease to view their behaviors as fixed and adapt their behaviors based on the situation. This is different from previous theories

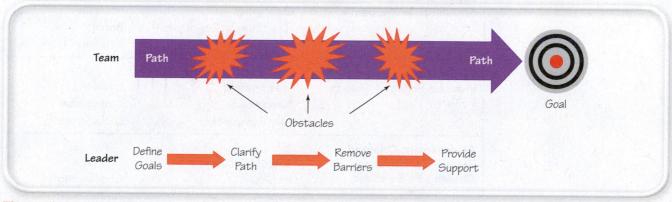

Figure 13-7
Path-Goal Theory Model
Sources: R. House, "Path-Goal Theory of Leadership: Lessons, Legacy, and a Reformulated Theory," *Leadership Quarterly* 7, no. 3 (1996): 323–352; model adapted from P. Northouse, *Leadership: Theory and Practice,* 4th ed. (Thousand Oaks, CA: Sage Publications, 2007).

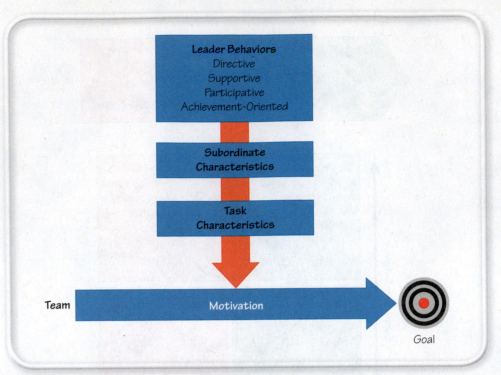

Figure 13-8

Path-Goal Theory Motivation Factors

Path-Goal Theory of motivation states that some leaders have a range of behaviors or styles that they can adapt to certain situations.

Sources: R. House, "Path-Goal Theory of Leadership: Lessons, Legacy, and a Reformulated Theory," *Leadership Quarterly* 7, no. 3 (1996): 323–352; model adapted from P. Northouse, *Leadership: Theory and Practice*, 4th ed. (Thousand Oaks, CA: Sage Publications, 2007).

that suggest that certain leaders have particular styles that apply to certain situations. This allows leaders to pursue more effective strategies actively in the current circumstance, as opposed to feeling helpless if their style is not appropriate for the scenario. So how do we put all of this together into a workable model that is useful in the business world? In Table 13-1, we suggest desirable leadership behaviors based on subordinate and task characteristics.

Table 13-1	Path-Goal Theory Model	
Leader Behavior	**Subordinate Characteristics**	**Task Characteristics**
Directive *Following up, Guiding, Consistency*	Inflexible Controlling	Unclear Complicated Vague Procedures
Supportive *Nurturing, Caring, Gentle*	Disgruntled Need Human Connection	Repetitive Boring Routine
Participative *Involved, Engaged, Sharing Power*	Independent Need Power Like Transparency	Unclear Ambiguous Lacks Structure
Achievement-Oriented *Sets High Expectations, Challenging, Energetic*	Success Focused Hopeful	Complex Challenging Ambiguous

Sources: R. House and R. Mitchell, "Path-Goal Theory of Leadership," *Journal of Contemporary Business* 3 (1974): 81–97; adapted from P. Northouse, *Leadership: Theory and Practice*, 4th ed. (Thousand Oaks, CA: Sage Publications, 2007), p. 134.

Contemporary Perspectives

Although the contingency perspective continues to inform our understanding of effective leadership, a number of contemporary perspectives on leadership have emerged in recent decades. Two of the more popular of these current views of leadership are the transformational/charismatic perspective and the empowering perspective.

Transformational/Charismatic Leadership In contrast to the transactional approach to leadership, which focuses on reward contingencies and catering to the immediate self-interests of followers, **transformational leaders** uplift and inspire their followers to higher levels of motivation and commitment by creating and communicating a charismatic vision.[46] These outcomes are achieved through three primary leader behaviors: idealized influence (charisma) and inspiration, intellectual stimulation, and individualized consideration. Idealized influence and inspiration tend to occur when leaders successfully envision a desired future, communicate how to move forward toward the future, and set high performance expectations while showing confidence and determination. Intellectual stimulation involves the leader's efforts to challenge followers be more creative and innovative in problem solving and decision making. Individualized consideration takes place when leaders attend to the developmental needs of their followers by supporting, coaching, and encouraging them to perform better. Although the concept of **charismatic leadership** has developed separately from transformational leadership, as inspired originally by the writings of Max Weber, these streams are increasingly converging and stabilizing into a single, unified paradigm.

Some of our most famous and successful contemporary leaders clearly exhibit the transformational/charismatic approach. For example, one well-known transformational leader is Sir Richard Branson, the founder and chairman of the Virgin company, who has founded over 360 companies under the Virgin brand and is one of the wealthiest businesspeople in the world. Born into prominence, Branson has some of the qualities of a "Great Man" as a result of his family's position and social stature. But Branson turned this personal good fortune into a multibillion-dollar fortune by being a transformational leader.

The leadership styles above assume a certain level of morality and goodness, but what happens when bad people become great leaders? A great leader with bad personal values is referred to as **pseudotransformational**.[47] This term describes a leader that is effective, yet their primary aims and goals are to seek personal power and wealth or cause harm or even death to others, such as dictators like Adolf Hitler, Benito Mussolini, and Saddam Hussein. These are extreme examples of wrongdoers. Indeed, the business world has many more examples of managers and executives making a difference by focusing on enriching others, and not just themselves.

Empowering Leadership Although the transformational/charismatic approach is perhaps the most popular leadership perspective today, another contemporary leadership perspective has been gaining popularity in recent years. An empowering leader encourages followers to take greater responsibility for their own behavior, resulting in a deeper level of commitment based on ownership.[48] Empowering leadership emphasizes follower self-influence rather than more traditional external control processes. Empowerment is particularly appropriate in today's dynamic organizations, marked by decentralized organizational structures and well-educated and highly skilled knowledge workers. Leaders can empower followers by:

- Fostering initiative and creativity
- Supporting individual decision making
- Giving fewer commands and orders
- Creating independence and interdependence while avoiding dependence
- Allowing mistakes and avoiding punishment
- Listening more while talking less
- Advocating and modeling self-leadership.[49]

Transformational leader A person who inspires employees, companies, and industries to innovate and evolve to achieve great goals.

Charismatic leadership A leadership style characterized by the ability to motivate employees to exceed expected performance through a leader's inspiring behaviors.

Paul Kane / Getty Images

Pseudotransformational A leader who is effective, yet their primary aims and goals are to seek personal power and wealth or cause harm to others.

Self-Leadership Many consider the ability to lead oneself effectively as a necessary prerequisite to leading others. The concept of *self-leadership* may be described as a process through which people influence themselves to achieve the self-direction and self-motivation necessary to perform.[50]

Self-leadership strategies are generally divided into three categories: behavior-focused strategies, natural reward strategies, and constructive thought strategies.[51] *Behavior-focused strategies* include self-observation, self-goal setting, self-rewards, self-correcting feedback, and self-cueing. Self-observation is the examination of behaviors in order to identifying those that need to be changed, enhanced or eliminated. This is done before specific goals and related reward contingencies are developed to energize and direct necessary behaviors. *Natural reward strategies* focus on the enjoyable aspects of task or activity and creating situations in which a person is motivated or rewarded by the task or activity itself. This strategy involves two primary approaches: building more pleasant and enjoyable features into a task or activity so that value is obtained from the task itself and it becomes naturally rewarding, and positively shaping perceptions of an activity by focusing on its rewarding aspects. *Constructive thought strategies* are aimed at reshaping certain key mental processes to facilitate more positive and optimistic thinking patterns and mental processes that can have a significant impact on an individual.

Mike Fuentes/Bloomberg / GettyImages

These strategies include identifying dysfunctional beliefs and assumptions and replacing them with more rational and constructive ones; examining self-talk, defined as what we tell ourselves in order to eliminate excessive negativity and pessimism; and visualizing successful performance or mental imagery, which involves symbolically experiencing behavioral outcomes prior to actual performance.

Herb Kelleher, founder of Southwest Airlines, provides a great example of an empowering leader who was able to create a company of self-leaders committed to sustaining the organization's fun-loving culture.[52] Kelleher founded Southwest Airlines as a low-cost, no-frills, customer-service-focused airline where employees and customers could enjoy themselves. Southwest has been so successful, in part, because the employees took ownership of Kelleher's founding vision. Kelleher is no longer involved in the day-to-day operations of the airline, having stepped down from his role as chairman of the board of directors in 2008, but the culture that he envisioned and helped to create lives on through a committed workforce. Kelleher, who can also be viewed as a transformational/charismatic leader, demonstrates that the various leadership approaches are not mutually exclusive and may, in fact, be blended effectively.

13.5 | *BEYOND TRADITIONAL LEADERSHIP*

13.5 | Appraise new and emerging leadership perspectives.

Transformational and empowering leadership approaches may dominate the current view of what constitutes effective leadership, but a number of new perspectives on leadership are emerging. We highlight three of them: servant leadership, shared leadership, and authentic leadership.

Robert Greenleaf (1904–1990), a former AT&T executive, devised a paradoxical view of an ideal leadership icon called a **servant leader**—one who focuses on the needs, objectives, and aspirations of team members to help them achieve organizational goals.[53] This icon demonstrates an evolution in leadership thought, where leaders now focus on followers and their situation to achieve the best results. This type of leader is ideally suited for the service industry, for the leader's style matches with the organization's mission and values. A convincing example of the power of a servant leader is Colleen Barrett, who was president of Southwest Airlines from 2001–2008. Southwest Airlines is the only airline to have posted profits for 35 consecutive years.[54] In an industry that contends with intense external political, social, and resource dynamics, such as terrorism, security regulations, and fuel prices, this was an impressive performance, led by Barrett.

How did she do it? It is not surprising that she offers the credit to the company's employees. This was revealed when asked about her philosophy of "proactive customer service to our employees," and she responded, "When we have employees who have a problem—or have employees who see a passenger having a problem—we adopt them, and we really work hard to try to make something optimistic come out of whatever the situation is, to try to make people feel good whatever the dilemma is that they're dealing with."[55] This is leadership. But are all leaders suited to this style of leadership? Is it possible that some leaders are more appropriate given the conditions of the team, challenges, and opportunities that their company faces?

Like servant leadership, shared leadership is quite different from more traditional leadership models, in which influence and decision making move in a top-down fashion from the traditional vertical leader to the follower. **Shared leadership** can be viewed as an interactive process that results in the distribution of leadership influence among group members for the purpose of achieving group or organizational goals or both.[56] Shared leadership is a collaborative process in which team members share key leadership roles, including transactional roles, transformational roles, directive roles, empowering roles, and social supportive roles. Shared leadership often takes place in conjunction with delegation processes. For example, one study found that extreme-action medical teams in emergency trauma centers engage in a system of shared leadership that includes a process of "dynamic delegation," whereby senior leaders on the medical team rapidly and repeatedly first delegate and then withdraw the active leadership role from more junior members of the team.[57] Consequently, shared leadership also generally involves employees engaging in effective self-leadership and responsible followership.

Finally, **authentic leadership** includes behaviors that encourage positive psychological capacities, an ethical climate, greater self-awareness, an internalized moral perspective, a balanced processing of information, and self-development.[58] Authentic leaders are aware of and trust their own emotions, motives, complexities, and abilities. They are unbiased and balanced in their processing of information, and consider multiple perspectives and inputs. They engage in behaviors that are true to themselves, staying focused by their own convictions and values while being unencumbered by the expectations of others and the desire to please them. Authentic leaders engage in relational authenticity and transparency, disclosing and sharing information about themselves openly, truthfully, and appropriately in their relationships with others. Harvard management professor and former Medtronic CEO Bill George is a keen proponent of authentic leadership, suggesting that the most effective leaders are those that find their "true north," an internal compass that serves as a guide through life and is founded on what is most important and meaningful.[59]

What do these leadership models really mean for today's 21st-century leaders? For the first time in history, communication is global on a virtual scale, with the inception of social networking sites, Twitter, blogging, video-sharing, and much more. Facebook, in particular, is arguably the Internet's most influential tool, as it brings massive numbers of people from different social groups together with one application, and on a worldwide scale. Advanced technology has given consumers, workers, and citizens a chance to be heard. In short, millions of people across the planet have been given a voice and the ability to communicate with others. But what does all this mean for today's leaders? It means that they need to adapt their leadership skills, reassess what it means to be a leader in the 21st century, and find different ways to engage with their teams on a virtual level and across all generations. Indeed, there is a whole new generation that has been brought up with tools like Facebook and Twitter, where freedom of speech and advanced technology is second nature to them.

Shared leadership A collaborative process in which team members share key leadership roles.

purpose of achieving group or organizational goals or both
■ Takes place in conjunction with delegation processes
✓ **Authentic Leader**—people who know themselves well and are able to stay true to their beliefs and values

Authentic leadership A style of leadership that includes behaviors that encourage positive psychological capacities, an ethical climate, greater self-awareness, an internalized moral perspective, a balanced processing of information, and self-development.

© Michael Ainsworth/Dallas MorningNews / Corbis

Research @ Work

Combat Training for Business Leaders[60]

Former Navy SEAL Rob Roy runs a leadership course called SOT-G that some may consider unconventional. Based on his military combat experience, Roy puts business leaders such as CEOs through their paces during a grueling, 80-hour course where they are tested to their limits. One of the first challenges that the clients face is a 2-mile midnight swim in the inky darkness. Roy believes that physical exercise in tough conditions unites groups, accelerates decision making, and encourages bonding. So, how does Roy define a great leader?

"Great leaders naturally think about the other guys first. That's how you create a sense of loyalty in an organization. Effective leadership is also about listening to people—after all, you won't always have the great ideas."

Roy believes the SEAL training that he has received is applicable to the business world, and particularly to business leaders who regularly make tough decisions: "In business, a great leader is someone who is going to

© Leo Mason / Corbis

step up at a difficult moment and make that next decision. He'll go into it blind, but people will follow him, because they'll know he always has their best interests in mind."

Critical Thinking in the Classroom

As a manager, how would you apply Roy's leadership training course to the business world?

Indeed, this generation often knows more about technology than their own leaders, resulting in clashes in the workplace and complex power issues.

The most cutting-edge leadership theorists have evaluated the effectiveness of the classic leadership icons in order to respond positively to these new conditions. They found that directive and "Great Man" leaders were often too "reliant on fear"; transactional leaders sometimes set a negative organizational culture of "what's in it for me"; and transformational leaders occasionally create unintended consequences of "discouraging independent thinking."[61] As the evolution of leadership theories discussed in this chapter reflects, new leadership models have emerged and continue to emerge, where the primary objective of leaders include "being a servant first," "being true to oneself," and "leading others to lead themselves."[62] As Julian Wales from the Upstream Fisheries case narrative proclaims, "We will be successful when our employees are leading themselves!"

Case**Snapshot**

Chapter 13 Case: Managers as Leaders:
Kazuhiro Tsuga, President of Panasonic Corporation
can be found on pg. 475

ADDITIONAL RESOURCES

KEY TERMS

Authentic leadership A style of leadership that includes behaviors that encourage positive psychological capacities, an ethical climate, greater self-awareness, an internalized moral perspective, a balanced processing of information, and self-development. (p. 343)

Behavioral perspective The behavioral perspective connects what managers do to their ability to influence others. (p. 334)

Charismatic leadership A leadership style characterized by the ability to motivate employees to exceed expected performance through a leader's inspiring behaviors. (p. 341)

Coercive power The influential ability to influence people through the threat of or actual negative consequences for undesired actions. (p. 329)

Contingency theory A way of thinking that matches the most suitable leadership style with a particular business situation. (p. 336)

Directive leadership involves providing specific, task-focused directions, giving commands, assigning goals, close supervision, and constant follow-up. (p. 330)

Empowering leadership A style of leadership that emphasizes employee self-influence processes rather than hierarchical control processes and actively encourages followers to take ownership of their own behaviors and work processes. (p. 330)

Expert power An influence that is derived from perceived knowledge, skill, or competence, such as a manager that is skilled in computer programming has expert power with a software development team. (p. 329)

"Great Man" leader A person born into a position of power and authority and seen by some as having a divine right to power. (p. 333)

Leadership A process of influence aimed at directing behavior toward the accomplishment of objectives. (p. 326)

Legitimate power The influence that a manager has because of his or her title inside an organization or status in a community. (p. 329)

Path-goal theory A theory that identifies leadership behaviors that motivate a team through clarification, support, and removal of barriers in pursuit of a goal. (p. 338)

Personal power Influence that is obtained by being perceived as likable and well-informed. (p. 329)

Positional power The influence that is granted because of a manager's type and ability to affect someone positively or negatively through resource allocation or disciplinary measures. (p. 329)

Power The ability to influence how others behave. Leaders have powers that are given and some that are earned. (p. 329)

Pseudotransformational leader A leader who is effective, yet their primary aims and goals are to seek personal power and wealth or cause harm to others. (p. 341)

Referent power An influence that is based on a manager's appealing traits or resources, such as charisma or the ability to offer an employee a promotion. (p. 329)

Reward power An influential ability to affect a team member positively through resources, preferred schedules, and additional status. (p. 329)

Self-leadership A process through which people influence themselves to achieve the self-direction and self-motivation necessary to perform. (p. 342)

Servant leader A person who focuses on the needs, objectives, and aspirations of team members to help them achieve organizational goals. (p. 342)

Shared leadership A collaborative process in which team members share key leadership roles. (p. 343)

Trait perspective A system of ideas that focuses on identifying effective leaders through personal characteristics that are difficult to or cannot be learned. (p. 332)

Transactional leadership focuses on the creation of reward contingencies and exchange relationships that result in a calculative compliance on the part of followers. (p. 330)

Transformational leadership involves creating and communicating a higher-level vision in a charismatic way that elicits an emotional response and commitment from the followers. (p. 330)

IN REVIEW

13.1 | Define leadership in a global context.

Leaders must understand how to effectively communicate, motivate, and achieve goals with team members with different cultural and ethnic backgrounds, ages, genders, and sexual orientations.

13.2 | Explain how managers gain or lose authority in teams and organizations.

A combination of both *positional powers*, which are granted because of a manager's type and ability to affect someone positively or negatively through resource allocation or disciplinary measures; and *personal powers*, which are obtained by being perceived as likable and well informed, determine a manager's capacity to have people listen when he or she is communicating and influence the team's actions when leading a team in pursuit of a goal. Understanding how to use both positional and personal powers effectively, thoughtfully, and judiciously is essential for managers.

13.3 | Distinguish among four basic types of leaders.

Directive leadership involves providing specific task-focused directions, giving commands, assigning goals, close supervision, and constant follow-up. This approach to leadership employs position power or legitimate power to exert influence over followers. *Transactional leadership* focuses on the creation of reward contingencies and exchange relationships resulting in a calculative compliance on the part of followers. The transactional leadership approach strives to reinforce desirable behaviors with rewards that are perceived to be equitable and attractive by followers. *Transformational leadership*, often contrasted with transactional leadership, involves creating and communicating a higher-level vision in a charismatic way that elicits an emotional response and commitment from the followers. *Empowering leadership* emphasizes employee self-influence processes rather than hierarchical control processes and actively encourages followers to take ownership of their own behaviors and work processes. This approach to leadership has been called "SuperLeadership" in popular media and has been defined as the process of leading others to lead themselves.

13.4 | Demonstrate the progression of leadership thought and practice.

The *"Great Man"* leader is a person that was born into a position of power and authority and seen by some as a divine right. The *behavioral perspective* connects what managers do and their ability to influence others. There are two primary behaviors that researchers have focused on within this perspective: *tasks* (behaviors that help team members achieve goals) and *relationships* (behaviors that enable team members to be satisfied with one another and their situation).

Leaders have two dominant sets of behaviors that predict success. *Consideration* refers to the behaviors that leaders exhibit to nurture employees by building trust, respect, and relationships among team members, and being generally likable. The second set is called *initiating structure*, which are behaviors that are oriented around achieving tasks, such as scheduling, prioritizing and organizing actions, and clarifying team member roles and responsibilities.

Leaders that took a personal interest in the needs of the team and emphasized interpersonal relationship building within team members, including themselves, were called *employee oriented*. And those that concentrated their behaviors more on task completion activities, such as scheduling, clarifying roles, organizing efforts, and defining team member responsibilities, were called *production oriented*.

13.5 | Appraise new and emerging leadership perspectives.

A *servant leader* focuses on the needs, objectives, and aspirations of team members to help them achieve organizational goals. *Shared leadership* can be viewed as an interactive process that results in the distribution of leadership influence among group members for the purpose of achieving group or organizational goals or both. *Authentic leadership* includes behaviors that encourage positive psychological capacities, an ethical climate, greater self-awareness, an internalized moral perspective, a balanced processing of information, and self-development. Authentic leaders are aware of and trust their own emotions, motives, complexities, and abilities.

SELF-TEST

13.1 | Define leadership in a global context.

1. Leadership is the process of _____ aimed at directing behavior toward the accomplishment of objectives.
   a. engagement
   b. motivation
   c. coercion
   d. influence

13.2 | Explain how managers gain or lose authority in teams and organizations.

2. Power is the ability to coerce.
   a. True
   b. False

3. List and define the five sources of power.

13.3 | Distinguish among four basic types of leaders.

4. Which of the following is *not* one of the four basic types of leaders?
   a. Directive
   b. Transformational
   c. Dictatorial
   d. Empowering

5. Transactional leadership involves creating and communicating a higher-level vision in a charismatic way that elicits an emotional response.
   a. True
   b. False

13.4 | Demonstrate the progression of leadership thought and practice.

6. The _____ perspective is a system of ideas that focuses on identifying effective leaders through personal characteristics that are difficult to obtain or cannot be learned.
   a. Trait
   b. Behavioral
   c. Contingency
   d. Cognitive

7. What are the four major components of emotional intelligence (EI)?

8. The Ohio State studies divided leadership behaviors into which of the following two categories?
   a. Employee oriented and production oriented
   b. Consideration and initiating structure
   c. Promotion and inhibiting
   d. Directing and engaging

9. List the five leadership styles shown on the Managerial Grid.

10. Fiedler's contingency theory matches the most suitable leadership style with a particular business situation.
    a. True
    b. False

11. What are the three contingency factors included in Fiedler's contingency theory?

12. The primary contingency factor in the situational leadership model is to be a follower _____.

13. What are the four categories of leader behavior according to the path-goal theory?

14. _____ leadership encourages followers to take greater responsibility for their own behaviors resulting in a deeper level of commitment based on ownership.
    a. Transformational
    b. Committed
    c. Responsible
    d. Empowering

15. List the three basic categories of self-leadership strategies.

13.5 | Appraise new and emerging leadership perspectives.

16. How is servant leadership different from many other leadership approaches?

17. _____ leadership can be viewed as an interactive process that results in the distribution of leadership influence among group members for the purpose of achieving group or organizational goals or both.
    a. Shared
    b. Distributed
    c. Decentralized
    d. Interactive

18. Authentic leadership includes behaviors that encourage positive psychological capacities, an ethical climate, greater self-awareness, an internalized moral perspective, a balanced processing of information, and self-development.
    a. True
    b. False

CHAPTER EXERCISE

The Missing Wrench*

It is nighttime, and a huge aircraft carrier is headed into the wind. Operations are in full swing, with planes being launched and recovered at the rate of one every 75 seconds. This is a training exercise that is being evaluated and scored by a team of external observers, including the carrier group admiral. The aircraft carrier captain is new to his position, having only been in command of the ship for about three weeks. Everyone is aware that the score on the exercise will reflect on his capabilities to lead the ship.

Eventually, the captain, the admiral, and the other observers retire to their quarters, while the operations continue into the night. There is a special tension among the crew, who know how important this operation is to their new captain. Meanwhile, down in the bowels of the ship, a young seaman, an apprentice mechanic, is finishing his shift and checking his tools off on a checklist as he returns them to their cabinet. Suddenly, he feels his stomach tighten. He is missing a wrench. He briefly considers forgetting about it and hitting the sack, but then thinks better of it and informs his chief petty officer. Within minutes, word of the missing wrench has gone up the chain of command, and the air boss orders the suspension of launch operations.

Now you may be wondering, "Why all this fuss about a missing wrench?" But the young seaman had been working on the flight deck earlier in the evening and may have left his wrench there. It could have possibly been sucked into an aircraft engine during launch and caused a crash. A walkdown of the deck is ordered. In a walkdown, officers and enlisted men walk shoulder to shoulder down the enormous deck looking for debris—in this case, the missing wrench. Because of this delay, the score for the exercise is ruined.

The next morning, a marine escorts the young seaman who lost the wrench to the bridge, where he stands at attention before the captain. The captain turns to face the young sailor who may be responsible for the failure of the exercise. He surveys the young man, takes a deep breath, and says . . .

What should the captain say? What would you say if you were captain?

Consider the following four possible reactions by the captain.

1. You screwed up! I'm going to make an example out of you. You'll stand trial for this. I'm going to throw your butt in the brig!

2. You're paid to do your job, and I expect you to do it right!

3. We must remember our mission! We're here to protect our country. Each one of us must do our job if we are to fulfill our mission!

4. I want to congratulate you for reporting that missing wrench. I know it would have been easy to ignore it, but you faced up to it and you did your duty. You did the right thing. I know you're the kind of person we can count on to make this ship the best in the navy.

Which of these statements do you think would be most appropriate for this situation? Why?

Match each of the numbered statements with one of the leadership types here by writing the appropriate number in the space provided.

_____ Transformational leadership involves creating and communicating a higher-level vision in a charismatic way that elicits an emotional response and commitment from the followers.

_____ Transactional leadership focuses on the creation of reward contingencies and exchange relationships, resulting in a calculative compliance on the part of followers.

_____ Empowering leadership emphasizes employee self-influence processes rather than hierarchical control processes and actively encourages followers to take ownership of their own behaviors and work processes.

_____ Directive leadership involves providing specific task-focused directions, giving commands, assigning goals, close supervision, and constant follow-up.

In fact, the actual captain in the situation responded with statement number 4. By the next day, his leadership response was known all over the ship. His crew was now 100 percent commited to their new captain, and he had a very successful tour of duty.

Additional Questions for Reflection

What might have happened if he had chosen another approach, say statement number 1 (a very traditional leadership reaction in a military context)? What would happen the next time someone lost a wrench? Would they report it? Is is possible to blend one or more of these approaches? If so, which two might work well together?

*This exercise was created based on a story contained in Henry P. Sims, Jr. and Charles C. Manz, *Company of Heroes: Unleashing the Power of Self-Leadership* (New York: Wiley, 1996).

SELF-ASSESSMENT

Self-Leadership*

For each statement, circle the number that best describes you based on the following scale:

Not at all Accurate	Somewhat Accurate	A little Accurate	Mostly Accurate	Completely Accurate
1	2	3	4	5

1. I establish specific goals for my own performance.
   1   2   3   4   5

2. I make a point to keep track of how well I'm doing at work.
   1   2   3   4   5

3. I work toward specific goals I have set for myself.
   1   2   3   4   5

4. I visualize myself successfully performing a task before I do it.
   1   2   3   4   5

5. Sometimes I picture in my mind a successful performance before I actually do a task.
   1   2   3   4   5

6. When I have successfully completed a task, I often reward myself with something I like.
   1   2   3   4   5

7. Sometimes I talk to myself (out loud or in my head) to work through difficult situations.
   1   2   3   4   5

8. I try to evaluate mentally the accuracy of my own beliefs about situations I am having problems with.
   1   2   3   4   5

9. I think about my own beliefs and assumptions whenever I encounter a difficult situation.
   1   2   3   4   5

Scoring:

Add the numbers circled above and write your score in the blank _____

Interpretation:

36 and above = You have very strong self-leadership skills. You are likely to be naturally effective at influencing and directing your own behaviors and thoughts toward accomplishing your goals.

19–35 = You have a moderate level of self-leadership skills. You may want to consider increasing your use of the self-leadership behavior-focused, natural reward–focused, and constructive thought strategies.

18 and below = You have room to improve your self-leadership skills. You will become more effective in accomplishing your goals and in leading others if you can first learn to lead yourself more effectively.

*Adapted from J. D. Houghton, D. Dawley, and T. C. DiLiello (2012). "The Abbreviated Self-Leadership Questionnaire (ASLQ): A More Concise Measure of Self-Leadership," *International Journal of Leadership Studies*, 7, 216–232.

SELF-TEST ANSWER KEY

1. d.
2. b; False. *Power* is the ability to *influence*. It may or may not be coercive.
3. *Legitimate power* refers to the influence that a manager has because of his or her title inside an organization or status in a community. *Reward power* is an influential ability to affect a team member positively through resources, preferred schedules, and additional status. *Coercive power* is what a manager uses to influence people through the threat of or actual negative consequences for undesired actions. *Referent power* is based on a manager's appealing traits or resources, such as charisma or the ability to offer an employee a promotion. *Expert power* is derived from perceived knowledge, skill, or competence, such as a manager, skilled in computer programming, who has expert power with a software development team.
4. c.
5. b; False. *Transformational* leadership involves creating and communicating a higher-level vision in a charismatic way that elicits an emotional response.
6. a.
7. self-awareness: the ability to be aware of our own emotions and make "gut decisions"; self-management: the ability to have power over one's own emotions; social awareness: the ability to be aware of, comprehend, and react to others' emotions; and relationship management: the ability to influence and cooperate with others, even through conflict.
8. b.
9. impoverished (1,1), authority-compliance (9,1), middle-of-the-road (5,5), country club (1,9), and team (9,9)
10. a; True
11. Leader-member relations, task structure, position power
12. Readiness or development level
13. Directive, supportive, participative, and achievement-oriented
14. d.
15. Behavior-focused, natural reward, constructive thought
16. It focuses on the leader serving the followers to meet their needs, objectives, and aspirations, rather than on the followers serving the leaders.
17. a.
18. a; True

Notes

CHAPTER FOURTEEN

UNDERSTANDING INDIVIDUAL BEHAVIOR

Learning Objectives

By the end of the chapter, you will be able to:

14.1 | Describe the dimensions of positive individual behaviors and its impact on organizational performance.

14.2 | Explain the characteristics of individual personalities and strength profiles.

14.3 | Explain how individual attitudes and beliefs affect team and organizational dynamics.

14.4 | Interpret how stress, deviance, and dysfunctional behaviors manifest and negatively affect team and organizational performance.

14.5 | Design a plan for maximizing individual behavior to change an organizational culture or performance positively.

ADDITIONAL RESOURCES

KEY TERMS
IN REVIEW
SELF-TEST
CHAPTER EXERCISE
SELF-ASSESSMENT
SELF-TEST
ANSWER KEY

JP Greenwood/Getty Images

INSIDE THIS CHAPTER

ManagementStory:
Featuring **Julian Wales**

14.1 | HOW INDIVIDUALS MAKE A DIFFERENCE

Abundance The conscious pursuit of purposeful infinite possibilities that are sustainable and stable over time.

Stress The physiological and emotional reactions experienced by individuals to excessive pressures or demands at work.

Absenteeism The frequent or habitual absence of employees from work.

Burnout A physical or mental reaction due to stressful and demanding working conditions.

Negative affectivity (NA) A general dimension of personality where an individual experiences negative mood states, such as anger, disgust, fear, and anxiety.

"When you get to my age, you'll measure your success in life by how many of the people you want to have love you actually do love you. That's the ultimate test of how you've lived your life."

—Warren Buffett

14.1 | Describe the dimensions of positive individual behaviors and its impact on organizational performance.

In Chapter 1, we learned about critical thinking, and the application of *Positive Psychology*. First introduced by Martin Seligman and Mihaly Csikszentmihalyi, Positive Psychology explores ways to help people recognize their positive traits or strengths, rather than their perceived weaknesses and failings, and nurture them to their full potential. The research field of Positive Psychology has made great strides in the past decade, especially with regard to understanding the behavioral factors associated with happiness. These researchers have suggested that we could all benefit from leading a life of **abundance**, which is the conscious pursuit of purposeful infinite possibilities that are sustainable and stable over time. This involves focusing our energies not just on ourselves, but also on the well-being of others. In fact, it can be argued that an organization could not exist without healthy, sustainable employee relationships.

Yet in economically tough times, when uncertainty is high and layoffs are prevalent, it can be challenging for managers to instill the message of Positive Psychology in the workplace, even at a time when it is most needed. During these periods of financial worries, work-related **stress**, the physiological and emotional reactions experienced by individuals to excessive pressures or demands at work, is more common.[1] Organizations with high levels of stressed-out employees tend to suffer from low productivity, higher turnover, and more accidents at work.[2] Another consequence of stress is **absenteeism**, the frequent or habitual absence of employees from work.[3] If the stress is consistent, employees may suffer from **burnout**, a physical or mental reaction due to stressful and demanding working conditions.[4]

Unhappy, stressed-out employees tend to display negative behaviors such as irritability, aggression, and frustration. **Negative affectivity (NA)** is a general dimension of personality where an individual experiences negative mood states, such as anger, disgust, fear, and anxiety.[5] In short, employees are simply not in the right mind-set to be more positive, and thus can be more challenging to manage. They are also less likely to make **contributions**, which are the quantifiable efforts produced by an employee based on that person's role and responsibilities.[6] However, in order to restore a good, healthy working environment, managers need to apply different

Edyta Pawlowska/Shutterstock

techniques, even under the most adverse circumstances, in order to encourage **Positive affectivity (PA)**, the outward display of affirming emotions, such as happiness, optimism, and encouragement.[7]

But how do managers help employees adapt and adjust their behaviors to improve relationships both inside and outside the workplace? Dave and Wendy Ulrich, the authors of *The Why of Work: How Great Leaders Build Abundant Organizations That Win*, believe that the application of six factors, or dimensions of abundance, have a significant effect on our behaviors, the way we relate to others, and organizational performance. The six dimensions of abundance are self-awareness, purposeful thinking, relationships of thoughtful candor, challenging work, moral courage, and joyful living.[8]

Self-Awareness

Self-awareness is the ability to look objectively at a circumstance and make subjective, principle-based judgment decisions simultaneously. This means that in order to remain objective about others, we must have a keen awareness of our own behavior. But as many of us tend to lean toward self-effacement, how do we develop an acute understanding of our strengths, talents, and skills? Sometimes it is easier to focus on the negative aspects of our selves, rather than our positive attributes. However, carrying out an objective analysis of ourselves eventually leads to the type of belief systems that we subscribe to and includes our values, the goals we aspire to, and what we would like to achieve in the future.

Similarly, we must also focus on our external relationships and how others perceive us—a process that can be quite difficult and sometimes is disruptive. It also involves the ability to listen to others. As behavioral research has shown, by practicing self-awareness, we become more adaptive to the environment around us.

Managers that practice the art of self-awareness are far more likely to obtain feedback from their employees, listen to other perspectives, encourage more open communication, and treat people fairly. They also act as role models in the area of personal development, which in turn is emulated by their staff. The culture of self-awareness in an organization cannot be underestimated—staff members who are more self-aware are more confident in their abilities, play to their own strengths and the strengths of others, and provide better customer service.

Purposeful Thinking

Purposeful thinking involves continually seeking pathways for possibilities and looking for opportunities to learn and grow. It means trying to achieve a balance between work life and personal life, while continually striving for goals. Many of us tend to dwell on the past and mull over the mistakes we have made and what we could have done better. However, purposeful thinking involves maintaining a healthy objective view of the past while focusing on making the future better. Managers who practice purposeful thinking continually strive forward, looking for ways for the organization to improve and grow.

Purposeful thinking is also linked to self-awareness; the more self-aware we are, the clearer our points of purpose will be. Sometimes this method can bring about some surprising results about the path you have chosen, why you have chosen it, and whether it is the right path toward a successful and abundant future.

Relationships of Thoughtful Candor

It is impossible to achieve our points of purpose without focusing our energies on our relationships with others. **Candor** is the quality of being open, frank, and sincere in speech or expression.

Being candid in a relationship involves honesty, fairness, and sincerity. In each situation, we must seek to hold ourselves responsible first, then others. Managers that work within a hierarchy can sometimes assign blame too quickly, rather than questioning the reasons behind the mistake in the first place. Displaying gratitude in a relationship can be

Contributions The quantifiable efforts produced by an employee, based on that person's role and responsibilities.

Positive affectivity (PA) The outward display of affirming emotions, such as happiness, optimism, and encouragement.

Self-awareness—The ability to look objectively at a circumstance and make subjective, principle-based judgment decisions simultaneously.

LECTURE ENHANCER:

14.1 How Individuals Make a Difference

✓ **Abundance** (leading a life of abundance)—the conscious pursuit of purposeful infinite possibilities that are sustainable and stable over time

✓ **Stress**—the physiological and emotional reactions experienced by individuals to excessive pressures or demands at work

✓ **Absenteeism**—the frequent or habitual absence of employees from work

✓ **Burnout**—a physical or mental reaction due to stressful and demanding working conditions

Purposeful thinking An approach that involves continually seeking pathways for possibilities and looking for opportunities to learn and grow.

Candor The quality of being open, frank, and sincere in speech or expression.

Challenging work Work that is comprised of two types of tasks: pleasureful and purposeful.

negative mood states, such as anger, disgust, fear and anxiety

Moral courage Taking a position against something or someone even though you know the outcome may be unpopular.

Self-efficacy The extent to which a person believes in his or her own competence regarding a process or task.

Risk The probability of loss or undesirable consequences.

Joyful living Feelings and emotions defined by interest, passion, curiosity, contentment, enthusiasm, satisfaction, and quality of life.

Perception The process by which individuals select, interpret, and organize information in the world around them.

Selective perception The process by which individuals accept information consistent with their values and beliefs, while screening out information that is not aligned with their own needs.

overlooked, particularly in the workplace. But in relationships of candor, we must consistently show gratitude for acts of kindness and fairness, and learn to forgive those that miss the mark.

Challenging Work

Challenging work is comprised of two types of tasks: pleasureful and purposeful. Pleasureful tasks provide an immediate feeling of joy and delight, with little effect on overall life satisfaction. The process of completing purposeful tasks gives us a sense of accomplishment, with lasting meaning.

Examples of pleasure tasks might include eating a delicious cake or making a high score on a computer game. However, purposeful tasks are more meaningful and satisfying, such as balancing a checkbook, organizing a workspace, or giving a great speech. The joy and delight is deferred and remembered. When we allow ourselves to become completely absorbed by a well-defined task and ignore any distractions or doubts, then we tend to lose our sense of time and all elements of self-consciousness in the pursuit of our goals.

Moral Courage

Moral courage is taking a position against something or someone even though you know the outcome may be unpopular. For example, breaking up a heated argument is a display of moral courage. A component of moral courage is **self-efficacy**, which is the extent to which a person believes in his or her own competence regarding a process or task.[9] If an individual has a high degree of self-efficacy, that person will be more motivated to take action and stand up for what he or she believes in.

Moral courage also involves taking **risks**, which is the probability of loss or undesirable consequences. Taking risks to protect others, taking steps to defend the values and belief systems of others, and going against the status quo are all examples of moral courage.

Within the workplace, there have been several recent examples of managers who have stood up against their organization to defend their rights and the rights of others. Typically, people who report the wrongdoing of an organization to higher authority figures or to the public are called *whistleblowers*. The greater the risks to self, such as financial insecurity, alienation, or ridicule, the greater the courage required.

Joyful Living

Joyful living can be described as feelings and emotions defined by interest, passion, curiosity, contentment, enthusiasm, satisfaction, and quality of life. Imagine an organization where every single employee subscribed to the theory of joyful living. What a happy place that would be! When we live joyfully, we can laugh openly, but never at the expense of others. We take pleasure in what we have rather than focusing on what we lack. Like the other dimensions of abundance, living joyfully involves focusing on the energies of others, where we can display enthusiasm and delight in others' accomplishments, even more than our own.

Joyful living is a measurable culmination of the other dimensions of abundance, providing the means for progress and motivation.

The Power of Perception and a Positive Approach

Perception, the process by which individuals select, interpret, and organize information in the world around them, is another critical way of understanding behavior.[10] Our personalities, beliefs, and values are all so diverse, and we tend to see things in different ways.

For example, one person might view getting a B on an exam as disappointing, whereas another might be delighted with the grade. Similarly, leadership teams might have differing perspectives that may prevent them from achieving a common goal. **Selective perception** is the process by which individuals accept information consistent with their values and beliefs, while screening out information that is not aligned with their own needs.[11] When receiving feedback, some people might focus on the positive and filter out the negative, or vice versa. By understanding the process of

XiXinXing/Shutterstock

selective perception, managers can provide feedback that focuses on the positive and use it as a way to improve performance.

Let's return to the Upstream Fisheries case narrative introduced in Chapter 13. We'll explore how Julian Wales manages the different personalities and perceptions of his team leaders in order to arrive at a solution to improve organizational performance.

In Chapter 13, we met Julian Wales, group leader for Upstream Fisheries, a global company that farm-raises fish using organic food and environmentally friendly practices. Julian has been asked to lead the Spanish branch of Upstream Fisheries, which has been suffering a decline in production levels. His role as leader is to motivate the team, promote sustainability, and generate results. So far, Julian has carried out a behavioral assessment test in an attempt to better understand the shift leaders he is working with. He also held a meeting to introduce a leadership typology, whereby each leader champions the company's mission, performance, and vision. Julian must continue to get to know the team in order to find ways of motivating them to boost productivity and produce successful results.

After the first meeting, Julian felt that he was making progress. The team seemed excited about the ideas he had presented. Julian believed the process had confirmed the extent of the leaders' **commitment**, which is the degree to which an employee is psychologically devoted to an organization or team.[12] As a follower of the six dimensions of abundance and a practitioner of self-awareness, he also felt the process had helped him grow and develop, and connect with the team. In fact, Julian had more **confidence**, which is a certainty about handling something that a person desires or needs to do,[13] in his leadership skills. Julian knew how to play to the strengths of the team and achieve results. He just hoped the others felt the same way.

As Julian reflected on the meeting, he was reminded of the best piece of management advice he had been given from a mentor—"Treat everybody the same, by treating them differently." He allowed himself to bask in the excitement of his elegant solution; after all, it wasn't easy to understand individual behaviors. Yet in one meeting, he had assessed the skills of each leader, and had defined their personality types, which would make them all the easier to manage.

From the initial round of results, it was clear that Liam and Vikas both had a **Type A** personality, which is a behavioral pattern where individuals tend to be ambitious, assertive, goal oriented, impatient, determined, highly organized, competitive, and aggressive.[14] Therefore, it was a "no-brainer" to assign them the more strategic champion roles of mission and vision. Maribel fell neatly into the category of **Type B**, which is a behavioral pattern where individuals tend to be more patient, relaxed, easygoing, and sensitive to the feelings of others.[15] She would make an excellent performance champion. However, as a leader, he also knows that if the "championing strategy" was going to be an effective solution, the work was only just beginning.

Max Johnson, the CEO of the company, has been repeating the mantra, "We need to foster abundance in a world of limited resources and scarcity, where the most limited resource and scarce commodity is positive thinking." This was all Julian needed to clarify his main objective: to support each team leader by enhancing positive behaviors and mitigating negative ones. To accomplish this, he needed to enter into a **psychological contract**, an informal expectation between employee and organization that determines quality and satisfaction, with the team leaders.[16] Julian knows that abundant organizations start from within—it is the people that create this type of culture. "This is easier said than done!" he thought.

In preparation for his next trip to Spain, Julian researched what enabled individuals and organizations to become "abundant," and how the six dimensions of abundance could be applied to the Upstream teams. First, he wanted to encourage himself and the team leaders to be more *self-aware*, to listen, and be conscious about how they formed opinions and attitudes toward ideas and others. This would open up communication further, and he hoped it would also unite the teams in their mission to achieve their goals. Second, he felt that the team leaders would do well by focusing on *purposeful thinking* and use this technique to set an example for their own teams. Vikas's team, in particular, has a tendency to focus on the past, and on how "boring" their jobs were. Vikas needs to teach his team about *points of purpose* to encourage them to look to the future and to contribute their ideas on how the organization could develop and grow.

✓ Contributions—the quantifiable efforts produced by an employee, based on role and responsibilities

✓ Positive Affectivity (PA)—the outward display of affirming emotions, such as happiness, optimism, and encouragement
➤ Six Dimensions of Abundance
1. **Self-Awareness**—ability to simultaneously look objectively at a circumstance and make subjective principle-based judgment decisions
2. **Purposeful thinking**— continually seeking pathways for possibilities and looking for opportunities to learn and grow

Commitment The degree to which an employee is psychologically devoted to an organization or team.

Confidence The certainty about handling something that a person desires or needs to do.

3. **Relationships of thoughtful candor**—the ability to self-organize and cultivate relationships that are aligned with purposeful thinking

Type A personality A behavioral pattern where individuals tend to be ambitious, assertive, goal oriented, impatient, determined, highly organized, competitive, and aggressive.

Type B personality A behavioral pattern where individuals tend to be more patient, relaxed, easygoing, and more sensitive to the feelings of others.

Psychological contract An informal expectation between employee and organization that determines quality and satisfaction.

4. **Challenging work**—comprised of two types of tasks: pleasureful and purposeful.
   ■ Pleasure tasks provide an immediate feeling of joy and delight, with little effect on life satisfaction. The process of completing purposeful tasks gives us a sense of accomplishment, with lasting meaning.
5. **Moral courage**—taking a position against something or someone even though you know the outcome may be unpopular

Stereotyping The tendency to ascribe characteristics or attributes to a particular group or individual unfairly.

When Julian reached his third dimension, *relationships of thoughtful candor*, he paused. How could he encourage the teams to be kind, honest, and express gratitude to one another without assigning blame? During the last meeting, among the joking and laughing, he thought he had detected an undercurrent of resentment; Vikas's team felt frustrated, as they were being micromanaged; Liam's team seemed happy with their leader but annoyed with the fish production process which seemed constantly in flux, and regularly complained to Liam about it; and Maribel, although clearly a popular leader, appeared to have frustrated some of her team members by putting them into positions where they felt out of their depth. Although Liam, in particular, went to great efforts to bond with his team by setting up a soccer team and organizing events at the pub, Julian made a note to keep an eye on the team morale. He wanted to ensure that the teams work together to come up with solutions rather than assigning blame.

The fourth point was *challenging work*. Julian believed that he has set some worthy challenges for the team leaders by assigning them to be champions of specific areas. He hoped that they will be inspired by their new roles and join their skills together to become one mighty, empowering leader.

The final two dimensions would be achieved if the leaders followed the first few steps; then they could strive to attain *joyful living*, where every employee would respect each other and take pleasure in the accomplishments of others. However, Julian also knew that a degree of *moral courage* would be needed to get them to the final stage, as there were sure to be a few bumps along the way.

14.2 | PERSONALITIES AND STRENGTHS

14.2 | Explain the characteristics of individual personalities and strength profiles.

In Chapter 11, we explored how organizations use psychometric tools during the interview process to obtain a better understanding of the strengths and styles of potential candidates. These tools are also a useful method of assessing job performance with regard to existing employees and help them form a reliable, objective view of their skills and attributes. They can also be helpful in opening a candid conversation between managers and employees about their feelings about the accuracy of the analysis.

Sure enough, Julian experienced the first of many challenges as soon as he arrived back at the Spanish branch. The first person to approach him was Maribel. "Julian, first I would like to say how much we all appreciate how you encouraged us to focus on our strengths. The leadership typology is inspiring, to say the least."

Julian smiled, but he sensed there was a "but" coming. Maribel went on, "But here is my issue. The way I am perceived around here is as the person who takes care of everyone, is sensitive to other people's feelings and 'gets things done.' In fact, every behavioral assessment test I have ever taken has revealed me as your average Type B.

"In contrast, Vikas and Liam are Type A personalities. From my perspective, the company assigns them with the more strategic and important work. The jobs you gave us based on the results of the behavioral test administered during the last meeting are a prime example of this. As a 'Type B' personality, I am assigned to be the 'performance champion,' the person who makes sure things are ticking along nicely; whereas Vikas and Liam champion 'mission and vision'—the more strategic side of the business.

"Although I have been classified as Type B over the course of my entire career, I don't necessarily agree with it. It's not that I totally disagree with your assessment; I just feel I have more to offer, and I don't want the company, and their classification of me, to limit my future growth and career opportunities."

Julian was taken aback. He had thought Maribel was happy with her champion role. And what about Vikas and Liam? Were they also experiencing doubts about the behavioral assessment? By aligning his team leaders with their perceived strengths, Julian needed to be sure that he is not **stereotyping**, which is the tendency to ascribe characteristics or attributes to a particular group or individual unfairly.[17] He was also concerned that he has unwittingly made limiting attributions to the team leaders. An **attribution** is an ascribed quality or characteristic that is related to a particular individual or situation.[18]

Julian told Maribel that he appreciated her perspective, and that he would take some time to think through the matter and come back to her with recommendations.

"Big Five" Personality Traits

As we explored in Chapter 13, researchers have spent years studying personality traits and how they apply to each individual. Although each theory is still debated, and there is little hard evidence to prove their accuracy, organizations tend to use the "Big Five" personality test as a means of evaluating and assessing their workers. The **"Big Five" personality traits** refers to the five broad domains of human psychology: openness, conscientiousness, neuroticism, extraversion, and agreeableness, as shown in Table 14-1.[19]

In turn, personality traits influence behaviors and **attitudes**, which are a person's or group's inclinations toward an idea or situation.[20] Managers have to take into account the wide range of **individual differences**, the variable psychological, behavioral, cultural, and physical dimensions that uniquely distinguish each team member.[21] There are three particular areas that managers focus on in relation to personality: locus of control, authoritarianism, and Machiavellianism.

Locus of Control **Locus of control** is the degree to which an individual or team feels in control of circumstances and outcomes.[22] Locus of control can be internal or external. For example, say that you have a final coming up; you might be nervous about it, but you know that if you study hard and focus on the subject matter, you stand a good chance of passing. This is *internal locus control*, where you feel that you are in control of your own fate. Conversely, you may think that the exam is too difficult and that no amount of studying will make a difference, and so you decide not to bother studying at all. This is an example of *external locus control*, which is a belief that there is nothing we can do to affect an outcome; we are simply pawns of our fate.

Typically, in the workplace, individuals with high levels of internal locus of control are easier to manage because they have an innate sense that their actions and behavior have a direct impact on results. In contrast, individuals with an external locus of control tend to blame everyone else for their lackluster performance and are more difficult to motivate.

Attribution An ascribed quality or characteristic that is related to a particular individual or situation.

"Big Five" personality traits The five broad domains of human psychology: openness, conscientiousness, negativity, extraversion, and agreeableness.

Attitudes A person's or group's inclinations toward an idea or situation.

Individual differences The variable psychological, behavioral, cultural, and physical dimensions that uniquely distinguish each team member.

Locus of control The degree to which an individual or team feels in control of circumstances and outcomes.

✓ **Attitudes**—a person or group's inclination toward an idea or situation.
✓ **Individual differences**—also known as the variable psychological, behavioral, cultural, and physical dimensions that uniquely distinguish each team member.
➤ Three Personality Focus Areas of Managers
  1. **Locus of Control**—the degree to which an individual or team believes it is in control of circumstances and outcomes
    ■ Can be internal or external
  2. **Authoritarianism**—the management philosophy that, by threat of punishment, power and legitimacy are required to produce superior results
    ■ Tend to be perfectionists and expect the same from others
  3. **Machiavellianism**—a pragmatic management philosophy that overlooks unethical and manipulative behavior to produce desirable results.
    ■ Has little respect for his subordinates, tends to take credit for their ideas, and rules with fear
• Focusing on Strengths
  ➤ Focusing on strengths is far more productive than honing in on and trying to "fix" weaknesses
  ➤ Table 14-1

Table 14-1	The "Big Five" Personality Traits
Openness	**Openness** is the ability to have fun and feel elation and delight. Open people have the capacity to foster diverse sharing of ideas and listen and learn from contradictory points of view.
Conscientiousness	**Conscientiousness** is when an individual exhibits thoughtfulness, organization, and responsibility in the pursuit of goals.
Neuroticism	Individuals high in **neuroticism** (or low in emotional stability) tend to be tense, moody, irritable, and anxious.
Extraversion	**Extraverted** people are generally outgoing, sociable, talkative, and able to get on well with others.
Agreeableness	**Agreeableness** describes the extent to which an individual relates to others by being trusting, forgiving, kind, affectionate, and cooperative.

Research@Work

The Big Five Personality Traits and Job Performance

Do personality traits really relate to performance at work, and if so how? Personality researchers Murray R. Barrick and Michael K. Mount have spent much of their careers addressing these and related questions. In one well-known study, Barrick and Mount reanalyzed 117 studies conducted over a nearly 40-year time span.[23] Their results indicated that the Big Five personality dimension of conscientiousness was a consistent predictor of job success for all occupational groups studied. In addition, their findings suggested that extraversion was a valid predictor across two major occupations: managers and salespeople. As you can imagine, both of these jobs involve significant interactions with other people.

Finally, they found that both extraversion and openness were valid predictors of training proficiency across all occupations studied. This result is likely based on the fact that people with these traits are more likely to be active,

engaged, and open to learning new things in a training situation.

More recently, Barrick and Mount, along with their colleague Ning Li, have expanded on their earlier work by presenting a model that suggests that personality traits shape purposeful goal strivings, experienced meaningfulness, and motivational processes, resulting in a number of predictable work outcomes, including job satisfaction, satisfactory task performance, and citizenship behaviors.[24] Based on these empirical findings and theoretical model, managers should carefully consider personality factors as they relate to important work outcomes.

Critical Thinking in the Classroom

How might an understanding of personality differences help a manager to be more effective in selecting, training, and motivating successful employees?

Authoritarianism The management philosophy that using the threat of punishment, power, and legitimacy is required to produce superior results.

Authoritarianism **Authoritarianism** is the management philosophy that using the threat of punishment, power, and legitimacy is required to produce superior results.[25] Authoritarian managers and leaders tend to be perfectionists and expect the same from others. The changing culture of organizations to a flatter structure has diluted the levels of authoritarianism that previously existed in hierarchical companies, resulting in a trend toward more equal employer/employee relationships.

Machiavellianism A pragmatic management philosophy that condones unethical and manipulative behavior if it produces desirable results.

Machiavellianism Another area of personality that managers focus on is **Machiavellianism**, a pragmatic management philosophy that overlooks unethical and manipulative behavior if it produces desirable results.[26] Typically, Machiavellian employees are tricky to spot. On the surface, they might be polite, well spoken, and good at negotiating; yet underneath, they are capable of lying to and manipulating others to get what they want. A Machiavellian leader has little respect for his or her subordinates, tends to take credit for their ideas, and rules with fear.

In an effort to come up with a clean, elegant, and swift decision, Julian realized that he may have arbitrarily put Maribel and the other team leaders in roles that were limiting to them and the organization. Perhaps he should not have jumped to conclusions so quickly; the last thing he wanted was to have the leaders lose faith in him and his leadership style. He decided to start the conversation over with the team leaders, beginning with an assessment of the "Big Five" Personality traits. He gave the team members an exercise where they were asked to rate the accuracy of each statement, from 1 (inaccurate) to 5 (very accurate). Typical statements included, "I like to be around other people"; and "I am very creative."

After getting everyone's permission to share the results, Julian convened a conversation to discuss the outcomes. Here are the results for each of the three team leaders . . .

Maribel	Liam and Vikas
Lower extroversion behaviors and motivation	**Higher extroversion behaviors and motivations**
Behaviors include at various levels	**Behaviors include at various levels:**
• Serious	• Outgoing
• Introspective	• Optimistic
• Task-oriented	• Selling
• Matter-of-fact	• Delegates authority
• Analytical	• Meets new people easily
• Imaginative	• Enthusiastic
• Reflective	• Empathetic
• Cautious around new people	• Socially poised
• Reserved	
Motivational needs include:	**Motivational needs include:**
• Opportunity for introspection	• Social interaction
• Recognition for technical/intellectual accomplishments	• Prestige/status
• Freedom from office politics	• Social recognition/acceptance
• Private/personal recognition	• Visible signs of position (titles, the right office, etc.)

Vikas's hardwiring as a natural extrovert is coupled with his need for control and decision making. When he is unable to convince others of his point of view, he can be perceived as negative. This is in direct contrast with Liam, who is sociable and driven by the need to be liked. Maribel is also accommodating, even though she is less likely to be open and share her experiences.

Julian was not surprised at the high levels of extraversion displayed by Liam. The previous test had described him as talkative, outgoing, and sociable. However, he didn't expect Maribel's results to show such low levels of openness, nor did he predict Vikas's results to have such high degrees of extraversion and neuroticism. The results were an interesting revelation for the group, especially the level of neuroticism shown in Vikas's assessment. The results of the first behavioral test that Julian had given them during the first meeting had shown Vikas to be a directive leader, who tended to micromanage his team, but had not suggested any neurotic tendencies. Not for the first time, Julian wondered about the accuracy of personality tests.

After an awkward silence, Vikas spoke up, with a little bit of defensiveness. "Personally, I think this exercise is destructive, because it focuses on the negative rather than the positive. Again, it pigeonholes us into certain categories and ascribes traits to us that I feel are inaccurate. If a person is told he is neurotic, then there is a danger that it will become self-fulfilling. If we have to complete these assessments, then why can't we do some that focus on our strengths?"

Julian looked around at the team and said, "What does everyone else think?"

Maribel spoke quickly. "I agree with Vikas. I consider myself a very open person in spite of what the test says. I am happy to complete another one based on my strengths."

Liam, the only leader who was happy with his results, nodded quickly. "If everyone else wants to do another one, that's fine with me," he said agreeably.

Julian left the meeting, more confused than ever. Maybe Vikas was right: perhaps the last behavioral test had been limiting. After all, what good was it to focus on the weaknesses of the team when he was trying to get them to work together as empowered leaders? He was also troubled by his own assumptions about the leaders. Was he guilty of defining their traits too quickly, before he had even had a chance to get to know them properly? This was an uncomfortable thought. As group leader, Julian knew that he should be setting an example to the other leaders as to how to manage and motivate their own teams. Yet, all he had taught them so far was to focus on people's weaknesses over their strengths. How could they be expected to lead and motivate their teams using this approach?

Morale took a dip after the Big Five test, and he needed to find a way of boosting the team, as well as finding a strengths test that he hoped would be deemed fair and accurate.

Focusing on Strengths

Following a couple of hours of research, Julian found just what he was looking for. Gallup, the research organization, had carried out a study suggesting that focusing on strengths was far more productive than honing in on and trying to "fix" weaknesses. Indeed, this is the core message of Positive Psychology: to develop and capitalize on skills in order to enhance work performance. Julian realized that he would need to spend more time observing the three leaders, taking mental notes, doing everything he could to identify their key strengths, and figuring out what made them tick.

Based on "in-depth interviews . . . of over 8,000 managers in over 400 companies," the Gallup Strengths Finder assessment, as shown in Table 14-2, provides individuals with a "signature of strengths" that identifies five dominant themes of talent excellence from 34 behavioral dimensions.[27]

The next day, Julian suggests that the group take the strength profile survey developed by Gallup, with a follow-up conversation in a restaurant the following week. He felt a more casual environment would be relaxing to the team and provide a pleasant ambience where they could discuss the results. The team approved the plan. Although arduous, Julian believed the exercises would yield significant results in the future. Table 14-3 shows the results from the Gallup Strengths survey for each team member.

Julian forwarded the strength survey results to the team with an invitation to attend dinner at a local restaurant. To boost morale, Julian arranged for a surprise guest to join them for dessert. He hoped by the end of the night, the team will have bonded further.

Table 14-2	The Gallup Strengths Finder
Achiever	Futuristic
Activator	Harmony
Adaptability	Ideation
Analytical	Inclusiveness
Arranger	Individualization
Belief	Input
Command	Intellection
Communication	Learner
Competition	Maximizer
Connectedness	Positivity
Context	Relator
Deliberate	Responsibility
Developer	Restorative
Discipline	Self-Assurance
Empathy	Significance
Fairness	Strategic
Focus	WOO (Winning Others Over)

Table 14-3	Strengths Survey Results

Vikas

Analytical
Loves collecting data and measuring results. He believes "what gets measured, gets done." Action requires thoughtful consideration.

Command
Extreme orientation toward goals. Once his mind is made up, he expects others to follow him without question, and he is quite comfortable with conflict.

Deliberative
Acts on a preconfigured set of beliefs. Some consider him to be dogmatic and overly rigid. He thrives on structure and controlled environments.

Discipline
Always on time at the beginning of shift and makes a point to do his "to-do" list before he goes home. Believes solutions come from hard work and stick-to-it-ness.

Responsibility
He is dependable and expects the same from others. Not one to push tasks off to others, he takes pride in being the hardest worker in every team. Trust is the most important thing in his relationships, and when that is lost, it takes him a long time to get it back.

Liam

Activator
Believes in the adage, "Begun is half done." He regularly comments to his team, "Let's stop talking about it and get it done." Not one for idle chatter.

Communication
Wants to be both understood and to understand others. He builds professional relationships on clear expectations and objectives.

Empathy
Sensitive; feels everything deeply. Laughs easily and frequently and is emotionally available to others. He constantly tries to put himself in others' positions.

Relator
He connects quickly with other people and feels most comfortable in the company of others. His builds friendships effortlessly in his personal and professional life.

Winning Others Over (WOO)
When you are around him, you feel like you are the only person in the world that matters. He offers compliments and praise as a way of garnering personal favor.

Maribel

Adaptability
Embraces change. She isn't deterred by barriers or obstacles and feels comfortable creating a new plan of action if something doesn't seem to be working. Mistakes don't bother her.

Connectedness
She believes that all actions have consequences, intended and unintended. Community and sustainability are important to her, as she sees the relationship of everyone to shared resources.

Futuristic
Always imagining a better tomorrow. She finds joy in using the latest technologies to redesign processes. Sees how the company can evolve to meet hypothetical market demands 5, 10, and even 20 years out.

Ideation
She trusts that the best solutions come from gathering as many diverse perspectives as possible. Constantly doodling and sketching in journals, she sees value in memorializing both good and bad ideas.

Maximizer
"Good enough" is a frustrating state. She thrives on continuous improvement and often referred to as a perfectionist. She is unwilling to stop "tweaking" until she believes that the absolute best solution has been implemented.

14.3 | ATTITUDES AND BELIEF SYSTEMS

14.3 | Explain how individual attitudes and beliefs affect team and organizational dynamics.

Sometimes individual attitudes and behaviors conflict with one another, leading to a state of **cognitive dissonance**, a psychological strain that occurs when a person is faced with two or more conflicting cognitions (e.g., beliefs, attitudes, or items of knowledge).[28] For example, say you have a boss whose views conflict with your own, yet the rest of the team seems to agree with everything he says. You can either try and adapt to his way of thinking and go along with the

LECTURE ENHANCER:

14.3 Attitudes and Belief Systems

✓ **Cognitive Dissonance**—a psychological strain that occurs

Cognitive dissonance The psychological strain that occurs when a person is faced with two or more conflicting cognitions (e.g., beliefs, attitudes, or items of knowledge).

when a person is faced with two attractive or negative options

- Co-aligning with Organizational Values
  ✓ Creativity—the ability to devise innovative ideas to meet the needs of a particular task or organizational goals

status quo, or you can speak your mind and tell him why you do not subscribe to his points of view. The first choice conflicts with your own belief system but doesn't rock the boat, whereas the second choice might cause friction among the team and damage interpersonal relationships.

Let's return to our case study and explore one leader's state of cognitive dissonance during the next team gathering.

The following Wednesday evening, the leadership team gathered at a local restaurant to discuss the strengths test results, and Julian's "champion strategy," with the team leaders focusing on mission, vision, and performance. Julian thought that the evening he has planned will be a fun and a well-deserved respite for the team, and he was looking forward to the arrival of the surprise guest he invited and the conversation that it will bring about.

Co-aligning with Organizational Values

It was clear from the beginning of the conversation at dinner that Maribel seemed satisfied with the assessment process. She believed that the strengths test truly summed up her personality—as someone who can lead as a visionary, rather than someone who simply supports others to get things done. She was also pleased that the test highlighted her **creativity**, which is the ability to devise innovative ideas to meet the needs of a particular task or organizational goals.[29]

Julian was happy with her response. Finally, the whole team was having a candid conversation about what makes the most sense for allocating their time and resources to increase the company's performance.

However, Liam wasn't as satisfied with the results. Although he was interested in the power of the strength-test tool, and its accurate portrayal of himself and the rest of the team, he couldn't help but notice that one member of the team wasn't as engaged as the rest of them. He decided to address Vikas and find out what was bothering him.

"Vikas, you haven't said much," Liam said, laughing. "Are you still mad about being assessed as neurotic? What happened? You used to be the most positive guy around here—everything was possible with you. You are turning into a curmudgeon!"

Vikas spoke up. "Maybe I think this is all a waste of time and company resources. Maybe I just want to do a good job for the next 10 years, get my pension, and buy a sailboat. To me there is more to life than this job!" With this proclamation, dessert arrived and with it, the evening's special guest.

Timothy Matthews is a successful British entrepreneur, world-renowned for the Internet media company he started and then sold to a large media company for $1 billion. Matthews was considered a bold visionary by many, but raised eyebrows when he announced his latest venture—a chain of restaurants! He opened Tim's Famous eatery with a revolutionary approach: each restaurant only serves food produced within a 100-mile radius of its location. Matthews calculated that if every locally owned restaurant in the world did this, the energy savings would be extraordinary—not to mention how much better the food would taste. His passion for sustainable fisheries was unparalleled, which eventually led him to consider opening a restaurant less than 10 miles from Upstream Fisheries.

While he believes in the Upstream founder's vision, Matthews has been critical of the results he has seen from the company. He thought that the local plant produced just enough to be considered "sustainable," and that they could do much more. Matthews has suggested a possible partnership, but only if Upstream Fisheries radically increases their productivity levels. Julian hoped that once Upstream improves its production levels, it would be considered a contender for providing fish to Matthews's new restaurant. And he hoped that this meeting would serve as a platform for future talks, as well as giving the team an opportunity to meet a valuable and important potential client.

After their introductions, Matthews, who would not be described as modest even by his best friends, gave each of the team leaders an autographed copy of his latest book, *Blue: The New Green Revolution*. The team, still recovering from Vikas's outburst, was subdued and gave Matthews a lukewarm reception. Matthews said, "I feel like I have just crashed a dull party. Why the long faces?"

Julian smiled politely, but just as he opened his mouth to change the subject, Vikas broke in: "Well, Timothy, I was just telling my colleagues here that I'm losing faith in the industry I am working in."

"What Vikas means is . . ." Julian interrupted, but he didn't get very far.

Creativity The ability to devise innovative ideas to meet the needs of a particular task or organizational goals.

"What *Vikas* means is," started Vikas, giving Julian a warning look, "This whole blue sustainability stuff is a sham, and I think we need to worry about protecting people first. Timothy, you know the power of money. Do you know that since we launched this insane sustainability initiative, our stock price has dropped by 50 percent? As I have quite a number of shares in this company, I was hoping I could cash them in on my retirement. If things keep plummeting, I won't be able to feed my family the basics, never mind sustainable fish! I have enough on my mind trying to figure out how to get out of this mess. Maybe you can afford the luxury of 'Blue Sustainability,' but how about the rest of us?"

Vikas finally caught himself. Julian, Maribel, and Liam look like deer frozen in the middle of a road at midnight with headlights barreling down on them—eyes wide open.

Matthews retorted, "Well, Vikas, that is certainly one way of looking at it. However, I see sustainable agriculture as a way of producing healthy food for consumers and animals without harming the environment, and as a method of supporting rural communities. It seems you and I have opposing views: you are looking at it from a corporate money-making perspective, but I see it as a way of ensuring the future of the planet. I never thought that ensuring that my grandchildren had fresh fish to eat 50 years from now was a luxury."

With that, Matthews stood up and walked out of the restaurant. Julian rushed after him to apologize. The rest of the team sat in awkward silence.

14.4 | STRESS, DEVIANCE, AND DYSFUNCTIONAL BEHAVIOR

14.4 | Interpret how stress, deviance, and dysfunctional behaviors manifest and negatively affect team and organizational performance.

"What just happened?" Julian thought as he drove back to his hotel from dinner. He had personally called Max Johnson to arrange for Timothy Matthews to join them for dessert, and Vikas had offended him before he even got a chance to start a conversation. If Matthews complained to Johnson about this, the potential partnership would be dead in the water. "I knew we had to improve the team bonding," Julian thought, "but I didn't realize one of the leaders was actually dysfunctional!"

When Julian got home that night, he wondered how he could manage a leader that so clearly demonstrated **dysfunctional behavior**,[30] signs of which include lack of commitment, lack of trust, fear of confrontation or conflicting opinions, a refusal to accept responsibility, and a tendency to focus on individual needs ahead of the team and the organization.

As far as Julian was concerned, Vikas had just ticked all the boxes off to qualify for dysfunctional behavior. By his own admission, he was not committed to Upstream or, more crucially, to its mission of abundance and sustainability. In all his years at Upstream, however, he had never once offered an opinion that suggested he was in conflict with the values of the organization or the other leaders. Julian was also concerned that Vikas appeared to be more worried about his own personal situation than the success of the organization. And to think he had made Vikas the mission champion! He wondered what he could have possibly been thinking.

Julian also contemplated how he was to manage a leader who had displayed such a high level of **deviance**, which is intentional behavior and attitudes that differ from or violate accepted social norms.[31] If Vikas was going to upset the status quo to such a degree, then he needed to find a way of instilling **positive deviance**, which is intentional behavior and attitudes that differ from the accepted social norms in an honorable way.[32]

Julian was worried about the impact that Vikas's rant was having on the rest of the leaders and on his own team. They already believed Vikas to be a bit "disconnected," but most likely his negative attitude would be detrimental to the work performance of the entire team. Julian knew he needed to nip this in the bud as quickly as possible, but he needed to calm down first.

Managing Stress

Julian spent all night trying to figure out a way to understand and deal with Vikas's astonishing behavior and had come up with nothing. To top it all off, he had to deal with Max Johnson, the CEO of Upstream Fisheries, who had received a call from Tim Matthews complaining about

LECTURE ENHANCER:

14.4 Stress, Deviance, and Dysfuntional Behavior

✓ **Dysfunctional behavior**—lack of commitment, lack of trust, fear of confrontation or conflicting opinions, a refusal to accept responsibility, and a tendency to focus on their own individual needs ahead of the team and the organization

✓ **Deviance**—the intentional behavior and attitudes that differ from or violate the accepted social norms

✓ **Positive deviance**—is the intentional behavior and attitudes that differ from the accepted social norms in an honorable way

• **Managing Stress**

• **Preventing Destructive Behavior**

✓ **General Adaptation Syndrome (GAS)**—a set of physiological reactions to long-term stress which can be grouped into three stages: alarm, resistance, and exhaustion

✓ **Citizenship**—a commitment to the overall functions of the team and organizational culture in order to improve performance

Dysfunctional behavior Actions that show a lack of commitment, lack of trust, fear of confrontation or conflicting opinions, a refusal to accept responsibility, and a tendency to focus on their own individual needs ahead of the team and the organization.

Deviance Intentional behavior and attitudes that differ from or violate the accepted social norms.

Positive deviance Intentional behavior and attitudes that differ from the accepted social norms in an honorable way.

Vikas's behavior. Johnson had apologized on Vikas's behalf and wanted to know why a staff member (let alone a team leader) had dared to speak to Matthews in such a disrespectful manner.

First thing in the morning, Julian decided to speak with Vikas about the situation. When Vikas knocked on his office door, Julian barely managed to keep it together. He stated, "Vikas, your behavior last night could potentially cost us millions of dollars. Why did you choose to offend a world-famous business personality and potential client?"

Vikas shuffled his feet and said nothing.

Julian said quietly, "What happened last night?"

"I don't know," Vikas offered, sheepishly. "I have been under a lot of stress lately, and it all erupted last night."

Preventing Destructive Behavior

Julian, still struggling to remain calm, said, "We need to schedule time to talk about this after we've both had some time to think. This behavior can never be repeated."

Before leaving Julian's office, Vikas turns and says: "Julian, I have been thinking about what Tim Matthews said to me. I haven't been having enjoying myself at work lately. Upstream Fisheries used to be one of the most important things in my life. Now, I dread coming in here every day. Not because of the people. Things haven't been so great at home. My wife is very ill; she had to give up her job, and with the plummeting performance of Upstream, I worry about my job security. For what it's worth, I am sorry for embarrassing you and the company last night."

After Vikas left, Julian felt he had more of an insight about what had caused Vikas's outrageous behavior the previous evening. He realized that Vikas's worries at home, as well as his resentment for the company's falling stock price, was having a festering negative impact at work. This had been the reason for his disengaged attitude at work and his misgivings about the core values, mission, and vision of the organization.

Vikas had not been aware of how much his mood had been affecting his team. He was responsible for the production line, and production was lower than it should be, which affected the performance of the whole organization. "Is it Vikas's behavior that is impacting the team's productivity?" Julian said to himself aloud. "And if so, how can I change the situation?"

The next day, Julian held a one-to-one meeting with Vikas, with the sole agenda of talking to him about his stress. From that meeting, Julian learned that Vikas was not only worried about the falling stock price of Upstream and its impact on his family's future, but also his own role in the low production levels versus the other fisheries around the globe. "I have tried everything to increase production in my area," Vikas said desperately. "I make charts, I tick boxes, and I follow every single move my team makes, yet we are still behind. I can't help but feel responsible for the organization's results. Maybe if it wasn't for me and my team, our stock price would have risen by now."

Julian was surprised that Vikas was blaming himself for the organization's problems, to the extent that it was causing him unprecedented levels of stress. He explained to Vikas about the impact of stress and **general adaptation syndrome (GAS)**, which is a set of physiological reactions to long-term stress that can be grouped into three stages: alarm, resistance, and exhaustion.[33] Vikas agreed that he has been feeling physically tense and wound up for some time, but now he just felt exhausted. Julian spent some time talking to Vikas about his problems at home, and directed him to human resources (HR), which would help him to alleviate his stress at home and at work through counseling, wellness programs, and taking more work breaks and time off.

At the same time, he was relieved to find that Vikas was more committed to Upstream than he had first thought. He had displayed a degree of **citizenship**, which is a commitment to the overall functions of the team and organizational culture in order to improve performance.[34] Next, he addressed Vikas's feelings of failure at work.

"Vikas, there is no one individual that is accountable for the performance of Upstream. We are all in this together, and it is our job to come up with solutions to make this company the best it can be."

"I would like to play a part in that, but to be honest, I don't think the personality tests we have been given describe me as a leader with the competence to have any real impact on

General adaptation syndrome (GAS) A set of physiological reactions to long-term stress that can be grouped into three stages: alarm, resistance, and exhaustion.

Citizenship In business, the commitment to the overall functions of the team and organizational culture in order to improve performance.

the organization. That's another reason I exploded at the dinner table; that strengths test described me as a real dictator and stick-in-the-mud," Vikas responded.

Julian was surprised again. Talk about selective perception! He took Vikas through the results again, pointing out how valuable his skills were and how the company depended on leaders like him to achieve success. At the end of the meeting, he assigned Vikas a task: "Over the next two weeks, I want you to work with the other leaders outside your shift to clarify your roles, and really think about what kind of leader you want to be. This will give you a chance to figure out what you and your team need to do to improve productivity."

Over the following weeks, Vikas worked with the other team leaders to come up with a solution to present to Julian. Maribel and Vikas, in particular, had lengthy conversations about their current roles, the sequence of personality tests, and how they feel about their "champion" assignments. Maribel told Vikas that she has learned a lot about herself and the way she manages others. "I have been a bit idealistic when it comes to assessing my team's capabilities. I think I have encouraged them to take on roles that extend them beyond their capacity, and then they resent me for it." Vikas replied, "Well, on my team, I assign tasks without really thinking about what my team is capable of. Maybe I need to get to know them better and see what they are really made of." Maribel said, "I think I have an idea . . ."

In the final analysis, with Julian's approval, Vikas and Maribel agreed to switch their champion roles, with Vikas as performance champion and Maribel as mission champion. This would give Vikas a chance to try a transactional style of leadership by becoming more engaged with the staff; and Maribel would now have more of an opportunity to devise and try new strategies in assigning tasks to her team.

Sure enough, over the coming weeks, Vikas found that he is enjoying being a transactional rather than a directive leader. By focusing on team performance, he began actively engaging in conversations with his staff. This personal engagement begins to transform Vikas's attitude.

14.5 | POSITIVE DEVIANCE AND PERFORMANCE

14.5 | Design a plan for maximizing individual behavior to change an organizational culture or performance positively.

Vikas was surprised at how much he enjoyed his role as performance champion. Not only was it encouraging him to engage more with his team, but it made him think about the type of leader he really wanted to be. For years, he had adopted a directive leadership style within a hierarchical structure, issuing commands to his subordinates, and watching them like a hawk to make sure they were performing well. When they made a mistake, he criticized them, and when they consistently did a good job, he made sure it was reflected in their financial reward at the end of the year. Yet, he could see now that his management style hadn't worked. In fact, it looked like his team barely managed to get through the day at all, so poorly did they view their role in the organization.

As Vikas became more engaged with his staff, he felt a change happening. His team members were more willing to come to him with ideas and communicate more openly. This was a good start, but he needed to maintain the momentum. A team's culture doesn't just change overnight; for all people to perform to the best of their abilities, a change of mind-set was badly needed.

Now that Vikas had become more motivated and engaged with his team, his next step was to transform the perceptions of their own work roles and work environment. Vikas was conscious that his team viewed their work as drudgery. So he met with his management team to talk about improving morale and creating a more positive and dynamic work environment.

After meeting with Julian, Vikas gave a lot of thought about his mood, his stress levels, and how they had affected the team. He tried his best not to bring his personal problems to work; in fact, he had never told anyone about his wife's illness or his financial concerns prior to his conversation with Julian. Yet, his refusal to confide in others resulted in isolation and resentment—not to mention an explosion in front of a valuable client. Perhaps he needed to take a leaf out of

LECTURE ENHANCER:

14.5 Positive Deviance and Performance

✓ **Emotional Intelligence (EI)—** the capacity to recognize and appreciate emotional responses in one's self and others

• **Purposeful Thinking & Change Management**
  ■ EI suggests that leaders get as much feedback as possible from their employees, peers, and bosses in order to improve their self-awareness and assess their levels of emotional impact
  ■ Managers who have insight into their own emotions and the feelings of others can inspire a greater degree of work performance

✓ **Inducements**—formal or informal agreements intended to entice positive or desirable behaviors

Maribel's book and practice the art of openness. He realized that he needs to know more about his own feelings and monitor his attitude accordingly to understand how it affected others. Only then would he be able to boost the mood of his team and lead them to success.

He took a few hours one each night to learn about the impact of mood on work performance. Vikas found that he was most inspired by the work of Daniel Goleman, on **emotional intelligence (EI)**, the capacity to recognize and appreciate emotional responses in one's self and others.[35] Vikas decides to work with his management team to ascertain the problems within his group, using the EI technique.

Purposeful Thinking and Change Management

Over the past few years, organizations have begun to apply the theory of EI in the workplace. The theory holds that managers who have insight into their own emotions and the feelings of others can inspire a higher quality of work performance. People that are more self-aware, optimistic, socially aware, and have the ability to build positive relationships with others generally have a high EQ. Good moods are contagious; if we smile and laugh, others will follow suit, according to the discoveries of EQ researchers. Yet, a good mood must also cater to the situation—if the company is being forced to eliminate a department and dismiss those employees, then it makes sense for the leader to be somber and respectful rather than outwardly happy and jocular.

EQ also suggests that leaders get as much feedback as possible from their employees, peers, and bosses to improve their self-awareness and assess their levels of emotional impact. No leader can make this assessment without help from others.

When Vikas sat down with his team, he asked them how they perceive him as a leader, with particular focus on his mood and behavior and how they affected the team. Nobody said anything. Eventually, Vikas managed to persuade them that they won't be fired if they tell him the truth. One manager tentatively told Vikas that he tended to mumble orders and then get frustrated if the team members asked him to repeat or clarify his demands. "OK, that's very useful," Vikas said. "That means I need to communicate more clearly with the team. What's next?"

Vikas's sensible attitude in response to that criticism served to open the floodgates, as the managers became more comfortable with giving him feedback. Another manager said, "It's just that the other teams seem to have more fun. Liam's team goes down to the pub and plays soccer, and Maribel's team has cake parties to celebrate reaching their goals. What do we have?"

As Vikas looked around at the team, he realized that he had not implemented any methods of motivating them or provided any **inducements**, which are formal or informal agreements intended to entice positive or desirable behaviors.[36] There had been no social engagements, no bonding opportunities, and no other rewards other than financial incentives, which, thanks to the slow economy, were becoming few and far between. In short, he hadn't spent any time getting to know them at all. Maybe if he understood his staff better, he would do a better job motivating them.

Throughout the meeting, Vikas made a concerted effort to be as accessible as possible. If he were being honest with himself, he was a little hurt about the way the staff viewed him—this process wasn't easy! However, he pushed away his pride and focused on the positive: he was learning more about himself and the team, and that was what really mattered.

By the end of the meeting, the team concluded that motivation and communication were sorely missed dynamics on the team. Vikas realized, more than ever before, that management is a "people" business, and managers who make the effort to get to know their teams and understand individual behaviors are more likely to secure commitment and loyalty, which in turn helps to generate more successful results. In the next chapter, we will explore how managers build highly functioning, motivated teams.

Case**Snapshot**

Chapter 14 Case: Understanding Individual Behavior: Millennials in the Workplace can be found on pg. 476

ADDITIONAL RESOURCES

KEY TERMS

Absenteeism The frequent or habitual absence of employees from work. (p.352)

Abundance The conscious pursuit of purposeful infinite possibilities that are sustainable and stable over time. (p.352)

Attitudes A person's or group's inclinations toward an idea or situation. (p.357)

Attribution An ascribed quality or characteristic that is related to a particular individual or situation. (p.357)

Authoritarianism The management philosophy that using the threat of punishment, power, and legitimacy is required to produce superior results. (p.358)

"Big Five" personality traits The five broad domains of human psychology: openness, conscientiousness, negativity, extraversion, and agreeableness. (p.357)

Burnout A physical or mental reaction due to stressful and demanding working conditions. (p.352)

Candor The quality of being open, frank, and sincere in speech or expression. (p.353)

Challenging work Work that is comprised of two types of tasks: pleasureful and purposeful. (p.354)

Citizenship In business, the commitment to the overall functions of the team and organizational culture in order to improve performance. (p.364)

Cognitive dissonance The psychological strain that occurs when a person is faced with two or more conflicting cognitions (e.g., beliefs, attitudes, or items of knowledge). (p.361)

Commitment The degree to which an employee is psychologically devoted to an organization or team. (p.355)

Confidence The certainty about handling something that a person desires or needs to do. (p.355)

Contributions The quantifiable efforts produced by an employee, based on that person's role and responsibilities. (p.353)

Creativity The ability to devise innovative ideas to meet the needs of a particular task or organizational goals. (p.362)

Deviance Intentional behavior and attitudes that differ from or violate the accepted social norms. (p.363)

Dysfunctional behaviors Actions that show a lack of commitment, lack of trust, fear of confrontation or conflicting opinions, a refusal to accept responsibility, and a tendency to focus on their own individual needs ahead of the team and the organization. (p.363)

Emotional intelligence (EI) The capacity to recognize and appreciate emotional responses in one's self and others. (p.366)

General adaptation syndrome (GAS) A set of physiological reactions to long-term stress that can be grouped into three stages: alarm, resistance, and exhaustion. (p.364)

Individual differences The variable psychological, behavioral, cultural, and physical dimensions that uniquely distinguish each team member. (p.357)

Inducements Formal or informal agreements intended to entice positive or desirable behaviors. (p.366)

Joyful living Feelings and emotions defined by interest, passion, curiosity, contentment, enthusiasm, satisfaction, and quality of life. (p.354)

Locus of control The degree to which an individual or team feels in control of circumstances and outcomes. (p.357)

Machiavellianism A pragmatic management philosophy that condones unethical and manipulative behavior if it produces desirable results. (p.358)

Moral courage Taking a position against something or someone even though you know the outcome may be unpopular. (p.354)

Negative affectivity (NA) A general dimension of personality where an individual experiences negative mood states, such as anger, disgust, fear, and anxiety. (p.352)

Perception The process by which individuals select, interpret, and organize information in the world around them. (p.354)

Positive affectivity (PA) The outward display of affirming emotions, such as happiness, optimism, and encouragement. (p.353)

Positive deviance Intentional behavior and attitudes that differ from the accepted social norms in an honorable way. (p.363)

Psychological contract An informal expectation between employee and organization that determines quality and satisfaction. (p.355)

Purposeful thinking An approach that involves continually seeking pathways for possibilities and looking for opportunities to learn and grow. (p.353)

Risk The probability of loss or undesirable consequences. (p.354)

Selective perception The process by which individuals accept information consistent with their values and beliefs, while screening out information that is not aligned with their own needs. (p.354)

Self-awareness The ability to look objectively at a circumstance and make subjective, principle-based judgment decisions simultaneously. (p.353)

Self-efficacy The extent to which a person believes in his or her own competence regarding a process or task. (p.354)

Stereotyping The tendency to ascribe characteristics or attributes to a particular group or individual unfairly. (p.356)

Stress The physiological and emotional reactions experienced by individuals to excessive pressures or demands at work. (p.352)

Type A personality A behavioral pattern where individuals tend to be ambitious, assertive, goal oriented, impatient, determined, highly organized, competitive, and aggressive. (p.355)

Type B personality A behavioral pattern where individuals tend to be more patient, relaxed, easygoing, and more sensitive to the feelings of others. (p.355)

IN REVIEW

14.1 | Describe the dimensions of positive individual behaviors and its impact on organizational performance.

The six dimensions of abundance include self-awareness, purposeful thinking, relationships of thoughtful candor, challenging work, moral courage, and joyful living. *Self-awareness* is the ability to look objectively at a circumstance and make subjective, principle-based judgment decisions simultaneously. *Purposeful thinking* involves continually seeking pathways for possibilities and looking for opportunities to learn and grow. *Candor* is the ability to self-organize and cultivate relationships that are aligned with purposeful thinking. *Challenging work* is comprised of two types of tasks: pleasureful and purposeful. Pleasureful tasks provide an immediate feeling of joy and delight, with little effect on overall life satisfaction. The process of completing purposeful tasks gives us a sense of accomplishment, with lasting meaning. *Moral courage* is taking a position against something or someone even though you know the outcome may be unpopular. *Joyful living* can be described as feelings and emotions defined by interest, passion, curiosity, contentment, enthusiasm, satisfaction, and quality of life.

14.2 | Explain the characteristics of individual personalities and strength profiles.

There are three particular areas that managers focus on in relation to personality: locus of control, authoritarianism, and Machiavellianism. *Locus of control* is the degree to which an individual or team feels in control of circumstances and outcomes. *Authoritarianism* is the management philosophy that using the threat of punishment, power, and legitimacy is required to produce superior results. *Machiavellianism* is a pragmatic management philosophy that overlooks unethical and manipulative behavior if it produces desirable results.

Focusing on strengths was far more productive than honing in on and trying to "fix" weaknesses. Develop and capitalize on skills in order to enhance work performance.

14.3 | Explain how individual attitudes and beliefs affect team and organizational dynamics.

Sometimes individual attitudes and behaviors conflict with one another, leading to a state of *cognitive dissonance*, a psychological strain that occurs when a person is faced with two or more conflicting cognitions (e.g., beliefs, attitudes, or items of knowledge).

14.4 | Interpret how stress, deviance, and dysfunctional behaviors manifest and negatively affect team and organizational performance.

Dysfunctional employees include lack of commitment, lack of trust, fear of confrontation or conflicting opinions, a refusal to accept responsibility, and a tendency to focus on their own individual needs ahead of the team and the organization. *Deviance* involves intentional behaviors and attitudes that differ from or violate the accepted social norms.

14.5 | Design a plan for maximizing individual behavior to positively change an organizational culture or performance.

Emotional intelligence (EI) is the capacity to recognize and appreciate emotional responses in one's self and others. EI can be used as a tool to help positively change a culture or performance. Managers who have insight into their own emotions and the feelings of others can inspire a greater degree of work performance. In addition, *inducements*, which are formal or informal agreements, intended to entice positive or desirable behaviors, may be used to help shape positive behavior and performance.

SELF-TEST

14.1 | Describe the dimensions of positive individual behaviors and its impact on organizational performance.

1. The outward display of affirming emotions, such as happiness, optimism, and encouragement, is known as:

   a. Positive affectivity (PA)
   b. Negative affectivity (NA)
   c. Abundance
   d. Burnout

2. Perception is the process by which individuals select, interpret, and organize information in the world around them.
   a. True
   b. False

3. Explain the difference between a Type A and a Type B personality.

14.2 | Explain the characteristics of individual personalities and strength profiles.

4. The tendency to ascribe characteristics or attributes to a particular group or individual unfairly is known as:
   a. A halo effect
   b. The fundamental attribution error
   c. Stereotyping
   d. Projecting

5. List and define the Big Five personality traits.

6. An internal locus of control is a belief that there is nothing we can do to affect the outcome; we are simply pawns of our fate.
   a. True
   b. False

14.3 | Explain how individual attitudes and beliefs affect team and organizational dynamics.

7. A psychological strain that occurs when a person is faced with two or more conflicting cognitions (e.g., beliefs, attitudes, or items of knowledge) is known as:
   a. Machiavellianism
   b. Cognitive dissonance
   c. Negative resonance
   d. A hindrance stressor

8. Creativity is the ability to devise innovative ideas to meet the needs of a particular task or organizational goal.
   a. True
   b. False

14.4 | Interpret how stress, deviance, and dysfunctional behaviors manifest and negatively affect team and organizational performance.

9. What are some of the signs of a dysfunctional employee?

10. _____ include intentional behaviors and attitudes that differ from the accepted social norms in an honorable way.
    a. Dysfunctional behavior
    b. Negative deviance
    c. Positive deviance
    d. Citizenship

11. Describe general adaptation syndrome (GAS).

14.5 | Design a plan for maximizing individual behavior to change an organizational culture or performance positively.

12. The capacity to recognize and appreciate emotional responses in one's self and others is known as:
    a. Emotional intelligence (EI)
    b. Optimism
    c. Agreeableness
    d. Empathy

13. Psychological contracts are formal or informal agreements intended to entice positive or desirable behaviors
    a. True
    b. False

CHAPTER EXERCISE

The Emotional Audit: Learning to Handle an Emotional Hijacking*

During the 2006 World Cup finals, in front of 28.8 million viewers worldwide, soccer role model Zinedine Zidane lost control of himself and headbutted Italy's Marco Materazzi. Zidane was ejected from the game, and France lost the World Cup. The incident led many to wonder, "What was he thinking?!" Well, maybe he wasn't thinking. Zidane was experiencing what some people have called an "emotional" or "amygdala" hijacking. The *amygdala* is the emotional part of the brain that controls the "flight or fight" response. When a person is threatened, the amygdala can respond with a rush of stress hormones that can flood the body and lead to irrational actions. In effect, your control over your emotions is temporarily hijacked. An emotional hijacking is characterized by a strong emotional reaction, a sudden onset, and a regret for one's actions later, after reflection.

An emotional audit is a tool that can help you maintain control over your emotions and reactions when you are experiencing an emotional hijacking. This strategy involves asking yourself a series of questions designed to help refocus activity away from the amygdala and engage other areas of the brain to gain more cognitive, emotional, and behavioral control. The emotional audit involves asking yourself a series of four questions. The first two access and label your thoughts and emotions, the third consciously appraises your intentions, and the final question examines your actions relative to your intentions. Here are the questions, along with the area of the brain they are engaged, according to the hypothesis:

1. What am I thinking? (Basal ganglia—integrates feelings, thoughts, and movements.)

2. What am I feeling? (Temporal lobes—emotional stability, "name it to tame it"; labeling effect.)

3. What do I want now? (Cerebellum—executive functions and cognitive integration.)

4. How am I getting in my own way? (Prefrontal cortex—learning from my mistakes.)

5. What do I need to do differently now? (Prefrontal cortex—executive functioning; planning; goal setting; insight; anterior cingulate gyrus—brain's gear shifter; sees options go from idea to idea.)

Instructions:

Think of a time recently when you feel that you were "emotionally hijacked." Briefly describe the situation, what triggered your emotional reaction, what you did, and what you regret.

_____

_____

_____

Now conduct an emotional audit on that experience by answering the following questions:

1. What was I thinking?

_____

2. What am I feeling?

_____

3. What did I want?

_____

4. How did I get in my own way?

_____

5. What should I have done differently?

_____

Practice applying the emotional audit technique when you feel that you are experiencing an emotional hijacking to help yourself control your emotions and possible reactions that you might regret later.

* Exercise inspired by Nadler, Relly, "What Was I Thinking? Handling the Hijack." *Business Management*, Issue 16; http://www.busmanagement.com/article/What-Was-I-Thinking-Handling-the-Hijack/.

SELF-ASSESSMENT

How Accurately Can You Describe Yourself?*

Describe yourself as you generally are now, not as you wish to be in the future. Describe yourself as you honestly see yourself, in relation to other people you know of the same sex as you are, and roughly your same age.

For each statement, check the circle that best describes you based on the following scale:

	Completely Accurate	Not at all Accurate	Somewhat Accurate	A little Accurate	Mostly Accurate
	1	2	3	4	5
1. Am the life of the party	O	O	O	O	O
2. Am interested in people	O	O	O	O	O
3. Am always prepared	O	O	O	O	O
4. Am relaxed most of the time	O	O	O	O	O
5. Have a rich vocabulary	O	O	O	O	O
6. Feel comfortable around people	O	O	O	O	O
7. Sympathize with others' feelings	O	O	O	O	O
8. Pay attention to details	O	O	O	O	O
9. Don't get stressed out easily	O	O	O	O	O
10. Have excellent ideas	O	O	O	O	O
11. Talk to a lot of different people at parties	O	O	O	O	O
12. Have a soft heart	O	O	O	O	O
13. Get chores done right away	O	O	O	O	O
14. Seldom feel blue	O	O	O	O	O
15. Have a vivid imagination	O	O	O	O	O
16. Start conversations	O	O	O	O	O
17. Take time out for others	O	O	O	O	O
18. Appreciate orderliness	O	O	O	O	O
19. Seldom feel blue	O	O	O	O	O
20. Am full of ideas	O	O	O	O	O

Scoring:

Extraversion (add items 1, 6, 11, 16 and write your score in the blank) _____

The extent to which you are outgoing, sociable, talkative, and able to get on well with others.

Agreeableness (add items 2, 7, 12, 17 and write your score in the blank) _____

The extent to which you are able to relate to others by being trusting, forgiving, kind, affectionate, and cooperative

Conscientiousness (add items 3, 8, 13, 18 and write your score in the blank) _____

The extent to which you exhibit thoughtfulness, organization, and responsibility

Emotional Stability (Neuroticism; reverse scaled) (add items 4, 9, 14, 19 and write your score in the blank) _____

The extent to which you are calm and relaxed rather than tense, moody, irritable, and anxious.

Openness to Experience/Imagination (add items 5, 10, 15, 20 and write score in the blank) _____

The extent to which you are able to have fun and feel elation and delight, foster a diverse sharing of ideas, and learn from contradictory points of view.

What was your strongest decision-making style? What are the advantages and disadvantages of this style?

What was your weakest decision-making style? What are the advantages and disadvantages of this style?

*These five scales were developed to measure the Big Five factor markers reported in the L. R. Goldberg, "The Development of Markers for the Big-Five Factor Structure," *Psychological Assessment, 4*, 26–42 (1992).

SELF-TEST ANSWER KEY

1. a.
2. a; True
3. A *Type A* personality is a behavioral pattern in which individuals tend to be ambitious, assertive, goal oriented, impatient, determined, highly organized, competitive, and aggressive. In contrast, a *Type B* personality involves a behavioral pattern in which individuals tend to be more patient, relaxed, easygoing, and more sensitive to the feelings of others.
4. c.
5. *Openness* is the ability to have fun and feel elation and delight. Open people have the capacity to foster diverse sharing of ideas and listen and learn from contradictory points of view. *Conscientiousness* occurs when individuals exhibit thoughtfulness, organization, and responsibility in the pursuit of goals. Individuals high in *neuroticism* (or low in emotional stability) tend to be tense, moody, irritable, and anxious. *Extraversion* is reflected in people who are generally outgoing, sociable, talkative, and able to get on well with others. Finally, *agreeableness* describes the extent to which an individual relates to others by being trusting, forgiving, kind, affectionate, and cooperative.

6. b. False. An *external* locus of control is a belief that there is nothing we can do to affect the outcome; we are simply pawns of our fate, while an *internal* locus of control is a belief that we are in control of our own fate.
7. b.
8. a; True.
9. Signs of dysfunctional employees include lack of commitment, lack of trust, fear of confrontation or conflicting opinions, a refusal to accept responsibility, and a tendency to focus on their own individual needs ahead of the team and the organization.
10. c.
11. *General adaptation syndrome (GAS)* is a set of physiological reactions to long-term stress which can be grouped into three stages: alarm, resistance, and exhaustion.
12. a.
13. a; False. *Inducements* are formal or informal agreements intended to entice positive or desirable behaviors.
    b; False.

Notes

CHAPTER FIFTEEN

COMMUNICATING AND MOTIVATING OTHERS

Learning Objectives

By the end of the chapter, you will be able to:

15.1 | Explain how managers use motivation and communication to achieve results.

15.2 | Understand how to apply communication to pursue and achieve goals efficiently and effectively.

15.3 | Describe how challenging work and goals motivate individuals and teams.

15.4 | Illustrate how positive reinforcement enables managers to motivate others to achieve superior results.

15.5 | Formulate and communicate a performance-based reward system that motivates individuals and teams to achieve organizational objectives.

ADDITIONAL RESOURCES

KEY TERMS
IN REVIEW
SELF-TEST
CHAPTER EXERCISE
SELF-ASSESSMENT
SELF-TEST
ANSWER KEY

JP Greenwood/Getty Images

INSIDE THIS CHAPTER

ManagementStory:
Featuring **Julian Wales**

Motivation An incentive or drive to complete a task, function, or idea.

15.1 | HOW MANAGERS ACHIEVE GREAT RESULTS WITH OTHERS

"If your actions inspire others to dream more, learn more, do more and become more, you are a leader."

—John Quincy Adams

15.1 | Explain how managers use motivation and communication to achieve results.

In Chapter 8, we explored the concept of goal setting, and how managers are able to motivate and inspire employees not only through financial incentives, but through igniting a sense of passion and pride in their work. So what is motivation? **Motivation** is an incentive or drive to complete a task, function, or idea.[1] Before the researchers Edwin A. Locke and Gary Latham began their experiment with loggers in Oklahoma, as discussed in Chapter 8, the only motivation given to these workers had been fear, intimidation, and low financial reward, giving rise to poor productivity and low morale. In an effort to prove that goal setting and motivation go hand in hand, the researchers devised a process whereby the loggers were supported by managers who gave them clear instructions, treated them fairly, and encouraged feedback. Because of this, the loggers felt more engaged with their work and proceeded to exceed all performance expectations.

© nycshooter/iStockphoto

Although many of us may not give much thought to as to why we get up in the morning, go to school or work, exercise, play sports, or engage in other social activities, the key driver is motivation.

What motivates a student to go to college or work hard to prepare for an exam? There might be a financial incentive involved, such as the promise of a good-paying job after graduation; or the student might be motivated by the desire for recognition, accomplishment, and even popularity if he or she performs particularly well. There is also the motivation that comes from knowing that education is the key to a more promising future. Yet all our behaviors are motivated by an intrinsic desire to do well; money might seem like a good motivator to pass an exam, but there also needs to be interest, a desire to learn, an aptitude to study, and innate passion to achieve the goal.

The same concept applies to managers and leaders within organizations: if motivation is high, then so is performance and productivity. To achieve optimal performance, managers need to understand what drives their employees in order to motivate them. Key to this process is **communication**, the act of transmitting information, thoughts, and processes through various channels.[2]

But with so many different personalities and behaviors within an organization, how do managers assess the underlying needs that motivate employees? The following theories of motivation have been applied to organizations worldwide and are still relevant today.

Communication The act of transmitting information, thoughts, and processes through various channels.

Maslow's Hierarchy of Needs

Developed by the psychologist Abraham Maslow in 1943, **Maslow's hierarchy of needs** suggests that people are motivated by a number of needs which are displayed in a hierarchy. These are physiological needs, safety needs, love/belongingness needs, esteem needs, and self-actualization needs.[3]

Physiological Needs These are basic items that we all need to ensure our survival, such as shelter, food, water, air, sleep, and warmth. In the workplace, for example, this translates in the need for a fair salary, which in turn provides the ability to feed, house, and clothe ourselves.

Safety Needs Once these physiological needs are satisfied, we need an environment that is safe, both physically and mentally. For example, in the production line of a manufacturing company, employees need to be reassured that every step possible has been taken in order to prevent any accidents with machinery. Employees also need to be mentally satisfied that their jobs are secure and that they are being provided with decent benefits.

Affiliation/Belongingness Needs These needs reflect our desire to be accepted by others and to find our place within certain working groups. Inherently, we want to foster good working relationships with our peers, managers, and coworkers in order to create a pleasant working environment.

Esteem Needs This is our need to be respected and appreciated by others. In organizations, most employees have a desire to be recognized, rewarded, and credited for hard work.

Self-Actualization Needs Sitting at the top of Maslow's hierarchy is our need for self-actualization. This means that we have an innate need for personal growth and self-development. Managers can aid the process of self-actualization in work environments by providing further training, assigning challenging goals, and encouraging creativity.

Esteem needs and self-actualization needs are particularly important and relevant for today's fluid workplace if organizations want to retain their staff. When managers communicate effectively with their teams, reward them sufficiently, and offer them opportunities for advancement, employees are more likely to attain a high level of job satisfaction, which encourages them to stay with an organization.

ERG Theory of Motivation

Maslow's theory has been challenged by a number of other scientists who have questioned the validity of the hierarchy of needs and their order of importance. The theorist Clayton Alderfer put forward a modification of Maslow's theory called the **ERG Theory of Motivation**, which sets out three categories of human needs relating to organizational behaviors: existent needs, relatedness needs, and growth needs.[4]

Existence needs describe our physiological and safety needs; relatedness needs reflect our desire for good relationships with others; and growth needs focus on our need for personal fulfillment, self-development, and accomplishment. Similarly to Maslow, Alderfer also laid out the needs in a hierarchical structure, but he believed that instead of moving up to the next need, one step at a time, that we can pursue different levels of needs simultaneously, moving up and down within the hierarchy depending on how well a particular need is satisfied at the moment.

Two-Factor Theory of Motivation

Another well-known theory of motivation was developed by Frederick Herzberg in the 1950s. The **Two-Factor Theory of Motivation**, also known as *motivation-hygiene theory* or

© skynesher/iStockphoto

ManagementStory:
Featuring Julian Wales

dual theory, is based on job satisfaction and/or job dissatisfaction and the extent to which attitudes influence outcomes.[5]

Following a series of interviews with hundreds of workers, Herzberg concluded that two factors influence employee behavior. The first he called *hygiene factors*, which include working conditions, wages, job security, and company policy. If employees considered any of these factors to be poor or below average, then the rate of job dissatisfaction was higher. The second set of factors he called *motivators*, which are the opportunities given to employees for personal growth, such as recognition, achievement, status, responsibility, and opportunity for advancement. When motivators are absent, employees experience a certain ambivalence toward their roles; however, if motivators are effective, then employees are highly stimulated and satisfied with their roles. Herzberg believed that managers needed to address the hygiene factors first in order to satisfy employees, before moving on to the next step of using motivators to meet their higher-level needs.

In this chapter, we will explore how the leaders at Upstream Fisheries use motivational and communication techniques in order to improve productivity and performance.

In Chapters 13 and 14, we followed the progress of Julian Wales, a group leader at Upstream Fisheries, a global company that farm-raises fish using organic food and environmentally friendly practices. Julian has been set a goal by Upstream's CEO to motivate the team and boost production levels. Thanks to the behavioral studies suggested by Julian, the team leaders have become more confident about their own strengths and how they can use their skills to motivate and communicate with others.

In particular, Vikas's and Maribel's satisfaction and performance start to increase; swapping their champion roles has proved to be a real motivator for them both, as they feel they are being challenged in new ways. As Vikas is now performance champion, he is responsible for overseeing the implementation of performance development and recognition systems in order to ensure financial and operational goal achievement. Maribel is now mission champion, and her role is to ensure that the company's mission, a commitment to sustainability, is not lost or mitigated because of daily operational challenges. Liam is a good motivator and communicator, and has not experienced any major personal changes. His team is doing well, and its success is crucial to the organization.

As Julian observes the three leaders in action, he realizes that his work in Spain is drawing to a close. He calls Max Johnson, CEO of Upstream Fisheries, and tells him that he is confident that the team leaders possess the skills needed to boost Upstream's performance and bring it in line with the other branches. Max agrees that it is time for Julian to depart and allow the leaders to do their work.

It is Saturday night, and Julian and the team go to the local restaurant—the place where Vikas had previously exploded at entrepreneur Tim Matthews, owner of a successful chain of restaurants called "Tim's Famous" —for their last get-together before he leaves. Worried about the falling profits at Upstream and the effect it would have on him financially, Vikas had taken his frustrations out on Matthews, shocking everyone with his behavior. The night had not ended well.

Once the appetizers are served, Vikas says, "I can't tell you all how much better I feel now than the last time we were here. Thanks for sticking with me and helping me believe in the potential of Upstream again. Julian, are you sure you can't stay around for a while longer?"

Julian responds, "No, it is up to all of you now. Thanks to your work in building interpersonal relationships with your teams, your team members appear to be reassured about their job security and are building stronger relationships with each other. These are good results, but remember, this is only the beginning. Great results will come only when you communicate and motivate with the passion, vision, processes, and discipline necessary to build a company worth believing in. When we do that, trust me, the financial results will come. What has worked with this team will work with your respective teams, if you let it." Following a relaxing evening with his team leaders, Julian drives to the airport and leaves them to continue the work they started together.

"This is our mission now." Liam says to the other team members. "Let's make it work."

15.2 | COMMUNICATING WITH OTHERS

15.2 | Understand how to apply communication to pursue and achieve goals efficiently and effectively.

Monday morning comes. The buzz of activity is palpable at Upstream Fisheries. Vikas, renewed with energy and focus, is visibly happy. Most of his team members return his smile, but they are quietly asking one another, "What's gotten into him?"

After the first two weeks, however, Vikas starts to get discouraged. He has introduced the team meetings where everybody is free to present ideas and initiatives regarding performance enhancement and provide feedback; he has set up regular one-to-one meetings to ensure the welfare of each member of the staff; and in keeping with their Spanish location, he has promised a "tapas party," where the team will be rewarded with delicious Spanish snacks if they reach their goals at the end of each month. Yet, although his staff seems more engaged than before, he is not fully convinced that they are aware of how important they are to the success of Upstream.

Vikas pulls out his cell phone and dials Julian's office number. "Hey, Vikas!" Julian says. "What's going on?"

Vikas replies, "I sure could use your help! I am getting a little discouraged. Although my team has become more open with me and is working better together, I'm not sure they fully understand the importance of their roles in achieving our goal to boost productivity within Upstream. What do you think I should do next?"

Julian chooses his words carefully, not wanting to discourage Vikas. "Well, have you told them what our goal is? Why what they do is so important? And how they can go from being good to great?"

Vikas says, "The Monday you left, I brought everybody into the large conference room and shared with them exactly what we had discussed."

Julian replies, "And what happened after that first meeting? How often have you discussed Upstream's mission—you know, the 'what, why, and how' for performance excellence"?

Vikas gets the point. "I guess that's the problem. I haven't mentioned our mission since that Monday . . ."

Julian says, "Don't worry about yesterday or the past two weeks or the past two years. No offense, but your team has had to deal with you for the past several years and they are probably unsure about the new you. Remember, if you don't maintain consistent communication with them, they will start reverting to their original perceptions of the old Vikas." After all, it is impossible to follow a leader who looks as if he doesn't want to climb the mountain that he's telling everyone else to climb. It is going to take a while before everyone is on board. Right now, the best you can do is to stay positive and communicate, communicate, and communicate. When you start getting tired of saying the "What? Why? How?" then you have only just begun to get the message across."

When Vikas ends the call, he sits deep in thought. Julian is right: a team is only as good as its leader. He needs to find a way of proving to his staff how passionate he is about Upstream's new vision and instill in them the same motivational forces he has gained to help attain their goals. To do this, he needs to refresh his knowledge about the communication process.

Process of Communication

One of the most widespread communication models used today is the Shannon-Weaver model, created by mathematician Claude E. Shannon in 1947, and later developed by Warren Weaver. The model is shown in Figure 15-1.

When we talk to people, face to face, there are two components at work: the sender (source) and the receiver. The sender transmits or encodes the message through a chosen communication channel, and the receiver must try and decode or interpret the meaning of the message that is being delivered. The receiver then provides feedback to the sender to ensure that the communication has been received and understood, and formulates a response where necessary.[6]

LECTURE ENHANCER:

15.2 Communicating with Others

- **Process of Communication**
  - ✓ Oral Communication—used to provide verbal discussions, ideas and processes; one on one or as a group in person (face to face)
  - ✓ Body (Nonverbal) Language—a person's facial and body movements that express communication and emotion without the use of words
- **The Communication Network**
  - ✓ Communication Networks—a system of resources used as a channel for communication such as internet or groups of people to connect
  - ✓ Communication Paradigms—modes of communication defined by the relationship between a single node and many nodes
    - One-to-One
    - One-to-Many
    - Many-to-One
    - Many-to-Many
  - ✓ Grapevine—an informal line of communication where information is passed on from one person to another
  - ✓ Gossip Chains—when several individuals manifest and spread generally inaccurate or misleading information throughout the organization
  - ✓ Cluster Chain—a group of people that disseminate information within their group
- **Increasing Efficiency and Effectiveness**
  - ➤ Ten Disciplines Necessary for Team Success
    1. Compassion
    2. Conscientiousness
    3. Forgiveness
    4. Gratitude
    5. Grit
    6. Humility
    7. Hypo-Egoic
    8. Mindfulness
    9. Openness
    10. Wisdom

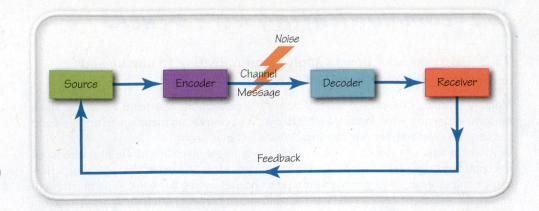

Figure 15-1
Shannon-Weaver Communications Model
The Shannon-Weaver model, a communications model showing the transmission of messages from sender to receiver.

Sometimes the flow of messages is interrupted by *noise*, which is anything that hampers communication between the sender and the receiver. Background noise, such as telephones ringing, construction work, or people talking loudly, can affect our ability to communicate. Noise also includes the use of unclear language, difficult vocabulary, and jargon, which may cause confusion and misunderstanding. Managers need to be aware of the impact of noise and take steps to ensure that the source of the disruption is eliminated.

Vikas knows that good communication skills are essential in the workplace in order to build successful relationships with others. He also knows there is room for improvement when it comes to his oral and written communication. In order to brush up and improve his skills, he considers the following communication channels.

Oral communication Provides verbal discussions, ideas, and processes, either one on one or as a group (face-to-face).

Oral communication is used to provide verbal discussions, ideas, and processes. This form of communication includes face-to-face discussion, (one-on-one or as a group) telephone conversations, presentations, speeches, meetings, conferences and lectures.

© Image Source/Corbis

Advantages Oral communication helps to build relationships, rapport, and trust; accelerates decision making and problem solving; and provides a forum whereby feedback is immediate and spontaneous.

Disadvantages The informal nature of oral communication may lead to vague or reckless statements that may result in confusion or misunderstanding. In addition, unless there is an attempt to record it, the information provided through the channel of oral communication can be unreliable, unstable and incomplete.

Written communication is where the sender writes emails, reports, memos, letters, and other documents; the receiver must interpret those emails the way they are intended.

Advantages Words can be carefully chosen and revised before sending; the message can be recorded and archived for future use; and the receiver has more time to interpret the message.

Written communication A system where the sender writes emails, reports, memos, letters, and other documents.

Disadvantages Written communication can be time-consuming, and it takes patience and skill to compose an effective message; it does not allow for spontaneous or immediate feedback; and the sender has no idea if the message will be correctly interpreted or even read by the receiver.

Electronic communication
A system that includes emails, Skype, videoconferencing, blogs, instant messaging, texting, and social networking.

Electronic communication includes emails, Skype, videoconferencing, blogs, instant messaging, texting, and social networking (LinkedIn, Twitter, Facebook, etc.).

Advantages Messages can be delivered instantly to a large audience across a global network; electronic communication is the speediest and most convenient way to deliver a long-distance message; messages can be sent and received from any location; and it is an effective way for groups to remain in touch (i.e., through social networking sites).

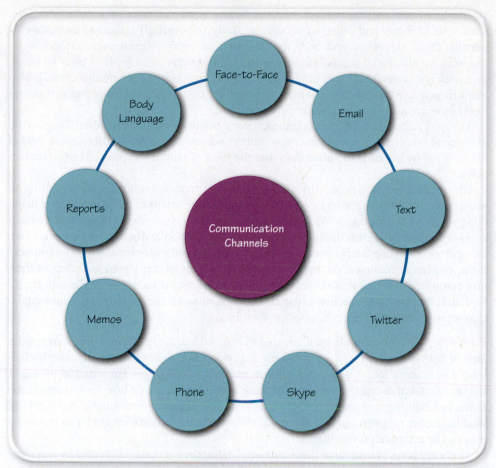

Figure 15-2
Types of Communication Channels
The many channels of communication at our fingertips.

Disadvantages Electronic communication can be hampered by technical problems, such as a computer crashing or a server breaking down; messages may be open to misinterpretation; and users may be vulnerable to security breaches by hackers and cyber criminals. The various forms of communication are shown in Figure 15-2.

Vikas's history as a communicator has been checkered, to say the least. Feedback from his management team has characterized his face-to face communication as brusque and impatient; his written communication as overly detailed but lacking in meaning; and his electronic communication as infrequent. Over the last few weeks, he has been working on his oral communication skills by trying to be more accessible to the team—listening to them, asking their opinions, and encouraging feedback, rather than just issuing orders. He has also been practicing his written skills by crafting documents and emails and running them by his fellow leaders for feedback before sending them out. An electronic communications course has also helped him to brush up on his social networking skills—he is even thinking about starting an Upstream Fisheries blog.

Yet something is missing. Although his team appears to agree with the new vision for the company, he gets the impression that they are just humoring him. Vikas notes that some people on his team tend to cross their arms when they see him approach and fail to make eye contact, both of which he perceives as defensive gestures. He hopes that through the initiatives that he has introduced and consistent communication from him, that they will become a bit more trusting and relaxed around him in time. However, Vikas knows that to communicate effectively with his team, he must choose the most optimal communication channels to deliver his messages.

Channel Richness With so many communication channels at our disposal, it is important that managers choose the most effective method to suit a given situation. **Channel richness** is the capacity to convey as much information as possible during the communication process. Face-to-face discussion is considered the richest form of communication, as it allows for direct personal contact, instant feedback, and immediate clarification. During

Channel richness The capacity to convey as much information as possible during the communication process.

Body (nonverbal) language
Consists of a person's facial expression and body movements that express communication and emotion without the use of words.

face-to-face conversations, we can also read certain nonverbal cues, such as facial expression, tone of voice, and other social signals. **Body (nonverbal) language** consists of a person's facial expression and body movements that express communication and emotion without the use of words.[7] Being able to read the signs and signals of body language increases our understanding of others, allowing for more effective communication. It also helps us perceive the effects of the messages that we are sending, and improves our awareness of the impact of our communication on others.

The next richest form of oral communication is the telephone conversation. Despite the absence of body language and direct eye contact, we are still able to gather a great deal of information by listening to verbal cues and the level of emotion expressed in the human voice.

Given the increasing popularity of electronic communication, it may be surprising to learn that many regard face-to-face and telephone conversations to be richer forms of delivering and receiving messages. Without verbal and facial cues, emails, texts, and instant messages are subject to a great deal of misunderstanding, especially when sensitive matters are being discussed. For example, sending an angry text or email will only cause more complications. Written communication, such as letters and memos, is considered less effective than oral communication, as it is slower, more impersonal, and does not allow for immediate feedback. It is far more effective to use face-to-face, or secondarily, telephone communication when dealing with difficult, emotive situations.

Barriers to communication
Obstacles that interrupt the flow of conveying and receiving messages.

Barriers to communication, illustrated in Figure 15-3, are obstacles that interrupt the flow of conveying and receiving messages. Every day, our ability to communicate is challenged by external forces, of which we may or may not be conscious. For example, we might not realize it, but distractions in the workplace have a big impact on how we communicate: noise, bad lighting, and uncomfortable chairs all interfere with communication. Similarly, working under pressure can also affect our ability to communicate effectively as messages may not be accurately transmitted.

There are ways to overcome these barriers. Distractions can be minimized by assessing the source of the problems and ensuring that they are fixed as a matter of high priority; and time management skills will also help managers to balance their workload more efficiently. Let's take a look at some more common barriers to communication and explore different ways to overcome them.

Figure 15-3
Barriers to Communication
Barriers to communication and ways to overcome them.

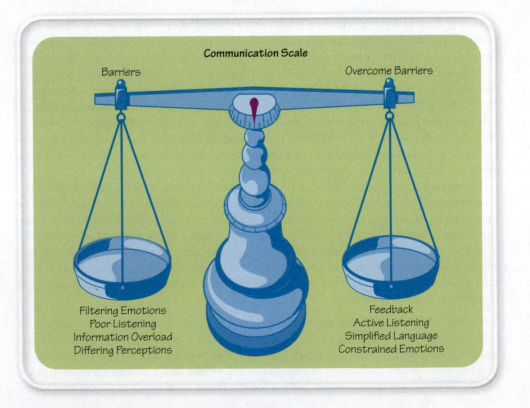

Filtering A message may be screened before being passed on to the receiver. For example, a manager may give his secretary or assistant a message to pass on to someone else. Before passing on the message, the secretary may screen the message for relevancy and clarity. While it is important to communicate clearly, sometimes filtering can interrupt the flow of communication, as the secretary may incorrectly eliminate information that he/she perceives as irrelevant. Filtering can be resolved by using simplified language and choosing a variety of communication channels to ensure the message is sent in its intended format.

Emotion Our mood can also affect communication. When we are stressed or experiencing high levels of anxiety, we may incorrectly perceive constructive criticism as a personal attack. Conversely, when we are relaxed and cheerful, we are more likely to accept advice and guidance, and perceive it as useful and constructive. To overcome emotional barriers, we must be aware of our feelings and try to constrain them when we communicate with others. We must also be mindful that there is a greater potential for misunderstanding and confusion during heightened emotional states.

Information Overload Sometimes we can become overwhelmed with the level of information around us and overlook or lose sight of important points, which leads to confusion and misinterpretation. Managers can eliminate or overcome barriers to communication by learning to prioritize their work more effectively to avoid becoming overwhelmed or overloaded by huge waves of information.

Differing Perceptions We often have a tendency to impose our own reality and project our own ideas, interests, and expectations onto other people and things. Making assumptions can lead to misconceptions, misunderstandings, and an eventual breakdown in communication. We can overcome this communication barrier by analyzing and questioning our assumptions for accuracy, and clarifying our perceptions by seeking constructive feedback from others.

Listening One of the chief barriers to communication is lack of attention, not really listening to what the other person is saying. This can lead to misunderstandings that can create tension and potentially damage working relationships. The ability to listen is one of the most important skills you can have as a manager.

Listening is the active effort to understand, learn, and obtain verbal information from others. Effective listening involves giving the speaker your full attention, avoiding distractions, not interrupting, reading body language and other nonverbal cues, and concentrating on what the other person is saying. You can also show the speaker that you are actively listening by maintaining eye contact, issuing short responses, and encouraging the speaker by smiling and nodding where appropriate. When formulating a response, be open and honest about what you have heard, and ask questions and provide feedback where appropriate.

Listening Across Global Networks With so many different ways to communicate, it is not surprising that some messages tend to get "lost in translation," certainly when it comes to communicating across the globe. Managers need to be proficient in communicating through global networks by actively listening, understanding culture and diversity, and teaching their teams the skills needed to work effectively in a virtual organization.

Communication Networks

A **communication network** is a system of resources used as a channel for groups of people to connect to each other, such as the Internet,.[8] While we could argue that the methods of communication have evolved immeasurably, from face-to-face communication, to sending letters through the mail, to the telephone, to the Internet, our innate need to communicate has not changed at all.[9]

Formal networks are not the only communication channels that managers need to work within; informal communication channels are also

> **Listening** The active effort to understand, learn, and obtain information from others.

> **Communication network** A system of resources used as a channel for groups of people to connect to each other, such as the Internet.

©Squaredpixels/iStockphoto

©Francesco Ridolfi/cultura/Corbis

powerful tools for spreading information. A **grapevine** is an informal line of communication where information is passed from one person to another.[10] Usually grapevines emerge in organizations where employees are not kept informed about what is going on by their management. Grapevines give rise to **gossip chains**, which is when several individuals manifest and spread generally inaccurate or misleading information throughout the organization.[11] Usually the gossip is spread by one or a few individuals to many coworkers and managers. In contrast, a **cluster chain** is a group of people that disseminate information within their group.[12] Regardless of how the information is communicated, it tends to spread very quickly throughout an organization, until the rumors are either proved to be true or false.

The main method that managers can employ to control rumors and gossip in an organization is through effective and consistent communication.

Grapevine An informal line of communication where information is passed from one person to another.

Gossip chain A format where several individuals spread information, which is sometimes false or misleading, through an organization.

Cluster chain A group of people that disseminate information within their group or cluster.

Increasing Efficiency and Effectiveness

Now that Vikas has been working tirelessly on his own methods of communication, he remembers how Julian advised him to use the leadership typology to achieve his goals within his own team. In order to become a more effective communicator and motivator, he studies the 10 disciplines that are necessary to lead his team to success.

Compassion A good leader must show compassion and care and respect others. They must have the ability to notice when others are going through a difficult time. This discipline especially rings true for Vikas, as he remembers how Julian showed him compassion when he told him about his wife's illness. Vikas makes a promise to himself that he will try and be more closely attuned to the behaviors of his employees; he vows that he will not let anyone suffer in silence.

Conscientiousness Conscientious leaders are aware of nuances in the environment and the behaviors of others. They are able to exercise self-control, tend to be good listeners, and are acutely aware of how their own actions impact others. Vikas knows that his team isn't fully on board with the new direction of the company, and he is conscious of his behavior over the years and doesn't blame them for being a little suspicious of the "new Vikas." By being aware of his own behavior, as well as the actions of others, he is confident that the team will eventually come around to the new vision.

Forgiveness Vikas must forgive himself for being a less-than-adequate leader by being too rigid with his team, and especially for losing his temper in front of an important potential client. His negativity has only served to isolate him and damage his relationships with others. Once he practices forgiveness for himself and others, he will achieve greater satisfaction in his personal and professional relationships.

Gratitude Vikas knows he has been lacking in this area. His directive style of leadership had been based on barking orders and issuing commands. Up to this point, the only "thank-you" he has ever given to his team was in the form of a small annual financial reward, which was getting smaller thanks to falling profits. He makes a promise to thank his team regularly when they have performed well, either orally or by a handwritten note.

Grit Most leaders adopt the discipline of grit; that is, they passionately persevere and are determined to achieve long-term goals and overcome obstacles along the way. From experience, Vikas knows that change does not happen overnight, but with a great deal of grit, he feels confident that his team will reach their organizational goals and achieve success.

Humility No leader works in a vacuum. Asking for help is essential when it comes to achieving goals. Vikas thinks that he should have confessed to his boss about his difficulties at home and at work sooner, instead of wrapping himself up in his own problems. He has learned a valuable lesson: to ask for help when he needs it, and to encourage others to do the same.

Hypo-Egoic Effective leaders will not allow their own ego to get in the way of achieving their objectives. This involves a hypo-egoic, or heightened level of self-awareness, for leaders to recognize when their actions are inhibiting others or are based on satisfying their own needs. Vikas notes, uncomfortably, that he has been guilty of letting his ego take over at times, particularly when he has micromanaged his team or snatched work away from them, believing that he "would be better off doing it himself." However, practicing the art of forgiveness helps him to avoid lingering too much on his past behavior and instead encourages him to look toward the future.

Mindfulness This is the ability to be aware of experiences that occur in the present moment. There is an expectation that leaders should provide quick solutions to complex problems in any given situation. In stressful times, the pressure on leaders to set a course of action is immense. However, making snap decisions and judgments without taking the time to form an honest assessment of the problem can sometimes fuel the crisis. As Vikas's behavioral test results have shown him to be measured and methodical, he believes he is already a mindful leader—maybe too mindful, in fact. He realizes that he must strike a balance between his dogmatic, rigid way of doing things and being more flexible when it comes to making decisions.

Openness As explored in Chapter 14, openness is the ability to have fun and experience elation and delight. Following his heart-to-heart conversation with Julian about his stress levels related to his problems at home and at work, Vikas is beginning to come around to the idea of being more open. He makes a list of bonding activities he believes will encourage the team to be more open with him and each other, such as trivia nights, and an Upstream Fisheries basketball team.

Wisdom Wise leaders demonstrate integrity, sound judgment, and moral courage and make principle-based decisions at the highest stage of morality. With every new situation, wise leaders will gain a deeper understanding of people or events, enhancing their ability to apply perceptions, judgments, and actions. Vikas knows that achieving true wisdom is a lifelong lesson, but one that he is willing to learn.

Over the next few weeks, Vikas puts each discipline into practice: he listens to his team members when they have a problem; he asks for their feedback regularly; he assigns them more responsibility and provides autonomy; and he thanks them personally when they achieve results. The trivia nights have been a huge success, and there is a lot of laughter the following day at work when the team members rehash the evening's events. Productivity is reaching stellar levels, and the CEO sent a note congratulating Vikas and his team for their excellent performance. Finally, Vikas feels that Upstream Fisheries is on the way up. Next, let's explore how the other team leaders are doing.

15.3 | POWER OF CHALLENGING WORK

15.3 | Describe how challenging work and goals motivate individuals and teams.

Months later, the Spanish branch of Upstream Fisheries has catapulted into becoming the number three performing facility in the company. It's an impressive improvement—they have moved up 25 places from their initial rank of 28th (and last) place. Meanwhile, Julian has continued to travel to underperforming facilities worldwide to implement his leadership strategies. The CEO, Max Johnson, announces that the organization will use the Spanish facility to test the company's latest advances in research and development (R&D)—a high honor, indeed. Because of Liam's consistent long-term performance, his team is selected to lead this effort.

Liam and his team are thrilled. Although they have been performing well, they have been frustrated with the system glitches that have affected their ability to identify the best yields of sustainable fish from the ponds. In particular, they have struggled with the systems that are supposed to measure the water temperature and levels of growth. This has led to "guesswork" when it comes to the production process, which has met performance expectations

LECTURE ENHANCER:

15.3 Power of Challenging Work

- **Expectancy Theory**
  - ➤ Introduced by Victor Vroom, 1964
    - ✓ individuals are more likely to be motivated and perform well if they expect to receive desired rewards
    - ✓ **Outcome**—the end result of a process or undertaking
    - ✓ **Valence**—individual attraction to the value of outcomes
    - ■ Effort-to-Performance Expectancy
    - ■ Performance-to-Outcome Expectancy
  - ➤ Porter-Lawler's Extension of Expectancy Theory
    - ■ *Intrinsic Rewards*
    - ■ *Extrinsic Rewards*
- **Goal-Setting Theory**
  - ✓ proposes that motivation will be increased by setting clear, challenging, specific goals where employees are fully committed, and encouraged to give feedback

so far, but the team knows it can do better. Liam can't wait for the experts from the R&D team to arrive. While he knows his team is capable of repairing the system glitches, he figures that the other team will do a quicker job. As soon as it is up and running, production will reach new heights, and profits will increase.

Shifting the Burden

In Chapter 3, we explored one of the concepts of Systems Theory, called Shifting the Burden. This is when short-term fixes are implemented instead of addressing the long-term, underlying problems. Because the "fixes" seem to be working, they are used repeatedly. But the fundamental problems still exist, so before too long, cracks begin to show, producing unwanted side effects further down the road. Let's see how Upstream Fisheries manages the system problems experienced by Liam's department.

The corporate office's R&D team launches a program called "Quick Fixes, Quick Results" as a way to refine production and increase profitability. The R&D team is placed in Liam's department for six months in order to fix the system glitches and improve the processes. They implement quick fixes that lead to immediate profit results. Liam, his team, and Upstream Fisheries management are delighted. While he has always been confident in his team, recently he has felt pressure because they were not performing to the best of their capabilities. Finally, with the fixes in place, they are better able to identify a higher yield and raise production levels.

However, after months of corporate office praise for the profit results, Liam notices a disturbing trend—there has been a 25 percent increase in absenteeism since the R&D team arrived six months before. When Liam consults his team about this trend, he is told that staff members no longer feel they are needed; automation has made the jobs too easy, and they are bored as a result. Apparently, a few members of his team don't see the point in showing up to work when they feel they aren't of any use. Furthermore, rumors are going around that people are going to be laid off because of these new processes, and this threat of job loss has led to even more absenteeism and apathy. To make matters worse, there have been two resignations since the R&D team left, the old system problems have begun to surface again, and there is not enough staff to remedy the issues.

Liam turns to Maribel for help. "I don't know what's happened to my team," Liam begins. "I thought fixing the system would make them as happy as it has made me, but now some of them are not showing up for work, two have resigned, and the remaining crew seems to be disengaged and uninterested in dealing with the resurfacing system problems. What do you think I should do?"

Maribel replies, "Since I switched roles with Vikas, I have been working on a vision for the next generation of the company. We're developing a program to help teams become more engaged, motivated, and challenged. I think if we work together, we can come up with some ways to get your team back on track again."

Liam and Maribel agree to sit down the next day to assess different motivational theories in order to work out a proper strategy for the teams.

Expectancy Theory

The next day, Maribel and Liam set aside two hours to devise their strategy for motivating their team members. Liam looks doubtfully at the number of management books Maribel has brought into the meeting room. "You seem to have carried out a lot of research," he says, trying not to look at his watch. He wonders if two hours will be enough.

Maribel laughs. "If we want to motivate our teams at Upstream, then we have to do our homework! And I have chosen a couple of motivational theories that I think we could apply right away."

Struck by her enthusiasm, Liam gives Maribel his full attention.

Maribel starts by discussing **expectancy theory**, first introduced by Yale University professor Victor Vroom in 1964. This theory, she explains, holds that individuals are more likely to be motivated and perform well if they expect to receive desired rewards.[13] In this sense, there is a relationship between expectancy and **outcome**, which is the result of a process or undertaking. However, not everyone's expectations are the same. Some people might value

Expectancy theory A theory that holds that individuals are more likely to be motivated and perform well if they expect to receive desired rewards.

Outcomes The results of a process or undertaking.

a raise over a promotion, and vice versa. This individual opinion of the value of outcomes is called a **valence**. According to expectancy theory, high or low motivation depends on the level of effort, performance, and reward expectations. So how do managers apply expectancy theory in the workplace?

Valence An individual opinion of the value of outcomes.

Effort-to-Performance Expectancy Maribel has learned that managers must instill in their employees a belief that the effort they put into their roles will result in high performance. If employees believe that they have the skills and abilities to perform well, then they have a high effort-to-performance expectancy and will be more motivated to work hard. Conversely, if they do not feel they have the ability to increase performance, expectancy will fall, as will their levels of motivation.

Performance-to-Outcome Expectancy Employees must also be reassured that successful performance will generate desired rewards or outcomes, according to Maribel's research. If the performance-to-outcome expectancy is high, then motivation will also be high. However, if there is no possibility of reward in spite of high performance, then motivation will be lower.

Managing the expectations of each individual employee enables managers to encourage motivation and high performance. Additional training and defined objectives can help support employees to achieve higher performance. Managers must listen to employees and assess their own perceived expectations of rewards. Often, there is a gap in organizations between what the employees believe they deserve and how their managers believe they should be rewarded. This leads to distrust, disappointment, and low motivation.

Porter-Lawler's Extension of Expectancy Theory Maribel then introduces Porter-Lawler's theory, which is similar to Vroom's theory in that it suggests that motivation depends upon the reward that individuals expect to receive for successfully completing a task.[14] However, Porter and Lawler also introduced additional factors to expectancy theory. First, they broke down the idea of reward into two categories: *intrinsic*, which means the positive feelings experienced by the individual as a result of achieving the task; and *extrinsic*, which are concrete rewards such as bonuses, promotions, and salary increases. According to this theory, individuals will be more motivated if they perceive the rewards as being fair and attractive.

Liam snaps his fingers. "I think I know what one of the problems is with my team. I didn't manage their expectations properly. Before the R&D team came in, everyone knew what they had to do and expected rewards for high performance, which I gave them verbally, or at least celebrated with them by taking them out to lunch. But when the new R&D team came in, I shifted my focus to what they were doing and lost track of my team. It was then that I think my team members lost their belief in their own skills and how necessary they were to the organization. No wonder they lost motivation—their leader wasn't present enough to acknowledge their hard work, tell them how important their roles were, or to notice the signs that they weren't satisfied or happy."

Maribel replied, "I think we can all agree, as leaders, that sometimes we get distracted and move in other directions, but the important thing is that we recognize and address the situation. That said, let's take a look at goal-setting theory and see how we can set some motivating goals for the team."

Goal-Setting Theory

In Chapter 8, we explored the concept of goal setting and its importance within an organizational setting. Introduced by Latham and Locke, goal-setting theory proposes that motivation will be increased by setting clear, challenging, specific goals where employees are fully committed and encouraged to give feedback.[15] So how do goals increase motivation? They help to focus our attention and encourage us to direct our efforts toward achieving a specific target. Goals also inspire us to create new plans and strategies that help us to become more invested in completing the task. When goals are achieved, we feel a sense of accomplishment and satisfaction, which increases our motivation for the next task.

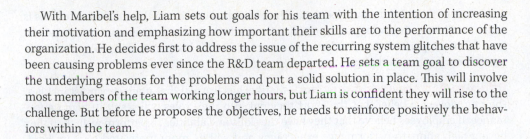

Glossary sidebar

Reinforcement theory A behavioral construct where individuals may be rewarded or punished based on the consequences of their behavior.

Behavior modification A method of shaping actions by the use of positive reinforcement.

Positive reinforcement A reward given to motivate a person or group which is usually stated verbally or with "pats on the back" and words of encouragement.

Avoidance learning A benefits theory, which postulates a behavior that is strengthened by the removal of negative statements or actions.

With Maribel's help, Liam sets out goals for his team with the intention of increasing their motivation and emphasizing how important their skills are to the performance of the organization. He decides first to address the issue of the recurring system glitches that have been causing problems ever since the R&D team departed. He sets a team goal to discover the underlying reasons for the problems and put a solid solution in place. This will involve most members of the team working longer hours, but Liam is confident they will rise to the challenge. But before he proposes the objectives, he needs to reinforce positively the behaviors within the team.

15.4 | REINFORCING POSITIVE BEHAVIORS

15.4 | Illustrate how positive reinforcement enables managers to motivate others to achieve superior results.

Introduced by behavioral psychologist B.F. Skinner, **reinforcement theory** is a behavioral construct where individuals may be rewarded or punished based on the consequences of their behavior.[16] Typically, organizations use three types of reinforcement schedules: A *fixed-interval schedule* reinforces behaviors after a set period of time; for example, employees might be paid weekly or once or twice a month, so long as they work during that pay period or interval. A *variable-interval schedule* is employed after a varying period of time to reward successful performance in the forms of bonuses, promotions, or other benefits.

Nina Leen/Time & Life Pictures /Getty Images

Finally, organizations might impose a *fixed-ratio schedule*, where a specific number of behaviors must be met before the reward is given; for example, a salesperson might have to sell a fixed amount of items before she is awarded a bonus. Like Vikas's team, Liam's team has only ever been awarded a small end-of-year bonus for their hard work. However, unlike Vikas, prior to the arrival of the R&D team, Liam always did his best to make up for the lack of financial reward by conducting team-bonding events to boost morale.

The practical application of reinforcement theory is **behavior modification**, which is a method of shaping actions by using positive reinforcement.[17] Liam is determined to reconnect with his team so he can manage their expectations and reintroduce **positive reinforcement**, which is a method used to motivate a person or group and is usually stated verbally with words of encouragement.[18] Liam also learns about **avoidance learning**, also called *negative reinforcement*, which is a behavior strengthened by the removal of negative statements or actions.[19]

Over the last six months, Liam realizes that he has unwittingly been practicing the art of **extinction**, which involves withholding praise or a positive reward, and vows to make up for this by bringing back his tried and trusted way of rewarding employees for high performance.[20]

Liam also remembers how motivated he felt when he learned the results of the Gallup Strengths test, the study suggesting that it is far more productive to focus on people's strengths than trying to "fix" their weaknesses. As far as he was concerned, it described his character and his skills perfectly. It also helped to reinforce his own self-belief and encourage him to be a better leader.

Guilt consumes Liam as he realizes how neglectful he has been in focusing on the strengths within his own team in favor of the R&D team. He had been too caught up with

Extinction A behavioral method that involves withholding praise or a positive reward.

the results generated by the R&D team. Liam needs to adopt a practice of **empowerment**, which is the sharing of decisions, information, and responsibility with others.[21] He sees now that the team had felt disempowered by the R&D team and believed that their skills were no longer needed. Liam is determined to communicate to them how important they are to Upstream, and he intends to give them the support and resources they need to deliver on future goals.

© Pedro Benavente/Demotix/Corbis

Behavior Modification

The following week, Liam calls a team meeting, determined to put his behavior modification learning into practice. As he looks around the room, he notices how empty it is. As a result of the resignations, they are two people down, and there is still a lot of work to be done. Still, he is confident that his team will pull together until he finds new hires, and he puts his anxiety aside and begins the meeting.

He apologizes for his own disengagement with the team over the previous six months, saying, "I am aware that I have been absent over the last few months, and I'm very sorry. But I know with this team's track record, we can overcome any obstacle. Now, I would like you to provide me with your feedback and let me know how you feel we can improve our performance going forward."

The team does not hold back; all the members tell Liam how bored and dissatisfied they have been and how unsure they are about the importance of their roles within Upstream. In response, Liam spends some time clarifying the roles and responsibilities of each member, and how important the performance of every person is to the success of the organization. He emphasizes that he will be there every step of the way to encourage them, track the team's progress, and give feedback to individuals. He reinforces their value to the company and restates the goals, mission, and vision of Upstream in an effort to align the aims of the organization with the team's own values. The team begins to get animated, making suggestions and introducing new ideas about how Upstream could become even more productive.

As Liam leaves the room, he is pleased with how the team has responded—they seem a little more motivated already.

Empowering Others

Over the next few weeks, Liam's team begins to come together once more. Liam set a goal of two months to find the underlying problems with the system and resolve the issues permanently in order to maintain an agreed level of performance. As promised, Liam assigns specific tasks to certain individuals and hands over a lot of the decision making to senior members of the team. Liam also makes good on his promise to reward his team for working longer hours; he frequently brings in a catered lunch or takes the entire team out to dinner after a hard day's work.

At the same time, their soccer team has suffered, as there doesn't seem to be enough hours in the day to practice or play matches. Many of his team members are too tired at the end of the day to play sports, anyway, so he decides to put soccer on the back burner for a while. In the meantime, Liam is busy interviewing replacement staff, but hasn't been able to find anyone who has the technical skills needed to work in his team. In the meantime, his staff is working longer and longer hours . . .

After one particularly long day, the team cracks. Liam notices a few people huddled in a group, deep in conversation. They do not look happy. As a spokesman for the team,

Empowerment The sharing of decisions, information, and responsibility with others.

LECTURE ENHANCER:

15.4 Reinforcing Postive Behaviors

✓ **Reinforcement Theory**—a behavioral construct where individuals may be rewarded or punished based on the consequences of their behavior
  ■ *Fixed-interval schedule*
  ■ *Variable-interval schedule*
  ■ *Fixed-ratio schedule*
✓ **Behavior Modification**—a method of shaping behaviors by using of positive reinforcement
✓ **Positive Reinforcement**—a method used to motivate a person or group and is usually stated verbally or with "pats on the back" and words of encouragement
✓ **Avoidance learning**—also called negative reinforcement, is a behavior strengthened by the removal of negative statements or actions.
✓ **Extinction**—withholding praise or a positive reward, and vows to make up for this by bringing back his tried and trusted way of rewarding employees for high performance
✓ **Empowerment**—the sharing of decisions, information, and responsibility with others
• **Empowering Others**

LECTURE ENHANCER:

15.5 Rewarding Performance

✓ **Reward System**—provides special recognition, prizes, and incentives for tasks, and jobs well done

✓ **Merit-based Rewards** are based on specific accomplishments with rewards given for achievement of specified measurements

✓ **Piece-rate Incentives** are awards or prizes given at a specific rate as accomplishments occur

✓ **Scanlon Plan**—recognizes and rewards individuals for collaboration, leadership, education and training given to another individual or group cohesively

Alejandro Desi, a longstanding member of staff approaches Liam, and tells them the reasons behind their dissatisfaction.

"Liam, we have been working longer and longer hours with no additional reward or compensation. A few free beers, while appreciated, are not enough to reward us for our performance. We are doing our best to make a profit for the company, but it comes to a point where we have to ask the question, 'What's in it for us?' I bet the executives in this company are being compensated handsomely for their contributions. We're not asking for much, but we need to be treated fairly."

Trying to disguise his disappointment (he had thought his motivational methods were really paying off), Liam promises Alejandro that he would think about what he said and get back to the whole team the following week.

15.5 | REWARDING PERFORMANCE

15.5 **Formulate** and communicate a performance-based reward system that motivates individuals and teams to achieve organizational objectives.

Reward system A theory that provides prizes, incentives for tasks and jobs well done, and special recognition.

© Larry Downing/Reuters/Corbis

Executive Compensation

The topic of executive reward and compensation has never come under so much scrutiny as it has over the last decade.[22] Bankrupt companies and unethical business practices have resulted in millions of people losing their houses, pensions, and financial security, while some business executives and CEOs have benefited from the economic downturn. This has led many organizations to revise their reward systems in order to distribute compensation more fairly and equitably.

A **reward system** provides special recognition, prizes, and incentives for tasks, and jobs well done.[23] Different organizations use a diverse number of methods to reward employees. **Merit-based rewards** are based on specific accomplishments, with rewards given for achievement of specified measurements.[24] For example, in the area of education, teachers might be awarded a bonus if their students perform well in their classes or on exams. **Piece-rate incentives** are awards or prizes given at a specific rate as accomplishments occur.[25]

It is common in the farming industry to use piece-rate plans by paying workers on the basis of the amount they produce; for example, a berry-picker might be paid according to the amount of berries he picks over a certain time period. Many public and private organizations have discovered the benefits of the **Scanlon plan**, which recognizes and rewards individuals for collaboration, leadership, education, and training given to another individual or group cohesively.[26] By being made a part of the firm's financial success, employees feel more motivated to work harder toward organizational goals.

Although Liam knows that Alejandro and the team have valid points about additional compensation, he doesn't have the authority to do anything about it. He remembers the mantra that Max Johnson, the CEO of Upstream, repeats at every Upstream event: "We need to foster abundance in a world of limited resources and scarcity, where the most limited resource and scarce commodity is positive thinking." Inspired by this concept, Liam calls Max directly to tell him the situation with his team. Max gives Liam permission to address the team and assess the sort of compensation and rewards that they are looking for.

Once Liam has gathered their feedback, Max asks that he devise a potential reward scheme to meet the needs of the team. If Max considers it a viable option, he will consider rolling out the scheme across all the branches of the Upstream organization. Liam is pleased with Max's

Merit-based rewards Positive reinforcement based on specific accomplishments, with rewards given for achievement of specified measurements.

Piece-rate incentives Awards and prizes given at a specific rate as accomplishments occurs, rather than all at one time.

Scanlon plan A system that recognizes and rewards individuals for collaboration, leadership, education, and training given to another individual or group cohesively.

Research @ Work

Equity Theory, Status, and Employee Theft

What are some of the ways in which employees might react to perceptions of inequity in the workplace? Researcher Jerald Greenberg has examined this question in a number of organizations and reports some interesting findings.

Greenberg studied employees in the underwriting department of a large insurance company who had been temporarily reassigned to the higher, lower, or equal status position of a coworker.[27] As equity theory would suggest, Greenberg found that relative to employees reassigned to equal status positions, employees reassigned to higher-status offices increased their performance (a response to overpayment inequity), while employees reassigned to lower-status offices decreased their performance (a response to underpayment inequity). This study is particularly noteworthy for being one of the few studies to show a response to overpayment inequity (most people do not have a problem with being overcompensated).

In a similar study, Greenberg examined workers in a manufacturing plant during a period in which pay had been temporarily decreased by 15 percent.[28] Greenberg found that, as compared with the pre- and post-reduction pay periods and with control groups with unchanged pay, workers experiencing the temporary pay cuts had significantly higher rates of employee theft. Employees were willing to steal from their company in order to restore their perceptions of fairness!

Critical Thinking in the Classroom

As a manager, how would you address a state of inequity within your team?

---

support but also worried about delivering such a tall order. What did he really know about reward schemes, anyway? He would have to listen very closely to his team, and enlist help from the other leaders.

First, Liam sets up a town-hall-style meeting for his team. After sharing Max's mantra, he asks them what the company can do to foster abundance. Liam decides to ask this question to someone specific. As Alejandro Desi has been quite forthright so far and has the reputation for giving honest answers to honest questions, he directs the question to him.

At first, Alejandro looks uncomfortable, but after a brief pause, he says, "I have been on staff here for over 20 years. Yet this is the first time anyone has ever asked me what I thought about our CEO's ideas about fostering abundance. Do you want my honest opinion?"

Liam nods his head encouragingly. This was just the sort of feedback he needed.

"I understand that we need to foster abundance in terms of fish sustainability; but what about our own personal abundance? Surely, as the CEO, it is easy to talk about abundance when you already have everything. I would like to continue working here until I retire in 10 to 15 years. When the stock goes up, so do the profits . . . but not for all of us. Of course it is only right that a large portion of the profits are invested back into the company, but it also seems that the investors, executive management, and Mr. Johnson also benefit more than we do. Don't get me wrong: money isn't everything. But I do regard the people at Upstream as my family; and healthy families are about fairness. I just feel that our efforts are not recognized sufficiently; and the small amount of compensation we receive does not justify the amount of work we put in."

The rest of the team nods their heads in agreement. Liam tells them that he wants everyone to be treated fairly too, and he promises that he will talk with the other leaders about devising a rewards scheme that suits everyone's needs.

Equity, Gainsharing, and Cooperatives

The next day, Liam fills Maribel and Vikas in on what has been happening with his team. "They do have a point," Maribel says. "They are working harder than ever, and need more of an incentive to keep motivated. And they need to be treated fairly."

- **Equity, Gainsharing, and Cooperatives**
  - ✓ **Equity Theory**—individuals are more motivated if they perceive they are being treated as fairly as their fellow workers or those in other firms
    - ■ a state of inequity can take place if one employee learns that another less experienced, and/or underperforming employee is receiving the same degree of compensation, thus putting the income-to-outcome ratio out of balance
  - ➤ Research at Work: Equity Theory, Status, and Employee Theft
  - ✓ **Stock Options**—company stocks given to employees as additional compensation or incentives, usually at a discounted price for a limited time
  - ✓ **Gainsharing program**—allows employees to share in any cost-savings made by the firm

Vikas says, "I have been thinking along the same lines too. The only financial reward I have ever given my team is a small bonus at year-end. Although I have recently introduced some after-work team activities to help the team bond, I can't help but feel it's not enough. Maybe a combination of fair financial compensation and bonding activities would be the best solution."

"But what is fair?" Liam asks. What are our options?"

Maribel smiles and says. "Well, Liam, I have an idea about this." She introduces the idea of **equity theory** which holds that individuals are more motivated if they perceive they are being treated as fairly as their fellow workers or those in other firms.[29] According to equity theory, we tend to base our perception on what is equal or fair by a ratio of inputs to outcomes. Inputs include experience, effort, qualifications, and interpersonal skills, while outcomes describe the expected result of the inputs, such as recognition, pay, benefits, and promotions. However, a state of inequity can take place if one employee learns that another less experienced and/or underperforming employee is receiving the same degree of compensation, putting the income-to-outcome ratio out of balance. If managers do not address this imbalance, employees will feel a sense of injustice, giving rise to a lack of motivation within the team. Managers need to devise reward schemes that are fair and satisfactory to employees.

By applying equity theory to the Upstream team, the three team leaders find that some of the workers are being paid more than others. Alejandro in particular is actually being paid less than some of the more recently hired staff, despite his 20-year service. Liam makes a note to address this imbalance with Human Resources (HR) immediately. Next on the list is the issue of **stock options**, which are company stocks given to employees as additional compensation or incentives, usually at a discounted price for a limited time.[30] Six months ago, the company's stock had fallen, throwing Vikas into a major panic about his family's future, but now it is a different story. Profits have soared recently, and so has the stock; all the employees should be rejoicing in their good fortune. However, on further investigation, they discover that only senior executives and a handful of long-term employees have been granted stock options. Surely it is only fair that everyone has the opportunity to benefit in the organization's success. Again, they make a note to address this issue.

Finally, the leaders feel like they are getting somewhere: if the state of inequity is resolved, then the employees will feel that they are being treated more fairly. But how can they put this into practice? Julie suggests the possibility of introducing a **gainsharing program**, which allows employees to share in any cost savings made by the firm.[31] This would means that everybody would have a "piece of the pie," based on Upstream's financial performance.

"I think this could work!" Liam says "As far as my team is concerned, once we have a solid system up and running, productivity will be through the roof, and the team will really be able to share in the benefits of their hard work!"

Vikas nods his head enthusiastically, "Productivity is already up in my area, so this would be a welcome reward for the team."

Maribel says to Liam, "I agree that it seems like a good idea, but your team needs to work together in order to improve the system; only then will productivity reach those new heights."

Liam agrees. His team had been through a rocky six months, with the arrival of the R&D team, followed by the resignations. . . . The staff he had left needed to work well together in order to get the department back on track.

Over the next few weeks, Liam and Maribel draw up a proposal for the reward schemes that they think are best suited to the needs of the Upstream workers. So far, they have received positive feedback from the teams; even Alejandro has agreed that the schemes, if implemented, would be fair and equitable. Two months later, the compensation schemes are signed off on by the CEO and applied to all the Upstream branches with great success. By sharing in the profits and being rewarded for good teamwork, the Upstream workers feel empowered and fairly compensated, that they are an integral part of the company, and that the work they do really matters.

Equity theory A system that holds that individuals are more motivated if they perceive they are being treated as fairly as their fellow workers or those in other firms.

Stock options Company stocks given to employees as additional compensation or incentives, usually at a discounted price for a limited time.

Gainsharing program A system that allows employees to share in any cost savings made by the firm.

Liam successfully recruits four new team members, providing much-needed assistance to the group. Thanks to the reward schemes and a boosted headcount, Liam's team is thriving. By focusing on the underlying problems of the system problems, they reach their goal of fixing the system glitches once and for all, ahead of schedule, and begin enjoying the financial and personal benefits of increasing the firm's profits through high levels of productivity. Furthermore, at the first-ever Upstream employee awards ceremony at the end of the year, organized by Maribel, Liam's team was awarded "team of the year," further boosting morale. Similarly, Vikas's and Maribel's teams continue to perform successfully, and they remain motivated by their leaders' passion and enthusiasm, as well as the new reward schemes put in place.

As discussed in this chapter, managers who really listen to their employees, encourage communication, and work hard to understand their needs will create an environment where employees feel valued and motivated. In the next chapter, we will explore how managers manage operations to ensure the smooth running of organizations.

CaseSnapshot

Chapter 15 Case: Communicating and Motivating Others:
Korean Air can be found on pg. 477

ADDITIONAL RESOURCES

KEY TERMS

Avoidance learning, A benefits theory, also called negative reinforcement, which postulates that behavior that is strengthened by the removal of negative statements or actions. **(p. 386)**

Barriers to communication Obstacles that interrupt the flow of conveying and receiving messages. **(p. 380)**

Behavior modification, A method of shaping actions by the use of positive reinforcement. **(p. 386)**

Body (nonverbal) language Consists of a person's facial expression and body movements that express communication and emotion without the use of words. **(p. 380)**

Channel richness The capacity to convey as much information as possible during the communication process. **(p. 379)**

Cluster chain A group of people that disseminate information within their group or cluster. **(p. 382)**

Communication The act of transmitting information, thoughts, and processes through various channels. **(p. 374)**

Communication network A system of resources used as a channel for groups of people to connect to each other, such as the Internet. **(p. 381)**

Electronic communication A system that includes emails, Skype, videoconferencing, blogs, instant messaging, texting, and social networking (using programs such as LinkedIn, Twitter, and Facebook). **(p. 378)**

Empowerment The sharing of decisions, information, and responsibility with others. **(p. 386)**

Equity theory A system that holds that individuals are more motivated if they perceive they are being treated as fairly as their fellow workers or those in other firms. **(p. 390)**

ERG theory of motivation A system that sets out three categories of human needs relating to organizational behaviors: Existent needs, Relatedness needs, Growth needs. **(p. 375)**

Expectancy theory A theory that holds that individuals are more likely to be motivated and perform well if they expect to receive desired rewards. **(p. 384)**

Extinction A behaviorial method that involves withholding praise or a positive reward. **(p. 386)**

Gainsharing program A system that allows employees to share in any cost savings made by the firm. **(p. 390)**

Gossip chain A format where several individuals spread information, which is sometimes false or misleading, through an organization. **(p. 382)**

Grapevine An informal line of communication where information is passed from one person to another. **(p. 382)**

Listening The active effort to understand, learn, and obtain information from others. **(p. 381)**

Maslow's hierarchy of needs A psychological theory that suggests that people are motivated by a number of needs, which are displayed in order. They are physiological needs, safety needs, love/belongingness needs, esteem needs, and self-actualization needs. **(p. 375)**

Merit-based rewards Positive reinforcement based on specific accomplishments, with rewards given for achievement of specified measurements. **(p. 388)**

Motivation An incentive or drive to complete a task, function, or idea. **(p. 374)**

Oral communication Provides verbal discussions, ideas, and processes, either one on one or as a group (face-to-face). **(p. 378)**

Outcomes The results of a process or undertaking. **(p. 384)**

Piece-rate incentives Awards and prizes given at a specific rate as accomplishments occurs, rather than all at one time. **(p. 388)**

Positive reinforcement A reward given to motivate a person or group which is usually stated verbally or with "pats on the back" and words of encouragement. **(p. 386)**

Reinforcement theory A behavioral construct where individuals may be rewarded or punished based on the consequences of their behavior. **(p. 386)**

Reward system A theory that provides prizes, incentives for tasks and jobs well done, and special recognition. **(p. 388)**

Scanlon plan A system that recognizes and rewards individuals for collaboration, leadership, education, and training given to another individual or group cohesively. **(p. 388)**

Stock options Company stocks given to employees as additional compensation or incentives, usually at a discounted price for a limited time. **(p. 390)**

Two-factor theory of motivation A theory, also known as "motivation-hygiene theory" or "dual theory," which is based on job satisfaction and/or job dissatisfaction and the extent to which attitudes influence outcomes. **(p. 375)**

Valence An individual opinion of the value of outcomes. **(p. 385)**

Written communication, A system where the sender writes emails, reports, memos, letters, and other documents. **(p. 378)**

IN REVIEW

15.1 | Explain how managers use motivation and communication to achieve results.

Motivation is an incentive or drive to complete a task, function, or idea. To achieve optimal performance, managers need to understand what drives their employees in order to motivate them. The key to this process is *communication*, the act of transmitting information, thoughts, and processes through various channels.

15.2 | Understand how to apply communication to pursue and achieve goals efficiently and effectively.

When we communicate with people, there are two components at work: the sender and receiver. The sender transmits the message, and the receiver must understand the message that is being delivered. *Channel richness* is the capacity to convey as much information as possible during the communication process. Face-to-face discussion is considered the richest form of communication. *Body (nonverbal) language* describes a person's facial expressions and body movements that express communication and emotion without the use of words. Being able to read the signs and signals of body language increases our understanding of others, allowing more effective communication. *Barriers to communication* include filtering, emotions, poor listening, information overload, and differing perceptions. Managers need to be proficient in communicating through global networks by understanding culture and diversity, and teaching their teams the skills needed to work effectively in a virtual organization. To become a more effective communicator and motivator, the following 10 disciplines are necessary for success: compassion, conscientiousness, forgiveness, gratitude, grit, humility, hypo-egoic, mindfulness, openness, and wisdom.

15.3 | Describe how challenging work and goals motivate individuals and teams.

If employees believe that they have the skills and abilities to perform well, then they have a high effort-to-performance expectancy and will be more motivated to work hard. Conversely, if they do not feel they have the ability to increase performance, expectancy will fall, as will their levels of motivation. Goal-setting theory proposes that motivation will be increased by setting clear, challenging, specific goals where employees are fully committed and encouraged to give feedback.

15.4 | Illustrate how positive reinforcement enables managers to motivate others to achieve superior results.

Behavior modification is a method of shaping actions by using positive reinforcement. *Positive reinforcement* is a method used to motivate a person or group and is usually stated verbally or with "pats on the back" and words of encouragement. Managers will reinforce their value to the company and restate the organizational goals, mission, and vision in an effort to align the aims of the organization with the team's own values

15.5 | Formulate and communicate a performance-based reward system that motivates individuals and teams to achieve organizational objectives.

A *reward system* provides special recognition, prizes, and incentives for tasks and jobs well done. Managers need to devise reward schemes that are fair and satisfactory to employees, and then draw up a proposal for the reward schemes that they believe are best suited to the needs of the workers.

SELF-TEST

15.1 | Explain how managers use motivation and communication to achieve results.

1. The act of transmitting information, thoughts, and processes through various channels is known as:
   a. Motivation
   b. Communication
   c. Negotiation
   d. Broadcasting

2. List and briefly describe the five levels in Maslow's hierarchy of needs.

3. Which of the following is *not* one of the three categories of human needs in Alderfer's ERG Theory of Motivation:
   a. Existence
   b. Relatedness
   c. Relaxation
   d. Growth

15.2 | Understand how to apply communication to pursue and achieve goals efficiently and effectively.

4. In the basic model of communication, the sender transmits or encodes the message through a chosen communication

channel, and the receiver must try and decode or interpret the meaning of the message that is being delivered.

    a. True

    b. False

5. Which of the following communication channels would include social networking (Facebook, LinkedIn, Twitter, etc.)?

    a. Oral communication

    b. Written communication

    c. Electronic communication

    d. Social communication

6. Body (nonverbal) language refers exclusively to the use of American Sign Language (ASL) in the communication process.

    a. True

    b. False

7. Which of the following is a barrier to communication?

    a. Feedback

    b. Simplified language

    c. Constrained emotions

    d. Differing perceptions

15.3 | Describe how challenging work and goals motivate individuals and teams.

8. Expectancy theory suggests high or low motivation depends on the level of _____, _____, and _____ expectations.

15.4 | Illustrate how positive reinforcement enables managers to motivate others to achieve superior results.

9. List and describe the three types of reinforcement schedules according to reinforcement theory.

10. Which of the following behavior modification tools involves withholding praise or a positive reward?

    a. Positive reinforcement

    b. Negative reinforcement

    c. Punishment

    d. Extinction

15.5 | Formulate and communicate a performance-based reward system that motivates individuals and teams to achieve organizational objectives.

11. _____, are based on specific accomplishments with rewards given for achievement of specified measurements.

    a. Merit-based pay

    b. Piece-rate incentives

    c. Seniority-based pay

    d. Scanlon plans

12. Equity theory holds that individuals are more motivated if they perceive they are being treated unfairly as compared to their fellow workers or those in other firms.

    a. True

    b. False

13. _____ allow employees to share in any cost savings made by the firm.

CHAPTER EXERCISE

How Should Merit Raises Be Allocated?*

Small State University is located in the eastern part of the United States and has an enrollment of about 8,000 students. The College of Business has 40 full-time faculty members and over 30 part-time professors.

The college is divided into five departments: Management, Marketing, Finance and Accounting, Decision Sciences, and Information Technology. Profiles of the Management Department faculty members are presented in Table 1. Management faculty are evaluated each year based on three primary criteria: teaching, research, and service. Teaching performance is based on student course evaluations over a two-year period. Service to the university, college, profession, and community is also based on accomplishments over a two-year period. Research is based on the number of journal articles published over a three-year period. Teaching and research are considered more important than service to the university. In judging faculty performance, the department chair evaluates each professor in terms of four standards: Far Exceeds Standards, Exceeds Standards, Meets Standards, and Fails to Meet Standards. The results of this year's evaluations are shown in Table 2.

This year, the state has agreed to give raises to state employees totaling 3 percent—$17,400 to the management department. Your task as department chair is to divide the $17,400 among the faculty members. Keep in mind that these raises will likely set a precedent for future years and that the professors will view the raises as a signal for what behavior is valued and what is not.

*This exercise developed by R. Bruce McAfee and Marian W. Boscia and was published in *Developments in Business Simulation and Experiential Learning*, Vol. 31, (2004): 116–119.

Table 1   Professor Profiles

Prof. Housman

55 years old; 25 years with the university; teaches Principles of Management mass sections; teaches over 400 students per year; has written over 40 articles and given over 30 presentations since joining the college; wants a good raise to catch up with others.

Prof. Jones

49 years old; 10 years with the university; teaches Human Resource Management and Organizational Behavior courses; stepped down as department chair three years ago; teaches about 200 students a year; has written over 30 articles and two books since joining the College; recently received an $80,000 grant for the college from a local foundation. Wants a good raise as a reward for obtaining the grant.

Prof. Ricks

61 years old; 6 years with the university; teaches Labor Relations and Organizational Development; stepped down as dean of the College of Business two years ago and took a $20,000 pay cut as a result; teaches about 180 students per year; has written only two articles in the last six years due to administrative duties; very active in the community and serves on several charity boards. Wants a good raise to make up for loss of $20,000 stipend.

Prof. Matthews

28 years old; new hire—only four months with the university; teaches Employee Relations and Compensation Management; just graduated with a Ph.D.; will teach about 110 students this year. To be competitive in the job market, the college needed to pay Prof. Matthews $87,000, plus provide a reduced teaching load for two years and a $6,000 per year summer stipend; none of the other faculty received this when they were first hired or subsequently; had two minor publications while a doctoral student, but none since joining the college. Wants a good raise to pay student loans and establish a new residence.

Prof. Karas

32 years old; 4 years with the university; teaches International Business and Honors sections of Management Principles; teaches about 150 students per year; won Teacher of the Year Award this year; published 12 articles in last four years; has been interviewing for a new job at other universities and may leave if good raise is not forthcoming.

Prof. Franks

64 years old: 18 years with the university; teaches Principles of Management and Human Resource Management; teaches about 150 students per year; principal advisor for management majors; has not written any articles during the last four years; plans on retiring within two to three years. Wants a good raise to enhance pension plan.

Table 2   Department Chairs Rating of Job Performance

Professor	Current Salary	Teaching	Research	Service
Housman	$82,000	Exceeds	Exceeds	Meets
Jones	$106,000	Exceeds	Far Exceeds	Exceeds
Ricks	$135,000	Meets	Meets	Far Exceeds
Matthews	$87,000	New Hire	New Hire	New Hire
Karas	$90,000	Far Exceeds	Exceeds	Meets
Franks	$80,000	Meets	Fails to Meet	Exceeds

SELF-ASSESSMENT

Listening Skills Self-Assessment*

For each statement, circle the number that best describes you based on the following scale:

Not at all Accurate	*Somewhat* Accurate	*A little* Accurate	*Mostly* Accurate	*Completely* Accurate
1	2	3	4	5

1. I give people my full attention and maintain eye contact when they are speaking.

   1   2   3   4   5

2. I maintain an attentive posture and respond with nonverbal cues to show that I am listening.

   1   2   3   4   5

3. I appreciate hearing other people's perspectives.

   1   2   3   4   5

4. I try to keep an open mind when I am listening.

   1   2   3   4   5

5. I can identify other people's emotions effectively when speaking with them.

   1   2   3   4   5

6. I can tell when someone is withholding information or not telling me the truth.

   1   2   3   4   5

7. I have good comprehension and recall of what is communicated to me.

   1   2   3   4   5

8. I ask for more information or ask follow-up questions as needed.

   1   2   3   4   5

9. I try to be patient and understanding when listening to people who are upset.

   1   2   3   4   5

10. I make others comfortable in sharing their feelings with me.

   1   2   3   4   5

11. I carefully evaluate the information that is shared with me.

   1   2   3   4   5

12. I let people know what I think of their message, even if I disagree with them.

   1   2   3   4   5

Scoring:

Add the numbers circled above: _____

Interpretation:

48 and above = You have outstanding listening skills that help you overcome communication barriers to be an effective communicator.

25 – 47 = You have moderate listening skills. You could improve some key aspects of your listening capabilities to become a more effective communicator.

24 and below = You need to make some substantial improvements in your listening skills in order to communicate effectively with others.

*Adapted from Zabava Ford, Wendy S., Andrew D. Wolvin, and Chung Sungeun, "Students' Self-Perceived Listening Competencies in the Basic Speech Communication Course," *International Journal of Listening* 14, (May 2000): 1.

SELF-TEST ANSWER KEY

1. b.

2. Physiological needs—These are basic needs that we all need to ensure our survival, such as shelter, food, water, air, sleep, and warmth. Safety needs—Once these physiological needs are satisfied, there is a need for a safe environment, both physically and mentally. Affiliation/belongingness needs—These needs reflect our desire to be accepted by others and to find our place within certain working groups. Esteem needs—These are our needs to be respected and appreciated by others. Self-actualization needs—These are innate needs for personal growth and self-development.

3. c.

4. a; True

5. c.

6. b; False. Body (nonverbal) language describes a person's facial and body movements that express communication and emotion without the use of words.

7. d.

8. effort; performance; reward

9. A *fixed-interval schedule* reinforces behaviors after a set period of time. A *variable-interval schedule* is employed after a varying period of time to reward successful performance in the forms of bonus, promotion, or other benefits. Finally, organizations might impose a *fixed-ratio schedule*, where a specific number of behaviors must be met before the reward is given.

10. d.

11. a.

12. b; False. Equity theory holds that individuals are more motivated if they perceive they are being treated *fairly* as compared to their fellow workers or those in other firms.

13. Gainsharing programs

PART SIX

Controlling

CHAPTER SIXTEEN

INFORMATION AND OPERATIONS

Learning Objectives

By the end of the chapter, you will be able to:

16.1 | Explain how managers use controls to operate organizational performance.

16.2 | Describe the different forms and types of information technologies that managers apply.

16.3 | Illustrate how managers use information and technology systems to create efficiencies and make more effective decisions.

16.4 | Identify the types of controls and the processes used by managers to measure and adapt organizational performance.

16.5 | Describe how managers effectively apply controls to influence performance, with both people and results.

ADDITIONAL RESOURCES

KEY TERMS
IN REVIEW
SELF-TEST
CHAPTER EXERCISE
SELF-ASSESSMENT
SELF-TEST
ANSWER KEY

INSIDE THIS CHAPTER

ManagementStory:
Featuring **Spencer Jones**

JP Greenwood/Getty Images

16.1 | HOW CONTROLS MAKE A DIFFERENCE

16.1 | Explain how managers use controls to operate organizational performance

> "Knowledge has to be improved, challenged, and increased constantly, or it vanishes."
>
> —Peter Drucker

Over the course of this textbook, we have explored several types of managerial functions such as planning, organizing, recruiting, strategic planning, goal setting, and decision making, all of which are essential to the success of an organization. Yet, in isolation, none of these functions guarantee success. In order for these functions to be effective and operations to run smoothly, managers must also implement a variety of controls. A **control** is a tool that helps managers use information to influence behavior and affect operational performance through greater efficiencies and effective decision making.[1] By exercising control, managers are better able to oversee activities and direct employees toward achieving organizational goals.

A major part of the role of the manager is to implement controls around specific areas within an organization, thereby regulating behavior and results. These include such controlling functions as guiding performance through company policies and procedures, carrying out regular performance appraisals, studying market conditions to regulate internal activities, and ensuring that employees share in the same vision, mission, and goals of the organization.

Although controlling functions are essential to the success of a company, controls do not have to be rigid. In today's fluctuating environment, managers need to adapt and refine operational controls accommodating new innovations and cutting-edge technologies. If organizations depend too much on inflexible controlling functions, they will be slow to respond to change, which will have a detrimental impact on future success.

Conversely, lack of control can easily lead to the demise of an organization. In the Dolphin Resort & Hotel case study, we explored how close the hotel came to bankruptcy because of poor management, a lack of performance reviews, and an absence of policies and procedures. As a result, the staff merely came and went, with no idea of the hotel's expectations of them, their roles in the company, or what needed to be achieved. General manager Chris Heppler established a number of controls that streamlined the operations of the hotel and led to it becoming the top choice for vacationers visiting the island.

The MPD case narrative discussed in Chapters 10, 11, and 12 also illustrated an out-of-control, bureaucratic organization. Paralyzed by the chain of command, along with rigid rules and regulations, the employees were too afraid to report problems to higher management for fear it would put their careers at risk. It was only when Chief Robin Richardson implemented controls based on employee feedback that the staff became more comfortable about reporting errors and suggesting improvements. The MPD also suffered from poor information systems, where data was not fed down to other departments in an efficient manner, leading to delays in crime resolution. Again, controls were put in place to ensure

---

Control A tool that helps managers use information to influence behavior and affect operational performance through greater efficiencies and effective decision making.

LECTURE ENHANCER:

16.1 How Controls Make a Difference

✓ **Control**—how managers use information to influence behavior and affect operational performance through greater efficiencies and effective decision making

➤ Lack of control can easily lead to the demise of an organization.

• **Types of Controls**
  ➤ Voices of Management: Don Hardenbrook
  ✓ **Standards**—models and examples of how items or tasks are expected to be executed
  ✓ **Preliminary Control (Planning Control)**—used as a preventative measure to identify potential deficiencies before they occur
  ✓ **Screening Control (Real time Control)**—used to take corrective measures based on feedback during a process should barriers arise
  ✓ **Post Action Control**—used to assess results after a process is complete in order to provide information for future planning

Voices of Management

Don Hardenbrook[2]
Founder, Leap Innovation LLC

Founded by Donovan Ray Hardenbrook, Leap Innovation LLC, based in Tempe, Arizona, provides sales, marketing, and leadership training, consulting, and coaching to small business owners. Donovan brings more than 28 years of experience in engineering, manufacturing, quality control, and product development in high-tech, utility, and aerospace industries.

"As a part of corporate management, we have always been taught and shown that inadequate internal controls often lead to substantial operating losses, especially when various auditors step in to review operating policies. To better prepare our team and overall organization, we continually monitor our control procedures. These control directives helps outmaneuver rivals and run a profitable business.

Our internal control process provides us with the right framework that fosters overall positive employee productivity and reins in waste. Over the years, I have learned that my company's performance standards should be aligned not only with overall organizational goals, but also with our company's reward and compensation plans."

Critical Thinking in the Classroom

As a manager, how would you ensure that controls are monitored within your organization? ∎

---

that the appropriate departments received the same information at the same time, resulting in a speedier reaction time and a decrease in crime.

Another symptom of an out-of-control organization is a lack of ethics and integrity. Employees who are not committed to a company may waste time deliberately or carry out their responsibilities in a half-hearted manner. In Chapter 15, we explored how Vikas's team at Upstream Fisheries lacked motivation and tended to do just enough to get by. The team members were also skeptical about Vikas's abilities as a leader. But once Vikas changed his rigid style of management and relaxed the number the controls he had implemented, his team became more motivated about and invested in achieving the goals of the company.

How do managers decide which controls to establish within an organization? In order to instigate proper controls, managers must set performance standards, measure performance, and ensure that any problems are addressed in a timely manner.

Types of Controls

Within every type of institution and organization, there is a need to implement certain types of operational controls. For example, say you worked as the managing editor of your weekly college newspaper. Your goal might be to collate all the information from your newspaper staff, ensure that it is accurate, meets cost expectations, and is free from errors before it goes to print or is published online.

Before the work on each new edition begins, you may set some **standards**, which are models and examples of how items or tasks are expected to be executed.[3] Clear standards help to clarify goals and establish performance levels for employees. For example, you might set such standards such as boosting circulation by 10 percent from the previous month, reducing production costs by 20 percent, or producing a 100 percent error-free document. By setting specific performance standards, staff will be invested in the goals of the newspaper and will work toward achieving those targets.

As we have explored, when beginning any type of project, managers must have a planning process in place. A **preliminary control (planning control)** is used as a preventative measure to identify potential deficiencies before they occur.[4] This means that managers must take corrective action before problems arise. As managing editor, you might read each article thoroughly in order to spot inaccuracies, incorrect grammar or syntax, or misspellings before the paper goes to print. During this whole process, you will also need to monitor and check in with your staff to ensure that they are carrying out their responsibilities effectively, and gain feedback in order to address and resolve any problems. This is called a **screening control (real-time control)**, which is used to take corrective measures based on feedback during a process should barriers arise.[5] For example, one of your reporters might be having

Standards Models and examples of how items or tasks are expected to be executed.

Preliminary control (planning control) A control used as a preventative measure to identify potential deficiencies before they occur

Screening control (real-time control) A control used to take corrective measures based on feedback during a process should barriers arise.

difficulties in acquiring permission from a source, which could put the whole story in jeopardy. As managing editor, you will need to resolve the issue before the paper goes to press.

Following a week of intensive effort by the entire newspaper staff, the paper finally goes to print. Yet, as managing editor, you cannot afford to relax; after all, everyone needs to get to work on next week's edition. Effective managers will carry out **post-action control**, which is used to assess results after a process is complete in order to provide information for future planning.[6] By gathering feedback and assessing that information, managers can take steps to improve results in the future. As you compare the figures from the previous month, you are pleased to find that circulation has risen. But costs are still higher than they should be, and there are still a few errors in a couple of the articles. You make a note to address these issues and establish the appropriate controls for the following week's publication.

In this chapter, we will explore how Spencer Jones, a systems programmer and analyst, helps to transform Providence Community Healthcare's delivery system through the management of controls and operations.

16.2 | INFORMATION, TECHNOLOGY, AND SYSTEMS

16.2 | Describe the different forms and types of information technologies that managers apply.

Community health centers were set up across the United States in the 1960s in order to provide high-quality preventative health care to a medically underserved population regardless of ethnicity, age, income, or ability to pay. Each center is governed by a board of directors, which is responsible for establishing program policies in line with federal, state, and local laws and regulations. The board meets once a month to make decisions about the future of the health center. With the global health-care industry growing at such a rapid pace, there is an urgent need for enhanced technology and automation.

Providence Community Healthcare, in the capital of Rhode Island, is a not-for-profit organization governed by a board of directors headed up by Michelle Zoe, the chief executive officer (CEO). Management executives oversee the core departments of the organization, such as human resources (HR), information technology, finance, clinical services, and administration. Providence is embarking on a number of new initiatives to improve health care and reduce the cost of care for its 5,000 patients. This will involve the implementation of new systems and technology, high-level training for employees, and better service. With a reputation for careless recordkeeping, old-fashioned systems, impractical treatment for patients, and underperforming staff, Providence needs to undergo a major transformation if it wants to compete successfully in the health-care industry.

When Spencer Jones started at Providence Community Healthcare in 2001, he was the only systems programmer and analyst on staff. In his previous role at a high-profile insurance company, he had been part of a vibrant technology team that regularly updated the company's systems to meet market expectations. Yet, in his role at Providence, he was expected to work in isolation, in the least technology-friendly environment he had ever come across. The health-care center didn't even have a company website. Spencer looked forward to the challenge ahead, but was also apprehensive about the amount of work that he would have to do in order to bring the health-care systems and employees up to speed with modern technology.

When Spencer joined Providence, the health-care industry as a whole was reluctant to adopt **information technology (IT)**, which involves the development, maintenance, and use of computer systems, software, and networks for the processing and distribution of data.[7] This was mainly because IT systems were regarded in the company culture as too complex and expensive. In general, nurses, physicians, and other staff were not encouraged to use systems to improve efficiency. Why invest in technology when practitioners could write and file everything by hand? However, this process only resulted in chaos: poor handwriting led to misinterpretation and mistakes; patient information was regularly lost or difficult to retrieve; health-care providers experienced delays when passing information to each other; and patients were often instructed to repeat tests because of miscommunication between different practitioners and providers. It was clear that training and a change of mindset was necessary to embrace health-care technology fully; but very few providers had chosen this path.

Spencer's primary role is to organize the chaotic and disparate forms of information. With the growing emphasis on the Health Insurance Portability and Accountability Act of 1996 (HIPPA; also known as the Privacy Act), a regulation that protects health information and monitors how health-care providers maintain that information, the demands and importance of his position are continuing to increase over time. With IT in the spotlight, together with the rising costs of health care, Spencer certainly has his work cut out for him to ensure that the systems at Providence meet certain protocols and HIPAA compliance standards.

© Jamie Kingham/cultura / Corbis

Types of Information

One of Spencer's main challenges is to sift through acres of data, which is information often found in numerical form. Spencer, with the help of some members of the administrative team, begins the difficult mission of pulling handwritten medical records from dusty filing cabinets and painstakingly entering them into a database. To gain easy access to the manual records, Spencer sets up his computer station in the dark, claustrophobic basement of the center, where all the files were stored. The level of information was astounding. Many of the files are incomplete, mixed up with other information, or have missing pages, which makes his life much more difficult. When he asks the administration staff about these discrepancies, they shrug their shoulders and blame staff members who had left Providence long ago.

Still, in spite of these frustrations, Spencer knows that this exercise will have to be completed in order for everyone in Providence to have access to the same **knowledge**, or information gained by an individual or team that is internalized.[8] If staff members are trained properly on the system, then there will be less room for carelessness and inefficiency.

Eventually, Spencer manages to implement an electronic patient records system sooner than even their for-profit competitors across the state of Rhode Island. Michelle Zoe, the CEO of Providence, encourages him to present the system to the board of directors who are extremely impressed with the new database. It will allow every staff member to have the same access to medical records and improve the overall efficiency of the center. Spencer has also devised a number of compulsory fields within each database that have to be completed before the user goes on to the next screen. This encourages staff to input the most accurate information possible regarding the patients' medical conditions. The directors immediately agree for the staff to be trained on the database as soon as possible.

Through this initiative, Spencer becomes known as the main **knowledge worker** on site, which is an employee who is known for the specific skills that he or she possesses, such as technology.[9] Suddenly, Spencer was in demand with staff members asking his opinion on improving systems and data tracking for their departments. It is not long before he is given another project: to use different areas of IT to organize information.

Organizing Information Using Technology and Systems

The database is up and running, and the staff, although apprehensive at first, like having accurate information at their fingertips. All employees are equipped with their own laptop computer or tablet and are attending additional training to get them up to speed on the latest technology. To ensure that the database is secure, Spencer builds a **firewall**, a software program designed to protect against unauthorized entry into a particular information system or personal computer.[10]

Knowledge Information gained by an individual or team that is internalized.

Knowledge workers Employees who are known for the specific skills they possess, such as technology.

Firewall A software program designed to protect against unauthorized entry into a particular information system or personal computer.

Yet, Spencer knows that for the database to be truly efficient, he needs to provide access to parties outside the center. This will mean that other organizations, such as hospitals and primary care providers that Providence interacts with regularly, will also be able to obtain the same, live medical information. Spencer decides to build an **extranet**, which is similar to the Internet but used primarily within a company for its employees and/or vendors.[11] This means that data is available only to users who have been given permission to share the information on the extranet. Through this initiative, providers such as hospitals and clinics are able to access medical information at the point of care, allowing patients to be treated more quickly and efficiently.

© Marje / iStockphoto

Here is a prime example of how this works. A Providence community center patient arrived at the emergency room (ER) with breathing difficulties and was unable to communicate with the doctors on duty. Instead of carrying out the usual, time-consuming tests to figure out what was wrong with her, the hospital was able to access her records and medical history instantly through the extranet. On discovering that the patient had chronic asthma, they were able to provide her with an inhaler and other medication. She recovered from the attack in a matter of hours.

Slowly but surely, the staff begins to report similar success stories regarding their patients. Indeed, some of the longstanding members often joke about the "olden days," when they could barely read each other's handwriting on a patient's files. They agreed that the digitization of data is the best thing to happen to Providence in a long time.

Spencer's star is on the rise. In 2007, he gets promoted to chief information officer (CIO). But there is no time to sit back and celebrate his new job. Although the center is improving its systems and patient service, there is still much to be done. For example, costs are still higher than they should be, and some patients are still not being treated as efficiently as they could be. Although most of the staff has embraced the new technology, some doctors are still resisting it, continuing to write manual records. This means that some data is not being entered into the database at all; rather, it is being stored in piles on doctors' desks, leading to disorganization and confusion.

Yet, Spencer can't be everywhere at once. He requests that HR arrange more training for the reluctant doctors, and then he focuses on the next challenge ahead.

Michelle Zoe assigns Spencer a new mission: to look at how information systems can help reduce overall health-care costs per patient, increase patient satisfaction, and shift the provider culture from reactive to proactive from managing disease to encouraging wellness. Spencer gets to work.

16.3 | MANAGEMENT INFORMATION SYSTEMS

16.3 Illustrate how managers use information and technology systems to create efficiencies and make more effective decisions

In his new role as CIO, Spencer knows that he has to shift his approach from simply organizing information into systems for easy access, to using these systems to identify challenges and opportunities in such a way that doctors, nurses, and the hospital administrators can make more effective decisions. He is confident that with the right systems in place, he will be able to find a way to reduce costs while continuing to elevate the quality of patient care in the community.

Spencer begins his research by looking at systems that have been successfully adopted by other health-care institutions. Inspired by the information he has found, Spencer implements a **management information system (MIS)**, which aids organizations to run more efficiently by incorporating people, technology, and information systematically.[12] The system records the center's operational activities, such as staffing, financial costs, workload, and patient care.

Yet, Spencer still needs to find a way of integrating the disparate business processes across a single platform. **Enterprise resource planning (ERP)** is a system that provides a flow of information to include accounting, manufacturing, customer relationship management, sales, and service.[13] In health-care terms, the system holds data from across all the departments, such as medical records, inventory, billing, HR, and staff scheduling information. Spencer has also included suppliers and other medical providers in the system, making the information as transparent and accessible as possible.

Now Providence employees, as well as external vendors, are able to view all the data associated with each aspect of the operation. This means that everyone is able to see how one action carried out in one area can affect another part of the organization, which aids in the decision-making process. For example, not long after the ERP is implemented, one manager in the financial department notices an inventory discrepancy. Every month, medical suppliers deliver a set amount of medications to the center, a lot of which go unused because not every patient requires a medication every month. The result is huge payouts for medication that is simply stored until it expires and has to be discarded. By spotting this expensive glitch, Providence managers are able to devise a plan to assess the medical needs of each patient and ensure that they have only the necessary medication in stock at all times. The result is lower inventory, which means lower costs, as well as the assurance that patients will be supplied with the medication they need when they need it.

Next, Spencer starts to implement an **executive support system (ESS)**, a management information system that uses internal and external data to aid the executive staff with their decision-making process with regards to organizational performance.[14] The ESS allows senior managers to gather and analyze financial and statistical data, including patient care, staffing levels, general accounting, and medical records. Data can be displayed in different formats such as graphic or tabular, depending on the user's requirements. In addition, rather than waiting for weekly or monthly reports, executives can instantly view the data in real time, allowing them to make speedier decisions.

When the ESS is rolled out to Providence executive management and its providers, the results are revolutionary. For the first time, managers can access live data that helps them make practical decisions for the organization. For example, HR workers now have access to staff time and attendance records, which help them recognize and address the problem of absenteeism and the cost of poor attendance to the organization. Similarly, the accounting staff are able to view real-time financial data and statements, which help them manage the budget more effectively.

Following on his research, Spencer notes that many medical institutions use **decision support systems (DSSs)**, which are computer-based information systems that help organizations with their decision-making processes.[15] In some clinics, DSSs aid doctors in making more accurate diagnoses. Such systems contain detailed health data, such as different types of diseases and conditions. When the doctor enters certain criteria, such as age, weight, gender, and symptoms, the system produces a list of options, based on probability, as to what could be the issue with the patient.

However, when Spencer presents the possibility of implementing a DSS to the board of directors, he is greeted with skepticism. Michelle Zoe leads the argument: "How can a computer do the work of a fully trained doctor?" she says. "Surely, treating patients is a human field. It not only relies on the vast wealth of knowledge gained over years of practice, but also on the good judgment of our doctors. A computer program should not be used to diagnose patients on the strength of some arbitrary data. Are you suggesting that this DSS will eventually replace medical practitioners in the future?"

Seeing that he has ruffled a few feathers, Spencer explains that DSSs have been adopted by some institutions to help doctors make better diagnostic decisions, not replace them. "It is by no means intended to be a substitute for years of expertise, but acts as an aid—an additional source of information when the doctor may be hesitant about a diagnosis," he says. But the board looks far from convinced.

To cement his argument further, Spencer reports a case where a patient was having unexplained chest pains. The doctor ordered a chest x-ray, which came up negative, and she prescribed a set of antibiotics. However, the patient felt no better; in fact, he started experiencing dizzy spells and a sharp pain in his left thigh. The doctor then input the patient's symptoms into the medical DSS, which suggested a possible thyroid problem. Following a few more tests, the patient was diagnosed with hyperthyroidism and promptly put on a corrective course of medication; subsequently, his symptoms disappeared.

✓ **Artificial Intelligence (AI)**—gives computers the ability to seemingly possess human intelligence and act accordingly to process information, in order to consider implementing the DSS

Executive support system (ESS) A management information system that uses internal and external data to aid the executive staff with their decision-making process with regards to organizational performance.

Decision support system (DSS) A computer-based information system that helps organizations with their decision-making process.

The board responds that it will need more evidence regarding the effectiveness of **artificial intelligence (AI)**, a software system that gives computers the ability to seemingly possess human intelligence and act accordingly to process information, before it will consider implementing a DSS.[16] Spencer agrees to find more statistical proof that DSS could be an essential tool to aid diagnostic decision making and promises to present it to the board at a future meeting.

Other than the board's reluctance to try DSS, Spencer feels that the meeting has been successful. Having effectively correlated all the data and implemented the majority of information systems, it is time for Spencer's next big challenge: to reduce patient costs while improving patient care.

16.4 | INFORMATION AND CONTROLS FOR OPERATIONS

16.4 | Identify the types of controls and the processes used by managers to measure and adapt organizational performance

Even though Spencer has all the data for Providence at his fingertips, he is more than a little overwhelmed by his latest task. How is he going to find the right areas to impose cost-cutting measures? The center is short-staffed as it is, so laying off employees to save money is out of the question.

From his research about other organizations, Spencer has found that some employers have implemented cost-cutting measures by raising medical insurance premiums for their own employees, in the hope that they will go to the hospital or visit a doctor only in the most extreme of circumstances. Spencer can't make sense of this at all. If people have a real medical problem but are put off by going to the hospital because it is too expensive, then surely that problem will escalate, eventually leading to longer hospital stays and more treatment, not to mention disgruntled and ailing employees? How would that approach impact company morale, and save costs?

As far as he can tell from the financial data, the level of expenditure seems to be absolutely necessary. Spencer knows that financial facts and figures are not his forte, so he makes a note to consult the accounting department to clarify the data he has uncovered.

Then one day, on a much-needed coffee break, Spencer reads a medical report in the *New Yorker*[17] that gives him a great idea. Suddenly he knows exactly what he needs to do to carry out Michelle's requests.

Spencer is inspired by Brenner's research and work. In the article, Brenner discusses how he managed to achieve everything that Spencer has been asked to do at Providence. If he is to model Brenner's approach, however, he knows that simply accessing medical records will not be enough. He needs to find out more about the financial situation at Providence before he can start trimming expenditures. He follows up on his note to communicate with the accounting department and arranges to meet with the most senior member the next day.

Types of Controls

The following day, Spencer meets with Joanne Donnelly, the **controller**, the chief accounting officer within an organization that helps control finances.[18] Spencer listens while Joanne begins by explaining her role and responsibilities within the organization.

She is responsible for accounting, insurance, operations, financial systems, and auditing. She gathers and analyzes data and creates financial reports, which help the board make financial decisions. Joanne also ensures that the Providence staff is in compliance with budgetary practices and financial policies. She sets up regular meetings with staff members to keep them up to date on all health-provider matters and is involved in the hiring and firing of employees.

Spencer explains to Joanne what he is trying to achieve: a reduction in costs while providing better patient care. Joanne asks Spencer why he isn't using his own creations to acquire this financial information: the management information systems. Spencer shrugs, "At this stage in

Research@Work

my career, I know my strengths and my weaknesses. Give me a computer and I will build an innovative program, but to be honest, financial facts and figures are way over my head."

Joanne replies, "Well, you might not believe me, but financial reporting is more interesting than people think, and fairly easy to understand. While people might say I have a boring job, I find it to be fascinating."

Doing his best to put his doubts aside, Spencer picks up a notepad and prepares to learn about finance. For the next couple of hours, Joanne brings Spencer through her responsibilities as a controller and explains the financial situation at Providence and how it is linked to other health-care providers.

Joanne begins by showing Spencer a variety of tools that she uses to control financial performance. First, she shows Spencer the latest **financial statement**, which is a summary that lists the revenue and liabilities for a company during a particular time frame.[20] Then, she brings him through the **balance sheets**, a type of financial statement that lists revenue, assets, and liabilities for a company during a particular time frame.[21] Finally, she produces an **income statement**, which is a summary of revenue gained during a specific time period, usually listed by month.[22]

Although Spencer is the first to admit he doesn't have a head for finance, one thing is obvious to him: Providence does not appear to be as financially healthy as it could be. Not wanting to appear too negative, he asks Joanne about the competition. Maybe Providence isn't the worst performer in Rhode Island. He says, "How do we compare with our competitors—the 'for-profit' providers on Rhode Island? Are they struggling as much as we are?"

Joanne explains the process of **ratio analysis**, which is a quantitative study of a company's financial statements within a particular collection of data.[23] "Every month, we run an analysis of our overall performance and use the results to compare our performance with our competition on Rhode Island." Joanne clears her throat before continuing: "I think it's fair to say we are lagging in almost every area."

Financial statement A summary that lists the revenue and liabilities for a company during a particular time frame.

Balance sheet A financial statement that lists revenue, assets, and liabilities for a company during a particular time frame.

Income statement A summary of revenue gained during a specific time period, usually listed by month.

Ratio analysis A quantitative study of a company's financial statements within a particular collection of data.

Spencer asks Joanne if last year's internal **audit**, a formal examination of a company, department, or individual's accounts or financial standing,[24] had shown any areas for improvement. Joanne responds: "Quite a few, actually. The additional problems we uncovered during the audit include poor inventory control, duplication of work, underuse of technology and machines, and a high level of absenteeism, to name a few. All of these problems are costing the company huge amounts of money."

"What does that say about our overall budget, then?" Spencer says, although he has a feeling he knows the answer.

One of Joanne's main responsibilities is to assess the company **budget**, a document that is used to predict revenues and expenditures during a certain period for financial forecasting.[25] She tells Spencer the hard truth—that Providence has been over budget every month for the last year, apart from the previous month, which remained stable.

Spencer is intrigued: "What made such a difference in last month's budget to bring it in line with revenues and expenditures?"

Joanne smiled, "Last month's budget is a clear reflection of the positive impact of your work here. Thanks to your new system, we have been able to reduce the amount of inventory we have with regard to medical supplies. That has significantly affected the bottom line, which means a sizeable reduction in costs."

Spencer had never expected to become particularly engaged with the finances at Providence, but now he saw that his work was having such a direct impact, he couldn't help but feel more enthusiastic. Yet, he had one more question on his mind: Wasn't it Joanne's job as controller to ensure that the budget remained stable every month? Trying to frame his question tactfully, he asks Joanne why there seems to be such fluctuation from month to month.

Joanne nodded, "Yes, the last year has been harder than most. Rising health-care costs across the U.S. means that our budget has taken a real hammering. Every health-care organization is bearing the brunt of this uncertain economic climate."

Spencer says, "I'm glad to hear that the inventory issue is having a favorable impact on the budget, but I also think that some of the other problems raised during the audit can also be addressed. For example, once the staff receives full training on the new systems and machines that should help to address the problem of underuse of resources and duplication of work."

Joanne nods, "I agree, but simply trimming expenditure here and there only makes a small difference; we need a more holistic solution to cut costs if we want to stay in the game."

Spencer said, "I might just have the solution you are looking for . . ."

He fills Joanne in about the findings made by family physician Jeffrey Brenner, as reported in the *New Yorker* article. Joanne says: "That's it! What we need to do is collate the financial data to assess which patients are having the greatest impact on our budget! If we can reduce the need for so many hospital visits, then we can actually reduce costs."

Spencer smiles; after carrying out so much of the IT work in isolation, he is relieved to finally have a partner in his search for answers.

Influencing Behavior Using Information and Controls

With the help of Joanne's financial reports and the management information system, Spencer is able to correlate the data from all the health providers in the area to assess patient cost, the number of emergency room visits, and the amount of staffing costs incurred. Within a couple of hours, using the hot-spotting technique, he has identified the chief patients in Rhode Island who would benefit from this program. Spencer arranges a meeting with Joanne to report his findings and to work out the potential financial savings incurred if the strategy succeeds.

After several minutes of silence as she reads the report, Joanne looks at Spencer with a glint in her eye. "Based on the data you have provided and my calculations, Providence could save over $15 million a year with this initiative, not to mention provide better, more personalized care."

Spencer is speechless. He had an idea that the plan would help cut costs, but not to this extent. He thanks Joanne and leaves the meeting, his head spinning. There is much to be done.

Later on, as he reflects on the *New Yorker* article, he realizes that cutting costs and paring down the budget is not just about hard facts and figures. If they are really going to make a difference in the health-care system, they will need to change the behavior and culture of the health-care providers for patients to receive the optimal and most cost-effective care available. The mindsets of health care workers, doctors, nurses, administrators, directors . . . in fact anyone involved in the health industry, will need to undergo a massive transformation. He realizes that only when attitudes change will cost reductions happen.

"It's not going to be easy," Spencer says out loud to himself. In his mind, playing with data and figures is a lot easier than trying to adjust behaviors and attitudes. Yet, if he wants to follow the example of Jeffrey Brenner, then he must put in as much effort as possible to get the support he needs and put his plan in action.

His next step is to come up with some imaginative solutions to provide care proactively for those patients identified via the hot-spotting method in order to reduce medical bills.

16.5 | MANAGING OPERATIONAL PERFORMANCE WITH CONTROLS

16.5 | Describe how managers effectively apply controls to influence performance, with both people and results.

To get the team on board with his goal, Spencer circulates the article on hot-spotting to his peers, along with a memo outlining his ideas.[26] After a lengthy meeting with Spencer, Michelle Zoe, the CEO of Providence Healthcare, recommends that he put together a medical team to implement operational controls that will identify and address the targeting patients. She instructs Spencer to come back the following week to present a detailed outline of the project for her approval. With the CEO's backing, the project takes off rapidly.

Spencer enlists the help of two of the nurses and four health workers at Providence. They go through the list of high-expense patients and make a plan as to how to better meet their needs and, in turn, save money. It is decided that the patients will continue to see the Providence doctors as usual, but the nurses and social workers will extend the level of care by communicating with the patients between visits. The hope was that the nurses could help resolve health matters over the phone or through quick home visits and prevent a trip to the hospital.

Each patient would have 24-hour access to the medical team, by phone, text messaging, and email. Always interested in the technical side of things, Spencer feels he could also empower patients by offering options such as videoconferencing at home, so they could have face-to-face contact with the team. He is also excited by the new telemetric devices on the market that are being tested to help patients monitor certain conditions at home. The devices transmit cardiac signals and display the results on a monitor. For example, cardiac patients could potentially use heart monitors to measure their own heart rates without having to go into a hospital unless they really needed to.

The new management information system will allow patients access to their own portal, which contains their medical records and other personal information. The portal electronically communicates this information between other health-care providers, resulting in better coordination. One of the roles of the health workers will be to teach the patients how to use this technology and ensure that they have the adequate computer equipment at home to carry out these functions. They will also help patients to manage their own care and devise appropriate pain management plans. The health workers will also assess the patient's lifestyle, living conditions, home safety, and social and family support, and provide referrals and other assistance where necessary.

The team compiles their plan into a presentation detailing the roles of the team, their main objectives, and the potential financial savings if they focus on helping to manage the care of the costliest patients. In a separate handout, they list the patients they intend to target. Michelle Zoe, the CEO, takes in all the information and then says, "I like your approach. It is well documented, and I agree that enhancing the care for these patients will make a real difference to their welfare, and result in cost savings. However, I just want to make something absolutely clear before I present this initiative to the board. In no way should the medical team recommend activities that would discourage people from coming to the ER."

She pauses as her eyes drift down the list of patients that Spencer has prepared.

"Take this 74-year-old patient, Barney, for example. According to your data, he has been averaging 3.4 ER visits a month for the past six months. That's not including the amount of visits he has paid to our doctors here at Providence; it also looks as if he gets an ambulance to his appointments here and the ER.

"Yet this report implies that only two of those visits were considered legitimate; one time he had pneumonia, and the second time he had cut his hand on a meat slicer. However, on the other occasions he has clearly been overusing the ER services. Your team needs to strike a balance as to when Barney has a legitimate cause to attend the ER, and when he can self-manage his own care. However, remember that if he feels put off by going to the ER, and he contracts another case of pneumonia and is not treated properly for it, there could be dire consequences for a man his age."

Spencer says, "I understand your point, and we will certainly tread carefully with all the patients on our list, and will in no way discourage them from paying hospital visits if they feel there is a real need."

The rest of the team nods in agreement.

Michelle replies, "I appreciate you taking the point on board, but I don't feel that we should start with all the patients on this list at once. So, I am suggesting a trial process to begin with, and then we will go from there."

The next day, Michelle tells the team that they have been given the go-ahead by the board to pilot the patient support program. The team agrees to test their controls on a small group of patients and assess the results before moving on to the other patients on their list. The first patient they choose is Barney, cited by Michelle during the previous meeting.

Five years ago, at the age of 69, Barney retired from a shipping company after a 30-year career. Last year, his wife of 52 years had suddenly passed away. It had been a week since Barney's last visit to ER. Spencer and one of the nurses on the team, Hazel, make a plan to pay Barney a home visit.

© Mark Bowden / iStockphoto

Barney lives in a modest Cape-style, three-bedroom house in a fairly isolated area, about a 30-minute drive from the Providence Healthcare center. Spencer notes the neatness of the lawn and the freshly painted siding of Barney's home. He is clearly a man who likes to take care of things. Before they even have a chance to knock on the door, it swings open, revealing a sturdy, healthy-looking man, dressed smartly in a sweater and slacks. Following a brief introduction, and an explanation of the reasons behind the visit, Barney invites Spencer and Hazel inside, guiding them toward a brightly lit, tidy living room.

Spencer hadn't been sure what to expect from this visit, but he sure hadn't thought he would find a man so sprightly and full of energy. Before they begin their discussion, Barney insists that they have some of the cake that he made that morning and homemade lemonade. Spencer and the nurse exchange a look—what on Earth could be so wrong with this man that he feels the need to go to the hospital so often?

It was time to find out.

"So, Barney; I hear you haven't been well lately," Spencer begins. "How are you feeling now?"

Barney replies, "I had a bout of pneumonia a couple of months ago that set me back, and I stupidly cut myself with a meat slicer, but the great staff down at the hospital soon sorted me out. They are a wonderful team down there, especially that nurse John Gailey. He is great company!"

Spencer makes a note to speak to John Gailey to find out more about Barney's situation.

"I'm really pleased that the team treated you so well in ER," Spencer says, carefully. "But are there any other reasons apart from those two visits that you felt warranted so many other trips to the emergency room?"

"Oh, it's just that I have this heart condition. I was diagnosed with it about 20 years ago, and it acts up now and then," Barney says, rubbing his chest.

Spencer tries to recall Barney's medical records, but he can't remember anything about Barney having a heart condition. He looks at the nurse for help, but she is similarly confused. Although he is not a medical man, Spencer thinks that he can ask a few of the right questions.

"Who diagnosed you so many years ago, and what are your symptoms?" he said, gently.

"Why, the same doctor that still works at your place in Providence; Dr. Aintree is his name. I had chest pains one day when I was at work at the shipping company, and I went to the doctor. He told me that I had to come back every three months for an examination."

Spencer is puzzled. Barney's "condition" certainly explained why he has been paying so many visits to Providence, as well as to the ER, but he doesn't know why his heart problem hasn't been entered in his medical records. It occurs to him that Dr. Aintree might be one of the doctors at Providence who is reluctant to use the new database to enter electronic records. "He probably has the rest of Barney's file buried beneath a pile of aging documents in the corner of his small office," Spencer thinks. Frustrated, Spencer makes a mental note to speak to Dr. Aintree when they get back to the center.

While Spencer is writing his notes, Hazel, the nurse, interjects, "And what results has Dr. Aintree given you, following these regular examinations?"

"Well, he just tells me everything is normal; but that I will still need regular check-ups for the rest of my life. Funny thing is, everything has been normal up until about six months ago. That's when I started experiencing some tightness in my chest and my heart starts pounding. That's when I dial 911," Barney says, ruefully.

"I understand why you feel the need to get to ER by ambulance when you are experiencing chest pains, but may I ask why you take the ambulance to your routine appointments at Providence?" Spencer asks.

"Well, I don't have any other way of getting to you from this house. I don't feel confident driving when I have chest pains, and the local bus service doesn't come within two miles of this place. As you can see, I'm a little isolated here. I don't have any children or neighbors to call on. Besides, I don't have the direct number for the clinic on hand," Barney responds.

Spencer decides this is a good time to tell Barney about the new initiatives that the health-care center is putting in place to improve the care for their patients. Barney is pleased to hear about the 24/7 direct access to the medical team, and he writes down the clinic's number so he has it on hand whenever he needs it. Barney is not so excited, however, about the technological initiatives suggested by Spencer. "Look, I'm an old man. Old dogs don't like new tricks. I just don't feel like I have the energy to deal with newfangled inventions. I have a computer, but I barely know how to switch it on. Maybe if my wife was here . . . She was always good at urging me on whenever I had doubts about something new. But, now . . . I simply don't have it in me."

Spencer is surprised to see such a transformation in Barney: the bright, sprightly man has suddenly aged before his eyes. He seems utterly defeated. "He's lonely," Spencer thinks.

Not wanting to push the subject, they end the visit, with Barney agreeing to call the medical team any time he needs to, day or night.

On the way back to the center, Spencer and Hazel discuss Barney's situation. They both agree that Barney, for all his energy and optimism, seems lonely. "His wife died only a few months ago; he doesn't have any kids, and he is alone in that house; no wonder he is feeling a little isolated," Hazel says. "I imagine he is still grieving."

"So what about the chest pains?" Spencer says. "Why haven't they been entered into his medical records?"

"That's something we need to ask Dr. Aintree," Hazel replies. "If the results keep coming back clear, I imagine his chest pains might be symptomatic of something else. Maybe he suffers from anxiety and doesn't know it or how to manage it."

"We'll just have to talk to Dr. Aintree and go from there," Spencer says, thoughtfully. "There is no point in presuming too much at this early stage."

When they get back to the center, they report their findings to Michelle, who is impressed with what they have discovered. When they tell her the reasons why Barney always gets an ambulance to his routine appointments, she looks thoughtful.

"I think I might have an idea about how to reduce the cost of our patients getting to and from Providence," she says. Spencer and the team listen while Michelle outlines her ideas for a transportation service for those patients who do not require urgent medical attention. She adds, "We could train some of our staff here at Providence, recruit new members to be the drivers, and purchase a few vans as transport. It would certainly cut the cost of ambulances, that's for sure."

Spencer thinks this is a great idea, but he has a question: "Do we have the budget for this?" he says, thinking of Joanne Donnelly, the controller, and the gloomy financial figures that she shared with him last week.

"I think I can persuade the board to make room for this initiative," Michelle smiles. "Leave it to me."

Next, Spencer pays a visit to the rest of the team to see what they have uncovered about Barney. The team has used the systems data to uncover an interesting pattern. On each visit to the ER, Barney has been seen by the same medical team for over 70 percent of his visits. Spencer picks up the phone and calls John Gailey, the nurse that Barney mentioned during their conversation.

John Gailey knows immediately who Barney is. "He is a lively man," he tells Spencer. "He has a great sense of humor and always asks if I have any new jokes. We have a lot of laughs together."

When Spencer asks John about Barney's chest pains, John hesitates. "Honestly? We can't find anything wrong with him in that area. Personally, I think Barney might be having anxiety attacks. As soon as he arrives at ER and we have a bit of banter, his symptoms subside almost immediately. Yet, Dr. Aintree keeps telling him to dial 911 as soon as he gets so much as a flutter. Maybe you should talk to Dr. Aintree directly."

"I intend to," Spencer replies, grimly. "But first, I need a favor . . ."

Spencer asks John to call Barney every other day to see how he is doing and to tell him a joke. John agrees. Soon, Barney's emergency room visits drop by 90 percent. John's calls, together with additional home visits and the comfort of direct access to the medical team, have made a huge difference to Barney's mental and physical health. He seems less sad and lonely and has not experienced any chest pains since they put the controls in place.

Although Spencer is pleased with the success of the cost-saving initiatives implemented at Providence Community Healthcare, he knows that there is much more work to be done. In the next chapter, we will explore how managers manage behavior and results through performance management.

Case**Snapshot**

Chapter 16 Case: Information and Operations:
Zipcar can be found on pg. 479

ADDITIONAL RESOURCES

KEY TERMS

Artificial intelligence (AI) A software system that gives computers the ability to seemingly possess human intelligence and act accordingly to process information. **(p. 406)**

Audit A formal examination of a company, department, or individual's accounts or financial standing. **(p. 408)**

Balance sheet A financial statement that lists revenue, assets, and liabilities for a company during a particular time frame. **(p. 407)**

Budget A document used to predict revenue and expenditures during a certain period for financial forecasting. **(p. 408)**

Control A tool that helps managers use information to influence behavior and affect operational performance through greater efficiencies and effective decision making. **(p. 400)**

Controller The chief accounting officer within an organization that helps control finances. **(p. 406)**

Decision support system (DSS) A computer-based information system that helps organizations with their decision-making process. **(p. 405)**

Enterprise resource planning (ERP) A system that provides a flow of information to include accounting, manufacturing, customer relationship management, sales, and service. **(p. 404)**

Executive support system (ESS) A management information system that uses internal and external data to aid the executive staff with their decision-making process with regards to organizational performance. **(p. 405)**

Extranet A system that is similar to the Internet but used primarily within a company for its employees and or vendors. **(p. 404)**

Financial statement A summary that lists the revenue and liabilities for a company during a particular time frame. **(p. 407)**

Firewall A software program designed to protect against unauthorized entry into a particular information system or personal computer. **(p. 403)**

Income statement A summary of revenue gained during a specific time period, usually listed by month. **(p. 407)**

Information technology (IT) The development, maintenance, and use of computer systems, software, and networks for the processing and distribution of data. **(p. 402)**

Knowledge Information gained by an individual or team that is internalized. **(p. 403)**

Knowledge workers Employees who are known for the specific skills they possess, such as technology. **(p. 403)**

Management information system (MIS) A tool that aids organizations to run more efficiently by incorporating people, technology, and information systematically. **(p. 404)**

Post-action control A control used to assess results after a process is complete in order to provide information for future planning **(p. 402)**

Preliminary control (planning control) A control used as a preventative measure to identify potential deficiencies before they occur **(p. 401)**

Ratio analysis A quantitative study of a company's financial statements within a particular collection of data. **(p. 407)**

Screening control (real-time control) A control used to take corrective measures based on feedback during a process should barriers arise. **(p. 401)**

Standards Models and examples of how items or tasks are expected to be executed. **(p. 401)**

IN REVIEW

16.1 | Explain how managers use controls to operate organizational performance.

Control is how managers use information to influence behavior and affect operational performance through greater efficiencies and effective decision making. By exercising control, managers are better able to oversee activities and direct employees toward achieving organizational goals. Managers need to adapt and refine operational controls to cater to new innovations and new technologies. If organizations depend too much on inflexible controlling functions, they will be slow to respond to change, which will have a detrimental impact on future success.

16.2 | Describe the different forms and types of information technologies that managers apply.

Information technology (IT) involves the development, maintenance, and use of computer systems, software, and networks for the processing and distribution of data. A *firewall* is used to protect against entry into a particular information system or personal computer. An *extranet* is similar to the Internet, but it is used primarily within a company for its employees and/or vendors.

16.3 | Illustrate how managers use information and technology systems to create efficiencies and make more effective decisions.

A *management information system (MIS)* aids organizations to run more efficiently by incorporating people, technology, and information systematically. *Enterprise resource planning (ERP)* is a system that provides a flow of information to include accounting, manufacturing, customer relationship management, sales and service. An *executive support system (ESS)* is a management information system that uses internal and external data to aid the executive staff with their decision-making process with regards to organizational performance. A *decision support system (DSS)* is a computer-based information system that helps organizations with their decision-making processes. Artificial intelligence (AI) is a software system that gives computers the ability to seemingly possess human intelligence and act accordingly to process information.

16.4 | Identify the types of controls and the processes used by managers to measure and adapt organizational performance.

A *financial statement* is a summary that lists the revenue and liabilities for a company during a particular time frame. *Ratio analysis* is a quantitative study of a company's financial statements within a particular collection of data. An *audit* is a formal examination of a company, department, or individual's accounts or financial standing.

16.5 | Describe how managers effectively apply controls to influence performance, with both people and results.

Managers can use cutting-edge control technologies such as videoconferencing and management information systems to empower employees and customers alike.

SELF-TEST

16.1 | Explain how managers use controls to operate organizational performance.

1. _____ is how managers use information to influence behavior and affect operational performance through greater efficiencies and effective decision making.
   a. Planning
   b. Recruiting
   c. Decision making
   d. Control

2. List and briefly describe the three basic types of control.

16.2 | Describe the different forms and types of information technologies that managers apply.

3. _____ involves the development, maintenance, and use of computer systems, software, and networks for the processing and distribution of data.

4. A(n) _____ worker is an employee who is employed for the specific knowledge that he or she possesses, such as technology.
   a. Data
   b. Information
   c. Knowledge
   d. Technology

5. The extranet is similar to the Internet but is used primarily outside a company for its customers and shareholders.
   a. True
   b. False

16.3 | Illustrate how managers use information and technology systems to create efficiencies and make more effective decisions.

6. A(n) _____ aids organizations to run more efficiently by incorporating people, technology, and information systematically.

7. _____ provides a flow of information to include accounting, manufacturing, customer relationship management, sales and service.
   a. Enterprise Resource Planning (ERP)
   b. Executive Support System (ESS)
   c. Decision Support System (DSS)
   d. Human Resource Planning (HRP)

8. Artificial intelligence (AI) gives computers the ability to seemingly possess human intelligence and act accordingly to process information.
   a. True
   b. False

16.4 | Identify the types of controls and the processes used by managers to measure and adapt organizational performance.

9. Which of the following is *not* a tool to control financial performance?
   a. Balance sheet
   b. Income statement
   c. Ratio analysis
   d. Human resources audit

10. An internal _____ is a formal examination of a company, department, or individual's accounts or financial standing, while a(n) _____ is used to predict revenues and expenditures during a certain period for financial forecasting.

16.5 | Describe how managers effectively apply controls to influence performance, with both people and results.

11. Which of the following is an example of a control technique used by some health-care providers to identify high-cost patients to provide additional personal care in order to reduce overall health care costs?
    a. Videoconferencing
    b. Hot-spotting
    c. Redlining
    d. Monitoring

CHAPTER EXERCISE

Post-action Contro

This exercise will help you to understand some of the limitations of post-action control. Your task is to count every "F" in the following text, answering immediately after reading the text only once.

FINISHED FILES ARE THE RESULT OF YEARS OF SCIENTIFIC STUDY COMBINED WITH THE EXPERIENCE OF YEARS . . .

How many did you get?

Did you find three?

There are actually six—believe it or not . . .

Seriously, go back and read the statement again carefully and try to find all six.

For some reason, the brain has a hard time processing the "F's" in the word "of." This exercise shows some of the possible challenges and limitations of using post-action control, especially if it is not used in conjunction with preliminary or planning control and screening or real-time control.

SELF-ASSESSMENT

Control Preferences Self-Assessment

How accurate are each of the following statements in describing your approach to completing an important written assignment such as a term paper? (Circle the most appropriate response.)

1. While composing my paper, I take my time and focus on accuracy so that I make few, if any, typographical errors.

    Accurate   Inaccurate

2. I correct typographical errors as they occur, not waiting to catch them in a final review.

    Accurate   Inaccurate

3. I use a spell-check function to ensure that my final paper is free of typographical errors.

    Accurate   Inaccurate

4. I try to write a mostly completed draft the first time, rather than writing a rough draft that I will revise later.

    Accurate   Inaccurate

5. I take notice of misspelled words, stopping to correct them, as I am writing my initial draft.

    Accurate   Inaccurate

6. I have a friend or relative proofread my final draft before I submit it.

    Accurate   Inaccurate

Scoring:

Statements 1 and 4 are indicators of a preference for preliminary or planning control, which involves taking preventative measure to identify potential errors before they occur. Statements 2 and 5 are indicators of a preference for screening or real-time control, which involves taking corrective measures based on feedback during a process. Statements 3 and 6 are indicators of a preference for post-action control, which is used to assess results after a process is complete and correct errors after they occur. Employing a healthy mixture of all three types of control may be the best policy for most situations.

SELF-TEST ANSWER KEY

1. d.
2. A *preliminary control (planning control)* is used as a preventative measure to identify potential deficiencies before they occur. A *screening control (real-time control)* involves taking corrective measures based on feedback during a process should barriers arise. A *post-action control* is used to assess results after a process is complete to provide information for future planning.
3. Information technology (IT)
4. c.
5. b; False. The *extranet* is similar to the Internet but used primarily *within* a company for its employees and/or vendors.
6. Management information system (MIS)
7. a.
8. a; True.
9. d.
10. Audit; budget
11. b.

Notes

_____

_____

CHAPTER SEVENTEEN

PERFORMANCE DEVELOPMENT

Learning Objectives

By the end of the chapter, you will be able to:

17.1 | Explain how managers connect facilities, processes, and people to control performance.

17.2 | Describe the context and standards through which managers control facilities.

17.3 | Illustrate how managers use processes to design, develop, and deliver quality products and services.

17.4 | Describe how managers work with team members to improve and adapt facilities and processes continuously.

17.5 | Show how managers connect facilities, processes, and people to achieve superior performance results.

ADDITIONAL RESOURCES

KEY TERMS
IN REVIEW
SELF-TEST
CHAPTER EXERCISE
SELF-ASSESSMENT
SELF-TEST
ANSWER KEY

JP Greenwood/Getty Images

INSIDE THIS CHAPTER

ManagementStory:
Featuring **Spencer Jones**

417

17.1 | HOW PERFORMANCE DEVELOPMENT MAKES A DIFFERENCE

17.1 | Explain how managers connect facilities, processes, and people to control performance.

> "It is an immutable law in business that words are words, explanations are explanations, promises are promises, but only performance is reality."
>
> —Harold S. Geneen

Performance development management spans a whole range of business activities, from systems performance to people performance to facility performance. Today's managers evaluate performance from a holistic perspective in order to deliver organizational improvement processes and strategies. This approach also ties in with the principles behind Systems Theory, first introduced in Chapter 3, whereby managers look at an organization as a fluid system composed of many different parts, all of which depend on each other. The role of managers is to look at these interconnected systems as a whole to understand the importance of each part and how it contributes to the organization. By understanding and analyzing how each part of the organization affects the other units, managers are able to introduce new innovative approaches to help the company achieve performance excellence.

As we have learned over the course of this book, a number of factors can affect organizational performance. For example, a poorly performing employee can affect the productivity of the rest of the team; and an ill-designed system can cause delays and financial loss if it is not fixed in a timely manner. Indeed, the very facility that we work from also can affect our performance. We may not be entirely conscious of it, but a badly lit, poorly ventilated, crumbling office building can have a severe impact on the way we work.

In this chapter, we will explore how Spencer Jones, the chief information officer (CIO) of Providence Community Healthcare, manages and controls performance by connecting the main fabric of the health center: its people, the processes they follow, and the facility from which they operate.

Connecting Space, Process, and People

In Chapter 16, we met Spencer Jones, a technology wizard who has implemented a series of databases and systems to improve efficiency at Providence Community Healthcare in the capital city of Rhode Island. Spencer has also introduced a new initiative to treat targeted patients—namely, the hot-spotting technique, which allowed the center to deliver higher-quality care for lower medical costs. In the next section, we will follow Spencer as he continues to revolutionize this approach to health care.

The successful pilot program of Spencer's initiative has proved that higher-quality health care and focused attention can help patients recover quicker and without as many visits to their doctor's office or the hospital, which curbs medical costs. As soon as the board gave

ManagementStory:
Featuring Spencer Jones

the plan the green light, Spencer and the medical team got to work focusing on the rest of the patients identified by the hot-spotting technique, with great success. The team conducted home-based assessments for each of the consenting patients, implemented treatment plans, provided administrative support in sorting out health insurance paperwork, set up training sessions to educate staff and patients on the latest technology to monitor certain health conditions, showed patients how to access their own unique patient portal, and assured patients that they will have access to the team 24 hours a day, 7 days a week. In addition, a newly implemented van service began to transport patients to and from their appointments at Providence, saving ambulance costs.

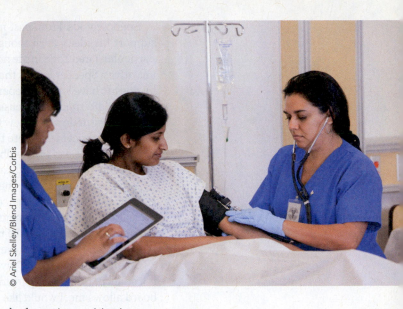

As a result of these efforts, the patients have begun to respond in ways the team and their health-care providers could never have imagined. The health of many of the patients are improving to such a degree that hospital visits dropped by over 60 percent in the space of six months, reducing costs by an impressive 40 percent. The van service also has had a major positive impact on the budget.

Now the success of Spencer's initiative has impressed the board of directors at Providence Community Healthcare and has even brought national attention to the small operation. The progressive initiative has been profiled in health-industry magazines, the contents of which have been picked up by national newspapers. The initial results of Spencer's information and the analytics team's efforts has an immediate positive impact on patient satisfaction, emergency room (ER) visits, and doctor and nurse satisfaction, while lowering health-care costs. As a nonprofit organization, the reduction of health-care costs translates into a financially healthier organization.

Spencer and his medical team are thrilled with the outcome of the initiative and pleased that they are receiving such favorable publicity for their efforts. But Spencer knows that there is much more to be done. As he is walking through the health center, he finds himself thinking about the dated condition of the facility and wonder what it would be like if Providence, like some of the for-profit providers in Rhode Island, was transformed into a state-of-the-art medical **facility**, a building designed and built to support a particular service or function.

> **Facility** A building designed and built to support a particular service or function.

Hazel, one of the nurses, comes up beside him and echoes his thoughts: "It's embarrassing, isn't it! Here we are promoting a brand-new initiative supported by the latest technology and launching it all from a rundown building with bad lighting and crumbling paint. What must journalists think when they come here to profile us—not to mention the thousands of patients we treat here. It's hardly a shining example of the future of the health industry!"

Spencer agrees with Hazel. If Providence is going to continue to make such great strides, its headquarters needs to look the part. Then, one day, out of the blue, something incredible happens.

Michelle Zoe, Providence Community Healthcare's chief executive officer (CEO), calls Spencer into her office and announces that she is going to retire. Spencer is surprised and disappointed; Michelle has been his chief supporter ever since he came up with the idea for the new initiative. He can't help but think how things might change when she leaves. But Michelle has a surprise for him. She tells Spencer that the board of directors wants to meet with him personally about potentially transitioning from the company's CIO to its most senior position of chairman and CEO. Spencer is speechless—in his wildest dreams, he had never expected to be considered for the CEO position. Before he can express his gratitude, Michelle adds:

"Congratulations, Spencer, for being considered as my replacement. Personally, I think you will make an excellent CEO, but it is not entirely up to me whether this appointment goes ahead or not. Although most of the board supports this internal recruitment decision, there are a few members who have their doubts, and they think a national search should be conducted for this critical role. It is up to you to share your vision with them and convince them otherwise."

Spencer nods. From past meetings with the board, he is aware that not all the members support his ideas, even though so far they have proved successful. One board member in particular, Jared York, made no pretense of his disapproval of Spencer and his "slow-burning" initiatives. Spencer knows that if he wants the CEO position, he will have to fight for it. But he doesn't have long to prepare—Michelle tells him that the board wants to meet with him later that afternoon to discuss the future of Providence Community Healthcare and what he would want to do as the new CEO.

When Spencer walks into the conference room, he is greeted with a mixture of smiles and polite nods. He can't remember the last time he felt so nervous. Before he can even begin, Jared York stands up and takes the floor, speaking as if Spencer is not even present.

Jared says, "Listen, we need sophisticated executive talent running the Community Healthcare center, and Spencer is a data and technology guy. Sure, he did a fine job running the patient care improvement project, but a project is not the same as running a company. I'm not sure Spencer has the right qualifications for the CEO position."

The room is silent, and everyone looks uncomfortable.

Spencer interjects, and says calmly, "Jared, I agree. The patient care improvement project is a small part of the opportunity, as we face an array of challenges in our organization. If the board allows me, I would like to share my vision of how I see the future of Providence Community Healthcare."

Jared sits down and gestures for Spencer to continue. The rest of the members turn their attention toward Spencer. He knows that this is his best opportunity to convince the board of his eligibility as the next CEO—he does not intend to waste it.

"With the board's support, I would follow a holistic process of planning, organizing, leading, and controlling performance to ensure Providence Community Healthcare's success into the future. That said, performance is as much about management as it is about a continuous development cycle of adaptability and improvement. Using the hot-spotting method is just one way of connecting our providers, patients, and the community and improving the care that our patients receive while saving money. My latest vision incorporates a whole coordinated series of projects, which I call "Performance Development for Our Community's Health." To translate this performance development vision into reality, I recommend a three-tier quality and innovation approach focused on 1) facilities, 2) processes, and, most important, 3) talent." To demonstrate his concept, he shows the board Figure 17-1.

One of the board members asks Spencer to elaborate on his three main approaches.

"In a nutshell, I think the center could do with some refurbishment; the last time it had a coat of paint was back in the early '90s," Spencer begins.

Figure 17-1
Performance Development for Our Community's Health
Performance includes management that incorporates continued adaptability and improvement.

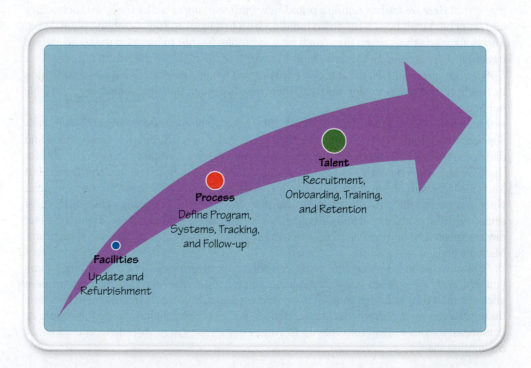

Talent
Recruitment, Onboarding, Training, and Retention

Process
Define Program, Systems, Tracking, and Follow-up

Facilities
Update and Refurbishment

The members agree. Everyone knows that Providence Community Healthcare needs an overhaul to bring it into the 21st century. Gaining confidence, Spencer continues to explain his vision. "We also need to bring the processes initially piloted on a limited basis for the patient care improvement program out into the community and provide the rest of our patients with the same level of health care and accessibility. And finally, we need to recruit more talent in order to provide these services."

Jared is the first to speak. "We, the board, need to meet and discuss how to move forward."

Following more questions from the board regarding how Spencer would implement his vision, he leaves the meeting, hoping that he has done everything he can to convince the board he is the most suitable candidate for CEO. There is nothing more he can do but wait.

A week later, York calls Spencer Jones and offers him the position of CEO—on an interim basis. He says, "You won over most of the board with 'your vision.' I guess now it is time for you to prove that you have what it takes to lead this organization. Recently, we received a very generous donation from one of our long-term patients. We are giving you a six-month trial period, and thanks to the donation, our full financial support to show us what you can do. If you do not perform to our expectations, we will recruit an external candidate for the position. Better get to work..."

17.2 | PHYSICAL SPACE AND FACILITIES MANAGEMENT

17.2 **Describe** the context and standards through which managers control facilities.

Hanging up the phone, Spencer feels a mixture of elation and dread. While he is thrilled that the board has assigned him to be the interim CEO and has agreed to fund his projects during this time, he is worried that he has only six months to bring his vision to fruition; otherwise the role will go to someone else.

Spencer knows exactly what he wants to do first: a full overhaul of the facilities. He believes that this will provide the most visual indication of change—everyone will know there is a new vision afoot.

Spencer considers the new facility's **layout** which is the design of space that specifies the workflow.[1] If they are going to be successful in recruiting new staff, more desk space will be needed, as well as additional space and facilities for the expanded staff. Of course, the gloomy reception area will need a whole new design to create the best impression for patients and visitors. But the facility is not just about an attractive design—it needs to act as a space that connects Providence Community Healthcare's providers, patients, and the broader community. But how can Spencer translate this vision into a plan?

The inspiration comes when Spencer least expects it—while shopping for his teenage son's birthday present, an iPhone. He knows that Apple Retail Stores have the most profitable retail concept, per square foot, in the world, but it wasn't until he was shopping in one did he realize why.

Facilities Layout

Spencer works with an architectural design firm to create a new layout and design for the facility. A key strategy for success is the center's **location**, which provides access to key market segments, including vendors and patients.[2] They all agree that the center is in a prime location for community access, especially now that the van service is underway. There is not one patient in Rhode Island who won't be able to conveniently get to the center.

Next, they discuss the appropriate layout in order to optimize **operational capacity**, which occurs when an operation is working at its maximum potential.[3] Spencer and the architectural team identify that the current layout does not make the best use of either space or operations. The doctors' offices, for example, are cramped and stuffy and don't have enough room for storage.

LECTURE ENHANCER:

17.2 Physical Space and Facilities Management

✓ **Layout**—the design of space which provides optimal work flow.

➤ Research at Work: The Apple Store Effect

■ *Organization identification*—the extent to which a person has a perception of "oneness" or "belongingness" relative to an organization

• **Facilities Layout**

➤ **Location** is important for a business that provides strategic access to all segments, vendors and vitality

✓ **Operational Capacity**—the capacity at which an operation is working at its full maximum of potential and successful execution

✓ **Fixed Position Layout**—one of three basic options for laying out a facility to produce goods, deliver services or process / product production all within a fixed position

✓ **Cellular Layout**—a combination of fixed positions and service elements

• **Technologies and Automation**

✓ **Operations Management**—a process (systems) built to assist in the daily activities of an operation

✓ **Automation**—occurs when manufacturing happens through an electronic devise that does not need continual operations support

✓ **Product-Service Mix**—the mix of the number of products provided vs. the services delivered

Layout The design of space in an organization that specifies the workflow.

• **Managing a Facility**

➤ The facilities manager may take on some of the roles himself but will also enlist other vendors to assist in the event of emergencies and natural disasters.

➤ Responsible for health and safety, security, air conditioning, heating, ground maintenance, lighting, and ensuring the facility is in compliance with environmental codes and corporate and regulatory standards

Location A characteristic of an organization that provides strategic access to all segments, vendors, and vitality.

Operational capacity The ability of an operation to work at its maximum of potential and successful execution.

Research@Work

The Apple Store Effect[4]

When the first Apple Retail Store opened in 2001, it didn't seem to make a lot of sense to customers. Prior to the opening of the Apple Retail Store, rival Dell had been successfully selling their computers directly to customers, first by mail and later online, while Gateway was in the process of closing its chain of struggling brick-and-mortar stores.

But more than a decade later, Apple Retail Stores have become a common sight in upscale malls, urban centers, and everywhere in between. These stores are the foundation of Apple's marketing strategy and have helped the company's market share grow steadily.

This is because Apple Retail Stores offer a different experience from other retail shopping outlets. Helpful, expert, and enthusiastic employees who wear colorful T-shirts emblazoned with the Apple logo seem to be more interested in living the Apple lifestyle than they are about selling Apple products. Their enthusiasm spreads to customers, who sometimes behave more like groupies—even going so far as to camp out in long lines for new product launches and promotions—than technology consumers.

Is it possible for other retail stores to replicate Apple's success in generating enthusiasm among their customers? In a recent study[5], researchers sampled employees from a chain of 306 women's apparel retail stores and examined the role of store managers in generating customer enthusiasm. They hypothesized that the more a store manager identifies with his or her organization, the more

that salespeople, and ultimately customers, identify with the organization, leading to higher financial performance for the store. "Organization identification" is the extent to which a person has a perception of "oneness" or "belongingness" relative to an organization. As predicted, the store managers' level of organizational identification influenced the employees' level of identification. This, in turn, influenced customers' identification with the brand, resulting in increased sales—the "Apple Store effect."

The implications of the study are obvious—managerial and employee identification is critical for building customer brand loyalty and increased sales. And according to these researchers, the identification must start at the top. The chain of influence starts with the CEO and trickles down through the various levels of management.

The late Steve Jobs, former CEO of Apple Inc., provided a perfect example of the trickle-down effect. When Jobs initially left Apple in the 1980s, the company lost market share. And when he returned about 10 years later, the company thrived again. Given the findings of the study, retail store executives and store managers would be well advised to consider the "Apple Store effect" as a critical tool for increasing customer loyalty and sales.

Critical Thinking in the Classroom

As a manager, how would you foster a sense of organizational identification among your employees and customers?

Fixed-position layout One of the three basic options for laying out a facility to produce goods, deliver services, all within a fixed position.

They agree on a **fixed-position layout** for the doctors' offices, which is one of three basic options for laying out a facility to produce goods and deliver services, all within a fixed position.[6] The offices will be designed to be roomier by implementing built-in storage to hold equipment, medical products, and patient files. The center's administrative unit will be given the task of ensuring that each office is fully stocked and organized neatly each day.

The rest of the center already operates on an open floor plan. The problem is the division of teams. Some employees are tucked away in corners, and because they have run out of space recently, some employees have been temporarily assigned to the windowless basement. Taking a walk through the office, the architectural team notes that many desks are empty during a certain part of the day. Spencer explains that these are the desks assigned to part-time employees, who occupy the desks only three days a week. The firm devises a plan where employees will rotate desks in order to conserve space, which means each staff member will have a desk, removing employees from the basement.

Cellular layout A combination of fixed positions and service elements.

For the open-plan office floor, the firm suggests a **cellular layout** which is a combination of fixed positions and service elements.[7] This means that the desks and machines would be grouped together in "cells," where employees carrying out similar roles would sit together and be cross-trained to run every machine there. This layout is fairly typical within manufacturing companies, where teams are responsible for the machinery in and output of each cell. For Providence Community Healthcare, this would mean that teams would work more closely together and learn collectively how to run the new systems that Spencer previously implemented. As each team member will share the same skills, Spencer hopes that they will be more motivated to work hard and come up with creative ideas to promote change and development.

Technologies and Automation

Thanks to Spencer's new systems, he is confident that Providence Community Healthcare is headed in the right direction with regard to **operations management**, the processes and systems built to assist in the daily activities of production.[8] He is also pleased by the new level of systems **automation**, which occurs when manufacturing happens through an electronic device that does not need continual operations support.[9] Yet, he also knows that as a manager, he needs to ensure that employees, stakeholders, and patients are satisfied with the new technology.

As the new CEO, he is expected to prove that the new operations are making a difference to Providence Community Healthcare itself, as well as the larger community. These results have everything to do with the **product-service mix**, which is the combination of the number of products provided (medical supplies) versus the services delivered (a reduction of waiting time).[10] If patients are seen quickly and provided with the appropriate medical treatment, then Providence will be able to build a brand based on its efficiency and high-quality care. As the center's reputation grows, more patients will be attracted to its services, leading to improved health in the community, a reduction of hospital bills, and fewer expenses for the center.

Managing a Facility

Spencer is excited about the renovation plans for Providence Community Healthcare. The architectural firm is also going to include such improvements as better lighting, floor-to-ceiling windows in the doctors' offices, a new, spacious parking garage, and a state-of-the art reception area. With the board's approval, Spencer will hire a facilities manager to oversee the new health center, who will be responsible for health and safety, security, air conditioning, heating, ground maintenance, lighting, and ensuring that the facility complies with environmental codes and corporate and regulatory standards. The facilities manager will enlist a number of vendors to assist in these tasks during emergencies and natural disasters.

17.3 | PROCESSES FOR MAKING QUALITY PRODUCTS AND SERVICES

17.3 | Illustrate how managers use processes to design, develop, and deliver quality products and services.

Spencer closely monitors the renovation to ensure that it incorporates the best use of space, time, and money. He also works closely with the architectural firm to ensure that they are adhering to the same organizational and environmental principles as the ones that he is working to instill in the Providence staff and management. These include keeping "lean" to avoid waste, managing inventory, maintaining a good relationship with suppliers, and minimizing any harmful effects on the environment.

Lean Manufacturing

In Chapter 2, we learned about the achievements of Henry Ford and Frederick W. Taylor. Both men succeeded in producing high-quality goods at a rapid rate. In both cases, **quality** measures product or service excellence minus the amount of defects.[11] Although

---

Operations management Processes and systems built to assist in the daily activities of production.

Automation The implementation of manufacturing through an electronic device that does not need continual operations support.

Product-service mix The combination of the number of products provided versus the services delivered.

LECTURE ENHANCER:

17.3 Processes for Making Quality Products and Services

- **Lean Manufacturing**
  ✓ **Quality**—measures product or service excellence minus the amount of defects
  ✓ **Lean Manufacturing**—the implementation of best practices to eliminate inefficiencies and waste while growing profit
  ✓ **Manufacturing**—a process where large goods are made typically by manual labor or large machinery
  ➤ The Main Principles of the Lean Approach
    ■ Using flexible and up-to-date technology
    ■ Educating employees on the methodology and philosophy of lean
    ■ Training employees in all areas
    ■ Instilling a sense of commitment
    ■ Shifting cultural values in order to embrace the lean model

- **Purchasing and Inventory Management**
  ✓ **Inventory**—defines the items and quantity in stock typically held in a warehouse or one designated area
  ✓ **Purchasing**—a process of buying goods or services to accomplish a goal
  ✓ **Just-In-Time (JIT) Method**—a production method to provide an item as needed vs. inventory sitting in stock

Quality A measure of product or service excellence minus the amount of defects.

Lean manufacturing The implementation of best practices to eliminate inefficiencies and waste while increasing profit.

Manufacturing A process where large goods are made, typically by manual labor or large machinery.

- Supply Chain Management
  ✓ Supply Chain Management—a network of interconnected businesses strategically aligned to provide product and service packages
  ➤ Often, points in the supply chain are linked by electronic communication so all parties can assess the level of inventory available, as well as being aware of where the goods are located at any given time.
- Aligning Products and Services

Inventory The items and quantity in stock typically held in a warehouse or one designated area.

Purchasing A process of buying goods or services to accomplish a goal.

Just-In-Time (JIT) Method A production method that provides an item as needed versus keeping inventory in stock.

Supply chain is a network of interconnected businesses strategically aligned to provide product and service packages.

the term *lean* wasn't around at the time, we could argue that these two innovative men were among the first to create a lean environment. **Lean manufacturing** is the implementation of best practices to eliminate inefficiencies and waste while increasing profit.[12] **Manufacturing** is a process where large goods are made, typically by manual labor or large machinery.[13]

More recently, Toyota and other manufacturers successfully applied the lean model, and other non-manufacturing companies followed suit. In a typical lean organization, there is a strict elimination of waste to make processes as flexible, efficient, and error-free as possible. In a lean company, there is a strong emphasis on quality.[14] For example, Toyota staff members are given full authority to halt operations during the manufacturing process if they find a problem. The process resumes only when the problem is addressed, preventing any future issues.

The main principles of the lean approach include using flexible and up-to-date technology, educating employees on the lean methodology and philosophy, training employees in all areas, instilling a sense of commitment, and shifting cultural values in order to embrace the lean model.

Purchasing and Inventory Management

Since Spencer began the patient care improvement initiative, he has been working to educate the Providence Community Healthcare staff about adopting a lean approach. An advocate of the lean approach, Spencer has been applying similar principles to Providence. He successfully reduced waste by cutting down the amount of unnecessary **inventory**, the items and quantity in stock typically held in a warehouse or one designated area[15] once he learned that the center was ordering too many medical products from suppliers. Spencer also needed to address the high level of **purchasing**, the process of buying goods or services to accomplish a goal.[16] Employees now follow a **just-in-time (JIT) method**, which provides an item as needed versus keeping an inventory sitting in stock.[17] This means that medical supplies are not delivered, or delivered only in small quantities, until the health center needs them. The result is less waste and reduced costs. The JIT approach is commonly used in both manufacturing and non-manufacturing companies to reduce cycle times, meet customer orders, increase quality, and add value.

But it is not just the inventory issue that has made a difference. Transitioning from manual to electronic records has decreased patient waiting times, as employees are able to obtain their patients' medical information quickly. Spencer has ensured that all the employees are trained on the new systems rather than just a few—that way, they have the skills necessary to cover for each other in the event of a worker's absence. He is aware that some of the more veteran doctors have been reticent when it comes to adopting the new technology, but he hopes that they will come on board over time, slowly but surely. Next, Spencer turns his attention to Providence Community Healthcare's suppliers, to ensure that they are meeting the organization's lean needs.

Supply Chain Management

Building a good relationship with suppliers is essential to the effective functioning of an organization. Organizations need to manage their costs to stay ahead of the competition. In turn, suppliers need to meet the demands of their customers and ensure that they have the right product, in the right quantity, at the right price. When Providence reduced the amount of inventory by ordering less from their suppliers, Spencer made sure that the managers of both parties collaborated to create an efficient, lean, supply process.

Supply Chain Management A **supply chain** is a network of interconnected businesses that are strategically aligned to provide product and service packages.[18] Companies rely on suppliers to produce high-quality goods as efficiently and cost-effectively as possible. Both suppliers and purchasers must work together in order to meet these goals. A manufacturing supply chain might include a flow of goods from the supplier to the manufacturer, which the manufacturer delivers to the warehouse; from the warehouse, the goods are delivered to retail stores, which are finally sold to the consumer. Often, these points in the supply chain are linked by electronic communication so that all parties can assess the level of inventory available, and be made aware of where the goods are located at any given time.

Aligning Products and Services While the renovation of the health center is underway, Spencer meets with his management team to design new service offerings intended to connect providers (nurses and doctors), patients, and the community. Why is the community a critical stakeholder for Spencer? He believes that Providence Community Healthcare should be primarily the community champion for proactive wellness, and then a provider of services for those who become ill.

In order to achieve this goal, Spencer needs to use the skills of the existing resources in Providence, such as doctors, nurses, and health-care workers, and recruit additional employees as well. He intends to recruit field nurses to work within the community, as well as field liaisons who can provide comfort and sympathy to patients. Patient care advocates will also be recruited to act as a link between the patient and their health-care providers. He hopes that the additional staff will help bring the community together and encourage them to embrace Providence's philosophy of living better by living healthier. Spencer devises a community wellness program, which he names "Proactive Providence." The goals of the program are as follows:

- The center goes to the community, rather than the community going to the center.
- Job profiles, ads, and descriptions will be created to attract new recruits.
- A "Proactive Providence" brochure, outlining the new facilities and the intentions of the wellness program, will be designed and sent to community members.
- "Patient care advocates" will work in the office part of the time but will spend most of their time with patients out in the community.
- Doctors and nurses will be retrained in the areas of leadership and management in order to manage the new recruits.
- Once trained, the new recruits will go out into the community and encourage members to take part in physical activities and wellness groups that focus on healthier living.
- The new recruits will carry out the duties originally initiated by the improved patient care medical team, only now on a much larger scale. Responsibilities will include training patients how to use the technology, making home visits, encouraging self-management, and providing social and administrative support.
- The wellness program will implement preventative health initiatives, such as designing nutritional programs to prevent or help treat obesity and type 2 diabetes.
- Providence Community Healthcare will take part in conferences and health forums nationwide to present and share information regarding the success of the program.
- Health providers will provide a forum for community members to provide feedback on their services and follow up on any issues that may need to be addressed. This willingness to be accountable will help to bond the community with their providers.

When Spencer presents the new initiative to the board, the response is quite positive. Most of the members seem enthusiastic about the new direction of Providence Community Healthcare and impressed with the ongoing renovations. Yet, toward the end of the meeting, Spencer's biggest critic, Jared York, drops a bombshell:

"So far, a rather large amount of our funds have been spent on the renovation. The pot is running out. How do you propose to pay the salaries of all these new recruits, not to mention benefits, vacation pay, and all the other additional costs?"

Spencer's stomach plummets. He hadn't read the fine print—he had thought that the donation would fund the whole operation, not just the renovation. Spencer is angry at himself; he should have nailed down exactly what the money was for and where it was going. Now he is in a real fix if he wants the program to go ahead. He tells the board that he will work closely with Joanne Donnelly, the controller, to figure out how the new program can be factored into the budget.

The next day, Spencer meets with Joanne in her office to work out what they can do with the remaining funds. Joanne takes Spencer through a plan that might just work in the short term.

Three months after Spencer and his team implemented the Proactive Providence Wellness Program, the results are lackluster. Providence is suffering from the Systems Theory archetype of underinvestment (previously discussed in Chapter 3), where organizations stop investing to avoid exposure to what is perceived as risky expenditure. Because of the tight budget, Spencer can only afford to hire contractors rather than full-time staff. Although they are less expensive, some of the contractors don't seem to have the same commitment to helping patients in the community and are often unsympathetic to their needs.

Adding to this difficulty, an unforeseen system breakdown keeps occurring, where patients can't access their medical records online, resulting in a flood of complaints. As Spencer doesn't have the budget to bring in a full-time information technology (IT) employee to fill his previous position, he simply fixes the problem himself each time it happens. However, one day when Spencer is out of the office, the system crashes. As the other employees have no idea how to fix the problem, the system remains out of use for hours, leading to more phone calls, delays, and confusion. From his knowledge of Systems Theory, Spencer realizes that Providence Community Healthcare has fallen into the trap of "shifting the burden" (outlined in Chapter 3), where underlying long-term solutions are ignored in favor of short-term fixes.

To top it all off, Spencer also recognizes that the organization is suffering from "drifting/eroding goals," another systems archetype (see Chapter 3). Since the program's implementation, performance levels have dropped and morale is low. Even the original medical team seems less enthusiastic about achieving its long-term goals. As Hazel, one of the nurses, says, "To us, these budget constraints imply a lack of faith by the board in what we are trying to achieve in the greater community. If our own board isn't supporting us, then what good are we going to do in the long term?"

Spencer agrees, but he knows that he has supporters on the board; he just needs to find a way out of this financial trap. He decides to tackle the problem head on at the following week's Proactive Providence six-month project review session with the board. The meeting will determine whether Spencer will be offered a permanent position as CEO of the health center.

As Spencer walks into the review session, the room seems divided. One side of the table is smiling, nodding, sending silent messages of "Don't worry—you've got this!" The other side of the table is emotionless, either giving him blank stares or scribbling in their notebooks. Before Spencer even sits down, one board member, Shelley Hinson, says, "Spencer, congratulations on a very successful six months. Not only have you successfully managed a complete overhaul of this facility, but under difficult budget constraints, you have implemented a communitywide program for transforming our focus from being a reactive to a proactive health-care provider. I know that there have been some stumbling blocks along the way, but I am sure you have plans to overcome these problems for the future, which we all look forward to hearing about."

Spencer is stunned. He never expected any acknowledgment for the achievements that he has made over the last six months—only the failures. Shelley's support is a small ray of hope. However, before he can respond, Jared steps in to dampen the mood.

"With all due respect, Shelley, I could not disagree more. Here we are, six months later, with an inexperienced CEO who has spent lots of money with no tangible results, apart from an expensive renovation. The renovation has eaten up the very generous funds we gave him, and the community program "Proactive Providence" is almost over budget. Spencer, would you mind sharing the results from that project's 90-day review?"

Spencer takes a deep breath and says, "I should probably sit down first and give everyone an update, including a plan for the future that Shelley requested."

Spencer outlines the projects that have defined his first 180 days in the position and assures the board that good results will come in time. He points out the lack of investment and outlines the potential results should the board consider allocating more funds to the project. If given the opportunity, he would like to implement the third tier of his vision—talent development which would involve hiring and training full-time staff to carry out the goals of the program.

After some further discussion, Spencer leaves the conference room. The board stays for hours, heatedly discussing Spencer's proposals and whether he should be appointed as CEO.

17.4 | ACHIEVING RESULTS THROUGH TALENT MANAGEMENT

17.4 Describe how managers work with team members to improve and adapt facilities and processes continuously.

Early the following morning, Spencer's cell phone rings. The display shows that board member Shelley Hinson is calling him. Catching his breath, he quickly answers.

"Congratulations, Mr. Chairman and CEO! I am so excited for you!" Shelley says.

It takes a moment to sink in, but after a few seconds, he realizes that all his hard work has paid off. He has done it! Before he can articulate his delight, Shelley continues, "As you can imagine, there were a few dissenting voices, but they were eventually overruled by the rest of us. So your first order of business will be to replace three board members that will be resigning tomorrow. But that's not all . . .

"Last year, before Michelle Zoe retired, we applied for a health care innovation grant. I just found out that we have been awarded a substantial grant to complete the rest of our program and initiatives. So, that means not only are you now Providence Community Healthcare's leader, but you have the support and funds to back your program. I look forward to working with you to make sure we are successful."

Spencer concludes the most exciting conversation of his life with a simple, "Thank you, Shelley. I appreciate everything you have done for me."

Spencer turns around to his wife, Elise, with a big smile and tears in his eyes. She throws her arms around him in celebration.

Dynamic Steering

Following a sleepless night full of excitement and anticipation, Spencer walks into the fully renovated facility knowing exactly what he has to do. Because of the problems over the last few months, the health center has become somewhat disjointed. The contractors and the permanent staff are constantly at odds with each other and work almost autonomously; the systems haven't been working at their optimal level, which has caused tension between the administrators and patients; and some of the doctors are still refusing to store patient data electronically. Spencer realizes he must enforce a process of **dynamic steering**, which occurs when an organization engages in incremental adaptation based on real-time feedback (in contrast to traditional predict-and-control steering methods) to push toward better engagement and overall productivity as outlined in Figure 17-2.[19]

This will involve focusing the administrators, doctors, nurses, and staff on the most important asset of the company—each other. They need to believe that they are the key to making the new Providence Community Healthcare a real triumph. Spencer believes that an emphasis on attracting, recruiting, and retaining the best possible team will be the most important determinant of the center's success.

In his first meeting as the official CEO, he calls the entire staff into the conference room and outlines a comprehensive plan to adapt and improve the company's facilities, processes, and services continuously by building authentic relationships of trust with each other and all the organization's stakeholders. Why is this so imperative? Spencer explains to the entire team that performance development is about meaningful, relevant, and timely feedback from all stakeholders. Without that feedback, continuous improvement and innovation is impossible. He then spends time answering questions and encouraging the staff to provide feedback on his suggestions.

Continuously Evolving Facilities and Processes

Spencer provides the following virtuous cycle for continuous improvement and innovation through employee engagement.

Selection and Recruitment In conjunction with the Human Resources (HR) department, Spencer works out a recruitment process (as described in Chapter 11) to identify

LECTURE ENHANCER:

17.4 Achieving Results Through Talent Management

- **Dynamic Steering**
  ✓ **Dynamic Steering**—where an organization senses and then directs processes as well as the tension between the two, in order to push towards better engagement and overall productivity
- **Continuously Evolving Facilities and Processes**
  - Selection and Recruitment
  - Onboarding
  - Building and Emotional Connection
  - Goal Alignment
  - Candid Conversations
  - Honest Appraisals (Formal and Informal)
  ✓ **Behaviorally Anchored Rating Scale (BARS)**—accurately rates employee performance based on specific behaviors relating to a particular role
  - Career Development
  - Leadership & Innovation
  - Compassion for All

Dynamic steering A process where an organization engages in incremental adaptation based on real-time feedback to push toward better engagement and overall productivity.

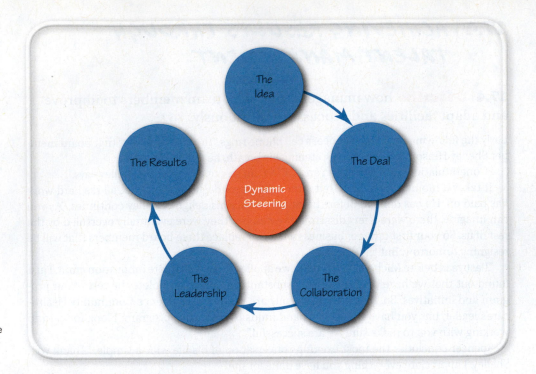

Figure 17-2
Dynamic Steering
The creation of an idea leads to a deal that initiates team collaboration under the guidance of leadership to generate successful results.

external talent, such as health-care workers and field officers, that they can recruit on a permanent basis. HR agrees to run ads in local newspapers, in health-care magazines and websites, and on the Internet and the company's extranet. HR is also assigned to find executive talent to replace the three board members who resigned shortly after being outvoted by the rest of the board.

With regard to internal recruitment, Spencer will identify the contractors to whom he would like to offer permanent positions. All external and internal applicants will be interviewed by Spencer and the management team and will be asked to complete a personality test. Selection will be based on the outcome of both the interviews and the tests.

Onboarding Successful candidates will go through a process of onboarding (defined in Chapter 11) designed by Spencer and HR. On their first day of work, new employees will be greeted by a HR representative, who will show them to their desks and give them a tour of the new facility. A new-hire welcome pack, containing an employee manual, employment forms, and gifts such as notepads and pens adorned with the company logo, will be prepared to speed up the administrative process. They will also be given a schedule of systems training and will be asked to attend a number of workshops to learn about the health center's mission of providing better care for patients.

Over the course of the first month, each new field officer will accompany an experienced member of the team on home visits in order to learn, on the job, how to behave toward patients and distribute information, help, and advice. The recruits will be given regular performance reviews and offered an opportunity to provide feedback in both group and one-to-one meetings.

Building an Emotional Connection In Chapter 13, we explored how leaders can use emotional intelligence (EI) to build relationships with their employees. This involves practicing self-awareness, as well as being aware of the feelings of others and the environment in which they work. By carrying out frequent appraisals, operating an open-door policy, providing an effective forum for feedback, and arranging for social evenings and team-bonding exercises, Spencer feels that he is doing his best to build awareness and form an emotional connection with employees.

Similarly, in their book *First, Break All the Rules: What the World's Greatest Managers Do Differently*, Gallup consultants Marcus Buckingham and Curt Coffman carried out a study of what talented employees need to thrive in the workplace, and how managers can find and maintain talent.[20] One of the

points that they introduce is the importance of having a "best friend" at work so that employees feel satisfied with their working culture. The theory holds that employees having someone at work or a manager who cares about them is essential in creating a happy work environment.

Goal Alignment Soon after his promotion to CEO, Spencer schedules a meeting with the entire staff to bring them in line with the goals of Providence Community Healthcare and attain a commitment from each employee. He begins by stating the organization's mission, vision, and values: to transform Providence Community Healthcare into the number one health-care facility in Rhode Island, with a reputation for innovation and the highest standard of patient care. To this end, he outlines a number of goals for the entire staff. He is pleased to find that they all seem to be listening attentively, but then he reaches a sticking point: systems training. Spencer states that all staff, with no exceptions, must enter medical data electronically into the database. Handwritten records no longer will be accepted.

A hand shoots up—it is Dr. Aintree, the doctor who for 20 years has been treating the first patient who participated in the patient care improvement initiative: Barney (whose situation is discussed in detail in Chapter 16). Dr. Aintree explains that he has been using the same manual method for over 25 years and has no intention of learning how to use technology at this point in his career. Spencer gently responds that every member, irrespective of their age or career longevity, will have to learn the new system. In fact, it is a nonnegotiable rule of the organization. Dr. Aintree is visibly angry and requests a private discussion with Spencer after the meeting. Spencer agrees and continues to the next goal.

Candid Conversations Spencer wants to promote relationships of candor among the staff (as covered in Chapter 14). He feels that over the past few months, employees have been quick to blame each other for certain problems. He wants to cultivate a working environment where everyone takes accountability and displays appreciation and gratitude toward each other rather than backstabbing and assigning blame.

Spencer uses this approach when he holds the private meeting that Dr. Aintree has asked for. By listening and remaining calm, he learns that the doctor has been struggling during the systems training sessions and is afraid that he doesn't have the skills necessary to use the new technology. In short, he is afraid of failing and humiliating himself in front of others. Spencer remembers that he has heard the "old dog—new tricks" argument before. He tells Dr. Aintree that Barney, his patient, has had similar misgivings about learning how to use a computer at home, and then he suggests that the two of them receive private training together. This way, they can encourage each other without the fear of "losing face." Dr. Aintree agrees, and Spencer proceeds to set up a series of training sessions to begin immediately.

Honest Appraisals (Formal and Informal) As part of the new mission, all Providence Community Healthcare employees will be given regular formal performance appraisals. They will consist of 360-degree reviews provided by management and peers, in conjunction with the Behaviorally Anchored Rating Scale (BARS), which accurately rates employee performance based on specific behaviors relating to a particular role.[21] The HR department has sent out surveys to the entire community so that patients can rate the treatment they are receiving from the field workers and the office staff. The feedback provided from the patients will also be included in the appraisals. Table 17-1 shows a couple of examples of BARS.

One of the HR managers brings Spencer's attention to several of these completed surveys. Over 20 patients in the community have complained that they have been called in to see one particular doctor for unnecessary treatment, resulting in higher medical costs. The doctor they have complained about is Dr. Aintree, Barney's longtime practitioner.

At his next appraisal, Spencer discusses the feedback with Dr. Aintree, who simply shrugs. He explains that he tells all the patients that they have a choice between attending regular appointments and putting their health at risk if they don't. Spencer cites Barney's case as an example of a patient who might not need so many follow-up appointments. Surprisingly, Dr. Aintree agrees that given Barney's state of improved health and lack of symptoms, it might be possible for him to self-manage his own health at home. Spencer feels that progress has been made. By the end of the discussion, Dr. Aintree agrees to reevaluate his patients who come in for regular check-ups and communicate with the health-care team in order to focus on those patients he feels would benefit from self-care.

With regard to informal appraisals, Spencer has established an open-door policy, which means that employees are able to seek informal advice and feedback from their managers

Table 17-1 Two Examples of BARS

Behaviorally Anchored Ratings Scale (BARS) Guide

1. Acceptance of Supervision – *Willingly accepts and follows instructions given by supervisor in the performance of duties; responds to training and coaching in a constructive manner.*

Rating	Possible Behavioral examples
Meets Expectation	• Readily accepts and completes assigned responsibilities • Attempts to improve performance following constructive criticism • Follows policies set by supervisor without reminder • Cooperates willingly with supervisor • Follows specific instructions
Exceeds Expectation	• Demonstrates exceptional ability to independently complete assigned responsibilities • Never complains about assigned tasks • Improves performance following constructive criticism • Knows and follows all policies set by supervisor
Does Not Meet Expectation	• Complains about assigned tasks; often questions supervisory requests • Fails to consistently follow all policies set by supervisor • Becomes upset when constructively criticized • Sometimes fails to follow specific instructions

2. Adaptability/Flexibility – *Adapts readily to new situations and changes in the workplace; works well under pressure; learns and functions well under widely different situations and circumstances.*

Rating	Possible Behavioral examples
Meets Expectation	• Readily adjusts to new situations and responsibilities • Easily handles a wide variety of tasks, sometimes concurrently • Readily comprehends new job related information • Performs well under widely different and/or changing circumstances
Exceeds Expectation	• Functions effectively under unusually high levels of mental or emotional stress • Capable of assisting other staff with change while maintaining regular personal workload • Conforms to changing demands with a positive attitude and skills
Does Not Meet Expectation	• Has difficulty adjusting to change in workload or assignments • Becomes nervous or upset under normal job stress • Loses composure under higher than normal stress level • Lacks patience when dealing with more than one assignment

LECTURE ENHANCER:

17.5 Managing for Excellence
- **Total Quality Management**
  ✓ **Total Quality Management (TQM)**—a long range, big picture process to assist companies in better overall total management for the entire organization
  ✓ **Productivity**—the measurement of quantity of product and services being produced
  ➢ TQM Tools:
    ✓ **Value-Added Analysis (related to TQM)**—provides core bare analysis of an item or process down to its raw costs vs. measurement to provide the most effective product or service

and peers whenever they want to discuss an issue. He hopes that both the formal and informal appraisal processes will help to reassure employees as to where they stand and reinforce the importance of their roles in the organization.

Career Development Spencer wants to encourage career development and provide additional training for employees who express an interest in moving into different roles. For example, one of the administrative assistants has informed him that she would like to become a field officer one day. Spencer agrees that she has the skills to make a fine officer, and he enrolls her in a program where she can attain the appropriate qualifications. Nurturing talent and ensuring employee satisfaction are two of his main goals.

Leadership and Innovation Providence Community Healthcare has traditionally operated within a hierarchical structure. The board and the CEO make decisions that filter down to management and the rest of the staff. Although Spencer perceives himself as someone who must lead by example, he also wants to instill the message that every single staff member is also a leader. They have the power to change processes, provide feedback, and innovate wherever possible. In short, Providence Community Healthcare is everyone's business.

Spencer knows that it is only by coming together that they will be successful in nurturing and growing the organization.

Compassion for All As Spencer goes through the virtuous cycle for continuous improvement and innovation, he lands on the most important point of all: compassion. He believes that no organization can be successful without compassion for all—especially a health-care center. The reputation of Providence hangs on the ability of its employees to be compassionate about each other, their patients, and all the members in the greater community. Only when they learn to care for each other will they succeed in bringing their goals to fruition. At every staff meeting, conference, and forum he attends, Spencer reinforces the importance of building a compassionate community. He fervently hopes that, one day, his dream for the center will come true.

17.5 | MANAGING FOR EXCELLENCE

17.5 | Show how managers connect facilities, processes, and people to achieve superior performance results.

One year later, Providence Community Healthcare is well on its way to becoming a national benchmark for service excellence in the health-care industry. With encouragement from the board, Spencer and his team work to improve services and operations continuously, now with the implementation of Total Quality Management (TQM) and Six Sigma practices.

Total Quality Management (TQM)

In Chapter 2, we were introduced to William E. Deming and his colleague, Joseph Juran, who presented the first philosophies of the quality movement. They believed that with continuous improvement, organizations would be able to improve their processes, methods, services, and/or products. Their ideas formed the basis of **Total Quality Management (TQM)**, which is a long-range, big-picture process to assist companies in better overall management for the entire organization.[22]

Managers who follow the TQM principles understand every detail about their business, how it operates, and how to motivate their employees. Some of the main aspects of TQM include striving for long-term solutions rather than short-term gains, rectifying errors and delays as quickly as possible, focusing on the customer as the main priority, continually improving systems and people performance, investing in ongoing training programs and workshops, building teams that are motivated to be innovative and creative, and creating an environment where all employees are involved in providing ideas and feedback.

Managers can also use certain TQM tools and techniques to improve service, quality, and **productivity**, which is the measurement of quantity of product and services being made.[23] The tools relating to TQM are as follows:

- **Value-added analysis** provides comprehensive study of an item or process to determine the overall value added to the customer to provide the most effective product or service.[24] This kind of analysis helps to identify and eliminate waste without affecting the customer.

- **Benchmarking** is information provided to mark a norm on the measurement scale of a product or service in the same *vertical market*, which is a group of similar businesses and customers.[25] Managers employ benchmarking to learn about how their competition carries out similar processes and activities. They draw from this knowledge and apply it to their own organization in the interest of improving products and services.

- **Outsourcing** occurs when the delivery of a product or services becomes valued as more profitable by using outside resources or systems versus internal resources, including human and capital assets.[26] Some organizations outsource some of their services or operations to other companies as a cost-saving exercise.

- **Cycle time** is the length of time that it takes to perform a function or task from beginning to end.[27] Enforcing control measures around product or operational cycles can result in improved efficiency, higher quality, and financial savings.

✓ Benchmarking (related to TQM)—information provided to mark a norm on the measurement scale of a product or service in the same vertical market

✓ Outsourcing (related to TQM)—occurs when the delivery of a product or services becomes valued as more profitable by using outside resources or systems vs. internal resources human and capital assets

✓ Cycle Time (related to TQM)—the length of time it takes to perform a function or task from beginning to end

• Six Sigma

✓ Six Sigma—a business management strategy designed to analyze the causes of defects using statistical methods

✓ Statistical Quality Control—the use of statistics that are monitored ongoing from production, for the sole purpose of determining production quality

✓ ISO 9000:2000—provides an exact measure of quality globally over a platform of systems

Total Quality Management (TQM) A long-range, big-picture process to assist companies in better overall total management for an entire organization.

Productivity The measurement of quantity of product and services being made.

Value-added analysis In TQM, an element that provides a core study of an item or process down to its raw costs vs. measurement to provide the most effective product or service.

Benchmarking In TQM, information provided to mark a norm on the measurement scale of a product or service in the same vertical market.

Outsourcing In TQM, an element that occurs when the delivery of a product or services becomes valued as more profitable by using outside resources or systems versus internal resources, including human and capital assets.

Cycle time In TQM, the length of time it takes to perform a function or task from beginning to end.

An advocate of TQM, Spencer has applied many of its principles to Providence Community Healthcare. Thanks to the recruitment of an IT specialist, the systems are running smoothly and reliably. Through regular training programs, all Providence employees have benefited from new skills. By encouraging feedback, the teams have come up with several innovative ideas to improve Providence and have presented more initiatives to eliminate waste and save on costs.

Six Sigma

Many service and manufacturing organizations also adopt the principles of **Six Sigma**, a business management strategy designed to analyze the causes of defects using statistical methods.[28] **Statistical quality control** is the use of statistics that are monitored from production on an ongoing basis for the sole purpose of determining production quality.[29] Originally introduced by Motorola and popularized by General Electric (GE), the Six Sigma philosophy has become one of the major contributors to TQM.

Organizations ensure that they are meeting certain standards by becoming certified by the International Organization for Standardization (ISO). The main standards that organizations strive to meet today include **ISO 9000:2000**, which provides an exact measure of quality globally over a platform of systems;[30] and **ISO 14000**, which provides total focus on the organization's environmental impact and quality.[31]

Thanks to Spencer's implementation of TQM and Six Sigma, as well as his commitment to environmental policies, Providence Community Healthcare has received both ISO 9000:2000 and ISO 14000 certifications.

Malcolm Baldrige Award

A year later, Spencer unveils his plan at the annual board meeting to apply for the prestigious Malcolm Baldrige Award for service excellence and quality. The **Malcolm Baldrige Award** is an annual award that recognizes performance excellence in U.S. companies and nonprofit organizations.[32] The award was established by the U.S. Congress in 1987 and named after secretary of commerce Malcolm Baldrige. It is presented by the president of the United States at a ceremony held in Washington, D.C. Winning organizations are selected on the basis of several criteria for performance excellence, including their ability to show **continuous improvement**, which is a process to strive for enhanced production on an ongoing basis by reevaluating processes on a frequent basis.[33] The seven health care criteria for performance excellence includes 1) leadership; 2) strategic planning; 3) customer focus; 4) measurement, analysis, and knowledge management; 5) workforce focus; 6) operations focus; and 7) results.

The application for the award states that health-care organizations must allocate over 50 percent of their staff members and/or budget to providing health care services directly to people.[34]

Spencer is confident that the excellent performance of Providence Community Healthcare will be acknowledged by the selection committee, and that the center has a good chance of being one of the national finalists. He waits frantically for the decision. One morning, a letter arrives from the Malcolm Baldrige Selection Committee addressed to "Spencer Jones, Chairman and CEO, Providence Community Healthcare." Spencer closes his eyes and tears open the envelope.

Case**Snapshot**

Chapter 17 Case: Performance Development: Telsa Motors can be found on pg. 480

ADDITIONAL RESOURCES

KEY TERMS

Automation The implementation of manufacturing through an electronic device that does not need continual operations support. (p. 423)

Benchmarking In TQM, information provided to mark a norm on the measurement scale of a product or service in the same vertical market. (p. 431)

Cellular layout A combination of fixed positions and service elements. (p. 422)

Continuous improvement A process to strive for enhanced production on an ongoing basis by reevaluating processes on a frequent basis. (p. 432)

Cycle time In TQM, the length of time it takes to perform a function or task from beginning to end. (p. 431)

Dynamic steering A process where an organization engages in incremental adaptation based on real-time feedback to push toward better engagement and overall productivity. (p. 427)

Facility A building designed and built to support a particular service or function. (p. 419)

Fixed-position layout One of the three basic options for laying out a facility to produce goods, deliver services, all within a fixed position. (p. 422)

Inventory The items and quantity in stock typically held in a warehouse or one designated area. (p. 424)

ISO 9000:2000 A standard from the International Organization for Standardization (ISO), which provides an exact measure of quality globally over a platform of systems. (p. 432)

ISO 14000 A standard from the International Organization for Standardization (ISO) with total focus on the organization's environmental impact and quality. (p. 432)

Just-In-Time (JIT) Method A production method that provides an item as needed versus keeping inventory in stock. (p. 424)

Layout The design of space in an organization that specifies the workflow. (p. 421)

Lean manufacturing The implementation of best practices to eliminate inefficiencies and waste while increasing profit. (p. 424)

Location A characteristic of an organization that provides strategic access to all segments, vendors, and vitality. (p. 421)

Malcolm Baldrige Award An annual prize that recognizes performance excellence in U.S. companies and nonprofit organizations. (p. 432)

Manufacturing A process where large goods are made, typically by manual labor or large machinery. (p. 424)

Operational capacity The ability of an operation to work at its maximum of potential and successful execution. (p. 421)

Operations management Processes and systems built to assist in the daily activities of production. (p. 423)

Outsourcing In TQM, an element that occurs when the delivery of a product or services becomes valued as more profitable by using outside resources or systems versus internal resources, including human and capital assets. (p. 431)

Productivity The measurement of quantity of product and services being made. (p. 431)

Product-service mix The combination of the number of products provided versus the services delivered. (p. 423)

Purchasing A process of buying goods or services to accomplish a goal. (p. 424)

Quality A measure of product or service excellence minus the amount of defects. (p. 423)

Six Sigma A business management strategy designed to analyze the causes of defects using statistical methods. (p. 432)

Statistical quality control The use of statistics that are monitored on an ongoing basis from production, for the sole purpose of determining production quality. (p. 432)

Supply chain is a network of interconnected businesses strategically aligned to provide product and service packages. (p. 424)

Total Quality Management (TQM) A long-range, big-picture process to assist companies in better overall total management for an entire organization. (p. 431)

Value-added analysis In TQM, an element that provides a core study of an item or process down to its raw costs vs. measurement to provide the most effective product or service. (p. 431)

IN REVIEW

17.1 | Explain how managers connect facilities, processes, and people to control performance.

There are a number of factors that can affect organizational performance. Managers look at an organization as a fluid system composed of many different parts, all of which depend on each other. A poorly performing employee can affect the productivity of the rest of the team, and an ill-designed system can cause delays and financial loss if it is not be addressed in a timely manner.

17.2 | Describe the context and standards through which managers control facilities.

Managerial and employee identification are critical for building customer brand loyalty and increased sales. "Organization identification" is the extent to which a person has a perception of "oneness" or "belongingness" relative to an organization. *Operations management* is a process (systems) built to assist in the daily activities of an operation *Product-service mix* is the mix of the number of products provided vs. the services delivered.

The manager will be responsible for health and safety, security, air conditioning, heating, ground maintenance, lighting, and ensuring that the facility is in compliance with environmental codes and corporate and regulatory standards.

17.3 | Illustrate how managers use processes to design, develop, and deliver quality products and services.

Lean manufacturing is the implementation of best practices to eliminate inefficiencies and waste while increasing profit. The *Just-In-Time (JIT) method* is a production method to provide an item as needed vs. inventory sitting in stock. *Supply chain*

management is a network of interconnected businesses strategically aligned to provide product and service packages.

17.4 | Describe how managers work with team members to improve and adapt facilities and processes continuously.

Dynamic steering is when an organization engages in incremental adaptation based on real-time feedback. Continuous improvement and innovation can be facilitated through employee engagement processes, including building emotional connections, goal alignment, candid conversations, honest appraisals, career development, leadership and innovation, and perhaps most important, compassion.

17.5 | Show how managers connect facilities, processes, and people to achieve superior performance results.

Total Quality Management (TQM) is a long-range, big-picture process to assist companies in better overall total management for the entire organization. Managers can also use certain TQM tools and techniques to improve service, quality, and productivity. *Value-added analysis* provides core study of an item or process down to its raw costs versus measurement to provide the most effective product or service. *Benchmarking* is information provided to mark a norm on the measurement scale of a product or service in the same vertical market. *Outsourcing* occurs when the delivery of a product or services becomes valued as more profitable by using outside resources or systems versus internal resources, including human and capital assets. *Cycle time* is the length of time it takes to perform a function or task from beginning to end.

SELF-TEST

17.1 | Explain how managers connect facilities, processes, and people to control performance.

1. The role of managers is to look at interconnected systems in isolation in order to understand the importance of each part and how they contribute to the organization.
   a. True
   b. False

17.2 | Describe the context and standards through which managers control facilities.

2. _____ is the design of space in order to provide optimal workflow.
   a. Facility layout
   b. Facility conceptualization
   c. Space optimization
   d. Workflow planning

3. A(n) _____ is when desks and machines are grouped together in "cells" where employees carrying out similar roles together and are cross-trained to run every machine there.

4. _____ refers to the processes and systems built to assist in the daily activities of an operation.

17.3 | Illustrate how managers use processes to design, develop, and deliver quality products and services.

5. The implementation of best practices to eliminate inefficiencies and waste while increasing profits is known as what?
   a. Quality manufacturing
   b. Lean manufacturing
   c. Excellence in manufacturing
   d. Process improvement

6. When material resources are not delivered until they are needed and/or are only delivered in small quantities, a(n) _____ approach to inventory is being used.
   a. As-needed
   b. Reduced cycle
   c. Small batch
   d. Just-in-time (JIT)

7. _____ involves a network of interconnected businesses strategically aligned to provide product and service packages.

17.4 | Describe how managers work with team members to improve and adapt facilities and processes continuously.

8. Incremental adaptation based on real-time feedback, as opposed to traditional predict-and-control steering methods, is known as _____
   a. Dynamic adaptation
   b. Incremental steering
   c. Dynamic steering
   d. Real-time adaptation

9. Which of the following is *not* one of the means for facilitating continuous improvement outlined in the chapter?
   a. Compassion
   b. Honest appraisals
   c. Candid conversation
   d. Maintaining traditions

17.5 | Show how managers connect facilities, processes, and people to achieve superior performance results.

10. Main aspects of Total Quality Management (TQM) include:
    a. Striving for long-term solutions rather than short-term gains
    b. Focusing on the customer as the main priority
    c. Continually improving systems and people performance
    d. All of the above

11. Benchmarking provides comprehensive analysis of an item or process to determine the overall value added to the customer to provide the most effective product or service.
    a. True
    b. False

12. When the delivery of a product or services becomes valued as more profitable by using outside resources or systems rather than internal resources, a company is said to be _____
    a. Outsourcing
    b. Insourcing
    c. Offshoring
    d. Open sourcing

13. Which of the following is *not* a process for managing or recognizing quality standards and acheivements within an organization?
    a. Six Sigma
    b. Operational capacity
    c. ISO 9000:2000
    d. Malcolm Baldrige Award

14. _____ involves a process of striving for enhanced production on an ongoing basis by reevaluating processes on a frequent basis.

CHAPTER EXERCISE

The Tennis Ball Exercise

This group exercise will help you to better understand the concept of continuous improvement.

General Instructions:

1. Form a group with other members of your class (7–10 members per group is a good size).
2. Your instructor will give your group three tennis balls.
3. You will play three rounds, stopping to answer some discussion questions after rounds 2 and 3.

Round 1 Instructions

1. The members of your group must stand in a circle.
2. One person starts with all three tennis balls.
3. Each person must touch each ball once.
4. All three balls have to start and stop at the same person.
5. You may not give the ball to a person standing next to you.
6. Two people may not touch the ball at the same time.
7. One person may not touch two or more balls at the same time.
8. A dropped ball is a quality defect, and you must start over.
9. The process that you develop must be repeatable, so be sure to practice it.
10. After a few practices, your instructor will time the process that you developed and record your time.

Round 2 Instructions

1. You must find a way to cut your time in half.
2. You must touch the ball in the same order as in Round 1.
3. You no longer have to stand in a circle.
4. Two people may not touch the ball at the same time.
5. One person may not touch two or more balls at the same time.
6. Again, your process must be repeatable.
7. After a few practices, your instructor will time your refined process and record your time.

Discussion Questions

1. What did you do to improve your process from Round 1 to Round 2?
2. Did you use just one person's idea, or did you combine ideas from several people?
3. Did you draw up a detailed plan, or did you just use trial and error?

Round 3 Instructions

1. You must find a way to cut your time in half again.
2. You may use *any* prop in the room.
3. You must touch the ball in the same order as in Round 1.
4. You no longer have to stand in a circle.

5. Two people may not touch the ball at the same time.

6. One person may not touch two or more balls at the same time.

7. As before, your process must be repeatable.

8. After a few practices, your instructor will time your newly refined process and record your time.

Discussion Questions

1. What did you do to improve your process from Round 2 to Round 3?

2. How can you apply this exercise to a work setting?

3. Do you think you could improve the process even further?

4. Did you use the identification and elimination of waste to help with your improvements?

SELF-ASSESSMENT

Continuous Improvement Self-Assessment*

For each statement, circle the number that best describes you based on the following scale:

Not at all Accurate	Somewhat Accurate	A little Accurate	Mostly Accurate	Completely Accurate
1	2	3	4	5

1. The quality of my work is important to success in my job or my schoolwork.

    1   2   3   4   5

2. Continuous improvement is essential to success in my job or my schoolwork.

    1   2   3   4   5

3. Looking for ways of improving how I do my job or schoolwork is important.

    1   2   3   4   5

4. To know that I made a contribution toward improving my effectiveness on my job or in my schoolwork would please me.

    1   2   3   4   5

5. I am strongly committed to total quality in my job or schoolwork.

    1   2   3   4   5

6. I am always looking for ways to prevent mistakes in my job or schoolwork.

    1   2   3   4   5

7. I put a lot of effort into thinking about how I can improve my effectiveness on my job or in my schoolwork.

    1   2   3   4   5

Scoring:

Add the numbers circled above: _____

Interpretation:

28 and above = You are highly concerned with quality and continuous improvement in your job or school work.

15 − 27 = You are moderately concerned with quality and continuous improvement in your job or school work, but you are likely to experience occasional quality lapses and miss opportunities for improvement.

14 and below = You have room to make substantial positive changes in your concern for quality work and your focus on continuous improvement.

*Adapted from Jacqueline A.-M. Coyle-Shapiro, "Changing Employee Attitudes: The Interdependent Effects of TQM and Profit Sharing on Continuous Improvement Orientation," *Journal of Applied Behavioral Science* 38, no. 1 (March 2002): 57–77.

SELF-TEST ANSWER KEY

1. b; False. The role of managers is to look at interconnected systems *as a whole* in order to understand the importance of each part and how it contributes to the organization.

2. a.

3. Cellular layout

4. Operations management

5. b.

6. d.

7. Supply chain management

8. c.

9. d.

10. d.

11. b; False. *Value-added analysis* provides comprehensive study of an item or process to determine the overall value added to the customer in order to provide the most effective product or service.

12. a.

13. b.

14. Continuous improvement

Notes

_____

_____

PART SEVEN

The Future of Management

Chapter 18 | Entrepreneurship and Innovation

CHAPTER EIGHTEEN

ENTREPRENEURSHIP AND INNOVATION

Learning Objectives

By the end of the chapter, you will be able to:

18.1 | Define the process of entrepreneurship and the role of managers as entrepreneurs.

18.2 | Describe the opportunities and challenges that affect growth for new ventures.

18.3 | Compare and contrast different types of ventures that entrepreneurs create.

18.4 | Explain how managers lead a creative process with individuals and teams.

18.5 | Outline how entrepreneurs use innovation to grow global opportunities.

ADDITIONAL RESOURCES

KEY TERMS
IN REVIEW
SELF-TEST
CHAPTER EXERCISE
SELF-ASSESSMENT
SELF-TEST
ANSWER KEY

JP Greenwood/Getty Images

INSIDE THIS CHAPTER

ManagementStory:

Featuring **Katy Johnson, Fred Arters, and Lisa Fang**

Entrepreneurs an individual that
plans, organizes, and leads high-risk
business opportunities with new
market value.

Entrepreneurial skills Capacities,
activities, and strengths that enable
individuals to manage successfully
in high-risk business environments.

Innovation A process that results
in new market value through the
creation of a product or service.

Innovation adoption curve A
staged model that describes
the evolution of an innovation's
acceptance with customers:
innovators, early adopters, early
majority, late majority, and laggards.

Innovators are the approximately
2 percent of a market's population
that initially uses and tests a new
product or service.

Early adopters The approximately
14 percent of a market's population
that uses a new product or service
after innovators have used and
tested it.

18.1 | HOW ENTREPRENEURSHIP MAKES A DIFFERENCE

18.1 | **Define** the process of entrepreneurship and the role of managers as entrepreneurs.

"I never perfected an invention that I did not think about in terms of the service it might give others . . . I find out what the world needs, then I proceed to invent."

—Thomas Edison

In the last decade, **entrepreneurs**, individuals who plan, organize, and lead high-risk business opportunities,[1] have changed the face of society, provided innovative ways to overcome global challenges, and transformed the way we live, communicate, and interact with each other. Entrepreneurs come in many shapes and sizes: from those that work within large companies, within the academic world, or those that build and launch their own businesses. Typically, these individuals have a high level of **entrepreneurial skills**, which are capacities, activities, and strengths that enable individuals to manage successfully in high-risk business environments.[2]

The role of the entrepreneur has become especially important during these financially turbulent times. Many of these businesspeople have contributed to economic development and growth by creating jobs, investing in communities, and making charitable donations. Successful entrepreneurs possess the skills, attitudes, and behaviors to change old, established systems for the better to benefit society and the greater community.

However, entrepreneurs do not achieve success overnight. One of the main challenges facing entrepreneurs is attracting customers to their products and services. So how do entrepreneurs encourage their customers to accept a new innovation? Here we can define **innovation** as a process that results in new market value through the creation of a product or service.[3]

In his 1962 book *Diffusion of Innovations*,[4] professor of sociology Everett Rogers devised an **innovation adoption curve**, a staged model that describes the evolution of an innovation's acceptance with customers, which he categorized as innovators, early adopters, early majority, late majority, and laggards. **Innovators** are the approximately 2 percent of a market's population that initially uses and tests a new product or service. Typically, these are young, affluent people who are willing to take risks to try or adopt a new product. We could say that the vast majority of Generation Y fit into this category, as they are more willing to embrace new technology than people from older generations often are.

The next wave to use a new innovation are **early adopters** , the approximately 14 percent of a market's population that uses a new product or service after innovators have used and

Voices of Management

Nesha Sanghavi[5]
Owner, University Girls Apparel

Nesha Sanghavi, owner of University Girls Apparel, knows firsthand both the challenges and exhilaration of being an entrepreneur. During her time as a student and cheerleader at West Virginia University (WVU), Sanghavi was impressed with the passion, enthusiasm, and sheer number of the fans that followed the university's sports teams. She also noticed that many women, like herself, would alter university-branded T-shirts by cutting sleeves and tying knots to make them look more feminine and fashionable. She began creating her own shirts by sewing university patches onto her own form-fitting, stylish shirts.

After graduating with a degree in finance and economics, she went to work as an investment analyst in Pittsburgh. But when her friends and acquaintances continued to request her homemade WVU gear, she began to contemplate a new career direction. "I was at my job in Pittsburgh for almost a year and felt like I had aged 10 years," Sanghavi explains. "One day, I asked myself if this is what I wanted to do for the rest of my life. I thought there had to be a better life than this. I'd always wanted to own a business and be an entrepreneur. So I thought, I need to do something that I love and am passionate about. That passion would be sports and fashion." She quit her job and enrolled in a two-year program at Parsons, The New School for Design in New York City, where she continued to refine her ideas for a women's line of fashionable, university-branded apparel. She also had the opportunity to complete an internship with the sports lifestyle company Puma at its world headquarters in Germany.

Sanghavi then faced the daunting tasks of obtaining licenses for university logos, securing a manufacturer for her line, and convincing retailers to carry her clothing.

She contacted a number of manufacturers but found no one who was willing to fulfill her company's relatively small orders. Finally, a family friend who operated a factory in India agreed to manufacture her clothing line. The University Girls Apparel collection includes fashionable women's styles that are trendy in the sportswear market, but are not as readily available in the collegiate market. The collection is designed for women to look and feel fashionable while supporting their team. Styles include dresses, baseball jerseys, T-shirts, hooded sweatshirts, and jackets, with feminine styling and details.

"These are styles that women of all ages, including myself, love to wear in their everyday lives,"

courtesy Nesha Sanghavi

Sanghavi states. "I wanted clothes that were trendy and fashionable, but were also made and fitted for real women of all sizes, not just students." Her company is currently licensed to sell branded apparel for 12 major universities, and she plans to expand to more than 50 in the near future.

"My big goal is to grow my line to represent all the major colleges in the country," she says. University Girls Apparel can be purchased online at www.UGapparel.com and at retail locations in several states. This entrepreneur's inspiration came from the loyalty and enthusiasm of sports fans who love to wear the colors of their school. "I love the idea of community within sports," she explains. "People are passionate about sports. It brings them together. I wanted to stay close to that." ■

UNIVERSITY GIRLS APPAREL

Courtesy Nesha Sanghavi/ UniversityGirls Apparel

tested it. Early adopters prefer to form their own opinions on whether to choose to adopt a new innovation.

Next is the **early majority**, which is the approximately 34 percent of a market's population that uses a product or service after early adopters have used it. These adopters tend to seek the opinions of early adopters as to the validity of the innovation.

The **late majority** describes the approximately 34 percent of a market's population that uses a product or service after the early majority has used it. Usually, this segment of the market is skeptical about an innovation and very slow to adopt it.

Finally, **laggards** are the approximately 16 percent of a market's population that is last to use a product or service. Typically, laggards are the part of the older generation that does not have much communication with the young innovators or early adopters.

We may not be aware of it, but many of the innovations that we use today on a daily basis would not have been possible without the influence of entrepreneurs. Every time we engage in social networking or use a search engine or an app, we are using technological innovations created by entrepreneurs. Indeed, many of the world's most successful technological companies, such as Microsoft, Facebook, and Google, were started by entrepreneurs. These companies began as **start-up companies**, which are newly formed organizations with limited or no operational history.[6] As the business landscape continues to evolve, and new global innovations come into play, there is more emphasis on **entrepreneurship**, activities associated with seeking opportunities that generate new value, with an array of unknown forces.[7]

Yet the **business model**, a proposed method for creating and sustaining market value, for start-up companies is constantly shifting and changing.[8] In this age of global communication and innovative technology, more and more entrepreneurs are coming together to start businesses, without relying on financial backing from other institutions. While many start-up companies depend on **venture capital**, funding that supports the starting and growing of high-risk business ventures, other entrepreneurs have found ways of raising their own funding.[9] This means that the future of the start-up is wholly in the hands of the entrepreneurs, giving them full ownership of the business without having to give up equity or intellectual property.

Josh Edelson/AFP / Getty Images

People, Processes, and the Ecosystem

As a result of the economic turbulence over the last few years, the tide has turned somewhat against capitalism. The massive imbalance between rich and poor and the inequity of power has caused many to question the effectiveness of a pure capitalist system on society. However, we can argue that a bigger and healthier capitalism may be possible if entrepreneurs, freelancers, and funders come together and independently run their own businesses. This would create an **entrepreneurial ecosystem** which is a set of stakeholders that are necessary to support the innovation and creation of new market value.[10]

Such workers could create market value by cooperating on *projects* (not just companies) that have recurring and sustainable revenues. This would mean that each participating stakeholder would enter into a financial sharing framework that enables each member to contribute unique value without having to sacrifice a portion of earnings, or a percentage of the business to outside institutions. But what would these entrepreneurial companies have to do to maintain their independence? They would need to fully embrace **creativity**, which is the process through which individuals and groups transform ideas into reality.[11] As we have seen over the course of this book, creativity helps with problem solving and innovation. Indeed, continuous innovation is the key to staying ahead of the competition and running a successful business model.

In this chapter, we will explore how three former university friends pool their entrepreneurial skills together to create an innovative start-up company.

Do you remember University of Texas (UT) students Katy Johnson, Fred Arters, and Lisa Fang from Chapter 4? Katy, who was a marketing and chemistry double major, joined a multinational electricity company, Reliable Energy, as a fuel marketing manager. Fred, a computer science major with a minor in management, started his career at a gaming company called Perfect Planet Interactive as a product coordinator. And Lisa, an information systems major with a minor in marketing, went to work for Hannah's, one of the world's largest online retailers, as an information technology (IT) project manager. It is five years later, and their lives are about to change.

Ben Johnson, Katy's grandfather, is an energy entrepreneur and investor. In recent years, along with energy billionaire T. Boone Pickens,[12] he has been supporting energy independence in the United States through natural gas innovations. The discovery of natural gas and domestic oil in North America has resulted in fewer imports from other countries. The hope is that by 2030, the United States will achieve total energy independence, leading to higher employment, a decrease in natural gas prices, and a reduction in power bills. However, there is controversy around the method used to extract the gas. *Fracking*, which is shorthand for "hydraulic fracturing," is the process of creating fractures in rocks by drilling and injecting fluid into the rocks in order to release oil and gas. Many environmental groups have held anti-fracking protests, arguing that the use of potentially harmful chemicals during the fracking process has caused small Earth tremors, pollution, and water contamination, among other environmental disruptions. In addition to the environmental concerns, anti-fracking supporters say that a heavy focus on nonrenewable energy detracts from the search for sustainable alternatives.

At the moment, the spotlight is on Bismarck, North Dakota, one of the nation's fastest-growing oil-producing states, with one of the lowest unemployment rates in the country. Katy's grandfather is interested in looking for opportunities to invest in the booming natural energy industry in North Dakota.

At a family event, Ben takes Katy aside and gives her some advice. "If I were your age, I would call all of my smartest friends and move to Bismarck, North Dakota. Give yourselves time to settle in and brainstorm until you come up with a great idea to take advantage of the economic opportunity there. With your background at Reliable Energy, you already have the knowledge and experience about the energy business—only this time, you will be focusing on domestic sources of natural gas and oil. Katy, this is the future—wouldn't you like to be a part of it? If you come up with an innovative way to approach this side of the business, then give me a call. I am always interested in investing in natural energy, and if your idea is better than anything else I am currently looking at, maybe I will put in a little angel funding."

Katy isn't quite sure what to say; after all, she has spent five years building up her career in one of the country's leading energy companies. Is she really going to consider starting all over, leaving behind a great job and good salary to relocate to a state she has never set foot in, to become an entrepreneur? But her grandfather's words ring through her head over and over. How many people have a chance of attracting an **angel investor**, individuals that provide entrepreneurs with funding and mentorship,[13] to invest in their ideas?

Wouldn't it be exciting to be part of something that groundbreaking? It would mean taking a huge risk, but she feels it is worth a discussion. She grabs her cell phone and calls the two smartest people she knows: her friends from UT, Fred and Lisa. She asks them, "How crazy of an idea do you think it would be to move to North Dakota together and start an exciting new business?"

Both Fred and Lisa are excited and intrigued. Although they are enjoying their current jobs, they both happen to be looking for a change, and agree that this is an opportunity worth pursuing. Following days of discussion, all three resign from their jobs. About two months later, they are set to move to North Dakota and embark on their adventure. The three college friends now find themselves in the middle of one of their generation's biggest economic opportunities. The only problem is that they have yet to figure out how to take advantage of it.

Entrepreneurial ecosystem a set of stakeholders that are necessary to support the innovation and creation of new market value.

Creativity A process through which individuals and groups transform ideas into reality.

> One of the main challenges facing entrepreneurs is attracting customers to their products and services.

✓ **Innovation**—a process that results in new market value, through the creation of a product or service

✓ **Innovation Adoption Curve**—a staged model that describes the evolution of an innovation's acceptance with customers which he categorized as innovators, early adopters, early majority, late majority, and laggards

■ **Innovators**—the 2% of a market's population that initially uses and tests a new product or service

■ **Early Adopters**—the 14% of a market's population that uses a new product or service after innovators have used and tested the offering

■ **Early Majority**—the 34% of a market's population that uses a product or service after early adopters have used the offering

■ **Late Majority**—the 34% of a market's population that uses a product or service after the early majority has used the offering

■ **Laggards** are the 16% of a market's population that uses a product or service last

✓ **Start-up companies**—newly formed organizations with limited or no operational history

✓ **Entrepreneurship**—activities associated with seeking opportunities that generate new value, with an array of unknown forces

Angel investor Individuals who provide entrepreneurs with funding and mentorship.

✓ **Business Model**—a proposed method for creating and sustaining market value

✓ **Venture Capital**—funding that supports the starting and growing of high-risk business ventures

● **People, Processes, and the Ecosystem**

✓ **Entrepreneurial Ecosystem**—a set of stakeholders that are necessary to support the innovation and creation of new market value

✓ **Creativity**—a process through which individuals and groups transform ideas into reality

ManagementStory:
Featuring Katy Johnson, Fred Arters, and Lisa Fang

18.2 | OPPORTUNITIES AND CHALLENGES THAT ENTREPRENEURS FACE

18.2 | Describe the opportunities and challenges that affect growth for new ventures.

Every new venture is faced with a certain amount of opportunities and challenges. Savvy entrepreneurs will always evaluate the criteria for growth and risk before establishing a start-up company. According to a study called "Global Entrepreneurship and the Successful Growth Strategies of Early-Stage Companies," carried out by the World Economic Forum,[14] there are five main growth accelerants and challenges that affect the performance of new ventures that Katy, Fred, and Lisa will need to consider before launching their new company.

Mark Graham/AFP / Getty Images

Growth Accelerants

1. Market Opportunity/Customers/Competitors Successful entrepreneurs are able to identify a market opportunity, or a gap in the market, in order to attract a diverse customer base. As the business grows, it becomes a serious competitor, possibly overtaking other competition operating in a similar market. For example, back in 1975, Bill Gates identified a need for "software that was increasingly easy to use and more powerful" and "a new kind of computer that was affordable, adaptable, and personal."[15] On the strength of these assumptions, Bill Gates revolutionized the personal computer industry forever.

2. Human Resources/People/Organization Culture In Chapter 13, we explored the importance of the "human side" of business. It cannot be underestimated how vital people are to the success of an organization, no matter how big or small. Indeed, it could be argued that this point should even come first within this category for growth accelerators. Successful start-up companies recognize the importance of attracting the best talent and nurturing that talent within the organizational culture. Google is an example of a thriving culture which, in spite of its growing size, still embraces the spirit of a start-up company: employees are encouraged to contribute ideas and feedback within a creative and inspirational environment. In fact, Google's culture was the inspiration behind the 2013 movie *The Internship*, although it is worth noting that the movie is a fictionalized, somewhat exaggerated, and comedic account of what it's like to work at Google. As we have seen, a happy employee is a productive employee. Methods such as *Positive Psychology* and *emotional intelligence* (EI) are becoming increasingly popular in helping to ensure the satisfaction of employees.

3. Product/Services/After-Sales Successful start-ups will have an excellent, innovative product and provide unparalleled customer sales and after-sales care. This is particularly relevant in the technology industry, where customers may struggle to use new products after purchase and rely on the customer care team to guide them through implementation and operation. Apple, in particular, is famous for its customer care, with cell phone and computer owners regularly rating it at the top of the American Customer Satisfaction Index (ACSI). Each Apple Retail Store is graced with a "Genius Bar," where customers are provided with help and support from members of the customer service team. This hands-on approach, together with real expertise and genuine care for its customers, has transformed Apple into one of the world's leading competitors in electronic and software products and personal computers.

4. Marketing/Branding Although this growth accelerant comes further down the list, many entrepreneurs might argue that a marketing and branding strategy should be designed before the company is even launched. Even with the right financial backing, brilliant innovative products, and a dedicated entrepreneurial team, a start-up will struggle if it doesn't try to stand out from the competition. These days, many growth companies use social networking, viral marketing, and word of mouth to advertise their services.

5. Research and Development/New Product Development A start-up has a good chance of experiencing rapid growth if it invests the appropriate amount of resources into its products. This means carrying out an exhaustive degree of research to ensure that products are designed to the highest quality specifications. Continuous research and development will help to main the product's position in the market and give rise to new product ideas. Netlogic Microsystems, a leader in semiconductor solutions, regularly invests a large portion of its profits back into research and development (R&D) to ensure that its products are among the highest-performing ones on the market.

Challenges to Growth

1. Human Resources/People/Organization Culture One of the most interesting aspects of the findings made by the World Economic Forum is how the category of Human Resources, People and Organizational Culture has actually served as a challenge to growth for start-up companies. This means that some fledgling businesses have struggled to attract and retain new talent. Miguel Santos, the cofounder and CEO of the start-up Technisys, states that the "[m]ajor challenge was attracting and retaining talented people."

Santos adds: "We are better at this for technical people than for the business side. We failed big time on one of our first senior management hires. He came from a major technology company. Great résumé. He did not understand and did not want to understand our start-up culture. We learned that a hiring with a bad outcome can not only freeze you but set you back."[16] So, not only is it important to find the right talent, but to find people that fit into the culture and embrace the mission of your company.

2. Market Opportunity/Customers/Competitors Some start-ups fail before they even get off the ground. This can be due to timing—where another company identifies a market opportunity sooner and captures a segment of the market before the other company is able to compete. However, even after start-ups are well established, entrepreneurs must retain and attract new customers consistently to stay ahead of the competition.

3. Company Financing And Liquidity No start-up will survive without the appropriate financing and **liquidity**, which is the measurement of available financial resources or the ability to convert an organization's assets into cash.[17] Many entrepreneurs are backed by venture capitalists, angel investors, and financial institutions. However, as described above, an entrepreneurial ecosystem emerges whereby more entrepreneurs are joining together to raise their own funds to support their businesses, resulting in greater autonomy and control of the business.

> **Liquidity** The measurement of available financial resources or the ability to convert an organization's assets into cash.

4. Operations Management/Systems Similarly, if the systems and operations don't work, there is little chance that the start-up will be in business for the long term. Even eBay experienced major system problems when it first launched its website. Brad Handler, the first in-house counsel for eBay, stated: "The site outages were a huge problem for eBay. The core issue was the failure to properly plan for the hypergrowth of the site. As long as the site was functioning, it was easy to ignore the engineering team's pleas that the site was running on Band Aids and fumes."[18] Many companies make the mistake of using "quick fixes," a symptom of "Shifting the Burden" (one of the systems archetypes discussed in Chapter 3) to keep systems running, but it is only a matter of time before the problem happens again, leading to costly repairs, and in some cases, a loss of customers.

Marcio Jose Sanchez / AP Photo

5. Top Management/Board When starting a growth company, many entrepreneurs look to hire executive managers with the right experience and contacts to make the company a success. While attracting the best talent is essential for any company, some start-ups have made expensive mistakes by paying top dollar to recruit outside executive managers from larger, more corporate companies, who simply "don't get" what the start-up is trying to achieve. In many cases, this has resulted in a power struggle, with the manager pushing the firm in one direction and the entrepreneurial team fighting to maintain the original vision. A young company that wants to hire an executive talent must first ensure that its new recruit buys into the direction and mission of the company.

Shortly after Katy, Fred, and Lisa arrive in Bismarck, Katy receives an encouraging phone call from her grandfather, "Remember, great opportunities come to those who solve the greatest challenges. Focus on what looks like it's broken!"

Although the city is enjoying economic prosperity and most of the residents work in oil-related jobs, the three entrepreneurs learn from local news reports that there aren't enough people to fill the number of jobs available.[19]

"That's it!" Katy says, excitedly to Fred and Lisa. "That's what's broken in North Dakota. One of the biggest problems I see here is that companies cannot find the right supply of employees to meet the demand." Fred and Lisa agree.

Keith Binns / iStockphoto

As they carry out more research, they find that there is huge competition between oil companies to find talent. Human Resource (HR) departments are under pressure to fill the thousands of job openings and fight for the right people to join their companies and stay. Katy calls her grandfather, explaining their breakthrough idea.

"There are thousands of jobs open here and companies are struggling to meet the demand. Our idea is to start a firm that communicates with potential employees across the country, and maybe even globally, about the opportunities here and connect them to employers. We will make a profit by charging a recruiting fee to the companies."

There is a moment of silence on the phone. Then Ben says, "That's the best you could come up with? A recruitment agency? If there is a shortage in talent in North Dakota, you can be sure that the energy companies are already in touch with the country's top recruitment firms. Are you three really going to try and compete with other established agencies when you have no experience trying to run that type of business? Didn't you tell me that Fred was a computer programming genius? You also told me Lisa managed a huge retailer's information systems. And you marketed fuel for Reliable Energy. You have to be innovative and think big. Let me know when you have an idea worth funding!"

Katy feels a bit discouraged at this critical feedback. But maybe her grandfather was right—maybe they hadn't thought the whole idea through . . . She realizes they hadn't figured out the **feasibility** of the venture, which is the degree to which a business venture is possible, given the availability of resources and technologies.[20]

Ben continues, "My one piece of advice now—go find the 10 most successful people in Bismarck and ask them what keeps them awake at night. If 5 of them say the same thing, solve that challenge—then you will have a company that's got a real chance at making it. You'll have your next idea when you have talked to those 10 people and start to understand everything about the opportunities and risks associated with doing business in the energy market."

The three college friends are deflated. But they knew there were opportunities waiting for them. It was just a matter of talking to the right people and coming up with the right plan.

> **Feasibility** The degree to which a business venture is possible, given the availability of resources and technologies.

Opportunities and Risks for New Ventures

It took a few weeks to convince the 10 most successful professionals in Bismarck to talk with Katy, Fred and Lisa about their companies' challenges. Trying to persuade the city's busiest and most prominent business leaders to talk to three unknown aspiring entrepreneurs proved to be a bit tricky. But they persevered by making polite calls to the professionals' personal assistants and sending follow-up emails to explain the reasons they wanted to meet with them. Slowly, doors began to open, and they were given some time with their chosen business executives. However, it was only following their ninth, and final, meeting that an idea began to spark. After they talked with Susan Richmond, CEO of ND Fuel Transportation Services, they finally discovered a challenge that they thought they could help solve.

As it turned out, Bismarck had the product, but not the right infrastructure. This meant that in spite of the large fuel supply available in Bismarck, combined with the strong demand for fuel, the infrastructure in place did not meet the demand; their transportation industry could not fulfill the expectations from both the fuel companies and independent refineries. Every day, Bismarck fuel companies were losing money by not meeting their clients' demands.

The three entrepreneurs are excited and relieved that they had finally identified a real gap in the market. Now they have to figure out how to transport the fuel to its destinations more quickly and efficiently, and improve customer service across the board.

The breakthrough idea arrives one night when the three friends are talking about their previous jobs and the interesting projects they had worked on. At his former company, Perfect Planet Interactive, Fred led a team that built a series of algorithms to help management understand the most popular features used within a game and how to cater to and anticipate the future interests of the game-players. This allowed the management team to refocus customer service efforts and resources associated with increased demand.

Fred, who was a bit of a science buff, had been inspired by scientific research conducted on bee colonies and ant farms, which showed that swarms of different species use their collective intelligence to find the shortest and most risk-free path to their destinations.[21] By using similar computer algorithms, Fred believes he can find a more efficient way for the trucks to deliver fuel on a timelier basis. This would mean working closely with the oil companies to create the most optimal route for trucks to get to their destination. The truck drivers would each be given a preprogrammed global positioning satellite (GPS) system, which would direct them along the quickest routes and provide an alternative route in the event of traffic jams, road accidents, or roadwork. Once Fred creates an algorithm based on a particular oil company's data, the entrepreneurs would be able to sell it to the company. If enough companies are interested, then the entrepreneurs might just have a successful business on their hands.

Katy and Fred are both excited about the idea for their new business, but Lisa is not so sure. She says, "Look, I like the idea. I know natural gas is big business right now. It's creating tremendous economic development in North Dakota and several other states. However, I'm uncomfortable with how the gas is being extracted and the potential effects it is having on the environment. There is a sign outside a house right down the block that reads: "Get the frack out of here!" There have also been some protests and demonstrations in the city . . . My concern is that by devising new, faster routes for oil companies, we are supporting a method of extraction as well as championing nonrenewable energy, both of which may prove to be real environmental concerns."

Katy replies, "Lisa, I understand where you're coming from, but our plan is simply to get that product to its destination faster."

Fred adds, "I agree with Katy, but I do think our business can promote sustainability."

"How?" Lisa says.

"Well, by optimizing the delivery routes, the trucks reach their destinations faster, which means they are using less fuel. As they are on the road less time, they will also emit fewer pollutants, which will help with air pollution. Our company will actually encourage oil businesses to use less fuel on their transport routes and reduce their carbon footprint," Fred replies.

Lisa thinks for a moment. "OK, I think you have made a good point, Fred, but I would like our company to be as socially responsible as possible."

"Let's do some research and see if our idea is viable, and then address ways in which we could be socially responsible. I think my grandfather will have some sound advice for us too," Katy says. However, before Katy runs the idea by her grandfather, she makes sure that the team

Danny Johnston / AP Photo

carries out extensive research to prove that their idea is worth investing in. This involves identifying the opportunities and risks for the new venture.[22]

Market Size First, the group focuses on market size. They agree that the energy boom in North Dakota has attracted a great deal of fuel companies, who are struggling to deliver their product and might be interested in their idea. They establish a list of the companies to approach with their idea, and discuss how they could potentially grow the market beyond North Dakota should they succeed. They reason that the larger the market size, the higher the growth potential of their new venture. Yet, before they proceed, they need to establish that no other company has captured a slice of the market by introducing a similar service.

Market Value Creation and Customer Adoption Next, they look at how their product can add value, and who will use it. This is **value creation**, which includes the activities and processes that increase the worth of a product or service.[23] "Well, that's straightforward," Lisa says. "The fuel companies will use our product to get fuel to their clients quicker and more efficiently." Fred says, "Agreed. But are they going to be so drawn in by the idea that they will be willing to pay for it?" The team spends the next few hours working the specifics, including the fees, charges, and financial implications of their new business.

Market Value Capture and Business Model The team has to include in their business model how much value of the market they can capture with their new venture. This depends on how much influence their company will have on the market and how effective their pricing strategy will be in comparison to any competitors they might have. Their business model will have to be both innovative and creative for them not to be undermined by their competition.

Management Team/People/Human Resources The team grows silent as they contemplate their next point. It involves evaluating their abilities. They needed to do some soul searching to figure out if all three of them have the skills, attitudes, and commitment necessary to lead the company to success, especially during turbulent times.

After a thoughtful discussion, the team concludes that they have the expertise and determination to work together, provided that they are all committed to the goals of the company. Lisa says, "After all, we will only attract talent if we behave as a top-rated company ourselves, and that means making money *and* being socially responsible." Katy and Fred agree, and the team moves on to their list of things to consider.

Discovery or Technical Feasibility Next, the team examines the extent of the breakthrough that they have made with regards to the transportation issue. Can it really work? Both Katy and Lisa expectantly turn to Fred. He explains that the "swarm" research carried out has proved that certain real-world operations can be made more efficient by imitating the actions of the collective groups of insects. "I have based my algorithms on this theory, and I believe the business is scalable as result." **Scaling** is the degree to which a company or its business model can grow, given the necessary resources.[24] It is now up to the team to prove to their potential clients that their innovation can be applied to transportation.

Financial and Liquidity The question of finances is one for Katy, as her grandfather is the one who will be providing the new venture with its initial funds—but only if he likes the idea. The team talks about how much they will need to set up and how long they must be in operation before they make a profit. They also talk about the possibility of going public in the future by initiating an **initial public offering (IPO)**, which is the first time a company sells its equity shares on the stock market.[25] This would be a great way of raising capital, generating publicity, and attracting attention to their products. But before they get too ahead of themselves, Katy needs to have that all-important conversation with her grandfather to ensure his financial commitment.

Value creation The activities and processes that increase the worth of a product or service.

Scaling The degree to which a company or its business model can grow, given the necessary resources.

Initial public offering (IPO) The first time a company sells it equity shares on the stock market.

Governmental/Political/Regulatory Here, the team believes that they have an advantage. The U.S. government has been pushing for environmental change and reform and has been supportive of natural energy. By making fuel transportation more speedy and efficient, they will be able to assist the fuel companies in reducing their carbon footprint. By carrying out research online, they do not believe that any regulations will inhibit the growth of their new venture.

Execution and Scaling The team knows that timing is everything. They need to execute the systems as soon as possible, secure clients, choose a location for the company, and get their finances in order.

Having identified the number of opportunities and risks, the team are confident that their new venture has a great deal of potential. Now, they face one more challenge—to convince Katy's grandfather that their venture is worth the investment. Katy takes a deep breath and picks up the phone . . .

18.3 | MANAGING AND LEADING NEW VENTURES

18.3 | Compare and contrast different types of ventures that entrepreneurs create.

In her nervousness, Katy begins talking without even saying hello. "Granddaddy, we have our new business. It's called Buzz Logistics! We are going to create algorithms that help fuel transportation companies get fuel to refineries faster and cheaper—potentially saving our customers millions of dollars each year in their own fuel costs."

"Good idea!" Ben says.

Katy and her grandfather talk for hours about the new venture, the research the team has carried out, the potential market, the risks and opportunities, and the business model that they have created.

"We would also like to make the business as socially responsible as we can," Katy adds, explaining Lisa's environmental concerns about fracking and nonrenewable energy, "but we're not quite sure how to go about it."

"How about when the business takes off, you invest a percentage of the profits in renewable energy such as wind and solar power?" Ben suggests. "That way, you are supporting the environment and investing in the future of the planet."

Katy likes the idea, and hopes Lisa and Ben will like it too.

Finally, Ben says, "I just have two more questions: how much do you need, and where do I send the check?" Katy gladly tells him what she needs him to do.

Having secured the funding, Katy meets with Fred and Lisa to give them the good news and to broach Ben's idea of investing some future profits in renewable energy. Both Fred and Lisa are delighted with the suggestion. Finally, all three entrepreneurs are fully committed and ready to get their company up and running. Buzz Logistics is officially a new business venture.

Different Strategies for New Ventures

Much like business strategies for mature companies, different strategic approaches can be categorized, which allows managers to better understand risks and conduct effective competitive analyses. Katy, Fred, and Lisa explore the eight different strategies for new ventures[26] to decide which one will suit the business model they have designed for Buzz Logistics:

An **aggregation venture** is a business strategy defined by acquiring, merging, and coordinating existing market products, services, and companies. This allows the company to achieve scale quickly and grow almost immediately, increasing revenues by capturing large market segments. However, immediate growth is not without its risks, as companies struggle to coordinate the different types of products, people, and companies they may acquire.

LECTURE ENHANCER:

18.3 Managing and Leading New Ventures

• **Different Strategies for New Ventures**
  ✓ **Aggregation Venture**—a business strategy defined by acquiring, merging, and coordinating existing market products, services, and companies
  ✓ **Discovery Venture**—a business strategy that seeks to invent a brand new product / service or find a new resource
  ✓ **New-Existing Venture**—a business strategy defined by offering an existing category of consumers a new product or service
  ✓ **New-New Venture**—a business strategy defined by offering a new category of consumers a new product or service, typically distinguished with higher-risk and higher-returns compared to "new-existing ventures"
  ✓ **System Change Venture**—a business strategy responding to a significant change in political environments, governmental legislations, and regulations
  ✓ **Transplant Venture**—a business strategy where an idea that achieves market success in one market region is transferred to other geographic markets
  ✓ **Value Chain Venture**—a business strategy that seeks to redesign or augment an offering in an existing business or management process
  ✓ **Wave Venture**—a business strategy defined by a systemic change in business and market environments

Aggregation venture A business strategy defined by acquiring, merging, and coordinating existing market products, services, and companies.

A **discovery venture** is a business strategy that seeks to invent a brand new product or service or find a new resource. New discoveries in the world of science, business, and medicine are being made all the time. However, continuous research needs to be carried out before the product can be brought to market.

A **new-existing venture** is a business strategy defined by offering a new product or service to an existing category of consumers. For example, many growth companies such as Apple have successfully introduced new products such as the iPhone and Mac to their existing customer base, as well as services such as the Genius Bar.

A **new-new venture** is a business strategy defined by offering a new category of consumers a new product or service, typically distinguished with higher risk and higher returns compared to new-existing ventures. This type of venture strategy carries more risks, as its success depends on attracting a new segment of the market with a brand new product. Facebook is an example of a successful new-new venture, as it introduced an original product that quickly captured a global market.

A **system change venture** is a business strategy responding to a significant change in political environments, governmental legislation, and regulations. Many start-up companies have benefited from governmental changes; for example, deregulation in the telecommunications industry has given rise to new competitors all over the world.

A **transplant venture** is a business strategy where an idea that achieves market success in one market region is transferred to other geographic markets. Again, this strategy is not without its risks. For example, when eBay tried to enter the Japanese market, it found that Yahoo had a stronger foothold. As a result, it was a challenge for eBay to initially establish a position in Japan.

A **value chain venture** is a business strategy that seeks to redesign or augment an offering in an existing business or management process, such as outsourcing of information technology and research. Some growth companies use this strategy to use technology as a differentiator in order to provide services to their clients.

A **wave venture** is a business strategy defined by a systemic change in business and market environments. Companies like Microsoft, Genetech, Google, and Facebook do not operate alone; rather, they work with a wide range of other companies that have also shared in their "wave" of success.

Following hours of discussion, the team decides that Buzz Logistics will be a value chain venture. This is because they will be using enhanced systems and technology to improve existing management processes in order to provide more efficient transportation services for their clients.

18.4 | MANAGING THE CREATIVE PROCESS

18.4 Explain how managers lead a creative process with individuals and teams.

"It was the best of times, it was the worst of times," thought Katy six months after they started the company. Word spread quickly after Buzz Logistics had signed up their first client, and now the majority of energy companies in North Dakota are using Fred's tailored algorithms; as a result, the company is expanding at an enormous rate. However, the three entrepreneurs have worked so hard in order to get the product delivered to their customers that they have ignored the need to build a cohesive team.

After a grueling, 80-hour week, Lisa puts her head in her hands and wails, "What are we going to do? We need more help!" Katy and Fred look equally exhausted.

Fred agrees, "I'm so exhausted and I feel like I'm chasing my tail. Our clients want us to come up with more and more creative solutions to their transportation problems, but I feel blocked. I have lost that 'in the zone' feeling."

For the first time since they started working together, the team feels a sense of hopelessness. They are overworked, stressed, and understaffed. More crucially, they have lost all sense of creativity and insight—the very two factors that inspired the inception of

Buzz in the first place. They need to address those critical areas if they want Buzz to be a success.

The Discipline of Creativity

In his book *Imagine: How Creativity Works*, Jonah Lehrer defines creativity as "an emergent property of people coming together."[27] He believes that tackling the ever-increasing rate of global challenges requires more than just one person. Indeed, rather than being born with the "creative gift," Lehrer argues that creativity is a science filled with thought processes that we are all capable of when working within the right kind of collaboration.

He also cites the work of Ben Jones, a professor of management at the Kellogg Business School who carried out a study on the production of scientific papers and patents over the last 50 years. Jones found that over 99 percent of scientific subfields have experienced increases in teamwork during this timeframe.[28]

Lehrer believes that the right group of people collaborating on a project gives rise to **meta-ideas** which are concepts that create, nurture, and support other concepts.[29] This means that sharing ideas inspires an inexhaustible supply of new ideas. Yet, in order to build the perfect creative team, each individual member must be invested in the creative process, be willing to take risks, not be afraid of sharing ideas, or receiving constructive criticism. In fact, Lehrer theorizes that constructive criticism is far more effective than brainstorming; rather than tearing people to shreds, he believes that criticism that is always backed up by a supporting or new idea sparks new creative processes.

Based on Lehrer's theory, we might conclude that individuals must be fully immersed in the creative process in order to achieve results. In other words, they must experience a sense of "flow." But what do we mean by "flow"? Let's look at that next.

Individual Creativity In Chapter 3, we explored the theory of Positive Psychology, founded by Martin Seligman and Mihaly Csikszentmihalyi. As a concept of Positive Psychology, Csikszentmihalyi also introduced the idea of **flow**, which is the experience of immersion and loss of time when an individual achieves an optimum balance of challenge, interest, and achievement.[30] The theory holds that once we allow ourselves to become completely absorbed by a well-defined task, we are able to ignore any distractions or doubts and fully focus on our goals, and lose all sense of time and self-consciousness. Csikszentmihalyi believes that if we find the right balance between our skills and the challenge of the task, we will become immersed in the most enjoyable of pursuits.

Eight Conditions for Flow in the Workplace[31] In order for individuals to experience flow in the workplace, they must be provided with the following working conditions. (You might find that some of the flow conditions subscribe to similar concepts outlined in the S.M.A.R.T. goals theory, as described in Chapter 8.)

1. **Clear Goals** Employees must be given clear, challenging goals that are aligned with their skill set and told exactly where their task fits in to the greater goals of the organization.

2. **Immediate Feedback** By providing timely feedback, employees will be reassured about their role in the process and are given the opportunity to adapt their behaviour where necessary. Delayed or limited feedback can be demotivating for employees as they will experience uncertainty about their own performance if they have no way of knowing the extent of their progress.

3. **A Balance Between Opportunity and Capacity** Employees are assigned challenging tasks that are achievable and within their capabilities.

4. **Deepened Sense of Concentration** Once individuals are confident of the goals they need to achieve, they may experience a high degree of concentration, which will allow them to delve more deeply into the task at hand.

5. **Living in the Present** When individuals are fully immersed in a task, they are completely working in the moment—thoughts about the past or the future do not interrupt their focus.

> **Eight Conditions for flow in the workplace**
> 1. Clear Goals
> 2. Immediate Feedback
> 3. A balance between opportunity and capacity
> 4. Deepened sense of concentration
> 5. Living in the Present
> 6. Personal Contact
> 7. Altered sense of time
> 8. Loss of ego
>
> • **Team Creativity**
> ✓ **Q-Level**—a measurement that determines the optimum level of group size and interaction to achieve successful creative output

Meta-ideas Concepts that create, nurture, and support other concepts.

Flow The experience of immersion and loss of time when an individual achieves an optimum balance of challenge, interest, and achievement.

6. **Personal Control** Achieving flow provides employees with a gratifying sense of personal control. They know exactly what they are doing and how they are going to achieve the task.

7. **Altered Sense of Time** When in the moment, individuals can lose all sense of time, even to the point where they forget to eat or sleep.

8. **Loss of Ego** Individuals can also experience a lack of self-awareness or self-consciousness; they are so wholly focused on achieving the goal that it becomes the only thing that matters.

The next challenge facing Katy, Lisa, and Fred is to expand their team and create a working environment that will provide an opportunity for growth and flow.

Team Creativity The three entrepreneurs set out to recruit employees to help with the burden of their ever-increasing workload. However, as the other companies in North Dakota have discovered, attracting talent is not easy. Seeking solutions to the company's plight, the team begins looking for creative solutions. In desperation, Katy, Lisa, and Fred hire temporary workers, software consultants, and contractors just to get them over the next "hump."

Soon, Buzz has over 50 employees, but only a handful of them are permanent. The new employees have such a high volume of work that they do not have a chance to communicate with each other. Katy tries to plan and organize team activities to encourage bonding, but nobody seems to have the time or interest in getting to know each other. Ironically, Buzz Logistics has become a logistical nightmare.

So, what has happened at this young company? The three entrepreneurs tried to solve the staffing problem with a short-term solution, but now they are challenged with a large group of people who simply don't collaborate or share ideas. They start to wonder—how should people work together?

When Katy, Fred, and Lisa sit down together to discuss the lack of team cohesion, they come to a startling realization: they themselves have all become too close by working so intensively together, which has stifled creativity. Their Q-levels are too high. None of them has any new ideas to bring to the table, and all three find themselves just going through the motions of fulfilling their obligations to the client base. Although they have hired new staff, the lack of collaboration has resulted in stagnation. Furthermore, during their discussion, the team realizes that they have fallen into the "Shifting the Burden" trap by hiring temporary employees to apply quick fixes to the running of their operations, instead of focusing on building a loyal staff committed to the welfare and future of Buzz Logistics.

Katy says, "We need to create an environment that encourages people to communicate with each other. Only then will we be able to foster a creative culture."

Over the next couple of months, the company moves to a new office building, where there is a large break room stocked with coffee, tea, and snacks, in the hopes of encouraging casual interaction, where employees can get to know each other and exchange ideas. Yet, much to her dismay, the staff simply uses the break room to grab a drink or snack which they bring back to their desks, without saying much to anyone else on the way.

Frustrated, Katy confides in her teammates, "What more can I do? I have set up this new break room with comfy couches and food, and nobody wants to go there and chat with other people. Where else do people run into each other if it's not in the break room?"

Lisa tentatively proposes, "How about the bathroom?"

Fred and Katy immediately burst out laughing—but then the idea sinks in, and the team grows thoughtful.

Katy says, "You know what, Lisa? I think that just might work."

The next day, Katy closes all the bathrooms in the building except for the ones near the break room.[32] At first, the employees are shocked and a few are annoyed; some of them have to walk quite a bit whenever they have to go to the bathroom but over time, casual encounters begin to spark communication and engagement.

Research@Work

Q-Levels and Teams

Brian Uzzi, a sociologist at Northwestern University, explored the ways in which people work together. Through his intensive study of Broadway musicals (from 1945 to 1989), Uzzi found that creative groups working together have a certain Q-level.[33] A **Q-level** is a measurement that determines the optimum level of group size and interaction to achieve successful creative output.[34]

For example, he found that teams comprising of close friends that collaborated on musicals had too high Q-levels; this meant that the friends were so close that they all shared similar ideas and thought processes, which stunted their ability to create new ones. Even with the greatest musical talent working together, a musical could suffer at the box office.

Uzzi also explored the effect of a team of strangers collaborating on a musical together. Perhaps, not so surprisingly, those musicals also tended to fail more often than not. According to Uzzi, this was because the artists had no foundation of having worked together in the past, and they struggled to communicate and exchange creative ideas. Uzzi described this group as having too low Q-levels, which meant that the team was simply not close enough to produce creative ideas.

So, what does the perfect creative team look like? According to Uzzi, the key is to find the Q-level sweet spot. His theory shows that the best Q-levels exist in teams that are comprised of both friends and new collaborators. Musicals that were produced by these sorts of teams tended to be the most successful. The friends had a good foundation to work from and further benefited from new team members who introduced new ideas.

© Jeff Christensen/Reuters / Corbis

Critical Thinking in the Classroom

As a manager, how would you ensure that your team had the highest Q-levels?

During the following months, Lisa and Katy pick up tidbits of information relayed by employees that helps to benefit the running of the company. One of these is a cost-cutting idea raised by one of the administrative staff who bumps into Lisa in the bathroom one day. The employee points out that the lights are always on in both the bathroom and the break room, even after hours, incurring unnecessary expense. Lisa is excited that a member of her staff feels comfortable enough to approach her with feedback, but she is disappointed that she didn't notice this herself. Given that they are working in the energy industry, and their investment in renewables, shouldn't Buzz Logistics be setting an example by making their own operations as energy-efficient as possible?

Lisa draws on her previous experience at Hannah's to install motion-sensor lighting in the bathroom and the break room so the lights come on only when the areas are in use, which saves electricity. In addition, she takes out the light bulbs in the vending machines,

Q-level A measurement that determines the optimum level of group size and interaction to achieve successful creative output.

which she learned at Hannah's was another unnecessary expense. The team also decided to have solar panels installed on the office roof as well. In an attempt to make Buzz Logistics more environmentally friendly, she sets up recycling bins and encourages the staff to operate in a paperless environment by converting as many documents as possible into digital form.

However, the biggest breakthrough in their plan to get people talking came one morning when Fred overheard a couple of software engineers, Leal and Kusum, chatting over coffee. At first, Fred was just pleased that the two members of staff had formed a friendship. But when he realized what they were discussing, he couldn't believe his luck. They were talking about what a shame was to see Buzz spending such large sums of money on software consultants, especially when their own college friends in California could program better and faster. A idea sparked in Fred's head: relying on expensive contractors was eating into the company's revenue—no wonder they were just about breaking even. They needed to come up with a new strategy to meet the growth in demand.

Fred races into Katy's office and throws out the idea of him moving to California. Katy, with panic in her voice, says, "What? You can't quit!!"

Fred quickly adds, "I don't want to quit! But I do think it would be a good idea to move to the San Diego area with software consultants Leal and Kusum, if they are up for it, and set up a California branch office. We'll have access to experienced programmers who we can hire and train. It will save us money and enable us to better meet the need of our customers. What do you think?"

They call Lisa into Katy's office to discuss the idea of expanding the company into California. After many questions and ideas are discussed, it is decided that with the help of Leal, Kusum, and their contacts, Fred will set up Buzz Logistics Research & Development in La Jolla, California, just outside of San Diego. The branch will be staffed primarily with college graduates who excel at programming. Save for a few key workers, the majority of the North Dakota temporary staff and consultants will be let go. Fred's California team will collaborate with the North Dakota office to create new, innovative market solutions in order to maintain Buzz Logistics' competitive advantage and a high level of customer service.

LECTURE ENHANCER:

18.5 Global Entrepreneurship and Innovation

• The Great 21st-Century Opportunity

18.5 | GLOBAL ENTREPRENEURSHIP AND INNOVATION

18.5 Outline how entrepreneurs use innovation to grow global opportunities.

On his arrival in California, Fred finds an ideal office space that he believes will be conducive to flow and help inspire new collaborations and ideas. He has learned from his experience at the Bismarck office that employees do not flourish when they are chained to a desk, worked too hard, or put under too much pressure to perform. Pursuing his belief that employees need to work under the right conditions to be creative, with the help of some local architects, he designs an office space to encourage employees who are struggling with a problem to take regular breaks by going for walks, lying down on couches placed by the windows, or simply playing an interactive video game.[35] In his experience, a relaxed mind is more likely to produce new ideas and find innovative ways to resolve problems.

With the help of Leal and Kusum's contacts, he offers formal, permanent roles to a team of 20 recent college graduates who are willing to live in or near La Jolla. The new team is made up of skilled programmers who work much faster and cost much less than the consultant team in North Dakota. Bursting with ideas, it is not long before the team begins to perform and produce new innovations.

Back in North Dakota, Katy and Lisa begin focusing on expanding their market opportunity by providing clients with IT solutions that can be delivered anywhere in the world. However, before they can roll out their solutions to their client base, they need to make sure that the systems at Buzz Logistics are fully functioning and up to date. The level of demand from clients means that they need to scale up their systems in order to take advantage of the growth that they are experiencing. The series of quick fixes employed by temporary staff has merely papered over the cracks. They need to address the underlying problems before they can grow as a business.

Over the course of a few months, Buzz Logistics puts the right measures in place to ensure that their existing systems are up to date and working, and implements new systems to facilitate growth. Adopting the right systems will provide a better communication network between the California and North Dakota offices, as well as allowing senior management to focus on key areas for growth and development.

Some of the management systems implemented include a financial budgeting and evaluation system to keep track of their revenues and expenses; a sales target and sales information pipeline system for collating the number of products that the firm sells over a certain period of time; and a new product system, which charts product development milestones. As a professional marketer, Katy knows the importance of marketing and branding to attract new business, as well as providing excellent customer service and building long-lasting relationships with clients. She ensures that Buzz Logistics implements management systems that can record and provide data on each of these key areas.

Buzz Logistics has also nurtured a culture and designed an organization structure where the most important asset is its people. The entrepreneurs have experienced firsthand the challenges of finding and attracting new talent. In such a fast-driven economy, they know that they need to invest and retain the right employees for their company continually. To support this belief, the company adopts several system applications, such as HR planning and evaluation systems. These systems help HR managers to outline strategic plans for the organization with regard to staffing and create a process whereby employees are encouraged to meet defined business goals.

The Great 21st-Century Opportunity

It is five years later. Buzz Logistics has become a global phenomenon and their strategies are being implemented by energy companies all over the world. The company has expanded internationally, and profits have gone through the roof, attracting even more investors. By constantly improving services and products for clients through continuous technological innovation, Buzz Logistics has attracted a large client base, as well as an enviable reputation for reliability and customer service.

Although the entrepreneurs have taken risks and experienced some dark times, they are proud of themselves for not giving up. Instead, they have succeeded in creating a fun corporate culture designed to inspire creativity and flow. As a result, their employees are motivated, empowered, and productive.

Now, the day they have been waiting for has finally arrived. Katy and Lisa are sitting in JFK Airport in New York waiting for Fred to arrive from California. They had arrived from the Bismarck office just a couple of hours earlier. They are both wearing yellow and black rugby shirts—the signature Buzz Logistics uniform. Katy is holding up a sign with a big "I" printed on it . . . and Lisa has a sign printed with a big "P." When Fred walks through the airplane's ramp tunnel, they both scream and run towards him for a group hug, and hand him a Buzz Logistics rugby shirt to put on. When he is dressed in the shirt, Lisa hands Fred a sign, which has a big "O" printed on it. Then Katy asks an exiting passenger if he wouldn't mind taking a picture of the three of them with her cell phone.

Getting into position, Katy says, "On the count of three . . . one-two-three . . . BUZZ LOGISTICS!" With this exclamation, the three friends and business partners raise their signs high in the air, spelling out "I—P—O." Katy immediately sends her grandfather the picture—because of his generous investment and the hard work of Katy, Lisa, and Fred, Buzz Logistics will have a big day tomorrow morning, when the team rings the NASDAQ starting bell, celebrating their IPO. All in all, the future looks pretty bright.

Throughout this text, we have explored many different aspects of management theory and investigated a variety of management scenarios based on real-life case studies from a critical-thinking standpoint. As you have learned, managers are leaders, decision-makers, goal-setters, role models, motivators, communicators, and entrepreneurs. We hope that during your future careers as managers, you will draw on the knowledge presented in this book by using critical thinking to guide you on your path toward achieving your own goals and the goals of organizations now and into the future.

Case**Snapshot**

Chapter 18 Case: Entrepreneurship and Innovation: Square can be found on pg. 481

ADDITIONAL RESOURCES

KEY TERMS

Aggregation venture A business strategy defined by acquiring, merging, and coordinating existing market products, services, and companies. **(p. 449)**

Angel investor Individuals who provide entrepreneurs with funding and mentorship. **(p. 443)**

Business model A proposed method for creating and sustaining market value. **(p. 442)**

Creativity A process through which individuals and groups transform ideas into reality. **(p. 443)**

Discovery venture A business strategy that seeks to invent a brand-new product or service or find a new resource. **(p. 450)**

Early adopters The approximately 14 percent of a market's population that uses a new product or service after innovators have used and tested it. **(p. 440)**

Early majority The approximately 34 percent of a market's population that uses a product or service after early adopters have used it. **(p. 442)**

Entrepreneur an individual that plans, organizes, and leads high-risk business opportunities with new market value. **(p. 440)**

Entrepreneurial ecosystem a set of stakeholders that are necessary to support the innovation and creation of new market value. **(p. 443)**

Entrepreneurial skills Capacities, activities, and strengths that enable individuals to manage successfully in high-risk business environments. **(p. 440)**

Entrepreneurship Activities associated with seeking opportunities that generate new value, with an array of unknown forces. **(p. 442)**

Feasibility The degree to which a business venture is possible, given the availability of resources and technologies. **(p. 446)**

Flow The experience of immersion and loss of time when an individual achieves an optimum balance of challenge, interest, and achievement. **(p. 451)**

Initial public offering (IPO) The first time a company sells it equity shares on the stock market. **(p. 448)**

Innovation A process that results in new market value through the creation of a product or service. **(p. 440)**

Innovation adoption curve A staged model that describes the evolution of an innovation's acceptance with customers: innovators, early adopters, early majority, late majority, and laggards. **(p. 440)**

Innovators are the approximately 2 percent of a market's population that initially uses and tests a new product or service. **(p. 440)**

Laggards are the approximately 16 percent of a market's population that is last to use a product or service. **(p. 442)**

Late majority describes the approximately 34 percent of a market's population that uses a product or service after the early majority has used it. **(p. 442)**

Liquidity The measurement of available financial resources or the ability to convert an organization's assets into cash. **(p. 445)**

Meta-ideas Concepts that create, nurture, and support other concepts. **(p. 451)**

New-existing venture A business strategy defined by offering a new product or service to an existing category of consumers. **(p. 450)**

New-new venture A business strategy defined by offering a new category of consumers a new product or service, typically distinguished with higher risk and higher returns compared to new-existing ventures. **(p. 450)**

Q-level A measurement that determines the optimum level of group size and interaction to achieve successful creative output. **(p. 453)**

Scaling The degree to which a company or its business model can grow, given the necessary resources. **(p. 448)**

Start-up company A newly formed organization with limited or no operational history. **(p. 442)**

System change venture A business strategy responding to a significant change in political environments, governmental legislation, and regulations. **(p. 450)**

Transplant venture A business strategy where an idea that achieves market success in one market region is transferred to other geographic markets. **(p. 450)**

Value chain venture A business strategy that seeks to redesign or augment an offering in an existing business or management process, such as outsourcing of information technology and research. **(p. 450)**

Value creation The activities and processes that increase the worth of a product or service. **(p. 448)**

Venture capital Funding that supports the starting and growing of high-risk business ventures. **(p. 442)**

Wave venture A business strategy defined by a systemic change in business and market environments. **(p. 450)**

IN REVIEW

18.1 | Define the process of entrepreneurship and the role of managers as entrepreneurs.

Entrepreneurs are individuals that plan, organize, and lead high-risk business opportunities with new market value. The role of the entrepreneur has become especially important during these financially turbulent times. Successful entrepreneurs possess the skills, attitudes, and behaviors to change old, established systems for the better in order to benefit society and the greater community. As the business landscape continues to evolve, and new global innovations come into play, there is more emphasis on *Entrepreneurship*, which are activities associated with seeking opportunities that generate new value, with an array of unknown forces.

18.2 | Describe the opportunities and challenges that affect growth for new ventures.

Successful entrepreneurs are able to identify a market opportunity, or a gap in the market with which to attract a diverse customer base. As the business grows, it becomes a serious competitor possibly overtaking other competition operating in a similar market. Successful start-up companies recognize the importance of attracting the best talent and nurturing that talent within an appropriate organizational culture.

Some start-ups fail before they even get off the ground. However, even after start-ups are well established, entrepreneurs must retain and attract new customers consistently to stay ahead of the competition. When starting a growth company, many entrepreneurs look to hire executive managers with the right experience and contacts to make the company a success. While attracting the best talent is essential for any company, some start-ups have made expensive mistakes by paying top dollar to recruit outside executive managers, which resulted in a power struggle, with the manager pushing the firm in one direction and the entrepreneurial team fighting to maintain the original vision.

18.3 | Compare and contrast different types of ventures that entrepreneurs create.

An *aggregation venture* is a business strategy defined by acquiring, merging, and coordinating existing market products, services, and companies. This allows the company to achieve scale quickly and grow almost immediately, increasing revenues by capturing large market segments. A *discovery venture* is a business strategy that seeks to invent a brand new product/service or find a new resource. A *new-existing venture* is a business strategy defined by offering an existing category of consumers a new product or service. A *new-new venture* is a business strategy defined by offering a new category of consumers a new product or service, typically distinguished with higher-risk and higher-returns compared to new-existing ventures. This type of venture strategy carries more risks as its success is dependent on attracting a new segment of the market with a brand-new product. *System change venture* is a business strategy responding to a significant change in political environments, governmental legislation, and regulations. A *transplant venture* is a business strategy where an idea that achieves market success in one market region is transferred to other geographic markets. A *value chain venture* is a business strategy that seeks to redesign or augment an offering in an existing business or management process, such as outsourcing of information technology and research. A *wave venture* is a business strategy defined by a systemic change in business and market environments.

18.4 | Explain how managers lead a creative process with individuals and teams.

The right group of people collaborating on a project gives rise to *meta-ideas* which are concepts that create, nurture, and support other concepts. This means that sharing ideas inspires an inexhaustible supply of new ideas. Constructive criticism is far more effective than brainstorming; rather than tearing people to shreds, he believes that criticism that is always backed up by a supporting or new idea sparks new creative processes.

To achieve a creative "flow" in the workplace, employees must be provided with the following work conditions: clear goals, immediate feedback, balance between opportunity and capacity, a deepened sense of concentration, living in the present, personal control, an altered sense of time, and loss of ego.

18.5 | Outline how entrepreneurs use innovation to grow global opportunities.

Entrepreneurs can expand their market opportunities by providing customers with innovative products and services. The Buzz Logistics case provides a good example of this process.

SELF-TEST

18.1 | Define the process of entrepreneurship and the role of managers as entrepreneurs.

1. Individuals who plan, organize, and lead high-risk business opportunities are known as:
   a. Venture capitalists
   b. Oligarchs
   c. Entrepreneur
   d. High-risk initiators

2. _____ is a process that results in new market value through the creation of a product or service.

3. List and briefly describe the five stages of the innovation adoption curve model.

18.2 | Describe the opportunities and challenges that affect growth for new ventures.

4. Which of the following is *not* a likely growth accelerant that can affect the performance of a new venture?
   a. Market opportunity
   b. Human resources
   c. Marketing/branding
   d. Stock dividends

5. No start-up will survive without the appropriate financing and _____, which is the measurement of available financial resources or the ability to convert an organization's assets into cash.

6. Value creation has to do with the activities and processes that increase the worth of a new venture's common stock.
   a. True
   b. False

7. The first time a company sells its equity shares on the stock market is known as:
   a. An initial public offering (IPO)
   b. An equity venture
   c. A stock option
   d. Angel investing

18.3 | **Compare** and contrast different types of ventures that entrepreneurs create.

8. A business strategy defined by acquiring, merging, and coordinating existing market products, services, and companies is:
   a. Aggregation venture
   b. Discovery venture
   c. System change venture
   d. Value change venture

9. A business strategy responding to a significant change in political environments, governmental legislation, and regulations is:
   a. Aggregation venture
   b. Discovery venture
   c. System change venture
   d. Value change venture

10. A business strategy that seeks to redesign or augment an offering in an existing business or management process, such as outsourcing of information technology and research is:
    a. Aggregation venture
    b. Discovery venture
    c. System change venture
    d. Value change venture

18.4 | **Explain** how managers lead a creative process with individuals and teams.

11. Meta-ideas are concepts that create, nurture, and support other concepts.
    a. True
    b. False

12. _____ is the experience of immersion and loss of time when an individual achieves an optimum balance of challenge, interest, and achievement.

18.5 | **Outline** how entrepreneurs use innovation to grow global opportunities.

13. By constantly improving services and products for customers through continuous innovation, entrepreneurs can establish a reputation for reliability and customer service.
    a. True
    b. False

CHAPTER EXERCISE

Creativity Exercise: The 30-Circle Test

Convert as many of the following circles into drawings as you can in 60 seconds.

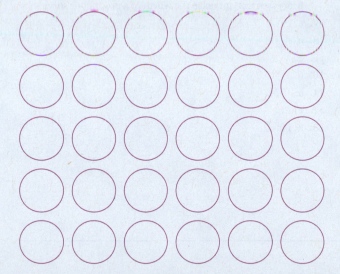

How did you do? Were you able to convert all 30 circles into pictures in 60 seconds?

The creator of this test, Robert McKim, an engineering professor at Stanford University, noted that many people choose to draw something, such as a smiley face, and then assume that they can't make any additional facial expressions. Consequently, they would then struggle in an effort to identify 30 different concepts to fill in the circles. One way to complete the task effectively is create quick variations on a single theme, like facial expressions. There was no rule stating that you couldn't draw 30 facial expressions in the circles—but it's a self-imposed constraint that many people place upon themselves!

SELF-ASSESSMENT

Entrepreneurial Skills Self-Assessment

For each statement, circle the number that best describes you based on the following scale:

Not at all Accurate	Somewhat Accurate	A little Accurate	Mostly Accurate	Completely Accurate
1	2	3	4	5

1. I believe that I control my own destiny.

    1   2   3   4   5

2. I have a high energy level.

    1   2   3   4   5

3. I have a strong need to achieve.

    1   2   3   4   5

4. I believe in myself and my ideas.

    1   2   3   4   5

5. Once I get an idea, I like to implement it as quickly as possible.

    1   2   3   4   5

6. It doesn't bother me if I don't have all the facts or information I need to make a decision.

    1   2   3   4   5

7. I believe that hard work and effort will be rewarded eventually.

    1   2   3   4   5

8. I enjoy working hard and expending effort toward my goals.

    1   2   3   4   5

9. It is important for me to accomplish my goals and objectives.

    1   2   3   4   5

10. I am a self-confident person.

    1   2   3   4   5

11. I am impatient when it comes to implementing my ideas.

    1   2   3   4   5

12. I am comfortable in situations that I do not fully understand.

    1   2   3   4   5

Scoring:

Add the numbers circled above: _____

Interpretation:

48 and above = You have outstanding entrepreneurial skills. You should consider carefully the possibility of becoming an entrepreneur.

25 − 47 = You have moderate entrepreneurial skills. You may want to consider the possibility of becoming an entrepreneur, although you may have a few characteristics that will make it challenging for you.

24 and below = You may want to consider working for an established company that will provide relative stability and lower risk than being an entrepreneur.

SELF-TEST ANSWER KEY

1. c.

2. Innovation

3. *Innovators* are the approximately 2 percent of a market's population that initially uses and tests a new product or service. *Early adopters* are the approximately 14 percent of a market's population that uses a new product or service after innovators have used and tested it. The *early majority* is the approximately 34 percent of a market's population that uses a product or service after early adopters have used it. The *late majority* are the approximately 34 percent of a market's population that uses a product or service after the early majority has used it. *Laggards* are the approximately 16 percent of a market's population that is last to use a product or service.

4. d.

5. Liquidity

6. b; False. Value creation has to do with the activities and processes that increase the worth of a product or service.

7. a.

8. a.

9. c.

10. d.

11. a; True.

12. Flow

13. a; True.

Notes

_____

_____

CASE STUDIES

Chapter 1 | MANAGEMENT IN THE 21ST CENTURY

Case Study: Facebook

Facebook. Google. Zappos. No longer do we idealize the stoic, steely gaze of the chief executive officer (CEO) toward a certain horizon. Today's leaders must be nimble, less the archer than the quick-footed ball player, ever mindful of the wild, unpredictable passes that come from seemingly anywhere—even from the bleachers. In the age of crumbling hierarchy and mass democratization of information, public opinion is no longer formed by a privileged few behind closed doors and subsequently doled out to the masses. Both inside the walls of company headquarters and beyond, the people lead, and the leaders follow.

Oft-covered in the media, Facebook is both a leader and trend-setter in the world of social media and Internet-based companies more broadly. Yet despite this unique stature, Facebook is also in many ways the quintessential example of a company plunging through the unsteady waters of change in the age of information—as true of more traditional business giants like Delta Airlines and General Electric (GE) as it is to a lesser but still significant extent to the corner mom-and-pop retail shop or restaurant. For better or worse, Facebook must constantly be sensitive to the whims and moods of at least three powerful "interest groups": its users (consumers), its advertisers (its bread and butter), and its own internal team, who shape the culture and to a large degree hold the fate of the company in its hands.

External Pressures

With close to 1 billion users (nearly one-seventh of the Earth's entire population), Facebook is still determining how to cultivate and turn a profit from such rich yet fickle soil. Facebook, valued at a still startlingly rich $55 billion at the end of 2012,* has often found itself caught between pleasing its users—cultivating the soil—and its advertisers, who keep the lights on and its shareholders happy (the company went public in May 2012). But change has always been part of Facebook culture; consider that since its founding in 2004, Facebook has altered its tagline nine times, reflecting not only the "start-up mindset" but a more fundamental (if essential) fiery reverence for constant, rapid evolution tempered by a corporate sensitivity to the external environment of public opinion.

Facebook has become a conduit for broad-based activism, often to its own detriment. Here are a few of many notable examples: Users were enraged after Facebook introduced Beacon in November 2007, an advertising system in which users' purchases or activities on some 40 partner sites were revealed to their Facebook friends. The company was forced to backpedal when more than 70,000 members organized a Facebook protest group led by political activist organization MoveOn.org, and discontinued Beacon in 2009 as a result. Nonetheless, Facebook acquiesced to a $9.5-million settlement in a class action lawsuit on behalf of 3.6 million of its users, which included an agreement to finance a "digital trust fund" of over $6 million for organizations that study online privacy. Facebook CEO Mark Zuckerberg publicly apologized in 2007, though the company never formally admitted to any wrongdoing.

In 2009, Facebook again changed its tune in response to public pressure. When the website made fundamental changes to its design and terms, more than 2.5 million joined a group on Facebook's own site called "Millions Against Facebook's New Layout and Terms of Service." At the time, Facebook had deleted a provision saying that users could remove their content at any time, and added new language stating that it could retain a user's content and licenses even after he or she cancelled the account. After briefly going on the offensive, Facebook agreed to withdraw these changes, with CEO Zuckerberg announcing, "We concluded that returning to our previous terms was the right thing for now . . . We need to make sure the terms reflect the principles and values of the people using the service."

Nor was 2012 immune from controversy. Kevin Systrom, a cofounder of the photo-sharing site Instagram, which Facebook purchased for $1 billion in April 2012, reacted within days of the outset of a mass protest over Instagram's announcement of changes to its service terms, which saw thousands of users, even *National Geographic* magazine, threatening to jump ship. Systrom apologized in a blog post, writing, "We've heard loud and clear that many users are confused and upset about what the changes mean . . . I'm writing this today to let you know we're listening and to commit to you that we will be doing more to answer your questions, fix any mistakes, and eliminate the confusion."[1] As Facebook and its growing family of subsidiaries continue their tightrope walk of pleasing users while courting advertisers, the Instagram embarrassment will surely not be the last of these struggles.

Internal Culture

The internal culture of Facebook is similarly indicative of management responding to new, fluid expectations of an empowered, opinionated group—its workforce. Even the workplace environment reflects a more open, less hierarchical mindset, a 57-acre campus (with a 22-acre expansion in the works) designed to please the masses of its 3,500+ employees rather than the tastes and whims of a privileged few. Gensler Architects was charged with "undesigning" this vast territory, leaving plenty of room for tree-shaded open spaces and amenities like sushi bars, barber's shops, and doctor's offices, a place in which long hours don't seem so draining, where "the employees are really happy to hang out," according to John Tenanes, director of global real estate for Facebook. The vibrant, stimulating environment is crafted to appeal to the company's diverse army of mostly young or young-ish professionals, who, like so many today, want—and expect—their career to contribute to quality of life rather than merely sustain life. It also allows for "ongoing experimentation for a culture that hasn't yet fully developed," reflected Tenanes, "We do not want to allow a rigid standards and approvals process where you end up with a cube farm and everyone is miserable."[2]

A freshly hired Facebook engineer provides an insider's account of the fluid acculturation and work process indicative of work and life under 21st-century management, "Before Facebook, I'd always been assigned to a team before my first interview at a company," wrote Ben Genzler in a Facebook post entitled "Bootcamp: Growing Culture at Facebook" in January 2010, reflecting on Facebook's preference to move new employees into positions *after* they demonstrated their strengths and preferences "live" in the Facebook team environment. "To think I had control over my own destiny at Facebook was at the same time empowering—and more than a little nerve-wracking!"[3]

Genzler was not alone. Since 2008, every new Facebook engineer—"from software engineers right out of college to engineering directors with Ph.Ds," according to a company video—is required to attend a six-week "boot camp." Described aptly by Mike Swift in the *San Jose Mercury News* in 2012 as "one part employee orientation, one part software training program, and one part fraternity/sorority rush," the idea is to teach newbies Facebook's technology and practices while, perhaps most important, indoctrinating them into its progressive, risk-taking, irreverent, and collaborative culture, where anyone can change the world, and indeed is expected to do so. Within days of beginning boot camp, for example, an engineer may be pushing out new software changes—live—to several million users. The reverence to a notion Zuckerberg has labeled "hacking" is one such principal instilled by this "trial by fire." Far from the nefarious connotation that the word *hacking* has earned in public discourse, "[hacking] is about being unafraid to break things in order to make them better," said Paul Buchheit, a Silicon Valley legend who was creator and lead developer of Gmail, and who was with Facebook from 2009 to 2010 after his startup FriendFeed was acquired. "The root of the hacker mind-set is 'There's a better way,' " he says, "Just because people have been doing it the same way since the beginning of time, I'm going to make it better."[4]

As technology becomes more complex and the public more savvy and discerning, Facebook, like all companies navigating the new management environment, must continue to become ever more nimble and responsive in its step—while somehow retaining the "soul" upon which it was founded. This is a delicate dance for any organization, even one as change-friendly as Facebook. . . . And perhaps the very fact that Facebook exudes dynamism from its core will allow it to continue to thrive. As David Kirkpatrick wrote in his 2010 book *The Facebook Effect*, "Facebook know[s] that things on the Internet are constantly changing at an extremely rapid rate, and the only way any organization can stay alive is to be unbelievably dynamic." Here's hoping Facebook can keep up with the breakneck speed of progress, of which they are at once conduit, creator, and subject.

*In January 2011, financial analyst Albert Babayev posited a "conservative" estimate of Facebook's 2013 market cap as around $224 billion.

Questions for Discussion

1. Chapter 1 discusses four "success factors" for organizations. Which of these factors do you see operating within Facebook?

2. Which of the four functions of management discussed in Chapter 1 stand out within this Facebook case?

3. Is Facebook an example of a "sustaining" type of management? Why or why not?

Sources

1. McGirt, Ellen, "Most Innovative Companies 2010: Facebook," *Fast Company*, August 24, 2012; http://www.fastcompany.com/mic/2010/profile/facebook; accessed January 2, 2013.
2. Swift, Mike, "Facebook Uses 'Hacker Bootcamp' to Train Engineers," *San Jose Mercury News*, April 18, 2012; http://www.standard.net/stories/2012/04/18/facebook-uses-hacker-bootcamp-train-engineers; accessed December 4, 2012.
3. Crum, Chris, "Facebook Provides a Look at Facebook Bootcamp," Webpronews, October 10, 2011; http://www.webpronews.com/facebook-provides-a-look-at-facebook-bootcamp-2011-10; accessed December 13, 2012.
4. Kumar, Nikhil, "U-turn for Instagram as it scraps controversial changes," *The Independent*, December 21, 2012; http://www.independent.co.uk/news/media/online/uturn-for-instagram-as-it-scraps-controversial-changes-8429430.html; accessed December 27, 2012.
5. Davison, Janet, "The Instagram dust-up: Is anything really free online?" CBC News, December 28, 2012; http://www.cbc.ca/news/technology/story/2012/12/27/f-instagram-social-media-terms-of-service-free.html; accessed December 27, 2012.
6. "Instagram, Facebook, and Media Controversies Lead of Social Media," Journalism.org, April 9–13, 2012; http://www.journalism.org/index_report/instagram_facebook_and_media_controversies_lead_social_media; accessed December 27, 2012.
7. Facebook blog, "Update on Terms," February 18, 2009; http://blog.facebook.com/blog.php?post=54746167130; accessed December 28, 2012.
8. Hoge, Patrick, "Zuckerberg Steams through Controversies," *Upstart Business Journal*, December 30, 2010; http://upstart.bizjournals.com/companies-executives/2010/12/30/zuckerberg-steams-through-controversies.html?page=all; accessed December 27, 2012.
9. Khan, Urmee, "Facebook Controversy over Right to Delete Personal Information," *The Telegraph*, February 17, 2009; http://www.telegraph.co.uk/technology/facebook/4680220/Facebook-controversy-over-right-to-delete-personal-information.html; accessed December 28, 2012.
10. Petterssen, Edvard, "Facebook's 'Beacon' Settlement Upheld in Privacy Lawsuit," Bloomberg, September 20, 2012; http://www.bloomberg.com/news/2012-09-20/facebook-s-beacon-settlement-upheld-in-privacy-lawsuit.html; accessed December 27, 2012.
11. Guynn, Jessica, "Judge Approves $9.5-million Settlement of Lawsuit over Facebook's Beacon Program," *Los Angeles Times*, March 18, 2010; http://articles.latimes.com/2010/mar/18/business/la-fi-facebook18-2010mar18; accessed December 27, 2012.
12. Taylor, Chris, "Facebook in 2013: More Growing Pains Ahead," Mashable, December 28, 2012. http://mashable.com/2012/12/28/facebook-predictions-2013/http://newsroom.fb.com/; accessed January 4, 2013.
13. Gertzfield, Ben, "Bootcamp: Growing Culture at Facebook," January 19, 2010; http://www.facebook.com/notes/facebook-engineering/bootcamp-growing-culture-at-facebook/249415563919; accessed December 13, 2012.
14. Weistein-Donator, Nathan, "Revised Facebook Campus Plans: More Rooftop Trees, Less Zigzags," *Silicon Valley Business Journal*, December 17, 2012; http://www.bizjournals.com/sanjose/blog/2012/12/revised-facebook-campus-plans-more.html; accessed December 28, 2012.

Chapter 2 | THE EVOLUTION OF MANAGEMENT

Case Study: Valve Corporation

Gabe Newell was a founder and is the CEO of Valve Corporation, a Bellevue, Washington–based video game maker founded by former Microsoft employees Newell and Mike

Harrington—or that's what it says on paper somewhere, anyway. Indicative of the loose, fluid structure (or lack thereof) at Valve, Greg Coomer, a designer and artist who was one of the first employees at Valve, said of Newell, "I think he's technically the CEO, but it's funny that I'm not even sure of that."

Pick a Desk and Run Around the Office

That's because Valve Corporation is not exactly, well, the archetypal vision of a "corporate" environment. Valve doesn't use formal titles, except in the hiring process so as to not scare away prospective applicants that might find the titleless work environment a bit peculiar. Here, desks move on wheels so that employees can relocate anywhere in the office and form work groups at a moment's notice. Employees also don't have strict job duties; they fill in where they think they can contribute the most. Valve has no formal bosses, pay is often determined by peers, and employees create their own schedules and workdays.

Valve personifies the trend of recent years to flatten out hierarchies within companies, reducing the role of middle management where information and processes can get clogged, enabling, in theory, a freer flow of communication and increased productivity. "When you're an entertainment company that's spent the last decade going out of its way to recruit the most intelligent, innovative, talented people on Earth, telling them to sit at a desk and do what they're told obliterates 99 percent of their value," states the now-famous employee handbook, which generated buzz in 2012 when it was leaked onto the Internet. "This company is yours to steer. Toward opportunities and away from risks."[5]

Valve developed Steam, an online service that is basically the iTunes of the video gaming world. Though some say it's overambitious, the 300-employee company is competing with Google to develop wearable computing—like video games played through goggles or glasses where you might literally see a zombie coming out of your own bathroom at home. Even competitors acknowledge that Valve is on the cutting edge of the industry. Valve is responsible for Half-Life—a game which has received numerous "Game of the Year" awards and is still widely regarded as influential among its peers; Half Life 2, Left 4 Dead, and Counterstrike, are among other wildly popular and industry-shaping games.

In other flat (also called "lattice") organizations, lines of communication are directly from one person to the other with no intermediary; there is no fixed or assigned authority; natural leadership is identified by those who follow; and objectives are set by the same employees who have to realize them. In many flat organizations, including Valve, associates decide how much they think their peers should be paid but are never allowed to vote for their own salaries. Teams at Valve also decide together if a team member isn't working out and should be let go.

"We don't have any management, and nobody 'reports to' anybody else," states Valve's employee handbook. Valve said it was rare that anyone chose to leave the company, and when someone did, it was often for something like a sick parent needing help.

There are challenges to the flat approach—like lack of accountability. Though the environment can trigger creativity and collaboration, some still leave for more traditional companies that feel more structured and organized. Retaining highly motivated individuals is critical for effectiveness within a flat organization. Discipline and motivation need to be off the chart, but unfortunately, the types of employees that a flat organization requires in order to thrive represent a small segment of the workforce. This type of structure does not work for everyone. Other challenges include talent management, appraising and motivating employees, and enforcing any policy the company might have. There is often a lack of standardization to ensure that salaries and benefits are competitive, internally and externally. Working in a flat organization may feel disorganized and chaotic, which, depending on the employee, can either be a great source of inspiration, or great frustration.

"I think of it as being a lot like evolution—messy, with lots of inefficiencies that normal companies don't have—but producing remarkable results, things that would never have seen the light of day under normal hierarchical management," said Michael Abrash, an engineer at Valve, "Almost by definition, it's a great place for the right sort of creative people to work."[6]

Questions for Discussion

1. What approaches to management discussed in Chapter 2 are best reflected within Valve?

2. In what ways is the humanistic approach to management in practice at Valve?

3. What would Chester Barnard and/or Jay Forrester have to say about the inner workings of Valve in terms of a balanced approach to management?

Sources

1. *Ramblings in Valve Time*, blog; http://blogs.valvesoftware.com/abrash/valve-how-i-got-here-what-its-like-and-what-im-doing-2/; accessed January 4, 2013.

2. Silverman, Rachel Emma, "Who's the Boss? There Isn't One," *The Wall Street Journal*, June 19, 2012; http://online.wsj.com/article/SB10001424052702303379204577474953586383604.html; accessed January 3, 2013.

3. Wingfield, Nick. "Game Player without a Rule Book," *The New York Times*, September 12, 2012; http://www.nytimes.com/2012/09/09/technology/valve-a-video-game-maker-with-few-rules.html?pagewanted=all&_r=0; accessed January 3, 2013.

Chapter 3 | CRITICAL THINKING FOR MANAGERS

Case Study: Airbnb

Share and share alike, and save while you're at it. It's the mantra—indeed, the way of life—behind the mammoth rise of social media and a plethora of recent companies and Internet groups, including Craigslist, Couchsurfing, Zipcar, Freecycle, Groupon, and dozens of others. In an increasingly connected and global world, where users outnumber resources yet are simultaneously beleaguered by an ongoing economic downturn, the "sharing economy" leverages consumers' hunger in ways that encourage them to maintain their lifestyles without pillaging their bank accounts. Airbnb has tapped into the budget traveler and vacationer's market to become one of Silicon Valley's most lauded, and imitated, successes. And unlike some of these imitators, it's got the financial flex to continue its globetrotting path of growth and innovation.

What is Airbnb? It's a bed and breakfast (BnB)–inspired site that links travelers with open rooms, or even apartments or homes, of private individuals in cities around the world (192 at current count). Traveling to Paris but can't afford the $125+ per night hotel room? Consider, instead, staying in Pierre's flat, for a much more palpable $60 per night. Or, say you're Pierre, and you just lost your job, or are looking to save up for a bigger place. Advertising your spare room on Airbnb and hosting a few strangers for a night or two might just be a great way to earn a few extra euros—just create your Airbnb listing, upload photos, answer a few questions, and agree to giving the company a 15 percent cut on your take. Airbnb is also an attractive alternative for traveling executives or those in transition, looking for or perhaps poised to start a new job in a new city, but lacking the finances, or maybe just the desire, to invest in a pricey hotel stay.

While not for everyone, Airbnb surely has captured a niche. It's entertained over 4.5 million bookings on 100,000 active listings in 192 countries—$500 million in transactions in 2011, says the privately held company. Venture funders, including Y Combinator, Greylock Partners, Sequoia Capital, Andreessen Horowitz, DST Global Solutions, and General Catalyst Partners, helped the company raise $119.8 million, with A-GRade Investments' partners, Ashton Kutcher and Guy Oseary, pitching in an additional undisclosed amount. Airbnb recently achieved Series B funding that valued the company at $2.5 billion. The company's CEO has boldly claimed that Airbnb will surpass Hilton in the number of rooms that it has filled by the end of 2013.

Airbnb has shown a willingness to invest for success. Early in the site's history (it was founded in San Francisco, California, in 2008 by Brian Chesky and Joe Gebbia, then-roommates who made their rent by selling cheap lodging on their air mattress to out-of-town guests), the company was having difficulty booking rooms due to users' substandard photos of their offerings. To mitigate the problem, the site began offering free professional photography services to thousands of its users. It's also introducing a new feature that includes neighborhood advice from thousands of seasoned reviewers and travel enthusiasts.

"We created a framework for keeping ourselves focused," said Chesky. "Most startups are only focused on growing faster. We realized that was the wrong thing to focus on solely—that would not make us a great company."[7]

Airbnb (and other members of the "sharing economy") have come under regulatory scrutiny as of late, but it seems that the movement is too strong, too relevant, and too great in number to be quashed any time soon.

Questions for Discussion

1. What, if anything, might disrupt the "sharing economy trend"? Is the sharing economy here to stay?

2. Assume that you were advising the new founders of Airbnb about how to continue the company's success. How could our discussion of critical thinking help you as you advise these two men?

Sources

1. Harrison, Lindsay, "Airbnb CEO Brian Chesky On Weighing Your Priorities," *Fast Company*, November 26, 2012; http://www.fastcompany.com/3003085/airbnb-ceo-brian-chesky-weighing-your-priorities; accessed December 10, 2013.

2. Fast Company Staff, "The World's 50 Most Innovative Companies," *Fast Company*, November 15, 2012; http://www.fastcompany.com/most-innovative-companies/2012/airbnb; accessed December 10, 2013.

3. Scwartz, Ariel. "How Airbnb's New Neighborhoods Feature Can Revive Local Economies," *Fast Company co.Exist*, September 13, 2012; http://www.fastcoexist.com/1680900/how-airbnbs-new-neighborhoods-feature-can-revive-local-economies - 1/5/2013; accessed December 10, 2013.

4. Lynley, Matthew, "Twelve Startups to Watch in 2013," *The Wall Street Journal*, January 12, 2013; http://blogs.wsj.com/digits/2013/01/02/twelve-startups-to-watch-in-2013/?KEYWORDS=airbnb.

Chapter 4 | ORGANIZATIONS AND CHANGE MANAGEMENT

Case Study: AstraZeneca

There was a day, not long ago, when the mighty pharmaceutical company seemed an unstoppable giant. Yet for those companies that resist diversification as the world seeks better, cheaper health care solutions, and with the "patent cliff" (which refers to loss of revenue when there is a drop in sales following the expiration of a patent) eroding beneath their feet, the prescription for restoring many of these former powerhouses to health is elusive.

The United Kingdom's second-largest drug maker AstraZeneca, founded in 1999 as a result of a merger between Swedish company Astra and British company Zeneca, has been scrambling to make changes to quell steep losses, tumbling stock prices, and shareholder panic, including the installment of a new CEO (Pascal Soriot) in June 2012. In October 2012, the company's net profit plunged by over half, to $1.53 billion from $3.48 billion. Revenue fell by 19 percent to $6.68 billion, due in large part to an 82 percent sales drop of Seroquel IR, its popular schizophrenia drug, in the United States, among other staggering defeats.

Tangled in the global trend of countries trying to decrease health care costs by allowing cheaper drugs to enter the market, among other things, over the next five years, legislative changes will see the drug maker losing patent protection on around 50 percent of its top-selling drugs, leaving its market vulnerable to generic, much cheaper competition. The patent loss includes Losec (known as Prilosec in the United States), which was once the world's best-selling drug, with sales reaching over $6 billion during its heyday in 2000; the breast cancer drug, Arimidex; and the U.S. patent on the popular antipsychotic medication Seroquel, which currently rakes in annual sales of almost $1.6 billion.

As if this weren't enough, other major cash cows are on the chopping block, too: in 2016, Crestor, Astra's biggest-selling drug, loses patent protection; the same is true in the United States in 2014 for Nexium, an acid reflux treatment.

The chips appear to be stacked against the traditional name-brand drug giants. Research and development ("R&D")—not to mention licensing, marketing, and launching a new drug—is a long and uncertain road that takes a mindboggling outpouring of time and money. A 2003 study by the consulting firm Bain & Company reported that the aggregate cost for introducing a new drug to market (including the money and elbow grease necessarily invested into versions that fail) was nearly $1.7 billion per drug. More recently, Matthew Herper of *Forbes* reviewed 15 years of financial statements from several major drug makers, including AstraZeneca. By Herper's estimate, AstraZeneca was able to bring only five drugs to market during this time, spending nearly $12 billion per drug.

Though it may represent a worst-case scenario, AstraZeneca is not suffering alone. Herper reported that GSK, Sanofi, Roche, and Pfizer all spent around $8 billion per drug that was approved (the most cost-effective drug-maker, Herper found, was Amgen, introducing nine approved drugs at the still-nothing-to-sneeze-at $3.7 billion per medicine). The challenges, including the lumbering timeline of the R&D process, mean that as patents expire, the losses aren't replaced rapidly enough by new drugs to boost the bottom line, a problem that generics don't have to face.

With Soriot at the helm, AstraZeneca is fighting back—but is it too little too late? The company has been accused of ignoring the future by resisting moves into consumer health care, generics, and niche drugs like some of its better-faring peers have done. During Soriot's predecessor's tenure, major acquisitions (including the $15.6 billion purchase of MedImmune, a Maryland-based biotechnology company, in 2007), served to beef up AstraZeneca's offerings in protein-based biologic drugs and included the lucrative nasal flu vaccine FluMist, but the growth was not significant enough to stop the bleeding by a very meaningful degree. Other moves have included mass layoffs and restructurings and slashing of overhead. But AstraZeneca's future is still uncertain.

Analysts now believe that more buyouts may be AstraZeneca's only option. Had AstraZeneca gotten its house in order a few years back, perhaps a mergers and acquisitions (M&A) strategy would not be so critical now. But as Navid Malik, an analyst at Cenkos, observed, "they needed revenues yesterday.... If you can't grow your way out of your problems, you buy your way out of them." He added, "Several single-digit billion-dollar deals don't solve short- to medium-term issues."[8]

"As expected, the company's financial performance in 2012 largely reflects the ongoing impact from the loss of exclusivity for several brands in key markets, as well as the challenges that confront the pharmaceutical industry as a whole," Mr. Soriot has said, "My priority is to restore the company to growth and scientific leadership."[9] Time will tell if Soriot follows analysts' advice and how AstraZeneca and other big drug companies will fare as the world of health care continues processing momentous change.

Questions for Discussion

1. What aspects of AstraZeneca's external environment are affecting its success?

2. If you were a top manager at AstraZeneca, what would you do to your internal environment to help you manage these external factors?

3. Can you think of an example of a company who failed because it did not consider important elements in its internal or external environment? Explain.

Sources

1. Hirschler, Ben, and Sinead Cruise, "Analysis: New AstraZeneca Boss Can't Dodge Taking Risks," *Reuters,* December 13, 2012; http://www.reuters.com/article/2012/12/13/us-astrazeneca-strategy-idUSBRE8BC0WT20121213; accessed December 15, 2012.

2. Walen, Jeane, and Benoit Faucon, "Counterfeit Cancer Medicines Multiply," *The Wall Street Journal*, December 31, 2012; http://online.wsj.com/article/SB10001424127887323320404578211492452353034.html?KEYWORDS=A; accessed January 5, 2013.

3. Kendall, Brent, "Cholesterol Drug's Patent Upheld," *The Wall Street Journal*, December 14, 2012; http://online.wsj.com/article/SB10001424127887324481204578179540572414544.html?KEYWORDS=AstraZeneca; accessed January 5, 2013.

4. Hodgson, Jessica, Marta Falconi, and Mimosa Spencer, "'Patent Cliff' Hits Europe Drug Makers," *The Wall Street Journal*, October 25, 2012; http://online.wsj.com/article/SB1000142405297020389740457807788234880942 0.html?KEYWORDS=AstraZeneca; accessed January 5, 2013.

5. Pollack, Andrew, "AstraZeneca CEO to Step Down," *The New York Times*, April 26, 2012; http://www.nytimes.com/2012/04/27/business/astrazeneca-ceo-to-step-down.html?_r=0; accessed January 6, 2013.

6. Telegraph Staff and Agencies, "AstraZeneca Sales Hurt by Patent Expiries," *The Telegraph*, October 12, 2012; http://www.telegraph.co.uk/finance/newsbysector/pharmaceuticalsandchemicals/9632470/AstraZeneca-sales-hurt-by-patent-expiries.html; accessed January 5, 2013.

7. Cooper, Rachel, "AstraZeneca is in need of radical surgery after chief David Brennan retires," *The Telegraph*, April 26, 2012; http://www.telegraph.co.uk/finance/newsbysector/pharmaceuticalsandchemicals/9229620/AstraZeneca-is-in-need-of-radical-surgery-after-chief-David-Brennan-retires.html; accessed December 10, 2012.

8. "Astrazeneca Seeks a Remedy for Its Patent Pain," *The Telegraph*, April 21, 2012; http://www.telegraph.co.uk/finance/newsbysector/pharmaceuticalsandchemicals/9218420/AstraZeneca-seeks-a-remedy-for-its-patent-pain.html; accessed January 7, 2013.

9. Hough, Jack, "Looking Beyond the Patent Cliff," *Barron's*, December 8, 2012; http://online.barrons.com/article/SB50001424052748703555704578157382328150460.html?mod=BOL_twm_fs#articleTabs_article%3D1; accessed December 10, 2013.

10. Herper, Matthew, "The Truly Staggering Cost of Inventing New Drugs," *Forbes*, February 10, 2012; http://www.forbes.com/sites/matthewherper/2012/02/10/the-truly-staggering-cost-of-inventing-new-drugs/; accessed January 3, 2013.

Chapter 5 | DIVERSITY IN A GLOBAL ECONOMY

Case Study: Zumba

Zumba isn't just a class that blends dance with exercise: it is billed as a "fitness-party," and what a party it has become. Zumba's creators and instructors have managed to see the Latin-dance style workout reach over 150 countries in just over 10 years. With over 14 million people taking at least one Zumba class a week, the company has generated enough dedicated instructors (numbering some 100,000) and followers to be named *Inc.* magazine's 2012 Company of the Year. The company has also extended its international brand into clothing, music, and charitable giving.

Beginnings

From its inception, Zumba has been a globally minded company. Founder Alberto "Beto" Perez hails from Cali, Colombia, and calls the creation of the now-worldwide fitness-party a "happy accident." After arriving at an aerobics class that he was set to teach, Perez realized he had forgotten the tape he intended to play for his class. Perez reached into his bag and pulled out some of his personal music—primarily salsa and merengue. Rather than count repetitions over the music, Perez allowed the music to take the class on a journey. Gone were stiff moves and students trying to imitate steps in lockstep. Perez served more as a liaison between his class and the music, allowing each student to have his or her own personal connection with it. Participants in the off-the-cuff class "couldn't stop smiling," Perez recalled.

Expansion

After experimenting with and honing his new fitness-party-style workout, Perez traveled to Miami, Florida, in 2001. There he met Colombian entrepreneurs Alberto Perlman and Alberto Aghion, with whom he created Zumba Fitness. The trio's goals were never small: they always wanted to "expand the brand all over the world." After selling hundreds of thousands of Zumba DVDs through Fitness Quest, Perez, Perlman, and Aghion made the decision to branch out into group instruction. By 2005, there were 700 trained and certified Zumba instructors. Business skyrocketed from there; according to Perlman, the company grew by a staggering 4,000 percent between 2007 and 2010.

How did Zumba see such dizzying growth in such a short time? Part of the answer lies in the company's philosophy. Zumba customers instructors have said the "joy" that the music and dance fitness-party brings them is infectious—they want to share it with others. Despite its growth, that "joy" still plays a major role in Zumba's business practices today. Staff members at the headquarters refer to it as "FEJ," or "Freeing, Electrifying Joy," and it affects every decision made. Zumba relies on creating "FEJ" in order to attract and retain customers and instructors.

Another reason for its rapid ascension is Zumba's faith and investment in a diverse cache of instructors. The Zumba Academy was created in 2005 to license new instructors, followed quickly by the Zumba Instructor Network (ZIN), a resource tool intended to turn instructors into entrepreneurs. The ZIN gives access to marketing materials, discounted workshops, music CDs and choreography DVDs, ways to earn money by selling Zumba apparel, and much more.

When expanding into new markets, Zumba doesn't seek out masters in business administration (MBAs). Instead, it hires top-tier, enthusiastic instructors and ensures that they have painstakingly cultivated marketing support. About half of Zumba's current annual earnings can be attributed to business outside the United States, but that figure is projected to grow considerably in the coming years.

Zumba "practitioners" demonstrate an almost cultlike fanaticism about the brand. Instructor Tania Carillo found Zumba to be the perfect way to blend culture from her native Mexico with her new home in the United States. "Through dance, people from different cultures and backgrounds can come together and forget their daily troubles," says Carillo. One woman who arranged a class to be conducted at work found it wonderful to see their "60+ clinic manager shimmying next to the 20-something nurses." One can find Zumba instructors across the world, each with a different story, but all of whom seem eager to describe that indescribable connection with the music and movement.

Zumba is becoming influential not only in the fitness industry, but also in entertainment. Music from across the globe is incorporated into Zumba classes, compilation CDs, conferences, and infomercials. Says CEO Perlman."Universal, EMI, Sony—they're calling us and saying, 'Can we put this song we're launching out on the ZIN network?' Because they know 14 million people are going to hear it."[10]

In order to appeal to as broad an audience as possible, Zumba executives have been careful to adjust their wares to the needs and norms of various global cultures. Marketing materials were sensibly "toned down" for markets in the largely more conservative-minded Middle East, for example. In Europe, infomercials focus less on weight loss and more on strength and endurance, which are more primary concerns there than in the United States.

Fitness fads come and go, but Zumba's growth and success is unprecedented, and it is sure to be a model for future fitness entrepreneurs.

Questions for Discussion

1. Diversity is the centerpiece of the mission of Zumba. Do you think this is true or false? Explain.

2. What lessons can future entrepreneurs learn from Zumba in terms of the importance of diversity to entrepreneurial ventures?

3. Can an organization be successful and not consider diversity as an important management issue?

Sources

1. "About Zumba," last modified January 15, 2013; http://www.zumba.com/about; accessed January 16, 2013.

2. Walters, Jennifer, "Meet Cata, Youngest Zuma Instructor in the World," Shape Your Life blog, May 25, 2012; http://www.shape.com/blogs/shape-your-life/meet-cata-youngest-zumba-instructor-world.

3. Andersen, Charlotte, "Real Women Reveal: How Zumba Changed My Life," *Shape*,; http://www.shape.com/fitness/cardio/real-women-reveal-how-zumba-changed-my-life; accessed December 28, 2012.

4. Buchanan, Leigh, "Zumba Fitness: Company of the Year," *Inc.*, December 4, 2012; http://www.inc.com/magazine/201212/leigh-buchanan/zumba-fitness-company-of-the-year-2012.html; accessed December 29, 2012.

Chapter 6 | ETHICS AND SOCIAL RESPONSIBILITY

Case Study: Chipotle

Sink your teeth into this: a whole-wheat wrap bursting with seasoned black beans, salsas made that morning, and grilled, locally grown chicken marinated overnight in spicy chipotle pepper adobo sauce. Sound like something reserved for the menu of a trendy downtown restaurant? Not anymore. Fast food and "fast casual" are getting in on the game of fresh, local, and in many cases, ethical foods.

The fast food industry in the United States serves up $200 billion in sales annually, and its fast-growing sister is the "fast casual" restaurant. While the definition is still somewhat up for debate, the fast casual style appeals to "current customer needs" by offering "a cheaper alternative to more expensive restaurants while offering customization and quality ingredients," according to Franchise Direct. In other words, for those folks watching their budget in tough times, yet who still have a hankering for good food without paying for the waiter and tablecloth service, the fast casual is the perfect in-between option. "The fast casual restaurant industry outperformed all other categories of the restaurant industry in 2009,"[11] reported Franchise Direct, and this fact has not escaped the attention of more traditional fast food purveyors. Eager for a taste of the fast casual market's success, Taco Bell recently introduced a "Cantina Bell" line developed by celebrity chef Lorena Garcia, with more upscale ingredients like black beans, fresh avocados, and cilantro dressing. Have a taste for an Angus beef burger smothered in aged cheddar? Prefer sea salt on your hand-cut fries, and an iced latte to wash it all down? Menu items like these are popping up with regularity on the menus of fast food stalwarts like Burger King, McDonald's, and Wendy's.

Pundits have speculated that the new direction of Taco Bell and others may put the heat on fast casual pioneers such as Chipotle, which is based in Denver and boasts a store opening almost every other day. Yet the latter offers something that Taco Bell (for now) does not: a conscience. Somewhat unusually, the company does all its advertising with an internal team, whose research indicated that "75 percent of its 800,000 daily customers came for the taste, value, and convenience of its food." While these numbers are encouraging, what's to say that customers can't find "taste, value, and convenience" elsewhere—especially with the traditional fast fooders stepping up their game? Chipotle needed something more; something that would earn not only dollars, but loyalty.

So Chipotle developed a marketing campaign that targets the soul as much as it does the stomach, emphasizing not just the healthful but ethical aspects of one's food choices. It's been introduced across an array of interesting media: an iPhone and Android game Pasture Pandemonium, currently in development; large-scale sustainable food festivals in cities like Chicago; and a two-minute animated film, *Back to the Start*, which portrays a family farmer deliberating between

factory farming and a more sustainable approach and the wide-ranging ramifications of each choice (the theme song of which is Willie Nelson's rendition of Coldplay's "The Scientist," downloadable on iTunes, with proceeds benefiting Chipotle's Cultivate Foundation). The narrative "humanized the devastating statistic that hundreds of families quit working their farms in the United States every week due to competition from big agriculture," wrote Danielle Sacks in *Fast Company*. Philanthropy has also played an important role. Jamie Oliver's Food Revolution and the Nature Conservancy are two recipients of over $2 million that the company has doled out in grants. In 2011, the foundation presented its first major award of $250,000 to Farm Aid, which was founded in the 1980s by Nelson and other celebrities to promote family farms.

In 2011, Chipotle's annual revenue rose to $2.2 billion, yet 2012's numbers were not quite as palatable, falling short of Wall Street's lofty expectations despite a quarterly profit increase of 20 percent from a year earlier. Just like the rest of us, Chipotle is struggling with rising food, beverage, and packaging prices, which may force the company to raise prices, a dicey decision during an economic downturn. And Chipotle's aggressive positioning as the sustainable, family-farm friendly alternative to fast food does not allow it to tinker with production costs as much as a Taco Bell or McDonald's might. "Today, even with 30,000 employees, the crew will come in the morning and see all this fresh produce and meats they have to marinate, rice they have to cook, and fresh herbs they have to chop," said CEO Steve Ells,

Many ingredients figure into Chipotle's recipe for continued success: consumer interest in the sustainable food movement, stiff competition from the Taco Bells of the world, and the economic climate within which all these uncertainties marinate. But the scent of change is in the air; some observers have argued that Chipotle's ethical model may put pressure on its competition to follow suit.

Questions for Discussion

1. Is Chipotle a socially responsible organization? Why or why not?

2. Some would argue that Chipotle is *not* socially responsible because its menu is full of very high-fat, high-calorie items, which encourages obesity. How would you respond to such critics?

3. If you were the CEO of Chipotle, what other socially responsible actions could you take to ensure the success of Chipotle in the long term?

Sources

1. Gasparro, Annie, "Chipotle Shares Sink on Outlook," *The Wall Street Journal*, January 4, 2013; http://online.wsj.com/article/SB100008723963 9044368410457806648403730132Ol.html?KEYWORDS=chipotle; accessed January 7, 2013.

2. Olson, Elizabeth, "An Animated Ad with a Plot Line and a Moral," *The New York Times*, January 4, 2013; http://www.nytimes.com/2012/02/10/business/media/chipotle-ad-promotes-sustainable-farming.html?_r=0; accessed January 6, 2013.

3. Sacks, Danielle, "The World's 50 Most Innovative Companies: Chipotle, For Exploding All the Rules of Fast Food," *Fast Company*, January 4, 2013; http://www.fastcompany.com/most-innovative-companies/2012/chipotle; accessed January 7, 2013.

4. "Fast Casual Restaurant Franchise Industry Report," *Franchise Direct*, http://www.franchisedirect.com/foodfranchises/2010foodfranchiseindustryreport/14/267; accessed January 8, 2013.

5. Jargon, Julie, "Fast Food Aspires to 'Fast Casual,'" *The Wall Street Journal*, October 10, 2012; http://online.wsj.com/article/SB10000872396390444657804578048651773669168.html?KEYWORDS=chipotle; accessed January 9, 2013.

Chapter 7 | *MAKING BETTER DECISIONS*

Case Study: Ticketmaster

In 2010, Ticketmaster found out the hard way that the entertainment industry is not, in fact, as recession-proof as it was once widely believed to be. The company, which sells tickets for live music, sports, and cultural events, and which represents a significant chunk of parent company's Live Nation Entertainment's business, saw a drop in ticket sales that year of a disconcerting 15 percent. Then there was the mounting negative press, including artist boycotts, the vitriol of thousands of vocal customers, and a number of major venues refusing to do business with Ticketmaster.

Yet 2012 has been more friendly to the company—under the leadership of former musician and Stanford MBA-educated CEO Nathan Hubbard, who took over in 2010 when Ticketmaster merged with Live Nation, the country's largest concert promoter. Third-quarter earnings were strong, with just under $2 billion in revenue, a 10 percent boost from the same period last year, driven largely by Live Nation's ticketing and sponsorship divisions. Ticketmaster was largely responsible as well, thanks to the sale of 36 million tickets worth $2.1 billion, generating $82.1 million in adjusted operating income, which translates to an increase of 51 percent for the year.

That's because Hubbard knows how to listen, and read the writing on the wall, "If we don't disrupt ourselves, someone else will," he said, "I'm not worried about other ticketing companies. The Googles and Apples of the world are our competition."

Some of the steps he took to achieve this included to the creation of LiveAnalytics, a team charged with mining the information (and related opportunities) surrounding 200 million customers and the 26 million monthly site visitors, a gold mine that he thought was being ignored. Moreover Hubbard redirected the company from being an infamously opaque, rigid and inflexible transaction machine for ticket sales to a more transparent, fan-centered e-commerce company, one that listens to the wants and needs of customers and responds accordingly. A few of the new innovations rolled out in recent years to achieve this include an interactive venue map that allows customers to choose their seats (instead of Ticketmaster selecting the "best available") and the ability to buy tickets on iTunes.

Hubbard eliminated certain highly unpopular service fees, like the $2.50 fee for printing one's own tickets, which he announced in the inaugural Ticketmaster blog he created.

Much to the delight of event goers—and the simultaneous chagrin of promoters and venue owners, who feared that the move would deter sales—other efforts toward transparency included announcing fees on Ticketmaster's first transaction-dedicated page, instead of surprising customers with them at the end, while consolidating others. "I had clients say, 'What are you doing? We've been doing it this way for 35 years,'" Hubbard recalled, "I told them, 'You sound like the record labels.'"

Social media is an integral part of listening, and of course, "sharing." Ticketmaster alerts on Facebook shows friends of purchasers who is going to what show. An app is in the works that will even show them where their concertgoing friends will be seated. Not that it's all roses for Ticketmaster—yet. Growth and change always involve, well, growing pains, and while goodwill for the company is building, it will take some time to shed the unfortunate reputation of being the company that "everyone loves to hate." Ticketmaster made embarrassing headlines in the first month of 2013 after prematurely announcing the sale of the president's Inaugural Ball and selling out a day early as a result, disappointing thousands. But as the biggest online seller of tickets for everything from golf tournaments to operas to theater to rock concerts, and with Hubbard's more customer-friendly focus, Ticketmaster should have plenty of opportunity to repent their mistakes.

Questions for Discussion

1. How did Ticketmaster's move toward greater transparency help its standing with customers? In what ways might transparency be potentially detrimental?

2. Ticketmaster transformed itself from a more client-friendly model (i.e., venue and promoter-geared) to a customer-friendly model (i.e., ticket purchaser-geared). How has this helped the company? How might it have harmed it?

3. If you were the CEO of one of the world's most "hated" companies, what would be your top three priorities in addressing your reputation issues?

4. Were the recent decisions that Ticketmaster's CEO made effective, according to the material in Chapter 7?

Sources

1. "Company Overview of Ticketmaster Entertainment, LLC," *Bloomberg Businessweek*, January 15, 2013; http://investing.businessweek.com/research/stocks/private/snapshot.asp?privcapId=89809; accessed January 16, 2013.

2. Sisario, Ben, "Live Nation Reports Strong Quarterly Earnings," *The New York Times*, November 5, 2012; http://mediadecoder.blogs.nytimes.com/2012/11/05/live-nation-reports-strong-quarterly-earnings/?ref=livenationinc; accessed January 9, 2013.

3. Salter, Chuck, "Ticketmaster: Rocking The Most Hated Brand In America," *Fast Company*, June 21, 2011; http://www.fastcompany.com/1761539/ticketmaster-rocking-most-hated-brand-america; accessed January 10, 2013.

4. Barenblat, Adam, "Ticketmaster CEO on Brand Hatred: 'People Want to Eat My Kids They're So Angry,'" *Fast Company*, November 10, 2011; http://www.fastcompany.com/1793541/ticketmaster-ceo-brand-hatred-people-want-eat-my-kids-theyre-so-angry; accessed January 7, 2013.

Chapter 8 | SETTING GOALS

Case Study: Spirit Airlines

Founded in 1964 as Clipper Trucking Co., within two decades Spirit Airlines was chugging through the skies as a tiny commercial airline connecting passengers between Florida and the Midwest. Yet by the 2000s, Spirit was near failure—a common story in the commercial airline business—until seasoned aviation executive and merciless cost-cutter Bill Franke stepped in in 2006 to buy the airline and then did something remarkable. Franke had honed his chops cutting costs as CEO of America West Airlines in the 1990s and was an early investor in ultra-low cost Ryan Air. Despite his detractors, Franke, along with his CEO, Ben Baldanza, put Spirit on a steadier (if frill-free) flight path, making it not only one of the few post-9/11 success stories, but also a trend-setter and model in a deeply challenged industry.

While larger carriers have suffered billions of dollars in losses and bankruptcies, Spirit was flying high last year with $289 million in earnings, 40 percent more per plane than any other domestic airline. The company is currently valued at about $1.63 billion, the same as U.S. Airways Group Inc., which is about nine times larger in terms of traffic. Despite its tiny size—Spirit carries just 1 percent of the nation's fliers on its 40-jet fleet—only two U.S. airlines have fared better: Southwest (with 692 Boeing jets) and Alaska Air Group Inc. (with 122 aircraft). While many airlines continue to cancel services, lay off employees, and cut corners to maintain minimal profitability, in 2011 Spirit's revenue soared 37.1 percent over the previous year. The airline also flew 15.2 percent more seats and added multiple routes.

So how did Franke and Baldanza transform a company once facing bankruptcy into the most profitable airline in the United States? By doing everything that was once deemed impossible, yet has since—thanks to Spirit's innovative example—become the industry standard. That means offering the cheapest tickets in the business and making everything—from water to boarding passes—a la carte. Spirit was the first U.S. airline to reintroduce a charge for checked luggage, which has since become commonplace.

Spirit has found its niche—the traveler who is ultra-budget conscious and is interested in little more than getting from A to Z at the cheapest possible price. It's that simple, and Spirit doesn't pretend to embody anything else—not comfort, not convenience, not service. Spirit's on-time performance is among the worst in the industry; its legroom is negligible at best, and (not surprisingly, considering its bare bones approach to travel), it has suffered more than a few PR disasters in recent years. These include irate, vocal customers like Jerry Meekins, a 76-year-old Vietnam vet with terminal cancer, who was denied a refund by Spirit after he was told by doctors that he had only months to live and couldn't fly (and so couldn't use his ticket); and a 2010 pilot strike that saw the airline grounded for 10 days.

Yet Baldanza seems unphased: "We just want to have the lowest price. That drives almost every other decision in the company: how many seats to have in the airplane, what times of day to fly, the kinds of cities we fly to, and so on."

With Spirit's enviable balance sheet, it's likely that more airlines will get on board with the nickel-and-diming scheme. It may be bad news for consumers, but it's good news to airlines that are struggling to make a profit in uncertain times.

Questions for Discussion

1. Spirit's number one goal seems to be "the lowest-price airline ticket." Is this a "S.M.A.R.T." goal? Explain.

2. Do you think this strategic goal will continue to be successful for Spirit?

3. If you were the CEO of Spirit, what goals would you add to ensure that the company prospers in the long run?

Sources

1. Nicas, Jack, "A Stingy Spirit Lifts Airline's Profit," *The Wall Street Journal*, May 11, 2012; http://online.wsj.com/article/SB10001424052702304749904577384383044911796.html?user=welcome&mg=id-wsj; accessed December 14, 2012.

2. Nicas, Jack, "Flying Spirit's 'Dollar Store in the Sky' to Profit," *The Wall Street Journal*, November 20, 2012; http://online.wsj.com/article/SB10001424127887324712504578131444166539174.html?KEYWORDS=spirit+airlines; accessed December 14, 2012.

3. Tuttle, Brad, "Uh Oh! Fee-Crazed Airlines Are the Most Profitable," *Time*, May 23, 2012; http://business.time.com/2012/05/23/uh-oh-fee-crazed-airlines-are-the-most-profitable/; accessed December 14, 2012.

4. Sharkey, Joe, "In a Changing Market, Low Prices vs. More Comfort," *The New York Times*, April 16, 2012; http://www.nytimes.com/2012/04/17/business/in-a-changing-marketlow-prices-vs-more-comfort.html?_r=0; accessed December 14, 2012.

5. "Southwest Corporate Fact Sheet," last updated October 18, 2012; http://www.swamedia.com/channels/Corporate-Fact-Sheet/pages/corporate-fact-sheet; accessed December 13, 2012.

6. "Aircraft Information," http://www.alaskaair.com/content/travel-info/fleet/737-900.aspx; accessed December 12, 2013.

Chapter 9 | DESIGNING STRATEGIES

Case Study: Big Bottom Market

After Michael Volpatt, a San Francisco public relations (PR) executive, bought a weekend home in Sonoma, California, he saw the potential for a great small business venture: A breakfast- and lunch-focused restaurant and specialty food store that also sold wines and locally made crafts in Guerneville, a small Sonoma town of about 6,500. So, between Volpatt and two business partners, they provided $100,000 to start up the business. After opening Big Bottom Market in July 2011, the business was bringing in a generous $20,000 per week, and $24,000 per week in August. Yet, come October, there was a drastic drop. By November, sales were down to a sobering $4,000 per week.

"We thought maybe we'd lose about 30 to 40 percent of our business," Mr. Volpatt said of his seasonal business located in a tourist mecca. But not 80 percent, "This is my first time at the rodeo, and I'll tell you, we were freaking out."

Seasonal Businesses Require a Special Strategy

Owning a company that brings in all its business during one season is challenging for multiple reasons. Depending on the nature of the business, it can be difficult to retain top-notch staff in only the busy season. How do you let good staff go and then get them back again? Or is it better to simply hire new staff every year? Also, when all the business is loaded into just one season, it can be very stressful—working long, laborious hours every day for a three- or four-month stretch, and when there's so much happening, it's easy to make mistakes. When the company depends on those three or four months to get it through the entire year, any mistake can be costly.

Depending on location, when the off-season is long, the biggest challenge for a seasonal business may be reminding the world that it's still there. This could be true of luxury bed and breakfasts, tucked away in quiet, secluded places, old historic buildings, or an outdoors destination off the beaten path. Another challenge—particularly if high season is the summer—is that strain can be put on family life. Children are in school nine months out of the year when parents have time, and then when the kids are on summer vacation and have time, the parents are busy. It's not so simple to plan family trips and the like.

Whatever the case may be, all seasonal businesses have one challenge in common: surviving the off-season, financially.

You Think You Know What You're Doing, and Then It All Goes Awry

Volpatt wasn't a total rookie at owning and investing, of course. He had owned his own PR firm for 10 years and had invested in real estate, including joint ownership of an apartment complex in St. Louis. Though the investment in Big Bottom Market was a dive into the unfamiliar world of retail and restaurants, Volpatt found a great chef to bring in a unique menu, plus a San Francisco mortgage broker who owned two popular Guerneville retail businesses to run the kitchen and market operations. Crista Luedtke was the hands-on owner of both Boon Hotel and Spa and Boon Eat and Drink and would surely be a huge asset.

Big Bottom Market was trendy yet relaxed—hardwood floors, barnboard, funky metal chairs around nine tables, a counter with stools, and a communal table. Word spread fast about Big Bottom's biscuits, and they became a hit. They included a variety of options: traditional biscuits, cheddar and thyme biscuits, ham and cheese biscuits, and a fun "sea biscuit" made with house-smoked salmon, capers, and pickled onions—not your ordinary biscuit fare. Also on the lunch menu were baguette sandwiches, soups, and salads. The biscuits were becoming a signature item, and Volpatt considered freezing and selling them elsewhere as part of the off-season strategy.

But then November hit and the bottom fell out for Big Bottom. "At the rate you guys are going," their accountant warned, "you're going to have to close your doors."

Finding Solutions

To respond immediately, Big Bottom closed its doors on slower days, Mondays and Tuesdays, and trimmed some of their staff of 20. The owners went on a crisis retreat and brainstormed the following ideas:

1. Mark down expensive wines and focus on bottles that cost $12 to $15 so that wine was more affordable. Locals—their off-season patrons—wouldn't pay as much as vacationers, the team reasoned.

2. Redirect marketing specifically toward the Guerneville community. They could create a new sandwich each month for a prominent Guerneville resident and start a promotion, like offering 15 percent off everything in the store as a designated "community day."

3. Stay open for dinner. A special three-course dinner on Wednesday nights for $20 was launched.

4. Add a catering component and take business beyond the building.

5. Start a Big Bottom food truck and sell food on the road, again taking sales beyond the store's walls. This way, there was opportunity for Big Bottom to continue building on its biscuit fame.

6. Do more of what works and tilt the business toward biscuits. The team thought to market their famous good as "the next cupcake" and sell it wholesale to leading local gourmet supermarkets. From there, Big Bottom could grow regionally—maybe even nationally.

Pundits advise that since no one really knows what will work, it makes sense to try multiple, complimentary ideas. Experts also say to look at the market to see what related products or services are still missing from the area. Sometimes those ideas are covert, like farm share pickup, catering classes, hosting food-writing groups during off-hours, local fundraising initiatives, cooking classes for kids, and the like. Other options are restructuring saving and spending—using money wisely during the high season so that it carries the business during the slow season.

In the end, Big Bottom Market decided to hold off on the truck and frozen food side of the business because for the time being, those ideas seemed a little off-message and too focused on capital. Instead, the new direction focused on maximizing the space between the four walls first. Big Bottom would concentrate on the wines, including getting more affordable ones on the shelves. It partnered with a local winery that made a specially branded bottle of red for them at $15 per unit that flew off the shelves. The three-course dinner for $20 on Wednesday nights was so successful they increased it to three nights per week in the summer. The team compromised on the catering idea by preparing large orders and allowing people to come pick them up. A popular boxed lunch program that targeted businesses was also begun.

Volpatt said, "We decided the keys to executive boardroom lunches are the executive assistants, the gatekeepers. So last fall I packed up 20 bags in my car and knocked on doors at large office parks in Sonoma County. Within two days we had our first order."

Big Bottom also started hosting winery-specific dinners and including vineyard logos on their menus, with the vineyards paying for advertising. One challenge that remains is continuing to provide excellent service to locals during the high season when all the tourists are back in town. But the plus is that they started making about $10,000 per week more during that summer compared to the summer before. That was money in the bank that helped Big Bottom weather the next winter season much more easily.

Big Bottom Market has become a go-to place for locals and visitors alike, earning recommendations in the *New York Times'* Travel section, among other high-profile accolades. Through focus, compromise, and innovation, Big Bottom appears to be here to stay, rain or shine, summer or winter.

Questions for Discussion

1. What would be the next strategy that you would implement at Big Bottom Market? Why?

2. Why do you think the team's decision to focus on increasing store-based revenue in their current market instead of expanding to new markets was successful? What would you have done differently?

3. What are the key aspects to consider when planning for the fiscal ups and downs that are inherent to seasonal and tourism-driven businesses?

Sources

1. Grossman, John, "A Seasonal Business Aims to Survive the Off-Season," *The New York Times*, June 11, 2012; http://www.nytimes.com/2012/07/12/business/smallbusiness/a-seasonal-business-aims-to-survive-the-off-season.html?pagewanted=2&_r=0&ref=casestudies&adxnnlx=1357784063-G2ufFd4R75DpN2x/3ATyVQ; accessed January 3, 2013.

2. Grossman, John, "A Tourist Dependent Business Decides to Reboot," *The New York Times*, July 18, 2012; http://boss.blogs.nytimes.com/2012/07/18/a-tourist-dependant-business-decides-to-reboot/; accessed January 3, 2013.

3. Schnuer, Jenna, "How to Survive the Peaks and Valleys of a Seasonal Business," *Entrepreneur*, November 28, 2011; http://www.entrepreneur.com/article/220714; accessed January 4, 2013.

4. Moran, Gwen, "4 Seasonal Business Survival Tactics," *Entrepreneur.com on MSNBC*, December 1, 2012; http://today.msnbc.msn.com/id/50037947/ns/today-money/t/seasonal-business-survival-tactics/#.UO9ZZ_K9uSo; accessed January 4, 2013.

Chapter 10 | STRUCTURING ORGANIZATIONS

Case Study: W. L. Gore and Associates

He was ready for anything—or so he thought. Dressed in his finest and armed with an MBA degree fresh off the press, Jack Dougherty walked in for his first day of work at Newark, Delaware–based W. L. Gore and Associates, the global fluoropolymer technology and manufacturing giant specializing in fabrics, medical implants, industrial sealants and filtration, signal transmission, and consumer products. But the company is perhaps best known as the maker of Gore-Tex.

But it turned out he wasn't ready for this: "Why don't you look around and find something you'd like to do," founder and CEO Bill Gore said to him after a quick introduction.

While many things have changed over the course of W.L. Gore and Associates' 50+ years in business, the late Gore stuck to his principles regarding organizational structure (or lack thereof), a legacy he passed down to subsequent generations of management. Gore wasn't fond of thick layers of formal management, which he believed smothered individual creativity. According to Gore, "A lattice (flat) organization is one that involves direct transactions, self-commitment, natural leadership, and lacks assigned or assumed authority."

In the 1930s, Gore received a bachelor's degree in chemical engineering and a master's degree in physical chemistry. During his career, he worked on a team to develop applications for polytetraflurothylene (PTFE), commonly known as Teflon. Through this experience, Gore discovered a sense of excited commitment, personal fulfillment, and self-direction. He followed computer and transmitter developments with interest, believing PTFE could serve as a type of insulator for them.

He was right. Gore spent nights awake with his son until he did what he had previously thought to be impossible: he created a PTFE-coated ribbon cable. It occurred to Gore that he might be able to start his own business producing insulated ribbon cable. So he left his career of 17 years, where he had stable income, and he and his wife mortgaged their house and took $4,000 out of savings to finance the first two years of his business. Though his friends advised him against taking such a risk, W. L. Gore and Associates was born in January, 1958. The basement of the Gore home was the company's first facility.

While no longer operating from a family basement (Gore boasts more than $2.5 billion in annual sales and 8,000 employees in over 50 facilities worldwide), the sense of informality has stuck. "It absolutely is less efficient upfront," said Terri Kelly, chief executive of W.L. Gore. (Her title is one of the few at the company.) "[But] once you have the organization behind it . . . the buy-in and the execution happen quickly," she added.

Structure and Management of Unstructure and Unmanagement

Even as Gore started to grow, the company continued to resist titles and hierarchy. It had no mission statement, no ethics statement, and no conventional structures typical of companies of the same size. The only formal titles were "chief executive" and "secretary-treasurer"—those required by law for corporations. There were also no rules that business units within the company couldn't create such structures, and so some of them did create their own mission statements and such. Many called Gore's management style "unmanagement."

What had started as 12 employees working in the Gore basement eventually evolved into a thriving company by the 1960s, with multiple plants. There were 200 employees working at a plant in Newark, Delaware. One day, Gore was walking around the plant, and it occurred to him that he didn't know all the employees there. Based on this realization, Gore established a policy that said no plant was to be larger than

150 to 200 workers per plant, to keep things more intimate and interpersonal. He wanted to "get big while staying small."

As the company grew, Gore also realized that there had to be some kind of system in place to assist new people on the job and to track progress. Instead of a formal management program, Gore implemented a "sponsor" program. When people applied, they were screened and then interviewed by associates. An associate who took a personal interest in the new associate's contributions, problems, and goals would agree to act as a mentor, or sponsor. The new hire's sponsor would coach and advocate for him, tracking progress, encouraging the person, and dealing with weaknesses while focusing on strengths. Sponsors were also responsible for ensuring that their associates were fairly paid. The result of all this focus on mentoring and the right-sized teams has cultivated a feeling of intimacy and appreciation that attracts and retains a strong workforce.

"You feel like you're part of a family," said Steve Shuster, part of Gore's enterprise communication team. "I have been working at Gore for 27 years, and I still get excited coming to work each day."

Questions for Discussion

1. What aspects of an "unmanagement" approach can you identify as potentially hazardous to overall productivity and profitability in a company the size of Gore? Why do you think Gore has been able to avoid these hazards?

2. What role do job titles play in the typical corporate hierarchy? What effect does the lack of mandated job titles seem to have on employee morale at Gore?

3. What is the relationship between the highly interpersonal nature of Gore's corporate structure and the level of loyalty and personal investment felt by employees?

4. Can you think of other companies that share Gore's atypical structure? What companies or industries in general do you think might benefit from an "unmanaged" style?

Sources

1. "Workplace Democracy at W.L. Gore & Associates," workplacedemocracy.com, July 14, 2009, http://workplacedemocracy.com/2009/07/14/workplace-democracy-at-w-l-gore-associates; accessed December 24, 2012.

2. "About Us," http://www.gore.com/en_xx/aboutus/culture/index.html.

3. Mayhew, Ruth, "Cons of a Lattice Organizational Structure," *The Houston Chronicle*, http://smallbusiness.chron.com/cons-lattice-organizational-structure-3836.html; accessed December 24, 2012.

4. Shipper, Frank, and Charles C. Man, "Classic 6: W.L. Gore & Associates," http://www.academia.edu/964711/Classic_Case_6_WL_Gore_and_Associates_Inc.; accessed December 26, 2012.

Chapter 11 | THE HUMAN SIDE OF MANAGEMENT

Case Study: Zappos.com

Shoe lovers, welcome to heaven. Zappos, the world's largest online shoe seller, offers a mindboggling array of shoes and merchandise, a free return policy, and extraordinary customer service reflected in its "Powered by Service" motto. While all these aspects helped create an Internet behemoth reaching $1 billion in sales in its eighth year of operation—making it one of the most successful Internet retailers in history, and culminating in a nearly $1 billion purchase by Amazon in 2009—it's the company's quirky policies (or in some cases, lack thereof) and emphasis on happiness and human connection that have earned it thousands of loyal customers and a regular presence on those ubiquitous media lists of the "Best Places to Work."

Zappos got its start in 1999 when its founder, Nick Swinmurn, pitched the idea of selling shoes online to venture capitalists Tony Hsieh and Alfred Lin, impressing upon the duo that "footwear in the U.S. is a $40 billion market" of which only 5 percent was being "sold by paper mail-order catalogs." While Hsieh admits that he had his doubts, shortly after the launch, he jumped on the opportunity to become co-CEO and began developing his "dream corporate culture" and people-centered management style not long after. Hsieh was at the time living comfortably from the sale of his previous start-up, LinkExchange, which the then-24-year-old sold to Microsoft for a sizeable $265 million in 1999. But while the lucrative buyout of LinkExchange was nothing to sneeze at, Hsieh says the real reason that he agreed to sell had nothing to do with price; it had everything to do with culture. Basing LinkExchange's hiring strategy on skills and expertise only, the company culture went from exuberant to downtrodden. By the time things really got going, "I just dreaded getting out of bed in the morning and was hitting that snooze button over and over again," Hsieh says. Hsieh pledged that he'd never run a company that way again, and became intrigued with creating a corporate culture that was everything his previous start-up was not.

Hsieh hit the mark with Zappos, which considers itself a customer service company that happens to sell online merchandise. With this emphasis on service—on people, internally and externally—it should be no surprise to hear Hsieh saying that Zappos will eventually move beyond retail to businesses such as hotels and banking, "I wouldn't rule out a Zappos airline that's just about the best customer service," Hsieh has said.

Something of a philosopher, Hsieh has used Zappos to test his theories on happiness, which Hsieh claims is what Zappos strives to provide, at its core. In his view, the secret is striking a balance among four basic human needs: perceived progress, perceived control, relatedness, and a connection to a larger vision. Zappos is his laboratory where this theory is tested.

But Zappos doesn't go about ensuring "happiness" in the typical way. Its salaries aren't great—they are often below market, in fact. With the notable exception of 100 percent of health care benefits paid for by Zappos, there are few bells-and-whistles perks for employees. There are, however, lots of great intangibles: nights out drinking with bosses and coworkers, for which Hsieh often tags along; a nap room; the interesting requirement that managers spend 10 percent to 20 percent of their time "goofing off" with their employees; an emphasis on fun and "weirdness," which ostensibly speaks to Zappos's greatest intangible benefit yet: the opportunity to express oneself in the workplace and feel empowered while doing it. There are no limits on the time a call center operator can spend on the phone with a customer, for example (the company made headlines in December 2012 with a record-breaking call that lasted 10½ hours), and no scripts to recite. And employees are empowered to make decisions—like offering refunds, or in one case, following up on a refund by sending flowers on the company tab to a customer whose husband died unexpectedly after she had ordered him a pair of shoes from Zappos—without adhering to a rigid playbook or consulting the higher-ups. Employees are encouraged to be individuals and treat their customers as such—not just as sales figures. All this contributes to what Hsieh calls the "wow" factor in customer service, which keeps his turnover low and his customers coming back while singing the company's praises to others, "Our philosophy has been that most of the money we might ordinarily have spent on advertising should be invested in customer service, so that our customers will do the marketing for us through word of mouth," said Hsieh.[12] In the beginning, this was a necessity for the cash-strapped company. Now, it's one of its greatest keys to success.

Of course, extending this much freedom to employees implies risk—and this is why Zappos goes to great lengths to make sure it hires the *right* employees, those who will fit within and contribute to its carefully crafted culture. There is intensive training, with a unique twist—at its conclusion, prospective employees are famously offered $2,000 (up from $100 when Hsieh came up with the idea in 2005), plus compensation for training hours, to quit. It's Hsieh's way of weeding out those who are in it for just the paycheck or the goodies—not the type he wants working for him. "We want people who are passionate about what Zappos is about— service. I don't care if they're passionate about shoes."[13]

At a 2009 conference in New York, Inc. reporter Max Chafkin recalls hearing Hsieh reflect on the widow who received flowers from Zappos thanks to a thoughtful and sympathetic call center rep. His voice cracking, his eyes slightly teary, Hsieh paused to regain his composure. "Stories like these are being created every single day, thousands and thousands of times," he said. "It's just an example that if you get the culture right, then most of the other stuff follows."

Questions for Discussion

1. What are the most successful elements of Zappos's human resource management approach?

2. Zappos does not create happy employees by paying them top wages. What does Zappos use besides salary to motivate its employees?

3. Would you be content working in such a Zappos culture? Why or why not?

Sources

1. "Meet Our Monkies," http://about.zappos.com/meet-our-monkeys/tony-hsieh-ceo; accessed December 29, 2012.
2. Chafkin, Max, "The Zappos Way of Managing," *Inc.*, May 1, 2009; http://www.inc.com/magazine/20090501/the-zappos-way-of-managing.html?nav=next.
3. Hsieh, Tony, "How I Did It: Zappos's CEO on Going to Extremes for Customers," *Harvard Business Review*, July 2010; http://hbr.org/2010/07/how-i-did-it-zapposs-ceo-on-going-to-extremes-for-customers/ar/1; accessed December 29, 2012.
4. Bryant, Adam, "On a Scale of 1 to 10, How Weird Are You?" *The New York Times*, January 9, 2010; http://www.nytimes.com/2010/01/10/business/10corner.html?pagewanted=all&_r=0; accessed December 29, 2012.
5. Rich, Motoko, "Why Is This Man Smiling?" *The New York Times*, April 8, 2011; http://www.nytimes.com/2011/04/10/fashion/10HSEIH.html?pagewanted=all&_r=0; accessed December 30, 2012.

Chapter 12 | MANAGING TEAM PERFORMANCE

Case Study: Pfizer

Discussions about the world's "happiest places to work" might bring to mind some now-famous companies like Zappos, Inc. and its focus on hiring only the right employees, or any number of technology-based upstarts creating unusual workspaces to foster creativity. The last industry that most people would likely bring up is the seemingly faceless world of pharmaceuticals. But 2013's number 1 ranking for happiest employees goes to Big Pharma's largest player. With annual revenue exceeding $64 billion, driven by over 100,000 employees, Pfizer not only ranks as the world's largest pharmaceutical company, it also employs the happiest workers, catapulting from the 11th spot in the previous year. What is it that makes the pharmaceutical giant's employees so happy?

As it turns out, it isn't drugs. Job satisfaction at Pfizer is the result of forward-thinking, innovative policies that seek to create a meaningful, engaging environment for colleagues (as Pfizer employees are called)—and one where those colleagues actually enjoy working with each other. The most prominent strategy used in creating such an environment is one of ownership. Pfizer CEO Ian Read pushed the ownership culture out to the company in 2012 with the goal of engaging each of the companies 100,000+ employees in improving the company for all its stakeholders, from consumers to shareholders. The ultimate goal was the creation of a work environment that was a birthplace not only of new products, but of new pathways leading to those products. In turn, this environment would be supportive of the employees within it, and would foster a deep sense of responsibility to fellow colleagues and every company stakeholder.

The idea of the ownership model was born of candid research within the company, with employees at every level. This research led to the creation of a corporate culture that fosters independent, innovative thinking, provides opportunity for growth and movement within the company, gives meaningful feedback to employees, and encourages responsible risk taking while placing a high emphasis on personal responsibility. In this model, failure is treated as an inevitability that provides an opportunity for learning or problem solving—and pharmaceutical research is no stranger to failure. By accepting failure and providing meaningful, constructive feedback, employees are encouraged to innovate, and innovation is something that Pfizer considers an imperative for continued success in a crowded industry.

The ownership model isn't the only aspect of Pfizer employment that leads to happy workers; the company has also taken great strides to ensure that its colleagues spend most of their time at work being able to focus on what they were actually hired to do. While at first glance this seems unnecessary or obvious, Pfizer's own reviews of employee activity found that a significant chunk of valuable time was spent on "support tasks," like creating Microsoft PowerPoint presentations or handling correspondence, instead of the appropriate use of the particular employee's talents and primary job roles. To address this issue, Pfizer turned to outsourcing, which goes far beyond the noisy call centers that that word typically conjures up. Pfizer employees can outsource presentations, data mining and analysis, document creation, scheduling, and other tasks so they can spend more time developing and implementing new research strategies, conducting research, and all the other tasks that ultimately allow Pfizer to remain a leading innovator in the industry. The result of this strategy is a tangible increase in productivity over shorter periods of time. This means a shorter path from idea to research to execution, not only for new products but for new business strategies as well.

Pfizer has worked hard to be an innovator, not only in the pharmaceutical development that sustains the bottom line but also in the creation of a corporate environment that is filled with happy, productive employees. The company's own stated outlook is that even in an industry driven by patents and products, "Pfizer's most important assets leave our building at the end of each workday." This company is a primary example of one that recognizes the value in having employees that believe in what they do and feel encouraged to produce high-quality, innovative work, not because they fear the consequences of underperforming but because they feel like a part of the company in a meaningful way. Pfizer's corporate policy treats employees as people rather than numbers, and the success of this strategy is evident in its continued reign as the largest pharmaceutical company in the world—and now as the happiest, too.

Questions for Discussion

1. Pfizer seems to be a group of teams within one large team. Do you agree with this statement?

2. What was the result of moving to an "outsource" model, both for the company as a whole and for individual colleagues?

3. Describe the "ownership model." How did Pfizer implement this model, and how did they ensure that it was more than just a token change in name only?

4. What are the tangible benefits for a company that creates a "happy" work environment? Are there any potential downsides to creating policies meant to ensure employee happiness?

Sources

1. The Career Bliss Team, "CareerBliss 50 Happiest Companies in America for 2013," Careerbliss, December 9, 2012; http://www.careerbliss.com/facts-and-figures/careerbliss-50-happiest-companies-in-america-for-2013/ - 1/10/2013; accessed January 11, 2013.

2. Breen, Bill, "The Thrill of Defeat," *Fast Company*, June 1, 2004; http://www.fastcompany.com/49239/thrill-defeat; accessed January 5, 2013.

3. Dishman, Lydia, "Secrets of America's Happiest Companies," *Fast Company*, January 10, 2013; http://www.fastcompany.com/3004595/secrets-americas-happiest-companies; accessed January 12, 2013.

4. Cohen, Adrienne, "Scuttling Scut Work," *Fast Company*, February 1, 2008; http://www.fastcompany.com/641153/scuttling-scut-work - 1/10/2013.

5. "Pfizer," *Forbes*, April 2012; http://www.forbes.com/companies/pfizer/; accessed January 12, 2013.

6. Pfizer Annual Report 2011; http://www.pfizer.com/investors/financial_reports/annual_reports/2011/colleagues.jsp; accessed January 12, 2013.

Chapter 13 | MANAGERS AS LEADERS

Case Study: Kazuhiro Tsuga, President of Panasonic Corporation

In 2012, headlines like "Panasonic Stock Tumbles" and "Panasonic Prepares for 'Garage Sale', to Axe 10,000 Jobs" were painfully commonplace. With a bloated portfolio and reduced consumer demand brought on by the global recession, Panasonic, Japan's largest commercial employer with over 300,000 on its payroll, was struggling to stay relevant. While foreign competitors like U.S.-based Apple and South Korea's Samsung Electronics were shining, Panasonic's shareholders were frustrated and looking for answers. In June 2012, Kazuhiro Tsuga, a longtime Panasonic man in R&D, with relatively little management experience, was tapped as the surprising choice to deliver as the Panasonic's freshly minted president.

So far, Tsuga seems undaunted by the challenges at hand. Perhaps it's because the 56-year-old is too busy with his company's "total makeover," with bold disruptions of its product line, management structure, and corporate culture as a whole, to notice. Over a series of frank videoconferences in late 2012, for example, Tsuga announced he was slashing middle managers' bonuses by a third. He would also scale back Panasonic operations—and workforce—dramatically. Weaker Panasonic units, among them light bulbs, bicycles, televisions, robotic hair washers, and air conditioners, were eliminated. Tsuga said that Panasonic would also be halting the sale of smartphones in Europe and stopping production of liquid crystal display (LCD) panels at its Malaysian and Czech plants. And those Panasonic subsidiaries failing to earn at least 5 percent margins have no place in Tsuga's new vision.

"Unless we take this step, whatever we say will be an empty promise," Tsuga later stated unapologetically at a press conference, appearing to buck the Japanese business norm of hanging on to weak units in tough times. Panasonic, Tsuga said, needed to readjust its business values. These had been shortsighted, putting too much focus on increasing revenue without prioritizing profit.

Manager Becomes Panasonic's Leader and Hope

It's Tsuga's "relative inexperience, along with his bluntness, [that] could be among his trump cards," wrote Tim Kelly of Reuters five months after Tsuga's ascension the same year. It wasn't until 2008, after all, that the longtime R&D man was appointed to his first senior managerial position at Panasonic, after joining the company in 1979. In the years that followed, Tsuga built a portfolio of patents. In 1986, he earned a master's degree in computer science from the University of California, Santa Barbara. But his shift away from research and toward leadership didn't take place until he was asked to lead talks with competitors and Hollywood studios on establishing the Blu-ray standard for DVDs. Just before Lehman Brothers collapsed and car sales tanked in 2008, Tsuga was also put in charge of automotive components. His zeal for cost-cutting and reducing middle management saw his struggling division return to profitability within a year.

"Tsuga honed the toughness that is indispensable to a manager," reflected an engineer that worked with him during that time, Noriko Fukuoka. And while his forthright nature may not have helped him climb the ladder in earlier years, ("he was not seen as someone pegged for the top," says an executive who worked with him early on, who asked to remain anonymous), it seems that his "tough love" is just what the doctor ordered in tough times.

Taking Back Leadership of the Industry

It's still too soon to say if Panasonic will be able to take back its leadership in the consumer electronics industry, but in the hands of its gutsy new president, there is reason for hope. He continues to show a fearlessness in making the tough decisions necessary for a company in crisis.

Tsuga is converting Panasonic, which he called "a loser in consumer electronics," into a company focused on energy-conscious technology, such as solar cell phones and energy-saving household systems. This may help set Panasonic apart from the pack. Sony, for example, is building its future around cameras, games, and mobile devices, while Sharp is focused on persuading companies such as Apple to use its latest power-saving screens.

"Japan's consumer electronic makers were great in the 1990s and then lost it," said Mitsuhige Akino, chief fund manager at Ichiyoshi Investment Management in Tokyo. All companies in the industry are now faced with the same challenge to restructure and "build products that will sell around the globe," he added.

Panasonic chose Tsuga because it was looking for a leader who was free from past practices and who could also act quickly and decisively in response to the rapid changes in the global market for consumer electronics. Their choice may pay off.

"Tsuga is an unusual person, and I mean that in a good way," said Tetsuro Li, chief executive of Commons Asset Management, a Tokyo fund that does not own Panasonic stock, "He looks like someone who can get things done."

Questions for Discussion

1. Which attributes does Tsuga possess that allow so many to believe that he is such a strong leader? Why do these attributes seem to be effective?

2. What did Panasonic need to change in order to stay in business? How did these realizations affect Panasonic's decision to choose Tsuga, someone with relatively little management experience, to be their new president?

3. What can be learned from Panasonic's business mistakes?

Sources

1. Kelly, Tim, "A New Style of Leadership at Panasonic," *The New York Times*, November 8, 2012; http://www.nytimes.com/2012/11/09/technology/09iht-panasonic09.html?pagewanted=all&_r=0; accessed January 12, 2013.

2. Kana Inagaki and Juro Osawa, "Panasonic Stock Tumbles," *The Wall Street Journal*, October 31, 2012; http://online.wsj.com/article/SB10001424052970204712904578089962887027962.html; accessed January 12, 2013.

3. Tim Kelly and Reiji Murai, "Panasonic Prepares for 'Garage Sale', to Axe 10,000 Jobs," *Reuters*, November 14, 2012; http://www.reuters.com/article/2012/11/14/us-panasonic-cfo-idUSBRE8AD0D120121114; accessed January 12, 2013.

4. Kelly, Tim, "Panasonic Cleans House with Writedowns, Sees $9.6 Billion Loss, *Reuters*, November 1, 2012; http://articles.chicagotribune.com/2012-11-01/business/sns-rt-us-panasonic-earningsbre8a003o-20121031_1_kazuhiro-tsuga-viera-tvs-panasonic-corp; accessed January 9, 2013.

5. Tetsushi Yamamura and Kazuki Kimura, "New Panasonic Head Wants to Reinvent Struggling Company," *Asahi Shimbum*, February 29, 2012; http://ajw.asahi.com/article/economy/business/AJ201202290057; accessed January 8, 2013.

Chapter 14 | *UNDERSTANDING INDIVIDUAL BEHAVIOR*

Case Study: Millennials in the Workplace

Welcome to the millennial-centered workplace. At Euro-RSCG, a PR firm, about 80 millennials (the generation born in the 1980s and 1990s), can be found wearing flip-flops, displaying tattoos, indulging in a rooftop happy hour, and using Facebook socially during work hours. The firm provides time off for volunteer work, and employees leave early on Fridays during the summer. Google offers a free juice bar, a yoga and Pilates room, and even reimbursement for a personal trainer. Chesapeake Energy boasts a 72,000-square-foot on-site gym for their employees; and when they are done with their workout, they can feel free to stretch out in one of its seven tanning beds or indulge in on-site Botox injections. DPR Construction's 17 offices feature wine bars, while workers in its Texas office can saunter into its saloon and tip a few back.

Millennials (also known as Generation Y) are demanding a work-life balance, "I have a girlfriend. I have family. I have friends. And these are all things that are very important, because we work to live and not the other way around," said Greg Housset, a millennial employee of Euro-RSCG. In the age of Facebook, Twitter, and text messaging, Generation Y is hyperconnected, has little patience for traditional hierarchy, and expects opportunities to "connect" in the workplace. According to MTV's "No Collar Workers" survey, 80 percent of millennials want regular feedback from their managers, but 75 percent really want mentors. Millennials tend to be motivated to work in a job that is meaningful, not just lucrative—where their ideas count and they can put their creativity to work.

A total of 81 percent of surveyed millennials think that they should have flexible work hours and make their own schedules, 70 percent said that they needed to have personal time off while on the job, and 79 percent thought they should be allowed to wear jeans to work. Many would like the option to work in the convenience of their homes, using technologies like Skype to telecommute when needed.

It can be trying for baby boomers (who are often the signers of millennials' paychecks) to entertain some of this generation's philosophies about the workplace. Especially during a time when unemployment and underemployment is high for teens and 20-somethings, a prevailing reaction among older employers seems to be, "beggars can't be choosers, right?" Some of the negative stereotypes associated with this generation include a sense of entitlement, laziness, and impatience. But like it or not, millennials are, in fact, the future. There are about 80 million millennials and 76 million baby boomers in the United States today. About half of those millennials are already in the workplace, and millions more follow each year. By 2025, three of every four workers will be millennials.

But Generation Y is not interested in "doing business as usual," and some are beginning to think Generation Y's philosophy might be very good for America. For instance, Marian Salzman, CEO of Euro-RSCG, asks her team of millennials questions and listens to their answers. She hasn't granted their every wish, like opening the firm a couple hours later every day or providing free meals, but she adjusts to the extent that she finds reasonable. Keeping employees happy makes them better at their jobs, and allowing them to play on Facebook sometimes, dress casually, take time off to volunteer, enjoy a rooftop happy hour three days per week, and have short workdays on Fridays during the summer are a few perks that keep employees happy.

"They're the new marketplace," Salzman said of her millennials, "They're the new brains. They come with all the new social media tools and tricks already embedded in them as natives." She later added, speaking to her fellow baby boomers, "You're not the smartest person in the room anymore. You may be the most experienced. You may be the wisest. You're not the smartest."

Salzman is learning to employ Generation Y's strengths to benefit the firm. She accomplishes this by listening to, and in many cases accommodating, their wishes. Other employers are now being advised on how to better manage millennials in the workplace. A few key tips for those managing the new generation: facilitate mentoring to allow for more cross-generational interaction, offer different working options like telecommuting or working off-site, and accommodate different learning styles. Keep employees engaged with educational and training opportunities and create recognition programs. Accommodate personal employee needs, and don't confuse generational traits with character flaws. And most of all, perhaps, provide the more democratic, transparent, and collaborative working environment that is fast becoming the norm of the modern workplace.

Questions for Discussion

1. Generation Y and Generation X tend to have conflicting expectations regarding workplace conduct. Discuss some of these differences.

2. How have some baby boomers attempted to better manage millennials?

Sources

1. Matchar, Emily, "How Those Spoiled Millennials Will Make the Workplace Better for Everyone," *The Washington Post*, August 16, 2008; http://articles.washingtonpost.com/2012-08-16/opinions/35490487_1_boomerang-kids-modern-workplace-privileged-kids; accessed January 2, 2013.

2. Kiisel, Ty, "GimmeGimmeGimme—Millenials in the Workplace," *Forbes*, May 16, 2012; http://www.forbes.com/sites/tykiisel/2012/05/16/gimme-gimme-gimme-millennials-in-the-workplace/; accessed January 3, 2013.

3. "How to Manage Different Generations," *The Wall Street Journal*, http://guides.wsj.com/management/managing-your-people/how-to-manage-different-generations/; accessed January 3, 2013.

4. Chernoff, Allan, "How One CEO Bends the Rules to Get the Most Out of Millennials," CNN.com, July 21, 2011; http://www.cnn.com/2011/US/07/21/millennials.managing/index.html; accessed January 5, 2013.

5. *The Week* Editorial Staff, "How Millennials Are Transforming the Workplace," *The Week*, August 24, 2012; http://theweek.com/article/index/232375/how-millennials-are-transforming-the-workplace; accessed January 4, 2013.

6. Seaoms, Kate, "13 Companies that Offer Amazing Perks," Newser, January 30, 2011; http://www.newser.com/story/110603/13-companies-that-offer-amazing-perks.html; accessed January 4, 2013.

7. Schwabel, Dan, "Millenials vs. Baby Boomers: Who Would You Rather Hire?" *Time*, March 29, 2012. http://business.time.com/2012/03/29/millennials-vs-baby-boomers-who-would-you-rather-hire/; accessed January 4, 2013.

Chapter 15 | COMMUNICATING AND MOTIVATING OTHERS

Case Study: Korean Air

Korean Air's highly publicized plane crash in Guam in August 1997, which killed 228 people, was one of many—too many. The crash rate was so disconcerting that in April 1999, both Delta Air Lines and Air France suspended their flying partnerships with Korean Air, and the U.S. Army forbade its personnel from using Korean Air. The airline nearly lost landing privileges in Canada.

It wasn't merely that training or resources were subpar. As discussed in Malcolm Gladwell's bestselling book, *Outliers*, there was something much more complex and nuanced contributing to the tragedies beneath the surface, and it had a lot to do with Korean culture and communication style. After transforming corporate communication style, the airline's safety record since 1999 has completely turned around. It's been crash free, has won awards including the "World's Most Innovative Airline" in the World Travel Awards (WTA) Grand Final Ceremony 2012, and is now a member of the prestigious SkyTeam alliance. It's now as safe as any other airline in the world.

The Vast World of Communication Styles

In cross-cultural psychology, "Hofstede's dimensions" are among the most widely used measurements to explore cultural differences. They are named after the Dutch psychologist Geert Hofstede, who traveled the world as a human resources professional to identify such things as how people from different countries go about solving problems, how they work together, and what their attitudes toward authority are. His questionnaires to analyze how cultures are different from each other were comprehensive, as was the database he created.

One of Hofstede's dimensions is what he called the Power Distance Index (PDI), which measures a given culture's attitude toward hierarchy and degree of respect toward authority. To create this index, Hofstede was concerned with questions like how frequently employees were afraid to express disagreement with their managers, how well respected older people were in a society, and how concerned members of an organization were with power being distributed equally. High-PDI countries hold those with power in high esteem, and there is a very clear distinction made between those with and without authority. Contrarily, powerful people in countries with low PDI will be more likely to downplay their authority—they renounce formal symbols or, for example, will take a streetcar to work, like Austria's prime minister, Bruno Kreisky. The United States, where President Barack Obama can be found playing basketball, is another low-PDI country.

Not so for South Korea, a classic example of high PDI. There are no fewer than six different levels of conversational address, for example, depending on the relationship between the addressee and the addresser. In *Outliers*, Gladwell helps explain Korean communication through the words of a Korean linguist, Ho-min Sohn:

All social behavior and actions are conducted in the order of seniority or ranking; as the saying goes, "chanmul to wialaykaita"; there is order even to drinking cold water.

Korean Air Flight 801

There were a few minor problems on Flight 801 destined for Guam, but none were singlehandedly responsible for the terrible plane crash that killed 228 people. Guam Airport has what is called a *glide scope,* which was not working at that time, a fact that the captain well knew. The glide scope is a beam of light that shines from the airport that the pilot can simply follow all the way down to the runway.

It was still possible to land without a glide scope, as 1,500 flights had done in the month that it was under repair. Yet there was a storm above the airport that night, not unusual for the tropical location. A visual approach was necessary to achieve a successful landing—one that was more challenging, required a great amount of coordination between pilot and control tower, yet was by no means impossible.

"They should have been coordinating. [The pilot] should have been briefing for the [DME] step-downs," said Brenner, a psychologist and investigator of the event, "But he doesn't talk about that. The storm cells are all around them, and what the captain seems to be doing is assuming that at some point he's going to break out of the clouds and see the airport. . . ."

It was 1 a.m., and the captain had been awake until 6 a.m. the night before, so fatigue was surely part of the problem. The three classic preconditions for an accident were all there: a minor technical malfunction, bad weather, and a tired pilot. However, there were three professionals in the cockpit, not just the captain. What were the other two doing?

Keeping in mind Korea's high PDI, as one Korean Air pilot put it, "The captain is in charge and does what he wants, when he likes, how he likes, and everyone else sits quietly and does nothing." So according to Flight 801's flight recorder transcript in the last 30 minutes before the crash, the first officer said to the captain, "Don't you think it rains more? In this area, here?" Gladwell translates this into American communication: *Captain. You have committed us to visual approach, with no backup plan, and the weather outside is terrible. You think that we will break out of the clouds in time to see the runway. But what if we don't? It's pitch black outside and pouring rain, and the glide scope is down.*

But Koreans don't speak to their superiors that way. The officer has hinted, and that is all that he thinks he can do. He won't mention weather again. The flight engineer says, "Captain, the weather radar has helped us a lot." Translated, Gladwell says the engineer is trying to underscore the first officer's comment. In other words: *This isn't a night where you can rely on just your eyes to land the plane. Look at what the weather radar is telling us: there's trouble ahead.*

There is a kind of beauty in the subtlety of Korean communication, Gladwell notes, but it does not work well in crisis communication. As the author puts it, "high-power distance communication works only when the listener is capable of paying close attention, and it works only if the two parties in a conversation have the luxury of time, in order to unwind each other's meanings. It doesn't work in an airplane cockpit on a stormy night with an exhausted pilot trying to land at an airport with a broken glide scope."[14]

After that terrible crash, Korean Air recognized they had a major problem. So in 2000, Delta Air Lines' David Greenberg was contracted by Korean Air to run their flight operations. The first decision he made was that everyone needed to learn and speak English in the cockpit. This is not a story about American cultural superiority or having higher competency than Korean culture, Gladwell says. Rather, this is about how different communication styles can alternatively be highly effective or absolutely devastating, depending on the context. If you wanted to remain a pilot at Korean Air, you had to speak English fluently.

"If you are trying to land at JFK at rush hour, there is no nonverbal communication," Greenberg said, "It's people talking to people, so you need to be darn sure you understand what's going on." In English, the Koreans would be free of the "sharply defined gradients" of Korean hierarchy. Instead, the pilots could participate in a culture and language with a very different legacy. While speaking in English, team members could be confident and motivated to speak up to their superiors.

The airline still has a way to go to shed its cloudy past. In January 2013, it dropped to number 56 of 60 airlines surveyed for safety by Germany-based Jet Airliner Crash Data

Evaluation Centre (JACDEC). The organization calculates its annual rankings based on crashes and serious near-accident incidents over the last 30 years, suggesting how long airline tragedies linger in the minds of the public. Nonetheless, things are continuing to look up since the airline's remarkable turnaround, as it's adding routes and continuing to earn glowing headlines. These make the Korean Airlines of today seem sky-miles away from its failures of the 1990s and earlier.

Questions for Discussion

1. What are some key elements of communication that you gathered from this case?

2. What are some of the potential internal and external (PR) dangers associated with mandating that the English language be spoken by nonnative English speakers?

3. How might a global company based in a high-PDI culture have a competitive edge over one founded on low-PDI cultural principles?

Sources

1. Gladwell, Malcolm, *Outliers: The Story of Success*. Aspen, CO: Little, Brown, and Company, 2008.

2. Wald, Matthew L., "Korean Airlines Faults Crew's Actions in Crash on Guam," *The New York Times*, March 26, 1998; http://www.nytimes.com/1998/03/26/us/korean-airlines-faults-crew-s-actions-in-crash-on-guam.html; accessed December 9, 2012.

3. Mace, William, "World's Safest Airlines Named," *The Sydney Morning Herald*, January 10, 2013; http://www.smh.com.au/travel/travel-news/worlds-safest-airlines-named-20130110-2cikq.html; accessed January 11, 2013.

Chapter 16 | INFORMATION AND OPERATIONS

Case Study: Zipcar

We live in a Zipcar economy—the "sharing economy," that is. Whether it's Airbnb, the free or housing swap section of craigslist, or the various "Freecycle" sites that have popped up in recent years, consumers seem ever more eager to swap, share, or give away what they have to offer in exchange for someone else's goods, a bit of extra cash, or maybe even a smidgen of good will. Robin Chase, the founder of Zipcar, was one of the early pioneers of the "sharing economy"— back before it was "cool." Chase says she was interested in using "excess capacity" to address a "sneaky goal": tackling global warming, "When we talk about sharing physical assets, that clearly has real implications for sustainability and environmental outcomes," says Chase, who left the company in 2003 to start Buzzcar another company that is trying to capitalize on excess capacity.

Zipcar offers an opportunity to rent out a car for both short and long periods, giving non-vehicle owners (especially city-dwellers) an economical way to haul their groceries home or perhaps take a relaxing, relatively inexpensive day trip with a loved one or friend. As the world's largest car-sharing network, in November 2012, Zipcar boasted 767,000 members

and 11,000 vehicles throughout the United States, Canada, the United Kingdom, Spain, and Austria.

But despite its popularity and demand for its services, Zipcar has yet to figure out how to turn a profit. Zipcar was purchased by Avis for a zippy $500 million in 2013, but its stock is faring far worse than investors had hoped (the company went public in April 2011). In 2012 alone, Zipcar has lost 39 percent of its value. Its success has been mixed at best. As this book goes to press, Avis Budget Group reported growth over its prior-year second quarter, with Ronald L. Nelson, Avis Budget Group Chairman and Chief Executive Officer, stating: "Zipcar continues to progress as planned, with both cost savings and incremental revenue opportunities being realized."

What went wrong—and right? Zipcar's timing is right, so it seems, capitalizing (or trying to) on the enmeshed trends of urbanites' declining car ownership rates, the growth of the "sharing economy," rising gas prices, a downturn economy, and increased consumer awareness of environmental issues. It's certainly good for cities: Zipcar users say they are less likely to purchase a car (and contribute to congestion, pollution, and parking issues), and more likely to bike, walk, or take alternate forms of transportation. The environmental benefits are undeniable—Zipcar claims that for every shared car, 15 privately owned cars are taken off the road, thus reducing CO_2 emissions. And of course, it's good for consumers. Car-sharing can eliminate a typical household's second-highest expense, saving $9,900 annually for every car eliminated.

While its purchase by Avis inevitably will affect Zipcar's bottom line, the reason for such disappointing returns, some argue, reflect fleet costs—maintenance, insurance, and parking, not to mention the price associated with attracting new customers, including that elusive, yet promising, European market. Competitors are nonetheless flooding the market, and the Avis purchase means that consumers aren't the only ones paying attention to Zipcar. In the hands of larger, more seasoned (and better-financed) owners, Zipcar's uncertain future is a bit brighter.

Questions for Discussion

1. What are some of the primary reasons that a popular, subjectively successful company like Zipcar can perform so poorly financially? How might you address those issues?

2. Is market expansion a good strategy to increase profitability for Zipcar? Why? What else can they focus on to increase the bottom line in established markets?

3. How could the company use the positive influence of Zipcar on the quality of urban life (less traffic, fewer cars, increased use of alternative transportation etc.) to turn a profit?

Sources

1. Berman, Denis K, "Zipcar: Entrepreneurial Genius, Public Company Failure," *The Wall Street Journal*, January 2, 2013; http://blogs.wsj.com/corporate-intelligence/2013/01/02/zipcar-entrepreneurial-genius-public-company-failure/?KEYWORDS=zipcar; accessed January 4, 2013.

2. Chapman, Lizette, "For Venture Firms, Zipcar Purchase a Profitable but Disappointing Exit," *The Wall Street Journal*, January 1, 2013; http://blogs

.wsj.com/venturecapital/2013/01/02/for-venture-firms-zipcar-purchase-a-profitable-but-disappointing-exit/?KEYWORDS=zipcar; accessed January 4, 2013.

3. Clendaniel, Morgan, "Zipcar's Impact on How People Use Cars Is Enormous," *Fast Company*, July 18, 2011; http://www.fastcompany.com/1768007/zipcars-impact-how-people-use-cars-enormous; accessed January 4, 2013.

4. "Avis Budget Group Profits Dip in Q2 2013," Breaking Travel News, August 8, 2013. http://www.breakingtravelnews.com/news/article/avis-budget-group-profits-dip-in-q2-2013/

Chapter 17 | *PERFORMANCE DEVELOPMENT*

Case Study: Tesla Motors

Being "ahead of the curve" is usually a positive adage, indicating that one has an eye on the future, ready for opportunities to present themselves, and poised to pounce—and profit—when the moment is right. But is it possible to be . . . *too* far ahead of the curve?

That's the (several) million-dollar question facing Tesla Motors, the California-based producer of high-end, luxury electric cars and powertrain components for electric cars, which despite great intentions and perhaps even greater expectations, has lost $290.2 million since its founding in 2003. The road for Tesla hasn't gotten smoother since then, unfortunately. In September, execs announced their outlook for a whiplash-inducing $200 million revenue shortfall in 2012, while confirming a full-year revenue forecast of between $400 million and $440 million, a downhill skid from the previous forecast of between $560 million and $600 million. As this book goes to press, things were looking more promising. Its 2013 second quarter showed revenue is growing better than expected, with shares jumping 14% to $153.20 in trading after it reported results. The stock has soared back up 300% year-to-date.

Tesla, like its more mainstream competitors, recognizes that as gas prices rise and the public's passion for environmentally sound products deepens, the market for electric cars is promising. It's also being spurred on by a federal mandate for a near-doubling of fleet average fuel economy by 2025, which has lit a fire in every competitor's belly to produce electric, hybrid, and otherwise fuel-efficient cars. Can Tesla offer enough amenities to woo consumers to choose to purchase their pricey, fully electric vehicles over the growing number of other options?

And while there's no doubt that Tesla is on the cutting edge, at what cost has it achieved that? In 2006, it introduced the world's first-ever fully electric luxury sports car, the Tesla Roadster, with a base price of $109,000. With the March 2009 introduction of the Tesla Model S, the first all-electric luxury car (priced at a more palpable $50,000 per vehicle), Tesla is slowly weaving its way from the high-end to the middle-of-the-road consumer market, which has long been its intention according to CEO Elon Musk. Sales of the Model S, according to the company, should hail the beginning of profitability for the beleaguered manufacturer.

Recent lawsuits from auto dealerships disputing Tesla's right to open company-owned dealerships (an infringement on state franchise laws, according to plaintiffs in New York and Massachusetts) have not made the forecast rosier either. Tesla, of course, is fighting back. Said Musk, "Automotive franchise laws were put in place decades ago to prevent a manufacturer from unfairly opening stores in direct competition with an existing franchise dealer . . . . We have granted no franchises anywhere in the world that will be harmed by us opening stores."

Tesla, like many green start-ups, is navigating a difficult economic landscape. Because such new, capital-intensive enterprises often depend on federal underwriting, Tesla has been stalled by the credit crisis. And meanwhile, the competitive landscape is becoming increasingly fast and furious, but that doesn't seem to rattle Tesla's CEO, "It's a mistake to draw parallels between electric vehicles," Musk said. The Model S was never intended to compete with mass market brands like Toyota and Chevrolet, who are experiencing their own fair share of difficulties, "Buyers for a Model S are buyers who would have otherwise bought an Audi A6 . . . a Mercedes E class . . . or a BMW 5 and 7 series." Whatever the outcome, Tesla's race toward profitability is sure to be a contest to watch.

Questions for Discussion

1. With its high-end offerings in a still-emerging market, did Tesla get into the "race" for success in the fuel-efficient market too soon, or perhaps too boldly? Why or why not?

2. In your view, was Tesla's opening of dealerships a miscalculated blunder or a calculated risk? Explain.

Sources

1. "Tesla Motors Inc.," *The New York Times*, June 29, 2010; http://topics.nytimes.com/topics/news/business/companies/tesla-motors-inc/index.html; accessed December 16, 2012.

2. Stenquist, Paul. "Tesla Model S Offers Lesson in Electric Vehicle Economics," *The New York Times*, June 25, 2012; http://wheels.blogs.nytimes.com/2012/06/25/tesla-model-s-offers-a-lesson-in-electric-vehicle-economics/; accessed December 16, 2012.

3. Gara, Tom, "After Winning Car of the Year, Tesla Raises Its Prices," *The Wall Street Journal*, November 29, 2012; http://blogs.wsj.com/corporate-intelligence/2012/11/29/after-winning-car-of-the-year-tesla-raises-its-prices/?mod=WSJ_qtoverview_wsjlatest; accessed December 15, 2012.

4. Jones, Kristin, "Tesla Posts Loss, but Production Ramps Up," *The Wall Street Journal*, November 5, 2012; http://online.wsj.com/article/SB10001424052970204349404578100991916095354.html?mod=WSJ_qtoverview_wsjlatest; accessed December 13, 2012.

5. White, Joseph B, "Tesla CEO Elon Musk Takes on Car Dealers," *The Wall Street Journal*, October 22, 2012; http://blogs.wsj.com/corporate-intelligence/2012/10/22/tesla-ceo-elon-musk-takes-on-car-dealers/?mod=WSJ_qtoverview_wsjlatest; accessed December 13, 2012.

6. White, Joseph B, "Tesla CEO Says New Models, Loans On Track," *The Wall Street Journal*, February 10, 2012; http://online.wsj.com/article/SB10001424052970203824904577213854167645844.html?mod=WSJ_qtoverview_wsjlatest; accessed December 14, 2012.

7. White, Joseph B, "Electric Cars Struggle to Break Out of Niche," *The Wall Street Journal*, September 25, 2012; http://online.wsj.com/article/SB10000872396390444358045780185100080605302.html?mod=WSJ_qtoverview_wsjlatest; accessed December 14, 2012.

8. "Tesla shares soar on earnings surprise," by Scott Martin, USA Today, August 13, 2013. www.usatoday.com/story/money/cars/2013/08/07/tesla.../2627739

Chapter 18 |
ENTREPRENEURSHIP AND INNOVATION

Case Study: Square

Square is the fastest-growing start-up in the history of start-ups, boasts its chief operating officer (and PayPal veteran) Keith Rabois. If you've visited a small or "pop-up" retailer lately, you have probably used Square's services to pay for your goods. Square is best known for its small, handheld credit card reader, which connects to a retailer's iPhone or Android and allows just about any business, no matter what size, to accept Visa, MasterCard, Discover, and American Express for payment—with no hassle, no upfront investment, and at a flat 2.75 percent fee per swipe. Jack Dorsey, its 35-year-old CEO, has applied his obsession for "elegance and simplicity" to the San Francisco, California–based company from its founding in 2009—the very same principles that inspired him to create Twitter in 2006. Dubbed by the *Wall Street Journal* as "a tech mastermind with the soul of an artist," Dorsey has long been fascinated with untangling mazes and bottlenecks, streamlining and even beautifying confusion. As a teenager, after long hours of listening to emergency radio convinced him that the ambulance service of St. Louis was terribly inefficient, Dorsey created a computer program to make it more effective. Dorsey has studied botanical illustration, fashion design, and massage therapy. He landed his first professional position after hacking into the server of the country's largest dispatch company and emailing the CEO, alerting him of both his server's security weaknesses and his desire for a job.

Dorsey felt compelled to cut through the mess of credit card fees and rules after one of his friends, a glassblower running his own small business, lost a $2,000 sale because a customer didn't have that much cash on hand. Prior to Square and its competitors, many small businesses like Dorsey's friend were unable to handle the monthly fees or web of confusing rules attached to a traditional credit card swipe machine. All that is changing, though, thanks to Dorsey's innovation. The technology allows customers of babysitters, Girl Scouts, tutors, contractors, artists, and all varieties of individual proprietors and mom-and-pop establishments the payment flexibility of a big-box store. Square also gives its users business analytics to understand their customers' spending habits.

Dorsey's is not the only game in town, though. Encouraged by Square's success, competitors are fast entering the market. The company raised $340 million in 2011 and an additional $200 million more recently, putting its implied valuation at $3.25 billion—a growth rate of 13.5 times in less than two years. It also more than doubled its number of users in 2012 and is processing $8 billion in annual payments. More than 1 million small businesses and individuals use Square to process credit cards—a following generated almost solely by word of mouth, for Square currently has no sales force or business-development team.

That may change, however, as the competitive environment heats up. Among just a few of those who promise strong rivalry are PayPal, Google, Groupon, Intuit, Pay Anywhere, and Bank of America, and perhaps Apple will get in the game soon. One thing is sure; mobile payments are here to stay, and they may just transform the industry—for small businesses, individuals, and big business alike. Starbucks is using Square for all credit- and debit-card transactions in its 7,000 U.S. shops, and others are sure to follow.

But Dorsey has shown a patience and focus that lends to continual honing and improvement of his technologies, which suggest that Square's future remains promising. As Twitter was gaining popularity in 2008, for example, Dorsey was steadfast in his focus on improving uptime versus revenue. His three guiding principles—simplicity, constraint, and craftsmanship—are more than just talk; they permeate his companies and their cultures. As does his dedication to innovation, which, to Dorsey, is simply about the inevitable process of progressively evolving, of building upon what is and making it better. "It's important to demystify the term. Innovation is just reinvention and rethinking. I don't think there's anything truly, organically new in this world. It's just mash-ups of all these things that provide different perspectives—that allow you to think in a completely different way, which allows you to work in a different way."

Questions for Discussion

1. What type of controls do you think will be important for Square as it continues to grow and expand?
2. How is Square using information and technology to create a business product that is appealing to customers?

Sources

1. Ankeny, Jason, "Jack Dorsey, CEO, Square/Executive Chairman, Twitter—Most Powerful People in Wireless," FierceWireless; http://www.fiercewireless.com/special-reports/top-25-most-powerful-people-us-wireless-2011/24-jack-dorsey-ceo-squareexecutive-chai; accessed January 12, 2013.
2. McGirt, Ellen, "The World's 50 Most Innovative Companies: Square," *Fast Company*; http://www.fastcompany.com/most-innovative-companies/2012/square; accessed January 11, 2013.
3. Stevenson, Seth, "Simplicity and Order for All," *The Wall Street Journal*, October 6, 2012; http://online.wsj.com/article/SB10001424052970204425904578072640691246804.html?KEYWORDS=%22Square+Inc%22; accessed January 7, 2013.
4. Rusli, Evelyn M, "Square Expects New Financing and a Loftier Value," *The New York Times*, July 24, 2012; http://dealbook.nytimes.com/2012/07/24/square-is-said-to-be-seeking-a-3-25-billion-valuation/; accessed January 13, 2013.
5. Duryee, Tricia, "Another Square Copycat: Bank of America Launches Mobile Payments," All Things D, November 12, 2012; http://allthingsd.com/20121112/another-square-copycat-bank-of-america-launches-mobile-payments/?KEYWORDS=%22Square+Inc%22; accessed January 14, 2013.

GLOSSARY

360-degree review Confidential feedback obtained from the performance appraisal about an individual provided by peers, subordinates, and supervisors that is intended to assess training and development needs. p. 292

Absenteeism The frequent or habitual absence of employees from work. p. 352

Abundance The conscious pursuit of purposeful infinite possibilities that are sustainable and stable over time. p. 352

Accommodative approach An approach to social responsibility in which an organization accepts responsibility and takes action in response to societal pressures. p. 156

Accountability An expectation that team members are responsible for their activities and must report outcomes transparently. p. 267

Acquisition When an organization purchases another organization or business in order to grow. p. 230

Action plan The specific actions, people, and resources needed to accomplish a goal. p. 218

Adaptive management An approach to decision making that requires managers to use critical thinking, collaboration, and reflection skills to make nonprogrammed decisions. p. 173

Administrative model A model of decision making that recognizes the limits of information, time, and individuals and seeks a satisficing rather than an optimum solution. p. 187

Administrative theory Identifies the functions of management in an organization and the principles needed to make sense of a complex set of organizational tasks. p. 35

Advocacy group A set of people dedicated to instituting change based on their concerns or interests. p. 93

Affiliation A person's perceived connection to a group, based on purpose, demographics, function, and other intangible dimensions. p. 309

Affirmative action A purposeful effort taken by an organization to create equal employment opportunities for minority groups and women. pp. 125, 290

Aggregation venture A business strategy defined by acquiring, merging, and coordinating existing market products, services, and companies. p. 449

Ambiguity Information about the situation, goals, or criteria that is incomplete or can be interpreted in multiple ways. p. 174

Analyzer A company whose strategies seek to maintain existing products and services while pursuing limited innovation. They often imitate or follow the proven success of prospector organizations. p. 231

Angel investor Individuals who provide entrepreneurs with funding and mentorship. p. 443

Appraisal The process of measuring and assessing an employee's performance objectively and providing feedback to that employee. p. 291

Articles of incorporation The legal agreement between shareholders and management that determines the fiduciary duty of management in operating the organization. p. 155

Artificial intelligence (AI) A software system that gives computers the ability to seemingly possess human intelligence and act accordingly to process information. p. 406

Association of Southeast Asian Nations (ASEAN) A cooperative organization of 10 countries in Southeast Asia established to promote economic, political, and social progress throughout the region. p. 119

Attitudes A person's or group's inclinations toward an idea or situation. p. 357

Attribution An ascribed quality or characteristic that is related to a particular individual or situation. p. 357

Audit A formal examination of a company, department, or individual's accounts or financial standing. p. 408

Authentic leadership A style of leadership that includes behaviors that encourage positive psychological capacities, an ethical climate, greater self-awareness, an internalized moral perspective, a balanced processing of information, and self-development. p. 343

Authoritarianism The management philosophy that using the threat of punishment, power, and legitimacy is required to produce superior results. p. 358

Authority The implicit and explicit power that a manager or employee has to fulfill an organizational function or role. p. 259

Automation The implementation of manufacturing through an electronic device that does not need continual operations support. p. 423

Autonomy The level of individual discretion that an employee has to make decisions. p. 265

Avoidance learning A benefits theory, also called negative reinforcement, which postulates that behavior that is strengthened by the removal of negative statements or actions. p. 386

Balance sheet A financial statement that lists revenue, assets, and liabilities for a company during a particular time frame. p. 407

Balancing correction A system behavior in which long-term problems are created through short-term fixes. p. 191

Balancing loop A reactionary force that seeks stabilization toward a stock level equilibrium, typically a goal or desired state. p. 63

Barrier to entry An obstacle that makes it difficult for an organization to enter a particular market or replicate a competitor's service and product offerings. p. 235

Barriers to communication Obstacles that interrupt the flow of conveying and receiving messages. p. 380

BCG Matrix A framework developed by the Boston Consulting Group for evaluating business units according to growth and market share. p. 237

Behavior modification A method of shaping actions by the use of positive reinforcement. p. 386

Behavior over time (BOT) diagrams A visual tool that allows managers to see the change in measurements across a span of time. p. 60

Behavioral management Understanding individual behaviors, decisions, and attitudes to motivate employees. p. 48

Behavioral perspective The behavioral perspective connects what managers do to their ability to influence others. p. 334

Behaviorally Anchored Rating Scale (BARS) A method that rates employee performance based on specific behaviors relating to a particular role. p. 292

Benchmarking In Total Quality Management (TQM), information provided to mark a norm on the measurement scale of a product or service in the same vertical market. p. 431

Benefits Non-monetary compensation in the form of health insurance, pensions, paid vacation, etc., which may vary from industry to industry. p. 290

"Big Five" personality traits The five broad domains of human psychology: openness, conscientiousness, negativity, extraversion, and agreeableness. p. 357

Body (nonverbal) language Consists of a person's facial expression and body movements that express communication and emotion without the use of words. p. 380

Bounded rationality Rational decision making that is limited by time, cognitive abilities, and available information. p. 187

Boycott An attempt by an individual or group to change the actions of an organization by convincing other consumers not to purchase its products or services. p. 93

Brainstorming Creating as many alternatives as possible, without making value judgments about any idea. p. 183

Broker A trusted intermediary that facilitates mutually agreed-upon outcomes for two or more parties. p. 261

Budget A document used to predict revenue and expenditures during a certain period for financial forecasting. p. 211

Bureaucracy A form of organization marked by division of labor, managerial hierarchy, rules and regulations, and impersonality. p. 34

Burnout A physical or mental reaction due to stressful and demanding working conditions. p. 352

Business model A proposed method for creating and sustaining market value. p. 442

Business plan The stated actions and goals that support the organizational strategy. pp. 211, 231

Candor The quality of being open, frank, and sincere in speech or expression. p. 353

Capacity refers to the financial and human resources available to the company, which will enable or hinder it to achieve goals. p. 237

Career surveys are questionnaires that employers use to assess employee satisfaction and career aspirations, in order to tailor development programs and project opportunities that support growth toward these goals. p. 291

Cellular layout A combination of fixed positions and service elements. p. 422

Centralized organization A design structure that relies on senior-level managers to collect information broadly, in order to make decisions on behalf of the entire company. p. 259

Ceremony An event that provides one or more stakeholders with a sense of purpose and meaning connected to the organization. p. 89

Certainty A situation in which a decision maker knows all the alternatives and their outcomes. p. 182

Chain of command A predefined structural order of authority that determines how decisions are made and communicated. p. 259

Challenging work Work that is comprised of two types of tasks: pleasureful and purposeful. p. 354

Change management Achieving goals by altering behaviors or processes in response to environment forces. p. 105

Channel richness The capacity to convey as much information as possible during the communication process. p. 379

Charismatic leadership A leadership style characterized by the ability to motivate employees to exceed expected performance through a leader's inspiring behaviors. p. 341

Citizenship In business, the commitment to the overall functions of the team and organizational culture in order to improve performance. p. 364

Classical model A normative model of decision making that leads to an optimal decision, assuming full availability of information, sufficient time, and rationality of the decision maker. p. 172

Cluster chain A group of people that disseminate information within their group or cluster. p. 382

Code of conduct An organization's guidelines for ethical behavior, also called a "code of ethics." p. 153

Coercive power The influential ability to influence people through the threat of or actual negative consequences for undesired actions. p. 329

Cognitive dissonance The psychological strain that occurs when a person is faced with two or more conflicting cognitions (e.g., beliefs, attitudes, or items of knowledge). p. 361

Cohesiveness The degree to which individuals in a working group exhibit loyalty and norm consistencies. p. 309

Collective bargaining The process of negotiation between employers and trade unions, usually with respect to pay, working hours, and working conditions. p. 276

Commitment The degree to which an employee is psychologically devoted to an organization or team. pp. 159, 355

Communication The act of transmitting information, thoughts, and processes through various channels. p. 374

Communication network A system of resources used as a channel for groups of people to connect to each other, such as the Internet. p. 381

Community principle Making decisions that contribute to the strength and well-being of the community. p. 152

Compensation Remuneration in salary or wages to reward employees for their work. p. 290

Competitive advantage The characteristics of an organization's products or services that distinguish it from competitors and provide an advantage in the marketplace. p. 231

Competitive analysis The process of assessing and monitoring the competition in order to design more effective strategies. p. 232

Competitive inertia A tendency to continue with competitive practices that had been successful in the past, even if they are less effective in the present. p. 237

Conceptual skills The ability to think through complex systems and problems. p. 21

Confidence The certainty about handling something that a person desires or needs to do. p. 355

Conflict Resistance or hostility resulting from two or more parties focusing on and attempting to reconcile differing opinions. p. 309

Conformity The situation where an individual or group adheres to organizational policies, procedures, cultural dynamics, and performance standards. p. 308

Contingency theory A management theory that states that different organizations, situations, and contexts require different approaches. pp. 48, 336

Continuous improvement A process to strive for enhanced production on an ongoing basis by reevaluating processes on a frequent basis. p. 432

Contributions The quantifiable efforts produced by an employee, based on that person's role and responsibilities. p. 353

Control A tool that helps managers use information to influence behavior and affect operational performance through greater efficiencies and effective decision making. p. 406

Controller The chief accounting officer within an organization that helps control finances. p. 406

Controlling The process of monitoring activities, measuring results and comparing them with goals, and correcting performance when necessary. p. 12

Conventional stage In Kohlberg's model, the stage of moral development in which the individual's moral decisions are based primarily on societal norms. p. 146

Cooperative system A kind of equilibrium in which organizations are effective and efficient when managers control and influence people's behaviors by modifying their motives. p. 49

Coordination The synchronization of an organization's functions to ensure efficient use of resources in pursuit of goals and objectives. p. 258

Core capabilities Activities and processes that an organization routinely does well in comparison to its competitors; also known as *core competencies*. p. 240

Corporate governance A compendium of policies intended to ensure transparency and fulfillment of duties to stakeholders. p. 261

Corporate social responsibility An organization's self-defined commitment to the health and well-being of the local and global community, beyond its legal obligation. p. 9

Cost leadership strategy A strategy in which an organization seeks competitive advantage by reducing production costs and therefore consumer prices. p. 232

Creativity The ability to devise innovative ideas to meet the needs of a particular task or organizational goals. p. 362

Critical thinking The ability to diagnose situations and predict patterns of behaviors, which result in better decision making. p. 4

Cross-functional team A formal, longstanding working group with representation from diverse divisions, departments, and levels of authority. p. 304

Cross-training Where team members freely share knowledge and provide peer-to-peer mentorship. p. 288

Crowdsourcing Employing the efforts of customers and the public to innovate and further an organization's mission. p. 93

Cultural intelligence A manager's or leader's ability to understand and make effective decisions based on cultural differences. p. 121

Cycle time In Total Quality Management (TQM), the length of time it takes to perform a function or task from beginning to end. p. 431

Decentralized structure A design structure that relies on all employees to collect and communicate information, in order to make decisions and recommend changes. p. 264

Decision support system (DSS) A computer-based information system that helps organizations with their decision-making process. p. 405

Decisional roles Managerial roles in which managers are responsible for making judgments and decisions based on available information and analysis of the situation. p. 14

Deep-level diversity The degree to which individuals in a group represent differences that cannot be seen, such as personalities, attitudes, values, and perspectives. p. 125

Defender A company whose strategies support stable growth and continual improvement of existing products and services. p. 231

Defensive approach An approach to social responsibility in which an organization accepts responsibility but does only the minimum required. p. 156

Delay Refers to the time a force, internal or external, takes to have an effect on system behavior. p. 62

Delegation When a manager grants power and authority to another team member. p. 258

Delphi technique A method of decision making in which a group of experts propose and question ideas until a consensus is reached. p. 184

Demographics Sociological characteristics, including age, gender, marital status, ethnicity, and geographic location, which affect buying habits, work ethic, work-life balance expectations, travel patterns, and disposable income. p. 102

Departmentalization A design structure that groups together processes and jobs based on functions, products, or customers. p. 264

Development Where managers help employees learn the skills necessary to carry out future roles. p. 288

Deviance Intentional behavior and attitudes that differ from or violate the accepted social norms. p. 363

Dialectical inquiry A method of decision making in which a proposal and a conflicting counterproposal are given equal consideration. p. 186

Differentiation The process through which managers divide labor based on tasks and functions. p. 257

Differentiation strategy A strategy in which an organization seeks competitive advantage by providing goods or services that are significantly different from the competition. p. 246

Direct foreign investment Buying existing or building new businesses in other countries. p. 119

Directional plan A general, flexible plan that provides guidelines for an organization's long-term goals. p. 212

Directive leadership involves providing specific, task-focused directions, giving commands, assigning goals, close supervision, and constant follow-up. p. 330

Disabilities Physical or mental impairments that substantially limit one or more of an individual's major life activities. p. 125

Discovery venture A business strategy that seeks to invent a brand-new product or service or find a new resource. p. 450

Discrepancy The difference between an inflow or outflow sum of flow, relative to an equilibrium or desired state. p. 64

Discrimination Treating individuals or groups unfairly or negatively based on their diversity traits, including sexual orientation, age, ethnicity, gender, or disability. p. 125

Distal goals Primary or long-term goals. p. 214

Distributed justice principle Making decisions that do not harm those who are already disadvantaged. p. 152

Diversification strategy A risk-reduction strategy in which an organization adds new kinds of goods, services, or business units. p. 230

Diversity The degree to which an organization represents different cultures. p. 125

Divisional organization A design structure that groups processes and jobs based on clearly defined market segments or geography. p. 265

Divisional strategy A strategy that determines how a business will compete in a particular industry or market. p. 230

Dynamic steering A process where an organization engages in incremental adaptation based on real-time feedback to push toward better engagement and overall productivity. p. 427

Dysfunctional behaviors Actions that show a lack of commitment, lack of trust, fear of confrontation or conflicting opinions, a refusal to accept responsibility, and a tendency to focus on their own individual needs ahead of the team and the organization. p. 363

Early adopters The approximately 14 percent of a market's population that uses a new product or service after innovators have used and tested it. p. 440

Early majority The approximately 34 percent of a market's population that uses a product or service after early adopters have used it. p. 442

Economy An orchestrated system of talent, resources, and money with the purpose to create and distribute products and services. p. 102

Effectiveness The level to which people or organizations achieve agreed-upon goals. p. 20

Efficiency Using the smallest amount of resources to achieve the greatest output. p. 20

Electronic communication A system that includes emails, Skype, videoconferencing, blogs, instant messaging, texting, and social networking (using programs such as LinkedIn, Twitter, and Facebook). p. 378

Emotional intelligence (EI) The capacity to recognize and appreciate emotional responses in one's self and others. p. 366

Employment-at-will The concept that employees can quit their jobs at any time without any reason, and employers can terminate employees at any time and without any reason. p. 280

Empowering leadership A style of leadership that emphasizes employee self-influence processes rather than hierarchical control processes and actively encourages followers to take ownership of their own behaviors and work processes. p. 330

Empowerment The sharing of decisions, information, and responsibility with others. p. 386

Enterprise resource planning (ERP) A system that provides a flow of information to include accounting, manufacturing, customer relationship management, sales, and service. p. 404

Entrepreneur an individual that plans, organizes, and leads high-risk business opportunities with new market value. p. 440

Entrepreneurial ecosystem a set of stakeholders that are necessary to support the innovation and creation of new market value. p. 443

Entrepreneurial skills Capacities, activities, and strengths that enable individuals to manage successfully in high-risk business environments. p. 440

Entrepreneurship Activities associated with seeking opportunities that generate new value, with an array of unknown forces. p. 442

Entropy The loss of social and market-based energy, leading to the decline of an organization. p. 49

Equal employment opportunity A principle stating that every employee has an equal right to advance in a company regardless of age, sex, race, disability, or color. p. 277

Equity theory A system that holds that individuals are more motivated if they perceive they are being treated as fairly as their fellow workers or those in other firms. p. 390

ERG theory of motivation A system that sets out three categories of human needs relating to organizational behaviors: Existent needs, Relatedness needs, Growth needs. p. 375

Eroding Goals archetype A systems pattern where managers impose short-term solutions, leading to the decline of long-term goals. p. 71

Escalation An increase in an organizational behavior as a direct response to a competitor's behavior. p. 149

Escalation archetype A systems pattern where two competing interests eventually take irrational actions against one another, resulting in a "lose-lose" situation. p. 73

Ethical dilemma A situation in which no choice is entirely right. p. 144

Ethics The moral principles, values, and beliefs that govern group or individual behavior according to what is right or wrong and what contributes to the balanced good of all stakeholders. p. 144

Ethnocentric An approach to international business in which management believes that people who share their cultural values make the best managers. p. 121

European Union (EU) A political and economic union of 27 European countries that share a common currency, the euro. p. 119

Executive support system (ESS) A management information system that uses internal and external data to aid the executive staff with their decision-making process with regards to organizational performance. p. 405

Expectancy theory A theory that holds that individuals are more likely to be motivated and perform well if they expect to receive desired rewards. p. 384

Expert power An influence that is derived from perceived knowledge, skill, or competence, such as a manager that is skilled in computer programming has expert power with a software development team. p. 329

Exponential growth or decay When a stock increases or decreases relative to its size, wherein the stock is self-multiplying. p. 65

Exporting The organizational process of creating products in one country and selling them in another. p. 119

External environments The specific and general factors outside an organization that can change how it operates. p. 90

External recruiting The process of creating a pool of qualified applicants outside the organization. p. 282

Externality A cost (negative) or benefit (positive) that occurs beyond the direct exchange between an organization and its stakeholders. p. 148

Extinction A behavioral method that involves withholding praise or a positive reward. p. 386

Extranet A system that is similar to the Internet but used primarily within a company for its employees and or vendors. p. 404

Facility A building designed and built to support a particular service or function. p. 419

Feasibility The degree to which a business venture is possible, given the availability of resources and technologies. p. 446

Feedback loop A reactionary force that causes fluctuations in behavior. (p. 63)

Financial statement A summary that lists the revenue and liabilities for a company during a particular time frame. p. 407

Firewall A software program designed to protect against unauthorized entry into a particular information system or personal computer. p. 403

First mover A company that gains competitive advantage by being the first to offer a new product or service, or to use a new cost-saving technology. p. 232

First-line managers Managers who direct daily activities for producing goods and services. p. 17

Fixed-position layout One of the three basic options for laying out a facility to produce goods and deliver services, all within an unchanging position. p. 422

Fixes That Fail archetype A systems pattern where managers use short-term fixes that result in long-term problems, typically significantly worse than the original challenge. p. 73

Flow The experience of immersion and loss of time when an individual achieves an optimum balance of challenge, interest, and achievement. p. 451

Focus strategy A strategy in which an organization concentrates on a specific target market and may use cost leadership and/or differentiation strategies. p. 246

Formal team A working group formed by an organization's management to achieve specific, agreed-upon strategies, plans, and outcomes. p. 303

Formalization The degree to which policies and procedures determine specific jobs and functions. p. 258

Free agents Independent workers who supply organizations with talent for projects or time-bound objectives. p. 268

Functional organization A hierarchal structure where employees are managed through clear levels of authority. p. 265

Functional strategy A strategy that determines how employees will implement and achieve a tactical plan. p. 230

Functional team A formal, longstanding working group organized around specific tasks, processes, or roles. p. 304

Gainsharing program A system that allows employees to share in any cost savings made by the firm. p. 390

General adaptation syndrome (GAS) A set of physiological reactions to long-term stress that can be grouped into three stages: alarm, resistance, and exhaustion. p. 364

General environment External forces that affect all organizations participating in an economy, where managers have little or no power to effect change. p. 97

Generalization An individual or group perspective that is formed through limited data or experiences. p. 308

Geocentric An approach to international business in which management seeks talent and best practices from all around the world. p. 121

Glass ceiling An invisible barrier that limits the opportunities for women and minorities to advance to upper-level positions. p. 125

Glass ceiling effect An invisible barrier that keeps women and minorities from moving up the corporate ladder, regardless of qualifications and achievements. p. 290

Global company An organization that has operations in multiple countries and its senior management decision making centrally located in one country. p. 119

Global Leadership and Organizational Effectiveness (GLOBE) A network of over 150 researchers from 62 cultures from around the world assembled to study cultural dynamics in leadership and management. p. 122

Global level of ethics The principles, values, and beliefs that are widely considered universal. p. 150

Goal commitment The motivation and determination needed to achieve a goal. p. 215

Gossip chain A format where several individuals spread information, which is sometimes false or misleading, through an organization. p. 382

Government activism Government's active role in "encouraging" business to behave in ways that are in the public interest through tax credits and other incentives. p. 96

Grapevine An informal line of communication where information is passed from one person to another. p. 382

"Great Man" leader A person born into a position of power and authority and seen by some as having a divine right to power. p. 333

Grievance A complaint made by an employee claiming unfair treatment. p. 287

Gross domestic product (GDP) The value of what a country produces on an annual basis, representing the size of its economy. p. 104

Groupthink A usually unconscious mode of group decision making in which individuals prioritize agreement over analysis. p. 182

Growth and Underinvestment archetype A systems pattern where managers reduce resource allocation to increase profits temporarily or to avoid risk, with the unintended consequence of losing its equilibrium in the marketplace. p. 77

Growth company An organization that increases its annual revenue faster than its competitors. p. 16

Growth strategy A strategy for increasing revenue, profits, market share, or territories. p. 238

Hero A real or imagined person who represents an ideal performer specific to the organizational culture. p. 90

Heuristics A set of informal rules used to simplify and expedite the decision-making process. p. 182

Hierarchy A vertically organized structure of power relationships, where the top level holds the most power and resources. p. 256

Human capital Employee skills and experience gained by education and training that increase the economic value for employers. p. 277

Human resource management (HRM, or HR) An organizational function that deals with people-related issues such as recruitment, performance management, benefits, training, employee motivation, safety, and administration, while ensuring compliance with employment and labor laws. p. 276

Humanistic approach A focus on the human side of management in response to negative worker response to scientific management principles. p. 44

Illusion of control Overestimating one's ability to control events and activities. p. 188

Imperfect duties Moral obligations that can be interpreted in different ways. p. 159

Importing The organizational process of acquiring products and services from another country. p. 119

Income statement A summary of revenue gained during a specific time period, usually listed by month. p. 407

Independent contractors Self-employed individuals or independent businesses that provide services to another entity. p. 280

Individual differences The variable psychological, behavioral, cultural, and physical dimensions that uniquely distinguish each team member. p. 357

Individual rights principle Making decisions that do not infringe upon the rights of other people. p. 152

Inducements Formal or informal agreements intended to entice positive or desirable behaviors. p. 366

Inflows Increase the value of a stock measurement. p. 60

Informal team A working group, generally not intended to be permanent, formed by team members to accomplish self-defined tasks and objectives. p. 303

Informational roles Managerial roles in which managers gather, assess, and communicate information to individuals and teams in support of the organization's values, mission, vision, and goals. p. 14

Information technology (IT) The development, maintenance, and use of computer systems, software, and networks for the processing and distribution of data. p. 402

Initial public offering (IPO) The first time a company sells it equity shares on the stock market. p. 448

Innovation A process that results in new market value through the creation of a product or service. p. 440

Innovation adoption curve A staged model that describes the evolution of an innovation's acceptance with customers: innovators, early adopters, early majority, late majority, and laggards. p. 440

Innovators are the approximately 2 percent of a market's population that initially uses and tests a new product or service. p. 440

Integration Horizontal coordination between functions, departments, and organizational activities. p. 257

Interactive engagement Collaborating with consumers to develop future products and services. p. 91

Internal environment The forces inside an organization that affect how the managers set expectations, how employees perform their roles, and how the company interacts with stakeholders and responds to external environments. p. 87

Internal recruiting The process of creating a pool of existing employees who may have the qualifications to fill required job vacancies in an organization. p. 282

Interpersonal roles Managerial roles in which managers build relationships with the people they work with and act as a public symbol for the many people that they represent. p. 14

Interview A meeting or conversation arranged to assess the qualifications of an individual and evaluate whether that person has the skills and abilities to do a job. p. 285

Intuitive decision A decision based on feelings, previous experience, and existing knowledge. p. 186

Inventory The items and quantity in stock typically held in a warehouse or one designated area. p. 424

ISO 9000:2000 A standard from the International Organization for Standardization (ISO), which provides an exact measure of quality globally over a platform of systems. p. 432

ISO 14000 A standard from the International Organization for Standardization (ISO) with total focus on the organization's environmental impact and quality. p. 432

Job description A written account of specific tasks, duties, and responsibilities required within a particular role p. 282

Joyful living Feelings and emotions defined by interest, passion, curiosity, contentment, enthusiasm, satisfaction, and quality of life. p. 354

Just-In-Time (JIT) Method A production method that provides an item as needed versus keeping inventory in stock. p. 424

Key performance indicators (KPIs) Measurements that managers identify as vital to the company's performance. p. 219

Knowledge Information gained by an individual or team that is internalized. p. 403

Knowledge workers Self-motivated workers that use a variety of skills to enhance their overall understanding of a particular subject or area. p. 280

Labor relations The relationship between management and the workforce. p. 276

Laggards are the approximately 16 percent of a market's population that is last to use a product or service. p. 442

Large organizations Organizations with more than 500 employees. p. 15

Late majority describes the approximately 34 percent of a market's population that uses a product or service after the early majority has used it. p. 442

Layout The design of space in an organization that specifies the workflow. p. 421

Leadership A process of influence aimed at directing behavior toward the accomplishment of objectives. p. 326

Leading The process of effectively motivating and communicating with people to achieve goals. p. 11

Lean manufacturing The implementation of best practices to eliminate inefficiencies and waste while increasing profit. p. 424

Legal principle Making decisions that follow both the letter and the spirit of the law. p. 152

Legitimate power The influence that a manager has because of his or her title inside an organization or status in a community. p. 329

Limits to Growth archetype A systems pattern where an external or internal force restricts the ability to expand a service or product offering. p. 69

Liquidity The measurement of available financial resources or the ability to convert an organization's assets into cash. p. 445

Listening The active effort to understand, learn, and obtain information from others. p. 381

Location A characteristic of an organization that provides strategic access to all segments, vendors, and vitality. p. 421

Locus of control The degree to which an individual or team feels in control of circumstances and outcomes. p. 357

Long-term plan A plan that covers time periods of a year or more and is used to achieve future goals. p. 210

Long-term principle Making decisions that support the long-term interests of yourself and your organization. p. 152

Machiavellianism A pragmatic management philosophy that condones unethical and manipulative behavior if it produces desirable results. p. 358

Malcolm Baldrige Award An annual prize that recognizes performance excellence in U.S. companies and nonprofit organizations. p. 432

Management The process of working with people and distributing an organization's resources to achieve goals efficiently and effectively. p. 6

Management by Objectives (MBO) A method of management in which management and employees agree to specific goals that are then used to evaluate individual peformance. p. 217

Management information system (MIS) A tool that aids organizations to run more efficiently by incorporating people, technology, and information systematically. p. 404

Management science Using statistics, mathematics, and other quantitative methods to improve efficiencies. p. 37

Management team A functional or cross-functional working group of managers formed to plan, organize, lead, and control organizational performance. p. 305

Managerial roles Organizational expectations that determine the actions of managers, including *interpersonal*, *informational*, and *decisional* roles. p. 14

Manufacturing A process where large goods are made, typically by manual labor or large machinery. p. 424

Market position An honest assessment about how the company competes in its industry. p. 237

Maslow's hierarchy of needs A theory proposed by psychologist Abraham Maslow that suggests that people are motivated by a number of needs, which are displayed in order. They are physiological needs, safety needs, love/belongingness needs, esteem needs, and self-actualization needs. p. 375

Matrix organization A design structure that facilitates horizontal integration and collaboration. p. 265

Means-ends chain An integrated series of goals in which the accomplishment of lower-level goals contributes to the achievement of higher-level goals. p. 215

Merit-based rewards Positive reinforcement based on specific accomplishments, with rewards given for achievement of specified measurements. p. 388

Meta-ideas Concepts that create, nurture, and support other concepts. p. 451

Middle managers Managers who direct the work of first-line managers and are responsible for divisions or departments. p. 17

Mid-size organizations Organizations with between 100 and 500 employees. p. 15

Mission An organization's central purpose intended to generate value in the marketplace (for-profit) or community (nonprofit) and which lasts for the life of the leader. p. 18

Moral courage Taking a position against something or someone even though you know the outcome may be unpopular. p. 354

Motivation An incentive or drive to complete a task, function, or idea. p. 374

Multi-domestic company An organization with operations in multiple countries and its senior management decision making distributed across the countries in which it operates. p. 119

Multinational corporation An organization with operations in multiple countries, usually more than 10,000 employees, and designs, develops, and sells products and services to customers all over the world. p. 16

Negative affectivity (NA) A general dimension of personality where an individual experiences negative mood states, such as anger, disgust, fear, and anxiety. p. 352

Negative entropy Social and market-based energy that builds or maintains a system. p. 49

Negotiation The process which two or more parties with differing objectives, desires, or perspectives go through to find a mutually agreeable solution. p. 312

Network organization A group of independent companies that organize themselves to appear as a larger entity. p. 262

New-existing venture A business strategy defined by offering a new product or service to an existing category of consumers. p. 450

New-new venture A business strategy defined by offering a new category of consumers a new product or service, typically distinguished with higher risk and higher returns compared to new-existing ventures. p. 450

Nominal group technique (NGT) A group decision-making process in which individuals rate proposed solutions and the total tally determines the final decision. p. 184

Nonprofit organizations Organizations that are required by the Internal Revenue Service (IRS) to reinvest all profits back into the organization, as opposed to distributing that money to investors or employees. p. 16

Nonprogrammed decision A decision based on reason and/or intuition in response to a unique situation that requires a tailored decision. p. 172

Norms Expectations implicitly or explicitly defined by a group that result in a consistent set of behaviors or beliefs. p. 308

North American Free Trade Agreement (NAFTA) An agreement between Canada, Mexico, and the United States intended to remove barriers to trade and investment. p. 119

Offshoring Moving a business process to another country. p. 131

Onboarding A new employee orientation where workers acquire the skills, knowledge and behaviors to aid transition into an organization. p. 287

Open systems Systems that have the power to change and be changed by external and internal forces. p. 50

Operational capacity The ability of an operation to work at its maximum of potential and successful execution. p. 421

Operational plans Plans that guide the day-to-day production or delivery of an organization's goods and services, and which enact a functional strategy. pp. 212, 230

Operations management Processes and systems built to assist in the daily activities of production. p. 423

Optimum decision The best possible decision given all the needed information. p. 172

Options-based planning A method of planning that preserves flexibility in contexts of uncertainty by investing in several alternative plans. p. 213

Oral communication Provides verbal discussions, ideas, and processes, either one on one or as a group (face-to-face). p. 378

Organic organization A highly adaptive structure defined by horizontal integration, distributed decision making, and employees with a high degree of generalization. p. 257

Organization An entity formed and structured to achieve goals. p. 15

Organizational chart A visual document that communicates how a company is organized. p. 261

Organizational culture A collection of beliefs that individuals and groups share to help their organization respond to environmental forces and changes. p. 87

Organizational strategy A corporate-level strategy that addresses the question "What business are we in?" and unites all parts of the organization. p. 230

Organizing The process of orchestrating people, actions, resources, and decisions to achieve goals. p. 11

Outcomes The results of a process or undertaking. p. 384

Outflows Decrease the value of a stock measurement. p. 60

Outsourcing (1) In Total Quality Management (TQM), an element that occurs when the delivery of a product or services becomes valued as more profitable by using outside resources or systems versus internal resources, including human and capital assets. p. 131 (2) Hiring an outside company to fulfill one or more of an organization's core functions. p. 131

Overload Behavioral and system strains that occur when expectations for positions or working groups exceed their capacity to perform. p. 307

Path-goal theory A theory that identifies leadership behaviors that motivate a team through clarification, support, and removal of barriers in pursuit of a goal. p. 338

Perception The process by which individuals select, interpret, and organize information in the world around them. p. 354

Perfect duties Moral obligations that are clearly articulated, such as a contract or verbal agreement. p. 159

Performance dashboard A visual representation of an organization's strategies and goals, which allow managers to track progress toward metrics and goals immediately. p. 218

Performance development Managing employee performance and assessing opportunities for growth and development. p. 290

Personal power Influence that is obtained by being perceived as likable and well-informed. p. 329

Piece-rate incentives Awards and prizes given at a specific rate as accomplishments occurs, rather than all at one time. p. 388

Planning The process of setting goals for the future, designing strategies, and deciding on the actions and resources needed to achieve success. p. 10

Policy A standing plan that describes how an organization and its members should respond to recurring or anticipated situations. p. 211

Policy-based analysis A method of problem analysis that isolates the variables in a system that can truly be addressed through management intervention p. 179

Polycentric An approach to international business in which management believes that managers from a particular country know best how to achieve results in that cultural context. p. 121

Positional power The influence that is granted because of a manager's type and ability to affect someone positively or negatively through resource allocation or disciplinary measures. p. 329

Positive affectivity (PA) The outward display of affirming emotions, such as happiness, optimism, and encouragement. p. 353

Positive deviance Intentional behavior and attitudes that differ from the accepted social norms in an honorable way. p. 363

Positive Psychology A field of psychology that helps people define and cultivate their personal strengths, so they can thrive and flourish with a sense of purpose through challenging work. p. 22

Positive reinforcement A reward given to motivate a person or group which is usually stated verbally or with "pats on the back" and words of encouragement. p. 386

Post-action control A control used to assess results after a process is complete in order to provide information for future planning p. 402

Postconventional stage In Kohlberg's model, the stage of moral development in which an individual's moral decisions are based primarily on what he or she believes is good for society as a whole. p. 146

Power The ability to influence how others behave. Leaders have powers that are given and some that are earned. p. 329

Preconventional stage In Kohlberg's model, the stage of moral development in which an individual's moral decisions are based primarily on self-protection or self-interest. p. 146

Preliminary control (planning control) A control used as a preventative measure to identify potential deficiencies before they occur. p. 401

Principle-based management A management style in which an organization proactively connects values and beliefs to behavior expectations, where all stakeholders are continuously made aware of these standards. p. 153

Prior-hypothesis bias Basing decisions on beliefs or assumptions despite evidence to the contrary. p. 186

Proactive approach An approach to social responsibility in which an organization goes beyond industry norms to solve and prevent problems. p. 155

Proactive engagement Creating a product or service as an alternative to enhance the customer's experience. p. 91

Problem-solving team A working group formed to minimize the negative impacts of a specific organizational challenge. p. 306

Procedure A standing plan that provides the specific steps to be taken as part of a recurring process or in response to a recurring situation. p. 211

Production blocking A loss in productivity during a brainstorming session because individuals are overwhelmed by the number of possibilities being generated. p. 182

Productivity The measurement of quantity of product and services being made. p. 421

Product-service mix The combination of the number of products provided versus the services delivered. p. 423

Professional employee organizations Organizations that offer employee management services to other companies. p. 132

Programmed decision A decision based on preestablished rules in response to a recurring situation. p. 172

Prospector A company that uses strategies for high-risk, fast growth through product and market innovation. p. 232

Proximal goals Short-term goals that increase individuals' ability to reach distal goals by providing motivation and feedback. p. 214

Pseudotransformational leader A leader who is effective, yet their primary aims and goals are to seek personal power and wealth or cause harm to others. p. 341

Psychological contract An informal expectation between employee and organization that determines quality and satisfaction. p. 355

Psychometric tools Questionnaires or tests that measure an individual's personality, intelligence, and aptitude. p. 282

Purchasing A process of buying goods or services to accomplish a goal. p. 424

Purposeful thinking -An approach that involves continually seeking pathways for possibilities and looking for opportunities to learn and grow. p. 353

Q-level A measurement that determines the optimum level of group size and interaction to achieve successful creative output. p. 453

Quality A measure of product or service excellence minus the amount of defects. p. 423

Quality circle A working group comprised of management and staff with the purpose of minimizing performance errors and variance. p. 306

Quantitative approach Applying objective methods to enhance decision making. p. 37

Ratio analysis A quantitative study of a company's financial statements within a particular collection of data. p. 407

Reactive approach A response to social responsibility in which an organization denies responsibility for social problems and responds only when legally required. p. 156

Reactive engagement Monitoring positive and negative customer feedback and improving the organization's products and services accordingly. p. 91

Reactor A company that does not follow a consistent strategy but just responds to changes in the environment. p. 231

Reasoned judgment A decision based on extensive information gathering, careful analysis, and generation of alternatives. p. 187

Recruiting The process of identifying the best applicants internally or externally for specific roles. p. 282

Referent power An influence that is based on a manager's appealing traits or resources, such as charisma or the ability to offer an employee a promotion. p. 329

Regional trading zones Zones established through trade agreements among several countries in which trade barriers are reduced or eliminated for member countries. p. 119

Regulations Rules set by external governing bodies that dictate standards and procedures for industries, businesses, and professionals. p. 94

Reinforcement theory A behavioral construct where individuals may be rewarded or punished based on the consequences of their behavior. p. 386

Reinforcing engine A system behavior indicative of growth coupled with an unintended consequence in another part of the system. p. 190

Reinforcing loops A self-multiplying reactionary force that amplifies change in a stock level. p. 63

Relational skills The ability to collaborate and communicate with others effectively. p. 21

Renewal strategy A strategy to address declining performance through retrenchment and regrowth. p. 247

Representative bias Generalizing from too small a sample size. p. 187

Resources The assets, people, processes, and capabilities of an organization. p. 237

Reward power An influential ability to affect a team member positively through resources, preferred schedules, and additional status. p. 329

Reward system A theory that provides prizes, incentives for tasks and jobs well done, and special recognition. p. 388

Rights The behaviors you can expect from others based on their duties. p. 159

Risk The probability of loss or undesirable consequences. pp. 184, 354

Ritual A formalized activity intended to communicate and teach the organization's culture. p. 89

Role A behavioral and performance expectation that is consciously or unconsciously defined by a group. p. 307

Role ambiguity Confusion that arises from an employee not understanding the expectations, intentions, or purpose of his or her position. p. 307

Role structure A prescribed set of behavioral and performance expectations for a position or job. p. 307

Rules and regulations Formal descriptions of how specific actions are to be carried out. p. 211

S.M.A.R.T. goals Goals that are specific, measurable, achievable, relevant, and time-bound. p. 204

Satisficing Choosing an acceptable solution rather than an optimal solution. p. 186

Scaling The degree to which a company or its business model can grow, given the necessary resources. p. 448

Scanlon plan A system that recognizes and rewards individuals for collaboration, leadership, education, and training given to another individual or group cohesively. p. 388

Scientific management Using a quantitative approach to analyzing and synthesizing the flow of work to maximize productivity. p. 37

Screening control (real-time control) A control used to take corrective measures based on feedback during a process should barriers arise. p. 401

Selection The process that assesses the level of skills and abilities possessed by an individual to perform a specific role. p. 282

Selective perception The process by which individuals accept information consistent with their values and beliefs, while screening out information that is not aligned with their own needs. p. 354

Self-awareness The ability to look objectively at a circumstance and make subjective, principle-based judgment decisions simultaneously. p. 353

Self-efficacy The extent to which a person believes in his or her own competence regarding a process or task. p. 354

Self-leadership A process through which people influence themselves to achieve the self-direction and self-motivation necessary to perform. p. 342

Servant leader A person that focuses on the needs, objectives, and aspirations of team members to help them achieve organizational goals. p. 342

Shared leadership A collaborative process in which team members share key leadership roles. p. 343

Shifting the Burden archetype A systems pattern, similar to "Fixes that Fail," where managers use short-term fixes that result in long-term problems, typically by using non-sustainable resources to address a challenge. p. 70

Short-term plan A plan that covers one year or less and is used to achieve short-term goals. p. 212

Single-use plan A plan developed to achieve a particular goal or in response to an event that is not expected to be repeated. p. 212

Six Sigma A business management strategy designed to analyze the causes of defects using statistical methods. p. 432

Skills The talents or abilities that enable a person to complete a particular task, interaction, or process effectively and efficiently. p. 20

Slogan A repetitive phrase intended to support an organization's culture, mission, vision, or values. p. 88

Small organizations Organizations with fewer than 100 employees. p. 15

Social entrepreneur Someone who starts a business for the dual purpose of profit and societal benefit. p. 157

Social integration The degree to which individuals in a group share and collaborate based on their unique perspective. p. 133

Social responsibility Proactive behavior by an organization for the benefit of society. p. 155

Socialization The processes by which individuals attain the knowledge, skills, cultural distinctions, and values to adapt to a group's norms. p. 309

Societal norms Society's expectations about how people (and organizations) should behave. p. 146

Sociocultural forces The behaviors and beliefs associated with demographic groups that comprise an organization's available talent and customers. p. 102

Soldiering A way that workers tested management by performing as slowly as possible, while giving their supervisors the impression that they were working fast. p. 37

Span of control The optimum number of direct reports that a person can manage effectively. p. 257

Specialization Focusing a group or individual's activities based on strengths, aptitudes, or skills. p. 258

Specific environment The industry-focused part of the external environment that directly affects an organization's operations and performance. p. 91

Stability strategy A strategy in which an organization focuses on processes, products, and services that will sustain it over the long term. p. 232

Stages of group development A four-stage process by which teams become more effective and efficient over time; the stages are Forming, Storming, Norming, and Performing. p. 308

Stakeholders Individuals or groups who have a direct interest in an organization's behavior and experience the effects of the company's management decisions. p. 148

Standardization A performance context where policies and procedures seek to create uniform results. p. 258

Standards Models and examples of how items or tasks are expected to be executed. p. 401

Standards of excellence An organization's highest expectations of behavior for all employees, including required and prohibited behaviors. p. 159

Standing plans Plans designed for repeated use in response to commonly occurring events. p. 211

Start-up company A newly formed organization with limited or no operational history. pp. 16, 442

Statistical quality control The use of statistics that are monitored on an ongoing basis from production, for the sole purpose of determining production quality. p. 432

Stereotyping The tendency to ascribe characteristics or attributes to a particular group or individual unfairly. p. 356

Stocks Materials or information that can be measured in a system. p. 60

Stock options Company stocks given to employees as additional compensation or incentives, usually at a discounted price for a limited time. p. 390

Story A narrative, usually fictionalized or enhanced over time, based on actual organizational experiences. p. 88

Strategic partnership An agreement between two or more organizations to share complementary resources to develop and sell products and services. p. 119

Strategy A plan of action for achieving goals. p. 230

Stress The physiological and emotional reactions experienced by individuals to excessive pressures or demands at work. p. 352

Stretch goal A goal that is almost unattainable and requires the full capacity of an individual, manager, team, or organization to accomplish. p. 214

Student organization An organization formed to engage students further in the college experience through academic, political, religious, sports, environmental, and social action. p. 16

Subsystem Smaller, interdependent systems that make up the whole system. p. 37

Success to the Successful archetype A systems pattern where two efforts compete for the same resources, and the more successful effort today gets more support, regardless of future potential of the competing effort. p. 74

Suppliers Entities that provide an organization with the external resources that it needs to operate, including money, materials, people, and information. p. 94

Supply chain is a network of interconnected businesses strategically aligned to provide product and service packages. p. 424

Surface-level diversity The degree to which individuals in a group represent differences based on visual cues, such as age, ethnicity, and gender. p. 125

Sustaining Seeing, analyzing, and designing systems to achieve long-term organizational, community, and environmental health. p. 13

SWOT analysis A method of assessing an organization's strengths, weaknesses, opportunities, and threats (abbreviated as SWOT). p. 239

Symbol An event, situation, object, person, or other artifact that provides greater meaning to the organization. p. 89

Symptomatic effects Observable behaviors related to underlying causal variables. p. 175

System change venture A business strategy responding to a significant change in political environments, governmental legislation, and regulations. p. 450

Systemic-based analysis A method of analyzing a problem that takes into account the array of all known variables associated with a problem and its symptoms, including behavior over time. p. 175

Systems archetypes Peter Senge's classification of common patterns of complex problems that managers encounter. p. 69

Systems thinking A methodology of analysis that managers use to understand interconnected cause-and-effect relationships that change organizational behaviors and dynamics. p. 59

Tactical plans Plans that cover an intermediate time scale and enact divisional strategies by allocating people and resources. pp. 212, 230

Talent The people who have the skills, knowledge, creativity, and relationships necessary to optimize an organization's performance. p. 92

Talent management A strategic, deliberate approach to attracting new highly skilled workers and developing the abilities of existing employees to meet current and future organizational objectives. p. 277

Task-based team a working group established to accomplish a specific objective, with a tightly defined time frame for completion. p. 306

Task-management system A combination of setting performance standards, selecting the best worker for the job, and building good relations between managers and employees. p. 37

Team A purposeful group formed to accomplish a project, task, or goal. p. 302

Teaming A process whereby an adaptive working group is formed to address unexpected environmental changes, challenges, and opportunities. p. 314

Technical skills The ability to perform job-specific tasks. p. 21

Telecommuting A work arrangement in which an employee is given flexibility in terms of work location, and often hours as well. p. 268

Theory X A negative view of the worker that states that people do not like to work; therefore, workers need to be coerced, told what to do, and intimidated. p. 47

Theory Y A positive view of the worker that states that people enjoy the mental and physical purpose that work provides; therefore, when participating in a group with a shared commitment, people will direct themselves and look for ways to expand their personal contributions and responsibilities. p. 47

Top managers Managers who set the organization's direction and make decisions that affect everybody. p. 17

Total Quality Management (TQM) A long-range, big-picture process to assist companies in better overall total management for an entire organization. p. 431

Tragedy of the Commons archetype A systems pattern where multiple efforts are competing for the same resource, where self-interest overrides a collective solution. p. 75

Training Teaching new or existing employees the skills necessary to carry out their roles and improve current job performance. p. 288

Trait perspective A system of ideas that focuses on identifying effective leaders through personal characteristics that are difficult to or cannot be learned. p. 332

Transactional leadership focuses on the creation of reward contingencies and exchange relationships that result in a calculative compliance on the part of followers. p. 330

Transformational leadership involves creating and communicating a higher-level vision in a charismatic way that elicits an emotional response and commitment from the followers. p. 330

Transplant venture A business strategy where an idea that achieves market success in one market region is transferred to other geographic markets. p. 450

Two-factor theory of motivation A theory, also known as "motivation-hygiene theory" or "dual theory," which is based on job satisfaction and/or job dissatisfaction and the extent to which attitudes influence outcomes. p. 375

Type A personality A behavioral pattern where individuals tend to be ambitious, assertive, goal oriented, impatient, determined, highly organized, competitive, and aggressive. p. 355

Type B personality A behavioral pattern where individuals tend to be more patient, relaxed, easygoing, and more sensitive to the feelings of others. p. 355

Uncertainty A situation in which a decision maker does not know all the alternatives and their outcomes. p. 182

Underlying causes The behaviors that lead to a desired or undesired symptomatic effect. p. 175

Unity-of-Command principle A philosophy that each employee reports to and is accountable to only one manager. p. 263

Utilitarian principle Making decisions that provide the greatest good to the greatest number (or the least harm to the fewest number). p. 152

Valence An individual opinion of the value of outcomes. p. 385

Value chain venture A business strategy that seeks to redesign or augment an offering in an existing business or management process, such as outsourcing of information technology and research. p. 450

Value creation The activities and processes that increase the worth of a product or service. p. 448

Value-added analysis In Total Quality Management (TQM), an element that provides a core study of an item or process down to its raw costs vs. measurement to provide the most effective product or service. p. 431

Values Beliefs that shape employee and organizational behaviors and are intended to be timeless. p. 18

Values-based management A management style in which the company's culture affects employee behavior in ways that are consistent with the organization's mission and values. p. 147

Variation The system-level changes that inevitably occur that may require individuals and groups to respond. p. 311

Venture capital Funding that supports the starting and growing of high-risk business ventures. p. 442

Vertical integration A method of diversification in which an organization begins producing its own supplies (backward integration) or takes on the distribution and selling of its products (forward integration). p. 247

Vertical organizational structure A structure, characterized by hierarchical authority and communication channels. p. 259

Virtual team A working group that conducts the majority of its collaborations via electronic communications. pp. 269, 306

Virtuous principle Making decisions that you would be publicly proud of. p. 152

Vision A description of an optimal future 1–10 years from now. p. 19

Wave venture A business strategy defined by a systemic change in business and market environments. p. 450

World Trade Organization (WTO) The organization responsible for global trade rules between countries. p. 119

Written communication A system where the sender writes emails, reports, memos, letters, and other documents. p. 378

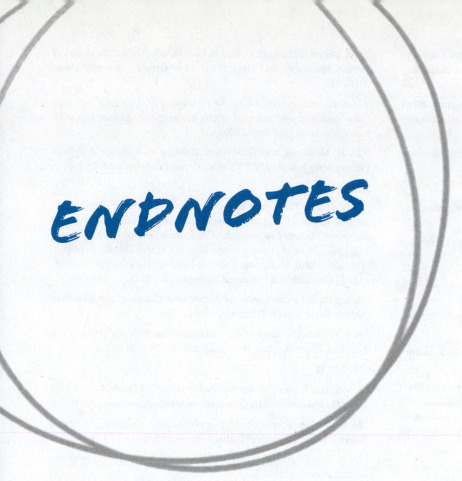

ENDNOTES

Chapter 1

1 John Chaffee, *The Thinker's Guide to College Success* (Boston: Houghton Mifflin College Division, 1999).

2 Abhijit Naik, "Tricky Riddles for Adults." http://www.buzzle.com/articles/tricky-riddles-for-adults.html. Accessed November 14, 2012.

3 *Are They Really Ready to Work? Employers' Perspectives on the Basic Knowledge and Applied Skills of New Entrants to the 21st-Century U.S. Workforce (2006)*. Study conducted by The Conference Board, Partnership for 21st-Century Skills, Corporate Voices for Working Families, and the Society for Human Resource Management.

4 B. Hagemann and J. M. Chartrand (2009). *2009 Trends in Executive development: A Benchmark Report [Technical Report]* (Oklahoma City: Executive Development Associates).

5 Deniz S. Ones, and Stephan Dilchert. "How Special Are Executives? How Special Should Executive Selection Be? Observations and Recommendations." *Industrial & Organizational Psychology 2*, no. 2 (June 2009): 163–170.

6 Elizabeth A. Jones et al., "National Assessment of College Student Learning: Identifying College Graduates' Essential Skills in Writing, Speech and Listening, and Critical Thinking." (National Center for Education Statistics, U.S. Department of Education, Office of Educational Research and Improvement, NCES 95-001, 1995), 14–16.

7 Content in this box is based on the following sources: M. Price, personal interview (November 10, 2009); D. Romero, "Surfing's Next Safari," *Entrepreneur* (July 2009), 24–27; http://www.firewiresurf-boards.com/technology.php?techid=tech#tech03.

8 D. Romero, "Surfing's Next Safari," *Entrepreneur* (July 2009): 24–27.

9 N. F. Koehn, *The Story of American Business from the Pages of the New York Times* (Boston: Harvard Business Press, 2009): 305.

10 D.K. Rigby, K. Gruver, and J. Allen, "Innovation in Turbulent Times," *Harvard Business Review* (June 2009): 79–86; G. H. Walker, N. A. Stanton, P. M. Salmon, and D. P. Jenkins (2008). A review of sociotechnical systems theory: A classic concept for new command and control paradigms. *Theoretical Issues in Ergonomics Science,* 9(6), 479–499; J. E. Kelly (1978). "A Reappraisal of Sociotechnical Systems Theory." *Human Relations,* 31(12), 1069–2000.

11 "Gives $10,000,000 to 26,000 Employees," *New York Times* (January 6, 1914) March 15, 2010, http://www.nytimes.com/learning/general/onthisday/big/0105.html.

12 J. Elkington, *Cannibals with Forks: Triple Bottom Line of 21st-Century Business* (Oxford: Capstone Publishing, 1997).

13 "Patagonia's History–A Company Created by Climber Yvon Chouinard and His Commitment to the Environment," *Patagonia,* http://www.patagonia.com/web/us/patagonia.go?slc=en_US&sct=US&assetid=3351.

14 L. Resnick, "Doing Well by Doing Good—Together," *The Huffington Post,* September 8, 2009, http://www.huffingtonpost.com/lynda-resnick/doing-well-by-doing-good_b_279545.html.

15 *Ibid.*

16 M. Friedman, *Capitalism and Freedom* (Chicago: The University of Chicago Press, 2002).

17 Statistics derived from *The 2008 Corporate Responsibility Report,* http://www.corporateregister.com/.

18 H. Fayol, *Industrial and General Administration* (Paris: Dunod, 1916).

19 B. Stone and S. Rosenbloom, "Price War Brews Between Amazon and Wal-Mart," *New York Times,* Nov 23, 2009, http://www.nytimes.com/2009/11/24/business/24shop.html?_r=2&scp=2&sq=amazon&st=cse.

20 A. Overholt, "Do You Hear What Starbucks Hears?" *Fast Company*, July 1, 2004, http://www.fastcompany.com/magazine/84/starbucks_schultz.html.

21 M. Vella, "How to Reenergize Starbucks," *Business Week* (February 20, 2008), http://www.businessweek.com/innovate/content/feb2008/id20080220_372003.htm.

22 E. Catmull, "How Pixar Fosters Collective Creativity," *Harvard Business Review* (September 2008): 64–72.

23 F. Beamer, personal interview, May 24, 2007.

24 "Pixar. How We Do It." Pixar website; http://www.pixar.com/howwedoit/index.html.

25 J. W. Heineman (2007). "Avoiding Integrity Land Mines." *Harvard Business Review,* 85(4), 100–108.

26 *Ibid.*

27 *Ibid.*

28 T. P. Pare, "Jack Welch's Nightmare on Wall Street," *Fortune*, September 5, 1994.

29 H. Mintzberg, *The Nature of Managerial Work* (New York: Harper & Row, 1973).

30 J. Battelle, *The Search: How Google and Its Rivals Rewrote the Rules of Business and Transformed Our Culture* (New York: Penguin, 2005); K. H. Hammonds, "How Google Grows . . . and Grows . . . and Grows . . ." *Fast Company*, March 31, 2003, http://www.fastcompany.com/magazine/69/google.html.

31 *Ibid.*

32 *Ibid.*

33 M. Lacter, "Talk About New Beginnings: How I Did It," *Inc. Magazine* (June 2007): 106–108.

34 J. Collins, *Good to Great and the Social Sector* (New York: HarperCollins, 2005).

35 *Teach for America*, http://www.teachforamerica.org/our-organization; accessed September 19, 2012.

36 See BCEC at Indiana University; available at http://www.indiana.edu/~bcec/.

37 This discussion is based on T. V. Bonoma and J. C. Lawler, "Chutes and Ladders: Growing the General Manager," *Sloan Management Review* (Spring 1989): 27–37.

38 Research and case studies on changing value systems can be found in P. Hemp and T. A. Stewart, "Change When Business Is Good," *Harvard Business Review* (December 2004): 60–70; and C. Zook, "Finding Your Next Core Business," *Harvard Business Review on Managing Through a Downturn* (Boston: Harvard Business School Publishing, 2009): 97–122.

39 Based on http://www.starbucks.com/aboutus and http://www.dunkinbrands.com/aboutus/.

40 Quoted in J. W. Robinson, *Jack Welch and Leadership* (New York: Random House, 2001).

41 L. Buchanan, "How I Did It: Margot Fraser," *Inc Magazine* (June 1, 2009), http://www.inc.com/magazine/20090601/how-i-did-it-margot-fraser.html.

42 *Ibid.*

43 M. Buckingham and D. O. Clifton, *Now, Discover Your Strengths* (New York: The Free Press, 2001).

44 P. A. Linley, S. Harrington, and N. Garcea, eds., *Oxford Handbook of Positive Psychology and Work* (New York: Oxford University Press, 2010), 145.

45 M. Csikszentmihalyi, *Flow: The Psychology of Optimal Experience* (New York: Harper Perennial, 2008); M. Seligman, *Authentic Happiness* (New York: Free Press, 2002).

46 D. H. Meadows and D. Wright, *Thinking in Systems: A Primer* (White River Junction, VT: Chelsea Green Publishers, 2008): 146.

Chapter 2

1 R. W. Paul, L. Elder, and T. Bartell, *California Teacher Preparation for Instruction in Critical Thinking: Research Findings and Policy Recommendations* (Sacremento, CA: Foundation for Critical Thinking, 1997); "A Brief History of the Idea of Critical Thinking," http://www.criticalthinking.org/pages/a-brief-history-of-the-idea-of-critical-thinking/408 (accessed November 1, 2012).

2 A. Smith, *An Inquiry into the Nature and Causes of the Wealth of Nations* (New York: E. P. Dutton, 1913).

3 N. F. Koehn, *The Story of American Business from the Pages of the New York Times* (Boston: Harvard Business Press, 2009): 4.

4 *Ibid.,* 9–11.

5 F. N. Stites, *Private Interest and Public Gain: The Dartmouth College Case, 1819* (Amherst, MA: University of Massachussetts Press, 1972).

6 M. Weber, *The Protestant Ethic and the Spirit of Capitalism,* trans. Talcot Parsons (London: Routlege, 1994): 173–174.

7 D. A. Wren, *The Evolution of Management Thought* (New York: Ronald Press, 1972): 228.

8 R. M. Weiss, "Weber on Bureaucracy: Management Consultant or Political Theorist?" *Academy of Management Review* 8.2 (1983): 142–148.

9 D. Wren, "Henri Fayol: Learning from Experience," *Journal of Management History* 1 (1995): 5–12.

10 H. Fayol, diary entry of July 19, 1898, in Frederic Blancpain, "Led Cahiers Inedits d'Henri Fayol," *Bulletin de l'Institute International d'Administration Publique* 28 (1973): 23.

11 H. Fayol and J. A. Coubrough, *Industrial and General Administration* (Geneva: International Management Institute, 1930).

12 "How Business Schools Began," *BusinessWeek* (October 19, 1963): 114–116.

13 C. Babbage, *On the Economy of Machinery and Manufactures* (London: Charles Knight, 1932): 208–213.

14 F. W. Taylor, *Shop Management* (New York: Harper & Brothers, 1903): 30.

15 *Ibid.*

16 C. Wrege and R. Greenwood, "The Early History of Midvale Steel and the Work of Frederick W. Taylor: 1865–1890," *Canal History and Technology Proceedings* 11 (1992): 145–176.

17 F. W. Taylor, *The Principles of Scientific Management* (New York: Harper & Brothers, 1911): 15–16.

18 F. B. Copley, *Frederick W. Taylor: Father of Scientific Management,* 2 vols. (New York: Harper & Brothers, 1923): 162–226.

19 Taylor, *Shop Management,* 149–176; Wren, *The Evolution of Management,* 126.

20 Taylor, *Shop Management,* 21.

21 Taylor, *The Principles of Scientific Management,* 149.

22 C. Graves, "Applying Scientific Management Principles to Railroad Repair Shops—The Santa Fe Experience, 1904–1918," in J. Atack, ed., *Business and Economic History*, 2d ed., vol. 10 (1981): 124–136.

23 H. Emerson, *Efficiency as a Basis for Operations and Wages* (New York: Engineering Magazine, 1911): 69.

24 Emerson, *Efficiency as a Basis for Operations and Wages*, 112.

25 N. Kranowski, "The Historical Development of Standard Cost Accounting Systems Until 1920," in E. N. Coffman, ed., *The Academy of Accounting Historians Working Paper Series* 2 (1979): 206–218.

26 A. L. Wilkins and N. J. Bristow, "For Successful Organization Culture, Honor Your Past," *Executive* 1, vol. 3 (1987): 221–229.

27 H. Emerson, *The Twelve Principles of Efficiency* (New York: Engineering Magazine, 1913): x–29.

28 A. Bedeian, "Finding the 'One Best Way': An Appreciation of Frank B. Gilbreth, the Father of Motion Study," *The Conference Board Record* (June 1976): 37–39.

29 H. S. Person, ed., *Scientific Management in American Industry* (Easton, PA: Hive Pub Co., 1972): 88–89.

30 F. B. Gilbreth and L. M. Gilbreth, *Applied Motion Study* (Easton, PA: Hive Pub Co., 1973): 207–273.

31 "The History of Quality—Overview," *American Society for Quality*, n.d., http://asq.org/learn-about-quality/history-of-quality/overview/overview.html; accessed May 27, 2013.

32 H. L. Gantt, *Work, Wages, and Profits*, 2d ed. (New York: Engineering Magazine, 1916): 154.

33 L. P. Alford, *Henry L. Gantt: Leading in Industry* (New York: Harper & Brothers, 1934): 207.

34 Wren, *The Evolution of Management*, 162.

35 W. Clark, "The Gantt Chart—I: Its Principles, Techniques, Application, and Use," *Management Engineering* 1 (August 1921): 77.

36 W. Clark, *The Gantt Chart: A Working Tool of Management* (New York: Ronald Press, 1922).

37 H. Ford, *My Life and Work* (New York: Cosimo Classics, 2007): 64–77.

38 "The History of Quality—Overview."

39 J. H. Heizer, "Determining Responsibility for Development of the Moving Assembly Line," *Journal of Management History* 4 (1998): 94–103. See also D. A. Hounshell, *From the American System to Mass Production, 1800–1932* (Baltimore: Johns Hopkins University Press, 1984): 249–253.

40 S. Greengard, "25 Visionaries Who Shaped Today's Workplace," *Workforce* (1997): 50–59.

41 M. F. Guillen and F. Mauro, "The Age of Eclecticism: Current Organizational Trends and the Evolution of Managerial Models," *Sloan Management Review* 36, vol. 1 (1994): 75–86.

42 E. W. Deming, *Out of the Crisis* (Cambridge, MA: Massachusetts Institute of Technology, 1986): 6.

43 A. Kleiner, *The Age of Heretics: A History of the Radical Thinkers Who Reinvented Corporate Management*, 2d ed. (San Francisco, CA: Jossey-Bass, 2008): 292.

44 J. Main, "How to Steal the Best Ideas Around," *Fortune* (October 1992): 102–106.

45 C. D. Wrege and R. M. Hodgetts, "Frederick W. Taylor's 1899 Pig Iron Observations: Examining Fact, Fiction, and Lessons for the New Millennium," *Academy of Management Journal* 43, vol. 6 (2000): 1287.

46 F. B. Copley, *Frederick W. Taylor: Father of Scientific Management*, vol. 2, 344.

47 J. M. Juran, "Early SQC: A Historical Supplement," *Quality Progress* 30, vol. 9 (1997): 74.

48 C. E. Snow, "Research on Industrial Illumination: A Discussion of the Relation of Illumination Intensity to Productive Efficiency," *Tech Engineering News* 8 (1927): 272, 282.

49 Wren, *The Evolution of Management Thought*, 285.

50 C. E. Turner, "Test Room Studies in Employee Effectiveness," *American Journal of Public Health* 23, vol. 6 (1933): 577–584.

51 R. G. Greenwood, A. A. Bolton, and R. A. Greenwood, "Hawthorne a Half a Century Later: Relay Assembly Participants Remember," *Journal of Management* 9, vol. 2 (1983): 217–231.

52 S. Highhouse, "The Brief History of Personnel Counseling in Industrial-Organizational Psychology," *Journal of Vocational Behavior* 55, vol. 3 (1999): 318–336.

53 J. H. Smith, "The Enduring Legacy of Elton Mayo," *Human Relations* 51.3 (1998): 221–249.

54 F. J. Roethlisberger and W. J. Dickson, *Management and the Worker: An Account of a Research Program Conducted by the Western Electric Company, Hawthorne Works, Chicago* (Cambridge, MA: Harvard University Press, 1939): 269.

55 E. Mayo, *The Human Problems of an Industrial Civilization* (New York: Routlege, 2003).

56 M. P. Follett, *The New State: Group Organization, the Solution of Popular Government* (London: Longmans & Green, 1918): 34.

57 *Ibid.*, 284.

58 M. P. Follett, *Creative Experience* (New York: The New State, 1924): 156.

59 *Ibid.*, 167–168.

60 D. McGregor and J. Cutcher-Gershenfeld, *The Human Side of Enterprise* (New York, McGraw-Hill, 2006): 48.

61 *Ibid.*, 49.

62 P. Sorensen and M. Minahan, "McGregor's Legacy: The Evolution and Current Application of Theory Y Management," *Journal of Management History* 17, vol. 2 (2011): 178–192.

63 T. Burns and G. M. Stalker, *The Management of Innovation* (London: Tavistock, 1961); P. R. Lawrence and J. R. Lorsch, *Organization and the Enviornment* (Boston: Harvard University Press, 1967); F. Luthans and T. Stewart, "A General Contingency Theory of Management," *Academy of Management Review* 2, vol. 2 (1977): 181–195.

64 Wren, *The Evolution of Management Thought*, 325.

65 W. B. Wolf, *The Basic Barnard: An Introduction to Chester I. Barnard and His Theories of Organization and Management* (Ithaca: New York State School of Industrial and Labor Relations, Cornell University, 1974).

66 C. Barnard, *The Functions of the Executive* (Cambridge, MA: Harvard University Press, 1964): 217.

67 L. von Bertalanffy, *General System Theory: Foundations, Development, Applications* (New York: George Braziller, 1968); F. E. Kast and J. E. Rosenzweig, *Contingency Views of Organization and Management* (New York: McGraw-Hill, 1973): 447–465.

Chapter 3

1 Donella H. Meadows and Diana Wright, *Thinking in Systems: A Primer* (White River Junction, VT: Chelsea Green Publishers, 2008), 11.

2 Peter Senge, *The Fifth Discipline* (New York: Doubleday/Currency, 1990), 42.

3 Senge, *Fifth Discipline*.

4 Senge, *Fifth Discipline*, 12.

5 Senge, *Fifth Discipline*, 3.

6 Content in this box is based on the following sources: M. Wood-head, personal interview (March 2012).

7 Meadows and Wright, *Thinking in Systems*, 18.

8 The preceding discussion on balanced systems and feedback loops is based on the following sources: Chester I. Barnard, *The Functions of the Executive* (Cambridge, MA: Harvard University Press, 1938); Jay W. Forrester, *Industrial Dynamics* (Waltham, MA: Pegasus Communications, 1961); Ludwig Von Bertalanffy, *General Systems Theory* (New York: George Braziller, 1968); Jay W. Forrester, *Principles of Systems* (Lawrence, KS: Allen Press Inc., 1968); Jay W. Forrester, "Market Growth as Influenced by Capital Investment," *Industrial Management Review* 9, no. 2 (Winter 68 1968): 83–105; Nancy Roberts, "Teaching Dynamics Feedback Systems Thinking: An Elementary View," *Management Science* 24, no. 8 (April 1978): 836–845; Jay W. Forrester, "System Dynamics and the Lessons of 35 Years" (Report D-4224-4, Cambridge MA, Massachusetts Institute of Technology, 1993); John D. Sterman, "Modeling Managerial Behavior: Misperceptions of Feedback in a Dynamic Decision-Making Experiment," *Management Science* 43, no.3 (March 1989): 301–335; Peter M. Senge, *The Fifth Discipline* (New York: Doubleday/Currency, 1990); Lawrence M. Fisher, "The Prophet of Unintended Consequences," *Strategy + Business*, no. 40 (Autumn 2005): 78.

9 Eric Knorr and Galen Gruman, "What Cloud Computing Really Means," *InfoWorld*, April 7, 2008, http://www.infoworld.com/d/cloud-computing/what-cloud-computing-really-means-031.

10 Mark Harris, "Inventing Facebook," *New York Magazine*, September 17, 2010, http://nymag.com/movies/features/68319/; Ben Mezrich, *The Accidental Billionaires: The Founding of Facebook, A Tale of Sex, Money, Genius, and Betrayal* (New York: Doubleday, 2009).

11 Bernard Golden, "Inside Amazon's Cloud: Just How Many Customer Projects?" *CIO Magazine*, September 29, 2009, http://www.cio.com/article/503570/Inside_Amazon_s_

12 Spencer Reiss, "Cloud Computing. Available at Amazon.com Today," *Wired*, April, 21, 2008, http://www.wired.com/techbiz/it/magazine/16-05/mf_amazon; Aaron Ricadela, "Amazon Looks to Widen Lead in Cloud Computing," *Bloomberg Businessweek*, April 28, 2010, http://www.businessweek.com/technology/content/apr2010/tc20100428_085106.htm; Jayant *Baliga*, Robert W. A. Ayre, Kerry Hinton, and Rodney S. Tucker, "Green Cloud Computing: Balancing Energy in Processing, Storage, and Transport." *Proceedings of the IEEE* PP 99, no. 1 (January 2011): 149–167.

13 Ratnesh Sharma, Tom Christian, Martin Arlitt, Cullen Bash, and Chandrakant Patel, "Design of Farm Waste-Driven Supply Side Infrastructure for Data Centers," *Proceedings of ASME 2010 4th International Conference on Energy Sustainability*, Phoenix, AZ (May 17–22, 2010).

14 *Ibid.*

15 Senge, *Fifth Discipline*.

16 *Ibid.*, p. 391.

17 *Ibid.*, p. 392.

18 *Ibid.*, p. 394.

19 *Ibid.*, p. 395.

20 *Ibid.*, p. 398.

21 Garrett Hardin, "The Tragedy of the Commons," *Science* 162, no. 3859 (December 13, 1968): 1243–1248.

22 *Ibid.*, p. 400.

23 Gary Hamel and Bill Breen, *The Future of Management* (Cambridge, MA: Harvard Business School Press, 2007).

Chapter 4

1 AIESEC, http://www.aiesec.org/.

2 R. Martin, "The Age of Customer Capitalism," *Harvard Business Review* (January–February 2010): 58–65.

3 M. Friedman, *Capitalism and Freedom* (Chicago: University of Chicago Press, 1962).

4 J. Welch, *Straight from the Gut* (New York: Warner Books, 2001); R. Slater, *Jack Welch and the G.E. Way: Management Insights and Leadership Secrets of the Legendary CEO* (New York: McGraw-Hill, 1999).

5 R. Martin, "The Age of Customer Capitalism," *Harvard Business Review* (January–February 2010): 58–65.

6 K. E. Weick, "Organizational Culture as a Source of High Reliability," *California Management Review* 29, no. 2 (1987): 112–127.

7 E. H. Schein, *Organizational Culture and Leadership*, 4th ed. (San Francisco: John Wiley & Sons, Inc., 2010)

8 T. E. Deal and A. A. Kennedy, *Corporate Cultures: The Rites and Rituals of Corporate Life* (Cambridge, MA: Perseus Books Publishing, 2000).

9 B. Z. Posner, J. M. Kouzes, and W. H. Schmidt, "Shared Values Make a Difference: An Empirical Test of Corporate Culture," *Human Resource Management* 24, no. 3 (1985): 293–309.

10 *Ibid.*

11 J. Campbell, *Hero with a Thousand Faces*, 3d ed. (Novato, CA: New World Library, 2008).

12 Associated Press, "Wal-Mart struggling with rising theft," *MSNBC*, June 13, 2007, http://www.msnbc.msn.com/id/19211630//.

13 S. Nwankwo, "Developing a Customer Orientation," *Journal of Consumer Marketing*, 12, no. 5 (1995): 5–15.

14 Manpower, "Manpower Inc. Annual Survey Reveals U.S. Employers Making Strides to Build Sustainable Workforces," *Manpower*; http://press.manpower.com/press/2013/talentshortage2013/.

15 E. Gordon, "The Global Talent Crisis," *The Futurist*, 43, no. 5 (September–October 2009): 34–39.

16 R. King, "Cisco Pays Big for New Ideas," *Bloomberg Businessweek*, Special Report, June 2, 2008; http://www.businessweek.com/technology/content/may2008/tc20080529_968185.htm.

17 J. Howe, "The Rise of Crowdsourcing," *Wired*, June 2006; http://www.wired.com/wired/archive/14.06/crowds.

18 Greenpeace International, "About Greenpeace"; http://www.greenpeace.org/usa/en/about/.

[19] CBC News, "Greenpeace 'Greenwashes' at BP Calgary HQ," *CBC News*, April 15, 2010; http://www.cbc.ca/canada/calgary/story/2010/04/15/calgary-bp-greenpeace-protest-oilsands.html.

[20] Entertainment Industry Foundation, "Stand Up 2 Cancer"; http://www.standup2cancer.org/.

[21] S. McNulty, "Exxon Shrugs off Effect of Moratorium," *Financial Times,* July 29, 2010.

[22] "Louisiana Oyster Laws 2008–2009"; http://www.lsu.edu/sglegal/pdfs/LouisianaOysterLaws2008.pdf.

[23] Based on U.S. Office of Management and Budget, "A New Era of Responsibility: Renewing America's Promise" (Washington, D.C.: U.S. Government Printing Office, 2009): 114–134.

[24] Motion Picture Association of America, "Frequently Asked Questions," http://www.mpaa.org/faq.

[25] T. Greene, "Self-regulation of mature video games works," *Ames 247*, April 21, 2011; http://www.ames247.com/2011/04/21/self-regulation-of-mature-video-games-works/.

[26] F. W. Abrams, "Management's Responsibilities in a Complex World," *Harvard Business Review*, 29, no. 3 (1951): 29–34.

[27] R. Reich, "Government in Your Business," *Harvard Business Review* (July–August 2010): 94–99.

[28] W. C. Kim and R. Mauborgne, *Blue Ocean Strategy* (Boston, MA: Harvard Business School Press, 2005).

[29] M. E. May, "How to Design a Flat Organization," *Open Forum*, August 6, 2009; http://www.openforum.com/idea-hub/topics/the-world/article/how-to-design-a-flat-organization-matthew-e-may.

[30] B. Kogut, "Designing Global Strategies: Comparative and Competitive Value-Added Chains," *MIT Sloan Management Review*, July 15, 1985; http://sloanreview.mit.edu/the-magazine/1985-summer/2642/designing-global-strategies-comparative-and-competitive-valueadded-chains/.

[31] P. Elmer-DeWitt, "Chart of the day: Apple's iPad and the 13 drawfs." Fortune, June 24, 2103; http://tech.fortune.cnn.com/2013/06/24/chitika-apple-ipad-share/.

[32] *Citizens United v. Federal Election Commission,* Findlaw; http://laws.findlaw.com/us/000/08-205.html; A. Liptak, "Justices, 5–4, Reject Corporate Spending Limit," *New York Times*, January 21, 2010; http://www.nytimes.com/2010/01/22/us/politics/22scotus.html?_r=1.

[33] J. Marcus, E. C. Kurucz, and B. A. Colbert, "Conceptions of the Business Society Nature Interface: Implications for Management Scholarship," *Business and Society* 49, no. 3 (2010): 402–438; J. Peloza, "The Challenge of Measuring Financial Impacts From Investments in Corporate Social Performance," *Journal of Management* 35, no. 6 (2009): 1518–1541; D. Etzion, "Research on Organizations and the Natural Environment," *Journal of Management* 33, no. 4 (2007): 637–654; L. Denning, "Power Investing: There's a Lot of Money to Be Made—and Lost—in the Energy Markets. Here's What You Need to Know," *Wall Street Journal*, September 13, 2010; http://online.wsj.com/article/SB10001424052748703846604575447762301637550.html.

[34] U.S. Census Bureau, "International Data Base (IDB)," U.S. Census Bureau website; http://www.census.gov/ipc/www/idb/world-popgraph.php; U.S. Census Bureau, "World Population Clock," U.S. Census Bureau website; http://www.census.gov/main/www/popclock.html; also see http://worldpopulationreview.com/world-population-2012/.

[35] *Ibid.*

[36] World Food Programme; http://www.wfp.org/hunger/stats; Media Centre, "1.02 Billion People Hungry: One Sixth of Humanity Undernourished—More Than Ever Before," *Food and Agriculture Organization of the United Nations*, June 19, 2009; http://www.fao.org/news/story/en/item/20568/icode/.

[37] American Experience, "Primary Sources: The 'Crisis of Confidence' Speech," *Public Broadcasting Service;* http://www.pbs.org/wgbh/amex/carter/filmmore/ps_crisis.html; Market Place, "Carter's Oil Crisis Warning Went Unheard," *American Public Media*, July 15, 2008; http://marketplace.publicradio.org/display/web/2008/07/15/carter; U.S. Energy Information Administration, "International Energy Outlook 2010," U.S. Energy Information Administration website; http://www.eia.doe.gov/oiaf/ieo/graphic_data_liquidfuels.html.

[38] United Nations Environment Programme, "The Green Economy Initiative," the United Nations Environment Programme website; http://www.unep.org/greeneconomy/.

[39] United Nationals Environment Programme, http://www.unep.org/greeneconomy/AboutGEI/WhatisGEI/tabid/29784/Default.aspx.

[40] Dow Chemical. "Understanding Our Water Risks—The GWT at Work," Last modified April 2010; http://www.wbcsd.org/web/projects/water/Dow.pdf.

[41] E. Beinhocker, I. Davis, and L. Mendonca, "10 Trends You Have to Watch," *Harvard Business Review* (July–August 2009): 55–60; "The Global Water Tool," World Business Council for Sustainable Development website; http://www.wbcsd.org/templates/TemplateWBCSD5/layout.asp?type=p&MenuId=MTUxNQ&doOpen=1&ClickMenu=LeftMenu=LeftMenu; and D. A. Lubin and D. C. Esty, "The Sustainability Imperative," *Harvard Business Review* (May 2010): 42–50.

[42] TED Conferences, LLC. "About TED"; http://www.ted.com/pages/view/id/5.

[43] "Jeff Han: Human-Computer Interface Designer," *TED: Ideas Worth Spreading:* http://www.ted.com/speakers/jeff_han.html.

[44] Mac Daily News, "Apple Awarded Huge 'Multi-Touch' Patent Covering iPhone, iPod Touch," *MacDailyNews*, January 26, 2009; http://macdailynews.com/index.php/weblog/comments/19885/.

[45] G. Hammill, "Mixing and Managing Four Generations of Employees," *FDU Magazine Online*, Winter/Spring 2005; http://www.fdu.edu/newspubs/magazine/05ws/generations.htm.

[46] D. Feldman and T. W. H. Ng, "Careers, Mobility, Embeddedness, and Success," *Journal of Management* 33, no. 3 (2007): 350–377; S. E. Sullivan, "The Changing Nature of Careers: A Review and Research Agenda," *Journal of Management* 25, no. 3 (1999): 457–484; W. B. Johnston, "Global Work Force 2000: The New World Labor Market," *Harvard Business Review* (March–April 1991): 115–127; S. Ashford and S. DeRue, "Five Steps to Addressing the Leadership Talent Shortage," *Harvard Business Review* (June 2, 2010); http://blogs.hbr.org/imagining-the-future-of-leadership/2010/06/5-steps-to-addressing-the-lead.html; S. A. Hewlett, L. Sherbin, and K. Sumberg, "How Gen Y & Boomers Will Reshape Your Agenda," *Harvard Business Review* (July–August 2009): 121–126; T. H. Davenport and J. G. Harris, *Competing Analytics: The New Science of Winning* (Boston: Harvard University Press, 2007); D. A. Ready and J. A. Conger, "Make Your Company a Talent Factory," *Harvard Business Review* (June 2007): 68–77.

[47] N. Jaimovich and S. Rebelo, "Can News About the Future Drive the Business Cycle?" *American Economic Review* 99, no. 4 (2009): 1097–1118.

[48] M. Arrington, "Apple Announces iPhone, Stock Soars," *TechCrunch*, January 2007; http://techcrunch.com/2007/01/09/apple-announces-iphone-stock-soars/; M. McNamarra, "Apple Stock Soars Thanks to iPhone," *CBSNews.com*, January 10, 2007; http://www.cbsnews.com/stories/2007/01/10/earlyshow/main2346856.shtml.

[49] Dow Jones Indexes, "Dow Jones Industrial Average," October 21, 2010; http://www.djaverages.com.

[50] NASDAQ, http://www.nasdaq.com.

[51] Standard & Poor's, "The S&P 500"; http://www.standardandpoors.com/.

[52] S. Klasen, "Inequality in Emerging Countries: Trends, Interpretations, and Implications for Development and Poverty Reduction," *Intereconomics* 44, no. 6 (2009): 360–363.

[53] Annabel Beerel, *Leadership and Change Management*. Thousand Oaks, CA: Sage Publications Ltd, 2009; Phil Merrell, "Effective Change Management: The Simple Truth." *Management Services* 56, no. 2 (Summer 2012): 20–23.

[54] John P. Kotter and Leonard A. Schlesinger. "Choosing strategies for change." *Harvard Business Review* 57, no. 2 (March 1979): 106–114.

[55] Kurt Lewin, *Field Theory in Social Science: Selected Theoretical Papers,* Dorwin Cartwright, ed. Oxford, U.K.: Harpers, 1951; Bernard Burnes, "Kurt Lewin and the Planned Approach to Change: A Re-appraisal," *Journal Of Management Studies* 41, no. 6 (September 2004): 977–1002.

[56] Kurt Lewin, "Frontiers in group dynamics: concept, method and reality in social science; social equilibria and social change." *Human Relations* 1, (1947): 5–41; Burnes, "Kurt Lewin and the Planned Approach to Change: A Re-appraisal."

[57] John P. Kotter, "Leading Change: Why Transformation Efforts Fail," *Harvard Business Review* 73, no. 2 (March 1995): 59–67.

[58] Donella H. Meadows and Diana Wright, *Thinking in Systems: A Primer* (White River Junction, VT: Chelsea Green Publishers, 2008), 145.

[59] Stacie A. Furst and Daniel M. Cable. "Employee Resistance to Organizational Change: Managerial Influence Tactics and Leader-Member Exchange," *Journal Of Applied Psychology* 93, no. 2 (March 2008): 453–462.

Chapter 5

[1] T. Moon, "Organizational Cultural Intelligence: Dynamic Capability Perspective," *Group & Organization Management* 35, no. 4 (August 2010): 456–493.

[2] J. H. Dyer, P. Kale, and H. Singh, "When to Ally and When to Acquire," *Harvard Business Review* 82 (July 2004): 108–115.

[3] "What Is the WTO?" World Trade Organization; http://www.wto.org/english/thewto_e/whatis_e/whatis_e.htm.

[4] J. Whalley, "Recent Regional Agreements: Why So Many, Why So Much Variance in Form, Why Coming So Fast, and Where Are They Headed?" *The World Economy* 31, no. 4 (April 2008): 517–532.

[5] L. H. Teslik, "NAFTA's Economic Impact," Council on Foreign Relations, available online at http://www.cfr.org/publication/15790/naftas_economic_impact.html.

[6] "About the EU," European Union; http://europa.eu/about-eu/index_en.htm.

[7] "UNASUR," Union De Naciones Suramericanas"; http://www.pptunasur.com/inicio.php?idiom=1.

[8] "About APEC," Asia-Pacific Economic Cooperation; http://www.apec.org/en/About-Us/About-APEC.aspx.

[9] "About ASEAN," Association of Southeast Asian Nations, http://www.aseansec.org/about_ASEAN.html; A. DeClouette and L. Migliore, "The Intersection of Corporate Governance Practices and National Culture in Emerging Markets." SSRN Working Paper Series 1 (December 2010).

[10] E. Fang, R. W. Palmatier, and K. R. Evans, "Goal-Setting Paradoxes? Trade-Offs Between Working Hard and Working Smart: The United States Versus China," *Journal of the Academy of Marketing Science* 32, no. 2 (2004): 188–202.

[11] R. Stroup, Email to C. Lattimer, September 17, 2010; January 31, 2010; and D. Kim, *Systems Archetypes II* (Waltham, MA: Pegasus Communications, 1994): 9.

[12] D. Kim, *Systems Archetypes II* (Waltham, MA: Pegasus Communications, 1994): 9.

[13] G. Kvedaraviciene and V. Boguslauskas, "Underestimated Importance of Cultural Differences in Outsourcing Arrangements," *Engineering Economics* 21, no. 2 (2010): 187–196.

[14] T. Jackson, "The Management of People Across Cultures: Valuing People Differently," *Human Resource Management* 41, no. 4 (2002): 455–475.

[15] P. C. Earley and S. Ang, *Cultural Intelligence: Individual Actions Across Cultures* (Stanford, CA: Stanford Business Books 2003); D. Thomas and K. Inkson, *Cultural Intelligence* (San Francisco: Berrett-Koehler, 2004).

[16] See also L. Žitkus and A. Junevičius, "Boundaries of Possible Solutions of Management Problems Caused by Cultural Interaction," *Engineering Economics* 51, no. 1 (2007): 44–49.

[17] P. C. Earley and E. Mosakowski "Cultural Intelligence," *Harvard Business Review* (October 2004), http://hbr.org/2004/10/cultural-intelligence/ar/1; C. Barnum and N. Wolniansky, "Why Americans Fail at Overseas Negotiations," *Management Review* (October 1989): 54–57; G. Ferraro, *Cultural Anthropology: An Applied Perspective*, 3d ed. (Belmont, CA: West/Wadsworth, 1998); J. Holt, "Gone Global?" *Management Review* (March 2000): 13.

[18] S. P. Douglas and H. V. Perlmutter, "Guidelines for Developing International Marketing Strategies," *Journal of Marketing* (April 1973): 14–23; H. V. Perlmutter, "The Tortuous Evolution of the Multinational Corporation," *Columbia Journal of World Business* (January–February 1969): 9–18; Y. Wind, S. P. Douglas, and H. V. Perlmutter, "Guidelines for Developing International Marketing Strategies," *Journal of Marketing* (April 1973): 14–23.

[19] G. Hofstede, "The Interaction Between National and Organizational Value Systems," *Journal of Management Studies* 22 (1985): 347–357; G. Hofstede, "The Cultural Relativity of the Quality of Life Concept," *Academy of Management Review* 9 (1984): 389–398.

[20] G. Hofstede, "Cultural Constraints in Management Theory," *Academy of Management Executive* 7 (1993): 81–94; G. Hofstede and M. H. Bond, "The Confucian Connection: From Cultural Roots to Economic Growth," *Organizational Dynamics* 16 (1988): 4–21.

[21] R. J. House et al., "Cultural Influences on Leadership and Organizations: Project Globe," *Advances in Global Leadership* 1 (Bingley, U.K.: Emerald Publishing Group, 1999): 171–233.

22 R.J. House, P. J. Hanges, M. Javidan, and P.W. Dorfman, eds., *Culture, Leadership, and Organizations: The GLOBE Study of 62 Societies* (Thousand Oaks, CA: Sage Publications, 2004).

23 M. Javadin and R. J. House, "Cultural Acumen for the Global Manager," *Organizational Dynamics* 29, no. 4 (2001): 289–305.

24 *Ibid*.

25 P. W. Dorfman, P. J. Hanges, and F. C. Brodbeck, "Leadership and Cultural Variation: The Identification of Culturally Endorsed Leadership Profiles," in *Culture, Leadership, and Organizations*, R. J. House et al., eds. (Thousand Oaks, CA: Sage Publications, 2004), 677.

26 *Ibid.*, 678.

27 J. Reingold, "Secrets of Their Success," *Fortune*, November 12, 2008, http://money.cnn.com/2008/11/11/news/companies/secretsof-success_gladwell.fortune/index.htm; M. Gladwell, *Outliers: The Story of Success* (New York: Little, Brown, & Co, 2008).

28 R. Yu, "Korean Air Upgrades Service, Image," *USA Today*, August 26, 2009, http://www.usatoday.com/money/companies/management/profile/2009-08-23-travel-airlines-korea_N.htm.

29 G. Hofstede, "Geert Hofstede Cultural Dimensions," Itim International; http://www.geert-hofstede.com/hofstede_dimensions.php.

30 D.A. Harrison, K. H. Price, and M. P. Bell. "Beyond Relational Demography: Time and the Effects of Surface- and Deep-Level Diversity on Work Group Cohesion," *Academy of Management Journal* 41 (1998): 96–107.

31 D.A. Harrison, K. H. Price, and M. P. Bell, "Beyond Relational Demography: Time and the Effects of Surface- and Deep-Level Diversity on Work Group Cohesion," *Academy of Management Journal* 41 (1998): 96–107; D. Harrison, K. Price, J. Gavin, and A. Florey, "Time, Teams, and Task Performance: Changing Effects of Surface- and Deep-Level Diversity on Group Functioning," *Academy of Management Journal* 45 (2002): 1029–1045; K. Wrenn and T. Mauer, "Beliefs About Older Workers' Learning and Development Behavior in Relation to Beliefs About Malleability of Skills, Age-Related Decline, and Control," *Journal of Applied Social Psychology* 34 (February 2004): 223–242; E. Sullivan and E.A. Duplaga, "Recruiting and Retaining Older Workers for the Millennium," *Business Horizons* 40 (November 12, 1997): 65; S. R. Rhodes, "Age-Related Differences in Work Attitudes and Behavior," *Psychological Bulletin* 92 (1983): 328–367; G. M. McEvoy and W. F. Cascio, "Cumulative Evidence of the Relationship Between Employee Age and Job Performance," *Journal of Applied Psychology* 74 (1989): 11–17.

32 M. E. Hellman, C. J. Block, and P. Stathatos, "The Affirmative Action Stigma of Incompetence: Effects of Performance Information Ambiguity," *Academy of Management Journal* 40, no. 3 (1997): 603–625; M. Selmi, "The Price of Discrimination: The Nature of Class Action Employment Discrimination Litigation and Its Effects," *Texas Law Review* 1 (April 2003): 1249; F. Neathey, S. Dench, and L. Thomas, "Monitoring Progress Toward Pay Equality," *Institute for Employment Studies Report on Behalf of the Equal Opportunities Commission*, 2003, http://www.equalityhumanrights.com/.../code_of_practice_equalpay.pdf.

33 J. N. Cleveland, J. Barnes-Farrell, and J. M. Ratz, "Accommodation in the Workplace," *Human Resource Management Review* 7 (1997): 77–108; A. Colella, R. L. Paetzold, and M. A. Belliveau, "Factors Affecting Coworkers' Procedural Justice Inferences of the Workplace Accommodations of Employees with Disabilities," *Personnel Psychology* 57 (2004): 1–23; F. Bowe, *Adults with Disabilities: A Portrait. President's Committee on Employment of People with Disabilities* (Washington, D.C.: U.S. Department of Labor, 1992); Louis Harris &

Associates, Inc., *The ICD Survey II: Employing Disabled Americans* (New York: Louis Harris & Associates, Inc. 1987); R. Greenwood and V. A. Johnson, "Employer Perspectives on Workers with Disabilities," *Journal of Rehabilitation* 53 (1987): 37–45.

34 M. Bendick Jr., C. W. Jackson, and V. A. Reinoso, "Measuring Employment Discrimination Through Controlled Experiments," in *African-Americans and Post-Industrial Labor Markets*, J. B. Stewart, ed. (New Brunswick, NJ: Transaction Publishers, 1997) 77–100; P. B. Riach, and J. Rich, "Measuring Discrimination by Direct Experimental Methods: Seeking Gunsmoke," *Journal of Post Keynesian Economics* 14.2 (1992): 143–150; A. P. Brief, R. T. Buttram, R. M. Reizenstein, and S. D. Pugh, "Beyond Good Intentions: The Next Steps Toward Racial Equality in the American Workplace," *Academy of Management Executive* 11 (1997): 59–72.

35 B. Reinhold, "Smashing Glass Ceilings: Why Women Still Find It Tough to Advance to the Executive Suite," *Journal of Organizational Excellence* (Summer 2005): 43–55; D. Jardins, "I Am Woman (I Think)," *Fast Company* (May 2005): 25–26; A. H. Eagly and L. L. Carli, "The Female Leadership Advantage: An Evaluation of the Evidence, *The Leadership Quarterly* 14 (2003): 807–834; S. Wellington, M. B. Kropf, and P. R. Gerkovich, "What's Holding Women Back?" *Harvard Business Review* 81 (2003): 82–111; E. Meyerson and J. K. Fletcher, "A Modest Manifesto for Shattering the Glass Ceiling," *Harvard Business Review* (January–February 2000): 127–136; S. Hewlett, A. B. Luce, and C. B. Luce, "Off-Ramps and On-Ramps: Keeping Talented Women on the Road to Success," *Harvard Business Review* (March 2005): 43–54.

36 M. Bertrand and K. Hallock, "The Gender Gap in Top Corporate Jobs," *Industrial & Labor Relations Review* 55 (2001): 3–21; J. R. Hollenbeck, D. R. Ilgen, C. Ostroff, and J. B. Vancouver, "Sex Differences in Occupational Choice, Pay, and Worth: A Supply-Side Approach to Understanding the Male-Female Wage Gap," *Personnel Psychology* 40 (1987): 715–744; L. M. Bajdo and M. W. Dickson, "Perceptions of Organizational Culture and Women's Advancement in Organizations: A Cross-Cultural Examination," *Behavioral Science* 45 (September 2001): 399–414.

37 N. Byrnes and R. Crockett, "Ursula Burns: An Historic Succession at Xerox," *Bloomberg BusinessWeek*, May 28, 2009, http://www.businessweek.com/magazine/content/09_23/b4134018712853.htm; A. H. Eagly and B. T. Johnson, "Gender and Leadership Style: A Meta-Analysis," *Psychological Bulletin* 108, no. 2 (1990): 233–246; A. H. Eagly and L. L. Carli, "The Female Leadership Advantage: An Evaluation of the Evidence," *Leadership Quarterly* 14 (2003): 807–834; G. N. Powell, "One More Time. Do Female and Male Managers Differ?" *Academy of Management Executive* 4 (1990): 68–75; R. P. Vecchio, "Leadership and Gender Advantage," *Leadership Quarterly* 13 (2002): 643–671.

38 T. A. Boe, "Gaining and/or Maintaining Employee Trust Within Service Organizations," Unpublished master's thesis, University of Wisconsin-Stout, August 2002, http://www2.uwstout.edu/content/lib/thesis/2002/2002boet.pdf; B. S. De Jong and T. Elfring, "How Does Trust Affect the Performance of Ongoing Teams? The Mediating Role of Reflexivity, Monitoring, and Effort," *Academy of Management Journal* 53, no. 3 (2010): 535–549; K. T. Dirks and D. F. Ferrin, "Trust in Leadership," *Journal of Applied Psychology* 87, no. 4 (2002): 611–628; D. C. Lau and R. C. Liden, "Antecedents of Coworker Trust: Leaders' Blessings," *Journal of Applied Psychology* 93, no. 5 (2008): 1130–1138.

39 I. LeBeauf et al., "Is Affirmative Action Still Necessary?" *Journal of Employment Counseling* 44, no. 3 (2007): 98–114.

[40] R. Fullinwider, "Affirmative Action," *The Stanford Encyclopedia of Philosophy* (Winter 2010), E. N. Zalta (ed.); http://plato.stanford.edu/archives/win2010/entries/affirmative-action/.

[41] U.S. Equal Employment Opportunity Commission, http://www.eeoc.gov/eeoc/index.cfm.

[42] "EEOC Reports Nearly 100,000 Job Bias Charges in Fiscal Year 2012," U.S. Equal Employment Opportunity Commission, January 28, 2013, http://www.eeoc.gov/eeoc/newsroom/release/1-28-13.cfm.

[43] U.S. Equal Employment Opportunity Commission, "Prohibited Employment Policies/Practices," http://www1.eeoc.gov//laws/practices/index.cfm?renderforprint=1.

[44] K. Wrenn and T. Mauer, "Beliefs About Older Workers' Learning and Development Behavior in Relation to Beliefs About Malleability of Skills, Age-Related Decline, and Control," *Journal of Applied Social Psychology* 34 (February 2004): 223–242; S. R. Rhodes, "Age-Related Differences in Work Attitudes and Behavior," *Psychological Bulletin* 92 (1983): 328–367.

[45] C. H. Loch, F. J. Sting, N. Bauer, and H. Mauermann, "How BMW Is Defusing the Demographic Time Bomb," *Harvard Business Review*, March 2010, 99–102.

[46] T. Mauer, and N. Fafuse, "Learning, Not Litigating: Managing Employee Development and Avoiding Claims of Age Discrimination," *Academy of Management Executive* 15, no. 4 (2001): 110–121.

[47] M. Toossi, "Labor Force Projections to 2020: A More Slowly Growing Workforce," *Monthly Labor Review*, January 2012; http://www.bls.gov/opub/mlr/2012/01/art3full.pdf; accessed May 30, 2013.

[48] C. H. Loch, F. J. Sting, N. Bauer, and H. Mauermann.

[49] *Ibid.*, 100.

[50] *Ibid.*, 102.

[51] J. H. Boyett, and J. T. Boyett, *Beyond Workforce 2000* (New York: Dutton, 1995); M. Toossi, "Labor Force Projections to 2014: Retiring Boomers," *Monthly Labor Review* (November 2005): 25–44.

[52] M. Morschhauser and R. Sochert, *Healthy Work in an Ageing Europe: Strategies and Instruments for Prolonging Working Life* (Germany: Federal Association of Company Health Insurance Funds, 2006); http://www.ageingatwork.eu/resources/health-work-in-an-ageing-europe-enwhp-3.pdf.

[53] Adapted from Bureau of Labor Statistics, "Employment Projections," last modified March 11, 2010; http://bls.gov/emp/ep_data_labor_force.htm.

[54] *Ibid.*

[55] M. Kenney, S. Massini, and T. Murtha, " Offshoring Administrative and Technical Work: New Fields for Understanding the Global Enterprise," *Journal of International Business Studies* 40, no. 6 (2009): 887–900.

[56] N. Checa, J. Maguire, and J. Barney, "The New World Disorder," *Harvard Business Review* (August 2003): 71–79; C. Bartlett, *Managing Across Borders*, 2d ed. (Boston: Harvard Business School Press, 1998).

[57] "Boeing Celebrates the Premiere of the 787 Dreamliner," Boeing press release, July 8, 2007; http://www.boeing.com/news/releases/2007/q3/070708b_nr.html.

[58] A. MacPherson and V. Vanchan, "The Outsourcing of Industrial Design Services by Large U.S. Manufacturing Companies," *International Regional Science Review* 33, no. 1 (2010): 3–30.

[59] S. Ray and K. Matsuda, "Boeing 787's Arrival at ANA Delayed to Third Quarter," *Bloomberg BusinessWeek*, January 19, 2011; http://www.businessweek.com/news/2011-01-19/boeing-787-s-arrival-at-ana-delayed-to-third-quarter.html.

[60] P. F. Drucker, "They're Not Employees, They're People," *Harvard Business Review*, February 2002, 70–77.

[61] *Ibid.*; M. Lapalme et al., "Bringing the Outside In: Can "External" Workers Experience Insider Status?" *Journal of Organizational Behavior* 30, no. 7 (2009): 919–940.

[62] G. Robinson and K. Dechant, "Building a Business Case for Diversity," *Academy of Management Executive* 11, no. 3 (1997): 22; R. A. Friedman and B. Holtom, "The Effects of Network Groups on Minority Employee Turnover Intentions," *Human Resource Management* 41, no. 4 (2002): 405–421.

[63] D. A. Thomas, "Diversity as Strategy," *Harvard Business Review*, September 2004, 98–108.

[64] *Ibid.*, 98.

[65] *Ibid.*, 100.

[66] *Ibid.*, 101.

[67] *Ibid.*, 103–108.

[68] "Our Commitment to Diversity," Kellogg Company, http://www.kelloggcompany.com/company.aspx?id=1464.

[69] E. Kearney, D. Gebert, and S. Voelpel, "When and How Diversity Benefits Teams: The Importance of Team Members' Need for Cognition," *Academy of Management Journal* 52 (2009): 581–598.

[70] W. E. Watson, K. Kumar, and L. K. Michaelsen, "Cultural Diversity's Impact on Interaction Process and Performance: Comparing Homogeneous and Diverse Task Groups, *Academy of Management Journal* 36 (1993): 590–602.

[71] A. Oshiotse and R. O'Leary, "Corning Creates an Inclusive Culture to Drive Technology Innovation and Performance," *Global Business and Organizational Excellence* 26, no. 3 (2007): 10.

[72] M. Janssens and J. M. Brett, "Cultural Intelligence in Global Teams: A Fusion Model of Collaboration," *Group & Organization Management* 31, no. 1 (2006): 124–153.

[73] O. C. Richard, "Racial Diversity, Business Strategy, and Firm Performance: A Resource-Based View," *Academy of Management Journal*, 43, no. 2 (2000): 154–177.

[74] R. J. Ely and D. A. Thomas, "Cultural Diversity at Work: The Effects of Diversity Perspectives on Work Group Processes and Outcomes," *Administrative Science Quarterly* 46. no. 2 (2001): 229–273.

[75] J. J. Distefano and M. L. Maznevski, "Creating Value with Diverse Teams in Global Management," *Organizational Dynamics* 29, no. 1 (2000): 45–63.

[76] M. J. Bittner, B. H. Blooms, and L. A. Mohr, "Critical Service Encounters: The Employees' Viewpoint," *Journal of Marketing* (October 1994): 95–106.

[77] R. W. Griffeth, P. W. Hom, and S. Gaertner, "A Meta-Analysis of Antecedents and Correlates of Employee Turnover: Update, Moderator Test, and Research Implications for the Next Millennium," *Journal of Management* 26, no. 3 (2000): 479; P. W. Hom and A. J. Kinicki, "Toward a Greater Understanding of How Dissatisfaction Drives Employee Turnover," *Academy of Management Journal* (October 2001): 975–987.

[78] A. DeClouette and L. Migliore, "The Intersection of Corporate Governance Practices and National Culture in Emerging Markets."

79 D. H. Meadows, *Thinking in Systems: A Primer*, D. Wright, ed. (White River Junction, VT: Chelsea Green Publishing, 2008).

80 A. P. Girlando and N. B. Eduljee, "An Empirical Investigation of the Malleability of Hofstede's Cultural Dimensions: The Case of the United States and Russia," *Journal of Transnational Management* 15, no. 3 (2010): 265–289.

81 D. Carl, V. Gupta, and M. Javidin, "Power Distance," in *Culture, Leadership, and Organizations*, 539.

82 D. Kim, *Systems Archetypes I* (Waltham, MA: Pegasus Communications, Inc., 1994).

83 A. I. Dudau and L. McAllister, "Developing Collaborative Capabilities by Fostering Diversity in Organizations," *Public Management Review* 12, no. 3 (2010): 385–402.

84 P. Rosenzweig, "Managing the New Global Workforce: Fostering Diversity, Forging Consistency," *European Management Journal* 16, no. 6 (1998): 644–652.

85 S. Pugh et al., "Looking Inside and Out: The Impact of Employee and Community Demographic Composition on Organizational Diversity Climate," *Journal of Applied Psychology* 93, no. 6 (2008): 1422–1428.

86 Drucker, "They're Not Employees, They're People."

Chapter 6

1 A. E. Tenbrunsel, "Misrepresentation and Expectaions of Misrepresentation in an Ethical Dilemma: The Role of Incentives and Temptations." *Academy of Management Journal* 41 (June 1998): 330–340.

2 A. C. Wicks, "An Introduction to Ethics," *University of Virginia Darden School Foundation* (January 12, 2009).

3 L. K. Trevinoand and K. A. Nelson, *Managing Business Ethics: Straight Talk About How to Do It Right* (New York: John Wiley & Sons, Inc. 1995): 4.

4 D. Ackman, "Enron the Incredible," *Forbes Magazine*, January 15, 2002, http://www.forbes.com/2002/01/15/0115enron.html.

5 K. Anderson, "How Enron Played the Media," *BBC News*, February 13, 2002, http://news.bbc.co.uk/2/hi/business/1817445.stm.

6 M. Swartz, "The Three Faces of Ken Lay," *New York Times*, May 21, 2006, http://www.nytimes.com/2006/05/21/opinion/21swartz.html.

7 The organization is now called Business for Social Responsibilty and has a broader scope.

8 " Company History," Ben & Jerry's website; http://www.benjerry.com/company/history/.

9 T. D. and L. E. Preston, "The Stakeholder Theory of Corporation: Concepts, Evidence, and Implications." *Academy of Management Review* 20 (1995): 65–91.

10 L. R. Young and M. Nestle, "Portion Sizes and Obesity: Responses of Fast-Food Companies." *Journal of Public Health Policy* 28 (2007): 238–248.

11 *Ibid.*

12 *Super Size Me.* DVD, Directed by Morgan Spurlock (Culver City, CA: Sony Pictures 2004).

13 "McDonald's UK Position on 'Super Size Me,'" McDonald's Corporation website; http://web.archive.org/web/20071012135323/http://mcdonalds.co.uk/pages/global/supersize.html.

14 Young and Nestle, "Portion Sizes and Obesity."

15 C. Meyer and J. Kirby, "Leadership in the Age of Transparency." *Harvard Business Review* (April 2010): 38–46.

16 Wicks, "An Introduction to Ethics."

17 *Ibid.*

18 P. M. Healy and K. G. Palepu, "The Fall of Enron." *Journal of Economic Perspectives*, 17.2 (2003): 3–26.

19 P. Patsuris, "The Corporate Scandal Sheet," *Forbes*, August 26, 2002, http://www.forbes.com/2002/07/25/accountingtracker.html.

20 "Five Years Under the Thumb: Sarbanes-Oxley," *The Economist*, July 28, 2007.

21 "UN at a Glance," United Nations website; http://www.un.org/en/aboutun/index.shtml.

22 "Global Compact Leaders' Summit 2010," United Nations website; http://www.un.org/News/Press/docs/2010/eco178.doc.html.

23 "United Nations Global Compact," United Nations website; http://www.unglobalcompact.org/.

24 L. K. Trevino, G. R. Weaver, and S. J. Reynolds, "Behavioral Ethics in Organizations: A Review." *Journal of Management* 32.6 (December 2006): 951–990.

25 L. T. Hosmer, "Trust: The Connecting Link Between Organizational Theory and Philosophical Ethics." *Academy of Management Review* 20 (1995): 379–403.

26 R. C. Soloman, *Ethics and Excellence* (New York: Oxford University Press, 1992).

27 J. E. Fleming, "Codes of Ethics for Global Corporations." *Academy of Management News* (June 2005): 4.

28 L. Ridgely, "Executive Interview: Lonnie J. Williams," *Contracting Profits*, November 2008; http://www.cleanlink.com/cp/article/Executive-Interview-Lonnie-J-Williams—10141.

29 J. B. McGuire, A. Sundgren, and T. Schneeweis, "Corporate Social Responsibility and Firm Financial Performance." *Academy of Management Journal* 31.4 (1998): 854–872.

30 D. Bornstein, *How to Change the World: Social Entrepreneurs and the Power of New Ideas* (New York: Oxford University Press, 2004); R. J. Bies, J. M. Bartunek, T. L. Fort, and M. N. Zald, "Corporations as Social Change Agents: Individual, Interpersonal, Institutional, and Environmental Dynamics." *Academy of Mangagement Review* 32.3 (July 2007): 788–793.

31 T. M. Jones, "Ethical Decision Making by Individuals in Organizations: An Issue Contingent Model." *Academy of Management Journal* 16.2 (1991): 336–395.

32 P. A. Heslin and J. Ochoa, "Understanding and Developing Strategic Corporate Social Responsibility." *Organizational Dynamics* 37.2 (2008): 125–144.

33 "Profiting from Social Responsibility," *Marketplace*, May 7, 2007, http://marketplace.publicradio.org/display/web/2007/05/07/profiting_from_social_responsibility/.

34 "About Us," Upstream 21 Corporation website; http://www.upstream21.com/about.

35 "About Certified B Corps," B Corporation website; http://www.bcorporation.net/about.

36 *Ibid.*

37 W. Bennis, D. Goleman, and J. O'Toole, *Transparency: How Leaders Create a Culture of Candor* (San Francisco: Jossey-Bass, 2008).

[38] H. H. Johnson, "Does It Pay to Be Good? Social Responsibility and Financial Performance." *Business Horizons* (November–December 2003): 34–40.

[39] J. A. Aragon-Correa and S. Sharma, "Contingent Resource-Based View of Proactive Corporate Environmental Strategy." *Academy of Management Review* 28.1 (2003): 71–88.

[40] D. Wheeler, B. Cobert, and R. E. Freeman, "Focusing on Value: Reconciling Corporate Social Responsibility, Sustainability, and a Stakeholder Approach in a Networked World." *Journal of General Management* 28.3 (2003): 1–28.

[41] C. Fishman, *The Wal-Mart Effect* (New York: Penguin Press, 2006): 4.

[42] J. D. Lord, "Wal-Mart Supercenter Market Share of Grocery Retailing in U.S. Metropolitan Areas." In *Wal-Mart World*, ed. S. D. Brunn (New York: Routledge, 2006): 55–66.

[43] A. D'Innocenzio and M. C. Jalonick, "Wal-Mart Gives Boost to Push for Healthier Food," *ABC News*, January 20, 2011; http://abcnews.go.com/Health/wireStory?id=12724782.

[44] L. S. Paine, R. Deshpande, J. D. Margolis, and K. E. Bettcher, "Up to Code: Does Your Company's Conduct Meet World-Class Standards?" *Harvard Business Review*, December 2005.

[45] D. Wells and M. Schminke, "Ethical Development and Human Resources Training: An Integrative Framework." *Human Resource Management Review* 11 (2001): 135–158.

[46] Wells and Schminke, "Ethical Development and Human Resources Training," 141.

[47] Ibid.

[48] Ibid.

[49] D. McFadden, "The Tragedy of the Commons," *Forbes*, September 10, 2001; http://www.forbes.com/asap/2001/0910/061.html; W. Cronon, *Changes in the Land: Indians, Colonists, and the Ecology of New England* (New York: Hill & Wang, 1983).

[50] D. H. Kim, *Systems Archetypes I* (Waltham, MA: Pegasus Communications, 1994): 7.

Chapter 7

[1] H. A. Simon, *Administrative Behavior* (New York: Macmillan, 1947): p. 82.

[2] D. A. Garvin and M. A. Roberto, "What You Don't Know About Making Decisions," *Harvard Business Review*, September 2001: 108–116.

[3] H. A. Simon, *The New Science of Management* (Englewood Cliffs, NJ: Prentice Hall, 1977).

[4] H. A. Simon, *The New Science of Management* (Englewood Cliffs, NJ: Prentice Hall, 1977).

[5] C. Kepner and B. Tregoe, *The Rational Manager* (New York: McGraw-Hill, 1965).

[6] P. Senge, The Fifth Discipline: The Art and Practice of the Learning Organization (New York: Doubleday, 1990).

[7] M. Masuch and P. LaPotin, "Beyond Garbage Cans: An AI Model of Organizational Choice," *Administrative Science Quarterly* 34 (1989): 38–67; R. L. Daft and R. H. Lengel, "Organizational Information Requirements, Media Richness and Structural Design," *Management Science* 32 (1986): 554–571.

[8] Source: B. Adler, personal interview, May 2011.

[9] Harich, Jack, "Change Resistance as the Crux of the Environmental Sustainability Problem," *System Dynamics Review* 26, no. 1 (January 2010): 35–72.

[10] Source: E. Dane and M. G. Pratt, "Exploring Intuition and Its Role in Managerial Decision Making," *Academy of Management Review* 32, no. 1 (2007): 33–54.

[11] S. Eilon, "Structuring Unstructured Decisions," *Omega* 13 (1985): 369–377; and M. H. Bazerman, *Judgment in Managerial Decision Making* (New York: Wiley, 1986).

[12] K. J. Arrow, *Aspects of the Theory of Risk Bearing* (Helsinki, Finland: Yrjo Johnssonis Saatio, 1965).

[13] R. D. Dimitroff, L. A. Schmidt, and T. D. Bond, "Organizational Behavior and Disaster: A Study of Conflict at NASA," *Project Management Journal* 36, no. 1 (2005): 28–38; J. K. Esser and J. S. Lindoerfer, "Groupthink and the Space Shuttle Challenger Accident: Toward a Quantitative Case Analysis," *Journal of Behavioral Decision Making* 2 (1989): 167–177.

[14] I. L. Janis, *Groupthink: Studies of Policy Decisions and Fiascoes* (Boston: Houghton Mifflin, 1982); C. P. Neck and C. C. Manz, "From Groupthink to Teamthink: Toward the Creation of Constructive Thought Patterns in Self-Managing Work Teams," *Human Relations* 47 (1994): 929–952.

[15] R. D. Dimitroff, L. A. Schmidt, and T. D. Bond, "Organizational Behavior and Disaster: A Study of Conflict at NASA," *Project Management Journal* 36, no. 1 (2005): 28–38; J. K. Esser and J. S. Lindoerfer, "Groupthink and the Space Shuttle Challenger Accident: Toward a Quantitative Case Analysis," *Journal of Behavioral Decision Making* 2 (1989): 167–177.

[16] M. Diehl and W. Stroebe, "Productivity Loss in Brainstorming Groups: Towards the Solution of a Riddle," *Journal of Personality and Social Psychology* 53 (1987): 497–509.

[17] E. Teach, "Avoiding Decision Traps," *CFO*, June 2004: 97–99; D. Kaheman and A. Tversky, "Judgment Under Uncertainty: Heuristics and Biases," *Science* 185 (1974): 1124–1131.

[18] M. H. Bazeman, *Judgment in Managerial Decision Making* (New York: Wiley, 1986).

[19] S. Kavadias and S. Sommer, "The Effects of Problem Structure and Team Diversity on Brainstorming Effectiveness," *Management Science* 55, no. 12 (2009): 1899–1913.

[20] J. E. Russo and P. J. Schoemaker, *Decision Traps* (New York: Simon & Schuster, 1989).

[21] K. Jenn and E. Mannix, "The Dynamic Nature of Conflict: A Longitudinal Study of Intragroup Conflict and Group Performance," *Academy of Management Journal* 44, no. 2 (2001): 238–251; R. L. Priem, D. A. Harrison, and N. K. Muir, "Structured Conflict and Consensus Outcomes in Group Decision Making," *Journal of Management* 21 (1995): 691–710.

[22] N. Dalkey, *The Delphi Method: An Experimental Study of Group Decision Making* (Santa Monica, CA: Rand Corp., 1989).

[23] D. M Schwieger, W. R. Sandberg, and P. L. Rechner, "Experiential Effects of Dialectical Inquiry, Devil's Advocacy, and Consensus Approaches to Strategic Decision Making," *Academy of Management Journal* 32, no. 4 (1989): 745–772; J. S. Valacich and C. Schwenk, "Devil's Advocacy and Dialectical Inquiry Effects on Face-to-Face and Computer-Mediated Group Decision Making," *Organizational Behavior and Human Decision Processes* 63, no. 2 (1995): 158–173; A. H. Van de Ven and A. L. Delbecq, "The Effectiveness of Nominal,

Delphi, and Interacting Group Decision Making Processes," *Academy of Management Journal* 17, no. 4 (1974): 605–621.

24 K. Girotra, C. Terwiesch, and K. T. Ulrich, "Idea Generation and the Quality of the Best Idea," *Management Science* 56, no. 4 (2010): 591–605; and L. E. Miller, "Evidence-Based Instruction: A Classroom Experiment Comparing Nominal and Brainstorming Groups," *Organization Management Journal* 6 (2009): 229–238.

25 P. Ingram and G. Bhardwaj, "Strategic Persistence in the Face of Contrary Industry Experience: Two Experiments on the Failure to Learn from Others" (paper presented at the annual meeting for the Academy of Management, Boston, 1997); J. M. Barnes, "Cognitive Biases and Their Impact on Strategic Planning," *Strategic Management Journal* 5 (1984): 129–137; P. E. Tetlock, "The Impact of Accountability on Judgment and Choice: Toward a Social Contingency Model," *Advances in Experimental Social Psychology* 25 (1992): 331–376.

26 R. O. Mason, "A Dialectic Approach to Strategic Planning," *Management Science* 13 (1969): 403–414.

27 E. Dane and M. G. Pratt, "Exploring Intuition and Its Role in Managerial Decision Making," *Academy of Management Review* 32 (2007): 33–54; M. H. Bazerman and D. Chugh, "Decisions Without Blinders," *Harvard Business Review*, January 2006: 88–97; C. C. Miller and R. D. Ireland, "Intuition in Strategic Decision Making: Friend or Foe in the Fast-Paced 21st Century," *Academy of Management Executive* 19 (2005): 19–30; E. Sadler-Smith and E. Shefy, "The Intuitive Executive: Understanding and Applying 'Gut Feel' in Decision-Making," *Academy of Management Executive*, 18, no. 4 (2004): 76–91; E. Jaffe, "What Was I Thinking? Kahneman Explains How Intuition Leads Us Astray," *American Psychological Society* 17, no. 5 (2004): 23–26; E. Dane and M. Pratt, "Exploring Intuition and Its Role in Managerial Decision Making," *Academy of Management Review* 32 (2007): 33–54.

28 Miller and Ireland, "Intuition in Strategic Decision Making: W. H. Agor, "The Logic of Intuition: How Top Executives Make Important Decisions," *Organizational Dynamics* 14 (1986): 5–18.

29 R. Cyert and J. March, *Behavioral Theory of the Firm* (Englewood Cliffs, NJ: Prentice Hall, 1963); J. G. March and H. A. Simon, *Organizations* (New York: Wiley, 1958); H. A. Simon, *Models of Man* (New York: Wiley, 1957): 196–205.

30 J. G. March, "Decision-Making Perspective: Decisions in Organizations and Theories of Choice," in A. H. Van de Ven and W. F. Joyce, eds., *Perspectives on Organization Design and Behavior* (New York: Wiley-Interscience, 1981): 232–233.

31 H. A. Simon, *Administrative Behavior* (New York: Macmillan, 1947).

32 S. P. Robbins, *Decide & Conquer* (Upper Saddle River, NJ: Financial Times/Prentice Hall, 2004).

33 R. Roll, "The Hubris Hypothesis of Corporate Takeovers," *Journal of Business* 59 (1986): 197–216.

34 M. Saunders, R. Mann, and R. Smith, "Constructs and Systems: Connecting Strategy Deployment and Performance Excellence," *Total Quality Management* 20, no. 1 (2009): 115–128; L. Bossidy and R. Charan, *Execution: The Discipline of Getting Things Done* (New York: Crown Business, 2002).

35 *Ibid.*, pp. 141–45, 178–179.

36 See also S. Markos and M. S. Sridevi, "Employee Engagement: The Key to Improving Performance," *International Journal of Business and Management* 5, no. 12 (2010): 89–96; B. Piersol, "Employee Engagement and Power to the Edge," *Performance Improvement* 46, no. 4 (2007): 30–33; B. Trahant, "Driving Better Performance Through Continuous Employee Engagement," *Public Manager* 38, no. 1 (2009):

54–58; J. C. Hughes and E. Rog, "Talent Management: A Strategy for Improving Employee Recruitment, Retention, and Engagement Within Hospitality Organizations," *International Journal of Contemporary Hospitality Management* 20, no. 7 (2008): 743–757.

37 Russo and Schoemaker, *Decision Traps*.

Chapter 8

1 See, for example, Gary P. Latham and Edwin A. Locke, "Goal Setting—A Motivational Technique That Works," *Organizational Dynamics* 8, no. 2 (September 1979): 68–80; Edwin A. Locke and Gary P. Latham, "Building a Practically Useful Theory of Goal Setting and Task Motivation: A 35-Year Odyssey," *American Psychologist* 57, no. 9 (September 2002): 705–717; Edwin A. Locke and Gary P. Latham, *A Theory of Goal Setting and Task Performance* (Englewood Cliffs, NJ: Prentice Hall, 1990); Ad Kleingeld, Heleen van Mierlo, and Lidia Arends, "The Effect of Goal Setting on Group Performance: A Meta-Analysis," *Journal of Applied Psychology* 96, no. 6 (November 2011): 1289–1304.

2 Taken from the Disney website, http://www.samples-help.org.uk/mission-statements/disney-mission-statement.htm.

3 Taken from the Starwood Hotels website, http://www.starwood-hotels.com/westin/index.html.

4 Gary P. Latham and J. James Baldes, "The "Practical Significance" of Locke's Theory of Goal Setting," *Journal of Applied Psychology* 60, no. 1 (February 1975): 122–124.

5 Lisa D. Ordóñez, Maurice E. Schweitzer, Adam D. Galinsky, and Max H. Bazerman, "Goals Gone Wild: The Systematic Side Effects of Overprescribing Goal Setting," *Academy of Management Perspectives* 23, no. 1 (February 2009): 6–16.

6 Edwin A. Locke and Gary P. Latham, "Has Goal Setting Gone Wild, or Have Its Attackers Abandoned Good Scholarship?" *Academy Of Management Perspectives* 23, no. 1, (February 2009):17–23.

7 Locke and Latham, 2002.

8 Peter Senge, *The Fifth Discipline* (New York: Currency, 1994), 154.

9 Locke and Latham, 1990.

10 Latham and Baldes, 1975.

11 Locke and Latham, 2002.

12 *Ibid.*

13 Gary P. Latham and Gerard H. Seijts, "The Effects of Proximal and Distal Goals on Performance on a Moderately Complex Task," *Journal of Organizational Behavior* 20, no. 4 (July 1999): 421–429.

14 Sim B. Sitkin, Kelly E. See, C. Chet Miller, Michael W. Lawless, and Andrew M. Carton, "The Paradox of Stretch Goals: Organizations in Pursuit of the Seemingly Impossible," *Academy of Management Review* 36, no. 3 (July 2011): 544–566.

15 Jonathan Gutman, "Means-end chains as goal hierarchies," *Psychology & Marketing* 14, no. 6 (September 1997): 545–560.

16 Ryan Hall, *Running with Joy: My Daily Journey To The Marathon* (Eugene, OR: Harvest House Publishers, 2011).

17 Edwin A. Locke, Gary P. Latham, and Miriam Erez, "The Determinants of Goal Commitment," *Academy of Management Review* 13, no. 1 (January 1988): 23–39.

18 George S. Odiorne, "Management by Objectives and the Phenomenon of Goals Displacement," *Human Resource Management* 13, no. 1 (Spring 1974): 2–7; Ronald C. Greenwood, "Management by Objectives: As Developed by Peter Drucker, Assisted by Harold Smiddy," *Academy of Management Review* 6, no. 2 (April 1981): 225–230.

[19] Tom Kawamoto and Bob Mathers, "Key Success Factors for a Performance Dashboard," *DM Review* 17, no. 7 (July 2007): 20–21; Ogan M. Yigitbasioglu and Oana Velcu, "A Review of Dashboards in Performance Management: Implications for Design and Research," *International Journal of Accounting Information Systems* 13, no. 1 (March 2012): 41–59.

[20] Robert S. Kaplan and David P. Norton, "Using the Balanced Scorecard as a Strategic Management System," *Harvard Business Review* (July 2007): 150–161.

Chapter 9

[1] Beard, Donald W., and Gregory G. Dess, "Corporate-Level Strategy, Business-Level Strategy, and Firm Performance," *Academy of Management Journal* 24, no. 4 (December 1981): 663–688; Hofer, Charles W., and Dan. E. Schendel, *Strategy Formulation: Analytical Concepts.* (St. Paul, MN: West Publishing Co., 1978).

[2] Barney, Jay, "Firm Resources and Sustained Competitive Advantage," *Journal of Management* 17, no. 1 (March 1991): 99; Barney, Jay B., "Resource-based theories of competitive advantage: A ten-year retrospective on the resource-based view," *Journal of Management* 27, no. 6 (November 2001): 643.

[3] Miles, Raymond E., Charles C. Snow, Alan D. Meyer, and Henry J. Coleman, Jr., "Organizational Strategy, Structure, and Process," *Academy of Management Review* 3, no. 3 (July 1978): 546–562; Shortell, Stephen M., and Edward J. Zajac. "Perceptual and Archival Measures of Miles and Snow's Strategic Types: A Comprehensive Assessment of Reliability and Validity," *Academy of Management Journal* 33, no. 4 (December 1990): 817–832.

[4] *Ibid.*

[5] Hitt, Michael A., R. Duane Ireland, and K. A. Palia, "Industrial Firms' Grand Strategy and Functional Importance: Moderating Effects of Technology and Uncertainty," *Academy of Management Journal* 25, no. 2 (June 1982): 265–298.

[6] Porter, M. E., *Competitive Strategy.* New York: Free Press, 1980; Dess, Gregory G., and Peter S. Davis, "Porter's (1980) Generic Strategies as Determinants of Strategic Group Membership and Organizational Performance," *Academy of Management Journal* 27, no. 3 (September 1984): 467–488.

[7] Miles et al., 1978; Shortell and Zajac, 1990.

[8] Gal-Or, Esther, "First Mover and Second Mover Advantages," *International Economic Review* 26, no. 3 (October 1985): 649; Lieberman, Marvin B., and David B. Montgomery, "First-Mover Advantages." *Strategic Management Journal* 9, *Special Issue: Strategy Content Research* (Summer 1988), 41–58; Lieberman, Marvin B., and David B. Montgomery, "First-mover (dis)advantages: Retrospective and link with the resource-based view," *Strategic Management Journal* 19, no. 12 (December 1998): 1111–1125.

[9] Jain, Akhil, Phone interview by Shelley Smith. Virginia Beach, VA, March 2012.

[10] Porter, Michael E., "How competitive forces shape strategy," *Harvard Business Review* 57, no. 2 (March 1979): 137–145; Porter, Michael E., "The Five Competitive Forces That Shape Strategy," *Harvard Business Review* 86, no. 1 (January 2008): 78–93.

[11] Porter, 1979; Barney, 1991.

[12] Gresov, Christopher, Heather A. Haveman, and Terence A. Oliva, "Organizational Design, Inertia, and The Dynamics of Competitive Response," *Organization Science* 4, no. 2 (May 1993): 181–208; Miller, Danny, and Chen Ming-Jer, "Sources and Consequences of

Competitive Inertia: A Study of the U.S. Airline Industry." *Administrative Science Quarterly* 39, no. 1 (March 1994): 1–23.

[13] Barney, 1991.

[14] Henderson, B. (1970) "The Product Portfolio," *BCC Perspectives* 66; Day, George S., "Diagnosing the Product Portfolio," *Journal of Marketing* 41.2 (1977): 29–38; Morrison, Alan, and Robin Wensley, "Boxing Up or Boxed In? A Short History of the Boston Consulting Group Share/Growth Matrix," *Journal of Marketing Management* 7, no. 2 (April 1991): 105–129; Wind, Yoram, and Vijay Mahajan, "Designing Product and Business Portfolios," *Harvard Business Review* 59, no. 1 (January 1981): 155–165; Srivastava, Ritu, and Ajay Prakash, "Growth-Share Matrix as a Tool for Portfolio Planning: Evidence from the Indian Telecommunication Services Industry," *IUP Journal of Business Strategy* 8, no. 2 (June 2011): 22–33.

[15] Hitt et al., 1982.

[16] Valentin, E.K., "SWOT Analysis from a Resource-Based View," *Journal of Marketing Theory & Practice* 9, no. 2 (Spring 2001): 54.

[17] Prahalad, C. K., and Gary Hamel, "The Core Competence of the Corporation," *Harvard Business Review* 68, no. 3 (May 1990): 79–91.

[18] Barney, 1991.

[19] Lajoux, Alexandra Reed, "M&A Due Diligence in the New Age of Corporate Governance," *Ivey Business Journal* 71, no. 3 (January 2007): 1.

[20] Robert S. Kaplan and David P. Norton, "Using the Balanced Scorecard as a Strategic Management System," *Harvard Business Review* (July 2007): 150–161.

[21] *Ibid.*

[22] Porter, M. E., *Competitive Strategy;* Dess, Gregory G., and Peter S. Davis. "Porter's (1980) Generic Strategies as Determinants of Strategic Group Membership and Organizational Performance."

[23] *Ibid.*

[24] Williamson, Oliver E., "The Vertical Integration of Production: Market Failure Considerations," *American Economic Review* 61, no. 2 (May 1971): 112–123; Arrow, Kenneth J., "Vertical Integration and Communication," *Bell Journal of Economics* 6, no. 1 (Spring 1975): 173–183; Harrigan, Kathryn Rudie, "Formulating Vertical Integration Strategies," *Academy of Management Review* 9, no. 4 (October 1984): 638–652; Harrigan, Kathryn Rudie, "Vertical Integration and Corporate Strategy," *Academy of Management Journal* 28, no. 2 (June 1985): 397–425.

[25] Pitts, Robert A., "Diversification Strategies and Organizational Policies of Large Diversified Firms," *Journal of Economics & Business* 28, no. 3 (Summer 1976): 181; Pitts, Robert A., "Strategies and Structures for Diversification," *Academy of Management Journal* 20, no. 2 (June 1977): 197–208; Kerr, Jeffrey L., "Diversification Strategies and Managerial Rewards: An Empirical Study," *Academy of Management Journal* 28, no. 1 (March 1985): 155–179.

[26] Hitt et al., 1982; Pearce II, John A., "Selecting Among Alternative Grand Strategies," *California Management Review* 24, no. 3 (Spring 1982): 23–31.

Chapter 10

[1] Recall our discussion from Chapter 2 of the influences of early management theorists, such as the writings of Mary Parker Follett and Elton Mayo and his colleagues' work with the Hawthorne Studies: F. J. Roethlisberger and W. J. Dickson, *Management and the Worker: An Account of a Research Program Conducted by the Western Electric Company, Hawthorne Works, Chicago* (Cambridge, MA:

Harvard University Press, 1939); E. Mayo, *The Human Problems of an Industrial Civilization* (New York: Routledge, 2003); M. P. Follett, *The New State: Group Organization the Solution of Popular Government* (London: Longmans & Green, 1918); M. P. Follett, *Creative Experience* (New York: The New State, 1924).

[2] See, for example, Lawrence, Paul R., and Jay W. Lorsch, "Differentiation and Integration in Complex Organizations," *Administrative Science Quarterly* 12, no. 1 (June 1967): 1–47.

[3] For two alternative perspectives on how this process takes place, refer to Child, John, "Organizational Structure, Environment and Performance: The Role of Strategic Choice," *Sociology* 6, no. 1 (January 1972): 1–22; Hannan, Michael T, and John Freeman, "The Population Ecology of Organizations," *American Journal of Sociology* 82, no. 5 (Mar., 1977): 929–964.

[4] Ostroff, Frank, and Douglas Smith, "The Horizontal Organization," *McKinsey Quarterly* no. 1 (March 1992): 148–168; Ostroff, Frank, *The Horizontal Organization: What the Organization of the Future Actually Looks Like and How It Delivers Value to Customers* (New York: Oxford University Press, 1997); Guttman, Howard M., "The New High-Performance, Horizontal Organization," in *The Organization of the Future 2: Visions, Strategies, and Insights on Managing in a New Era* (San Francisco, CA: Jossey-Bass, 2009) 268–281.

[5] Burns, Tom, and Stalker G. M., *The Management of Innovation* (London: Tavistock Publications 1961); Morand, David A., "The Role of Behavioral Formality and Informality in the Enactment of Bureaucratic versus Organic Organizations," *Academy of Management Review* 20, no. 4 (October 1995): 831–872; Zanzi, Alberto, "How Organic Is Your Organization? Determinants of Organic/Mechanistic Tendencies in a Public Accounting Firm," *Journal of Management Studies* 24, no. 2 (March 1987): 125–142.

[6] Entwisle, Doris R., and John Walton, "Observations on the Span of Control," *Administrative Science Quarterly* 5, no. 4 (March 1961): 522–533; Ouchi, William G., and John B. Dowling, "Defining the Span of Control," *Administrative Science Quarterly* 19, no. 3 (September 1974): 357–365; Udell, Jon G., "An Empirical Test of Hypotheses Relating to Span of Control," *Administrative Science Quarterly* 12, no. 3 (December 1967): 420–439; Urwick, Lyndall F. "The Manager's Span of Control," *Harvard Business Review* 34, no. 3 (May 1956): 39–47; Urwick, L. F., "V. A. Graicunas and the Span of Control," *Academy of Management Journal* 17, no. 2 (June 1974): 349–354.

[7] Although this concept can be traced back through antiquity, Adam Smith was one of the first to write in detail about the idea of specialization in 1776: Smith, Adam. *The Wealth of Nations*, edited by C. J. Bullock. Vol. X. The Harvard Classics (New York: P.F. Collier & Son, 1909–1914); published online by Bartleby.com, 2001; www.bartleby.com/10/. For a more recent academic overview of the concept and its applications in modern organizations, see Shepard, Jon M., "Functional Specialization and Work Attitudes," *Industrial Relations* 8, no. 2 (February 1969): 185–194.

[8] See, for instance, Peters, Gangolf, "Organisation as Social Relationship, Formalisation, and Standardisation: A Weberian Approach to Concept Formation," *International Sociology* 3, no. 3 (September 1988): 267–282.

[9] Wickesberg, Albert K., "Determining Relative Degrees in the Delegation of Executive Authority," *Journal of the Academy of Management* 1, no. 1 (April 1958): 18.

[10] Information for Chief Lanier's bio was obtained from the website of the Metropolitan Police Department, Washington, D.C.; http://mpdc.dc.gov/mpdc/cwp/view,a,1230,Q,561417,mpdcNav,%7C,.asp; accessed September 6, 2012.

[11] Simpson, Richard L., "Vertical and Horizontal Communication in Formal Organizations," *Administrative Science Quarterly* 4, no. 2 (September 1959): 188–196; Aoki, Masahiko, "Horizontal vs. Vertical Information Structure of the Firm," *American Economic Review* 76, no. 5 (December 1986): 971.

[12] Fayol, Henri, *General and Industrial Management* (trans. C. Storrs; London: Sir Isaac Pitman & Sons, 1949); Wren, Daniel A., Arthur G. Bedeian, and John D. Breeze, "The Foundations of Henri Fayol's Administrative Theory," *Management Decision* 40, no. 9 (October 2002): 906; Zábojník, Ján, "Centralized and Decentralized Decision Making in Organizations," *Journal of Labor Economics* 20, no. 1 (January 2002): 1.

[13] Davis, Stanley M., "Two Models of Organization: Unity of Command Versus Balance of Power," *Sloan Management Review* 16, no. 1 (Fall 1974): 29–40; Fayol, *General and Industrial Management*; Wren, Bedeian, and Breeze, "The Foundations of Henri Fayol's Administrative Theory."

[14] Donaldson, Thomas, "The Epistemic Fault Line in Corporate Governance," *Academy of Management Review* 37, no. 2 (April 2012): 256–271; Estes, Robert M., "The Emerging Solution to Corporate Governance," *Harvard Business Review* 55, no. 6 (November 1977): 20–164; Judge, William Q., Thomas Weber, and Maureen I. Muller-Kahle, "What Are the Correlates of Interdisciplinary Research Impact? The Case of Corporate Governance Research," *Academy of Management Learning & Education* 11, no. 1 (March 2012): 82–98; Westphal, James D., and Edward J. Zajac, "The Symbolic Management of Stockholders: Corporate Governance Reforms and Shareholder Reactions," *Administrative Science Quarterly* 43, no. 1 (March 1998): 127–153.

[15] Chandler, Jr., Alfred D., "Origins of the Organization Chart," *Harvard Business Review* 66, no. 2 (March 1988): 156–157.

[16] Miles, Raymond E., and Charles C. Snow, "Network Organizations: New Concepts for New Forms." *McKinsey Quarterly* no. 4 (September 1986): 53–66; Miles, Raymond E., and Charles C. Snow, "The New Network Firm: A Spherical Structure Built on a Human Investment Philosophy," *Organizational Dynamics* 23, no. 4 (Spring 95 1995): 5–18.

[17] Gannon, Martin J., and Frank T. Paine, "Unity of Command and Job Attitudes of Managers in a Bureaucratic Organization," *Journal of Applied Psychology* 59, no. 3 (June 1974): 392–394; Davis, "Two Models of Organization"; Fayol, *General and Industrial Management*; Wren, Bedeian, and Breeze, "The Foundations of Henri Fayol's Administrative Theory."

[18] Fayol, *General and Industrial Management*; Wren, Bedeian, and Breeze, "The Foundations of Henri Fayol's Administrative Theory"; Zábojník, "Centralized and Decentralized Decision Making."

[19] Concepts presented in the following discussion are taken in part from these sources: Anand, N., and Richard L. Daft, "What Is the Right Organization Design?" *Organizational Dynamics* 36, no. 4 (November 2007): 329–344; Duncan, Robert, "What Is the Right Organization Structure? Decision Tree Analysis Provides the Answer," *Organizational Dynamics* 7, no. 3 (Winter 1979): 59–80; Galbraith, Jay R., *Designing Complex Organizations* (Reading, MA: Addison–Wesley, 1973); Galbraith, Jay R., *Organization Design* (Reading, MA: Addison-Wesley, 1977); Galbraith, Jay R., "Matrix Organization Designs," *Business Horizons* 14, no. 1 (February 1971): 29.

[20] For additional background information on the protests, see Bingham, Amy, "Wall Street Protests Expand to D.C. to 'Take Back Our Country,'" *ABC News,* October 6, 2011; http://abcnews.go.com/blogs/politics/2011/10/wall-street-protests-expand-to-d-c-to-take-back-our-country/; accessed November 15, 2012.

[21] *Ibid.*

[22] Davidson, Paul, "Temporary Workers Reshape Companies, Jobs," *USA Today,* October 13, 2010.

[23] *Ibid.*

[24] *Ibid.*

[25] Davidson, "Temporary Workers"; Pink, Daniel H., *Free Agent Nation: The Future of Working For Yourself* (New York: Warner Business Books, 2001).

[26] Davidson, "Temporary workers."

[27] Pfeffer, Jeffrey, "Why Free Agents Don't Feel Free," *Business 2.0* 7, no. 9 (October 2006): 78.

[28] *Ibid.*

[29] Meinert, Dori, "Make Telecommuting Pay Off," *HR Magazine* 56, no. 6 (June 2011): 32–37.

[30] *Ibid.*

[31] *Ibid.*

[32] Leonard, Bill, "Managing Virtual Teams," *HR Magazine* 56, no. 6 (June 2011): 38–42.

Chapter 11

[1] Salvatore, Paul, Daniel Halem, Allan Weitzman, Gershom Smith, and Lan Schaefer, "How the Law Changed HR," *HR Magazine* 50, (December 2, 2005): 47–56.

[2] See, for example, Dyer, Lee, and Donald P. Schwab, "Personnel/Human Resource Management Research," in *Industrial Relations Research in the 1970s: Review and Appraisal,* Thomas A. Kochan, Daniel J. B. Mitchell, and Lee Dyer, eds. (Madison, WI: Industrial Relations Research Association, 1982), 187–220; Ferris, Gerald R., Wayne A. Hochwarter, M. Ronald Buckley, Gloria Harrell-Cook, and Dwight D. Frink, "Human Resources Management: Some New Directions," *Journal of Management* 25 (1999): 385–415; Wallace, Jr., Marc J., "Methodology, Research Practice, and Progress in Personnel and Industrial Relations," *Academy of Management Review* 8, no. 1 (January 1983): 6–13; Wright, Patrick M., and Wendy R. Boswell, "Desegregating HRM: A Review and Synthesis of Micro and Macro Human Resource Management Research," *Journal of Management* 28, no. 3 (May 2002): 247–276.

[3] Hogler, Raymond, "Exclusive representation and the Wagner Act: The structure of federal collective bargaining law," *Labor Law Journal* 58, no. 3 (Fall 2007): 157–169; Levy, Beryl Harold, "Collective bargaining under the Taft-Hartley Act," *Harvard Business Review* 26, no. 4 (July 1948): 468–479; Robbins, E. C., "Collective Bargaining Under the Wagner Labor Act," *Harvard Business Review* 15, no. 4 (Summer 1937): 393.

[4] Goodman, Jon Prooslin, and William R. Sandberg, "A Contingency Approach to Labor Relations Strategies," *Academy of Management Review* 6, no. 1 (January 1981): 145–154; Krell, Eric, "The Rebirth of Labor Relations," *HR Magazine* 54, no. 2 (February 2009): 57–60; Suntrup, Edward L., "Labor Relations: Development, Structure, Process," *Academy of Management Review* 5, no. 3 (July 1980): 480–482.

[5] Burns, John E., "Equal Employment Opportunity Under Federal Civil Rights Act," *Industrial Management* (August 1965) 1; Konrad, Alison M., and Frank Linnehan, "The Implementation and Effectiveness of Equal Opportunity Employment," *Academy of Management Best Papers Proceedings* (August 1992): 380–384; Marshall, Ray, "Equal Employment Opportunities: Problems and Prospects," *Labor Law Journal* 16, no. 8 (August 1965): 453–468; Vertreace, Walter, "Equal Employment Opportunity: Mission Accomplished, or Dream Deferred?" *Black Collegian* 40, no. 2 (January 2010): 57–60.

[6] Donahue, Kristen B, "Time to Get Serious About Talent Management," *Harvard Business Review* 79, no. 7 (July 2001): 6–7; Handfield-Jones, Helen, Ed Michaels, and Beth Axelrod, "Talent Management," *Ivey Business Journal* 66, no. 2 (November 2001): 53.

[7] See the following for recent discussions on generational differences at work: Dries, Nicky, Roland Pepermans, and Evelien De Kerpel, "Exploring Four Generations' Beliefs About Career: Is 'Satisfied' the New 'Successful?'," *Journal of Managerial Psychology* 23, no. 8 (2008): 907–928; Hansen, Jo-Ida C., and Melanie E. Leuty, "Work Values Across Generations," *Journal of Career Assessment* 20, no. 1 (February 2012): 34–52; Shaw, Sue, and David Fairhurst, "Engaging a New Generation of Graduates," *Education & Training* 50, no. 5 (2008): 366–378.

[8] Crook, T. Russell, Samuel Y. Todd, James G. Combs, David J. Woehr, and David J. Jr. Ketchen, "Does Human Capital Matter? A Meta-analysis of the Relationship Between Human Capital and Firm Performance," *Journal of Applied Psychology* 96, no. 3 (May 2011): 443–456; Goode, Richard B, "Adding to the Stock of Physical and Human Capital," *American Economic Review* 49, no. 2 (May 1959): 147; Mincer, Jacob, "Investment in Human Capital and Personal Income Distribution," *Journal of Political Economy* 66, no. 4 (August 1958): 281–302; Ployhart, Robert E., Chad H. Van Iddekinge, and William I. Mackenzie Jr., "Acquiring and developing human capital in service contexts: The interconnectedness of human capital resources," *Academy of Management Journal* 54, no. 2 (April 2011): 353–368.

[9] See, for example, Golden, Karen A., and Vasudevan Ramanujam, "Between a Dream and a Nightmare: On the Integration of the Human Resource Management and Strategic Business Planning Processes," *Human Resource Management* 24, no. 4 (Winter 1985): 429–452; Lengnick-Hall, Cynthia A., and Mark L. Lengnick-Hall, *Interactive Human Resource Management and Strategic Planning.* New York: Quorum Books, 1990; Rowden, Robert W, "Potential Roles of the Human Resource Management Professional in the Strategic Planning," *SAM Advanced Management Journal* 64, no. 3 (Summer 1999): 22.

[10] Heshizer, Brian, "The New Common Law of Employment: Changes in the Concept of Employment at Will," *Labor Law Journal* 36, no. 2 (February 1985): 95–107; Radin, Tara J., and Patricia H. Werhane, "Employment-at-Will, Employee Rights, and Future Directions for Employment," *Business Ethics Quarterly* 13, no. 2 (April 2003): 113–130; "Employment at Will," *Dictionary of Human Resource Management* (January 2001): 100.

[11] Bates, Steve, "A Tough Target: Employee or Independent Contractor?" *HR Magazine* 46, no. 6 (June 2001): 68; also recall our discussion from Chapter 10 regarding flexible workforce arrangements, which include temporary workers, free agents, and independent contractors: Davidson, Paul, "Temporary Workers Reshape Companies, Jobs," *USA Today,* October 13, 2010; Pink, Daniel H., *Free Agent Nation: The Future of Working For Yourself* (New York: Warner Business Books, 2001).

[12] Boudreau, John W., and Sara L. Rynes, "Role of Recruitment in Staffing Utility Analysis," *Journal of Applied Psychology* 70, no. 2 (May

1985): 354–366; Rynes, Sara L, "Recruitment, Job Choice, and Post-hire Consequences," in *Handbook of Industrial and Organizational Psychology* 2d ed., Vol. 2, Marvin D. Dunnette and Leaetta M. Hough, eds. (Palo Alto, CA: Consulting Psychologists Press) 399–444; Rynes, Sara L., and John W. Boudreau, "College Recruiting in Large Organizations: Practice, Evaluation, and Research Implications," *Personnel Psychology* 39, no. 4 (Winter 1986): 729–757; Taylor, M. Susan, and Thomas J. Bergmann, "Organizational Recruitment Activities and Applicants' Reactions at Different Stages of the Recruitment Process," *Personnel Psychology* 40, no. 2 (Summer 1987): 261–285.

[13] Bangerter, Adrian, Nicolas Roulin, and Cornelius J. König, "Personnel Selection as a Signaling Game," *Journal of Applied Psychology* (October 31, 2011); Fleishman, Edwin A, "Some New Frontiers in Personnel Selection Research," *Personnel Psychology* 41, no. 4 (Winter 1988): 679–701; Guion, Robert M, "Employee Selection: Musings About Its Past, Present, and Future," in *Handbook of Employee Selection* (New York: Routledge/Taylor & Francis Group, 2010), 943–957; Guion, Robert M, "Changing view for personnel selection research," *Personnel Psychology* 40, no. 2 (Summer 1987): 199–213; Guion, Robert M, "Some Virtues of Dissatisfaction in the Science and Practice of Personnel Selection," *Human Resource Management Review* 8, no. 4 (Winter 1998): 351. Guion, Robert M, "Personnel Assessment, Selection, and Placement," in *Handbook of Industrial and Organizational Psychology,* 2d ed., Vol. 2 (Palo Alto, CA: Consulting Psychologists Press, 1991), 327–397; Schmidt, Frank L., and John E. Hunter, "The Validity and Utility of Selection Methods in Personnel Psychology: Practical and Theoretical Implications of 85 Years of Research Findings," *Psychological Bulletin* 124, no. 2 (September 1998): 262–274.

[14] Bayo-Moriones, Alberto, and Pedro Ortín-Ángel, "Internal Promotion Versus External Recruitment in Industrial Plants in Spain," *Industrial & Labor Relations Review* 59, no. 3 (April 2006): 451–470; Chan, William, "External Recruitment Versus Internal Promotion," *Journal of Labor Economics* 14, no. 4 (October 1996): 555–571; Friedman, Stewart D, "Why Hire from Within? Causes and Consequences of Internal Promotion Systems," *Academy of Management Best Papers Proceedings* (August 1991): 272–276; Waldman, Michael, "Ex Ante Versus Ex Post Optimal Promotion Rules: The Case of Internal Promotion," *Economic Inquiry* 41, no. 1 (January 2003): 27–41.

[15] Bayo-Moriones and Ortín-Ángel, "Internal Promotion versus External Recruitment"; Chan, "External Recruitment Versus Internal Promotion"; Kong-Pin, Chen, "External Recruitment as an Incentive Device," *Journal of Labor Economics* 23, no. 2 (April 2005): 259–277; Schwan, Rolf, and Joseph Soeters, "The Strategy of Vacancy-Filling from Internal and External Labor Market Sources: An Empirical Assessment of the Recruitment Strategy of Different Types of Organization," *Scandinavian Journal of Management* 10, no. 1 (March 1994): 69–85; Werbel, James D., Lynda Jiwen Song, and Shifu Yan, "The Influence of External Recruitment Practices on Job Search Practices Across Domestic Labor Markets: A Comparison of the United States and China," *International Journal of Selection and Assessment* 16, no. 2 (June 2008): 93–101.

[16] See, for example, Bakker, Shawn, "Psychometric Selection Assessments," *HR Professional* 26, no. 3 (April 2009): 21; Joubert, Tina, and Hendrik J. Kriek, "Psychometric Comparison of Paper-and-Pencil and Online Personality Assessments in a Selection Setting," *South African Journal of Industrial Psychology (SAJIP)* 35, no. 1 (December 2009): 78–88.

[17] See, for instance, Stybel, Laurence J, "Managing the Inner Contradictions of Job Descriptions: A Technique for Use in Recruitment," *Psychologist-Manager Journal* 13, no. 2 (April 2010): 105–110.

[18] "The Questions You Should and Shouldn't Ask in a Job Interview," *Forbes* (July 6, 2012), accessed September 2, 2012; http://www.forbes.com/sites/jacquelynsmith/2012/07/06/the-questions-you-should-and-shouldnt-ask-in-a-job-interview/.

[19] Eder, Robert W, and Gerald R. Ferris, *The Employment Interview: Theory, Research, and Practice* (Thousand Oaks, CA: Sage Publications, Inc., 1989); Huffcutt, Allen I., "An Empirical Review of the Employment Interview Construct Literature," *International Journal of Selection and Assessment* 19, no. 1 (March 2011): 62–81; McDaniel, Michael A., Deborah L. Whetzel, Frank L. Schmidt, and Steven D. Maurer, "The Validity of Employment Interviews: A Comprehensive Review and Meta-analysis," *Journal of Applied Psychology* 79, no. 4 (August 1994): 599–616.

[20] Schmidt and Hunter, "The Validity and Utility of Selection Methods"; McDaniel et al., "The Validity of Employment Interviews."

[21] For a recent review of employer-employee grievance processes, see Walker, Bernard, and Robert T. Hamilton, "Employee-Employer Grievances: A Review," *International Journal of Management Reviews* 13, no. 1 (March 2011): 40–58.

[22] Arnold, Jennifer Taylor, "Ramping up Onboarding," *HR Magazine* 55, no. 5 (May 2010): 75–78; Bauer, Talya N., and Berrin Erdogan, "Organizational Socialization: The Effective Onboarding of New Employees," in *APA Handbook of Industrial and Organizational Psychology, Vol 3: Maintaining, Expanding, and Contracting the Organization,* (Washington, D.C.: American Psychological Association, 2011) 51–64; Snell, Alice, "Researching Onboarding Best Practice," *Strategic HR Review* 5, no. 6 (September 2006): 32–35.

[23] "The 10 Commandments of On-Boarding," Career Builder.com, accessed April 21, 2012; http://www.careerbuilder.com/jobposter/small-business/article.aspx?articleid=ATL_0192ONBOARDINGTIPS_s.

[24] Colquitt, Jason A., Jeffrey A. LePine, and Raymond A. Noe, "Toward an Integrative Theory of Training Motivation: A Meta-analytic Path Analysis of 20 Years of Research," *Journal of Applied Psychology* 85, no. 5 (October 2000): 678–707; Goldstein, Irwin L, "Training in Work Organizations," In *Handbook of Industrial and Organizational Psychology,* 2d ed., Vol. 2 (Palo Alto, CA: Consulting Psychologists Press, 1991) 507–619; Salas, Eduardo, Janis A. Cannon-Bowers, Lori Rhodenizer, and Clint A. Bowers, "Training in Organizations: Myths, Misconceptions, and Mistaken Assumptions," In *Research in Human Resources Management,* Vol. 17 (Greenwich, CT: Elsevier Science/JAI Press, 1999) 123–161; Tannenbaum, Scott I., and Gary Yukl, "Training and Development in Work Organizations," *Annual Review of Psychology* 43, no. 1 (February 1992): 399.

[25] Forray, Jeanie M, "Management and Leadership Development," *Academy of Management Learning & Education* 9, no. 1 (March 2010): 145–147. Tannenbaum and Yukl, "Training and Development."

[26] Ellis, Aleksander P. J., and Matthew J. Pearsall, "Reducing the Negative Effects of Stress in Teams Through Cross-Training: A Job Demands-Resources Model," *Group Dynamics: Theory, Research, and Practice* 15, no. 1 (March 2011): 16–31; Marks, Michelle A., Mark J. Sabella, C. Shawn Burke, and Stephen J. Zaccaro. "The Impact of Cross-Training on Team Effectiveness," *Journal of Applied Psychology* 87, no. 1 (February 2002): 3–13.

27 For an overview of the ADDIE training model, see Allen, W. Clayton, "Overview and Evolution of the ADDIE Training System," *Advances in Developing Human Resources* 8, no. 4 (November 2006): 430–441.

28 *Ibid.*

29 Bell, Myrtle P., "Changing Attitudes Toward Affirmative Action: A Current Issue that Calls for Action," *Academy of Management Best Papers Proceedings* (August 1997): 438–442; Harrison, David A., David A. Kravitz, David M. Mayer, Lisa M. Leslie, and Dalit Lev-Arey, "Understanding Attitudes Toward Affirmative Action Programs in Employment: Summary and Meta-analysis of 35 Years of Research," *Journal of Applied Psychology* 91, no. 5 (September 2006): 1013–1036; Ruderman, Marian N, "Affirmative Action: Does It Really Work?" *Academy of Management Executive* 10, no. 3 (August 1996): 64–65; Taylor, Marilyn L, "Implementation of Affirmative Action: A Preliminary Identification of Impetus and Enabling Factors," *Academy of Management Proceedings* (August 1979): 272–276.

30 Federal Glass Ceiling Commission, *Solid Investments: Making Full Use of the Nation's Human Capital* (Washington, D.C.: U.S. Department of Labor, November 1995): 4.

31 Gerhart, Barry, and George T. Milkovich, "Employee Compensation: Research and Practice," in *Handbook of Industrial and Organizational Psychology*, 2d ed., Vol. 3 (Palo Alto, CA: Consulting Psychologists Press, 1992) 481–569; Gerhart, Barry, and George T. Milkovich, "Organizational Differences in Managerial Compensation and Financial Performance," *Academy of Management Journal* 33, no. 4 (December 1990): 663–691; Zhu, Kejia, "Pay Dispersion-Performance Relationship in High-Tech Firms: A Holistic View of the Compensation System," *Academy of Management Annual Meeting Proceedings* (August 2008): 1–6.

32 Dulebohn, James H., Janice C. Molloy, Shaun M. Pichler, and Brian Murray, "Employee Benefits: Literature Review and Emerging Issues," *Human Resource Management Review* 19, no. 2 (June 2009): 86–103; Harris, Michael E., and Laurence S. Fink, "Employee Benefit Programs and Attitudinal and Behavioral Outcomes: A Preliminary Model," *Human Resource Management Review* 4, no. 2 (Summer 1994): 117; Yamamoto, Hiroshi, "The Relationship Between Employee Benefit Management and Employee Retention," *International Journal of Human Resource Management* 22, no. 17 (October 15, 2011): 3550–3564.

33 Shuck, Brad, "Four Emerging Perspectives of Employee Engagement: An Integrative Literature Review," *Human Resource Development Review* 10, no. 3 (September 2011): 304–328; Shuck, Brad, and Thomas G., Reio, Jr., "The Employee Engagement Landscape and HRD: How Do We Link Theory and Scholarship to Current Practice?" *Advances in Developing Human Resources* 13, no. 4 (November 2011): 419–428.

34 See, for example, Frank, Fredric D., Richard P. Finnegan, and Craig R. Taylor, "The Race for Talent: Retaining and Engaging Workers in the 21st Century," *Human Resource Planning* 27, no. 3 (July 2004): 12–25; Harter, James K., Frank L. Schmidt, and Theodore L. Hayes, "Business-Unit-Level Relationship Between Employee Satisfaction, Employee Engagement, and Business Outcomes: A Meta-analysis," *Journal of Applied Psychology* 87, no. 2 (April 2002): 268–279.

35 Hastings, Rebecca R, "Study: Supervisors Drive Employee Engagement," *HR Magazine* 56, no. 8 (August 2011): 22.

36 Xu, Jessica, and Helena Cooper Thomas, "How Can Leaders Achieve High Employee Engagement?" *Leadership & Organization Development Journal* 32, no. 4 (2011): 399–416.

37 *Ibid.*

38 Hastings, "Study: Supervisors Drive Employee Engagement."

39 *Ibid.*

40 *Ibid.*

41 For a recent study examining employee attitude surveys, see Mueller, Karsten, Manuel C. Voelkle, and Keith Hattrup, "On the Relationship Between Job Satisfaction and Non-response in Employee Attitude Surveys: A Longitudinal Field Study," *Journal of Occupational and Organizational Psychology* 84, no. 4 (December 2011): 780–798.

42 Bailey, Caroline, and Clive Fletcher, "International Performance Management and Appraisal: Research Perspectives," In *Handbook of Research in International Human Resource Management* (New York: Taylor & Francis Group/Lawrence Erlbaum Associates, 2008) 125–143; Bretz, Robert D., Jr., George T. Milkovich, and Walter Read, "The Current State of Performance Appraisal Research and Practice: Concerns, Directions, and Implications," *Journal of Management* 18, no. 2 (June 1992): 321; Catano, Victor M., Wendy Darr, and Catherine A. Campbell, "Performance Appraisal of Behavior-Based Competencies: A Reliable and Valid Procedure," *Personnel Psychology* 60, no. 1 (Spring 2007): 201–230.

43 Bracken, David W., and Dale S. Rose, "When Does 360-Degree Feedback Create Behavior Change? And How Would We Know It When It Does?" *Journal of Business & Psychology* 26, no. 2 (June 2011): 183–192; Hazucha, Joy Fisher, Sarah A. Hezlett, and Robert J. Schneider, "The Impact of 360-Degree Feedback on Management Skills Development," *Human Resource Management* 32, no. 2/3 (Summer–Fall 1993): 325–351.

44 Atkin, Robert S., and Edward J. Conlon, "Behaviorally Anchored Rating Scales: Some Theoretical Issues," *Academy of Management Review* 3, no. 1 (January 1978): 119–128; Maiorca, Joseph, "How to Construct Behaviorally Anchored Rating Scales (BARS) for Employee Evaluations," *Supervision* 58, no. 8 (August 1997): 15; Schwab, Donald P., III, Herbert G. Heneman, and Thomas A. DeCotiis, "Behaviorally Anchored Rating Scales: A Review of the Literature," *Personnel Psychology* 28, no. 4 (Winter 1975): 549–562.

Chapter 12

1 Our definition is based upon the following sources: Stewart, Greg L., Charles C. Manz, and Henry P. Sims, *Team Work and Group Dynamics* (New York: John Wiley and Sons, 1999); Guzzo, Richard A., and Marcus W. Dickson, "Teams in Organizations: Recent Research on Performance and Effectiveness," *Annual Review of Psychology* 47, no. 1 (February 1996): 307; Ilgen, Daniel R., John R. Hollenbeck, Michael Johnson, and Dustin Jundt, "Teams in Organizations: From Input-Process-Output Models to IMOI Models," *Annual Review of Psychology* 56, (2005): 517–543.

2 See, for example, Bell, Bradford S., and Steve W. J. Kozlowski, "Collective Failure: The Emergence, Consequences, and Management of Errors in Teams," in *Errors in organizations* (New York: Routledge/Taylor & Francis Group, 2011) 113–141.

3 Stewart, Manz, and Sims, *Team Work.*

4 See, for instance, Aubé, Caroline, and Vincent Rousseau, "Interpersonal Aggression and Team Effectiveness: The Mediating Role of Team Goal Commitment," *Journal of Occupational and Organizational Psychology* 84, no. 3 (September 2011): 565–580; Durham, Cathy C., Don Knight, and Edwin A. Locke, "Effects of Leader Role, Team-Set Goal Difficulty, Efficacy, and Tactics on Team Effectiveness," *Organizational Behavior and Human Decision Processes* 72,

no. 2 (November 1997): 203–231; Hu, Jia, and Robert C. Liden, "Antecedents of Team Potency and Team Effectiveness: An Examination of Goal and Process Clarity and Servant Leadership," *Journal of Applied Psychology* 96, no. 4 (July 2011): 851–862.

[5] *Ibid.*

[6] Latham, Gary P. and J. James Baldes, "The "Practical Significance" of Locke's Theory of Goal Setting," *Journal of Applied Psychology* 60, no.1 (February1975): 122–124.

[7] Uhl-Bien, Mary, and George B. Graen, "Individual Self-Management: Analysis of Professionals' Self-Managing Activities in Functional and Cross-Functional Work Teams," *Academy of Management Journal* 41, no. 3 (June 1998): 340–350.

[8] Uhl-Bien and Graen. "Individual Self-Management"; Likert, Rensis, "Improving Cost Performance with Cross-Functional Teams," *Management Review* 65, no. 3 (March 1976): 36; Randel, Amy E., and Kimberly S. Jaussi, "Functional Background Identity, Diversity, and Individual Performance in Cross-Functional Teams," *Academy of Management Journal* 46, no.6 (December 2003): 763–774.

[9] Blindenbach-Driessen, Floortje, "The Effectiveness of Cross-Functional Innovation Teams," *Academy of Management Annual Meeting Proceedings* (August 2009): 1–6; Peelle, Henry E., III, "Appreciative Inquiry and Creative Problem Solving in Cross-Functional Teams," *Journal of Applied Behavioral Science* 42, no. 4 (December 2006): 447–467.

[10] Hu and Liden, "Antecedents of Team Potency and Team Effectiveness"; Sonnentag, Sabine, and Judith Volmer; "What You Do for Your Team Comes Back to You: A Cross-Level Investigation of Individual Goal Specification, Team-Goal Clarity, and Individual Performance," *Human Performance* 23, no. 2 (April 2010): 116–130.

[11] Antoni, Conny, and Guido Hertel, "Team Processes, Their Antecedents and Consequences: Implications for Different Types of Teamwork," *European Journal of Work and Organizational Psychology* 18, no. 3 (September 2009): 253–266; Cooley, Elizabeth, "Training an Interdisciplinary Team in Communication and Decision-Making Skills," in *Human Resource Development Review: Research and Implications* (Thousand Oaks, CA: Sage Publications, Inc, 1997) 247–266; Wagstrom, Patrick, James D. Herbsleb, and Kathleen M. Carley, "Communication, Team Performance, and the Individual: Bridging Technical Dependencies," *Academy of Management Annual Meeting Proceedings* (August 2010): 1–7.

[12] Joni, Saj-nicole A., and Damon Beyer, "How to Pick a Good Fight," *Harvard Business Review* 87, no. 12 (December 2009): 48–57; Parayitam, Satyanarayana, and Robert S. Dooley, "The Relationship Between Conflict and Decision Outcomes: Moderating Effects of Cognitive- and Affect-based Trust in Strategic Decision-Making Teams," *International Journal of Conflict Management* 18, no. 1 (2007): 42–73; Simons, Tony L., and Randall S. Peterson, "Task Conflict and Relationship Conflict in Top Management Teams: The Pivotal Role of Intragroup Trust," *Journal of Applied Psychology* 85, no. 1 (February 2000): 102–111.

[13] Anthony, William P., and Don D. Daake, "The Roles of a Facilitator in Top Management Team Decision Making: Promoting Strategic Group Consensus and Information Use," in *Advances in interdisciplinary studies of work teams: Team leadership, Vol. 3* (Greenwich, CT: Elsevier Science/JAI Press, 1996) 239–251; Flood, P. C., Hannan, E., Smith, K. G., Turner, T., West, M. A., & Dawson, J., "Chief Executive Leadership Style, Consensus Decision Making, and Top Management Team Effectiveness," *European Journal of Work and Organizational Psychology* 9, no. 3 (September 2000): 401–420.

[14] Lerner, Jennifer S., and Philip E. Tetlock, "Accounting for the Effects of Accountability," *Psychological Bulletin* 125, no. 2 (March 1999): 255–275; Marx, Leslie M., and Francesco Squintani, "Individual Accountability in Teams," *Journal of Economic Behavior & Organization* 72, no. 1 (October 2009): 260–273.

[15] Khan, Mohammad Saud, "Role of Trust and Relationships in Geographically Distributed Teams: Exploratory Study on Development Sector," *International Journal of Networking & Virtual Organisations* 10, no. 1 (January 2012): 40–58; Simons and Peterson, "Task Conflict."

[16] Aubé and Rousseau, "Interpersonal Aggression"; Bishop, James W., and K. Dow Scott, "An Examination of Organizational and Team Commitment in a Self-Directed Team Environment," *Journal of Applied Psychology* 85, no. 3 (June 2000): 439–450; Pearce, Craig L., and Pamela A. Herbik, "Citizenship Behavior at the Team Level of Analysis: The Effects of Team Leadership, Team Commitment, Perceived Team Support, and Team Size," *Journal of Social Psychology* 144, no. 3 (June 2004): 293–310.

[17] Carson, Jay B., Paul E. Tesluk, and Jennifer A. Marrone, "Shared Leadership in Teams: An Investigation of Antecedent Conditions and Performance," *Academy of Management Journal* 50, no. 5 (October 2007): 1217–1234; Pearce, Craig L., Jay A. Conger, and Edwin A. Locke, "Shared Leadership Theory," *The Leadership Quarterly* 19, no. 5 (October 2008): 622–628. Pearce, Craig L, "The Future of Leadership: Combining Vertical and Shared Leadership to Transform Knowledge Work," *Academy of Management Executive* 18, no. 1 (February 2004): 47–57.

[18] Bishop and Scott, "An Examination of Organizational and Team Commitment"; Gerard, Robert J, "Teaming Up: Making the Transition to a Self-Directed, Team-Based Organization," *Academy of Management Executive* 9, no. 3 (August 1995): 91–93. Millikin, John P., Peter W. Hom, and Charles C. Manz, "Self-Management Competencies in Self-Managing Teams: Their Impact on Multi-team System Productivity," *The Leadership Quarterly* 21, no. 5 (October 2010): 687–702.

[19] Iverson, Annette M, "Best Practices in Problem-Solving Team Structure and Process," in *Best Practices in School Psychology IV (Vol. 1, Vol. 2)* (Washington, D.C.: National Association of School Psychologists, 2002) 657–669; Postrel, Steven, "Islands of Shared Knowledge: Specialization and Mutual Understanding in Problem-Solving Teams," *Organization Science* 13, no. 3 (May 2002): 303–320.

[20] See, for example, Stewart, Manz, and Sims, *Team Work and Group Dynamics*; Joshi, Aparna, Niti Pandey, and Guohong (Helen) Han, "Bracketing Team Boundary Spanning: An Examination of Task-based, Team-level, and Contextual Antecedents," *Journal of Organizational Behavior* 30, no. 6 (August 2009): 731–759.

[21] Gregerman, Ira B, "Introduction to Quality Circles: An Approach to Participative Problem-Solving," *Industrial Management* 21, no. 5 (September 1979): 21; Griffin, Ricky W, "Consequences of Quality Circles in an Industrial Setting: A Longitudinal Assessment," *Academy of Management* Journal 31, no. 2 (June 1988): 338–358; Munchus III, George, "Employer-Employee Based Quality Circles in Japan: Human Resource Policy Implications for American Firms," *Academy of Management Review* 8, no. 2 (April 1983): 255–261.

[22] Kirkman, Bradley L., Benson Rosen, Paul E. Tesluk, and Cristina B. Gibson, "The Impact of Team Empowerment on Virtual Team Performance: The Moderating Role of Face-to-Face Interaction," *Academy of Management Journal* 47, no. 2 (April 2004): 175–192; Malhotra, Arvind, Ann Majchrzak, and Benson Rosen, "Leading Virtual Teams," *Academy of Management Perspectives* 21, no. 1

(February 2007): 60–70; Montoya-Weiss, Mitzi M., Anne P. Massey, and Michael Song, "Getting It Together: Temporal Coordination and Conflict Management in Global Virtual Teams," *Academy of Management Journal* 44, no. 6 (December 2001): 1251–1262.

[23] See, for instance, Lorge, Irving, and Herbert Solomon, "Individual Performance and Group Performance in Problem Solving Related to Group Size and Previous Exposure to the Problem," *Journal of Psychology: Interdisciplinary and Applied* 48 (July 1959): 107–114; Sharma, Monika, and Anjali Ghosh, "Does Team Size Matter? A Study of the Impact of Team Size on the Transactive Memory System and Performance of IT Sector Teams," *South Asian Journal of Management* 14, no. 4 (October 2007): 96–115.

[24] Table adapted from Jaques, David, and Gilly Salmon, *Learning in Groups: A Handbook for Face-to-Face and Online Environments,* 4th ed. (New York: Routledge/Taylor & Francis Group, 2006), p. 11.

[25] Latané, Bibb, Kipling Williams, and Stephen Harkins, "Many Hands Make Light the Work: The Causes and Consequences of Social Loafing," *Journal of Personality and Social Psychology* 37, no. 6 (June 1979): 822–832; Steiner, Ivan D, "Models for Inferring Relationships Between Group Size and Potential Group Productivity," *Behavioral Science* 11, no. 4 (1966): 273–283.

[26] Steiner, Ivan D., and Joan S. Dodge, "Interpersonal Perception and Role Structure as Determinants of Group and Individual Efficiency," *Human Relations* 9, (1956): 467–480.

[27] Ghorpade, Jai, Jim Lackritz, and Gangaram Singh, "Personality as a Moderator of the Relationship Between Role Conflict, Role Ambiguity, and Burnout," *Journal of Applied Social Psychology* 41, no. 6 (June 2011): 1275–1298; Organ, Dennis W., and Charles N. Greene, "Role Ambiguity, Locus of Control, and Work Satisfaction," *Journal of Applied Psychology* 59, no. 1 (February 1974): 101–102; Pearce, Jone L, "Bringing Some Clarity to Role Ambiguity Research," *Academy of Management Review* 6, no. 4 (October 1981): 665–674.

[28] Malik, Muhammad Imran, and Abid Usman, "Role Overload, Job Satisfaction and Their Effect on Layoff Survivor's Job Retention and Productivity," *Interdisciplinary Journal Of Contemporary Research in Business* 2, no. 11 (March 2011): 427–440; Santora, Joseph C., and Mark Esposito, "Dual Family Earners: Do Role Overload and Stress Treat Them as Equals?" *Academy of Management Perspectives* 24, no. 4 (November 2010): 92–93; Tordera, Nuria, Vicente González-Romá, and José María Peiró, "The Moderator Effect of Psychological Climate on the Relationship Between Leader-Member Exchange (LMX) Quality and Role Overload," *European Journal of Work and Organizational Psychology* 17, no. 1 (March 2008): 56–72.

[29] Stewart, Manz, and Sims, *Team Work.*

[30] Goncalo, Jack A., and Michelle M. Duguid, "Follow the Crowd in a New Direction: When Conformity Pressure Facilitates Group Creativity (and When It Does Not)," *Organizational Behavior & Human Decision Processes* 118, no. 1 (May 2012): 14–23; Kiesler, Charles A, "Attraction to the Group and Conformity to Group Norms," *Journal of Personality* 31, no. 4 (December 1963): 559; Prapavessis, Harry, and Albert V. Carron, "Sacrifice, Cohesion, and Conformity to Norms in Sport Teams, *Group Dynamics: Theory, Research, and Practice* 1, no. 3 (September 1997): 231–240.

[31] Bonebright, Denise A, "40 Years of Storming: A Historical Review of Tuckman's Model of Small Group Development," *Human Resource Development International* 13, no. 1 (February 2010): 111–120; Tuckman, Bruce W, "Developmental Sequence in Small Groups," *Psychological Bulletin* 63, no. 6 (June 1965): 384–399; Tuckman, Bruce W., and Mary Ann C. Jensen, "Stages of Small-Group Development

Revisited," *Group & Organization Studies* 2, no. 4 (December 1977): 419–427.

[32] Amason, Allen C., and Harry J. Sapienza, "The Effects of Top Management Team Size and Interaction Norms on Cognitive and Affective Conflict," *Journal of Management* 23, no. 4 (1997): 495–516; Celani, Anthony, and Kevin Tasa, "We're All in This Together: Examining Associations Between Collectivistic Group Norms, Collective Efficacy, and Team Performance," *Academy of Management Annual Meeting Proceedings* (August 2010): 1–6; Chatman, Jennifer A., and Francis J. Flynn, "The Influence of Demographic Heterogeneity on the Emergence and Consequences of Cooperative Norms in Work Teams," *Academy of Management Journal* 44, no. 5 (October 2001): 956–974; De Jong, Bart A., and Katinka M. Bijlsma-Frankema, "When and How Does Norm-based Peer Control Affect the Performance of Self-Managing Teams?," *Academy of Management Annual Meeting Proceedings* (August 2009): 1–6; Taggar, Simon, and Robert Ellis, "The Role of Leaders in Shaping Formal Team Norms," *The Leadership Quarterly* 18, no. 2 (April 2007): 105–120.

[33] Behfar, Kristin J., Randall S. Peterson, Elizabeth A. Mannix, and William M. K. Trochim, "The Critical Role of Conflict Resolution in Teams: A Close Look at the Links Between Conflict Type, Conflict Management Strategies, and Team Outcomes," *Journal of Applied Psychology* 93, no. 1 (January 2008): 170–188; Jiatao, Li, and Donald C. Hambrick, "Factional Groups: A New Vantage on Demographic Faultlines, Conflict, and Disintegration in Work Teams," *Academy of Management Journal* 48, no. 5 (October 2005): 794–813; Von Glinow, Mary Ann, Debra L. Shapiro, and Jeanne M. Brett, "Can We Talk, and Should We? Managing Emotional Conflict in Multicultural Teams," *Academy of Management Review* 29, no. 4 (October 2004): 578–592.

[34] Fullagar, Clive J., and David O. Egleston, "Norming and Performing: Using Microworlds to Understand the Relationship Between Team Cohesiveness and Performance," *Journal of Applied Social Psychology* 38, no. 10 (October 2008): 2574–2593; van Woerkom, Marianne, and Karin Sanders, "The Romance of Learning from Disagreement. The Effect of Cohesiveness and Disagreement on Knowledge Sharing Behavior and Individual Performance Within Teams," *Journal of Business and Psychology* 25, no. 1 (March 2010): 139–149; Wendt, Hein, Martin C. Euwema, and I. J. Hetty van Emmerik, "Leadership and Team Cohesiveness Across Cultures," *The Leadership Quarterly* 20, no. 3 (June 2009): 358–370.

[35] Jackson, Susan E., Veronica K. Stone, and Eden B. Alvarez, "Socialization Amidst Diversity: The Impact of Demographics on Work Team Oldtimers and Newcomers," *Research in Organizational Behavior* 15, (June 1992): 45; Lawson, Benn, Kenneth J. Petersen, Paul D. Cousins, and Robert B. Handfield, "Knowledge Sharing in Interorganizational Product Development Teams: The Effect of Formal and Informal Socialization Mechanisms," *Journal of Product Innovation Management* 26, no. 2 (March 2009): 156–172.

[36] Carney, Michael, Eric R. Gedajlovic, Pursey P.M.A.R. Heugens, Marc Van Essen, and J. (Hans) Van Oosterhout, "Business Group Affiliation, Performance, Context, and Strategy: A Meta-analysis," *Academy of Management Journal* 54, no. 3 (June 2011): 437–460; Shi, Weilei, Livia Markoczy, and Gregory G. Dess, "The Role of Middle Management in the Strategy Process: Group Affiliation, Structural Holes, and *Tertius lungens*," *Journal of Management* 35, no. 6 (December 2009): 1453–1480.

[37] For a detailed discussion of groupthink, see Janis, Irving. L., "Groupthink". *Psychology Today* 5 (6) (November 1971): 43–46, 74–76; Janis, Irving. L., *Victims of Groupthink: a Psychological Study of Foreign-Policy Decisions and Fiascoes.* Boston: Houghton Mifflin

(1972); Janis, Irving. L., *Groupthink: Psychological Studies of Policy Decisions and Fiascoes.* Boston: Houghton Mifflin (1982).

[38] *Ibid.*

[39] Janis, *Groupthink;* Moorhead, Gregory, Richard Ference, and Chris P. Neck, "Group Decision Fiascoes Continue: Space Shuttle Challenger and a Revised Groupthink Framework," *Human Relations* 44, no. 6 (June 1991): 539–550.

[40] Janis, *Victims of Groupthink.*

[41] Janis, *Groupthink.*

[42] Ntayi, Joseph Mpeera, Warren Byabashaija, Sarah Eyaa, Muhammed Ngoma, and Alex Muliira, "Social Cohesion, Groupthink, and Ethical Behavior of Public Procurement Officers," *Journal of Public Procurement* 10, no. 1 (March 2010): 68–92.

[43] See, for example, Thompson, Leigh, Erika Peterson, and Susan E. Brodt, "Team Negotiation: An Examination of Integrative and Distributive Bargaining," *Journal of Personality and Social Psychology* 70, no. 1 (January 1996): 66–78.

[44] Behfar et al., "The Critical Role of Conflict"; Von Glinow et al., "Can We Talk, and Should We?"

[45] See, for instance, Ruiz Ulloa, Bianey, C, and Adams, Stephanie G, "Attitude Toward Teamwork and Effective Teaming," *Team Performance Management* 10, no. 7/8 (November 2004): 145–152.

[46] Materials in this section are adapted from Manz, Charles C., Christopher P. Neck, James Mancuso, Karen P. Manz, *For Team Members Only: Making Your Workplace Team Productive and Hassle-Free* (New York: AMACON, 1997) 136–138.

[47] Houghton, Jeffery D., Neck, Christopher P., & Manz, Charles C, "We Think We Can, We Think We Can, We Think We Can: The Impact of Thinking Patterns and Self-efficacy on Work Team Sustainability," *Team Performance Management* 9, (2003): 31–41.

[48] Latané, Williams, and Harkins, "Many Hands Make Light the Work"; Steiner, Ivan D, "Models for Inferring Relationships Between Group Size and Potential Group Productivity," *Behavioral Science* 11, no. 4 (1966): 273–283.

[49] These strategies are adapted from Thompson, Leigh L., *Making the Team: A Guide for Managers,* 4th ed. (Upper Saddle River, NJ: Prentice Hall, 2011) 31–34.

[50] Thompson, "Making the Team"; Gross, Steven E., *Compensation for Teams: How to Design and Implement Team-Based Reward Programs* (New York: AMACON, 1995).

Chapter 13

[1] For a review of leadership research, see House, Robert J., and Ram N. Aditya. "The Social Scientific Study of Leadership: Quo Vadis?" *Journal of Management* 23, no. 3 (1997 Special Issue 1997): 409; Jago, Arthur G., "Leadership: Perspectives in Theory And Research." *Management Science* 28, no. 3 (March 1982): 315–336.

[2] Speigel, Jan Ellen, "Faith in Granola Earned Its Makers Millions," *New York Times Online* (Jan 27, 2008); http://www.nytimes.com/2008/01/27/nyregion/nyregionspecial2/27granolact.html?_r=1 ; accessed March 1, 2010.

[3] Hesse, Monica, "Get Bear Naked!" *On Tap*; http://www.ontaponline.com/article/10105; accessed February 16, 2010.

[4] Sources include K. Flatley, personal interview (February 2007); Monica Hesse, "Get Bear Naked!" *On Tap;* http://www.ontaponline.com/article/10105 (accessed February 16, 2010); "Our Story" *Bear Naked,* http://www.bearnaked.com/story.htm (accessed February 16, 2010). "Kelly Flatley: Co-Founder" *Bear Naked* website; http://www.bearnaked.com/press/company_info/kelly_flatley.pdf; accessed February 16, 2010; Jessica Harris, "Bear Naked Ambition: The Inside Start-up Story," *CNNMoney.com* (February 6, 2008); http://money.cnn.com/2008/02/05/smbusiness/bear_naked.fsb/index.htm, accessed February 16, 2010.

[5] "Our Story" *Bear Naked;* http://www.bearnaked.com/story.htm; accessed February 16, 2010.

[6] K. Flatley, personal interview (February 2007).

[7] Matthews, H. Scott, and E. Williams, "Telework Adoption and Energy Use in Building and Transport Sectors in the United States and Japan," *Journal of Infrastructure Systems* 11, no. 1 (March 2005), 21–30; Lister, K., and T. Harnish, *Undress For Success—The Naked Truth About Making Money at Home* (Hoboken, NJ: John Wiley & Sons, 2009).

[8] Inspired by Northouse, P., "Three Shifts, Three Supervisors," *Leadership: Theory and Practice,* 4th ed. (Thousand Oaks, CA: Sage Publications, 2007), p. 138.

[9] French, J. R., and B. Raven, *The Bases of Social Power,* D. Cartwright, ed. (Ann Arbor, MI: Institute for Social Research, 1959).

[10] *Ibid.*

[11] *Ibid.*

[12] "William Clay Ford, Jr." media.ford.com; http://media.ford.com/article_display.cfm?article_id=93; accessed February 11, 2010.

[13] Cabadas, Joseph, *River Rouge: Ford's Industrial Colossus* (St. Paul, MN: Motorbooks International, 2004).

[14] "William Clay Ford, Jr.," Wikipedia; http://en.wikipedia.org/wiki/William_Clay_Ford,_Jr.; accessed February 11, 2010.

[15] Manz, Charles C., and Henry P. Sims Jr., "SuperLeadership: Beyond the Myth of Heroic Leadership," *Organizational Dynamics* 19, no. 4 (Spring 1991): 18–35.

[16] See, for example, Pearce, Craig L., and Henry P. Sims, Jr, "Vertical Versus Shared Leadership as Predictors of the Effectiveness of Change Management Teams: An Examination of Aversive, Directive, Transactional, Transformational, and Empowering Leader Behaviors." *Group Dynamics: Theory, Research, and Practice* 6, no. 2 (June 2002): 172–197; Pearce, Craig L., Henry P. Sims Jr., Jonathan F. Cox, Gail Ball, Eugene Schnell, Ken A. Smith, and Linda Trevino, "Transactors, Transformers, and Beyond," *Journal of Management Development* 22, no. 4 (April 2003): 273; Manz, Charles C., and Henry P. Sims, Jr., *The New SuperLeadership: Leading Others to Lead Themselves* (San Francisco: Berrett-Koehler, 2001).

[17] Weber, Maximillan, "The Nature of Charismatic Authority and Its Routinization," in *Theory of Social and Economic Organization,* A. R. Anderson and Talcott Parsons, trans. (New York: Free Press, 1947).

[18] Manz and Sims, *The New SuperLeadership.*

[19] Stoghill, R. M., *Handbook of Leadership: A Survey of Theory and Research* (New York: Free Press, 1974).

[20] Mann, R. D., "A Review of the Relationship Between Personality and Performance in Small Groups," *Psychological Bulletin* 56 (1959), pp. 241—270.

[21] Lord, R. G., C. L. DeVader, and G. M. Alliger, "A Meta-analysis of the Relation Between Personality Traits and Leadership Perceptions: An Application of Validity Generalization Procedures," *Journal of Applied Psychology* 71 (1986): pp. 402–410.

22 *Ibid.*

23 Machiavelli, Niccolò, *The Prince,* Quentin Skinner and Russell Price, eds. (Cambridge, U.K.: Cambridge University Press, 1988).

24 Walter, Ekaterina, "Top 7 Qualities of Women Leaders," *Huffington Post* (January 22, 2013); http://www.huffingtonpost.com/ekaterina-walter/leadership-qualities-women_b_2491203.html?utm_hp_ref=tw; accessed February 2, 2013.

25 Goleman, D., *Emotional Intelligence: Why It Can Matter More Than IQ* (New York: Bantam, 1995); Goleman, D., *Working with Emotional Intelligence* (New York: Bantam, 1998).

26 Hemphill, J. K., and A. E. Coons, *Leader Behavior: Its Description and Measurement (Research Monograph No. 88)* (Columbus, OH: Ohio State University, Bureau of Business Research, 1957).

27 *Ibid.*

28 Cartwright, D., and A. Zander, *Group Dynamics Research and Theory* (Evanston, IL: Row, Peterson, 1960); Katz, D., and R. L. Kahn, "Human Organization and Worker Motivation," in *Industrial Productivity* (Madison, WI: Industrial Relations Research Association, 1951); Likert, R., *New Patterns of Management* (New York: McGraw-Hill, 1961).

29 Bowers, D. G. and S. E. Seashore, "Predicting Organizational Effectiveness with a Four-Factor Theory of Leadership," *Administrative Science Quarterly* 11 (1966): pp. 238–263.

30 Kahn, R. L., "The Prediction of Productivity," *Journal of Social Issues* 12 (1956): pp. 41–49.

31 Blake, R. R., and J. S. Mouton, *The managerial Grid* (Houston, TX: Gulf Publishing Company, 1964).

32 *Ibid.*

33 Byrnes, Natalie, and Roger O. Crockett, "Ursula Burns: An Historic Accession at Xerox," *Business Week* (May 28, 2009); http://www.businessweek.com/magazine/content/09_23/b4134018712853.htm; accessed February 11, 2010.

34 Hoffmann, Katie, "Xerox's Burns Takes Reins During 'Daunting' Time (Update 2)," *Bloomberg.com* (May 22, 2009); http://www.bloomberg.com/apps/news?pid=20601204&sid=azEm34Pezz54; accessed February 15, 2010.

35 Morris, Betsy, "Xerox's Dynamic Duo," *Fortune* (Nov 19, 2007); http://money.cnn.com/magazines/fortune/fortune_archive/2007/10/15/100536857/ (accessed February 11, 2010).

36 Fiedler, F. E., "A Contingency Model of Leadership Effectiveness," in L. Berkowitz, ed., *Advances in Experimental Social Psychology,* Vol. 1 (New York: Academic Press, 1964), pp. 149–190; Fiedler, F. E., *A Theory of Leadership Effectiveness* (New York: McGraw-Hill, 1967); Fiedler, F. E., and J. E. Garcia, *New Approaches to Leadership: Cognitive Resources and Organizational Performance* (New York: Wiley, 1987).

37 Example inspired by Northouse, P., *Leadership: Theory and Practice,* p. 114.

38 Fiedler, F. E., "A Contingency Model of Leadership Effectiveness,"; Fiedler, F. E., *A Theory of Leadership Effectiveness* (New York: McGraw-Hill, 1967); Fiedler, F. E., and J. E. Garcia, *New Approaches to Leadership.*

39 "Xerox at a Glance," Xerox website, http://www.xerox.com/about-xerox/company-facts/enus.html (accessed February 11, 2010).

40 Blanchard, K. H., *SLII: A Situational Approach to Managing People* (Escondido, CA: Blanchard Training and Development, 1985).

41 *Ibid.*

42 House, R. J., "A Path-Goal Theory of Leader Effectiveness," *Administrative Science Quarterly* 16 (1971): pp. 321–328.

43 Indvik, J., "Path-Goal Theory of Leadership: A Meta-analysis," in *Proceedings of the Academy of Management Meeting* (Briarcliff Manor, NY: Academy of Management, 1986): pp. 189–192.

44 Northouse, P., *Leadership: Theory and Practice,* 4th ed. (Thousand Oaks, CA: Sage Publications, 2007): p. 128.

45 House, R. J., and R. R. Mitchell, "Path-Goal Theory of Leadership," *Journal of Contemporary Business* 3 (1974): pp. 81–97.

46 Bass, Bernard M., "Two Decades of Research and Development in Transformational Leadership," *European Journal of Work & Organizational Psychology* 8, no. 1 (March 1999): 9–32; Conger, Jay A., "Charismatic and Transformational Leadership in Organizations: An Insider's Perspective on These Developing Streams of Research," *Leadership Quarterly* 10, no. 2 (Summer 1999): 145.

47 Bass, B. *The Ethics of Transformational Leadership* (Westport, CT: Praeger, 1998), pp. 169–192.

48 Manz, Charles C., and Henry P. Sims, Jr., SuperLeadership: Beyond the Myth of Heroic Leadership." *Organizational Dynamics* 19, no. 4 (Spring 1991): 18–35; Manz and Sims, *The New SuperLeadership*; Pearce, Craig L., and Henry P. Sims, Jr. "Vertical Versus Shared Leadership as Predictors of the Effectiveness of Change Management Teams: An Examination of Aversive, Directive, Transactional, Transformational, and Empowering Leader Behaviors." *Group Dynamics: Theory, Research, And Practice* 6, no. 2 (June 2002): 172–197;

49 Manz and Sims, *The New SuperLeadership.*

50 Neck, Christopher P., and Jeffery D. Houghton, "Two Decades of Self-Leadership Theory and Research," *Journal of Managerial Psychology* 21, no. 4 (June 2006): 270–295; Neck, Christopher P., and Charles C. Manz, *Mastering Self-Leadership: Empowering Yourself for Personal Excellence*, 6th ed. (Upper Saddle River, NJ: Pearson, 2013).

51 *Ibid.*

52 Manz and Sims, *The New SuperLeadership.*

53 Greenleaf, R. K., *The Servant as Leader* (Newton Centre, MA: Robert Greenleaf Center, 1970).

54 Esterl, M., "Southwest Airlines CEO Flies Uncharted Skies," *The Wall Street Journal* (March 25, 2009); http://online.wsj.com/article/SB123793884639232193.html; accessed on February 15, 2010.

55 "Southwest Airlines' Colleen Barrett Flies High on Fuel Hedging and 'Servant Leadership,'" *Knowledge@Wharton* (July 9, 2008); http://knowledge.wharton.upenn.edu/article.cfm?articleid=2006; accessed February 11, 2010.

56 Carson, Jay B., Paul E. Tesluk, and Jennifer A. Marrone, "Shared Leadership in Teams: An Investigation of Antecedent Conditions and Performance," *Academy of Management Journal* 50, no. 5 (October 2007): 1217–1234; Pearce, Craig L., and John A. Conger, *Shared Leadership: Reframing the Hows and Whys of Leadership* (Thousand Oaks, CA: Sage Publications, 2003).

57 Klein, Katherine J., Jonathan C. Ziegert, Andrew P. Knight, and Xiao Yan, "Dynamic Delegation: Shared, Hierarchical, and Deindividualized Leadership in Extreme Action Teams," *Administrative Science Quarterly* 51, no. 4 (December 2006): 590–621.

58 Avolio, Bruce J., and William L. Gardner, "Authentic Leadership Development: Getting to the Root of Positive Forms of Leadership," *Leadership Quarterly* 16, no. 3 (June 2005): 315–338; Walumbwa, Fred O., Bruce J. Avolio, William L. Gardner, Tara S.

Wernsing, and Suzanne J. Peterson, "Authentic Leadership: Development and Validation of a Theory-Based Measure," *Journal of Management* 34, no. 1 (February 2008): 89–126.

[59] George, Bill, *True North: Discover Your Authentic Leadership* (San Francisco: Jossey-Bass, 2007).

[60] Content in this box was taken from Markowitz, Eric, "Training CEOs to be Better Leaders," *Inc.* (October 2012); http://www.inc.com/magazine/201110/former-navy-seal-rob-roy-on-training-ceos.html; accessed: November 26, 2012.

[61] Manz and Sims, *The New SuperLeadership*.

[62] Neck and Houghton, "Two Decades of Self-Leadership Theory."

Chapter 14

[1] Eriksen, Charles W., Richard S. Lazarus, and Jack R. Strange, "Psychological Stress and Its Personality Correlates," *Journal of Personality* 20, no. 3 (March 1952): 277; Hunter, Larry W., and Sherry M. B. Thatcher, "Feeling the Heat: Effects of Stress, Commitment, and Job Experience on Job Performance," *Academy of Management Journal* 50, no. 4 (August 2007): 953–968; Lazarus, Richard S, "A Laboratory Approach to the Dynamics of Psychological Stress," *Administrative Science Quarterly* 8, no. 2 (September 1963): 192–213.

[2] Avey, James B., Fred Luthans, and Susan M. Jensen, "Psychological Capital: A Positive Resource for Combating Employee Stress and Turnover," *Human Resource Management* 48, no. 5 (September 2009): 677–693; George, Halkos, and Bousinakis Dimitrios, "The Effect of Stress and Satisfaction on Productivity," *International Journal of Productivity & Performance Management* 59, no. 5 (May 2010): 415–431; Kirkcaldy, Bruce D., Rüdiger Trimpop, and Cary L. Cooper, "Working Hours, Job Stress, Work Satisfaction, and Accident Rates Among Medical Practitioners and Allied Personnel," *International Journal of Stress Management* 4, no. 2 (April 1997): 79–87; Wunder, R. Stephen, Thomas W. Dougherty, and M. Ann Welsh, "A Casual Model of Role Stress and Employee Turnover," *Academy of Management Proceedings* (August 1982): 297–301.

[3] Biron, Michal, and Peter Bamberger, "Aversive Workplace Conditions and Absenteeism: Taking Referent Group Norms and Supervisor Support into Account," *Journal of Applied Psychology* (March 5, 2012); Hausknecht, John P., Nathan J. Hiller, and Robert J. Vance, "Work-Unit Absenteeism: Effects of Satisfaction, Commitment, Labor Market Conditions, and Time," *Academy of Management Journal* 51, no. 6 (December 2008): 1223–1245; Keller, Robert T., "The Role of Performance and Absenteeism in the Prediction of Turnover," *Academy of Management Journal* 27, no. 1 (March 1984): 176–183.

[4] Cordes, Cynthia L., and Thomas W. Dougherty, "A Review and An Integration of Research On Job Burnout," *Academy of Management Review* 18, no. 4 (October 1993): 621–656; Dunford, Benjamin B., Abbie J. Shipp, R. Wayne Boss, Ingo Angermeier, and Alan D. Boss. "Is Burnout Static or Dynamic? A Career Transition Perspective of Employee Burnout Trajectories," *Journal of Applied Psychology* 97, no. 3 (May 2012): 637–650.

[5] Brief, Arthur P., Michael J. Burke, Jennifer M. George, Brian S. Robinson, and Jane Webster, "Should Negative Affectivity Remain an Unmeasured Variable in the Study of Job Stress?" *Journal of Applied Psychology* 73, no. 2 (May 1988): 193–198; Holtom, Brooks C., James P. Burton, and Craig D. Crossley, "How Negative Affectivity Moderates the Relationship Between Shocks, Embeddedness, and Worker Behaviors," *Journal of Vocational Behavior* 80, no. 2 (April 2012): 434–443.

[6] See, for example, Lepak, David P., Jennifer A. Marrone, and Riki Takeuchi, "The Relativity of HR Systems: Conceptualising the Impact of Desired Employee Contributions and HR Philosophy," *International Journal of Technology Management* 27, no. 6/7 (May 2004): 639–655.

[7] Czajka, Joseph, "The Relation of Positive and Negative Affectivity to Workplace Attitudes," *Academy of Management Best Papers Proceedings* (August 1990): 201–205; Kaplan, Seth, Jill C. Bradley, Joseph N. Luchman, and Douglas Haynes, "On the Role of Positive And Negative Affectivity in Job Performance: A Meta-analytic Investigation," *Journal of Applied Psychology* 94, no. 1 (January 2009): 162–176; Watson, David, and Kristin Naragon, "Positive Affectivity: The Disposition to Experience Positive Emotional States," in *Oxford Handbook of Positive Psychology* (2d ed.), (New York: Oxford University Press, 2009) 207–215.

[8] For a more detailed overview of these dimensions, see Ulrich, Dave, and Wendy Ulrich, *The Why of Work: How Great Leaders Build Abundant Organizations That Win* (New York: McGraw-Hill, 2010).

[9] See, for instance, Bandura, Albert, "The Explanatory and Predictive Scope of Self-Efficacy Theory," *Journal of Social and Clinical Psychology* 4, no. 3 (1986): 359–373; Bandura, Albert, "On the Functional Properties of Perceived Self-Efficacy Revisited," *Journal of Management* 38, no. 1 (January 2012): 9–44; Schmidt, Aaron M., and Richard P. DeShon, "The Moderating Effects of Performance Ambiguity on the Relationship Between Self-Efficacy and Performance," *Journal of Applied Psychology* 95, no. 3 (May 2010): 572–581.

[10] For a more in-depth overview, see Howard Bartley's classic text on this subject: *Principles of Perception,* 2d ed. (New York: Harper & Row, 1969).

[11] See, for example, Massad, Christopher M., Michael Hubbard, and Darren Newtson, "Selective Perception of Events," *Journal of Experimental Social Psychology* 15, no. 6 (November 1979): 513–532; Mosak, Harold H., and Frederick J. Todd, "Selective Perception in the Interpretation of Symbols," *Journal of Abnormal And Social Psychology* 47, no. 2 (April 1952): 255–256.

[12] See the following sources for a detailed overview of organizational commitment: Allen, Natalie J., and John P. Meyer, "Construct Validation in Organizational Behavior Research: The Case of Organizational Commitment," In *Problems and Solutions in Human Assessment: Honoring Douglas N. Jackson at Seventy* (New York: Kluwer Academic/Plenum Publishers, 2000) 285–314; Meyer, John P., and Natalie J. Allen, "A Three-Component Conceptualization of Organizational Commitment," *Human Resource Management Review* 1, no. 1 (Spring 1991): 61.

[13] See for example, Stajkovic, Alexander D, "Development of a Core Confidence–Higher-Order Construct," *Journal of Applied Psychology* 91, no. 6 (November 2006): 1208–1224.

[14] Caplan, Robert D., and Kenneth W. Jones, "Effects of Workload, Role Ambiguity, and Type A Personality on Anxiety, Depression, and Heart Rate," *Journal of Applied Psychology* 60, no. 6 (December 1975): 713–719; Ganster, Daniel C., John Schaubroeck, Wesley E. Sime, and Bronston T. Mayes, "The Nomological Validity of the Type A Personality Among Employed Adults," *Journal of Applied Psychology* 76, no. 1 (February 1991): 143–168; Watson, Warren E., Tracey Minzenmayer, and Matt Bowler, "Type A Personality Characteristics and the Effect on Individual and Team Academic Performance," *Journal of Applied Social Psychology* 36, no. 5 (May 2006): 1110–1128.

[15] Keenan, A., and G. D. M. McBain, "Effects of Type A Behavior, Intolerance of Ambiguity, and Locus of Control on the Relationship

Between Role Stress and Work-Related Outcomes," *Journal of Occupational Psychology* 52, no. 4 (December 1979): 277–285; Rosenberger, Lisa M., and Michael J. Strube, "The Influence of Type A and B Behavior Patterns on the Perceived Quality of Dating Relationships," *Journal of Applied Social Psychology* 16, no. 4 (1986): 277–286.

[16] Lambert, Lisa Schurer, "Promised and Delivered Inducements and Contributions: An Integrated View of Psychological Contract Appraisal," *Journal of Applied Psychology* 96, no. 4 (July 2011): 695–712; Rousseau, Denise M., *Psychological Contracts in Organizations: Understanding Written and Unwritten Agreements* (Thousand Oaks, CA: Sage Publications, Inc, 1995); Rousseau, Denise M, "The Individual-Organization Relationship: The Psychological Contract," In *APA Handbook of Industrial and Organizational Psychology, Vol. 3: Maintaining, Expanding, and Contracting the Organization* (Washington, D.C.: American Psychological Association, 2011) 191–220.

[17] Bodenhausen, Galen V., and Jennifer A. Richeson, "Prejudice, Stereotyping, and Discrimination," in *Advanced Social Psychology: The State of the Science* (New York: Oxford University Press, 2010) 341–383; Schneider, David J., *The Psychology of Stereotyping* (New York: Guilford Press, 2004).

[18] Malle, Bertram F, "Attribution Theories: How People Make Sense of Behavior," in Derek Chadee (Ed.), *Theories in Social Psychology* (Wiley-Blackwell, 2011) 72–95; Weiner, Bernard, "Reflections on the History of Attribution Theory and Research: People, Personalities, Publications, Problems," *Social Psychology* 39, no. 3 (September 2008): 151–156.

[19] For more detailed reviews of the Big Five personality perspective, refer to Barrick, Murray R., and Michael K. Mount, "The Big Five Personality Dimensions and Job Performance: A Meta-analysis," *Personnel Psychology* 44, no. 1 (Spring 1991): 1–26; John, Oliver P., Laura P. Naumann, and Christopher J. Soto, "Paradigm Shift to the Integrative Big Five Trait Taxonomy: History, Measurement, and Conceptual Issues," In *Handbook of Personality: Theory and Research*, 3d ed. (New York: Guilford Press, 2008): 114–158.

[20] Bem, Daryl J. *Beliefs, Attitudes, and Human Affairs* (Oxford, England: Brooks/Cole, 1970); Fishbein, Martin, and Icek Ajzen, "Attitudes and Opinions," *Annual Review of Psychology* (1972): 487–544.

[21] See, for example, Chernyshenko, Oleksandr S., Stephen Stark, and Fritz Drasgow, "Individual Differences: Their Measurement and Validity," In *APA Handbook of Industrial and Organizational Psychology, Vol. 2: Selecting and Developing Members for the Organization* (Washington, D.C.: American Psychological Association, 2011) 117–151; Martins, Luis L., and Charles K. Parsons, "Effects of Gender Diversity Management on Perceptions of Organizational Attractiveness: The Role of Individual Differences in Attitudes and Beliefs," *Journal of Applied Psychology* 92, no. 3 (May 2007): 865–875; Judge, Timothy A., Christine L. Jackson, John C. Shaw, Brent A. Scott, and Bruce L. Rich. "Self-Efficacy and Work-Related Performance: The Integral Role of Individual Differences," *Journal of Applied Psychology* 92, no. 1 (January 2007): 107–127.

[22] Fournier, Geneviève, and Chantale Jeanrie, "Locus of Control: Back to Basics," in *Positive psychological assessment: A handbook of models and measures*, (Washington, D.C.: American Psychological Association, 2003) 139–154; Wang, Qiang, Nathan A. Bowling, and Kevin J. Eschleman, "A Meta-analytic Examination of Work and General Locus of Control," *Journal of Applied Psychology* 95, no. 4 (July 2010): 761–768.

[23] Barrick, Murray R., and Michael K. Mount, "The Big Five Personality Dimensions and Job Performance: A Meta-Analysis," *Personnel Psychology* 44, no. 1 (Spring 1991): 1–26.

[24] Barrick, Murray R., Michael K. Mount, and Ning Li, "The Theory of Purposeful Work Behavior: The Role of Personality, Higher-Order Goals, and Job Characteristics," *Academy of Management Review* 38, no. 1 (January 2013): 132–153.

[25] Bergum, Bruce O., and Donald J. Lehr, "Effects of Authoritarianism on Vigilance Performance," *Journal of Applied Psychology* 47, no. 1 (February 1963): 75–77; Duckitt, John, "Authoritarianism and Dogmatism," in *Handbook of Individual Differences in Social Behavior* (New York: Guilford Press, 2009) 298–317.

[26] Drory, Amos, and Uri M. Gluskinos, "Machiavellianism and Leadership," *Journal of Applied Psychology* 65, no. 1 (February 1980): 81–86; Jones, Daniel N., and Delroy L. Paulhus, "Machiavellianism," in *Handbook of Individual Differences in Social Behavior* (New York: Guilford Press, 2009) 93–108; Kessler, Stacey R., Adam C. Bandelli, Paul E. Spector, Walter C. Borman, Carnot E. Nelson, and Lisa M. Penney, "Re-examining Machiavelli: A Three-Dimensional Model of Machiavellianism in the Workplace," *Journal of Applied Social Psychology* 40, no. 8 (August 2010): 1868–1896.

[27] For more detailed information on the Gallup Strengths Finder assessment, see Rath, Tom. *Strengths Finder 2.0* (New York: Gallup Press, 2007).

[28] Cooper, Joel, "Cognitive Dissonance Theory," in *Handbook of Theories of Social Psychology (Vol. 1)*, (Thousand Oaks, CA: Sage Publications Ltd, 2012) 377–397; Festinger, Leon, *A Theory of Cognitive Dissonance.* (Stanford, CA: Stanford University Press, 1957); Festinger, Leon, "Cognitive Dissonance," *Scientific American* 207, no. 4 (1962): 93–107.

[29] See, for instance, Amabile, Teresa M., *Creativity in Context* (Boulder, CO: Westview Press, 1996). Hennessey, Beth A., and Teresa M. Amabile, "Creativity," *Annual Review of Psychology* 61, no. 1 (February 2010): 569–598.

[30] See the following for two examples of papers examining dysfunctional behavior in organizations: Cole, Michael S., Frank Walter, and Heike Bruch, "Affective Mechanisms Linking Dysfunctional Behavior to Performance in Work Teams: A Moderated Mediation Study," *Journal of Applied Psychology* 93, no. 5 (2008): 945–958; MacKenzie, Clíodhna, Thomas N. Garavan, and Ronan Carbery, "Understanding and Preventing Dysfunctional Behavior in Organizations: Conceptualizing the Contribution of Human Resource Development," *Human Resource Development Review* 10, no. 4 (December 2011): 346–380.

[31] Berry, Christopher M., Deniz S. Ones, and Paul R. Sackett, "Interpersonal Deviance, Organizational Deviance, and Their Common Correlates: A Review and Meta-analysis," *Journal of Applied Psychology* 92, no. 2 (March 2007): 410–424; Witt, L. A., and Martha C. Andrews, "The Predisposition to Engage in Interpersonal Deviance at Work," *Academy of Management Annual Meeting Proceedings* (August 2006): F1–F6.

[32] Leavy, Brian, "Leading Adaptive Change by Harnessing the Power of Positive Deviance," *Strategy & Leadership* 39, no. 2 (March 2011): 18–27; Stebbins, Robert A, "Tolerable, Acceptable, and Positive Deviance," In *The Routledge Handbook of Deviant Behavior* (New York: Routledge/Taylor & Francis Group, 2011) 24–30.

[33] Laforge, Hubert, Mario Moisan, Francice Champagne, and Maurice Seguin, "General Adaptation Syndrome and Magnetostatic Field: Effects of Sleep and Delayed Reinforcement of Low Rate," *Journal of Psychology* 98, no. 1 (January 1978): 49; Selye, Hans, "The General-Adaptation-Syndrome in its Relationships to Neurology, Psychology, and Psychopathology," in *Contributions Toward*

Medical Psychology: Theory and Psychodiagnostic Methods, Vol. 1 (New York: Ronald Press Company, 1953) 234–274.

34 Organ, Dennis W., *Organizational Citizenship Behavior: The Good Soldier Syndrome*. (Lexington, MA: Lexington Books/D. C. Heath and Com, 1988); Ozer, Muammer, "A Moderated Mediation Model of the Relationship Between Organizational Citizenship Behaviors and Job Performance," *Journal of Applied Psychology* 96, no. 6 (November 2011): 1328–1336; Smith, C. Ann, Dennis W. Organ, and Janet P. Near, "Organizational Citizenship Behavior: Its Nature and Antecedents," *Journal of Applied Psychology* 68, no. 4 (November 1983): 653–663.

35 Goleman, Daniel. *Emotional Intelligence*. (New York: Bantam Books, Inc, 1995); Goleman, Daniel, Richard Boyatzis, and Annie McKee. *Primal Leadership: Realizing the Power of Emotional Intelligence* (Boston: Harvard Business School Press, 2002); Salovey, Peter, and John D. Mayer, "Emotional Intelligence," *Imagination, Cognition and Personality* 9, no. 3 (1989): 185–211.

36 Irving, P. Gregory, and Samantha D. Montes, "Met Expectations: The Effects of Expected and Delivered Inducements on Employee Satisfaction," *Journal of Occupational & Organizational Psychology* 82, no. 2 (June 2009): 431–451; Lambert, Lisa Schurer, "Promised and Delivered Inducements and Contributions: An Integrated View of Psychological Contract Appraisal," *Journal of Applied Psychology* 96, no. 4 (July 2011): 695–712.

Chapter 15

1 For an overview of work motivation theory, refer to the following: Kanfer, Ruth, "Work Motivation: Advancing Theory and Impact," *Industrial and Organizational Psychology: Perspectives on Science and Practice* 2, no. 1 (March 2009): 118–127; Kanfer, Ruth, Gilad Chen, and Robert D. Pritchard, *Work Motivation: Past, Present, and Future*. (New York: Routledge/Taylor & Francis Group, 2008); Landy, Frank J., and Wendy S. Becker, "Motivation Theory Reconsidered," *Research in Organizational Behavior 9*, (January 1987): 1.

2 For a general introduction to the field of organizational communication, refer to the following: Hargie, Owen, and Dennis Tourish, *Auditing Organizational Communication: A Handbook of Research, Theory and Practice* (New York: Routledge/Taylor & Francis Group, 2009); Harris, Thomas E., and Mark D. Nelson. *Applied Organizational Communication: Theory and Practice in a Global Environment*, (3d ed.) (New York: Taylor & Francis Group/Lawrence Erlbaum Associates, 2008); May, Steve, and Dennis K. Mumby, *Engaging Organizational Communication Theory and Research: Multiple Perspectives*. (Thousand Oaks, CA: Sage Publications, Inc., 2005).

3 Maslow, A. H, "A Theory of Human Motivation," *Psychological Review* 50, no. 4 (July 1943): 370–396.

4 Alderfer, Clayton P, "An Empirical Test of a New Theory of Human Needs," *Organizational Behavior & Human Performance* 4, no. 2 (1969): 142–175; Schneider, Benjamin, and Clayton P. Alderfer, "Three Studies of Measures of Need Satisfaction in Organizations," *Administrative Science Quarterly* 18, no. 4 (December 1973): 489–505.

5 Herzberg, F., Mausner, B., & Snyderman, B. *The Motivation to Work* (2d ed.) (Oxford, U.K.: John Wiley, 1959); Herzberg, Frederick, "One More Time: How Do You Motivate Employees?" *Harvard Business Review* 81, no. 1 (January 2003): 87–96.

6 Berlo, D. K., *The Process of Communication* (New York: Holt, Rinehart, & Winston, 1960); Shannon, C. E., & Weaver, W., *The Mathematical Theory of Communication* (Urbana, IL: University of Illinois Press, 1949).

7 Beattie, Geoffrey. *Visible Thought: The New Psychology of Body Language* (New York: Routledge, 2004); Gifford, Robert, "The Role of Nonverbal Communication in Interpersonal Relations," In *Handbook of Interpersonal Psychology: Theory, Research, Assessment, and Therapeutic Interventions*, (Hoboken, NJ : John Wiley & Sons Inc., 2011) 171–190.

8 Krackhardt, David, and Lyman W. Porter, "The Snowball Effect: Turnover Embedded in Communication Networks," *Journal of Applied Psychology* 71, no. 1 (February 1986): 50–55; Monge, Peter R., and Eric M. Eisenberg, "Emergent Communication Networks," in *Handbook of Organizational Communication: An Interdisciplinary Perspective* (Thousand Oaks, CA : Sage Publications, Inc., 1987) 304–342; Shane, Barry, "Open and Rigid Communication Networks: A Reevaluation by Simulation," *Academy of Management Proceedings* (August 1978): 339–343.

9 *Ibid.*

10 See, for example, Mishra, Jitendra, "Managing the Grapevine," *Public Personnel Management* 19, no. 2 (Summer 1990): 213; Nicoll, David Cathmoir, "Acknowledge and Use Your Grapevine," *Management Decision* 32, no. 6 (August 1994): 25; Smith, Bob, "Care and Feeding of the Office Grapevine," *Management Review* 85, no. 2 (February 1996): 6.

11 Davis, Keith, "Management Communication and the Grapevine," *Harvard Business Review* 31, no. 5 (September 1953): 43–49.

12 *Ibid.*

13 Vroom, Victor H., *Work and Motivation* (New York: Wiley, 1964).

14 Porter, L. W., & Lawler, E. E., *Managerial Attitudes and Performance* (Homewood, IL: Richard D. Irwin, Inc., 1968).

15 See, for example, Gary P. Latham and Edwin A. Locke, "Goal Setting—A Motivational Technique That Works," *Organizational Dynamics* 8, no. 2 (September 1979): 68–80; Edwin A. Locke and Gary P. Latham, "Building a Practically Useful Theory of Goal Setting and Task Motivation: A 35-Year Odyssey," *American Psychologist* 57, no.9 (September 2002): 705–717; Edwin A. Locke and Gary P. Latham, *A Theory of Goal Setting and Task Performance* (Englewood Cliffs, NJ : Prentice-Hall Inc., 1990); Ad Kleingeld, Heleen van Mierlo, and Lidia Arends, "The Effect of Goal Setting on Group Performance: A Meta-Analysis," *Journal of Applied Psychology* 96, no. 6 (November 2011): 1289–1304.

16 Skinner, B.F., *Contingencies of Reinforcement: A Theoretical Analysis* (Englewood Cliffs, NJ: Prentice-Hall, 1969).

17 See, for example, Babb, Harold W., and Daniel G. Kopp. 1978, "Applications of Behavior Modification in Organizations: A Review and Critique," *Academy of Management Review* 3, no. 2: 281–292; Miltenberger, Raymond G, "Behavior Modification," In *Handbook of Clinical Psychology, Vol. 2: Children and Adolescents* (Hoboken, NJ: John Wiley & Sons Inc., 2008) 626–652; Pedalino, Ed, and Victor U. Gamboa, "Behavior Modification and Absenteeism: Intervention in One Industrial Setting," *Journal of Applied Psychology* 59, no. 6 (December 1974): 694–698; Schneier, Craig Eric, "Behavior Modification in Management: A Review and Critique," *Academy of Management Journal* 17, no. 3 (September 1974): 528–548.

18 See, for instance, Wiard, Harry, "Why Manage Behavior? A Case for Positive Reinforcement," *Human Resource Management* 11, no. 2 (Summer 1972): 15–20; Wiegand, Douglas M., and E. Scott Geller, "Connecting Positive Psychology and Organizational Behavior

Management: Achievement Motivation and the Power of Positive Reinforcement," *Journal of Organizational Behavior Management* 24, no. 1–2 (2004): 3–24.

[19] See the following for a discussion of the differences between positive reinforcement, negative reinforcement, and punishment: McConnell, James V, "Negative Reinforcement and Positive Punishment," *Teaching of Psychology* 17, no. 4 (December 1990): 247; Michael, Jack, "Positive Psychology and the Distinction Between Positive and Negative Reinforcement," *Journal of Organizational Behavior Management* 24, no. 1–2 (2004): 145–153.

[20] Refer to the following for an overview of the extinction concept: Falls, William A, "Extinction: A Review of Theory and the Evidence Suggesting That Memories Are Not Erased with Nonreinforcement," in *Learning and Behavior Therapy*,. Needham Heights, MA : Allyn & Bacon, 1998) 205–229.

[21] Conger, Jay A., and Rabindra N. Kanungo, "The Empowerment Process: Integrating Theory and Practice," *Academy of Management Review* 13, no. 3 (July 1988): 471–482; Seibert, Scott E., Seth R. Silver, and W. Alan Randolph, "Taking Empowerment to the Next Level: A Multiple-Level Model of Empowerment, Performance, and Satisfaction," *Academy of Management Journal* 47, no. 3 (June 2004): 332–349; Spreitzer, Gretchen M, "Psychological, Empowerment in the Workplace: Dimensions, Measurement, and Validation," *Academy of Management Journal* 38, no. 5 (October 1995): 1442–1465.

[22] See, for example, Dillon, Karen, "The Coming Battle over Executive Pay," *Harvard Business Review* 87, no. 9 (September 2009): 96–103; Ignatius, Adi, "CEO Pay Is Up! Is That Good?" *Harvard Business Review* 89, no. 7/8 (July 2011): 14; Kaplan, Steven N, "Are U.S. CEOs Overpaid?" *Academy of Management Perspectives* 22, no. 2 (May 2008): 5–20.

[23] Fay, Charles H., and Michael A. Thompson, "Contextual Determinants of Reward Systems' Success: An Exploratory Study," *Human Resource Management* 40, no. 3 (Fall 2001): 213–226; Kerr, Steven, "Reward Systems: Does Yours Measure Up?" *Harvard Business School Press Books* (October 2008): 1.

[24] Pearce, Jone L., William B. Stevenson, and James L. Perry, "Managerial Compensation Based on Organizational Performance: A Time Series Analysis of The Effects of Merit Pay," *Academy of Management Journal* 28, no. 2 (June 1985): 261–278; Terpstra, David E., and Andre L. Honoree, "Merit Pay Plans in Higher-Education Institutions: Characteristics and Effects," *Public Personnel Management* 38, no. 4 (Winter 2009): 55–77.

[25] Dickinson, Alyce M., and Kirk L. Gillette, "A Comparison of the Effects of Two Individual Monetary Incentive Systems on Productivity: Piece Rate Pay Versus Base Pay Plus Incentives," *Journal of Organizational Behavior Management* 14, no. 1 (1993): 3–82; Gibbons, Robert, "Piece-Rate Incentive Schemes," *Journal of Labor Economics* 5, no. 4 (October 1987): 413.

[26] Geare, A. J, "Productivity from Scanlon-type Plans," *Academy of Management Review* 1, no. 3 (July 1976): 99–108. White, J. Kenneth, "The Scanlon Plan: Causes and Correlates of Success," *Academy of Management Journal* 22, no. 2 (June 1979): 292–312.

[27] Greenberg, Jerald, "Equity and Workplace Status: A Field Experiment," *Journal of Applied Psychology* 73, no. 4 (November 1988): 606–613.

[28] Greenberg, Jerald, "Employee Theft as a Reaction to Underpayment Inequity: The Hidden Cost of Pay Cuts," *Journal of Applied Psychology* 75, no. 5 (October 1990): 561–568.

[29] Adams, J. Stacy, "Towards an Understanding of Inequity," *Journal of Abnormal and Social Psychology* 67, no. 5 (November 1963): 422–436; Polk, Denise M, "Evaluating Fairness: Critical Assessment of Equity Theory," in *Theories in Social Psychology* (Wiley-Blackwell, 2011) 163–190.

[30] Brandes, Pamela, Ravi Dharwadkar, and Diya Das, "Understanding the Rise and Fall of Stock Options Compensation: Taking Principal-Agent Conflicts to the Institutional (Battle)field," *Human Resource Management Review* 15, no. 2 (June 2005): 97–118. Sesil, James C., and Maya K. Kroumova, "Broad-based Stock Options: Before and After the Market Downturn," *International Journal of Human Resource Management* 18, no. 8 (August 2007): 1471–1485.

[31] Arthur, Jeffrey B., and Christopher L. Huntley, "Ramping Up the Organizational Learning Curve: Assessing the Impact of Deliberate Learning on Organizational Performance Under Gainsharing," *Academy of Management Journal* 48, no. 6 (December 2005): 1159–1170; Arthur, Jeffrey B., and Dong-One Kim, "Gainsharing and Knowledge Sharing: The Effects of Labour-Management Co-operation," *International Journal of Human Resource Management* 16, no. 9 (September 2005): 1564–1582; Bullock, R. J., and Edward E. Lawler, "Gainsharing: A Few Questions, and Fewer Answers," *Human Resource Management* 23, no. 1 (Spring 1984): 23–40.

Chapter 16

[1] Koontz, Harold, "Management Control: A Suggested Formulation of Principles," *California Management Review* 1, no. 2 (Winter 1959): 47–55; Merchant, Kenneth A, "The Control Function of Management," *Sloan Management Review* 23, no. 4 (Summer82 1982): 43–55; Ouchi, William G., "A Conceptual Framework for the Design of Organizational Control Mechanisms," *Management Science* 25, no. 9 (September 1979): 833–848.

[2] Donovan Ray Hardenbrook, personal interview (October 2011).

[3] Koontz, "Management Control"; Ouchi, "A Conceptual Framework."

[4] Koontz, Harold, and Robert W. Bradspies, "Managing Through Feedforward Control," *Business Horizons* 15, no. 3 (June 1972): 25.

[5] *Ibid.*

[6] *Ibid.*

[7] Collins, Rosann Webb, "Communications Policy and Information Technology: Promises, Problems, and Prospects," *Academy of Management Review* 28, no. 4 (October 2003): 673–675; Hak Chong, Lee, "On Information Technology and Organization Structure," *Academy of Management Journal* 7, no. 3 (September 1964): 204–210; Ping, Wang, "Chasing the Hottest IT: Effects of Information Technology Fashion on Organizations," *Academy of Management Annual Meeting Proceedings* (August 2007): 1–7.

[8] See, for example, Arikan, Andaç T., "Interfirm Knowledge Exchanges and the Knowledge Creation Capability of Clusters," *Academy of Management Review* 34, no. 4 (October 2009): 658–676; Nag, Rajiv, Kevin G. Corley, and Dennis A. Gioia, "The Intersection of Organizational Identity, Knowledge, and Practice: Attempting Strategic Change via Knowledge Grafting," *Academy of Management Journal* 50, no. 4 (August 2007): 821–847.

[9] See, for instance, Drucker, Peter F., "Knowledge-Worker Productivity: The Biggest Challenge," *California Management Review* 41, no. 2 (Winter 1999): 79–94; Reinhardt, Wolfgang, Benedikt Schmidt, Peter Sloep, and Hendrik Drachsler, "Knowledge Worker Roles and Actions—Results of Two Empirical Studies," *Knowledge and Process Management* 18, no. 3 (July 2011): 150–174.

[10] See the following for recent discussions of data security and firewall technology: Frolick, Mark N., "A New Webmaster's Guide to Firewalls and Security," *Information Systems Management* 20, no. 1 (Winter2003 2003): 29; Smith, Roger, "Computing Beyond the Firewall," *Research Technology Management* 53, no. 3 (May 2010): 64–65.

[11] See, for example, Ling, Raymond Rihao, and David C. Yen, "Extranet: A New Wave of Internet," *SAM Advanced Management Journal* 66, no. 2 (Spring 2001): 39; Sanna, Laukkanen, Sarpola Sami, and Kemppainen Katariina, "Dual Role of Extranet Portals in Buyer-Supplier Information Exchange," *Business Process Management Journal* 13, no. 4 (July 31, 2007): 503–521.

[12] See, for example, Li, Chan, Gary F. Peters, Vernon J. Richardson, and Marcia Weidenmier Watson, "The Consequences of Information Technology Control Weaknesses on Management Information Systems: The Case of Sarbanes-Oxley Internal Control Reports," *MIS Quarterly* 36, no. 1 (March 2012): 179–204; Saunders, Carol Stoak, "Management Information Systems, Communications, and Departmental Power: An Integrative Model," *Academy of Management Review* 6, no. 3 (July 1981): 431–442.

[13] See, for instance, Basoglu, Nuri, Tugrul Daim, and Onur Kerimoglu, "Organizational Adoption of Enterprise Resource Planning Systems: A Conceptual Framework," *Journal of High Technology Management Research* 18, no. 1 (September 2007): 73–97; Robert Jacobs, F., and F.C. "Ted" Weston, "Enterprise Resource Planning (ERP)—A Brief History," *Journal of Operations Management* 25, no. 2 (March 2007): 357–363.

[14] See, for example, Elangovan, K., V. Selladurai, and S. R. Devadasan, "Maintenance Quality Policy Statement: Its Research, Design, and Executive Support System," *International Journal of Technology, Policy, & Management* 6, no. 3 (June 2006): 237–255; Friedman, Mark, and Paul Munter, "Creating an Excel-based Executive Support System," *Journal of Corporate Accounting & Finance (Wiley)* 15, no. 5 (July 2004): 53–59.

[15] Chatzimouratidis, Athanasios, Ioannis Theotokas, and Ioannis N. Lagoudis, "Decision Support Systems for Human Resource Training and Development," *International Journal of Human Resource Management* 23, no. 3 (February 2012): 662–693; Hogue, Jack T., "A Framework for the Examination of Management Involvement in Decision Support Systems," *Journal of Management Information Systems* 4, no. 1 (Summer 1987): 96–110; Power, Daniel J., "Understanding Data-Driven Decision Support Systems," *Information Systems Management* 25, no. 2 (Spring 2008): 149–154.

[16] See the following for a more detailed overview of this topic: Chang, Alec, Michael Leonard, and Jay Goldman, "Artificial Intelligence: An Overview of Research and Applications," *Industrial Management* 28, no. 6 (November 1986): 14; Goel, Ashok K., and Jim Davies, "Artificial Intelligence," in *The Cambridge Handbook of Intelligence* (New York: Cambridge University Press, 2011) 468–482.

[17] Gawande, Atul, "The Hot Spotters," *The New Yorker* 86, no. 45 (January 24, 2011): 40–51.

[18] See, for example, Messmer, Max, "The Role of the Controller," *Management Accounting: Official Magazine of Institute of Management Accountants* 80, no. 8 (February 1999): 16; Vafeas, Nikos, "Is Accounting Education Valued by the Stock Market? Evidence from Corporate Controller Appointments," *Contemporary Accounting Research* 26, no. 4 (Winter2009 2009): 1143–1174.

[19] Gawande, "The Hot Spotters."

[20] For a more detailed overview of basic accounting control mechanisms, see Weygandt, Jerry J., Paul D. Kimmel, and Donald E. Kieso, *Accounting Principles,* 10th ed. (New York: Wiley, 2011).

[21] Ibid.

[22] Ibid.

[23] Ibid.

[24] Ibid.

[25] Ibid.

[26] Gawande, "The Hot Spotters."

Chapter 17

[1] Matai, Rajesh, S. P. Singh, and M. L. Mittal, "Facility Layout Problem: A State-of-the-Art Review," *Vilakshan: The XIMB Journal of Management* 7, no. 2 (September 2010): 81–106; Zijlstra, Emma, and Mark P. Mobach, "The Influence of Facility Layout on Operations Explored," *Journal of Facilities Management* 9, no. 2 (April 2011): 127–144.

[2] See, for example, Kumar, Rajanikar, Vijay Manikrao Athawale, and Shankar Chakraborty, "Facility Location Selection Using the UTA Method," *IUP Journal of Operations Management* 9, no. 4 (November 2010): 21–34.

[3] See, for instance, Bendoly, Elliot, and Frederick Kaefer, "Linking Technological Compatibility and Operational Capacity Constraints to Communication Technology Adoption," *Journal of Electronic Commerce in Organizations* 1, no. 2 (April 2003): 1–13; Liu, Liming, Xue-Ming Yuan, and John J. Liu, "Operational Capacity Allocation for Unreliable Module-based Assembly Systems," *European Journal of Operational Research* 155, no. 1 (May 16, 2004): 134.

[4] The content in this research box is taken from Coget, Jean-Francois, "The Apple Store Effect: Does Organizational Identification Trickle Down to Customers?" *Academy Of Management Perspectives* 25, no. 1 (February 2011): 94–95.

[5] Lichtenstein, Donald R., Richard G. Netemeyer, and James G. Maxham, "The Relationships Among Manager-, Employee-, and Customer-Company Identification: Implications for Retail Store Financial Performance," *Journal of Retailing* 86, no. 1 (March 2010): 85–93.

[6] For an overview of the classic types of facility layouts, see Kundu, A., and P. K. Dan, "The Scope of Genetic Algorithms in Dealing with Facility Layout Problems," *South African Journal of Industrial Engineering* 21, no. 2 (November 2010): 39–49. El-Shaieb, A.M., "A Bayesian Approach to the Selection of the Classical Type of Layout," *Industrial Management* 18, no. 4 (July 1976): 19.

[7] Ibid.

[8] For a detailed overview of operations management, refer to Reid, R. Dan, and Nada R. Sanders, *Operations Management*, 5th ed. (New York: Wiley, 2013).

[9] Lipstreu, Otis, and Kenneth A. Reed, "A New Look at the Organizational Implications of Automation," *Academy of Management Journal* 8, no. 1 (March 1965): 24–31; Megginson, Leon C, "Automation: Our Greatest Asset—Our Greatest Problem?" *Academy of Management Journal* 6, no. 3 (September 1963): 232–244.

[10] See, for example, Lee, Jinkook, "A Key to Marketing Financial Services: The Right Mix of Products, Services, Channels, and Customers," *Journal of Services Marketing* 16, no. 3 (June 2002): 238.

[11] Anderson, John C., and Manus Rungtusanatham, "A Theory of Quality Management Underlying the Deming Management Method," *Academy of Management Review* 19, no. 3 (July 1994): 472–509; Spencer, Barbara A, "Models of Organization and Total Quality Management: A Comparison and Critical Evaluation," *Academy of Management Review* 19, no. 3 (July 1994): 446–471.

[12] Barker, R. C., "The Design of Lean Manufacturing Systems Using Time-based Analysis," *International Journal of Operations & Production Management* 14, no. 11 (November 1994): 86–96; Ramesh, Varun, and Rambabu Kodali, "A Decision Framework for Maximising Lean Manufacturing Performance," *International Journal of Production Research* 50, no. 8 (April 15, 2012): 2234–2251.

[13] See, for instance, Goldhar, Joel D., and David Lei, "Variety Is Free: Manufacturing in the Twenty-First Century," *Academy of Management Executive* 9, no. 4 (November 1995): 73–86; Youndt, Mark A., Scott A. Snell, Jr., James W. Dean, and David P. Lepak, "Human Resource Management, Manufacturing Strategy, and Firm Performance," *Academy of Management Journal* 39, no. 4 (August 1996): 836–866.

[14] Anderson and Rungtusanatham, "A Theory of Quality Management."

[15] See, for example, Crandall, Richard E., and William "Rick" Crandall, "Managing Excess Inventories: A Life-Cycle Approach," *Academy of Management Executive* 17, no. 3 (August 2003): 99–113; Thompson, Howard E, "Forecasting Errors, Diversification, and Inventory Fluctuations," *Academy of Management Journal* 9, no. 1 (March 1966): 67–77.

[16] See for instance, Kerkfeld, Dieter, and Evi Hartmann, "Context-Dependency of Purchasing and Supply Management: An Empirical Institutional Theory Approach," *Academy of Management Annual Meeting Proceedings* (August 2010): 1–6.

[17] Hall, Jr., Ernest H, "Just-In-Time Management: A Critical Assessment," *Academy of Management Executive* 3, no. 4 (November 1989): 315–318; Petersen, Peter B, "The Misplaced Origin of Just-In-Time (JIT) Production Methods," *Academy of Management Proceedings & Membership Directory* (August 1999): A1–A6.

[18] For more information, see Hugos, Michael H., *Essentials of Supply Chain Management,* 3rd ed. (New York: Wiley, 2012); Kaynak, Hale, and Ivan Montiel, "The Relationship Between Sustainable Supply Chain Management and Sustainable Performance: An Integrated Framework," *Academy of Management Annual Meeting Proceedings* (August 2009): 1–6.

[19] See, for instance, Robertson, Brian J., "Holocracy: A Complete System for Agile Organizational Governance and Steering," *Agile Project Management Advisory Service, Executive Report* 7, no. 7 (2006): 1–21.

[20] Buckingham, Marcus, and Curt Coffman, *First, Break All the Rules: What the World's Greatest Managers Do Differently* (New York: Simon & Schuster, 1999).

[21] Atkin, Robert S., and Edward J. Conlon, "Behaviorally Anchored Rating Scales: Some Theoretical Issues," *Academy of Management Review* 3, no. 1 (January 1978): 119–128; Schwab, Donald P., III, Herbert G. Heneman, and Thomas A. DeCotiis, "Behaviorally Anchored Rating Scales: A Review of the Literature," *Personnel Psychology* 28, no. 4 (Winter 1975): 549–562.

[22] Douglas, Thomas J., and William Q. Judge, Jr., "Total Quality Management Implementation and Competitive Advantage: The Role of Structural Control and Exploration," *Academy of Management Journal* 44, no. 1 (February 2001): 158–169; Waldman, David A., "The Contributions of Total Quality Management to a Theory of Work Performance," *Academy of Management Review* 19, no. 3 (July 1994): 510–536.

[23] See, for example, Miller, Katherine I., and Peter R. Monge, "Participation, Satisfaction, and Productivity: A Meta-Analytic Review," *Academy of Management Journal* 29, no. 4 (December 1986): 727–753.

[24] See, for instance, "Partial List of Quality Improvement Models," *Quality Progress* 37, no. 7 (July 2004): 34.

[25] Longbottom, David, Richard Mayer, and James Casey, "Marketing, Total Quality Management, and Benchmarking: Exploring the Divide," *Journal of Strategic Marketing* 8, no. 4 (December 2000): 327–340; Spencer, Michael S., and Arvinder P. S. Loomba, "Total Quality Management Programmes at Smaller Manufacturers: Benchmarking Techniques and Results," *Total Quality Management* 12, no. 5 (August 2001): 689–695.

[26] Barthélemy, Jérôme, "The Seven Deadly Sins of Outsourcing," *Academy of Management Executive* 17, no. 2 (May 2003): 87–98; Franceschini, F., M. Galetto, A. Pignatelli, and M. Varetto, "Outsourcing: Guidelines for a Structured Approach," *Benchmarking: An International Journal* 10, no. 3 (June 11, 2003): 246.

[27] See, for instance, Hodgetts, Richard M., Fred Luthans, and Sang M. Lee, "New Paradigm Organizations: From Total Quality to Learning to World-Class," *Organizational Dynamics* 22, no. 3 (Winter 1994): 4–19; Ittner, Christopher D., and David F. Larcker, "The Performance Effects of Process Management Techniques," *Management Science* 43, no. 4 (April 1997): 522.

[28] Laureani, Alessandro, and Jiju Antony, "Standards for Lean Six Sigma certification," *International Journal of Productivity and Performance Management* 61, no. 1 (2012): 110–120; Xingxing, Zu, Lawrence D. Fredendall, and Tina L. Robbins, "Organizational Culture and Quality Practices in Six Sigma," *Academy of Management Annual Meeting Proceedings* (August 2006): F1–F6.

[29] Followell, Roy F., and John S. Oakland, "Research into the Use of Statistical Quality Control in British Manufacturing Industry. Part I," *Quality & Reliability Engineering International* 1, no. 2 (April 1985): 85–92; Fuqua, Donovan O, "No Belts Required: The Advantages and Limitations of Statistical Quality Control," *Army Logistician* 41, no. 4 (July 2009): 54–57.

[30] Costa, Micaela Martínez, and Ángel Rafael Martínez Lorente, "ISO 9000:2000: The Key to Quality? An Exploratory Study," *Quality Management Journal* 14, no. 1 (January 2007): 7–18. Lundmark, Erik, and Alf Westelius, "Effects of Quality Management According to ISO 9000: A Swedish Study of the Transit to ISO 9000:2000," *Total Quality Management & Business Excellence* 17, no. 8 (October 2006): 1021–1042.

[31] Angel Del Brio, Jesús, Esteban Fernández, Beatriz Junquera, and Camilo José Vázquez, "Joint Adoption of ISO 14000-ISO 9000 Occupational Risk Prevention Practices in Spanish Industrial Companies: A Descriptive Study," *Total Quality Management* 12, no. 6 (September 2001): 669–686; Vastag, Gyula, "Revisiting ISO 14000 Diffusion: A New "Look" at the Drivers of Certification," *Production & Operations Management* 13, no. 3 (Fall 2004): 260–267.

[32] Garvin, David A, "How the Baldrige Award Really Works," *Harvard Business Review* 69, no. 6 (November 1991): 80–93; Kathawala, Yunus, Dean Elmuti, and Laura Toepp, "An Overview of the Baldrige Award: America's Tool for Global Competitiveness," *Industrial Management* 33, no. 2 (March 1991): 27.

[33] Hsin Hsin, Chang, "The Influence of Continuous Improvement and Performance Factors in Total Quality Organization," *Total Quality Management & Business Excellence* 16, no. 3 (May 2005): 413–437; Tanco, Martin, Ricardo Mateo, Javier Santos, Carmen Jaca, and Elisabeth Viles, "On the Relationship Between Continuous

Improvement Programmes and Their Effect on Quality Defects: An Automotive Case Study," *Total Quality Management & Business Excellence* 23, no. 3/4 (March 2012): 277–290.

[34] Taken directly from the Baldrige Award application form: http://www.nist.gov/baldrige/publications/upload/Baldrige_Award_Application_Forms.pdf.

Chapter 18

[1] See, for example, Webster, Frederick A., "A Model for New Venture Initiation: A Discourse on Rapacity and the Independent Entrepreneur," *Academy of Management Review* 1, no. 1 (January 1976): 26–37; Webster, Frederick Arthur, "Entrepreneurs and Ventures: An Attempt at Classification and Clarification," *Academy of Management Review* 2, no. 1 (January 1977): 54–61.

[2] See, for instance, Brockhaus, Robert H., "Risk Taking Propensity of Entrepreneurs," *Academy of Management Proceedings* (August 1976): 457–460; Mescon, Timothy S., and John R. Montanari, "The Personalties of Independent and Franchise Entrepreneurs, An Empirical Analysis of Concepts," *Academy of Management Proceedings* (August 1981): 413–417; Schere, Jean L., "Tolerance of Ambiguity as a Discriminating Variable Between Entrepreneurs and Managers," *Academy of Management Proceedings* (August 1982): 404–408.

[3] Ahlstrom, David, "Innovation and Growth: How Business Contributes to Society," *Academy of Management Perspectives* 24, no. 3 (August 2010): 11–24; Damanpour, Fariborz, "Organizational Innovation: A Meta-Analysis of Effects of Determinants and Moderators," *Academy of Management Journal* 34, no. 3 (September 1991): 555–590.

[4] Rogers, Everett M., *Diffusion of innovations*. (New York: Free Press, 1962).

[5] Elkin, Alicia Ann, "The Right Fit," *West Virginia University Alumni Magazine* 48, no. 1 (2012): 43; McCadam, Jess, "Former WVU Cheerleader Starts Clothing Line," *West Virginia Illustrated* (December 4, 2011); Robinson, Julie, "Football Fans Show Passion with Fashion," *The Charleston Gazette* (August 27, 2011).

[6] See, for example, Archibald, T. W., L. C. Thomas, J. M. Betts, and R. B. Johnston, "Should Start-up Companies Be Cautious? Inventory Policies Which Maximise Survival Probabilities," *Management Science* 48, no. 9 (September 2002): 1161–1174; Dotzler, Fred, "Follow-On Financings of Portfolio Companies: Issues for Investors and Start-Up Companies," *Journal of Private Equity* 15, no. 3 (Summer 2012): 9–11.

[7] Shane, Scott, and S. Venkataraman, "The Promise of Entrepreneurship as a Field of Research," *Academy of Management Review* 25, no. 1 (January 2000): 217–226; Zahra, Shaker A., and Mike Wright, "Entrepreneurship's Next Act," *Academy of Management Perspectives* 25, no. 4 (November 2011): 67–83.

[8] See, for example, Bornemann, Malte, "Performance Implications of the Business Model and the Moderating Effects of the Environment," *Academy of Management Annual Meeting Proceedings* (August 2009): 1–6.

[9] Bygrave, William D., and Jeffry A. Timmons, "Venture Capital at the Crossroads," *Harvard Business School Press Books* (July 1992); De Clercq, Dirk, Vance H. Fried, Oskari Lehtonen, and Harry J. Sapienza, "An Entrepreneur's Guide to the Venture Capital Galaxy," *Academy of Management Perspectives* 20, no. 3 (August 2006): 90–112.

[10] Cohen, Boyd, "Sustainable Valley Entrepreneurial Ecosystems," *Business Strategy and the Environment* 15, no. 1 (January 2006): 1–14; Malecki, Edward J., "Connecting Local Entrepreneurial Ecosystems to Global Innovation Networks: Open Innovation, Double Networks, and Knowledge Integration," *International Journal of Entrepreneurship & Innovation Management* 14, no. 1 (July 2011): 36–59.

[11] See, for instance, Amabile, Teresa M., *Creativity in Context*. (Boulder: Westview Press, 1996); Hennessey, Beth A., and Teresa M. Amabile, "Creativity," *Annual Review of Psychology* 61, no. 1 (February 2010): 569–598.

[12] Mullaney, Tim, "Energy Independence Isn't Just a Pipe Dream," *USA Today*, May 16, 2012: News Section, 1.

[13] Degennaro, Ramon P, "Angel Investors: Who They Are and What They Do; Can I Be One, Too?" *Journal of Wealth Management* 13, no. 2 (Fall 2010): 55–60; Mitteness, Cheryl, Richard Sudek, and Melissa S. Cardon, "Angel Investor Characteristics That Determine Whether Perceived Passion Leads to Higher Evaluations of Funding Potential," *Journal of Business Venturing* 27, no. 5 (September 2012): 592–606.

[14] *Global Entrepreneurship and the Successful Growth Strategies of Early-Stage Companies: A World Economic Forum Report* (New York: World Economic Forum USA Inc., 2011).

[15] *Ibid.*, p. 35.

[16] *Ibid.*, p. 40.

[17] For a more detailed overview of basic concept of liquidity, see Weygandt, Jerry J., Paul D. Kimmel, and Donald E. Kieso, *Accounting Principles*, 10th ed. (New York: Wiley, 2011).

[18] *Global Entrepreneurship*, p. 40.

[19] See the following for an overview of the economic situation in Bismark, ND, at the time of the case narrative: MacPherson, James, "ND Oil Boom City Reaping Prosperity, Problems," *Associated Press*, May 22, 2012; http://www.businessweek.com/ap/2012-05/D9UU498G0.htm.

[20] Justis, Robert T., and Barbara Kreigsmann, "The Feasibility Study as a Tool for Venture Analysis," *Journal of Small Business Management* 17, no. 1 (January 1979): 35–42; Spiller, Richard, Robert A. Peterson, and Roger A. Kerin, "Project Feasibility Analysis: A Guide to Profitable New Ventures," *Journal of Marketing Research (JMR)* 14, no. 4 (November 1977): 621.

[21] Miller, Peter, *The Smart Swarm*. (New York: Avery, 2010); Miller, Peter, "Swarm Theory," *National Geographic* 212, no. 1 (July 2007): 126–147.

[22] The opportunities and risks reviewed in the following paragraphs are taken from *Global Entrepreneurship*, pp. 11–13.

[23] See, for example, Johannessen, Jon-Arild, and Bjørn Olsen, "The Future of Value Creation and Innovations: Aspects of a Theory of Value Creation and Innovation in a Global Knowledge Economy," *International Journal of Information Management* 30, no. 6 (December 2010): 502–511; O'Cass, Aron, and Liem Viet Ngo, "Examining the Firm's Value Creation Process: A Managerial Perspective of the Firm's Value Offering Strategy and Performance," *British Journal of Management* 22, no. 4 (December 2011): 646–671.

[24] See, for instance, Gupta, Hari M., and José R. Campanha, "Firms Growth Dynamics, Competition, and Power-Law Scaling," *Physica A* 323, no. 1–4 (May 15, 2003): 626; Sutton, John, "The Variance of Firm Growth Rates: The 'Scaling' Puzzle," *Physica A* 312, no. 3/4 (September 15, 2002): 577.

[25] See, for example, Fischer, Harald M., and Timothy G. Pollock, "Effects of Social Capital and Power on Surviving Transformational Change: The Case of Initial Public Offerings," *Academy of Management Journal* 47, no. 4 (August 2004): 463–481; Heeley, Michael B., Sharon F. Matusik, and Neelam Jain, "Innovation, Appropriability, and the Underpricing of Initial Public Offerings," *Academy of Management Journal* 50, no. 1 (February 2007): 209–225.

[26] The following typology of eight strategies is based on materials in *Global Entrepreneurship*, p. 10.

[27] Lehrer, Jonah. *Imagine: How Creativity Works* (New York: Houghton Mifflin Harcourt, 2012).

[28] Lehrer, *Imagine*; Wuchty, Stefan, Benjamin F. Jones, and Brian Uzzi, "The Increasing Dominance of Teams in Production of Knowledge," *Science* 316, no. 5827 (May 18, 2007): 1036–1039.

[29] Lehrer, *Imagine*.

[30] Csikszentmihalyi, Mihaly. *Finding Flow: The Psychology of Engagement with Everyday Life.* (New York: Basic Books, 1997); Nakamura, Jeanne, and Mihaly Csikszentmihalyi, "Flow Theory and Research," in *Oxford Handbook of Positive Psychology*, 2d ed. (New York: Oxford University Press, 2009) 195–206.

[31] These eight conditions are based on materials in Csikszentmihalyi, Mihaly, *Good Business: Leadership, Flow, and the Making of Meaning* (New York: Penguin, 2003).

[32] This incident was inspired by the Steve Jobs anecdote found in Lehrer, *Imagine*, pp. 149–152.

[33] Uzzi, Brian, and Jarrett Spiro, "Collaboration and Creativity: The Small World Problem," *American Journal of Sociology* 111, no. 2 (September 2005): 447–504; Lehrer, *Imagine*.

[34] Uzzi and Spiro, *Collaboration and Creativity*.

[35] See, for example, Hutton, Elizabeth, and S. Shyam Sundar, "Can Video Games Enhance Creativity? Effects of Emotion Generated by Dance Dance Revolution," *Creativity Research Journal* 22, no. 3 (July 2010): 294–303; Also inspired by 3M's culture, as mentioned in Lehrer, *Imagine*.

Case Studies

[1] See Kumar, Nikhil, "U-turn for Instagram as It Scraps Controversial Changes," *The Independent*, December 21, 2012; accessed December 27, 2012.

[2] See Weistein-Donator, Nathan, "Revised Facebook Campus Plans: More Rooftop Trees, Less Zigzags," *Silicon Valley Business Journal*, December 17, 2012; accessed December 20, 2012.

[3] See Gertzfield, Ben, "Bootcamp: Growing Culture at Facebook," January 19, 2010; accessed December 13, 2012.

[4] See McGirt, Ellen, "Most Innovative Companies 2010: Facebook," *Fast Company*, August 24, 2012; http://www.fastcompany.com/mic/2010/profile/facebook; accessed January 2, 2012.

[5] See *Ramblings in Valve Time*, blog; accessed January 3, 2013.

[6] See *Ramblings in Valve Time*, blog; accessed January 4, 2013.

[7] See Harrison, Lindsay, "Airbnb CEO Brian Chesky on Weighing Your Priorities," *Fast Company*, November 26, 2012; http://www.fastcompany.com/3003085/airbnb-ceo-brian-chesky-weighing-your-priorities; accessed December 10, 2012.

[8] See Cooper, Rachel, "AstraZeneca Is in Need of Radical Surgery After Chief David Brennan Retires," *The Telegraph*, April 26, 2012; accessed December 13, 2012.

[9] See Telegraph Staff and Agencies, "AstraZeneca Sales Hurt by Patent Expiries," *The Telegraph*, October 12, 2012; accessed December 10, 2012.

[10] See Buchanan, Leigh, "Zumba Fitness: Company of the Year," *Inc.,* December 4, 2012; accessed December 29, 2013.

[11] See "Fast Casual Restaurant Franchise Industry Report," *Franchise Direct*; accessed January 4, 2013.

[12] See Hsieh, Tony, "How I Did It: Zappos's CEO on Going to Extremes for Customers," *Harvard Business Review*, July 2010; accessed December 27, 2012.

[13] *Ibid.*

[14] See Gladwell, Malcolm, *Outliers: The Story of Success.* Aspen, CO: Little, Brown, and Company, 2008.

NAME INDEX

SUBJECT INDEX

ORGANIZATION INDEX

FEATURES